IN SEARCH OF THE
LOST TESTAMENT
OF ALEXANDER THE GREAT

IN SEARCH OF THE
LOST TESTAMENT
OF ALEXANDER THE GREAT

DAVID GRANT

Matador
9 Priory Business Park,
Wistow Road, Kibworth Beauchamp,
Leicestershire. LE8 0RX
Tel: 0116 279 2299
Email: books@troubador.co.uk
Web: www.troubador.co.uk/matador
Twitter: @matadorbooks

PB: ISBN 978 1785899 522
HB: ISBN 978 1785899 539

British Library Cataloguing in Publication Data.
A catalogue record for this book is available from the British Library.

Printed and bound by CPI Group (UK) Ltd, Croydon, CR0 4YY
Typeset in 11pt Aldine401 BT by Troubador Publishing Ltd, Leicester, UK

Matador is an imprint of Troubador Publishing Ltd

CONTENTS

'The Macedonia of Alexander has disappeared, almost without a trace. Its older capital Aegae is a malaria-ridden site and nothing more... The tombs of the Macedonian rulers, where Alexander had thought to be gathered to his fathers, have never been found; his own capital, Pella, is a mass of shapeless ruins...'[1]

Albert Olmstead, 1948

'Half a century after the start of systematic, large-scale excavations, the huge labour by archaeologists, who have dragged from the earth ruins hidden in the past, and the patient work of all the scholars, who have concentrated the expertise on their finds, have revealed an inhabited land that had been *terra incognita* and given a face to the people, enigmatic until that point, whom Alexander led to the ends of the earth.'[2]

Miltiades Hatzopoulos, 1996

PRESS RELEASE

REMAINS OF PHILIP II, FATHER OF ALEXANDER THE GREAT, CONFIRMED FOUND

10 October, 2014, by April Holloway for *Ancient Origins*

'Buried beneath a large mound located in the village of Vergina in northern Greece, an archaeological excavation carried out in 1977 by Greek archaeologist, Manolis Andronikos, uncovered a spectacular tomb holding the remains of ancient Macedonian royalty.

The historically important tomb has been the subject of intense debate ever since, dividing archaeologists over whose cremated remains were housed inside two golden caskets – Philip II, father of Alexander the Great, and one of his wives; or Philip III Arrhidaeus, Alexander's half-brother, who assumed the throne after Alexander's death, with his wife Eurydice.[3] *Discovery News* reports that, finally, the most detailed and extensive study ever conducted on the remains has settled the decades-old argument, confirming the bones indeed belong to the Macedonian King Philip II.

The 'Great Tumulus', as it came to be known, over 330 feet in diameter and 40 feet tall at the centre, was found to contain three primary burial sites. Tomb I, which was looted, contained fragmentary human remains believed to belong to three individuals.[4] The main chamber of Tomb II, measuring approximately 15 feet by 15 feet by 17.5 feet high, around which the debate is centered, contained relatively complete cremated remains of a male, which had been placed within a golden larnax (chest) bearing an embossed starburst, the emblem of the Macedonian royal family, and the remains of a female in the antechamber, wrapped in a golden-purple cloth with a golden diadem. Also within the burial chamber were a gilded silver diadem, an iron helmet, an elaborate ceremonial shield, an iron and gold cuirass, and two small ivory portrait heads believed to represent Philip II and Alexander. Tomb III contained a number of silver vessels and a silver funerary urn with the bones of an adolescent believed to be Alexander IV of Macedon, son of Alexander the Great.

Numerous studies have been published concerning the relatively intact human remains found in the twenty-four-carat gold casket in Tomb II. A study published in the journal *Science* in 2000, for example, concluded that the remains could not be Philip II as they did not bear traces of injuries that Philip supposedly suffered during his lifetime. Then, a study released in 2010 conversely stated that the remains must be Philip II as a notch in the eye socket is consistent with a battle wound received by Philip II at the siege of Methone in 355/354 BCE, years before he died.[5]

To settle the score once and for all, an extensive anthropological investigation was launched to fully analyse more than 350 bones and fragments found in the two golden caskets. The research team, led by anthropologist Theodore Antikas, utilised X-ray-computed tomography, scanning electron microscopy, and X-ray fluorescence, to uncover any pathologies, activity markers, or trauma that could lead to the identification of the remains.

The results revealed features in the bones not previously seen or recorded. Antikas explained that the skull showed signs of sinusitis, which may have been caused by an old facial trauma, such as the arrow that is known to have hit and blinded Philip II at the siege of Methone.[6] Furthermore, there are signs of chronic pathology on the surface of several rib fragments, which are believed to be linked to Philip's trauma when he was struck with a lance around 345 BC. Finally, the bones reflect a fully-fleshed cremation, which disproves the theory that the remains belong to Philip III Arrhidaeus who had been buried for some time before being exhumed and cremated.

The analysis also revealed that the remains of the female in the antechamber are consistent with a female warrior and horse-rider, aged thirty to thirty-four. This find rules out the wife of Philip III Arrhidaeus, who was under twenty-five.[7] Furthermore, a major fracture in her left tibia, causing leg shortening, explains the presence of a pair of Scythian greaves, in which the left side is shorter than the right. This indicates the Scythian weaponry and armour must have belonged to the female occupant of the tomb. Antikas told *Discovery News* that: 'No Macedonian king other than Philip II is known to have had relations with a Scythian.'

AUTHOR'S NOTE

Discovery News also reported on further revelations that additionally shed light on Tomb I. During the study being undertaken by Antikas' team, a young archeologist working on his thesis at Vergina found three wooden crates in a storage place filled with bone fragments and artefacts from Tomb I: three plastic bags containing well over one hundred bone fragments never before studied. Until then, Tomb I had been thought to hold solely a male, female and infant. But the seventy identified bones suggest the chamber held at *least* seven individuals: an adult male, a female, a child, four babies aged eight-ten lunar months and one foetus of six and a half lunar months. Antikas believes: 'This find disproves every previous hypothesis of historians and archaeologists alike that Tomb I was intended for Philip II and his last wife.' *Discovery News*, October 10, 2014.

The two small ivory portrait heads found in Tomb II and believed to depict Philip II and Alexander.

'Do not bury my bones apart from yours, Achilles
But let them lie together, just as we were raised in your house…
So may the same vessel contain both our bones
The golden amphora, which your lady mother gave you.'

Homer *Iliad*[8]

EXCAVATING HOMERIC HEROES: AUTHOR'S COMMENTARY

The ancient city of Aegae where the royal tombs are located dates back to the 7th century BCE; it became Macedonia's first capital after it was conglomerated from a collection of villages into a city in the 5th century BCE. Aegae was eventually supplanted by a new capital at Pella in the 4th century BCE but retained its status as the spiritual home and burial ground of the Macedonian kings.

Both settlements were partially destroyed by Rome in 168 BCE following the Battle of Pydna when Macedonia was finally defeated, and a landslide buried the older capital in the 1st century, after which it was uninhabited. The name 'Aegae' ceased to be used and its history was grazed over by goats and sheep and survived in oral legend only, while papyri and faded vellums told of a former city of kings. Only a nearby early Christian basilica built from the stones of the ancient ruins marked the forgotten location. In the 1920s, on what had once been the southeast side of the Macedonian royal palace, Greek refugees from the Euxine Pontus region of Asia Minor founded the village of Vergina, and the still unidentified fallen stones were used as masonry in the new houses.[9]

Supervised excavations at what turned out to be the founding city of the Argead (otherwise, Temenid) dynasty go back to the 1860s when a dig by French archaeologist, Léon Heuzey, sponsored by Napoleon III, revealed a Macedonian tomb next to the village of Palatitsia, 'the small palaces', a name that hinted tantalisingly at its former significance, though it was erroneously thought to be the site of the ancient city of Valla. In the 1930s, Konstantinos Romaios, a professor of archaeology at the Aristotle University of Thessaloniki, revealed a further tomb, but as Albert Olmstead's above despondent summation affirms, as late as 1948 archeologists still had not pinpointed the location of Aegae.

Between 1958 and 1975 excavations in the area were extended by Georgios Bakalakis and Fotis Petsas, the antiquities curator (from 1955-65). Professor Manolis Andronikos, a pupil of Romaios, eventually became convinced the so-called Great Tumulus, *Megali Toumba*, must house the tombs of the Macedonian kings. But it was the British historian, Nicholas Hammond, who first voiced the idea (in fact in 1968) that the ancient ruins lying between Vergina and Palatitsia (rather than those at the town of Edessa) were in fact the lost city of Aegae, a contention that was not immediately accepted.[10]

After initial disappointment in 1977 when shafts were sunk through the centre of the mound (where remains of a stoa and/or cenotaph tumulus, might have nevertheless been found) with some 60,000 cubic feet of earth removed, and while preparing an access ramp on the southeast perimeter for works planned the following season, Andronikos stumbled across gold, literally: two royal tombs were finally revealed.[11] Tombs I and II had originally been buried together under a single low tumulus with Tomb II at its centre; Tomb III, close by, was discovered the following year. Andronikos was exposing what is now referred to as the 'royal burial cluster of Philip II', Alexander's father.[12]

The precious articles found within suggested to Andronikos that in the 'monumental death chamber' of Tomb II, 'laid on an elaborate gold and ivory deathbed wearing his precious golden oak wreath' – which features 313 oak leaves and 68 acorns – King Philip II had been 'surrendered, like a new Heracles, to the funeral pyre'.[13] For the flesh-boned cremation (the evidence lies in the colour, warping and minute forms of bone fractures) which took place soon after its occupant's death (distinct from 'dry-boned' which takes place long after death when flesh has rotted away) revealed traces of gold droplets, a clue that the king was placed on the pyre wearing his crown. A more recent analysis suggests that in the *holokautoma*, the total incineration, his body was wrapped in an asbestos shroud to help separate the bones from the pyre debris.[14]

Within the Great Tumulus of Aegae, Andronikos discovered some 'forty-seven complete or nearly complete *stelae*' [commemorative stone slabs] representing commoners' graves dating back to the second half of the 4th century BCE. Since his death in 1992, the Eucleia and Cybele sanctuaries, the acropolis and vast necropolis with graves dating mostly to the Early Iron Age (1,000-700 BCE), and the northeast gate, have all been revealed, along with the royal palace, which is now considered to be the largest building in classical Greece. Occupying 41,259 square feet, it is three times the size of the Athenian Parthenon. Archeologists have unearthed the fortress walls, more cemeteries with more sanctuaries and over 1,000 identified graves in total, besides the burial clusters of royal women and earlier Temenid kings (clusters 'B' and 'C'), including the Heuzey and Bella clusters closer to Palatitsia. All in all, some 500 tumuli have been exposed covering over 900 hectares between Vergina and Palatitsia and they reveal the extent of the ancient city, which, with its suburbs, covered some 6,500 hectares.[15]

Having survived numerous battles, skirmishes, city sieges and hostile alliances against him, Philip's death was sudden and unexpected. Intending to show the Greek world his impressive enhanced religious capital at Aegae with its revolutionary palace design that would have been visible from afar as visitors crossed the plains below, and when entering its older amphitheatre at which the tragedies of the resident Euripides must have once been heard, Philip was stabbed at the wedding of his daughter, Cleopatra, in 336 BCE. It was nothing short of a 'spectacular, world-shaking event'. Unearthing in 1977 what is thought by many to be his tomb was no less dramatic and it has since been dubbed the 'discovery of the century'.[16]

Philip's funeral had been overseen by a grief-stricken, or perhaps a quietly elated, king-in-the-waiting, Alexander the Great.[17] His bones appear to have been washed in emulation of the rites described in Homer's *Iliad* in which Achilles' remains were similarly prepared before being steeped in wine and oil. After cremation the bones were carefully collected and placed in the twenty-four carat gold chest or larnax weighing 11 kilograms, in a similar manner to the burial rites of Hector and Patroclus, and they were possibly covered in a soft purple cloth.[18] However, the discovery of traces of the rare mineral huntite and Tyrian purple (porphyra) hint that Philip may in fact have been cremated in an elaborate funeral mask.[19]

The remains of bones and trappings of four horses have been found in what appears to have been a purifactory fire above the cornice. Along with two swords and a *sarissa* (pike), they were left to decay in a (now collapsed) mud brick structure above the tomb. Some scholars believe the remains include the mounts of Philip's assassins and/or his famous chariot horses. Once again, this would have followed the funerary rites Homer described for Patroclus.[20] The Macedonian burial tradition, clearly following a heroic template, may have influenced Plato when he was writing his *Laws* which outlined the ideal burial in an idealised state.[21]

What are believed by some scholars to be Philip's remarkable funerary possessions provide a testament to a warrior king: a sword in a scabbard and a short sword, six spears and pikes of different lengths, two pairs of greaves, a throat-protecting gorget besides the aforementioned ceremonial shield ('completely unsuitable to ward off the blows of battle', according to Andronikos), body armour and the impressive once-plumed iron helmet.[22] The weaponry is representative of a soldier who fought in both the Macedonian cavalry *and* infantry regiments.[23] In front of the sarcophagus in the main chamber were found the remains of a wooden couch decorated with five (of fourteen finally recovered) chryselephantine miniature relief figures thought (by some) to represent the family of Philip II.[24]

Winthrop Lindsay Adams insightfully stated back in 1980 that the contents of the antechamber of Tomb II are 'crucial to identification of the king in the main chamber'.[25] And the contents are fascinating; they include a Scythian gold *gorytos*, the distinct two-part quiver that traditionally held arrows (seventy-four were found) often poison-tipped and unleashed by a compact powerful Scythian compound bow. This is suggestive of a warrior woman whose identity we probe further in the epilogue. The *gorytos*, along with the exquisite items retrieved from the main chamber of Tomb II, are now on display in the Archaeological Museum at Vergina; the gold wreaths and the diadem have been described as the most beautiful pieces of jewellery of the ancient world.

Osteoarchaeological studies on the bones of the two individuals from Tomb II, one of the longest and tallest of the chamber tombs at Aegae, have led to conflicting conclusions, as the press release made clear.[26] But as Antikas' 2014 report points out, the '… cremains had been studied insufficiently and/or misinterpreted, causing debates among archeologists and anthropologists for over three decades.'[27] Fortunately, the last thirty years have witnessed significant advances in bioarchaeology. Working on behalf of the Aristotle University Vergina Excavation, Prof. Antikas explains that from 2009 to 2014 osteological and physiochemical analyses backed by CT and XRF scans (X-ray-computed tomography, scanning electron microscopy and X-ray fluorescence) have provided new theories regarding age, gender, paleopathology and morphological changes to the bones which are now catalogued by 4,500 photos.

Although the new investigations employed the latest tools in the science of physical anthropology that the earlier examinations of teams had not benefitted from in the 1980s, the technology has not yet put an end to the debate. In 2008, and *prior* to the highly scientific post-mortem by Antikas' team in 2014, the Greek historian, Dr Miltiades Hatzopoulos, summarised the background to the previous research: 'The issue has been obscured by precipitate announcements, the quest for publicity, political agendas and petty rivalries…'[28] The summation sounds remarkably like the motives of the agenda-driven historians who gave us Alexander's story.

Yet the Great Tumulus at Aegae, built from layers of clay, soil and rock, and thrown up by unknown hands labouring under a still-unnamed king, seems to have protected some of its finest secrets from historians and looters, both from the marauding Gauls and the invading Romans, who carted everything they could back to Italy following Macedonia's defeat.[29] No doubt there is much more still to be discovered; the recent excavations at the Kasta Hill *polyandreion* (communal tomb) at Amphipolis some 100 miles from Vergina and the newly unearthed tombs at Pella and Katerini, remind us we have only unearthed a fragment of classical Macedonia, and, we suggest, no more than fragments of the story of Alexander himself.

FORGERY AND PHILOLOGY: THE BAG OF TRICKS PLAYED UPON THE DEAD

'O wicked Fortuna,
Fickle as falling leaves, harsher than tigers,
More savage than the deadly Hydra, crueler
Than any monster, fearsome as Tesiphone,
why do you cut the prince's flowering years
before his day?'[30]

The *Alexandreis* of Gautier de Chatillon

'It is indeed true that the archaeologist has succeeded in exacting from dumb, cold marble or crustated metal, the interesting story of contemporaneous achievements... while their very nature possessed well-nigh all the elements of absolute authenticity, this is far from being the case with written records. For in their transmission from century to century they are all but certain to become distorted or adulterated.'[31] In his *Literary Fraud Amongst the Greeks* published in 1894, Alfred Gudeman saw value in ruins and inscriptions and yet nothing more than 'disturbing agencies' in the literature he sensed had misplaced the truth. But as Gudeman pointed out, the better, or perhaps the worse, part of 'history' *has* come down to us through written sources.

Literature and archaeology do, however, collaborate occasionally, and both the surviving texts and Babylonian cuneiform tablets recorded that on the 10th, or more likely the 11th, of June in the year 323 BCE in the 114th Olympiad, or the year 5,176 according to The *Greek Alexander Romance*, King Alexander III of Macedonia died in Babylon in his thirty-third year; with him died his extraordinary eleven-year campaign that changed the face of the Graeco-Persian world forever.[32]

Some 2,340 years on, five barely intact accounts survive to tell a hardly coherent story. At times in close agreement, though frequently in opposition, they conclude with a contradictory set of suspicious claims and death-scene rehashes. One portrayed Alexander dying silent and intestate; he was Homeric and vocal in another, whilst a third detailed his Last Will and Testament though it is attached to the end of a book of romance. Which account do we trust?

Since the Rennaisance, and sped along by new techniques developed over the past two centuries, classical scholars, and philologists in particular, have dedicated themselves to separating the 'historical' out of the total written evidence Gudeman was so suspicious of. The quest has solicited contemplations from some of the greatest minds of the ages: the philosophers, priests, politicians, antiquarians and polymaths attempting to unlock the gates of the past. In their own way each of them appreciated that the relationship between 'what actually took place' and 'what is recorded to have taken place' is an uneasy one; some went further and concluded that duplicity of one kind or another, subtle or overt, is endemic to the narrating of 'history', so that falsifications and the forensic method to unravel them compete on every page.

'Forgery and philology fell and rose together in the Renaissance, as in Hellenistic Alexandria'; it is an observation that gives this book much of its momentum, for Alexander's eponymous city *was* a key ingredient in the birth of his story, which, with some justification, we could term his 'legend'.[33] Moreover, it was during the Renaissance that Alexander was extracted once more from the moth-eaten scrolls and decrepitated manuscripts that had been hidden in 'leaky rat-ridden monastery attics'; they were, thought the collector Poggio Bracciolini (1380-1459), 'looking up at him for help' like 'friends in a hospital or a prison'.[34]

The 'legend' and the manuscripts have brought us three competing witnesses all the way from Babylon in June 323 BCE, as the testimony they contain potentially originated with men who were there. The first comes in the form of the *'Journal'*, which documented Alexander's final twelve-day decline. The *Journal* detail was allegedly extracted from the official campaign diary, the *Ephemerides* (plural: day-to-day records, *in toto* a single diary) and it is found in the final pages of the biographies of the Roman-era historians Arrian (ca. 86-160 CE) and Plutarch (ca. 46-120 CE), as well as in the *Historical Miscellany* of the Roman antiquarian Aelian (ca. 175-235 CE).[35]

The *Journal*'s dry, laconic and deadpan prose sits in stark contrast to the vivid portrayals of pre-death portents appearing in the biographers' previous pages, and it makes no reference at all to a transfer of power; Alexander was, it claimed, comatose and speechless through his final two days and nights. Known for his attention to detail and meticulous military planning, the *Journal* implied the dying Argead king employed none of these famous faculties, leaving neither a Will nor any succession instructions for either the Macedonian kingdom or the newly conquered

Asian empire. It was this state of affairs, assumed historians, that led to infighting immediately after, and soon to Macedonian 'civil war'.[36]

It was left to what we term the '*Pamphlet*' to provide a more detailed and colourful account of Alexander's death. This apparently partisan political document is thought to have originated in the first decade of the Successor Wars waged by Alexander's generals for their share of the divided empire. The *Pamphlet* alleged there was nothing natural, or even supernatural, to Alexander's death, for it revealed a conspiracy to poison him at an impromptu banquet thrown by a prominent court friend. Many attendees were implicated, including the king's royal Bodyguards corps and his closest Companions, whilst six of the guests were cited as innocent and ignorant of the plot.[37]

The *Pamphlet* explained the motives behind the assassination and the poison used. It detailed the drafting and then the reading of a lucid Last Will and Testament in which Alexander distributed the empire to the *megistoi* ('great men', the most prominent men at court) as his end approached. This was not a formal 'partitioning' or breaking up of the newly-conquered lands, but rather the regional governance of an intact empire on behalf of his son (or sons). The Will bequests were listed beside commemoratives and donations to leading cities and religious sites, and Alexander paired the surviving royal women with carefully chosen generals to secure the safety of his sons, born or still *in utero*, for they were the future of the Argead (or Temenid) royal line.[38] In fact, the Will stands as a voice of reason against the backdrop of competing narratives in which anarchy and treasonous power plays otherwise dominated the scene.

Some indeterminate years later, this *Pamphlet*-originating detail was most likely absorbed by the quasi-historical *Historia Alexandri Magni*, as it was titled in the oldest surviving manuscripts. This highly rhetorical and eulogistic template of Alexander's deeds was erroneously once credited to the official campaign historian, Callisthenes, and hence is often still termed a 'Pseudo-Callisthenes' production.[39] It soon absorbed the *thaumata*, 'wonders', that were attaching themselves to Alexander and in time it metamorphosised into something of a book of fables, popularly referred to today as the *Greek Alexander Romance*, a multicultural depository of traditions that grew up around the king.

In this literary environment, Alexander's death was not immune to the encroaching *fabulae* and the *Romance* texts we read today conclude with him addressing Bucephalus, his warhorse standing obediently by his bed. Once the *Pamphlet* detail had been wholly subsumed by the *Romance*, Alexander's testament became something of a pariah and unworthy of further consideration. As a result, the biographies, monographs, universal histories and academic studies over the past two millennia have concurred on one key issue: Alexander the Great died intestate and never made a

Will. The irony, a positive one for our contention, is that these fanciful romances, so welcomed in the Middle Ages and translated into myriad languages, significantly outsold them all.

Unlike the rejected Will, the plot to poison Alexander was too alluring to send into exile. This conspiratorial section of the *Pamphlet* was swept up by mainstream history and it became a colourful adornment to the closing pages of the Roman-era Vulgate accounts (Vulgate here suggesting a 'popular' or 'widely-accepted' genre) represented by the surviving texts of Curtius Rufus (likely published mid-1st century CE), Diodorus (toponymic *Siculus,* literally the 'Sicilian', published between 60 and 30 BCE) and Gnaeus Pompeius Trogus (late 1st century BCE) whose work is preserved in an epitome by the otherwise unknown writer, Justin (likely 3rd century CE). Their textual similarities point to a common, if not exclusive, source, and many scholars conclude that was the earlier Alexandria-based historian Cleitarchus, a likely contemporary of Alexander's veterans or their sons.[40]

According to the Vulgate tradition, Alexander's final words left his kingdom (not specifically the 'empire') 'to the strongest' or 'most worthy' of men.[41] The dying king was still sufficiently lucid to add that he foresaw the wars of succession that would follow, and he cynically referred to them as his 'funeral games'.[42] With this Alexander was recalling the posthumous Homeric contests honouring the fallen heroes of Troy, those Achilles had held for Patroclus in the *Iliad*, for example, when the late-Mycenaean world seemed perennially at war, and it was a funerary tradition upheld in Macedonia.[43] The highly rhetorical epitome of Justin was more lucid on the import of the 'games': Alexander '… could foretell, and almost saw with his eyes, how much blood Macedonia would shed in the disputes that would follow his death, and with what slaughters, and what quantities of gore, she would perform his obsequies.' Curtius' account went on to paint a picture of Persian mourning and dissent amongst the assembled generals, where Justin clearly suggested the Macedonians were glad to see Alexander go.[44]

The rumours of conspiracy reverberated far and wide; even Arrian and Plutarch, adherents to the *Journal* silence and dismissive of Vulgate claims, felt duty-bound to report it. When closing his narrative, Plutarch reported that some five years after Alexander had been embalmed, his mother, Olympias, exacted revenge on the architects of the assassination by 'putting many men to death'.[45] Diodorus and Curtius believed that historians had dared not write of the plot when the men at the heart of the conspiracy were still fighting to become *primus inter pares* in their bid for the Macedonian throne or control of the Asian empire (or both), and 'whatever credence such stories gained, they were soon suppressed by the power of the people implicated by the rumour'. More specific was the claim (possibly in the *Pamphlet* itself) that Onesicritus, the court philosopher and campaign historian, deliberately avoided naming the banquet guests for fear of personal reprisals.[46] The *Pamphlet* was clearly virulent and one of our aims is to identify its still anonymous author in our bid to navigate back to Alexander's original Will.

VIVA ENIM MORTUORUM IN MEMORIA VIVORUM EST POSITA[47]

The texts available for autopsy have been termed 'both many and few'; many accounts of Alexander were written but only a few survive as coherent narratives. More often than not our knowledge is reliant upon fragments from philosphers, antiquarians, poets, politicians and propaganda pamphleteers, whose accounts range from the sound and sober, to the downright suspicious and the outright fabrication.[48] When summing up this corpus of contradictory evidence in his 1973 biography, Robin Lane Fox stated that he knew of 1,472 books and articles analysing the subject, but that did not deter him from adding his own account. Written with a remarkable degree of acuity when publishing at the age of twenty-seven, Lane Fox advised that his methodology was not pretending 'to certainty in Alexander's name'.[49]

This remains the state of affairs, for when weighing up the probabilities of what might have actually happened, including plausible impossibilities and implausible possibilities, we still do, and perhaps always will, rely heavily upon the five cohesive biographies that date to the Roman era. Their authors represent an eclectic mix of social and ethnic backgrounds: Greek, Gallic, Greek-Sicilian, Bithynian and Italian, each writing under the scrutiny of a Rome now dominating the former Hellenistic world that had coalesced around the kingdoms of Alexander's successors, the *Diadokhoi*.[50] Written from the distance of some 300 to 450 years after the events they portrayed, these texts were themselves compiled from a corpus of earlier sources. Apart from surviving fragments, *all* of this earlier material from the Hellenistic era (popularly defined as the period between Alexander's death in 323 BCE and the battle of Actium in 31 BCE) has been lost. Indeed, without the infrequent references to these archetypal sources that are strewn sparingly across the classical library, the parental Alexander historians would otherwise be unknown, and many are surely still buried in unmarked graves.

Thanks to Karl Müller's five-volume *Fragmenta Historicorum Graecorum* published between 1841 and 1870, and Felix Jacoby's incomplete *Die Fragmente der griechischen Historiker* published in 1929, today's scholars can identify almost 400 fragments directly relating to Alexander from some thirty 'lost' writers whose works ranged from serious biography to propaganda pamphlets by the 'good, sound and important' and 'the world's greatest liars'; paradoxically, those traits often combine in the same source.[51] They were translated into English by Charles Robinson (published 1953) and Lionel Pearson followed with a profiling of these lost texts in his influential *The Lost Histories of Alexander the Great* (1960). But source identifications remain problematic; after historians had sifted through the fragments to identify the truly original reporting from regurgitated *testimonia*, many were deemed paraphrases and others were labelled 'spuriously assigned'.[52]

It would be logical to expect a linear deterioration in the accuracy and detail of this material through time, and it would be reasonable to suppose that the most lamentable losses will always be those compiled by Alexander's senior staff, the eyewitnesses we define as the 'primary sources', or more specifically, 'court sources', who, as the title suggests, frequented the king's palace and campaign headquarters. Yet that would be an oversimplification, for evidence suggests that the magnet of political ambition and the realities of survival in a world torn apart by rivalries, along with the powerful hand of sponsorship that any publication would have required, perniciously drew fabrication, omission, exaggeration and agenda into the first generation texts. 'Truth' is, after all, the first casualty of war.[53]

Plutarch, a voracious collector of detail who paired twenty-two greats in his *Lives of Noble Greeks and Romans* (otherwise known as *Parallel Lives*), named twenty-four sources in his profiling of Alexander, and he provided a sober warning on early material in general:

> So very difficult a matter is it to trace and find out the truth of anything by history, when, on the one hand, those who afterwards write it find long periods of time intercepting their view, and, on the other hand, the contemporary records of any actions and lives, partly through envy and ill-will, partly through favour and flattery, pervert and distort truth.[54]

This raises a larger philosophical conundrum: what indeed is 'history', and how *is* the literary evidence to be detached from the 'historical'? With straightforward Indo-European etymological roots in 'to see', 'to know', or 'to gain knowledge from', the simplicity of the word 'history' hides an epistemological complexity with which the answer has evolved. Although Cicero (106-43 BCE), charismatically reminded us that *Viva enim mortuorum in memoria vivorum est posita* – 'The life of the dead is set in the memory of the living' – he rather damagingly considered that orators alone should be entrusted with the care of the past. The solemn Thucydides (ca. 460-395 BCE) saw history as 'philosophy teaching by examples', a metaphysical slant we might today term 'historiosophy',[55] whilst the ever-wary Polybius (ca. 200 BCE-118 BCE) in his language of officialdom, provided a more familiar warning: 'Readers should be very attentive to, and critical of, historians, and they in turn should be constantly on their guard.'[56]

More recently, less florid definitions have perpetuated an ever more cynical historiographical perspective in which our knowledge of the past has been likened to a '… damn dim candle over a damn dark abyss.'[57] But for all the erudition and seasoned metaphysical debate, Samuel Butler provided the most useful insight for our particular purpose: 'Though God cannot alter the past, historians can.'[58]

The forensic and systematic analysis of extant sources is epitomised in the word '*Quellenforschung*'. The research was developed most prominently through philological scholarship in Germany in the 18th and early 19th centuries, and is now a broad-based discipline for peeling the historical onion (often with tears) of its *täuschung* (deception) and *fälschung* (forgery). Although philology 'nourishes itself on the erosion of history',[59] in searching for the 'infallible criterion of truth' – arrived at by what Brian Bosworth terms an 'almost Cartesian principle' (finding a reliable source as a yardstick for the credibility of the rest)[60] – the methodologies for tearing apart and reconstructing ancient texts were not always wholly successful:

> The German scholars of the 18th and 19th centuries were masters at creating and accepting elaborate hypotheses, some of which rested, like inverted pyramids delicately balanced, on a single point of evidence. Many of them found it easy to believe three impossible things, or more, before breakfast.[61]

Nonetheless, new textual interpretations and the associated hermeneutical uncertainties soon gave rise to categorisations of pseudohistory, cryptohistory, and historical revisionism, as methodological flaws came under scrutiny when the rules of textual interpretation were shifted by the so-called 'fathers of historiography'. The challenges posed by the surviving classical texts generated a further 19th century debate, *Altertumswissenschaft* ('science of antiquity'); this questioned whether any study of the classical past ought to include *solely* written works or *all* cultural material (as Alfred Gudeman sensed) including archeological and numismatic evidence, for example.[62]

The 20th century saw the rise of the social sciences that were soon pulled into historical interpretations, and thereafter every historian needed to be a multidisciplinarian: an 'economist, sociologist, anthropologist, demographer, psychologist' and a 'linguist', pushing the *Altertumswissenschaft* debate into wholly new dimensions.[63] Enlightened philologists further considered that any truly complete appraisal should include Egyptian, Old Persian and Arabic texts for a wider perspective still. Tertullian (ca. 160-225 CE), the 'father' of Western theology and born in a Rome-humbled Carthage, had long before taken a similar line on barbarian texts in his *Apology*, when he proposed that the '… archives of the most ancient nations… Egyptians, Chaldeans and Carthaginians' were needed to establish proofs.[64]

Despite this enlightenment, there remained a distinct absence of *heteroglossia* in the recording of Alexander's deeds, save in the multi-cultural romances. As Macaulay concluded of the Greeks, they: 'borrowed nothing. They translated nothing. We cannot call to mind a single expression of any Greek writer earlier than the Age of Augustus, indicating an opinion that anything else worth reading could be written in any language except his own.'[65] So Alexander's mainstream history remained an almost exclusively Graeco-Roman affair, paradoxical, when we consider that most of his adult life was spent campaigning in Asia Minor, Phoenicia, Egypt, Babylonia, the far-flung provinces of the eastern Persian Empire, and what the Greeks liberally referred to as India.[66]

The last fifty years, in particular, have seen a proliferation in academic studies that relate in some way to Alexander and his successors, as a new generation of scholars has been at work on autopsying what we have.[67] Luckily, today we enjoy the benefits of advanced historiographical methodologies to help us frisk sources for weapons of deceit, or as Joseph Speyer commented, we live in a time when objectivity has replaced subjectivity and philology replaced rhetoric.[68] The study of the past has become a multi-disciplined process; the core principles of its method have evolved to six-and seven-step checklists that probe probability laws,[69] at times relying on simple maths, and at others on advanced linguistic algorithms employed by cliometricians. The ancillary disciplines of *Quellenforschung* now include papyrology, palaeography, linguistic palaeontology, osteoarchaeology, codicology, iconography, numismatics, epigraphy and even space-archaeology – the 'total' evidences available, all of which are being brought to bear on the evidence. Papyri and parchment palimpsests (re-used scrolls or book pages) and even the bones at Aegae are undergoing multi-spectral imaging to reveal their historical and actual DNA, processes that the Renaissance philologists could never have conceived of.

But if the raw disciplines of *Quellenforschung* are designed to be immune from bias, the operators employing them are not, and many scholars have pondered on how we unconsciously rewrite the past. One of their conclusions: 'By and large, the historian will get the kind of facts he wants. History *is* interpretation. The belief in a hard core of historical facts existing objectively and independently of… the historian is a preposterous fallacy, but one which it is very hard to eradicate.'[70] This serves as a reminder to: 'cherish those who seek the truth, but to beware of those who find it'.[71]

The path of my investigation, the 'backstory' to the history of the life and death of Alexander and his remarkable successors, follows my own voyage of discovery into an ocean of anecdotes, testimony and propaganda in which the tides of scholarly opinion on Alexander drift. Any author delving into the murky waters of *Quellenforschung* soon realises just how frail are the facts behind the life of the man on whom the late Hellenistic era bestowed the epithet 'Great'.[72] And it reminds us how little we really know about the campaigning Macedonian king. Moreover, when sources are analysed impartially, there appears evidence that those who *did* know, the eyewitness historians who campaigned beside him, had much invested in keeping it that way.

After reading the available texts, both the ancient testimony and modern reconstructions, I too was dissatisfied with conclusions drawn to date and suspicious of an opacity that ought to have been black and white. Any study of the period does inevitably begin with the eyewitness historians, though they are often provided with a cursory, or even dismissive, accreditation in all but dedicated technical studies, principally because their archetypal accounts have vanished without exception. As a result, we heap too much expectation on the shoulders of the few tenderly revered and now scholar-chaperoned derivatives from the Roman era, though they represent second or third hand testimony, or hearsay further removed. Whilst readers may well be familiar with the names attached to these narratives, I was more interested in the 'when', 'how' and 'why' their books emerged, and in asking them a number of awkward questions and in looking them in the eye.

When we appreciate how far removed these Roman-era accounts were, both chronologically and culturally, from both their early Hellenistic-era histories (with whom they nevertheless courted and interbred) and the events of Alexander's day, a synthesis of his tale seems inevitable. Alexander's deeds remain no less impressive for that, but the themes and imagery interwoven into these portrayals are less unique than they first appear. As a result, this book captures the essence of my first thesis on the subject in which I voiced a rather fulsome polemic:

> As a rule, the orphaned, crippled, raped, betrayed, bankrupted, tortured and the left-behind had no historical voices. The eyewitness accounts of gnarled veterans, dispossessed townsfolk and mercenaries forced to resettle in the distant mud-brick Alexandrias at the ends of the empire, and the half-caste children conceived when the Macedonians swept through, had no forum nor papyrus for expression either. In Alexander's day, and through the Hellenistic era, kings did, and those sponsored by kings did, and ultimately it is their voices we hear.

As a historiographical *koinos topos* – a conventional rhetorical theme – it is certainly not new and is perhaps best summed up with a quote from a study aptly named *Rethinking History*: 'Put simply, history is never for itself; it was always for someone.'[73] Agenda-laden historians writing under royal or imperial patronage and protection are not difficult to find. But when the archetypal historian behind an account was himself *porphyrogennetos*, born in the royal purple, we must further question his partiality and the resulting lack of censorship.[74] But if we challenge the veracity of the few sources we have and those who fit this category, we would be undermining the very fabric of 'Alexander' and that would render decades, or even millennia, of historical interpretations redundant. If our platform of trust is gone, what is it that remains?

Smouldering beneath the embers of Alexander's still romantic ash is hot scholarly debate on every other aspect of his life and influence. At times scathing in peer critique, and evidently cyclical in opinion, arguments often fall into familiar furrows and risk losing their momentum when straightjacketed by the accepted boundaries of *communis opinio*. We may, as Demosthenes would have termed it, be 'boxing like barbarians'.[75] One of the results is that historians have adopted the 'standard model' of Alexander's intestacy and its effect on the Graeco-Macedonian world. This is a conclusion I found paradoxical when the footprints of his testament are still visible in texts. When triangulated back to its source, the rejection of the Will appears, once more, contrived. Put simply, the standard model doesn't quite work and much 'dark matter' remains undetected, to use a cosmographical analogy.

But whilst '… there is nothing so ridiculous that some philosopher has said it', there remains much to sensibly say about Alexander if we *are* prepared to radically rethink what we have, for 'the mistake is to believe the past is dead.'[76]

With no academic background, I represent the countless and curious 'self-educated' (and originally 'self-indoctrinated') readers who have over the past two millennia consumed Alexander with an appetite that never felt satiated. I graduated from an easy grazer of information, to an inquisitive browser of competing sources, to a chewer of contentious fat, and on to a voracious devourer of the still unexplained, in my own *gradus ad Parnassum* and a correspondent Masters degree, with a thesis built around the testament of Alexander the Great.[77] This book retraces the path of that ascent, and it was substantially written to answer my *own* questions about the era. The journey took me in many unexpected directions, some oblique, but all relevant to the heart of the investigation, and all retained here. I soon learned that fundamental to any understanding of Alexander's legacy is the twenty-three-year reign of his extraordinary father, Philip II, and the first twenty-three-year story of Alexander's equally remarkable successors who fought no less spectacular warfare for their piece of the vastly expanded Macedonian-governed empire.[78]

When adapting my thesis to a book, I decided to subordinate commercial considerations to freedom of expression and dump the rigidity of scholarly norms along the way; I did not shorten it, simplify it, or sterilise my style. Moreover, I attempted to inject some new momentum by challenging common notions and making little attempt at sidestepping the resulting controversy. Above all, I wanted to open up the themes under scrutiny in a broader way to try and bridge the divide between the academic studies by the subject specialists (some of which require advanced knowledge) and the more accessible and broader-based narratives on the era, as Alexander remains behind a 'poetic institution'.[79]

Widening the field of debate also provided the opportunity to expand on the rarely discussed influences at work on the writings of the period. As 'all roads lead to Rome', I soon found myself wandering through the conscience of its republic and the excesses of its imperium. But Alexander's legacy radiated further and wider still; into the metamorphose literature of the Middle Ages and the newly curious Renaissance, when authors and scribes with their diaskeuastic fingers attempted to rekindle the classical past, but more often than not they transported Alexander still further from his literary and historical origins.

In 1953 Charles Alexander Robinson published his 'fresh study of the entire ancient evidence', whilst wryly noting his shock at having promised to 'supply this Alexander harmony *shortly*'... back in 1932; Robinson never completed the second edition. His quoting from the preface of WW Tarn's 1948 study – 'The history of Alexander has never received much help from new material...' – reminds us that the new material was not so different from the old.[80] It is what we do with it that can make a fundamental change.

This book has likewise been long in the making, a decade or more of stolen moments and contemplations on the subject. Each was organically born, as I had not set out to challenge anyone or anything, and I would have been more than content to know Alexander's story had been faithfully captured on the original papyri and *pergamena*. But to borrow a phrase from Tacitus belonging to his *Annals*: '*maior e longinquo reverentia*'. Although everything *did* look reverently preserved when viewed from afar, on closer inspection I discovered that was simply not the case. So I set about radically rebalancing and recalibrating my investigative scales, lest I was seduced into weighing up too faithfully, too literally, or too unquestioningly, the testimony from the past.[81]

George Grote's 'first principles' of Greek history see the subject as '... essential to the formation of the liberal mind, but in its turn the liberal mind is religious in examining the evidence.'[82] True to his proposition, I soon realised that if I was to liberate my own thinking on the matter and pose a credible challenge to accepted interpretations, I would need to examine much more than the brief closing pages laid down by Alexander's early biographers, those who found, and those who wished us to find, Alexander 'guilty' of dying intestate. As any jury knows, guilt can only be established when the supporting evidence is beyond reasonable doubt. So here we bring the subject of historical fraud, duplicity and political manipulation into the vortex of our case, out of which emerges one unavoidable verdict: after these 2,340 years, the Last Will and Testament of Alexander III of Macedonia needs to be extracted from 'romance' and reinstated to its rightful place in mainstream history: Babylon in June 323 BCE, the gateway of the gods.

Virgil once asked the question: 'Why should fear seize the limbs before the bugle sounds?' I now think I know, and I sign this off with some trepidation knowing a phalanx of sharp and critical blades shall soon be marching in close-order my way.[83]

'History is a bag of tricks we play upon the dead,' remarked Voltaire.
To which the sophistic answer would be:
'On the contrary, history is a bag of tricks
the dead have played upon historians.'

The author

THE ART OF THE CORRECT SACRIFICE

Greek scholar and anthropologist, Dr Theodore Antikas, encouraged me to allow, as far as possible, the Greeks and Macedonians their onomastic 'identity', naming them on paper as they might have been hailed in the agora, rather than using the anglicised transliterations we have become accustomed to reading now.[84] And that *was* my initial aim. But as any author attempting this approach has discovered, the result is an unsatisfactory compromise; moreover, Attic, Aeolic, Doric, Ionic and the common *lingua franca* of Hellenistic *koine*, with its short vowels and diphthongs, might each have rendered different phonemic results (for this reason I have avoided using diacritics). In addition, Greek proper names were often Latinised in literature before becoming anglicised in, for example, the early *New Testament* translations that gave us many of today's forms, and this can leave us in macaronic territory.

Some of the enduring characters of our past need no help, for their names have remained steadfast despite the alchemy of vernacular languages: Curtius, Cato, Claudius, Eumenes, Demosthenes and Diogenes are relevant examples. Others have not: Ploútarchos (Πλούταρχος), a victim of a voiceless velar fricative, was Latinised to 'Plutarchus' (he had no complaint; he became a Roman citizen with *ius honorum*) and it has since been anglicised to the further-cropped 'Plutarch'.[85] In Pella, the seat of government of the late Macedonian Argead kings, we would have found Philippos not Philip, Alexandros not Alexander, and his boyhood friend and general, Ptolemaios, rather than Ptolemy. In their absences on campaign, the king's regent, Antipatros, written in English as 'Antipater' today, oversaw the kingdom, while in Athens (Athenai), the most populated city in the Mediterranean at the time, the metaphysical world lay at the feet of the broad-shouldered Platon (Plato) and his pupil, the remarkable polymath Aristoteles, better known to us as Aristotle.[86]

As for the epithets we now attach to the colourful dynasts of the Hellenistic era, I have been more faithful to the original Greek form, so they are written in italics to stress just that and to serve as a reminder that they *are* in fact just epithets (rather than formal patronymics, for example). So we see Antigonus II *Gonatas* (an epithet that possibly stemmed either from his birthplace, from being 'knock-kneed', or even from the name of the protective iron knee plate)[87] and Demetrius *Poliorketes*, and it is debatable whether these titles (some or all) would have been formally attached to, or recognised by, the individuals themselves during their own lifetimes. Alexander himself had to wait even longer for *Megas* – 'Great', *Magnus* in Latin – to be added to his name.[88] The Ptolemies: Ptolemy I *Soter* and Ptolemy II *Philadelphos* (308-246 BCE, 'sibling-loving' and here referring to his sister, Arsinoe II, whom he married in Phaoronic style), for example, *may* well have been so titled during their lives (or soon after) as they *were* distinguished by epithets, though numbering them in a dynastic line is a modern (but useful) convention.

In Roma to the Latins, the city of perhaps a million souls in its heyday, Livy started life as Livius when writing in the day of Octavianus (Octavian, later 'Augustus'), and Pliny signed as Plinius, and he dedicated his book to the new *princeps*, Titus, the son of Vespasianus, our Vespasian.[89] Yet Greeks were still influential in the Roman literary world where we would have encountered the influential Arrianos, rather than Arrian, Appianos, now shortened to Appian, and the more melodious Herodianos as opposed to today's Herodian. Convention has, nevertheless, left us with original Latinised forms such as Ammianus Marcellinus, a Greek who unusually chose to write in Latin (perhaps to more convincingly segue Tacitus). That result might have seemed unfair to the Roman lyric poet Horatius whose name we spell, without his consultation, a starchy 'Horace', or in Victorian England as 'Horatio' even. Each chronicled, or poetised, a part of Rome's own story whilst Strabon (Strabo), the apparently squint-eyed geographer, walked the unrecognisable ruins of a Novum Ilium which were believed by many (not Strabo) to cover legendary Troy – Troia or Ilios to the Greeks.[90]

I have also used familiar spellings for place names for historic cities and regions that no longer carry the name today (Cilicia not Kilikia, Cappadocia not Kappadokia, though is its still informally called Kapadokya in Turkey today) and I maintained the more common Latinised forms for locations in Greece (thus Laurium not Lavrion, Phalerum not Phaleron, and Cape Taenarum rather than Tainaron). To attempt any reversion of Persian and Egyptian titles would have required a whole chapter dedicated to toponymic uncertainty and more exotic fonts besides, for their consonants are not the same as ours and their vowel sounds are regionally distinct; the result would be, to quote TE Lawrence tacking the issue in his *Seven Pillars of Wisdom*, 'a washout for the world'.[91]

For consistency and for copyright considerations when using published quotes and longer extracts from the extant accounts, I have therefore remained with the accepted orthography for handling Greek and Latin textual imports into English, unless italicised. Nevertheless, translations of ancient texts through the ages yielded vastly different outcomes as vernacular languages were evolving and depending on whether the secondary historians, medieval scribes and even modern writers, were metaphrasing (a 'word by word' attempt at translation), paraphrasing (translation with 'latitude') or imitating ('the liberty to forsake' both 'words and sense'), as John Dryden would have termed it. This is a theme I have emphasised in detail in the chapter titled *The Precarious Path of Pergamena and Papyrus*, to give the reader a sense of the linguistic drift that plays a part in the investigation. The challenge of achieving the desired translation outcome – more often than not a compromised middle ground – has been appropriately termed 'the art of the correct sacrifice'.[92]

Below is short concordance with additional and relevant examples of how the original Greek, Latin, or Latinised Greek names (including Hellenised Persian names), have been rendered into the modern alphabet, beside the familiar anglicised forms appearing in the book.

I have not included examples in which a soft 'C' has simply supplanted 'K' (Socrates-Sokrates, Cleopatra-Kleopatra) or where 'U' replaces 'O' (Antigonus-Antigonos, Hieronymus-Hieronymos), or both (Seleucus-Seleukos, Craterus-Krateros, Cleitarchus-Kleitarchos).

Names as they appear in this book	Greek/Latin form in the modern alphabet	Names as they appear in this book	Greek/Latin form in the modern alphabet
Aeacides	Aiakides	Hecataeus	Hekataios
Aelian	Ailianos	Lucan	Lucanus
Aesop	Aisopos	Lucian	Lucianus
Aeschines	Aiskhines	Meleager	Meleagros
Aeschylus	Aiskhulos	Menander	Menandros
Achilles	Akhilleus	Ovid	Ovidius
Cassander	Kassandros	Pindar	Pindaros
Cyrus	Kyros	Pompey	Pompeius
Darius	Dareios	Porphyry	Porphyrios
Epicurus	Epikouros	Thucydides	Thoukydides
Euclid	Eukleides	Timaeus	Timaios
Hesiod	Hesiodos	Virgil	Vergilius

LIGHTING DIM CANDLES IN THE DARK ABYSS: ACCESSING THE EVIDENCE

For the benefit of those wishing to retrace my investigative steps, bibliographical citations with explanatory details are provided as chapter endnotes. I have kept these as brief as practically possible following Goralski's logic: 'The impact of and value of a paper is measured by the amount of material mentioned in it that you no longer have to read, rather than the other way around.'[93]

Ideally, for readers who do not have the classical texts covering events either side of Alexander's death, I would have reproduced them here. But their length and the associated copyright restrictions made this impractical. The increasing availability of texts online, however, provides a solution. The relevant extracts are numbered (T1) to (T27) and they are referred to at pertinent points in the chapters, with links to them provided below. Here I have used their popular English titles, though in the bibliography I have given their Greek or Roman names as well.

A more detailed discussion of these ancient authors can be found in chapters titled *Hierarchic Historians and Alexandrian Alchemy* and *Classicus Scriptor, Rhetoric and Rome*, with a focus on the anonymous *Pamphlet* and the *Journal*, which become our central witnesses, in chapter titled *Guardians and Ghosts of the Ephemerides*.

A general and more comprehensive list of Alexander sources can be found at:
www.attalus.org/info/sources.html
https://sites.google.com/site/alexandersources/home

SECTION 1: THE *PAMPHLET*

(T1) The content of the *Pamphlet* as preserved at the end of the *Metz Epitome*.
The relevant section is 87-123; a translation at:
https://sites.google.com/site/alexandersources/romance-and-other-sources/liber-de-morte

A recommended comparison is the translation in W Heckel and JC Yardley, *Alexander the Great: Historical Sources in Translation,* Blackwell Publishing, pp 281-289. This publication appears in the bibliography as Heckel-Yardley (2004).

(T2) The content of the *Pamphlet* as it appears in Recension A of the *Greek Alexander Romance*.
The relevant section is 3.30-3.34; translation at www.attalus.org/translate/alexander3d.html
The full *Greek Alexander Romance* can be accessed at www.attalus.org/info/alexander.html

A recommended comparison is the *Greek Alexander Romance* translation and commentary by R Stoneman, Penguin Books, 1991, pp 148-156. This publication appears in the bibliography as Stoneman (1991).

SECTION 2: THE *JOURNAL*

(T3) The *Journal* detail as it appears in Arrian *Anabasis*.
The relevant section is 7.25.1-7.26.1; translations at:
https://sites.google.com/site/alexandersources/arrian/arrian7b
https://en.wikisource.org/wiki/The_Anabasis_of_Alexander/Book_VII/Chapter_XXV

(T4) The parallel *Journal* detail as it appears in Plutarch *Life of Alexander*.
The relevant section is 76.1-77.1; translation at:
http://penelope.uchicago.edu/Thayer/E/Roman/Texts/Plutarch/Lives/Alexander*/10.html

(T5) Additional *Journal* detail appears in Aelian *Historical Miscellany*.
The relevant section is 3.23; translations at:
https://sites.google.com/site/alexandersources/minor/aelian---varia-historia
http://penelope.uchicago.edu/aelian/varhist3.xhtml

SECTION 3: ALEXANDER'S DEATH ACCORDING TO THE VULGATE GENRE

(T6) Diodorus *Library of World History.*
The relevant section is 17.116.1-118.4; translation at:
http://penelope.uchicago.edu/Thayer/E/Roman/Texts/Diodorus_
Siculus/17F*.html

(T7) Curtius *History of Alexander the Great of Macedon.*
The relevant section is 10.5.1-10.5.7 translations at:
www.attalus.org/info/curtius.html
https://babel.hathitrust.org/cgi/pt?id=mdp.39015008158407;seq=525

(T8) Justin's epitome of Gnaeus Pompeius Trogus *Philippic History.*
The relevant section is 12.13-12.15; translations at:
www.forumromanum.org/literature/justin/english/trans12.html
www.attalus.org/translate/justin11.html#12.1

The Vulgate detail was also briefly (and dismissively) mentioned by Plutarch and Arrian, though their biographies were not Vulgate-genre accounts.

(T9) Arrian *The Campaigns of Alexander.*
The relevant section is 7.27-7.28; translations at:
https://sites.google.com/site/alexandersources/arrian/arrian7b
https://en.wikisource.org/wiki/The_Anabasis_of_Alexander/Book_VII/
Chapter_XXVII

(T10) Plutarch *Life of Alexander.*
The relevant section is 77.2-77.5; translation at:
http://penelope.uchicago.edu/Thayer/E/Roman/Texts/Plutarch/Lives/
Alexander*/10.html

SECTION 4: THE INFIGHTING AT BABYLON FOLLOWING ALEXANDER'S DEATH THAT LED UP TO THE BABYLONIAN SETTLEMENT AND THE FORMAL DISTRIBUTION OF THE EMPIRE

(T11) Curtius *History of Alexander the Great of Macedon.*
The relevant section is 10.5.7-10.10.20; translations at:
www.attalus.org/info/curtius.html
https://babel.hathitrust.org/cgi/pt?id=mdp.39015008158407;view=1up;seq
=535

(T12) Justin's epitome of Gnaeus Pompeius Trogus *Philippic History.*
The relevant section is 13.1-13.4; translations at:
www.forumromanum.org/literature/justin/english/trans13.html
www.attalus.org/translate/justin1.html

(T13) Diodorus *Library of World History.*
The relevant section is 18.2-18.4; translation at:
http://penelope.uchicago.edu/Thayer/E/Roman/Texts/Diodorus_
Siculus/18A*.html

(T14) Arrian *Events After Alexander* **as précised in Photius** *Library of History* – **(***Myriobiblion* **or** *Bibliotheke***), Codex 92.**
A translation at:
www.livius.org/sources/content/arrian/arrians-events-after-alexander-
photius-excerpt/

(T15) Photius' précis of Dexippus' epitome of Arrian *Events After Alexander***, Codex 82.**
A translation at:
www.tertullian.org/fathers/photius_03bibliotheca.htm#81

SECTION 5: THE DIVISION OF THE EMPIRE FOLLOWING THE SETTLEMENT AT BABYLON

(T16) Diodorus *Library of World History.*
The relevant section is 18.2.1-18.5; translation at:
http://penelope.uchicago.edu/Thayer/E/Roman/Texts/Diodorus_
Siculus/18A*.htm

(T17) Arrian *Events After Alexander* **as précised in Photios'** *Library of History* **(***Myriobiblion* **(or** *Bibliotheke***), Codex 92.**
Translation at:
www.livius.org/sources/content/arrian/arrians-events-after-alexander-
photius-exce rpt/

(T18) Photius précis of Dexippus' epitome of Arrian *Events After Alexander***, Codex 82.**
Translation at:
www.tertullian.org/fathers/photius_03bibliotheca.htm#81

(T19) Curtius *History of Alexander the Great of Macedon.*
The relevant section is 10.6.1-10.9.21; translations at:
www.attalus.org/info/curtius.html
https://babel.hathitrust.org/cgi/pt?id=mdp.39015008158407;seq=563

(T20) Justin's epitome of Gnaeus Pompeius Trogus *Philippic History.*
The relevant section is 13.4-13.24; translations at:
www.forumromanum.org/literature/justin/english/trans13.html
www.attalus.org/translate/justin1.html

SECTION 6: PRE-DEATH PORTENTS

(T21) Plutarch *Life of Alexander.*
The relevant section is 73-75; translation at:
http://penelope.uchicago.edu/Thayer/E/Roman/Texts/Plutarch/Lives/
Alexander*/10.html

(T22) Diodorus *Library of World History.*
The relevant section is 17.112.1-17.116.7; translation at:
http://penelope.uchicago.edu/Thayer/E/Roman/Texts/Diodorus_
Siculus/17F*.html

(T23) Arrian *The Campaigns of Alexander.*
The relevant section is 7.16.5-7.24.4; translations at:
https://sites.google.com/site/alexandersources/arrian/arrian7b
https://en.wikisource.org/wiki/The_Anabasis_of_Alexander/Book_VII/
Chapter_XVI

(T24) Justin's epitome of Gnaeus Pompeius Trogus *Philippic History.*
The relevant section is 12.13.1-12.13.6 translations at:
www.forumromanum.org/literature/justin/english/trans12.html
www.attalus.org/translate/justin11.html#12.1

SECTION 7: ALEXANDER'S 'LAST PLANS'

(T25) Diodorus *Library of World History.*
The relevant section is 18.4.1-18.4.6; translation at:
http://penelope.uchicago.edu/Thayer/E/Roman/Texts/Diodorus_
Siculus/18A*.html

NOTES

1. Quoting AT Olmstead *History of the Persian Empire*, 1948, pp 523-533, published posthumously; he died in 1945.
2. Quoting MB Hatzopoulos *La Macédoine: Géographie, historique, Langue, Cultes et croyances, Institutions.* (Travaux 2) De Boccard, 2006, p 93, as translated in Briant (1974) p 167. The juxtapositioning of the two extracts was inspired by Briant (1974) pp 166-167.
3. As examples of the early papers on the Vergina tombs after Andronikos' finds see Andronikos (1981, 1984 and 1987), Hammond (1978), Musgrave (1991), Barr-Sharrar (1991), Carney (1991), Adams (1991), Borza (1991); a comprehensive list of studies on the cremains is given in Antikas-Wynn Antikas (2014) *Introduction.*
4. Tomb I contained the inhumed (non-cremated) remains of a man, a woman and a baby; discussion in Musgrave (1991) pp 7-8; see Antikas' report below which contradicts the number. In the 1980s Professor Musgrave was only provided with less than ten per cent of the total bone fragments now known to exist (see author's note below); his conclusions of what he had were correct; three individual humans. The belief that the remains belonged to only three individuals was wrong; see *Postscript: The Return to Aegae* at the end of the book for discussion.
5. The wound received at Methone was almost twenty years before Philip died; Justin 7.6.14 (and mentioned without place or date at Plutarch 3.2).
6. The skull showed signs of maxillary and frontal sinusitis.
7. See Musgrave (1991) p 5 footnote 12 and Carney (1991) p 18 footnote 4 for arguments on the ages of Eurydice and her mother Cynnane.
8. Homer, *Iliad* 23.83-84,91-92. For the significance of the amphora, see *Iliad* 24.73-77. The bones of Achilles and Patroclus finally lay together in a gold amphora; *Odysseia* 24.73-77.
9. Vergina had formerly been two settlements, Koutles and Barbes.
10. As an example see the report in *The Free Lance Star*, 10 December, 1977, in which Prof. Demetrios Kanatsoulis (and Fotis Petsas) refute the claim that Vergina was Aegae.
11. Hammond *Tombs* (1991) p 78 for the stoa and cenotaph tumulus at the centre of the Great Tumulus.
12. Andronikos-Fotiadis (1978) p 35 for the history of the early excavation. Hammond *Tombs* (1991) p 75 for the original tumulus covering Tombs I and II. Hammond *Tombs* (1991) p 78 for the stoa remains.
13. Quoting from the official website of the Polycentric Museum of Aegae.
14. As reported in Antikas-Wynn Antikas, 2014, p 3 and p 4; Plinius had reported on the properties of asbestos being known to the Greeks.
15. For the area covered by Aegae and the size and structure of the royal palace see Lane Fox (2011) chapter 15; Hammond (1978) p 332 stated 300 tumuli but much work has been done since.
16. Quoting Hammond (1978) p 339 on 'world-shaking event'.
17. Diodorus 17.2.1 confirmed Alexander 'dedicated himself' to his father's funeral.
18. Andronikos-Fotiadas (1978) for the state and preservation of the bones and blue colouring suggesting the presence of purple cloth and Hammond (1978) p 350 for discussion; see *Iliad* 24.72 and 24.795-796 for similar treatment.
19. Director of Research and Head of the Laboratory of Archaeometry at the Democritus Institute, Giannis Maniatis, who conducted the analysis, believes that these residues are from a mask 'of complex design, using laminated fabric that is found for the first time in Macedonia, meticulously crafted from six or seven layers of huntite and porphyra, and which Philip wore during religious ceremonies, possibly as high priest of the Orphic mysteries.' Quoting Archaeology News Network.
20. Homer *Odyssey* 24.72 for the treatment of Achilles' bones, *Iliad* 24.795-6 for Hector's burial and purple cloth and *Iliad* 23.171-76 for Patroclus' larnax. Hammond (1978) p 337 for the horse remains and Andronikos-Fotiadis (1978) p 36; Hammond (1991) p 95 and Hammond *Tombs* (1991) p 76 and for the suggestion that the assassins' remains were found above the tomb. Justinus 9.7.11 and 11.2.1 for corroborating evidence. Hammond (1978) p 337 for the chariot horses suggestion; see also Antikas (2002) *Horse and Heroes in the Tomb of Philip II*, Minerva 12(1): pp 46-49. As Carney (2006) pp 85-96 points out, the mistreatment of the bodies of the dead featured prominently in the *Iliad*; 22.395-404 for Achilles' maltreatment of Hector, 23.20-3 and 24.14.21 as the most notable examples. The later 'over-mound' is itself resonant of Achilles' wish that the burial tumuli of both him and Patroclus be so covered following his own funeral; *Iliad* 23.245 ff, following the observation in Hammond (1978) p 333.
21. Plato *Laws* 947d-e; discussed in Hammond *Tombs* (1991) p 73 and Hammond (1991) p 54; the tombs he describes are remarkably similar to the Vergina finds. It was not unique; the tomb of King Seuthes III of the Odrysian kingdom in Thrace and only discovered in 2004,

exhibits similar burial rites, though he did marry a Macedonian wife and was long exposed to Macedonians under Lysimachus.

22. Hammond (1989) p 219 quoting M Andronikos. Arrian 1.11.7, Diodorus 17.18.1 suggested Alexander had taken the 'strongest of the panoplies' from Troy, which hardly fits the ornate shield description; the remains of two further shields were found: Borza-Palagia (2007) p 113 for the remnants of three shields.

23. Hammond (1989) p 218 following the report of Andronikos for the list of weapons and armour and Andronikos-Fotiadis (1978) for fuller list; a gold myrtle wreath, diadem and second larnax were also found in the antechamber.

24. Fredericksmeyer (1981) pp 331-332 for the chryselephantine statues and the total numbers; Lehman (1980) points out many such heads have been discovered elsewhere blurring any argument that they directly represented the statues Philip commissioned at Olympia. Chryselephantine is amalgam of ivory and gold leaf, often studded with precious stones.

25. Quoting Adams (1980) as it appears in Antikas-Wynn Antikas (2014) *Paleopathology*.

26. Tomb II measures in total (externally) 9.5 x 4.46 x 5.3 metres high: 31.35 x 14.7 x 17.5 feet.

27. Quoting Antikas-Wynn Antikas (2014) *Introduction*. Hammond (1991) p 98 for external dimensions.

28. Hatzopoulos' report, from which this quote is extracted, appeared in *Tekmeria*, Volume 9, pp 91-118, 2008 and is provided in full in Antikas-Wynn Antikas (2014) *Introduction*.

29. Discussion of the Great Tumulus in chapter titled *Lifting the Shroud of Parrhasios*. It is thought by some scholars to have been constructed by Lysimachus, Macedonian king ca. 285 BCE (so Hammond (1991) p 78) or Antigonus II *Gonatas* the king of Macedonia from ca. 277 to 239 BCE, who witnessed the damage inflicted on the more exposed tombs in the necropolis by marauding Gauls in 274/3 BCE. He regained control of Aegae the following year and a fourth tomb discovered in 1980 may therefore be his. Following Carney (2002) p 108 for the association with *Gonatas* with the Great Tumulus at Vergina. This covered smaller earlier tumuli housing the tombs of the kings. Carney-Ogden (2010) pp 119-121 for Tomb III discussions. Adams (1991) p 28 for the format of the Great Tumulus. Plutarch *Pyrrhus* 26.6 for the earlier looting by Gallic mercenaries. Borza-Palagia (2007) p 82 footnote 5 for detail of Tomb IV and its dating. Also see Andronikos-Fotiadis (1978) p 35 for *Gonatas'* own tomb and his rationale for building the Great Tumulus.

30. The *Alexandreis* of Gautier de Chatillon, verses 2.195-200.

31. Gudeman *Greeks* (1894) p 52.

32. Full chronological discussion in Depuydt (1997) pp 117-135, Hannah (2005) p 95, Stoneman (1991) p 159. Arrian 7.28.1 for the Olympiad reckoning. The dating sources are cuneiform tablet BM 45962 and the later tablet, BM 34075, a fragment of a Babylonian astronomical diary for 323/2 BCE. It included a note for 29 Ayyaru that 'the king died'. The Summer Palace might better be termed the 'Outer Palace' for its defensive nature, see discussion in Reade (2000) p 203.

33. Quoting Grafton-Blair (1998) p 32.

34. See chapter titled, *The Precarious Path of Pergamena and Papyrus* for more on Poggio Bracciolini.

35. Following Hammond *Journal* (1989) p 158 for the singular use of '*Journal*'. Detailed discussion on the *Journal* in chapter titled *Guardians and Ghosts of the Ephemerides*.

36. Curtius 10.7.1-3 and 10.9.20 used the term *bellorum civilium Macedonibus* when describing the first at Babylon following Alexander's death.

37. Detailed discussion of the Pamphlet in chapter titled *Guardians and Ghosts of the Ephemerides*. For the importance of the *symposia* at the Macedonian court see Thomas (2007) pp 82, 87, 97 and Borza (1995) pp 159-169, F Pownall's discussion in Carney-Ogden (2010) pp 55-63. Heckel (1988) p 10 for the guest list. Full conspiracy text in the *Metz Epitome* 87-101 and *Romance* 31-32.

38. Argead was the hereditary tribal name of the royal line dating to the 7th century BCE Macedonian king, Perdiccas I. The Macedonian royal line retained its hereditary name, Temenid, allegedly stemming from Temenus of Argos, an alleged ancestor of Perdiccas I; Herodotus 8.137 More detail in chapter titled *The Reborn Wrath of Peleus' Son*.

39. Fraser (1996) p 206 for discussion on its title. The original name of the archetypal text is unknown; detailed discussion in chapter titled *Mythoi, Muthodes and the Birth of Romance*. Pseudo-Callisthenes is the popular alternative name though the work was attributed to other notable writers; also discussion in Fraser (1996) p 206 and detailed discussion in chapter titled *Mythoi, Muthodes and the Birth of Romance*.

40. Textual similarities which argue for a common Vulgate source discussion in Bosworth (1983) p 156 and in JE Atkinson (1994) p 25 with a useful summary of earlier studies in Brown (1950) citing the works of Müller, Schwartz and Jacoby in particular.

41. Diodorus 17.117.4 and Arrian 7.26.3 for *toi kratistoi* from *kratistos*: 'the strongest or noblest'. Latin interpretation of that from Curtius 10.4.5 *qui esset optimus* (the 'best') and *dignissimus* (broadly the 'most worthy') from Justin 12.15.

42. For the funeral games or contests see Curtius 10.5.5, Diodorus 17.117.4, Arrian 7.26.3 reporting 'other historians'. Justin (so we assume Trogus) 12.15.6-8 gave a darker more expansive account of the disputes and slaughter that the dying Alexander expected would follow.

43. *Iliad* 23. Some scholars believe the Homeric funeral games (pre 1200 BCE) led directly to the founding of the Pan-Hellenic athletics contests, the Olympic, Pythian, Isthmian and Nemean Games. Roller (1981) pp 107-119.

44. Quoting from Justin 12.15, translation by Rev. J Selby Watson, 1853; Curtius 10.6-10.10 and Justin 13.1 for the sentiment in Babylon.

45. Plutarch 77.2. Olympias' actions are detailed by other historians and discussed in later chapters.

46. For Onesicritus' fear see *Metz Epitome* 97. A *komos* was the traditional Macedonian drinking party or symposium. The theme of 'fearful historians' is reiterated in the Vulgate texts at Curtius 10.10.18-19, Diodorus 17.118.2, Justin 12.13.10.

47. Cicero *Philippicae* 9.5: 'The life of the dead is set in the memory of the living'.

48. The 'many and few' sentiment echoes that of Stewart (1993) p 1.

49. Lane Fox (1973), Preface, p. 11

50. Historians consider the Hellenistic era commenced variously at the Battle of Gaugamela when Darius III was displaced, at Darius' death, or at the death of Alexander in 323 BCE, or at the Battle of Ipsus in 301 BCE; and it ended when Rome's republic became 'empire' after the Battle of Actium in 31 BCE, or when it absorbed the last Hellenistic kingdom of Egypt (Aigyptos to the Greeks) after the Battle of Alexandria, 30 BCE.

51. For the numbers of fragments and writers, see Wilken (1967) and quoting from the Introduction by E Borza p XXV.

52. Reemphasising the observation made in Bosworth-Baynham (2000) p 3.

53. The saying has been attributed to Aeschylus as well as a host of modern politicians.

54. Plutarch *Pericles* 15, translation by J Dryden, 1683.

55. Livy 1.1.34, Dionysius of Heraclea (or Pseudo-Dionysius) *Ars Rhetorica* 11.2, quoting Thucydides. 'Historiosophy' is a term coined by Gershom Scholem. 'Solemn' was Cicero's description of Thucydides in the fragmentary *Hortensius*; see Dominik (1997) p 36.

56. Polybius 16.14.6-8. Polybius' exact dates of birth and death are unknown. An 'early' school proposes he was born ca. 208 BCE and died in the mid-120s BCE and a 'late' school proposes ca. 200 or 186 to 116 BCE. Discussion in Eckstein (1992).

57. Possibly originating with WS Holt, professor of history at Washington University, or Charles Beard, cited in a communication by RF Smith, *American Historical Review* 94, October 1989, 1247.

58. Samuel Butler *Erewhon Revisited Twenty Years Later, Both by the Original Discoverer of the Country and by His Son*, 1901, chapter 14. It was the Athenian tragic poet Agathon who is said to have quipped, 'even the gods cannot change the past'.

59. Robinson (1953), Jacoby (1926-1958), Müller (1853-1870).

60. Quoting Heller-Roazen (2002) p 151.

61. Following and quoting Bosworth *A in the East* (1996) p 32.

62. Quoting Grafton (1990) p 69.

63. Winckelmann's 1764 *History of the Art of Antiquity* pushed the *Altertumswissenschaft* (science of antiquity) argument into new territory, as did the philological arguments of Freidrich August Wolf (1759-1824) articulated in his *Darstellung der Altertumswissenschaft*.

64. Quoting Braudel (1969) p 68 for discussion of the social sciences being drawn into historiography, including Henri Berr's *Revue de synthèse historique* of 1900.

65. Tertullian *Apology* 19.2.5-6, full text in Fortenbaugh-Schütrumpf (2000) p 127.

66. Quoting Macaulay (1828).

67. Discussion on Scaliger's work on Berossus and Manetho in Grafton (1990) pp 100-102.

68. Speyer (1971) following discussion by Grafton (1990) p 70.

69. Garraghan (1946), McCullagh (1984) and Shafer (1974) for examples of the method checklists referred to.

70. Carr (1961) p 12 and Carr (1987) p 23, in the incomplete second edition of the 1961 treatise.

71. A statement credited to both Voltaire and André Gide: *Croyez ceux qui cherchent la vérité, doutez de ceux qui la trouvent.*

72. The first recorded use of the epithet 'Great' came from the Roman playwright Plautus in the *Mostelleria* 775 in ca. 200 BCE. It may of course have been in use before but Greek literature did not employ it and was somewhat more hostile to his memory.

73. Quoting K Jenkins *Rethinking History*, Routledge, London 1991, p 21.

74. An honorific of the Byzantine age literally meaning 'born in the purple' and stemming from the Tyrian murex trade in purple dye.

75. Demosthenes *Philippic* 1.40. He was alluding to the reactive boxing style of barbarian boxers who are always one step behind their opponents' moves and strategy, and here elating it to

Athens' amateurish opposition to Philip II of Macedonia.

76. Cicero *Epistolarum ad Atticum*, 9.10.4 and *de Divinatione*. Quoting Highet (1949) p 455.

77. 'Steps to Parnassus', the highest peak in central Greece; it has come to depict a long steep path of learning or instruction; a thanks to Professor Carol Thomas for inspiring me to use it.

78. That is twenty-three years from Alexander's death in 323 BCE to the aftermath of the Battle of Ipsus in 301 BCE.

79. Quoting M Pallottino in his 1957 review of DH Lawrence's 1927 *Etruscan Places*, Olive Press, London, pp 13-14, including the reference to a 'poetic intuition'; following its use by Barker-Rasmussen (2000) *The Etruscans*, Blackwell Publishing.

80. See discussion in Robinson (1953) Preface p VII, quoting Tarn (1948).

81. Tacitus 1.47.

82. Following Momigliano (1966) p 70.

83. Virgil *Aeneid* 11.376.

84. Quoting the terminology from the preface of Stewart (1993) p XXXV. Prof Theodore Antikas' education includes degrees in veterinary science and in law, politics, economics and a PhD in medicine. He is the author of books on classical Greece including a study of Poseidippus of Pella.

85. See Hamilton (1971) Introduction: Plutarch had been granted Roman citizenship with possibly an honorary Roman consulship and also a Greek magistrate and archon in his municipality.

86. According to Diogenes Laertius *Plato* 4, Plato was so named by his wrestling coach because of his broad shoulders; *platon* means 'broad' in Attic Greek.

87. Discussion on the epithet *Gonatas* in Iossif-Chankowski-Lorber (2007) p 418.

88. The first recorded use of the epithet 'great' came from the Roman playwright Plautus *Mostelleria* 775 in ca. 200 BCE. It may of course have been in use before but Greek literature did not employ it and was somewhat more hostile to his memory; more in chapter titled *The Rebirth of the Wrath of Peleus' Son*.

89. The census of Augustus in his own *Deeds of Divine Augustus* 15 dating to 5 BCE recorded 320,000 adult plebs in the city to whom he paid 240 *sestertii* each; accounting for women, children, slaves and non-citizens, the population may well have exceeded 1 million.

90. Strabo's original name is unknown, though in Greek *strabon* means 'squint-eyed'. Strabo stated, upon visiting the alleged site of Troy , known as Ilium to the Romans, 'This is not the site of ancient Ilium, if one considers the matter in accordance with Homer's account'; Strabo 13.1.27, translated by HC Hamilton and W Falconer, published by Henry G Bohn, London, 1854. Strabo 13.1.1 and at 13.1.38 he additionally voiced the view that no trace remained; see chapter titled *Classicus Scriptor, Rhetoric and Rome* for further detail.

91. TE Lawrence *Seven Pillars of Wisdom*, Doubleday reprint 1991, p 21; its use inspired by the same in *A Companion to Science, Technology, and Medicine in Ancient Greece and Rome*, Wiley, 2016, Introduction p 6.

92. Quoting Wolfgang Schwaderwaldt in the Bryn Mawr Classical Review. June 2010, review of Mindt N (2008) *Manfred Fuhrmann als Vermittler der Antike: ein Beitrag zu Theorie und Praxis des Ubersetzens*. Transformationen der Antike, Bd5, Berlin, New York, p 3.

93. Quoting Goralski (1989) p 83.

HISTORIANS: WHEN THEY LIVED

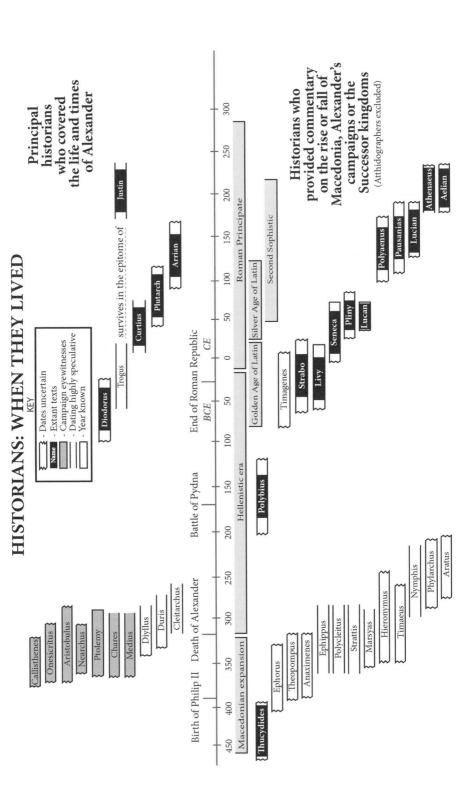

Principal historians who covered the life and times of Alexander

Historians who provided commentary on the rise or fall of Macedonia, Alexander's campaigns or the Successor kingdoms
(Atthidographers excluded)

KEY

Name

- Dates uncertain
- Extant texts
- Campaign eyewitnesses
- Dating highly speculative
- Year known

survives in the epitome of

Callisthenes
Onesicritus
Aristobulus
Nearchus
Ptolemy
Chares
Medius
Diyllus
Duris
Cleitarchus
Justin
Trogus
Diodorus
Curtius
Plutarch
Arrian

Ephorus
Theopompus
Anaximenes
Ephippus
Polycleitus
Strattis
Marsyas
Hieronymus
Timaeus
Nymphis
Phylarchus
Aratus
Polybius
Timagenes
Strabo
Livy
Seneca
Pliny
Lucan
Polyaenus
Pausanias
Lucian
Athenaeus
Aelian

Thucydides

Macedonian expansion
Hellenistic era
Golden Age of Latin
Silver Age of Latin
Roman Principate
Second Sophistic

Birth of Philip II   Death of Alexander   Battle of Pydna   End of Roman Republic

BCE   CE

450 400 350 300 250 200 150 100 50 0 50 100 150 200 250 300

1

THE REBORN WRATH OF PELEUS' SON

Would Alexander have been content to die without making a Will and without planning for a succession?

Historians have been trying to unveil the man behind the legend for the past two millennia, and the opinion of every age has, to some degree, reshaped Alexander III of Macedonia.

What did it mean to be descended from the Macedonian royal house with an elite Greek education? What was Alexander's relationship with his father, his men, their high-ranking generals, and with his entourage of court 'friends', diviners, philosophers and poets? And what part did Homer, Herodotus, Xenophon, and Aristotle's view of the barbarian Persian Empire play in his character development?

We look at Alexander's policy, his behaviour and mindset on campaign to question whether this correlates with the man who allegedly declined to recognise his sons as heirs and failed to provide succession instructions to his generals.

'My vast army marched into Babylon in peace; I did not permit anyone to frighten the people of Sumer and Akkad. I sought the welfare of the city of Babylon and all its sacred centres. As for the citizens of Babylon, upon whom he [Nabonidus] imposed a corvée, which was not the god's wish and not befitting them, [1] relieved their weariness and freed them from service. Marduk, the great Lord, rejoiced over my deeds.'[1]

The Cyrus Cylinder

'A man, he shunned humanity; it seemed
A trifle to stand highest among mortals.'[2]

Gautier de Chatillon *Alexandreis*

'… the gods and heroes begrudge that a single man in his godless pride should be king of Hellas and Asia, too.'[3]

Themistocles, Herodotus *Histories*

Babylon, mid-June 323 BCE, the 'gateway of the gods'; an ancient city already two millennia old and which, according to legend, was founded by the Mesopotamian deity, Marduk.[4] This was now the Macedonian campaign capital and the staging point for the planned expeditions to Arabia and westward to the Pillars of Heracles. Inside the lofty baked-brick and bitumen-bound walls, the city had become a hive of activity with trepidatious envoys arriving from nations across the known world, those conquered and those expecting to be.[5] Prostrated in the Summer Palace of Nebuchadnezzar II on the east bank of the Euphrates, wracked by fever and having barely survived another night, King Alexander III, the ruler of Macedonia for twelve years and seven months, had his senior officers congregate at his bedside.[6] Abandoned by Tyche who governed fortune, and the healing god Asclepius, he finally acknowledged he was dying.[7]

Growing fear and uncertainty filled the portent-laden air. Priests interpreted omens, livers and entrails as whispered intrigues and newly divulged ambitions filled heavy sweat-soaked nights. Life signs were tenuous; the king's breathing was almost imperceptible. Finally, Alexander, born under the watch of two eagles that signified two great empires, and birthed from a womb sealed with the image of a lion,[8] was publicly pronounced dead and the prophecy of the Chaldean seers came to pass.[9]

The ancient city founded over 1,000 years before the legendary fall of Troy was a fitting stage for the death of the king who had conquered the empire of the Persian Great Kings and vanquished their progeny, for Alexander had married daughters of both Darius III (king 336-330 BCE) and Artaxerxes III Ochus (king 359/358-338 BCE). The backdrop was no mud-brick town in the eastern regions the Greeks loosely termed

'India', or windswept pass in the upper satrapy of Bactria, or, as the Greek historian Plutarch put it, 'that nameless village in a foreign land must needs have become the tomb of Alexander', but the greatest opulence the world had to offer.[10] It was appropriately theatrical and it was uniquely 'Alexander' and yet the reporting is wholly unconvincing as a conclusion to his story. Alexander's final days should have provided us with the rich and colourful imagery we read in the campaign accounts, for by mid-summer 323 BCE, warships, grain ships, pack animals, cavalry mounts and Indian elephants were being prepared for a new Arabian expedition, while the citadel guarding wealth the Greeks had never imagined was being mined for funds to pay what had become a multinational army.

Gossiping eunuchs, concubines and wives frequented the Summer Palace of Nebuchadnezzar II (Naboukhodonosor to the Greeks, reigned ca. 605-562 BCE). Bodyguards, physicians, slaves, scribes, cooks, tasters and royal pages filed through anterooms filled with waiting ambassadors who brought dispatches from distant lands at the borders of the known world. According to Plutarch, the palace was now full of 'soothsayers (*magoi*), seers (*manteis*), sacrificers, purifiers (*kathartai*) and prognosticators'; by-products of the king's late obsession with death-harbouring portents.[11] As events had already shown on more than one occasion, it was the seers and doctors, fearful of providing inaccurate divinations or ineffective prognoses, who had the most to lose: their lives.[12] So no doubt spells (*epoidai*) and incantations (*epagogai*) had been covertly cast as complex fears and political intrigues manifested themselves in dark corridors as Alexander's health continued to deteriorate. Indeed, the surviving texts ought to have replicated the drama captured in the final chapter of the *Cyropaedia* of Xenophon (ca. 430-354 BCE), the vivid and laudatory portrayal of the former Persian Great King.[13]

Cyrus the Great (reigned 559-530 BCE) becomes significant to our case, for Alexander inherited the Achaemenid Empire he had founded and he appears to have become an admirer. The *Cyropaedia,* which can be broadly translated as 'the education of Cyrus', laid out the perfect death for a king of kings.[14] Surrounded by the loved and faithful, Cyrus distributed his kingdom to his two sons, making sure no ambiguity or conflict would arise. According to Xenophon, both he and Darius I left enduring traditions that included oral testaments and farewell speeches of enlightened and benevolent words. They rounded off careers that had already become immortal, and Cyrus' ended his with: 'Now I must leave instructions about my kingdom, that there may be no dispute among you after my death.'[15] Although Cyrus' final hours were, in fact, the encomiastic overlay of a Greek historian, Alexander had about him all that was required to do the same, along with a prolonged illness that provided sufficient time. According to the surviving mainstream accounts, he failed in every respect, even when, as one tradition claims, he was being pressed by his generals to announce a successor. We are left wondering what truly took place at Babylon, and who Alexander had become, for it is not only accounts of his death that conflict, but opinions of his life.

According to Aristotle, Zoroastrianism and the Magi of the East believed there are two 'first principles' in the world: 'A good spirit and an evil essence; the name of the first is Zeus or Ahura Mazda, and the other Hades or Ahriman.' This dualism could have featured in any introduction to the life of Alexander so divergent is his character portrayal within the Vulgate genre.[16] Written in vastly different times, two books became required reading for the American founding fathers as a lesson and warning on the nature of governance: Machiavelli's *The Prince* and Xenophon's *On the Education of Cyrus*, copies of which remain today in the US Congress Library. Like the Magi's opposed spirits, they represent the two faces of man: one promoting rule by fear and the other by benign enlightenment, and each book had its place in the evolving profile of the Macedonian king.

One of the leitmotifs of Alexander's story is his belief in his own divine and heroic origins. Yet he also had mortals to emulate and one of them *was* Cyrus the Great. Two centuries before him – tradition suggests October 29th 539 BCE – Cyrus stood on the steps of the ziggurat of Etemenanki, the 'Cornerstone of the Universe', and dedicated to the god Marduk in his newly conquered Babylon.[17] Rejecting the slavery and loot which was his by Victor's Justice, he purportedly made an address which is widely regarded as the first charter of human rights. In 1879 a clay cylinder was unearthed at Babylon and it recorded the complete address previously known to us only from the biblical references in the *Book of Ezra*, chapter one. A copy of the so-called Cyrus Cylinder now sits in the halls of the United Nations Secretariat Building in New York.[18]

Portrayed as politically astute, in the first years of the campaign at least, Alexander III chose to emulate Cyrus when in 333 BCE he too entered Babylon for the first time via the ancient Processional Way having just defeated Darius III. He respected personal freedoms as well as local religious rights, and surviving cuneiform inscriptions found in the city's astronomical diaries captured a part of the declaration: 'Into your houses I shall not enter.'[19] Alexander even sought to repair the Esagila Temple whose golden statue had been melted down by Xerxes upon his hasty return from Greece following defeat at Plataea in 479 BCE, a battle whose aftermath saw Greeks conducting annual sacrifices to their dead in Plutarch's day, some 600 years on.[20] This, along with the adoption of Persian customs and his inheriting a still largely unified Persian Empire, had led some modern commentators to even refer to Alexander as 'the last of the Achaemenids'.[21]

The 22.5 cm clay Cyrus Cylinder, inscribed with Akkadian cuneiform, tells of Cyrus' conquest of Babylon in 539 BCE and the capture of King Nabonidus. The account details Cyrus' benevolence and tolerance, which followed a long tradition of Mesopotamian victory declarations. Discovered in 1879, it resides in the British Museum.

THE *THEOGONIA* OF THE ELUSIVE COMPARANDUM

Whether Alexander displayed a genuine Graeco-Oriental spirit unique for his time, or simple political expediency, is perennially debated, but few men in history have been subjected to so many post-mortems through the ages; his body of literature was bruised by, or benefited from, the ebbs and flows of the philosophical movements and social tides that washed back and forth across the 'universal Comparandum', as Alexander has been termed.[22]

In his *Prior Analytics* Aristotle proposed that it is possible to deduce a person's character from their physical appearance, though the contradictions found in the descriptions of Alexander render any conclusion suitably ambiguous.[23] We are told that though he was of average height, he was striking and menacing even, with a melting glance of the eyes. His breath and skin, according to the *Memoirs* of Aristoxenus of Tarentum (a pupil of Aristotle), exuded a sweet odour, but they were the by-products of his hot and fiery temperament, so his contemporary, Theophrastus (ca. 378-320 BCE), believed. His voice was described as harsh yet also femininely high-pitched; he sported a gold leonine-mane with *anastole* in the heroic style, but he chose to remain beardless; this became a new vogue for him *and* his men.[24] Alexander appears to have been heterochromatic, with one pupil black and the other grey, and his widely reported neck tilt suggests torticollis (wry neck). His teeth were asserted to be sharp and pointed like those of a snake, but this comes from the *Greek Alexander Romance* with its many serpent associations.

Clearly, many of the descriptions, like other detail relating to his life, come down to us from the Roman era and from anonymous, dubious and romanticised sources with little court authentication.[25] Yet it is not Alexander's physiognomy but his character and mindset that remain the more elusive, despite the best attempts of *Quellenforschung* to unmask the man behind the rhetorical veil. Modern historians soon discovered they lacked the vocabulary to cope with him, and word hybrids like *verschmelzungspolitik* appeared to describe what some have romantically believed was his 'policy of racial fusion'.[26] So perhaps we should try and appreciate how Alexander III originally viewed *himself* in the light of his unique and privileged, though hazardous, Macedonian heritage and upbringing.

Some modern scholars accept that the origins of the ethnic, *Makedones*, approximated 'men from the highlands' or even 'high-grown men', though the ancient authors that shepherded Greece out of the Dark Ages proposed a more colourful, though conflicting, genesis.[27] Hesiod's *Theogonia* (likely 7th century BCE) and the *Catalogue of Women*, a supposed continuation that was attributed to him in antiquity, were cosmogonies that provided the archetype of mythical genealogical claims, though they made little of nationalist distinctions and some of this early material was even influenced by the religious doctrine of Babylonia and Mesopotamia, including the *Epic of Gilgamesh*.

In Hesiod's legends (and those attached to him) the origins of tribal Greece and Macedonia started with Deucalion who bore a son, Hellen, from whom the 'Hellenes' were derived. He in turn bore three sons who became the founders of eponymous tribes: Aeolus, Dorus, and Xuthus who bore Ion and (according to other writers) Achaeus. By Zeus, Deucalion's daughter, Thyla, produced two sons, Magnes, and Macedon who 'rejoiced in horses'; Magnes journeyed south into Thessaly and Macedon remained in the region of Mount Olympus and Pieria, the heartland of what was once Emathia, the 'prehistoric name for the cradle of the Macedonian kingdom'. A fragment of the *Makedonika* of Marsyas of Pella (broadly contemporary with Alexander) informs us that it was the two sons of Macedon, Amathus and Pieria, who became the eponymous founders of these two regions.[28]

But whether Alexander considered himself 'Macedonian' in the tribal sense of the word is open to question; he was in any case half-Epirote through his mother, and he likely embraced a more Aristotelian definition of identity approaching '*to Hellenikon*'. To Herodotus (ca. 484-425 BCE) the 'Hellenes' were a people bound together by blood, speech, religion and a common mode of living. Of course if your tribe was lucky enough to appear on Homer's Catalogue of Ships which listed the assailant fleet to Troy, then your 'Greekness' – or allegiance to Hellas at least – was beyond question, though the *Iliad* appears to have portrayed the Trojans as Greek-speaking as well.[29]

In the Homeric epics, the ethnonyms and endonyms of early tribal appellations were not always easy to follow; the 'long-haired Achaeans' (*Akhaiwoi* in ancient Greek, *Akaiwasha* to the Hittites) that followed Achilles to war are at times ethnically distinct, and in other cases they represented the total *ethne* of mainland Greece.[30] The Catalogue of Ships itself presented the diversity of the invading 'Achaean' army heading to Asian shores; Homer declared (sometime in the 9th century BCE, debatably): 'For I could not count or name the multitude who came to Troy, though I had ten tongues and a tireless voice, and lungs of bronze as well.'[31] In the *Illiad* and *Odyssey*, the *Danaoi* (or Danaans, possibly the *Danuna* mentioned in Hittite and Egyptian records) and 'Argives' were repeatedly cited in some collective tribal fashion representing the invading Greeks ked by Agamemnon.[32]

As with all else he touched, Alexander's teacher, Aristotle, attempted to bring some rationalisation to the 'pre-history' of Greece after the fall of Mycenaean civilisation; he described 'ancient Hellas' as being occupied by *Selloi* (Zeus' priests, likely an alternative of *Helloi*) and *Graikoi*, who later became known as the homogenised *to koinon ton Hellenon*, which we might loosely term a 'Hellenic commonwealth'.[33] The *Periegetes Hellados* of Pausanias (ca. 110-180 CE), his unique *Guide to Greece* (though a Greece whose northern boundary was the pass at Thermopylae) in the form of a straight-talking guide interwoven with the history, architecture and ancient Greek myths, mentioned that an inscription by Echembrotus dating to the 48th Olympiad (584 BCE) employed the term 'Hellenes' in a dedication to Heracles at the Amphictionic Games.[34] A similar dedication at Delphi celebrating victory over Persia credited another Pausanias as the leading general of this ethnic group; it was a unity further endorsed at the fourth Panhellenic Games in which 'non-Hellenes' could not participate in any of the disciplines.

Plato (ca. 428-348 BCE) believed the most 'Greek of the Greeks' were the Athenians, and in the dialogue of the *Menexenus* (attributed to him), Aspasia, the mistress of the Athenian statesman Pericles, (ca. 495-429 BCE) proposed *only* Athenians were pure and free from barbarian blood.[35] According to Herodotus, Athenians (and other pre 'pre-Hellenised' tribes) were once Pelasgians, arriving through migration, or the autochthonic inhabitants.[36]

Clearly, there had been no original Pan-Hellenic name for what became the Greek homeland, populated as it was with at least two major tribal migrations, the first by the Ionians and Aeolians (perhaps 16th century BCE, if so, this coincided with the emergence of what we now term the Mycenaean civilisation) and later the Dorians (11th century BCE), though from exactly where (and why) they came is unknown.[37] These racial exoduses took place in mytho-historical eras between which the mysterious 'Peoples of the Sea' (perhaps including Greek tribes) caused such destruction around the Eastern Mediterranean in the late 13th century BCE. But questions and theories of population displacement go back further; new studies of the sudden flooding of the land basin that is now the Black Sea (expanded from a lake ca. 8,400 years ago) suggest the resulting refugees became the farmers of Macedonia and northern Greece, a theory some scholars link to the true origins of the deluge behind Noah's legendary ark, or perhaps to the myth of Deucalion and Pyrrha.[38]

A fragmented *synoikismos* (synoecism) – a population amalgam – existed through the Helladic period and Greek Dark Ages (ca. 1100-850 BCE) before the city-state culture of the Archaic period (ca. 800-480 BCE), and it resulted in a *dioikismos* of independent communities in which *symbola*, the rudimentary agreements between pairs of states, nevertheless, provided a basis for trade and law between the ethnic groups.[39] Tribal identity was then far more relevant than today's homogenised terms, possibly because linguistic palaeontology *does* provide overwhelming evidence of a 'pre-Greek' population inhabiting the region: the names Corinth (Korinthos), Knossos, Larissa, Samos, Mycenae (Mykenai) and Olympus even, are thought to be of pre-Hellenic construction. The name Cadmus (Kadmos), the legendary Phoenician founder of Thebes who introduced the alphabet into Greece, is also considered pre-Greek.[40]

The Latin term *Graecus* and the land of *Graecia* developed later, perhaps from the *Graikoi* who assisted the citizens of Euboea to migrate to Cumae in Italy through Epirus in the 8th century BCE; they were from the ancient city of Graia linked to Tanagraia, the daughter of Asopus (and so to the eponymous city of Tanagra and to Oropus), by Hesiod, Homer, Aristotle and Pausanias after them. According to Aristotle and the *Parian Chronicle* it was the *Graikoi* who were the renamed Hellenes, though early attachments still restricted them to Epirus and the Dodona region and its Homeric links to the age of Odysseus and Achilles. Hesiod referred to this region as *Hellopia* and Stephanus of Byzantium later named Graikos as the son of Thessalus the woodcutter who was first shown the shrine at Dodona dedicated to the cult of Zeus Naos.[41]

In time, the Romans, whose early continuous contact *was* likely with northwestern Greece, came to term Hellenes (now meaning *all* Greeks) *Graeci*.[42] In return, the Greeks were partly responsible for the widening use of the appellation *Italia*; it stemmed from the Latin for 'land of calves' or 'cattle' (calf, *vitulus*), thus *Vitalia*. Lacking a 'v' in their alphabet, the Greeks in southern Italy settled on a name that spread north from Calabria and was eventually adopted by Rome itself. Some 600 years on from Alexander's day, both the Greeks and the Italians of the Eastern Roman Empire were to become grouped together as the *Rhomaioi, Romhellenes* and the *Graecoromans* of a new Byzantine Empire.

Outside Greece's borders were the *barbaroi*. The verb *barbarizein* described the imitation of non-Greek sounds and followed Homer's use of *barbarophonoi* for those of incomprehensible speech.[43] In Plato's view, much of it adopted by Aristotle, barbarians were 'more servile in their nature than the Hellenes, and the Asiatics more than the Europeans', and thus they 'deserve to be slaves', though curiously, Aristotle put this differentiation down to climate; in his *Politics*, Aristotle even seems to have implied that the Macedonians, alongside the Celts and Scythians, were barbarians too, whilst Isocrates (ca. 436-338 BCE) likened the Greek-barbarian divide to nothing short of that between mankind and beasts.[44]

The 'closed world' of some 750-1,000 introspective and independent mainland Greek *poleis*, city-states (originally 'strongholds'), had acted as a natural buffer to the integration of barbarians and to the concept of national monarchy as well, unlike the development of Greece's northern neighbours.[45] But the need for foreign commodities meant a *polis* could never remain totally isolated, thus the appearance of 300 or so Greek settlements overseas where they had to live side-by-side with the indigenous population and probably developed a less xenophobic attitude as a result.

The Greeks, and later the Romans, repeatedly referred to all northern barbarian tribes (including the Goths) as 'Scythians' or 'Thracians'.[46] Thucydides considered the Acarnanians, Aetolians, Epirotes – the northern Greek tribes – and Upper Macedonians (more akin to the *ethne* of the Epirotes, thus Molossic) as barbarians, though he did distinguish 'proper Macedonians' (the 'Lower Macedonians') from the Balkan tribes to the north (as did Ephorus of Cyme ca. 405-330 BCE); it was these upper cantons (including Paeonia, Pelagonia, Lyncestis, Orestis, Eordaea, Elimea, Tymphaea and Almopia) that Alexander's father, Philip II, effectively absorbed into a 'greater Macedonia'.[47] Polybius (ca. 200-118 BCE), who once *implied* the Romans were a tribe of *barbaroi* as part of a (long) rebuttal to his forerunner, the historian Timaeus (ca. 345-250 BCE), provided a more nuanced distinction of ethnicity, and it appears that by his day (the 2nd century BCE) the widespread use of Hellenistic *koine* (a dialect) *had* begun to break down the ancient divides.[48]

Defying the older Homeric-era definitions, Alexander may indeed have been an original *kosmopolites*, a self-declared 'citizen of the world', a term that first became attached to Diogenes the Cynic who he famously met in Corinth. For political purposes Alexander might have presented himself as *philhellenos,* the cognomen taken by his Temenid predecessor, King Alexander I (ruled ca. 498-454 BCE), though the titles *Proxenos* and *Euergetes* ('guest-friend' and 'benefactor') granted by Athens to King Archelaus I (ruled Macedonia 413-399 BCE, his name broadly meaning 'leader of men'), were hardly likely to have come Alexander's way now that Greece was garrisoned.[49] Macedonia itself had been infused with foreign settlers through tribal and city state migrations and the displacement of war: when Mycenae was destroyed by Argos, over half the population relocated to Macedonia on the invitation of Alexander I.[50] Justin summed up Philip II's own empire forging and repopulating in more recent times:

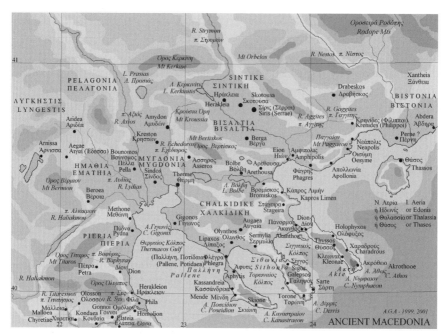

The cantons of ancient Macedonia.

> On his return to his kingdom, as shepherds drive their flocks sometimes into winter, sometimes into summer pastures, so he transplanted people and cities hither and thither, according to his caprice... Some people he planted upon the frontiers of his kingdom to oppose his enemies; others he settled at the extremities of it. Some, whom he had taken prisoner in war, he distributed among certain cities to fill up the number of inhabitants; and thus, out of various tribes and nations, he formed one kingdom and people.[51]

If, as a result, Alexander's view on *ethne* was even something more eclectic that defied autochthonous norms, it was his ancestral Greek origins that would have rooted him in a distinct cultural upbringing with its vow to excellence and a particular honour code that backboned the Homeric sagas.

But there remains an ongoing philological contention over the original language of the Macedonians, and this stems in part from dialogues within the Alexander histories. As far as Thucydides was concerned, the region had previously been culturally backward ('a majority of unwalled villages federated into *ethne*') and probably linguistically distinct from the population to the south that spoke the more refined *Attikoi* (Attic) dialect of Greece.[52] This is backed up by Curtius' description of the trial of Philotas, the son of Alexander's prominent general, Parmenio, for it suggested 'legal' procedures were conducted in a tongue (or dialect at least) distinct from the Greek that Alexander's top echelons apparently spoke.[53] Philotas replied that he wished to use the language Alexander had adopted (*aedem lingua*), rather than the *patrius sermo* that Curtius' Latin text referred to, in order that the greatest number of soldiers could understand his defence; the 'mother tongue', Philotas stated, had become obsolete because of the wider dialogue with foreign nations. As Edward Anson concluded, Philotas' practical retort indicates the Macedonians could understand Attic Greek more easily than Greeks could grasp Macedonian.[54] The common 'adopted' dialect being referred to (*aedem lingua*) *was* most likely akin to Hellenistic *koine* (which became known as 'Macedonian' Greek) rather than Attic Greek, for the Ionic dialect (with perhaps an admix of others) which was later infiltrated by Macedonian, *was* the basis of the *lingua franca* prevalent in much of the early Hellenistic world.[55]

Plutarch believed that in cases of extreme emergency Alexander did beckon his Bodyguards in *makedonisti*, so 'in the Macedonian tongue'.[56] The contention is backed up by a fragment found at Oxyrhynchus (Egypt) by archaeologist Annibale Evaristo Breccia in 1932; it described the clash between Eumenes of Cardia (the former royal secretary, now a governor and general in the post-Alexander world) and the Molossian noble, Neoptolemus, in the early Successor Wars during which Xennias, 'a man of Macedonian speech', was sent out to intimidate the opposing ranks.[57] Of course the claim may have been made by a historian emphasising Eumenes' Greek disadvantage, and the historian Hieronymus, his client, cannot be discounted as the architect of that. We have a similar anomaly in Plutarch's *Life of Eumenes* when the Macedones were portrayed as saluting their fever-ridden general: '... they hailed him at once in their Macedonian speech, caught up their shields, beat upon them with their spears, and raised their battle-cry...'[58]

But noting statements from the Roman chronicler Livy (64/59 BCE-17 CE) and earlier from Herodotus that Greeks and Macedonians shared a common tongue, and with scant references in the texts to *makedonizein*, 'to speak Macedonian', scholars remain split on the case for a national language. A middle ground concludes that the Upper Macedonia cantons to the north and west, which Hatzopoulos terms 'the cradle of the Macedonian *ethnos*', were linguistically distinct from the Lower Macedonian heartlands, the flat fertile plain bordering the Thermaic Gulf, which included Bottiaea (possibly settled by Cretans in the Late Bronze Age ca. 1300 BCE) and Pieria.[59] The upper cantons had perhaps adopted the harsh Doric of northwest Greece as suggested by the Pellan Curse Tablet.[60]

If taken at face value, episodes suggest that any diglossia that *had* existed in Macedonia rested with the nobility, and not with the peasant-conscripted infantry. Yet a formal approbation, national war cry, or a judicial procedure such as the trial described above, may indeed have followed archaic procedures rooted in the old tribal dialect that retained (or shared) elements of Illyrian, Phrygian and Thracian, which were evidenced by the lexicographer Hesychius of Alexandria in the 5th century.[61] As a parallel, we might note that the judicial language of Solon's legislative reforms of 5th century BCE Athens was sufficiently archaic to cause interpretive problems for later classical-era scholars.

The graves unearthed at Vergina dating back to the 5th century BCE indicate inhabitants had certainly adopted Hellenic *names* by then; of the 6,300 inscriptions found in the former state borders, ninety-nine per cent were written in Greek. In contrast, Hatzopoulos notes that 'a relatively high percentage of the names attested in the neighbouring lands conquered after 479 BCE are of pre-Greek origin'; this suggests the vanquished were not immediately displaced and for a time retained their ethnicity.[62] But there can be no doubt that Macedonia, though regionally discrete and perhaps tribally distinct, was by the 5th century BCE certainly a part of the Greek cultural milieu,[63] by which point it is likely that foreign policy and out-of-state business was conducted in Attic Greek, though Attic Greek, in turn, would be infiltrated by elements of Macedonian in time.[64]

If we need any proof that the reform-minded Macedonian monarchs like Alexander I, Perdiccas II (reigned ca. 448-413 BCE) and Archelaus I were modelling their cultural sophistication on Greece, we only have to recall that the great tragedian Euripides, Hippocrates of Kos (ca. 460-370 BCE) the 'father of western medicine', the revered Pindar of Thebes (ca. 518-433 BCE), the dithyrambic poet Melanippides and Bacchylides the lyric poet, Choerilus the epic poet and Agathon the tragic poet along with his lover Pausanias, were all invited to stay at the royal court at Aegae or at the new capital at Pella. So was the musician Timotheus, alongside Zeuxis who captured life on canvas like none before him, and the historian Hellanicus of Mytilene who as colourfully captured lives on parchment.[65]

Foreign *hetairoi* (high-ranking court friends) were given substantial tracts of land in Macedonia and many ended up drinking at *symposia*, the banquets (*komoi* or *deipnoi*) typical of the Macedonian court.[66] Guests typically relaxed on the Greek-styled couch, the *kline*, and famously downed their wine neat, *akratos*, and judging from the outcomes they consumed more than the Spartans' daily ration of two *kontylae* per soldier which had helped to wash down their notorious *melas zoomos*, Sparta's black bean soup (with boiled pork, blood and vinegar) that Leonidas, Alexander's stricter teacher, might well have introduced him to as a youth.[67]

Herodotus is thought to have 'stayed with the king of the Macedonians in the time of Euripides and Sophocles' (ca. 480 and 497-406 BCE respectively), whilst Aristotle's own father, Nicomachus, had been a state doctor to Amyntas III (reigned 393/392-370 BCE), the father of Philip II.[68] Although Socrates (ca. 470-399 BCE) is said to have declined an invitation to the state, Euphraus, the philosophising student of Plato, visited and taught at the court of Perdiccas III, Philip's older brother; it was, in fact, Euphraus who advised Perdiccas to give the teenage Philip II a district to cut his teeth in governance.

The Greek comedy playwrights of the period made references to the lavish Macedonian court banquets and weddings that were the envy of the Athenians. Actors, such as the celebrated Neoptolemus and Philocrates were even sent as diplomats to Philip, so aware were they of his *philanthropia* to performers; in this particular case, as a precursor to what is now termed the 'Peace of Philocrates' of 346 BCE, the anti-Macedonian Athenian orator Demosthenes accused the *hypocrites* (actor) Neoptolemus of 'acting' in the best interest of Philip rather than Athens. Opposing Demosthenes to the end of his career, the Macedonia-friendly orator Aeschines, also present as part of the embassy, was a former actor himself.[69]

The emerging power of Macedonia had hardly gone unnoticed; Plato certainly took an interest and Thucydides appears to have been an admirer of the growing state (he owned property in the Strymon basin); the historians Theopompus and Anaximenes of Lampsacus (ca. 380-320 BCE), possibly encouraged by Isocrates, spent time at the Pellan court of Philip II, as, of course, did Aristotle who would uniquely influence his son; Aristotle's student Theophrastus (who became an expert on plants) was to later advise on land reclamation nearby.[70] The Argead kings, if not quite ready to adopt the 'people power' of *demokratia*, had ambitions on becoming civilised in all other ways, especially now that the 'Aegean façade' of Lower Macedonia had integrated itself into the 'international, economic, diplomatic and cultural world of its times'.[71]

This newly 'united' and monarchic Macedonia was a 'sub-Homeric enclave' in which citizens started adding *Makedon* to their names as a sign of a national identity, suggesting there existed an extraordinary legal homogeneity under the late Argead kings. This was something of a paradox to a still-fragmented Greek mainland, a state of affairs epitomised by the almost simultaneous call from Isocrates for Philip II to lead a 'Panhellenic' expedition against 'barbarian' Persia, and a reply from Demosthenes which rallied Athens to oppose the 'barbarian' Macedonian king.[72]

Something of that paradox resurfaced in Alexander who was mentally fused to the past through *syngeneia* (kinship) and lineage to the heroes of Hellas and the venerated kings of antiquity: 'For what is the worth of human life, unless it is woven into the life of our ancestors by the records of history?'[73] He was acutely aware of being *porphyrogennetos* with an illustrious crossbreeding, and just as mindful of how that imagery could be exploited. 'Alexander' broadly translates as 'repeller' or 'defender' of men, and it was a name fit for cause.[74] He appears to have genuinely believed in his alleged descent from heroes, and his training had been far more illustrious than the *encyclios paideia,* the general classical Greek education. The poems of the Trojan Epic Cycle became his Omphalos, or as Alexander liked to term them, his 'campaign equipment' or *viaticum.*[75] But surely the keenest blade in his Homeric arsenal was Odysseus' declaration: 'Let there be one ruler and one king!'[76]

Alexander's birth was heralded as divine. Hegesias the Magnesian (fl. ca. 300 BCE), founder of the 'Asiatic style' of composition, proposed that the great fire at Ephesus in 356 BCE could be explained on the basis that the goddess was absent from her temple attending his delivery, for the events had apparently coincided; Plutarch wasn't impressed with the connection, terming it 'a joke flat enough to have put out the fire'.[77] Yet Parmenio's defeat of the Illyrians and Philip's recent capture of Potidaea, along with the victory of his racehorse at the Olympic Games, made the day Philip heard that a son had been born to him, indeed seem rather auspicious.

Alexander's mother, Olympias, initiated into the Dionysiac mysteries of the Clodones and Mimallones (the Maenads, 'raving ones', of Greece linked to Orpheus whose grave was located in Macedonia), was from the Molossian tribe of Epirus.[78] Through her, Alexander managed to claim Aeacid descent from Achilles, whose son, Neoptolemus (also known as Pyrrhus of the Pyrrhidae), according to legend, had once ruled the region.[79] Through him, and as popularised in the *Andromache* of Euripides who spent his final years in Macedonia, Alexander was also a descendant of Hector's widow, the Trojan princess Andromache, who became Neoptolemus' concubine and gave birth to Molossus, the founder of the eponymous Epirote tribe; the ancestry linked Alexander to both the attackers and defenders of Troy.[80] As a result, as Bosworth points out, he did not view Trojans as barbarians but as 'Hellenes on Asian soil', which rather underpins Homer's own linguistic treatment of Priam's men and Dardanus' mythological roots. In Alexander's invasion of Asia, the united blood of Achilles and Priam would finally campaign together.[81]

Arrian associated Alexander with the hero Perseus, the son of Zeus, and the father of both the Persian race and the Greek Dorians through Heracles; this helps explain the similarities between the Greek *Succession Myth* and the Babylonian equivalent, the *Enûma Elis*.[82] From his reading of Herodotus, Alexander would have been aware that King Midas, adopted by the childless Gordias, and the founder of the Phrygian dynasty, was said to have emerged from a region of Macedonia though the Roman geographer, Strabo (literally, 'squint-eyed', 64/63 BCE-24 CE), thought the Phrygians, originally Bryges or Brigians, were a Thracian tribe. Midas' wealth came from mining iron ore until he was expelled by the semi-mythical Caranus ('Billy-goat'), 'the founding father of Macedonia' who in legend reigned ca. 808-778 BCE. The Gardens of Midas at the foot of Mount Bermion still carried his name in Alexander's day.[83] This dominant Phrygian tribe, which migrated across to Asia Minor (ca. 800 BCE, though claims dating to as early as 1200 BCE suggest they broke Hittite power), inhabited the early tombs at Aegae found under some 300 of the tumuli, and it is worth noting that in Euripides' *Helen* the Trojans are referred to as 'Phrygians'.[84]

The opening lines of Plutarch's biography additionally managed to trace Alexander's descent (through the Heraclid line of his father) back to the 'founding father', Caranus, who originally hailed from Argos and invaded Macedonia 'with a great multitude of Greeks'.[85] This enabled Alexander to trace his lineage to the Argive Heracleidae and back to Danaus and the Danaans who shipped to Troy, the heritage Isocrates had assigned to Philip.[86] Other Heraclids included the kings of Sparta and the Aleuadae dynasty of Larissa in Thessaly (Heracles' supposed birthplace), and so by definition their relatives, care of their common forefather, Heracles *Patroos*.[87]

Euripides, once described as 'the first psychologist', had a different idea altogether: to please his reform-minded host, he proposed it had been an earlier Archelaus, a son of Temenus, who anticipated the Temenids, encapsulating the new proposition in a play aptly named *Archelaus*.[88] Adding to the thickening founding fog was a parallel belief that the etymological roots of the Argeads lay in 'Argives' who were Dorians in Greek tradition, as this challenged the claims that the stemma actually derived from 'Argaeus' the son of King Perdiccas I, or, according to later writers, a son of Macedon.[89] Appian (ca. 95-165 CE), writing later from the safe distance of Roman Alexandria, more controversially claimed that the true origins of the name of the Macedonian royal clan might have stemmed from a far more rural Argos in the Macedonian canton of Orestis; if so, it had been expediently hidden beneath layers of court-sponsored propaganda.[90]

Hellanicus of Mytilene, who also spent time at the Macedonian court (probably in the reign of Archelaus), positioned a Macednus (not Macedon) as the son of Aeolus, so from the direct line of Hellen with ancestry to the Aeolians and Dorians, thus firmly 'Hellenic'; Herodotus, who treated geography and ethnology as one, supported the Dorian links and claimed that Alexander I, the first Argead to mint coins, had convinced the adjudicating *hellanodikai*, the official judges from Elis, of his Peloponnesian Argive roots so that he might compete in the Olympic Games; his entry resulted in victory in the furlong foot race ca. 495 BCE. It has been more recently suggested that the increasingly pro-Hellenic stance of the Macedonian court resulted in the kings adopting the Greek names conspicuously found on the Vergina graves.[91]

To anchor down these polymorphic lineages, Philip and Alexander minted a new bimetallic currency system, stamping images of Zeus crowned with laurel and Apollo on gold *Philippeioi*, while Heracles appeared on silver tetradrachms; and here, anew, was *allos houtos Heracles*, the hero 'reborn', as the Greek proverb suggested.[92] Philip's 'sacred wars' in Greece in Apollo's name had already forged the attachment and the imagery of success was stamped on his coinage in both the Attic and Thraco-Macedonian standards for circulatory effect: it included Philip's three chariot victories at the Olympic Games showing a youth on horseback and, suitably, a chariot.[93]

The first of Alexander's own silver coins; a tetradrachm struck sometime between ca. 335-29 BCE. Minted in Pella, it still displays the laureate head of his father, Philip II. On the obverse is a nude youth holding a palm frond and reins on horseback with a *kantharos* (a deep double-handed drinking vessel) below. Images provided with the kind permission of the Classical Numismatic Group. Inc. www.cngcoins.com.

A late Alexander tetradrachm minted at Sardis, the well-guarded treasury, under its governor Menander ca. 324 BCE. It bears a head of Heracles wearing a lion skin, and Zeus *Aetophoros* ('Eagle-bearer') with a club is seated on the obverse.

Philip and Alexander had commissioned portraits and bronzes by Lysippus and Euphranor before the planned Persian campaign. The family statues Philip commissioned from Leochares and erected in chryselephantine (or possibly marble) in the circular Philippeion in the precinct of Zeus at Olympia suggest the early birth of the Argead public relations machine, as well as an attempt of reconciliation with a then alienated son and wife.[94] Epic lineages were ever sought after by kings and their court poets, but here the Argeads were creating a new *Succession Myth*, and as history was to show, they became every bit as brutal as the Titans from whom they professedly descended.[95]

Backed by this useful polytheism, these heritages implied a telegony in which their combined traits and bloodlines would converge and meet in a new demigod: Alexander himself. They gave him his *entelekheia*, the vital force that completed him and then compelled him to Persia in his father's stead. Although heritages were clearly often fused, confused and conveniently manipulated, the one ancestor that Alexander was never able to comfortably integrate into his developing persona *was* his own father, Philip, murdered at Aegae when Alexander was aged twenty, for he had provided the legitimacy that Alexander needed, but not the identity he ultimately sought. And as a recent study concluded, once the memory of Philip began to develop into nostalgic myth, Alexander lost control over its subordination to him.[96]

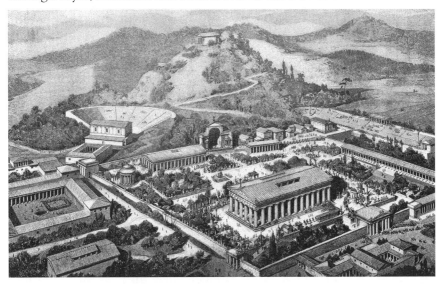

A reconstruction of ancient Olympia from Pierers Universal-Lexicon, 1891. The circular building in the left corner is the Philippeion housing the statues of Philip's family.

'THE GIVER OF THE BRIDE, THE BRIDEGROOM, AND THE BRIDE'[97]

There were both immediate and lingering rumours that Alexander had played a part in his father's death, and they, in turn, were fuelled by Philip's accusations of Olympias' infidelity (so claimed Justin, who also stated that Philip divorced her – Arrian claimed he 'rejected' her), and that would have been tantamount to Philip disowning his son.[98] Badian went as far as suggesting the previous rift between the prince and king had resulted in Philip favouring Amyntas Perdicca, the son of his older brother, Perdiccas III, in the line of succession; Philip had ostensibly 'managed' Amyntas' kingship due to his nephew's youth and more recently he had married him to his daughter, Cynnane, Alexander's half-sister.

Plutarch believed the Macedonians themselves were inclining to Amyntas *and* to the sons of Aeropus of Lyncestis (who had a claim to the throne through an older branch of the royal house) at Philip's death. Alexander had two of the latter (Heromenes and Arrhabaeus) immediately executed, and soon after, Amyntas as well, to secure his position. The exception was the superficially compliant third son of Aeropus, Alexander Lyncestis, married to a daughter of the now all-important Antipater, previously Philip's foremost general and the regent in his absences.[99] Plutarch summarised the court position at the time:

> All Macedonia was festering with revolt and looking toward Amyntas and the children of Aeropus; the Illyrians were again rebelling, and trouble with the Scythians was impending for their Macedonian neighbours, who were in the throes of political change; Persian gold flowed freely through the hands of the popular leaders everywhere, and helped to rouse the Peloponnese; Philip's treasuries were bare of money, and in addition there was owing a loan of two hundred talents...[100]

Along with 'the accomplices in the murder' who were summarily executed on Alexander's orders 'at the tumulus of Philip', those upon whom regicidal suspicion fell (genuine or contrived) would have suffered a similar fate, either publicly, or behind the scenes.

Several events which took place in close succession contributed to the patricidal finger pointing: Philip had recently married Cleopatra, the young niece (Diodorus and Justin said 'sister') of the influential Macedonian baron, Attalus, who had prayed for a 'legitimate heir' from the union; that was a barbed reminder to Alexander, who apparently threw his goblet at him during the court banquet where the toast was made, that he was half Epirote, or indeed a product of Olympias' infidelity.[101] Philip had his sword drawn as he lurched drunkenly towards his unapologetic son who then called into question his father's ability to lead the invasion of Asia. The incident precipitated the flight of Olympias to her home in Epirus, while Alexander journeyed to Illyria, probably to his friend and ally, the Agrianian king, Langarus. That is exactly where you would go to raise a hostile force to oust a Pellan king, for the Illyrians had managed exactly that before.[102]

The teenage Cleopatra was now pregnant with Philip's heir; she gave birth to a daughter, Europa, just days before Philip's death and there was *possibly* an earlier son named Caranus; they were murdered by Olympias, probably with the blessing of Alexander (despite claims otherwise), within the year.[103] Moreover, at the time of the wedding of Philip and Cleopatra, Alexander had reached throne age, eighteen.

The rift between Alexander and his father appears to have run deeper still. In preparation for his invasion of Asia, Philip had (earlier) reached out to Hermias of Atarneus (with whom Aristotle had resided), and to Pixodarus of the Carian Hecatomnid dynasty – the 'grandest' in the Eastern Mediterranean and influential in Lycia – to arrange a royal marriage for an alliance on the coast of Asia Minor. Perhaps when still in his self-imposed exile in Illyria, Alexander had undermined the proposed pairing of his half-witted half-brother, Arrhidaeus, to Pixodarus' daughter, by offering himself instead; it was Parmenio's son Philotas who possibly revealed the plot to Philip, and he was apparently a marked man thereafter.[104] Some have interpreted from the episode that Alexander already had plans to lead the invasion of Asia in his father's stead. His recent impetuous founding of Alexandropolis in 340 BCE (when Philip was busy besieging Byzantium) after campaigning in Thrace at the age of just sixteen, was a testament to the prince's own ambition, and it may have left his father wary despite Plutarch's claim that he 'was excessively fond of his son, so that he even rejoiced to hear the Macedonians call Alexander their king, but Philip their general.'[105]

Justin painted a more hostile picture of court affairs: after the initial rift with Philip, Olympias urged her brother, Alexander Molossus, now the Epirote king, to declare war; it would have been an opportune moment with Philip's most effective generals, Parmenio and Attalus (Cleopatra's uncle), absent in Asia with a significant part of the royal army which was establishing a bridgehead for the invasion. At this point Alexander's envoy, Thessalus, was to be found in Corinth potentially seeking military Greek support for the prince. Philip's *oikos* (household) was clearly in trouble, and only the diplomacy of Demaratus of Corinth managed to reconcile father and a son who then became Master of the Royal Seal.[106]

Astute as ever in a political crisis, Philip paired Alexander's sister, Cleopatra, to Molossus to stave off any Epirote threat; he 'disarmed him as a son-in-law', as Justin put it.[107] Nevertheless, he sent Alexander's *philoi* (closest court friends) including Ptolemy (the future Egyptian dynast), Nearchus, Laomedon and Harpalus (with his older brother Erygius) into exile. Those broadly coeval with Alexander were *syntropoi* (literally 'those eating together') who would later become the *megistoi*, the 'great men', who frequented his court. Staging the wedding would be the last performance of Philip's twenty-three-year reign, for he was stabbed by Pausanias of Orestis upon entering the amphitheatre at Aegae.[108] The day signified Alexander's arrival; it was perhaps even a day he orchestrated himself. Alexander took up the reins of power as keenly as he is said to have mounted his Thessalian warhorse, Bucephalus, and he and Olympias didn't hesitate in executing the rivals for the throne, most likely along with their families and their political backers as well.[109]

Pausanias was pursued by Alexander's close court friends, Perdiccas and Leonnatus, and by the royal page Attalus, and was conveniently murdered before he could be questioned; the murderer and his pursuers were all from the canton of Orestis and both Perdiccas and Leonnatus became Alexander's personal Bodyguards, *Somatophylakes*, on campaign.[110] Pausanias had allegedly confronted Alexander with the same grievance he had previously taken to Philip – sexual assault – and he received, as Alexander's reported reply, the line from Euripides' *Medea*: 'the giver of the bride, the bridegroom, and the bride'; it hinted of a triple murder in the making, and one that did come to pass (at Philip's death, Alexander executed the 'giver', Attalus, and Olympias murdered the bride, Cleopatra). Justin claimed Olympias had arranged the getaway horses for the assassins.[111]

Possibly to distance himself from any further implication of guilt, Alexander 'took every possible care over the burial of his parent' at a time when he needed all the support he could muster.[112] Within two years, and having 're-subdued' Greece, Thrace and the Balkans, Alexander crossed the Hellespont (*Hellespontos*, 'Sea of Helle'), today's Dardanelles (named after Dardanus), in his father's place, and he bolstered support for the invasion by claiming Philip's assassins were backed by Persian gold. We will never know if Alexander fully dismantled the stigma of parricide, but an alleged oracular reply at Siwa some three years on, confirming *all* Philip's killers had been punished, sounds suspiciously like a contrived vote on his own innocence, though it was peculiarly exonerating to the still-at-large Persian Great King as well.[113]

The two previous invasions of Greece by Persia under Darius I (ended 490 BCE) and his son Xerxes I (ended 480 BCE) had not been sudden appearances of Persian power and influence in Europe. Macedonia of the 6th century BCE was, as Borza termed it, a 'dependency of the Persian Empire', after which the autonomous vassal kingdom was formally occupied as Darius' forces under Mardonius spread west across the Hellespont in 492 BCE. The occupation and the tribute lasted until 479 BCE when Xerxes was forced to withdraw after three decades of Persian control which had nevertheless helped their client kings, Amyntas I, and then his son Alexander I, subjugate a hinterland that would become 'Upper Macedonia'; also absorbed were lands to the west into an expanded Lower Macedonia.

Alexander I had prudently and ingeniously managed to play a 'double game with great skill'; chosen by Mardonius to offer seductive terms to Athens to fracture Greek resistance, he provided the Persians with support at Plataea, yet timber for the Greek fleet, and he covertly spied for the allied forces to warn them of imminent Persian attack, eventually falling on a large body of the retreating Asiatic army.[114] Macedonia's hinterland and the Athos peninsula provided much-needed wood (pine, silver fir and four types of oak) to the Athenian shipbuilding trade and alliances (often short) with Athens were driven by this dependence.[115] To counter any suggestion of exploitation in the war, Alexander I next dedicated a golden statue of himself at Delphi and Olympia, with the result that Pindar termed him 'the bold scheming son of Amyntas'. His son, Perdiccas II, was to change sides even more frequently in the Peloponnesian War (431-404 BCE); a century and a half later a no less scheming Philip II played a similar diplomatic game and was once aligned with Artaxerxes III, sending expediently supportive messages to the Persian court.[116]

Persian occupation left its mark on Macedonia and perhaps on Alexander III as well; the term 'satrap' we see in the campaign histories relating to Alexander's regional governors, stemmed from the Achaemenid rule of an empire managed through client kings and officials who maintained the *pax Persika*. It has been proposed that the late Argead tradition of enrolling royal pages (*paides basilikos,* 'informal hostage sons' of the Upper Macedonian nobles), as well as the formal polygamy of the Argead (and Molossian) kings, who had their own military units of 'friends' (*hetairoi*), were also of Persian origin, and some commentators argue that the *melophoroi*, the golden apple-bearing Persian Immortals, were the inspiration behind the Macedonian *agema* of the hypaspists, the royal guard.[117] *Somatophylakes*, the king's personal Bodyguards, as well as *chiliarchos*, likened to post of the Achaemenid *hazarapti* (a second-in-command who also had administrative and diplomatic responsibilities like chief usher and the king's intermediary with messengers) and reintroduced by Alexander (and occupied by his closest companion Hephaestion, and assumed by Perdiccas after him), were titles or roles adopted (or adapted) from the Persian courts, it is believed. Even the position of the king's cupbearer had its origins with the Achaemenid kings.[118]

Compared to the 'old guard' command – the seasoned campaigners and infantry generals Alexander inherited from his father – the Bodyguards represented a class of relatively young equestrian aristocrats expected to adhere to the *kalos kagathos* of classical Greece, the Homeric-rooted code of virtue and honour.[119] In fact the Homeric poems have been termed nothing less than the *Bible* of the Greeks containing 'the germs of all Greek philosophy'.[120] Alexander's Bodyguard corps emerged from the *syntrophoi* raised at the king's court in Pella, the 'city of stone'.[121] If broadly coeval, they too would have been familiar with, or even educated with Alexander under the tutelage of Aristotle. Along with other trusted generals and leading landowners, they formed the noble 'cavalry' class of Macedonia, which attended the *synedria*, the gatherings of the king's Privy Council and advisers. In the absence of what we might today term a 'middle class', Macedonian nobles commanded both the cavalry and the infantry battalions that were formed from tenant farmers and herders who responded to the king's call, and who made up a professional standing army that first appeared under Philipp II.[122]

Hellas, and especially Macedonia, had been fascinated with tales of the Persian dynasty with its fabled court wealth which still pulled influential strings across the Aegean; at one time over 300 Greeks frequented the Achaemenid court and some even attended the Great Kings as physicians. Inscriptions dating to the reign of Darius I confirm the presence of Ionian and Carian stonecutters working on the new palace constructions, and the Greek cities of the Asia Minor seaboard acted as information conduits and contact points with the Persian administration.[123]

It is no wonder, then, that the Greeks had tried to link the ancient East with their own mythology once they appreciated its greater antiquity; they accepted African and Asian origins for the ancestries established by Medea, Perseus and the Achaeans, which appears a paradoxical sociality considering their proud autochthonism.[124] Cadmus, Pelops, Danaos and Aegyptus all arrived in Greece from Asia and Egypt in the founding myths.[125] As Nietzsche put it, '... Their culture was for a long time a chaos of foreign forms and ideas – Semitic, Babylonian, Lydian and Egyptian – and their religion a battle of all the gods of the East...' Xerxes had exploited just that when he too reminded Greece of the Persian-Perseus link when garnering Argive support for his pending invasion.[126]

In Greek literature the term 'Persian' was employed loosely, as was its geographic and dynastic association. In the Alexander histories we see the Great King's vassals referred to as Iranian, Asiatic and Oriental, as well as Median, beside Persian. Cyrus and Darius I were additionally termed kings of Assyria (often shortened to 'Syria' by Diodorus), the breadth of which might unite Assyrian Nineveh, Mesopotamia (Greek in origin, from *mesos* 'middle' and *potamos* 'river') and Babylonia. The ambiguity has caused much confusion for historians;[127] Herodotus and Xenophon used 'Assyria' when referring to regions as diverse as Anatolia to the Black Sea and the Aramaic Mesopotamian lands, where Curtius at times referred to the region of 'Lydia' in a manner that recalled the old kingdom of the expanded state, thus Asia Minor west of the Halys river.[128] Unable to untwine these knotted threads, we will defer to simply using 'Persian' when regional appellations and ethnographies remain less than well defined, and refer to their inhabitants as 'Asiatic' where their origins are mixed or contested.

Herodotus, faced with the task of combining 'oriental dynasties with Greek genealogies in the first attempt at international chronology',[129] and Ctesias, himself a physician to Great King Artaxerxes II (Artaxšaçā in Old Persian), argued over the conflicting traditions behind the Achaemenid dynasty founded by Cyrus I and which endured from 539 to 330 BCE, ending with Alexander's defeat of Darius III. Originally named 'Artashata' in Persia and Kodommanos (Latinised, Codommanus) to the Greeks, 'Darius' originated as something approximating 'Darayavaus of the haxamanisiya' in Old Iranian. Yet the founder of the line, Achaemenes, was as mythical as Romulus, the legendary founder of Rome. Cyrus the Great was an Elamite described as half-Median – Xenophon confirmed his Median roots through Astyages and his Perseidae origins from Cambyses[130] – though 'Cyrus' is a Latinised-Greek derivative descended from Old Persian (Kūruš) with Elamite and Assyrian overtones, the meaning of which is still debated, though Plutarch claimed it was the Persian word for 'sun'.[131]

The tombs at Naqsh-e Rustam (close to Persepolis), and that identified as Darius I's, in particular, among other less-legible inscriptions at the necropolis, along with the relief at Behistun (Bastagana in Persian, 'place of god'), are rich in multi-lingual engravings referring to the conquests of the Great Kings. Cuneiform syllabary often placed Elamite beside Akkadian as well as Old Persian – the languages that later transmuted into the more broadly used Parsi and written in Aramaic script.[132] Like the bilingual and trilingual stone inscriptions of the Ptolemies, these provide us with 'rosetta stones' of rare linguistic clarity.[133]

To the Persians the Hellenes were *Yauna*, Ionians, though it seems *Yauna takabara* specifically referred to Macedonians and possibly because of their distinctive felt hats, the traditional flat *kausiai*, that would now be seen across the empire as Alexander's army marched east.[134]

The 50 x 82 feet Behistun Inscription of Darius I carved sometime in his reign ca. 522-486 BCE. The multi-lingual texts in Old Persian, Elamite and Babylonian recorded Darius' lineage and battles through the upheaval caused by the deaths of his predecessors, Cyrus the Great and his son, Cambyses.

ATHLIOS PAR' ATHLIOU DI' ATHLIOU PROS ATHLION: THE GRUDGING FACE OF FEALTY

Scholars have noted that from the beginning of the Asian campaign Alexander 'acted not merely as a conqueror, but as the rightful heir' to the Persian royal line.[135] Quite possibly he saw the Asian hinterland as a 'Pantheon' for installing the legend that would underpin the new *anabasis*, his journey into the Asian interior. In Tarn's opinion 'the primary reason that Alexander invaded Persia was, no doubt, that he never thought of not doing it; it was his inheritance', as were the vast lands that lay across the Hellespont.[136]

'Persuasion through words is not a characteristic of kings but of orators',[137] and as early as 330 BCE, as Alexander ventured into the heart of the Persian Empire, Demosthenes' *On the Crown* made a scathing declaration to Aeschines, the *philomakedon*, on the extent of Macedonian continued domination in Greece.[138] Having subdued Greece in the wake of his father's death, Alexander was confirmed as *hegemon* (literally the 'dominant one'), or in the military context, *strategos autokrator*, of the League of Corinth,[139] a federation which represented *to koinon ton Hellenon*, the community of Greeks and their Defenders of the Peace. He inherited two seats on the Amphictionic Council and life archonship of the Thessalian League, as Philip had before him, deftly holding measuring scales in one hand and a dagger in the other, like Themis and her divine justice.[140] For the Macedonian court at Pella was 'freeing' Greece from the Persian yoke and yet holding the sword of Damocles over the *kyria ekklesia*, the treasured assembly meeting that kept Athenian *demokratia* (literally 'people power') alive and vocal from the Pnyx.[141]

He left behind him a smouldering resentment despite the oath sworn by its members under the Treaty of the Common Peace, the *Koine Eirene*:

> I swear by Zeus, Gaia, Helios, Poseidon and all the gods and goddesses. I will abide by the common peace, and I will neither break the agreement with Philip, nor take up arms on land or sea, harming any of those abiding by the oaths. Nor shall I take any city, or fortress, nor harbour by craft or contrivance, with intent of war against the participants of the war. Nor shall I depose the kingship of Philip or his descendants...[142]

The oath went on to list all the member states and the 'peace' was watched over by a Macedonian garrison positioned on the heights of the Acrocorinth and Chalcis which were described by Polybius as two of the 'Three Fetters of Greece' (Demetrias in Thessaly became the third), as well as at the Cadmea, the citadel of Thebes.[143] More garrisons would soon appear under Alexander's regent, Antipater. The real meaning of Greek loyalty, however, was epitomised by Athens' contribution to the Macedonian-led war effort: the city-state supplied no more than 600

The natural auditorium of the hill of the Pnyx in the foreground and the view across to the Acropolis.

cavalrymen and twenty triremes from a fleet of over 300 in commission.[144] So it is no surprise to read that of the fifty-two attested satraps Alexander appointed to govern the newly acquired Persian satrapies, only three were Greek and none of them came from the mainland, a clear sign of continued distrust. Of Alexander's eighty-four identified *hetairoi* just nine were Greek, which illustrates the reality of the 'Panhellenic' crusade.[145] And only thirty-three Greeks were associated with any *military* command from a list of 834 officers (principally Macedonians) identified in the accounts of Alexander's decade-long campaign.[146]

In the first major pitched battle in Asia at the Granicus River in the summer of 334 BCE, the Macedonians slaughtered some 18,000 of perhaps 20,000 'warlike and desperate' Greek mercenaries at the conclusion of the engagement, or so we are led to believe from cross-referencing Arrian's claims with Plutarch's. Four Persian satraps and three of Darius' family also fell. Any Greeks rounded up (Athenians, Thessalians and Thebans) were sent back to hard labour camps in Macedonia. But we should once again be cautious with the numbers, for this has the distant feel of the propaganda of the on-campaign historian Callisthenes, in the form of a lesson to Hellas and the Corinthian League; modern interpretations suggest 5,000 mercenaries might have been killed.[147] But Alexander was to have a more effective stranglehold on Greek dissent: he soon controlled the corn supply routes from Egypt and trade through the Hellespont to the Kingdom of Bosphorus and its commercially favourable grain contracts. The Black Sea ports remained the largest grain producer and Greece required 'more imported corn than any other nation', a vulnerable state of affairs, as Demosthenes voiced.[148]

Nevertheless, obtaining the approbation of Athens, Plato's 'Hellas of Hellas', seems to have weighed heavy on Alexander's mind, or in the mind of those who crafted his public relations machine, for the ethnic divide that separated Macedonians and Greeks persisted through the campaigns.[149] When the Great King's palace at Persepolis burned and 'prosperity turned to misery', it was for Athens that revenge was reportedly being extracted.[150] In Bactria, Callisthenes had apparently needed to remind his king that it was to the dominion of 'Hellas' that Asia was being added (though this may be posthumous Greek spin for it was woven into Callisthenes' rejection of *proskynesis*, the prostration before the king that emulated Persian court protocol).[151] And in India ('lands east of the Persian Empire', much took place in modern Pakistan), Onesicritus claimed Alexander commenced battle with King Porus (a derivative of his Hellenised name) of the Paurava region, broadly the Punjab, with the cry: 'O Athenians can ye possibly believe what perils I am undergoing to win glory in your eyes.'[152]

We do sense that Alexander, an honorary Athenian citizen (as Philip had become following the victory at Chaeronea in 338 BCE which brought Greece to its knees), wished to be acknowledged for allowing the city its democratic heart, but he knew in order to do so Athens would need to be hemmed in by pro-Macedonian oligarchs, a situation that left the Pella-salaried Aristotle in a precarious position. It is difficult to say whether Alexander genuinely admired Athens' constitutional ideals, or whether he shared the jaundiced view of Xenophon and, in particular, the exiled Alcibiades (ca. 450-404 BCE), on its unique governmental system once they became exiles of the state: 'As for democracy, the men of sense among us knew what it was, and I perhaps as well as any, as I have more cause to complain of it: but there is nothing new to be said of a patent absurdity.'[153] Thucydides credited Alcibiades with a speech that extolled the virtues of conquest, and that would have been easier for Alexander to comprehend: 'We cannot fix the exact point at which our empire shall stop… and we must scheme to extend it', for 'if we cease to rule others, we are in danger of being ruled ourselves.'[154]

No doubt as a part of his education syllabus in the Temple of the Nymphs at Mieza, Aristotle had credited the tight formation of the hoplite phalanx with the forging of a cooperative ethos that made a Greek *polis,* and so *demokratia,* possible, and yet his *Athenian Constitution* detailed its bureaucratic drag: Athens attempted to employ 7,000 jurymen, 1,600 archers, 1,200 knights, 500 council members, 500 arsenal guards, 700 other resident officials with 700 more overseas, 12,500 hoplites (in time of war) and twenty coastal vessels with 2,000 crew; all on an annual income of not much over 1,000 talents once the silver production from the silver mines at Laurium tapered off. Few of the potential new revenue streams suggested in Xenophon's *Poroi* (or *Peri Prosodon*, broadly 'ways and means', or 'revenues') had ever been introduced. It was in this environment that *leiturgia* (the root of 'liturgies') evolved, requiring the wealthier citizens to assume the funding of onerously expensive public activities in return for an honorific; almost one hundred liturgical appointments existed for festivals alone and these increased under the *Diadokhoi*. What the constitution failed to mention was the additional cost of a slave ratio of perhaps three to one serving the citizens in Athens.[155]

Conceivably, with the dichotomies of Aristotle's *Politics* fighting in his head, Alexander adopted an erratic policy that turned the cities in his path into an eclectic mix of 'loyal' democracies, oligarchies, tyrannies and indefinable in-betweens.[156] Philip's advanced expeditionary force under Parmenio, Attalus and Amyntas had done much the same through 336/335 BCE and some of the alliances they formed were inherited by Alexander, though townsfolk had been sold into slavery by his predecessors too.[157] Although Philip's foray into Asia Minor had found receptive ears in a few Greek cities, others living symbiotically with the Great King's satraps under the King's Peace of 387/6 BCE (otherwise known as the Peace of Antalcidas, which had once maintained Spartan supremacy in Greece) just saw trouble ahead.

ISOCRATES' IDEOLOGICAL INVASION, ALEXANDER'S ARGEAD ADVENTURE

Unlike Xenophon who had his Theban friend, Proxenus, to act as a *proxenos* and broker relations with Cyrus the Younger, Alexander had received no formal invite to Asia.[158] He did, nevertheless, have Isocrates' famous 'persuasion through words'. How influential was his early plea for *koinonia*, a commonality of purpose, remains conjecture, for it had failed to unite Greece against the Macedonian threat. As well as reaching out to Philip II, the Athenian rhetor had courted the fourteen-year-old Macedonian prince through correspondence; Isocrates' letter praised Alexander's *philanthropos*, his *philosophos* and his *philathenaios*, the love of Athens.[159] The *Rhetoric to Alexander*, possibly written around 340 BCE by Anaximenes, suggests the prince was indeed a political target in his malleable teens.[160] Isocrates had challenged Philip to Heraclean efforts, but his rousing words, more sycophantic than practical on the Pellan-strained budget, might have resonated deeper with the young self-assured Alexander:

> Be assured that a glory unsurpassable and worthy of the deeds you have done in the past will be yours when you shall compel the barbarians – all but those who have fought on your side – to be serfs of the Greeks, and

when you shall force the king who is now called Great to do whatever you command. For then will naught be left for you except to become a god.[161]

Xenophon and his working colleague, King Agesilaus of Sparta, had shared Isocrates' view, though the deep-rooted resentment of Sparta's supremacy in the wake of the Peloponnesian War made her leadership of any Panhellenic force impossible. Moreover, Sparta had been aided by Cyrus the Younger in the last years of the conflict, a state of affairs that earned the pro-Spartan Xenophon his exile from Athens.[162] Since then, military supremacy had passed to Thebes under the remarkable generals Epaminondas, Pelopidas and Pammenes (died 364, 362, 356 BCE respectively), whose military reforms had led victory at Leuctra in 371 BCE over Sparta which was either deliberately excluded by Philip from the League of Corinth, or was standing aloof in a display of *xenalasia*.[163] When Thebes was destroyed by Alexander in 335 BCE, Isocrates' decades-old call for the invasion of Persia fell upon the new Macedonian *hegemon*.

When Alexander picked up the challenge, to obtain the funding for the expedition that would extend his rule beyond the bounds the gods and heroes approved of – so Themistocles had warned – he had been forced to borrow some 800 talents and at a loan rate that probably reflected the risk to the capital from (we assume) the Macedonian aristocracy.[164] He exempted Macedonians from tax to consolidate his position after Philip's death and was now dishing out crown lands to secure further funds, though Perdiccas, the future *Somatophylax*, is famously said to have declined any such security, joining Alexander with a simpler trust in his 'hopes for the future'.[165] Curtius and Arrian claimed the king still carried a debt of 500 talents from his father; this may have been derived from a court source who had wished to reinforce the non-pecuniary notion of loyalty of the state soldiers crossing to Asia, if it was not an allusion to the similar plight of the younger Cyrus in Xenophon's *Anabasis*.[166]

The alleged 60 or 70 talents remaining in the royal coffers at Philip's death would have covered the wages of the 30,000 or so mixed infantry Alexander crossed to Asia with for only a few meagre weeks without additional plunder coming their way, discounting the far higher remuneration the cavalry would have expected; Duris of Samos (date of birth uncertain, possibly as late the 330s BCE), calculated Alexander had funds sufficient for thirty days and Onesicritus claimed he owed 200 talents besides.[167] The 800 newly borrowed talents would have maintained the expedition for no more than a further several months, and, as a result, Alexander was forced to disband his 160-ship navy (costing perhaps 250 talents a month) after the siege of Miletus due to financial constraints; his continued mistrust of his Greek naval officers in the face of 400 Phoenician ships still in Persian employ possibly played a part.[168] Although the treasury at Sardis would yield to him and Tarsus would be captured intact (giving him his first mint), and no doubt his adoptive mother, Queen Ada of Caria, made available funds from her stronghold of Alinda, the pressure was on for a confrontation that would prise the Persian treasury open.[169]

As Alexander pressed on down the coast of Asia Minor, cities and synoecisms that refused immediate obeisance were ransomed, garrisoned, destroyed and pillaged, or occasionally pardoned on the promise of good behaviour. For apart from a few Greek cities on the Aegean seaboard, these were *not* members of the League of Corinth, and thus they were fair game, despite any ancient Ionian League affiliations.[170] Non-Greek communities (those in Lycia, for example) could expect no terms at all; essentially their fate lay in the manner in which they treated the Macedonian advance.

Some cities failed to comply from the outset; others did, and then revolted. More than twenty cities came under siege, and Alexander (if not Philip II before him), and not Demetrius the son of Antigonus, should have earned the epithet *Poliorketes*, the Beseiger.[171] When they did finally fall, Greek, Macedonian or local resident governors were installed (or reinstalled) with *nomographoi* to draft new laws and 'correct' those that had been already been drafted or imposed by the *koine sympoliteia,* the federal state body that oversaw their interests.[172] In Miletus, Alexander was even nominally elected (or self-appointed) as *stephanephoros*, chief magistrate, for the year 334/333 BCE. There was no Thucydidean Melian Dialogue to weigh up arguments of alignment or neutrality; as Solon (ca. 638-558 BCE) had once been warned: 'Written laws, are just like spiders' webs; they hold the weak and delicate in their meshes, but get torn to pieces by the rich and powerful.'[173] In fact Solon had himself departed Greece for ten years to avoid being called to task for the decrees that backfired in the wake of his own reforms.[174]

In the view of Tarn, Alexander's behaviour was justifiable; he pointed out that the state of affairs in Asia Minor, specifically relating to these years, required extraordinary measures because the outcome of the war with the Great King was still far from certain.[175] We have an equally conspicuous *apologia* by Arrian: Alexander's '… instructions were to overthrow the oligarchies and install democracies throughout, to restore their own local legislation in each city, and to remit the tribute they had been paying to the barbarians.' This appears to overlook the key objective of the arrangement: the tribute (*phoros*) was now redirected to the Macedonian regime.[176]

In truth, all political ideologies suited Alexander's direction and in isolation each of them worked, for a while. A number of inscriptions preserve the essence of Macedonian *machtpolitik* and none better than Alexander's *Letter to the Chians*, thought to have been written sometime between 334 and 332 BCE. The decree provided for the return of exiles to the island (including the historian Theopompus) with a 'democratic' constitution to be reinstated, and yet it demanded that all judicial disputes be referred directly to Alexander. Though Tarn argued this was the 'decent thing' to stop the civil strife, Chios, a member of the Corinthian League (as was Lesbos), was forced to donate twenty fully-crewed and funded triremes to the war effort, and the island was summarily garrisoned at its own expense – though the occupiers were termed a 'defence force'.

To accomplish what he did, and to hold it together with limited military resources, required the threatening charisma and his exploitative genius Alexander had inherited from his father. But it was not a sustainable policy; loyalty was fickle, garrisons were vulnerable to being overrun and so were his regional governors. But it was a salutary lesson on Macedonian-style freedom; the Common Peace was, as Badian noted, an 'aggressive peace'… 'governed by the will of one man'.[177] And so in Alexander's Homeric adventure the 'liberation' from Persia was to become a very mixed blessing.[178]

The cynical Diogenes, watching from occupied Corinth, is said to have summed up the campaigning king, his regent then in Athens, and his messenger (named Athlios) who had just arrived in the city, with, '*athlios par' athliou di' athliou pros athlion*'. This broadly (and here with poetic licence) translates as 'wretched son of wretched sire to wretched wight by wretched squire'.[179] The mixed signals broadcast by this new order in the Eastern Mediterranean seaboard had to be weighed up against the certainty of annihilation if Alexander's ambition was stifled.

The confrontation that would finally access significant funds from the Persian treasury came with the second major pitched battle with the Great King's army beside the Pinarus River at Issus in Cilicia in November 333 BCE, near the strategic border 'gates' that separate Cilicia from Upper Syria. Demosthenes was hoping that Alexander, the *meirakion* (stripling) that held Greece under his thumb, would be 'trampled under Persian hooves'.[180] The result was quite different: Darius fled in the face of Alexander's penetrating charge in his direction despite the spirited defence of his nobles, forcing him to eventually abandon his chariot, shield and bow, along with his family and his harem of 329 concubines. Further hauls at nearby Damascus included hostile Spartan and Athenian envoys and some 2,600 talents of coined money, 500 pounds of wrought silver and 7,000 loaded pack animals.[181]

Some 100,000 infantry and 10,000 of Darius' cavalry were reportedly slain, though Justin clarified that 40,000 were actually taken prisoner. Only 300 Macedonian infantry and 150 cavalry fell, claimed Diodorus who incongruously added, '… the cavalry on both sides was engaged and many were killed as the battle raged indecisively because of the evenly matched fighting qualities…' The Persians had additionally '… launched at Alexander such a shower of missiles that they collided with one another in the air'; the source behind the figures (Arrian's text suggests it might be Ptolemy) was obviously expecting readers to conclude that few arrows had found their mark. Curtius more plausibly added that that 4,500 of Alexander's men were additionally wounded.[182]

The battle at Issus may have been the first instance in which the Macedonian infantrymen were provided reason to question Alexander's motives as well as their own position in the scheme of things. In a pre-battle address to his troops, Alexander encouraged the Illyrians and Thracians to loot and pillage but there is no mention that any wealth filtered down to his Macedonian regulars. All this was, however, buried beneath the grander themes of post-battle chivalry that saw the captured Persian women embraced as Alexander's own.[183]

Keeping royal hostages alive on the pretext of bargaining for a larger prize was supportable. But Alexander assured Darius' captive daughters that he would provide dowries for their marriages and find them suitable husbands – himself and Hephaestion as it turned out – for he married Stateira and Hephaestion married Drypetis at Susa in 324 BCE. Alexander further promised to bring up Darius' young son as his own and to show him royal honour.[184] Had Alexander's regular soldiers known of the outcome, it is doubtful they would have put their lives on the line at Issus, despite Diodorus' claim that Alexander '…won universal recognition throughout his own army for his exceeding propriety of conduct', behaviour that Diodorus hoped would echo through the future ages.[185]

Some 8,000 Greek mercenaries had made good their escape in the cover of darkness.[186] Up to this point, more Greek mercenaries had fought *for* Darius III than in the invasion force; it was a state of affairs captured by an earlier Theban proclamation: 'Anyone who wished to join the Great King and Thebes in freeing the Greeks and destroying the tyrant of Greece [Alexander] should come over to them.'[187] Those behind the Theban revolt were attempting to revive a Boeotian confederacy, one supposedly disbanded in 386 BCE (and again in 336 BCE).[188] Some 50,000 mercenaries might have eventually found their way into the Great King's ranks, and if captured the punishment for their 'treachery' was bound to be harsh; many were exiles of their city-states care of Philip's earlier campaigns.[189]

The next major campaign episode, the drawn-out siege of Tyre in 332 BCE and the slaughter that followed, warned of the consequences of continued opposition to Alexander's war machine; after the Macedonian envoys had been cast from the walls which were finally breached some seven months later, 8,000 civilians were massacred in Tyre itself and 2,000 were reportedly crucified along the beach. Alexander had now destroyed both cities of the Phoenician Cadmus.[190] The Greeks had always viewed the aquiline-featured *Phoinikes* (Phoenicians, though they still termed themselves Canaanites) with suspicion. They were shrewd and cunning traders who had settled at Aradus, Byblos, Berytus, Sidon and Tyre some

2,000 years before, and who furtively slipped in and out of Mediterranean ports after offloading their cargoes; no doubt their merchandising contacts were secretly coveted by the Greeks, and Herodotus all but blamed them for starting the Trojan War.[191]

Habitually settling on coastal islands into a loose Phoenician federation, here at Tyre, some 600 yards of maritime arrogance separated them from the shore; Alexander set about building a mole 200-feet wide so that '... they too would understand they belonged to the mainland.'[192] He had already proven it could be done; Clazomenae had been joined to the coast with a permanent causeway a year or so before. The siege at Tyre requiring an estimated 28,000-plus tons of grain to feed the attackers, probably accounting for many of the support ships from Rhodes and the other 'allies' who watched on as a seaborne competitor was being battered into submission.[193] It is the silted-over remains of Alexander's mole that joins the city to the mainland today.

Accounts of the military ingenuity employed against the Phoenician mother-city spanned many colourful pages. The artillery knowledge Philip's engineers had gained from the innovations of Dionysius I of Syracuse, and which had been employed in the sieges Philip II brought to bear on Olynthus, Perinthus and Byzantium, was passed down to Alexander who had already used it well at Miletus and Halicarnassus (Bodrum in Turkey).[194] The taking of the city became a challenge that inspired the Thessalian, Diades ('the man who took Tyre', successor to Polyidus, a siege engineer for Philip) to invent and further develop movable towers (*phoretoi pyrgoi*), wheeled rams (*arietes*), drills (*trypana*), cranes (*korakes*), possibly 'belly shooters' (*grastraphetes*) and the new rock-hurling torsion catapults, the *katapeltai Makedonikoi*.

Arrian provided a description of the catapult-carrying warships, *mechanophorai nees,* which bombarded the walls. This in turn required the defenders to employ fire-throwers of bitumen, sulphur and other combustibles, as well as spoked spinning wheels to deflect the incoming projectiles, while red-hot sand was poured down into the armour of Alexander's men.[195] The siege technology would pass down the generations through the lost writing of Diades himself and into the descriptions of Agesistratus and Athenaeus' *Mechanicus*, through Ctesibius' *Construction of Artillery,* Biton's *Construction of War-machines and Artillery*, into the new catapult technology in Polyidus' *On Machines*, Heron's treatises *Belopoeika* and *Cheiroballistra*, and to the extant treatise of Aeneas Tacticus' *Defence of Fortified Positions* (written soon after ca. 357 BCE) which survived along with Vitruvius' three chapters on artillery for the Roman army to exploit.[196]

This was a far cry from the honour code of the 'spear-famed lords of Euboea' who apparently banned missiles in the early Archaic 'mythistorical' Lelantine War ca. 700 BCE, and it renders the opening lines of Heron's *Belopoeika* (*On Arrow-Making*) somewhat paradoxical: 'Artillery-construction has surpassed argumentative training… and taught mankind how to live a tranquil life.'[197] The Tyrian siege was a tense, bitter, drawn-out and expensive delay in Alexander's progress. Yet the city's eventual fall and the tribute to the dead is afforded a single line by Plutarch and Justin, less than a quarter-page by Arrian, and a meagre half-page by Curtius who provided the most detailed account (some thirty Loeb edition pages) of the siege.[198] Despite the Phoenician priests roping down and nailing Tyrian Apollo to his pedestal, with proposals to reinstate the Carthaginian tradition of sacrificing a freeborn son to Canaanite El (Cronus to the Greeks, Saturn to the Romans), the gods joined Alexander, and the Phoenician city that had survived a thirteen-year siege by Nebuchadnezzar II two and a half centuries before (585 through 572 BCE), was finally taken.[199]

But what immediately became of the precious Tyrean murex purple dye trade that fetched its weight in silver, giving us the Byzantine honorific *porphyrogennetos,* 'born in the purple', is unreported.[200] The murex divers reappeared some years later when transferred to fleet maintenance in the planned dockyards at Babylon, but neither recorded is the lingering hatred engendered by the sale of a reported 15,000 to 30,000 survivors (7,500 may be more plausible) into slavery with additional refugees flooding the Mediterranean.[201] The enigmatic Phoenician ships of Tarshish, a fleet that once defied the summer sailing season the Greeks adhered to, were never mentioned again and with them surely disappeared some of the closely guarded knowledge of safe anchorages, freshwater sources, trading outposts and the mineral deposits of Northern Europe and the tin islands of Britain, now accessed by sea since the Etruscans took control of the overland routes through France.[202] The Phoenician-exploited silver deposits at Tartessus (possibly Tarshish) had been known to the Greeks and coveted since Colaeus the Samian explorer and merchant was reportedly blown off course when voyaging to Egypt ca. 638 BCE.[203]

Alexander's (alleged) simultaneous declaration of war on the 500-year-old Carthage merited a few words from Curtius and does not feature in any other extant account.[204] Carthaginian envoys were present in Tyre (though Alexander gave them safe passage, according to Arrian) and Justin curiously recorded the presence of a Hamilcar Rhodanus in the campaign entourage; he had been sent by Carthage to gather information about Alexander's intentions, probably before the Macedonian king entered Mesopotamia. This detail does not appear elsewhere either, and was perhaps scooped up by Trogus at Gallia Narbonensis.[205] Carthage, by now more famous for its export of carpets and pillows to Greece according to the comedian Hermippus, was obviously expecting the worst after the Tyrian sun god was renamed Apollo *Philalexander*; the unfortunate Hamilcar was executed upon his return to Carthage for allegedly plotting against the city.[206]

'THOU WILT NOT BE ZEUS MERELY BECAUSE THOU GRASPEST THE THUNDERBOLT.'[207]

Although Aristotle's influential writings had cautioned that 'a youth is an unsuitable student of civil philosophy', his most famous pupil was setting out to change the world.[208] Alexander did not wish to simply conquer, he wanted to seduce, and whether vainglorious, visceral, or carefully calculated propaganda, this is where the thaumaturge, Callisthenes, *did* come in, for a while. After the sieging and storming of Gaza, the route was now clear for the invasion of Egypt where Alexander's legend could truly be developed.

Amongst the *thaumata* that must have proliferated Callisthenes' account, we hear of sacred springs coming to life and the Pamphylian Sea parting to allow the Macedones to navigate a narrow rocky coastal track; presumably this report was compiled with Alexander's blessing and it was later swept up by the poet Menander (ca. 342-290 BCE), an associate of Theophrastus and Demetrius of Phalerum, his once pupil:[209]

> How Alexander-like, indeed, this is; and if I seek some one,
> Spontaneous he'll present himself; and if I clearly must
> Pass through some place by sea, this will lie open to my steps.[210]

Arrian explained the Pamphylian phenomenon in less divine terms; the coastal road could only be negotiated when a north wind blew, otherwise the route would be submerged. But aquatic feats were far from original, and miraculous water-crossings were a symbol of legitimacy when attached to campaigning kings. Xenophon's *Anabasis* credited the Euphrates with yielding to Cyrus the Younger who waded across its span, and Cyrus the Great enjoyed a notable revenge when diverting the River Gyndes for the impiety of swallowing his warhorse. More pertinent to Alexander's cause we have Xerxes' triumphant bridge across the Hellespont and which briefly joined Europe and Asia in a hubristic defiance of prevailing doctrine, though combining the empires *was* Xerxes' destiny claimed the banished Athenian, Onomacritus.[211] Inevitably, the *Romance* gave Alexander power over dangerous water when he crossed the River Stranga when it froze every night, enabling him to meet, and then make good an escape from, Darius at Persepolis.[212]

Alexander *was* establishing his own romance, even in his life. Callisthenes, along with Anaxarchus (ca. 380-320 BCE), had annotated Aristotle's copy of Homer's *Iliad* (the 'Recension of the Casket'), an editing possibly spurred on by Aristotle's (now-lost) *Homeric Problems*, which had highlighted the epic's inconsistences; Alexander is said to have kept the edited scrolls close.[213] Reliving the epic *Iliad*, in which the 'temporal boundary between the ages of myth and history is in fact a fuzzier, less distinct line than appears at first glance', was a role that suited Alexander, who took a firmly euhemeristic stance when tracking down his heroes.[214] He believed he was following in the footsteps of Heracles and Dionysus the conqueror of the Orient, and with a sense of the *arete* and *aidos*, the honour and duty, that the homage would have bestowed; ominously Aidos, the goddess of reverence and respect, was the companion goddess of Nemesis, who stood for indignation and retribution. Euripides' description of Dionysus, with his juxtaposed qualities and polysemousness, was peculiarly relevant to Alexander: he was both the 'most terrible' and 'most gentle', crossing male and female as well as things Greek with foreign.

Euripides' *Bacchae*, written at Pella ca. 407 BCE (posthumously premiered in Athens in 405 BCE) and possibly inspired by Macedonian court behaviour (or from the legacy of the Phrygian occupation of Macedonia), claimed Dionysus had travelled through Bactria, the likely home of Alexander's wife, Roxane. When we consider that Alexander had named his first son Heracles, we might wonder if he would have named his second son Dionysus had he recovered at Babylon.[215] Euripides' tragedy also portrayed the god of wine and ritual madness (whose divinity was here being rejected) as bringing destruction upon the ancient city of Thebes, and this could help explain why Euripides remained in the Macedonian king's favour.

Alexander's appointment of Antipater's son, Iolaos, as his chief cupbearer (*archioinochooi*) perhaps recalled Euripides' lines in the *Herakleidai*: 'You have heard of me, I think. I am Iolaos, known as the right hand man of Heracles.'[216] Of course, on campaign Iolaos served as an informal hostage to ensure the regent's loyalty back home. But this hypostatic union of the present and the past would have proven more politically useful than Aristotle's Peripatetic penchant for rational classifications, or Thucydides' subordination of the past to the present that had eliminated the fingers of the divine,[217] for where Herodotus' scrolls gave Alexander the glories of Greece, Thucydides' had captured only the misfortunes of the day.[218]

The Macedonian king paid homage to the gods – 'an immortal aristocracy' – and in return they were expected to accept his notion of *isotheos*, his equality to them. But Alexander also knew 'the gods helped those who helped themselves',[219] for the adage *syn Athena kai kheira kinei*, 'Athena is with you, but you too need to move your hands', made it clear the deities favoured men of action.[220] And so Alexander sacrificed to the River Danube before negotiating its crossing, and to Protesilaus whose tomb at Elaios had been plundered by Xerxes. He may have even once (earlier) sacrificed at Aulis near Thebes as Agamemnon had done on the way to the Trojan War; the Spartan Agesilaus was once denied the privilege, so pushing Greece towards the Peloponnesian War.[221]

Alexander observed the rites to Poseidon and the Nereids before sailing the narrows of the Hellespont and he made oblations to Priam and Athena when arriving at the 'small cheap' temple of Athena on the alleged ruins of Troy; the ceremonies reminded everyone why Philip had declared war on Persia – to exact retribution for her profanation of Greek temples.[222] Alexander had adopted the role of a new Protesilaus, the hero from the *Iliad*, and he was the first of the coalition army to set foot on Asian soil after hurling his spear to it to denote *chora doryktetos*, a spear-won prize. He was duly crowned by his sailing master and enthusiastic entourage.[223] If, as it was claimed, he had learned the *Iliad* scrolls *apo narthekos,* by heart, it would have required the memorising of 15,693 standardised lines of dactylic hexameter. Alexander is said to have kept the epic under his pillow along with a dagger, and if this might have been Onesicritus' own rendering of an 'armed philosopher king', it nevertheless appears symbolic of the mindset of the man.[224]

When seeking the blessing of Artemis in her sanctuary at Ephesus, propitious-looking entrails were even paraded around Alexander's camp in hepatoscopic triumph; the superstitious troops were unlikely to complain at ceremonies of *sphagia* (signs derived from bloodletting, usually by cutting the throat), for all received a share of the sacrificial meat.[225] Before battle at Issus, Alexander offered to Thetis and once again he followed Achilles' own pre-battle ritual; in Egypt, Apis was honoured and in Babylon, Bel, as well as those deities suggested by the Chaldean priests.[226] Alexander was clearly hedging his polytheistic bets and courting gods linked to both ancestral friend and enemy, besides those Ammon had chosen for him. He was now undermining both Aristotle and Euripides, for both had espoused the superiority of the Greeks and their gods over barbarians in no uncertain terms.

Hesiod had summed-up his *Works and Days* with: 'Well with god and fortune is he who works knowledge of all this, giving the immortals no cause for offence, judging the bird-omens and avoiding transgressions.'[227] And yet Alexander's rant at his seer, Demophon, whether historic or allegorical, captured something of the contradiction within his piety: 'when I have before my eyes such important matters and not the entrails of animals, what could be a greater hindrance to me than a superstitious seer?' In this particular instance, in Mallia in India, his ignoring the signs was ill advised; Demophon cautioned him against battle and Alexander almost lost his life.[228] Yet even the revered Chaldeans were not above reproach: 'the best of prophets is the one who guesses right', Alexander reminded them, alluding to another line from a now lost Euripides tragedy.[229] Prediction was a dangerous business with the Macedonian king, and the seers would have recalled that Alexander ordered the crucifixion of the diviner who presided over the 'favourable' entrails on the day his father was stabbed to death at Aegae, though this would have been the perfect veneer of outrage from an only superficially grieving son.[230]

Philip had himself once sought oracular advice and he received a typically cryptic response: 'Wreathed is the bull. All is done. There is also the one who will smite him.'[231] He and any reader of Herodotus should have been aware of the misadventure of Croesus (reigned ca. 560-546 BCE) when interpreting his favourable-looking answer: the Delphic Oracle had told the Lydian king that if he invaded Cappadocia a mighty empire would fall; the already-prosperous Croesus never considered that it might be his own.[232] Wealth, as Aristophanes portrayed it, is blind; an avowed acquaintance of Aesop, Croesus nevertheless failed to heed his Fable of the Mule: every truth has two sides.

The oracles of Delphi, Dodona and Didyma did not disappoint with their ambiguous predictions given, according to Theopompus, in verse.[233] The priestess Pythia who Alexander himself dragged by force from the *adyton*, the inaccessible temple chamber, to extricate the reply he coveted on an 'inauspicious day', learned of his particular brand of piety the hard way.[234] Alexander should have known that the god of Delphi neither revealed, nor concealed, but just 'hinted' the truth.[235] The Pythia is said to have spoken only in a frenzied gibberish caused by the vapours arising from the Kerna below; in hindsight, it would have been more profitable to have assaulted the *prophetai*, the temple priests employed to interpret her responses.[236]

Less ambiguous was the result of the encounter with the Gordian Knot, 'Fate's silent riddle' that vexed all-comers in Phrygia. A famed waggon stood on the acropolis of the palace of Gordius and Midas and had been dedicated to Sabazios, a god the Greeks associated with Zeus. Midas tied it to a post with an impossibly intricate knot; oracular prediction held that whoever unravelled it would become the king of Asia.[237] Eyewitnesses variously reported that Alexander, driven by his *pothos*, yearning, either impetuously sliced through the ancient rope in frustration, or, as Aristobulus claimed, he cunningly unyoked the pin of the cart to which it was bound. This appears to be face-saving propaganda to hide an embarrassing performance – what Justin described as 'a false interpretation of the oracle'– even though thunder is said to have followed signifying the approval of the gods.[238]

'How is it to be decided whether the more dramatic or the more prosaic version of a story is the original one? The question of historical probability may be irrelevant: no one can really hope to know what actually happened at Gordium any more than one can say what song the Sirens sang.'[239] But as Robert Graves noted, Alexander's brutal cutting of the knot ultimately

Alexander and the riddle of the Gordian Knot. A line engraving from 1899 after a drawing by André Castaigne.

'... ended an ancient dispensation by placing the power of the sword above that of religious mystery.'[240] Any priestesses attending the oracle obviously knew nothing of the dangers of toying with Alexander's piety.

If Alexander was an acolyte to divine and heroic doctrine, he was no hollow dreamer, and in him legend was bound up in practical military method; so Homer sat beside Xenophon in the campaign tent. Alexander sought bodily protection from what had been presented to him as the 'shield of Achilles' at Troy, and he would have absorbed lessons on cavalry command from Xenophon's *Hipparchicus*.[241] To lead his men Alexander would have learned from Jason of Pherae whose exemplary behaviour Xenophon portrayed as unswerving self-restraint.[242] The lessons of fighting in Asia could already be learned from Xenophon's *Anabasis* (in particular the need for a sizeable cavalry force, which Xenophon and Cyrus lacked), and in his father's day stories and advice stemming from Spartan-led forays into Asia were surely absorbed by Philip as he planned his own campaign. So Alexander was no trailblazing 'Columbus', even if much geographical knowledge of the East remained shrouded in uncertainty; he was, as Bosworth proposed, more a 'Hernán Cortéz', the *conquistador* who brought down a civilisation and changed a newly opened old world forever.[243]

Neither was Alexander short on irony in victory, it seems. Following the battle at Issus, the Macedonians had received envoys from the freshly defeated Darius III, the 'antagonist to Alexander's genius' who reportedly spoke some Greek; with them came, reportedly, the offer of a huge ransom for the return of the Great King's captured family and *possibly* a concession to divide the Persian Empire at the Halys River (or Euphrates – sources conflict: there may have been as many as three separate offers).[244] What appear monochrome correspondences between the kings in the campaign accounts were reborn with much colour in the *Romance*.[245]

According to Diodorus, Alexander hid the Great King's olive branch and replaced it with a fabricated letter containing far less benign terms so his generals would reject them.[246] Certainly, if left to his Companions and the veteran Parmenio, 'the best tactician of his generals', the Macedonian war machine would have settled for a truce, for under the terms of Darius III's alleged peace offer, Alexander could have shared Asia with the Great King as his son-in-law.[247] Here the fate of the world turned on a singular response dictated in a campaign tent in Cilicia (or northern Mesopotamia), proving the course of history *can* indeed turn on the toss of a tetradrachm.

This particular episode does not appear in the texts of Arrian or Plutarch; if it *was* genuine, perhaps their 'court' sources have felt the charade was best hushed-up. But according to Curtius, Alexander chose an envoy curiously named Thersippus to carry his terse rejection back to the Persian king.[248] We know from Plutarch, who in turn took it from Heracleides, that it was a certain Thersippus who ran to Athens after the defeat of Darius I at Marathon some 160 years before.[249] Having just defeated his namesake (Darius III), and now encamped at Marathus, Alexander appears to have chosen a high-ranking man of exactly the same name to deliver his reply.[250]

Anyone sceptical of the associations that Alexander or his press corps were attempting to make, should recall that the previous battle at the River Granicus in May 334 BCE had been fought (it was claimed) on the anniversary of the fall of Troy;[251] Duris reckoned that took place exactly 1,000 years (to the month, Thargelion) before in 1,334 BCE.[252] The Granicus bordered the Anatolian Troad: the messages being sent out were clear. Although the Macedonian kings never campaigned in the Macedonian May-moon month of Daisios (traditionally a month of harvest-gathering), Alexander inserted a *second* month of Artemisius in the calendar, corresponding to the moon of April, to pull it off.[253] He was by then aged twenty-one and perhaps ten months.

Just a year earlier, the house of Pindar had remained untouched when Alexander flattened Thebes when it revolted upon receiving false reports of his death; the city's downfall was apparently heralded in by portents including a fountain running with blood. He released the relatives of those who had once hosted his own father (as a hostage) but some 6,000 Thebans were reportedly executed and 30,000 prisoners were sold into slavery to fund the cost of the campaign.[254] Although the *andrapodismos* (deportation and enslavement) ended 800 years of continuous occupation at Thebes, Alexander, nevertheless, paid homage to a fifty-two-year career that saw Pindar's *epinikia,* his victory odes, honour winners at the Olympic, Isthmian, Nemean and Pythian Games.

Besides, it was Pindar who introduced Zeus-Ammon, the hybrid god who became attached to Alexander's own divinity, to Greece in his *Pythian Ode 4*; Pindar dedicated a cult statue in 462 BCE to the sanctuary on the Cadmea, having seen the god being worshipped on his visit to Cyrene in

Libya.[255] A 'mean spirited' Thebes had fined her homebred celebrity 1,000 drachmas for his *Pythian Ode 1* in which the enemy, Athens, was praised for her defence against Xerxes' naval assault.[256] The costly lines read:

> I will earn
> the praise of Athens by singing of Salamis
> and of Sparta by making my theme
> the battles beneath Cithaeron
> where the curved-bow Medes strive and were crushed…[257]

Furthering any nostalgic attachment, Pindar had also written an encomium of the campaigner's predecessor, the flamboyant Alexander I who was termed a traitor by Demosthenes for his part in assisting the Persian advance at a time when Themistocles was insightfully persuading Athens to spend its rich silver finds of 483 BCE (from the mines of Maronia in Laurium) on a new Athenian fleet of 200 triremes – the fleet that helped smash Persian naval power at Salamis in 480 BCE. Athens theatrically recompensed Pindar ten-fold for the Theban fine.[258]

With these past incursions in his mind, Alexander minted coins depicting the Persian defeat at Salamis before himself confronting the might of her empire; it was a message to the Great King and an announcement of intention. Spoils from the battle at Gaugamela, the 'camel's house' (otherwise named Arbela),[259] that saw Darius III finally toppled from power in 331 BCE, were even sent to Croton in Sicily as compensation for her naval expense in that earlier epic defence of Greece.[260] Alexander's declaration of war on Carthage at the siege of Tyre in 332 BCE, if indeed it ever took place, was possibly motivated by its part in Xerxes' pincer movement generations before than its blood ties with the Phoenician mother-city then under siege.[261]

If Athens was unlikely to have granted him an early apotheosis for facing the Achaemenid threat, Alexander received the divine response he surely sought at the Ammonium at the Libyan Desert oracle of Siwa after being welcomed into Egypt by the native population that had been under the Persian yoke. The very public divine 'private reply', which suggested he was the son of Zeus-Ammon, was most likely crafted with Callisthenes' help, though if the priests of the sanctuary expected that Alexander would next proclaim himself pharaoh, then his immortality could hardly be denied.[262] The outcome *was* an avowed confirmation of his immortal blood and it readied him for the march ahead into the Asian interior.[263] The divinity was later ridiculed by Marcus Terentius Varro (ca. 116-27 BCE) in a work titled *Orestis or A Treatise on Insanity*[264] and satirised by Lucian (ca. 125-180 CE) who captured something of the dilemma and the real political agenda in his *Dialogues of the Dead*:

Philip: 'You cannot deny that you are my son this time, Alexander; you would not have died if you had been Ammon's.'

Alexander: 'I knew all the time that you, Philip, son of Amyntas, were my father. I only accepted the statement of the oracle because I thought it was good policy.'

Philip: 'What, to suffer yourself to be fooled by lying priests?'

Alexander: 'No, but it had an awe-inspiring effect upon the barbarians. When they thought they had a God to deal with, they gave up the struggle; which made their conquest a simple matter.'[265]

Alexander's *pothos* (desire or yearning) to journey through the desert and consult the deity, a god now with ties with both the East and West, was less unique than Callisthenes' account might have suggested.[266] The oracle was well known to the Greeks through their intermediaries in Cyrene, the lush 'spring' city consecrated to Apollo in Libya that had left its mark on Pindar.[267] Founded by famine-threatened settlers from Thera (Santorini) in 631 BCE and the birthplace of Eratosthenes (ca. 276-194 BCE) and Callimachus (ca. 310/305-240 BCE), Cyrene, along with its port, Apollonia, became a major centre of maritime trade and was minting its own coinage since the last quarter of the 6th century BCE on the Athenian standard. It was also the home to Aristippus' (ca. 435-356 BCE) hedonistic brand of philosophy, which produced a treatise titled *On Ancient Luxury,* which provided Diogenes Laertius with much doxographic *scandaleuse.*[268]

Plutarch explained that Cimon, who waged incessant war on Persia a century before, had also sent messengers to the Siwan oracle to obtain answers from Zeus-Ammon, and the Spartan commander Lysander, too, at the end of the 5th century BCE. Each was following in the windblown footsteps of Cambyses II (ruled 529-522 BCE) who reportedly lost a 50,000-strong army in a sandstorm (their remains were possibly discovered in 2012), and those of Heracles and Perseus before him.[269] Alas, Cimon did not live to receive his reply, but the emotional footprints were certainly there for Alexander to step into.

Cementing the foundations of Alexander's own apotheosic myth, and one appropriately born in Egypt, was the priest's allegorical slip of the tongue from 'O, Paidion' ('O, my son') to 'O, pai Dios' ('O, son of God', thus Zeus). We should recall that Alexander's forefather, Danaus, who settled in Argos, was in myth the son of Belus, the legendary king of Egypt; Alexander was stepping into yet another ancestral homeland.[270] We have no evidence of formalities to proclaim him pharaoh at this time except claims in the *Romance*, and, in any case, the more enduring epitaph was to be the founding of the city of Alexandria.[271] But to quote de Polignac's study of the Macedonian 'myth': 'Alexander stands at the crossroads of a Greek legend born out of the Libyan pilgrimage and the ancient Egyptian tradition of the pharaoh's divine conception…'[272]

As the Macedonian war machine advanced from Egypt into the heart of the Persian Empire, Alexander cited revenge as his mantra: it was unifying, uncomplicated, profitable and legitimate. Being *semeiotikos* when it suited him – observant of portentous signs – and having sacrificed to Phobos to bring terror to the enemy, he finally slept deeply late in the night before the battle at Gaugamela dated to 1ˢᵗ October 331 BCE. This may have been propaganda to counter the effect on morale of an ominous lunar eclipse,[273] for Curtius gave the impression that the phenomenon occurred 'right on the brink' of the final confrontation with Darius III, whereas Arrian, Plutarch, and tableted Babylonian observations, placed the eclipse some eleven days earlier; modern astronomical calculations point to the night of 20ᵗʰ September.[274] A source (the most obvious being Cleitarchus following Callisthenes' original propaganda) was obviously attempting to coincide the phenomenon that swallowed the 'far shining Goddess Selene' with the final toppling of the Achaemenid Empire.[275] Alexander's Egyptian diviners managed to spin the eclipse as portentously positive, and his seer, Aristander, who rode out in front of the ranks 'wearing a white mantle and crown of gold', pointed to a propitious eagle soaring overhead to motivate the Macedonian-led army.[276]

The Persians interpreted the eclipse differently: Herodotus claimed the Magi regarded the moon as the symbol of Persia; the Great King's soldiers knew it and fear permeated their ranks. Babylonian astronomical diaries additionally recorded 'deaths and plague occurred'; two days later a meteorite was seen 'flashing to earth' with two consecutive nights of 'falls of fire' along with an ominous reference to a dog being burned. Finally, there was 'panic in the camp'; by the time the armies faced off, there was apparently little confidence left on the Persian side of the plain.[277]

The morning of the battle, Alexander rode at the head of his royal cavalry *agema* (the king's own brigade) wearing a gleaming helmet fashioned by Theophilus, a sword of 'astonishing temper' from the king of the Citeans, an ornate Rhodian belt crafted by Helicon 'the ancient', and a thick linen *thorax* belonging to Darius himself, captured with booty at Issus two years before; the cuirass must have been far too large for Alexander (as was Darius' throne) though the effrontery of its bearing must have humiliated the Persian king.[278] Plutarch's rundown of the panoply is once again steeped in the *Iliad*; Alexander was now adorned with not just an ancestry that combined the gods of friend and foes, but with their panoply and weapons too.[279]

Alexander's return of the statues of the two tyrant slayers, Harmodius and Aristogeiton, from Susa to Athens soon after (where tyrannicides could find refuge, according to Callisthenes), and his burning of Persepolis, the Persian ceremonial capital modelled on Nineveh, echoed his continued retributions for those earlier Persian invasions of Greece.[280] As a 'political

No. -330 (BM 36761) Rev.

No. -330 (BM 36761) Obv.

Babylonian cuneiform tablet BM 36761 which formed part of the astronomical diaries recording the defeat of Darius at Gaugamela and Alexander's entrance into Babylon. With permission and © of The Trustees of the British Museum.

act' the destruction of the palace, the ceremonial home of Persian power, was defensible and it signified a regime change from the Achaemenids to the Argeads.[281] But Alexander had other reasons to be angry; mutilated Greeks had been encountered nearby (if reports are genuine and not designed to justify what came next) and despite his defeat at Gaugamela, Darius III was still on the loose.

Alexander would have additionally been aware of the rising tension within the Hellenic League in Greece which had recently resulted in a coalition led by Agis III of Sparta and an eventual battle with the Macedonian home army at Megalopolis in which the Greeks were funded by Persian gold. Alexander had himself sent funds to his regent, Antipater, to counter the accumulating threat (though probably too late to have had an effect). The message being sent from Persepolis was clear: if Alexander could now torch the Persian heartlands he could certainly burn Athens and the Peloponnese. On the other hand, Hellas was still supposed to rejoice in seeing the *hegemon* of the League of Corinth executing 'Greek' revenge. The result was, nevertheless, lamentable and Alexander is said to have regretted destroying the royal precinct, which was now, as Parmenio pointed out, his own property.[282]

The new conqueror of Asia was still pandering to the image Greece demanded, or rather the image he desired Greece demand of *him*: her long-awaited avenging hero with due cause and grievance. To cap it off he had Apelles paint him as Zeus wielding a thunderbolt to open a path to the gods.[283]

'OF WILD SYCOPHANTS AND TAME FLATTERERS'[284]

With the defeat of Darius, Alexander was effectively on the path to becoming the Great King of Persia, *Shahansha*, a title that came with connotations of divine approbation, even if it did not suggest the ruler was a god himself.[285] Heracles achieved his divinity through nobility of soul alone, though it arrived posthumously and thanks to the oracle at Delphi.[286] Being far less patient than his ancestral hero, Alexander knew true immortality lay in the lifetime recording of his deeds, 'monuments more durable than bronze', to quote Horace's *Odes*.[287] And so his campaign retinue included writers, philosophers, poets and classical antiquarians, and an unparalleled retinue of intellectuals: scientists, surveyors (*bematistes*), engineers and Aristotle-educated *hetairoi* recording the developing detail. And we should not forget the exiles that attached themselves to the mobile court. This was a proto 'Scipionic Circle', a group reminiscent of the scholars and philosophers Scipio Aemilianus (185-129 BCE) famously gathered about him two centuries later in Rome. Pondering the entourage in Asia, Cicero once questioned: 'How many historians of his achievements are said to have been with Alexander?'[288]

Inevitably, the group housed the fawning camp followers whose traits Diogenes likened to the 'worst biters' in nature: 'of wild beasts, the sycophant, and of tame animals, the flatterer'.[289] 'So great is the power of flattery, and nowhere greater, it seems, than among the greatest people.'[290] The court poetasters, including Agis of Argos, Choerilus of Iasus and Cleon of Sicily, were noteworthy amongst the *kolakeutikoi* (sycophants) who proffered Homeric comparisons to Alexander and encouraged Achaemenid-style *proskynesis*, full body prostration in front of the king.[291] And there were more besides, those Curtius referred to as 'the other dregs of their various cities', for the mobile Macedonian court and its *symposia*, which followed the Homeric tradition of strengthening bonds through the ritualistic feasting of the commander with his men, were the perfect venues to practise *he rhetorike techne*.[292] And no doubt some of the noise was *menoeikes* to Alexander, soothing words for a searching soul.[293] His early tutor, Lysimachus, had understood the prince in this respect; he took to referring to himself as 'Phoenix', to Alexander as 'Achilles' his pupil, and to Philip as 'Peleus' his father who had, in fact, befriended the hero Heracles.[294]

Alexander's relationship with these writers reflected the paradox in him, and to quote a further fable attributed to Aesop: 'We often despise what is most useful to us.'[295] He recognised the utility of their artful prose for his pro-Greek press corps, and yet despised his own reliance upon them to produce a truly timeless history – 'Some men are better served by their bitter-tongued enemies than by their sweet-smiling friends; because the former often tell the truth, the latter, never.'[296]

If there *is* any truth behind the late-sourced anecdotes preserving the king's scorn of Choerilus, who was apparently paid a gold coin for each quality verse he wrote, Alexander held a dim view of their efforts. Choerilus' epic 'excremental poetry' *had* inevitably likened Achilles to Alexander, whose reported response to the poet was less than enthusiastic: 'By the gods, I would rather be Homer's Thersites, than *your* Achilles.' Thersites was the dull-witted, bow-legged fool whose 'unbridled tongue' had branded the hero a coward in the *Iliad*; he was eventually slain by Achilles for mocking his grief over Penthesilea, the dead Amazon queen.[297] The *Romance* developed a variant in which Agamemnon took the place of the warrior.[298] But in Alexander's case, what none of the king's entourage trailing around the Persian Empire fully appreciated was that he *did* see himself as both Agamemnon and Achilles, the king that led a flotilla to war and its most eminent warrior who fought *dia promakhōn*, in the foremost of the ranks.

Curiously, when considering the possible origins of this episode, the Athenian demagogue, Demades, captured after the Athenian defeat at Chaeronea, had apparently accused the drunken Philip II of playing the 'Thersites' role when fate had, in fact, cast him as the Mycenaean King.[299] Once described as 'the wreckage of a shipwrecked state', it was Demades who finally obliged Alexander with a proposal of divine honours, though his *On the Twelve Years* (ca. 326 BCE, and if truly attributable to him) had laid the groundwork for his later *apologia* to a hostile Athens for his proposing the same status for Philip II in 338 BCE.[300]

Alexander may even have been guilty of meddling in the affairs of his literary entourage; Anaximenes, the historian on campaign with the Macedonians and the likely author of the *Rhetoric to Alexander*, circulated a work in the literary style of Theopompus, the accomplished Chian chronicler who may have recently returned from exile. Copies of Anaximenes' *Trikaranus,* a work deliberately hostile to Athens, Thebes and Sparta, were dispatched to each city with the result that Theopompus was unwelcome in much of Greece.[301] The mischief-making was obvious to those in the know yet the *Trikaranus* misled notable later historians; Josephus (Yosef Ben Matityahu 37-ca. 100 CE), Lucian and Aristides all referred to it as a genuine Theopompian work.[302]

Theopompus' authentic history of Greece had undermined the tradition of Athens' glorious past, and it justified the new Macedonian supremacy that the historian had himself benefited from. Yet his *Philippika*, a history spanning the years 359-336 BCE and completed (we believe) shortly before Alexander's death, included foul-language derogatory remarks about Philip II. It also painted a picture of degenerate behaviour at the Macedonian court (and even Alexander's court, if a letter concerning his friend, Harpalus, is genuine).[303] This explains why

Theopompus was termed a 'prosecutor' rather than a historian, despite the attempts he had made to widen the telling of history with ethnology, geography, mythography and digressions that ventured away from the habitual focus on war and politics.[304]

Theopompus' hostility, which suggests that he too, amongst many others, did not believe Alexander would return from his Eastern campaigns alive, was captured by a disapproving Polybius who was: '… indeed astonished at this writer's extravagance.'[305] He painted Philip's *hetairoi* as a 'band of debauchees assembled from across Hellas'; his Companions were 'whores', soldiers were 'harlots' and Philip's men-slayers were 'men-sodomisers by habit'. This reads as something of a paradox, for Theopompus simultaneously portrayed Philip as nothing less than the second founder of the Macedonian nation after Caranus. Theopompus is further alleged to have published a sophistical treatise on Alexander that balanced an encomium with polemic, so we may even posture that Alexander endorsed Anaximenes' literary subterfuge.[306]

STORM-TOSSED BY CHANGING FORTUNE: THE EMERGING RAPACIOUS *MONOLYKOS*

Alexander dismissed his Greek allies at Ecbatana in Media, the summer residence of the Archaemenid kings, soon after Darius' defeat at Gaugamela, and this suggested that the League of Corinth was being excluded from his future campaigning; quite possibly the recent news of Peloponnesian support for the Spartan revolt of King Agis had a part to play. Alexander was sufficiently practical, however, to offer the units he discharged employment as mercenaries, but as they no longer represented a city-state in that capacity, formal Greek participation in the subjugation of Asia was over.[307]

The rhetorical war of revenge against the Achaemenid kings was over too and a personal crusade began; even Isocrates had only envisaged the conquest of Asia Minor. If Alexander no longer needed Greek political support, neither did he need a historian obsequious to her demands; raw conquest was something the sophist Callisthenes would have found difficult to tame on his pages and his arrest came soon after.[308] 'The cloven hoof' had shown itself, but for a time Alexander's troops were carried along on the adrenaline of battle and loot, and by the knowledge that their tight and disciplined formations resulted in comfortingly few casualties, if numbers are to be believed.[309] But the 'old guard' generals who headed what was substantially his father's army, still influentially commanded by Parmenio and his sons, would soon be supplanted by Alexander's own generation of 'friends'.[310]

So what had now become of the Isocrates' grand ideal, which latterly implored Philip to lead a Panhellenic army against Persia?[311] Well, on one hand, Isocrates, then in his late nineties, took it with him when he starved himself to death shortly after defeat at Chaeronea while reportedly reciting lines from a Euripides play.[312] And there is an added irony here too, for it was that battle in Boeotia that finally enabled Philip to take the leadership of the League at Corinth and so advance his invasion plans. Isocrates, it seems, didn't foresee the true price of conquest or the cost of a unified Greece, for he had not lived to see the total destruction of Thebes.[313] The Sicilian historian Timaeus, who 'turned his back' on Alexander and his *Diadokhoi* when 'steeping himself in a past age of civil liberties', gave a usual scathing summation: he quipped that Alexander needed fewer years to conquer Persia than Isocrates had taken to write his *Panegyric*.[314]

We may speculate whether Alexander, at that point, saw his own personal Bodyguards, traditionally seven in number, as the *Epigonoi* in the *Thebaid,* the 'seven against Thebes' who were sons of Argive heroes, when he oversaw the city's destruction in 335 BCE; its *Hieros lochos*, the Theban Sacred Band, had been annihilated by him and his Companion Cavalry in the charge at Chaeronea three years before. But following the landscape-changing battle at Gaugamela, Alexander's *Somatophylakes* would now be better considered as 'seven against the False Smerdis', for a final hurdle separated him from his own Great Kingship: the still-at-large pretender Bessus, the satrap of Bactria.[315] It took a further year to track down the renegade who proclaimed himself a new Great King, Artaxerxes V;[316] yet the eventual capture and execution of Bessus heralded in Alexander's own troubled reign. He was twenty-seven when he effectively became the first European 'Great King' of the Persian Empire.

The Vulgate genre presented Alexander as a king 'storm-tossed by changing fortune' and the transformation is nowhere better exhibited than in Curtius' polemical artistry.[317] Initially, 'fortune was with him at every turn and so even his rashness had produced glorious results'; it was a rhetorical high point from which Alexander was to slide.[318] Even before victory at Issus Alexander reportedly 'feared Fortuna'.[319] He murdered the innocent Sisines due to misguided suspicions, and he left infantry stragglers for the approaching enemy to mutilate; when the Persians found them they 'succumbed to a frenzy of barbarian ruthlessness'.[320]

From the alleged crucifixions following the siege of Tyre, to a 'foreign mode of behaviour' that saw him drag the still-breathing Baetis, the *phrourarchos* (here, a garrison commander) of Gaza, behind his chariot in the fashion of Achilles, whilst putting all men to the sword, dark clouds had been gathering.[321] Gaza, the spice capital of Syria, fell, and 500-talents' weight of frankincense and a hundred of myrrh headed back to Alexander's austere tutor, Leonidas, so that he could stop 'dealing parsimoniously with the gods'. Somewhat paradoxically, the incident involving the cruel treatment afforded to Baetis (possibly traceable back to Hegesias) is regularly challenged, whereas the crucifixions at Tyre are not.[322]

A 'recklessness that could have spelled defeat' preceded Curtius' statement that: 'The blood of thousands was paying for the grandiose plans of one man who despised his country, and who had deluded ideas about aspiring to heaven.' Curtius' fifth chapter highlighted Alexander's liaisons with courtesans and an inexcusable fondness for drink, though, in his defence, Heracles had himself been a notoriously heavy imbiber and Dionysus was the god of wine (Liber or Bacchus to the Romans). These degenerative themes, repeated by Curtius throughout the next five books, are a far cry from the sexual abstinence and organisational brilliance that Plutarch and Arrian extended further into their coverage.[323] Alexander had, as Timaeus would have phrased it, run aground into luxury.[324]

Callisthenes, who may have concluded the same, might have reported on one final post-Gaugamela episode before he was executed, and it occurred in Sogdia sometime in 329 BCE. Ptolemy and Aristobulus bypassed it, saving Arrian the trouble of justifying what was possibly the most troubling crime Alexander would commit: the massacre of the Branchidae. Eulogistic scholars such as Tarn have tried to dismiss the historicity of the event, though Callisthenes' deliberately inaccurate rendering of its background argues that it actually took place.

Callisthenes claimed that the clan of the Branchidae, who were the keepers of the ancient shrine of Apollo at Didyma near Miletus, 'gave over the treasuries of the gods to the Persians' when Xerxes was planning his advance upon Greece (483 BCE onwards) some 150 years before.[325] Herodotus, however, had made it clear that the Persian plundering of the temple was punishment for the earlier Ionian revolt against Darius I, which ended in 494 BCE; moreover, the oracle had not been rebuilt by Xerxes' day.[326] But following Callisthenes, Strabo claimed the Branchidae themselves sacked the temple before being granted a safe haven in Bactria beyond the Oxus River by Darius I to protect them from Greek retributions.

Alexander had symbolically reconsecrated the temple at Didyma in 334 BCE, and some five years later he located, by chance, the new settlement of the Branchidae (a site possibly rediscovered in 2014) when campaigning in the upper satrapies. The population, still Greek-speaking and retaining Hellenic customs, came out to greet him. Alexander had their city surrounded and reportedly massacred them to the last man to punish them for their ancestral betrayal, reportedly urged on by the Milesians in his entourage. As Curtius described it: 'Everywhere there was butchery; neither their common language, nor prayers, nor olive branches held out to the attackers were able to prevent the cruelty.'

The city and its groves were razed to the ground. Yet by suggesting the Branchidae had treacherously sided with Xerxes, Callisthenes was, it appears, trying to justify (perhaps deliberately poorly) the crime that made its way into the pages of Diodorus, Strabo, Curtius and into Plutarch's *Moralia*; the polemic in the latter two suggests that Cleitarchus characteristically saw the darker consequences of the episode as well.[327] Despite his thinly veiled spin on the morality of retribution in the name of Greece, it may have been the point at which Callisthenes rebelled. He died soon after, and here, in Bactria, what the Macedonians saw were the descendants of Greeks being massacred when an Asiatic (Roxane) was being wed by their king.

The campaign magic and its love of honour, *philotimia*, died in what have been termed Alexander's 'three catastrophes': the trial and execution of Philotas in Drangiana (autumn 330 BCE); the murder of his general, Cleitus, at Maracanda in Bactria (Samarcand, winter 328/7 BCE); and the *proskynesis* debacle that preceded the arrest of the official campaign historian (possibly as late as 327 BCE). Callisthenes may have been required to write in eulogistic tones but he is also credited with: 'For my part, I hold Alexander for any mark of honour that a man may earn; but do not forget that there is a difference between honouring a man and worshipping a god.'[328]

This was a distinction, a limitation, and an apotheosic rejection that Alexander could not tolerate, just as he could not accept a Cleitus who revered him and yet who maintained that Philip, his *mortal* father, was responsible for the foundation of his success – a father whose life Alexander was claiming he had once saved.[329] The sword arm of 'Black' Cleitus, whose sister had been Alexander's wet-nurse, saved Alexander's life at the battle at the Granicus River, but it was now the unwelcome arm of his father's old guard generals sabotaging his metamorphosis from a carousing Macedonian warlord to demigod.[330]

'Alas what evil customs reign in Hellas' was Black Cleitus' accusation on the back of Alexander's boasting; it was a line taken from Euripides' *Andromache*, supposedly quoting Peleus the father of Achilles.[331] It was fatal; Alexander ran Cleitus through with a spear, though he blamed his murderous frenzy on the vengeful wrath of Dionysus that was brought to bear for his sacking of Thebes.[332] But Cleitus had been right; the 'rudder's guidance and the curb's restraint' that Sophocles propounded and Plutarch once saw in Alexander's early education under Aristotle, were by now long abandoned in the dust of Asia.[333] As Justin phrased it: 'The father had laid the foundations of the empire of the world, the son consummated the glory of conquering the whole world', and yet the son exceeding father 'in both his virtues and his vices'.[334] At Cleitus' death in the upper satrapies, Alexander was probably aged twenty-eight, but the tragedy of the episode may have been instructive; after the customary withdrawal, fasting and weeping to the gods at Opis several years later, Alexander did place his father *first* when summing up royal achievements to appease his mutinous men, so the sources inferred.[335]

After the controversial execution of the popular veteran general, Parmenio, who, until he fell under the shadow of suspicion at Philotas' trial, had been a demonstrably loyal *strategos*, Alexander censored letters home; when the couriers were a sufficient distance from the camp, he ordered them opened and read to fathom the army's opinion of his actions and continued eastward campaigning. Damning reports were destroyed, the malcontents identified and then brigaded into the *ataktoi*, the 'disciplinary unit'; his plan was, allegedly, to destroy them or settle them in distant colonies at the empire's edge.[336] This was not the first censorship; we are told Alexander had previously demanded that Antigone spy on Philotas, her lover already under suspicion.[337] Although Curtius permitted the reader a vote on the outcome of Philotas' trial, he condemned Alexander's execution of Callisthenes as nothing short of 'barbarous'.[338]

'Alexander fixed his gaze on him [Philotas]. The Macedones are going to judge your case,' he said. 'Please state whether you will use your native language before them.'[339] The unfortunate Philotas, now the most prominent commander of the Companion Cavalry, was being tried for treason. Alexander mocked Philotas for rejecting their native tongue, a harsh repost in the circumstances. In Curtius' rendering of the trial, Bolon, a common soldier, also reprimanded Philotas for needing an interpreter to listen to men speaking his own language; this was perhaps a rhetorical device to highlight Philotas' aloofness from the common infantryman and their rustic virtue, for he had grown, according to Curtius, vulgar in extravagant living.[340] The treatment of Alexander in the extant Roman-era accounts is peppered with rhetorical devices.

The decapitation of Parmenio at Ecbatana in late 330 BCE, and Alexander's use of Darius' own signet ring *and* his harem, symbolised a metamorphosis complete, as Hermolaus' defence speech at the trial of the 'conspiring' pages had neatly articulated.[341] Parmenio may have never been forgiven for his 'sluggish' performance at Gaugamela which ultimately led to Darius' escape, depriving Alexander of the long-dreamt of opportunity of seeing the Great King prostrated before him, unless this was once again Callisthenes' handiwork at the general's expense.[342]

The trial of Parmenio's son, Philotas, nevertheless acts as a litmus test for the political pH of each narrator and their underlying sources, in this case through the reporting of a plot on Alexander's life led by a court *hetairos*, Dymnus.[343] As far as Curtius was concerned, Philotas' torture after a sham trial in front of a hastily convened Common Assembly of Macedones, and his subsequent sentencing and execution, formed an integral part of Alexander's moral decline that was painted in tragic biographical tones that typified the Vulgate genre.[344] Although Plutarch also saw a conspiracy *against* an innocent Philotas too, at this point the dispassionate Diodorus still saw Alexander 'stumbling into a base action quite foreign to his goodness of nature'; Arrian almost bypassed the affair altogether, as no doubt had his principal source, Ptolemy. After all, the removal of the prominent Bodyguard, Demetrius, on the suspicion of collusion with the plotters, provided the opportunity for Ptolemy to occupy the resulting vacant post of *Somatophylax*.[345] Indeed, at Alexander's death, the *Somatophylakes* were transformed from Bodyguards to successors, the *Diadokhoi*, who governed regions of the newly expanded empire; by then they would include Perdiccas, Leonnatus, Ptolemy, Aristonus, Lysimachus, Seleucus, Peucestas, and possibly Eumenes.

Cleitarchus, writing later in Ptolemaic Alexandria, sensibly appears to have kept Ptolemy off the list of commanders summoned to coordinate a covert action against the accused.[346] And soon after the trial, the acquitted Amyntas, a prominent (though arrogant) son of Andromenes, a *syntrophos* of the Pellan court and one of the king's *hetairoi*, died conveniently (some might say 'mysteriously', for he had too much support for an open conviction).[347] Yet both trials – that of Callisthenes with the pages, and Dymnus with Philotas – along with the death of Alexander Lyncestis (Antipater's son-in-law) who had been held in captivity for years after falling under suspicion of offering his services to Darius, would have caused widespread panic in the ranks, for Macedonian law seems to have demanded the death of *all* who were related to those deemed guilty of treason.[348]

This series of episodes represented a dark period for Alexander, though blacker was still to come. Holt calculates that the Macedonian campaigns in Bactria and Sogdia through 328/9 BCE (much of it absent from Arrian's account and dealt with more fully by Curtius) had already left 100,000 dead, including women and children, whilst 7,000 Macedonians are estimated to have perished there. Deaths from wounds, illnesses and disease had surely taken more allied troops than any eyewitness source would have been prepared to admit. When Alexander departed the region he had to leave behind a defence force with garrisons that might have totalled 20,000 'peacekeepers'.[349] Curtius claimed he actually tried to conceal the disastrous outcome, '... threatening with death those who came back from the battle, if they revealed what had happened.'[350]

The 'Vulgate Alexander' was now more Ahriman than Ahura Mazda, and more the stuff of the Spartan Crypteia than king portrayed in Xenophon's *Cyropaedia*.[351] The wolf that the priestess Pythia predicted would guide the Macedonian conqueror to the Persians (Apollo-Lyceus that appeared on Macedonian coinage?), had finally crept out of Alexander himself;[352] as far as Demosthenes was concerned, this was the *monolykos*, the rapacious 'arch wolf of Macedonia', he had warned of years before.[353]

> It was at this point that Alexander lost control of his passions that his self-restraint and continence, supreme virtues at the height of good fortune, degenerated into arrogance and wantonness… he began to rival the loftiness of the Persian court, equal to the power of the gods.[354]

Alexander was criticised for slapping Asiatics on the back and marrying into the Persian royal line the Macedonians had fought to topple in battle, and he slept with the 'prostitute' eunuch, Bagoas, who had convinced him to execute Orsines, 'the noblest of Persians'.[355] Even the apologist Arrian, in an unconscious attempt at physiognomy, commented in his so-called 'great digression' on moral turpitude that it was 'regrettable that a descendent of Heracles' traded Macedonian garb for 'the median dress and the Persian mitre… when he was victor and they the vanquished.'[356]

But objection on campaign had become dangerous, and the relationship between the Macedonian commander-in-chief and his men-at-arms, which traditionally permitted *isegoria* – freedom of speech – was dissolving. Alexander began to see his kingship as a personal sovereignty more than an organ of state and any word against it was deemed mutinous. Finally, Curtius claimed his 'friends regarded him as the enemy'.[357] Alexander's own brand of court politics had been a one-way diplomacy: unstoppable, inflexible, unflankable and unforgiving as his phalanx; there was no neutral and Alexander recognised no reverse gear at all.

If Alexander had 'systematically exploited the tensions of his court', he had finally become part of them himself;[358] the passage in Aelian's *Varia Historia* is likely apocryphal but may, nonetheless, preserve a core of truth:

> Alexander son of Philip is said to have been very jealous of his friends and suspicious of them all, though not for the same reasons. He disliked Perdiccas for being a natural solder, Lysimachus because he was renowned as a general and Seleucus for his bravery. Antigonus' ambition troubled him, and he disliked Antipater's ability in leadership, and he was suspicious of Ptolemy's cleverness and feared Atarrhias' insubordination, not to mention Peithon's revolutionary character.[359]

Of course, this type of epitomised *scandeleuse*, and the Vulgate character portrayal along with its sibling offshoots, was a literary and rhetorical package deal: the philosophical and moral viatica were all thrown in so that they are now impossible to separate from the core of unimpeachable detail. But somewhere buried beneath Arrian's steadfast *apologia*, Plutarch's moralising 'pottages' (as Macaulay termed them), Trogus' troubled king which gave us Justin's jaundiced précis overlaid on Cleitarchus' kingly model of reverse transfiguration artfully re-rendered by Curtius in moralistic Rome, lies the *real* Alexander, who pushed himself, his men, and *tyche* to the limits of the imagination and on towards the great encircling ocean.

THE ILLUSIVE *OIKOUMENE:* A RIVER TOO FAR

We can only try to approximate the psychological processes at work on Alexander through the latter part of the campaign, fettered as we are today by the concept of infinity. To the learned community of his day the world must have seemed intellectually tameable and truly all knowable, despite the *apeiron* (the 'indefinite' or 'boundless') of Anaximander (ca. 610-525 BCE) and the paradoxes of Zeno of Elea (ca. 490-430 BCE) who first pondered them. Plutarch claimed Alexander had wept when the campaign philosopher, Anaxarchus, proposed innumerable worlds existed: 'Is it not worthy of tears,' he said, 'that, when the number of worlds is infinite, we have not yet become lords of a single one?'[360]

But would Ephorus, Herodotus or Diodorus have embarked on 'universal' history unless they believed its boundaries *could* be encompassed in their pages? One cannot help but imagine that Aristotle felt, given a long life, he could wrap his arms around the sum total of the physical and metaphysical world and house it in a treatise. Indeed he tried; Cicero reported Aristotle '… could see that, since great advances had been made in so few years, philosophy would be completely finished in a short time.'[361] If ever completed, it would have anticipated the so-called speculum literature of the Middle Ages, the single compendia encompassing the supposed sum of all knowledge.

So it was with Alexander, whose geography, or the geography he chose to believe in, *was* finite; for him the *Oikoumene,* the whole inhabited world, was engulfed by an endless Stream of Ocean mentioned by Hesiod, Homer and Herodotus.[362] Psychologically, it magnified his ambitions, for this perspective made even the aim of becoming *kosmokrator* possible despite Herodotus' warning of the things he had heard: 'I know of no river of Oceanus existing, but I think that Homer or one of the poets who were before him invented the name and introduced it into his verse.'[363]

In India, Alexander did witness crocodiles in the Hydaspes (the Jhelum River) and what appeared to be Egyptian beans in the Acesines River; thinking he had discovered the source of the Nile in India, he prepared for a river voyage that would take him back to Egypt. Knowledge, it is said, is the enemy of faith, and Nearchus' report captured the reality and disappointment once things became clear. Alexander soon realised such a journey was impossible, for Strabo, quoting Nearchus' *Indike,* explained,

'… for great rivers stand in between, and fearsome streams; first, Ocean into which all the Indian rivers empty…' As Green put it, the '… diplomatic lie had been nailed, once and for all, by the brute facts of geography.'[364]

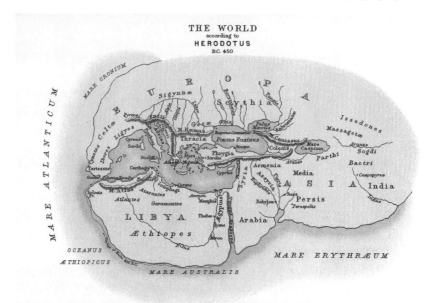

A map of the known world drafted according to Herodotus' geographical descriptions ca. 450 BCE. When the Macedonians arrived in India they started to appreciate the boundless East with the Ganges clearly referenced in extant texts. Whether the land of the Seres (China) was mentioned to them we can only speculate.

There were additional reports arriving of the River Ganges, some four months to the east, and probably tales of lands beyond from the traders they encountered or from remnants of the reports of Scylax of Carianda who (debatably) explored the Indian river systems for Darius I ca. 515 BCE.[365] This gave rise to a spurious tradition that Alexander even reached the Ganges' banks.[366] The Roman Empire was to learn the true scale of things with the arrival of silk from the Seres and through Egyptian commerce to the south and Parthian trade routes to the north.[367] But when Alexander departed Europe he enjoyed a cartographic naivety stemming from maps and notions dating back to Ephorus and Hecataeus' *Periodos Ges* (or *Periegesis*, broadly *World Survey*) based on Anaximander's design, an *Iliad* and *Odyssey* that looked to the East no further than Colchis on the Black Sea (today's southern Georgia), Xenophon's *Anabasis* which had turned back at the Tigris, a Pseudo-*Periplous* which advanced nowhere east of Phoenicia, and a *Persika* from Ctesias which contradicted the claims of both Herodotus *and* Xenophon.[368]

Eudoxus of Cnidus' no-longer extant *Tour of the Earth* and Aristotle's *Meteorologica* apparently proved no more help locating Oceanus, supposedly just beyond the Punjab if his distances were correct. Alexander was confounded; upon returning to Babylon in 323 BCE he sent shipwrights to the Hyrcanian Sea (the Caspian) to find its source and determine exactly where it connected to the encircling stream, which was becoming as illusive as the rising *pneuma* of priestess Delphian Pythia.[369] Tarn, dampening any suggestion that Alexander was hell-bent on conquering the world, saw the planned Arabian expedition as another 'voyage of discovery'.

As Alexander ventured ever eastward, Aristotle's declaration that Greeks were born to rule through a superior Hellenic civilisation was being severely undermined by epigraphy and by Alexander himself. The stele listing the Laws of Hammurabi, dating back 1,500 years, proclaimed the sophistication of Babylonian civil codes at a time when Greece was learning to smelt iron, presumably from the Ideaen Dactyls of Mount Ida.[370] In India the Macedonians encountered Brahmin sages whose material simplicity made Diogenes' Corinthian barrel and loincloth appear an extravagance, and whose truth-twisting sophistry matched any Athenian prosecutor.[371] Pythagoras, who had been captured at the school of Egyptian mysteries by Cambyses II and ferried as a prisoner to Babylon to the presence of Chaldean prophets, already knew it, of course, some two centuries before, and yet the hellenocentric Aristotle must have been disturbed at the reports arriving in Athens. The campaigning 'student' may have dumped his former teacher when he caged Callisthenes in favour of a far more eclectic philosophy born of a much wider Peripatus.[372]

It follows that Alexander's belief codes, rooted in Greek propaganda, must have perished at some point in the odyssey that took him beyond the Indus, and this may well have contributed to his gradual orientalisation, or as his men thought, 'barbarisation', his poignant retort to the Hellenic lie. What the Macedonians encountered next left Pyrrho of Elis demonstrably sceptical, despite (or possibly because of) the 10,000 gold pieces Alexander is said to have offered him at their first meeting.[374] For if any illusion of campaigning glory still carried any currency, India crashed the exchange rate. Victory was tarnished as the highly choreographed battles on open plains were replaced by poisoned arrowheads, snakebites, dysentery and monsoon mud. Rain rusted what shining metal was left in panoplies, and pike heads, swords blades and spear tips were of weatherable iron, and tougher steel (though still weatherable) was almost unheard of in Europe at that time.[375] Cavalry officers were now climbing scaling-ladders, and the orderly phalanx formation turned into street-to-street fighting with religious fanatics; when the walls were finally scaled, honourable surrender became nothing less than mass slaughter.[376]

The 2.25-metre tall diorite column in the shape of an index finger recording the Laws of Hammurabi, the sixth Babylonian king, dating to ca. 1750s BCE. Discovered in 1901, the inscription in Akkadian commences with a record of his deeds and then details the 282 laws defining his Babylonian social order. Perhaps originally erected at Sippar, it was discovered on the site of ancient Susa. Xenophon's eulogistic tribute to Cyrus commented that the 'Persian laws try, as it were, to steal a march on time, to make their citizens from the beginning incapable of setting their hearts on any wickedness or shameful conduct whatsoever.' Now in the Louvre, Room 3, Mesopotamia.[373]

Alexander had finally marched a river too far and his army refused to follow him further east; as Bosworth pointed out, the court propaganda that saw him as '… superhuman, had long ago worn thin amongst the men upon whose efforts his godhead rested.'[377] By now, Alexander had been faced with '… storms, droughts, deep rivers, the heights of the Birdless Rock [Aornus], the monstrous shapes of savage beasts, an uncivilised manner of life, the constant succession of petty kings and their repeated treachery.'[378] Alexander's near-death wound in the city of the Mallians in today's southern Punjab would only reinforce their doubts; Alexander was not *aniketos* (invincible) after all.

The beginning of the Mallian episode has the ring of Philip's siege of Methone (354 BCE) when he withdrew the scaling ladders once his men had climbed the wall 'leaving the assailants no hope of safety but in their courage', though here played in reverse. Two ladders had collapsed leaving Alexander himself exposed upon the citadel wall; furious with the hesitation of his men (who had recently threatened to mutiny), he jumped down the enemy side whereupon he was attacked and almost killed.[379] Lucian satirically captured the state of affairs again: (father to son) 'You were passing for a God; and your being wounded, and carried off the field on a litter, bleeding and groaning, could only excite the ridicule of the spectators…' Nevertheless, Alexander's 'miraculous' healing, as Brian Bosworth has pointed out, rivalled that of Ares in the *Iliad* when 'divine *ichor* flowed' and yet it healed as 'swiftly as fig-juice thickens milk that curdles when stirred'.[380]

But Phegeus' well-calculated report (with Porus' affirmation) of two great rivers and the 200,000 strong army of Xandrames with its 2,000 chariots and 400 war elephants that lay directly in their path, probably had the desired effect,[381] and Alexander may have been as relieved as his men to be retracing his steps at last, for the recent clash with Porus and his 'city of elephants' had shaken the Macedonian army.[382] Bucephalus had been run through at the grand old horse-age of thirty and the gods had finally punished the new Bellerophon for attempting to ride his Pegasus up Mount Olympus, and like the fabled slayer of monsters, Alexander had tumbled back to Earth.[383]

He remained haunted, perhaps for the very first time, by an ambition unaccomplished, and neither was he able to give the superficial impression to the world that had he had fulfilled it. If his two-day sulk on the banks of the Hyphasis (now the Beas River in Northern India) was reminiscent of Achilles' own tented isolation, it was again a well-worn picture; the Spartan general Clearchus had done the same to avert mutiny under Cyrus. The Hyphasis may have been the boundary of the empire of Darius I; if the troops knew it, they would have considered their job completed.[384]

Alexander's next instructions were similarly theatrical, if they are to be believed. Sensing that he may never return, he ensured his men paid for their dissent; he commanded that twelve stone altars some 50 cubits high (approximately 75 feet) be built to Olympian gods, and he set about exaggerating the stature of the 'giants' who erected them: oversized weaponry, equipment, couches, and beds were left behind. The altars were apparently still standing in Plutarch's day before the Hyphasis changed its course. Curtius concluded of the whole affair: 'He was preparing to leave posterity a fraudulent wonder.'[385] Alexander had already, and somewhat symbolically, destroyed Cyra, the city that marked the furthest foundation of Cyrus' earlier empire, and these altars were to be the new eastern boundary marks.[386] Arrian, thus we assume his favoured source, Ptolemy (and perhaps Aristobulus too), was predictably silent on any suggestion of 'fraud', focusing their texts on memorials to 'victorious progress' instead.

But this time victory came at a price. The 'commoner' Coenus, whose family had received significant land in Macedonia, had spoken out on the dissatisfaction of the regular infantryman in what became an immortal speech.[387] He was a brother-in-law of the executed Philotas as he had married one of Parmenio's daughters, whose previous husband was most likely the also executed Attalus.[388] The incompliant Coenus was precariously placed; now a distinguished infantry *hyparchos* who had sarcastically congratulated Alexander for giving 1,000 talents to the Indian rajah of Taxila, he next pointed out the poor condition of his men and their weapons in India. He too, suspiciously, died a few days later on the banks of the Acesines (today's Chenab); Alexander is said to have adorned his 'grief' with, 'It was for the sake of a few days that Coenus had made his long harangue, as if he alone were the one who would see Macedonia again.'[389]

The retracing of steps westwards ceased at the River Hydaspes when Alexander ordered the famous 1,800-vessel flotilla to be built on which they would head south to the sea; he, like Achilles, would do battle with a river, or at least emulate Scylax's voyage of discovery. In the rapids at the confluence of the Hydaspes and Acesines, he certainly fought for survival, and once more at the delta of the Indus when tides never imagined nearly scuttled the whole fleet. On the voyage, Alexander's men would embark upon the most bloody campaigning to date, while a young Chandragupta (Sandrokottos to the Greeks), who reportedly once approached Alexander for help, watched on as he planned his own Indian dominion.[390] But aware that Darius I had conquered the Indus Valley, Alexander could do no less, and he attempted to extract the veneer of fealty from the river-bordering tribes.

We may doubt that he knew that some 2,000 years earlier a great Indus Valley civilisation had existed; it was once twice the size of that of Egypt and Mesopotamia and it was only discovered in the 1920s along with the dry beds of the once great Saraswati River. A thousand settlements, the largest at Mohenjo-Daro and Harappa, extending over 500,000 square miles, once proliferated the fertile basin with some one million inhabitants with an elaborate and unrivalled system of drainage and sanitation, and a still-undeciphered script.[391]

Blind to that ancient past, Arrian, we imagine drawing principally from Ptolemy (though with a weather-eye on Cleitarchus when information was scant) littered his fifth and sixth chapters with terms associated with the carnage that followed no fewer than sixteen times from the aftermath of the Hydaspes battle with Porus, through the slaughter in Mallia, to Alexander's flotilla finally arriving at the Indus Delta: translations give us 'crushed', 'cut down', 'put to death', 'subdued', 'attacked unarmed men', 'onslaught', 'massacred', 'enslaved', 'trapped', 'stormed', 'plundered' and 'hanged'.[392] Campaigning in Gedrosia added to the death toll and Diodorus recorded that: 'Every spot was filled with fire and devastation and great slaughter.'[393]

Remarkably, Arrian recounted this period in an easy and matter-of-fact way despite the enemy casualties (reportedly) falling in the tens of thousands. But this was typical of Arrian's stoic principles: 'never say an action is bad', and so the death count was simply labelled 'high'. Tarn, in a similarly characteristic stance, claimed Cleitarchus 'had a taste for inventing, or adopting inventions of, massacres', though did agree that the period was 'unique in its dreadful record of mere slaughter'.[394] Then again, we must recall that 'India' had become a byword for *thauma* and the exaggeration of scale; living dragons, 300-year-old elephants and 200-foot-long serpents epitomised the inflation of misunderstood fact.[395] The twelve oversized temples and numbers attached to the massacres may simply be its by-product, and after all, chronic policy failure was rarely reported as simply that.

The river-based 'campaign' took seven months, and once the fascinations of the Indus delta had been left behind and sacrifices to Tethys and Oceanus had been made, the army was to suffer from Alexander's worst decision of all: the crossing of the arid Makran desert region of Gedrosia.[396] Arrian provided another sanitised rationale for the disastrous choice of route:

> It was not that Alexander chose this route unaware of its difficulty (only Nearchus claims this), but because he had heard that no one had yet succeeded in getting an army through the region safely. Semiramis had travelled this route on her forced retreat from India, but locals reported that even she made it through with twenty survivors from the entire army, and Cyrus the son of Cambyses suffered the same with only seven to tell the tale.[397]

Alexander was evidently lost to the West and he was being consumed by the East; it was Cyrus and the Assyrian queen who occupied his nostalgia. Babylon had seduced, India had scarred, and finally Gedrosia attempted to swallow the Macedonian-led army. The desert did not step aside in obeisance as the sea had in Pamphylia, and the 'yearning' (*pothos*) Nearchus attributed to the choice of route looks like the cover-up of another huge blunder that 'proved fatal to a large proportion of the army'; 'most were lost in the sand, like sailors lost overboard at sea'.[398] Notably many must have been Greek mercenaries.[399] Of the 125,000 infantry and 15,000 cavalry Alexander once commanded in India, Plutarch believed one-quarter survived (though he didn't directly attribute the loss to this disaster alone). These overall numbers appear grossly exaggerated (even accounting for a 'moving state' of non-combatants) but it was, nevertheless, a devastating outcome.[400]

The despondent king soon began executing misbehaving officials who must have doubted he would return; 'In short, the whole empire was in turmoil, and an atmosphere of instability prevailed everywhere', claimed Plutarch.[401] Curtius reported that over 600 transgressors were executed in Carmania for malversation, including the scapegoat administrators Alexander pinned blame on for the poor Gedrosian logistics; the death list included Persian satraps and common soldiers alike, as well as the four men Alexander had earlier enlisted to murder Parmenio, one of them Coenus' brother.[402] The ever-trustworthy general, Craterus, brought two Persian nobles who had planned to revolt to Alexander in chains, whilst Leonnatus had suffered heavy losses when attacked by local tribes. At this point there was still no news of whether Nearchus' fleet had survived its journey; the disaster could be greater still.

Harpalus, Alexander's boyhood companion and now the *gazophylax* (treasurer) in Babylon who had probably colluded in the maladministrations, saw the writing on his accounts ledger and summarily fled for the second time; he received a lukewarm reception in Athens despite the honorary citizenship the city had bestowed on him for supplying much-needed grain.[403] 'He dreaded his master, who had by then become an object of terror even to his friends'; the executed Cleander (the brother of Coenus) was surely one of them for he had held a similar treasury role in Media, and both men heralded from the canton of Elimea in Upper Macedonia.[404] The state of affairs prompted Apollodorus, the *strategos* overseeing the government of Babylon, to request his brother, the seer Pythagoras, to divine for him whether he was also in danger now that the king was returning.[405]

At Opis (or Susa, there is some chronological uncertainty) Alexander received a long-overdue reality check in the form of a second (or third) troop mutiny.[406] Having infiltrated the Companion Cavalry with Persians as early as 329 BCE, Alexander had nevertheless refrained from arming and equipping them in Macedonian style. But the arrival at Susa of 30,000 *epigonoi,* the cadets representing the next generation of Asiatic soldiers, was a step too far for the veteran infantrymen whose unique status with their king was being undermined. According to Diodorus, the *epigonoi* were to 'serve as a counterbalance to the Macedonian phalanx', which implied Alexander's lack of trust in his domestic ranks; perhaps it also pointed at their dispensability now the Achaemenid threat was gone.[407]

'Foreigners' now carried Macedonian lances in place of the thonged javelins of their native lands, a Persian battalion of Silver Shields was formed (previously an elite hypaspist unit), and Arrian suggested that even the *melophoroi*, the golden apple-bearing Immortals, had been assimilated, though he predictably saw this as Alexander prudently distancing himself from chauvinism.[408] Persian cavalry, in small numbers, had been serving with the army since 330 BCE, but here we have the first signs of dissent from the king's own mounted units which were being diluted by 'barbarian' regiments from Bactria, Sogdia, Arachosia, Zarangiana (Drangiana), Areia, Parythaea (Parthia) and the elite Euacae from Persia; as a result a fifth hipparchy (cavalry squadron) emerged.[409]

Young Persian nobles had also augmented the Royal Guard, the *agema*, which was now, tellingly, under Alexander's personal command; the king was, it must have appeared, handing back the empire to the Persians.[410] As Briant notes: 'Of the twelve satrapies conquered and reorganised between 331 and 327 BCE, only one, Arachosia was given to a Macedonian (Menon); all others, at least initially, had been bestowed on Iranians'; even former Persian plotters (Nabarzanes) were pardoned, though they relinquished their military power and then saw their sons enrolled in

Macedonian ranks as hostages for good behaviour.[411] In Alexander's wedding of Roxane he effectively gained a 'detainee', for this helped ensure the troubled regions of Bactria and, or, Sogdia, remained 'loyal'.

The face of the original expeditionary force had changed beyond recognition; the core of the royal army 'became increasingly less Macedonian – perhaps only a sixth of the entire force – and behaved more mercenary itself.'[412] When Alexander announced his intention to demobilise up to 10,000 veteran soldiers and return them to Macedonia, including those unfit for future campaigning, the assembled men (probably those due to leave *and* those scheduled to remain) expressed their discord, shouting back something along the lines of 'go to war yourself then, together with your father Zeus-Ammon'; Alexander's public rejection of his 'terrestrial father', Philip II, had clearly offended those who had once fought under him. The disquiet was suppressed by the drowning of thirteen ringleaders, by Persians no less, a traditional Babylonian retribution though also a Macedonian punishment for those committing sacrilege.[413]

The mutiny at Opis (or Susa), when veterans were discharged, was the second, or arguably the third, revolt in three years.[414] So where did the loyalty, the *esprit de corps* and *eunoia* (goodwill) to the king now come from except within Alexander's own personal guard? Where was the implicit *pistis*, trust, in their commander-in-chief? The answer looks increasingly pecuniary; the new *homonoia* came in the form of a talent of silver per discharged man; this equated to approximately 57 lb (26 kg) of silver, the equivalent of 6,000 drachmas which would have amounted to something like sixteen years of an infantryman's generous pay.[415]

On top of that, Alexander pledged the repayment of years of accumulated debt, a settlement that '… was received not more thankfully by the debtors than by the creditors.' Rather than be burdened with hauling waggons of silver into India, Alexander had kept the captured wealth in the Persian treasuries at Susa and Ecbatana; unable to pay his men in coin, a huge backlog of payments must have accumulated, and that in turn would have filtered down to camp provisioners and service providers.[416] But what was once monetary munificence was now little short of a bribe; according to Cicero, this was not the first time Alexander had imprudently used wealth to garner support:

> Philip takes his son Alexander sharply to task for trying by gifts of money to secure the goodwill of the Macedonians: 'What in the mischief induced you to entertain such a hope,' he says, 'as that those men would be loyal subjects to you whom you had corrupted with money?'[417]

There followed the announcement that Alexander would fix the royal seat in Asia, and dissent once more filled the air.[418] But by now the greater part of Alexander's adult life *had* been spent east of the Hellespont. Chaldeans from Babylonia, Indian gymnosophists, Phoenician shipwrights and traders, and embalmers from Egypt complemented the Macedonian entourage.[419] The inner circle at the court *symposia* included Thessalians, Cretans, Cypriots and royal Asiatics. His first wife, Roxane, was Bactrian, or perhaps Sogdian ('another Briseis for a new Achilles' suggested Curtius), and he had attachments to Carian and Persian 'mothers', adopted by one, and adopting the other.[420] Alexander was not a man longing to return to the provincial pastures of Pella, whose harbour and natural port was in any case (evidence suggests) beginning to silt up.[421]

The arrival of the Macedonian army at Susa in early 324 BCE saw the *en masse* marriages of Macedonian soldiers to Asian brides in a great celebratory pavilion, a venue that itself paralleled the *apadana*, the marquee-style audience hall of Achaemenid tradition.[422] Arrian summed up Alexander's intentions: he was offering his *megistoi* to 'the *noblest* of Persian and Median blood'.[423] Performing at the weddings, and possibly capturing the truer sentiment of the betrothed Macedonians officers, were the tragic actors Aristocritus, Athenodorus and Thessalus, though none of the *neogamoi*, the newlyweds, dared voice their dissent.[424] The event evidenced a practical reality rather than the more fanciful stoic notions that were later attached to it: Alexander *was* initiating plans for a hybrid aristocracy. His *Somatophylakes* and other distinguished officers, some ninety-two in total, were to produce a future generation of half-Asiatic governors that would maintain his legacy across the vast empire.[425] And it is here that we may insert Badian's final assessment: Alexander was 'essentially not interested in a future without himself', a presence that was to be extended through his own half-caste sons who would be accepted as overlords of this new environment.[426]

Had Darius been captured alive, we might even conjecture that Alexander would have followed the example he later set with Porus in India: reinstating him as a 'client king' to manage an eastern Argead realm, and in the process reuniting him with a family Alexander had all but adopted himself; he did bring Darius' brother, Oxyathres, into the fold of court *hetairoi* and even into his Bodyguard corps.[427] And we sense that Alexander would have relished the moment of this grand and poignant gesture, which may explain why he levied such a cruel sentence on Darius' murderer, Bessus, who was delivered to him naked in a collar, with nose and ears then cut off, and summarily crucified.[428] Pure altruism would not have been behind his partial reinstatement, for practically speaking it would have saved him a huge administrative burden, and where possible and when suitably compliant, we know Asian satraps *were* reconfirmed. Moreover, Alexander 'will certainly have understood that his work could not last unless he made use of the Achaemenid model'.[429]

Alexander had made sure that Darius was buried in the royal sepulchre of the Achaemenids close to Persepolis.[430]

The Macedonian rank and file was bewildered by Alexander's adoption, admiration, and preservation of so much he had conquered, just as the Spartan hoplites under Lysander had questioned why Pausanias voted against destroying Athens at the end of the Peloponnesian War (which nevertheless marked the end of the creativity of the Greek city-state). Pausanias was tried and finally exiled for his pacifist policy, though Plutarch credited the lines of Euripides' *Electra* with saving the day, for upon hearing them, '… all were moved to compassion, and felt it to be a cruel deed to abolish and destroy a city which was so famous, and produced such poets.' But Athens' Long Walls were pulled down and its fleet was burned to the melancholy sound of the flute.[431] But in Alexander's case, the simple truth is that he did not so much *defeat* the Persian Empire as become subsumed by it.

The army finally returned to Babylon in late 324 BCE, by which time troops were cynical, friends had been executed and close Companions were dead. How did this affect the ever-campaigning king? Lane Fox insightfully stated 'nothing is harder, than to appreciate Alexander after Hephaestion's death', for the former *chiliarchos* – Alexander's *alter ego* – had died in Ecbatana earlier in the year.[432] A decade before, and in more hopeful times, Darius' mother, Sisygambis, had unwittingly mistaken Hephaestion for the king due to his height.[433] The king's immortalised reply – 'he too is Alexander'– implied a true *homoousios* in which they shared the same essence. If Aristotle's definition of 'a single soul dwelling in two bodies' held true here, Alexander had lost his more temperate half, and any remaining *sophrosyne*, moderation, was lost along with him.[434]

'To lighten his sorrow', after reportedly destroying the temple to Asclepius at Ecbatana and shearing the manes of his horses and mules in a Homeric mourning, Alexander embarked on a 'blood-soaked hunt' of the Cossean tribes from the youths upwards; Plutarch termed it a 'sacrifice to the shades of his dead friend.'[435]

In contrast to the earlier Asiatic appointments, by the time Alexander returned to Babylon, tellingly, only three Persians still held office.[436] The new administration was never the Graeco-Oriental *homonoia* many believe he attempted to bring about. Within this new administrative model Alexander relied on resettled mercenaries, principally Greeks, to keep peace across the empire. Curtius proposed that: 'Alexander… was thinking that Asia could be held by an army of modest size because he had distributed garrisons in many places and filled his new cities with settlers eager to preserve the *status quo*.'[437] But Isocrates had long before alerted Philip to the prospect of these wandering and destitute fighters searching for new employment, advising him to plant them in colonies on the empire borders to thwart any dangerous build-up.[438] Even Calanus, the resident Indian gymnosophist, had demonstrated to Alexander, with a stiffened hide laid on the floor, that unless you controlled the centre, the edges of the empire would always rise up in opposition.[439]

Polybius ominously concluded that tyrant-employed mercenaries are superior to those recruited by democracies.[440] But Iphicrates' advice to hire a 'mercenary soldier fond of money and of pleasures, for thus he will fight the more boldly to procure the means to gratify his desires', did not contemplate a life on the far banks of the Indus, or the wolf-packed forests of Hyrcania ('wolf-land'), despite the raising of the mysterious so-called Wall of Alexander erected in the region.[441] These garrisoneers were supposed to become what the Romans broadly termed *limitanei*, frontier soldiers. They were farmers of *kleroi*, land grants in the Athenian-style *kleroukhia* that established a new colony with political dependence on the mother city.

Those in settlements furthest from home inevitably degenerated into local militia when regular 'state' contact became infrequent. The policy was a huge overestimate of their enthusiasm and stability; some 3,000 of these settlers in *katoikiai*, military settlements or colonies, had already revolted upon rumour of Alexander's death in Mallia. Others murdered Philip, the satrap of the expanded Indian provinces east of the Indus.[442] Demaratus of Corinth had been wasting his tears on the fallen Hellenes who, he lamented, had been deprived of the 'great pleasure' of seeing Alexander finally sit on Darius' throne; he, like Isocrates, appears to have held a far too utopian view of the 'Panhellenic' invasion of Persia.[443]

Alexander had issued an edict to his Asian satraps in 326 BCE ordering them to disband their own hired armies in anticipation of trouble, just as the Persian King Artaxerxes III Ochus had soon after his accession in 358 BCE, for by now over 100,000 mercenaries (if cited numbers can be believed) had seen service with the Macedonians and were stationed across the empire; many of them *had* once been in the pay of Darius III.[444] 'Partly for the sake of gaining fame, and partly wishing to secure many devoted personal followers in each city to counter the revolutionary movements and seditions of the Greeks', Alexander followed up with the Exiles Decree that was read aloud at the 324 BCE Olympic Games (July 31st-August 4th), and which must have broadly coincided with the trouble at Opis or Susa.[445]

The edict, unconstitutional as it turned out, *was* partly motivated by the need to repatriate these itinerant soldiers and to gain a core of support in the Greek cities. The decree was particularly onerous for Athens which had turfed out the native residents of Samos and made the island a cleruchy in 366/365 BCE, following which the Samian exiles may have journeyed to Sicily (amongst other locations, Iasus, for example) where the historian Duris may have been born.[446] We even have the lengthy *diagramma* (legislation) drafted by the city of Tegea in Arcadia to deal with the complicated property and civil laws surrounding the returnees.[447] The re-emergence of up to 20,000 political outcasts in Greece was to cause huge property conflict, though Antipater was instructed to act against any city resisting. In this Antipater was precariously placed, for the decree undermined his own political architecture and perhaps Alexander was aiming to achieve just that, for Craterus was already journeying home through Asia with orders to take over the regency.[448]

The Athenian commander Leosthenes, ironically the son of an exile once given sanctuary *by* Philip II, and singled out for the sacred duty of leading the Greek forces by a newly vocal and ever-hostile Hyperides, another of the so-called 'Ten Attic Orators', was offering wandering mercenaries an alternative: a home at Taenarum in southern Laconia. Here the seeds of the Lamian (originally 'Hellenic') War against Macedonia were being irrigated by covert Athenian sponsorship, along with an alliance with Locris, Phocis and Aetolia using 50 of the talents from the Athenian treasury that now housed, thanks to the earlier arrival of Alexander's defecting treasurer, Harpalus, a further 700 talents guarded on the Acropolis.[449] The 22,000 or so gathering soldiers of fortune (some 8,000 of them formerly employed in Asia by Alexander) should, however, have thought twice about the chthonic implication, for it was here at Taenarum that Heracles discovered the entrance to Hades; a *nekyomanteion*, a 'drawing place of ghosts', was located nearby as well as the Death Oracle of Poseidon and its temple of sanctuary.[450]

Hyperides, who was quite accustomed to representing for a fee, argued to keep the balance of Harpalus' stolen gold to fund 'his' war, fermenting an already explosive brew. Demosthenes, who had been positively mute for the previous six years, and who had been appointed Athens' representative, *archetheoros*, for the 324 BCE Olympic Games, was now planning to meet, or had just returned from meeting, Alexander's general, Nicanor of Stagira (*possibly* Aristotle's nephew and soon-to-be son-in-law) at Olympia. Demosthenes now voted against the move. We can only speculate on the repercussions Nicanor threatened both him and Athens with if Harpalus and his funds were not handed over.

Demosthenes was nonetheless accused (by Hyperides, Stratocles and Deinarchus) of taking a commission; 350 talents went missing and so did Harpalus himself to a death in Crete at the hand of one of his Spartan associates, Thibron, while being chased across the Aegean by Alexander's agent, Philoxenus. After the Areopagus concluded its investigation and made its accusations (the result possibly guided by accusations from Harpalus' captured steward), Demosthenes, the recipient of a gold crown in 340 BCE and again in 338 BCE at the Great Dionysia for his services to the state, was eventually forced to seek sanctuary on the island of Calauria.[451]

Alexander's well-documented requests for divinity had accompanied the Exiles Decree. Demosthenes, surely heeding those warnings from Nicanor, declared: 'Alexander can claim to be the son of Zeus and Poseidon as well for all we care;'[452] certainly by 370/371 BCE Athens had a cult of Zeus-Ammon, Alexander's alleged father, and that would have been an obvious target as a place to leave votives for the new Pella-born deity.[453] The pro-Macedonian Demades warned the arguing Athenians that they were so concerned with the gods above that they would lose the earth below.[454] And they almost did, immediately following the arrival of reports of Alexander's death in Babylon; the city fined Demades 10 talents and deprived him of his citizenship, and Leosthenes was killed enforcing the blockade at Lamia; his 'towering cypress tree' bore no fruit except a poignant funeral oration by Hyperides.[455]

THE ETERNAL QUEST FOR THE SPHINX

With the backdrop of turmoil in both Greece and the Asian empire, the final months of Alexander's life are difficult to decipher, as we are left with the image of a man painted in sfumato, and the court sources appear to have been remarkably light on coherent detail through this period, when the rapidly concluding biographies degenerated into local reports of portents, prophecies and funeral pyres. So it is difficult to establish who or what Alexander had become. Eugene Borza proposed that every historian needs to deal with *three* incarnations of the Macedonian king: the 'mythological-romanticised', Alexander the 'historical', and 'Alexander the man'.[456] They are of course inseparable despite *Quellenforschung*'s best efforts. Besides, 'the original author of the myth was often Alexander himself'.[457]

There can be no doubt that he was, on the whole, incomprehensible to the average man of his age; simply put, Alexander was a maverick. Can we reconcile the king who paired eighty officers with Asiatic brides at the Susa mass weddings with the campaigner who forbade them and soldiers to take their half-caste offspring back to Macedonia?[458] Can we explain why Persepolis was burned when Cyrus' tomb and the Esagila Temple were repaired? And can the Alexander who ran Cleitus through be the same tyrant who let the ever-hostile Demosthenes outlive him? The latter may have been down to the influence of his agent, Aristion, who had enjoyed a friendship with Hephaestion,[459] and yet the long arm of Antipater and his oligarchs could have easily silenced the anti-Macedonian *logographos* years before.[460]

If Alexander was misunderstood, he himself may have failed to grasp the subtleties of those around him when journeying off the road Aristotle would have bade him follow. The elite education Philip had arranged for his son was not void of controversy itself; Alexander allegedly took

Aristotle to task for disseminating his 'exclusive' knowledge and learning to anyone but him: 'Thou hast not done well to publish thy acroamatic doctrines; for in what shall I surpass other men if those doctrines wherein I have been trained are to be all men's common property?'[461]

Plutarch claimed that in a letter sent to his regent, Antipater, Alexander threatened to bring Aristotle to account for his role in Callisthenes' treason, but how far their relationship had truly deteriorated remains conjecture.[462] Nevertheless, we doubt Aristotle would have performed *proskynesis* at the campaign court despite knowing what had befallen his relative. Alas, he left us no opinion of the great Macedonian conquest; Aristotle's essay titled *Alexander, or On the Colonists*, which was associated with his *On Kinship* and similarly dedicated to Alexander, is lost, and here he might have critiqued what he heard of the new overseas *poleis*.[463]

Precariously based in Athens as a *philomakedon* (or rather an employee of its king), Aristotle had to condone the presence of Macedonian-installed oligarchs in Greece while managing a philosophical school founded under a *demokratia* in which, according to Aristotle's *Athenian Constitution*, 'the poor, with their wives and children, were "enslaved" to the rich'. The limits of Aristotle's own creativity must have been tested when he attempted to pair the conqueror of Asia with the *pepaideumenos* (learned) prince he had taught in the Temple of Nymphs at Mieza. The recurring dichotomies in his writings, and what Diogenes Laertius described as a 'double criterion of truth', along with the 'dual structure of politics, morality and ethics', were probably a result of his uncomfortable position.[464] In his *Politics* Aristotle appreciated that some monarchies can neither be described as absolute nor constitutional, and this is no doubt how he avoided passing judgment on *Makedonon Politeia*.[465] If genuinely attributable to him, his disquisition on monarchy hinted that he and Alexander may have philosophically shadow-boxed on which of his five subcategories of kingship Alexander had actually established, encroaching as it did on 'absolute rule' as far as it fitted into the 'heroic'.[466]

If these complexities defied easy explanation, the Platonist and Peripatetic classifications did not advance the case. Plato determined there are four species of justice, two divisions of law, four of nobility and four of perfect virtue.[467] They seek absolute definitions for Alexander's mercurial character when there was clearly an evolution. The abstemious prince who fought at Chaeronea could hardly be the king who enjoyed nightly *komoi* (Macedonian-styled court banquets which often descended into drinking binges) at Babylon dressing variously as Ammon, Artemis and Hermes, a point even the admiring Tarn reluctantly conceded.[468] Nietzsche apparently took delight in discovering that at his death the solemn Plato was found to be reading the light-hearted Aristophanes. He concluded the philosopher has a sphinx-like nature; isn't it just possible Alexander did too?[469]

But just as 'great natures exhibit great vices also, as well as great virtues', mythology provided us with both a Theban winged Sphinx with malevolent riddles, and an Egyptian Sphinx endowed with benevolent strength.[470] Opinion on which inhabited the conqueror depends entirely on the position of the onlooker.

While guessing like Oedipus on the changing nature of man, we recall that the corpus of fragments collected by Jacoby and Müller is exclusively of Graeco-Roman descent and opinion.[471] What of the opposing view expounded by the Persian, Phoenician, Egyptian and Babylonian accounts? We have no idea what Berossus, the Chaldean priest of Bel-Marduk, actually wrote about Alexander in Babylon; writing just a generation later, the twenty-two quotations or paraphrases of his work and the eleven statements about him in classical sources suggest he was prolific in astronomical and philosophical references to Chaldeans, though to what extent is represented a *history* of events remains unknown.[472] The 'barbarian' accounts that *are* extant remember history quite distinctly. Controversial Zoroastrian claims in the *Book of Arda Viraf*, the religious texts written in 'Middle Persian' or Pahlavi, paint Alexander as that thoroughly evil spirit:

> But afterward, the accursed evil spirit, the wicked one, in order to make men doubtful of this religion, instigated the accursed Alexander, the Roman, who was dwelling in Egypt, so that he came to the country of Iran with severe cruelty and war and devastation; he also slew the ruler of Iran, and destroyed the metropolis and empire, and made them desolate.[473]

This may be later Sassanid-era spin (with specious ethnic attachments) but it surely captures the ancient tones of the regions Alexander had once devastated, and were they not just as entitled to their reflections in order to balance the total tradition?

Surely Porus, the 7-foot tall ruler of Paurava, had scribes in India recording the Macedonian onslaught. What did Alexander's 'most loyal vassal', as Arrian termed him, *really* think of the short godless invader who killed two of his sons at the Hydaspes River?[474] What did Manetho's *Aegyptiaca* (ca. 285 BCE) make of the Macedonian rule of the Ptolemies written from the perspective of a subjugated priest of Ra based at Heliopolis?[475] Manetho's *Criticism of Herodotus* gives us a hint of his views on Greeks coveting the oriental past for themselves. Nevertheless it was Herodotus' account, and not Manetho's pages and neither those of Berossus, that remained 'the standard authority' on the prehistory of Egypt and Babylonia, from a Western perspective at least.[476]

THE ARTISTIC ANACYCLOSIS

Even in Western eyes Alexander metamorphosed, through the Hellenistic Age and the rise and fall of Rome, then through the so-called European Dark Ages and then the Renaissance that rediscovered the Hellenistic philosophies once more. As Polybius, Tacitus and the Annales school of historians proposed, the canvas of history *is* cyclical. Renaissance France of the 16th and 17th centuries reviled Alexander and much of the polemical tone was surely inspired by Curtius' account, for the National Library of France had printed ten editions of his texts before 1550.[477] Nicolas de Soulfour's 1629 *L'Alexandre françois* proposed: 'Alexander, in order to acquire the title 'Great', ceased to be just and did not hesitate to appropriate the empires of the others or lay unjust hands on the treasures of all the world, to increase his own glory.'[478] And though King Karl XII of Sweden (ruled 1697-1718) thought he *was* Alexander reborn when campaigning brilliantly in his Great Northern War in the Baltic, Nicolas Beauzée, in 1781, suggested Alexander '… had no other motive than his own vanity, no right on his side other than that he could seize with his sword, no rule other than that dictated by his passions.'[479] Durante degli Alighieri (ca. 1265-1321), whom we refer to mononymously as simply 'Dante', ultimately consigned Alexander to the inferno.[480]

But the popes, Alexander VI in particular and the Borgia line especially, had inclined to the opposite view, decorating the Vatican with his likeness and charging their contemporaries to 'behave like Alexander, in dealing with the kings of the East'.[481] Louis XIV, the 'Sun King' (1683-1715), fashioned himself on the conqueror, commissioning paintings and a set of prints from Charles Le Brun named *Battles of Alexander*; even Mehmet II, who ended the Byzantine Empire when conquering Constantinople, adopted the iconography of the Macedonian.[482] The political philosopher Montesquieu in his 1748 *De l'Esprit de Lois* (*On the Spirit of the Laws*) saw an enlightened policy of infrastructure improvement and racial integration in Alexander's maritime plans and his Graeco-Persian intermarriages.

It has been proposed that 'murderers are allowed to kill if to the sound of a trumpet', and so Machiavelli's *Why the Kingdom of Darius, conquered by Alexander, did not rebel against his successors after his death* was tolerant of Macedonian brute force too.[483] He also forgave and even lauded the Borgias' cruel reign when discussing 'whether it is better to be loved or feared', and he found Hannibal's 'inhuman cruelty wholly responsible'.[484] Machiavelli (1469-1527) had in fact borrowed much from Polybius' anacyclosis and theories of mixed constitutions along with stoic credits to Fortuna, when outlining his own city state models.[485] The Florentine is remembered as 'Machiavellian' when he was in many ways a model

Renaissance man: a humanist trained in grammar, Latin and rhetoric, a musician, playwright, diplomat and a political scientist who published an *Art of War.*

A reading of Machiavelli's *Discorsi* (on the first ten books of Livy) reveals a true republican, and his statement that 'no prince is ever benefited by making himself hated' should be juxtaposed beside the cruelty he advocates, perhaps satirically, in *The Prince* – a 'cynical, amoral' work that once again ended up on the *Index Librorum Prohibitorum*, the papal list of banned works first issued in 1559 under the directorship of Pope Paul IV.[486] We should not forget that Machiavelli had been tortured 'with the rope' before retiring in exile and each evening 'entering the courts of the ancients', as he himself described his fascination with, and immersion into, the classical world.[487] The cruelty must have left its mark and tarnished his sense of 'civil virtue'. He died at age fifty-eight, though not before the Church of Santa Croce in Florence afforded him the epitaph *tanto nomini nullum par elogium,* 'no eulogy would be adequate to praise so great a name'.

Where Gustav Droysen saw a 'Bismarck' in Alexander in the 1870s,[488] Tarn, born into privelege in 1869 and writing on the subject through to 1948 in the heyday of the League of Nations, represented Alexander's campaign somewhat differently: he saw in him that 'utopian' mission to bring unity or 'brotherhood to mankind'.[489] Schachermeyr published in 1949 and as a result saw the 'mixing of cultures' as a dangerous 'chaos of blood', rejecting Tarn's ideals completely.[490] Ernst Badian, writing in 1958 in the aftermath of Jewish persecution, considered Alexander a ruthless totalitarian tyrant where Peter Green, who published his brilliant but cynical account in the liberal 1970s, was simply disillusioned and failed to see any higher ideals at all. He nevertheless conceded that Alexander was, '… perhaps, taken all in all, the most incomparable general the world has ever seen.'[491]

In contrast, Lane Fox's charismatic 1973 biography has been labelled a 'last great gasp' of the Alexander 'romance'. But a historiophotic romantic genre does still persist when summing up his military achievements;[492] even Polybius allowed Alexander some divinity when recognising his soul had, 'as all admit, something of the superhuman in it'.[493] Hammond's influential source studies have been branded as: 'A misguided attempt to turn back the clock of Alexander studies to the time when WW Tarn dismissively rejected the fruitful work of German *Quellenforschung,* in an attempt to lay the foundations for his Alexander, the Nice.'[494] As one commentator proposed, Tarn's thematic approach '… has tended to cow originality into silence, because of the mass of erudition underlying that study.' And it has been said that the studies of 'Droysen, Berve, Tarn, Schachermeyr and Badian have both added to our understanding and multiplied uncertainties' attached to the Macedonian king.[495]

But to attempt to attach to Alexander the simplistic and polarised behavioural notions of 'good' or 'bad', or to label him 'benevolent' or 'evil', would be as anachronistic as concluding that Demosthenes, or any one of the Ten Attic Orators, was (in our sense of the word) a democrat or a republican, monarchist or anarchist, on the basis of the few speeches ascribed to them. Nevertheless, few men from our classical past, perhaps with the exception of the equally mercurial Alcibiades, termed 'in spirit brilliant' by Diodorus and 'the least scrupulous' of human beings by Plutarch, *have* been so variously summed-up and decanted.[496] Alexander remains, as Heuss aptly put it, 'a bottle which could be filled with any wine'.[497]

These many 'vintages' have been readily captured in oils and tapestries – enduring propaganda that pitted the brush and weave against the pen. An *ekphrasis* in late-medieval art was reasserted throughout the Renaissance merging contemporary and classical themes as effectively as an *auctor supplementorum* filled manuscript gaps.[498] Paying due attention to the intolerances of the Holy Roman Empire, the tale of Alexander was already something of an iconograph that was sufficiently alluring to divert the attention of great painters from the safe career of biblical depictions. The result was colourful tapestries depicting the *Tales of Alexander* and canvasses named *Les Reines de Perse aux pieds d'Alexandre* (1660-61, better known as *The Tent of Darius*), *Alexander at the Tomb of Cyrus*, *Alexander and Porus* (1673) and *Alexander the Great and the Fates* (ca. 1667), whilst the 17th and 18th centuries saw a still wider artistic proliferation of the theme.[499]

Albrecht Altdorfer's *The Battle of Alexander at Issus* painted in 1529 and commissioned by Duke Wilhelm of Bavaria, was influenced by both the recently published *World Chronicle* of Hartmann Schedel (1440-1514) and Curtius' account of the engagement.[500] A civic officer of some repute with connections at the imperial court, Altdorfer had announced the expulsion of Jews from the city and sketched the synagogue before its destruction. He interrogated Anabaptists, appointed Protestant ministers and he shunned 'spiritual accessories'. The fermenting Turkish push towards Vienna threatened apocalyptic events, and it is against this background that Altdorfer's canvas depicted a dark turning point in history, thus his rendering of Issus has been described as a 'cosmic Armageddon'.

A tablet within the picture emphasised the Persian death toll while soldiers wear turbans in Turkish style and women wear feathered toques in the fashion of the German court. Their presence is a likely allusion to Curtius' description of the capture of Darius III's royal family, a scene depicted in Paolo Veronese's equally anachronistic *The Family of Darius before Alexander* (1565-70). What Duke Wilhelm IV finally received from Altdorfer was a depiction of a world 'dominated in equal parts by new ideas and medieval tradition'. The conquering Napoleon, a clear admirer of Alexander's military genius, had the painting relocated to Paris and hung in his bathroom.

Alexander was not alone in artful transformations; Hannibal, Mark Antony and Cleopatra were all synthesised and resyncronised to the artists' own era. Lorenzo Castro's *The Battle of Actium* painted in 1672,[501] probably inspired by a new English translation of Virgil's *Aeneid,* revealed a thoroughly Baroque interpretation. The triremes and quinqeremes of Antony and Octavian resemble squat Dutch fluyts; soldiers wear plumed *galea* which look more *Pickelhaube* than Roman, and Cleopatra is garbed in a 17th century gown. *Hannibal Crossing the Alps*, a fresco by Jacobo Ripanda from ca. 1510 at the Palazzo del Campidoglio (Capitoline Museum) in Rome, is similarly structured with little regard to historical accuracy; the Carthaginian general is astride an elephant in what appears an Ottoman turban.

In all these ideological hybrids, however, one episode has remained literarily and artistically stable: the rendering of Alexander's death. In no portrayal of his passing, from the illuminated manuscripts of the 1330s to the unfinished *The Death of Alexander the Great* by Karl Theodor von Piloty (he died in 1886), do we see sight of a testament or the reading of a Will, not even in those depictions taken straight from the *Romance.*

THE POISONED TRAGEDIAN AND THE CONSCIENCE OF ACHILLES

If Athenaeus' testimony is accurate, Alexander was launching himself into an animated recital from Euripides' *Andromeda* at Medius' *komos* in Babylon just days before he died, as Perseus the saviour we would imagine. Medius of Larissa, whose close relationship with Alexander might stem from the assistance the Thessalian royal Aleuadae line had provided to his grandfather, Amyntas III, allegedly called the impromptu party with the specific intent of facilitating the poisoning of the king. Alexander was toasting his guests in unmixed wine; Ephippus claimed his usual cup held 2 *choes* (12 pints which verged on a *krater,* so mixing-bowl-sized) and so it was redolent of the cup of Nestor, so large it was a challenge to lift. We do not know how much Alexander had imbibed that night but the tenth *krater* signified madness and unconsciousness, according to a fragment of a play from Eubolus (*floruit* 370/60s BCE).[502] Euripides seems to have been the choice verse for fevered men; Lucian claimed that when an epidemic hit the population of Abdera, the pale ghost-like citizens recited Perseus' lines over, mimicking Archelaus' performance seen earlier that summer. Apparently it was only stopped by the onset of frost.[503]

How symbolic was the *Andromeda* for Alexander, and how symbolic is this recital for our argument? We might wonder who played opposite him at Medius' banquet, for an extant line from the now lost tragedy proposed: 'I forbid the getting of bastard children. Though, not at all inferior to legitimate ones, they are disadvantaged by law. You must guard against this.'[504] We may hope for his counterpart's sake that Alexander avoided the subject of offspring, for within two weeks of his final gulp, the argument over succession, and which child, or children, would inherit the Macedonian kingdom, almost resulted in civil war.[505]

Aside from his professed silence in the *Journal* and his succession failure in the Vulgate accounts, what did Alexander *truly* contemplate in the fevered days before he died? He must have recalled the Chaldean warning not to enter the city, the advice that diverted him past the now barely inhabited Borsippa, if this is historical and not part of later *thauma* that attached itself to his death (T21, T22, T23, T24). Or, perhaps he regretted heeding Anaxarchus who advised him to ignore it, though the philosopher's belief in innumerable worlds might at last have seemed appealing.[506] Reflecting that most of the Aeacid line had died before the age of thirty, did the first Macedonian 'Great King', now with one young son (two, if Justin's unlikely episode with Cleophis is true), a pregnant wife, an illustrious family and the wealth of Croesus, complain that Tyche and Asclepius had treated him unkindly?[507] Asclepius had no explaining to do for he was termed 'the blameless physician', but surely the Homeric and Iliadic comparisons finally came back to haunt Alexander.[508] The *Iliad,* which (it has been proposed), like Statius' epic poem, was perhaps once named the *Achilleid* due to its focus on the hero,[509] opened with:

> Sing Goddess, the wrath of Peleus' son, Achilles and its devastation,
> that caused the Achaeans loss on bitter loss and hurled many warrior
> souls down into the house of Hades.[510]

Through Alexander's final hours, as he 'exchanged life for an eternal battle line' (as Hyperides phrased it), and when fever-wracked and sweat-soaked in Nebuchadnezzar's bedchamber, did he think of the warriors *he*, like Achilles (whose name stems from 'grief') had cast into the underworld, or had he conveniently become a believer in the Pythagorean immortal soul?[511] Did Alexander expect to meet Cronus breathing the upper air of Aether in the Elysian Fields, or on Hesiod's *Makaron Nesoi*, the Isles of the Blessed?[512] And we wonder whether he requested Zeus to consider himself and Hephaestion as new *Dioscouri* and immortalise them *both*.[513]

The Persian Great Kings buried clay cylinders inscribed with a record of their deeds in the corners of significant city buildings. Where were Alexander's, and where was his golden commemorative statue on the Babylonian plain?[514] If he had truly inherited the pharaonic titles 'Horus the Strong', 'the beloved of Ammon', and 'Son of Ra', as a Luxor inscription suggests, he would have also been introduced to the Egyptian

Book of the Dead.[515] Alexander would have known that he would fail many of the thirty-six denials and that would have hindered his journey to the Egyptian gods, demigods and spirits of the dead.[516] In which case, he might have simply considered little more than the words of Themistocles, 'the subtle serpent of Hellas', after the Persian defeat: '… the gods and heroes begrudge that a single man in his godless pride should be king of Hellas and Asia, too.'[517]

Perhaps Alexander was contemplating Themistocles' own fate: a hero at Marathon and the *real* (if not official) commander of the Greek forces at the naval battles at Artemisium and Salamis, and in Plutarch's opinion 'the man most instrumental in achieving the salvation of Hellas', his arrogance saw him ostracised to Argos (as the 190 inscriptions on excavated *ostraka* testify). Themistocles then ventured to the sanctuary of Alexander I of Macedonia, before, ironically, gaining Persian employ, for Athens had a habit of exiling and poisoning her best.[518]

The eyewitness authors would have us believe that none of these introspections, regrets, the blood guilt (*alastoria*) and the pleas to the gods of Olympus, Egypt and Esagila, made their way to Alexander's fever-cracked lips as his men gathered around him. Was the king who had been quoting 'the most tragic of the poets' about to acquiesce to another silent tragedy, leaving the last lines of his own play unwritten, or to be penned by those about him?[519] We propose not, for Alexander was a manipulator of men, Pythia, diviners and their gods; he exploited imagery of the past and he attempted to change the present; he was more likely to have been disdainfully churning over Themistocles' challenge on impiety the moment he left Pella. And whether truly *verschmelzungspolitik* or a purely practical initiative, the mass weddings at Susa made it clear that Alexander was setting out to manipulate the future as well.

As it has been pointed out, the very existence of Alexander's lavish funeral hearse and its unchallenged construction at Babylon over two full years is evidence enough that he requested burial somewhere else.[520] The 12 by 15-foot bier that departed Babylon, vividly described by Diodorus, was so heavy that special shock-absorbing axles had to be designed and a team of road menders and mechanics employed to accompany its slow but loud advance.[521] Mysteriously, a spectacular sarcophagus was found in Sidon in 1887 and now has pride of place in the Istanbul Archaeology Museum. One scholar commented: 'It is tempting to see its scaled roof, running vine garlands, guardian lions, and long narrative friezes, as an homage to Alexander's hearse, which must have passed close by the city in 321 BCE but nothing can be proved',[522] though the frieze clearly depicts the Macedonian king and Hephaestion.

The sarcophagus is now popularly accredited to Abdalonymus, the 'rags to riches' King of Sidon, but that has been recently challenged;

Laomedon, the displaced satrap of Coele-Syria, has been proposed as its alternative inhabitant.[523] Forensics now reveal that the Pentelic Marble sarcophagus was brightly painted in polychromatic style with evidence of gold plating; this is not inconsistent with the 'hammered gold' in Diodorus' description of Alexander's hearse.[524] And so we might be forgiven for wondering whether Ptolemy left the ponderously heavy cask in Syria in his hurried flight back to Egypt after kidnapping Alexander's body, if it weren't for a panel which appears to depict the murder of Perdiccas which took place a year or so later.[525]

If Alexander had genuinely envied Achilles in having Homer to preserve him, he might have equally taken solace in the speech Thucydides provided to Pericles:

> Rather, the admiration of the present and the succeeding ages will be ours, since we have not left our power without witness, but have shown it by mighty proofs; and far from needing a Homer for our panegyrist, or other of his craft whose verses might charm, for the moment, only for the impression, which they gave to melt at the touch of fact we have forced every sea and land to be the highway of our daring, and everywhere, whether for evil or for good, have left imperishable monuments behind us.[526]

But in Alexander's case the monuments had not been built; no new Acropolis with a Propylaia or Erektheion adorned Asia's rocky outcrops. The new eponymous cities listed in the epitome of Stephanus of Byzantium's *Ethnica* (6th century) and in the *Romance*, were, more often than not, simply Asiatic settlements refounded.[527] They appear little more than mud brick forts ('and a market'), or a forced synoecism of smaller settlements into a larger hastily walled town, and, moreover, through the campaign decade much had been destroyed. One of the many new Alexandrias (of perhaps fourteen, and with the exception of the new city in Egypt, all of them east of the Tigris) had been founded on the River Jaxartes (today's Syr Darya flowing through Uzbekistan and Kyrgyzstan); the population of three existing 'cities' *was* resettled here at Alexandria Eschate (the 'Furthest') and yet a wall 6 miles in circuit was completed in just seventeen days.[528]

This does not represent a true attempt at architectural permanency, despite Arrian's statement about its intended greatness and the 'splendour of its name'. Neither did the settlements (rather, fortresses) of Boucephala and Nicaea on the banks of the Hydaspes, for these were significantly damaged by heavy monsoon rain soon after being established. As Tarn put it, 'he left his arrangements in India an unfinished sketch, to be sponged off the canvas the moment he died.'[529] None were monuments to an empire any more than Hadrian's ditch and palisade *limites* at Rome's furthest borders were; Alexander's infrastructure is simply redolent of military occupation rather than empire building. The speech Xenophon crafted for Cyrus in the *Cyropaedia* had called for just that, fortresses along the way, or his men risked becoming sailors on a sea that left open and hostile water behind them.[530]

Twelve altars to the Olympian gods at Alexander's 'world's end' now existed, sculptures by Lysippus of the twenty-five Companions who fell at the Granicus River had been erected at Dion, and 'Alexander's Steps' had been cut into Mount Ossa in Thessaly (they are still visible); we must include the mole at Tyre and the causeway at Clazomenae as 'construction projects', though both were simply necessities of aggressive siege warfare. But there was little else to show; no lofty gardens or new palaces with stone carvings that graced Assyrian reliefs.[531] Even his treasurer, Harpalus, seems to have outdone him in Babylon for an 'expensive' monument (perhaps a temple) to Pythionice had already been erected for his dead courtesan.[532]

There were no new aqueducts, permanent bridges or a new road network that we know of, just the flotsam and jetsam of campaign necessity and a mercurial nostalgia for a Great King's tomb; even the harbour construction at Babylon and removal of weirs on the Tigris and Euphrates appear more motivated by military requirements (for the fleet heading to Arabia) than for agricultural purposes.[533] Although Alexander retained Achaemenid administration structures, whether they could be maintained under garrison conditions and thinly spread Macedonian authority is questionable. So was this the skilled and pragmatic adaptation to circumstances that Briant, for one, credits to him, or the tired and insufficiently imaginative solution from a warrior who simply coveted the Persian throne? Perhaps Alexander realised, like Hannibal would later do in Italy, that you cannot truly 'own' or keep a whole begrudging country or empire suppressed – when it had been gained by military conquest – when you are ethnically foreign.

'Positive Hellenism', which was to see safe trading routes, *real* cities constructed and Greek amphitheatres nestling in the foothills of the upper and eastern Persian provinces, came later with the Successor kingdoms, when Greeks settled by choice and not coercion in the newly opened up Asiatic world. Aramaic would then give way to *koine*, the patois of the Western conquerors, and even the Babylonian calendar was synchronised to that of Macedonia.[534] But with the exception of Silk Road commodities and dwindling Persian gold, and camels exported to Macedonia and Egypt with hydraulics and irrigation expertise – as well as the appearance of leprosy that was probably imported from India with Alexander's returning veterans – this was predominantly one-way traffic and not a permanent cultural exchange. It was something of a reversal of the old world order in which the Persian Empire saw little need of Greek goods in the interior. Yet even in this more stable environment, the Greeks themselves continued to show a great apathy for learning foreign tongues or homogenising their existence. The one significant exception, however, was in the growing *entrepôt* of Alexandria in Egypt.

The statement that 'Alexander was essentially a destroyer, not a creator' epitomises the view of many historians, old and new; even Tarn thought he was 'fortunate in his death' as 'the real task was yet before him.'[535] The conclusion that he '... was better able to cope with war than with peace', repeated in many guises, was a weakness Alexander might have even recognised himself. 'Augustus heard Alexander at the age of thirty-two years had subdued the greatest part of the world and was at a loss what he should do with the rest of his time. But he wondered why Alexander should not think it a lesser labour to gain a great empire than to set in order what he had got.'[536]

In the opinion of the Roman emperor Augustus (ruled 27 BCE-14 CE), 'for Alexander conquest and *arete* were all, the dull but essential business of administration held no charms for him.'[537] Is the appraisal unfair? We could argue that had he lived a decade longer we might have evidence of a grand infrastructure emerging across Asia, and yet his desire to head west from Babylon when the East was still so fragile and recently won, clearly suggests otherwise. It is perhaps understandable then that Alexander's original Will might have sought to address this: demanding construction of grand mausoleums, temples and chryselephantine statues in his name, a dying man's compensation for the lack of stone mortared during his life. The Wills detailed in the *Romance* and at the end of the *Metz Epitome* (*Epitoma Metensis*, possibly 4th or 5th century CE), a later Latin précis which recounted campaign events through 330 to 325 BCE, request just that (T1, T2).

We opened the chapter with an extract from the words carved into the Cyrus Cylinder, but this timeless and benevolent imagery has its flip side too. It was the Shah of Iran in 1971 who referred to its declaration as 'the first bill of human rights' when dedicating a copy to the United Nations; the Pahlavi regime was exploiting the relic as a symbol of 2,500 years of continued Persian monarchy. But Cyrus' true mindset must be considered in a more sober context, for he had just defeated the much-hated Babylonian king, Nabonidus, at Opis, slaughtering the retreating army and capturing a great haul of loot; Babylon was his for the taking.

The inscription on the cylinder, hardly original in Mesopotamia, was standard conqueror's rhetoric. Along with the *Nabonidus Chronicle,* it positioned Cyrus' capture of the city as an invitation from the local god, Marduk, in the same way that Nabopolassar (Nebû-apal-usur, ca. 658-605 BCE) had recorded and justified his actions at Nineveh seventy years before.[538] Cyrus' 'restraint' was a political necessity if he was to unify his new empire, and there is no archaeological evidence suggesting the reconstruction of any building, or the repairing of Mesopotamian temples during his reign.[539] Even Xenophon's encomiastic *Cyropaedia* contradicted the claims on the cylinder, providing an altogether darker version of events:

> Cyrus sent squadrons of cavalry down the different roads with orders to kill all they found in the street, while those who knew Assyrian were to warn the inhabitants to stay indoors under pain of death...When all was done he summoned the Persian priests and told them the city was the captive of his spear and bade them set aside the first fruits of the booty as an offering to the gods and mark out land for sacred demesnes...[540]

The legends that Alexander fed off were clearly open to question. Arrian doubted that either Heracles or the ivy-wreathed Dionysus, the 'Lord of the Triumph', had really visited India; he was after all in Hades bringing Euripides back to life.[541] And according to the *Cypria*, a book of the early Homeric Cycle, the invading Greek fleet heading for Troy made a navigational error and landed at Theuthrania some miles south, fighting an inconclusive battle before noting their mistake.[542] After nine years besieging the city, a disheartened Agamemnon proposed sailing home with: 'Cut and run! Sail home to the fatherland we love! We'll never take the broad street of Troy.' Helen was, in any case, not in the city; she was stranded for a decade in Egypt while the Greeks battered the Ilion walls.[543] Herodotus' verdict on it all:

> It seems to me that Homer was acquainted with this story, and while discarding it, because he thought it less adapted for epic poetry than the version which he followed... If Helen had been at Troy, the inhabitants would, I think, have given her up to the Greeks, whether Alexander [Paris] consented to it or not.[544]

We may be equally dubious about the much-debated concept of *verschmelzungspolitik* that was so fulsomely anticipated in Plutarch's *Moralia* with its 'philosophic commonwealth' and 'one great loving cup'.[545] Arrian's account of 'the international love-feast' at Susa, which espoused a 'union of purpose between Macedonians and Persians and partnership in empire', along with Curtius' rendering of Alexander's indignant harangue to his troops that preceded it with further calls for *homonoia* and *koinonia* ('harmony' and 'fellowship') – must have played their part in the notion. The phraseology Curtius used implied the Macedonian king sought to erase the national distinctions of his soldiers: 'It is neither unbecoming for the Persians to copy Macedonian customs nor for the Macedonians to imitate the Persians'; this was an equalising sentiment that was perhaps perpetuated by the frequent references in Roman rhetoric to Alexander's breaking the bolts of the doors of the earth. Yet this admirable notion has been described as nothing more than a '… romantic comfort blanket thrown by later Hellenistic writers over a by now wobbling Isocratic crusade.'[546]

Curtius did, however, have his reasons for rebroadcasting such a theme: he was espousing the benefits of a Roman imperialism (we suggest in Nero's rule, 54-68 CE) which was by then rapidly swallowing up a good portion of the known world.[547] Some historians such as Droysen argued that a breakdown of cultural barriers *was* part of Alexander's grand design, and it is hard to refute the man who first coined the term 'Hellenistic', though, ironically, he saw the outcome of the cultural movement as positive to the spread of Christianity but to little else.[548] Tarn more cautiously stated: 'The germs of certain phenomena of Hellenism begin to appear before Alexander.'[549] Mausolus and his Hecatomnid predecessors had, for example, already established a Greek-orientated cultural foothold at Halicarnassus in Caria in the previous century, and Hermias' philosophical experiment in government at Assus (in the Troad) ought to be mentioned too, though perhaps it was too perfect a concept to escape Persian curiosity;[550] he was tortured to death in Susa giving his son-in-law, Aristotle, something to ponder on after his prudent return to Macedonia from a too-close-by Lesbos.[551]

But it remains highly unlikely that Alexander had such elevated pretensions, and the speech re-rendered by Curtius surely attempted nothing more than to deliver something of a morale-boosting *epipolesis* (akin to a pre-battle speech) in the face of a military mutiny.[552] The Greek allusion to a common purpose, *homonoia*, is, as one scholar put it, a phantom that should be laid to rest.[553]

As even the harshest critics have, we must acknowledge Alexander's military prowess and credit him with a coercive campaign genius, for with the exception of Procles of Carthage who rated Pyrrhus of Epirus (died 272 BCE) the better tactician, Alexander is hailed as history's most successful general. According to Appian, even Hannibal agreed and Scipio too, reluctantly; Livy, Appian and Plutarch repeated the story of Scipio and Hannibal meeting at Ephesus some years after the formative battle at Zama in 202 BCE, and it was here that they questioned each other on their respective military rankings. Polybius rated leaders by the plots and mutinies they attracted or steered clear of, but where Hannibal had remained conspiracy-free, Scipio, whose deeds were later immortalised by Petrarch (who took a dim view of Alexander) in his poem *Africa*, had not been free from controversy himself. Scipio's near death illness led to a mutiny of his troops at Sucro in Spain, though the grievances were familiar: soldiers demanding back pay and a larger share of the plunder.[554]

Less fortunate than Pompey the 'Great' (106-48 BCE), and though perhaps *megalopsychos* ('great souled') in spirit, Alexander had no spontaneous elevation by his men to *Megas* and had to wait centuries for Rome to propose the epithet *Magnus*.[555] But Pompey had Cicero arguing for him, where Demosthenes, to whom Cicero was often compared, was on the opposing team in Alexander's day. Aeschines, the 'old sprain' who might have proposed the honorific, had been shamed to retirement on Rhodes despite his 'Three Graces' (eloquent speeches), and was no doubt attacking his nemesis in absentia from his new school of rhetoric, for Demosthenes clearly had the upper hand in Athens.[556]

The close temporal proximity of the deaths of Alexander and Demosthenes, with the equally influential Aristotle, each within the successive years 323-322 BCE, has been termed 'one of the most marvellously significant synchronisms in the history of civilisation', for it emphatically marked the end of a productive period of Greek genius. It is indeed a wonder that three of history's most brilliant individuals breathed the same air and with fates that were intertwined. The list becomes even more remarkable if we include Diogenes the Cynic who was said to have died on the same day as the Macedonian king.[557]

To these we may add the *Somatophylax* Leonnatus (322 BCE), Alexander's acting chiliarch Perdiccas (321 BCE), the regent-in-waiting Craterus (321 BCE), the court philosopher Anaxarchus (320 BCE) alongside the Macedonian regent Antipater (319 BCE) and Alexander's vocal opponent Hyperides who died in 322 BCE on Antipater's orders. Both Theopompus and his opponent, Anaximenes, died within these years taking their *Hellenika* and *Philippika* with them, and there followed '… a period when anecdote and fable gradually came to usurp the place of truth'.[558] And this sums up well the environment in which the tales of Alexander's life, and his death, were first put to papyrus, as it becomes apparent when reviewing the historians who gave us the 'universal comparandum'.

The Alexander herm ca. 330 BCE following the bronze of Lysippus; perhaps the statue with a bronze lance described by Plutarch *Moralia* 360d. For a time this was the only known portrait of Alexander, an identification made possible from the still legible frontal inscription. It is potentially a work that comes closest to Lysippus' original. Unearthed at Tivoli in 1779 it was first gifted to Napoleon by Azara who organised the excavation. It was dedicated to the Louvre in 1803, or after, by Napoleon who was then First Consul, as confirmed by an inscription on the right side.

NOTES

1. An adaption of the transcription from H Schaudig *Die Inschriften Nabonids von Babylon und Cyrus' des Großen*, Münster, 2001, *The Prince of Peace* 24, 25 and 26. The translation is a modified version of M Cogan's published in WH Hallo and KL Younger *The Context of Scripture. Vol. II: Monumental Inscriptions from the Biblical World*, 2003, Leiden and Boston.
2. Gautier de Chatillon *Alexandreis* 3.307-312.
3. Herodotus 8.109-110 for Themistocles' warning that no king should rule Asia and Hellas too.
4. Curtius 5.1.24 reported that 'most have believed' Babylon was founded by Belus (alternatively, Marduk), and he added that they were wrong and it was Semiramis; see chapter titled *Babylon Cipher and Rosetta Stone* for more on its founding.
5. Curtius 5.1.16 described the Babylonian walls as bitumen cemented, using the bitumen stream that poured from a cavern at nearby Mennis.
6. Diodorus 17.117.5 stated twelve years and seven months, Arrian 7.28.1 stated twelve years and eight months; a discussion of the calculation of the length of reign can be found in the Loeb Classical Library 1963 edition, p 467 footnote 5.
7. The Summer Palace might better be termed the 'Outer Palace' for its defensive nature; see discussion in Reade (2000) p 20.
8. Justin 12.16.5 for the eagles and Plutarch 2 for Philip's dream that he sealed Olympias' womb with the image of a lion before his son's birth.
9. Arrian 7.16-17 and 7.22.1 for the Chaldean warning to Alexander not to enter Babylon.
10. Quoting Plutarch *Moralia* 327b, translation from the Loeb Classical Library edition, 1936.
11. Plutarch 75.1. 'Magi' comes from the Old Persian name for 'priest'; Collins (2008) p 54.
12. The doctor treating Alexander's closest companion, Hephaestion, had been executed for failing to cure him the previous year: Arrian 7.14.4, Plutarch 72.3. Alexander executed the seer who predicted a propitious day when his father was murdered; Hammond (1994) p 176 for discussion; a fragment of the report of the trial following Philip's death is preserved.
13. Xenophon *Cyropaedia* 8.7.6 provided a vivid account of Cyrus' deathbed speech attended by his sons and generals.
14. As an example of the admiration, Alexander had Cyrus' tomb repaired and punished those he suspected of tomb-raiding. Discussed in detail in chapter titled *Lifting the Shroud of Parrhasius*.
15. Xenophon *Cyropaedia* 7.6.9 translated by HG Sakyns 2009, Gutenberg e-book project.
16. Aristotle *Magikos* fragment 6 cited in Diogenes Laertius book 1 Prologue, section 8-9 *On Philosophy*. Aristotle's lost work, *On the Pythagoreans*, is also said to have discussed the Magi and, or, magic. See discussion in Chroust (1964) p 572 and Momigliano (1977) pp 18-19.
17. With calendar changes and recalibrations it is not possible to support the exact dating of this event to the modern calendar with any certainty, despite the accuracy of astronomical observations.
18. Scholars disagree on whether the text on the Cyrus Cylinder really portrays a tolerant regime; see discussion in Kuhrt (1983) pp 83-97 and below.
19. The tablets are labelled BM 36761 and 36390. For full discussion see Polcaro-Valsecchi-Verderame (2008) pp 55-64. Sprague de Camp (1972) p 141 for a description of the Processional Way.
20. Arrian 3.16.4,7.17.2, Diodorus 2.9.9, Strabo 16.1.5 for the destruction; Xerxes melted down the gold statue of Marduk for his depleted treasury. Plutarch *Aristides* 21.2 reported on the sacrifices taking place by the Plataeans in his day.
21. Following P Briant, *Rois, tributs et paysans: études sur les formations tributaires du Moyen-Orient ancient*, Pu Franc-Comtoises, 1989, p 330; discussed in Briant (1974) pp 183-184; the contention was also re-asked as a question by R Lane Fox in 2007.
22. Quoting Bosworth (2004) p 553.
23. Aristotle *Prior Analytics* 2.27.
24. Alexander's beardless tradition discussed by VA Troncoso in Carney-Ogden (2010) pp 13-24; Plutarch *Moralia* 180a-b claimed Alexander ordered his men to shave before battle. See Athenaeus 6.260d-261a and 13.565a-b for references to the beardless fashion. Plutarch 4.1-4 for his sweet odour, neck tilt, melting eyes and fair complexion. Aelian 12.14 for his menacing or alarming appearance.
25. Stewart (1993) pp 341-350 and Carney-Ogden (2010) p 13 for other citations on Alexander's appearance. Plutarch 4.1-7, Plutarch *Moralia* 53D and Pyrrhus 8.1 for Alexander's hair, smell, harsh voice. For his teeth *Romance* 1.13.3. Plutarch 4 for the *Memoirs* of Aristoxenus.
26. The word literally means 'policy of fusion' and was first used by Droysen in his *Geschichte Alexanders des Grossen* (1833) to describe Alexander's supposed plan.
27. Roisman-Worthington (2010) p 89 ff for origins of *Makedones*, and following Anson (1984).
28. For the influences absorbed by Hesiod, see discussion in West (2008) Introduction vii. See

discussion in Roisman-Worthington (2010) p 16 for the origins of the name 'Macedon' from *The Catalogue of Women,* a work once attributed to Hesiod and dating to the 7th or 6th century BCE. Herodotus 7.127.1, 7.128.1, 7.131 for the heartland of Macedonian in the regions of Mt Olympus and Pieria as well as Emathia and Bottiaea. Strabo 7.7.11, Pliny 4.17 Justin 7.1 for the older, perhaps Bronze Age name for Macedonia, Emathia. Quoting Hatzopoulos (1996) p 239 on Emathia. For Marsyas FGrH 135-136, F13; discussed in Hatzopoulos (1996) pp 240-241.

29. The Catalogue of Ships is found in Homer's *Iliad* 2.494-759. Herodotus 2.154.2, Thucydides 2.68.5, Xenophon *Cyropaedia* 2.3 all stress the commonality of the Greek language; discussed in Anson (2004) p 205 ff.

30. Both Herodotus and Pausanias were more specific in the identification. For example Pausanias 7.1.5 links Achaeans to the inhabitants of Argolis and Laconia being displaced by the Dorian invasion.

31. Quoting *Iliad* line 484-5.

32. The collective *Akhaioi* was used almost 600 times in the *Iliad*, the *Danaoi* almost 140 times and Argives some 182 times to denote the Greek where *Hellenes* appeared only once.

33. Aristotle *Meteorologica* 1.14.

34. Pausanias 10.7.6. The Amphictionic League represented an ancient association of tribes with obscure origins.

35. For Aspasia's contention see Plato *Menexenos* 245d.

36. Herodotus 1.57.3, 1.58.1; quoting E Anson from Roisman-Worthington (2010) p 15 for 'Greek of Greeks'. Anson (2004) p 193 for Pelasgians. In myth Pelasgos the son of Zeus and Niobe *was* an Arcadian.

37. Herodotus 1.56.3 suggested the Dorians inhabited northern Greece before migrating south.

38. Following C Thomas in Roisman-Worthington (2010) p 65.

39. Snodgrass (1967) p 48 for discussion of the end of the Greek Dark Age. Finlay (1973) p 161 for the emergence of the *symbola.* As examples, Polybius 5.104.1, 7.9.3, 7.9.5, 7.9.7, 9.37.7, 38.3.8 Also Polybius 18.18.1 suggested the 'Greeks' used the *sarissa* and not specifically or exclusively Macedonians. It is highly unlikely all Greece used the *sarissa.*

40. Discussion of the pre-Greek population and the non Indo-European vocabulary that survived into Greek in Mallory (1989) pp 66-72. Herodotus 5.58-5.59.1 for the Cadmus and founding of Thebes. RSP Beekes *Etymological Dictionary of Greek,* Brill, 2009, p 614 for the pre-Greek etymology of Kadmos.

41. Pausanias: Boeotia 20-24. Aristotle *Meteorologika* 1.14. *Parian Chronicle* entry 6: 'From when Hellen (Ἕλλην) [son of] Deuk[alion] became king of [Phthi]otis and those previously called Graikoi were named Hellenes.' Strabo 7.328 for the *Hellopia* of Hesiod. Stephanus of Byzantium *Ethnika* for Graikos' origins. Homer *Odyssey* 14.327 for Odysseus' visit to Dodona; *Iliad* 16.233 for Achilles praying to Zeus of Dodona; Malkin (1998) pp 149-150 for discussion. Carney (2006) p 91 for the cults of Dodona.

42. Aristotle originated from Euboea which perhaps explains his earlier reference. For the various clues to the etymology of *Graecus* see Homer 2.498, Pausanias 5, Aristotle *Meteoroligica* 1.352a.

43. Homer *Iliad* 2.867.

44. Loosely attributed to Aristotle *Politics* 3.14, 1285a.20, but more likely emanating from his 'school'. *Politics* 7.1324b for the Macedonian reference as 'barbarians' and 1333b38-34a1 for the barbarians deserving their fate; Finlay (1973) pp 156-157 for discussion. Aristotle *Politics* 1327b 23-28 for the climate discussion. Isocrates *Panathenaicus* 12.163. Also see the earlier view at Plato *Republic* 470c-471a; see Tarn 1 (1948) p 9 for discussion.

45. Hansen (1999) p 55 for the estimated 750 *poleis* and Roisman-Worthington (2010) p 93 for 1,000 poleis.

46. Dexippus, for example, termed the Goths 'Scythians' in his *Skythika.*

47. Thucydides referring to tribes as barbarian at 1.5.3, 1.6.6, 1.47.3, 1.50.3, 2.68.9, 2.80.5, 2.81-82, 3.112.7, 4.124.1, 4.126.3, 4.127.2. He did occasionally distinguish Macedonians from barbarians, as did Ephorus at 16.4.2, 5.71-2. Thucydides 2.99.2 for the distinction of tribes. Hammond argued 'barbarian' was used in a cultural not linguistic sense, considering they all spoke dialects of Greek; HGL Hammond, *Ancient Macedonia-Deductions and explanation of the term 'Barbaroi',* published in Ancient Macedonian Ethnicity, Language, Linguistics, Modern Historians, February 2010. Hatzopoulos (1996) p 479 for Upper Macedonians being more ethnically akin to Epirotes.

48. Polybius 12.4b 2-3, further discussion in Champion (2000) pp 425-444.

49. Herodotus 8.144.2 defined what it was to be Hellenic. Diogenes Laertius *Diogenes* 6.63 for Diogenes' use of *kosmopolites.* Roisman-Worthington (2010) p 93 for *philhellenus.* The epithets were granted after Archelaus provided much-needed timber for the Athenian fleet after disaster at Syracuse in 413 BCE.

50. As pointed put by Anson (2103) p 17 following Pausanias 7.25.6.

51. Justin 8.5-6.
52. Thucydides referring to tribes as barbarian at 1.5.3, 1.6.6, 1.47.3, 1.50.3, 2.68.9, 2.80.5, 2.81-82, 3.112.7, 4.124.1, 4.126.3, 4.127.2. He did occasionally distinguish Macedonians from barbarians, as did Ephorus at 16.4.2, 5.71-2. Thucydides 2.99.2 for the distinction of tribes. Hammond argued 'barbarian' was used in a cultural not linguistic sense, considering they all spoke dialects of Greek; HGL Hammond, *Ancient Macedonia-Deductions and explanation of the term 'Barbaroi'*, published in Ancient Macedonian Ethnicity, Language, Linguistics, Modern Historians, February 2010. Hatzopoulos (1996) p 479 for Upper Macedonians being more ethnically akin to Epirotes. Quoting Hatzopoulos (1996) p 101 following Thucydides 1.5.1 for 'villages federated into *ethne*'.
53. A thorough study on the issue of a distinct Macedonian language or dialect in Anson (2004) pp 191-231.
54. Anson (2004) p 208.
55. Athenaeus 3.122a for Attic adopting elements of Macedonian; discussed in Anson (2004) p 209.
56. Plutarch 51-52 for the Black Cleitus episode in which Alexander demanded his Bodyguard turn out 'in the Macedonian tongue'. See Borza (1999) pp 42-43 who saw this as a strong case that Macedonians did have a distinct language.
57. Papyrus PSI 12: 1284. See Goralski (1989) pp 95-96 for full transcription of the fragment and Bosworth (1978) for full discussion.
58. Plutarch *Eumenes* 14.5.
59. See Bosworth (1978) p 236 for Macedonian being considered a wholly separate language in Alexander's day and Anson (2004) pp 191-231. Livy 31.29.15 and Herodotus 5.22 each claimed Greeks and Macedonians spoke the same language. Livy could have followed Herodotus who might have simply meant the educating or leading Macedonians were able to understand Greek. Andronikos concluded in 1984 that the names on the gravestones at Vergina unequivocally confirm the Macedonians were a Greek tribe. Hammond *Philip* (1994) for fuller discussion on dialects of Macedonia. Quoting Hatzopoulos (1996) p 77 and p 209. Hammond (1991) p 12 for Cretan immigrants in Bottiaea.
60. Roisman-Worthington (2010) p 95 for discussion of the Pellan Curse Tablet and its Doric linguistic style; Hammond suggested Aeolic; Anson (2004) p 210 for discussion.
61. Roisman-Worthington (2010) p 93 for the influences in Macedonian and p 94 for Hesychios.
62. Andronikos concluded in 1984 that the names on the gravestones at Vergina unequivocally confirm the Macedonians were a Greek tribe. Anson (2013) p 19 for the Greek inscriptions. Quoting Hatzopoulos (1996) p 173 for the pre-Greek names.
63. Following the point made by Anson (2013) p 18.
64. Athenaeus 3.122a for Attic adopting elements of Macedonian; discussed in Anson (2004) p 209.
65. See Billows (1990) p 21 for discussion on the development of the Macedonian court. Hammond (1994) p 43 for discussion of the notable artists invited to the Macedonian court.
66. Aelian 13.4 for Euripides and Agathon; how late in the reign of Archelaus Pella was founded in disputed. Athenaeus 6.261a for the land grants to foreign *hetairoi*.
67. Borza (1995) for the Spartan troop ration of wine; 2 *kontylae* was approximately 1 pint.
68. Discussion of Herodotus visiting Macedonia in Hammond (1996) p 67 citing the *Suda* FGrH 4T 1, ca. 455 BCE.
69. Demosthenes *On The Peace* 5.7-8.
70. Discussed in Wilkins-Hill (2006) p 45 citing Aristophanes *Frogs* 85, Anaxandrides *Protesilaus* frag. 41 and Mnesimachus *The Horsebreeder* where Macedonian luxury is referred to. WS Greenwalt in Carney-Ogden (2010) p 155 for Euphraus at Pella. Flower (1994) p 22 for the presence of Theopompus and Anaximenes. Photius claimed Isocrates influenced the content and style of their works: Flower (1994) pp 42-43 though rejected by him. Hammond (1991) p97 for Theophrastus' role.
71. Quoting Hatzopoulos (1996) p 468 on Macedonia's integration.
72. As examples of nationalistic calls, Demosthenes 3.24, 9.31-32, Isocrates *To Philip* 5.154. Green (1974) p 6 for 'sub-Homeric' enclave.
73. Quoting Cicero *Orator* XXXIV, translation from *Routledge Dictionary of Latin Quotations* 2005 p 284.
74. Alexander is derived from *alexein*, to defend against or repel, and *andros* the genitive of the noun for 'man'.
75. Omphalos is literally 'navel' though also a sacred stone such as at the oracle at Delphi. Lenden (2005) p 36. For Alexander's reference to the poems of Homer as 'campaign equipment' see Plutarch *Moralia* 327f or *Fortune* 4.
76. Homer *Iliad* 2.204 for the wording of Odysseus to quell an uprising in the Greek camp.
77. Plutarch 3.6. Strabo 14.648 credited Hegesias with founding the Asian style of composition. Cicero *Letter XXXV: ad Atticum* 6.1 branded him a 'silly writer'.

78. For Olympias' association with the Dionysiac mysteries see Plutarch, 2.5-6, Athenaeus 13.560 ff, Polyaenus 4.1. Pausanias 9.30.7 for Orpheus' grave.

79. Plutarch 1 gives us Alexander's Aeacid descent on his mother's side from Neoptolemus, and Justin 17.3. Neoptolemus was also known as Pyrrhus; Plutarch *Pyrrhus* 1-1-4 for his origins and Pausanias 1.11.1, 2.23.6 for Neoptolemus rule of the Molossians; Anson (2004) p 211 for detail, also Carney (2006) p 5. The mythical association is confirmed by Pindar in his *Nemean Odes* 4.51-53 and 7.38-38. See Arrian 1.11-12 for Alexander's sacrifice to Priam to avert anger against the family of Neoptolemus.

80. Molossus inherited Epirus after the death of Helenus, the son of Priam.

81. Quoting and following the observation of Bosworth (1988) p 39.

82. For Perseus see Arrian 3.3.2. Also discussed in Thomas (2007) p 200. At Herodotus 7.150 Xerxes claimed the Persians were descended from Perseus whose father was Danae's son, Perseus. The full text is 'Men of Argos, this is the message to you from King Xerxes. Perseus our forefather had, as we believe, Perseus son of Danae for his father, and Andromeda daughter of Cepheus for his mother; if that is so, then we are descended from your nation.' Thus Xerxes claimed to be of the same blood as the Greeks. Heracles was a Perseid four generations after Perseus, so claimed Isocrates in the *Busiris* 8.36.

83. Justin 7.1.6 for Midas' expulsion. Herodotus 1.14 for the son of Gordias, and at 8.138.3 he mentioned the Gardens of Midas in Macedonia. It is certain Alexander would have read Herodotus, for Aristotle had and it would have surely been an educational study topic; see Aristotle *Rhetoric* 1409a 27 where Aristotle opened with 'Herodotus of Thurii hereby publishes the results of his enquiries.' Callisthenes FGrH 124 F 24 for Midas' wealth coming from iron ore, cited in Hammond (1994) p 5. Hammond (1996) for discussion of early Macedonia and Midas' dynasty and (1991) p 31 for early genealogies. Strabo 7.3 for origins of the Phrygians; Herodotus 7.73 for Bryges and 8.138 for their coexistence with Macedonians.

84. Euripides *Helen* lines 39, 109 as clear examples. Graves (1955) p 283 for the earlier date and Hittite power.

85. Lineage discussions in Hammond (1996) and in Roisman-Worthington (2010) pp 1-39, Green (1970) pp 20-21, Hammond (1993) pp 5-6, Hammond (1991) pp 12-13, Plutarch 1 and in Greenwalt (1985). Plutarch 2.1 for Caranus founding the Argead line (with similar claims in Satyrus FGrH 631 F1, Theopompus FGrH 115 F 383 and Marysas FGrH 135-6 F14; Roisman-Worthington (2010) p 128. Herodotus 5.22.1, 7.73 and 8.137.8-9 for the link from Temenus to King Perdiccas of Macedonia; Justin 7.1.6 for Caranus' invasion and the re-founding of Aegae. Diodorus 7.17 for Caranus' Argive origins. There is in fact uncertainty of the lineage of the early kings of Macedonia; discussed in Greenwalt (1985) pp 43-49. Thucydides 2.99.3 and Herodotus 8.137-9 reported on the Temenid origins from Argos.

86. Arrian 2.5.9 confirmed Alexander's descent from the Argive Heracleidae. Isocrates *To Philip* 32: 'Argos is the land of your fathers.' Also Isocrates *To Philip* 115 for his descent from Heracles.

87. Hammond (1994) p1 for discussion of the Spartan and Aleuadae connections.

88. Quoting Jaeger (1939) p 347 for Euripides exploiting rhetorical device and for 'the first psychologist'. See Green (1996) pp 69-71 for the Temenid line and its ascendancy over the Argead line. Athenaeus 12.537d recorded that Nicobule said: 'In his last dinner, Alexander in person acted from memory a scene from the *Andromeda*; perhaps he favoured the poet for his Macedonian links.' Greenwalt (1999) p 164 ff, quoting Hammond for Euripides' play and the development of the Caranus myth. Temenus was the alleged ancestor of King Perdiccas I; Herodotean tradition has it he ruled Macedonia in the early or mid-7th century BCE.

89. Justin 7.2.2-4 for Perdiccas' son Argaeus and St Stephanus of Byzantium for the son of Macedon; Polyaenus 4.1 for Argaeus' deeds and Herodotus 8.137-139 for the Macedonian line. Anson (2013) p 14 for additional detail. See Borza (1995) pp 114-115 for the etymology of Argead and history of the Argives.

90. Appian *Syrian Wars* 63. Also see discussion of links to Argos and Orestis in Jarde (1997) p 324 ff. Orestis had formerly been part of the Molossian tribal region of Epirus. The other tribal coalitions were Thesprotians and Chaonians; Hammond (1994) p 120.

91. Herodotus 5.22 for the story that Alexander 1 of Macedonia was allowed to compete after proving his Argive roots; Justin 7.2.13-14. Macedonians were at that time not permitted to enter the games and only allowed Greeks to compete. Herodotus' treatment of geography and ethnology following discussion in Jaeger (1939) p 382. FGrH 4 F-74 for Hellanicus' claim see Roisman-Worthington (2010) p 16 for discussion and Anson (2004) p 200 and p 90 (Engels). Apollodorus *Chronica* 3.8.1 also followed the contention of Hellanicus of Mytilene.

92. Stewart (1993) p 277 for the Greek proverb and its use. Hammond (1994) p 158 for Philip's coinage. Roisman-Wilkinson (2010) pp 50-51 for the bimetallic minting in the Attic and Chalcidian standards.

93. See Carney-Ogden (2010) pp 70-71 for the titles credited to Philip after the Sacred Wars against

the defilers of the Temple of Apollo at Delphi. For stamping his coins with his chariot victories, Plutarch 4.8-9; Roisman-Worthington (2010) p 52 for the imagery stamped: youth on horseback and chariot. On the reverse of the silver stater appeared a bearded horseman in cloak and hat raising a hand in salutation. Also for Philip's coinage carrying iconography of his Olympic victories see discussion by O Palagia in Carney-Ogden (2010) p 33. Anson (2004) p 213 for detail of Philip's three victories in 356 BCE, 352 BCE and 348 BCE.

94. The statues were to be of himself, his parents Amyntas and Eurydice, Olympias and Alexander; Pausanias 5.17.4 (states, probably incorrectly, that Eurydice was the wife of Arrhidaeus), 5.20.9-10. Scholars debate whether the Eurydice being referred to was his mother or last wife, niece of Attalus, otherwise named Cleopatra (Arrian 3.6.5 for the rename of Cleopatra to Eurydice); discussed by O Palagia Carney-Ogden (2010) pp 33-41; p 38 for the marble argument identity of Eurydice. Alexander and Olympias had fled Macedonia to Epirus and Illyria following Philip's wedding to Attalus' niece, Cleopatra; O Palagia therefore suggests including them in the family statues was an act of reconciliation; Carney-Ogden (2010) p 37; however if Eurydice was his new young wife Philip was walking a dangerous path. The Philippeion description comes from Pausanias 5.20.9-10 and is discussed in Carney (1995) p 380.

95. The *Succession Myth* related the cruel lineage of the Titans from the primordial Uranus and Gaia. Cronus, the youngest son, killed his father Uranus, who prophesized a similar fate for the line of Cronus who swallowed his own children whole to evade that fate. Only the youngest son, Zeus, survived. Refusing to free his sibling from Tartarus, the fiery abyss, his wife, Rhea and mother, Gaia, conspired against Cronus; Cronus coughed up the three children whereupon Zeus freed them from Tartarus, and so started a war between he and Cronus lasting ten years which eventually saw Zeus take his place amongst the gods. Whilst Ouranus is generally considered the first god of the sky with Gaia as his wife, Hesiod's *Theogonia* 126 ff cited him as the son of Gaia, Mother Earth. For its link to the Babylonian creation myth, *Enûma Elis*, see discussion in West (2008) Introduction xii.

96. Following the observation from Sabine Müller in Carney-Ogden (2010) p 31.

97. Euripides *Medea* 288; mentioned at Plutarch 10.6.

98. Justin 9.5.9 for claims of adultery and mention of divorce (also 9.7.1), Arrian 3.6.5 for 'rejection'; Carney (2006) p 11 believed Justin may have sourced that from the *Romance*. Justin 9.7.1 for the divorce and Plutarch 10.6 for suspicions falling on Alexander.

99. Badian (1963) pp 245-6 for the suggestion of Philip favouring his nephew over Alexander. Plutarch *Moralia* 327c-d for the preference of Amyntas and the sons of Aeropus. Curtius 6.9.17, Justin 12.6.4. Arrian 1.25.2, Justin 11.2.2 for Lyncestis' show of support for Alexander. Arrian 1.25.1 for the murder of two of the three sons of Aeropus.

100. Plutarch *Moralia* 327c-d.

101. Diodorus 17.2.3, Justin 9.5.9 for 'sister'.

102. Diodorus 16.93.7 for Attalus' prominence at court and Curtius 8.8.7 for Alexander's distrust and lack of forgiveness for Attalus' comment that Cleopatra may produce a 'legitimate' heir to the throne; Plutarch 9.7-9, Satyrus fr.5, *Romance* 1.21.1, Justin 9.7.3 for the banquet at which Attalus insulted Alexander. Plutarch 9.4-11 for events that led to the flight of Alexander and Olympias. Also Justin 9.7.5 for Alexander in Illyria. Athenaeus 13.557e, Diodorus 17.2.3 for Cleopatra's daughter; Justin 9.7.2 for Cleopatra giving birth to a daughter *and* a son; see Lane Fox (2011) p 385 for discussion. Some consider that Alexander had Illyrian blood himself: Carney (2006) p 90 for Philip's Illyrian blood through his mother Eurydice, though contested. Plutarch *Moralia* 14b-c and Libanius through the *Suda* stated Eurydice was Illyrian of the Taulanti tribe but Eurydice's father, Sirrhas, was probably of Lyncestian (so Upper Macedonian) origin, which makes sense when considering his recent defeat at Illyrian hands.

103. Justin 11.2.3 alone claimed Alexander killed a brother (Caranus, should read 'half-brother') by his 'mother-in-law' thus we assume Cleopatra, which suggests a second child. Justin 9.7 and Satyrus via Athenaeus 13.557e claimed Cleopatra had a daughter, Europa. Heckel (2006) p 78 argues, Justin's claim this should be ignored. Diodorus 17.2-5, Curtius 7.1.3,8.4.2, Justin 12.6.14 for the murder of Attalus. Justin 9.7.12, Pausanias 8.7.7, Plutarch 10.8 for the murder or mistreatment of Cleopatra.

104. Plutarch 10.1-2 for the Pixodarus episode. Plutarch 10.3 for the implication that Philotas revealed the plot; detailed below.

105. Plutarch 9.1-4 for Alexander's campaign in Thrace, the founding of the city and events that followed.

106. Following the proposals of S Ruzicka in Carney-Ogden (2010) pp 4-11 for the importance, timing and implications of the Pixodarus affair. Justin 9.7.7 for Alexander's plans to overthrow his father and Plutarch 10.4 for Thessalus' presence on Corinth; Philip demanded he be returned in chains. Demaratus' role at Plutarch 9.12-14, *Moralia* 197c.

107. Justin 9.7.

108. Diodorus 16.1.3 stated a twenty-four-year reign; the additional year depends upon whether he initially acted as regent for his nephew, Amyntas, or immediately proclaimed himself king.

109. Curtius 6.11.20 and 8.6.28 clearly (though uniquely) stated Macedonian law demanded the death of all those related by blood to the guilty party, though here no trial or Assembly meeting was held; see chapter titled *The Reborn Wrath of Peleus' Son* for more on the purge. Justin 9.7.7 claimed Alexander was aware of the plot to kill Philip.

110. Plutarch 10.5, Arrian 3.6.5 for the exile of Alexander's friends. For Philip's death see Diodorus 16.91.2-.94.4, Justin 9.7, Plutarch 10.6-7; Heckel (2006) p 194 for other sources, Heckel (2006) p 197 and Heckel *Somatophylakes* (1978) for their inter-relationships. Diodorus 16.94.4 and Justin 9.7.9-12 for the death of Pausanias, the slayer of Philip. Justin claims he was caught alive and hung on a cross. He had been pursued by Attalus, Perdiccas and Leonnatus who killed him even though he was reportedly helpless after tripping and falling to the ground. This suggests they may have been covering up a plot to kill Philip. Both Perdiccas and Pausanias were from Orestis. Attalus (much) later became Perdiccas' brother-in-law. Justin 9.7.10-13 alleged that Olympias put a gold crown on the crucified Pausanias after she returned from Epirus, scattering his ashes on Philip's grave and providing him with a tomb of his own. See Hammond (1978) pp 339-349 for discussion of the veracity of events.

111. Euripides *Medea* 288; mentioned at Plutarch 10.6. Justin 9.7 for the mounts.

112. Quoting Diodorus 17.2.1; discussed in Hammond (1978) p 339.

113. Diodorus 17.51.2-3, Curtius 4.7.28 for the oracle's answer on Philip's assassins. For the journey to Siwa see Diodorus 17.49.2-52.7, Arrian 3.4-5, Curtius 4.7.8-4.89, Plutarch 26.3-27.11, Justin 11.11.1-13, Strabo 17.1.43, *Itinerarium Alexandri* 48-50.

114. Herodotus 5.17-21 for Macedonia first accepting Persian dominance. For more on Xerxes' invasion, and Macedonian complicity, see Hammond (1991) pp 14-19 and quoting Hammond p 17 for 'double game'. Herodotus 9.31.5 for support for Persian at Plataea.

115. Meiggs (1982) pp 43 and 47 for timber types. Perdiccas II would also construct a treaty with Athens on the promise of timber.

116. Justin 7.4.1-3 for Xerxes placing Alexander I in command of an expanded Lower Macedonia, stemming from the marriage of Bubares, a Persian ambassador, to his sister. Demosthenes 4.48 reported Philip II sending envoys to Artaxerxes III in 351/350 BCE; this may have reconciled Artabazus, taking refuge in Macedonia, with the Great King. Hammond (1994) p 57 for discussion. Demosthenes 6.11 termed Alexander I a traitor. Herodotus 7.173, 8.34, 8.136-144, 9.44-45 for Alexander I's participation in the Persian invasion. In the wake of the Persian Wars lower Paeonia with Pella, Ichnai, Mygdonia beyond the Axius (Thracian) and territories to the Strymon river were added to the kingdom: Hatzopoulos (1996) p 106. Hammond (1991) pp 16-19 for the politics of the Persian occupation.

117. Anson (2013) p 55 for Persian origins of the hypaspist corps; discussion in chapter titled *Sarissa Diplomacy: Macedonian Statecraft*. Pausanias 10.19.9 ff suggests one explanation of why the Persian guardsmen named 'Immortals' as casualties were immediately replaced to keep the number static. Borza (1980) cited in Anson (2013) p 52 and pp 53-55 for polygamy discussion of Persian origins including the *agema* of the hypaspists, *Somatophylakes* and *paides basilikos*; pp 58-59. Heckel-Jones (2006) p 11 for the observation that the pages were from Upper Macedonia and Roisman-Worthington (201) pp 447-448 for the origins of 'Friends' units. The Persian chiliarch who commanded the 10,000 Immortals and was second only to the Great King. The term traditionally meant 'commander of a thousand men', but the Persian usage was adopted; Heckel (2006) pp 32-48 for discussion.

118. Atkinson (2009) p 178 and Collins (2001) pp 260-261 proposed *chiliarchos* was the equivalent post of the Achaemenid *hazarapati*, the king's second in command; Collins (2001) p 266 for cup-bearer. Diodorus 11.69.1, 18.48.4-5 ('…the post and rank of chiliarch had been brought to fame and glory under the Persian kings.') and Nepos *Conon* 3 for the Persian chiliarchy, also Diodorus 18.48.4-5 gives an explanation as 'second in command'. Arrian *Events After Alexander* 1.3 and 1.38 for Perdiccas and Cassander holding the post.

119. The aristocratic code of conduct in classical Greece was termed the *kalos kagathos*; discussion in Jaeger (1939) p 4.

120. Quoting Jaeger (1939) p 53 for the Homeric epics containing the germs of all Greek philosophy. The importance of the Homeric epics in the mindset of the Greeks discussion in Lendon (2005) p 36.

121. 'Pella' translated as 'stone' in ancient Macedonian, or perhaps 'stone enclosure' from the Doric *apella*. Livy 44.46 for the description of Pella. Strabo 7 fragment 20 did mention its position on the River Axius.

122. Discussion of *hetairoi* and the *synedrion* in Billows (1990) pp 19-21 and p 246 for discussion of the *synedrion* and its function. Quoting Anson (2014) p 4 for the make-up of the common infantry.

123. M Boyce *A History of Zoroastrianism* Volume II (1982), Brill, p 171 for the Greeks at the Persian

court. Boardman (1964) pp 102-110 for Greek presence at the Persian court. Democedes and Ctesias were doctors at the Achaemenid court later.

124. Cook (1983) pp 1-2 and pp 25-28. Medea was the daughter of the king of Colchis in the Southern Caucasus, present Georgia. Perseus' wife was Andromeda, of Ethiopian origin, and through their nine children they established the line of Mycenae. The Achaeans have been linked to both the Hittites (through the similarity of *Akhaioi* and *Ahhiyawa* of Hittite texts) as neighbours in the region of Troy and thus to the Trojans.

125. Plato's *Menexenus* termed Cadmus, Pelops, Danaus and Aegyptus 'by nature barbarians'...who nevertheless 'pass as Hellenes'.

126. Quoting Nietzsche *On the Use and Abuse of History for Life*, translation by A Collins, 1909. Herodotus 7.150. Xerxes claimed the Persians were descended from Perseus to gather support from the Argives for their invasion of Greece.

127. Discussed in Dalley (1994) p 47. Herodotus 1.179 and Strabo 16.1.16 included Babylon in Assyria.

128. Curtius 3.4.1, 4.5.7-8, 11.5, 7.8.18 for the broader use of 'Lydia'; discussed in Anson (1988) p 474.

129. Herodotus 1.107-195. Quoting Momigliano (1966) p 213.

130. Dalley (2013) p 190 for Cyrus' Elamite origins. Xenophon *Cyropaedia* 1.2.1-2 for his median and Perseidae roots.

131. Plutarch *Artaxerxes* 1.2 for 'sun'.

132. Dalley (2013) for the Assyrian architecture of Persepolis modelled on Nineveh. Full discussion in RG Kent *The Oldest Old Persian Inscriptions*, University of Pennsylvania Press, 1946, pp 1-10.

133. Examples of Ptolemaic inscriptions include the Canopus Stone of 238 BCE of Ptolemy III *Euergetes*, the Memphis Stele ca. 218 BCE by Ptolemy IV, and the Rosetta Stone itself, erected by Ptolemy V *Epiphanes* in 196 BCE.

134. Roisman-Worthington (2010) pp 87 and 343-344 for *Yauna*. *Takabara* means 'wearing shields on their heads'. The epithet possibly refers to the shield-shaped flat hat, the *kausia*.

135. Quoting Bosworth (1988) p 229.

136. Quoting Tarn 1 (1948) p 8.

137. Strabo 9.2.40 and following its citation by Shipley (2000) p 36.

138. Demosthenes *On the Crown* 270; the excerpt heads chapter titled *Sarissa Diplomacy: Macedonian Statecraft*.

139. For discussion on the League of Corinth see Hammond-Griffith (1979) p 639. Also Heckel (2006) p 349 for the significance of the role of *hegemon*. See Bosworth-Baynham (2000) pp 98-99 for the significance and origination of the league, a successor to the Hellenic League of 480 BCE.

140. Diodorus 16.89.3 for the Common Peace. Justin 11.3 uniquely mentioned the same inherited position in the Thessalian League. Other citations to the Common Peace at Diodorus 17.4, Arrian 1.1.1, Justin 11.2.5, Plutarch 14.1. Anson (2013) p 102 for the Amphictionic Council seats; he controlled the seats in the name of Thessaly too; p 132 for the life archonship of the Thessalian League.

141. The *kyria ekklesia* was an assembly meeting in Athens held ten times each year to vote on city and state issues on the rocky hill known as the Pnyx which acted as a natural auditorium.

142. Translation from the inscription still surviving in Athens.

143. Polybius 18.11.3-7 stated 'fetters' was a term first used by Philip V of Macedonia. Following Anson (2014) p 142 and the observations in Worthington (2000) p 97 for the strategic value of these cities.

144. Diodorus 17.22.5 for the twenty triremes Athens provided from a navy of 400; Blackwell (1999) p 50 and Green (1970) p 89 for discussion of the total Greek contribution of men.

145. Anson (2103) p 25 quoting Stagakis for the eighty-four *hetairoi*.

146. See Anson (2004) pp 244-245 for discussion of the Greeks who held satrapal governorships under Alexander during the campaign and military commands.

147. Arrian 1.16.2-3 and Plutarch 16.12-15; Arrian 1.14.4 suggested there was a similar number ('little less') of mercenaries to the Persian cavalry stated at 20,000, and that all died bar 2,000 prisoners; 1.16.2. The Macedonians allegedly lost only eighty-five cavalry and thirty infantry (less according to Aristobulus, so claimed Plutarch). Modern interpretations suggest more like 5,000 mercenaries were present; discussion in Parke (1933) p 180, Green (1974) p 179 and in detail pp 499-500.

148. Finlay (1973) p 162 for the trade with the Kingdom of Bosphorus. Demosthenes against *Leptines* 31-3 for Greek corn imports.

149. As examples where Macedonians are distinguished from the allied Greek forces under Alexander see Arrian 4.11.8, 7.4.5, Plutarch 47.9, Diodorus 18.56.1-3.

150. Diodorus 17.70.6.

151. Arrian 4.11.7.

152. As reported by Plutarch 60.6, translation from the Loeb Classical Library edition, 1919.

153. The speech of Alcibiades at Thucydides 6.89.6 translated by Richard Crawley, Project Gutenberg, 2009. Xenophon's attitude to democracy discussed in R Warner (1949) p 8 and in Warner (1966) p 9 ff.

154. Thucydides 6.18.

155. See discussion of Aristotle's linking the phalanx with the Greek *polis* in Lenden (2005) p 44. Aristotle *Athenian Constitution* 24.3 for the breakdown of city employees and discussed in Finlay (1973) p 173. For Athenian income in the time of Socrates and the Peloponnesian War see Xenophon *Anabasis* 7.1.27. This had not significantly changed by Alexander's day. See discussion in Roberts (1984) p 74. For confirmation of Athens' annual income in the time of the *Diadokhoi* see Athenaeus 12.542g, where he alleged Demetrius of Phalerum spent most of Athens' 1,200 talents income on parties rather than the army or city administration; confirmed by Aelian 9.9 but this was some years later. Athenaeus 6.20 for the census of Demetrius of Phalerum (313 BCE) recording slave numbers at 400,000; Hyperides estimated 150,000 including mining district slaves; both seem excessive. The population was given at 84,000 (313 BCE) and 172,000 estimated in 431 BCE; 100,000 is an extrapolated number for Aristotle's day; numbers discussed in Kamen (2013) p 9. Finlay (1973) p 151 for the liturgy system.

156. See chapter titled *The Wrath of Peleus' Son* for more on the dichotomies within Aristotle's *Politics*.

157. Parmenio sold the population of Grynium into slavery in 335 BCE; Diodorus 17.7.8.

158. Coincidentally, a *proxenos* was a public guest-friend, a type of ambassadorial relationship where 'a person who, in his own city, assisted citizens from another city that had appointed him *proxenos* of its citizens', quoting the explanation of Hansen (1999) p 403. A *proxenos* might formally introduce his guest-friend to the assembly or magistrates of the host city. Here Xenophon would in return have been a *widioxenos,* an invited guest-friend. Xenophon *Anabasis* 1.1.2. Proxenus was a friend of Xenophon and already with Cyrus. He invited Xenophon to Sardis with a promise to introduce him to the Persian prince.

159. Isocrates *Letter 5* (of nine extant letters), discussed in Worthington (2007) p 73.

160. Originally credited to Aristotle but more recently to Anaximenes of Lampsacus; discussed in Worthington (2007) pp 104-120. Quintilian refers to Anaximenes in his *Institutio Oratio* 3.4.9 and the reference *may* be to the *Rhetoric to Alexander.*

161. Isocrates *To Philip*, II 3.5, translation by G Norlin.

162. Diogenes Laertius 2.58, Xenophon *Anabasis* 7.7.57 for Xenophon's own exile; discussed in Warner (1966) p 12.

163. Justin 9.5 for the Spartan's position: 'stood aloof'. The Lacedaemonian *xenalasia* laws were designed to preserve Spartan 'purity' of customs and bloodlines by banning its citizens from travelling outside the state and foreigners from entering, except in religious festivals and on state business.

164. Herodotus 8.109-110 for Themistocles' warning that no king should rule Asia and Hellas too; the text heads the chapter.

165. Justin 11.5.5, Plutarch 15.3-5, *Moralia* 342d-e for the handing out of land grants. For Alexander's financial position pre-loan see Plutarch 15.1-3, Curtius 10.2.24 and Arrian 7.9.6 for his borrowing 800 talents. For interest rates see Bellinger (1979) p 37. Athenian interest rates were typically anywhere between twelve per cent and eighteen per cent depending upon the venture; risky maritime loans were higher still; see Tarn (1927) p 115. Also see Archibald-Davies-Gabrielson (2005) p 145 and Tarn's comments in Bury-Barber-Bevan-Tarn (1923) p 115.

166. For Philip's debt see Plutarch *Moralia* 327d and Plutarch 15. Duris suggested the Macedonians had sufficient money for thirty days campaigning where Aristobulus claimed Alexander had 70 talents in total, whilst Curtius 10.2.24 and Arrian 7.9.6 claimed 60 talents. Pearson (1960) pp 90-92 for discussion and the allusion to Cyrus the Younger and his plight detailed in Xenophon's Anabasis.

167. See Hammond-Atkinson (2013) footnote to 7.9.6; 1 talent was sufficient to pay 6,000 Athenian hoplites for one day; whether a formal wage was being paid to Macedonian soldiers is uncertain but as Greek mercenaries arrived in the ranks, remuneration must have been broadly equalised. Plutarch 15.1-3 and *Moralia* 327d-e for the various statements of the campaign funds; Aristobulus stated 200 talents debt with only 70 talents with Alexander on campaign.

168. Rodgers (1937) p 21 for the estimate of 250 talents a month. Tarn 1 (1948) p 14 reckoned the army would have cost 200 talents per month with another 100 for the Graeco-Macedonian fleet.

169. Arrian 1.20.1 for the disbanding of the Macedonian navy. Heckel-Jones (2006) pp 20-21 for soldiers' pay rates. Plutarch 17.1 Diodorus 17.21.7, Arrian 1.17.3-8 for the treasury at Sardis. Green (1974) pp 192-193 for discussion of the fleet disbandment; they were costing 100 talents per month. For Tarsus see Arrian 2.4.2-6, Curtius 3.4.14-15, Justin 11.8.1-2.

170. See Arrian 1.17-1.29 for clearest examples of his eclectic administrations and treatment of captured cities. Sardis was garrisoned and its treasury turned over despite its submission (1.17.3-

8) and a tribute levied upon the city; Ephesus was pardoned (1.17.10-12), no other action was 'taken at this time'; Magnesia and Tralles, like Ephesus, were returned to 'democracies' (1.18.1-2) but we may assume tribute was to be paid to the Macedonians for the privilege, as well as to their temples. Miletus was besieged and the defenders killed in the city (1.19. 1-7), those who swam to safety were pardoned; cities between Miletus and Halicarnassus were taken by assault (1.20.2), Halicarnassus was besieged (1.20.4-1.23.6) and (the citadel?) razed to the ground; what remained was garrisoned. In Lycia Termessus, Pinara, Xanthus, Patara and Phaselis and thirty smaller towns initially submitted but the terms are unknown (1.24 5-6). Aspendus was initially left ungarrisoned but it paid the price of 50 talents' contribution, along with horses, to the campaign expenses (1.26.2-3) but rebelled and hostages were taken and the levy increased to 100 talents (1.27.1-5). Side submitted but was garrisoned (1.26.4-5). The Pisidian cities were attacked (including a force of Telmessians (1.27.6-1.28.8) though what terms were levied upon them is not mentioned: probably tribute and garrisons.

171. Full discussion of Alexander's siegecraft in Kern (1999) pp 201-335. *Poliorketes* translated as 'the besieger of cities'. Philip besieged six cities between 357 and 354 BCE (Amphipolis, Pydna, Potidaea, Pagasai, Methone, Olynthus) and more after; Gabriel (2010) p 91.

172. For discussion on *nomographoi* see O'Neil (2000) pp 424-431. They were specially qualified men entrusted to draft new laws for the polis as well as to record existing legal codes.

173. Thucydides 2.34-2.46 inserted a fictional dialogue that pitched Melos' claim for neutrality with Athenian aggression, forcing them to side against Sparta or be destroyed. Plutarch *Solon* 5; state of affairs recalling a warning the Scythian Anacharsis once gave to Solon in Athens.

174. Herodotus 1.29, Plutarch *Solon* 25.1 for Solon's departure; as an example of the backfiring decrees, learning that he was about to cancel all debt, his friends took out loans to purchase land; suspected of complicity, Solon was forced to cancel all debts to himself. His friends never paid up: Plutarch *Solon* 15.

175. Tarn (1948) p 200 ff for discussion of the state of affairs with the Greek cities of Asia Minor; Mytilene is an example of a harbour city that did enter the League of Corinth, as well as Tenedos; Tarn 1 (1948) p 31.

176. Arrian 1.18.2 for the tribute due to the Persians now redirected to Alexander; here referring to Aeolian and Ionian cities in Hellespontine Phrygia under his new *strategos,* Calas.

177. Tarn 1 (1948) p 34 and Tarn (1949) p 213 for his arguments on intervention in Chios. For a full translation of the letter see Heckel-Yardley (2004) pp 87-88. For dating discussion see Heisserer (1973). Blackwell (1999) p 38 footnote 18 for Chios being a member of the Common Peace and p 39 for the quote from Badian. Anson (2013) p 133 quoting Badian on the 'will of one man'.

178. Following the comments in Heckel-Yardley (2004) p 87; Briant (1974) pp 78-79 for Chios' position in the League.

179. Diogenes Laertius 6.44 *Diogenes*. The messenger's name was Athlios, which in Greek meant 'wretched' or 'miserable', so this is a play on names, implicating Philip, Alexander and Antipater to whom the message was being sent. Translation from CD Yonge 1853, Bohn's Classical Library.

180. Aeschines *Against Ctesiphon* 164, discussed in Worthington (2000) p 93.

181. See chapter titled Lifting the Shroud of Parrhasius for money on the captive lists at Issus and Damascus. Curtius 13.13.16 for the sums secured.

182. Diodorus 18.36.6 and 17.33.3 for the missiles; Diodorus did add that the collisions made the missile impact weaker, but clearly the numbers are questionable. Arrian 2.11.8 suggested Ptolemy was the source of the numbers. Curtius 3.11.27 corroborates the numbers but added that 4,500 of Alexander's men were wounded. Curtius stated 504 wounded, 32 infantrymen killed and 150 cavalrymen. Justin 11.9 for casualty and prisoner numbers.

183. Curtius 3.10.9 for Alexander's encouragement to the Thracians and Illyrians; 3.12.1-13 for his treatment of the Persian women.

184. Diodorus 17.38.1-3 for the promised dowries and also Justin 11.9.10-11.10.4. Hephaestion married Drypetis at Susa, Alexander 'wanting to be uncle to his children'; see Arrian 7.4.5.

185. Diodorus 17.38.3-7 for his eulogy to Alexander's behaviour.

186. Arrian 2.13.1 for mercenary escapees.

187. It is reckoned Darius had 20,000 Greek mercenary infantry at the Granicus and Alexander 10,000 according to Arrian 1.12.8 and 1.14.4. Also at Issus Darius had 30,000 Greek mercenaries facing 10,000 according to Arrian 2.8.6 and a fragment of Callisthenes from Polybius 12.17-18 has 30,000 mercenaries facing the Macedonians. Diodorus 17.9.5 for the Theban proclamation.

188. Arrian 1.7.10-11 stated that the Theban exiles who incited Thebes to revolt against Alexander in 335 BCE were members of the Boeotian Confederation that had supposedly been disbanded with the King's Peace (or Peace of Antalcidas) in 386 BCE.

189. Anson (2004) p 235 for discussion of the exiled mercenaries. Curtius 5.11.5, Pausanias 8.52.5 for 50,000 and discussed in Parke (1933) pp 179-185, Green (1974) p 157 footnote; a similar

figure was given by Pausanias 8.52.5 but for returning mercenaries under Leosthenes before the Lamian War. Arrian 1.16.6-7 for their fate if captured.

190. Arrian 2.24.4 stated 8,000 dead civilians. Curtius 4.2.15 for the treatment of the envoys. Curtius 4.4.10-21 stated 6,000 civilians were killed and 2,000 crucified. Diodorus 17.46.4 stated 7,000 with 2,000 crucified. Legend had it that Cadmus, son of King Agenor of Tyre, founded Thebes; Herodotus 5.58-5.591.

191. Herm (1975) p 25 for the self-identification as Canaanites and pp 52-63 for the Amorite-Canaanite migrations that saw the cities settled. Herodotus recorded that Phoenicians carried off Io, daughter of the king of Argos. In retaliation the Greeks abducted Europa from Tyre and so Paris stole Helen from Sparta.

192. Curtius 4.2.5 for Alexander's threat to make Tyre 'a part of the mainland'. Diodorus 17.41.5 for the width of the mole.

193. Engels (1978) p 55 for the grain requirement of the siege.

194. Snodgrass (1967) p 111 for Dionysius' siegecraft.

195. Tarn (1948) p 39 for 'the man who took Tyre'. For the siege engines see Plutarch 25.5; Justin 12.2.14; Arrian 2.21-22. Vitruvius 10.13.3. See summary of sources in Heckel (2006) p 111. Full discussion on the siege engines of Diades in Whitehead-Blyth (2004) pp 85-90. Hammond (1994) p 133 for Polyidus' ingenuity and his *On Machines*. Diodorus 16.74.2 for machines used at Perinthus; Gabriel (2010) pp 91-92 for discussion on the 'belly shooters' and *katapeltai Makedonikoi*. Diodorus 17.43.1-2 and 17.45.3 for the spinning spoked wheels used in defence and Diodorus 17.44.4 for fire-throwers. Arrian 2.22.6 and 2.23.2 for the machine-carrying ships; discussed in Murray (2012) p 177. Philip's use of artillery discussed in Keyser (1994). Examples at Diodorus 16.53 and 16.54.3-4 (Olynthus), 17.74.2-76.4 (Perinthus), 16.77.2-3 (Byzantium). For Alexander's siege of Miletus, Arrian 1.18.3-19, Diodorus 17.22.1-3, Plutarch 17.2; Diodorus 17.24.1 for the transfer of siege equipment from Miletus to Halicarnassus, and Arrian 1.20.8-1.22.2, Diodorus 17.24.6-17.26.6 for the siege and use of catapults. For catapults at Tyre see Arrian 4.21.1-2, 4.22.6-23.1, Curtius 4.3.24-26, Diodorus 17.41.3-4, 17.43.1-2,17.43.7-17.44.5, 17.45.3-4.

196. Marsden (1971) pp 1-14 for discussion of artillery sources.

197. Thucydides 1.15.3, Herodotus 5.99 for what we now name the Lelantine War; Strabo 10.1.12 for the banning of missiles; discussed in Lenden (2005) p 17 and quoting Archilochus 3. Quoting Heron's *Belopoeika* introduction 72 in Marsden (1971) p 19.

198. Curtius' account spans 4.2.1-4.4.21.

199. The previous siege was mentioned in the *Old Testament* books of *Jeremiah* 27:3-11 and *Ezekiel* 26:7-14. Curtius 4.3 23 for the child sacrifice tradition; it was well known in Greece, see Fears (1976) p 218 footnote 26 for other sources.

200. Athenaeus 12.526 for the value of Tyrean purple dye, citing Theopompus.

201. Arrian 7.19.4 for the murex divers. Arrian 2.24.5 stated 30,000 were sold into slavery at the fall of Tyre, whereas Diodorus 17.46.4 stated 13,000 with 2,000 crucified and Curtius added that 15,000 were smuggled to safety. So 30,000 seems an aggregate total. Tarn 1 (1948) p 7 and footnote 2 calculates 7,500 slaves from the resulting 440 talents; Tarn terms Diodorus' 30,000 a stereotyped figure and Tarn 1 (1948) p 40 suggests the result had no effect on the world slave market; p 40.

202. There are many references to Tarshish in the *Old Testament* as well as other trading posts and sources of silver. Boardman (1964) pp 210-217 for the mineral trading.

203. Boardman (1964) p 213 for Colaeus' journey and return with a horde of silver. *Kings* 1.10.22 and *Ezekiel* for references to the ships of Tarshish; discussed in Herm (1975) p 95. Tarshish was *possibly* Tartessus near Cadiz.

204. Curtius 4.18. Various conflicting sources place the founding of Carthage around 825 BCE; Josephus *Against Apion* 1.18 placed Dido's departure in the seventh year of Pygmalion, her brother, quoting Menander the Phoenician historian.

205. Arrian 2.24.5 for the Carthaginian envoy with Darius. Justin 21.6.1-7, Orosius 4.6.21, Frontinus *Stratagemata* 1.2.3. Trogus did record the founding of Carthage and its links to the early Tyrian kings.

206. Diodorus 17.46.6 for the renaming of Tyrean Apollo. Hermippus fr 63 K-A for the fragment mentioning Carthage's exports.

207. Quoting Plutarch *Themistocles* 29.5; the lines credited to Artaxerxes II's cousin Mithropaustes in the time of Themistocles' exile in Persia.

208. Aristotle *Ethics* 1.1.

209. See Robinson (1953) p 69 for the fragment. It is recorded as a miracle in the *Romance* 1.28. Strabo 17.1.43 (following Callisthenes) for the sacred spring at Branchidae, dry for some 160 years, flowing again once Alexander arrived.

210. Plutarch 17 quoting the poet Menander, translation from the Loeb Classical Library edition,

1919. Arrian 1.26.1 also recorded the incident and mentioned the relation of the winds; Plutarch implied Alexander gave a more sober description of the event.

211. Xenophon *Anabasis* 1.4.17-18 and Herodotus 1.189-190 for the feat of Cyrus the Great and 7.33-36 and 7.54-57 for Xerxes' bridging the Hellespont. Onomacritus the oracle monger had been banished from Athens by editing the prophecies of Musaeus; discussed in chapter titled *The Precarious Path of Pergamena and Papyrus.* As for prevailing doctrine, see Herodotus 8.109-110 for Themistocles' warning that no king should rule Asia and Hellas too.

212. Arrian 1.26.1-2; Plutarch 17.6-8. *Romance* 2.14-16 for the River Stranga episode.

213. Strabo 13.1.27 and Plutarch 8.2, Plutarch *Moralia* 327f and Pliny 7.29.108 for the casket *Iliad*.

214. Quoting Romm (1988) p 5.

215. Following the observation and discussion in Wilkins-Hill (2006) p 168 for Dionysus' traits. Stewart (1993) p 79 for discussion of Dionysus and his origins. Euripides *Bacchae* 13-22 for Dionysus hailing from Bactria. Whilst Ephippus did not include Dionysus in the list of gods Alexander impersonated, it does not mean he was excluded from the king's psyche; Athenaeus 12.537e. Moreover the Ptolemies visibly associated Alexander with Dionysus; discussion in Stewart (1993) p 238. Following Carney (2006) p 99 for the inspiration for the *Bacchae.* Hammond (1991) p 12 for the suggestion that Phrygians introduced the worship of Dionysus.

216. Euripides *Herakleidai* lines 88-89, based on the translation by R Gladstone from *Euripides I, The Complete Greek Tragedies,* edited by D Grene and R Lattimore, The University of Chicago Press, 1955.

217. See discussion of Thucydides in Momigliano (1966) p 130.

218. Following the descriptions and observations of Momigliano (1966) p 134.

219. Quoting Jaeger (1939) p 10 for 'an immortal aristocracy'. *Heracles and the Waggoner,* a fable attributed to Aesop for the 'gods help those who help themselves'.

220. For example *Iliad* 22.273; Athena stepping in to recover Achilles' spear in his battle with Hector at Troy.

221. Protesilaus' grave was plundered by Artacytes, a satrap under Xerxes during the invasion of Greece; Herodotus 9.116-120, 7.23. Xenophon *Hellenika* 3.4.2-5, Plutarch *Agesilaus* 6.6-11 for the abortive attempt to sacrifice at Aulis.

222. Diodorus 17.17.3, Justin 11.5.12 for the sacrifices at Troy. Diodorus 16.89.2 for Philip's declaration of war and the causes. Strabo 13.1.25-26 described the temple as 'small and cheap'.

223. When Alexander disembarked from the first ship to land on Asian shores, he cast his spear into the soil to claim it by spear; Diodorus 17.17.2, Justin 11.5.10. Robbins (2001) p 67 and Arrian 1.11 for Alexander's sacrifice to Protesilaus before crossing the Hellespont and for his disembarkation as the first to set foot of the invading force again on Asian soil, and subsequent crowning.

224. Plutarch 8.2 quoting Onesicritus' claim that Alexander kept a dagger and the *Iliad* under his pillow.

225. Following Heckel's footnote to Curtius 3.8.22, footnote 55, p 274, Penguin Classics 2001 edition. Arrian 1.11.1-2, Diodorus 17.16.3-4, Plutarch *Moralia* 1096b, Athenaeus 12.538c, 539d for the sharing of sacrificial meat. The noun, *sphagia,* is cognate with the verb *sphazein,* 'to pierce the throat'; Hanson (1991) p 197 ff.

226. Polyaenus 4.3.14 for Alexander having the sacrificial bodies carried through the camp if the omens were positive. *Iliad* 18 for Achilles' sacrifice before fighting Hector. Arrian 3.1.4 for Apis and Egyptian gods and 3.16.5 for Bel.

227. Hesiod *Work and Days* lines 825-828.

228. Curtius 9.4.29.

229. Arrian 7.16.6 for Alexander's reply to the Chaldeans warning him not to enter Babylon. This appears to come from a Euripides fragment 963 in Nuake's edition of collected fragments; see Hammond-Atkinson (2013) footnote 22 for Arrian 7.16.6 p 3.

230. Hammond (1994) p 176 for discussion; a fragment of the report of the trial following Philip's death is preserved.

231. Diodorus 16.91.2 for the reply Philip received from the Pythia.

232. Herodotus 1.53. The reply from the Delphic Oracle warned Croesus that if he invaded Cappadocia, a mighty empire would fall. He did not consider that it might mean his own. Cicero *De Divinatione* 2.116 believed Herodotus made up the story.

233. According to Plutarch, Aesop journeyed to Delphi on a diplomatic mission for Croesus; a fatal one, as it turned out, for he insulted the Delphians who threw him off a cliff; Plutarch's references to Aesop appeared in *On the Delays of Divine Vengeance.* Flower (1994) p 162; Theopompus claimed oracular replies were still given in verse not prose in his day.

234. Plutarch 14.4. Apparently Alexander visited on an 'inauspicious' day when replies were forbidden.

235. Plutarch *Moralia* 404d or *De Pythiae Oraculis* 21.

236. Diodorus 16.26.1-4 described the frenzied state of the Pythia and the priests who interpreted her

responses. Plutarch *Moralia* 437c recorded that the hallucinogenic state was induced by vapours from the Kerna spring arising from fissures in the rock. Modern scholars have questioned this and suggested she spoke coherently.

237. Arrian 2.3.1 for the acropolis location and Justin 11.7.3-4 for the dedication. 'Fate's silent riddle' as it was described in the *Alexandreis* of Gautier de Chatillon 2.99. The waggon or chariot was fastened to its yoke by the bark of the cornel tree. See Plutarch 18, Arrian 2.3, Curtius 3.1.14, Justin 11.7.3 for biographical sources narrating the episode.

238. Justin 11.7.16.

239. Quoting Pearson (1960) p 157.

240. Graves (1955) p 282

241. For Achilles' shield Arrian 6.8.3, and Arrian 2.7.8 for Alexander's confirmed familiarity with Xenophon; full discussion in McGroaty 2006 who concludes Arrian's statement is not proof that Alexander actually read Xenophon. Xenophon's *Hipparchicus* advised the pointing forward of the lance between the horses' ears to make the approaching cavalry appear more fearsome; discussed in Hornblower (1981) p 198.

242. Xenophon's *Hellenika* 6.1.14-16 eulogised Jason's character. Using the date and title in Hammond (1994) p 11 for Aeneas' book. Hammond (1994) pp 133-134 for Polyeidos and siegecraft.

243. Bosworth's comparison to Cortez in Bosworth-Baynham (2000) pp 23-49.

244. Quoting Diodorus 17.6.3 on Darius' genius. According to Curtius 5.11.5 Darius III had some knowledge of Greek. Three distinct offers from Darius were recorded in the extant accounts and confusion between dates exists. Justin 11.12.1-2, Arrian 2.14-15 and Curtius 4.1.7-14 stated Darius demanded Alexander withdraw from Asia after Issus. Arrian mentions no financial offer for the return of the royal family. Arrian 2.25.1 cited the Euphrates, not Halys. The offer of marriage to Barsine and the division of empire is positioned in Curtius after the capture of Tyre. See Curtius 4.5.1-8 and Justin 11.12.3-3. The third offer comes after Alexander departed Egypt and sometime before Gaugamela. See Diodorus 17.39.1-3, 17.54.1-6, Curtius 4.11-12, Arrian 2.25-26, Justin 11.12.7-16, Plutarch 29.4. Some scholars such as Briant (1974) p 52 doubt Darius ever made such an offer.

245. *Romance* 2.14-15 and 2.22 for examples of the embellished correspondence between Alexander and Darius.

246. Diodorus 17.39.1-3 alone recorded the forgery.

247. Curtius 4.13.4 for Parmenio and his tactical ability. Chapter titled *The Rebirth of the Wrath of Peleus' Son* for more on the truce being offered by Darius III to divide the Persian Empire. For Darius' peace offering(s) and Alexander's rejection, see Curtius 4.11.1-14, Arrian 2.25.1, Plutarch 29.7-9 and Diodorus 17.54.

248. Thersippus is mentioned as the envoy in Curtius 4.1.14 and he confirmed the camp was at Marathus at 4.1.6.

249. Lucian *Pro Lapsu* 3 has 'Philippides'. Plutarch *Moralia: De Gloria Atheniensium* 3 stated it was either Thersippus of Erchea, or Eucles, who ran to Athens with news of the victory at Marathon. Lucian's name appears to have been taken up by Robert Browning into Pheidippides.

250. See Heckel (2006) p 264 for discussion. Thersippus seems to have survived the incident, no doubt because Alexander had Darius' family as hostages and was later honoured by the Nesiotic League for services to Philip and Alexander.

251. Plutarch 8.2; Arrian 1.11.5 and 15.7-9.

252. Callisthenes, Ephorus, Damastes, Phylarchus and Duris agreed Ilium fell on the 24th of Thargelion (May-June); confirmed in Plutarch *Camillus* 19.7; others claimed 12th or 22nd; see Pearson (1960) pp 60-61 and full discussion in Lincoln (2002) pp 1-18. Fragments from ancient historians suggest the following dates BCE: Duris 1334, *Life of Homer* 1270, Herodotus ca. 1240, Cleitarchus 1234, Dicearchus 1212, *Parian Chronicle* 1209, Thrasyllus 1193, Timaeus 1193. Apollodorus and the so-called *Canon of Ptolemy* also dated the fall of Troy; Eratosthenes and his disciples (Apollodorus, Castor, Diodorus, Apollonius, Eusebius) 1184/3; Sosibius 1171, Phanias ca. 1129, Ephorus ca. 1135; detail taken from Mylonas (1964) p 353.

253. Plutarch 16 for Alexander changing the name of the month of Daesius (May-June) to a second or 'long' Artemisius (April).

254. Plutarch 13 for the Theban link to Dionysus. Aelian 12.57 for the portents heralding on the destruction of Thebes, though the Thebans assumed they signaled the end of the Macedonians. Aelian 13.7 for the exemption from slavery of the families of Philip's former hosts and the numbers of dead and captured.

255. Pausanias 9.16.1 for the description of the sanctuary and its roots. Pausanias 3.18.2, 8.32.1, 10.13.3 for the worship of the god in other parts of Greece. Pindar *Pythian* 4.29 for the reference to Zeus Ammon. Herodotus 1.46, 2.32,52.6 for references to Ammon being equated to Zeus; discussion in Anson (2013) p 97. Early links to Zeus refuted by Tarn (1948) pp 348-351 who nevertheless confirms the presence of a cult to Ammon in Athens before 371/370; Tarn 1 (1948) p 42.

256. Thebes was termed 'mean spirited and greedy' in the *Suda* A518.1. The preservation of Pindar's house was mentioned at Arrian 1.9.10. See discussion in Nisetich (1980) pp 10-11. Whilst Eustathius claimed the fine was 1,000 drachmas, Isocrates claimed 10,000.

257. Pindar *Pythian 1*, lines 75-80, translation from Nisetich (1980) p 9 though replacing Persians with Medes.

258. Pindar *Pythian 1* lines 62-72. Finlay (1973) p 172 for the importance of the naval industry at Athens. Quoting Borza (1995) p 115 on the 'flamboyant' Alexander I.

259. Plutarch 31.7 related the story of the naming of Gaugamela, the 'camel's house'. Dalley (2013) p 97; the name may derive from the Gomela River. Arrian 6.11.5-6 for the actual location of Gaugamela and its relation to Arbela some 500 or 600 stades away (the Attic stade was equivalent to 185 metres or 610.5 feet, whereas the Olympic stade to 176 metres or 580.8 feet). Herodotus 2.6 has a stade at 600 Greek feet (a *parasang* was equal to 30 stades); discussed in Gershevitch-Fisher-Boyle (1968) p 628.

260. For the Salamis coins see Stewart (1993) pp 159-160. See Plutarch 34 for his gifts to Croton.

261. Curtius 4.4.18; for additional siege detail Curtius 4.4.13-17, Arrian 2.24.3-6.

262. For the journey to Siwa see Diodorus 17.49.2-52.7, Arrian 3.4-5, Curtius 4.7.8-4.89, Plutarch 26.3-27.11, Justin 11.11.1-13, Strabo 17.1.43, *Itinerarium Alexandri* 48-50.

263. See Bevan (1927) p 13 for discussion. Recognition of the pharaoh or kings as the son of Ammon-Ra had been common practice since the second millennium.

264. Varro's letter discussed in Pearson (1955) p 447.

265. Lucian *Dialogues of the Dead* 12, translation from *Lucian, Complete Works*, Delphi Classics, 2016, p XIV.

266. According to Strabo 17.1.43 Callisthenes stated Alexander received, uniquely, spoken words from the priests confirming that he was the son of Zeus, whereas nods and signs were used elsewhere. See full discussion of the various versions from Plutarch, Arrian, Diodorus and Justin in Hammond (1993) pp 58-60. Anson (2013) p 97 for the origins of Zeus Ammon.

267. De Polignac (1999) p 4 for notoriety of the city. Herodotus 4.171 for details of its founding.

268. Diogenes Laertius *Aristippos* 1.96; 2.23 and 48-49; 3.29-32; 4.19; 5.3-4 and 39; 8.60 for its hedonistic references. Boardman (1964) p 137 for Cyrenian coinage.

269. Herodotus 3.25.3, 26.1-3, Plutarch *Cimon* 12.5 and Plutarch 26.12 mentioned Cambyses' earlier journey; Arrian 3.3.1 and Strabo 17.1.43 mentioned that Alexander knew Perseus and Callisthenes stated Heracles had visited the oracle before him. See also Robinson (1953) pp 62-63.4. For discussion on Heracles and Perseus see Bosworth (1988) p 281. The remains of the 50,000-strong army that vanished in 525 BCE were reportedly discovered in 2012 by Angel and Alfredo Castiglioni after thirteen years of research and desert expeditions; report at http://news.discovery.com/history/archaeology/cambyses-army-remains-sahara.htm

270. The slip of the tongue was recorded in Plutarch 27, though this is hardly likely. *Hypostaseis* is a substance in which a god could exist in different forms. Strabo 17.1.43 indicated Callisthenes stated the oracle's reply confirmed Alexander as the son of Zeus. Diodorus 1.28.1-4 for the journeying of Belos and Danaos from Egypt.

271. *Romance* 1.32 for the inscription of founder being associated with Alexandria; discussion of its significance in Carney-Ogden (2010) p 127. Only the *Romance* 1.34.2 claimed Alexander was given the title of pharaoh. Discussed in Anson (2013) p 104 and Tarn (1948) p 347 accepts this as proof Alexander became pharaoh.

272. De Polignac (1999) p 6.

273. Plutarch 32 for Alexander sacrificing and his deep sleep.

274. Curtius 4.10.1-8 for the eclipse and interpretations. Discussion in Hammond (1993) pp 269-270 and Pearson (1960) p 162 with footnote 70. The time between the eclipse and the battle (eleven days) Plutarch 31.8, Pliny 2.180 though 'some days' before battle in Arrian 3.7.6. Polcaro-Valsecchi-Verderame (2008) pp 55-64 for discussion of the dating of the eclipse. The Babylonian cuneiform tablet recording the eclipse is referred to as BM 36761 along with 36390. Modern calculations place the eclipse after sunset on the 20th September 331 BCE whereas the battle commenced on 1st October 331 BCE.

275. The Goddess Selene represented the Moon in Greek mythology and was termed 'the far shining' in the *Homeric Hymns*.

276. Plutarch 33.2 for Aristander riding before the lines at Gaugamela.

277. Herodotus 7.37. A translation of the relevant cuneiform table in the British Museum, using extracts from Sachs-Hunger (1988). It somewhat backs up Diodorus' account at 17.60.2-4 that Darius himself did not order a retreat, but that the ranks around him collapsed, perhaps due to the earlier drop in morale following the celestial portents. The panic in the camp is strangely dated to the 11th of the month (in the sixth month of Darius) when the battle took place on the 24th, with the eclipse reportedly preceding it on the 13th. Yet the same entry recorded or suggested the armies were encamped opposite one another. This actually suggests Curtius'

source might have been correct and the battle actually took place eleven days earlier.

278. Plutarch 32.5-6 for the run down of Alexander's panoply. Borza *Tombs* (1978) pp 112-113 for the Tomb II helmet, which in turn matches the image on the so-called Porus Medallion.

279. For example the *Iliad* 11.16 ff; discussed in Mossman (1988) p 88.

280. Arrian 4.10.3-4 for the alleged dialogue between Philotas and Callisthenes on tyranny. For the return of the statues see Arrian 3.16.7-8. Valerius Maximum claimed Seleucus returned the statues.

281. Anson (2013) pp 153-156 for the discussion of the themes behind the burning of Persepolis. Curtius 5.5.5-24, Diodorus 17.69.2-9, Justin 11.14.11-12 for the mutilated Greeks.

282. Arrian 6.30.1 for Alexander's later regret. See Borza (1995) pp 220-229 for discussion of possible motives for burning Persepolis.

283. Aelian 2.3, Pliny 32.95, 35.16.12 for the painting by Apelles.

284. 'Of wild beasts the sycophant, and of tame animals the flatterer' attributed to Diogenes of Sinope, according to Diogenes Laertius, *Diogenes* 6.

285. For examples of divine approbation of being chosen by the gods at *Ezra* 1.2 for Cyrus declaration, and the wording on the *Nabonidus Chronicle*, discussed below.

286. Discussed in Bosworth-Baynham (2000) p 101. Xenophon had proposed Heracles had achieved a divinity due to the nature of his soul. For Heracles' posthumous elevation to hero see Arrian 4.10.5-7, Diodorus 4.29.1, 5.15.3.

287. Horace *Odes* 3.301 claimed of his own poetry 'I have built monuments more durable than bronze.'

288. Cicero *Pro Archias Poeta (In Defence of Archias the Poet)* Exodium 24.

289. Diogenes Laertius 6.50 *Diogenes*.

290. Plutarch *Moralia: How to tell a Flatterer from a Friend* translation by AR Shilleto, digireads publishing 2011.

291. Herodotus 1.134 gave a detailed description of *proskynesis*. See discussion in Stewart (1993) p 13 quoting Curtius 8.5.7-8. Plutarch 45.1 and Curtius 6.6.3 did suggest Alexander initially restricted mandatory *proskynesis* to Asians. Also Arrian 4.9.9, 10.5.12, 6, Curtius 8.5.5-24, Plutarch 54.2-6 for the introduction of *proskynesis* and the repercussions.

292. Curtius 8.5.8.

293. Plutarch *Phocion* 2.2 described the use of *menoeikes* as something soothing and yielding to the soul.

294. Plutarch 5.8 for Lysimachus' Homeric comparisons.

295. Attributed to Aesop *The Hart and the Hunter.*

296. Cato's advice from Cicero *Laelius De Amicitia* 24.

297. Homer *Iliad* 2.212 translated into English blank verse by William Cowper, published by Project Gutenberg, edition 1860. For Penthesileia see chapter titled *Mythoi, Muthodes and the Birth of Romance*.

298. Curtius 8.5.8 for Choerilus' presence with Alexander and *Romance* 1.42. For Alexander's payment to the poet see Pomponius Porphyrio's commentary on Horace' *Epistles* ii. 1.232-4. Also Horace *Ars Poetica* 357 for the derision of Choerilus as *poeta pessimus.*

299. Diodorus 16.87.1-2 for Demades chiding Philip. Hammond (1994) p 156 rejects it ever happened.

300. Plutarch *Phocion* 1.1. Demades discussed Pearson (1960) p 206; for the proposal of divine honours see Athenaeus 6.251b, Aelian 5.12. He was fined by Athens for the proposal. For the authenticity of Demades' *On the Twelve Years* see discussion by VJ Gray in Marasco (2011) p 19 ff.

301. Pausanias 6.18.2. Also Josephus *Against Apion* 1.24, Lucan *Pseudologos* 29, Aelius Aristides *To Rome* 51; Flower (1994) p 22 footnote 36 for other traditions concerning the *Trikaranus*. Dionysius of Halicarnassus *On Composition* 4 thought Anaximenes of Lampsacus 'weak, unconvincing' and 'four-sided'.

302. Lucian *A True History* 2.20 and discussed in Gudeman *Greeks* (1894) p 67.

303. Discussion of Theopompus' (and Ephorus') treatment of Athens vs. Philip in Carney-Ogden (2010) pp 72-73. Theopompus wrote a scathing letter about Harpalus' behaviour (and Alexander's *hetairoi*); recorded at Athenaeus 595a-c.

304. 'Prosecutor' from Lucian *How to Write History* 59. Flower (1994) p 161 on Theopompus' digressions. Further Cicero thought Theopompus 'bitter' and Nepos thought him (and Timeus) 'most malicious' (*maledicentissimi*).

305. Polybius 8.9.1-3 translation by ES Shuckburg, Macmillan 1889. Polybius' own astonishment actually superseded the above extract from Theopompus.

306. Justin 7.1.12 for Philip's status as the second founder. Polybius 8.9.6-13 and his reference to Theopompus' *Philippics*. Reiterated at Athenaeus 10.435b-c and quoting Theopompus' fragment F225 in Flower (1994) pp 185-186. Flower (1994) p 24 for Theopompus' exile and p 38 for

Theopompus' encomium to Philip and Alexander. Theopompus' comments also discussed in Pearson (1960).

307. Arrian 3.19.5-6 Diodorus 17.76.3, Curtius 6.2.17 for the dismissal of allies. Blackwell (1999) p 55 for discussion of the Peloponnesian contingent; some were members of the league. For more on the revolt of Agis and battle at Megalopolis see chapter titled *Sarissa Diplomacy: Macedonian Statecraft*.

308. Following discussion in Atkinson (1963) pp 126-127.

309. For 'cloven hoof' see Robinson (1953) p 7 referring to Tarn's (1948) p 98 commentary. All the extant accounts confirm otherwise unheard of battle death and casualty ratios in favour of the Macedones. While this is certainly an exaggeration, light casualties are a recurring message against heavy enemy losses. As examples for Issus see Arrian 1.16.2 for Persian cavalry losses and 1.16.4 for Macedonian cavalry losses and 2.11.8 for Persian losses; where only mounted troop numbers were mentioned, Plutarch 20.11-13, Curtius 3.11.27. For Gaugamela see Arrian 3.15.6 for losses on both sides, Diodorus 17.61.3, Curtius 4.16.26. See Pearson (1969) p 156 and footnote 41 for discussion of Arrian's statement on casualty numbers, relating them to Companions only where Aristobulus and Justin claimed these were the total killed.

310. Nicanor had commanded the Guards Brigade of hypaspists until he died in Areia, Philotas the Companion Cavalry until executed, Hector drowned in the Nile; Parmenio's brother Asander had governed Lydia.

311. Isocrates *To Philip* 16.

312. Pseudo-Plutarch *Isocrates*, Pseudo-Lucian *Makrobioi* 23 with a similar tradition in Dionysius of Halicarnassus *Attic Orators*, *Life of Isocrates* 3.2, Pausanias 1.18.1, Flavius Philostratus *Lives of the Sophists* 17. Other corroborating claims in anonymous 'lives' remain.

313. See Bosworth-Baynham (2000) p 97. Michael Flower suggested the destruction of Thebes and the restoration of Plataea were symbolic of Panhellenic policy.

314. Timaeus fragment 139 cited by Shipley (2000) p 263 and quoting Momigliano (1977) p 46 on Timaeus' attitude.

315. According to the Behistun Inscription (as well as Herodotus, Justin and Ctesias), in 522 BCE Gaumata, allegedly a Magus from Media, impersonated Bardiya the brother of Cambyses II (son of Cyrus the Great) who was campaigning in Egypt. Bardiya had been secretly murdered by Cambyses before he departed and Gautama seized the throne for some seven months. Greek tradition called him Smerdis and then the 'False Smerdis' once the background to his usurpation was revealed. The various reports of the episode conflict, as do names and his legitimacy. The imposter was stabbed to death in September 522 BCE by seven Persian nobles who had discovered his true identity.

316. For the capture and execution of Darius by Bessus and Nabarzanes see Curtius 5.9-12 and 5.13.15-25, Arrian 3.21.1-10, Diodorus 17.73.2 and for Bessus' final capture see Curtius 7.15.19-26 and 36-38, Arrian 3.29.6-3.30.5 Also Arrian 3.25.3 for his proclaiming himself king.

317. Curtius 4.14.21 for Alexander describing the Macedonian army as 'storm-tossed by changing fortune'.

318. Curtius 3.6.18 for attributions to fortune. For the episode with Sisines, Curtius 3.7.11-15.

319. Curtius 3.8.20 for Alexander fearing Fortuna on the eve of the battle at Issus.

320. Curtius 3.8.15 for Persian ruthlessness.

321. Curtius 4.6.29 for Baetis' treatment. 'Batis' amended to 'Baetis' following Pearson (1960) pp 247-248. The treatment of Baetis is reminiscent of Virgil's *Aeneid* 4.6.29. Arrian 4.2.4 for the treatment of captured men at Gaza.

322. Quoting Plutarch 25.8; also Pliny 12.62, Plutarch *Moralia* 179e-f. Discussion of Hegesias as a source of the Baetis episode in Pearson (1960) p 247; see chapter titled *Sarissa Diplomacy: Macedonian Statecraft* for more on the siege of Tyre. The crucifixions were reported by Curtius 4.410-21 so this may be a rhetorical device but his total casualty numbers, 6,000 killed and 2,000 crucified, tie in with 8,000 total at Arrian 2.24.4.

323. For the 'blood of thousands' 4.10.3-4; the descriptions of the burning and plundering of Persepolis, 5.6.1-8 and 5.7.1 for Curtius' claims on drink and courtesans. For Alexander coping with war better than peace, 6.2.1.

324. A phrase coined by Timaeus; Flower (1994) p 166 for discussion.

325. Quoting Strabo 14.1.5.

326. Herodotus 6.19.

327. The sources of the Branchidae episode are Curtius 7.5.28-35, Diodorus 17, table of contents (a lacuna swallowed the text), Strabo 11.11.4, 14.1.5, Plutarch *Moralia* 557b. Discussion of its historicity in Tarn (1949) pp 272-275, also Tarn *Classical Review* 36, 1922, p 63 and Parke (1964).

328. Arrian 4.11.2, translation by A de Selincourt, Penguin Books edition, 1958.

329. Bosworth *A in the East* (1996) pp 100-110 for a good discussion of the Cleitus incident and Alexander's search for divinity and *proskynesis* its adoption or rejection by his men. Hermolaus

accused Alexander of much the same – rejecting his father; see Arrian 4.14.2, Curtius 8.17.1 ff. Arrian 8.1.24-25 for the claim to have saved Philip in battle.

330. Arrian 1.15.8, Plutarch 16.11, Diodorus 17.20.7 for Cleitus' part at the Granicus battle. For the role of Lanice, Cleitus' sister, see Curtius 8.1.21,8.2-9, Arrian 4.9.3, Aelian 26, Athenaeus 4.129a, *Romance* 1.13, Julius Valerius 1.17.

331. Euripides' *Andromache* line 683 is referred to by Plutarch 51.8. See Bosworth-Baynham (2000) p 101 for further discussion.

332. Plutarch 13.4 for Alexander attributing Cleitus' death to Dionysus' wrath. For Cleitus' death see Curtius 8.1.49 ff, Plutarch 50-51, Arrian 4.8.6-9, Justin 12.6-7, Lucian *Dialogues of the Dead* 12.

333. Plutarch 7.2.

334. This comes from Justin's lengthy digression that compared father to son from 9.7.13-21.

335. Arrian 7.9.2, Curtius 10.2.12, Diodorus 17.109 for Alexander praising the virtues of his father.

336. Diodorus 17.80.4 and Polyaenus 4.3.19 for the censoring of letters; Curtius 7.2.35; Justin 12.5.8 also for the *ataktoi* unit and (Justin) for its fate. Strabo claimed Alexander told his men he planned three years of further campaigning and wanted to know the true feelings of his men. Curtius 7.2.35 suggested they were openly unhappy at the death of Parmenio.

337. Plutarch 48-49 for Antigone spying on Philotas.

338. Curtius 8.8.21-23 for Callisthenes' character portrayal and innocence.

339. Curtius 6.9.33-37.

340. Curtius 6.8.3 and 6.11.3-4; Anson (2004) p 208 for discussion and following Anson for 'aloofness'.

341. Curtius 7.2.32 for Parmenio's decapitation; the head was sent to Alexander. Diodorus 17.77.7 and Justin 12.3.11-12 for Alexander's adding concubines to his retinue. Justin 12.3.9-10 for Alexander wearing Darius' diadem. For Hermolaus' speech and the themes it captured see Arrian 4.14.2, Curtius 8.7.1 ff.

342. Plutarch 33 described the reports of Parmenio as 'sluggish' and 'dispirited'.

343. Plutarch *Caesar* 66. For full details of the Philotas affair see Curtius 6-7.1-6.8.21, Diodorus 17.79, Plutarch 49.3-12, Arrian 3.26.1-2, Justin 12.5.1-3.

344. Baynham (1989) pp 171-180 for a good discussion on the themes underlying the Philotas affair.

345. Arrian 3.27.5 for the arrest of Demetrius whose post Ptolemy subsequently filled. Curtius 6.7.15 and 6.11.35-38 claimed he was named guilty by a witness. Curtius 6.11.10 and 6.11.38 for the custom of stoning.

346. Curtius 6.8.17 named Hephaestion, Craterus, Coenus, Erygius, Leonnatus and Perdiccas as those summoned to coordinate the plans against Philotas.

347. Arrian 3.27.3 for Amyntas' death during an insignificant siege. Curtius 7.1.18 for Amyntas' own argument that he was innocent of colluding with Philotas. For Amyntas' arrogance see Curtius 7.1.15.

348. Curtius 6.11.20 and 8.6.28 clearly (though uniquely) stated Macedonian law demanded the death of all those related by blood to the guilty party. For the execution of Alexander Lyncestis see Curtius 7.1.5-9, Diodorus 17.80.2, Justin 12.14.1; the captured Persian Sisines allegedly carried correspondence from Lyncestis to Darius.

349. Holt (2005) p 107. Bosworth (1988) p 238 for the defence force.

350. Curtius 7.7.39.

351. Plutarch 48-49. Plutarch *Lycurgus* 28.3-7 for Crypteia references. The Crypteia has been credited with anything from a secret role of the Ephebia to spy on helots, to a secret police force.

352. Plutarch 37.1-2. Apollo Lyceus, the wolf-like deity gave its name to the Lyceum in Athens. The wolf had appeared on the coins of King Amyntas II; Hammond (1991) p 51.

353. Plutarch *Demosthenes* 23.5. Also Plutarch 37 for the story that the priestess Pythia had predicted a wolf would guide Alexander on his march against the Persians. Whether the stories were connected remains unclear. Demosthenes was referring to one of Aesop's fables; sheep stood up to wolves when allied with dogs until the dogs promised peace in return for abandoning the alliance.

354. Curtius 6.6.1-2.

355. At Susa in 325 BCE Alexander married Stateira or Barsine, daughter of Darius III as well as Parysatis, daughter of Artaxerxes Ochus. The troop mutiny at Opis followed. See Arrian 7.4-5. Curtius 10.1.25-37 for the behaviour of Bagoas.

356. Arrian 4.7.4 based on the translation by M Hammond, Oxford World Classics, 2013 edition. The so-called 'great digression' takes place between 4.7.4 and 4.15 and includes digressions on Alexander's orientalism, his murder of Cleitus, Callisthenes and the conspiracy of the pages.

357. Curtius 6.2.2.

358. Quoting Bosworth-Baynham (2000) p 18.

359. Aelian 14.47a. Atarrhias was a prominent hypaspist commander who may have served Cassander after Alexander's death; Heckel (2006) p 60 for details of his career.

360. Quoting Plutarch *Moralia* 466d-e, or *On Tranquility of Mind*.

361. Cicero *Tusculan Disputations* 3.28.69, translated by CD Younge, published by Project Gutenberg, 2005.
362. Arrian 5.26.1 gave a description of Alexander's geographical belief in this encircling Stream of Ocean.
363. Herodotus 2.23. *Kosmokrator*: ruler of the world.
364. Strabo 15.1.25 quoting Nearchus' *Indike*, translation from Pearson (1960) p 123. Green (1974) p 405.
365. Arrian 5.26.1 included a reference to the Ganges in Alexander's speech to the mutinous men at the Hyphasis River, claiming it was a comparatively small distance away. Strabo 15.1.42 however claimed Nearchus reported it was a four-month march to the Ganges through India. It remains unclear if Scylax sailed down the Indus or Ganges; Herodotus 4.44; Aristotle *Politics* 7.14.2 for early references to him; Strabo 12.4.8, 13.1.4, 14.2.20 for later references.
366. Plutarch 62.2, Diodorus 2.37 Strabo 15.1.35 (c702) quoting a letter of Craterus to his mother for the Ganges tradition; see Fears (1976) p 217 for discussion.
367. The Seres were inhabitants of Serica, the land of silk, so China. Strabo 11.11.1 first referred to them though their whereabouts and cultivation method remained unknown, as evidenced by Pliny 20 *The Seres,* when he referred to the woollen substance as forest-derived.
368. Ephorus espoused a simplified view that the known world was bordered by Scythians to the North, Ethiopians to the South, Celts to the West and Indians to the East; discussion in Pearson (1960) Introduction p 13. Hecataeus' description of the Earth was the first geographical treatise to include a map and corrected the earlier map of Anaximander who produced the first world map around 550 BC in his treatise *On Nature*. Xenophon's *Anabasis* turned back northwest at Cunaxa, close to Babylon, following the Tigris to the Black Sea. Ctesias' *Persika* contradicted both Herodotus and Xenophon and is preserved in fragments in Diodorus, Athenaeus, Photius and Plutarch. The *Periplous* that survives is attributed to Pseudo-Scylax of Carianda. Scylax is mentioned by Herodotus at 4.44 and may itself have been influenced by Phileas of Athens, the Greek navigator; see discussion in Shipley (2011). How close the extant *Periplous* is to the original is conjecture. Green (1974) p 404 and footnote 108 for Aristotelian geography; *Meteorologica* 362b 19-23 for relative distances.
369. Arrian 7.16.1-4 for the mission to Hyrcania.
370. The stele of Hammurabi is a black diorite stone discovered by J De Morgan and V Scheil during their excavations at Susa in 1901-1902. The fifty-one columns of cuneiform text were written in Akkadian. It is now in the Louvre. It dates to around 1790 BCE and already continues a royal tradition of laying down legal codes, with similarities to earlier *stelae*, for example the Code of Urukagina, as early as 2350 BCE. The text comprises a long list of civil codes, sophisticated in their social applications. See M Van de Mieroop (2005) pp 99-111. In contrast, almost all Greek legal code developed after 600 BCE; I. Arnaoutoglou, *Ancient Greek Laws, A Sourcebook,* Routledge Press, London, 1998. Diodorus 17.7.3-4 explained that the Ideaen Dactyls of Mount Ida were the first to work iron.
371. Arrian 7.1-2 references to Dandamis the Wise Man and Plutarch 64 for Brahmin sophistry.
372. Plutarch 8 recorded a gradual estrangement between Alexander and Aristotle; the Peripatus was part of the Lyceum. The building had colonnades, *peripatoi*, though which Aristotle would walk whilst teaching, earning him the title *peripatetikos*, hence peripatetic. Whilst the link is attractive, the term *peripatetikos,* of walking, was likely already in use; Diogenes Laertius *Aristotle* 4 for the origins of the name.
373. Xenophon *Cyropaedia* 1.2.3.
374. Pyrrho of Elis founded the *Skeptikoi* movement. According to Plutarch *Moralia* 331e, Sextus Empiricus recorded in his *Adversus Mathematicus* that Alexander gave the philosopher 10,000 gold pieces on the first meeting.
375. Steel blades have been found elsewhere that pre-date Alexander, most notably in India (Seric steel), produced by the hands-on crucible technique. There is little or no evidence of steel being manufactured for weapons or armour in Europe at this time. *The Periplous of the Erythrean Sea* 6 describing the trading route from the Red Sea to India, and broadly dated to the 1st century, made reference to the Greeks importing steel and iron from India. And Pliny 34.145 referred to the Seres of China making 'true steel', though this has been challenged, as it is the only known reference linking the Seres to steel manufacture. India was the most likely origination point. See full discussion in Schoff (1915). See the argument for India in Srinivasan-Sinopoli-Morrison-Gopal-Ranganathan (2009). A form of mild steel was however found on the helmet and cuirass in the so-called tomb of Philip II at Vergina; Hammond (1994) p 180.
376. Curtius 9.8.15 records that 80,000 Indians were slaughtered in the area of King Sambus, according to Cleitarchus. Arrian 5.24.7-8 recorded that 17,000 men were slaughtered and 70,000 more at Sangala. As an example of crucifixion, Arrian 6.17.1-2 and Curtius 9.8.16 for the punishment of Musicanus.

377. Following Bosworth A in the East (1996) p 108; past tense used as Bosworth related his comment to the Bactrian campaign of 328/7 BCE and soon after the imposition of *proskynesis*.
378. Plutarch *Moralia* 327c. The Birdless Rock refers to the Rock of Aornus.
379. For Alexander's entry into the Mallian city and subsequent wounds see Arrian 6.8.4-6.13.5, 6.28.4, Curtius 9.4.26-9.5.30, Diodorus 17.98.1-17.100.1, Plutarch 63.5-13. Curtius 9.4.15 for the mutinous behaviour before entering Mallia.
380. Polyaenus 4.2.15 for Philip's siege of Methone. Bosworth *A in the East* (1996) pp 60-65 for discussion of Alexander's wound in Mallia. *Iliad* 5.900-904 for Ares' wound and recovery. Arrian 6.9.1-2 for Perdiccas' surgery.
381. For Xandrames' army see Diodorus 17.93.2, Curtius 9.2.3; Plutarch 63 has 200,000 infantry, 80,000 cavalry, 8,000 chariots and 6,000 elephants. For Phegeus' report of the army facing them Diodorus 17.93-12, Curtius 9.1.36-9.2, *Metz Epitome* 68.
382. Diodorus 17.87.5 described Porus' army with its elephants resembled the towers of a city.
383. Zeus sent a gadfly to sting Pegasus and dismount Bellerophon for attempting to fly on Pegasus up Mount Olympus, presumably to become a god. Bellerophon was crippled and died a hermit. For his fate see Pindar *Olympian Odes* 13.87-90 and *Isthmian Odes* 7.44, Apollodorus *Bibliotheke* 2.3.2; Homer's *Iliad* 6.155-203 and 16.328, Ovid *Metamorphoses* 9.646. Plutarch 61.1 for Bucephalus' age.
384. Arrian 5.28.1-3, Curtius 9.3.16-19, Plutarch 62.5-8. Roisman (2012) noted where Achilles refused to fight and abandoned the Greek army, Alexander wanted to fight and had been abandoned *by* his army. Tarn 1 (1948) p 98 for the suggestion that the Hyphasis was Darius' boundary with India.
385. For the differing descriptions of the altars and 'oversized' artefacts see Justin 12.8.16-18, Plutarch 62; Arrian 5.29.1; Diodorus 17.95.1-3. Plutarch claimed the 'present day' kings of the Praesii still sacrificed on the altars when crossing the river. Arrian never mentioned any oversized construction. Xenophon *Anabasis* 1.3 for Clearchus' handling of the Greek mercenaries. Quoting Curtius 9.3.18-19.
386. Strabo 11.11.14 for Alexander's destruction of Cyra; discussion in Pearson (1960) pp 94-95.
387. Hatzopoulos (1996) p 336 for the tracts given to Coenus family over two generations. Coenus (Koinos) loosely translates as 'common'. Curtius 9.3.3-15, Arrian 5.27.2-9 for Coenus' speech.
388. Heckel (2006) p 91 and p 62 for the family history of Coenus, Attalus and Parmenio. Justin 1.5.1 for the death of Attalus' family.
389. Curtius 9.3.20, translation based on the Loeb Classical Library edition, 1946. Curtius 8.12.10-18 for Coenus' comment in Taxila.
390. Arrian 5.29.2. Diodorus 17.97.3 stated that after navigating the dangers of the Indus-Acesines, Alexander reflected that he had emulated Achilles in doing battle with a river, referring to the *Iliad* 21.228-282. Alexander would have believed from Herodotus 4.44 that Scylax journeyed down the Indus and then west to the Persian Gulf. Plutarch 62.9 for Sandrokottos meeting Alexander.
391. The Indus Valley civilisation unearthed in the 1920s appears to have matured through 2,600-1,900 BCE.
392. Arrian 5.21.6, 5.23.5, 5.24.3 (500 dead when retreating), 5.24.4 (17,000 deaths, 70,000 prisoners), 5.24.7-8, 6.6.3, 6.6.6, 6.7.1-4,6.7.6,6.8.3, 6.8.8,6.11.1,6.16.1-2,6.16.5,6.17.1-2,6.18.1,6.21.4-5. Specific numbers of dead were not recorded for most operations but the numbers we do have make it clear than tens of thousands died.
393. Diodorus 17.104.6-7 for the Gedrosian campaign.
394. Arrian's *Epictetou Encheiridion 45 (Manual of Epictetus)*, *Do Not say it is Bad*, preserved the Stoic doctrine of Epictetus. Tarn (1948) p 127 and Tarn *Alexander the Great Volume I, Narrative*, 1948, p 103.
395. Aelian 16.39 for dragons; Strabo 15.1.43 for 300 and 500-year-old elephants; Strabo 15.1.28 for the impossibly long snakes.
396. Plutarch 66 for the length of the seven-month voyage down the Hyphasis-Indus.
397. Arrian 6.24.2.
398. Arrian 6.24.4 and 6.25.3.
399. Diodorus 17.95.4-5 recorded the arrival of 30,000 Greek allied and mercenary infantry and 6,000 Greek cavalry just prior to the journey down the Indus. Alexander sent around 10,000 mercenaries home with Craterus and Polyperchon (Arrian 7.12.4) before crossing the desert, so these new recruits must have comprised a large percentage of the remaining numbers that made the desert journey.
400. Arrian 6.24.4 termed the crossing 'fatal' to a large proportion of the army. Plutarch 66.4 stated he lost over seventy-five per cent of his 120,000 men and 15,000 cavalry; the numbers are suspiciously high and may include Leonnatus' contingent and the garrisons left behind; Green (1974) p 435 suggests 85,000 marched through the desert, surely most non-combatants.

Nearchus' *Indike* suggested that was the size of the whole army that accompanied Alexander down the Indus, not the Gedrosian contingent. Tarn suggested 8,000-10,000 and not more than 30,000 entered India; Tarn 1 (1948) p 84. See discussion in Arrian 6.24, Penguin Classics edition, 1971, p 336 footnote 46. Semiramis was, according to Greek legend, the wife of King Ninus of Assyria. Tarn 1 (1948) p 84 for 'moving state'.

401. Quoting Plutarch 68, translation by I Scott-Kilvert, Penguin Classical Library, 1973.

402. Curtius 10.1.1-9, Arrian 6.27, Plutarch 68.2-3, Justin 12.10.8. Those arrested included Sitacles, Cleander, Heracon and Agathon who had been charged with murdering Parmenio. Whilst non-confirmed, they were presumably executed. Cleander was likely Coenus' brother; Heckel (2006) p 85.

403. Harpalus was Alexander's boyhood friend and treasurer in Babylon. Diodorus 17.108.6, Curtius 10.2.1, Arrian *Events After Alexander* 1.16, Plutarch *Demosthenes* 1-2 for Harpalus' flight. For his friendship with Alexander Arrian 3.6.5, Plutarch 10.4.

404. Quoting Plutarch *Demosthenes* 25. Bosworth (1971) p 124 for Cleander and Harpalus and following Heckel (2006) p 130 for Harpalus' involvement with Cleander, Sitacles, Heracon and Agathon.

405. Arrian 7.18.1-3 for the episode involving Apollodorus.

406. The actual chronology of the Pasargadae, Opis and Susa chain of events, including the mutiny, debt repayment and weddings is uncertain; see discussion in Robinson (1953) p 5 footnote 8 and Olbrycht (2008) pp 237-239; what amounted to the start of a mutiny when the flotilla approached Mallia is mentioned. At Curtius 9.4.15 ff.

407. For the dissent caused by the arrival of the Asian *epigonoi,* Diodorus 17.108.1-3, Arrian 7.6.1, Plutarch 71.1, Justin 12.11.4.

408. Diodorus 18.108.3 and Arrian 7.6.5 for the reissued weaponry. For the Persian Silver Shields see Arrian 7.11.3 and 7.29.4 for the Golden Apple-Bearers. Arrian 7.29.4 for the supportive statement on chauvinism.

409. Curtius 7.3.4 for the 200 Persian horsemen present since 300 BCE. Also Arrian 3.24.1 for the first use of *hippakontistai*, mounted skirmishers, who appear to be locally recruited. Arrian 7.6.3-4 for the resentment from the Companion Cavalry and its dilution and 7.6.4 for the reference to barbarians in the ranks. For the various positions they held and regiments they were divided into see Arrian 7.11.1-3, Diodorus 17.109.3, 17.110.1; fuller discussion in Olbrycht (2008) p 246.

410. Justin 12.12.3 ff for the 1,000 Persian bodyguards and sentiment that he trusted them as much as Macedonians at Diodorus 17.110.1 Plutarch 71.4.

411. Quoting and following Briant (1974) pp 113-112. Curtius 8.5.1 regarded the Asiatic *epigonoi* as 'hostages'.

412. Discussion of the mercenary tendencies in Carney (1996) pp 19-44.

413. For the demobilisation of veterans to be escorted home under Craterus, Justin 12.11.4, 12.7, Arrian 7.12.1, Diodorus 17.109.1, 18.4.1, 18.16.4, Curtius 10.10.5. Full discussion in Hammond (1991) p 146. For the insult thrown at Alexander see Plutarch 71.1, Diodorus 17.109.2. Following the observation in Olbrycht (2008) p 240 for the rejection of Alexander's 'terrestrial father'. For Alexander's resulting fury, Diodorus 17.108.3, Arrian 7.8.3, Justin 12.11.6. Curtius 10.2.3 for the executions. Drowning as a means of execution was documented in Babylonia; see Olbrycht (2008) p 243 for discussion and p 245 for the alleged request by those sentenced to be killed by Macedonians and not foreigners; Curtius 10.4.1-3. Hammond (1994) p 48 for the punishment for sacrilege, here referring to the aftermath of the Battle of the Crocus Field when 3,000 prisoners were supposedly drowned.

414. Curtius 9.4.15 for the beginnings of a mutiny before entering Mallia; an Assembly gathering had to be called.

415. This assumes the Attic talent was being referred to. See chapter titled *The Tragic Triumvirate of Treachery and Oaths* for pay rates. 1 talent = 6,000 drachmas = 36,000 obols, equivalent to 6 obols per day for sixteen years; most infantrymen received 4 per day. Top pay would equate to 1/10 of a talent per man per year.

416. The hypaspists remained loyal at Susa/Opis enabling Alexander to round up the ringleaders; Arrian 7.8.3. For the repayment of debt see Curtius 10.2.8, Diodorus 17.109.2 and quoting Justin 12.11.2-4. For the talent per man see Arrian 7.12.2. More details follow in this chapter. Where the debt repayment took place remains debatable, possibly Susa and before Opis to soften the blow of the planned dismissal of veterans. Following the observation of Roisman (2012) pp 41-44. Diodorus 17.71.2, Strabo 15.3.9 for leaving the treasury behind (except a basic float); cf Curtius 5.6.9.

417. Cicero *De Officiis* 2.15.

418. Curtius 10.2.12 for his new Asian capital, and for the mutiny Arrian 7.8.1-7.12.4, Diodorus 17.108.3, 17.109.103, Plutarch 71.1-5, Justin 12.11.5-12.12.10, Curtius 10.2.8-10.4.2.

419. Aristobulus' account of the sophists at Taxila captured by Arrian 6.22.4-8 included reference to

Phoenicians 'who had been following the expedition in search of trade' collecting spikenard, myrrh, gum and other roots.

420. Ada was reinstated as satrap of Caria and she adopted Alexander; see Arrian 1.23.8. Alexander addressed Sisygambis, Darius' mother, in terms that suggest he adopted her as his second mother; see Curtius 5.2.22. Curtius 8.4.26 for the comparison to Briseis and Achilles; see Homer *Iliad* 2.688-694 for the capture of Briseis. Plutarch 21.7-9. Roxane was Bactrian or Sogdian; the campaign and siege of the so-called Rock of Sogdia, the Rock of Sisimithres (Chorienes) and the Rock of Ariamazes are confused; see Heckel (2006) pp 241-242 and 187 for identifications and Heckel (1987) p 114 for discussion. Barsine and Parysatis were from Persian royal lines, see Arrian 7.4.4-7 The prominent non-Macedonian drinking partners mentioned at Alexander's final *komos* were Medius from Thessaly, Heracleides the Thracian, Ariston of Pharsalus, Nearchus the Cretan and Stasanor, a Cypriot; Heckel (1988) p 10 for a further list of those present. Holcias may have been Illyrian (see chapter titled *The Silent Siegecraft of the Pamphleteers*) and Lysimachus was originally Thessalian but became a naturalised Macedonian; Heckel (2006) p 153.

421. Greenwalt (1999) for the strategic position of Pella and its silting problems.

422. For discussion of the Achaemenid tradition of the great royal tent see Albrycht (2008) p 234 and Briant (1974) p 128.

423. Arrian 7.4.6.

424. Aristocritus had supposedly acted for Pixodarus and Thessalus for Alexander in his own failed bid to marry the daughter of the Carian dynast. Plutarch 10.1-4 for Thessalus' mission to Pixodarus and Athenaeus 12.538f for his performance at Susa, along with Athenodorus and Aristocritus.

425. Arrian 7.4.6 stated eighty marriages in total, whereas Chares cited ninety-two; see Athenaeus 12.538b-539a. Arrian's statement came after his naming key personnel and could have been designed to exclude them.

426. Badian (1964) p 203. Arrian *Events After Alexander* 1.2; see Arrian 6.28.4 for the previous seven, who became eight with Peucestas. Hephaestion had died in 324 BCE. Eumenes may have been elevated after that; see chapter titled *The Tragic Triumvirate of Treachery and Oaths*.

427. Plutarch 43.7, Curtius 6.2.11 for Oxyathres' *hetairos* status; Diodorus 17.77.4, Curtius 7.5.40, *Metz Epitome* 2 for his enrolment into the Bodyguards.

428. Arrian 3.30.5 for Bessus' capture and arrival naked in a collar. For the cruel end administered to Bessus see Diodorus 17.83.9, Curtius 7.5.40-42 and 7.5.43, Arrian 30.30.5 and 4.7.3. Curtius stated he was crucified though other traditions have him beheaded and torn apart by recoiling trees.

429. Quoting E Will and discussed in Briant (1974) p 184.

430. Diodorus 17.73.3; Arrian 3.22.1, Justin 11.15.15, Plutarch *Moralia* 343b, Pliny 36.132 for Darius' royal burial.

431. Pausanias was pro dual hegemony and peaceful co-existence with Athens, whereas Lysander was for harsher treatment; see discussion in Cartledge (2003) pp 200-201. The lines come from Plutarch *Lysander* 15.3-4.

432. Lane Fox (1973) p 436.

433. Arrian 2.12.6-8, Curtius 3.12, 15-17, Justin 11.9.12, Diodorus 17.11.4.2 (implied at 17.114-34 also) for Alexander's reply. The Persian Queen Mother Sisygambis, mistook Hephaestion for Alexander on account of his height. Plutarch 21.6 for Darius' height: 'the tallest man in the Persian Empire' thus kings were supposed to be so.

434. Diogenes Laertius *Aristotle*.

435. Quoting Plutarch 72 for Alexander's sacrifice to the shades of Hephaestion and 'blood-soaked hunt'. Plutarch *Pelopidas* 34.2 for the shearing of horses and mules, Arrian 7.14.5 for the references to the temple of Asclepius in Ecbatana.

436. Following the observation in Briant (1974) p 126 for the three remaining Persian governors.

437. Curtius 10.2.8.

438. A theme running through Isocrates' *Philippos*.

439. Plutarch 65 related how Calanus threw hide on the ground and stepped around its edges observing how the opposite edge rose up. The demonstration was supposed to show Alexander that he needed to concentrate his weight on the centre if he was to keep the empire under control.

440. Polybius 11.13.

441. Plutarch *Galba* 1 for Iphicrates' advice. Alexander 6.17.4 gave Hephaestion orders to populate fortified cities on the far banks of the Indus in the land of Musicanus; the Macedonians had ravaged the area and Musicanus had been crucified. Presumably the settlers included mercenaries or there was little point; Arrian 6.21.5 and 6.22.3. Hyrcania, renowned for its thick forests, translated as 'land of wolves'. Remains of a so-called 'Wall of Alexander' exist, though it

cannot specifically be identified as a campaign defence. It is positioned in modern Golestan, a northern region of Iran and separates the region from Turkmenistan.

442. For Philip's governorship and rapidly expanding provinces, Arrian 5.8.3, 5.20.7, 6.2.3,6.4.1, 6.14.3, Plutarch 60.16. For his death Arrian 6.27.2 and Curtius 10.1.20. For the revolt of 3,000 mercenaries, Curtius 9.7.1-11.

443. Plutarch 37.4 and 56.1 alleged Demaratus burst into tears for the Hellenes who fell in battle before seeing Alexander throned.

444. Plutarch 68.3 stated the empire was in chaos. See Diodorus 17.106.2 and 17.111.1 for his decree that all satraps disband their mercenary forces as a result. Griffiths (1935) p 39 for the 100,000 mercenary numbers. Parke (1933) p 196 for Artaxerxes Ochus' ordering provincial governors to dismiss their mercenary recruits.

445. For the timing of the drafting of the Exiles Decree see Bosworth (1988) p 221 and Blackwell (1999) pp 14-15.

446. Unconstitutional as votes of the League were needed to change its laws and as the return of exiles was banned under the terms of the League of Corinth; following the observation in Worthington (2000) p 102. A useful discussion in Bosworth (1988) pp 220-228. Diodorus 18.8.7 for the Athenian occupation of Samos. See Kebric (1977) p 3 for discussion of Samos' loss of freedom and p 4 for possible Sicilian exile and p 19 for Iasus.

447. Bagnall-Derow (2004) pp4-6 for the Tegean *diagramma*.

448. Diodorus 18.8.2-7 for its aftermath.

449. Diodorus 17.111.3 for Athens authorising Leosthenes to recruit mercenaries and 18.9.1 for the sum of 50 talents he was provided with. Pausanias 1.25.5 for his appointment as commander-in-chief of Greek forces following Alexander's death. Diodorus 18.9.12 for the alliance with Locris, Phocis and Aetolia. Anson (2014) p 29 for the amassed 18,000 talents at Athens. See chapter titled *The Wrath of Peleus' Son* for discussion of Harpalus' flight; Harpalus left Asia with 5,000 talents and when turned away by Athens he reentered the city a second time with 700 talents; Blackwell (1999) pp 11-31 for sources and discussion.

450. Pausanias 8.52.5 gave 50,000 soldiers but Diodorus 18.9.1 for 8,000 dismissed satrapal mercenaries, 18.9.5 for 7,000 Aetolians, 5,000 Athenian foot, 500 horse and 2,000 mercenaries. Heracles is said to have found the entrance to the underworld at Cape Taenarum (also known as Cape Matapan) in his final labour to capture Cerberus. Four locations were associated with the oracles of the dead, Taenarum, Heraclea Pontica, Acheron in Threspotia and Avernus in Campania; discussion in Ogden (2001). For reference to the Temple of Poseidon, Diodorus 11.45.4, Pausanias 3.25.4; discussed in Anson (2014) p 30.

451. For Demosthenes' lack of political activity between 330 and 324 BCE see discussion in Worthington (2000) pp 93-94. The accusations against Demosthenes embodied in Plutarch *Demosthenes* 25-26, Hyperides *Against Demosthenes*; also Pseudo-Plutarch *Hyperides*, also Plutarch *Phocion* 21, Athenaeus 8.342f. Demosthenes was probably not guilty of stealing the gold but perhaps guilty of freeing Harpalus; see discussion in Worthington (2000) p 105 and he was in fact attempting to appease Alexander so he could argue for a repeal of the Exiles Decree. For Harpalus' death see Diodorus 17.108.8, 18.19.2, Curtius 10.2.3, Arrian *Events After Alexander* 1.16, Strabo 17.3.21, Pausanias 2.33.4-5. For Nicanor's possible ties to Aristotle see Diodorus 18.8.3 (Stagira), *Aristotle* by G Grote, John Murray, 1880, footnotes 23-24 and Heckel (2007). Blackwell (1999) pp 14-31 for a good summary of events and pp 18-19 for Philoxenus' identity; he captured Harpalus' steward and extracted a list of bribed Athenians; Pausanias 2.33.4-5.

452. The request for divine honours from Athens is most colourfully recorded in Aelian 2.19 and 5.12, Plutarch *Moralia* 804b and 842d, Polybius 12.12b.3, and Pausanias 8.32.1 mentions what is considered to be a shrine at Megalopolis dedicated to Alexander, housing a statue of Ammon. Discussed in full in Blackwell (2006). Hyperides *Against Demosthenes* 31 and Deinarchus *Against Demosthenes* 94 for Demosthenes proposing divine honours. Yet Timaeus (see Polybius 12.12b.3) suggested Domosthenes had voted *against* divine honours though the timing is uncertain; see Blackwell (1999) p 151 ff for discussion.

453. Tarn 1 (1948) p 42 for discussion of the presence of a cult to Ammon in Athens before 371/370.

454. Discussed in Worthington (2000) p 105. Demades' quip is preserved in Valerius Maximus 7.2.13.

455. Athenaeus 6.251b, Aelian 5.12 for Demades' fine, Plutarch *Phocion* 26.2. Diodorus 18.18.1-2 for his losing citizenship. Plutarch *Phocion* 23.2 reported that Phocion likened Lesothenes' inciting speeches to a cypress tree, large and towering but bearing no fruit. See chapter titled *Babylon: the Cipher and Rosetta Stone* for Leosthenes' statement on Macedonian disarray following Alexander's death from Plutarch *Moralia* 336e-f. Hyperides *Funeral Oration* 6 or *Hyperides over Leosthenes and his Comrades in the Lamian War* for the eulogy to Leosthenes.

456. Quoting Borza from Wilken (1931) Introduction p IX.

457. Quoting De Polignac (1999) p 3, translation by Ruth Moriss.

458. For Alexander's refusal at Opis to let veterans return to Macedonia with their Asiatic children,

Arrian 7.12.2 and for the eighty marriages at Susa, Arrian 7.4.6, and 7.4.8 for the 10,000 total Macedonians who had married Asian wives, a suspiciously high number.

459. According to Aeschines *Against Ctesiphon* 162 and Marsyas FGrH 135/6 F2, Demosthenes sent Aristion to Hephaestion to secure 'immunity and reconciliation' from Alexander. See Heckel (2006) p 110 for further discussion.

460. See Worthington (2000) p 101 for a summary of Demosthenes' activity in 323/4.

461. Plutarch 7.7; translation from the Loeb Classical Library edition, 1919. Acroamatic: those to be disseminated orally only, implying only the elite initiates were worthy of hearing them.

462. Plutarch 55. The letter had allegedly been sent to Antipater, the regent in Macedonia.

463. Aristotle discussed in Thomas (2007) p 197. These lost works, supposedly dedicated to Alexander, discussed in Ober (1998) p 348.

464. Aristotle *Athenian Constitution* 2.2. Quoting the introductory note prepared by Ian Johnston for students in Liberal Studies and Classics classes at Malaspina University-College, Nanaimo, BC, Canada, released May 1999. Diogenes Laertius *Aristotle* 13 for the 'double criterion of truth'. Athenaeus 9.398e for Aristotle's grant from Alexander, though when this was made is uncertain.

465. Aristotle *Politics* 3.1285a-b, translated by Benjamin Jowett 1885. WS Greenwalt in Carney-Ogden (2010) pp 115-163 for discussion on Aristotle's position on Macedonian politics.

466. Aristotle *On Monarchy* only permitted absolute monarchy if the ruler was intelligent and enlightened beyond his subjects to the extent that a man exceeds an animal's intelligence. For the five subcategories see Aristotle *Politics* 3.1284b35-1285b33; discussed in Roisman-Worthington (2010) p 380.

467. Diogenes Laertius *Plato* 81-90.

468. Athenaeus 12.537e cited Ephippus as claiming Alexander dressed as Ammon, Artemis and Hermes. Tarn (1948) p 97.

469. Blackburn (2006) p 18.

470. Plutarch *Demetrius* 1.7.

471. Oedipus answered the 'many footed' riddle of the sphinx and thereby avoided strangulation. His answer was that man was born on all fours, walked with two feet in life and ended with three, when a walking stick was required. Recorded by Apollodorus *Library* 3.5.8. This was a standardisation of an extremely old legend and probably represents just one possible version of the riddle.

472. Berossus' *Babylonaika* was written around 290-278 BCE for King Antiochus *Soter*, son of Seleucus. It is not extant, but a number of classical writers referenced it in their works. See discussion of the dating of Berossus in Pearson (1960) p 231; he dated Berossus' writing to between 293 and 281 BCE. Drews (1975) p 50 ff for Berossus' contribution to 'history'.

473. Excerpt from the *Book of Arda Viraf* (alternately *Arda Wiraf* or *Wiraz*) 3-7, a Zaroastrian religious text from the Sassanid era, written in Middle Persian; translation from CF Horne *The Sacred Books and Early Literature of the East, Volume VII: Ancient Persia*, 1917.

474. Seven feet if the Attic cubit was being referred to; at 18.25 inches it was longer than the Macedonian cubit of 14 inches. Diodorus 17.88.4, Arrian 5.19.1, Plutarch 60.12 agreed King Porus was over seven feet tall, i.e. 5 cubits. Tarn (1948) p 170 suggests the Macedonian cubit was being referred to. Arrian 5.18-19. Diodorus 17.89.1 reported that two of Porus' sons were amongst the 12,000 Indian dead.

475. Verbrugghe-Wickersham (2000) for discussion of the writings of Berossus and Manetho and their influence.

476. Quoting Momigliano (1966) p 134.

477. Following the details in Hadjnicolaou (1997) for the printed editions in France.

478. Nicolas de Soulfour *L' Alexandre francois,* 1629.

479. Quotation from N Beauzée *Histoire d' Alexandre Ie Grand par Quinte Curce*, 1781.

480. Dante *The Divine Comedy: Inferno,* Circle 7, Canto 12.

481. Rodrigo Borgia took the title Alexander VI in admiration. He, and later Alessandro Farnese, pope from 1534 to 1549 under the name Paul III, decorated the Vatican apartments with scenes from Alexander's life. See discussion in Hadjinicolaou (1997).

482. Avcioğlu (2011) p 126 for emulation of Alexander by Louis XIV and Mehmet II.

483. Following Voltaire *Rights,* 1771.

484. Machiavelli *The Prince* chapter 17.

485. See discussion of Machiavelli's use of Polybius' political theories in McGing (2010) pp 215-216 and Brouwer (2011) pp 111-132.

486. Nicolo Machiavelli *Discorsi (Discourses on first ten years of Titus Livy),* translated by Ninian Hill Thompson, 1883, 13.19.

487. Discussed in Hale (1961) p 139.

488. Droysen (1877); detailed discussion of biographer opinions in Green (1974) p 481 ff.

489. Tarn (1948).

490. Schachermeyr (1944).
491. Badian (1958), Green (1974) p 487.
492. Green (1974) p 487. Lane Fox's view appears to have influenced Oliver Stone's 2004 movie to which he consulted; discussed by G Nisbet in Carney-Ogden (2010) pp 217-231; 'historiophotic' was a term coined by Hayden White in 1988 in his *Historiography and Historiophoty*, American Historic Review 93, to describe the 'representation of history' and our thoughts about it in visual images and filmic discourse.
493. Polybius 12.23.5.
494. Heckel (1993), final page of the review.
495. Atkinson (1996) pp xvi and p 218, and Atkinson (1963) p 125.
496. Diodorus 13.68.5 and Plutarch *The Comparison of Alcibiades with Coriolanus* 6.
497. A good summary of the relative views of these modern historians is given in Baynham (1998) pp 63-66.
498. *Ekphrasis* derives from the Greek 'out' (ek) 'to speak' from *ekphrazein,* and a term often used to capture the rhetorical devices in artistic expression. See chapter titled *The Precarious Path of Pergamena and Papyrus* for discussion of medieval text supplements.
499. *Alexander at the Tomb of Cyrus* by Giovanni Benedetto Castiglione, ca. 1650, *Alexander and Porus* by Charles Le Brun (1619-1690), *Alexander the Great and the Fates* by Bernadino Mei (ca. 1612-1676) *The Tent of Darius* by Charles Le Brun was originally titled *Les Reines de Perse aux pieds d'Alexandre.*
500. Displayed at the Alte Pinakothek, Munich.
501. Now at the Maritime Art collection in Greenwich.
502. Alexander recited from the *Andromache* at Medius' *komos;* see Athenaeus 12.537b, fragment on Robinson (1953) p 89. Athenaeus 10.44p for the size of Alexander's drinking cup and *Iliad* 11.632-637 for Nestor's cup; Diodorus 17.117.1 also term the cup 'huge'. Discussed by F Pownall in Carney-Ogden (2010) p 64. The fragment is from Eubolos' *Semele* of *Dionysus.*
503. Lucian *How to write History* 1-2.
504. Fragment 141, for full discussion of the Euripides' fragments, see translation and discussion in Collard-Cropp-Gilbert (2004) p 153.
505. Discussed at length in the chapter titled *Babylon: the Cipher and Rosetta Stone.*
506. Justin 12.13.3-7 for the Magi warning and Alexander's diversion past the 'uninhabited' Borsippa; the Babylonian surviving documents however suggest Borsippa was still a trade centre, see Bosworth (200) p 220 for detail. Also Arrian 7.16.5-7, Plutarch 73.1 and Diodorus 112.2-5 who terms them Chaldeans as opposed to Magi. Plutarch *Moralia* 466d or *On Tranquility of Mind* for Anaxarchus' belief in innumerable worlds following Democritus' school.
507. Justin 12.15.1-3 for his reflection that most of his line died before reaching thirty. See chapter titled *Mythoi, Muthodes and the Birth of Romance* for detail of Cleophis. Arrian 7.14.5; Alexander is said to have destroyed the shrine of Asclepius at Ecbatana at Hephaestion's death, complaining to envoys from Epidaurus that Asclepius had 'not treated me kindly, for he did not save my friend I valued as my own life'; translation by A de Selincourt, Penguin edition, 1958.
508. Homer *Iliad* 11.518 for Asclepius 'the blameless physician'; better 'faultless' or 'capable'.
509. Jaeger (1939) p 47 for the *Achilleid* discussion; some scholars believe the original title. Statius wrote an unfinished *Achilleid* as a life story of the hero in the 1st century.
510. Homer *Iliad* 1.1.
511. Quoting from *Hyperides over Leosthenes and his Comrades in the Lamian War.*
512. For references to the Elysian Fields see Homer *Odyssey* 24.5-9 and Virgil *Aeneid,* 6.54. For Pythagorean belief in immortality see Riedweg (2002) p 37. Hesiod termed the Elysian Fields the Fortunate or Blessed Isles, which were, like the Elysian Fields, supposedly located at the western edge of the Earth.
513. Castor and Pollux, or Polydeuces, were the Dioscouri, twin brothers yet of different fathers; Castor was immortalised by his father, Zeus, and begged him to let Pollux (son of the mortal Tyndareus of Sparta) share his immortality with him. Alexander did sacrifice to them; see Plutarch 50 describing the death of Cleitus.
514. The *Book of Daniel* 3.1 described a golden statue erected by Nebuchadrezzar II on the plain of Dura near Babylon. It was purportedly 90 feet tall.
515. The Egyptian titles are discussed in de Mauriac (1949) p 112 quoting FA Wright *Alexander the Great,* 1934, pp160-161. Also Anson (2013) p 105 for the inscriptions.
516. For details of the *Book of the Dead* see Casson (2001) *Egypt* pp 116-117. For the progression of gods see Manetho's *Dynasties of Gods, Demigods, and Spirits of the Dead* as preserved in Eusebius' *Kronographia.*
517. Herodotus 8.109-110. Plutarch *Themistocles* 29.3; Artaxerxes II's reference to Themistocles as a 'subtle serpent'.
518. *Ostraka* were potsherds inscribed with the names of those to be banished; used by citizens casting the vote. Plutarch *Themistocles* 7.

519. Aristotle *Poetics* 13.1453a 27-30 termed Euripides 'the most tragic of the poets'.
520. Full description of the funeral hearse in Diodorus 18.26-28.
521. Diodorus 18.27.3-4 for the axle design and 18.28.1 for the team of road menders. The funeral carriage was such a spectacle that spectators from nearby cities flocked to witness its passing; loud due to the bells attached to the sixty-four mules. Stewart (1993) p 216 for its dimensions.
522. Stewart (1993) p 294.
523. See Heckel (2006) p 315 and text note 383 for Judeich's view that Laomedon was the original occupant. K Schefeld convincingly made a case that the coffin was constructed before Abdalonymus' reign; see his review of Brunilde Sismondo Ridgway in the *American Journal of Archaeology* 73.4, October 1969, p 482. Anson suggested Alexander's original sarcophagus would have been shipped up the Euphrates to Thapsacus and overland from there to Alexandria; see Anson (1986) p 213. Anson (2013) p 150 for the background to Abdalonymus; Curtius 4.1.16-26, Diodorus 17.47.1, Justin 11.10.7-9 for the Vulgate story.
524. Diodorus 18.26-28.
525. Chapter titled *Lifting the Shroud of Parrhasius* for Perdiccas' role in Syria and his possible links to the sarcophagus. As Heckel-Jones (2006) p 91 points out, there is no proof, only supposition, that this depicts the murder of Perdiccas.
526. Thucydides 2.41 from Pericles' panegyric to the Athenian dead, translated by Richard Crawley, 1910, based on the earlier translation by Cannop Thirwall and published by JM Dent and Sons.
527. Fraser (1996) pp 1-46 for discussion of the Alexandrian lists of the cities of Alexander. Modern excavations suggest the new 'Alexandrias' were little more than renamed Asiatic cities.
528. Justin 12.5.13 for Alexandria on the Tanais, also Strabo 11.7.4 and Plutarch *Moralia* 2.352e, 341c; discussion in Pearson (1960) Introduction p 14. The Jaxartes was later misidentified as the Tanais, the modern Don in Russia and then considered the boundary of Europe and Asia. Anson (2013) p 183 for 14 Alexandreias. Plutarch *Moralia* 438e claimed Alexander established seventy settlements and a minimum of six named after himself. Justin 12.5.12-13 claimed 13 cities (unnamed) were founded in Bactria and Sogdia alone. Green (1974) p 412 for 'and a market'.
529. Arrian 4.1.3-4 for the intentions for Alexandria Eschate and 5.29.5 for the damage by monsoon rains. Quoting Tarn 1 (1948) p 100.
530. Xenophon *Cyropaedia* 6.1.16.
531. For the twelve monuments see Arrian 5.29.1-3, Diodorus 17.95; Curtius 9.3.19. Diodorus stated 75 feet high, i.e. 50 cubits. Arrian 1.16.4 for the twenty-five Companion statues later taken to Rome in 146 BCE. For the bronze statues at Dion, Arrian 1.16.4, Plutarch 16.8, Velleius Paterculus *Roman History* 1.11.3-4. Polyaenus 4.23 for the steps in Mt. Ossa.
532. Theopompus wrote a scathing letter about Harpalus' behaviour (and Alexander's *hetairoi*); recorded in Athenaeus 595a-c. Diodorus 17.108.5 referred to it as an expensive tomb of the Attic type'; Flower (1994) pp 260-261 for discussion.
533. Arrian 7.7.7 for the removal of weirs; also Strabo 15.3.4, 16.1.9 ff; here the restrictive nature of the cataracts on trade is mentioned though it was clear Alexander's navy could not sail downriver either. The sentiment reiterates Bosworth (1988) p 159.
534. See Hannah (2005) pp 91-94 for discussion on the recalibration of the Babylonian calendar.
535. Quoting Billows (1990) pp 5-6 and Tarn 1 (1948) p 121.
536. Plutarch *Apophthegms* or *Sayings of Kings and Commanders* 207D8, based on the translation by E Hinton, William W Goodwin, Little Brown and Co., Boston, 1878.
537. Quoting Green (1970) p 258.
538. Van der Mieroop (2004) Part 1, p 3.
539. Winn Leith (1998) p 285.
540. Xenophon 7.5.31.
541. Arrian 4.28.2 and 5.1-3 for his doubt surrounding the legends of Heracles and Dionysius and India, and Arrian 6.28.2 for the epithet Lord of the Triumph. According to Aristophanes' *Frogs* Dionysus visited Hades to bring Euripides back to the living, so disenchanted was he with the state of Athenian tragedians. 'Ivy-wreathed' following the *Homeric Hymn* to Dionysus.
542. See discussion in Robbins (2001) p 91.
543. Herodotus 2.120 gave the alternative version of Helen's Egyptian captivity.
544. Herodotus excerpted from Book 2.116 and 2.120, translation by George Rawlinson, Everyman's Library 1910. *Iliad* 9.26 and 14.74-81 for Agamemnon's plea.
545. See discussion in Tarn (1923) pp 26-27 citing Plutarch *Moralia* 329c or *Fortune* 6. See Tarn (1948) pp 399-449 for his full treatise on 'brotherhood'. Bosworth-Baynham (2000) pp 97-135 for a detailed discussion of Panhellenism. 'Loving cup' came from Eratosthenes and referred to the drinking cup used at the Opis reconciliation ceremony and formerly belonging to Darius; see Tarn 1 (1948) p 116.
546. Arrian 7.11.8-9, Oxford World Classics edition, 2013, translation by M Hammond. Curtius 10-

3.10-14 which likely echoed Roman themes and Curtius' vocabulary; see discussion in Atkinson (2000) pp 134-139, Bosworth *A in the East* (1996) pp 2-4 for Plutarch's influence on later interpretations of Alexander's racial intentions. As examples of the use of breaking barriers or doors, Seneca *Epistle* 119.7 *'mundi claustra perrumpit'*, Lucretius *De Rerum Natura* 1.70 ff *'effringere portarum claustra'*. For discussion of the literal meaning of the Greek *homonoia* see de Mauriac (1949) pp 104-114.

547. See chapter titled *Comets, Colophons and Curtius Rufus* for discussion of Curtius' identity and publication period.

548. Droysen (1877) p 4.

549. Quoting from Tarn-Griffith (1952) p 1.

550. See discussion by Grimal (1965) p 5.

551. Diogenes Laertius *Aristotle*. Also Athenaeus 15.696a. Hermias of Atarneus ruled Assus and was a student of Plato. He invited philosophers to study there. Aristotle had been there for three years and had married Hermeias' niece, Pythias.

552. An *epipolesis* was a troop review, typically pre-battle, in which a rousing speech was given to boost morale.

553. Quoting Thomas (1968) p 258.

554. Pausanias 4.35.4 for identification of Procles and his dating see Hernandez (2009). Livy 35.14, Appian *Syrian Wars* 10-11, Plutarch *Flaminius* 21 for the meeting at Ephesus; Livy and Plutarch recorded different opinions on rankings. According to Appian, Hannibal and Scipio met at the court of Antiochus III. He preserved their discussion on who was considered the greatest of generals. However the meeting, as Baynham (1999) pp 19-20 explains, is historically unlikely. Plutarch *Pyrrhus* 8.2 confirmed Hannibal's opinion, rating Scipio second and himself third. McGing (2010) pp 96-97 for discussion of Polybius' attitude to treason and plots. Lucian *Dialogues of the Dead* 25 embellishes the conversation through third parties. The relation of the *Alexandreis* to the *Africa* discussed in Townsend (1996) Introduction p 17.

555. The first recorded use of the epithet 'great' came from the Roman playwright Plautus *Mostelleria* 775 in ca. 200 BCE. It may of course have been in use before but Greek literature did not employ it and was somewhat more hostile to his memory.

556. Plutarch *Moralia* 840c-d for the founding of a school of rhetoric, and Plutarch *Aeschines* for his fate. Aeschines may have been at Ephesus until Alexander's death.

557. This is unlikely to be true and yet is suggests a death sufficiently close to the date to have made the claim that appeared in Plutarch *Moralia* 717c, Diogenes Laertius *Diogenes* 11. The *Suda* claimed the same.

558. Quoting Gudeman *Greeks* (1894) p 57.

2

SARISSA DIPLOMACY: MACEDONIAN STATECRAFT

Would Alexander's generals have permitted their king to die without formally recognising their right to govern the new empire?

The most prominent of Alexander's Bodyguards and Companions became kings and governors of vast regions of the former Persian Empire and beyond. They were schooled in the diplomatic and military revolution of Philip and Alexander and were immersed in their irrepressible brand of Macedonian statecraft.

We review the rise of the Macedonian military machine that swept all before it to highlight the extraordinary careers of the *Diadokhoi* whose dynasties survived until the arrival of Rome. Then we ask: would these ambitious and talented men have acquiesced to Alexander leaving them nothing but the challenge of fighting it out for a fragment of an empire they had battled for a decade to acquire?

'Aeschines, if you can name any person under the sun, Greek or barbarian, who remains unharmed by the dominance of Philip, first, and now of Alexander, well so be it.'[1]

Demosthenes *On the Crown*

'Tyche and Philip were master of the deeds. Things turned out not as we prayed, but as Philip did.'[2]

Aeschines *On the False Embassy*

'It is a general rule of human nature that people despise those who treat them well, and look up to those who make no concessions.'[3]

Thucydides *The Peloponnesian War*

'… it is no longer proper to count these exceptional men a part of the state; for they will be treated unjustly if deemed worthy of equal status, being so widely unequal in virtue and in their political ability: since such a man will naturally be as a god among men… but there can be no law dealing with such men as those described, for they are themselves a law…'[4]

Aristotle *Politics*

'An old saying has been handed down that it is not men of average ability, but those of outstanding superiority who destroy democracies.' Diodorus was quoting an adage that had its roots in the advice shared by the late-7th century tyrants of Miletus and Corinth: 'Slay the tallest stalks to protect the crop', a lesson more colourfully articulated by Livy in a warning from the legendary Tarquin the Proud, the last king of Rome: crop the tallest poppies to stave off revolt.[5] And as Aristotle was carefully reminding Athens in his chapter headed *Politics,* the tallest of them all *were* Philip and Alexander: the 'lions among the hares'.[6]

Aristotle's *Athenaion Politeia*, one of many political treatises attributed to him, appears to have been constructed when Alexander was campaigning deep in Asia (if not before). His enthusiasm for Solon's reforms of 594/3 BCE and those that followed – which laid the foundations of the republic if not actually sowing the seeds of democracy – seems to have waned, however, by the time Aristotle's *Politics* appeared.[7] For by then, the civil and political community in Athens, the *koinonia politike,* operating through the Assembly, the Council and the Areopagus (though still incorporating much of the Solonian Constitution) was under the thumb of Aristotle's client and patron: the Macedonian monarchy. Philip II, 'as if looking from a watchtower', had attacked liberties across Greece, and now his former general, Alexander's regent Antipater, was strangling any notions of true political freedom; the fire of democracy had all but been snuffed out in the Athenian prytaneion.[8]

Aristotle's argument – that an exceptional individual is naturally above state law – may have been written to justify the very existence of the remarkable father and then his campaigning son on his 'undemocratic' Eastern campaign. For by now, the Graeco-Persian world revolved around the 'star of Macedonia', as Curtius referred to him, as history generally attributes the maelstrom that swept from Pella through the Persian heartlands to Alexander alone.[9] Yet that would be a hugely flawed conclusion. Allocate a part of the storm to his father who galvanised Macedonia into a cohesive spear-won military state with an army able to campaign in both summer and winter (until then a uniquely Spartan ability due the enslaving of the Messenians, the 'helots'), and credit a further share to his gifted companions, and you have a more accurate picture of the energies at work in that turbulent generation.[10] Moreover, we have evidence that by 323 BCE the sun was beginning to set on the Pellan imposter who slept in the Great King's bed, for contrary to the utopian vision Onesicritus may have espoused in his *Alexandrou Paideia*, Alexander's empire may have been something approaching a dystopia at the time of his death.

The Macedonian conquest of the East is better remembered than the extraordinary period that followed because it was the more easily understood, like the stark-chiselled emotions and clean-sculpted motives that underpinned war in the *Iliad*. Alexander's *anabasis* had shape, direction and cause, operating under the banner of 'revenge for the earlier Persian invasions of Hellas', just as Philip's brief foray into Asia had been punishment for the 'profanation of temples'.[11] To this grievance Alexander had added accusations of the Persian gold backing assassination of his father. The Successor Wars lacked these public-relations-friendly soundbites and yet they were perpetuated by a group of mighty personas almost unparalleled in history: the new Myrmidons of a reborn Achilles.[12]

In a sense, the first generation of *Diadokhoi* were the *true* offspring of Alexander, or as Justin termed them, 'the many Alexanders of Macedonia', a uniquely privileged generation of 'prefects who became princes'.[13] They had learned their trade alongside their king, some as *syntrophoi* at the Pellan court, and as a cohesive unit they proved unstoppable in the decade that saw the Macedonian military machine advance as far as India. Its leadership became a true meritocracy: the unfortunate had fallen in battle, the non-performers had been sidelined, the indiscreet and loose-tongued were executed, and the frailer constitutions died on the march. Those who survived both the campaign *and* Alexander, were tough, brutal, ambitious, and most importantly, they proved to be cunning politicians.

On few occasions could a circle of men so influential to the fate of an empire have congregated in a single assembly hall or king's campaign pavilion. Perhaps only the Roman Senate attended at once by Julius Caesar (100-44 BCE), Mark Antony (83-30 BCE), Cicero, Crassus (ca. 115-53 BCE), Clodius (ca. 93-52 BCE), Pompey the Great (106-48 BCE), Lucullus (ca.118-56 BCE) and Cato the Younger (95-46 BCE) could compare. But as Cicero warned: 'The shifts of Fortune test the reliability of friends'.[14] They *were* friends at times, drinking at 'Lucullan' banquets that had replaced the Macedonian *symposia*.[15] And they became bitter enemies, as Alexander's Bodyguards had before them, for 'there is no fellowship inviolate, no faith is kept, when kingship is concerned'.[16]

MARRIAGE *KATA POLEMON*: THE POLITICS OF SURVIVAL[17]

The story of the rise of Alexander and the *Diadokhoi* began with Philip II, possibly the twenty-fourth king of the Argead line (the historicity of the early founding kings is uncertain) who, according to Demosthenes' orations from the auditorium of the Pnyx, united '… the functions of a general, a ruler and a treasurer…' He saw Philip as the absolute autocrat: commander and master of everyone and everything.[18] If Plutarch considered Cicero as the first 'professional' politician to commit himself seriously to such a job, it was simply because he did not biograph Philip whom Cicero himself rated above his ambitious son:[19] 'Philip, king of Macedonia, I observe, however surpassed by his son in achievements and fame, was superior to him in affability and refinement. Philip, accordingly, was always great; Alexander, often infamously bad.'[20]

In 359 BCE Philip, at the young age of twenty-three, was 'forced by the people to take on the kingship', as his nephew Amyntas IV, the son of his older brother Perdiccas III, was just a child; Philip, who had already administered a region of Macedonia in Perdiccas' reign, may have initially acted as Amyntas' regent, but he soon declared himself king in his own right.[21] At this point he was threatened on all fronts and by five 'would-be usurpers' that included three half-brothers.[22] Paeonians were pillaging in the north, and Illyrian forces, which had recently killed Perdiccas III along with 4,000 of his men, occupied Upper Macedonia with a history of installing puppet kings at Pella. Both Philip's father and his brother had been expelled by the Illyrians (Philip was once their hostage at around the age of twelve) and the still independent upper cantons could form an alliance against him at any time, spurred on by foreign interference or funded by the Persian purse.

Thessaly had already thrown out her Macedonian garrisons thanks to the Theban general-statesman Pelopidas, and King Berisades of Thrace was supporting the claim of the pretender Pausanias (of unknown royal connections) to the Macedonian throne, until blocked by the intervention of the Athenian general, Iphicrates. Not long before, and even closer to home, Ptolemy of Alorus (from another branch of the Argead house), allegedly had Philip's second brother, Alexander II, assassinated and installed himself as regent (some say king) with a complicit Queen Eurydice (Philip's mother), until Perdiccas III had him murdered in 365 BCE. The Argead house was as precariously placed as King Perdiccas II had been back in the 430s-420s BCE when similarly beset by enemies on all sides, and when the formidable young Illyrian king, Bardylis, had first appeared.[23] Even Philip's own father, the calculating King Amyntas III, had started paying tribute to stave off invasion in 390s BCE.

The Greek city-states dominated the coastal cities of Macedonia and Thrace, and Athens desperately wanted to regain control of the Macedonian-garrisoned Amphipolis (they would try to by installing the elderly compliant Argaeus on the throne – his second attempt). The strongly walled Amphipolis, founded as Ennea-Hodoi ('Nine Ways') by Athens in 465 BCE, bridged the Strymon River, control of which provided access to valuable timber resources and pitch extraction. The city had been deemed impregnable, that is until Philip began his siege in 357 BCE in the guise of reclaiming a once Heraclean – thus an Argead – possession, as the legendary family line traced itself back to the hero.[24] Philip proclaimed it 'independent' but in his own style: the pro-Athenian leaders were banished and it became a key Macedonian stronghold thereafter.

It was this challenging environment, in which the previous three Macedonian kings had died in just ten years, which forced Philip to resort to consorting for survival. He immediately commenced what would become a 'longstanding practice of fighting war through marriage', as Satyrus put it.[25] Six of Philip's seven wives we know of, 'a harem for political purposes', were all of noble families or from royalty dynasties surrounding the Macedonian state: Audata of the Dardanian Illyrian line of Bardylis (we *assume* she was his daughter or niece), Meda of the Getae line of King Cothelas in Thrace, Philinna and Nicesipolis of noble Thessalian lines (possibly of the Aleuadae and of Jason of Pherae), Phila of the Elimeote royal family, Alexander's mother Olympias of the Molossian royal family of Epirus, and a *possible* wife from the line of King Ataias of the Danube-region Scythians.[26] Philip's final marriage to Cleopatra, the niece of the Macedonian baron Attalus, would have been similarly calculated to provide political stability at home before he set off to campaign in Asia, though a true 'love match' was mentioned by Plutarch and Athenaeus.[27]

Philip would frequently display the unique political astuteness that was epitomised by these marriages, as well as his guile and understanding of men and their superstitions. He had, for example, once marched a coalition army to war by '... ordering all his soldiers to assume crowns of laurel as if under the leadership of a god.'[28] In his calculated dealings with Greece, Philip had manipulated affairs so that he was operating under the auspices of the Amphyctionic Council in the Third Sacred War against the Phocian defilers of Apollo's sanctuary and was eventually given Phocis' two seats on the council. The Macedonian *hegemon* was now representing the justice of thirteen Greek peoples and under the blessing of a god, a cause possibly aided by Theopompus' publishing of *On the Funds Plundered from Delphi*.[29]

Although branded a slayer of Greek democracy after his victory at Chaeronea in 338 BCE, Philip had, nevertheless, become the archon of Thessaly for life, protector of shrines for the Hellenic and Amphictionic Leagues, and he was voted *promanteia* (broadly 'privilege of priority at ceremonies') in 346 BCE by the Delphians who erected a statue in the sanctuary of Apollo where he also presided over the Pythian Games; Philip was truly the consummate politician.[30] The Macedonian king's manipulative arsenal of weapons had included, to quote Fredericksmeyer, '… diplomacy, bribery, intimidation, deceit, subversion, sabotage, assassination, marriage, betrayal, war – and on occasion, he even scrupulously kept his promise.'[31]

Philip's success was well epitomised in Isocrates' call to him, rather than Spartan leadership, to head the Panhellenic invasion of Persia in his *Address to Philip*. His evidently clear intention to accept Isocrates' challenge spurred Artaxerxes III Ochus to arms and his invasion of Phoenicia and Egypt followed (345-343 BCE) providing immediate employment for many Greek mercenaries. Philip agreed to a non-aggression pact with the Persian Great King, apparently to buy himself time. But by the early 340s Philip had already more than trebled the size of his realm, ruling over the 'old' and 'new' kingdoms he would successfully integrate; the self-governing cantons of Orestis, Lyncestis, Tymphaea and Elimea came into the Pellan fold, and a fair degree of autonomy was at first permitted.[32] Although 'the possessions of the Macedonian kings were always more extensive than the lands inhabited by Macedonian citizens',[33] Philip now controlled everything to the immediate north of Hellas in a domain described as 'the first large land-empire in the history of Europe'.[34] It was a state of affairs that saw Athens align with Artaxerxes: gold crossed the Aegean and the city-states armed themselves; the battle at Chaeronea was one of the inevitable bloody results.

In 336 BCE Philip arranged the marriage of Alexander's sister, Cleopatra, to King Alexander Molossus of Epirus, the brother of Olympias who had been elevated and 'housed' by Philip at Pella for eight years. It was another political bond following Molossus' informal 'hostageship', though this time it had been arranged to outmanoeuvre Olympias herself, for she appears to have repudiated him in some way after his recent marriage to the niece of Attalus.[35]

Cleopatra's wedding festival, possibly coinciding with the annual *panegyris* that marked the beginning of the Macedonian New Year (autumn equinox), was to be a grand media event before the assembled (and now humbled) Greek world, and it was clearly designed to showcase Macedonia's newly acquired wealth and rapidly extending power. A statue of Philip was paraded after those of the twelve Olympian gods, a statement that at the least suggested he had their divine approval. Perhaps it implied still more; gone were the days following battle at Chaeronea when he had a slave call out thrice every morning, 'Philip you are human', to bring him down to earth.[36] But human enough he was and Philip was stabbed to death.

What Alexander inherited from his father was a formidable war machine and a network of alliances, even if continued border threats and treasury limitations restricted the size of any army that could be immediately transported to Asia. Philip had to rewrite the rules of engagement to avoid the fate of his predecessors and complete the military reforms that were probably initiated by his elder brothers.[37] At the head of his command chain was Antipater, veteran general and the leading statesman in Macedonia in the king's absence; he would become Alexander 'general over Europe'.[38] Left in Macedonia with a modest force of 1,500 cavalry and 12,000 infantry, probably from the more predictable Lower Macedonian cantons (Pieria and Bottiaea), he was variously referred to as the 'regent' (though neither Greek nor Latin have *direct* equivalents for that role) and *strategos*, thus a military administrator who was the caretaker, *epimeletes*, of the kingdom.[39]

Elsewhere Antipater is cited as holding a *hegemonia*, a regional or league command, whilst Plutarch suggested he, and the young Alexander before him, shared authority as a *kurios*, or one of the guardians of power, when Philip was on campaign.[40] In fact it seems more likely that Antipater shared power with Olympias while Alexander was in Asia – Antipater in a military capacity and she administratively as figurehead of the Argead royal house – before an irrevocable rift between them saw her take up residence in Epirus once more.[41] The title of Alexander's widowed mother is never specifically stated, though her *basileia,* regal authority, required little explanation; even Athens had shuddered to open captured correspondence between her and her king.[42]

Operating under Antipater were lesser governors and officers or *hyparchoi*, though this title later became a utility word denoting a variety of positions.[43] The terms relating to the relative *authoritas* attached to the Macedonian court nobles were employed less than clinically by the secondary sources, because Polybius, Diodorus, Livy, Curtius, and Arrian after them, were employing the phraseology associated with the 'class orders' at the Hellenistic courts and command structure of the Roman armies of *their* day.[44] The frequent use of the almost interchangeable titles of *strategos, prostates* (protector), *epimeletes* and *epitropos* (guardian or steward) that are peppered through the accounts of the Macedonian campaigns, still pose a challenge to definitive judgments on hierarchy.[45]

The Successor Wars are even less easily deciphered as self-elevations and unauthorised titular proclamations added further speculation to the legitimacy of roles, most visibly post-315 BCE when the 'royalists' who had sided with Perdiccas had finally been wiped out. Some of the ambiguity dissipated, however, once Alexander's line was all but terminated (ca. 309/308 BCE), and when the title 'king', *basileus*, an honorific inherited from obscure and possibly non-Indo-European origins adopted by Bronze-Age Greeks, was formally assumed by the dominant *Diadokhoi* (ca. 307 BCE onwards).[46]

THE *PEZHETAIROI* AND THE ARGEAD ANVIL

The 'Macedonian revolution' was perhaps the most comprehensive modernisation and development of Hellenic warfare since Mycenaean times. The archaic soldiers of Homeric days, who wore boar-teeth-and-tusk helmets and loose bronze panoply as exhibited in the Dendra find, were protected by the body-sized ox-hide figure-of-eight shields, or the later *dipylon* that adorned the pottery from the period – that is, when warriors were not depicted in 'heroic nudity'.[47] Shaft-grave finds at Mycenae dating to the so-called 'Palace period' (roughly 1450-1350 BCE) reveal elaborate Minoan-influenced weaponry with flint and obsidian blades from Egypt and Cycladian Melos; this represented an attempt to improve on softer bronze when iron was still rare and its production a Hittite monopoly.[48]

Defensive armour plating was found in a single warrior chamber tomb in May 1960 at Dendra close to Mycenae. It dates to the Mycenaean Palace period (1450-1350 BCE). The elaborate cuirass consisted of front and rear plate with neck guard, shoulder and arm guards. The plates are strung together with the widest at the bottom to facilitate leg movement. It has been compared to armour made for Louis XIV over 3,000 years late. A boar-tooth-and-tusk helmet is partially intact.[49]

At Mycenae we see the first signs of the armour of the Late Helladic period (1550-1050 BCE) including the heavy 'bell' corselet or the cuirasses of bronze plates joined at the sides, out of which would eventually emerge the classical *hoplites*.

Hoplites were armed with a spear (or two), short-sword (*xiphos*), a lighter 'muscle-cuirass' with *pteryges* (forming a protective skirt for the thighs) and a hardy bronze helmet, commonly of the menacing Corinthian design; this was a panoply apparently 'codified' between 725 BCE and 675 BCE.[50] For defence they carried the robust 3-foot-wide Argive wood-core shield (*hoplon*, though the plural, *hopla*, was often used for 'arms' in general), typically adorned with tribe-denoting letters or the symbols of their patron deity. This was now wielded more firmly by a rigid armband (the *porpax*) and leather grip (*antilabe*).[51]

The advances in Greek metalworking that enabled the more widespread production of hammered bronze helmets, which were increasingly lightened towards the *pilos* type, also led to the 'mass production' of bronze for facing the protective *hopla*. As a result, on the battlefield individual duels were superseded by the phalanx in which warriors advanced as an almost impenetrable wall of shields and spears. Hoplite warfare followed an extraordinary rigid framework that lasted for more than 300 years during which cavalry were never used as a shock weapon but were largely marginalised to guarding flanks and for harassing manoeuvres.

A Greek hoplite fighting a Persian on an Attic terracotta amphora dating to ca. 480-470 BCE. The *porpax* and *antilabe* of the Argive shield are clearly visible. Spears were thrust both underhand and overhand at shoulder height when in phalanx formation. The hoplite wears a *thorax* rather than a muscle cuirass, bronze greaves and horsehair-crested helmet with brim suggesting some Thracian or Phrygian influence. Metropolitan Museum of Art, New York, Rogers Fund 1906, online collection. www. metmuseum.org.

The formerly 'rigid' hoplite battle order had certainly started to evolve in Greece in the generation of Philip II which witnessed Epaminondas' victory at Leuctra in July 371 BCE when a reinforced fifty-deep infantry 'wedge', headed by the Sacred Band under Pelopidas, broke through the 'invincible' Spartan crescent phalanx. Until then Sparta had dominated

A Corinthian bronze hoplite helmet dating to ca. 700-500 BCE. The nose-guard and cheekpieces of the undecorated crestless helmet left only the eyes and mouth of its wearer exposed. The small holes around the edge anchored a leather lining that would have been sewn inside. Each close-fitting helmet of this type had to be custom made. Some finds have been 'killed' or rendered unusable by bending the cheekpieces outward, a distortion common among helmets found dedicated in sanctuaries, including those at Aegae.

set-piece battles with its hoplite formation that had mastered complex battleground manoeuvres such as the 'forward-bend' (*epikampe*), 'counter-march' (*exeligmos*) and 'back-wheel' (*anastrophe*). The era also saw Iphicrates' reforms which adopted a more unified approach to employing the different elements of a fighting force; he likened the phalanx to the 'chest and breastplate' of the whole 'body' of the army, with the cavalry representing the feet and the light-armed troops the hands.[52] But Philip's Macedonian war machine was about to revolutionise things further.[53]

Thucydides and Xenophon provided a picture of the early composition of the Macedonian army in the reign of Perdiccas II (which overlapped with the years of the Peloponnesian War, a conflict which had itself shaken up tactical thought) and in the era of Amyntas III: it comprised a small accomplished corps of heavy cavalry (who were nevertheless principally used as skirmishers, not in shock tactics), a modest number of hoplites, and a more numerous force of light troops from domestic tribes or client princes, and still organised by tribe as Nestor advised in the *Iliad*.[54] Between their reigns, King Archelaus I had intensified the reforms by building strongholds, defensive walls and new roads that carried both cavalry and infantry across an increasingly urbanised state.[55]

Philip's innovation saw a major change in the tactics of both foot soldiers *and* horsemen, lethal when working in unison, with the cavalry contingent increased five-fold compared to its strength under his predecessors.[56] His understanding of the *techne* of war had created a new cohesion that linked all parts of Iphicrates' 'body' together; the result was that the sum of the whole assaulting army was greater than the sum of those specialist parts. This became the 'blueprint' of Hellenistic warfare, which, together with his particular style of *metis*, his martial savvy and military cunning, was irrepressible.[57]

Philip's brigades of 'upper class' Companion Cavalry, perhaps originally some 600 in number, were later organised into eight territorially identified squadrons (*ilai*) of usually 200 horsemen, the most prestigious of which was the purple-cloaked and double-strength king's royal squadron (later capped at 300), the *ile basilike*; this was the vanguard *agema* which held a position of honour in the battle formation; the 1,800 cavalry that Alexander crossed to Asia with are thought to have been sectioned more or less this way, though Alexander later employed a command rotation that saw relative positions move.[58]

The unit numbers increased in Asia when two or more *ilai*, each commanded by an *ilarches*, formed a *hipparchiai* under the command of a *hipparchos,* with the larger squadrons later divided into two *lochoi* (companies) as new recruits arrived and units were amalgamated. However, vaguer references to 'light' and 'heavy' cavalry and to unit depth makes definitive cavalry assessments tricky, when, for example, the administrative infantry unit of one hundred, the *hekatostyes*, became interchangeable with *lochoi* after Darius fell in 331 BCE; it was a term Arrian seems to have used for an 'undifferentiated mass' that included non-Macedonians as well. Anaximenes' *Philippika* used a similar identification for unspecified infantry units.[59]

The Companion Cavalry and their manoeuvrable spear (*xyston*), and no doubt the *sarissophoroi* – the mounted lancers with longer thrusting spears – were by now practising flying wedges; Aelian Tacticus (2nd century CE) suggested a 200-man *ile* was comprised of four forty-nine-men *tetrarchiai* that rode in these formations, each under the command of a *tetrarchos*.[60] The Thessalian cavalry's versatile diamond (rhomboid) developed by Jason of Pherae may have played a part in its refinement, though Thracian and Scythian horsemen also reportedly deployed in wedges.[61] The wedged front (*embolon*) was a disposition which, according to Arrian, could uniquely penetrate a hoplite phalanx, defying the belief that cavalry were unable to attack organised infantry head on; Alexander may have spearheaded such a charge to penetrate the Theban Sacred Band at Chaeronea. But despite Arrian's claims, it remains more reasonable that wedges exploited weak points or gaps in an infantry line.[62]

It was at Chaeronea in Boeotia that the new Macedonian secret infantry weapon was also rolled out in front of the Greek world, when the eight-deep Greek allied ranks (including Athenians, Boeotians, Achaeans, Chacidians, Epidaurans, Corinthians and Megarans) fell on the armour-penetrating double-length infantry Macedonian pike. The Athenians, who had not fielded a land army in over twenty years for a major set-piece battle, were stunned.[63] And from then on the policies of Philip and Alexander were propagated most devastatingly through the shaft of the Macedonian *sarissa*.

The early development of the *sarissa* (literally a 'hafted weapon') is poorly documented. Diodorus claimed Philip had been inspired by the *pyknosis* – compact order – of the phalanx Homer alluded to at Troy, though this could equally have portrayed a traditional hoplite *synaspismos*,[64] the ultra-tight formation with overlapping shields, though much of the Homeric fighting was either peltast-styled or single combat rather than in disciplined ranks. But in the *Iliad* Hector's spear was described as being sufficiently long and 'far-shadowing' to be wielded with both hands.[65] Iphicrates had already lengthened the spears and swords of his men considerably (perhaps a necessity when he fought in Egypt), creating the lighter crescent-shaped-shield-bearing peltasts (named after the lighter shield, *pelta*) who defeated the shorter-sworded Spartans. Evidence suggests Thracians had also carried longer thrusting spears.[66]

The seeds of an idea to neutralise the traditional hoplite phalanx may have even been planted when Philip was a hostage at Thebes in his teens; he was in the hallowed company of the great generals Pammenes, Epaminondas and Pelopidas, themselves military innovators (of the infantry wedge) as well as accomplished philosophers. Alexander II, Philip's brother, had also been acquainted with Pelopidas (who had arbitrated for his mother in the regency, or kingship, of Ptolemy of Alorus, and assisted in ridding the kingdom of the pretender, Pausanias) and ideas may have filtered down. But 'when Epaminondas and Pelopidas prevailed, they did not kill anyone, nor did they enslave cities', claimed Plutarch.[67] Philip had innovated differently; thousands fell at Chaeronea and cities were later garrisoned.[68]

The period spent at Thebes was in fact Philip's second hostage term due to the immediate pressures on his older brothers, and it stood him in good stead. Given a regional command by Perdiccas III when he was just eighteen, he had Antipater and Parmenio drill the regiments with a precision never witnessed before when he himself became king. Philip hardened his men with forced marches over 300 stades (approximately 34 miles) during which they carried their own panoply and rations for thirty days; this still-waggonless army (and chariotless after Philip's run-in with the oracle of Trophonius) could out-range any opposition, while punishments of flogging and execution were levied on the undisciplined and any deserters.[69] Philip would have used the equivalent of *hoplomachoi*, seasoned hoplite tutors, but now trained in the new arts of the *sarissa* phalanx and its supporting parts.[70]

Similar loose references to infantry guards units as 'hoplites', 'light' and 'heavy' foot soldiers (which may have included skirmishers, slingers and peltasts), and to 'wedges', 'oblique phalanxes' and 'compact formations', provide challenging definitions.[71] Nevertheless, each unit would have been trained in the new Macedonian fashion to perfect complicated manoeuvres, including the oblique advance that created gaps in the enemy line and into which the cavalry wedges would fly with devastating effect.

According to Theopompus, the tallest and strongest infantrymen had been originally enrolled in the king's elite *agema* of the *pezhetaroi* ('foot Companions') who were once more generally referred to as the king's *doryphoroi* ('spear bearers'), though they later developed into the *hypaspistai* ('shield bearers').[72] Hypaspists were used on special missions that required a fast response and potentially hand-to-hand combat, but when involved in set-piece battles, led by an *archihypaspistes* with unit commanders below him, they were positioned closest to the king.

Like the Companion Cavalry they were retained all year round as the nucleus of a professional army. As instigated by his elder brother, Philip was now inviting the infantry into the former cavalry-dominated 'friendship' with the king in the form of elite personal brigades (generically, *epilektoi*) recognised by their privileged position on the right of the line in battle.[73] The king and his 'Companionate' would worship Zeus *Hetairos* and their status as 'friends' was reaffirmed at a festival of the *Hetairideia*. Hypaspist numbers grew from perhaps 800 initially under Philip to a corps of some 3,000 from which the king's personal infantry guard of 1,000 had been selected, though their panoply and weapons remain much disputed.[74]

Hypaspists were likely equipped as mobile hoplites (possibly carrying smaller shields) with laminated linen corselets worn since Homeric times (*linothorakes,* perhaps now with iron plates inside, as Pausanias thought linen was only good for hunting) and traditional 8-foot spears (if not also extended).[75] Their outfitting would again emulate elements of Iphicrates' reforms, and the association with the great Athenian general is fully understandable; Philip's father had ca. 386 BCE adopted Iphicrates, who was later to come to the aid of his mother Eurydice (ca. 367 BCE); according to the claim of Aeschines, Philip had known the innovating general since, literally, a babe in his arms.[76]

Under Alexander, either by the battle of Gaugamela in 331 BCE, or after the Macedonians returned from India (if not early in the Successor Wars, again, sources are ambiguous), an elite hypaspist brigade emerged – the Silver Shields (*Argyraspides*) – and they played a central role in the balance of power in the first eight years after Alexander's death.[77] Certainly Alexander's campaigning in the mountainous upper and eastern satrapies required a new mobile type of fighting; Diodorus mentioned a reorganisation of the army after the defeat of Darius III at Gaugamela, and this followed restructuring at Sittacene earlier in the year.[78] It is possible that an 'upper' and 'lower' canton mix was wisely being maintained when incorporating the new recruits, though the depopulation of the former by this overseas enlistment reduced the threat of a domestic uprising at home. Philip had himself initiated a programme of integration (and forced exchange) of the citizens of Lower and Upper Macedonia, and surely for similar reasons.

The foot-Companions, *pezhetairoi*, now re-emerged as the pike-bearers, the 9,000 strong heart of the infantry at the centre of the Macedonian battle line.[79] It was these phalangites who had been armed with *sarissai* and they initially formed up in manoeuvrable ten-by-ten boxed formations under Philip in what replicated Achaemenid order, with the ten-deep files (*dekades*) under the command of *dekadarches*. The unit depth was later increased to sixteen more in line with deepest traditional Greek phalanx formation (a doubling of its traditional eight).[80] In the *sarissa* ranks, sixteen files formed a *syntagma* of 256 men under a *lochagos*, and in turn, six *syntagmata* formed a *taxis* of 1,536 regionally-distinct infantrymen commanded by *taxiarchoi* originally selected from their local aristocrats (Perdiccas the Orestians and Lyncestians, Coenus the Elimeans, and Polyperchon the Tymphaeans, for example). Once again, '*taxis*' appears to have become a general term used for a major infantry command.[81] Later, in the Asian campaign, *chiliarchiai* of 1,024 men were frequently referred to, half of which had been a *lochoi* (or *pentakosiarchia*) of 512, charge of which represented a new intermediary command.[82]

Arrian's unique references to the so-called infantry ranks of *asthetairoi*, often interpreted as 'Close Companions', who would have occupied a position of honour and who seemed to hail from the cantons of Upper Macedonia, have sparked enormous debate: the prefix, '*ast*', has been variously interpreted as stemming from '*aristoi*', '*astoi*', '*asth*' or '*assista*', suggesting either 'best', 'townsman', 'star' or 'renowned', and here thought to refer to their geographical origins, shield adornment, or reputation. But were they the elite brigades of *pezhetairoi* – pike-bearers – or part of the more mobile *hypaspistai* and as lightly clad as the figures depicted on the Alexander Sarcophagus?[83] The term employed by Arrian, the 'so-called' *asthetairoi*, may suggest a non-contemporary tag or an earlier less-formal epithet. If the latter, these unique brigades may have been multi-role versatile units designed to form flying columns and protect *pezhetairoi* flanks (linking up with cavalry) and rear in set-piece battles; mercenary *thureophoroi* were employed in similar roles in the later Hellenistic armies.[84] Moreover, under this interpretation they could double, with other hypaspists, as fast mobile infantry on special missions where slow, inflexible pike-bearing brigades could not be usefully deployed.

When recounting events of 316 BCE and the mounted brigades of

Antigonus *Monophthalmos*, Diodorus additionally made a single mention of what might have been a cavalry equivalent, the *asthippoi* (which, however, varies between the manuscripts Parisinus gr. 1665 and Laurentianus 70,12), though this is usually amended to *amphippoi*, 'two-horse men', as Diodorus believed, in which case they were possibly a specialist squadron of the Tarentine cavalry.[85] But some scholars maintain that this *hapax legomenon* refers once more to 'closest cavalry' of an elite *agema*.

What is surprising is the lack of any reference to shield-bearing cavalrymen, who, for practical reasons, would have been equipped with a smaller, lighter *aspis* ('*asphippoi*'?); certainly carrying a shield would have been a distinction, as it appears (again from images, as well as texts) that the cavalry units depicted were *generally not* equipped with such protection, though the melees in which Alexander and his Companion Cavalry found themselves, with archers and missile-throwers concentrating on them, indicate he and his royal squadron must have had more protection than *linothorakes*. Scythian horsemen did carry small *pelta*-styled shields, as had the legendary Amazons.[86] Furthermore, we do still need some equipment identifier for the elusive 'heavy' cavalry, and in this light it is perhaps noteworthy that the *sarissophoroi*, cavalry equipped with the longer and heavier lance – the obvious contenders – disappeared from texts around 329 BCE.[87]

At Philip's death, Alexander became the commander-in-chief of a force that included some 1,800 Macedonian cavalry and a similar number of Thessalian horsemen with mounted auxiliaries, with 24,000 infantrymen, as well as engineers, speciality troops and mercenaries in pay; by the time he crossed to Asia he had under arms a total of some 32,000 infantry and 4,500 cavalry.[88] At the heart of this conglomerate army was the *sarissa*-bearing phalanx. What *does* remain clear amongst the varied weaponry and brigades listed on both sides of the Hellespont, is that the *sarissa* had developed into a deadly two-handed pike that outreached any hafted weapon in the Graeco-Persian world; its leaf-shaped blade could penetrate both shield and armour and nothing could withstand a phalanx frontal assault. The Macedonians now had a 'first-strike' capability that would become decisive.[89]

Fittingly, as the symbol of Alexander's ambition, the length of the *sarissa* is still controversially debated, though it is clear it was far longer than the traditional spear, *dory*, with its bronze 'lizard-killer' butt, *sauroter*, we first read of in the *Iliad*.[90] Depending upon whether ancient writers had adopted the attic cubit (cubit stems from the Latin *cubitum*, elbow, possibly *pechys* in Greek) or the *bematistes*' (map-makers') Macedonian cubit, the cornel (male cherrywood) shaft, or more likely a pike made of ash (Achilles' spear was of Pelion ash), may have been as long as 18 feet in Alexander's ranks, and it might have even varied in length to ensure sufficient blades protruded. A pike-head lodged in the wall of Tomb II at Vergina (after its wood shaft rotted away) suggests it had been at least 16.5 feet long.[91]

Evidence points to the *sarissa* being practically assembled in two halves and joined by an iron-coupling device; it was tapered towards the blade to balance it and reduce its overall weight, resulting in a gripping position closer to the butt.[92] In the hands of strictly drilled *pezhetairoi*, *sarissai* created an impenetrable 'porcupine' of blades (Curtius termed it an 'immovable wedge') that effectively rendered the classic *othismos aspidoon,* the traditional Greek shield-shoving tactic of the hoplite phalanx, redundant.[93]

Assuming the blades from a maximum of five ranks protruded through the Macedonian front, a disciplined system must have been developed whereby the exhausted front lines, which presented pikes horizontally, and the fresher rear lines with *sarissai* held vertically, could interchange during battle. Polybius, following Callisthenes, described how Alexander's phalanx formations reduced from thirty-two, to sixteen, to eight ranks deep as they approached enemy lines. The three rear ranks (whose blades would not reach past the front) were either on stand-by to relieve the front – it has been suggested that they possibly threw javelins using a free hand, but this seems impractical – or they were ready to extend the line in the way the deep-order *pezhetairoi* fanned out for battle at Issus; Arrian's *Tactics* suggested the rear ranks could manoeuvre through the intervals (the gaps between each man were perhaps 6 feet in 'open order' – though less than 2 feet in close order) to double the length of the front.[94]

With both hands employed in wielding the long pike, an eye had to be kept by the rear on possible infiltration, and this would have required agile lightly armed auxiliaries to dispatch any interlopers. Demosthenes confirmed the presence of *epikouroi* ('fighters alongside'), including archers, mercenaries and other auxiliary troops in the army's composition, making it very clear this was no longer one-dimensional warfare.[95]

The penetrative result of the *sarissa* ranks must have been devastating against soldiers sporting a leather or linen cuirass, though pike-bearers were relatively unprotected; they carried the smaller shield, the *pelta* or *aspis*, likely slung over their shoulder, then to the chest when engaging the enemy, and held in place by a *telamon*, a neck strap. In addition, *pezhetairoi* were issued a short sword (*kopis* or curved *machaira*), possibly to deal with any of the still dangerous wounded they were walking over or in case the line should break. There is mixed evidence for their protective corselets; the lighter (and cooler) *linothorax* seems to have been initially worn, though later in the campaign a *hemithorakion* (half-cuirass) was mentioned, suggesting backs were no longer protected.

An illustration, dating to ca. 1886, of Alexander's operation against Thracians in 335 BCE. The leaf-shaped blades of *sarissai* from five front ranks of the *pezhetairoi* could protrude, as Polybius reported, and the right side of the image captures the terror of the 'porcupine' of blades that an approaching line would be faced with when points would be variously aimed at the vulnerable necks and groins of the enemy infantry or in this illustration cavalry.[96]

Depictions we have show phalangites arrayed in Phrygian-styled and lighter *pilos* helmets, and Polybius additionally (and curiously) claimed that *sarissai* in upright position were effective in deflect incoming missiles.[97] The pike-bearers, then, were not 'heavy infantry' as such (as hoplites had been 'heavy' in shield and armour), except in the scale of the pike, and yet the king's confidence in their formation was never betrayed.[98] The bristling Macedonian phalanx became the proverbial 'anvil' on which the *exelasis*, the charge by Alexander's 'heavy' cavalry, dealt the decisive hammer-blow.

The Persian Great Kings still relied on intimidation and their 10,000 famed Immortals to cow the empire's satraps into submission. Yet Xenophon's *Anabasis* had already exposed Persian weakness in the face of well-organised Greek hoplites despite vastly superior Asiatic numbers, and this must have encouraged the Macedonian-led coalition when crossing the Hellespont. Persian satraps had hired Greeks as crack regiments and as bodyguards for just this reason, as Cyrus the Younger had in Xenophon's day.[99] But if the Greeks' heavy *hoplon* was unable to parry a *sarissa* assault, then the *gerrhon*-bearing (wicker-shielded), felt-capped, shorter-speared Persians, or even the Cardaces present at Issus and likened by Arrian to 'hoplites', did not stand a chance; this was akin to warfare against the

A Bronze Phrygian helmet ca. 350-300 BCE typical of those worn by the Macedonian *sarissa* bearers, the *pezhetairoi*, though the Thracian type is also mentioned. The helmet was formed from two sections with a riveted horizontal seam where the crown joins the bowl. The high crown afforded some shock protection against downward blows. This example has additional ear and jaw protection from the hinged face guards, with a neck guard at the rear.

unshielded (*anhoploi*).[100] As the Athenian general, Charidemus, had fatally warned a doubting Great King at Susa when in exile following the fall of Thebes, Darius' host might be 'glittering with gold and silver' but it now faced the iron and bronze of *real* soldiers; 'the hardiest and most warlike of Europe against the laziest and effeminate of Asia'.[101]

Mnesimachus, a comic poet of Philip II's day, had already spread effective propaganda: Macedonians dined on honed-up swords and swallowed blazing torches, they desserted on broken arrowheads and splintered spear-shafts; for pillows they used shields and breastplates and they wreathed their brows with catapults.[102] His lyrical description captured their formidability, for the *sarissa* phalanx of Philip, and then Alexander, would deal out death in victor-vanquished ratios still unheard of, if we are to trust even the most conservative of our sources' conflicting estimates. The total enemy numbers are of course questionable, but if Xerxes had brought 'millions' of troops to face the Greeks at Thermopylae, then 'interested' historians, those present at the battles or at the courts of participants, could hardly credit Alexander with facing less. Curtius pondered: 'Who counts troops at the moment of victory or flight?' This was perhaps stated with some irony, for a few paragraphs earlier he had listed the casualty numbers at Issus.[103] But following his second defeat in Cilicia in 333 BCE and noting the devastating effect of the *sarissa,* Darius apparently ordered an increase in the length of Persian swords and spears as well.[104]

Above any other feature of Alexander's army, the *sarissa* came to represent the indomitable face of Macedonian might. National unity was now significantly lubricated by the goldmines of Crestonia, Mygdonia (formerly occupied by the Thracian Edones), Damastion and Thrace, as well as silver from Mount Pangaeum now flowing into the state coffers at 1,000 talents a year (equivalent in value to 300,000 gold pieces) since Crenides, renamed Philippi, fell to Philip in 356 BCE. With the dissolution of the Chalcidian League after Olynthus fell in 348 BCE, new mineral deposits were won.[105] Iron ore, lead, molybdenum, magnetite, huntite, chrome and copper were mined for income and to pay for the accessories of war; this was an essential resource, because in the absence of any significant middle class, the infantry had to be armed, outfitted, housed and fed by the state. Although there is no firm evidence that Philip had formally remunerated his infantrymen, Curtius and Diodorus suggested 2-3 drachmas per day were paid to state levies, but when this commenced is unclear; of course the king additionally had the spoils of war to call upon to reward his men.[106]

Philip's new phalanx design was, in any case, a cheaper option than units of fully panoplied hoplites, enabling him to outfit a greater percentage of the recruiting pool of perhaps 30,000 men of fighting age in his consolidated Macedonia. Indeed, a spear butt-spike has been unearthed inscribed with the letters MAK suggesting the weapon *was* Macedonian government issue; comparison can be made with Athens where the state issued a hoplite shield and spear at the completion of the *ephebia*, the compulsory military training of eighteen to twenty-year-old citizens in garrison at the Piraeus.[107]

WHEN 'THE PRESTIGE OF OLD REFLECTS UPON THE PRESTIGE OF THE PRESENT'

The Macedonian *sarissa* worked its way inexorably through the Persian heartlands and in the set-piece battles with Darius III. Yet the upper satrapy revolts, which saw increasing mountain warfare, were a different affair altogether, and it was here that Alexander suffered his first setbacks, conspiracies and the resulting trials. But it was in India that the slackening tide finally turned and where the campaign bordered on disaster for both him and his battle-weary men. The king's popularity was in retrograde motion by which time the stature of Alexander's own Bodyguards – 'autocrats within their own armies long before the assumption of royal title' – along with the most prominent of his pan-provincial *strategoi* and the generals under them, were hugely influential, both regionally and amongst their own men.[108]

The one-eyed Antigonus had governed much of Asia Minor for over a decade by the time Alexander returned to Babylon, with talented satraps and officers about him. Parmenio had been vested with a pivotal administrative role at Ecbatana in Media, guarding the royal treasury and keeping communication and supply routes open between Asia Minor and the Near East. If he had survived the banquet at which Alexander ran him through, Black Cleitus might have assumed a similar role from Bactra (the capital of Bactria, modern Balkh) to govern the upper satrapies. And in Alexander's vanguard the voice of Craterus resounded loudly with the veterans.[109] These top-tier commanders, along with the Silver Shields veterans and their popular infantry officers, remained the conservative face of a Macedonian authority, which, for many of the rank and file, represented a far more coherent and attractive order than Alexander's increasingly indecipherable behaviour and erratic policy towards those he conquered.

As Macedonian regent and *hegemon* in Pella, Antipater had ably governed Greece, Thessaly, Illyria, Epirus, the upper cantons and neighbouring tribes for more than a decade in Alexander's absence, and his 'home army' may well have preserved a nationalist spirit that Alexander's troops in Asia were to lose, for in Macedonia it was still Philip II the army nostalgically recalled, and it was probably his *heroon*, not Alexander's, they saw standing at Aegae.[110]

In 331 BCE Antipater had crushed King Agis III of Sparta at Megalopolis, the city founded by the Arcadian League with Epaminondas' support; it was here that the 'prestige of old reflected upon the prestige of the present'. In the wake of defeat at Issus and following Alexander's rejection of his peace terms, Darius III had been trying to rouse Greece into an uprising against Macedonia; his envoy, Pharnabazus, was courting King Agis who had to sail to Halicarnassus in a single trireme to raise his money for a war that was ever more reliant upon mercenaries, in this case 8,000 escapees from Issus who had later seen action in Egypt. Lycurgan law prohibited Sparta's free citizens from engaging in moneymaking activity, whilst its *xenalasia* barred foreigners from entering the state (also denying its citizens the right to exit), so the reliance on Persian gold is not difficult to understand. Antipater received 3,000 talents from Alexander in Asia with which to equip a force to meet the threat, though whether it arrived in time has been questioned.[111]

Megalopolis was a significant victory, though Alexander deprecatingly labelled it a 'battle between mice' when he heard the outcome in Ecbatana in Media.[112] Antipater had been faced with a revolt by Memnon in Thrace at the same time, probably not coincidentally, and a substantial Macedonian army under Corrhagus, his *strategos* in the Peloponnese, had recently been annihilated.[113] If that threat was not enough, Alexander had just stripped his regent of more new recruits. The 'never more violent conflict' with Sparta took the lives of 5,300 of the 22,000 arrayed in their ranks, half of which were mercenaries; Curtius claimed hardly anyone returned to the Spartan camp without a wound. Some 3,500 of Antipater's 40,000 troops fell; this was a death toll larger than the Macedonian casualty numbers provided at the three major battles Alexander fought against Darius in Asia.[114]

The technique of grabbing hold of the *sarissa* with two hands to render it useless was still a generation away, and a defeated Sparta was finally forced to join the League of Corinth and its oath of non-aggression towards Macedonia.[115] The previously unwalled city would soon have a ditch and palisade, something unthinkable in Xenophon's day in which King Agesilaus II had been questioned on the lack of fortification; as a reply he simply pointed to his men.[116] A century after Alexander, by 222 BCE and the battle at Sellasia, Sparta would itself convert to the Macedonian style of warfare under Cleomenes III.[117]

Curtius alleged: 'Alexander was often heard to say that Antipater took upon himself the state of a king, that he was more powerful than a prefect ought to be, and that he was puffed up by the rich spoil and fame of his Spartan victory while he claimed as his own all that the king had given him.'[118] Although this may be polemical material added later by anti-Macedonian, or more targeted anti-Antipatrid hostility, it clearly suggests the extent of the regent's influence at home.[119]

Antipater's influence would increase following Alexander's death and the challenge that came when Greece tested his resolve in the Lamian War. Following a setback when initially outnumbered whilst waiting for reinforcements from Asia, and after a siege in the town of Lamia some 6.25 miles north of Thermopylae – where the Greek commander Leosthenes was nevertheless killed – Antipater finally met the Greek allied forces at Crannon in 322 BCE; supporting them were elements of the Thessalian cavalry, originally Antipater's allies by virtue of the legacy of Alexander's giving each of them a talent bonus when he dismissed them at Ecbatana. Their experience had already taken its toll; their recent defeat of the newly returned Leonnatus, who fought bravely in the region's swampy terrain, saw '... the first major defeat for Macedonian cavalry in over thirty years.'[120]

Although the Thessalian brigade bettered their Macedonian counterparts at Crannon, Antipater's overwhelming numbers, which had been boosted by the arrival of Craterus and 1,500 cavalry with 11,000 mixed infantry including 6,000 veterans who left Macedonia with Alexander twelve years before, saw the Greeks treating for peace. Their terms were initially refused, and the Thessalian cities were stormed one by one as Antipater and Craterus made their way south towards Athens.[121]

Following defeat at Lamia and abandoned by its allies, Athens was soon to suffer a further blow to her democratic heart. Antipater had seen his fill of Alexander's experiment in managing democracy from afar and he effectively turned its government into a plutocracy. Under the old system, citizens were still divided into the four property classes that emerged under Solon's reforms, regardless of their production. Antipater's new constitution demanded a property qualification of 2,000 drachmas, effectively disenfranchising 22,000 Athenian citizens and leaving just

9,000 'qualifying' voters in a city now garrisoned at Piraeus; estimates suggest the number of male citizens in the city had already dropped from some 60,000 in the day of Pericles to 30,000 by the time Demosthenes had first rallied the population against Philip.[122] The new regime was a far cry from Pericles' egalitarian declaration: 'Neither is property a bar, but a man may benefit his city whatever the obscurity of his condition.'[123]

Ploutos and *penia*, wealth and poverty, were once again at war. Those who were ostracised either emigrated or fled to Thrace with Antipater's encouragement, though they too were summarily branded 'warmongers and disturbers of the peace'.[124] The principal beneficiaries were the incorruptible Phocion *ho chrestos* ('do good'; he had turned down Leosthenes' military post) and the highly purchasable Demades, who, until he was implicated in plotting with the royalist Perdiccas in Asia, enjoyed Antipater's support; he managed to convince the Athenian Assembly to sentence the newly reconciled Hyperides and Demosthenes to death.[125] Demosthenes had once warned Phocion that he might be killed some day if the people became irrational. Phocion responded with: 'Yes, however, they would kill you if they came to their senses'; it seems they did.[126]

The Macedonian garrison entered the city while the celebration of mysteries was in progress and while the gods '... looked down with indifference upon the most grievous woes of Hellas.'[127] Although Antipater's son, Cassander, would halve the voting qualification in 318/317 BCE (to those possessing more than 10 *minae*, 1,000 drachmas) when garrisoning Munychia in the face of Polyperchon's promise of freedom, a democracy that had lasted in various guises from 507 BCE to 322 BCE, was now dead.[128] The panel of 6,000 male citizens over the age of thirty who had taken the solemn Heliastic Oath (which pledged impartiality), so providing the city with annual jurors (*diskastai*) at the People's Court with its annual magistrates and legislators (*nomothetai*), were subordinated to the law of the Macedonian pike. *Eisangelia*, denunciation, and the resulting charges of treason, now hovered over any loose recalcitrant tongues.[129]

IN THE WAKE OF THE WRATH OF PELEUS' SON

A famous Roman aphorism was used well by Tacitus: 'They plunder, they slaughter, and they steal; this they falsely name Empire, and when they create a desert, then they call it peace';[130] it is a disillusioned speech that could have been written in hindsight of the Macedonian campaign in Asia. Few men in history were ever universally loved to the point where they could rule out assassination, and as Demosthenes' opening oration declared, fewer still could have been as widely resented, feared and hated, outside his own campaign headquarters as Alexander by 323 BCE.[131]

With Alexander's passing, '… the civilised world, which had never before known only one master, now found itself in a novel situation, that of knowing no master at all.'[132] Momentum was lost and his fragile *sarissa*-enforced statecraft began to implode. The vacuum united everyone who had suffered his policies in quiet dissent, including the *pezhetairoi* who had carried the pikes on their shoulders for some 170,000 stades.[133]

The theme of the years either side of Alexander's death was uncertainty, both in Greece and Asia. The Persian Empire at its height had enjoyed an annual income of 30,000 talents, and sources suggest Alexander and his hubristic new order spent over 50,000 talents, equivalent to fifty years of Athenian total revenue, in his extravagant last two years.[134] Some 10,000 had repaid soldiers' personal debts, gold crowns were handed out at Susa (though surely not the 15,000 talents-worth claimed by Chares) and a further 10,000 talents paid off veterans, with a similar sum destined for temple restoration in Greece; presents, weddings dowries and a research grant of 800 talents to Aristotle added to the bill, as well as payments to orphaned children and their promised education.[135]

The compliant rajah of Taxila had even been given 1,000 talents and Harpalus had fled to Athens with a further 5,000 from the treasury, equating to some 140 tons in silver or 14 tons of gold, which alone (if in gold) would have required a minimum of thirty ships to transport it.[136] In comparison, the sacking of ancient Thebes in 336/5 BCE had apparently only yielded 440 talents, though this number probably related to the sale of prisoners alone.[137] Some 180,000 talents had reportedly been captured from Persian treasuries (estimated by Engels at some 7,290 tons of gold and silver) during Alexander's campaign, possibly the equivalent of one hundred billion dollars today; it would have been sufficient to run Athens and the Aegean for two centuries. Justin suggested 50,000 talents remained at Alexander's death.[138]

By summer 323 BCE and through the months preceding it, projects had been underway for an ornate funeral pyre for Hephaestion costing a further 12,000 talents, gargantuan Babylonian dockyards and the construction of 700 warships.[139] Opulent dinners with 600 to 700 Companions allegedly ran to 100 minae, if Ephippus is to be believed; that is 10,000 drachmas or well over a talent per meal. Once again, this appears an emulation of the Great King's dining arrangements, though these negative images painted by Ephippus might have been written to reinforce Greek bitterness during the Lamian War.[140] Alexander had appointed a Rhodian, Antimenes, to upkeep the roads in the region and he had already imposed a previously unenforced ancient duty of ten per cent on imported goods, a levy that must have been hugely unpopular; it was no doubt required to fund these heady projects in the face of a waning treasury.[141] This points to the collapse of the Achaemenid tax-raising network, which saw serfs paying great landowners, who in turn paid satraps who collected for the Great King; it was clear that the treasuries across the empire would soon be bled dry.[142]

The regional *strategoi*, and the king's Bodyguards above them who were impatient to administer a chunk of the new empire, knew it, and a confrontation was inevitable, though whether that was resolved with a poisoned cup we may never establish. Evidence suggests the common Macedonian would have considered the state treasury as a wealth *safeguarded* by the kings *for* the people, and that their tax revenues were similarly the property of a state they had a voice in through their representative landlords and nobles at the Common Assembly of Macedones. If so, Alexander's continued extravagance would have increased the resentment at Babylon from the men who had not yet been provided bonuses or anything more then a soldier's basic remuneration.[143]

In Alexander's wake, manpower drains, commodity price rises and famines resurfaced. The early years of the campaign saw little new coinage issued, for Philip II's gold staters, *Philippeioi*, and his silver tetradrachms had already become an international medium used from what is now Romania and Italy in the West, to Syria in the East, while bronze coinage was used for local transactions, the latter only possible under a stable and established monetary regime. But Alexander struck enormous quantities of what was expected to become the new reference currency in the late campaign. It is estimated that from 330 BCE onwards, after raiding the Persian treasuries, Alexander minted some 4,680 tons of silver in the form of *to basileion nomisma*, the king's coinage; this was an enormous circulation increase, with some coins remaining in use for up to a century. Unsurprisingly, an unusually large issue was minted in 324/323 BCE. But as time would show, the economies of his successors were no less ambitious, and they too needed trading platforms based on *nomisma*, metal-based money.[144]

By 301 BCE and the 'Battle of the Kings' at Ipsus, the cost of living had tripled over the previous century; wheat prices had risen from 2 drachmas per artaba (27 litres, a dry measure used in Persian and Egypt) in 404 BCE to 10 drachmas around 300 BCE, and oil prices had trebled.[145] The dramatist, Menander, suggested that any man whose land was mortgage-free was 'lucky', and overbearing loans at Ephesus, a city ruined by its continued support for Demetrius *Poliorketes* against Lysimachus in the *Diadokhoi* Wars, led to a suspension of ordinary law, so that palliative measures were invoked to stop the collapse of interest payments and other property obligations.[146]

Some 30,000 'campaign' talents, discounting gifts and bonuses, are reckoned to have re-crossed the Hellespont. The tombs at Emathia, Pieria and the 'Great Tomb' at Lefkadia display the extraordinary resources of even the undistinguished officer who made it home alive, despite the claims by Curtius that: 'The army which had defeated so many rich nations took from Asia more prestige than booty.'[147] This was, nevertheless, private wealth and not a state resource that could have more positively contributed to the nation's infrastructure. We have evidence that the quantity of 'unearned' wealth dumped on Macedonia had been hugely inflationary too, destabilising and devastating the rural markets that saw gold-to-silver ratios drop from (approximately) 15:1 to 10:1, when supply of manufactured goods could often not meet the demand. Philip's expansion of the mines at Mount Pangaeum, which had once provided the Athenian Peisistratus (died ca. 527 BCE) with much of his wealth, and the associated *argyrokopeion*, the gold mint at Amphipolis, had already contributed to the inflationary trend.[148]

A more obvious cause of upheaval in Macedonia itself was the ongoing recruitment campaigns that saw some 33,800 or more men-in-arms shipped to Asia, besides the 14,000 Macedonians Alexander had originally departed with; in total this may have equated to something like one in eight of every adult eligible for military service.[149] And we should not forget that in 334 BCE Alexander Molossus of Epirus, Alexander's uncle (and brother-in-law through his marriage to Cleopatra), simultaneously invaded Italy with an army that further depleted regional manpower. Little of this economic upheaval was ever recorded in the mainstream narratives; the fate of men and battles took precedent from Homer and Herodotus onwards, when the social causes that led to war were marginalised by all but Thucydides.[150] Yet a whole world order *was* changing and the Argead regime of the generation of Philip and Alexander was to blame.

Alexander's absence in Asia had been a mixed blessing for Athens. The city-state, paradoxically, enjoyed something of a *pax makedonika* with some prosperity returning between 330-324 BCE under the stewardship of Lycurgus who implemented prudent financial restraints, and who by 330 BCE had replaced the previous temporary structures that held the plays performed at the Great Dionysia with an enlarged stone theatre; it was the city's new 'tragic' heart that may have held as many as 17,000 spectators overlooking its three bronze statues of Euripides, Sophocles and Aeschylus (ca. 525-455 BCE). Most likely with the help of the newly pro-Macedonian statesman Phocion, Lycurgus does appear to have silenced Demosthenes, whose 'good luck' motto on his shield at Chaeronea had clearly not performed.[151]

Ironically, this period of relative stability enabled Athens to amass as much as 18,000 talents that would later be used for waging war against Macedonia.[152] But the years 330-326 BCE had also seen Greece in the grip of a series of acute grain famines, throwing Athens' thirty-five *sitophylakes* and *sitonai*, the corn guardians and corn buyers, into turmoil. Egyptian

Cyrene, the most important city of the pentopolis of five settlements in the republic of Cyrenaica (Libya) and a vital grain centre for Athens, is recorded as sending 1,200,000 Attic *medimnoi* (230,000 bushels) of corn to Greece, including 72,600 to Olympias and 50,000 to Cleopatra in Macedonia and Epirus.[153] But Cleomenes, Alexander's governor administering the Arabian portion of Egypt east of the Nile Delta with the financial responsibility of *arabarchos* (monetary administrator or revenue collector), refused to allow grain ships to leave his ports without a crippling imposition of duty which only increased Athenian hostility, resulting in negative portrayals of him that were (spuriously) attached to both Demosthenes and Aristotle.[154]

But trade routes had opened up, wider-spread Greek law rationalised and harmonised transactions, piracy was suppressed by the *Diadokhoi* navies and Macedonians spent coin on Greek expertise and luxury goods; 'capitalism' flourished at both state and private enterprise level though it would also lure Greeks overseas, and with it there appears to have been widespread emigration from Greece in the half century after the fall of the Archaemenid regime.[155] This was no doubt accelerated by the drop in local mercenary rates of pay that had steadily fallen from as much as 8 obols per day ca. 400 BCE when fewer soldiers of fortune were for hire, to perhaps as little as 4 obols at Alexander's death. The remuneration was never extravagant even in cheaper non-inflationary times; paupers on state benefit in Athens received 2 obols per day, and the stipend for jury duty paid twice this, or more.[156] It was a clear example of supply and demand and now better employment opportunities were beginning to present themselves in the newly Hellenised lands of the *Diadokhoi*.

CITY-TAKERS WITH BRONZE-BEAKED SHIPS, AND NO ORDINANCES OF JUSTICE: THE RISE OF THE MYRMIDONS[157]

At Alexander's death in 323 BCE his Bodyguards and leading generals had to pick up the pieces. They, alongside the foremost infantry battalion officers at Babylon, had voiced their opinions, in one form or another, in the Assembly of Macedones convened to decide on the fate of empire governance and Alexander's last wishes and instructions. But by now, as events were to prove, the *Somatophylakes* were too authoritative in their own right to be subservient to their peers, and though alliances of necessity pockmark the Successor Wars, they were forged only to preserve the independence they had by then achieved and to bring down a mutual threat.

Any persisting veneer of Agread loyalty vanished following the short-lived treaty known as the 'Peace of the Dynasts' of 311 BCE:

... Cassander, Ptolemy, and Lysimachus came to terms with Antigonus and made a treaty. In this, it was provided that: Cassander be general in Europe until Alexander, the son of Roxane, should come of age; that Lysimachus rule Thrace, and that Ptolemy rule Egypt and the cities adjacent thereto in Libya and Arabia; that Antigonus have first place in all Asia, and that the Greeks be autonomous. However, they did not abide by these agreements, but each of them, putting forward plausible excuses, kept seeking to increase his own power.[158]

Cassander abandoned his 'plausible excuses' when he had Alexander IV and Roxane executed in spring 310 BCE, 'a move welcomed by all the successors who had aspired to the kingship'. Alexander IV was, after all, pledged in marriage to Deidameia, the daughter of the Molossian Aeacides and the sister of Pyrrhus of Epirus. This could have revived an Epirote-Macedonian dynastic superpower like that of Philip II through Olympias, and one promised by the marriage of their daughter, Cleopatra, to Alexander Molossus.[159]

Soon after, Cassander orchestrated the murder of Alexander's elder son, Heracles, by his mistress Barsine, reportedly the half-Greek daughter of the renowned Artabazus (son of the Achaemenid princess Apame) and his Rhodian bride. Some five or six years before the mighty clash of powers at Ipsus, these super-governors – Cassander, Lysimachus, Ptolemy, Seleucus and Antigonus – who by now were reporting to no one but themselves, began to declare themselves kings, or to behave as such.[160] Thereafter, the new dynasts would be raising and retaining what became their own revenues, rather than nominally collecting them for the Pellan regime.[161] As it has been poignantly noted, Ptolemy's early rejection of *epimeletia* to the kings following Perdiccas' death in Egypt (320 BCE) was, 'in a quiet way, an *early* declaration of independence'.[162]

Cornelius Nepos provided a suitable summation of this first generation of the successors:

... nor did they care to perform what they had originally promised, namely, to guard the throne for Alexander's children; but, as soon as the only defender of the children was removed [Eumenes], they disclosed what their real views were. In this iniquity the leaders were Antigonus, Ptolemy, Seleucus, Lysimachus, and Cassander.[163]

Antigonus was, most likely, the first satrap to openly reveal his empire-wide ambitions, as well as the first to grant himself and his son *basileia*, in 307-306 BCE; this effectively coincided with the commencement of the Fourth *Diadokhoi* War, which was emphatically ended at Ipsus in 301 BCE. The regal proclamations supposedly came at Athenian request; Demetrius had recently 'freed' Athens from Cassander (307 BCE), though his crown was sealed by his naval victory at Salamis on Cyprus in 306 BCE. Demetrius had allegedly fought alone on the stern of a galley against an enemy boarding party in a battle in which 12,800 of Ptolemy's men were taken prisoner after the annihilation of half of his army.[164] The crowning of his father was formalised when Aristodemus of Miletus, 'the boldest flatterer of all the courtiers', arrived and declared: 'Hail King Antigonus!'[165]

Seleucus declared himself a king when he heard the news, and Ptolemy and Lysimachus (who, along with his son, married two of Ptolemy's daughters) were not slow to follow with their royal declarations, though it is highly likely that they were addressed as kings some years before in their own domains.[166] Agathocles, the tyrant of Sicily, who started life as a mercenary solder, followed suit, proving that anyone can wear purple; a few years on he was offering his daughter, Lanassa (the name of Heracles' granddaughter), to Pyrrhus to safeguard his regal future along with a dowry of Corfu (Korkyra). King of Epirus intermittently from 306 BCE, Pyrrhus would marry the daughters of both Illyrian and Paeonian kings.[167]

The title 'basileus' was soon to be emphasised by a newly manifested festival, the basileia.[168] These kingships had unique connotations when attached to the early Diadokhoi; it was more a 'term of office' than 'head of state', for the 'state' was – as epitomised by Demetrius' tidal career 'now waxing, now waning' – a notional region with ever-shifting borders and displaced campaign headquarters.[169] Demetrius was, uniquely, a king without a country for much of his career until the six years following 294 BCE when he finally ascended the throne of Macedonia as King Demetrius I and reunited the previously divided state once more. By then, however, he was not unanimously popular and had to defend his intriguing in a Common Assembly, whose attendees only agreed to his kingship 'due to their lack of a better man…'[170] But even the royal women were now being referred to as basilissa, koine Greek for 'queen', once married to the new Hellenistic kings who were 'officially monogamous' (a view which is challenged) despite the 'many mistresses they might maintain'.[171]

Demetrius Poliorketes, the charismatic son of Antigonus Monophthalmos, delighted in hearing revellers propose that only he and his putative father were true kings (though Plutarch recorded that he was, in fact, Antigonus' adopted nephew), whereas Ptolemy was merely an admiral, Lysimachus a treasurer and Seleucus nothing more than 'a commander of a squadron of elephants', thus an elephantarchos.[172] Seleucus' beasts had been a widely publicised gift from Chandragupta (probably in 303 BCE), but that appears to have been a face-saving initiative to camouflage his failed invasion of India, following which he had been forced to cede his easternmost provinces to the Indian dynast.[173] All laughed at their new titles except Lysimachus, for treasurers were traditionally eunuchs, though Seleucus' own 'spectacularly successful' naval operations with the Ptolemaic fleet were being marginalised with his new epithet.[174]

The *Diadokhoi* were, however, walking a tightrope of acceptance, but being adept politicians who could have shown Cicero a thing or two, they continued to milk their association to the dead conqueror, even the hostile Cassander, who, though was never destined to acquire any of Asia (apart from an expeditionary force to Cappadocia and, arguably, some authority in Cilicia, briefly governed by his brother Pleistarchus), managed to control Macedonia for almost twenty years.[175] After he had orchestrated the execution of Olympias at Pydna in 316/315 BCE, irreverently 'throwing her body out without burial' (he possibly also removed her statue from the Philippeion at Olympia), Cassander took Alexander's half-sister, Thessalonice, as his bride.[176]

Next came *Diadokhoi* associations to Alexander in literature and art. Apelles' paintings had captured the gradual divinity in the Macedonian king's profile from youthful victor, to hero, and then to god.[177] And if the Pellan poet, Poseidippus, accurately described Lysippus' sculpting skill, itself a poetic *mimesis* in bronze, there did indeed exist a powerful imagery at work:

> Lysippus, Sicyonian sculptor, daring hand, learned artisan,
> Your bronze statue has the look of fire in its eyes,
> That one you made in the form of Alexander, The Persians deserve
> No blame. We forgive cattle for fleeing a lion.[178]

Alexander's approved team – the painter Apelles, the sculptor Lysippus and the gem engraver and goldsmith Pyrgoteles – had been effective for the Argeads and now they would be newly employed.[179] Lysippus, who had criticised Apelles for painting Alexander wielding a thunderbolt rather than a spear (that being the more glorious), was commissioned to sculpt King Seleucus.[180] Ptolemy hired Antiphilus, an alleged hostile rival of Apelles, to paint him in a hunt; Antiphilus' canvas of a youthful Alexander and Philip with Minerva, also painted at Ptolemy's court, reinforced the suggestion of 'a family unit' and would have supported the rumours of Ptolemy's parentage; the appearance of the Ptolemaic eagle symbol may also have been designed to signify Argead roots.[181] Philoxenus of Eretria even painted a battle scene at either Issus or Gaugamela for Cassander who had been absent from both conflicts; this was *possibly* the model for the famous Pompeii mosaic (unearthed in 1831) that now resides in the National Museum of Archaeology in Naples.[182]

Not to be outdone, monuments commissioned by Seleucus and Antigonus, and erected by the Eleans, appeared at Olympia beside Alexander and Philip.[183] In fact, Plutarch and Polybius both record a tradition being circulated: Antigonus and his descendants also came from the same line as Philip II; Herodian recorded that Antigonus, like Alexander, '... imitated Dionysus in every way, even wearing a crown of ivy instead of the Macedonian hat or the diadem and carrying the thyrsus instead of a sceptre.'[184] An inscription first published just a few decades ago and dating to the latter half of the 3rd century BCE, further confirmed that one of the Ptolemies (a Lagid) and Antiochus (a Seleucid) were additionally addressed as descendants of Heracles and the Argeads.[185]

Ptolemy erected a bronze equestrian statue to Alexander, symbolising *alexikakos* the national protector, and it remained a landmark in Alexandria for a thousand years, reminding the population that the 'saviour', *Soter*, had been his true heir.[186] Sometime later he constructed the Tychaion, dedicated to the goddess of fortune; it adjoined the Mouseion (the home of the Muses) that housed additional Argead portraits. Seleucus commissioned a statue to the goddess Tyche in his new capital of Antioch; in this both successors had possibly been stimulated by Demetrius of Phalerum's *Peri Tyches*, published sometime around 310 BCE.[187] In the shadows of these living gods, the poetic *Idylls* of Theocritus (*floruit* ca. 270 BCE) and the *mimiamboi* (mimes) of Herodas (a younger contemporary, both 3rd century BCE), felt duty-bound to remind their audience in verse that the common man (and now more prominently, woman) and the challenges and routines of commonplace life, did still, in fact, exist.

Cicero knew that 'endless money formed the sinews of war' and it was never truer than now.[188] For a time, Alexander's image was retained on the head of the *Diadokhoi* coins and the major denominations minted by Seleucus, including gold staters and silver tetradrachms that maintained Alexander's imperial currency type. These personal likenesses still carried the clean-shaven and leonine-maned look of the conqueror and they were often adorned with bulls' and rams' horns recalling Dionysus and Ammon, or struck with Heracles wearing a lion's scalp.[189] These were mythological and divine associations that Alexander perpetuated himself at the court *symposia*, imagery that was likely reenergised once Cleitarchus' colourful campaign account entered circulation a generation on.[190] As Olga Palagia argues: 'The Successors used lion hunt imagery as a means of underlying and legitimising their share in his empire'; it represented their part in that subjugation of Persia and was perhaps a gesture to Heracles *Kynagidas*, the tutelary deity of the hunt.[191]

From the *Diadokhoi* there soon emerged an inevitable image-fusion of 'the king they had served', and 'the king they had themselves become', for they and their *epigonoi* had to relate to the mixed ethnicities now under their regal wings. Seleucus in particular had to appeal to veteran Macedonian campaigners – the Greek garrison troops he inherited from Antigonus after the battle of Ipsus – and yet he also needed to connect psychologically with his multi-ethnic Asiatic ranks. They included the half-caste sons of the campaigners whose education Alexander planned to fund when envisioning them as future replacements for their veteran fathers.[192] Seleucus, who retained an Achaemenid-style administration, went on to portray Alexander in an elephant-scalp headdress as a symbol of his hybrid army.

Lysimachus, once reportedly blundering into Alexander's spear – a wound staunched by the king's bloody diadem which, according to Aristander, portended a troubled future reign[193] – justified his association as a 'treasurer' by minting at his new capital, Lysimachia, built on the site of the demolished Cardia; it was itself greatly damaged by an earthquake twenty-two years later.[194] As the new king of Thrace and its bordering lands, Lysimachus also churned out coins from Sestus, Lampsacus, Abydus, Sardis and from other new mints established across the Asia Minor satrapies he acquired from Antigonus after Ipsus, with most denominations showing the winged goddess Nike, Lysimachus' well-earned victory motif.

But once their own dynasties were securely established following the uncertainties preceding kingships, the *Diadokhoi* had their *own* likenesses minted in addition to Alexander's to propagate their cults and to lure Hellenic trade and Greek settlers eastward.[195] True Ptolemaic numismatic independence came with the legend *Alexandreion Ptolemaiou* (the Alexandrine of Ptolemy) on which the dynast's own heavy-set jaw entered circulation sometime around 304 BCE in his 'dual kingship' of Egypt, though gold staters still carried Alexander in a chariot pulled by four elephants.[196] Ptolemy had established a Graeco-Macedonian administration in Alexandria but maintained a traditional Egyptian model in the Nile valley and delta. Outside these regions metal commerce was revolutionary, as coinage was not used in rural Egypt where raw commodities, manufactured goods, or metal exchanged by weight (uncoined), were traded instead. The exceptions were the Greek trading posts and their *prostatai*, the administrators in charge of the ports, but even then coin was predominantly used for the payment of foreign mercenaries.[197]

Lysimachus announced his independence by striking his own lion's forepart device in 303 BCE, and Seleucus added the anchor symbol at his new mints at Susa, Ecbatana and Seleucia-on-Tigris; the anchor, said to be visible on Seleucus' thigh, was allegedly a divine birthmark carried through the generations.[198] It has been argued that the strategic positioning of his new cities in otherwise rural areas was to propagate a coined monetary economy as quickly as possible where commodity-based trading was still the norm, rather than for any military initiative. This was especially true of the Seleucid East where tax rates on agriculture soon rose to fifty per cent in order to restock the treasuries that had been pillaged in the earlier campaigns. The greatest advantage, however, was that coin struck in gold and silver, often referred to as *chrysion* and *argyrion*, was non-perishable, it could be hoarded, and it was more stable than commodities (as Aristotle observed), so in universal demand.[199]

The new legal tender being introduced by the *Diadokhoi* soon saved 2 grams of silver in negotiations; the 17.62-gram tetradrachm was now reduced to the Rhodian weight of 15.50 grams to cover the manufacture cost; Ptolemy was the first to adopt the new standard in 310 BCE when it seems he banned foreign money from circulating in Egypt. Thus imports became cheaper where exports were taxed as usual. Electrum coins, like the early Lydian currency and later the staters from Cyzicus, Phocaea and Mytilene, were cautiously traded as they could not be assayed until Archimedes' discovery of specific gravity, causing much head scratching for the *metronomoi*, the inspector of weights and measures, the *daneistes* (moneylenders), the *trapezitai*, the official bankers and their *kollybistikai trapezai*, exchange banks.[200]

Greeks *were* wary of coins being traded at a higher nominal than intrinsic (bullion) value, especially when bronze was being minted, and today it is still possible to see bankers' 'test cuts' on the edges to reveal the inner material, as forgers were known to cover copper with silver plate. Ptolemy II *Philadelphos* introduced bronze in Egypt around 260 BCE, and later copper drachmas appeared with Roman domination of the Mediterranean, though its exchange rate to a silver equivalent was to plummet from 60:1 to as low as 625:1, until Roman annexation of Egypt stopped the inflationary crisis.[201]

Herodotus believed that hard gold and silver currency *had* originated in Lydia with Gyges or his son, probably in the 7th century BCE; once again this most likely stemmed from the king's need to pay mercenaries, whereafter its usage gradually spread.[202] But now, in the new *Diadokhoi* kingdoms, currency was overlaid with propaganda that carried motifs fashioned to humiliate opponents. Short on land-based success, and too young to have exploited his own association with Alexander, Demetrius depicted Poseidon with a trident and a ship's prow to recall his victory at Salamis, a motif that suggested his thalassocracy. So even the successor coins, each displacing the popular Persian gold daric in Asia, were not free from what has been termed 'antique spin'.[203]

Over the 250 years that stretched from Alexander's accession in 336 BCE through to the close of the Hellenistic era, some ninety-one mints produced 'Alexander's coinage' (twenty-six in his own lifetime); a Roman quaestor of Macedonia even reintroduced his image on new coins struck sometime around 90 BCE, though possibly this was specifically to pay the local population to fight against the mutual Pontic threat. The last Alexander-styled coin of the Hellenistic era was churned out at Mesembria (on the Thracian coast, now Bulgaria) around 65 BCE.[204]

A Ptolemy I *Soter* tetradrachm minted at Alexandria ca. 300-285 BCE showing his own likeness: a diademed head, an aegis around the neck and an eagle standing on a thunderbolt on the obverse. The eagle may be connected to Aelian's statement of rumours that Ptolemy was an illegitimate son of Philip II.[205] Images provided with the kind permission of the Classical Numismatic Group. Inc. www.cngcoins.com.

A Seleucus I *Nikator* tetradrachm minted at Seleucia-on-Tigris ca. 296-281 BCE showing the strength of his elephant corps. The laureate head of Zeus and Athena brandishing a spear with shield in a quadriga of elephants on the obverse.

A Demetrius *Poliorketes* tetradrachm minted at Salamis ca. 306-285 BCE celebrating his naval victory over Ptolemy. It displays Nike with a trumpet and stylus on a ship's prow, with Poseidon with trident and arms in a mantle on the obverse.

A bronze coin with the legend 'of King Lysimachus' with a leaping lion and spearhead. Numismatists are divided on whether the head in Attic crested helmet depicts a young male or the goddess Athena.

'Royal mints' and what we might term 'state banks' (*demosiai trapezitai*) funded an arms race that saw the construction of ever more ambitious ships for the swelling *Diadokhoi* fleets. It was in this environment that sophisticated banking tools must have evolved, such as credit arrangements alongside commodity commitments, because transporting large quantities of coin from one treasury or sanctuary to another was simply impractical.[206]

The trireme ('three', Greek *trieres*, Roman *triremis*), probably the first ship to be pulled by oars at three levels, had been the mainstay of Mediterranean navies; they were generally increased in size to what the Romans later termed quadriremes ('fours'), and quinqueremes ('fives') in the Syracusian and Carthaginian styles, though larger denominations may refer to the rower per oar (a system later termed *alla scaloccio*) rather than to the number of decks of oarsmen.[207] The positioning of oarsmen to avoid the clashing of strokes was aided by a *parexeiresia*, an overhanging outrigger, though the exact configuration of even the ubiquitous trireme is still debated; some scholars believe a *trieres* refers to three men seated on a single bench, each pulling an independent oar (a system later known as *alla sensile*).[208]

The cost of maintaining a fleet of the magnitudes we read of in the *Diadokhoi* Wars would have been a huge undertaking: ships were manned by conscripted citizens, not slaves, who were in any case expensive to upkeep. Powering them would have been the *thranitai, zygitai*, and *thalamitai* (or *thalamioi*), the upper, middle, and lower deck rowers in a three-tiered design. An Athenian trireme would have required over 10,000 drachmas per year (1.5 to 2 talents) to run, before accounting for the wages of its fighting contingent at something like 4 to 6 obols per man per day.[209]

Possibly as a response to Ptolemy sending Antigonus a package containing a large fish and green figs ('master the sea, or eat these'),[210] each now commissioned *kataphraktos* (armoured) polyremes: the 'eights' (*okteres*), 'nines' (*enneres*) and finally the 'tens' (*dekeres*) that were soon seen floating around the Eastern Mediterranean. Alexander had shown them the way, for he had ordered wood for 700 'sevens' (*hepteres*), and according to the *Naturalis Historia* of Pliny ('The Elder', 23-79 CE), he had once built a 'ten' from trees cut from the forests of Lebanon.[211] By 314 BCE Antigonus commanded 240 warships which included ninety that allegedly had four banks of oars, ten of them 'fives', three with nine 'orders' of oarsmen, and ten ships housing ten.[212] To repel them, and as described in the accounts of Demetrius' famous siege of Rhodes (305-304 BCE), thick floating booms of squared logs with iron plates and spikes, the *phragma* or *kleithron*, were often deployed to block their path into harbours, whilst more elaborate pontoon barriers, *zeugmata*, were constructed from vessels planked together.[213]

The showman in Demetrius commissioned more ambitious ships still, the *megista skaphe*: 'fourteens', 'fifteens' and 'sixteens' (*hekkaidekereis*), some of them catapult-prowed and shooting arrows or stones.[214] They were 'much admired by his enemies as they sailed past', though historians are, once again, still at odds over the intricate rowing arrangement these titans must have employed.[215] Plutarch attempted to describe them:

> … up until this time, no man had seen a ship of fifteen or sixteen banks of oars … However, in the ships of Demetrius their beauty did not mar their fighting qualities, nor did the magnificence of their equipment rob them of their usefulness, but they had a speed and effectiveness which was more remarkable than their great size.[216]

Following the defeat of Antigonus at Ipsus in 301 BCE, and after Asia Minor and Syria had been torn apart by those vying for the pieces, the treasury at Cyinda still yielded 1,200 talents to Demetrius, throwing him a fleet-building lifeline in well-forested Cilicia.[217] Here he celebrated his new family ties with Seleucus who married his daughter, Stratonice, aboard a ship with thirteen banks of oars, and Demetrius soon occupied Cilicia, possibly with Seleucus' consent. According to Plutarch, the marriage was prompted by the alliance formed between Lysimachus and Ptolemy (from the aforementioned marriages to Ptolemy's daughters).[218]

The Cilician aggression earned Demetrius the denunciation of the provincial governor, Cassander's brother Pleistarchus, who then took refuge with Lysimachus who now controlled all of Asia Minor north of the Taurus range. Having already seen the Chersonese ravaged by Demetrius, Lysimachus invaded Cilicia by land, but he cordially asked Demetrius to give him a demonstration of his naval power and Demetrius obliged; this is just one of the episodes that captures the mercurial and perplexing relationships between the warring *Diadokhoi*.[219]

The new fleet enabled Demetrius to cling on to his garrisoned Greek cities as well as Ephesus, Sidon, Tyre and Cyprus, for a while, the latter harbours posing a threat to Ptolemaic Egypt.[220] And some years on, after a revival in Greece (starving Athens into submission in 295 BCE with his remaining fleet of 300 ships) and his increasingly autocratic and unpopular kingship in Pella (294-288 BCE) – when his darkest hours were approaching that would see him expelled from Macedonia after his soldiers deserted to Lysimachus and Pyrrhus – Demetrius was still able to (plan to) lay keels for 500 new ships. He soon raised an army of 98,000 men with 12,000 cavalry; 'all wondered at not just the multitude, but at the magnitude' of the force with which he planned to re-conquer 'Antigonid' Asia Minor. Demetrius' behaviour leaves us in no doubt that in the minds of the *Diadokhoi*, at least, state property and monarchy indeed belonged to the man with the crown and not to 'the people'.[221]

The recruiting numbers still sound incredible today, though we know Greek league cities were fined if they did not produce their levy of soldiers, and surviving details of those fines suggest Demetrius was prepared to pay well above the average for a Greek hoplite.[222] Even pirates were being employed for their naval experience, though notably this was principally for action against Rhodes, 'their special enemy'.[223] Yet a fleet of 500 ships would have required thousands of talents per year if crews were to be retained throughout winter; this was an impossible undertaking for even the former dominant naval powers of Athens and Rhodes, restricting these ambitious navies to the former-Persian-Empire-coffered *Diadokhoi* alone.

Commissioned sometime after 289 BCE, Lysimachus built a mammoth ship at Heraclea, the *Leontophoros* ('Lion Bearer', denoting his new symbol); it was possibly a catamaran that required 1,600 rowers and its construction may have been funded by the hidden Thracian treasure hoard revealed to him ca. 285 BCE.[224] Detail of the 'super dreadnought' was recorded in Photius' epitome of Memnon's *History of Heraclea*:

> … in this fleet were some ships, which had been sent from Heraclea, six-bankers and five-bankers and transports, and one eight-banker called the Lion-Bearer, of extraordinary size and beauty. It had one hundred rowers on each line, so there were eight hundred men on each side, making a total of sixteen hundred rowers. There were also twelve hundred soldiers on the decks, and two steersmen.[225]

Demetrius' son, Antigonus II *Gonatas* (ca. 319-239 BCE), under threat from all sides and by then unsurprisingly short on funds, needed twenty-four years to build a riposte, his 'sacred *triremos*', a ship possibly larger still and built at Corinth. It secured victory at Kos (ca. 258 BCE) over Ptolemy II *Philadelphos* who was now assisting Athens after the Chremonidean War (ca. 267-261 BCE). He had himself been busy constructing a 'twenty' and two 'thirties' in a fleet comprising four 'thirteens', two 'twelves', fourteen 'elevens', thirty 'nines', thirty-seven 'sevens', five 'sixes' and seventeen 'fives'.[226] A surviving papyrus detailed Ptolemy II's instructions to fell 500 acacia, tamarisk and willow trees to provide the breastwork of his 'long ships'. The fleet included twice as many smaller ships, with more than 4,000 in total in the Aegean.[227] The bloated nautical appetites culminated in Ptolemy IV *Philopatros* (reigned 221-204 BCE) building a *tessarakonteres*, a giant 280 cubit-long (perhaps 410 feet) 'forty', allegedly requiring 4,000 rowers and 400 additional crew to ferry a further 2,850 armed men to war.[228]

Despite Plutarch's enthusiasm for the performance of Demetrius' fleet, there is little evidence that these later huge and unwieldy warships remained dominant at sea, and smaller agile vessels were more practical for most naval operations: the fast *lembos* and the light *hemiolia* and *myoparones* of the pirates, for example, or the *trihemioliai* the Rhodians used to counter them, because their nimble shallower-draughted ships could usefully navigate up rivers.[229] The behemoths were probably also too slow to catch opponents in ramming or close-quarter manoeuvres, in which a *dorudrepanon* ('spear-sickle') might be used to cut enemy rigging, and they would have been vulnerable to the 2-metre long Athlit-style ram (*embolos*) sheathed in bronze that typically featured on the bows of triremes.[230] Certainly the tactical manoeuvres used effectively by the Rhodians such as the *diekplous*, *periplous* and *anastrophe*, designed to shear away oars and punch a hole in enemy lines, outflank and expose vulnerable sterns with a quick avoidance turn, must have fallen by the wayside when two giants met.[231] The Hellenistic naval arms race was about prestige above functionality; this was floating court propaganda.

The construction techniques were soon applied to pleasure barges; Athenaeus described the *Syracusia* launched ca. 240 BCE and which had been designed by Archimedes for Hieron II (ca. 308-215 BCE) the Greek king of Syracuse who was his friend and possibly his cousin. It came complete with eight armed towers and catapults, gardens, a bathhouse, gymnasium and a temple to Aphrodite: the summit of Hellenistic extravagance. To construct the Syracusia, wood sufficient for sixty quadriremes was cut from Mount Etna and it took 300 craftsmen over a year to build it. A folly too large to dock anywhere but Alexandria, the unwieldy giant was gifted to Ptolemy III *Euergetes* ('Benefactor', reigned 246-222 BCE) and renamed *'Alexandris'*.[232] Guiding the ship to her final resting place was the Pharos, the lofty lighthouse that had been designed by Sostratus of Cnidus and which took twelve years to build on Pharos Island; standing for over sixteen hundred years, it has been aptly described as nothing short of more Ptolemaic 'propaganda in stone'.[233]

The Roman Emperor Caligula, clearly looking back with admiration to Alexander and his successors, was inspired by what he read and determined to have the final say in water-borne excess that outshone even Cleopatra's

300-foot-long barge on which she seduced her Roman suitors in its gardens, grottoes, porticoes and bedrooms. Caligula built the previously unparalleled barges that were recovered by Mussolini from the lake known to the Romans as Diana's Mirror, now Lake Nemi, when he drained it through 1928 to 1932. These were nothing less than floating palaces with underfloor heating, libraries, temples and mosaics; excavations suggest the barges must have been cripplingly costly, no doubt a part of the reason why the new emperor taxed lawsuits, weddings and prostitution, and auctioned gladiators' lives at Colosseum games.[234]

A reconstruction of the Pharos in Alexandria. Engraving by F Adler, 1901.

CULTS, HEROES, SAVIOURS AND GODS: THE FINAL METAMORPHOSIS

Alongside the *Diadokhoi* coinage, portraits and naval power, emerged the encouragement of cult worship, a development termed a '… servile, despicable flattery, the product, not of any religious feeling, but of scepticism.'[235] By the end of the 4th BCE 'the heroisation of living men was no longer a paradox' and liturgies proliferated.[236] In November 311 BCE, officially the seventh year of the reign of King Alexander IV, Ptolemy erected the Satrap Stele commemorating the victory by the 'Great Viceroy' (himself) over Demetrius at Gaza the previous year (though the never-mentioned Seleucus was at Ptolemy's side); it described the Egyptian satrap-soon-to-be-king as '… strong in two arms, wise in spirit, mighty among men, of stout courage, of firm foot and resisting the furious.'[237] It went on to eulogise his fighting ability, his restoration of Egyptian statues and temples, and it firmly placed Ptolemy in the pantheon of Egyptian gods and beside Alexander himself. The rhetoric must have recalled the eulogies he would have read on the Babylonian royal cylinders, or the inscription Onesicritus claimed to have seen on the tomb of Darius I; indeed, the descendants of Seleucus did have stone cylinders carved to tell their stories in the tradition of the Persian Great Kings.[238]

Demetrius, who modelled himself on Dionysus, and who now sported a many-coloured cloak depicting the heavens, was described by Plutarch as '... amorous, bibulous, warlike, munificent, extravagant, and domineering.'[239] Upon entering Athens by chariot in 307 BCE, he turned the rooms of the Parthenon behind the statue of Athena into his lodging and became legendary for his womanising; he was 'not a very suitable guest for the virgin goddess', counselled the devout Plutarch.[240] But the Hellenistic kings no longer feared impiety for they were becoming demi-gods themselves; when Demetrius returned 'democracy' to the Athenians, he and his father were hailed as God Saviours. Plutarch captured the moment: 'They decreed Demetrius and Antigonus should be woven into the sacred robe, along with those of the gods; and the spot where Demetrius first alighted from his chariot they consecrated and covered with an altar, which they styled the altar of Demetrius Alighter.'[241]

Enthused by the delivery of 150,000 *medimnoi* of grain – possibly from Antigonus' grain-producing estates in Asia in an attempt to bypass the Ptolemaic monopoly – and now that Athens had sufficient timber for one hundred new ships, the city set about naming games, hymns and even a month, Demetrion, after the liberator (at the expense of the Athenian month of Munychion).[242] The city extended its traditional ten tribes to include two new orders: the Antigonis and the Demetrias, with the extravagant and fawning Stratocles proposing many of the obsequies that included golden statues.[243] By 'championing the case of the Greek cities', the League of Islanders and then Scepsis erected altars and a cult statue to Antigonus from 311/310 BCE onwards; Samos, Delos and Sicyon followed with cults and games thrown in honour of both father and son.[244] By 307/6 BCE the tide of approbation saw them attempt to unite Greeks under a new coalition, and by 302 BCE Antigonus and Demetrius, exploiting the anthem of 'freedom' once more, drafted their charter of a new Hellenic League (we have it in fragments) that would conveniently continue waging war against Cassander.[245]

Even philosophy did not escape their control; the historian Hieronymus (ca. 350s-250s BCE) who wrote a unique eyewitness account of these *Diadokhoi* Wars, now a long-time client of the Antigonids, witnessed the suppression of the Lyceum and its Peripatus as well as the competing Academy under a decree from Demetrius requiring all such schools to have a licence; the Lyceum had previously been supported (and no doubt milked for philosophical approbation) by Cassander's regime, and this recalls Aristotle's friendship with his father. It was Demosthenes' nephew, Demochares, who was involved in the proposal to expel *all* philosophers from Attica, preferring oratorical eloquence over dangerous ideas that might undermine any continued veneer of Athenian democracy; it was a stance that seems to have been threaded through his own 'rhetorical and combative' writing.

Demetrius of Phalerum, the recently deposed philosopher-statesman installed in Athens by Cassander, had, apparently, behaved in just as depraved a fashion as *Poliorketes*, and he eventually fled to Ptolemy in Egypt after a decade in power.[246] The learned polymath secured himself a legacy, if not a happy end, for the 'gracelid' statesman was historically deemed to have been a 'tyrant' in the city of Athena.[247] Fortune's movements, as Euripides knew, are indeed inscrutable;[248] some 300 (or more) statues that the city had once dedicated to him were summarily pulled down when he departed (some were allegedly turned into chamber pots).[249]

Although Plutarch reported 'the government was called an oligarchy, but in fact, was monarchical, for the power of Demetrius of Phalerum met with no restraint', Strabo suggested Demetrius 'did not put an end to democracy but even restored its former power' during his tenure of Athens. Once a student of Theophrastus, Demetrius certainly supported the Peripatetics (and they reciprocated) and Cicero, Diodorus and Diogenes Laertius spoke positively of him.[250] Peter Green more soberly concluded that the years of his rule '… are chiefly remarkable as evidence for what was liable to happen when a philosopher-king got a hand in real life.'[251] Demetrius was, nevertheless, sentenced to death *in absentia*.[252]

The eventual reinvasion of Asia Minor by Demetrius *Poliorketes* in 287/6 BCE, after being ousted from Macedonia, saw the city of Priene devastated when it held out for Lysimachus; when he finally managed to relieve it a cult was established and a bronze statue erected in Lysimachus' image following Samothrace's lead.[253] As for the heroisation of Seleucus, in Syria where he tried to breed elephants, and in the deeper regions of his empire, Seleucus' own cult came to hail him as Zeus *Nikator* ('Victor'). It was here that his propaganda team claimed his mother, Laodice, conceived him with Apollo; his aforementioned anchor device allegedly depicted the carving on the ring gifted to her by the god for her compliance in the union.[254] It may well have been at this point that the story of his retrieving Alexander's diadem in the marshes of Babylon was spread, for that augured in his 'vast kingdom'.[255] Seleucus' son, Antiochus I, gained a cult at Ilion after having come to terms with the Ionian League,[256] and toasts were now being drunk from drinking vessels named the 'Seleucis' and (previously) the 'Antigonis'; divine honours, sacrifices and even the linen headband 'diadems' were overshadowed as *stephanephoria* adorned the wreath-clad heads of the *Diadokhoi*.[257]

The grateful Rhodians bestowed the epithet *Soter* ('Saviour') upon Ptolemy for his part in lifting the siege of Demetrius, whose discarded *Helepolis* ('city-taker'), a nine-story armoured siege tower mounted with torsion catapults, helped fund the construction of their iron-framed and bronze-plated Colossus erected close to the harbour entrance.[258] After consulting the oracle at the sacred precinct at Siwa, a Ptolemaion was built in the Rhodian capital whereafter Ptolemy was worshipped as a new deity at the annual festival. By 279 BCE he was posthumously deified at home in Alexandria at the first festival of Ptolemaia.[259]

An artist's impression of the siege of Rhodes by Demetrius *Poliorketes* in 305-304 BCE showing his famed *Helepolis* ('city-taker'), the nine story armoured siege tower. The year-long siege failed to take the city and the left behind siege engine helped fund the construction of the bronze-plated Colossus built close to the harbour entrance. The strategic importance of Rhodes' harbours, navy and ship building facilities saw the island courted and invaded through the Successor Wars.

How regally sanctioned were the epithets 'city-taker' (*poliorketes*), 'saviour' (*soter*), 'benefactor' (*euergetes*) that became attached to the Hellenistic kings, and whether they were simply popular *sobriquets* that stuck or were home-grown Ptolemaic devices (in the case of the latter two), remains open to debate, but few of them made it to their coinage; this is perhaps indicative that the kings themselves held loftier pretensions.[260] In this environment it is likely the *isegoria* that saw common infantryman slap the king on the back, or even take him to task, probably disappeared, though Polybius suggested it resurfaced in the leaner days in Macedonia before its eventual fall to Rome.[261]

In stark contrast, 'the European at heart' Cassander, who had seen little of Asia but who knew his local market, appears to have shied away from the loftier regal attachments, refusing the diadem and signing official correspondence without royal title. Cassander had nevertheless buried King Philip III (Arrhidaeus) in the style befitting a 'royal' successor, so in the eyes of the Macedonians he actually 'reigned' from that point onwards, and probably from the time of his marriage to Thessalonice; he certainly presided over the Nemean Games dedicated to Heracles, suggesting he was broadcasting *basileia*, though only bronze coinage was ever struck with his own name.[262]

If conservative Macedonia had not itself been ready for the oriental-style godhead, Cassander didn't hesitate in joining the other *Diadokhoi* in the establishment of their eponymous cities and those of their wives and sons.[263] So there emerged Thessalonica, a *synoikismos* of twenty-six smaller (and no doubt unwilling) towns, and Cassandreia. The perennially ill Cassander had expediently named two of his sons (by Thessalonice) Philip and Alexander 'to establish a connection with the royal house', for, as Carney points out, he was the 'first non-Argead to attempt the permanent rule of Macedonia rather than maintaining an existing hereditary role'.[264]

Ironically, though somewhat symbolically in the context of Cassander's role in the *Pamphlet* (T1, T2), their third son, Antipater (married to a daughter of Lysimachus), murdered Thessalonice for the favour she showed to the younger Alexander (married to a daughter of Ptolemy), though not before she had seen the two of them become kings (297-294 BCE) who fought over what soon became a Macedonia divided at the River Axius, care of Pyrrhus' annexation of the western cantons closest to Epirus.[265] Both of Cassander's remaining sons were to eventually die at the hands of Demetrius *Poliorketes* and Lysimachus when advancing their own designs on the throne. It brought the first conflict to Macedonian soil since Cassander consolidated his position some twenty years before; by 294 BCE the power once wielded by the house of Alexander's former regent, Antipater, was finally spent.[266] Demetrius lasted on the throne until Lysimachus and Pyrrhus invaded from east and west in 288 BCE; once more the nation that had ruled from Epirus to India was domestically cut in two.

In Asia there emerged the eponymous successor cities of Ptolemais, the various Lysimachias, Apameas, an Arsinoea (at Ephesus' expense), the Antigoneas, Seleucias, Laodiceas and others which formed part of the Seleucid Syrian stronghold. Seleucus would eventually found more than fifty settlements, naming nine of them after himself, three after his wife and Antiochia was named after his father; even ancient Achaemenid Susa was renamed Seleucia-on-the-Euleaus.[267] Some *were* synoecisms, others *katoikiai*, military colonies like Alexander's earlier settlements. Antigonus had destroyed much of Seleucus' former capital at Babylon in the brutal Mesopotamian campaign of 310-309 BCE, so the sweetest moment for his heirs must have been transferring the population of Antigonus' former capital, Celaenae (along with a Jewish population), to the close-by Apamea (often referred to with the epithet *Kibotos*, chest or coffer, suggesting its wealth) established by his son, Antiochus I.[268]

This was not the first major post-Alexander resettlement in the empire: Seleucus had already dismantled Antigonea in Upper Syria with its seventy-stade perimeter to found Antiochia, now full of resettled veterans.[269] The site is probably identifiable with Thapsacus, the principal Euphrates River crossing of antiquity, a settlement that was possibly renamed Zeugma in the Roman period.[270] Additionally, around 304 BCE, Antigonus had been planning to synoecise the Ionian League cities of Lebedos and Teos as part of his grand infrastructure plan (Lysimachus later moved the population of Lebedos to Ephesus in 292 BCE). In fact, Antigonus had ironically furrowed the hard-tilled ground in which Seleucus planted his own empire, a point often overlooked by history. Antigonus' Hellenisation of Asia Minor and Syria formed what has been termed a 'bridge between Philip and the Achaemenids' in which his administrative reforms, city building, and colonisation had achieved far more than Alexander had managed in his tenure of Persia.[271]

Only Egypt remained untrampled by the *Diadokhoi* Wars although its overseas possessions were tugged at from all sides. Of all the original generals who governed a fragment of Alexander's empire, only Ptolemy and the old regent Antipater (and *possibly* Polyperchon who followed him) died in bed of what *appear* to be natural causes.[272] Arguably, Demetrius *Poliorketes* joined them, though in somewhat different circumstances; after one reversal of fortune too many, he submitted himself to Seleucus' mercy and requested '… a petty empire among the barbarians in which he might end his days.'[273] His son, Antigonus II *Gonatas*, pleaded for his life, while Lysimachus offered 2,000 talents for his immediate execution; a supposedly indignant Seleucus (now Demetrius' *elder* son-in-law) had him quarantined in luxury in the Syrian Chersonese until he drank himself to death in 283 BCE.[274] As with his father before him, and as perhaps for all the *Diadokhoi* who had accompanied Alexander on campaign, a kingdom in Asia was irresistible and more attractive than Macedonia itself.

'O CHILD OF BLIND AND AGED ANTIGONUS, WHAT ARE THESE REGIONS WHITHER WE ARE COME?'

Demetrius is said to have reflected upon his greatest reversals of fortune with, 'my flame thou fannest, indeed, and thou seemest to quench me, too', recalling a tragic line from Aeschylus. He should have stuck to the sea where his power was unmatched: as an ancient proverb warned, 'For useless is a dolphin's might upon dry ground.'[275]

Viewed from afar, Demetrius' efforts to re-establish himself across the Aegean look ill-conceived and futile; his disgruntled troops, being dragged to the East in one last bid for supremacy, are said to have confronted him with lines adapted from Sophocles' *Oedipus at Colonus*: 'O child of blind and aged Antigonus, what are these regions whither we are come?'[276] And yet there must have been a core of lingering support for him through his father's veterans in Asia Minor, moreover, he partook of a generation that knew it took no more than a lucky javelin strike, a penetrating cavalry charge or a defecting crack regiment to alter the fate of an empire. Demetrius was buried in *his* eponymous city in Thessaly and his five, or possibly six children, took his line down to King Perseus (reigned 179-168 BCE) who was finally subdued by Rome.[277]

Ptolemy I *Soter* passed away in the same year as Demetrius, 283 BCE, when his own Will was surely read out; Alexander's general, biographer and rumoured half-brother knew full well that no king leaves his life's work with a quip 'to the strongest', and that no father quoted the curse of Oedipus to sons holding sharpened swords.[278] He nominated power not to his eldest son, Ptolemy *Keraunos* ('Thunderbolt'), who was conceived with Cassander's sister, Eurydice, but to his already co-regent second son, Ptolemy II *Philadelphos*, who had been co-ruler since 285 BCE. Some years earlier, *Philadelphos* had murdered another half-brother (again born to Eurydice), who may well have been in league with *Keraunos*, for inciting the Cypriots to revolt.[279]

Ptolemy I *Soter* may have married Eurydice as early as 322 BCE, and he appears to have had repudiated her (or sidelined her, if not formally divorced her) by 316 BCE in favour of Berenice, Eurydice's lady-in-waiting who 'had the greatest influence and was foremost in virtue and understanding'; Pyrrhus had cunningly singled her out for his affections when he was a hostage in Egypt, knowing she held sway with Ptolemy.[280] Berenice was, nevertheless, still from the Antipatrid house; her paternal grandfather was the brother of Antipater. The displaced Eurydice, who was based at Miletus in Caria by 287 BCE, had brokered a useful alliance with Demetrius *Poliorketes* by offering him her daughter, Ptolemais; she had been pledged to him as early as in 298 BCE, supposedly on the instigation of Seleucus when he married Demetrius' daughter, Stratonice.[281]

Following the accession of Ptolemy II *Philadelphos* in 282 BCE, the rebuffed *Keraunos* was forced to seek a career with Lysimachus, then married to *Philadelphos*' sister, Arsinoe; with the alliance came the use of his navy which was later put to good use against Antigonus II *Gonatas* in 280 BCE. After a series of dynastic intrigues in Thrace that saw Lysimachus execute his own son – the popular heir apparent Agathocles (*Keraunos*' brother-in-law) – *Keraunos* next sought employ with the still ambitious though aged Seleucus, a position from which he could potentially launch his bid for Macedonia *or* Egypt.[282]

Seleucus saw an opportunity to intervene in Thracian politics, perhaps noting the recent defeats Lysimachus had suffered at the hands of the Getae, as well as the waning support for his regime after Agathocles' death; Seleucus was, no doubt, also influenced by the pleas of assistance from Agathocles' widow, Lysandra, a daughter of Ptolemy I *Soter* and Eurydice.[283] Seleucus and Lysimachus, the former Bodyguards of Alexander and once colleagues in arms, faced off at Curopedion near Sardis in 281 BCE in the 'last major battle of the *Diadokhoi*'. The Thracian dynast, once married himself to a sister of Cassander (Nicaea), and who had by then tragically lost fifteen children, was by now seventy-four, and Seleucus was seventy-seven, though both still 'had the fire of youth and the insatiable desire for power'.[284] Lysimachus was felled by a javelin and left to rot on the battlefield until a Pharsalian, curiously named Thorax, saw to his burial. The identification is curious because a same-named Thessalian (from Larissa) is said to have stood over Antigonus at Ipsus twenty years before.[285]

The temporary vacuum in Asia Minor allowed Philetaerus, Lysimachus' resourceful eunuch general, to establish the Attalid dynasty at Pergamum on the cone-shaped mountain peak that had acted as a treasury for 9,000 of Lysimachus' talents. Destined to build a great library and enter into isopolity with strategically aligned cities, Pergamum was now watched over by Athena, Demeter, Heracles and son, and no doubt by the heirs of Seleucus with whom Philetaerus had intrigued.[286]

Lysimachus' widow, Arsinoe, encouraged to marry her half-brother, Ptolemy *Keraunos*, following Persian and Phaoronic custom, was clearly dissatisfied at his growing power; she conspired against him and it precipitated his retaliatory murder of her two youngest sons. She fled to Egypt and married her own full-brother, Ptolemy II, becoming Queen Arsinoe II and triggering the use of his epithet, *Philadelphos*.

Ptolemy *Keraunos*, then based at Lysimachia, showed his gratitude to Seleucus by murdering him and having the army pronounce him King of Macedonia based at the new capital, Cassandreia. He lasted two years and was decapitated in the Gallic invasions in 279 BCE; Eurydice's second son, Meleager, lasted two months until he was forced to relinquish the crown. Antipater *Etesias*, the son of Cassander's brother, soon followed them with a reign lasting just forty-five days – 'as long as the Etesian Winds blew'. There followed an interregnum in which Sosthenes become *strategos* and *de facto* ruler of Macedonia from 279-277 BCE (he was possibly a former general of Lysimachus with no ancestral or dynastic claim to the throne) until he was overwhelmed by the still-at-large Gauls under Brennus. The next few years saw an 'independent' Cassandreia fall to the 'bloody' tyrant Apollodorus (through 279-276 BCE) the leader of a local proletariat revolt.[287]

The turmoil in Macedonia through the period of incursions by the Celtic Gauls, during which even Athens lost her shackles for several years, enabled Antigonus II *Gonatas* to make a bid for the throne. Pyrrhus' absence in Italy and a significant victory by Antigonus against the once 'great expedition' of Galatae (reportedly once as large as 150,000 infantry and perhaps 15,000 cavalry, though now decimated and reduced in number to 15,000 infantry and 3,000 horsemen) near Lysimachia in 277 BCE, when *Gonatas* was probably returning from a peace treaty in Asia Minor with Antiochus I (Seleucus' son, and which included marriage to his daughter), gave him a foothold back in Macedonia that would eventually herald in a reign that saw him on the throne to the age of eighty.[288]

Antigonus was, nevertheless, temporarily displaced by Pyrrhus who defeated him at the Aous River in 274 BCE, at which point his authority was restricted to the coastal cities whilst Pyrrhus controlled Aegae, a lamentable period that witnessed the plundering of the royal tombs by his Gallic mercenaries. The Epirote, who died at Argos in 272 BCE, was surely paying for their services with the promise of royal loot, a sad state of affairs when considering that he had fought alongside Antigonus' father (Demetrius *Poliorketes*, by then Pyrrhus' brother-in-law) at Ipsus.[289] Notably, *Gonatas* had previously retained a significant Gallic contingent himself and he was to rely on their services again; this was the precursor for Pyrrhus hiring his own Gauls.[290] Allegedly making little attempt to stop the plundering at Aegae, Pyrrhus was perhaps testing King Perdiccas I's prophecy that held: 'As long as the relics of his posterity should be buried there, the crown would remain in the family.'[291]

This extremely compressed and necessarily simplified summary of the intrigues within intrigues of the Macedonian royal lines through the two decades between the 'Battle of the Dynasts' at Ipsus in 301 BCE, and the national divisions following the final gasp of the first generation Successor Wars at Curopedion in 281 BCE ('the plain of Cyrus'), portrays a period 'lacking none in dishonorable comparison', and yet it was a period in which all the heads of the *Diadokhoi* kingdoms became related to one another.[292] Plutarch's *Life of Demetrius* and *Life of Pyrrhus* paint a vivid picture of the Hellenenistic world as one extended family at war, when fathers were challenged by jealous sons and intriguing daughters whose internecine rivalries and alliances were secured by a 'labyrinthine' series of intermarriages. The era that followed was just as dynastically toxic as the *epigonoi* of the Successors commenced their bids to become *primi inter pares*, with much of its early detail neatly captured in Nepos' *De regibus Exterarum Gentium*.[293]

Plutarch soberly reflected on the extraordinary state of affairs, possibly following the sentiment of Duris who was likely responsible for much of the *scandaleuse* attached to the period:

... so utterly unsociable a thing, it seems, is empire, and so full of ill-will and distrust, that the oldest and greatest of the successors of Alexander could make it a thing to glory in that he was not afraid of his son, but allowed him near his person lance in hand... Many killed their mothers and wives... as for the killing of brothers, like a postulation in geometry, it was considered as indisputably necessary to the safety of the reigning prince.[294]

Euripides had forewarned: 'There is a something terrible and past all cure, when quarrels arise 'twixt those who are near and dear';[295] this had truly become what Hesiod and Ovid (43 BCE-ca.18 CE) described as the bloody 'age of iron', when 'loyalty, truth and conscience went into exile'.[296]

THE ECLIPSE OF ALEXANDROCENTRICITY

In *The Prince*, Machiavelli titled his fourth chapter *Why the Kingdom of Darius, conquered by Alexander, did not rebel against his successors after his death.* It supposedly illustrated how a principality, once conquered, is easily held if all are subservient to the monarch. He was, however, unconsciously arguing that Alexander's successors, those who 'ruled securely', represented his second of two scenarios: nobles whose authority was *already established* independent of their king's. Machiavelli may have been inspired by Polybius who first voiced the suspicion that an 'Alexandro-centric' universe was in fact contrived, for he too considered much of the credit for Alexander's success was due to Philip II and that retinue of 'helpers and friends':[297]

> ... one could scarcely find terms adequate to characterise the bravery, industry and in general, the virtue of these men who indisputably by their energy and daring raised Macedonia from the rank of petty kingdom to that of the greatest and most glorious monarchy in the world.[298]

Polybius, influencing (or influenced by) the Stoic Panaetius (ca. 185-110 BCE),[299] appears to have inspired Trogus too, for between brooding images of Macedonian dissent, his epitomiser, Justin, retains an otherwise unlikely encomium to the *Diadokhoi*:

> Nor did the friends of Alexander look to the throne without reason; for they were men of such ability and authority, that each of them might have been taken for a king. Such was the personal gracefulness, the commanding stature, and the eminent powers of body and mind, apparent in all of them, that whoever did not know them, would have thought that they had been selected, not from one nation, but from the whole earth. Never before, indeed, did Macedonia, or any other country, abound with such a multitude of distinguished men; whom

Philip first, and afterwards Alexander, had selected with such skill, that they seemed to have been chosen, not so much to attend them to war, as to succeed them on the throne. Who then can wonder, that the world was conquered by such officers, when the army of the Macedonians appeared to be commanded, not by generals, but by princes?[300]

Justin also captured the resulting conundrum: 'Their very equality inflamed their discord, no one being so far superior to the rest, that any other would submit to him.'

Despite the remarkable *Diadokhoi* and their ambitious offspring, Macedonian superiority did pass irrevocably west in 190 BCE when the brothers Scipio *Asiaticus* and *Africanus*, along with their ally, Eumenes II of Pergamum (ruled 197-154 BCE, Polybius would later delicately argue his cause), defeated Antiochus III of the Seleucid line at the Battle of Magnesia in Lydia.[301] Some believe that Hannibal, seeking sanctuary from a common foe, was present at the conflict that would, just a decade after the conclusion to the Second Punic War (ended 201 BCE), give Rome passage to Alexander's former empire. If Hannibal *was* in Lydia it didn't affect the outcome: the 15,000-talent war indemnity levied on Antiochus was crippling, as was the loss of much of Asia Minor. The Seleucids never recovered and Rome soon became the undisputed power in the Near East.

As the Seleucid Empire fragmented, the legacy of Alexander's conquest did manage to hold out in the former eastern and upper satrapies in the form of Graeco-Bactrian kingdoms in the dynasties of Diodotus *Soter*, Euthydemus and Eucratides 'the Great' (broadly spanning 250-125 BCE). These principalities were centred in Bactria-Sogdia, Margiana and Arachosia, and in the Graeco-Indian kingdoms they fought to the east, extending into the Punjab until the close of the Hellenistic era. No doubt the descendants of the less rebellious Greek mercenaries settled by Alexander had participated in their founding, providing a cohesion that saw an uninterrupted arrival of Silk Road traders in the Levant.

Ai Khanoum on the Oxus River at the northern border of Afghanistan (possibly the site of 'Alexandria on the Oxus' or perhaps the later city of Eucratidia established ca. 280 BCE), and other recently excavated sites, have revealed Corinthian columns and tiles, huge Greek theatres, amphorae and sculptures, inscriptions and coin hoards with striking images, as well as textual evidence of Platonist philosophical doctrines. They paint a picture of remarkable Hellenic tenacity in the face of Parthian expansion and nomadic hoards, the southward migrations of the Scythians and the tribes of the Yuezhi from Central Asia (modern northwestern China).[302] In 1909 inscriptions on the Heliodorus Column in central India, dating to ca. 113 BCE and Graeco-Indian rule of King Antialcidas *Nikephoros* ('victorious'), were fully deciphered; Heliodorus had been a Greek ambassador to Taxila in the modern Punjab.[303]

Perplexingly, back across the Hellespont, having crushed every opponent from the Balkan kingdoms to the southern Greece *poleis*, and every tyrant, king or satrap from Asia Minor to the Indus Valley tribes, the Macedonians were said to be 'shocked' at the brutality of the Roman war machine, and yet awed by the precision and arrangement of its military camp; wounds caused by Roman slashing weapons, in particular, were gruesome compared to the more familiar puncture wounds from spears and lances.[304] Although Rome was already conducting brisk business in slaves exported from captured Greek cities, what the Macedonians witnessed in the First Macedonian War of 212/211 BCE under King Philip V – who ascended the throne at just seventeen and who was himself responsible for the mass suicide of women and children in the city of Abydus – was confusing. The cruelty, discipline, efficiency and organisation were not the traits that coexisted in the usual 'barbarians' threatening the Pellan kings. But by now 'the day of the professional long-service Macedonian army' was over; it was 'once again a levy of farmers called up when needed'. Macedonia was weary of war, the nationalistic fervour of the generations before had passed, and Greece aggregated itself into confederacies and new leagues in the face of Macedonian frailty.[305]

Rome *was* looking formidable; Hannibal had been defeated in 202 BCE and the young charismatic Philip V, likened to Alexander but loved throughout Greece (before turning into 'a savage tyrant', according to Polybius),[306] was forced into the Second Macedonian War (200-197 BCE) which concluded at Cynoscephalae in Thessaly in 197 BCE, when the *sarissa* ranks finally broke. Thessaly was lost to the Senate's legions espousing a familiar refrain: 'the protection of Greek freedom'. The ratio of Macedonian cavalry to infantry had also decreased from its employment in Alexander's early campaign army, perhaps again due to financial restraints, though this reduction in numbers exposed the vulnerable flanks of the pike phalanx. The Macedonian defeat, which included a 1,000-talent indemnity, had been portentously 'predicted' by an earthquake the year before.[307]

King Perseus faced Rome in the Third Macedonian War twenty-six years later (171-168 BCE), but like Philip V before him, he could only muster a modest core of *stratiotai politikoi*, home-grown citizen soldiers, so that Gallic, Thracian and Illyrian mercenaries were to be found in greater proportions in the ranks. The eclectic composition was not unique; Gauls even made it into the Ptolemaic armies of Egypt, some surely coming from the kingdom of Galatia formed after Gallic marauders made their way to Asia Minor in the wake of their earlier invasion of Thrace and Macedonia. With them had come the wider use of lighter and cooler chainmail, which replaced breastplates in hotter climes, and there arrived the infantry regiments of *thureophoroi* who fought with far larger oval shields that may have been inspired by Celtic or even Italian design.[308]

After successes in Thessaly in 171 BCE and inconclusive campaigning after, came the battle at Pydna on 22nd June 168 BCE announced by a further prodigy.[309] To raise support for an invasion, Rome had lodged complaints against Perseus with the Delphic Amphictionic League. The date of the battle at Pydna (and the city's exact location) is once again disputed following controversy over a lunar eclipse, a *sine qua non* when reinforcing how formative a clash of arms had been.[310]

Plutarch recorded that: 'Taking command of the [Roman] forces in Macedonia, and finding them talkative and impertinently busy, as though they were all in command, Aemilius Paullus issued out his orders that they should have only ready hands and keen swords, and leave the rest to him.'[311] Their trust was well placed; according to Livy, the general had wisely employed the lettered tribune, Gaius Sulpicius Gallus, to explain the celestial phenomenon in scientific terms to the troops who had been clashing bronze utensils and waving firebrands at the heavens 'to avert fear'.[312] Gallus' speech must have been well received for he was inspired to write a book on eclipses which no doubt came to reside in the first ever library in Rome, stocked with scrolls from Perseus' collection that would soon be liberated from Pella.

The bristling ranks of the *sarissa* bearers were still *kataplektikos* (broadly, 'awe inspiringly intimidating') and the most terrifying ever seen by the highly educated and Greek-speaking Lucius Aemilius Paullus '*Macedonicus*' whose father had died at Cannae fighting Hannibal, for even now the Macedonian two-handed pike and its leaf-shaped blade could still (Plutarch believed) pierce Roman shields and armour. How the battle commenced is not clear though it is said Paullus waited for the sun to shine in enemy eyes, or he provoked the Macedonians to attack when entrails were not sufficiently propitious for him to do so himself; Livy blamed a skirmish over an escaped horse for the start of full-scale fighting.[313]

Although the Macedonians initially had the better of it on level ground, the pike-bearers' tight formation, essential to success, was eventually prised open by uneven terrain they unwisely advanced on, by Roman flanking maniples, and by elephants; Macedonian morale finally fell once Perseus and his cavalry fled the field on the pretext of sacrificing to Heracles within the city walls.[314] After the Macedonian king made good his escape with his ally, King Cotys (and his Odrisaeans on his tail), there was little to stop Rome marching on the capital. According to Livy's unique description, the site for Pella's fortifications had been chosen well:

> It stands on a hill which faces the south-west, and is surrounded by morasses, formed by stagnant waters from the adjacent lakes, so deep as

to be impassable either in winter or summer. In the part of the morass nearest to the city the citadel rises up like an island, being built on a mound of earth formed with immense labour, so as to be capable of supporting the wall, and secure against any injury from the water of the surrounding marsh. At a distance it seems to join the city rampart, but is divided from it by a river, and united by a bridge; so that if externally invaded it has no access from any part, and if the king chooses to confine any person within it, there is no way for an escape except by that bridge, which can be guarded with great ease.[315]

Strabo reported that the lake-fronted city, already the largest in Macedonia in Xenophon's day, lay some 120 stades (approximately 14 miles) from the Thermaic Gulf up the still navigable Ludias River fed by an offshoot of the River Axius.[316] But centuries before, when King Archelaus first surveyed the site, it was probably rather closer to being a seaport: sufficiently maritime for trade (and loading timber and pitch for Athenian ships) and yet protected from an invading fleet.[317] But despite Livy stating 'it can be guarded with great ease', the stone capital at Pella, and the spiritual capital at Aegae (some 19 miles from Pydna as the crow flies) were pillaged and largely destroyed.[318]

Perseus fled from Pella to Amphipolis and then on to Galepsus in Thrace by sea. But at Amphipolis, 'lacerated by his misfortunes' and having slain his two treasurers in Pella, he initially let his badly needed Cretan supporters take riches worth 60 talents; he subsequently demanded the return of 'certain objects made from the spoils captured by Alexander'. Perseus '… lamented to his friends that through ignorance he had suffered some of the gold plate of Alexander the Great to fall into the hands of the Cretans, and with tearful supplications he besought those who had it to exchange it for money.'

An extraordinary passage in Justin dealing with Antigonus II *Gonatas*' seduction of the Gauls (who were 'struck with the vast quantity of gold and silver set before them') before battle near Lysimachia in 277 BCE, and those in Diodorus and Plutarch detailing the aftermath of Perseus' defeat, provide evidence that a still substantial hoard of riches from Alexander's campaigns must have remained in the Pellan vaults; astoundingly, it appears that even in the ruinously expensive Successor Wars the Macedonian kings dared not coin the conqueror's gold and silver campaign spoils from Persia.

Perseus sought sanctuary in the temple of the Dioscuri in Thrace with his brother-in-law and son. Somewhat less remarkably, Perseus' royal pages abandoned him on the Roman promise of freedom and property. King Perseus had no choice but to turn himself in.[319] The Macedonian 'play had been performed'; the woollen *clamys* of the new *provincia Macedonia* finally bowed to the Roman toga, and the *sarissa* now took second place to the *gladius* and the *scutum*, which slew 20,000 Macedonians on the day with a further 11,000 taken prisoner. The gleaming silver shields of the *Argyraspides* had long before dulled to the bronze of the *Chalkaspides* and white of the *Leukaspides*, and Greek celestial superstition kneeled to cosmic practicality.[320] Livy claimed only one hundred Romans died, though the wounded count was far higher; these are victor-vanquished ratios resonant of Alexander's battles with Darius III.[321]

Whilst Livy stated that Macedonia was (initially) to remain 'free' and with her mines unexploited, the country was divided into four civic regions (*merides*) and half of the royal tribute was now directed to Rome; in addition, all nobles and their children over fifteen years of age were to be shipped to Italy.[322] Cicero was clearer on the consequences: mines *were* confiscated and over 5,600 talents, equivalent to some fifty-six years of tribute now set at 100 talents per year, ended up in Rome; the riches, he claimed, 'did away with the need for a tax on property… for all time to come'. Although Diodorus focused on Aemilius' lenient treatment of the defeated, Polybius captured the more calamitous detail: some 150,000 of the inhabitants of allied Epirus were sold into slavery and seventy cities were destroyed.[323]

The remaining Macedonian-governed domains of the Ptolemies and Seleucids were under the threat of direct occupation too. As blades met at Pydna, Antiochus IV *Epiphanes* ('god manifest', though Polybius used *Epimanes*, 'the mad one', due to his eccentric behaviour) proclaimed himself king of Egypt to conclude the Sixth Syrian War; Polybius had been chosen as part of the Achaean embassy to Antiochus a decade before when in his early twenties.[324] Alexandria, surrounded by hostile troops, appealed to Rome which sent no army but the solitary Gaius Popilius Laenas as ambassador to demand the Seleucid withdrawal; standing alone in Antiochus' path, he drew his famous line in the sand about the Seleucid king standing outside the besieged city. Antiochus requested time to consider his position, but Popilius demanded an answer on withdrawal before he stepped over the line, or he would deem it a declaration of war on a 'friend' of Rome.

Surely recalling that his predecessor, Antiochus III (then an ally of the Greek Achaean League), had been defeated at Magnesia twenty-two years before, *Epiphanes* quickly withdrew, allowing the previously hostaged Ptolemy VI *Philometor* (his nephew who had previously asked for help from the Achaean League) and his wife Cleopatra II (Ptolemy's sister in Pharaonic style), along with his younger brother Ptolemy VIII *Euergetes* II (nicknamed *Physkon,* 'potbelly' or 'sausage' for his obesity, ca. 182-116 BCE), to jointly rule. Even Greek cities like Lampsacus, close to the ruins of Troy, appealed to their 'kinsmen' in 'the Rome of Aeneas' for protection against their Seleucid overlords. Clearly, all including the 'indolent' Egyptian pharaohs, now knew the consequences of facing the legions of Rome.[325]

The great era of the Hellenistic warships of the Successors passed once Rome termed the Mediterranean *mare nostrum*, 'our sea', in which Rhodes and then the new Rome-protected clearinghouse of Delos became preeminent in trade (particularly in slaves), necessitating the minting of new coinage for the expanded market; the Delian sanctuary of Apollo became a prolific moneylender as a result. Ptolemaic Egypt lost out commercially to Syria as the traditional caravan routes were now terminating in Phoenicia and Palestine, and a Rome-backed Attalid Pergamum began to eclipse even Alexandria.[326]

By 146 BCE Macedonia finally became an official Roman province and Lucian would later describe Pella (ca. 180 CE) as 'insignificant, with very few inhabitants'.[327] The *Koinon Makedonon*, the nation's traditional Common Assembly, became a Roman-supervised *concilium* although the new masters did learn the Greek language to administer their spoils, whereas the Greeks showed little interest in Latin.[328] As one scholar put it, the Hellenes had given the world a culture, now Rome would establish a civilisation.[329] Greece would not see her freedom again until 1832.[330]

Aemilius Paullus, the architect of the victory at Pydna, was the father of the also-present seventeen-year-old Scipio Aemilianus, blood stained and 'carried away by the uncontrollable pleasure of the victory...' He would oversee the fall of Carthage in 146 BCE, the same year wealthy Corinth was plundered, by which time Rome had become something of a museum of Greek art and antiquities; even the twenty-five bronze equestrian statues Alexander had Lysippus fashion in memory of the Companions who fell at the Granicus River battle would be collected from Dion by Quintus Caecilius Metellus '*Macedonicus*'.[331]

Escorted back to Rome after victory at Pydna were 250 waggons of booty, a chained King Perseus, and Metrodorus the Athenian philosopher as a tutor for Aemilius Paullus' sons.[332] Also taken were 1,000 notable Achaeans as good-behaviour hostages;[333] they included Polybius, the politically-connected cavalry commander (*hipparchos*) from Megalopolis in Arcadia, and who, as a member of the Achaean League (in fact second-in-command), was technically in league with the Italians (since 198 BCE when the league abandoned Philip V, a former ally), though he was on the wrong side of the equally hostile Callicrates and his policy of 'abject subservience and obsequiousness to Rome'.[334] For Polybius' father had advocated strict neutrality in the Roman war with Macedonia and he was a victim of that political divide, thus deemed of suspect loyalty.[335]

Now in his early thirties, Polybius would also educate Paullus' sons; he soon perfected for the Roman legions a telegraphic aid that sent messages by torches and which came to be known as the Polybius Square. During the next seventeen eventful years as a hostage in Rome (despite at least five pleas by the Achaean League for his return to Greece), or on the march with Roman generals which included a stint in Africa, he rubbed shoulders with senators and influential families and completed his military *Tactics*; it prompted Scipio and his brother to petition the city praetor that he be allowed to remain there for good. In return, Polybius' diplomacy is said to have 'stayed the wrath' of the Romans against a now toothless Greece, and in particular against the Achaean League which was also disbanded in 146 BCE following a disastrous (and ill-reported) short war with Rome.[336]

Recalling the battle at Pydna when he later penned his *Histories*, and summing a fate that saw King Perseus die in prison in Rome, Polybius claimed the last ever *dynastic* Macedonian king recalled a prophecy that the goddess Fortuna favoured the Macedones only until she favoured others:

> So then often and bitterly did Perseus call to mind the words of Demetrius of Phalerum. For he, in his treatise on Fortuna, wishing to give men a striking instance of her mutability asks them to remember the times when Alexander overthrew the Persian Empire, and speak as follows: 'For if you consider not countless years or many generations, but merely these last fifty years, you will read in them the cruelty of Fortune. I ask you, do you think that fifty years ago either the Persians and the Persian king or the Macedonians and the king of Macedon, if some god had foretold the future to them, would ever have believed that at the time when we live, the very name of the Persians would have perished utterly – the Persians who were masters of almost the whole world – and that the Macedonians, whose name was formerly almost unknown, would now be the lords of it all? But nevertheless this Fortune, who never compacts with life, who always defeats our reckoning by some novel stroke; she who ever demonstrates her power by foiling our expectations, now also, as it seems to me, makes it clear to all men, by endowing the Macedonians with the whole wealth of Persia, that she has but lent them these blessings until she decides to deal differently with them.' And this now happened in the time of Perseus. Surely Demetrius, as if by the mouth of some god, uttered these prophetic words.[337]

Demetrius' words were repeated almost word for word by Diodorus and also précised by Livy.[338] So no one in Rome could fail to acknowledge Alexander's part in its own conquest of the East, but as Polybius sensed, and as Diodorus, Nepos, and Plutarch knew from their own research of the era, the remarkable *Diadokhoi* who became the first Hellenistic kings, had inherited more than a knowledge of *sarissa* drills and flying wedges from their Argead mentors: they had learned Macedonian statecraft.

Had Alexander's own ambition never ventured beyond the expanded borders established by his father, these Pellan court aristocrats may have contented themselves with governing one of the ancient feudal cantons of Upper or Lower Macedonia.[339] The more ambitious of them might have become condottieri working for a tyrant or satrap in Asia Minor. But Alexander had set the bar high, and in the process he infused his court *hetairoi* with a vision far grander than domestic state affairs or seasonal campaigning to pocket gold darics. For they had come to harbour a self-belief that emanated from their part in his great journey, resulting in talented satraps who coveted kingdoms, not the ephemeral wealth of serving the remaining Argead line. It was an ambition that, according to Justin, left Fortune inspiring them 'with mutual emulation for their mutual destruction'.[340] Their transformation to purple and the wearing of *stephanephoria* was irreversible and an idea as intoxicating as Alexander himself.

What *is* beyond doubt is the ambition, ruthlessness and tenacity of Alexander's successors. If their king's last words in Babylon had truly rejected a continuation of his line and had cynically invited them to slug it out for the throne, diadems would have adorned the *Diadokhoi* and their coins more than a decade before they did.

The Tyche of Antioch, a Roman copy of a bronze by Eutychides, a pupil of Lysippus, dating to ca. 300 BCE and the founding of the city of Antioch by the Seleucids. The goddess of fortune is portrayed in mural crown sitting on a rock by the Orontes River represented by a swimming boy, while holding stalks of grain signifying prosperity. The depiction proved so popular that it was copied by a number of cities and on coins. Her divine roots were however obscure: Hesiod related Tyche to Tethys and Oceanus, whereas Pindar claimed she was the most powerful sister of the Three Fates. Now in the Galleria dei Candelabri, Vatican Museum.

NOTES

1. Demosthenes *On the Crown* 270.
2. Aeschines *On the False Embassy* 118.
3. Thucydides 3.39.5.
4. Aristotle *Politics* 3.1284a.
5. Diodorus 19.1 for the saying. 'Slay the tallest stalks to protect the crop' is rooted in Aristotle *Politics* 3.1284a, and also Herodotus 5.92 ff; in Herodotos' version it is Thrasybulus giving the advice to Periander, and the reverse in Aristotle's rendering. Livy 1.54.
6. Aristotle *Politics* 3.1284a; the text continued '… indeed a man would be ridiculous if he tried to legislate for them, for probably they would say what in the story of Antisthenes the lions said when the hares made speeches in the assembly and demanded that all should have equality.'
7. The dating of the *Constitution of the Athenians* is uncertain as themes relating to the 330s and 320s BCE *appear* to be present; the work may even have been a later student compilation. Aristotle's *Politics* appeared sometime between his return to Athens in 335 BCE when he founded the Lyceum, and before 323 BCE.
8. Quoting Justin 8.1.1-3 on Philip's oppression of Greek liberty. The prytaneion was the room in which the central hearth housing sacred fire was kept. Each city-state, or even town, had one and it came to represent the town hall or magistrates' office. Thucydides 2.15 and Aristotle's *Politics* referred to the prytaneion of Athens where the archons resided, though its location is uncertain and may have changed through time.
9. Curtius 9.6.8.
10. Demosthenes *Second Olynthiac* 8.11, 9.50 and 18.235 for Philip's campaigning ability. As the Spartans used enslaved helots to farm their land, they were free to campaign throughout the year, religious festivals aside.
11. Diodorus 16.89.2 for Philip's declaration against Persia.
12. The Myrmidons were a legendary race commanded by Achilles and renowned as skilled warriors. *Iliad* 1.179-180 for the Myrmidons being referred to as Achilles' *hetairoi*.
13. Justin 13.1-4 commented that after Alexander's death the Bodyguards became princes instead of prefects.
14. A loose translation of the sentiment in Cicero *Laelius De Amicitia* 17.64, for example the Loeb Classical Library edition, 1923, translates this as 'When Fortune's fickle the faithful friend is found'.
15. Lucullas became so renowned for his banqueting that we now use 'Lucullan' when referring to 'lavish' or 'gourmet'. Plutarch *Lucullus* claimed be had a budget of 50,000 drachmas for nightly dining.
16. Quoting Ennius from Cicero's *De Officiis* 1.7.
17. '*Kata polemon*', broadly 'to do with war'; see I Worthington in Carney-Ogden (2010) p 171 and footnote 29 for a discussion of its use.
18. Demosthenes *First Olynthiac* 1.4; discussed in Anson (2013) p 19. The list of Macedonian kings traditionally includes legendary names such as Caranus, but additional uncertainty exists over whether Philip's nephew, Amyntas IV, briefly came to the throne or whether Ptolemy of Alorus had, or simply acted as regent.
19. As indicated at Plutarch *Cicero* 7.1-2. Cicero *De Officiis* 1.26.
20. Cicero *De Officiis* 1: *Moral Goodness* 90.26, translation from the Loeb Classical Library edition, 1913.
21. Musgrave-Prag-Neave-Lane Fox (2010) section 9.1.3 for Amyntas IV's possible reign. Justin 7.5.9 for the people demanding Philip take on the kingship.
22. Green (1974) p 22 for the five usurpers.
23. Diodorus 14.92.3-4, 14.19.2, 16.6.2 for Illyrian incursions, and following Anson (2013) p 44. Diodorus 16.2.4-5 for the death of Perdiccas III and his losses. Hammond (1991) pp 25-30 for a summary of Perdiccas' challenges. After the death of King Amyntas III in 370/369 BCE, Ptolemy of Alorus, a possible envoy to the king (an alliance with Athens in 375-373 BCE mentioned the name) and possibly the son of Amyntas II (Diodorus 15.71.1; thus descended from the line of Menelaus, son of Alexander I) started a liaison with Amyntas' widow, Eurydice, and he may in fact have married her and ascended to the throne. In 368/367 BCE Ptolemy allegedly assassinated Alexander II (Diodorus 16.2.4 and 15.71.1-2 but Demosthenes *On the False Embassy* 19.194-95 stated an Apollophanes was executed for the murder) after less than two years on the throne (Diodorus 15.60.3 stated 1 year), and became guardian (*epitropos*) for the immature Perdiccas III (Aeschines *On the Embassy* 2.29, Plutarch *Pelopidas* 27.3), a role that saw him become regent of the kingdom until Perdiccas killed him in 365 BCE and then reigned for five years (Diodorus 15.77.5). Diodorus 15.71.1, 15.77.5, Eusebius *Kronographia* 228, stated Ptolemy was in fact

basileus, king, for three years, but the use of the demotic, Alorus, and the absence of coinage in his name, speak otherwise. Moreover his marriage to Eurydice (Justin 7.4.7, Aeschines 2.29) and previously to her daughter, Eurynoe (Justin 7.4.7-7, 7.5.4-8 stated Ptolemy and Eurydice were lovers even then), suggest he needed legitimacy his heritage did not provide. According to Justin, the intrigue was revealed by Eurynoe. Why Eurydice intrigued with Ptolemy remains unclear (Justin 7.5 claimed she had previously plotted against Amyntas who spared her for the sake of their children); it may have been to undermine Alexander II, or the line of Amyntas on behalf of a foreign regime, or simply lovers intriguing to put Ptolemy in power, even above her sons. However, neither Diodorus nor Plutarch included her in any plotting with Ptolemy, so her involvement may be fiction; Carney (2006) p 90 argues that there is evidence she was a loyal and devoted mother. Pelopidas, who had already driven the Macedonian garrisons installed by Alexander II from Thessaly, was called in to arbitrate (Plutarch *Pelopidas* 26.3, Diodorus 16.67.4). Pelopidas was offered, or took, hostages for good behaviour, including Philip II.

24. Iphicrates (in 368-365 BCE) and Timotheus (in 363, 360 and 359 BCE) had both tried to take the city without success. Carney-Ogden (2010) p 74 for Heracles' former possession of the city, according to Speusippus. Hatzopoulos (1996) p 184 argues Amphipolis remained 'theoretically independent' after the siege; epigraphic evidence suggests a high Ionic Greek population remained. See chapter titled *The Rebirth of the Wrath of Peleus' Son* for more on Heraclid origins of the Argeads.

25. Athenaeus 13.557 for Satyrus' comment.

26. Quoting Fredericksmeyer (1981) p 334 on 'harem for political purposes'.

27. Plutarch 9.4, Athenaeus 13.557d declared it a love match. Anson (2013) p 53 for discussion. Athenaeus 13.557b-e for a rundown of Philip's wives and the political motivation behind the marriages.

28. Justin 8.2 for the laurel crowns.

29. Diodorus 16.95.2-5 suggested that Philip was more proud of his strategy and diplomatic successes then his valour in actual battle. For Philip's guile see discussion in Thomas (2007) p 83. Justin 8.2.3-5 for Philip leading a coalition of Macedonians, Thessalians and Thebans. The Amphyctionic Council represented thirteen Greek peoples; Anson (2013) p 71. Flower (1994) pp 36-37 for Theopompus' book on the Sacred War stolen artifacts.

30. Diodorus 16.60.1-4 for Philip and the Amphyctionic League. Hammond (1994) pp 168-169 for Philip's expeditionary force and its treatment of cities.

31. Fredericksmeyer (1990) p 305 as quoted in Gabriel (2010) p 2.

32. Hatzopoulos (1996) p 476 for the expansions under Philip. According to Thucydides 2.99.2 these Upper Macedonian regions were self-governing previously; detail in Anson (2004) p 214 and p 221 for ongoing autonomy.

33. Quoting Hatzopoulos (1996) p 204.

34. 'Everything north of Hellas' was an observation by Justin 7.2.13-14 and quoting Hammond (1994) p 137.

35. Justin 9.7.2-7 for the hostility between Olympias and Philip and him painting a picture that Philip's assassination was contrived by Olympias. See chapter titled *The Reborn Wrath of Peleus' Son* for fuller discussion of the intrigues of Olympias and Alexander in the final years of Philip's reign.

36. Diodorus 16.92.5 for the display of wealth in the procession of statues of the twelve Olympian gods and a thirteenth of Philip that preceded the wedding; following the conclusion of Anson (2013) p 91. Hatzopoulos (1996) p 272 for the wedding coinciding with the *panegyris*. Aelian 8.15 for the slave calls. Carney (2006) pp 1001-101 and footnote 131 for varying views on Philip's quest for divinity.

37. Discussion by AB Bosworth in Carney-Ogden (2010) p 99 for the development of the foot companions under the sons of Amyntas.

38. Diodorus 17.17.5, 17.118.1, 18.12.1 for the implication that Antipater was general of Europe; presumably this meant Greece and a 'greater' Macedonia comprising the control of Thrace, Epirus, Illyria and adjacent conquered regions; see Blackwell (1999) p 36 footnote 10 for discussion.

39. Diodorus 17.17.3-5 for the total troop numbers accompanying Alexander to Asia and left in Macedonia, some 12,000 infantry and 1,500 cavalry; Anson (2013) p 44 for discussion.

40. Discussed in Carney (1995) pp 370-371 quoting Diodorus 17.118.1 for *strategos* and 17.17.5 for *hegemonia*. Plutarch 9.1 for the *kurios* role Alexander held under Philip II and 68.3 for suggesting a non-exclusive power of Antipater in Alexander's own absence. Fuller discussion in Anson (1992).

41. Full discussion of Olympias' role and her relationship with Antipater in Blackwell (1999) pp 81-131.

42. Plutarch *Demetrius* 22.1 for the captured correspondence. They allegedly opened all of Philip's

letters except one from Olympias, which they returned to him unopened.

43. Quoting the definition in Arrian 3.16.10, Penguin Books edition, 1971, p 174, editor's footnote 42.

44. Hornblower (1981) pp 34-35 and pp 76-80 on the Hellenistic use of terms associated with Alexander's army and general staff. Livy 44.41.2 for Livy's confusing use of *caertracti* for peltasts; discussed in Snodgrass (1967) p 123. Also see Sekunda (2012) pp 11-12 for Livy's military terminologies.

45. The various titles are presented and discussed in Carney (1995) p 373 and fuller discussion in Anson (1992) pp 39-41.

46. For the origins of *basileus* see Sihler (1995) p 330.

47. The armour was discovered in a chamber tomb at Dendra near Mycenae in May 1960. This shield design was termed *dipylon* after the group of vases depicting them found at the Dipylon Cemetery in Athens. Similarly the Corinthian helmet is found on Corinthian pottery and mentioned at Herodotus 4.180.

48. Snodgrass (1967) p 14 ff for Mycenaean shaft-grave funds, armour and weaponry. The Hittite monopoly on iron production discussed in Snodgrass (1967) p 36.

49. The comparison made in Snodgrass (1967) p 24. The Louis XIV armour is exhibited in the Musée D'Artillerie in Paris.

50. Hoplites were frequently depicted as holding two spears in 7th century works of art, perhaps for throwing and for thrusting; discussed in Hanson (1991) p 16; p 65 for the 'codification'. The cuirass would have been worn over a *chitiniskos*, a linen tunic to stop chaffing; Anderson (1970) p 25.

51. Snodgrass (1967) p 48 ff for the development of the hoplite and p 67 for shield designs.

52. Quoting Plutarch *Pelopidas* 2.1 for the analogy to the body and Snodgrass (1967) p 49 for 'rigid framework'.

53. For the respective formations of the Thebans and Spartans at Leuctra, see Plutarch *Pelopidas* 22-23, Xenophon *Hellenika* 6.4.12 (6.4.14 for their shoving the Spartans back), 6.4.17; Spartan manoeuvres at 4.2.20, 4.3.18, 6.5.18-19 and discussed in Hanson (1991) p 104. There is some confusion on where the Sacred Band hit the Spartan line as they appear to have run ahead of the Theban advance to catch the Spartans off-guard; some scholars suggest they hit the Spartan flank. Devine (1983) p 204 for the infantry wedge. The traditional phalanx face-off arrangement disappeared in favour of oblique advance, refusals and deliberate retreats, as later employed by Philip and Alexander. The death toll in battle also rose from such strategies where 'shock assaults' were used. Diodorus 15.52-56 detailed the battle at Leuctra but did not mention the Sacred Band, curious when he referenced the Carthaginian Sacred Battalion in the same book.

54. *Iliad* 2.362.

55. Thucydides 2.100.5, Xenophon *Hellenika* 5.2.38-5.3.6 for cavalry use in the Macedonian state and following the summation of Hatzopoulos (1996) p 267. Thucydides 2.100.2 for Archelaus' reforms; discussed in Hatzopoulos (1996) p 469.

56. Following Anson (2013) p 44 for the increase in cavalry numbers.

57. Quoting Lane Fox (2011) p 377 for 'blueprint of Hellenistic warfare'.

58. Tarn (1948) pp 138-139 for the origins of the Companion Cavalry. Sekunda (1984) p 5 for 600 in number originally. Arrian 6.21.3 seems to have used the term Close Companion as the elite corps of the Companion Cavalry, thus the royal *agema* as per Arrian 4.24.1. The numbers given by Diodorus 17.17.4 and Arrian 6.14.4 suggest the royal squadron was doubled in size and later possibly trimmed at 300; Eumenes and Antigonus had units of 300 with them at Paraetacenae; Diodorus 19.29.5, 19.28.3. The purple cloaks suggested by the Alexander Sarcophagus and Diodorus 17.77.5; discussed in Sekunda (1984) p 17. Arrian 1.14.6, 1.28.3, 5.13.4 for the suggestion of 'daily' positions of command; following Hatzopoulos (1996) p 244 for the observation. 'Upper class' was a term attached to cavalry under Alexander by Anaximenes of Lampsacus; FGrH 72 F 4.

59. Arrian 4.24.1 and 4.24.2 for *ilai* making 1 *hipparchaia*. Arrian 6.27.6 and 7.24.4 for *hekatostyes*. Sekunda (1984) p 31 for the infantry reforms in Asia and B Bosworth in Carney-Ogden (2010) pp 94-102 for *hekatostyes* and *lochoi*. Anaximenes FGrH 72 F4 from Harpocration's *Lexikon*.

60. Markle (1977) proposed 120-men wedges and discussed in Gabriel (2010) p 219 though Sekunda (1984) p 14 refers to Aelian Tacticus for forty-nine men. Aelian Tacticus 39.2-6 credited Philip with the development of the wedge; this probably means 'refinement'. Arrian 3.18.5 mentioned a *tetrarchia* of cavalry. The *tetrarchia* discussed in Roisman-Worthington (2010) p 453.

61. Aelian Tacticus 18.2-4, Asclepiodotus *Tactics* 7.2-3 and 7.6.7 for the wedge development by the Scythians and Thracians and Jason's development of the diamond formation. Devine (1983) for the origins of the wedge infantry and cavalry formation in detail and Lenden (2005) pp 98-102 for the Rhombus formation and its advantages.

62. Arrian *Tékhne Táktika* 16.6 ff for the wedge formation adopted by Philip, cited in Gabriel (2010)

pp 76-77, and Markle (1977) p 339. Gabrielson (1990) pp 84-85 for discussion of Alexander's cavalry action at Chaeronea.

63. Hammond (1994) pp 148-150 and Gabriel 2010 pp 214-222 for in depth analysis of the battle. Green (1974) p 74 for Athens' inactivity.

64. *Pynknosis* is an 'intermediary' compactness in which phalangites were separated by perhaps 3 feet and *synaspismos* represented a more closely packed order.

65. Diodorus 16.3.2 and *Iliad* 13.131 ff for the compacted ranks at Troy; see the discussion in Lenden (2005) p 11. Hector's spear was described in the *Iliad* 6 as 11 cubits (16 feet) long and held with both hands. The *Iliad's* allusion of peltast-styled fighting discussed in Lenden (2005) pp 96-97.

66. Anson (2013) p 47 for the Thracian thrusting spear. The relative shortness of the Spartan sword discussed in Anderson (1970) p 38; they carried spears of course as well. Snodgrass (1967) p 110 and p 127 for Iphicrates' military reforms based on Diodorus 15.44.4, Nepos *Iphicrates* 1.3-4 where it was claimed that Iphicrates doubled the length of spears; Diodorus 15.44.3 stated they were extended by half their length. Also Anderson (1970) pp 130-131 for Iphicrates' lengthening weapons and the rationale.

67. Plutarch *Comparison of Pelopidas with Marcellus*. Devine (1983) p 204 for Epaminondas' infantry wedge used at Leuctra. Plutarch *Pelopidas* 26.3 for his arbitration in Macedonia. Justin 7.5 for Epaminondas being an 'eminent' philosopher.

68. AB Bosworth in Carney-Ogden (2010) p 99 for Alexander II's friendship with Pelopidas. Diodorus 16.2.1-4 for Philip being handed to the Thebans by the Illyrians with whom he had been a child hostage and being schooled with Epaminondas under a Pythagorean teacher. Following Diodorus 16.2.2, Loeb Classical Library edition, 1952, footnote 4: since Philip was born ca. 383 BCE he was an infant when given to the Illyrians. Justin 7.5.1 stated that Philip was ransomed by Alexander II and later sent by him as a hostage to Thebes. However at Diodorus 15.67.4 likewise has Alexander II sending him to Thebes, as does Plutarch *Pelopidas* 26.4. Some modern historians agree that Ptolemy of Alorus, paramour and later husband of Eurydice, the widow of Amyntas III, was the monarch who sent Philip to Thebes, basing their account on Aeschines *False Embassy*, 2.26 ff, which placed Philip at the court of Ptolemy. Pelopidas who had already driven the Macedonian garrisons installed by Alexander II from Thessaly, was called in to arbitrate (Plutarch *Pelopidas* 26.3, Diodorus 16.67.4) and he may have demanded hostages for good behaviour, including Philip II. Philip, aged fourteen or fifteen, was probably in Thebes throughout 368-365 BCE. See discussion by Hammond (1991) p 58 and Hammond (1980) pp 53-63. Plutarch *Pelopidas* 26.5 termed Philip an 'emulator' of Epaminondas with whom he was said to be educated by a Pythagorean; this conflicts with the claim that Philip lodged in the house of Pammenes (Plutarch *Pelopidas* 26.5, Diodorus 15.94.2, 16.34.1-2) and Epaminondas was surely too old to have been educated with Philip. Diodorus 15.39.2 for Epaminondas' education. See discussion in Billows (1990) p 30. Many scholars reject this and claim Philip was too young in his hostage period to have been significantly influenced; full discussion in Hammond (1997). Justin 8.5.1-3 for Philip's hostage time with the Illyrians. Diodorus 18.86.5 for the overall numbers of dead and captured at Chaeronea.

69. Polyaenus 4.2.10 for the forced marches of Philip and Frontinus 4.1.6 for the rations; Heckel-Jones (2006) p 12 for discussion. Frontinus 4.1.6 for the waggonless army; discussion in Gabriel (2010) pp 85-86. Frontinus 4.2.4 and Aelian 14.48 for flogging and execution; Roisman-Worthington (2010) p 451 for discussion. The oracle at Trophonius in Boeotia warned Philip to be on his guard against a chariot; he avoided them thereafter; Aelian 3.45.

70. Plato *Laches* 181-183d for an example of the demonstration of the *hoplomachia*; discussed in Hanson (1991) p 29.

71. Confusion stems from the Roman-inspired '*cohors*' (a cohort, but here perhaps a *chiliarchia*). Latin sources further complicate our understanding of battle order with units and commands labelled *armiger* and *custos*, as well as *corporis* for the bodyguard corps of nobles (perhaps 200; royal hypaspists, or former royal pages) and the seven elite members of the *hypaspistai basilikoi*, the king's *Somatophylakes*. Heckel *Somatophylakes* (1978) p 224, Sekunda (1984) p 9 for the Latin derivatives associated with the corps of perhaps 200. Curtius 3.12.3 for *cohors*. Curtius 4.21.9 mentioned a body of 700 bodyguards. Curtius 5.2.3-5 for nine chiliarchs being appointed. Devine (1983) p 206 for the terms relating to infantry formations. Arrian 1.11.7-8 suggested the hypaspists carried the king's weapons, taken from Troy, into battle; as Peucestas allegedly carried the shield from Troy at Mallia, then he is credibly a former royal hypaspist of perhaps 200 elites.

72. Theopompus FGrH 115 F 348 and Diodorus 16.93.1 for references to Philip's *doryphoroi*. A summary of the arguments on the panoply of the king's guard in Anson (2013) pp 50-51 and by Anson in Carney-Ogden (2010) pp 81-90; p 81 for shield sizes. The term hypaspists may be alternatively used for 'armour-bearer' or 'esquire'; see Milns (1971) p 186. Their attested mobility on long forced marches suggests they might have been more lightly armed than the rest of the phalanx; their activities detailed at Arrian 1.27.8, 2.4.3, 3.23.3, 4.28.8; Milns (1971)

pp 187-188 for discussion of armour and equipment and Heckel-Jones (2006) pp 17-18. The hypaspists seem to have numbered 1,000 under Philip in an army of 10,000 infantry and were expanded to 3,000 under Alexander when he left for Asia; he had 12,000 infantry in total, 9,000 of which were pikemen; discussion in Anson (1985) p 248 and Heckel-Jones (200) pp 30-31. Arrian 1.11.8 stated the hypaspists carried Alexander's sacred shield from Troy into battle; hardly a role for anyone but a hoplite-equipped infantryman.

73. Anson (2004) pp 227 and 229 for the possible, or misunderstood, expansion of the *hetairos* relationship outside of these elite units. We do not read of Philip in cavalry units and he may well have preferred an infantry position for himself. Hammond (1991) p 44 for the military reforms of Alexander II.

74. Theopompus FGRH 115 F-225 for the number at 800; discussed in Hatzopoulos (1996) p 29 and Anson (2004) p 228. The number 3,000 was *possibly* later raised to 4,000 (as per Berve) and as suggested in Curtius 5.1.40 and Arrian 3.16.10. Milns (1971) argues against this.

75. Pausanias 1.21.7; the limited use of linen discussed in Anderson (1970) p 23.

76. Plutarch *Pelopidas* 2 for Iphicrates' hoplite reforms. Aeschines *On the Embassy* 2.28 claimed Eurydice placed her two surviving sons in Iphicrates' arms when pleading for his support as her stepson.

77. Anson (1988) summarises the arguments about the origin of the Silver Shields, whether it was shortly after the Macedonians returned from India or early in the Successor Wars; at Diodorus 19.28.1 and 19.40.3 they are mentioned as distinct from hypaspist units. Curtius 8.5.4 and Justin 12.7.4 suggested Alexander's fighting force was adorned with precious ornaments and shields plated with silver as they entered India, i.e. after capturing the Achaemenid treasuries. Also Tarn (1948) p 116 ff and pp 151-152 for the origins of the unit. Tarn's contention was that *Argyraspides*, first mentioned at the battle of Gaugamela, was simply the elite *agema* of the hypaspists renamed by Hieronymus who misled later historians. He likewise sees this as proof that Curtius used Diodorus. Diodorus 18.57.2 stated they were distinguished because of the brilliance of their armour. Confusion is thrown in by the mention at Arrian 7.11.13 of a Persian *Argyraspides* regiment and earlier mention of the Silver Shields at Gaugamela at Diodorus 17.57.2 and Curtius 4.13.27, yet by then considerable wealth had already been captured from Darius' baggage train at Issus and Damascus. The identification may have additionally been retrospective by historians, as it seems the regiment was renamed during the Indian campaign; see discussion in Roisman-Worthington (2010) p 455. Sekunda (2012) pp18-19 for varying shield sizes found dating to the period.

78. Diodorus 17.65.4 and Curtius 5.2.2-7 for the Sittacene reorganisations. E Anson in Carney-Ogden (2010) p 93 for the reorganisations at Sittacene.

79. Diodorus 17.57.2, Curtius 4.13.28 for the upper canton names attached to the infantry battalions. Hammond (1991) p 70 for the size of Philip's army when he died. Heckel-Jones (2006) p 10 and pp 30-31 for 9,000 *pezhetairoi*.

80. Heckel-Jones (2006) p 43 for the arrangement of the phalangites. Curtius 5.2.3 for the suggestion of *pentakosiarchos*; discussion in Milns (1971) pp 188-189. *Hekatostyes* discussed by B Bosworth in Carney-Ogden (2010) pp 94-102. Roisman-Worthington (2010) p 448 for the increase in size of *dekades* and its origins, as well as *lochoi* used for one hundred infantry.

81. Hatzopoulos (1996) p 450 for the general use of *taxis*. Anson (2004) p 215 for examples of regional battalion leaders.

82. Curtius 5.2.3 for the new commands of 1,000 versus 500.

83. Heckel-Jones (2006) p 10 and pp 30-31 for 9,000 *pezhetairoi* and the distinction arguments between them and *asthetairoi*. Hammond (1994) p 150 along with Bosworth suggests the *asthetairoi* units were comprised of Upper Macedonians (derived from *astya*, the towns) where the *pezhetairoi* came from the old kingdom, i.e. the ancient heartlands. Heckel (1988) p 321 for identity discussion and differing views; Bosworth suggests the title 'closest companions'. In Carney-Ogden (2010) pp 88-89 Anson suggests the '*asth*' stood for 'star' referring to the star motif on their shields. Their mobility is convincingly argued for and applied at Arrian 4.23.1, 4.218.8. Arrian 2.23.2 and 4.23.1 for examples of 'Close Companions'. Arrian 2.23.3-4, 3.11.9-12, 3.25.6, 4.23.1 for use and deployment. Whilst an apparent *hapax legomenon*, as Milns (1981) p 354 points out, six variants of *asthetairoi* appeared in Arrian *Anabasis*. Roisman-Worthington (2010) pp 457-458 for the evidence on the Alexander Sarcophagus.

84. More on the *thureophoroi* below.

85. *Asthippoi* (or *amphippoi*) appear at Diodorus 19.29.2; the suggestion was that these cavalrymen rode a pair of horses with the rider jumping from one to the other when a mount was exhausted, in the style of the Tarentines who followed Philopoemen; see Livy 35.28.8. Aelian 38.3 was clear that they were nomadic archers who exchanged mounts. Both titles, *asthippoi* (or *amphippoi*) and *asthetairoi* could be Hieronymus-sourced (if Arrian was back-forming names). See Milns (1981) and Hammond *Cavalry* (1978) for possible identifications and derivation of the name.

86. Diodorus 17.20.3 stated Alexander carried a shield, and his survival in close action at 17.60.2, Plutarch 16.4, Arrian 1.2.6, when spears were being hurled against him, suggests the same. Anderson (1970) p 113 for Amazon and Scythian cavalry shields.

87. Hammond *Cavalry* (1978) and Milns (1981) p 351 for the disappearance of *sarissophoroi*.

88. Diodorus 17.17.3-5 for troop numbers crossing to Asia. Following the Loeb Classical Library edition, (1963), 17.17.4 footnote 4: Diodorus is our only source for the detailed troop list of Alexander. Justin 11.6.2 gave 32,000 foot and 4,500 horse; Plutarch 15.1 cited 30,000-43,000 foot and 4,000-5,000 horse; Arrian 1.11.3 stated 'not much more than' 30,000 foot and 5,000 horse. Plutarch *Moralia* 327d-e (*De Fortuna aut Virtute Alexandri* 1.3) stated Aristobulus stated 30,000 foot and 4,000 horse, Ptolemy 30,000 foot and 5,000 horse, and Anaximenes 43,000 foot and 5,500 horse.

89. Plutarch *Aemilius* 19.2 and 20.2 for the ability of the *sarissa* to penetrate shields and armour. 'First-strike' capability quoting Milns (1971) p 188. Plutarch *Aemilius* and Diodorus 17.84.4 for the shield and armour piercing ability of the sarissa.

90. The Greek *dory* had a sharp point at the counterpoint known as a *sauroter*, literally 'lizard killer', or alternatively the *sturax* or *ouriachos* (see Hanson (1991) p 71), which anchored the spear securely to the ground and could be used as a secondary blade if, for example, the spear snapped in two or the enemy lay on the ground. Homer *Iliad* 10.153 for the first reference to the *sauroter*.

91. Anson (2013) and Sekunda (2012) pp 15-16 reject cherrywood in favour of the much lighter ash. Theophrastus *Enquiry into Plants* 3.12.1-2 reported that the male cherry tree grew up to 12 *ells* (or 12 cubits thus 18 feet) high, the length of the longest *sarissa* but did not specifically state this wood was used; in fact the shape of the trees and its low split point argues against it, unless the sarissa was assembled in two parts. The Roman Statius stated ash instead. Pliny 16.84 detailed the advantage of using ash being lighter and more pliable than cornel; a contention made by Statius; see Sekunda (2001) for discussion. Homer *Iliad* 19.390 and 4 47 for references to ash; discussed in Hanson (1991) p 22 ff. For the debate on the length of the *sarissa* see Sekunda (2012) pp 15-17; also Markle (1997) pp 323-329; Rahe (1981) pp 84-87; Mixter (1992) p 21 ff, Manti (1992) pp 77-91. Hatzopoulos (1996) p 268 states 3.5 to 4.5 metres for the *sarissa* length. Also see Polybius 18.28 and 31 for a description of the phalanx and lengths of pikes. See full discussion of the longest recorded *sarissai* in Delbrück (1920) pp 402-406. Polyaenus 2.29.2 stated that by 300 BCE the length had been increased to 16 cubits or 24 feet to 26 feet. Hammond (1991) p 7 for the Tomb II pike-head.

92. Andronikos (1970) proposed the two-part *sarissa* construction. Heckel-Jones (2006) p 14 for the iron coupling device.

93. Curtius 3.2.13.

94. Polybius 12.19.6 for a description of the thinning formation at the Battle of Issus; discussed in Sekunda (1984) p 23. Javelin throwing using the free right hand suggested by Diodorus 17.100.6-7 and Curtius 917.19-21 though this relies on the evidence in a single hand-to-hand combat; the suggestion is that all *pezhetairoi* bore javelins but perhaps more practically only the rear uncommitted ranks. Arrian *Tactics* 5 for the manoeuvre; discussed in Anderson (1970) p 101 ff.

95. Demosthenes *Third Philippic* 49. *Epikouroi* can be broadly interpreted as 'professional auxiliaries'.

96. The terror of the sight of the advancing phalanx as reported in Plutarch *Aemilius* 19.2. Polybius 18.29-30 for a description of the phalanx formation. Arrian 1.1.7-10 for the operation in which carts were rolled down on the Macedonian phalanx which allegedly used shields while lying flat to let the carts pass over, if the ranks could not be parted fast enough.

97. Sekunda (2012) p 20 for the helmets of the *pezhetairoi*. Whilst its exact construction method is still debated, the *linothorax* was mentioned at Herodotus 2.182, 2.529, 2.830, 3.47, 7.63, at Livy 4.19.2-4.20.7 and at Strabo 3.3.6; 13.1.10. 'Soft' armour was also known as *spolas* and could have been a thickly woven tunic, the *exomis*. Sekunda (1964) p 31 for the half-cuirass. Plutarch *Aemilius* 19.1-2 for the suggestion (unclear) that shields were slung to the chest when the *sarissa* phalanx advanced. Polybius 18.30 for the *sarissai* deflecting missiles.

98. Snodgrass (1967) p 117 for discussion of the *sarissa* phalanx armour. Shields were described as 8 hands or approximately 2 feet wide. Heckel-Jones (2006) p 15 for discussion of the *pezhetairoi* corselets, if any. Polyaenus 4.3.13 did suggest the *hemithorakion* was issued to those who had fled in battle to make their backs vulnerable. Heckel-Jones (2006) p 17 for the short sword. Sekunda (2012) argues for a handle on the shield rather than a neck strap but this would have put great stress on the left arm when holding the *sarissa*, as well as being presented at an awkward angle.

99. Polybius 3.6-7. Agesilaus' Spartan incursion in Persia is mentioned alongside Xenophon's march through the Persian Empire. As an example of the Greek bodyguards, four hundred hoplites deserted to Cyrus from the army of Abrocomas, satrap of Phoenicia, as the campaign against Artaxerxes II began. Discussion in Parke (1933) p 26.

100. For Persian military attire see Herodotus 7.61 and discussion in Cook (1983) pp 101-107.

Snodgrass (1967) p 102 for a comparison of the armour of the Greeks and Persians. Arrian 2.8.6 and Strabo 15.3.18 for Cardaces; their descriptions conflict; Tarn (1949) pp 180-182 for discussion.

101. Curtius 3.3.26-28 for his description of the Persian army and 3.2.13-16 for Charidemus' description of the Macedonians. Justin 11.13.11 for 'glittering with gold and silver'. Quoting Arrian 2.7.5 for warlike Europe and lazy effeminate Asia.

102. Fragment of Mnesimachus' *Philip*, translation from Green (1974) p 39.

103. All the extant accounts confirm otherwise unheard of battle ratios in favour of the Macedonians. Whilst this is certainly an exaggeration, light casualties are a recurring message against heavy enemy losses. As examples, for Issus see Arrian 1.16.2 for Persian cavalry losses, 1.16.4 for Macedonian cavalry losses and 2.11.8 for Persian losses where only mounted troop numbers were mentioned. Compare to Plutarch 20.11-13 and Curtius 3.11.27. For Gaugamela see Arrian 3.15.6; for losses on both sides, Diodorus 17.61.3, Curtius 4.16.26. Pearson (1969) p 156 and footnote 41 for discussion of Arrian's statement on casualties, relating them to Companions where Aristobulus and Justin claimed these were the total killed.

104. Diodorus 17.53.1 for the lengthening of the Persian weapons. As an example of the troop numbers credited to the Persians at Thermopylae see Herodotus 7.186 and compare to Arrian 3.8.4, Diodorus 17.53.3 and Plutarch 31.1 who reported one million soldiers (or more) faced the Macedonians at Gaugamela. Only Curtius 4.12.13 gave a sensible count at 245,000. Curtius 3.11.7 for his comment on counting losses and 3.11.27 for his exact numbers of deaths on both sides.

105. Green (1974) p 31 for the 300,000 gold pieces.

106. See Green (2007) p 11 and Borza (1995) pp 40-43 for gold and silver production. Also Hammond-Atkinson (2013) notes to Arrian 7.9.3 p 319 for discussion of the captured mines. They were also referenced in Justin 8.3.12-13. Hammond *Philip* (1994) p 5 for additional goldmines, p 5 and p 31 for other mineral resources and p 39 for 1,000 talents a year. Drawing from Diodorus 16.8.7, Demosthenes *First Olynthiac* 18.235. Hammond (1991) p 14 for the former Edones. Heckel-Jones (2006) pp 21-22 for Macedonian soldier pay rates. Curtius 5.1.45, Diodorus 17.64.6 for the lower numbers.

107. Following Anson (2013) p 18 for state provisioning. Sekunda (1984) p 28 and Heckel-Jones (2006) p 18 for MAK inscribed on a *sarissa* butt. Hatzopoulos (1996) p 267 for the absence of a middle class. Hatzopoulos (1996) p 268 for the 30,000 recruit estimate. Aristotle *Athenian Constitution* 42.3 for the training of the ephebes.

108. Quoting Hornblower (1981) p 211.

109. For Cleitus' appointment as *strategos* of Bactria and Sogdia see Curtius 8.1.19-21.

110. Following the observation by Griffiths (1935) p 39 for the nationalist spirit of Antipater's men. See epilogue titled *The Return to Aegae* for more on the *heroon*.

111. Curtius 6.1.8 for the 'prestige of old and present'. Agis was able to raise 30 silver talents from Persia and eight thousand Greek mercenaries from Crete; see Arrian 2.13.4-6, Curtius 4.1.38-40, Diodorus 17.48.1. Alexander sent Antipater 3,000 talents for the war, Arrian 3.16.10 for the funds. The total casualty numbers discussed in Adams (1985) p 83 and following his observation. Xenophon *Spartan Constitution* 7.1-5 for Lycurgus' ban on moneymaking activity. The Spartans used mercenaries as early as the battle of Megalopolis in 331 BCE; Parke (1933) p 201 for discussion of mercenary numbers.

112. Plutarch *Agis* 15.4 for a 'battle of mice'.

113. Diodorus 17.62.6-17.63 for Memnon's revolt and the battle. Aeschines 3.165 (*Against Ctesiphon*) for Corrhagus' defeat.

114. Plutarch *Agesilaus* 15.4 for the 'mice' label. Curtius 6.1.17-19 went as far as claiming Alexander resented the victory as it detracted from his own glory, perhaps supporting Plutarch's statement. Arrian 2.13.4 for Agis' journeying to Siphnos in a single trireme where he met Pharnabazus and Autophradates. Parke (1933) p 201 for discussion on the mercenary numbers at Megalopolis.

115. Curtius 6.1.7-16 for the violence of the conflict at Megalopolis citing losses as 3,500 Spartans and 1,000 Macedonians. Diodorus 17.63.3 for 5,300 Spartans and 3,500 of Antipater's troops. Cleonymus advised his Spartans to grab the *sarissa* to neutralise its effect, Polyaenus 2.29.2. Diodorus 17.62.5 for Memnon's revolt in Thrace. Griffiths (1935) p 318 for discussion of the widespread use of the *sarissa* and the Macedonian style of fighting. The statement from Polybius 18.18.1 is ambiguous whilst suggesting all Greece adopted the *sarissa* though it had been shortened to 14 cubits (21 feet) from an extended 16; Polybius 18.29.2; Sekunda (2012) p 13 for discussion.

116. Pausanias 1.13.6 for Sparta's defences against Pyrrhus of Epirus. Agesilaus' reply comes from Plutarch *Spartan Sayings*.

117. Plutarch *Cleomenes* 11.2 and Snodgrass (1967) p 127 for Cleomenes' reforms and use of the pike; Polybius 18.18.3 for the general use of the *sarissa* by Sparta.

118. Curtius 10.10.14-15.
119. Plutarch 74.2-4 for complaints arriving from Greece and Alexander's treatment of Cassander. Justin 12.14.4 for complaints from Olympias. As far as *Pamphlet*-originating allegations, complaints from Greece about the regent *were* linked to Alexander's ill treatment of Cassander in Plutarch's account. Any of this could have spawned such hostile anecdotal material.
120. For Lamia see Diodorus 18.14.4-18.15.4 and quoting Adams (1996) p 31.
121. Plutarch 42.3, Diodorus 17.74.1-4, Arrian 3.19.5 for the dismissal of the Thessalian cavalry. Arrian 5.27-28 for Coenus' speech in which he allegedly claimed the Thessalians were dismissed as their heart was no longer in their work. Diodorus 18.16.4 for Craterus' numbers. Diodorus 18.17.1-4, Plutarch *Phocion* 26.1 for events at Crannon.
122. Diodorus 18.18.1-6 and Plutarch *Phocion* 28.4 for the political reform in Athens and 24.144 for 22,000 population though Diodorus 18.8.5 and Plutarch *Phocion* 28.7 for 12,000 disenfranchised; discussion in Hansen (1999) p 107 and p 55 for the population of Athens.
123. Thucydides 2.37.1 for Pericles' declaration.
124. Diodorus 18.18.4-5, Plutarch *Phocion* 28.7; discussed in Hansen (1999) p 107 and Worthington (2000) p 107. Finlay (1973) for discussion of *ploutos* and *penia* in the Greek economy.
125. *Chrestos*, 'do-good', an epithet Phocion gained. Nepos *Phocion* 2.2 Arrian *Events After Alexander* 1.13 for Demades' call for the death of Demosthenes.
126. Plutarch *Phocion* 9.5.
127. Quoting from Plutarch *Phocion* 28-29 for the arrival of the garrison; also 31.2-3, 32.4-10, Diodorus 18.64.5, Nepos *Phocion* 2.4-5.
128. Diodorus 18.74.3 for the 10 *minae* qualification.
129. The 6,000 were comprised of 600 from the ten tribes; Aristotle *Athenian Constitution* 63.2.
130. Tacitus *On the life and character of Julius Agricola* 30.
131. Referring to the chapter heading polemic that appeared in Demosthenes *On the Crown* 270.
132. Quoting Griffith (1935) p 38.
133. It was reckoned the Macedonians had walked 12,000 miles by the time they reached the Hyphasis River; discussion in Thomas (2007) p 19. By their return to Babylon this has obviously increased by perhaps 9,000 miles to approximately 21,000 in total, thus stades. TA Dodge, cited in Heckel-Jones (2006) p 20, calculated the infantryman that had campaigned with Alexander in both Europe and Asia had marched some 20,870 miles. Engels (1978) p 12 however suggested waggons were not used and the *sarissa* would have been portered much of the way.
134. Justin 13.1 for 30,000 annual income. For confirmation of Athens' annual income see Athenaeus 12.542g where it was alleged Demetrius of Phalerum spent most of Athens' 1,200 talent income on parties rather than the army or city administration. Confirmed by Aelian 9.9. Adams (1996) p 33 argues for 600 talents.
135. Following the discussion in Adams (1996) p 33 and Tarn (1948) p 131 for the sums spent in the last two campaign years. Arrian 7.5.3, Justin 12.11.1 for the 20,000 that went to settle debts though this might be a combination of debt and veteran bonuses, each 10,000; Arrian 7.12.2 for the 1 talent bonus paid to each of the 10,000 retiring veterans. Curtius 10.2.10, Plutarch 70.3 stated that of the 10,000 talents laid out for debt repayment, only 130 remained. Diodorus 17.109.2 stated 'a little short of 10,000'. Athenaeus 9.398e for Aristotle's grant though when this was made is uncertain. Chares claimed the crowns were valued at 15,000 talents but this appears scandal (Athenaeus 12.538a-539b). Athenaeus 9.398e for Aristotle's grant.
136. Blackwell (1999) pp 13-14 footnote 13 for the relative weights of Harpalus' stolen talents. Curtius 8.12.16, Plutarch 59.5 for the gift to Taxiles (otherwise Omphis or Ambhi).
137. Athenaeus 4.148.d-f quoted Cleitarchus' account, which gave the figure of 440 talents amassed after the sacking of Thebes, a city described as 'mean spirited and stingy'. Diodorus 17.14.4 related that figure to the sale of prisoners but alluded to much wealth being plundered besides.
138. Justin 13.1. For the estimates of sums captured see Lane Fox (1973) p 437 and Cook (1973) p 228. For the estimate of 180,000 talents see Strabo 15.3.9. Green (2007) p 62 for the modern (1970s/80s) value calculation and Adams (1996) p 33 for the two centuries of Athenian and Aegean income. Adams (1996) p 33 for Athens' 600 talent annual income a century before. Engels (1978) p 79 for the estimate of tonnage of bullion.
139. Arrian 7.14.8-10 and Plutarch 72.3 for the cost of Hephaestion's funeral and Diodorus 17.115-116 for the 12,000-talent cost. Curtius 10.1.19 for warship numbers.
140. Plutarch 23.9-10 and Athenaeus 4.146c-d for the dining expenses of 100 minas. 1 mina was worth 100 drachmas according to Aristotle *Constitution of the Athenians* 10.2. It has been calculated that a mina was equal to approximately 1/60 of a talent. Plutarch confirmed 10,000 drachmas. According to the *Persika* of Ctesias or Heracleides, the Great King's daily food supply could feed 15,000 people. Following Pearson (1960) p 16 for the link to propaganda and the Lamian War.
141. Pseudo-Aristotle *Oikonomika* 2.1352 for the ten per cent import duty.
142. Tarn 1 (1948) p 30 for the probable working basis of the tax collecting regime.

143. Discussed in Hatzopoulos (1996) p 431 ff, and citing Arrian 7.9.9, Curtius 10.6.23, with other examples of the view that common Macedonians regarded wealth as a state commodity at Arrian 1.27.4, Diodorus 16.71.2. For the repayment of debt see Curtius 10.2.8, Diodorus 17.109.2 and quoting Justin 12.11.1-4.

144. Bellinger (1979) p 9 for the success of Philip's currency. Archibald-Davies-Gabrielson (2005) p 59 for the new minting by Alexander, the tonnage of silver and the *Diadokhoi* and p 46 for the standards of Philip and p 65 for bronze coinage. Hammond (1994) p 138 for coin hoard finds. Also Wheatley (1995) pp 438-9 and following Wheatley on the 'unusually large issue' minted for 'grandiose plans'. Hammond (1991) p 72 for Philip's currency.

145. For money in circulation see Archibald-Davies-Gabrielson (2005) pp 59 and 65. Cuneiform tablets from the Esagila Temple confirm high commodity prices when Alexander's troops were in Babylon. Commodity information was also provided by Babylonian cuneiform tablets; see Geller (1990) p 1. Tarn (1927) p 115 for the fall in the value of the drachma, pp 98, 103 and 110 for the prices of wheat and oil. For the tripling in the cost of living see Adams (1996) pp 36-37.

146. For the strife at Ephesus see Tarn (1923) p 130 according to Phylacus. Also discussed in Finlay (1973) p 143. Bagnall-Derow (2004) pp 19-23 for the surviving provisions.

147. Curtius 10.2.11 for the suggestion that the Macedonian troops left Asia with little in the way of booty.

148. Philip's mines at Mount Pangaeum discussed in Green (2007) p 63 and the gold to silver ratio fluctuations in Bellinger (1979) p 31. Adams (1996) pp 30-37 for the estimation of 31,000 talents being 'dumped' on the home market during this period. Silver coins found at Amphipolis however suggest the ore came from various mines, not just Pangaeum; Roisman-Worthington (2010) p 53.

149. For the numbers of 'home grown' Macedonians sent to Asia for Alexander's campaign see discussion in Anson (2013) p 160 and in Adams (1985) p 79. Anson (2013) p 70 for population discussion; some 250,000 to 375,000 Macedonians might have been eligible for service from a total population estimate of 1 to 1.5 million.

150. Discussed in Grant (1995) p 57. Momigliano (1966) pp 116-12 for the treatment of war and constitutional matters by historians.

151. Athens and the *pax makedonika* discussed by Worthington (2000) pp 100-101. Demosthenes was notably quiet during this period and restrained his invective against Macedonia until after Lycurgus died in 324 BCE. Plutarch *Demosthenes* 20.2 for the shield motto.

152. Anson (2014) p 29 for the amassed 18,000 talents at Athens; quoting Plutarch *Moralia* 841c.

153. Aristotle *Athenian Constitution* 51.3 for the corn guardians. Finlay (1973) pp 169-170 for discussion of the corn famine.

154. Arrian 3.5.4 and Curtius 4.8.5 for the famines and Pseudo-Aristotle *Oikonomika* 2.1352a for the duty imposed. Aristotle termed Cleomenes 'an Alexandrian' but this might simply relate to his residency. Heckel (2006) p 88 for Cleomenes' responsibilities. Blackwell (1999) pp 89-91 for discussion of the grain shipments to Olympias and Cleopatra. As Blackwell (1999) pp 96-97 points out, the shipments to the Argeads may not relate to these same years. Cleomenes' dubious commodity and financial activity is mentioned in Pseudo-Aristotle *Oikonomika* 2.1352a-1353 and Pseudo-Demosthenes *Against Dionysodorus* 56.7-8.

155. Discussion of Greek economic revival in Rostovtzeff (1936).

156. Discussed in Shipley (2000) p 39. Due to the lack of detail on whether pay included *misthos* – basic pay, as well as *siteresion* – ration allowance – makes the total remuneration comparisons uncertain. Griffiths (1935) p 356: Isocrates was clear that ca. 400 BCE there were few or no mercenaries readily available. Adams (1996) p 35 for the 2 obols cost of jury duty compensation in the 5th century BCE rising to 6 obols by the end of the 4th century BCE. Griffiths (1935) pp 297-316 for discussion of mercenary pay rates. Also Bellinger (1979) p 30 for the pauper and juror pay at Athens; also Miller (1996) p 35.

157. Author's play on the lines from Homer *Iliad* 1.238f quoting from Plutarch *Demetrius* 42.5 and relating to Demetrius *Poliorketes'* behaviour that offended the Greeks; translation from the Loeb Classical Library edition, 1920. The full lines are: '… and Homer speaks of kings as receiving from Zeus for protection and safe-keeping, not city-takers nor bronze-beaked ships, but ordinances of justice.'

158. Diodorus 19.105.1-2.

159. For Cassander's execution of Alexander IV and Roxane see Diodorus 19.105.3, Justin 15.2.5, Pausanias 9.7.2, *Heidelberg Epitome* FGrH 155 F2-3. Anson (2014) p 149 for the dating of the event; also Adams (1991) p 30: Diodorus dated it to the archon year of 311/310 BCE whilst the *Parian Chronicle* dated its knowledge or announcement to 310/309 BCE. Plutarch *Pyrrhus* 4.3 for the pledge in marriage to Deidameia.

160. Diodorus 20.53.1-4, Justin 15.2-3 for the declaration of kinships. See discussion on the dates of early kingship amongst the successors in Bosworth-Baynham (2000) pp 229-235. Ptolemy was

likely a self-styled king several years before as he was referred to as 'king' in various episodes. Also see discussion in Hadley (1969) p 146. For the dating of the death of Heracles see Carney-Ogden (2010) p 118 and for his identity see chapter titled *Lifting the Shroud of Parrhasius*.

161. Tarn (1921) p 19.

162. Diodorus 18.36.6-7 for Ptolemy's proposal that Peithon and Arrhidaeus become guardians, or rather 'administrators, *epimeletai*, of the kings rather than himself. Quoting Grainger (2007) p 104 for 'quiet independence'; author's italics. The date of Perdiccas' death is backed up by the *Babylonian Chronicle* extract BM 34, 660 Vs 4 though still disputed; see Anson (2003) for discussion.

163. Nepos 13, translation by Rev. JS Watson, George Bell and Sons, London, 1886.

164. For the battle, Diodorus 20.47-52, Justin 15.2; discussion in Hadley (1974) pp 55-56. Griffiths (1935) p 111 for the calculation that total Ptolemaic forces might have numbered 32,000. Plutarch *Demetrius* 17.5 claimed 12,800 men were taken prisoner; presumably deaths accounted for the balance of 16,000 lost. Diodorus 20.52.1-2 for Demetrius' defence of his ship.

165. Plutarch *Demetrius* 10.3 for the Athenians being first to pronounce Demetrius and Antigonus kings and 18.1 for the 'multitude' as opposed to just Athenians using the title 'kings'. Plutarch *Demetrius* 17.2-18 for Aristodemus hailing Antigonus king after victory at Salamis and his flattery.

166. Plutarch *Demetrius* 17.2-6 and 18.2-4 for the assumption of kingships confirming they had first been addressed as kings in their own domains before the Greeks addressed them as such; also Diodorus 20.53.2, Appian *Syrian Wars* 54. See Bosworth-Baynham (2000) pp 229-235 for further discussion on the declarations of kingship. For discussion on the origins of *basileus* see Mallory (1989) p 67. It should be noted that Lysimachus was Thessalian, but his father Agathocles, along with his five brothers, had been granted Macedonian citizenship. He was educated at Pella and thus considered a Macedonian by the rank and file.

167. Plutarch *Pyrrhus* 9.1 for Pyrrhus' marriages.

168. The festival mentioned and discussed in Carney (1995) p 376.

169. Plutarch *Demetrius* 45.3.

170. Following the observation in Carney (1995) p 371 and Anson (2014) p 175 for 'king without a country.' Anson (2014) p 178 and footnote 13 for chronological dating to 294 BCE. Justin 16.1.10-18 and Plutarch *Demetrius* 37.2-4 for the Assembly.

171. Quoting Carney (2000) p 227 and discussion of the use of *basilissa* on pp 227-228; the Attic form was *basileia*. Pausanias 1.6.8 seems to undermine Ptolemy's monogamy at least by claiming he was married to Eurydice and Berenice at the same time; suggested at Plutarch *Pyrrhus* 4.4 too, though 'wives' does not necessarily require marriage in parallel.

172. Plutarch *Demetrius* 2.1 suggested there existed rumours that Demetrius was in fact adopted by Antigonus at an early age. Plutarch *Demetrius* 25.4-5 for the titles afford the *Diadokhoi*.

173. Scott (1928) p 150 quoting Phylarchus and Plutarch *Demetrius* 25. The gift of elephants from Chandragupta is recorded in Plutarch 62.4, Appian *Syrian Wars* 55, Strabo 15.2.9, Justin 15.4.11-21.

174. Plutarch *Demetrius* 25.5 for Lysimachus' anger at the title of 'treasurer'. See Bosworth (2002) p 215 for a discussion of Seleucus' 'spectacularly successful' naval operations against Antigonus in 314/314 BCE. For Seleucus' collusion with Ptolemy see Diodorus 19.56.1, 19.62.1-9, 19.64, 19.75.2, 19.80.3, 19.83.1 and 4, 19.85.3-19.86.4.

175. Stewart (1993) p 234 for Cassander's coinage depicting Alexander and (or as) Heracles; also Miller (1991) pp 49-55.

176. For Thessalonice's heritage see discussion in Heckel (2006) p 265 and for further detail Carney (1988) p 386 and p 387 for the discussion of her continued spinsterhood; also chapter titled *The Silent Siegecraft of the Pamphelteers*. For her forced marriage see Diodorus 19.52.1 and 19.61.2, Pausanias 8.7.7, Justin 14.6.13, Carney (2006) p 104 for the site and once fragmentary inscription marking Olympias' tomb near Pydna; further discussion in Edson (1949). Quoting Plutarch *Moralia* 747f-748a. Diodorus 17.118.2 (and Porphyry FGrH 2.260 3.3) claimed Cassander 'threw her body out without burial'. Following the proposal of O Palagia in Carney-Ogden (2010) p 41 for Cassander's removal of Olympias' statue from the Philippeion.

177. See Stewart (1993) pp 52-59. The three-stage elevation from youth to god was proposed by Himmelmann in 1989 in *Herrsher und Athlet: Die Bronzen vom Quirinal*, Milan p 57-58.

178. Quoting Poseidippus from a recently discovered epigram from the Milan Papyrus. The full title of the papyrus is Papyrus Milano Vogl. VIII 309.

179. Pliny 7.125 and 37.8 stated that only Apelles, Lysippus and Pyrgoteles were allowed to make likenesses of Alexander.

180. Discussed in Pollitt (1972) p 174. Plutarch 4 also suggested Apelles painted Alexander with too ruddy a complexion. Plutarch *Moralia* 335a, Plutarch 4.3 for the thunderbolt.

181. The rivalry was recorded by Lucian *on Calumny* 59.15 but appears a jest or a misidentification with a later painter. Carney-Ogden (2010) p 129 for the roots of the Ptolemaic eagle. See

discussion in Baynham (1998) p 85. Baynham suggested Ptolemy may have started the rumour himself in his history.

182. Pliny 35.110 for Cassander's painting; Borza *Tombs* (1987) p 111 for discussion of its later copy. Discussed in Stewart (1993) p 30 following descriptions in Pliny books 34-36.
183. Stewart (1993) p 279 for the monuments at Olympias.
184. Plutarch *Aemilius* 12, Polybius 5.10 for the suggestion that Antigonid kings were from Alexander's line. Herodian 1.3.3.
185. Hammond (1991) p 31 for the inscription.
186. See discussion in Stewart (1993) p 230 and following Stewart (1993) p 235 for *Alexikakos*; p 245 for the portraits in the Tychaion.
187. For the dating of Demetrius' *Peri Tyches* see discussion in Bosworth-Baynham (2000) p 299; Demetrius stated the fifty-year rise of Macedon, which would logically date from Philip II's reign from ca. 360 BCE, suggesting it was written around 310 BCE. Polybius gave further guidance stating that Demetrius published some 150 years before the end of the Third Macedonian War culminating in the battle at Pydna in 168 BCE. It is a very loose triangulation but suggests Demetrius' work was one of the first treatises to deal with Alexander in a meaningful philosophic way.
188. Cicero *Philippicae* Oration 5.5.
189. Hadley (1974) pp 50-65. Discussion by VA Troncoso in Carney-Ogden (2010) pp 21-22 on the *Diadokhoi* unshaven imagery and emulation of Alexander on coins.
190. Athenaeus 12.537e cited Ephippus as claiming Alexander dressed as Ammon, Artemis and Hermes. In particular the wearing of purple raiment and slit sandals with Ammon-style horns 'just as the god's'. Stewart (1993) p 319 for the observation that once the Vulgate template was circulating, the imagery attached to Ammon was most likely reinvigorated.
191. Borza-Palagia (2007) p 97.
192. The *epigonoi* referenced here are distinct from the 30,000 Asiatic soldiers who had been trained and armed in Macedonian style. Here sons of Macedonian soldiers are being referred to under the same general heading as 'offspring'. Diodorus 17.110.3 for their education funding, Justin 12.4.1-11 for Alexander's payment to men with Asiatic offspring, Arrian 7.4.8 and Plutarch 70.3 for the newlyweds receiving gifts. For Alexander considering them replacements for their fathers see Arrian 7.12.3, Plutarch 71.9, and Curtius 8.5.1. Full discussion in Roisman (2012) p 58.
193. Appian *Syrian Wars* 64; Justin 15.3.11–14. See Heckel (2006) p 155 for opinion of these later fabrications to Lysimachus' story.
194. Justin 17.1.1-3 for the destruction of Lysimachia.
195. For the assumption of the titles of kings and coin images see Bellinger (1979) pp 86-87.
196. For the design on the Ptolemaic gold staters see Erskine (2002) p 175.
197. Quoting Adams (1996) p 30. The appointments described in Arrian 3.5.2-3 give a hint of the complexity of the administrative structure Alexander was employing in managing Egypt. Boardman (1964) p 131 for *prostatai*.
198. Justin 15.4 for the origins of the Seleucid anchor symbol; compare to Appian *Syriaka* 56. For the anchor device see Hadley (1969) p 143.
199. Following GG Aperghis in Archibald-Davies-Gabrielson (2005) pp 27-40 and p 37 for tax rates and pp 52-53 for *argyrion* and *chrysion*; Aristotle *Nicomachean Ethics* 5.1133b for his comment on coined money.
200. For coinage essays see Cunningham (1884) and Stewart pp 314-323. The Attic tetradrachm standard of 17.62 grams was replaced with the Rhodian weight of 15.50 grams by Ptolemy in 310 BCE and the other successors followed; see discussion in Bellinger (1979) p 2 and p 86 and Archibald-Davies-Gabrielson (2005) p 46. Also discussed in Stewart (1993) p 241; Ptolemaic coin hoards suggest few or no foreign coins were in circulation in Egypt thereafter. Hadley (1974) pp 50-65. Finlay (1973) p 167 for the electrum dilemma. Electrum was available naturally from the silt of the River Pactolus, which flowed through Sardis and which may have started the trend, though controlled gold and silver ratios became the norm.
201. Meijer-Nijf (1992) p 62 for discussion of the new bronze coinage and the associated suspicion. Bellinger (1979) p 1 for the early Lydian coinage and its bullion value. Rostovtzeff (1936) p 244 for copper drachmas in Egypt.
202. Herodotus 1.94 for the origins of Lydian currency and the resulting trade. Bellinger (1979) p 1 for the suggestion that currency commenced in Lydia with court payment to mercenaries. Aristotle however claimed coins were introduced by Damodice of Cyrme, the wife of King Midas. Julius Pollux *Onomasticon* 9.83 summarised the traditions; Xenophon too credited the origins to Lydia.
203. Green (2007) p XXXVII though this is disputed and arguments have been put forward that the Poseidon coins actually belonged to Antigonus *Doson*. See Hammond-Walbank (1988) p 594.
204. Roisman-Worthington (2010) p 52 for the twenty-six mints operating in Alexander's lifetime.

Stewart (1993) pp 328-330 for the last Alexander coinage.

205. Carney-Ogden (2010) p 129 for Aelian's version of Ptolemy's illegitimate birth.

206. Archibald-Davies-Gabrielson (2005) pp 144-149 for royal banks and lending systems.

207. The Greek *triereis* stemmed from three tiers of oars though larger number-denominated ships probably corresponded to numbers of oarsmen per oar. Aristotle credited the Carthaginians with building the first *quadriremes;* Diodorus credited Dionysius of Syracuse with inventing the *hexareis.* Full discussion of ship design in the Hellenistic era in Casson (1971).

208. Full discussion of the trieres arrangement in Morrison-Coates-Rankov (2000) p 8 ff and p 131 for name derivations and p 161 ff for the outrigger.

209. Murray (2012) pp 189-190 for the cost of running a trireme. Mercenary pay was generally 4 obols per day (a drachma was 6 obols). However between 400 and 350 BCE the pay rate had fallen from possibly as much as 8 obols to 4; Griffiths (1935) p 297. Cavalry might be paid several times this sum when including provisions for their mounts. Discussion in Champion (2014) p 184.

210. Athenaeus 8.333 a-b.

211. Curtius 10.1.19. Murray pp 269-278 for the sources and texts referring to 'sixes' to 'tens'.

212. Diodorus 19.62.8-9 for Antigonus' fleet.

213. Diodorus 20.85.2 for a description of the floating booms. Murray (2012) p 135, p 176 and p 290 ff for further description of the harbour defences and booms.

214. Diodorus 20.83.1; Murray (2012) pp 279-282 for sources and texts citing the largest ships (16s to 40s).

215. Plutarch *Demetrius* 20.4. Murray (2012) p 145 for description of the catapults employed.

216. Plutarch *Demetrius* 43.4.

217. Plutarch *Demetrius* 32.1 for his raiding the 1,200 talents from Cyinda. Xenophon *Hellenika* 6.1.11 and Theophrastus *Enquiry into Plants* 5.2.1 for Macedonian timber being sourced by Athens.

218. Plutarch *Demetrius* 31.3-4.

219. Plutarch *Demetrius* 20.4 for the display of naval power to Lysimachus.

220. Plutarch *Demetrius* 32.2 for the ship with thirteen banks of oars and 31.4-32.3 for Pleistarchus' activity.

221. Plutarch *Demetrius* 43-44 for Demetrius' shipbuilding and new army.

222. Griffiths (1935) p 300 for discussion of the fines levied on Greek cities and p 309 for Demetrius' pay.

223. For the pirates in the employ of the *Diadokhoi* see Ormerod (1997) pp 12-123 citing Diodorus 20.82, 20.83, 20.97, 20.110 and Polyaenus 4.6.18. Quoting Griffiths (1935) p 52 for the pirates operating against Rhodes for Demetrius *Poliorketes* 'special enemy'.

224. Lysimachus did not acquire control of Heraclea until 289 BCE. See Tarn (1910) p 211. Casson (1971) p 110 for the reference to its possible catamaran-like structure. Diodorus 21.13 for the treasure hoard.

225. Photius' epitome of Memnon's *History of Heraclea* Book 13; Murray (2012) pp 171-172 for further discussion of the 'super-eight' *Leontophoros.*

226. Murray (2012) p 8 for discussion on the naming protocol and the corresponding numbers.

227. For a discussion of the battle at Kos see Casson (1971) pp 138-139. Athenaeus 5.203d for the fleet make-up. Bagnall-Derow (2004) p 250 for the papyrus text for the felling of trees.

228. As described by Athenaeus 598c and Plutarch *Demetrius* 43.4.

229. Ormerod (1997) p 29 for the *hemiolia* and *myoparones.*

230. Plato *Laches* 183d for the use of the spear-sickle; discussed in Hanson (1991) p 24.

231. Full discussion of the seafaring warfare manoeuvres in Whitehead (1987) and Lazenby (1987). See Thucydides 2.89.8 for a description of the manoeuvres. Murray (2012) p 32 ff and p 52 for image and description of the Athlit-styled ram.

232. The ship was described in Athenaeus 5.40-44 drawing from the earlier description of Moschion of Phaselis.

233. The Moor, Idrisi visited Alexandria in 1115 and reported that the Pharos still stood; Vrettos (2001) p 33 for discussion. It probably fell in the earthquake of 1365 though by 1165 a small mosque had replaced the beacon at its summit.

234. Cassius Dio 59.10 for the financial crisis; also Suetonius *Caligula* 37-41 for Caligula's fundraising schemes and expenditure; Cassius Dio 59.15 for the redirected Wills.

235. Quoting Lattey (1917) p 327.

236. Quoting from Bosworth-Baynham (2000) p 129.

237. For a full transcription of the stele found in Cairo in 1871, now referred to as the Satrap Stele, see Bevan (1927). Diodorus 19.81.5,19.81.4,19.85.3, 19.75.2,19.80.3 for the suggestion that Seleucus fought beside Ptolemy in a joint command at Gaza and for events surrounding it. McKechnie (1999) pp 53-54 for discussion on Ptolemy position and recognition of year seven of King Alexander IV.

238. Dalley (2013) p 125 for an image of the cylinder inscription of Antiochus and Stratonice. Strabo 15.3.8 for Onesicritus' wording from Darius' tomb: 'I was friend to my friends; as horseman and bowman I proved myself superior to all others; as hunter I prevailed: I could do everything'; translation from Pearson (1960) p 165.

239. Plutarch *Demetrius* 41.4.

240. Plutarch *Demetrius* 24.1 for his womanising and 1.7 for his character traits. Plutarch *Demetrius* 10.13-22 for the lodging.

241. Plutarch *Demetrius* 10.13-22 for his retaking of Athens and his honours. Plutarch *Demetrius* 10.4; every fifth year at the Panathenaic festival a sacred robe was carried in solemn procession and deposited with the goddess Athena on the Acropolis. On it were represented the exploits of the goddess, particularly in the Battle of the Giants; quoting footnote 8 from the Loeb Classical Library edition, 1920.

242. Plutarch *Demetrius* 10.13-22. Diodorus 20.46.4, 150,000 *medimnoi* is about 230,000 bushels of grain. Billows (1990) p 287 for Antigonus' grain industry.

243. The extension of the Athenian tribes discussed in Habicht (1999) p 68. Plutarch *Demetrius* 11-12 for the activity of Stratocles.

244. Diodorus 20.102.1-4 for the divine honours from Sicyon; for the honours paid by Scepsis and the League of Islanders see Bagnall-Derow (2004) p 8; fuller discussion in Scott (1928). Quoting Bagnall-Derow (2004) pp 8-9 and for Scepsis' reply. Kebric (1977) p 5 for Samos' festival to the Antigonids.

245. Diodorus 20.46 for the efforts of 307/6 BCE, Diodorus 20.102 and Plutarch *Demetrius* 25 for the charter of the Hellenic League's fragments in Bagnall-Derow (2004) pp 16-18.

246. Athenaeus 542b-e described the depraved behaviour of Demetrius of Phalerum who had 1,200 talents at his disposal. Quoting Momigliano (1977) p 44; pp 43-45 for discussion of Demochares. For Demetrius of Phalerum's exile there are many sources, most fully accounted in Plutarch *On Exile* 7 601F-602A, Cicero *On Ends* 5.19.53-54, Plutarch *How to tell a Flatterer from a Friend* 28 69 C-D; full texts in Fortenbaugh-Schütrumpf (2000) pp 75-81. However upon taking Athens, Demetrius *Poliorketes* allowed Demetrius to be escorted safely to Thebes before he journeyed to Egypt; Plutarch *Demetrius* 9.2.

247. Pausanias 1.25.6 called him a tyrant. Athenaeus 539e-f for Diyllus' statement that Demetrius was known as 'gracelid'; full text in Fortenbaugh-Schütrumpf (2000) p 35.

248. Euripides *Alkestis* line 780.

249. Strabo 9.1.20 and also Plutarch *Political Precepts* 27 820E; see full citation in Fortenbaugh-Schütrumpf (2000) p 65. In contrast Pliny 34.12.27 recorded 360 statues were destroyed. Favorinus reported 1,500 statues were pulled down in one day; see Fortenbaugh-Schütrumpf (2000) p 65 for full text. For chamber pots see Plutarch *Moralia* 820e.

250. Plutarch *Demetrius* 10.2. Strabo 9.1.20 full citation in Fortenbaugh-Schütrumpf (2000) p 53. Demetrius controlled Athens from 317-307 BCE. Fortenbaugh-Schütrumpf (2000) p 333 for the positive sources.

251. O'Sullivan (2009) p 5 quoting Peter Green.

252. Plutarch *Phocion* 35.2.

253. Bagnall-Derow (2004) pp 24-26 for honours to Lysimachus.

254. Justin 15.4 for the origins of the Seleucid anchor symbol; compare to Appian *Syriaka* 56.

255. Arrian 7.22.5, Appian *Syrian Wars* 56 for Seleucus and the diadem in the marshes near Babylon.

256. Hadley (1974) p 58 and Justin 15.4.1-6 for Laodice's union with Apollo. Bagnall-Derow (2004) pp 32-33 for Ilion's decree and pp 41-42 for the Ionian League.

257. Plutarch *Aemilius* 33 for a description of the drinking bowls. Full discussion of Hellenistic deification in Scott (1928) pp 137-166.

258. Pausanias 1.8.6. There is still a debate whether he gained the epithet *Soter* due to his actions at the Rhodian siege. The first mention of the title comes from coins issued by Ptolemy *Philadelphos* in 263 BCE. See discussion in Green (2007) p 45. Details of the *Helepolis* in Diodorus 20.48.2; for the siege of Rhodes, see Diodorus 20.91.1-4 and Plutarch *Demetrius* 20.5-21.2 where it is suggested the Rhodians actually asked Demetrius to leave them some siege engines 'to remind them of his power as well as their own bravery'.

259. Diodorus 20.100.1-4 for Rhodian honours. De Polignac (1999) p 7 for the Alexandrian festival of Ptolemaia.

260. See discussion on Hellenistic epithets in Iossif-Chankowski-Lorber (2007). Technically an epithet suggests a name 'imposed upon' or 'added to' from the Greek *epithetos*.

261. Polybius 5.27.5-7 suggests the Macedonians took Philip V to task over his treatment of a commander.

262. Plutarch *Demetrius* 18.2. 'European at heart' is quoting Errington (1990) p 147. Miller (1991) p 51 for the observation that Cassander's 'state burial' of Philip III was a declaration of *basileia*; Polyaenus 9.10.1 and George Syncellus *Ekloge Chronographias* 504 ff. Miller (1991) p

53 for Cassander presiding over the Nemean Games. Roisman-Worthington (2010) p 53 for Cassander's coinage.

263. Following the argument of Lattey (1917) p 330 on 'godhead'.

264. Diodorus 19.52.1-2, Justin 14.6.13, *Heidelberg Epitome* FGrH 155 F2.4 Diodorus 19.61.2 for Antigonus' accusation that the marriage was forced upon Thessalonice. Quoting Diodorus 19.52.1. Quoting Carney (1991) pp 20-21.

265. A third son, Philip, was too ill to govern Macedonia for long and soon died of tuberculosis. Events well covered in Plutarch *Demetrius* 36.1-2.

266. For Antipater's murder by Lysimachus and Alexander's death by Demetrius, the principal sources are Plutarch *Demetrius,* 36.1-37.3, Plutarch *Pyrrhus* 6.2-7.1, Pausanias 9.73-4, Diodorus 21.7.1, Justin 16.1.5, Eusebius 123.1.

267. Anson (2014) p 127 for the fifty settlements of Seleucus. Strabo 12.8.15 and Livy 38.13.5 for the founding of Apamea. Appian *Syrian Wars* 57 stated Seleucus *Nikator* named three cities after her; also Strabo 16.2.4. Archibald-Davies-Gabrielson (2005) p 29 ff for other Seleucid cities; Ammianus Marcellinus 14.8.6, Appian *Syrian Wars* for other estimates of city numbers.

268. Hornblower (1981) pp 114-115 for Antigonus' campaign that destroyed parts of Babylon. Josephus 12.3-4 for the relocation of the Jewish population.

269. Diodorus named Seleucus' new city Seleucia, but it is more likely Antiochia, named after his father. See Diodorus 20.47.6 and footnote 4 in the Loeb Classical Library edition, 1954. Diodorus 20.47.5 for the size and founding of Antigonea.

270. Thapsacus discussion in Gawlikowski (1996) pp 123-133.

271. Following observation and discussion in Billows (1990) p 323. Bagnall-Derow (2004) pp 11-15 for Antigonus' letters to Teos.

272. Peucestas may have been active at the court of Demetrius *Poliorketes* and died of natural causes, but he did not play a major role in events; see Heckel (2006) p 205 for discussion and sources. Nepos 21 *Of Kings* 3 did claim *Philadelphos* killed his father but this appears hearsay and is preceded with 'it is said'.

273. Plutarch *Demetrius* 47.4 for his pleas. Plutarch *Demetrius* 50.2 for Demetrius' final surrender and 50-52 for his subsequent decline to death. Also Diodorus 21.20.1 for Lysimachus' offer of 2,000 talents to have Demetrius killed.

274. Diodorus 21.20 for Lysimachus' offer of 2,000 talents for the death of Demetrius.

275. Plutarch *Demetrius* 35.2, translation from the Loeb Classical Library edition, 1920.

276. Sophocles *Oedipos epi Kolono* 1f, following Plutarch *Demetrius* 46.5, translation from the Loeb Classical Library edition, 1920. The original lines were: 'O child of a blind and aged sire, Antigone, what are these regions?'

277. The Syrian Chersonese may have been Apamea or not inconceivably Triparadeisus as game parks were referred to. Diodorus 21.20.1 named it Pella though that seems to have become a general term for an enclosed settlement of stone, hence the derivation of the name; in Doric Greek 'pella' is 'stone'. Plutarch *Demetrius* 53.4 for his line extending down to Perseus. Plutarch *Demosthenes* 3.2 for the proverb.

278. The significance of Euripides' lines relating to the curse of Oedipus (from *Phoenician Women* credited to Euripides) discussed in chapter titled *Hierarchic Historians and Alexandrian Alchemy*.

279. Pausanias 1.7.1 for *Philadelphos'* murder of another half-brother by Eurydice.

280. Quoting Plutarch *Pyrrhus* 4.4. Some scholars use the term 'repudiated' when recognising that Ptolemy favoured Berenice; whether divorce actually took place is an open question, as, in fact, is the formal monogamy of the *Diadokhoi*. Pausanias 1.6.8 stated Antipater sent Eurydice to Ptolemy in Egypt; this was, it appears, sometime before his death in 319 BCE, and could have been as early as 322 BCE once Ptolemy was installed in Egypt, and not necessarily after Triparadeisus. Pausanias 1.6.8 does suggest a parallel marriage with Eurydice and Berenice, and Plutarch *Pyrrhus* 4.4 mentions 'wives' in the plural but not specifically parallel marriages.

281. Plutarch *Demetrius* 32.3 and with more explanation at 46.3; the chronology and who instigated the marriages at which point is unclear. It could be interpreted that only at the earlier date of the pledge did Ptolemy I *Soter* approve of the union. Bosworth (2002) p 263 footnote 66 for its dating.

282. Agathocles was married to another of Ptolemy's daughters, Lysandra, hence he and *Keraunos* were brothers-in-law (also by virtue of Lysimachus' marriage with Arsinoe II).

283. Diodorus 21.11-13 for Lysimachus' defeats and capture at the hands of the Getae. For the waning support of Lysimachus after Agathocles' death see Justin 17.1.1-4, Memnon FGrH 434 F5.7, Polyaenus 8.57. Pausanias 1.10.4-5 for Lysandra's pleas.

284. Quoting Justin 17.1 and 17.2 for Lysimachus' loss of fifteen children.

285. The javelin is recorded by Memnon *History of Heraclea* 7-9. Appian *Syrian Wars* 10.64 for the reference to Thorax burying Lysimachus. Plutarch *Demetrius* 29.5 for the mention of Thorax at Antigonus' death at Ipsus.

286. Strabo 13.4.1 for the background to Philetaerus and the description of the mountain summit

of Pergamum. Strabo 13.4.1 and Pausanias 1.10.4 for Philetaerus' intriguing with Seleucus. Bagnall-Derow (2004) p 120 for the isopolity between Pergamum and Temnos as an example. Justin 26.5 ff for the decapitation of *Keraunos*.

287. Apollodorus ruled an 'independent' Cassandreia from 278 to 276 BCE until the city was captured by Antigonus *Gonatas*; see Diodorus 22.5.1-2, Polyaenus 6.7.1-2.

288. Gallic numbers at the battle based on Justin 25.1, though his version of their defeat is quite different. Pausanias 10.19.9 stated 152,000 infantry and 20,400 cavalry, Diodorus 22.9.1 stated 150,000 infantry and 10,000 cavalry and Justin 24.6 stated 150,000 infantry and 15,000 cavalry were under Brennus' command.

289. Discussed in Brown (1947) pp 685-686 drawing from Tarn (1923). Plutarch *Pyrrhus* 4.3 for Pyrrhus' part supporting Demetrius at Ipsus. Pausanias 1.9.7-8 for Hieronymus' accusation that Lysimachus plundered the graves and scattered the remains of the Aeacids. Momigliano (1977) pp 41-43 for Athens through the years of the Celtic invasion. Demetrius married Pyrrhus' sister Deidameia soon after the death of Alexander IV (ca. 309 BCE).

290. Polyaenus 4.6.17, Plutarch *Pyrrhus* 26.3 for the Celtic contingent under *Gonatas*.

291. Justin 7.2.4-6 for the prophecy.

292. Quoting Green (2007) p 81.

293. Nepos *De regibus Exterarum Gentium* 3.1-3. See discussion in Shipley (2000) p 14. The original name may well have been *de exellentibus ducibus exterarum gentium* (*The Book of the Great Generals of Foreign Nations*) whilst an early manuscript attributed the work to Aemilius Probus; see Geiger (1979) for explanation.

294. Plutarch *Demetrius* 3.3-5. Quoting Bagnall-Derow (2004) p 101 for 'labyrinthine'. Kebric (1977) pp 56 ff for Plutarch's reliance on Duris.

295. Euripides *Medea* lines 619-620, translation by EP Coleridge, 1910, Internet Classics Archive.

296. Ovid *Metamorphoses* book 1 lines 128-131, Hesiod *Work and Days* lines 109-201 for the ages of men.

297. Discussed in Bosworth-Baynham (2000) pp 294-296.

298. Polybius 8.10.5-6.

299. Cicero *De Officiis* 2.5 recorded that Panaetius had commented: '… Alexander, who he says could not have achieved so great success without the support of other men.'

300. Justin 13.1, translation based on Rev. JS Watson, published by Henry G Bohn, London, 1853.

301. Polybius 28.7.8-14 explained that he had delivered a long speech to the Achaean League in favour of restoring honours to King Eumenes II of Pergamum.

302. Polybius 10.49 for the Seleucid-Graeco-Bactrian war of 210 BCE. Polybius 11.34.2-5 for the nomadic hoards and founding of the Graeco-Bactrian dynasty. Justin 41.1-7 for the fragmentation of the Seleucid Empire and the Graeco-Bactrian Graeco-Indian wars. Justin 15.4 for Diodotus' rule. Also Strabo 11.11.1 and 21.21.1 for the extending power of the Greeks in Bactria. For the coin hoards see Holt (1996). Boardman-Griffin Murray (1986) p 422 for the Platonist finds.

303. Originally reported in the *Journal of the Royal Asiatic Society (JRAS)*, London, 1909, pp 1053-1055.

304. Hanson (1991) pp 26-27 for the comparison of wounds.

305. The Macedonian opinion of Rome's war machine discussed in Champion (2000) p 428; King Philip V was reported by Livy 31.34.8 as shocked at the brutality and organisation of Rome's army. Polybius 7.10.7-12 for Callicrates' activity and Polybius' own exile. Polybius 16.30-31 for the suicide of women and children at Abydus. Bagnall-Derow (2004) pp 68-69 for the fragments of Rome's alliance with the Aetolian League. Polybius 4.2.5 and 4.24.1-3 for Philip's youth, repeated in chapters 2,3,5; McGing (2010) p 97 ff. See Polybius 18.28-31 and 44 for the subsequent collapse of Macedonian authority over Greece.

306. Polybius 11.7.8 and 11.12 for Greek opinion of Philip V. Polybius 4.77 for his lamenting that Philip turned into a tyrant; translation from McGing (2010) p 33 and also p 154 for a further rundown of Polybius opinions of Philip V.

307. Justin 30.4.4 for the earthquake associated with the rise of Rome. The reduction in cavalry was also apparent at the battle at Sellasia in 222 BCE when infantry-cavalry ratios had dropped from 6:1 in Alexander's day to 25:1; E Anson in Carney-Ogden (2010) p 84.

308. Quoting Griffiths (1935) p 65 and p 78 for the status of the citizen soldier and the foreign soldiers in the 2nd century BCE Macedonian ranks. Full discussion of dwindling Macedonian troop numbers in Adams (1996) pp 303-31. There is some evidence Etruscans were familiar with chainmail in the 3rd century BCE. Lenden (2005) p 154 for *thureophoroi*.

309. Justin 33.1.7 for the prodigy.

310. For Pydna see Plutarch *Aemilius* and the most complete coverage is provided by Livy 44.40-42 drawing from Polybius. For the lunar eclipse see Livy 44.37.8 and Aemilius Paullus 17.7. The exact site of Pydna has not yet been discovered; Diodorus 18.49.2 claimed it was moved inland ca. 410 BCE but Olympias' attempt to escape her siege by ship (19.50.4, Polyaenus 4.11.3) suggests it was re-established back on the coast, possibly close to modern Makriyialos.

311. Plutarch *Galba* 1.2, translation by J Dryden, 1683. This recalls Plutarch *Phocion* 25.1 in which Phocion is said to have uttered 'how many generals I see, and how few soldiers' when preparing for battle and receiving advice from all ranks.
312. Livy 44.7. Plutarch *Aemilius* 17. Also see Casson (2001) p 66 for discussion of the eclipse.
313. Plutarch *Aemilius* 19.2 and 20.2 for the ability of the *sarissa* to penetrate shields and armour. Livy 44.40-42 related that a horse or mule got loose when being watered and a clash over its recovery precipitated the start of the battle; Livy added that reports claimed Paulus deliberately let the horse loose as a provocation, as entrails proved unpropitious unless Macedonians struck the first blow.
314. Plutarch *Aemilius* 19 recorded many differing outcomes, cowardly and otherwise, for Perseus' retirement to the city. Bagnall-Derow (2004) p 82 for Rome's complaint against Perseus.
315. Quoting Livy 44.46 for the description of Pella.
316. Xenophon *Hellenika* 5.2.13.
317. Strabo 7.20, 7.23; discussed in Greenwalt (1999); Theophrastus *Enquiry into Plants* 5.2.1 detailed the value of Macedonian wood.
318. Livy 44.46 for the description of Pella after the Romans entered and sacked it. Pella was used by the Romans as a provincial base, so the basic city structure must have remained largely intact.
319. Justin 25.1-2, Diodorus 30.21-22, with similar commentary in Plutarch *Aemilius* 23-24; 23.3 for 'lacerated by misfortunes'; Plutarch claimed Perseus was carrying 50 talents of riches with him; 23.9 for his regret. Livy 45.6/7-9 for the Royal Pages.
320. Livy 44.40.5-6 for the *Chalkaspides* and *Leukaspides*.
321. 'Play had been performed' taken from Plutarch *Demetrius* 53.4 as his summation of Demetrius' career. Valerius Maximus 2.2.2 recorded that Roman magistrates across the empire refused to speak in Greek, holding that 'they held that in all matters the Greek cloak should bow to the Roman toga'. Roisman-Worthington (2010) p 252 for the start of the *provincia*. Livy 44.40-42 for the battle and 44.40.8 for the fate of the Rome-allied Palignians which suggest death numbers must have been far higher.
322. Livy 45.32.3 for the shipment of nobles to Italy.
323. Diodorus 30.22-24 for Aemilius' lenient treatment though this is almost identical to Polybius 29.20 and Livy 45.7.4. Cicero *De Officiis* book 2 (*Expediency*) 22 and Plutarch *Aemilius* 38.1. Here 'for all time to come' meant until his own day. Polybius 30.15 reported seventy Epirote towns were sacked and 150,000 people were sold into slavery. Also Livy 45.29.4-32 for the outcome; discussed in Hatzopoulos (1996) pp 43-46 and p 222; Cicero *De lege agrarian* 1.2.5 for confiscation of state mines.
324. Polybius 24.6 for his ambassadorial role, 26.1.7 for the 'mad man'.
325. Polybius 29.27.4, Livy 45.12.4 ff for Popilius Laenas. Polybius 29.23-25 for Egyptian calls for help to the Achaean League under the command of Polybius and his father. Quoting Polybius 39.7.7 on indolence, actually attributed to Ptolemy *Philometor*. Boardman-Griffin-Murray (1986) p 372 for Lampsacus' appeal to Rome's common ties with Troy for protection.
326. Rostovtzeff (1936) p 242 for the new trading environment. Archibald-Davies-Gabrielson (2005) p 151 for the banking role of Delos.
327. Polybius 31.2.12, 31.17.2, 35.4.11 for the discord in Pella. Lucian *Alexander the false Prophet* 6 for Pella's fate.
328. Rome's abolishment or otherwise of the Assembly discussed in Hatzopoulos (1996) pp 353-355.
329. Braudel (1969) p 189 on culture and civilisation.
330. In the Greek War of Independence, the Ottoman Empire finally recognised Greek independence in 1832, though the London protocol of 1830 declared Greece free and under her protection.
331. Velleius Paterculus *Historiae* 1.11.3-5 for the bronzes known as the 'Granicus Monument 'being taken to Rome.
332. Pliny 25.135 for the appointment of Metrodorus. Plutarch *Aemilianus* 22.7 for Scipio's deeds at Pydna. Plutarch *Aemilius* 23-24 for Perseus fleeing.
333. Pausanias 7.10.7-12 for the 1,000 hostages.
334. Quoting McGing (2010) p 133 on Callicrates' policy to Rome.
335. Polybius 28.6.9 for his Achaean command. Polybius 24.8-10 for his presence in Rome pleading his case. In contrast Polybius' father, Lycortas, believed the Achaean League should state its case and relied on Roman common sense to be reasonable with demands. Rome wanted the Achaeans onside against Macedonia as evidenced by their embassy at Polybius 28.3-7, and 30.13 for the political motivation.
336. Polybius 45.6-47.4. Polybius admitted Cleoxenus and Democleitus had conceived the torch system, though he perfected it. The alphabet was broken into five lines and referenced by numerals 1-5 of each axis. McGing (2010) p 142 for discussion of the dating of Polybius' *Tactics*. Polybius 31.23 for Scipio's petitioning. Quoting from an inscription seen by Pausanias; Momigliano (1977) p 68. Polybius was uniquely in Rome (31.23.5) whereas other hostages were

in provincial towns. McGing (2010) p 140 for his probable presence in Africa in 151/150 BCE. Polybius 38.10.8-10 for the reasons for the war of 146 BCE; he returned to Rome in 145/144 BCE to plead the league's case, Polybius 39.8.1.

337. Polybius 29.21.1-9, translation from the Loeb Classical Library edition, volume VI, 1922-2.
338. This extract is repeated almost word for word at Diodorus 31.10.1-2 and shortened in Livy 55.9.2.
339. Perdiccas and Craterus were from Orestis, Leonnatus from Lyncestis, and Polyperchon from Tymphaea, Ptolemy from Eordaea, and Seleucus from Europus.
340. Justin 13.1.

3

HIERARCHIC HISTORIANS AND ALEXANDRIAN ALCHEMY

What influenced the testimony of the eyewitness historians and what were their personal agendas? More specifically, did they have an interest in burying Alexander's Will?

The eyewitness historians – those on campaign with Alexander and those who stood beside his deathbed – provided testimony that spawned all later interpretation of events, though their accounts have since disappeared. The conflicting fragments we have suggest that they were constructed around highly personalised agendas.

These men were persuaded by their king to journey to lands few Europeans had ever seen, to partake in warfare on a scale history had rarely witnessed, and to scheme beyond the range of any tyrant or politician. In the life-changing, philosophy-challenging, world-shaping process, they were inspired by their campaign contributions to become 'historians' who appear to have acknowledged few literary restraints or rules of reputational engagement.

Here we review these archetypal sources, for the sum of the parts of their literary output *was* the Alexander the world would remember in the centuries thereafter.

'It is a naive belief that the distant past can be recovered from written texts, but even the written evidence for Alexander is scarce and often peculiar.'[1]

Robin Lane Fox *Alexander the Great*

'One should not look for thoughtful, or even consistent, characterisations any more than one looks for sincerity or accuracy… the mistake has commonly been made of trying to divide Alexander's historians into two classes, favourable and unfavourable.'[2]

Lionel Pearson *The Lost Histories of Alexander the Great*

'A history in which every particular incident may be true may on the whole be false.'[3]

TB Macaulay *History*

Disenchanted with the legacy of the literary output of these historians of old, the Roman-era satirist Lucian, whose essays have been described as forming a bridge between the dialogues of philosophers, the fantasy of Aristophanes and the criticisms of the satirists, wrote a parody appropriately named *A True History* to drive his point home. It was written in the thick of the Second Sophistic (broadly 54-230 CE), a period that recalled Rome's nostalgia for all things Greek. Although Lucian proposed a historian's mind should be 'like a mirror' – so reflecting events as they truly appeared – he was well aware of the cracks in the glass too.[4]

Besides proposing a trip to the moon, the Blessed Island and the Morning Star, and possibly drawing inspiration from the fantasy of Antonius Diogenes' *The Wonders Beyond Thule*, Lucian's satire on historicity ridiculed the writers who gave fantastical events a little too much credence.[5] Amongst his victims were Homer, Herodotus and Ctesias' *Indike* along with his twenty-three book *Persika* (history of Persia, the books appeared in the early 4th century BCE), which, considered together, formed the backbone of Alexander's knowledge on Asia. Lucian, a self-proclaimed barbarian (most likely ethnically Assyrian), summed up his introduction with: 'When I come across a writer of this sort, I do not much mind his lying, the practice is much too well established for that, even with professed philosophers; I am only surprised at his expecting to escape detection.'[6]

What becomes clear from the fragments of these lost accounts is that these ancient authors have never lacked attitude and agenda, and they showed little hesitation in criticising their literary forerunners, either for the sake of self-promotion, or to hamstring a rival. In fact it has been proposed that: 'The contentious spirit of Greek historians can be considered a significant catalyst in the development of Greek historiography.'[7] But that might be a touch encomiastic for the state of literary affairs, for when Hecataeus, the Milesian geographer and mythologist of the 6th BCE, complained: 'I write these accounts as they seem true to me, for the stories told by the Greeks are various and in my opinion absurd', he was apparently not offering posterity a methodology to better them.[8] We know that historians who were broadly contemporary with Alexander and his father, such as Theopompus of Chios and Anaximenes of Lampsacus, and probably Duris of Samos too, even used their prologues and prefaces to attack their peers. As Momigliano put it: 'The Greek and Romans were not apt to kneel in silent adoration before their own classical writers.'[9]

Less contentious are the few brief references we have to the period of Alexander's immediate successors, the *Diadokhoi*, in, for example, a fragment of the *Parian Chronicle* (otherwise known as the Parian Marble) compiled ca. 264/3 BCE which cover events from 336 to 302/1 BCE, as well as the Babylonian *Chronicle of the Successors,* a fragmentary cuneiform tablet that now resides in the British Museum.[10] A further inscription found at Scepsis recording the contents of a letter from Alexander's one-eyed general, Antigonus *Monophthalmos*, to the Greek cities of Asia Minor, is an enlightening insight into the state of affairs and a fragile peace of 311 BCE that did not last. *Stelae* like these are, epigraphically speaking, primary witnesses too *if* they were inscribed by contemporaries; moreover, they have little room for the rhetoric that we find interwoven into manuscripts, a contention that would hold true were it not for the Egyptian Satrap Stele (erected in 311 BCE) which essentially reads as Ptolemaic propaganda in stone.[11] As Sir Mortimer Wheeler reminded us in what serves as a useful warning on archaeological evidence: 'The archaeologist is digging up, not *things*, but *people*'.[12]

So here we take a closer look at the background of the 'people': those who preserved the tale of the Alexander we just attempted to survey. They became kings, or the generals and court favourites of kings who were themselves veterans of the campaigns, and their recollections were the stock for the secondary and tertiary stews served up in the 500 years that followed, a few of which survive on the classics menu of today.

Strabo considered that 'who wrote about Alexander preferred the marvellous to the true', and even Arrian, who looked to court sources for reliable detail, summed up his frustration with pessimistic lines: 'So, we see that even the most trustworthy writers, men who were actually with Alexander at the time, have given conflicting accounts of notorious events with which they must have been perfectly familiar.'[13] So we are standing on uncertain ground with the historians who both educated Alexander, and as those who educated us on him. It is in this light we need to adjudicate on what we read today, recalling the sobering advice: 'Study the historian before you begin to study the facts.'[14]

It has been proposed that Alexander's contemporaries, the men who accompanied their king on his *anabasis*, the campaign 'up country' through the Persian Empire, wrote for their own 'literary' purposes rather than for any higher 'historical' ideals.[15] But as products of a brutal and cataclysmic age, when royal sponsorship was key to survival, they were inevitably partial and self-interested and this is why their commentaries frequently conflict. Their retrospective words in ink, sharper-tongued than a Greek logographer, slashing reputations like scythed chariots and removing textual entrails like the blade of a deft diviner, were capable of obscuring the truth like a total eclipse, leaving us one more example of 'history eavesdropping on legend'.[16]

THE INDISCREET PHILOSOPHER – 'A SAGE BLIND TO HIS OWN INTERESTS'

We start with Callisthenes the son of Demotimus of Olynthus, as he was the first to put pen to ink in Alexander's name. Callisthenes was appointed by Alexander as what amounted to 'official' campaign historian, most likely through the influence of his relative, Aristotle, who reputedly warned his protégé on his indiscreet tongue when quoting lines from the *Iliad*, here poetically translated as: 'Alas! My child, in life's primeval bloom, such hasty words will bring thee thy doom.'[17] Plutarch reported an ulterior motive for Callisthenes joining the Macedonian adventure: it was to convince Alexander to re-settle his native city, Olynthus, destroyed by Philip II in 348 BCE for its part in sheltering the king's half-brothers, both of whom were destined for the axe.[18] In fact Callisthenes was following Aristotle's lead with this request, for he had likewise petitioned Philip to restore his birthplace, Stagira, destroyed in the same year when Macedonian forces annexed the Chalcidian Peninsula.[19]

Callisthenes was now mandated to toe the Argead corporate line; his new role was more akin to front-line reporting by a journalist employed by a state newspaper: a Macedonian Party *Pravda*. Although his account was to be a political manifesto, it became something of a biographic encomium that attempted to embody ideals that would appeal to Greek consumption.[20] Callisthenes had already proven himself an able historian having completed a *Hellenika* (Greek history from ca. 387-357 BCE), a *Periplous* (circumnavigation) of the Black Sea, and *On the Sacred War* (which may have assisted Philip's cause in that conflict in Greece), amongst other works, before joining Alexander.[21] He, like Theopompus, Anaximenes, Ephorus of Cyme and other writers of the 4th century BCE, attempted more than one literary genre.[22]

We can assume that aside from the sycophantic and semi-hagiographic content displayed in surviving fragments, his *Praxeis Alexandrou* (*Deeds of*

Alexander), if indeed this was his title, was on the whole coherent and valuably replete with dates, names, and numbers, even if a work of lower quality than his previous publications, as he himself admitted; when questioned on why his *Hellenika* was superior Callisthenes is said to have replied: 'Because I wrote it when I was hungry, and the other work when I was well fed.' That is until he was arrested and reportedly kept in a cage after losing favour on campaign.[23] Possibly anecdotal, and yet suitably cynical, this retort was preserved in the *Gnomologium Vaticanum*, a Byzantine collection of chestnuts by ancient Greek philosophers and other exploitable sources.

Callisthenes was employed at a turning point in history. Philip II had defeated the Greek alliance at the battle at Chaeronea and Alexander had levelled Thebes after which he enforced his father's edicts: the Boeotian League (headed by Thebes) was abolished and the Greek city-states had already been reorganised into an uneasy alliance in the form of the Hellenic League, more commonly referred to as the League of Corinth and its imposition of a Common Peace. The notion of 'freedom', underpinned by Isocrates' calls for Greek unity in an environment where perennial city-state war was crippling the land, was now revived in a war of revenge on the Persian Great King, Darius III, and Callisthenes performed his part. His description of the Battle of Gaugamela and which ended Achaemenid rule, has been termed 'nothing short of a Pan-Hellenic set piece'.[24] It was the last major battle the campaign historians would ever witness.

Callisthenes reportedly proposed, in Thucydidean style: 'In attempting to write anything one must not prove false to the character, but make the speeches fit both the speaker and the situation'; it dovetailed neatly with his contention that 'history' was 'philosophy teaching by example'.[25] But Polybius later warned, writing as he was when Macedonia fell to Rome, 'discursive speeches destroy the peculiar virtue of history',[26] and many we read in classical accounts do appear self-constructed, much like the dialogues that formed almost twenty-four per cent of Thucydides' *History of the Peloponnesian War* in which speech and narrative is bound together as firmly as in the *Iliad*.[27] This questions the extent to which words defined our history or events truly defined the words.

But self-righteous statements of method on reconstructed dialogues like these, repeated in various guises throughout Greek and Roman history, at once reveal an epideictic addiction and its supposed antidote, although *mimesis*, the 'imitation of characters and emotions', *was* considered a virtue of historical prose style.[28] But rather than narrowing the corridor of artistic license, this implicitly widened the path for a *logos pseudes*, untrue discourse, for the character and situation were both the historian's to originate. In the case of Callisthenes, by merging didactic discursions into his history with antiquarian scholarship, he was now writing in 'an almost rhetorical' manner, according to Cicero, who termed him a 'hackneyed piece of goods'; Polybius thought Callisthenes' statements were simply 'absurd'.[29]

Extant fragments of Callisthenes' campaign account reveal a systematic denigration of the influential old guard general Parmenio who was executed on Alexander's orders in late 330 BCE.[30] Knowing when Parmenio died, and supposing when Callisthenes followed him (conflicting reports make exact dating impossible, but no later than 327 BCE), we have our *termini* within which this latter part of his work might have been released. Campaign-related detail is limited and not all *testimonia* we have is necessarily first-hand.[31] Fragments contain geographical digressions on Asia Minor linking sites to Homeric legend, and they do not suggest a coherent or progressive campaign log; they may, in fact, be taken from Callisthenes' earlier works.

A Thucydides he was not, but Callisthenes' book *was* official, vetted and, we assume, sanctioned by Alexander before publication, and thus not easily contradicted by his contemporaries. Moreover, written in 'real time', it was a veritable campaign atomic clock when personal memories faded, as well as an invaluable spinal column for new flesh to be grafted onto. So modern historians remain vexed by the paucity of references to Callisthenes in the extant sources. Why do the histories we have, based on the books by Alexander's contemporaries such as Ptolemy and Aristobulus, stay silent on his contribution? In the case of Ptolemy's testimony the answer is easily deduced: citing Callisthenes as the source would have undermined his own eyewitness position, and furthermore, the tactless sophist had been controversially executed in his presence and possibly with Ptolemy's encouragement.[32]

Hemmed in on one side by his philosophical precepts, and with an ever more censorious king the other, Callisthenes should have trodden carefully when sermonising on campaign, as Aristotle warned.[33] Yet it appears he did not, for according to Arrian he tactlessly claimed that Alexander and his exploits (along with a share of divinity) would be forgotten without him and his pen.[34] His aphorism has undertones of the more cynical quip: 'Any fool can make history, but it takes a genius to write it.'[35] Callisthenes had 'kept his superfluous wit but had thrown away his common sense' and that may have spelled the end.[36] But his reminder proved prophetic and with him went valuable detail no one has since recovered.

As a result, it appears that only a few key episodes from Callisthenes' campaign account survived for the Roman-era historians to consult. Moreover, Arrian's references to him come with second-hand wrappings, such as: '… it is said that Callisthenes the Olynthan…' and '… the following remark of his, if indeed it has been correctly recorded…'. Hammond puts this down to Arrian's disdain for the Olynthan and yet Plutarch only twice cited Callisthenes as a source, and he too, like Arrian, could have extracted through an intermediary.[37] He is not named as a source at all in the Vulgate genre. If we require further proof that his history disappeared early on, we simply need to recall that the *Greek Alexander Romance*, still popularly referred to as a Pseudo-Callisthenes production, was at some point (in its earlier less fabulous form) credited to him; this was a misattribution only possible in the absence of the original. But it equally suggests that Callisthenes' reputation as a marvel-maker, propagated by those few encomiastic episodes, was established at the outset.[38]

Callisthenes was finally arrested for his reputed part in a plot involving the *paides basilikoi*, the king's royal pages (some of whom were his students) to assassinate Alexander.[39] It was a huge eyewitness conundrum and one that demanded some form of public relations initiative, executed as the historian was with little evidence of guilt.[40] The episode and its outcome, and the speeches couched within, neatly set the tone for the criticism of the conqueror that were to soon emanate from Greece: Alexander, the once model student, had lost his way in the East and had now become a tyrant.[41]

Arrian noted the disunity in the reports of Callisthenes' death and as Lane Fox points out, he ultimately experienced 'five different deaths' on Alexander's orders.[42] Callisthenes' incomplete book has an uncertain demise as well, for it disappeared from the corpus of history too gracefully for comfort, with his only epitaph appearing in the *On Grief* of Theophrastus (a former student of Aristotle and his successors at the Lyceum) which observed that Alexander misused the good fortune sent his way. But this was something of a leitmotif of Hellenistic biography; even the Persian Great King, Darius III, was portrayed as pondering fortune's vicissitudes in his addresses to his troops before his final battle at Gaugamela.[43]

Callisthenes' position was surely compromised from the start; his disapproval of Alexander's adoption of Persian court protocol, his lack of tact and alleged morose silences (we assume biting his tongue when witnessing indigestible episodes) led Alexander himself to brand the sophist 'a sage who is blind to his own interests', or so Plutarch claimed.[44]

THE CYNICAL *EPIPLOUS*

Onesicritus of Astypalea (in the Greek Dodecanese) in many ways appears to have been Callisthenes' successor, and he *might* have been summoned to replace him at the mobile campaign court.[45] This remains a surprisingly undeveloped theory when considering that the first references to Onesicritus appear after Callisthenes' death. It has been suggested that Alexander didn't require a 'political historian' after Darius had been overthrown, for the initial propaganda mission had by then been fully accomplished. But it is doubtful that the Macedonian king, set to campaign to the world's end, was prepared to let his future deeds go entirely unrecorded.

Onesicritus was a student of Diogenes the Cynic (as were his sons) whom Alexander reportedly admired, and this might have propelled his credentials to the top of the application pile.[46] He and Callisthenes had benefited from dialectic training (reasoned truth through discourse) and philosophical teaching, so perhaps we should refer to them as 'philosophers with a penchant for history' rather than the reverse. The amalgam was never likely to have produced a straight-talking narrative, though Onesicritus was certainly the more tactful of the two men; his survival speaks for his political dexterity because the Cynics, and *possibly* the Peripatetics (followers of Aristotle's school of philosophy taught at the Lyceum), were a significant part of that decidedly hostile picture later painted of Alexander.[47] The new Stoic followers of Zeno of Citium (ca. 334-262 BCE, from Cyprus), who was fortuitously shipwrecked to a career in Athens, look to have been influential too in the shaping of Alexander's legacy in the generation after his death, for they retrospectively blamed him for the rise of the cults and kingships of his successors that saw their schools censored and closed.[48]

In his 1953 translation of the extant fragments of the campaign histories, Robinson noted the chapters in which the sources appeared 'thin' on campaign detail. More recently a scholar probed into the existence of 'a lacuna of nearly six months in the chronicle' of a total 'missing year' broadly coinciding with this period.[49] Even formative episodes involving Alexander's meeting with his first wife, Roxane, and her father, Oxyartes, suffered from these conflicts, and if we can trust the anonymous *Metz Epitome*, the birth and loss of a first child by Roxane fell into the reporting gap as well.[50]

Callisthenes was executed at some indeterminate point after the battle at Gaugamela in September 331 BCE, possibly in Bactria and as late as 328/327 BCE, though he had already been under arrest for some time before his death.[51] The clear lack of synchronicity between the court-sourced account of Arrian (who principally drew from Ptolemy and Aristobulus), and the Cleitarchus-derived Vulgate profiling of the eastern campaign, broadly relating to the period between the winters spanning 329/328 and 328/327 BCE, does suggest the absence of front-line reporting.[52] If Onesicritus was called out to replace Callisthenes (before or after his eventual execution), and factoring in the distance a 'recruitment message' and its response had to travel – from the eastern Persian satrapies to Greece and back again – Onesicritus may not have arrived until Alexander was already in the upper satrapies (covering today's northern Afghanistan, Pakistan, Tajikistan and Uzbekistan), to which some fragments linked to him refer, or perhaps even preparing to enter India through the Khyber Pass.[53]

The blurring of detail suggests that the official campaign *Ephemerides*, from which the brief *Journal* of Alexander's illness and death was allegedly extracted (T3, T4, T5), must themselves have been far from perfectly preserved. Plutarch reported that the tent of Eumenes of Cardia had caught fire, or rather was set on fire by Alexander as a prank in India.[54] In his regret Alexander made every effort to assist Eumenes, who held the role as the royal *hypomnematographos* (the diary-keeping secretary), in retrieving correspondence from the generals and regional governors. By this stage a 'tent' was more likely a significant pavilion of enclosures that housed the campaign secretariat; much was obviously lost and its recovery was essential to the administration of the newly acquired empire.

Although we remain uncertain of when his account commenced, elements of Onesicritus' work appear to have survived intact for Roman period autopsy. Aulus Gellius (ca. 125 to post 180 CE) claimed his manuscripts were available when he arrived at Brundisium (modern Brindisi) in Italy and made his way to Rome along the Via Appia, and he linked Onesicritus' texts to the many *fabulae* cheaply on sale in the streets.[55] Once again, his account or what survived of it appears to have been select titbits rather than a cogent and chronologically organised campaign history.

Onesicritus was keen to preserve the wonders of the East, and some twenty-one of the surviving thirty-eight fragments do refer to India, the 'third part of the world' as it was labelled; he was, for example, the very first Greek to detail a sighting of cotton plants.[56] And it was here in India, on the very edges of the Persian Empire, that he was keen to see Alexander accepted as the 'first armed philosopher' by the *gymnosophistai* (literally 'naked sophists'), the Brahmin sages they encountered, though this approach was steeped in Platonist doctrine. Perhaps it captured something of an idealistic self-reflection as well as an attempt to align the Indian dogma with that of the Cynic school.[57] Strabo's branding him the 'chief pilot of fantasy' was no doubt a play upon his attested role as pilot, *kybernetes*, of the fleet dispatched from the Indus to the Persian Gulf, or his position as helmsman of the royal barge on the Hydaspes-Indus river flotilla.[58]

These were roles that earned Onesicritus an immortal place in the *Greek Alexander Romance*. His involvement with the Brahmins hints that he was something of a spokesperson for the king's propaganda machine on ascetic matters. If new tribes and nations were to be encountered as the Macedonian-led army made its way south towards the sea, a court philosopher and councillor on the metaphysical might win them over more effectively than a soldier and a spear, for the Indian campaign had become mired in blood.[59] And this may also explain his presence with Nearchus on the naval expedition of supply and discovery through the Persian Gulf; Onesicritus' own account of that voyage did not survive, though extracts appeared in the *Naturalis Historia* of Pliny.[60]

Onesicritus' book of wonders and Eastern exotica seems to have dovetailed neatly with Callisthenes' earlier colour, but we have no idea how one account met and greeted the other. If its title is accurate – *Alexandrou Paideia, The Education of Alexander* – it was a latter-day *Kyrou Paideia* (*Cyropaedia*), we assume in the style of Xenophon's eulogy of Cyrus the Great.[61] And that is not promising, for Xenophon rendered the deaths of his idols unrecognisable; he did, however, warn his readers in his *Hellenika* (his Greek history down to 362 BCE) which commenced without any introduction at all to give the impression of a seamless continuation of Thucydides' work (which closed in 411 BCE): 'I shall pass over those actions that are not worth mentioning, dealing only with what deserves to be remembered.' And that is tragic, as the works of Xenophon represent Greek historical literature for the entire 4th century BCE, and that legacy has been stripped of the *Athenaion Politeia,* the *Athenian Constitution,* once credited to him but now attributed to a still anonymous author we term the 'Old Oligarch' due to its anti-democratic tone.[62] Yet Xenophon's statement on 'deserved' history was reused by a much admiring Arrian, and it inevitably leads to questions on what Onesicritus may have selectively bypassed too.[63]

Once again, Arrian's references to Onesicritus verge on the dismissive, and they additionally fail to confirm he actually read his original campaign account;[64] his rejection of Onesicritus' claims to naval authority, for example, looks to be sourced from Nearchus.[65] Even Plutarch's references to the Cynic-trained historian leave us unsure whether he had a copy of his *The Education of Alexander*. Certainly a retort from Lysimachus, Alexander's prominent Bodyguard who became king of Thrace and the adjacent lands after his death, and which questioned the philosopher's credibility over an 'Amazon affair', did not come from Onesicritus' own manuscript, for that would have been wholly self-incriminating.[66]

Gellius' statement on plentiful 'Onesicritus' material on sale, as Pearson observed, may once again refer to something other than the biography of Alexander, and his campaign account may have followed Callisthenes' into oblivion rather earlier than we assume. The meagre length of Diogenes Laertius' doxography on the philosopher from Astypalea certainly indicates he found little biographic detail worth extracting, though his opinion of Onesicritus' work in comparison to that of Xenophon's, probably explains why: 'Onesicritus, as is to be expected of an imitator, falls short of his model.'[67]

Callisthenes and Onesicritus were the principal spin-doctors on campaign with Xenophon possibly inspiring them *both*, for his earlier *Anabasis* (in fact it became more of a *katabasis*, a march 'out to the coast') had detailed a previous Greek military venture in the Persian hinterland; as Plutarch commented on his legacy: 'Xenophon became his own history.' Here, on campaign with Alexander, it appears once again that partiality was never a compromising factor. Eunapius (born ca. 346 CE), the Sardian sophist-cum-historian, later made the proposition that: 'Alexander the Great would not have become "great" if there had been no Xenophon.'[68] Could this have been what he meant?

THE CRETAN *ARCHIKYBERNETES*

Nearchus son of Androtimus, a Cretan by birth but a citizen of the newly Macedonian city of Amphipolis, was a *syntropos* raised at the Macedonian court and one of the coeval *hetairoi* of the young Alexander. Other *philoi* were principally Macedonians of noble birth and veteran officers from Philip's military ventures, though highborn Asiatics controversially entered the ranks later in Alexander's campaign.[69]

Nearchus had reputedly once been exiled from Pella along with Ptolemy (as well as Laomedon and his brother, Erygius, and Harpalus who may have been a nephew of Philip's wife Phila) for his part in the Pixodarus affair, most likely in 337 or early 336 BCE in the final years of Philip's reign, though the veracity of the episode has now been called into question.[70] If true, the exile suggests Nearchus was amongst the few who were truly trusted by the then teenage Alexander.

By 334/333 BCE, with Philip II dead and Alexander's own invasion force in control of much of Asia Minor, Nearchus was appointed as governor of Lycia and Pamphylia, thus he became a prominent *strategos* (general or military governor of a region) with a pan-provincial brief. The role most likely required his naval experience to deny any Persian flotilla access to the numerous harbours on that rugged coastline, and potentially (with the navarch Amphoterus) to deal with pirates, the scourge of the Eastern Mediterranean since Homeric times when the Cilician coast, Skyros and the Thracian Chersonese (peninsula) were notorious for piracy; in fact as early as 380 BCE Isocrates' *Panegyrikos* had laid out how Greek mercenaries were to deal with the freebooters (harshly).[71] Additionally, the Persian fleet had commenced naval attacks in the Aegean in 333 BCE so that Athens needed well over one hundred ships to protect the grain shipments arriving from Egypt. Nearchus' post, crucial to watching Alexander's back, lasted some six years until 328 BCE when he was called to the East with new recruits once the naval threat had subsided with the end of Archaemenid rule.[72]

Nearchus became an accomplished commander of light infantry as well as a *trierarchos* of the Indus-Hydaspes flotilla, an esteemed role that would have seen him relieved of significant funds by Alexander to equip a troop barge without the benefit of bottomage.[73] He finally became admiral of the sea fleet and he recorded the unique two-and-a-half-month 1,700-mile *paraplous,* a coastal voyage of the Erythrean Sea (alternatively named the Red Sea by some sources) from the Indus delta to the mouth of the Euphrates, a route that allegedly (and mistakenly) provided him with calculations that 'proved' he crossed the Tropic of Cancer and the Equator.[74] His *Indike* (or *Indica,* broadly 'about India') took a swipe at his co-pilot, Onesicritus, along the way, for they clashed on claims of nautical authority and who bore the title *nauarchos* and *archikybernetes,* chief helmsman and admiral, and thus who was potentially *epiplous,* vice-captain, to the other.[75]

Nearchus' lost work, though substantially preserved in Arrian's book of the same name (*Indike*), was most likely written in old Ionic dialect in the style of Herodotus, and his geographical digressions on rivers, monsoons and floods were rooted in Herodotean tradition as well as his own understanding of Skylax's similar journey almost two centuries before.[76] Nearchus appears to have sensibly bypassed the land campaign in his memoirs in favour of Indian geography (in Herodotean style), customs and military organisations; he may have concluded his book at a point before Alexander's death in Babylon as Arrian deferred to Aristobulus for detail on the fleet preparations being carried out there at the time. But he was certainly present; Plutarch and Diodorus claimed Nearchus warned Alexander against entering the city due to adverse portents the Chaldean priests had observed (T21, T22).[77]

Ernest Badian, the renowned Austrian-born classical scholar, commented that Nearchus, who uniquely had a major achievement of his own amongst the officers of Alexander, '… shines like a good deed in the admittedly naughty world of Alexander historians.'[78] An earlier summation by Lehman-Haupt considered the conclusion to his sea voyage (as it was portrayed by Arrian) unsurpassed '… in loyalty and depth of penetration into human personality.'[79] Yet much of it appears 'epic adornment' inspired by the *Odyssey,* whilst the extensive list of thirty-three trierarchs (officers commanding, and funding, a trireme; here twenty-four Macedonians, eight Greeks and one Persian) he provided reads like the Catalogue of Ships from the *Iliad.*[80] Nearchus *was* most likely attempting to emulate the notoriety of the *Periplous* of Pseudo-Skylax and possibly Phileas of Athens; ultimately his account ended up as another 'philosophical geography'.[81]

Strabo grouped Nearchus alongside Onesicritus, Deimachus (mid-3rd century BCE) and Megasthenes, who also wrote an *Indike,* as someone who could not avoid the obligatory *mirabilia* in his work. On the other hand,

Arrian, perhaps unsurprisingly in light of his own same-named book, considered Megasthenes a 'distinguished writer'; he had, in fact, held an ambassadorial role under Alexander's Bodyguard and dynast, Seleucus, to the Mauryan court of Chandragupta some years after Alexander's death.[82]

Crowned at Susa for his loyal service (as was Onesicritus), Nearchus played a prominent part in the Successor Wars in which his legacy was significant.[83] He was usefully employed by Antigonus *Monophthalmos* until the battle at Gaza in 313/312 BCE, at least, where he was cited as one of the advisers to Antigonus' son, Demetrius *Poliorketes*. Nearchus was in his middle forties by then (assuming he was broadly coeval with Alexander) and he was never mentioned thereafter. If he perished in the disastrous outcome when 'most of Demetrius' friends fell... the majority of which were cavalry or men of distinction', then he must have published his book in the unattested years before his attested Successor War activity (ca. 318 BCE) and possibly as early as 320 BCE, supported by the fact that it *may* have been referred to by Theopompus (who cited 'authors of *Indike*'), who was thought to have died that year on the orders of Ptolemy.[84]

A plate subtitled *Nearchus leading on his followers against the monster of the deep*, from Jules Verne's *Celebrated Travels and Travellers, Exploration of the World*, 1882. The narrative accompanying the image reads 'just as they entered the Persian Gulf they encountered an immense number of whales, and the sailors were so terrified by their size and number, that they wished to fly; it was not without much difficulty that Nearchus at last prevailed upon them to advance boldly, and they soon scattered their formidable enemies.' This follows the detail in Arrian's *Indike*. Made available by the Internet Archive/Canadian Libraries via Project Gutenberg.

THE MACEDONIAN PHARAOH

Arrian's principal court source, Ptolemy I *Soter*, the putative son of Lagus of Eordaea, lies at the heart of our suspicions of the suppression of Alexander's Will and features prominently in later chapters. His mother, Arsinoe, was a former concubine of Philip II and possibly from a lesser branch of the Argead royal house. This fostered the rumour that Ptolemy was Alexander's half-brother, a loud whisper Ptolemy may have propagated himself.[85] As Pausanias put it in his *Guide to Greece*: 'The Macedonians consider Ptolemy to be the son of Philip, the son of Amyntas [Philip's father], though putatively the son of Lagus, asserting that his mother was with child when she was married to Lagus by Philip.'[86] This could explain why Ptolemy had the controversial Theopompus executed when he inherited governance of Egypt, for the Chian chronicler had conspicuously damned Philip and his court.[87]

In 330 BCE Ptolemy became one of the *Somatophylakes basilikos*, the king's seven personal Bodyguards, after which his prominence continued to grow, in his own account of the campaign at least.[88] A statement from Curtius – that 'he was certainly no detractor of his own fame' – suggests Ptolemy's self-promotion had not gone unnoticed (though such wording was not unique and similar statements appeared in the Roman narratives of Livy and Tacitus).[89] A *syntropos* at the Pellan court, Ptolemy was, and always had been, one of those destined to exert influence over men if he showed loyalty, military acumen and political agility. Certainly the latter two were on display until he died at age eighty-four.

Waldemar Heckel, a leading Alexander scholar who 'has made the prosopography of the late 4th century his special preserve', neatly summed up the problem we face when interpreting the texts citing Ptolemy's campaign contribution: 'Much of what we know about his career in Alexander's lifetime derives from Arrian and, ultimately, from Ptolemy himself'; yet we have just thirty-five fragments of his writing.[90] A parallel autopsy of Xenophon's *Hellenika* articulates the challenge of dealing with a self-documenting source: it 'thus requires delicate handling by the historian. What it says, and the way it says it, is always to be weighed against what it does not say, and the reason why it does not'; certainly Ptolemy appears to have avoided commenting on Alexander's darker episodes, for they in turn blackened him by the close association.[91]

By the time Ptolemy published his campaign account, his unchallengeable position as king and pharaoh of Egypt provided him with the power to manipulate character portrayals; those who opposed him in the Successor Wars no doubt suffered a *damnatio memoriae* as a consequence. Others were simply not spoken of; the *anonymae* remain, to quote Heckel, '... like the unhappy souls of Asphodel, on the marches of historical and prosopographic studies.'[92] It was a far more enduring victory than any under arms, but for all that, Ptolemy's campaign history appears to have been a dry and pedestrian military-focused affair that failed to ignite the Roman imagination, and it was less widely read than, for example, Cleitarchus' more colourful account.[93]

Recalling the guidance to historians offered by Voltaire – 'A historian has many duties. Allow me to remind you of two that are important. The first is not to slander; the second is not to bore…' – it seems Ptolemy was, in fact, guilty of both.[94] Modern studies including those by Strasburger, Badian, and more recently Errington, have conceded Ptolemy was unreliable. Fritz Schachermeyr concluded he got what he wanted from 'a lie, a fraud, and an intentional omission' just as Badian noticed his 'mixture of *suppressio veri* and *suggestio falsi*'.[95] Peter Green simply branded Ptolemy 'a conniving pragmatic old shit'.[96]

A FLATTERING TECHNICIAN, A GOSSIPMONGER *EISAGGELEOS* AND MERCENARY REMINISCES

The second of Arrian's 'court' sources, Aristobulus, lived to old age, beyond ninety, supposedly commencing his writing when he was a tender eighty-four, a literary achievement that was not, however, unique: Isocrates' output was prolific through his eighties and nineties and we encounter a number of long-lived historians and philosophers in the classical texts.[97] We have no title for Aristobulus' book, and the sixty-two genuine-looking fragments provide no chapter numbers, so we cannot gauge its length.[98] His interest in river systems and flood plains and his accurate descriptions of monuments (some he was tasked to repair) as well as the siege of Tyre reveals a technical eye with a geographical slant and leads scholars to believe he was employed as a technician or engineer on campaign.[99] Like Nearchus and Onesicritus, he was eager to recount the colour of India, though apparently without the blatant exaggerations and the overt *thauma*. But the gods still had their place in Aristobulus' reckoning and their divine intervention always fell on the side of his king, that is until Alexander's ill-omened return to Babylon in 323 BCE (T21, T22, T23, T24).[100]

Aristobulus also appears to have avoided the negative campaign episodes and he airbrushed those he could not completely erase; if not a fully-fledged 'flatterer' (*kolakeutikos*) of Alexander, then he might be termed an 'apologist'. Lucian claimed that a newly penned chapter that Aristobulus was reading aloud was tossed overboard by Alexander in an apparent rejection of its portrayal of him slaying elephants with a single javelin throw.[101] But this sounds contrived (if not exaggerated), for Onesicritus was afforded a similar retrospective in the pages of Lucian's *How to Write History*.[102] Yet to become truly Homeric, a king had to be seen fighting *monomachia*, in single combat. The episode does, nevertheless, confirm that Aristobulus enjoyed a well-known intimacy with Alexander, as well as a tradition that he was an unreliable historian. But as Pearson noted, Aristobulus' literary approach falls into no easy category.[103]

Aristobulus' post-campaign activity remains unattested, and this is unsurprising because he did not hold a military command; few engineers, architects or city planners were ever referred to in the histories except perhaps in siege situations or concerning noteworthy funerary constructions.[104] His birthplace is uncertain though Plutarch, Lucian and Athenaeus linked him to the city of Cassandreia; this had led to one theory that proposes he was a supporter of Cassander who retired to his eponymous city founded in 316 BCE on the ruins of Corinthian Potidaea which also lay on the Chalcidian Peninsula.[105] But there is no further evidence of his return to Europe after Alexander's death. Aristobulus could equally have worked for Ptolemy through the Successor Wars; Alexandria would have been *the* place to be for an already-established engineer, for the new city was one of the largest civic construction projects ever undertaken, though Cassandreia was a significant other.[106] A generation later, the ever-advancing Alexandrian building site was described by the poet Theocritus as having 'everywhere army-boots and men in military cloaks'.[107]

Although his was not an uncommon name, the one possible link to his post-campaign service is the 'Aristobulus' cited as Ptolemy's high-ranking diplomat operating in Asia Minor to negotiate the so-called 'Peace of the Dynasts' in 311 BCE. The connection is offered in name alone but we would expect him to have been offered some prominent service – and especially in a role that involved dealing with former campaign comrades (as this envoy would have) – if he truly did not commence his writing until an octogenarian.[108] The proposal is not conflicting; a career with Ptolemy, whose interests were aligned with Cassander much of the time (he had sons by Cassander's sister and was allied with him against the threat from Antigonus), followed by retirement to Cassandreia, is supportable for Aristobulus. Moreover, Diodorus suggested much of the population that survived Philip's destruction of Olynthus was absorbed by Cassandreia, as were other smaller towns, so the city's footprint and notoriety would have grown fast.[109] For a brief period, from 281-279 BCE, Cassandreia even became a 'Ptolemaic' city in the Macedonian kingship of Ptolemy *Keraunos*, the passed-over son of Ptolemy I *Soter*.[110]

A change of employer, as well as city, was not unique. If finally publishing from Cassandreia as a noteworthy resident, Aristobulus' similarly extensive service would have been so associated in retrospective literary citations; certainly the city officials would have appreciated the public relations opportunity. Although the identification of Aristobulus' employer and location is not essential to our case, the influences exerted upon him by Cassander, who controlled Macedonia for some twenty years and who lay at the nefarious heart of the rumours of Alexander's poisoning, alongside the influence of an already-published book by Ptolemy who enjoyed absolute rule of Egypt, cannot be underestimated.

Evidence of that influence may still be traceable, for Arrian concluded his *Anabasis* with a phrase suggesting that Aristobulus had no more to offer on Alexander's death than that claimed by the *Journal*, and, moreover, that corroborated with Ptolemy's account (T3).[111] If Ptolemy (as we will argue) was the originator of this supposed *Ephemerides* extract, which denied that any formal succession took place at Babylon, then Aristobulus could not easily have provided Alexander with anything more than that silent, intestate and conspiracy-free death, despite what he might have witnessed there or heard after the event.[112]

Furthermore, as a writer living in the political and military sphere of influence of either these dynasts, Aristobulus would have been extremely sensitive when making references to Roxane and her son, Alexander IV, or to Alexander's older son, Heracles, each of whom had been executed on Cassander's direct orders or through his political reach. But no matter how well disguised a suppression is, clues always remain and 'whilst silence is not necessarily an admission, it is not a denial either'.[113] As it has been pointed out, Aristobulus certainly 'was not encumbered by the truth'.[114]

Chares of Mytilene on Lesbos has to be considered a primary or 'court' source, penning his *Historiai peri Alexandron* in ten or more books. As *eisaggeleos,* the royal usher or chamberlain to the king, he could not resist capturing court gossip he was uniquely well placed to hear. Some nineteen fragments remain, principally in Athenaeus' *Deipnosophistai* and Plutarch's *Lives,* and they range from lucid eyewitness memoirs of court ceremony to what are clearly tinsel-covered anecdotes.[115] The vivid descriptions of regal excesses suggest he published under a later patronage that must have been tolerant of its content; a location on Lesbos under Antigonus' sphere of influence might support that supposition.[116] There is no guarantee, however, that the fragments are fully representative of Chares' work as a whole, and unlike the unrestrained accusations of alcoholism credited to Ephippus of Olynthus, he was careful not to directly slander Alexander or his Companions.[117]

Medius the son of Oxythemis from Larissa, host of the fatal party at which Alexander was reportedly poisoned, was possibly a member of the Thessalian Aleuadae royal house, and Anaximenes of Lampsacus, a Hellespontine city notable for its philosophers and historians, resided within Alexander's inner circle; both dipped their reeds into self-serving ink.[118] Anaximenes, possibly a pupil of Diogenes of Cynic, supposedly composed an epic poem and histories of Greece and Philip II, as well as a *Rhetoric to Alexander*; these disappeared without a trace despite his notoriety.[119] Fragments strewn through the Roman-era texts of Pliny, Strabo, Plutarch, Aelian and Athenaeus suggest Polycleitus of Larissa may have been a contemporary author, and although he did not accompany the Macedonians, we already know Theopompus had much to say (some of it negative) about Macedonian court life.[120]

Aristoxenus of Tarentum (a pupil of Aristotle) gave Plutarch a physical description of Alexander, and Marsyas from Pella, the half-brother to Antigonus and a naval commander at the battle at Salamis in 307/6 BCE, authored another now lost *The Education of Alexander* and a *Makedonika* in ten books that captured detail of the early campaign;[121] his was, almost uniquely, a Macedonian history written by a Macedonian, whereas the thirteen other authors we know of who chronicled the rise of the nation were conspicuously not.[122] Eugene Borza, the 'Macedonian specialist', concluded that, 'like the Carthaginians and the Spartans, the Macedonians are among the silent people of the ancient Mediterranean basin', referring to the lack of literary output from these once dominant powers. This might be a little over-generalised, for we know that either Alexander's regent, Antipater, or perhaps an Antipater of Magnesia, wrote a historical work titled *On the Deeds of King Perdiccas in Illyria* (a former Macedonian king), and we know there once existed a *Ta peri Alexandron* by a Philip of Pella. We also have fifteen fragments of a *Makedonika* by the native Theagenes (possibly written in the Hellenistic era) whose works may have perished when Rome and her broadsword waded into the marshes bordering Pella.[123]

References to Idomeneus of Lampsacus, a friend of Epicurus, suggest an anecdotal work in the style of Duris (whom he likely knew) had once existed, and the *Suda* suggested another contemporary, Menaechmus of Sicyon, wrote a history of the campaign. Strabo captured an additional snippet of the sea voyage back from India by Androsthenes of Thasos who was a prominent crewmember under Nearchus' command.[124] A few of the titles attached to these lost works are tantalising: Ephippus' *On the Death* (or *Funeral*) *of Alexander and Hephaestion,* and Strattis of Olynthus' *Five Books on the Royal Diary* are mouth-watering names for our enquiry but so far they remain no more than that.[125]

These writers no doubt constituted the corpus that Arrian, Diodorus and Curtius later referred to under the frustrating collectives of 'some historians', 'other writers', or even, 'so they say'; the indeterminate in-betweens that still elude identification and dating, leaving us wondering if the snippets that feature in Plutarch's multi-sourced biographies, or in the still-anonymous *Oxyrhynchus Papyri* XV 1798 found in Egypt and which looks to have been copied from a detailed archetypal history, reincarnates any of them accurately or substantially.[126]

A five-column fragment of the *Oxyrhynchus Papyri XV 1798*, probably dating to the late 2nd century CE preserving otherwise unknown details relating to Alexander's campaign from the death of Philip II to the prelude to the battle at Gaugamela. Now housed at the Papyrology Rooms, Sackler Library, Oxford, it was first published by Grenfell and Hunt in 1922. There are similarities to both Curtius' book and the *Romance* with evidence of epitomising.[127]

We should not forget the verbal material that birthed rumour, hearsay and anecdote that crept into Alexander's tale. Tarn identified what he termed a 'mercenary source' which we postulate was not an individual but a recycling factory of information from soldiers of fortune and campaigners settling in the provinces in the Successor War years, some seeking sanctuary and others seeking silver. According to Tarn, this incendiary bundle included the reminiscences of a soldier who fought *for* the Persian king. Political discharge was just as surely emanating from Cape Taenarum to the south of Athens, the gathering ground for returning Greek mercenaries who were employed to good, or arguably poor, military use, in the Lamian War of 323-322 BCE, when Greece attempted to shake off its Macedonian shackles immediately after Alexander's death.[128] Both locations were magnets for campaign veterans on either side of the Persian-Macedonian divide; they had stories to tell and grudges to settle in the choppy wake of Macedonia's continued domination of Greece.

THE FUNERAL GAMES HISTORIAN AND THE SAMIAN TYRANT

When Alexander died, his remarkable group of generals assumed control of the Macedonian-governed empire, and it was at this point Hieronymus of Cardia[129] commenced his account of the years that saw them rise and fall. Professedly living to a remarkable age of 104, Hieronymus first supported Eumenes, and then served three successive generations of the Antigonid dynasty; Antigonus *Monophthalmos* and his son Demetrius *Poliorketes*, and finally his grandson, Antigonus II *Gonatas*, Hieronymus' lengthy career saw him operating in Asia Minor, the eastern provinces, Greece, and finally in Macedonia, and alliances were fluid within those years. We do not know the title of his work with any certainty, though the Romanised Josephus and Dionysius of Halicarnassus (published from 7 BCE onwards) who described it as 'long winded and boring', suggested it was called *A History of the Diadokhoi* (successors), or *Epigonoi* (broadly meaning 'offspring' or 'sons of').[130]

Hieronymus' 'post-Argeadia', which, in its scope, most obviously followed on from the *Philippika* of Theopompus but which was also neatly sequelled the monographs on Alexander, was a unique work that unified Greek, Macedonian and Asian contemporary history through his unique eyewitness testimony. Hieronymus' 'elitist' approach once again focused on the deeds (*praxeis*) of kings, generals and their statesman alone, with little space on the pages for the plight of the common man,[131] an 'aristocratic bias' in historical writing that goes back to the *Iliad* and the *Odyssey*. But the narrative, ending sometime after the death of Pyrrhus of Epirus in 272 BCE, captured at least fifty-two years of war reporting through one of history's most dramatic and metamorphic eras.[132]

Like Ptolemy, Hieronymus' affiliations and the vicissitudes of his career are central to our debate on the fate of the Will and to the portrayals of the characters that both buried and exhumed it. Yet 'strictly speaking, we do not possess a word' of his original material.[133] The eighteen or nineteen fragments we have (one is dubious), less than five pages of text in all, make any evaluation of Hieronymus' work rather speculative, that is unless we are prepared to accept that his account is preserved reasonably intact in the more expansive sections of books eighteen to twenty-two of Diodorus' *Bibliotheke* (*Library of History*, known in Latin as the *Bibliotheca historica*) of the Roman era and which deal with the same years; a reasonable conclusion considering Diodorus' utilitarian method.[134]

Though it was criticised by Dionysius, Hieronymus' work was a unique and invaluable account of the decades that may have been less thoroughly chronicled otherwise because of the instability. A number of Hellenistic and Roman-era historians extracted detail for their biographies of his contemporary generals and statesmen and Hieronymus' books was précised to various degrees in 'universal' histories of the period.[135] Hieronymus himself is said to have criticised the writing of his broad contemporary, Duris of Samos, for its hostility towards Macedonian affairs, which in turn appears to betray Hieronymus' own political partiality;[136] it has even been suggested that he published, once again in old age, in response to Duris' critical books, though he must have diarised events and sketched out his narrative years before.[137] Hieronymus would have had an intimate knowledge of the nature of the death of Alexander (through the testimony of Eumenes, amongst others) and we believe he had a hand in the provenance and the birth of the *Pamphlet*; so, like Ptolemy and the royal secretary Eumenes, Hieronymus reappears in later chapters in a significant way.[138]

The anti-Macedonian Duris was termed 'tyrant' of the island of Samos, but we should beware of the despotic label; in the pre-Hellenistic era a *turannos* had carried no ethical censorship or connotation of 'tyranny', but rather it meant the sole ruler (at the head of a plutocracy, for example) who used unconventional means, and, moreover, it was a position that could be inherited.[139] Duris had been watching events from close by after the family's return from exile (the Samians were exiled from their island by Athens from ca. 366/365 BCE to 322/321 BCE) and he wrote at the time when Samos was 'gradually swallowed up by Macedonian warlords.' Duris apparently modelled his *Makedonika* in twenty-three or more books on the style of Herodotus and Hellanicus (ca. 480-395 BCE) the logographer and historian from Mytilene on Lesbos. The son of Kaios (possibly the tyrant of Samos before him), Duris was a self-proclaimed descendant of the Athenian Alcibiades, famous for his unconventional military tactics in the latter Peloponnesian War and his close relationship with Socrates.

Duris' history covered the period from the Battle of Leuctra in 371 BCE to the battle of Curopedion in 281 BCE, at least, and he too had to carefully navigate through the political reefs and shoals of the *Diadokhoi* shores. His work appears to have been a highly anecdotal *scandaleuse* that targeted luxury and extravagance, if the thirty-six fragments are indicative, though we cannot say with any certainty (Hieronymus' alleged criticism aside) how slanted his account was to any one regime. He certainly had cause to hate Athens as much as the continued Macedonian upheaval, and though he was perhaps younger than the first generation of *Diadokhoi*, he would have met certain of them (Antigonus, Demetrius and Lysimachus, for example) as part of his family's governance of an island that came under their respective (or attempted) control.[140]

Here the 'contentious spirit' of Greek historians raises its head once more. Plutarch implied Duris was untrustworthy and yet we know he frequently borrowed his detail for his own biographical works.[141] Dionysius of Halicarnassus viewed his arrangement as completely faulty, where Duris himself criticised both Theopompus and Ephorus, who was himself accused at a banquet (according to Porphyry) of stealing 3,000 of his lines from the works of Daimachus, Callisthenes and Anaximenes. Ephorus, whose thirty-book history dealt with events from ca. 1069

BCE to 341 BCE, could, in fact, have had an inside track and featured most prominently in the story of Alexander had he wanted, for Plutarch claimed it was he who was initially invited to join the Macedonians as the official historian, possibly for the compliments he had already afforded Philip II.[142] Ephorus wisely declined and saved himself much trouble, for he liked to draw a sharp line between the mythical and the historical, and that was a methodology unlikely to have pleased Alexander.[143]

But to Duris, these historians were concerned with merely 'writing' and not with *mimesis* or *hedone*, imitation or pleasure. This, too, rather reveals *his* own literary agenda, and it suggests he believed 'tragic' history (typified by Alexander's Vulgate genre) was an imitative art, thus not distinct from poetry, as Aristotle proposed it should be.[144]

THE *QUELLENFORSCHER*'S PHANTOM

> No one can glance through the thirty-six fragments of Cleitarchus without being struck by one thing, how little we really know about the writer who in modern times has been magnified into such an influential and far-reaching source in the Alexander story, and has attracted to himself most of the flotsam brought down by that somewhat muddy stream or streams, the so-called Vulgate.[145]

Tarn's opening commentary from his study of Cleitarchus captures an unfortunate dilemma: though his influence on the Vulgate tradition has now been established, the extent of that sway, and the original shape of Cleitarchus' book, remains nothing short of a mystery; he is as Badian mused, 'the *Quellenforscher*'s phantom.'[146]

Based in Alexandria (according to Philodemus) in the final years of older campaign veterans or in the early years of their offspring, Cleitarchus composed the first syncretic biography of Alexander by fusing primary material in circulation with the gossip, rhetoric and those negative philosophical tones emanating from Greece.[147] The fermentation vat of Alexandria did the rest in that tumultuous, creative, and yet dangerous period for historians and dynasts alike.

Many veterans found their way to new employment in Egypt, for the Ptolemies knew, as did all of the *Diadokhoi*, that you needed a hard core of Macedonian soldiers to face Macedonian-led satrapal armies, and no standing Asiatic contingent of the time had proved able to withstand an assault by its unique phalanx. So the *klerouchoi* (cleruch) system of incentive and remuneration became all-important in attracting new 'settlers' who formed a 'state within a state' in Egypt, Greek mercenaries and Macedonian former campaigners alike. Under this arrangement land was allotted on condition of continued military call-up and no doubt the enrolment of their sons into the state army.[148] This may explain why

Cleitarchus was able to garner more eyewitness detail (as Thucydides had for the Peloponnesian War) than Arrian could obtain from his revered but long-dead and 'sanitising' court sources.[149]

The result was the most influential Greek biography of Alexander that would circulate in the Roman Republic some two centuries on. Cleitarchus became the template, if not the whole pattern, for the Latin Vulgate, even if he was at times, as Cicero thought, entertaining with 'pretty fictions' and a 'better orator than historian', a claim that somewhat undermined Cicero's own canon on the subject. Although the Roman rhetorician Quintilian (ca. 35-post 96 CE) considered him 'brilliantly ingenious but notoriously untrustworthy',[150] Cleitarchus, nonetheless, appears to have been a talent that eclipsed the eyewitness histories written without his flair, for neither Ptolemy and Aristobulus, nor Nearchus and Onesicritus, had benefited from any formal literary training or previous journalistic experience that we know of.

Cleitarchus' father, Deinon, came from Colophon in Lydia, one of the cities claiming to be the birthplace of Homer and one later destroyed by Alexander's former Bodyguard, Lysimachus. Deinon had been a colourful historian who based himself in Egypt and produced a non-extant history of Persia (a *Persika*) that was praised by Cornelius Nepos (ca. 110-24 BCE) and much referenced in Athenaeus' *Deipnosophistae* and Plutarch's biography of Artaxerxes II.[151] The *Persika*, however, frequently contradicted Ctesias who was resident at the Persian court from ca. 415-387 BCE, though, according to Plutarch, he too '… put into his work a perfect farrago of extravagant and incredible tales… often his story turns aside from the truth into fable and romance.'[152] Deinon's son, it seems, was born in the same mould, setting out to 'improve on the facts'.[153] Alexandria was to become a centre of creative reporting and elements of Deinon's work might well have found their way into his son's book, especially detail concerning Babylon and a Persia Cleitarchus may never have visited himself.

The acquaintance of Ptolemy I *Soter* with the philosopher Stilpo of Megara, whom he (unsuccessfully) invited to Egypt around 307 BCE, suggests Cleitarchus, who is attested to have studied under Stilpo, would himself have been personally acquainted with Ptolemy or his son, Ptolemy II *Philadelphos*, in the years that followed.[154] Ptolemaic authority, whilst progressive in terms of architecture, the arts and trade, was also ruthless, and the new Macedonian dynasts proved to be manipulative politicians.[155] So it would have been impossible for Cleitarchus to publish a work under Alexander's former *Somatophylax* or his son unless it was politically benign and did not undermine Ptolemy's claims on the nature of Alexander's death, as portrayed in the *Journal* with which Ptolemy closed his book. And like Aristobulus, Cleitarchus would have been unable to recount any lingering rumours or suspicions concerning Alexander leaving a Will with succession instructions.

If the Ptolemaic regime could not control or regulate the *inbound* flow of information available to Cleitarchus in Alexandria, the repeated flattering of Ptolemy we see in the Vulgate texts (especially the closing chapters) indicates the historian was prudently sensitive with the *outbound* production and its references to the dynast.[156] The burgeoning city would have been full of scurrilous propaganda and allegations emanating from a patchwork of personal campaign memories, and if this and the accusations which originating in the *Pamphlet* could not be rebroadcast in the original form, it could be cloned, cropped and grafted by Cleitarchus onto a suitable root. If he published sufficiently late for the alleged participants in the plot to poison Alexander to have died, he *would* have been able to incorporate the lingering rumours and colourful story of regicide, for the allegations exonerated Ptolemy from guilt. Moreover, by then the earlier Ptolemaic alliances with those damned in the *Pamphlet* were over. So where the books of Ptolemy and Aristobulus had ended as wholly quarantined affairs, the swelling of Cleitarchus' final chapter still posed no threat to the Egyptian dynasts.

But a more malevolent Alexander did, nevertheless, appear; Cleitarchus *may* have been influenced by Theopompus' earlier harsh moralising on the Argead court, as well as the earlier negative Peripatetic-school noises (as proposed by Tarn and others, though we have little actual evidence) that were originally aired from Athens under the protection of Cassander's shield. For through the period 317-307 BCE, Cassander installed as his administrator (later termed a 'tyrant' too) Demetrius of Phalerum, a student of Theophrastus, in a role that was 'in theory an oligarchy, but in practice a monarchy'. We should note, however, that Stilpo, Cleitarchus' philosophy teacher, had himself been influenced by Diogenes the Cynic whose movement had little good to say about the Macedonian king.[157] It is not impossible that tragic elements of Duris' *Samian Chronicle*, if not his later Macedonian-centred history, also infiltrated Cleitarchus' account, if it was published sufficiently late.[158]

Besides these influences in circulation, disgruntled veterans and their offspring reared on stories of the campaign sagas, may well have recalled the gradual deterioration in Alexander's behaviour when the troubled campaign was quagmired in the East. Like many who had taken part in the decade-long invasion and subjugation of the Persian Empire, veterans surely faced the dilemma of wanting to be associated with, and yet disassociated from, select episodes of the story. As time passed, the second generation Ptolemies had nothing to lose from seeing a more tarnished image of Alexander manifest itself, as this in turn highlighted their own 'benign' rule, and '... not every monarch has an interest in preserving the immaculate purity of their predecessor's reputation.'[159] Thus the compromised, politicised and carefully re-characterised template of what we term the Roman-era Vulgate genre of Alexander was born.

The stature of Cleitarchus' biography of Alexander – as a conduit between the earlier eyewitness histories and the later Roman-era derivative accounts – helps us address an inconvenient reality: the dividing line between primary sources (eyewitnesses) and the secondary historians who drew from their testimony, is often indistinct. If Ptolemy and Aristobulus were influential on campaign, they were nevertheless writing some decades after the events they were inking on papyrus, and though the 'real organ of history is memory', these aged court sources must have leaned on either personal memoirs, *hypomnematismoi*, or on other already published eyewitness accounts to complete their own books. For we have detailed descriptions (if often contradictory) of the rank-by-rank battle orders, troop numbers, section commanders and the intricate manoeuvres in the rivers, valleys and plains at the Granicus, Issus, Gaugamela and the Hydaspes River, as well as the numerous skirmishes and sieges in mountain passes and 'unassailable' rocks of the upper satrapies of the Persian Empire.[160]

Significantly more military actions had taken place in the Successor Wars, probably before Ptolemy and Aristobulus published, some eclipsing even these in complexity and others in strategic importance to the survival of the *Diadokhoi*. Whilst Lucian did refer to a collection of letters to and from Ptolemy, suggestive that he maintained communication with Seleucus at least, these veteran luminaries would have wished to consult any surviving logs from the campaign *Ephemerides*, alongside any extracts they still had of Callisthenes' history, as far as it went.[161] And it didn't go far; the contradictions between Ptolemy and Aristobulus that Arrian cited are frequent; some are minor and some relate to the most fundamental of detail.[162]

The earlier published accounts of Onesicritus, Chares and Nearchus *were* already in circulation, so Ptolemy and Aristobulus would have been able to extract from them, but the result, like Cleitarchus' book, would have effectively been another syncretism. Moreover, a century ago Eduard Schwartz re-asked a question linked to an observation Polybius had once made:[163]

> For since many events occur at the same time in different places, and one man cannot be in several places at one time, nor is it possible for a single man to have seen with his very own eyes every place in the world and all the peculiar features of different places...[164]

Pearson more sarcastically added: 'Indeed, it is hard to imagine how history could have been written at all in ancient times, except by men with great powers of memory.'[165] He also doubted Xenophon could have taken notes on the so-called 'march of the ten thousand' from which he created his *Anabasis* (and there are gaps), or that Nearchus could have kept a useful log on his almost fatal sea voyage. The latter seems a little unfair; even the Indus-Hydaspes fleet had a secretary, Evagoras, and surely the sea fleet did too.[166] But the relative value of a 'primary' source to a 'secondary' offspring is not always as clear as the label suggests, rendering the definition of 'tertiary sources' even more opaque.

In these circumstances the Roman expression, *rem ad triarios redisse*, comes fittingly to mind. It broadly translates as 'it has come to the third rank' and it came to suggest a military last-resort situation. A legacy of the Etruscans and the reforms of Camillus (ca. 446-365 BCE), the class-based ranks within the Roman legion positioned the inexperienced *hastati* in the front row in battle, the more heavily armed *principes* in the second row, and the veteran *triarii* behind them on whom the first ranks would fall back if unable to break the enemy line.[167] It was a system that served Rome well until faced with less conventional generals like Hannibal. In attempting to break the secrets of the primary sources, *Quellenforschung* is often similarly challenged as so little early material survived. Secondary sources are thin on the ground, and it is often left to the tertiary sources – the thrice or more removed historians – to defend a story; so figuratively speaking, *Quellenforschung* is often relying on the texts of the *triarii* too.

The consequences of this are not always disastrous, for we are also faced with the myopic symptoms of long-sighted historical perspective, an apparent contradiction in terms explained by Hornblower's comment: 'Proximity as well as distance, can distort the vision.'[168] Historians in the thick of things might be compromised by their direct involvement. In contrast, later historians, and even coetaneous writers compiling from the 'privileged' position of 'reflective' distance and even exile, often provided a more holistic and balanced narrative, if not entirely free from bias. Xenophon, Thucydides and Hieronymus, as well as the Greek Sicilian historian Timaeus and Polybius who followed them, all commenced or completed their historical writing in forced *absentia*.[169]

Exile, by definition, obliged the authors to live in the sphere of an opposite, or at least neutral, regime, and Plutarch provided insight into its result: '...ostracism was not a penalty, but a way of pacifying and alleviating that jealousy which delights to humble the eminent, breathing out its malice into this disfranchisement.'[170] Thucydides, who had been banished from Athens, was sufficiently self-aware to explain:

> It was also my fate to be an exile from my country for twenty years after my command at Amphipolis; and being present with both parties, and more especially the Peloponnesians by reason of my exile, I had leisure to observe affairs more closely.[171]

Here again 'distance' (though we do not know to where he journeyed, potentially amongst Athenian allies and enemies) apparently enabled 'closer' observation. Thucydides' own failure to relieve Amphipolis when under assault by the Spartan Brasidas in 424/423 BCE, and his two decades of expulsion that followed, made him question life deeply; his prose has been described as retaining a 'bitter austere gravity' with a 'ruthless, condensed brooding astringency' born of that displacement.[172] Xenophon, similarly exiled from Athens, went further in a quest for (the façade of) neutrality, for there is evidence that he originally published the *Anabasis* under the *nom de plume* 'Themistogenes of Syracuse' to provide the allusion of impartiality to events he himself participated in or orchestrated.[173]

Should we therefore value refugee reportage over that of the statesman-historian who dispossessed him of his home? And do we credit the account of the embattled general with more authenticity than the narrative of the civilian onlooker? Which primary is 'prime' material and which is primed by the threat of war, 'the continuation of politics by other means', according to Von Clausewitz?[174] The answer to the last question if of course both, and these questions bring us back to Alexandria in the vibrant and dangerous years that saw the insoluble and permanent dyes of Alexander's first blueprints stain papyrus.

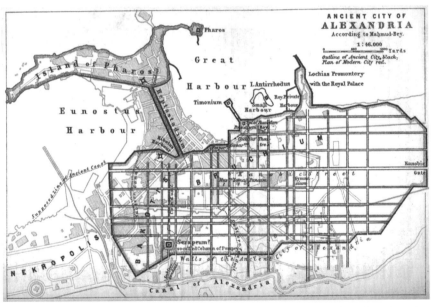

A layout of Alexandria in the time of Ptolemy II *Philadelphos*, showing the Pharos lighthouse centre top. According to Philo, the city was laid out in five major quarters: the Brucheion or royal quarter; the gymnasium quarter; the Soma; the Museion quarter; and Rhacotis, in an overall grid layout of the city. To the south of the canal lay Lake Mareotis. From K Baedeker *Egypt, handbook for travellers. pt. 1. Lower Egypt, with the Fayum and the peninsula of Sinai*, 1885. From Travelers in the Middle East Archive (TIMEA). http://hdl.handle.net/1911/9303.

OBSCURUM PER OBSCURIUS: THE BIRTH OF AN ALEXANDRIAN LITERARY MONOPOLY

The conflicts that frequently appear in the extant accounts, many of them relating to names, numbers, and relative chronology, suggest that neither Callisthenes' official account *nor* the *Ephemerides* from which the *Journal* was supposedly extracted, survived to the Roman period, except in fragments and through second or third-hand *testimonia*. If they had survived, no contradictory reporting should ever have appeared, for together they would have provided a near perfect campaign log, whilst any archetypal inaccuracies would have been uniformly carried forward.[175] Further, and to quote Robinson's 1953 study of the source problem: 'Since agreement ends with the arrest of Callisthenes, however, it is evident that historians had the facts of the expedition through Callisthenes, and not directly from the Ephemerides.' Relating to the troubled reporting post-327 BCE, Robinson went on to conclude: 'Therefore the Ephemerides for both the first and second divisions [his way of carving up campaign chronology] were probably lost before any account except that of Callisthenes was written.'[176]

The conclusion to be drawn here is that the books of the Alexandrian and possibly Cassandreian-influenced historians – Ptolemy, Aristobulus and Cleitarchus – dominated the Roman-era perceptions of Alexander, and, in turn, the Roman-era derivatives are the basis of the interpretations we make today. One result is that modern scholars believe (to quote Pearson) that: 'The history of events after his [Alexander's] death is intelligible only on the assumption that he made no Will.'[177] Yet that contention falls apart if we are prepared to accept that those blueprint histories were specifically fashioned to give credence, or serve obeisance, to claims of intestacy and Alexander's failure to clarify his succession.

If Ptolemy and Aristobulus were at the foundation of Arrian's court-sourced biography (as Arrian himself stated on his opening page), and if Cleitarchus' book substantially templated the Vulgate-genre accounts, our suggestion of an 'Alexandrian' monopoly seems to hold. The combined tradition carried forward by these three historians became a robust pesticide on the tenuous roots of any mention of a succession attempt by Alexander; it was a Hellenistic literary inheritance tax that foiled his estate planning. And this is our suggested publication order for these three influential books: Ptolemy first, then Aristobulus, and lastly Cleitarchus, a discussion not without contention and discord.

We do not have space here to cite the full extent of previous arguments and they are in any case inconclusive, but a few serve to illustrate the disparity of opinion.[178] Gustav Droysen's 1833 biography of Alexander employed newly developing critical methods at work on the 'great men' of history and in 1877 he proposed that Cleitarchus' book had been in circulation before those of Ptolemy and Aristobulus, a view later backed up by Eduard Schwartz.[179] The 'early' view was broadly supported by a 1921 article by Felix Jacoby proposing a date of ca. 300 BCE, with Helmut Berve, whose 1926 *Das Alexanderrei auf prosopographischer* provided additional prosopographic perspective on the command structures within the Macedonian army, following suit. Since then many scholars have concurred, believing Cleitarchus published within twenty years of Alexander's death.[180]

In contrast, Tarn saw the order as Aristobulus, then Ptolemy, with Cleitarchus writing last, after Ptolemy's death and possibly as late as 260 BCE. Tarn further believed Cleitarchus had little later impact on the Vulgate genre and on Curtius in particular, whose principal source therefore remained *obscurum per obscurius*.[181] Like Tarn, Pearson argued that Cleitarchus used Aristobulus as a source, while other scholars have proposed publication in instalments, so straddling the dating divide. Hammond, for example, proposed Ptolemy circulated his account between 320 to 295 BCE, with chapter-packets being issued at intervals (as did Livy three centuries later), though the earlier end of this dating conflicts with Arrian's claim that Ptolemy was a 'king' when he published, for this suggests a *terminus post quem* of 305 BCE.[182]

Although the geographical arguments, titular dissections, and acquaintance evidences that underpin the chronology debate each fall short of 'proof', the mantra for those concluding Cleitarchus published first is his report of the alleged heroics of Ptolemy in a gruesome battle against a city of the Mallians in India when Alexander found himself alone inside the city wall.[183] The episode was treated rather vocally by both Arrian and Curtius who both went to the trouble of uncharacteristically describing Cleitarchus, and also Timagenes who wrote later in Alexandria (he was captured by Romans ca. 55 BCE), as 'careless' and 'gullible', when on the whole he forgave source discrepancies, and more so if they were inclined to flatter Alexander.[184]

The interpretation born of this critique is that when Ptolemy stated in his own book that he was not present at the battle (as he apparently did), he was making a deliberate, and thus later, correction to Cleitarchus, whose account placed Ptolemy in the thick of the fighting and saving the king's life; this was supposedly (just one version of) how Ptolemy gained the title *Soter*, 'Saviour'. But if that correction, or even the total wording of the polemic against Cleitarchus, originated with Ptolemy, we would have expected Arrian and Curtius to be more specific on its origin; had they not, their own mirror critique would have appeared a rather obvious and unimaginative plagiarisation. Moreover, as Tarn pointed out: 'Ptolemy never contradicted anybody; things he believed to be wrong he usually omitted altogether…'[185] And clearly Ptolemy could not have been including Timagenes in any rebuttal, for his *Universal History* was a product of a much later and begrudging Augustan Rome.[186]

A reverse interpretation seems more valid. Curtius and Arrian knew all about conflicting accounts; Arrian recounted numerous other discrepancies in a matter-of-fact way.[187] Here, however, their parallel chastisement of Cleitarchus indicates Ptolemy had published his version of events *first* in which he claimed to have been absent from the battle. That would have been, as they voiced, a careless and egregious contradiction for Cleitarchus (and later Timagenes) to have made. It further suggests that there existed in the Roman era an unambiguous certainty on the publication order, which argues for a gap of some years between Cleitarchus' and Ptolemy's publication dates. But it does confirm Cleitarchus' desire to eulogise the memory of the founder of the Ptolemaic dynasty.

In this interpretation it follows that Curtius must have read Ptolemy's book to have criticised Cleitarchus in this way (which argues for his Vulgate archetyping), and it is also highly suggestive that Arrian read Curtius (who we believe published, more or less, a century before him) and he thought the didactic value of Curtius' criticism too good to pass up, for their wording is unique and strikingly similar.[188] The campaigns in India and the voyage down the Hydaspes-Indus were nothing short of wholesale slaughter and so not easily captured by Nearchus, Onesicritus, Ptolemy and Aristobulus – the court sources at the heart of policy decisions or complicit in some way in their implementation. As Curtius' account and Arrian's narrative remain in close agreement on major place names here, it does suggest to their parallel (self-admitted) use of Cleitarchus at this point, for he had garnered testimony that originated outside court sources – campaign veterans, for example – and that filled their reporting gaps.[189]

A final, though rather cynical, possibility does need voicing: Ptolemy *was* present at the battle but he felt the whole Mallian affair, like the earlier reported massacre of the Branchidae in Sogdia (or Sogdiana), was too gruesome to be a part of, when, as even Arrian reported, many unarmed men were slaughtered and 'neither women, nor children were spared'. So Ptolemy spirited himself away on an expedition elsewhere.[190] That would have additionally exonerated him from failing to protect Alexander, for other accounts had claimed it was the future Bodyguard, Peucestas (or Leonnatus) in his role as one of the *hyperaspisantes* who reportedly held a shield above his fallen king.[191] Somewhat suspiciously, Ptolemy did provide a most detailed description of Alexander's wound which issued 'both blood and breath', but perhaps Critobulus (or Critodemus), the attending physician, recorded his work patching up his king; the description points to a lung piercing and yet it is at odds with other statements in which the arrow lodged in Alexander's breastbone.[192]

One unnamed writer used by Arrian claimed that Perdiccas, prominent among the king's Bodyguards, cut out the arrow blade; the source is unlikely to have been Cleitarchus, for reading between the lines of Curtius' closing narrative of events at Babylon, it appears Cleitarchus was rather hostile to Perdiccas who had by then assumed the role of the king's *chiliarchos* (chiliarch, here denoting second-in-command), in contrast to his laudatory treatment of Ptolemy.[193]

ANOTHER HELEN, ANOTHER TROY

A further formative event in the chronology debate beckons parallel autopsy. It concerns Thais, the Athenian courtesan who became Ptolemy's mistress, the mother of three of his children, and according to Athenaeus, eventually his wife.[194] Vulgate texts credited Thais with instigating the fire that burned the palace of Persepolis to the ground in a bacchanal that took place in May 330 BCE. The royal complex completed ca. 518 BCE by Darius the Great was no more, and the firing was supposedly the conclusion to a drunken Dionysiac affair, though it came some months after the Macedonians had arrived in the city (in December 331/January 330 BCE). Quite in contrast, Arrian claimed the burning was a political decision and no accident, and so it is argued, once again, that Ptolemy, Arrian's principal source, had corrected Cleitarchus on the matter.[195]

A reconstruction of the royal palace at Persepolis, ceremonial capital of the Achaemenids, depicted before Alexander burned it to the ground, by the renowned Iranologist Charles Chipiez (1835-1901).

But surely Ptolemy had little choice when adopting the reporting line he did, for he could hardly have implicated his mistress, or wife, in a regrettable incident in which '... the enormous palaces, famed throughout the whole civilised world, fell victim to insult and utter destruction.'[196] Arrian's sanitised version stems from here, so the 'political decision' appears a scapegoat for an act that might have been arrived at under the influence of alcohol. Cleitarchus' narrative, captured most vividly by Diodorus and Curtius, does paint Thais as a somewhat heroic and patriotic figure who urged Alexander to avenge Xerxes' burning of the Temple of Athena in her own native city, Athens, so the two accounts are not as irreconcilable as they first appear.[197]

Her Dionysiac revelry was possibly setting out to emulate Herostratus, the Greek arsonist whose blaze at the Temple of Artemis at Ephesus was supposed to bring him immortal fame; this was an infamous inferno portentously linked to Alexander's birth.[198] If Cleitarchus published his book late, however, in the reign of Ptolemy II *Philadelphos*, Thais' heroic imagery would have suited a dynasty that had propelled her children into prominent positions in the Successor Wars.[199] The portrayal became immortal through Shakespearean-era plays and John Dryden's 1697 *Alexander's Feast: or the Power of Music*:

> Thais led the way
> To light him to his prey
> And like another Helen, fired another Troy

A further pointer to a late Cleitarchean publication date would be Onesicritus' alleged reading of his own account aloud to the Thracian dynast 'when he was king':

> And the story is told that many years afterwards Onesicritus was reading aloud to Lysimachus, who was now king, the fourth book of his history, in which was the tale of the Amazon, at which Lysimachus smiled gently and said: 'And where was I at the time?'[200]

Jacoby believed this suggested: 'Onesicritus stood on the same footing with Lysimachus as Cleitarchus did with Ptolemy.'[201] But the episode sounds as suspicious as Aristobulus' river recitation even though some scholars believe it indeed captured a key date marker: the publishing when the *Diadokhoi* were crowned.

The earliest date Lysimachus could have been referred to as 'king' was 305 BCE, by which time Onesicritus might have been in his seventies. But he had no obvious reason to publish so late as he took no active part that we are aware of in the Successor Wars.[202] As it has been firmly established that Cleitarchus took detail from Nearchus' book,[203] which itself appears to have been published after Onesicritus' work (judging by his criticism of Onesicritus' claims), and if the Lysimachus episode *did* portray the reading of a freshly completed chapter by Onesicritus (the fourth book in this case, probably of eight),[204] it is likely Cleitarchus published a good number of years after 305 BCE for Onesicritus to have completed his subsequent chapters, and for Nearchus to have published between them.[205]

And yet this all hangs on the reference to 'kingship'; this could have just as credibly meant 'when Lysimachus had established himself in Thrace', and there is no further evidence the reading came from Onesicritus' newly inked scrolls. Furthermore, as we will see, the *Diadokhoi acted* as kings soon after leaving Babylon in 323 BCE. If the claim that Onesicritus was fearful of naming the supposedly guilty guests at Medius' banquet *did* originate with the *Pamphlet* (T1), Onesicritus may in fact have published before anyone else.[206]

WHEN 'FEAR DRIVES OUT THE MEMORY'[207]

Tarn brings our attention back to Diodorus' comments (T6) on other 'fearful historians' who avoided commenting on Cassander's reported part in the regicide at Babylon (T1, T2).[208] If, as Tarn logically concluded, this 'fear' can only refer to writers publishing *before* Cassander's death in 297 BCE, then Cleitarchus, who *did* detail the plot to poison Alexander and Cassander's alleged central role, must have published later, assuming he was the common source behind these Vulgate allegations.

More convincing still is a first publication after Cassander's sons had been killed (by 294 BCE) and his nephews too (by 279 BCE with the death of Ptolemy *Keraunos*), as well as his former brothers-in-law who had sons by his sisters: this category included Ptolemy I *Soter* himself who died in 283 BCE and Lysimachus who died in 281 BCE, the year in which the still-dangerous Seleucus, *possibly* named as a Babylon plotter, was also killed.[209] After then, those who *might* have defended the reputation of Cassander and his extended family, and theirs by association, were gone. It is in this environment, logically focusing on the period after 280 BCE, that the rebroadcasting, without repercussions, of the *Pamphlet* allegations of poison and regicide would have first been possible by a historian seeking fame without the fear of execution.

Aristobulus' penchant for the portentous further pushes out the Cleitarchean publication date. It was Aristobulus who reported the presence of the mysterious Syrian prophetess when the royal pages made an attempt on Alexander's life, and he was additionally the source for the supernatural episodes and divinations heralding Alexander's death, the detail the Vulgate accounts picked up on along with other corroborating augural detail (T21, T22, T23, T24).[210] As we have no indication that the Roman-era Vulgate historians used Aristobulus directly, we assume their source was once again Cleitarchus.[211] But for him to have read Aristobulus, who commenced his book in his eighties (or at least 'late' in life) and who was yet sufficiently young to complete challenging assignments for Alexander on campaign, once more suggests Cleitarchus published his book later than many scholars have concluded.

A final dating clue involves the emergence of Rome, as, according to Pliny, Cleitarchus claimed a Roman deputation visited Alexander at (or on the way to) Babylon, presumably sent to pay homage to the Macedonian king and avert his expansionist eye.[212] Arrian named Aristus of Cyprus and Asclepiades (who is otherwise unknown) as the historians behind the detail (though he referenced 'other writers' too when discussing Italian delegations), and it was accompanied by suspicious pro-Roman ambassadorial propaganda: Alexander recognised the 'proud freedom of their bearing' and with 'greatness prophesised for their country'.[213]

No Roman legation was mentioned by Diodorus, whose Sicilian origins suffered in the Roman politics of his troubled day, though it has been argued that he may have omitted the detail for political expediency, writing as he was in the dangerous Roman era of the Second Triumvirate (43-33 BCE), and when Antony and Cleopatra, the last ruler of the Macedonian dynasty in Egypt, still posed a threat. Tarn accused later authors, including Trogus (as evidenced in the epitome of Justin), of inventing embassies from *all* the lands by then subject to Rome – though not to Macedonia centuries before – as paying tribute to Alexander.[214] And many scholars do still uphold the anonymity of the Latin city in Cleitarchus' day, but that is on the premise that he published *early*. The contention falls apart, however, if he published in the 270s, and, moreover, if we analyse Rome's ascent, its 'anonymity' is clearly questionable.

Polybius believed (possibly duped by Fabius Pictor's propaganda) that as early as 509 BCE Rome had already signed a treaty with Carthage (a modern scholar suggests 348 BCE), but certainly by 338 BCE, the year of Philip II's victory at Chaeronea, Rome had reached an accord with the Italian states that had revolted in the Second Latin War; the dissolution of the Latin League was a major step towards Rome's pre-eminence in the Italian peninsula.[215] And that is unlikely to have gone unnoticed overseas; the south of Italy and Sicily were populated by many Greek colonies that were trading with mainland Greece.

The discrediting of Cleitarchus' claim of Roman ambassadors additionally ignores the significance of Livy's recording the peace treaty between Alexander Molossus of Epirus (Alexander's uncle and brother-in-law mentioned in the extract above) and Rome in 332 BCE, a year or two before Molossus was killed in Italy.[216] His death, apparently fulfilling a prediction from the oracle at Dodona, was mourned by the conqueror in Asia who threw three full days of funeral games, so communications were intact.[217] Strabo additionally believed that Alexander (though which one is not clear), and later Demetrius *Poliorketes*, petitioned Rome to take steps against the piracy of Antium in which they were apparently participating (or perhaps simply tolerating).[218]

After Molossus' misadventure in Italy almost a decade before Alexander's death in Babylon, Rome surely watched the rise of Macedonian power with interest, noting how easily the Adriatic was being crossed by its westward-looking Epirote neighbour on the pretext of protecting Tarentine interests in Italy. What *is* accepted is that the Lucanians and Bruttians (and Samnites) who felt the Epirote blade and successfully turned it back on the Molossian king, *did* wisely send a delegation to 'apologise' to Alexander, and Arrian further stated that 'other writers' claimed Italy was a future target for the Macedonian war machine.[219] So it is not impossible, in fact, that the Latins did too. Trogus' generalised list of ambassadors at Babylon also included 'some from Italy' and Diodorus' reference to 'those who dwell around the Adriatic' *may* well have been meant (guardedly) to include Rome.[220]

Although a Rhodian trade negotiation with Rome dating to 306 BCE is widely regarded as the city's first known formalised contact with a Greek (rather than Epirote) state,[221] the rhetorical *On the Soul* by Heracleides of Pontus (died ca. 310 BCE), the Greek philosopher-astronomer and 'inventor' of a pre-Homeric literary ancestry, had already claimed Rome was founded as a 'Greek city'; a later tradition even held that a Corinthian, Demaratus, sired Tarquinus Priscus the fifth king of Rome, parts of whose first Cloarca Maxima, the great sewer that drained the marshes and gave the city her forum (constructed ca. 600 BCE), is still functioning today.[222] Moreover, both Hecataeus (ca. 550-476 BCE) and Hellanicus had detailed the legends of Rome's founding some two centuries (or more) earlier.

Closer to Alexander still, the sack of the city by the Gauls under Brennus in ca. 387/386 BCE was known, it seems, in Aristotle's school.[223] His successor, Theophrastus, the Greek historian Callias of Syracuse (3rd century BCE), as well as Timaeus and the poet Lycophron in his *Alexandra* (likely written pre-264 BCE at the court of Ptolemy II *Philadelphos*) also touched on the rising presence of Rome; the city was certainly not the *agnotos*, 'unknown', that her absence from early Hellenistic history suggests.[224] And just forty-three years after Alexander's death the dispatches of Pyrrhus were broadcasting Rome's presence to the Hellenistic world in no small way; Hieronymus most likely had a hand in that when using Pyrrhus' memoirs.[225] So the whole chronological debate is rather questionable. Whether Pliny was correct in naming Cleitarchus or not, and regardless of whether Cleitarchus himself was lying about events at Babylon, if he *was* publishing as late as the 270s

BCE, the name of Rome, which invaded Sicily in 264 BCE, would have been ringing in the ears of the second-generation *Diadokhoi*, and the idea of the city's submission or allegiance to the Macedonian king may have been useful propaganda for the Ptolemies.

IPSUS: FINESPUN VERSES FROM THE QUIET MIND

The digression on publication dates does have particular relevance to the fate of Alexander's testament and the literary monopoly we touched on above, because if Ptolemy had led the publishing order, and if the *Journal* extract did originate with his book, his was indeed the 'Cranmer's *Bible*' of the day that opposed any 'heretical' belief in Alexander's Will and its succession instructions. But how early could Ptolemy himself have published to head that influential hierarchy? Well, as Hammond postulated, he might have steadily drafted his account over the years in which he was expanding his influence from Alexandria, releasing critical extracts for propaganda purposes to justify his evolving policy; Callisthenes may have established this approach for Alexander as the Asian campaign progressed.

Yet with the epic battle at Ipsus in 301 BCE there finally came a world without Antigonus *Monophthalmos*, the charismatic general who had challenged for, and once gained, supremacy in Asia (though never Egypt). The former *Somatophylakes*, kings in the waiting for much of that time, had been hemmed in by his tactical brilliance and by his sway with the veteran Macedonians. With his defeat at Ipsus, the Antigonid storm passed, and if the squalls from his equally charismatic son, Demetrius *Poliorketes*, had not quite settled, the horizon in Asia extended.[226]

Before then, powerful and well-informed enemies resided close by (Coele-Syria and Phoenicia changed hands repeatedly) and an invasion of Egypt was only ever a Nile Delta crossing away. Ptolemy's grip on power was still tenuous and alliances were not yet consummated with marriages between the *Diadokhoi* outside Macedonia; those were not the years in which to publish a web of deceit, for dangerous repercussions were likely. If Ptolemy had read his Euripides, he would have known of a pertinent wisdom: 'Silence in season, speech where speech is safe';[227] and, moreover, as Ovid later poetised, 'fine-spun verses come from a tranquil mind'.[228] But even then: 'There are truths which are not for all men, nor for all times.'[229]

The great 'Battle of the Kings', as Ipsus was labelled, removed much clutter from Ptolemy's desk and it provided the victors with a pool of battle-hardened veterans that Antigonus had kept in arms. The outcome was a tribute to Ptolemy's powers of persuasion, for neither he nor his army turned up to fight on the Phrygian plain. Where possible he preferred to manipulate the nemesis of his rivals from afar; this was a classic example of an *actio in distans* that left Seleucus and Lysimachus to represent his interests alongside an expedition force Cassander had sent. Philip II was always said to have been 'prouder of his grasp of strategy and diplomatic successes than his valour in actual battle'; his rumoured son was following his lead.[230]

Although it appears that in the longer term Ipsus 'created more tensions than it resolved',[231] galvanised by Demetrius *Poliorketes'* still-intact ambition, the trio of Alexander's former Bodyguards, Ptolemy, Seleucus and Lysimachus, avoided self-destruction for the best part of the next twenty years, each living into their eighties.[232] That is not to say they didn't intrigue, use their intermarriages nefariously, or, in fact, sponsor some of the most famous generals in history to undermine their opponents. Responding to Seleucus' occupation of Coele-Syria in the wake of Ipsus when governance of the empire was again reviewed, Ptolemy allegedly commented on the quiet revenge he may one day extract: 'For friendship's sake he would not for the present interfere, but would consider later how best to deal with friends who chose to encroach.'[233] And that might just have been carried out through the medium of his book.

In the view of many historians, the battle at Ipsus represented the *true* beginning of the Hellenistic era, when the landscape of the empire was reshaped by 'agreement' rather than by brute force for the very first time.[234] In the following decades superpowers emerged and around them the Eastern Mediterranean and former Persian Empire gravitated for generations to come. The kingdoms of Seleucus, Ptolemy and Lysimachus (and Antigonus before them) riveted Asia, Egypt and Macedonia together as never before, propagating Greek culture and language eastward, perhaps in a way Alexander had originally conceived, though now without the Argead Star (more commonly known as the Vergina Sun) stamped on state correspondence.

Perhaps we should finish by asking why the long-lived Seleucus and Lysimachus declined to publish campaign accounts and stake their own claims to heroics and a share in Alexander's success, for they became kings with great tales to tell and no doubt with their own hatchets to bury deep. Possibly it was because Ptolemy ended his account at Alexander's death, and until then, his pages had treated them fairly enough, if perhaps not 'frequently' enough, for their liking, for Ptolemy's reluctance to attribute credit to Alexander's other nobles has long been recognised.[235] But for all we know, Seleucus and Lysimachus were felled halfway through writing their memoirs in old age with primed court historians ready to dictate to. But manuscripts, diaries, journals, libraries and official correspondence disappeared without a trace in the face of defeat in battle, giving the impression that a literary desert had existed at their court. Along with treasuries, wives, generals and their men, chattels, ships and cities, literary ordnance was also seized, so the history of the vanquished slipped into the folio of the victor.

After occupying Antigonus' former 'empire' that spanned Asia Minor, Lysimachus did set about repairing the crumbling walls of what he believed was Troy, suggesting he harboured something of a 'caretaker' role for the Homeric past, no doubt for propaganda purposes. According to a fragment from Memnon's history of Heraclea Pontica, preserved in an epitome by Photius,[236] Lysimachus exiled a certain Nymphis from Thrace; he appears to have written a work titled *Concerning Alexander, the Diadokhoi and the Epigonoi*, and this may suggest Lysimachus was sensitive to the subject as a whole, marrying as he once did into the Antipatrid house, whose figurehead through much of the Successor Wars, Cassander, had murdered Alexander's mother and two sons.[237] Or, perhaps after thirty years of bloody campaigning, these giants of the age were simply content to rule in their own name with their dynasties unfolding before them, though they were themselves to witness, and even orchestrate, the death of a number of their own children.[238]

The result is that the hierarchic historians – the Alexandrian-Cassandreian-linked trio of Ptolemy, Aristobulus and Cleitarchus – *were* overwhelmingly influential in fixing the chemical formula of Alexander's compound. Although we may be accusing them of gross historical manipulation, so that 'the challenge of the historical Alexander was therefore refused', they themselves would have thought quite differently on the matter, for the known world was itself in flux: geography, astronomy, the calendars, philosophy, scientific classification and even currencies were all being replaced, reorganised and recalibrated.[239] The present was finally obscuring the earlier preoccupation with the Homeric past, for Heraclean tasks were being presented to the new generation of kings.

So we doubt Cleitarchus lay awake over passages that captured Alexander's darker hues, and surely Ptolemy wasted no sleepless nights over his manipulative methodology that may have inserted a self-serving *Journal* extract into his closing pages. If, as Cicero reminds us, the duty of every historian is to the future, then they simply shifted that obligation to their *own* paths ahead. Polybius later commented upon the state of the historians writing in the late Argead era: '… because there are so many various conditions and circumstances, yielding to which men are prevented from uttering or writing their real opinions.'[240] It appears the following years were no less constraining.

Aristotle reasoned that men are by nature political animals, historians the more so it seems.[241] The great Peripatetic philosopher was also the originator of the adage: 'Libya always bears something new.'[242] If revenge is best served cold, then free from having to pander to the image of men he despised, Ptolemy served up Alexander from the shores of Libya (which, for the Greeks, broadly meant 'northeast Africa') subtly garnished with omission and delicately seasoned with new deceits.

Lucian's *How to Write History* stated: 'My belief is that when actions are finished and done with, not even Clotho [the Spinner] can unspin them, nor Atropus [the Unchanging] change them back.'[243] It was perhaps once again laced with sarcasm, for it naively ignores the state of affairs that led Lucian to publish his own *True History*: the spin and the undetectable 'change' from the primary historian himself. But here, at the dawn of the Hellenistic Age, the result was literary alchemy and Alexandria was the historian's alembic, a recycling factory of rumour, grudges as well as retrospective fraud. And its resident historians appear to have been dealing in both bags of guile.

NOTES

1. Lane Fox (1973) Preface p 11.
2. Pearson (1960) pp 240-241.
3. Macaulay (1828).
4. Lucian *How to Write History* 51.
5. Lucian *A True History* 1.12. Quoting Highet (1949) p 304 for Lucian's unique approach.
6. Lucian *A True History* 1.4, translation by HW Fowler and FG Fowler, Clarendon Press, Oxford, 1905. Lucian referred to himself as 'Assyrian' rather than of Greek or Roman descent. He also claimed his native language was a foreign tongue, probably Syriac, a form of Aramaic; see his comment in Lucian *The Double Indictment* 27. For a summary of Lucian's career see the introduction by AM Harmon to *The Works of Lucian* in the Loeb Classical Library edition, 1913. Lucian, from Samosata on the banks of the Euphrates (in modern Turkey), entered imperial service late in life.
7. Quoting Hornblower (1981) p 234.
8. Hecataeus *Genealogies* FGH 1 F 1, cited in Boardman-Griffin-Murray (1986) pp 216-217.
9. Momigliano (1966) p 128. Walbank (1962) p 3 for polemic appearing in prefaces. For Duris' criticism of Ephorus and Theopompus see Kebric (1977) p 39.
10. Discussion of the steles in Bosworth (2002) pp 20-24 and pp 241-242. For a detailed transcription of the Satrap Stele, see Bevan (1968) pp 28-32; its propaganda discussed in Marasco (2011) pp 70-72.
11. See chapter titled *Sarissa Diplomacy: Macedonian Statecraft* for more on the Satrap Stele.
12. M Wheeler, *Archaeology from the Earth,* Harmondsworth, Penguin Books, 1956 p 13; its use inspired by Musgrave-Prag-Neave-Lane Fox (2010): People and Archaeology.
13. Strabo 2.1.9, 15.1.28, Arrian 4.14.3, translation by A de Selincourt, Penguin Classics edition, 1958; his jibe was aimed at Ptolemy and Aristobulus, and specifically at their reporting of Callisthenes' death.
14. Carr (1987) p 24. The original 1961 publication of EH Carr's *What is History?*, which challenged the notion of a historian's objectivity, stirred up a hornets' nest of criticism following the series of lectures behind it; he sagely added this quote in his 1987 update.
15. Following and quoting Pearson (1960) pp 86-78.
16. Following Pernot (2005) p 7 quoting Victor Hugo.
17. His 'official' role confirmed at Arrian 4.10.1, Plutarch *Sulla* 36. Callisthenes was a relative according to the *Suda* and a great nephew according to Plutarch 55.8; he was the son of Hero, niece of Aristotle. Callisthenes' father had married Aristotle's older sister, Arimneste, mother of Hero. Diogenes Laertius termed him 'kinsman'. Seneca *Suasoria* 1.5 called him 'cousin'. *Iliad* 18.95 quote from Diogenes Laertius *Aristotle* 6, translation by CD Yonge.
18. Plutarch 53.1 for Callisthenes' motives and Justin 8.3.9-11 for the Olynthian intrigue. Philip had already executed a third half-brother and the other two by Gygaea, his stepmother, and Amyntas, his father, were destined for the same.
19. Diogenes Laertius *Aristotle* 6 for both his and Callisthenes' petitions to Philip.
20. Atkinson (1963) pp 125-126 for discussion of Callisthenes' political role.
21. Pearson (1960) p 25-27 for discussion of the fragments of Callisthenes' works. The *Suda* also accredited him with a *Persika*. Barber (1993) p 133 for the quality of Callisthenes' work. Robinson (1953) pp 45-77 for other possible publications including a *History of Thrace* and a *Makedonika* that may or may not be distinct from the *Hellenika*. Diodorus 14.117.8, 16.14.4 stated Callisthenes' ten-book Greek history ended in the fourth year of the 105th Olympiad, the year in which Philomelus the Phocian despoiled the temple at Delphi.
22. Following Flower (1994) p 40 for the multi-genre trend.
23. *Gnomologium Vaticanum* 367 for Callisthenes' riposte. The fragments that attest to Callisthenes' caging collected in Robinson (1953) pp 52-53; citations came from Ovid, Plutarch and Strabo as well as eyewitness historians. Pearson (1960) p 33 for discussion on the title of Callisthenes' work.
24. Curtius 3.10 and Justin 11.9.3-6 cited Alexander's multi-national encouragement to his allied force. Plutarch 33.1 mentioned Callisthenes 'seeking to win the favour of the Hellenes'. The 'pan-Hellenic set piece' quotes Bosworth-Baynham (2000) p 112.
25. Pearson (1960) p 31 for discussion quoting the Vatican *Gnomologos* 367. Full citation in Robinson (1953) p 54. Dionysius of Halicarnassus *On Thucydides* 36. Discussed in Pitcher (2009) p 105. Also in the *Art of Rhetoric* 11.2.19-21 of Pseudo-Dionysius, referring to Thucydides 1.22.4 and his contention that the reading of history should be profitable.
26. Polybius 12.25b.
27. For the reference to narrative and epic in the *Iliad* see Pernot (2005) p 1. Grant (1995) p 47 for twenty-four per cent comprising speeches.

28. Thucydides imitation of Herodotus discussed by JL Moles in Gill-Wiseman (1993) p 100. Gray (1987) p 468 for discussion of mimesis, and quoting Dionysius of Halicarnassus *ad Pompeium Geminum* 18 (776) as it appears in Gray (1987).

29. Cicero *De Oratore* 2.58; full text in Robinson (1953) p 55. Quoting Pearson (1960) p 250 for the merging of 'rhetorical history and antiquarian scholarship.' Polybius 12.12.b and 17-22.

30. For examples of the treatment of Parmenio see Tarn (1921) p 24; this appears to have infiltrated the Vulgate, examples at Curtius 4.9.14-15, 4.13.4 and 4.7-9; also Arrian 3.10.1-2 and Plutarch 31.11-12.

31. The collected fragments can be found in Robinson (1953) pp 45-77.

32. Arrian 4.14 suggested both Aristobulus and Ptolemy deliberately implicated Callisthenes in their texts. Certainly they were not apologetic. Curtius 8.6.22 suggested Ptolemy brought Callisthenes' involvement to Alexander's attention.

33. Aristotle was reportedly aware of the danger of Callisthenes' outspokenness in front of Alexander; Diogenes Laertius 5.4-5.

34. Arrian 4.10.1-2.

35. Oscar Wilde *The Critic as Artist* Part 1, 1891.

36. Robinson (1953) p 46 for the fragment relating to Aristotle's purported joke on wit and common sense.

37. At Plutarch 33, Callisthenes is mentioned twice; Plutarch *Aristeides* 27.2 mentioned Callisthenes as a source but this is clearly not from his account of Alexander; Pearson (1960) pp 72-74.

38. Stoneman (1991) p 28 for discussion of the possible more sober archetype of the *Romance* texts. Also Fraser (1996) pp 210-226 for the earliest form of the *Romance*.

39. For Callisthenes' alleged part in the pages' conspiracy see Plutarch 55.3-5, Arrian 4.12.7, 4.13.3-4, 14.1 and 8.6.24-25, Curtius 8.7.10, 8.6.8, 8.8.21, Justin 12.7.2. There are five conflicting reports of how he died; see chapter titled *The Damaging Didactic of the Classical Death* for fuller explanation.

40. Plutarch 55 claimed letters were circulating to Craterus, Attalus and Alcetas in which Alexander stated the pages had no accomplices, a contention supported by Arrian 4.14.1.

41. The underlying themes and speeches surrounding the Hermolaus affair discussed by S Müller in Carney-Ogden (2010) pp 26-27.

42. Arrian 4.141-4 for the reporting disunity of the eyewitness sources. Lane Fox (1980) p 307.

43. Diogenes Laertius *Theophrastus* 1.5.44. Atkinson (1996) p 135 for citation on fortune. However the treatise may not have been about Callisthenes, just dedicated to him. Curtius 4.4.19 for Darius' long speech prior to the battle at Gaugamela when fortune's changing blessings are pondered.

44. Pearson (1960) p 25 for discussion of his being referenced as a 'sophist'. Plutarch 53.2 for the quote and Callisthenes' superior sophistry that earned him the hatred of the Macedonians.

45. Heckel (2006) p 183 assumes he was with the campaign earlier, citing Diogenes Laertius *Onesicritus*. However this remains uncertain as this text simply suggested 'he accompanied Alexander' with no dating reference. It does not confirm Onesicritus 'set out' with Alexander. Onesicritus' family may have been from Aegina, according to Diogenes Laertius 6.84. For discussion see Heckel (2006) p 183 and Pearson (1960) p 85 and in depth in Brown (1949) p 1 ff, 4, 24. He was a student of Diogenes the Cynic; see Plutarch 65.2, Strabo 15.1.65, *Metz Epitome* 331e.

46. Diogenes Laertius *Onesicritus* 6.75-76, Plutarch 65.2, Plutarch *Moralia* 331e, Strabo 15.1.65 for Onesicritus' association with Diogenes the Cynic.

47. Tarn 1 (1948) p 82 and Tarn (1948) p 97 for discussion of the Peripatetic treatment of Alexander. The hostile tradition to Alexander from the Peripatetics is challenged by Badian (see Borza (1995) pp 179-182 and Milns (1966) p 499 as there is little evidence to prove this. Aristotle founded the Lyceum in Athens in 335/334 BCE. It took its name from Apollo-Lyceus, the god incarnated as a wolf, and was initially a gymnasium and meeting place. The building had colonnades, *peripatoi*, though which Aristotle would walk whilst teaching, earning him the title *peripatetikos*, hence peripatetic. Whilst the link is attractive, the term *peripatetikos,* of walking, was likely already in use; Diogenes Laertius *Aristotle* 4 for the origins of the name.

48. Diogenes Laertius *Zeno* 4-5 related a different version of a story that Zeno was shipwrecked at Athens and thus began his own philosophical movement thereafter. Tarn (1949) pp 93-98 for discussion of the peripatetic portrait of Alexander.

49. Robinson *The Ephemerides of Alexander's Expedition* (1953). The missing year discussed in full in Bosworth (1981) relating to the lack of synchronicity through 329/328 and 328/327 BCE.

50. Conflicts best summarised in Heckel (2006) p 187 for Oxyartes and p 250 for Sisimithres, where the possible meeting with Roxane took place after the capture of the Rock of Chorienes, or after the siege of the Rock of Sogdia. The sons that Curtius attributed to Oxyartes, Roxane's father, appear in fact to belong to Chorienes. Even Oxyartes' governorship and territorial claims are uncertain. Also Bosworth (1981) pp 29-32 for discussion of conflicting reports from this period.

Metz Epitome 70 recorded that Roxane bore a child that died in its infancy; its narrative runs, broadly, from July 330 to July 325 BCE.

51. Heckel (2006) pp 76-77 for a summary of the conflicting deaths recorded by Curtius, Arrian, Chares, Aristobulus and Ptolemy and references to either Bactria or Bactra (the regional capital, modern Balkh) in Zariaspa.

52. For the dating of Callisthenes' death and the termination of his writing, see Robinson (1953) Preface pp viii-xi.

53. Robinson *The Ephemerides of Alexander's Expedition* (1953) Introduction p 11 and pp 70-71. Fragments of Onesicritus' work do relate the curiosities of Sogdia and Bactria, though this could be hearsay and does not prove he was there. For the relevant fragments see Robinson (1953) pp 152-153. Likewise the Amazon affair was probably considered 'essential' reporting though Onesicritus might have arrived after the event; Plutarch 46 for Onesicritus' version.

54. Plutarch *Eumenes* 2.3.

55. For Onesicritus' reputation as a purveyor of marvels, see discussion in Pearson (1960) p 86, citing Aulus Gellius 9.4.1-3.

56. Brown (1949) p 7 for the fragments relating to India. Brown (1949) p 89 for the reporting on cotton; Herodotus had more vaguely referred to the plant's 'wool' as a fruit and p 7 for the surviving fragments of Onesicritus in Strabo 15.1.63-65.

57. The 'philosopher in arms' is distilled from Onesicritus' own narrative preserved by Strabo 15.1.58-66. Various other texts including, most notably, Plutarch 64-65, described dialogues between Alexander and the sages. Onesicritus referred to India as 'a third part of the world', suggesting his view that it was a distinct continent, possibly as a PR move to help explain Alexander's decision to turn back west at this point. Discussion in Pearson (1960) p 95.

58. Strabo 15.1.28 discussed by Pearson (1960) pp 83-111 and p 98 for Onesicritus' place in the *Romance*, referring to Strabo 15.1.58-66 and the description of the Indian wise men or gymnosophists and the philosophical dialogues.

59. Sphines became known as 'Calanus' after '*kale*' the word he addressed the Macedonians with; Plutarch 65.5; Heckel (2006) p 74 suggests Kalyana as its possible origin. The Indian campaign discussed further in chapter titled *The Reborn Wrath of Peleus' Son*.

60. Brown (1949) p 108 for discussion of Pliny preserving Onesicritus' account of the coastal voyage.

61. Pearson (1960) pp 87-89 for discussion on the title of Onesicritus' work.

62. Xenophon's legacy discussed in Flower (1994) p 42.

63. Discussion on the reference to Xenophon's lack of introduction in McGing (201) p 61. Xenophon *Hellenika* 4.8.1. Compare with Arrian Preface 1.1-2, discussed further in chapter titled *Classicus Scriptor, Rhetoric and Rome*.

64. There are four references to Onesicritus, two that indicate he was the original source of detail; see Robinson (1953) pp 149-166.

65. Arrian 6.2.3. In contrast the *Suda* N117 claimed it was Nearchus who lied about his role of admiral of the fleet.

66. Plutarch 46.4-5 for the episode involving Onesicritus and Lysimachus.

67. Pearson (1960) pp 84-87 for discussion; other third-party references can be found in Diogenes Laertius *Onesicritus* 6.84-85; Aulus Gellius 9.4; Strabo 2.1.9; Arrian 6.2.3-4, 7.5.6, 7.20.9; these are pro-Nearchus suggesting they came from Nearchus' own account. Quoting Diogenes Laertius *Onesicritus* 6.84.

68. Plutarch *Moralia* 345c or *de Gloria Atheniensium*. Eunapius *Lives of the Sophists* VS 1.453. A *katabasis* more ominously denotes a trip down to the underworld.

69. Anson (2004) p 42 also Borza (1995) pp 166-167 for the use of *hetairoi* and *philos* for the inner circles of the Macedonian court.

70. Arrian 3.6.5 for confirmation of his exile and Plutarch 10.1-4 and Arrian 3.6.5-6 for the alleged Pixodarus affair that led to Philip banishing them. Hammond *Philip* (1994) pp 173-4 suggests the whole affair was the 'malicious fiction' of Satyrus' *Life of Philip*. However for a different interpretation see Carney-Ogden (2010) pp 4-11. Chapter titled *The Reborn Wrath of Peleus' Son* for more on the Pixodarus affair.

71. Ormerod (1997) p 14 and p 108 for Cilician piracy. Ormerod (1997) p 119 for Isocrates *Panegyricus* 115.

72. Following the arguments cited in Pearson (1960) pp 114-115 surrounding Nearchus' naval expertise. Piracy was still rife and Alexander had tasked his admiral Amphoterus with clearing the seas of them; Curtius 4.8.15. *The Hymn to Apollo* 452-5 from the anonymous *Homeric Hymns* mentioned the hazards of pirates. Thucydides 1.5 also described their plundering. Demosthenes 17 explained how the Athenian fleet needed a further one hundred ships to escort Athens' grain fleet; Blackwell (1999) pp 95-96 for discussion.

73. For Nearchus' role commanding mercenaries and light-armed troops see Arrian 4.7.1 and 4.30.5-6. For his role at the Hydaspes-Indus see Arrian *Indike* 18.1-11 the fleet. Trierarchies

were expensive and often didn't return capital to those obligated under the Athenian system of 'liturgy'. It came with the obligation to fit out and provision a naval ship. Bottomage or bottomry was a form of hypothecation using as security the 'bottom' or keel of a ship, and thus its cargo, to guarantee a loan. As an example Diogenes *Zeno of Citium* 13 is said to have arrived in Athens with 1,000 talents and lent it on bottomry; also Demosthenes *Against Phormio* 7-8 for examples.

74. 1,700 miles according to Pliny 6.96-100. Apparently Nearchus and Onesicritus concurred on the distance. Arrian *Indike* 18.10 and 18.14 for Nearchus role on the Indus. The Erythrean Sea is literally the 'Red Sea' though the Greeks loosely extended its use for the Persian Gulf and Indian Ocean. Curtius 8.9.14 and 10.1.13-14 claimed the name 'Red' came from King Erythrus who also featured in Strabo 16.3.5, Pliny 6.13.28, 19.1.2, Arrian *Indike* 37.3. Engels (1978) p 13 for the calculation of the length of Nearchus' voyage.

75. Pearson (1960) p 83 for discussion on the nautical conflict with Onesicritus and p 15 for Nearchus' observations for crossing the tropics and equator. Other titles for his work are suggested by Pliny and Strabo; full discussion in Badian (1975) pp 157-159. Arrian 6.2.3 suggested Onesicritus lied about his and Nearchus' relative authority and at 7.20.9 outlined a disagreement. There is evidence Nearchus slandered Onesicritus as evidenced in Arrian's *Indike*. See discussion in Heckel (2006) p183. For discussion of *epiplous* see Berthold (1984) p 44.

76. Arrian penned his *Indike* in Ionian dialect, which suggests Nearchus had too. Pearson (1960) pp 112-149 for discussion of Nearchus' emulation of Herodotus, the *Odyssey* and even Pseudo-Scylax's *Periplous*. Herodotus 4.44 claimed Scylax ventured down the Indus and west to the Persian Gulf.

77. Arrian 7.19.3-6 for Nearchus' warning, Plutarch 73, Diodorus 17.112.3; discussed in Pearson (1960) p 116.

78. Closely following Badian (1975) p 148.

79. Discussion in Badian (1975) pp 147-148 quoting CF Lehman-Haupt.

80. Arrian *Indike* 18.1-11 for the list of trierarchs and Homer *Iliad* 2.494-759 for the catalogue of ships. Tarn 1 (1948) p 101 for the ethnic breakdown.

81. Quoting Pearson (1960) p 135 for 'epic adornment' and Shipley (2011) for a 'philosophical geography', referring to Pseudo-Scylax' *Periplous*. The *Periplous* was attributed to a 'Pseudo-Scylax' for it was supposedly compiled by the 6th century BCE Greek navigator mentioned at Herodotus 4.44 and yet its knowledge base appears to be that of a much later age, perhaps the mid 330s BCE and with direct connections to Athenian teaching. It was nevertheless widely known and perhaps inspired Alexander to send a fleet on a voyage of exploration of the southern coasts of 'his' new empire. It is likely Alexander still harboured the desire to find a coastal route back to Egypt; see Strabo 15.1.25 and Alexander's short-lived belief that the source of the Nile was to be found in India. The *periplous* of Hanno the Carthaginian was likely by now in circulation too; Pearson (1960) p 139.

82. Strabo 2.1.9. For examples of the *mirabilia* see Badian (1975) p 148. Deimachus was Megasthenes' successor at the Mauryan court in India.

83. Arrian 7.5.6 recorded that all the Bodyguards were crowned with the addition of Onesicritus.

84. Diodorus 19.85.1 for the death of 'most of Demetrius' friends'. Peithon son of Agenor is cited as the most distinguished of them, which may suggest Nearchus may have survived. Heckel (2006) p 171 for discussion of Nearchus' birth date. Nearchus' whereabouts from Babylon to his reemergence working under Antigonus some four or five years later are unknown. An episode in Polyaenus 5.35 is undated (possibly 318 BCE) though he was operating under Antigonus by 317/316 BCE, as suggested by Diodorus 19.19.4-5 Plutarch 76.3 portrays Alexander listening to Nearchus' account of the sea voyage; it hints, but does not necessarily prove, he might have already completed a written account. See Flower (1994) p 34 for a *possible* reference (in Strabo 1.2.35) to the authors of an *Indike* by Theopompus who is reckoned to have died ca. 320 BCE.

85. Quoting Heckel (2006) p 235 for Arsinoe's possible royal roots. For the rumour of parentage see Curtius 9.8.22 and Pausanias 1.6.2, but it is rendered unlikely by the claim in Pseudo-Lucian *Makrobioi* 12 that Ptolemy was eighty-four when he died, thus born in 367 BCE when Philip II was only sixteen. Also see discussion in Heckel 1992 p 222. The authorship of the *Makrobioi* is however disputed and other commentators variously assigned it to a 'pseudo' compiler.

86. Pausanias 1.6.2.

87. See below and chapter titled *Sarissa diplomacy: Macedonian Statecraft* for Theopompus' treatment of the Pellan court; Photius reported that Ptolemy wished Theopompus dead; discussion in Flower (1994) p 12.

88. Arrian 3.27.5. Heckel (2006) p 351 pointed out that the term *Somatophylakes* is occasionally used in the general sense and hypaspists were at times being referred to, i.e. the king's personal infantry corps. Diodorus 17.61.3, Curtius 4.16.32, Arrian 3.15.2 for references to Hephaestion commanding the undefined bodyguard corps. We restrict its usage to the Bodyguards alone. Also discussion in Chugg (2009) pp 14-18 citing specific examples where the term was more broadly

used and also Tarn (1948) p 138. Heckel *Somatophylakes* (1978) p 224 for the Latin derivatives.

89. Curtius 9.5.21. Bosworth (1983) p 157 noted the similarity with Livy 34.159 and Tacitus 11.11.3; see chapter titled *Comets, Colophons and Curtius Rufus* for more on Tacitus' emulation of Curtius – it is a contentious point and some scholars argue the opposite.

90. Heckel (1992) p 222 and Marasco (2011) p 59 for the thirty-five fragments. Quoting G Shipley's review of Heckel (1992) in *The Classical Review*, New Series 49, no. 2, 1999, pp 480-482, on his prosopography.

91. Quoting G Cawkwell in Warner (1966) p 43.

92. Quoting Heckel (1987) p 114.

93. Discussion of the military slant in Ptolemy's account in Pearson (1960) p 196. Pearson (1955) p 436 for lack of interest in Ptolemy's book in Rome.

94. The quotation is attributed to Voltaire without reference to a specific work. It appears to be an aggregation of two or more quotes: 'All styles are good except the boring kind' from *L'Enfant prodigue: comédie en vers dissillabes* (1736), Preface, and 'We should be considerate to the living; to the dead we owe only the truth' from his *Letter to M. de Grenonville* (1719).

95. Citing Roisman (1994) pp 373-374; bias in Ptolemy's history is well covered by Errington (1969) and also by Pearson (1960) pp 188-211. For the reference to Badian, see Roisman (1994) p 374 who sees less propaganda than some others in Ptolemy's history.

96. Citation from J March, D F Kennedy, J Salmon, T Wiedemann, BA Sparkes, P Walcot, *Greece and Rome*, 2nd Series, Vol. 41, No. 2, 1994 pp 220-255 and also Ellis (1994) p 60: private letters of Professor Peter Green to WM Ellis.

97. Flower (1994) p 62 for discussion of Isocrates' late output.

98. Pearson (1960) p 154.

99. Pearson (1960) p 151 for his technical roles and examples on p 161; his account of the siege of Tyre was praised by Menander *Oration* 27.6 ff; Brunt (1974) p 66 for discussion.

100. Pearson (1960) p 186 for divine intervention, including the Siwa episode. For the journey to Siwa see Diodorus 17.49.2-52.7, Arrian 3.4-5, Curtius 4.7.8-4.89, Plutarch 26.3-27.11, Justin 11.11.1-13, Strabo 17.1.43, *Itinerarium Alexandri* 48-50.

101. Lucian *How to Write History* 12. See Pearson (1960) p 150 who rejects the veracity of Lucian's reference.

102. Lucian *How to Write History* 40-41.

103. See discussion in Pearson (1960) pp 150-151 for discussion on Aristobulus' flattery and pp 156-157 for discussion of his possibly sanitised reporting of the Gordian Knot episode. Following Pearson (1960) p 263 for the conclusion that Aristobulus fell into no obvious category.

104. The various accounts of the siege of Tyre are a good example where engineers were mentioned, and Hephaestion's death for architects, for example.

105. See Robinson (1953) pp 205-243 for fragments citing Cassandreia. Tarn argues Kos; discussion in Pearson (1960) p 106 and Pearson (1960) p 151. Plutarch *Demosthenes* 23.6 cited him as a Cassandreian. See full career discussion in Pearson (1960) pp 150-187. Arrian 6.29.4-6.30 for his engineering role suggested by the task of restoring Cyrus' tomb. Heckel (2006) p 46 assumes Aristobulus returned to Europe, but there is little evidence.

106. Cassander's brother Alexarchus founded the city of Uranopolis at the same time; Athenaeus 3.98d-e.

107. Theocritus *The Festival of Adonis* 15.6 cited in Erskine (2002) p 165.

108. The letter from Antigonus to Scepsis for the reference to an Aristobulus who appears to have been a representative of Ptolemy in the so-called 'Peace of the Dynasts'. See citations by Bosworth-Baynham (2000) pp 231-232 and Heckel (2006) p 46. A late publication date for Aristobulus' work is supported by Arrian's detailing of the divination of Pythagoras the seer in which Aristobulus is mentioned as the source, and it suggests the engineer-historian published after the Battle of Ipsus in 301 BCE, for Arrian also recounted the fate of Antigonus *Monophthalmos* who perished at the battle; it is inconclusive as Arrian used Hieronymus for this period.

109. Diodorus 19.52.1-3 for the founding of Cassandreia.

110. See chapter titled *Sarissa Diplomacy: Macedonian Statecraft* for detail on *Keraunos'* career.

111. Arrian 7.26.3. The interpretation of the Greek has been debated, but it seems clear the *Journal* had nothing more to say about events after Alexander's death.

112. Ptolemy's link to the *Journal* discussed in chapter titled *Guardians and Ghosts of the Ephemerides*.

113. Quoting Cicero *Paulus* L17.

114. Heckel (2006) p 46.

115. See Robinson (1953) pp 77-86 for translations of the assembled fragments.

116. Until the battle at Ipsus in 301 BCE Lesbos was most prominently under the control of Antigonus or his supporters. Thereafter the Ptolemies assumed control.

117. Robinson (1960) p 86 for Ephippus' accounts of the *symposia* that led to the downfall of Hephaestion and Alexander.

118. Billows (1990) p 400 for Medius' possible Aleuadae roots at Larissa.
119. Pearson (1960) p 244 for discussion of Anaximenes' background and pp 68-70 for Medius; p 243-245 for Anaximenes' work, citing Pausanias 6.1.8 and Diodorus 15.89.3 for Anaximenes' *Hellenika* and *Philippika*.
120. Pearson (1960) pp 70-78 for Polycleitus. Polybius 8.9.1-4 claimed Theopompus denigrated Philip II's behaviour at court; see Pearson (1960) p 18 for discussion.
121. *Suda* M 227 and Plutarch *Moralia* 182c for Marsyas' relations to Antigonus, and Diodorus 20.50.4 for his command at Salamis; Robinson (1953) p 166 for the fragments. Pearson (1960) pp 253-254 and Kebric (1997) pp 43-44 for discussion of Marsyas' career and work. Plutarch 4.4 for Aristoxenus' description.
122. The reference to thirteen possible historians that wrote histories of Macedonia is taken from Roisman-Worthington (2010) p 7.
123. Roisman-Worthington (2010) p 24 for full citation from Borza's *Before Alexander: Constructing Early Macedonia*, 1999, Claremont, p 5. Quoting Carol Thomas' introduction to Eugene Borza's *Makedonika* for 'Macedonian specialist'. The title of Antipater's book in FGrH 114 T1 from the *Suda*, Marsyas and Philip of Pella in FGrH 135-6; see Marasco (2011) p 45 for discussion of Antipater's identity and the opinion of C Bearzot on misidentification. Roisman-Worthington (2010) pp 85-86 for Theagenes.
124. Kebric (1997) p 42 for discussion of Idiomenias' work. Pearson (1960) pp 250-251 for discussion of Menaechmus' work. Brown (1949) p 106 for the account of Androsthenes mentioned in Strabo 16.32 (citing Athenaeus 3.93b). His role in the Hydaspes-Indus fleet mentioned at Arrian *Indike* 18.4.6. Billows (1991) pp 334-337 for Duris' fragments and style.
125. Athenaeus 4.146c for the title of Ephippus' book. Pearson (1960) is rightly dubious about the corruption of the title and suggested it could equally have been titled *Five Books of Diaries on the exploits of Alexander*. Bosworth *A to A* (1988) p 181 discussed the issue and reminds us many attributions made in the *Suda* are questionable. Strattis of Olynthus was cited in the *Suda* as the author of *Five Books of Commentary on the Diary* (*Ephemerides*). The title is probably corrupt. Pearson (1960) p 260 suggested the dating but Hornblower p 252 rejected it noting many people called themselves Olynthians much later. Nevertheless we may assume Strattis was born before Olynthus' destruction by Philip II in 348 BCE, making him a possible contemporary and eyewitness to campaign events, whilst the destruction of his city would have explained any hostile reporting. Pearson (1995) p 437 suggests the attachment to Olynthus was to reinforce the authenticity of forged diaries.
126. See Bosworth-Baynham (2000) p 287 for discussion; as examples Arrian 7.15.4-6 mentioned two further little known Alexander historians, Aristus and Asclepiades, and Plutarch 46.1-3 mentioned six otherwise unknown historians, including Ister, Antigenes, Anticleides, Philo the Theban and Philip of Theangela. Pearson (1960) p 255 for the *Oxyrynchus Papyri* XV 1798.
127. Discussion in Pearson (1960) pp 255-257.
128. Tarn (1948) proposed the source was a Greek working *for* Darius, see discussion in Atkinson (1963) p 133.
129. Hornblower (1981) pp 5-7 and Heckel (200) p 139 for the dating of Hieronymus.
130. Anson (2004) pp 3-4 for the lost title. Discussion of Dionysius' opinion in Hornblower (1981) pp 246-248. Detail discussed of Hieronymus' account in chapter titled *The Tragic Triumvirate of Treachery and Oaths*.
131. For Hieronymus' approach see chapter titled *The Tragic Triumvirate of Treachery and Oaths* and in particular Roisman (2012) p 18 and pp 9-30 for a discussion of the bias in Hieronymus.
132. Bosworth (1990) p 330 for discussion of the period covered by Hieronymus and see chapter titled *The Tragic Triumvirate of Treachery and Oaths*.
133. Quoting Hornblower (1981) p 16. None of the eighteen or nineteen fragments are direct quotations of Hieronymus.
134. Brown (1947) p 691 for discussion and referring to Jacoby's *Die Fragmente der griechischen Historiker* which collected the fragments. See chapter titled *Classicus Scriptor Rhetoric and Rome* for more on Diodorus' method and use of sources. Diodorus' books eighteen and twenty-two survive in fragments and yet the era they covered suggest they too would have used detail from Hieronymus who detailed events down at least to the death of Pyrrhus in 272 BCE.
135. Hieronymus' history provided material for Pausanias, Polyaenus (2nd century) and Appian (ca. 95-165 CE), as well as for the biographies of Eumenes and the Athenian statesman Phocion (ca. 402-318 BCE) written by Nepos and Plutarch. His narrative was the foundation of Plutarch's *Lives* of Demetrius *Poliorketes* and Pyrrhus of Epirus (ca. 319-272 BCE), and Hieronymus was the template for several books of Trogus' *Philippic History*, though Duris' overlapping account is surely woven into these biographical portraits too, sourced directly or indirectly. Hieronymus' was substantially the material behind Arrian's *Events after Alexander*, parts of which exist as an epitome in the encyclopaedic *Myriobiblion* (also named *Bibliotheke*) of Photius who précised a

parallel work by Dexippus (ca. 210-273 CE), the Athenian historian and hero of the Gothic invasion of 262 CE. The *Vatican Palimpsest* (or *Codex*) contains two extracts from Arrian's seventh follow-on book and the *Gothenburg Palimpsest* houses a fragment from the tenth, all ultimately stemming from Hieronymus' account, as does the *Heidelberg Epitome*. For Pausanias, Polyaenus, Appian (*Syrian Wars*) and Dionysius using Hieronymus, see discussion in Hornblower (1981) pp 71-74 and Rozen (1967) p 41. Nepos used Hieronymus for his part of his biography of Eumenes and Phocion. Determining how much of the detail Trogus drew directly from Hieronymus, or through Diyllus, is confused by Justin's compression of detail; see discussion in Heckel-Yardley (1997) pp 3-5. For the length of Hieronymus' work see Hornblower (1981) pp 97-102. Further fragments of Dexippus' book can be found in the *Excerpta de Sententiis*, a work commissioned by Constantine VII of Byzantium around 900 CE and transmitted in palimpsest *Vaticanus graecus 73* in the Vatican Library. Anson (2014) p 10 for a useful summary of Photius' work and the two palimpsests. *Gothenburg Palimpsest* discussion in Roisman (2012) p 147.

136. See discussion in Green (2007) p xxvii and Billows (1990) p 333-337 and quoting Kebric (1977) p 9.

137. Kebric (1977) p 46 for the proposition that Hieronymus published in response to Duris' account. For his career and dating see Kebric (1977) pp 1-5. The conclusions are refuted by Billows (1990) pp 333-336 who sees no evidence of the use of Duris. Diodorus is reckoned to have drawn from Duris rather than Hieronymus for detail that appears in book 19 concerning Agathocles, the tyrant of Syracuse; the logic being that Duris had published a so-named book and had possibly been born in Sicily-Kebric (1977) p 4. Whilst Timaeus, who harboured a special grudge against the tyrant, is a strong contender as a source, as are the pro-Tyrant Callias and Antander (brother to Agathocles) – all mentioned by Diodorus himself (21.16-18) – several episodes found in Plutarch are specific to Eumenes' career, and Duris must be a prime candidate for each. The absence of these episodes from Diodorus suggests the possible strategic omission by Hieronymus, who may well have been involved in their provenance; a point of some significance to our investigation. Hieronymus' method and bias discussed in chapter titled *The Tragic Triumvirate of Treachery and Oaths*. Perdiccas' enforcement of Alexander's Exiles Decree allowed Samians to return to Athens-dominated Samos but Polyperchon overturned this in 319 BCE and returned the island to Athens after which they turned to Antigonus for support: Kebric (1977) pp 4-5.

138. Chapter titled *The Tragic Triumvirate of Treachery and Oaths* for detailed discussion of Hieronymus' role in the Successor Wars.

139. Kebric (1977) pp 7-9 for discussion of Samian plutocracy.

140. See Kebric (1977) p 37 for discussion of Duris' style and emulation and pp 10-11 for the fragments; p 19 ff for his political stance. He is thought to have taken much material on Egypt and Africa from Herodotus. Billows (1990) p 333-335 for the length and dating of Duris' work. Some sixteen of the thirty-six fragments appear in Athenaeus *Deipnosophistae*. Diodorus 15.60.6 confirmed where Duris' history commenced. Duris was personally familiar with Antigonus, Demetrius and Lysimachus; Kebric (1977) p 81.

141. Plutarch *Demosthenes* 23.4, *Pericles* 28 and *Alcibiades* 32 for Duris' unreliability; also Photius *Myriobiblion* 176. Plutarch *Eumenes* 1.1 for his confirmation that he was drawing from Duris for Eumenes' background.

142. Plutarch *Moralia* 1043d. Hammond (1994) p 189 for discussion of Ephorus' treatment of Philip and his excellence appearing in the early chapters of Diodorus' book 15. Flower (1994) Introduction p 1 for discussion of the scope of Ephorus' history; 1069 represented the return of the Heracleidae.

143. Strabo 9.3.11. Strabo suggested Polybius was in agreement.

144. FGrH 76 F1 for the fragment of Duris; cited in full in Gill-Wiseman (1993) p 184. *Mimesis* and its use discussed in Gray (1987) and following Gray for history as an 'imitative art', Aristotle's *Poetics* saw a separation of the disciplines. Grafton (1990) p 78 for Ephorus stealing 3,000 of Duris' lines, see FGrH 70 Ephorus T 17.

145. Tarn (1948) p 43.

146. Quoting Badian (1975) p 164.

147. Cleitarchus was 'Alexandrine' according to Philodemus *De Sublimate* 3.2 (FGrH 137 T 9). Bosworth (1992) p 2 however considered the evidence tenuous.

148. 'State within a state' quoting Bagnall (1976) p 4.

149. The comparative lack of information in Arrian's account, for example, compared to the Vulgate for the period after 328 BCE, discussed in Bosworth (1981).

150. Cicero *Brutus* 43. Cleitarchus was popular in Rome and he was cited as a source by Diodorus, Plutarch, Strabo, Athenaeus and Diogenes Laertius, to name a few. Quintilian 10.1.74-5. Cicero *Brutus* 11.42. Cicero had proposed that orators alone should be entrusted with the care of the past. For other criticisms see Pearson (1960) p 153 footnote 21.

151. Deinon's account was rich in Persian court customs, as inferred by a fragment in Athenaeus 2.67a. Plutarch *Artaxerxes* mentioned Deinon nine times as an information source; we assume Deinon's *Persika* was being referenced. Nepos *Conon* 5 for his praise of Deinon.

152. Quoting Plutarch *Artaxerxes* 1.2 and 6.6, translation from the Loeb Classical Library edition, 1926; Ctesias had in fact called both Hellanicus and Herodotus liars.

153. Quoting Pearson (1960) p 213. Ctesias appears a preferred source as he was resident at the Persian court; Diodorus 2.125, 2.129-137 for Ctesias' capture and service under Artaxerxes II.

154. Diogenes Laertius *Stilpo* suggested Stilpo 'won over' Cleitarchus, detaching him from his previous teacher of Aristotle of Cyrene. See discussion in Bosworth (1996) p 2. As Bosworth (1996) points out, the meeting would have taken place in Greece not Egypt. For more on the philosophy and influences of Stilpo see Brown (1950) pp 136-137.

155. Ptolemy's manipulative or even ruthless character is well demonstrated. As examples: his murder of Cleomenes, a local governor or treasurer, see Pausanias 1.6.3; for the forced suicide of Polemaeus, a defecting nephew of Antigonus' and who had become 'presumptuous' see Diodorus 20.27; and his annexation of Coele-Syria after a failed bribe, Appian *Syrian Wars 52* and Diodorus 18.43.2.

156. For the flattery still visible in Curtius' account of the Babylonian settlement onwards see chapter titled *Babylon: the Cipher and Rosetta Stone.*

157. For Cleitarchus' use of Theopompus see Pearson (1960) Introduction p 19. Following Tarn (1948) p 127 for the proposal of Peripatetic polemic and p 297 for 'under Cassander's shield'. Athenaeus 10.435b-c for an example of Theopompus' treatment of the Macedonian court under Philip II. Brown (1950) for discussion of Diogenes' influence over Stilpo, and thus Cleitarchus. Brown (1950) p 153 disputes there is any proof of Cleitarchean hostility towards Alexander. Flower (1994) pp 98-116 for Theopompus' treatment of Philip and pp 166-167 and pp 169-183 for his moralising. Quoting Plutarch *Demetrius* 10.2 of the Athenian regime. Pausanias 1.25.6 termed Demetrius a 'tyrant'.

158. See Kebric (1977) p 36 ff for Duris' influence on other historians and p 79 for the early publication of the *Samian Chronicle*; Theopompus is not proposed but if the *Samian Chronicle* was published before Samos was occupied by Ptolemaic forces in 281 BCE, then it is possible Samos' struggle under Alexander's *Diadokhoi* influenced Cleitarchus, assuming he published late.

159. Quoting Bosworth (1971) p 112.

160. Quoting Spengler on 'organ of history' and cited in Brown (1962) p 257.

161. Lucian *Pro lapsu inter salutandum* 10; discussed by C Bearzot in Marasco (2011) p 46.

162. In Arrian's account he cited, or implied, there had been discrepancies between Aristobulus and Ptolemy at 2.3.7 (implied), 2.4.7 (implied), 3.3.6, 3.4.5, 3.30.5, 4.3.5, 4.5.6 (implied), 4.13.5 (implied), 4.14.3-5, 5.14.3 (implied), 5.20.2.

163. *E Schwartz Arrian* no 9 in Pauly-Wissowa Real Encyclopedia I, 1894. See discussion in Brunt (1975) p 23.

164. Polybius 12.3.4c 4-5.

165. Pearson (1960) p 194.

166. Arrian *Indike* 18.9 for Evagoras' role.

167. Polybius 6.19-28 and 6.40 gave a fulsome description of their uses and arms.

168. Quoting Hornblower (1980) p 153.

169. Noted by Hornblower (1981) p 234. Polybius and Hieronymus could have returned to their native lands but had by then become influential to regimes elsewhere.

170. A view supported by Momigliano and quoted in full in Grant (1995) p 70. Plutarch *Themistocles* 22.3.

171. Thucydides 5.26.5-6, translation from Strassler (1996).

172. Grant (1995) p 19.

173. The *nom de plume* discussed in Pitcher (2009) p 4. See Xenophon *Hellenika* 3.1.2 for his attribution to Themistogenes and Plutarch *Moralia* 345c, *de Gloria Atheniensium* for the revealed identity. The *Suda* compiler(s) assumed Themistogenes of Syracuse was a separate author.

174. Von Clausewitz *On War*, published posthumously. Originally *Vom Kriege*, 3 volumes, Berlin, 1832-34.

175. Robinson (1953) believed Callisthenes himself drew from the diaries as did later historians, yet paradoxically he believed the 'thin sources' in 327-326 BCE were due to Eumenes' loss of the documents in a tent fire rather than Callisthenes' death. This is paradoxical for while Callisthenes is mentioned as a source in later works, the *Journal* is never mentioned aside from the fragment dealing with Alexander's death.

176. Quoting Robinson (1953) Itinerary, pp 70-71.

177. Quoting Pearson (1960) p 261.

178. A summary of the earlier chronology debate is given in Pearson (1960) pp 152-154, pp 172-173 and pp 226-233; also Brown (1950).

179. Droysen *Geschichte Alexanders des Grossen 1833*. Fused with later 1836-42 work on Alexander's successors as *Geschichte des Hellenismus,* Gotha, Perthes, 1877-87.
180. Bosworth more recently proposed that Cleitarchean publication was as early as 310 BCE, citing the research of Badian, Prandi and Schachermeyr who believed it was published within twenty years of Alexander's death (thus before 303 BCE). Bosworth (2002) p 43 citing G Droysen (1877) *Geschichte des Hellenismus*, Gotha; E Schwartz, *Aristobulus*, Pauly-Wissowa, R.E. II, 911 ff, 1957, H Berve (1926), Hamilton (1961), Prandi (1996) p 28. Jacoby Pauly-Wissowa R. E. XI, 622 ff, 1921. Heckel (1988) p 2 for Schachermeyr's view.
181. Tarn (1948) p 101 described the relationship between Curtius and Cleitarchus' underlying source as *obscurum per obscurius,* though on pp 124-125 he did concede Trogus' use of Diodorus and a common source.
182. Hammond (1993) p 195 citing the earlier research by Goukowsky. Pearson (1960) pp 212-242 for the profile and dating of Cleitarchus and in particular his use of Aristobulus. Arrian *Preface* 1.2 for his claim that he wrote when a king. As with the claim that Lysimachus was a king when Onesicritus read aloud to him, we do not need to take this too literally; both *became* kings. See chapter titled *Sarissa Diplomacy: Macedonian Statecraft* for the dating of regal proclamations by the *Diadokhoi.*
183. The geographical argument is based on Cleitarchus' comment on the relative sizes of the Black and Caspian Seas; see Tarn (1948) pp 16-29 and his use of Patroclus' geography. The titular argument surrounds Ptolemy's investiture with the title *Soter.* The chronology argument is based around Cleitarchus' time studying with Stilpo of Megara. Well summarised in Pearson (1960) pp 212-242 and Brown (1950) pp 137-139 and Hamilton (1961). For Alexander's entry into the Mallian city and subsequent wounds see Arrian 6.8.4-6.13.5, 6.28.4, Curtius 9.4.26-9.5.30, Diodorus 17.98.1-17.100.1, Plutarch 63.5-13. Curtius 9.4.15 for the mutinous behaviour before entering Mallia.
184. Arrian 6.11.8 and Curtius 9.5.21 for their polemics on other historians reporting the events, including Timagenes and Cleitarchus.
185. Tarn (1948) p 27.
186. 'Begrudging' because Timagenes fell out with both Caesar and Augustus and was banished from court; see Seneca, *On Anger* 3.22-23. Timagenes originally arrived in Rome as a slave in 55 BCE; discussed in Hamilton (1961) p 456.
187. See Robinson (1953) pp 183-243 for the fragments, especially in Arrian, detailing their conflicting accounts.
188. Arrian 6.11.8 and Curtius 9.5.21 for the lines referred to. For Curtius' likely publication date see chapter titled *Comets, Colophons and Curtius Rufus.*
189. See discussion of the similarities in Robinson (1953) *The Ephemerides* pp 69-71.
190. Arrian 6.6.3 for the slaughter of unarmed men and Arrian 6.11.1 for the women and children. For the massacre of the Branchidae see chapter titled *The Rebirth of the Wrath of Peleus' Son.*
191. Arrian *Indike* 19.8; *hyperaspizantes* are hypaspists who protected their king or colleague with a shield. Plutarch 63.5 has Limnaus instead of Leonnatus in the role but this could be a manuscript corruption. An *aspis* is a small light shield though a larger *hoplon*-style shield is implied.
192. See discussion in Hammond (1993) pp 268-9 citing Arrian 6.10.2 who in turn cited Ptolemy as his source. For Leonnatus' actions see Arrian 6.4.3 and Curtius 9.4.15; for Peucestas' actions, Curtius 9.5.14-18, Arrian 6.9.3, 10.1-2, 11.7-8, 6.28.4, Diodorus 17.99.4. The arrowhead was allegedly four fingers in breadth; Plutarch *Moralia* 341C gave Aristobulus' equally detailed account of the wound. Curtius 9.5.24-28 for Critobulus' role; this is the same name as Philips' physician at the siege of Methone 28 years before; Pliny 7.37; Arrian 6.11.1 called him Critodemus.
193. Chapter titled *Babylon: the Cipher and Rosetta Stone* for discussion of Cleitarchus' respective treatment of Perdiccas and Ptolemy and Arrian's belief, probably from Ptolemy, that Alexander never replaced Hephaestion's chiliarchy. Collins (2001) pp 270-273 for discussion of the chiliarch's peripheral roles.
194. Athenaeus 13.576e.
195. Briant (1974) p 108 for the chronology of Persepolis' fall, looting and burning. Plutarch 37.6 mentioned a four month stay. Diodorus 17.72 and Curtius 5.7.3-7 embodying Cleitarchus' version of events; Justin 11.14.10 is too brief for any analysis. The report of Strabo 15.3.6 and Arrian 3.18.12 didn't mention Thais but focused on Alexander's political decision to please the Greeks. Plutarch 38 reported both versions. Arrian 6.30.1 claimed Alexander regretted his action upon returning to Persepolis on his way back to Babylon after the Indian campaign.
196. Diodorus 18.70.3, translation from the Loeb Classical Library edition, 1963.
197. Plutarch 38.2-5 captured the heroic theme but commented that her speech urging on Alexander was not in keeping with her place. Diodorus 17.72 followed closely clearly putting Thais in the lead role. Athenaeus 13.576d-e confirmed Cleitarchus was his source for the reporting of the fire.
198. Plutarch *Alexander* 3.5. Valerius Maximus *Memorable Deeds and Sayings* 8.14.5 recorded that

the arsonist of Ephesus was found. The Ephesians decreed that his name never be recorded, according to Aulus Gellius 2.6.18. It was Strabo 14.1.22 who revealed it. Originally the name had been preserved by Theopompus in his *Philippika,* but that work is now lost. See Plutarch 3.5 for the links to Alexander's birth.

199. Athenaeus 13.576e. A daughter, Eirene, married Eunostus of Soli, King of Cyprus, and a son by Thais fought at Salamis in 307/6 BCE against the Antigonids according to Justin 15.12. Bosworth (1996) p 3 disagrees that Cleitarchus would have dared change Ptolemy's version of events at Persepolis.

200. Plutarch 46.4-5, translation from the Loeb Classical Library edition, 1919.

201. Following Jacoby's statement in Brown (1949) p 6.

202. Heckel (2006) p 183 and Pearson (1960) pp 84-85 for discussion on Onesicritus' age.

203. Discussion in Pearson (1960) pp 224-225 for Cleitarchus' use of Nearchus.

204. Brown (1949) p 7 for the comparison of the length of Onesicritus' work with that of Xenophon's *On the Education* of Cyrus, its model which was similarly divided into eight books, as was the *Anabasis* of Arrian. Pearson (1960) pp 83-84 for discussion of Nearchus' criticism of Onesicritus, citing Arrian 7.20.8-10 and *Indike* 32.9-13. A more specific rebuttal of Onesicritus' claims appears at *Indike* 3.5 and Strabo 15.1.12.

205. See discussion on the relative chronology of Nearchus' and Onesicritus' publication dates in Brown (1949) pp 4-5, Pearson (1960) p 84 and in Brown (1950) pp 5-7. Plutarch 46.4 for the reference to Lysimachus. Heckel (2008) p 7 brings to our attention the fact that the *Journal* claimed Nearchus read an account of his voyage to Alexander in his final days in Babylon, thus suggestive that he published soon after. However the *Journal* citations are spurious and reading excerpts from a diary does not imply an immediate publication when events that followed were so calamitous.

206. See chapter titled *The Silent Siegecraft of the Pamphleteers* for further discussion.

207. Thucydides 11.87, cited by Plutarch in *Moralia* 333c or *Fortune* 12.

208. Tarn (1948) p 4 citing Diodorus 17.118.2.

209. Though Ptolemy I *Soter,* the Egyptian dynast, had married Cassander's sister Eurydice in 321/320 BCE, he was to repudiate her in 317 BCE in favour of Berenice, Eurydice's lady-in-waiting who 'had the greatest influence and was foremost in virtue and understanding'; Plutarch *Pyrrhus* 4.4. Pyrrhus singled her out for his affections knowing she held sway with Ptolemy. Berenice was nevertheless of the Antipatrid house; her paternal grandfather was the brother of the regent Antipater, the father of the accused Cassander. Cassander's own sons were exploited by Pyrrhus the 'Eagle of the Epirotes' (Plutarch *Pyrrhus* 10.1), and executed by Demetrius and Lysimachus for their internecine intrigues; by 294 BCE the power once wielded by the house of Antipater, the former regent, and his offspring, was finally spent; see Plutarch *Pyrrhus* for Pyrrhus' relations with the sons of Cassander – though he had provided aid to one brother (Alexander) against the other (Antipater), he ultimately made both pay. Moreover, Ptolemy II *Philadelphos,* who succeeded his father in 282 BCE (he had been co-ruler with his father from 285 BCE), put to death his half-brother by Cassander's sister, Eurydice, who was based at Miletus in Caria by 287 BCE where she formed a dynastic alliance with Demetrius *Poliorketes,* Cassander's old enemy (Eurydice offered her daughter, Ptolemais, to Demetrius in 298 BCE – Plutarch *Demetrius* 32 and 46). *Philadelphos* allegedly murdered his half-brother for inciting the Cypriots to revolt (Pausanias 1.7.1); the half-brother might have been in league with Ptolemy *Keraunos,* another son of Eurydice, to oust *Philadelphos.* Lysimachus, once married to another of Cassander's sisters, Nicaea, died at Curopedion in 281 BCE. Eurydice's eldest son, Ptolemy *Keraunos* (thus Cassander's nephew), who had been passed over for the kingship in Egypt, died in the Gallic invasions in 279 BCE, and her second son, Meleager, followed him soon after. Between them they had held the Macedonian throne for less than three years (281-279 BCE) at the court based at Cassandreia. Antipater *Etesias,* the son of Cassander's brother, soon followed them as his reign lasted just forty-five days – 'as long as the Etesian Winds blew'. For Seleucus' possible *Pamphlet* guilt see chapter titled *The Silent Siegecraft of the Pamphleteers.*

210. Arrian 4.13.5-6, also Curtius 8.6.16 for the Syrian prophetess. See further discussion of Aristobulus as source of the portentous in chapter titled *The Guardians and Ghosts of the Ephemerides.*

211. There is a lacuna in point in Curtius' account preceding Alexander's death, but Justin (so we assume Trogus) and Diodorus captured the supernatural detail. Hammond (1998) pp 420-421 assumes Curtius drew directly from Aristobulus for some portentous incidents, but he could equally have taken the detail from Cleitarchus. And Curtius never mentioned Aristobulus as a source elsewhere.

212. Cleitarchus' reference to the embassy from Rome was recorded by Pliny 3.57-58; many scholars doubt Rome could have sent the embassy as early as 323 BCE, whereas in Cleitarchus' day Rome was clearly on the rise, which argues for a late-Cleitarchean publication date. Refuted by

Tarn (1948) pp 22-23 who believes Pliny was mistaken in identifying Cleitarchus as its source.

213. Arrian 7.15.4-6 for the embassies to Babylon and sources behind them. He was doubtful on the report; Aristus is further mentioned as a historian of Alexander in Athenaeus 10.10 and Strabo book 15.

214. Well summed up by Tarn (1949) pp 374-378; see Justin 12.13.1 for Trogus' list of embassies.

215. Polybius 3.22. Momigliano (1977) p 104 for discussion; the Pyrgi Tablets relating to ca. 500 BCE suggest an Etruscan-Carthaginian relationship which may be the basis of Polybius' claim.

216. See Justin 12.2.12-13 and Livy 8.17.10 for the peace treaty with Rome in the Varronian years, so 332 BCE. The date of the death of Alexander of Epirus is uncertain though Livy 8.24.1 credited it to the year of the founding of Alexandria, thus 332/1 BCE, yet Livy dated these events to 326 BCE, so uncertainty remains. Alexander Molossus had married Alexander's sister, Cleopatra, his own niece.

217. Justin 12.3.1 for the funeral games. Justin 12.2.2-4 and 12.1.14-15 for the oracle of Dodona that warned Alexander to beware of the city of Pandosia and the river Acheron.

218. Strabo 5.3.5, Memnon FGrH 434 F.

219. In Arrian 7.15.4-6 the Tyrrhenians, alongside Lucanians and Bruttians, were reported to be sending ambassadors to Babylon and this could have referred to Etruscans or other Latins bordering the Tyrrhenian Sea. Arrian 7.1.3 for the alleged plans to campaign in Sicily and Italy.

220. Diodorus 17.113.2, Justin 12.13.1.

221. Chugg p 11 for a discussion of Rome's emergence after Pyrrhus' campaigns, and for the Rhodian trade discussion see Berthold (1984) p 80.

222. For Tarquinus' heritage Pliny 35.152, Livy 1.34, Dionysius of Halicarnassus 3.46; discussed in Boardman (1964) p 202. Whether the original *Cloarca Maxima* was all subterranean or an open canal remains debated. It was certainly built over by later Rome.

223. Plutarch *Camillus* 22.2-3. The date of the sacking of Rome is often stated as 390 BCE based on the faulty Varronian chronology. This stems from Heracleitus' claim that Hyperboreans descended on a Greek city named Rome; Aristotle apparently credited Camillus as its saviour.

224. Pliny stated that Theophrastus was the first foreigner to write about Rome in detail, though Theopompus had mentioned the capture of Rome by Gauls; discussion in Pearson (1960) p 233. The coverage of Rome in Timaeus and Callias came from their associations with Agathocles, tyrant of Syracuse; Diodorus 21.17.1-4 for their relative positions; Momigliano (1977) pp 52-55 for discussion.

225. Hieronymus' portrayal of Pyrrhus necessarily brought Pyrrhus' clashes with Rome into his narrative and thus he was one of the earliest Hellenistic authors to bring Rome into mainstream Hellenic history. See discussion in Hornblower (1981) pp 71-72. Dionysius of Halicarnassus *Roman Antiquities* 1.5.8 claimed Hieronymus was the first historian to give an account of Rome and Timaeus the second. Yet an 'account' might suggest the definition of something fuller than the mention of an embassy; perhaps something of a background history to their origins, which fits Hieronymus' style. Discussion in Tarn (1948) pp 22-23.

226. See chapter entitled *The Tragic Triumvirate of Treachery and Oaths* for Antigonus' career.

227. Euripides *Ino* fragment 413.2 quoted by Plutarch *On Exile* 16 and *Moralia* 506c.

228. Ovid *Tristia* 1.1.39.

229. Quoting Voltaire *Treatise on Toleration*, 1763 and *Letter to François-Joachim de Pierre, Cardinal de Bernis*, 1761.

230. Diodorus 19.95.3, translation from the Loeb Classical Library edition, 1963.

231. Quoting Bosworth *From A to A* (1988) p 266 and for full discussion pp 260-270.

232. According to Pseudo-Lucian *Makrobioi* 10-13, Lysimachus was over eighty when he died, Ptolemy eighty-four and Seleucus eighty.

233. For the opening of hostility between Ptolemy and Seleucus post-Ipsus see Diodorus 21.5-6.

234. See discussion in Green (2007) p 46.

235. Discussed in Errington (1969) p 233.

236. Memnon's work is preserved in an epitome by Photius FGrH no. 434 F 7.3 and detailed the city's history and the influences upon it, dating from the tyranny of Clearchus (ruled 364-353 BCE) to the city's capture by Rome in 70 BCE.

237. Discussed in Bosworth-Baynham (2000) p 287. See Billows (1990) p 339 for sources.

238. See chapter titles *Sarissa Diplomacy: Macedonian Statecraft* for more on the fate of the children.

239. Discussed in Boardman-Griffin-Murray (1986) p 234.

240. Polybius 8.8.8-9, translation from the Loeb Classical Library edition, vol. III, 1922-1927. See discussion in Walbank (1962) p 4.

241. Aristotle *Politics* 1.1253a2-3 proposed that men are by nature political animals.

242. Aristotle *Historia Animalium*, 2.7. Aristotle actually wrote: 'On the whole, the wild animals of Asia are the fiercest, those of Europe the boldest, and those of Libya the most varied in form.' Later authors turned this into a well-used adage.

243. Lucian *How to Write History* 38.

4

MYTHOI, MUTHODES AND THE BIRTH OF ROMANCE

What are the origins of the *Greek Alexander Romance* and does the book contain any historical truths relevant to our investigation?

The *Greek Alexander Romance* is, in one form or another, one of the most influential and widely read books of all time; it has birthed a whole literary genre on the Macedonian king.

Where and when did it first appear and what did it originally look like? Which earlier accounts did it absorb and what is its relationship to the mainstream Alexander histories? Most importantly, does it contain unique factual detail?

We take a closer look at the best-selling book of fables in which Alexander's testament sits most conspicuously. We review the perennial propensity for writers to 'romance' and highlight some of the iconic episodes in history that have been misinterpreted as a result.

'In their narratives they have shown a contempt for the truth and a preoccupation with vocabulary and style, because they were confidant that, even if they romanced a bit, they would reap the advantages of pleasure they gave to their public, without the accuracy of their research being investigated.'[1]

Herodian *History of the Empire from the Death of Marcus Aurelius*

'… the uncomfortable fact remains that the *Alexander Romance* provides us, on occasion, with apparently genuine materials found nowhere else, while our better-authenticated sources, *per contra,* are all too often riddled with bias, propaganda, rhetorical special pleading or patent falsification and suppression of evidence.'[2]

Peter Green *Alexander of Macedon*

'Historical, or natural, truth has been perverted into fable by ignorance, imagination, flattery or stupidity.'[3]

Sir William Jones *On the Gods of Hellas, Italy and India*

In 1896 the historian and orientalist, Sir Ernest Alfred Thompson Wallis Budge, proposed only one country could be the birthplace of Alexander's story, and that country was Egypt.[4] Its new city, 'Alexandria-by-Egypt', as the Greeks came to differentiate it from the conqueror's many eponymous settlements, was to become a centre for syncretistic literature and the likely birthplace of the *Corpus Hermeticum,* the *Sibylline Oracles, The Wisdom of Solomon*, the *Septuagint* with its reputed seventy-plus translators, and its *Alexandrian Canon* too. Much of the detail that eventually filled the *Suda* most likely had its origins in the vibrant metropolis whose creative environment recycled apocrypha onto papyrus in the Hellenistic Age. And we have grounds to believe one of its earliest and most successful productions was to metamorphosise into the *Greek Alexander Romance*.[5]

As antiquities adviser to the British Museum, Budge was exploring the origins of the various Ethiopic *Romance* recensions, and he stumbled on something of a basic truth: the nations humbled by Alexander, he reasoned, would not so quickly record their own downfall.[6] Only one place immediately prospered in the aftermath of the Macedonian campaigns, and that *was* Egypt. The propitious interpretation of Alexander's seer, Aristander, which deflected embarrassment at Alexandria's mapping-out when birds flocked to eat the barley-meal being used as the boundary marker, had provided a founding prophecy: the new city, which bears the inscription *ktistes*, founder, against Alexander's name in the *Romance*, would feed the world.[7]

Cleomenes' posthumous bank balance of some 8,000 talents, a legacy of over-zealous and quasi-autonomous tax collection, probably had the greater part to play, though its fate was now underpinned by the talisman that was

Alexander's body.[8] Egypt's new heart, Alexandria, established by the harbour settlement of Rhacotis, originally established to fend off Greek pirate attacks on the Nile Delta, was becoming something of a 'new Heraclion'; it was fostered into maturity by the Bodyguard, Ptolemy I *Soter*, who, within two decades of taking up his post, would proclaim himself a king.[9]

ALEXANDER THE TWO-HORNED BEAST

Macaulay proposed history 'is under the jurisdiction of two hostile powers: the Reason and the Imagination', and, he added, never equally shared between them.[10] This was particularly the case in ancient Attic Greek where the stories of the past were literally *mythoi*, and the segregation between myth, legend, and the factual past was a soft border blurred by Homeric epics and Hesiod's *Theogonia*, which permitted a coeval interaction between men, heroes, and gods. Scholars have even pondered that 'the absence of a clear distinction between factual and fictional discourse' in the influential dialogues of Plato, 'far from being idiosyncratic, may reflect a larger feature of Greek (or ancient) thinking'.[11] Even Thucydides, who claimed to have sacrificed 'entertainment value' (*hedone*) in order to dispense with *to muthodes,* the mythical elements in his work, nonetheless interlaced his texts with self-constructed speeches which reintroduced just that.[12] But the results *were* 'immortal' and the legends live on; as the habitually terse Sallust (ca. 86-35 BCE) reasoned, 'these things never were, but are always'.[13]

We will illustrate how fraud entwined itself around the most momentous of historical episodes, but once a deliberate deceit is discovered, the truth is more often than not revealed. When an episode is adorned in the colourful robes of romance, however, we are on less firm ground, for truth and fiction may have been wedded in a ceremony that rendered them lifelong partners: 'There are many occasions in the story of Alexander when it is hard to be sure just where history ends and romance begins.'[14] To quote Michael Wood on the problem: 'We are accustomed to believing that fiction can tell both truths and untruths… poets have a (highly visible) stake in the notion, but so do historians and philosophers and scientists.' In which case it is '… misleading to contrast the so-called "historical biographies" with the legendary lives.'[15] And this better equips us to appreciate how the *Pamphlet* and Alexander's Will, along with many other genuine campaign episodes, came to be bedfellows with the *Greek Alexander Romance*.

Separating the historical from the *fabulae* has indeed proved no easy task, for material was added through a gradual process of accretion. Analysis of the *Romance* manuscripts was made easier once the composite 1846 *editio princeps* of Müller had been printed in Paris, for it provided a continuous non-lacunose text.[16] Adolf Ausfeld's 1894 *Zur Kritik des Griechischen*

Alexanderromans and his treatise of 1901, with that of Kroll in 1907, attempted to reconstruct the lost *Romance* archetype and started probing into the mysteries behind 'peculiarities' within the main narrative and the testament of Alexander sitting in its last chapter. Merkelbach's 1954 study, *Die Quellen des Griechischen Alexanderromans*, articulated the challenge of detecting the underlying sources, and alongside them developed an influential corpus of German studies that set the forensic standard for a modern reassessment of what we might term the 'quasi-historical' Macedonian king.[17]

Attributing the *Romance* in its earliest form to a single author or date remains impossible, but evidence suggests that both the unhistorical and the quasi-historical elements were in circulation in the century following Alexander's death. The oldest text we know of today, recension 'A', is preserved in the 11th century Greek manuscript known as Parisinus 1711; the text is titled *The Life of Alexander of Macedon* and 'this most closely resembles a conventional historical work', though any factual narrative is only a 'flimsy continuum' to which other elements were attached. Recension A, whilst 'ill-written, lacunose, and interpolated', is nevertheless the best staging point scholars have when attempting to recreate an original (usually referred to as 'α' – alpha) dating back some 700 or 800 years (or more) before the extant recension A.[18] We cannot discount an archetype that may have been written even earlier still, in the Ptolemaic era; if Callisthenes was once credited with its authorship

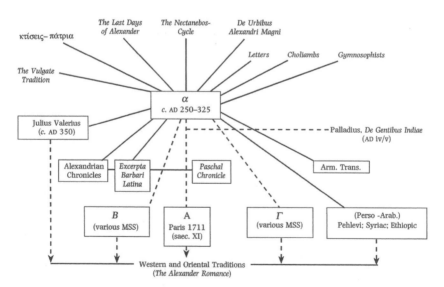

The Alexander *Romance* stemma from recension 'α', which may itself be an embellished descendent of an earlier archetype. Provided with the kind permission of Oxford University Press and copied from PM Fraser *Cities of Alexander the Great*, Clarendon Press (1996).

(thus 'Pseudo-Callisthenes'), the prevailing belief must have been that it emerged in, or soon after, the campaigns. Through the centuries that followed, the *Romance* evolved and diversified into a mythopoeic family tree whose branches foliaged with the leaves of many languages, faiths and cultures; more than eighty versions appeared in twenty-four languages.[19]

The Hellenistic world saw exotic tales arriving from the fabled lands of Kush to the south of Egypt and from the distant East, carried down the Silk Road with the help of the settlements Alexander had founded or simply renamed along its route. According to Strabo, who studied in Egyptian Alexandria, the 'city' of Alexandria Eschate ('the furthest') in the Fergana Valley had brought the Greek settlers and the Graeco-Bactrian Kingdom into contact with the silk traders of the Han dynasty of the Seres (the Chinese, who lived to age 300, claimed Pseudo-Lucian) as early as the 3rd century BCE.[20] Within 200 years the Romans would have a voracious appetite for silk and they obtained cloth through the Parthians who most likely encouraged the belief that silk grew on (or as) trees.[21] Pliny dispelled that myth and described the role of the silkworm, and yet the Senate issued edicts in vain to prohibit the wearing of silk due to the trade imbalance it caused; one decree was based on accusations of immodesty for the way silk clung to the female form. In Pliny's reckoning, India, China and the Arabian Peninsula extracted 'from our empire 100 million sesterces per year – that is the sum which our luxuries and our women cost us…'[22]

Ptolemaic Egypt had fostered trade eastward as far as India with the help of Arabs and Nabateans, and the resulting contact fertilised Hellenistic literature. But, paradoxically, much of the geographical knowledge of the former Persian East was lost in the period between Megasthenes' eyewitness reports from India in the generation after Alexander (ca. 290s BCE) and the *Parthian Staging Posts* of Isidore of Charax in the 1st century CE, principally due to the collapse of the Seleucid Empire and its dynasty established by Alexander's former Bodyguard, Seleucus.[23]

It was a millennium later that Marco Polo's twenty-four-year adventure and travelogue opened up knowledge of the East once more. His account appeared under a number of titles including *Livre des Merveilles du Monde, The Book of the Marvels of the World*, first published in the descendant of Old French (*langues d'oïl*), and *Il Milione* written in Italian, which brought back stories of Cathay and Kublai Khan, lending further colour to developing European fables. The authorship of what we have come to name *The Travels of Marco Polo* is, in fact, contested, as is its *original* transcribed language; tradition holds that Polo dictated the book to a romance writer, Rustichello da Pisa, while in prison in Genoa between 1298 and 1299, and we would assume in Italian. Rustichello had already written a work in French, *Roman de Roi Artus* (*Romance of King Arthur*), and certainly much interpolated material was included, so we might speculate how much of Polo's original detail remained unsullied in the hands of an established story-philanderer. The oldest manuscripts differ widely in content and length, and what we read today has been 'standardised' like other romances and the *Iliad*.

The *Greek Alexander Romance* was similarly developed. As examples of the genre offspring we have the Latin *Epitome* of Julius Valerius (probably 4th century) and the *Historia de Preliis Alexandri Magni* (*The Wars of Alexander the Great*) of Archpriest Leo of Naples (10th century), first put to print in 1487 and giving rise to a whole new generation of re-renderings of the story. With over 200 surviving manuscripts, the *Historia de Preliis* drew much inspiration from Curtius' history of Alexander, as did the *Alexandreis siva Gesta Alexandri Magni*, a Latin poem in epic-style dactylic hexameter by the theologian Gautier de Chatillon (ca. 1135-post 1181), with a similar Curtian ten-book layout and much credit paid to the goddess Fortuna.[24] The verses were so popular that they displaced the reading of ancient poets in grammar schools.[25] De Chatillon's production, 'a tissue of other texts' (Virgil, Lucan, Ovid, Horace and Claudian among them), could not avoid alluding to the recent death of Thomas Beckett (1170) and the failures of the first Crusades; it even housed the crucifixion of Jesus some three and a half centuries out of context.[26] De Chatillon was fluid with his metre, ranging back and forth between dactylic hexameters, iambics and trochaics; fortunately these provided a stylistic rhythm that identified much of the imported syncretism.[27]

The *Alexandreis* had other siblings and more distant relatives too: the distinctive *Li romans d'Alixandre*, for example, fed by the 'alexandrine' verses of Lambert de Tort, and the *Mort Alixandre* credited to Alexandre de Bernay, alongside the *Roman d'Alexandre* by Albéric de Pisançon which was the possible source of the German *Alexanderlied* (ca. 1130) of Lamprecht 'The Priest'.[28] These were hugely influential in the Middle Ages and they were amongst the earliest texts translated into the vernacular literature that emerged in the Renaissance. Like the oil paintings of the period, they were cultural palimpsests, absorbing textual supplements and stylistic elements from other classical works as well as the iconography of their day. The *Alexandreis* has the Macedonian king and his men fighting in chainmail with axes and broadswords against Arabs who fled in terror, scenes more representative of crusaders than ancient Greek hoplites; we additionally read of Spanish, Teutonic, Gallic and Flemish envoys arriving at Babylon to pay homage to the Macedonian king.[29] If Tarn's criticism of 'invented embassies' is indeed correct, then *every* age wished to communicate with the Macedonian ruler of the Graeco-Persian world.[30]

The Saracen threat from the Ottoman Empire loomed large in the minds of the romance writers, and it led to the emergence of vivid characters born out of fear or misplaced hope. In 1165 the *Letters of Prester John* entered circulation; this was an epistolary fantasy that convinced Pope Alexander III of the existence of a lost Nestorian Christian kingdom somewhere in central Asia.[31] The character's provenance might be found in the *Historia Ecclesiastica* of Eusebius (ca. 260-340 CE), the Bishop of Caesarea, and the fabled Prester John and his Christian outpost was an alluring enough idea for the Portuguese to venture to Ethiopia in search of his kingdom.[32] He, and the appropriately named legendary Gates of Alexander, were supposedly constructed to hold back the pagan hordes, imagery with direct parallels in the Arabic *Qur'an*. The gated wall at the world's end was in fact the narrow geographical feature that formed the Caspian Gates.

Josephus may have played a part in the legend, for in his *Jewish Wars* he claimed Alexander had indeed blocked the pass with huge iron gates.[33] That is somewhat ironic as Josephus had expounded: 'It is often said that the Greeks were the first people to deal with the events of the past in anything like a scientific manner… but it is clear that history has been far better preserved by the so-called barbarians.'[34] He added: 'Nevertheless, we must let those who have no regard for the truth write as they choose, for that is what they seem to delight in.'[35] But the fantasy was seductive and 'breaking the bolts' or the 'gates' of the earth had been a popular Roman *locus* (Greek, *topos*) when Alexander was under the knife.[36]

A map titled *A Description of The Empire of Prester John, Also Known as the Abyssinian Empire*. Produced in Antwerp in the 1570s by Abraham Ortelius, it outlined Prester John's fabled empire with both real and imagined names. Ortelius' *Theatrum Orbis Terrarum* is regarded as the first atlas and was the most expensive book ever printed. Nevertheless, some 7,300 copies were printed in four editions from 1570 to 1612.

At the height of the Crusades it was alleged that John, the supposed Presbyter of Syria, had re-taken the city of Ecbatana.[37] Yet much of Middle Age literature *was* about historical alchemy and Prester John was just one base metal alloyed with the superstitions and apprehensions of the age. But for an influential time he was as real as Alexander had been in the minds of *his* chroniclers and he became a regular feature in medieval texts. His legend was finally laid to rest when his mythical kingdom was removed from maps by the German Orientalist Hiob Ludolf (1624-1704) who exposed the seductive fancy for what it was.

Today in Greece the best-known *Romance* derivative is the *He Phyllada tou Megalexantrou*, first published in Venice in 1670 and never out of print through the three centuries that followed. The text represented the first attempt to 'fix' the fluid *Romance* recensions in circulation. Emerging 'from the Byzantine preoccupation with the classical past', the conflicts between the former Eastern Roman Empire and Ottoman Turks were inevitably dragged into the story.[38] The *Phyllada* portrayed Alexander as the protector of Greek Orthodox Christian culture, and ultimately as *kosmokrator*, the ruler of the world.

Through the romance genre Alexander's story finally infiltrated the East in a more permanent way than his own military conquest managed to. He entered the *Qur'an* texts, reemerging as Dhul-Qarnayn, the 'two-horned' who once again raised unbreachable gates to enclose the evil kingdoms of Yâgûg and Mâgûg (Gog and Magog) at the world's end; the reincarnation, with roots in the Syriac version of the *Romance*, had its earlier origins in the silver tetradrachms issued by Alexander's successors that depicted him with rams' horns. A Persian *Romance* variant was the *Iskandernameh* and alongside it Armenian and Ethiopian translations circulated imbuing the tale with their own cultural identities. An interesting textual 'rediscovery' appeared in the 8th century Syriac *Secretum Secretorum*; it included what was purported to be Aristotle's lost doctrine on kingship dedicated to Alexander.[39]

Ironically, it was not a Greek book, but the *Lives of the Physicians* (1245/46) by Ibn Abi Usaib'a (ca. 1203-1270), that preserved much of Aristotle's biographical detail, and yet it hardly merits a mention in debates on Peripatetic scholarship. Neither does the *Kitab al-Fehrest* of Ibn al-Nadim (died ca. 998 CE), a remarkable compendium of pre-Islamic text he himself described as 'an index of all books of all nations'.[40] Where Western texts vanished with the fall of Rome and with the torching of private collections and libraries at Pergamum and Alexandria, '… most of the surviving Greek literature was translated into Arabic by 750 CE; Aristotle became so widely studied that literally hundreds of books were written about him by Arabic scholars.' Even his Will survived intact in the writing of An-Nadim, Al-Qifti and Usaib'a.[41] The *Muqaddimah* of Ibn Khaldun (1332-1406), a universal history rich in new political, economic and historiographical theory, much of it again influenced by Aristotle's ideas, only reappeared in the West in the 19th century, as the *Prolegomena*. Trade with the Muslim world had flourished through Constantinople, but the voices of these authors are rarely heard west of the Hellespont; 'East is East, and West is West, and never the twain shall meet.'[42] There was however one exception to this cultural irreconcilability: Alexander himself, a historic genre not as separable from romance as we might imagine.

Many parallels to the Alexander romance corpus have appeared in literature: the rabbinic *aggadah* for example, with its folklore, historical anecdotes and moral exhortations dressed like biblical parables with attendant mythical creatures. We have the *Norse Sagas* which recapture a similar legendary past, and *Beowulf*, the Anglo-Saxon poem (ca. 1,000) of Scandinavian pagan legends and heroic exploits that emerged at the end of the Dark Ages when barbarism still triumphed over classical civilisation.[43] However, the enduring tale of King Arthur has the most significance for us, and somewhat predictably, Alexander and Arthur crossed paths in the 14th century French romance, *Perceforest*. Stock to Greek playwrights was the storm at sea, a neat mechanism for a dramatic location shift and one reused, for example, effectively in Shakespeare's *The Tempest*. *Perceforest* upheld the tradition, and Alexander was swept off course to a mythical visit to Britain.[44]

Transformed by Malory into *Morte D'Arthur* (ca. 1470), the Arthurian canon dominated British historiography for centuries. The ancient sources behind the legends of Brut, Arthur and his knights, have disappeared, leaving us in the dark on their identities, real or imagined.[45] Malory penned the Arthurian romance based on the earlier account of Geoffrey de Monmouth, whose *Historia Regum Britanniae* (ca. 1135) and Chrétien de Troyes' French 'grail' romances, appeared in the mid-12th century. The debate on Monmouth's work goes on regarding the extent to which it was purportedly derived from early Welsh or Breton manuscripts of an Archdeacon Walter. As early as 1190 the historian William of Newburgh declared of Monmouth's work, which traced the lineage of English kings back to Troy, '… only a person ignorant of ancient history would have any doubt about how shamelessly and impudently he lies in almost everything…' He followed with:

> … it is quite clear that everything this man wrote about Arthur and his successors… was made up, partly by himself and partly by others, either from an inordinate love of lying, or for the sake of pleasing the Britons.[46]

Any truth behind the identity of Arthur is lost and his very existence is questioned. Yet so was the existence of Troy until Heinrich Schliemann claimed to have dug it up in 1873 in his search for King Priam's treasure. Whether part of Mycenaen legend, or steeped in historical fact, Troy still faces the same hurdle as Plato's (or Solon's) Atlantis, Arthur's Camelot and the once-ridiculed 4th century BCE journey by the explorer Pytheas to Thule.[47] In the case of the 'biblical-only' Hittites, we were ignorant of the existence of a once-great empire for three millennia until Hattusa, the capital, was stumbled upon in 1834 and yet it defied identification for almost another century until detailed tablets were finally translated.[48] If the Vandals, Visigoths, Franks or Huns and the later Arabic invasions had between them managed to destroy every library in Europe, leaving Wallis Budge and the British Museum only with exotic Ethiopian *Romance* redactions, would we be able to say with any *certainty* that Alexander had really existed?

To some extent, Rome participated in the rise of both the romances of Arthur and Alexander: the fall of the Roman Empire, which saw the loss of the libraries that guarded primary historical testimony, allowed for a further metamorphosis in Alexander's story, and Rome's abandonment of Britain set the scene for Arthur's legend to emerge. For when sheep began to graze in Rome's Field of Mars, European history entered a millennium that put more stock in colourful fables than the accounts of, for example, the pedantic and stoic Arrian, whose *Anabasis* fell out of circulation until the Renaissance as a result. The change in biographical slant was not sudden and character portrayals were remodelled over time: compare the no-nonsense Sallust with Plutarch's didactic profiling a century on, then place them beside the biographies of the *Scriptores Historiae Augustae* penned perhaps a further two centuries later.[49]

These controversial texts, first termed *Scriptores Historiae Augustae* by Isaac Casaubon (1559-1614), are a remarkable collection of source-rich documents of 'dying Paganism'. In this self-labelled *mythistoricis*, the biography of Alexander Severus (ruled 222-235 CE) is an 'awkward imitation' of the *Cyropaedia*, according to Edward Gibbon.[50] It is appropriate, then, that the Latin *romanice scribere* – to write in a 'romance language' – formed the origins of 'romance'.[51] These biographies were supposed to pick up where Suetonius' *Lives of The Twelve Caesars* ended, a logical claim if ever the biographies of Nerva (emperor 96-98 CE) and Trajan (emperor 98-117) are found. The compendium, like the equally vexatious and still anonymous two sections (of three) of the *Origo gentis Romanae*, provides unique biographical details of late emperors (spanning 117-284 CE) presented as a corpus of texts by six historians written during the reigns of Diocletian (ca. 245-311 CE), the emperor who managed to push the barbarians back over Rome's borders, and Constantine (272-337 CE).[52]

Possibly the works of a single 'rogue scholiast', the authenticity and accuracy of the *Scriptores Historiae Augustae* are hotly debated, but it remains the sole account of a period when little other information exists. Debate on its dating and origins continues, and though the compilation is lucid at times, with some 130 supporting documents cited as the 'evidence', the web of home-spun sources descends into fable and rhetorical flights of fancy, heading in the direction of full-blown romance.[53] Nevertheless, the *Scriptores* were used as a source in Gibbon's *The History of the Decline and Fall of the Roman Empire* (published 1776-1789), a treatise not short on irony (and a little plagiarism), and which concluded that the social process underpinning the title had been '… the greatest, perhaps, and most awful scene in the history of mankind.' Gibbon's research method was initially widely praised for he opened with:

> I have always endeavoured to draw from the fountain-head; that my curiosity, as well as a sense of duty, has always urged me to study the originals; and that, if they have sometimes eluded my search, I have carefully marked the secondary evidence, on whose faith a passage or a fact were reduced to depend.[54]

Momigliano was scathing of the impression Gibbon attempted to perpetuate about his methodology and his pedantic footnotes, summing up his use of the *Scriptores* with: 'Theirs was an age of forgeries, interpolations, false attributions, tendentious interpretations. It would be surprising if the *Historia Augusta* should turn out to be more honest than the literary standards of the time required.'[55] Yet is it just another example of where 'romance' had clearly infiltrated 'history' with a dividing line we cannot readily see today.

EUHEMERISING THE TESTAMENT

In attempting to extract Alexander's Will from his *Romance* we are in fact taking a euhemeristic stance: treating what has been deemed mythical as an echo of historical reality. This is an appropriate moment to introduce Sir Isaac Newton into our contemplations, for his tendentious views as a deeply religious euhemerist could not be easily revealed in his lifetime, and neither could the twenty years he dedicated to heretical alchemy in his search for the Philosopher's Stone. Newton's *Chronology of Ancient Kingdoms Amended* was posthumously published in 1728; it was an exegesis in which he employed his mathematical erudition to recalibrate the events of antiquity to bring them 'safely' into the chronology proposed by Archbishop James Ussher. It may have inspired the publication of the multi-authored *The Universal History from the Earliest Account of Time to the Present*, which also 'found', or forged, 'correlations between the *Bible* and classical worlds'.[56]

Newton's book dated the Creation to 4004 BCE, following which he placed Noah's flood in 2347 BCE and shifted the fall of Troy from an Eratosthenes-supported date of 1183/4 forward to ca. 904 BCE, arguing that even the most ancient of extra-biblical historical references were post-1125 BCE.[57] His euhemerist hermeneutics (here meaning the study of the interpretation of ancient biblical texts) positioned all gods and heroes as factual kings, and he too viewed myths as historically inspired;[58] in the process Newton credited atomic theory to one Mochus the Phoenician whom he supposed was the biblical Moses. Newton modestly summed up his introduction with: 'I do not pretend to be exact to a year: there may be errors of five or ten years, and sometimes twenty, and not much above.'

The full title of Newton's publication included the prefix, *A Short Chronicle from the First Memory of Things in Europe, to the Conquest of Persia by Alexander the Great.* It was presented with a covering letter to the Queen from John Conduitt who claimed 'Antiquity' had benefited from '… a sagacity and penetration peculiar to the great Author, dispelling that Mist, with which fable and error had darkened it.' Newton's treatise, consciously or otherwise, supported the methodology of the 1623 *On the Plan and Method of Reading Histories* by Digory Whear, and ironically so, for Newton is better remembered for the weighty gravitas of his *Philosophiae Naturalis Principia Mathematica,* whose publication was delayed when poor sales of the *History of Fishes* almost bankrupted the Royal Society.[59]

Newton's gravitational masterpiece was based on Kepler's astronomically unpopular law of planetary motion, and that too is ironic, for Kepler, who held the conviction that God had a geometric plan for the universe, fell foul of the *Index Librorum Prohibitorum*, as did the texts of Galileo with whom he collaborated. Although Kepler's first publication, the *Mysterium Cosmographicum,* attempted to reconcile a heliocentric solar-system with biblical geocentrism, his refusal to convert to Catholicism (and dispense with elliptical orbits) ultimately sealed his fate, despite his imperial patronage in Prague. He was banished from Graz where his last astronomical calendar was publicly burned, and his mother was accused of witchcraft, an allegation backed up by spurious claims that his *Somnium*, the first attempt at 'science fiction', had referred to demonic themes. In 1626 the Catholic Counter-Reformation placed his library under lock and key.[60] In Newton's case, as one author has commented in his study of his lesser-known euhemerist life, 'the hunter turned prey' when his scientific discipline produced more myths than it dispelled.[61]

While we are on the matter of euhemerism, it looks wholly suspicious that it was Cassander, the regent's son accused of ferrying to Babylon the poison bound for Alexander, who employed Euhemerus, the founding 'mythographer', at his Macedonian court.[62] One result was Euhemerus' utopian land of Panchaea (surely Platonist in origin), though his employer, Cassander, displayed few of the qualities found on the idealised

Indian Ocean island paradise.[63] Could Euhemerus have been tasked with attempting an ironical role-reversal: that of explaining away a damaging 'truth' – Cassander's part in the alleged plot – as nothing more than a myth propagated by a scurrilous pamphleteer? Euhemerus' principal work was his *Sacred History*.[64] So was it perhaps he, without the reverence his title suggested, who tossed the *Pamphlet* Will and conspiracy into the final chapter of an early redaction of the *Greek Alexander Romance*?

Many euhemeristically inclined historians accept that romances may be built around a folklore that preserved elements of genuine historicity, a stance Ennius found useful when linking Rome's foundations to Troy.[65] Others more cautiously see myths as 'symbols of permanent philosophical truths', and the Greek legends as natural cyclical processes forever recurring.[66] If an echo of reality has indeed been captured, these lodestones may still be camouflaged by the incredible. It's worth re-quoting Peter Green's conclusion on the issue, though he never linked his observation to Alexander's Will:

> … the uncomfortable fact remains that the *Alexander Romance* provides us, on occasion, with apparently genuine materials found nowhere else, while our better-authenticated sources, *per contra,* are all too often riddled with bias, propaganda, rhetorical special pleading or patent falsification and suppression of evidence.[67]

Other 'legends' may have similarly been built around misplaced or forgotten events. Jason's journey in the Argo and the legend of King Solomon's Mines may all be aggregates of real journeys distilled from explorers' travel logs along exotic trading routes; the latter inland to the metropolis of Manyikeni in the land of the city of 'Great Zimbabwe' through the port of Kilwa in modern Tanzania – termed the finest and most handsomely built towns by Ibn Battuta (1364-ca. 1369) – its name already changed to 'Quiloa' (as the Portuguese called it) by Milton in *Paradise Lost*. Solomon's legendary mines were perhaps in the lost Land of Punt, 'Ta netjer' ('God's land'), believed by the people of Egypt to be their ancient homeland. According to biblical references, Phoenician ships traded down the African coast, visiting Ophir at the end of the Red Sea and bringing back 'gold and silver, ivory, and apes and peacocks' for Solomon; it was a famed trading city of 'stones of gold' that has been variously linked to Great Zimbabwe, Sofala in Mozambique (in Milton's *Paradise Lost*) and Dhofar in Oman.[68]

Under Ptolemy II *Philadelphos*, in the generation immediately after Alexander, Greek influence extended to Elephantine, an island in the Upper Nile that marked the boundary with Ethiopia (in Greek: 'the land of men with burnt faces'), though the Satrap Stele erected in 311 BCE appears to reference an earlier Nubian campaign of 312 BCE under

Ptolemy I *Soter* who may have stationed garrisons at Syene (Aswan). Elephantine (the Greek name for Pharaonic Abu at Aswan), previously used by Alexander as a deportation centre, was perhaps an early centre of the ivory trade when Ptolemaic commerce started to penetrate the African interior; Herodotus had apparently visited the trading post ca. 430 BCE. Commercial ties with the kingdom of Kush with its capital at Meroe (in today's Sudan) had flourished after Persian expeditions attempted to subdue it, and references to its Nubian ruler, Queen Candace, and to its regional wealth appeared in biblical references.[69]

A curiosity with the source of the Nile and reason for its annual flooding was a common investigative and well established theme in Greek scholarship since the time of Herodotus, and it reappeared in Aristotle's now lost treatise, *De Inundatione Nili* (as titled in a medieval Latin translation); he finally pinned the phenomenon on the Ethiopian summer rains, as Democritus, Thrasyalces and Eudoxus of Cnidus had proposed before him.[70] Aristobulus apparently touched on the problem too, and a tradition even existed in Roman times (through Seneca's description and Diodorus' polemic on the issue, for example) that Callisthenes claimed Alexander had commissioned an expedition to Ethiopia to ascertain the truth. If so, it could explain the reported presence of Ethiopian ambassadors in Babylon.[71]

State-employed elephant hunters would disappear into the African interior for months at a time once the Seleucids cut the Ptolemies off from their supply of Indian war elephants; they would return with animals never before seen and which became 'objects of amazement'. There were reports of snakes 100 cubits long (approximately 150 feet) large enough to devour bulls and oxen and even bring elephants down.[72] A live 30-cubit-long python was delivered to Ptolemy II *Philadelphos*, according to Diodorus, and once exhibited it became a court showpiece.[73] To quote Bevan's 1927 summation of the second Ptolemy:

> He was a parallel to Solomon in his wealth, surpassing that of any other king of his time… Perhaps it was less the real Solomon to whom Ptolemy II was a parallel than the ideal Solomon portrayed in the Book of Ecclesiastes – the book written by some world-weary Jew at a date not far off from Ptolemy's time. Ptolemy, too, was a king who had 'gathered silver and gold and the peculiar treasure of kings and of provinces', who got him 'men-singers and women-singers, and the delights of the sons of men, as musical instruments, and that of all sorts', who had 'proved his heart with mirth and enjoyed pleasure', who had 'made great works and builded him houses'…[74]

This approaches the fabled tones of Polo's description of Shangdu (Xanadu) and the summer court of Kublai Khan that was immortalised in poetry by Samuel Taylor Coleridge. Although Solomon existed historically, two millennia hence, will history be able to differentiate between Rider Haggard's Allan Quatermain and his real-life model, the British explorer and hunter, Frederick Courtney Selous – who 'led a singularly adventurous and fascinating life, with just the right alternations between the wilderness and civilisation' – in the fictional search for Solomon's mines?[75]

THE *MUTHODES* OF MIEZA AND PROPAGANDA OF PELLA

Chimeral characters frequent the most influential of 'historical' episodes, and nowhere more vividly than when early classical Greece emerged from its Dark Age.[76] In the *Iliad* the 1,186 troop transporters comprising the Greek flotilla to Troy (the Catalogue of Ships; a number frowned upon by Thucydides) may in fact represent a hundred late Bronze Age and Mycenae-led invasions across the Aegean; it was the start of an ongoing saga continued in the *Aethiopis, Ilias Mikra (Little Illiad)*, the lost *Iliou Persis, The Sack of Ilium, Nostoi, Odyssey* and the *Telegony* which completed the Epic Cycle.[77] Hittite texts suggest the invading *Ahhiyawa* (linguistic links

to the *Akhaioi,* the Achaeans, *are* hard to dismiss) may have been Mycenaen Greeks based in coastal Asia Minor who were fighting for control of Wilusa, likely the Hittite name for Troy.[78]

Some of the underlying imagery, if not its application, is sound. There is much evidence, for example, that the legend of the Wooden Horse of Troy started life as an Assyrian-style battering ram, for many were ornately horse-headed in design and fully enclosed to house and protect the men who inched them forward to the walls.[79] On the other hand, the now lost *On Rhetoric According to Homer* by Telephus of Pergamum exposed the

A photo of Wilhelm Dörpfeld and Heinrich Schliemann at the Lion Gate of Mycenae ca. 1884/5.

narratives within the Trojan epics for what they really were: flights of epideictic fancy that reinforced the dominant value systems underlying the tale: the *aidos* and the *nemesis* that framed honour and revenge.

Whether there ever was a 'Homer' is doubtful, whether blind as one tradition claimed, or indeed far-sighted and as many as seven cities staked their claims as his home: Cyme, Smyrna, Chios, Colophon, Pylos, Argos, and Athens.[80] In one view, 'the works ascribed to Moses and Homer were libraries', and 'to deprive a library of an author would be to consign it to the realm of the anonymous';[81] 'Homer was a sort of shorthand for the whole body of archaic hexameter poetry.'[82] As with the thirty-three poems comprising the *Homeric Hymns*, a collection of different authors from many periods coalesced into something approximating a genre; the epics were collected into a 'book' sung by the *Homeridai*, the guild of the 'sons of Homer' that kept the ancient accounts alive orally at the Panathenaia.[83] Certainly the *Life of Homer* (one of many 'lives') by a Pseudo-Herodotus betrays the fictional traits of a later age.[84] The still anonymous *Greek Anthology* proposed more divine origins: 'Whose pages recorded the Trojan War and of the long wanderings of the son of Laertes? I cannot be sure of his name or his city. Heavenly Zeus, is Homer getting the glory for your own poetry?'[85]

The Roman poet Horace (65-68 BCE) coined the term 'Homeric Nod' in his *Ars Poetica* to describe the continuity errors Homer repeatedly made through the *Iliad*, and this perhaps supports the 'multiple-author' theory over a single compiler of the epic of prehistory.[86] Today the corpus

A gypsum wall panel relief from the palace of Tiglath-Pileser III (reigned ca. 744-727 BCE) at Nimrud dating to ca. 730 BCE, showing an Assyrian battering ram in front of the walls of a city under siege. The fully enclosed and wheeled battering ram may be the inspiration for the legend of the Trojan Horse. The panel is now in the British Museum. BM 118903.

of literature contained in the *Homeric* or *Trojan Epic Cycle*, or rather in its *scholia*, the critical and explanatory commentary in the margins, has spurred its own investigative science: Neoanalysis.[87]

Herodotus' semi-mythical battle between the champions of Sparta and Argos in the mid-6th century BCE at Thyrea described a single sun-baked blood-soaked day which might in fact have similarly recalled many campaigning seasons that witnessed similar hoplite clashes on the plains of Lacedaemonia in the heart of 'the dancing floor of Ares.'[88] Reminiscent of a gladiatorial arena, the format at Thyrea, designed to limit casualties, allocated victory to the last man standing, in this case a lone Spartan who committed suicide for fear that his valour would be questioned in the face of the deaths of all his comrades. But the outcome of the battle reads more like a tutorial on the prevailing warrior honour code. Some 300 in number from each city, the Thyrean champions are reminiscent of the elite *Hieros lochos*, the Theban Sacred Band, the shock troop corps of paired lovers that Alexander annihilated in 338 BCE, and whose remains were likely discovered in the 19th century.[89]

The battle at Chaeronea remains well attested, as does Philip's harsh treatment of Boeotian soldiers who left their crack unit isolated: Boeotian corpses had to be purchased by their relatives, and captives were ransomed or sold into slavery. But was the Theban Sacred Band, a unit modelled on Spartan example, really annihilated to the last man as texts record, as a total of 254 skeletons were excavated from the tomb guarded by the Lion of Chaeronea? 'Perish any man who suspects that these men either did or suffered anything that was base', exclaimed Philip II upon seeing their corpses after the battle.[90] Perhaps the more poignant testament to their

The 20-foot tall Lion of Chaeronea as it appeared ca. 1907 in *Outlines of European History*, after earlier repairs and reconstruction of the fragments in 1902. According to Pausanias, the original statue was erected to guard the graves of the Theban Sacred Band who fell at the battle in Boeotia between Mt Helicon and Mt Parnassus. There is no surviving inscription. Excavation of the quadrangular enclosure revealed the remains of 254 corpses laid out in seven rows. Similar statues and a communal tomb (*polyandreion*) have been found at Thespiae and Amphipolis.[91]

bravery is a tumulus 230 feet around and some 23 feet high that bears witness to the *polyandreion,* the mass grave, of their Macedonian attackers who were inhumed with their weapons.

But monuments to valour date further back. The battle at Marathon in 490 BCE clearly epitomised Greek *arete* and *aidos,* the classical codes of valour and duty. However it was likely Thersippus, or more popularly Eucles, and not the *hemerodrome* (day-runner) Pheidippides (famed by the 1879 Robert Browning poem of the same name) who delivered the news of victory at Marathon to the expectant Athenians; the proud motto of such messengers (in fact of their Persian counterparts) read, '… and neither snow nor rain nor heat nor night holds back from the accomplishment.'[92] According to Plutarch, Eucles was a self-sent messenger who arrived in full armour from the battle he fought in himself. The Athenian Pheidippides (or Philippides, according to Lucian) apparently ran to Sparta to request help *before* the battle commenced, and he met the god Pan on the way, for legend had it that the god's cave in the Parthenian ridge overhanging Tegea, was en route. In fact it was Euchidas, running the route to Delphi, who allegedly died on the spot.[93] An amalgam of truths with popular fiction is what we recite today, when 'eager to adopt and adorn the fable', writers embellished the subject 'as if it were the soil of a fair estate unoccupied'.[94]

Sparta's own heroic holding of the pass against Xerxes' Persian horde is itself shrouded in legendary misattribution, for the 4,200 reported defenders at Thermopylae are widely bypassed in eulogies that alone immortalise the alleged 300 Spartans who led them, though the numbers given by Herodotus (who claimed to know the 300 by name) are open to question (perhaps short by 700 or more in total), as is the Spartan-led night attack on Xerxes' tent mentioned by Diodorus who was likely drawing from Ephorus, who in turn took this detail from an unknown source.[95]

And this leads us to the exemplar of a laconic retort by Leonidas to the Great King's demand that the Greeks hand over their arms: *molon labe* – 'you come and take them'. It is a bold riposte, and yet one taken from the *Apophthegmata Lakonika, Laconian Sayings*, attributed to Plutarch (now grouped with his *Moralia*) and compiled over 500 years after the event. Moreover, the historical pragmatist would ask: if the defenders died to the last man, could a Greek have recorded Leonidas' reply? The son of the seer, Megistias, sent home the penultimate day, is a possible contender, and the exiled Spartan king, Demaratus (ruled 515-491 BCE), who accompanied the Persians on the north side of the Hot Pillars (the literal translation of *Thermo Pylai*) is perhaps a stronger candidate, though we should recall, when dealing with Spartan legend, that Lycurgus (ca. 390-324 BCE), the forefather who supposedly gave Sparta its polity, has been termed nothing more than a 'benevolent myth'.[96]

The lyric poet Tyrtaeus (likely 7th century BCE) was probably more responsible for the militarisation of the Spartan constitution, if we can believe the claims in the *Suda*; his military elegies certainly encouraged the nineteen-year Messenian Wars that led to their enslavement of the helots, if the fragments we have are indicative of its overall tone and despite the Attic propaganda that described the poet as 'a lame Athenian schoolmaster'.[97]

What did Alexander himself conclude about *his* sources 2,300 years ago when carrying Herodotus and the philosopher-edited *Iliad* into an Asia he only knew from their scrolls or from Aristotle's teachings at Mieza?[98] When Alexander finally joined battle with Darius III, where were Herodotus' famed 10,000 'Immortals' (a description unique to him), the Great King's elite royal guard that the Macedonians expected to face? The answer is probably reincarnated in the *melophoroi*, so-called Apple Bearers, who were named after the fruit-like counter-weights on their spear butts, for Herodotus had most likely confused the Persian term 'Anûšiya' with 'Anauša', which simply meant 'Companion'.[99] Herodotus himself is said to have quipped: 'Very few things happen at the right time, and the rest do not happen at all. The conscientious historian will correct these defects.' But who can find the comedic lines within the historian's work? It was in fact Mark Twain who attributed the words to him in the preface to *A Horse's Tail*.[100]

Given time and propagated convincingly enough, this may well become a 'genuine' metaphrase that will further tarnish Herodotus' reputation, for no historian has been more maligned (perhaps because he was a barbarophile) than the 'father of history' from Halicarnassus 'who attempted to open up the gates to the past'. Plutarch penned a *De Heroditi Malignitate* (*On the Malice of Herodotus*), which has been termed literature's 'first slashing review';[101] the attack may have been in part due to Herodotus' religious cynicism that offended the deeply pious Priest of Apollo, and the negative picture he painted of Plutarch's fellow Boeotians.[102] Valerius Pollio, Aelius Harpocration and Libanius followed suit with declamatory texts against the *Histories*, and Aristotle branded Herodotus a 'teller of myths' above anything else.[103] Perhaps the greatest disservice paid to him was a two-book epitome of the *Histories* by Theopompus.[104]

Herodotus, 'who blended the empirical attitude of the scientists with the rhapsode's love of praising famous men', nevertheless, offered in defence to the accusation, 'that he sometimes wrote for children and at other times for philosophers': 'My business is to record what people say, but I am by no means bound to believe it, and let this statement hold for my entire account.'[105] The *apologia* was a popular prenuptial in the marriage of the *historikon* and *mythistoria*. He nevertheless remains unique; as Momigliano concluded simply: 'There was no Herodotus before

Herodotus', moreover, 'he was more easily criticised than replaced'.[106]

This, in turn, draws us by the bridle and halter to Alexander's breaking of Bucephalus, the king's Thessalian warhorse which was probably named after its ox-head branding (*boos kephale*). The rendering of the story fitted the overall encomiastic portrayal of the young prince: he was a Bellerophon mounting a wild Pegasus that could be only tamed by him before an incredulous Macedonian court and an elated horse-dealer, Philonicus. Yet the event, which 'abounds in circumstantial detail and dramatic immediacy', was preserved by Plutarch alone, as was Alexander's quizzing of Persian envoys on military detail at an even younger age, for this anticipated, and set the tone for, his later invasion of Asia.[107] Did Onesicritus' hagiographical *The Education of Alexander* (or Marsyas' book of the same name) provide the models, or did Plutarch, in his 'quiet naivety', find this detail in the epistolary corpus he uniquely referred to on some thirty occasions?[108] Surely neither source was reliable. Was the Bucephalus episode an allusion to the metaphor in Plato's *Phaedra* which likened the untamed horse to an unruly youth who must be broken by an education, *paideia*, itself steeped in Homeric values? In which case it is fully understandable why Bucephalus 'was born to share Alexander's fate' in the *Romance*.[109]

The careers of Plutarch, Callisthenes, Demosthenes and Aristotle, each influential to Alexander's story, have also given birth to a spurious epistolary corpus in their name. Plutarch seems to have had unique access to a folio of correspondences to and from Alexander, so numerous that he commented: 'In fact it is astonishing that he [Alexander] could find time to write so many letters to his friends.'[110] Confirmation that a collection once existed, possibly collated as a book, came with the discovery of papyri in Hamburg, Florence and Oxyrhynchus in Egypt, though suspiciously 'there is no trace of them earlier than Cicero's *De Officiis*' which referred to *epistulae Philippi ad Alexandrum et Antipatri ad Cassandrum et Antigoni ad Philippum filium*;[111] the title suggests there once existed a corpus of letters between Philip and Alexander, and correspondence between Antipater, Cassander and Antigonus *Monophthalmos*, the remarkable Macedonian 'one-eyed' general.

Arrian also referred to the collection and it is likely a common source was behind the tradition.[112] Plutarch's folio was even more specific; those letters written to Alexander's mother, Olympias, were 'private', and only Alexander's closest friend, Hephaestion, was permitted to read them. Nevertheless, the detail we garner from them appears, in hindsight, to be fictitious. The authenticity of one of Plutarch's own works remains just as vexatious; a Greek manuscript attributed to him and titled *Pro Nobilitate, In Favour of Noble Birth*, resurfaced as recently as 1722 and was not convincingly discredited until the late 1900s. Yet separating deliberate imposters from well-meaning 'impostures' is not always achievable.[113] And so the authenticity of similar correspondence by the philosophers Plato, Speusippus (Plato's nephew, ca. 408-338 BCE), Archytas (428-347 BCE) and the influential rhetorician Isocrates, whose pleas for an invasion of Persia arguably motivated Philip II (and then Alexander) to launch his Asian campaign, is still debated.[114] But the composition of such letters, in emulation of the great minds of the past, was a part of Greek classroom preparatory exercises, *progymnasmata*.

Some thirty-plus letters concerning Alexander made their way into the *Greek Alexander Romance*, a publication unique in ancient fiction in the breadth of its epistolary 'pseudo-documentarism'. Examples range from what Merkelbach termed *wunder-briefe* to the almost credible, a state of affairs that epitomises the whole *Romance*.[115] Plutarch may have been unwittingly incorporating letters that had no historical foundation into his own biographies, perhaps fooled by the freehand-form of their intimacy when no stylistic baseline for comparison existed. They may have even originated, convincingly, with a court scandalmonger such as Chares, the king's chamberlain. So the argument about the 'truth' revolves around the degree of trust we place in the instincts of our secondary sources and *their* immunity to seduction.

The association of the authorship of *Romance* with the campaign historian Callisthenes (besides other historians) reminds us that we commonly place credit where none is due, when the real architects of events may disappear without a trace. With a superficial knowledge of characters and the events attached to them, we risk, once again, creating our own *modern* 'romances' when regurgitating the tale. We habitually lay down Mercator-like projections on history's prosopographic *terroir*; but this is a one-dimensional mapping that distorts both the shape and the scale of contributions, for the truth lies hidden in contours and grottos time has flattened out.

Examples proliferate the classical accounts: Pythagoras' theorem still bears his name, yet the triplets had already been in use in Babylon and Egypt for over 1,500 years before his day, since the Middle Bronze Age in fact.[116] If Porphyry is correct, Pythagoras took his knowledge of geometry from Egypt, arithmetic from Phoenicia, astronomy from Chaldeans, and principles of religion from the Magi too,[117] which is no doubt why Plato is said to have paid the exorbitant sum of 100 minas to purchase three books of Pythagorean doctrine by Philolaus of Croton.[118] Plutarch's *Symposiacs* provided further detail of his teachings but these were penned some 500 years later using notes left behind by the polymath's inner circle, the *mathematikoi* and *akousmatikoi,* the 'learners' and 'listeners'.[119]

Pythagoras' association with the newly 'discovered' geometry was in fact first made by Cicero in his *On the Nature of the Gods*. Cicero had been a political survivor *par excellence*, until Mark Antony presented Octavian with his proscription list, but without his 800 extant letters would we have known he was a giant of the Julian age? Or would his bit part of just nine lines in Shakespeare's *Julius Caesar* have swayed us otherwise? If it was not for Petrarch's discovery of the Ciceronian epistolary collection, *ad Atticum*, in Verona in 1345, which contained such a wealth of detail that Nepos had believed there was little need for a history of that period,[120] we would only have half the correspondence; inevitably some of the corpus does appear less than genuine.[121] Petrarch, whose epic but unfinished *Africa* – a poem perhaps written as a reply to the *Alexandreis* of Gautier de Chatillon and written in the style of Virgil's *Aeneid* – was so excited about his find that he compiled a letter to the long-dead Cicero to tell him (and to Livy too). And could either Cicero, or Julius Caesar even, have made the historical grade if not for Apollonius Molon's lessons in Rhodian rhetoric?[122]

If the inscriptions found at Nineveh have been deciphered correctly, the so-called Archimedes Screw was also in use centuries before Archimedes 'stumbled' upon the idea.[123] And on the subject of water management, De Lesseps' canal at Suez remains a wonder of the industrial revolution, but Aristotle, Diodorus, Strabo and Pliny each placed an original channel linking the two oceans (though indirectly and via a different route) in the time of the Egyptian pharaohs. The first excavations *possibly* commenced with Merenre I of the Sixth Dynasty in the late third millennium BCE, though sources better corroborate the early efforts of Sesostris (ca. 1878-1839 BCE, probably identifiable with Senusret III).[124] Re-excavation of the watercourse had commenced around 600 BCE, centuries before Alexander crossed the Nile, which was named the Aegyptus River in antiquity, though in Greek mythology Aegyptus was a descendent of the river-god Neilus.[125]

Pharaoh Necho II (ruled ca. 610-595 BCE) stopped construction of the waterway when an oracle warned him he was 'working for the advantage of a barbarian', though by then, according to Herodotus, some 120,000 Egyptians had died in the construction efforts. Another tradition picked up by Aristotle more practically suggested that engineers had advised against contaminating the freshwater Nile with salt, for the channel linked the Red Sea (thought to be at a higher level than Lower Egypt) to the river and not directly to the Mediterranean.[126] The canal was finally completed by Darius I whose inscription commemorating the project survives to this day; according to Herodotus the waterway was sufficiently wide for two triremes to pass and Ptolemy II *Philadelphos* had it re-excavated to the Bitter Lakes using navigable locks and sluices to prevent the in-flow of seawater; it was known as the 'Ptolemy River'.

Excavated papyri do reveal a remarkable irrigation system in the Fayyum basin south of Memphis, which drained marshland that was otherwise uninhabitable and reclaimed valuable settlement areas for

Egyptians and Hellenic mercenaries alike through to the mid-3rd century BCE.[127] Rome would later benefit from the engineering feat and Trajan extended the canal system with a branch known as the Amnis Trajanus, which joined the Nile somewhere close to Memphis (which was some 12 miles south of modern Cairo). Remnants of an ancient East-West canal *were* indeed found by Napoleon's cartographers in 1799 along with an emaciated Alexandria with barely 6,000 inhabitants; Napoleon reincarnated the idea of putting it back into service, though the canons of the British navy did not allow him the opportunity.[128]

Rome's own enigmatic past is not beyond question. The 'legend' of Coriolanus (5th century BCE), a vivid narrative of a hero turned enemy, was scooped up by Livy, Plutarch and Dionysius, amongst others. Although Plutarch confidently afforded him a lineage (and a nickname) and a fifty-page biography, the consular *fasti* (official records) never mentioned Coriolanus at all, yet they record the siege of Corioli and the Volscian uprising that supposedly made him.[129] Was he a figure invented to warn the Senate of the unbridled power of popular generals and kings, or a representation of aristocratic tyranny over the city's plebeian interests? For these themes were prominent in the early days of Rome; Livy recorded the fall of the Etruscan city of Veii, which was alienated by the remaining tribes for its abhorrent adherence to monarchy.[130]

It is worth noting that new linguistic investigation suggests the Etruscans, to whom Rome 'owed much of its civilisation', may well have been refugees from fallen Troy (Herodotus reported they emigrated from Lydia in Asia ca. 1,000 BCE), though Augustus, Naevius, Ennius (ca. 239-169 BCE) and Virgil (70-19 BCE) would be mortified to hear it. Certainly, some of the paintings on the walls of Etruscan tombs (6th century BCE), somewhat Greek in style, have Phrygian and Lycian points of comparison. Etruscan offerings (7th century BCE) have been found at Olympia, suggesting continuous early contact with Greece.[131] Trosia, the Greek name (alongside Ilium) for the city of Priam, resonates with similarity to the frequent Hittite and Egyptian references to Turush and Trusya that appeared in 14th and 15th century BCE documents, and thus, it is suggested, to later Tros or Trus, the supposed roots of the names 'Etruria' and 'Etruscans'. What was once a fanciful notion is now backed up by the identification of genetic similarities,[132] though as one historian noted of the Etruscan civilisation and its supposedly indecipherable texts: 'I don't think there is any field of human knowledge in which there is such a daft cleavage between what has been scientifically ascertained and the unshakable belief of the public...'[133] But the same could perhaps be stated, of course, of Alexander himself.

THE INCOMPARABLE COMPARANDUM AND THE NEW SACK OF ILIUM

Alexander's character portrayal survives as a Graeco-Roman amalgam that is analysed against the backdrop of ever-changing contemporary ideals. But the comparisons inevitably made are not always digestible. Texts are unambiguous that Caligula (alternatively Gaius, 12-41 CE) was something of a monster who paraded himself in Alexander's breastplate, which he claimed was taken from the now-lost Alexandrine sarcophagus.[134] But are we troubled, or inspired, by Alexander's own heroic emulation? For he relieved the guardians of the Temple of Athena at Troy of Achilles' shield, or so he believed. The deeds are comparable but the men are not, and so we revile the one while admiring the Homeric homage being paid by the other. If Schliemann had not staked his claim to Troy in 1868, the value we place on what we deem 'court' sources may have been quite different, for Arrian, for one, claimed Alexander found the site easily enough upon beaching at the Troad and sacrificing at the tombs of his heroes, where Strabo stated little identifying evidence of the site remained.[135]

Alexander's own Homeric shield-coveting might have been inspired by tales of Pythagoras, who, through eternal transmigration, claimed to be a reincarnation of a Trojan hero. He was, he believed, Euphorbus, who had been cut down by Menelaus in the fight over Patroclus' body, a story put to verse in Ovid's *Metamorphoses*, a 'compendium of myth' written in the dactylic hexameter of the Epic Cyle. Unlike the Socratic belief that all knowledge of a previous life was washed away with each rebirth, Pythagoras had been, he claimed, granted eternal memory as part of the gift from Mercury. As 'proof' of his past when inhabiting the reincarnated body of Hermotimus, he apparently went to the (original) territory of the Branchidae and tracked down the beaten shield (by now worn down to the ivory) that Menelaus had retrieved from the battlefield and dedicated to the temple of Apollo.[136] Whether Pythagoras or Alexander truly believed they had the genuine defensive armour of the Trojans is a matter of conjecture, but in Alexander's case that would have meant that the *hoplon* he actually used in battle was more than 800 years old; what he had retrieved from the Athena's temple was surely a symbolic talisman rather than a functional shield.[137]

Alexander also shared intriguing parallels with the Roman emperor Nero, who should feature prominently in any chapter dedicated to the vivid hues of romance. An open admirer of the Macedonian conqueror, Nero formed an elite personal unit staffed exclusively by men over 6 feet tall and he named it The Phalanx of Alexander the Great;[138] according to the *Suda*, an Alexander of Aegae was even employed as one of Nero's tutors.[139] The excesses and colour that epitomised Nero's imperium became legendary and fascinated the citizens of an expanding empire.[140] Everyone related to something of the emperor, and paradoxically, besides the havoc he wrought, the populace remained curiously nostalgic for Nero's eccentricities. Even his choice of a 'proud whore' as second wife (Poppea Sabina) must have appealed to those outside the elite patricians and *nobiles*. Dio Chrysostom recorded their enthusiasm: '... for so far as the rest of his subjects were concerned, there was nothing to prevent his continuing to be emperor for all time, seeing that even now everybody wishes he were still alive. And the great majority believe that he still is...'[141]

Chrysostom's final line brings us to the most significant parallel with Alexander: the 'false' Neros that appeared. For many *did* believe he never committed suicide but rather lived on in obscurity; at least three imposters presented themselves as the living emperor over the next twenty years and with subjects ready to accept them.[142] Cassius Dio (ca. 155-235 CE) reported that in 221 CE, a century and a half on, a mysterious person appeared at the Danube with an entourage and claimed to be Alexander the Great. Entranced by the apparition (an *eidolon* to the Greeks), none dared to oppose his progress; on the contrary, they provided him with food and lodging. After performing nocturnal rituals and burying a wooden horse, he disappeared once more.[143] As for Nero, it was the developing *Sibylline Oracles* that took the thespian emperor to the realms of apocalyptic legend through to the *City of God* of Augustine of Hippo (354-430 CE, also

A 17th century sculpture of Nero at the Musei Capitolino, Hall of Emperors, Rome. A part of it is original giving form to the reconstruction. Suetonius provided a vivid description of the emperor: 'He was about the average height, his body marked with spots and malodorous, his hair light blond, his features regular rather than attractive, his eyes blue and somewhat weak, his neck over thick, his belly prominent, and his legs very slender... he was utterly shameless in the care of his person and in his dress, always having his hair arranged in tiers of curls.'[145]

known as 'Saint Augustine'), which criticised the portrayal of him as the Antichrist, and like Alexander, Nero entered the folklore of the Middle Ages.[144]

Nero had forced his teacher, Seneca ('the Younger', ca. 4 BCE-65 CE), and his teacher's nephew, the celebrated poet Lucan, to commit suicide, claiming they both had a part in the Pisonian plot to remove him.[146] In fact Nero simply wished to put an end to Seneca's criticism of his increasingly bizarre behaviour following his alleged murder of his own mother, Agrippina; Nero claimed that Seneca had amassed the remarkable (and highly suspicious) sum of some 300,000,000 *sestertii* in just four years under his patronage.[147] The *Apocolocyntosis* (loosely translated as the 'pumpkinification') *of the Divine Claudius*, flattering to Nero and *possibly* written by Seneca shortly after Claudius' death (in 54 CE), suggested this Stoic teacher once held high hopes for his new 'radiant-faced' Nero. Alas, after some promising years, the trappings of *imperium* saw the 'new star' begin to fade. The demise of Lucan, once an imperial friend and holding a questorship and augurate at a remarkably early age, stemmed ultimately from the republican sympathy embedded within the later books of his *De Bello Civili*.[148] This led to the banning of his poetry, including the *De Incendiis Urbis*, *On the Burning of the City*, in which Lucan termed Nero a tyrant, and that paralleled his critique of the conquering Alexander. Lucan was forced to open his veins at the age of twenty-five.[149]

The parallel here is Callisthenes, Alexander's own outspoken historian. He had opened promisingly for Alexander too; seas parted and the gods took due notice of their favourite new son. However, his distaste for Alexander's oriental adoptions, divine pretensions and perhaps, finally, the wholesale slaughter of the defenceless Branchidae, saw him forget Aristotle's warnings and he let loose his indiscreet tongue. He too was executed on the king's orders; according to one tradition, quite possibly again stemming from Greek polemic emanating from the Peripatetic school, Callisthenes was first caged for some years and dragged around in chains before being tortured. Perhaps he saw it coming: once offered undiluted wine at a court *komos*, he reportedly declined with, 'I do not wish to drink Alexander's cup and then need the cup of Asclepius', the healing god.[150] The comparison with Nero is rarely made but the crime was ultimately the same.

Philosophers *were* the bane of kings, emperors and even democracies, as was Diogenes the Cynic of Sinope. Alexander visited the barrel-bound philosopher in Corinth in 334 BCE shortly after the destruction of Thebes, and he enquired if there was anything that Diogenes desired. In the legendary anecdote captured by Plutarch (and others), Diogenes asked Alexander to step aside as he was blocking his sun.[151] Tradition claims that this prompted the Macedonian king to confide to his companions that '… if he were not Alexander he would like to be Diogenes.' The unlikely dialogue, probably the output of the Diogenes' Cynic school, ought to be shadowed in historical reality.[152] Superficially impressive in its hauteur as his reply was, any biography of Diogenes would not be complete without mentioning his public behaviour, which included defecation and masturbation, leading Plato to brand him (and Diogenes to brand himself, for that matter) a dog, *kynos,* the root of the word 'cynic'; it was behaviour supposed to emphasise his objection to 'regressive' civilisation.[153]

A former slave captured by pirates, and one charged with debasing (or defacing) the local currency at his native Sinope (a charge carrying severe penalty),[154] Diogenes had found the clay barrel (or urn) in which he slept in the Temple of Cybele. He might have been the *first* true 'citizen of the world', *kosmopolites,* a concept the *Stoikoi* later took up when Rome was indeed assimilating much of the known world.[155] But there were, in fact, a number of traditions floating around involving Alexander and the 'dog' he so admired. Plutarch's *Moralia* claimed Diogenes expired on the same day as Alexander, whilst another writer has him brought before Philip II after the Athenian defeat at Chaeronea; when questioned on his identity Diogenes replied he was 'a spy, to spy upon your insatiability' following which his amused captor set him free.[156] A further story, which proliferated in later works, claimed Alexander found the philosopher rummaging through a pile of bones; when asked why, Diogenes replied: 'I am looking for the bones of your father, but cannot distinguish them from those of a slave.' No doubt allegorical too, it bears the hallmarks of Lucian's *Menippus*, a dialogue featuring the 3rd century Cynic-satirist whose style he often imitated,[157] and it remains highly unlikely that the 'mad Socrates', as Plato called Diogenes, would have been worthy of Alexander's continued esteem.[158]

THE GIRDLE OF HIPPOLYTE

Plutarch was always creative when dealing with a scandal. In a campaign episode that featured the legendary Amazons he named fourteen different sources that either confirmed, or repudiated, Alexander's affair with their tribal queen, Thalestris. Superficially, the incident is quaint and much developed in the *Romance*, however, for our study, it is a tutorial on the grey matter between the black and white.[159] Of those sources cited, five declared for the meeting, and nine, according to Plutarch, maintained it was a fiction. Notably, one of the five was Onesicritus, supposedly an eyewitness to the event. Another was Cleitarchus who likely followed Onesicritus' lead. Surprisingly, one of the nine doubters was Chares the royal usher who had an interest in court *scandaleuse*; Ptolemy and Aristobulus also came down on the side of invention.[160]

Plutarch named six historians who are little known or unique to this passage and their responses, it seems, confirmed it either happened, or it did not. But we need to tread carefully, for in the same passage Plutarch confirmed Alexander *did* write to his Macedonian regent to report his meeting with a Scythian king who offered him his daughter. Moreover, the Macedonians were indeed close to Amazon country, the relevant part of southern Scythia attached to the legend popular since the *Iliad*. Scythian 'warrior women' *are* known to have existed; modern excavation of burial sites prove female warrior bands operated amongst the Sacan nomads, and Amazonomachy (art depicting Greeks fighting Amazons, often equipped with light battle-axes), much of it based on Heracles' Ninth Labour, adorned everything from the Parthenon, the Painted Stoa and the Temple of Zeus at Olympia.[161] Although Plutarch saw the presence of the Scythian king as a vindication of the doubters, it nevertheless confirmed that an event that broadly approximated the reports could have in fact taken place.

Arrian recorded the presence of embassies from various Scythian tribes as Alexander progressed through Asia; when reporting that Atropates, the satrap of Media, sent one hundred women *dressed* as Amazons to the Macedonian king, he reminded us of their frequent appearances in the *Histories* of Herodotus, which recounted Heracles' task of bringing the girdle of their queen, Hippolyte, back to Greece. Arrian concluded with: 'I cannot believe that this race of women never existed at all, when so many authorities have celebrated them.'[162] But regardless of their historicity, if Alexander was presenting himself as a new Achilles, as sources appears to confirm, then the hero needed an encounter with his own Penthesilea, the legendary Amazon queen who turned up to defend Troy and take on the famed warrior.[163] That Alexander seduced an Amazon where Achilles stabbed her instead, did not lessen the romantic parallel. The spectacular shield found in Tomb II at Vergina may in fact bear the imagery of that legendary Trojan encounter as its centrepiece in ivory and gold.[164]

So can we blame Onesicritus for what may amount to a modest embellishment of truth inspired by the Median episode? Upon hearing Onesicritus recount the episode, Lysimachus' cynical quip – 'Where was I then?' – may have been targeted at the thirteen-day tryst Alexander allegedly enjoyed with the queen (assuming Onesicritus covered that too) and not at the meeting itself.[165] Furthermore, Lysimachus' criticism appears singular, which might suggest that on the whole Onesicritus narrated events that were supportable. That itself appears misleading, for we have examples of far more fabulous claims from him concerning the wonders of India: living dragons, three-hundred-year-old elephants and 200-feet-long serpents among them.[166] So we in turn may ask: 'Where were *all* the Macedonians *then*?'

Another of Alexander's famous liaisons involved Cleophis, the mother of the Indian dynast, Assacenus, and whose robust defence of Massaga (today's Swat region of Pakistan) brought her to Alexander's attention.

Latin tradition (only) portrayed Alexander as impressed with her beauty and Justin went as far as claiming he fathered a son with her, also named Alexander, with Cleophis retaining her position through ongoing sexual favours; Curtius simply stated she bore a so-named child. The historicity of the story is, however, clouded by Alexander's massacre of the mercenary contingent of Massaga which 'stained his career'; if, on the other hand, this dishonourable conclusion was Roman-era scandal from Trogus or Timagenes, and recalling Cleopatra's similar seduction of Julius Caesar and Mark Antony, the Cleophis affair may well have inspired the legend behind Alexander's affair with Candace of Meroe in the *Romance*.[167]

Clearly, this genre of 'romantic' material, based on the seductions of, and by, the Macedonian king, has endured in the 'mainstream' accounts. Should 'romances' then be so easily dismissed and relegated behind their 'serious' counterparts? Our point, illustrated from various angles, is that the dividing line between fiction and fact is subtle, like the 'all-too-narrow isthmus' Lucian proposed marked off 'history from panegyric'.[168] And it was often muddied over by the debris of romance, leaving us guessing if we are dealing with plausible impossibilities, or rather, implausible possibilities.

THE KALEIDOSCOPIC BIRTH OF THE LEGEND

What made Alexander's story so ripe for 'romancing' when, as an example, the life of Julius Caesar – paralleled with Alexander's in Plutarch's *Lives* – was not? Certainly without the *thauma*, the marvels developed by the fabulously inclined biographers, Ptolemy's sober military treatise would not have provided sufficient flammable tinder either. It required hagiographies and panegyrics to blow on the fire, and a death in distant Babylon, not on the steps of the Theatre of Pompey in a no-nonsense and fractious Rome. Strabo sensed it when he wrote of Alexander historians: 'These toy with facts, both because of the glory of Alexander and because his expedition reached the ends of Asia, far away from us.'[169] Caesar had in fact stood before the statue of the Macedonian with its outstretched arm in the Temple of Heracles (now Roman Hercules) at Gades, modern Cadiz, when he was quaestor of Hispania Ulterior; vexed at his comparatively slow progress to greatness, he is said to have sighed impatiently. The statue remained standing until the 12th century by which time Arab authors proposed Alexander had himself excavated the Straits of Gibraltar.[170]

Both Caesar and Alexander had understood the need to lay their achievements down in writing when fresh, pliable, and untarnished by partiality and the reasoned balance of hindsight. Alexander had Callisthenes and Onesicritus on the spot to do the job, whereas Caesar himself penned his own Gallic War diaries, '… incomparable models for military dispatches. But histories they are not…' There are ten surviving manuscripts of Caesar's commentaries on the war in Gaul and none of them mentioned the estimated one million slaves taken between 58-51 BCE.[171] But *Quellenforschung* would rule both approaches unfair, a partiality uniquely manifested when the recorder of the episodes was either employed by their architect, or the architect himself; as far as Caesar's *Commentarii*, as Wilkes points out, they 'acquired authority in later years, not because they were invariably more reliable' but because his followers 'could allow no other version to prevail'.[172] Nevertheless, Cicero praised them for their simplicity, straightforwardness and grace, and he found them 'stripped of all rhetorical adornment', so much so that it 'kept men of any sense from touching the subject'.[173] Had Caesar wanted an enduring romance, it seems he ought to have outsourced to an author in Egypt.

Highly readable romances *were* more easily assimilated than the more challenging and often lengthy classical histories, in much the same way that Cleitarchus' Alexander eclipsed the primary sources it subsumed. This was something of a literary Oedipus complex, when the parental work is rejected by the collusion of later sibling texts that were drawn to the story. But it remains impossible to pinpoint Alexander's *Romance* equivalent of 'Chrétien de Troyes', the first writer to mention the Arthurian Holy Grail.[174] Yet, as with the *jongleurs*, the Middle Age troubadours who kept Arthur in circulation, and the authors of the *Four Continuations* who diversified and accessorised the tale, there was probably no single influence that gave the *Romance* its birth, and there would have been a number of 'pre-texts', as Fraser termed them, behind the first edition.[175]

Pearson aptly noted that: 'The distinction between different streams of the tradition is an artificial one… nor is there any fixed rule that a story acquires new miracles or discards them as it grows older: the methods of mythological criticism are not applicable to anecdotes about historical personages.'[176] He was referring to what he termed 'the historical, the rhetorical, the philosophical, the political and the purely romantic publications'.[177] But if the kaleidoscope of colourful protomatter behind the *Greek Alexander Romance* coalesced into focus for a moment, we would likely see Callisthenes' *Praxeis Alexandrou* with its apotheotic spice, Onesicritus' encomium on education replete with the quasi-utopian land of Musicanus (likely a tribe, not a king) and Brahmin sophistry, with Chares and Polycleitus of Larissa, and even Ctesias, in the melting-pot beside them.[178]

Much of their writing had already been synthesised by Cleitarchus into an early colourful account that laid the foundations of the quasi-historical texts that added *dramatikon* and *plasmatikon*, the drama and exaggeration. Toss in the epistolary corpus that Plutarch (and to an extent

Arrian) believed was genuine for extra biographical seasoning (some of it appears to have exonerated Callisthenes from guilt), and then simmer with Nearchus' own Indian *mirabilia* before baking it in the ovens of the *Kynikoi* and *Stoikoi*.[179] We might further season it with Demetrius of Phalerum's *On Fortune*, for it linked God, man and the mercurial nature of divine intervention, and this may also have infiltrated Cleitarchus' texts. The Nectanebo cycle and the Alexandrian Lists were each condiments ground in, and the result, a rich new Hellenistic recipe for the Macedonian king, was 'now not about who Alexander was, but what Alexander meant'.[180]

If all this gave us the cast and the plot, the unique cultural diversity of Alexandria, where Alexander's body now resided, tuned up a script which claimed the corpse's final resting place was apparently prompted by an oracle of Babylonian Bel-Marduk; the god demanded his interment in Memphis, though the local priests thought otherwise.[181] The most influential element was Egypt, as Wallis Budge, an expert in this genre, sensed; *The Demotic Chronicle*, *The Dream of Nectanebo* and *Romance of Sesonchosis* (Alexander is supposed to have declared himself the 'new Sesonchosis'), and many more of the themes that were regurgitated in the *Romance* originated here.[182] Budge's famous acquisition of the Egyptian *Book of the Dead* for the British Museum was a fitting triumph for his career, for he himself was a believer in the paranormal and the occult; perhaps it was a result of his friendship with H Ryder Haggard, whose gothic fantasies recalled genealogies that traced lineages back to the generals of Alexander the Great.[183]

In Hellenistic Alexandria, where Eratosthenes was to place the Prime Meridian when carving up the Earth in longitudinal lines, 'magic' *was* the watchword; the compressed air water pumps and musical instruments of Ctesibius (*floruit* ca. 270 BCE) and later the mechanical devices of Heron (ca. 10-70 BCE) mysteriously opened temple doors and turned visitors into cult believers, anticipating the 'golden age of automata' by almost two millennia.[184] The *Book of Thoth* (a god paralleled to Greek Hermes) inspired the *Corpus Hermeticum,* the book of knowledge in which wisdom was fermented with alchemy, prophesy and prayer-spells. The new arts in thaumaturgy, along with the influential local Jewish predilection for narrating tales, provided a suitably atmospheric set. Josephus, the Jewish scholar, claimed that Alexander had visited Jerusalem, linking him to the Persian Empire-destroying prophecy of the *Book of Daniel*; Ptolemy I, when taking Judea in his Syrian campaigns, ferried captives (many of them willing) back to Egypt to bolster its creative population, and the Jewish Quarter in the eastern section of Alexandria, governed by an ethnarch, became almost as large as the Greek.[185] Scholars estimate that the Jewish population may have comprised ten per cent of the population of Egypt (which was perhaps five million in total) and possibly twenty-five per cent of the population of Alexandria estimated by Diodorus to be 300,000 in his day, excluding slaves.[186]

'For a time, Alexander is lost to the practical, political and military world of the West, having been subsumed into an oriental idyll. His eventual return to the "Western" world is only accomplished with the growth of humanistic studies.'[187] That reality check arrived with *Quellensforschung* when the irreconcilability of East and West was finally put under the microscope, and when any mystique that survived through the Renaissance was finally extinguished. As TB Macaulay neatly put it: 'History commenced among the modern nations of Europe, as it had commenced among the Greeks, in romance.'[188] Macaulay's rather prejudiced methodological treatise, *History*, was published in the *Edinburgh Review* in May 1828 to great critical acclaim, although his *History of England* was described as 'a sad testimonial to the cultural regression of our times';[189] so much then for one of history's own methodological guards. An elitist Europhile, as firmly as Aristotle had been a bigoted xenophobe, Macaulay, nevertheless, provided a relevant historiographical summation that is particularly apt:

> A history in which every particular incident may be true may on the whole be false… the changes of manners and morals, the transition of communities from poverty to wealth, from knowledge to ignorance, from ferocity to humanity – these are, for the most part, noiseless revolutions. Their progress is rarely indicated by what historians are pleased to call important events. They are not achieved by armies, or enacted by senates. They are sanctioned by no treaties, and recorded in no archives…

Of course those 'noiseless revolutions' include the 'important events' that have so far evaded detection: the deceptions, manipulations, interpolations and recreations that remain in history's pockets. For in the 'headlong, dramatic, breathless rush of its narrative', as Braudel termed it, history often fools us into rushing past subtler detail too.[190] In this context it is paradoxical that historians have not further questioned why Alexander has been credited with three conflicting deaths.

One of our chapter-heading quotations comes from Sir William 'Oriental' Jones, who relied on Newton's earlier treatise on biblical chronology when developing his own euhemerist views. As did the *Romance* texts, Jones managed to find a common ground for East and West, though his notions were initially considered politically dangerous to a world that clung to the divide. In his 1786 speech to the Asiatic Society of Bengal, he successfully proposed, for the first time, that many European languages, some of them already identified by Renaissance scholar, Joseph Scaliger (1540-1609), had a common ancestry and additionally shared their roots with certain Asiatic languages; this was a theory already advanced by James Parsons in 1767 in his *The Remains of Japhet, being Historical Enquiries into the Affinity and Origins of the European Languages.* Yet that publication, as the title might suggest, was too tedious to merit serious attention. Jones further argued that these linked languages descended from a lost common ancestor, which, thanks to Thomas Young, we now term 'Indo-European'.[191] Thus he paved the way for further studies into, and an appreciation of, the common heritage and migrations of the Indo-European peoples; no publication has absorbed, or been absorbed by, more of those diverse peoples than the various recensions of *The Greek Alexander.*[192]

A sharp, coherent, and confidently structured Last Will and Testament sits at the conclusion to the *Metz Epitome* and the *Romance* (T1, T2), in contrast to unlikely Vulgate deathbed noises (T6, T7, T8) and the silence of the *Journal* (T3, T4). Have the wrong historical bodies been attached to the wrong biographical heads? If so, how could such a wholesale misinterpretation occur? In part, the question has already been answered: because Alexander's story had its provenance in Alexandria. 'Legends and lies about Alexander were given currency by authors who had actually seen him or accompanied his expedition: there had been no Thucydides to strangle such monsters at birth.'[193] The conqueror of Persia may have bemoaned that he had no Homer to immortalise him, but equally his politics never would have permitted a Thucydides, a Polybius, or even a Tacitus, to set the record straight.

No attempt has been made to reincarnate Alexander's *original* Will, principally because few historians have given credence to the idea that it ever existed, and yet Alexander's intestacy is the mytheme in his mythology, for the testament was too tenacious a tradition to disappear completely. The *Pamphlet* resurrected it, Curtius claimed other historians had mentioned it, Diodorus clearly linked the testament to Rhodian guardianship, and the preservers of the *Metz Epitome*, along with the compiler of the *Kronika Alexandrina*, preferred it over Alexander's alleged silence and his incendiary last words.[194] Nevertheless, Curtius branded the Will nothing more than an imposter, and on the whole the Roman-era historians wrapped their cloaks against the uneasy breeze it arrived upon, deeming it nothing more than romantic driftwood floating past. So it was boat-hooked aboard and into the safe haven of the *Greek Alexander Romance* in whose final chapter still lay a welcoming and empty bed. Truth and romance make unlikely bedfellows, and yet in Alexander's story they never slept apart.

NOTES

1. Herodian 1.1-3, translation by CR Whitaker, London, 1969-70 and quoted in Pitcher (2009) p 40.
2. Green (1974) p 479.
3. Sir William Jones *On the Gods of Hellas, Italy and India* 3.320-322, 1784. Discussion of Jones' work in Lincoln (2002) pp 1-18.
4. Wallis Budge (1896) p VI. Also see Stoneman (1991) pp 14-16 on early Alexandrian literature.
5. Stoneman (1991) pp 8-10 for Egyptian origins of the *Romance*. The *Septuagint* derived its name from the seventy-plus translators who, ancient tradition tells us, worked on the manuscripts; see Casson (2001) p 35. For discussions of the various origins of the *Septuagint* see Jobes-Silva (2001), for the *Corpus Hermeticum* see Copenhaver (1992), Sundberg (1958) pp 205-226 for the *Alexandrian Canon*.
6. A sentiment more recently restated by Momigliano (1966) p 116. Budge's work was published as the *Life and Exploits of Alexander the Great. Ethiopic Histories of Alexander by Pseudo-Callisthenes and other Writers.*
7. Aristander's prophecy is detailed at Arrian 3.1.2, Aelian 12.64 (though here after Alexander's death). Other 'seer' prophecies regarding the city appear at Curtius 4.8.6, Plutarch 26.5-6 and Strabo 17.1.6.
8. Diodorus 18.14.1. Ptolemy apparently found 8,000 talents in the treasury amassed by Cleomenes' tax collections. Cleomenes was eventually executed by Ptolemy, possibly for his Perdiccan sympathies. Heckel (2006) pp 88-89 for 'over-zealous tax collection'.
9. Formerly Heraclion (also known as Thonis) was the dominant seaport positioned on the Nile Delta. Heracles, Paris and Helen are all associated with the city. The city was lost until recent excavations confirmed its legendary status. In ancient texts Heraclion was mentioned by Diodorus 1.9.4, Strabo 17.1.16 and Herodotus 2.113 amongst others.
10. Macaulay (1828).
11. Quoting C Gill in Gill-Wiseman (1993) p 41.
12. Herodian 1.1.3 for a further example. Herodian's *History of the Empire from the time of Marcus* claimed that the portraits of previous imperial biographers were romanced 'because they wanted to give flattering praise to an emperor or a city of a private individual' and yet he, like Thucydides reconstructed their speeches.
13. Sallust *Of Gods and the World* IV. Quintilian 4.44-45 termed Sallust 'terse'.
14. Quoting Pearson (1960) p 9.
15. Quoting Wood from Gill-Wiseman (1993) Prologue xiii and de Polignac (1999) p 3 quoting Goukowsky.
16. Following Stoneman (1991) p 10 on 'a process of accretion'.
17. Müller combined recensions A and B to create a continuous text; see Fraser (1996) pp 205-227 for a useful summary of the *Romance* recensions. Heckel (1988) pp 2-3 for 'peculiarities' and a useful summary of Ausfeld's work.
18. Quoting Stoneman (1991) p 28. Fraser (1996) pp 205-207 for discussion of the origins of the recension A manuscript, p 206 for 'ill-written, lacunose, and interpolated', and p 210 for 'flimsy continuum'.
19. Tarn 1 (1948) p 144 for the numbers of versions and languages.
20. Strabo 11.11.1 reported the expansion of the Hellenistic kingdoms and expeditions that might have travelled as far as the Seres (China) and the Phryni. Pseudo-Lucian *Makrobioi* 5 for living to 300. The Seres were inhabitants of Serica, the land of silk, so China. Strabo 11.11.1 first referred to them, though their whereabouts and cultivation method remained unknown, as evidenced by Pliny 20 *The Seres,* when he referred to the woollen substance as forest-derived.
21. Seneca *Phaedra* and Virgil *Georgics* both referred to silk as a 'tree'. Pliny 11.76 corrected them.
22. Seneca *Declamations* volume 1 for the Senate's edict. Pliny 12.84 for the trade imbalance figure.
23. The loss of geographical knowledge discussed in Fraser (1996) p 86 ff. Pliny named Isidore as 'Dionysius' of Charax.
24. The dactylic hexameter was the poetic meter of the majority of Latin verse of the medieval period, as well as of Homer, Virgil and the Silver Age of Latin; discussion in Townsend (1996) Introduction xxiii. Discussion of the manuscripts and print history of the *Alexandreis* in Townsend (1996) Introduction xi.
25. Discussed in Townsend (1996) p 15 quoting Henry of Ghent's statement on the popularity of the *Alexandreis.*
26. Gautier de Chatillon *Alexandreis* book 3, verses 400-407 and quoting Townsend (1996) Introduction xviii and xxiii.
27. Details of the interpolation authors from discussion in Townsend (1996) p 18.

28. The tradition behind the *Li romans d'Alixandre* discussed in Highet (1949) pp 56-57.
29. The medieval imagery pervades the whole *Alexandreis* poem but good examples of the military adornments can be found in the *Alexandreis* at 4.600-620 and for the envoys 10.265-280.
30. See chapter titled *Hierarchic Historians and Alexandrian Alchemy* for Tarn's criticism of the Roman authors that invented contemporary embassies at Babylon.
31. Full discussion in R Silverberg *The Realm of Prester John*, Ohio University Press, 1996.
32. Eusebius *Historia Ecclesiastica* 3.34.4.
33. Josephus *Jewish Wars* 7.4
34. Josephus *Against Apion* 1.3, 1.11.
35. Josephus 20.8.3.
36. As 'gate' examples Seneca *Epistle* 119.7 '*mundi claustra perrumpit*', Lucretius *De Rerum Natura* 1.70 ff '*effringere portarum claustra*'.
37. As related by Otto of Freising in his *Chronicon*, edited by GH Pertz, *MGH SSRG*, Hanover: Hahn, 1867, VII, 33, pp 334-35; translated by James Brundage in *The Crusades: A Documentary History*, Marquette University Press, Milwaukee 1962.
38. Quoting Stoneman (2012) Introduction p ix, and full discussion through pp xii-xxix. He *Phyllada tou Megalexantrou* is closest to the Middle Greek *Romance* recension.
39. Discussed in Townsend (1996) p 17.
40. Cited in Fortenbaugh-Schütrumpf (2000) p 315 drawing from I During *Aristotle in the Ancient Biographical Tradition*, Studia Graeca et Latina Gothoburgensia, Goteborg, 1957, p 215 and pp 233-234.
41. Quoting Harris (1999) p 78 and Chroust (1970) p 630 for Aristotle's Will in Arabic.
42. R Kipling *Barrack Room Ballads,* 1892. Herodotus' accounts of the Persian invasions illustrated the constant mistrust and friction between East and West. In Greek legend Helle drowned in the strait when fleeing her stepmother, Ino, to Colchis with her brother Phryxus on a golden-fleeced ram; referred to by Pindar, Herodotus, Aeschylus, amongst others.
43. *Beowulf* survives in a single anonymous manuscript residing in the British Library, known as the *Nowell Codex*; following Highet (1949) p 81 for the definition of the Dark Ages.
44. The *Perceforest* link following Roussineau (2001) and the parallels with Arthurian tales discussed in Spencer (2002) pp 207-208.
45. Thorpe (1966) p 17.
46. William of Newburgh *Historia rerum Anglicarum*, Book 1, Preface.
47. Polybius 34.5-7 (and confirmed by Strabo 2.4.1-2) ridiculed Pytheas' journey having himself sailed out of the Pillars of Hercules and questioning sailors on their opinion; Scipio had likely given Polybius a ship to explore beyond the Pillars of Hercules (straits of Gibraltar) after the fall of Carthage; McGing (2010) p 144. Timaeus nevertheless believed Pytheas' account according to Pliny 37.36. His hostility appears unfounded; discussed further in chapter titled *Lifting the Shroud of Parrhasius*. Plutarch *Solon* 31.3-32.1 recorded that Solon was embarking on a work about Atlantis using information he heard from the men of Sais, but this may be Plato's own imagination at work, 'eager to adopt and adorn the fable'… 'as if it were the soil of a fair estate unoccupied'. Diodorus 3.54-55, 56.1 and 60-61 for one example of the legend of the Atlantians.
48. See discussion of Hittite finds in Wood (1985) chapter 6.
49. In a passage of the *Quadriga tyrannorum* the *Historia Augusta* accuses Marius Maximus of being a producer of a 'mythical history' or *mythistoricis*. See Syme (1971) p 76 for discussion.
50. See Momigliano (1966) p 40 for discussion of Gibbon and the *Historia Augusta*.
51. Following Syme (1971) p 279. The connection is that the tales in the vernacular languages derived from Latin were usually about chivalric adventure, hence 'romance'.
52. Following the dates in Momigliano (1966) p 145 and Momigliano (1977) p 121 for the *Origo gentis Romanae*.
53. See Pitcher (2009) p 29 for discussion on the spurious sources used by the *Historia Augusta*; also Syme (1971) and Baynes (1926). Momigliano (1966) p 147 for the 130 documents cited and their breakdown and groupings. Quoting Momigliano (1966) p 145 and pp 143-166 for the authenticity of the *Historia Augusta*. His full dissection of the *Historia Augusta* can be read in Momigliano (1954) pp 22-46.
54. Gibbon (1776 to 1789) Volume 1 p xvii. Gibbon's work was first to give the reader detailed subtext, the precursor to the modern use of footnotes; for his use of the *Historia Augusta* see introduction by Leckie (1906). For Gibbon and source analysis see Momigliano (1966).
55. Gibbon's own testimony in Preface to Volume 4, in Womersley (1994) p 520. The implausibilities within the *Historia Augusta* are also discussed in Pitcher (2009) p 153. The quote is from Momigliano (1954) p 23.
56. Quoting from Mallory (1989) p 9. The work was published broadly between 1736 and 1765. It was a multi-authored compendium of contributions.
57. Callisthenes, Ephorus, Damastes, Phylarchus and Duris agreed Ilium fell on the 24th of

Thargelion (May-June). Full discussion in Lincoln (2002) pp 1-18. Apollodorus and the so-called *Canon of Ptolemy* also dated the fall of Troy. Fragments from ancient historians suggested the following dates BCE: Duris 1334, *Life of Homer* 1270, Herodotus ca. 1240, Cleitarchus 1234, Dicearchus 1212, *Parian Chronicle* 1209, Thrasyllus 1193, Timaeus 1193, Eratosthenes and his disciples (Apollodorus, Castor, Diodorus, Apollonius, Eusebius) 1184/3; Sosibius 1171, Phanias ca. 1129, Ephorus ca. 1135; detail taken from Mylonas (1964) p 353.

58. Full discussion in B Lincoln (1987) pp 1-18.
59. Whear's methodology discussed in chapter titled *Classicus Scriptor, Rhetoric and Rome.*
60. Caspar (1993) pp 308-328 and for the sentencing of Kepler's mother, pp 300-301.
61. Quoting Lincoln (2002) p 17.
62. Full discussion of Euhemerus' whereabouts in Winiarczyk (2013) p 3.
63. Discussed in Thomas (1968) p 259. Euhemerus wrote his *Sacred History* and expounded his 'rationalising method of interpretation', known as Euhemerism, at the court of Cassander. He treated mythology as a reflection of real historical events, reshaped over time and according to the social mores of the day. See discussion in Brown (1946) pp 259-274 and chapter titled *Mythoi, Muthodes and the Birth of Romance.*
64. Most of what we know about Euhemerus' work is preserved in references in Diodorus 5.41-46 and 6.1.
65. Rome's use of Euhemerism discussed in Walbank (1981) p 219.
66. Quoting and following Highet (1949) p 520.
67. Green (1974) p 479.
68. Milton *Paradise Lost* 11.399-401. See Kings 1.9:28, 1.10.11, 1.22.48, Chronicles 1.29: Chronicles 2. 8:18; 9:10 for expeditions to Ophir and the recurring mention of gold. CEV Crawford *Treasure of Ophir*, Skeffington and Son Ltd, 1929 for the link to Dhofar.
69. Herodotus 2.29.1-2; following Burstein (1976) p 142; *Job* 28.19 as example of biblical references.
70. Herodotus 2.17-34 for digression on the mysteries of the Nile.
71. Burstein (1976) pp 135-136 for Aristotle's lost work on the Nile floods. Aristotle's *Meteorologika* touched on Ethiopian rains and p 137 ff for the expedition. Strabo 15.1.17-19 for Aristoboulos' text on Nile floods. Arrian 7.15.4 for Ethiopian ambassadors. Seneca *Naturales Quaestiones* 4a, *De Nilo* 2.11. Diodorus 1.37 covered previous opinions which he attacked as inventions.
72. Diodorus 1.37 and 3.36 for Ptolemy II *Philadelphos* journeying to the Upper Nile and into Ethiopia. Bagnall-Derow (2004) p 250 for a papyrus detailing the elephant hunters. The length of the Attic cubit is not established for certain.
73. Diodorus 3.36.1 for 100-cubit-long snakes, 3.36 for the length of the live python at Alexandria, 3.39.9 for the ability of the pythons to devour bulls, oxen and bring down elephants. For Ptolemy's hunting expeditions 3.36-39. The Attic cubit at 18.25 inches was longer than the Macedonian cubit of 14 inches. Arrian 3.2.7 for the deportation of pro-Persian tyrants from the Aegean islands to Elephantine.
74. See full discussion of the comparison between Solomon and Ptolemy II *Philadelphos* in Bevan (1927) pp 76-78.
75. This appeared as an epitaph by Theodore Roosevelt in the *American Museum Journal*, volume 18, no. 5, 1918, pp 321-330, some months after Selous had been killed in January 1917.
76. The Greek Dark Age is deemed to have ended ca. 750 BCE when the first alphabetic inscriptions appeared.
77. See discussion of the Epic Cycle in Shelmerdine (1995) p 2. For the catalogue of ships that set sail for Troy see Homer *Iliad* 2.494-759. Thucydides 1.10.4 for his suspicions of Herodotus' numbers and fidelity.
78. Discussion in Wood (1985) p 147 and fuller discussion of the Ahhiyawa in Bryce (1977) who links them to the Trojans but with Greek affiliations.
79. The Siege of Lachish wall relief in Sennacherib's palace at Nineveh clearly shows different types of siege engines.
80. From the Planudean Appendix to the *Greek Anthology* 16.298; discussion in J Martinez (2011) p 15.
81. Quoting Borchardt (1986).
82. Quoting West (2008) Introduction xx.
83. By the 6th century BCE the Homeric epics and *Homeric Hymns* were recited at the festival of Panathenaia in Athens; Shelmerdine (1995) p 8.
84. Full discussion on the authenticity of the lives of Homer in Allen (1912) pp 250-260.
85. Author's transmission of the anonymous *Greek Anthology* 16.293.
86. Horace *Ars Poetica* lines 358-359. Mistakes can be reviewed in Homer's *Iliad* at book 5 lines 576-579 and book 13 lines 643-665. Fitzgerald (1998) p xii for the multiple-author theory behind the *Odyssey.*
87. Neoanalysis is the study of the relationship between the two Homeric epics and the extent to

which Homer made use of earlier poetic material and vice versa.

88. So-called due to the innumerable battles fought in the Peloponnese, thus the 'dancing floor of Ares', the god of war.

89. Herodotus 1.82 for the battle of champions and 1.82.8 for the last survivor. The factual basis of myths is discussed in Wood (2005). Jason's journey it is suggested is a tale of Greek colonisation of the Black Sea coast. For the battles at Thyrea see discussion in Lenden (2005) p 11. The remains of the Sacred Band are said to lie beneath the Lion of Chaeronea; excavation revealed 254 skeletons laid out in seven rows; Pausanias 9.40.10 reported that there was no inscription on the lion monument which represented a common grave for the Thebans. Strabo 9.2.37 also reported a 'public tomb' was erected near the battlefield; Hanson (1991) p 43 for discussion.

90. Hammond (1989) p 217 and (1994) p 217 for discussion of the tumulus excavations at Chaeronea and weapons found in the tumulus. A 'trophy' to the dead was confirmed at Diodorus 16.86.6. Plutarch *Life of Pelopidas* 18.5 for Philip's words. Lenden (2005) p 109 for Theban emulation of Spartan lovers standing side by side.

91. Pausanias 9.40.10.

92. Herodotus 8.98 for the motto though here relating to the Persian messaging system.

93. A *hemerodrome* was literally a 'day runner', a messenger employed to bear news from one city to another. Pheidippides is mentioned in Herodotus 6.105-107 as the messenger sent to Sparta; in Lucian's *A Slip of the Tongue in Greeting* 3 and Pliny 7.20.84 he is named Philippides. The poem of the same name by Robert Browning in 1879 suggested Pheidippides died upon delivering a victory speech at Athens. There is no historical basis for that. The tradition goes back through Lucian to Plutarch and before him to Heracleides of Pontus. Plutarch *On the Fame of the Athenians* 347c named him Thersippus or Eucles who expired on the spot in full armour. Euchidas is said to have died after running to Delphi; see Frost (1979) pp 159-163.

94. Quoting Plutarch *Solon* 32.1; he was actually referring to Plato's (and Solon's) Atlantis.

95. For a discussion of numbers see Flower (1998). Herodotus 7.202-203 mentioned 3,100 varied Peloponnesians and 1,100 from Thebes (400) and Thespiae (700), the largest contingent from a single Greek city. Herodotus 7.205.2 only mentions the 300 Spartans chosen by Leonidas but later quotes an epitaph at 7.228.1 suggesting 4,000 Peloponnesians fought in the battle, including 3,000 other Greeks, thus 1,000 Lacedaemonians were present but as 700 departed before the battle only 300 were ever mentioned; Diodorus 11.4.5 suggested 1,000 Lacedaemonians as did Isocrates *Panegyrikos* 90, *Archidamas* 99, so Herodotus may well have been at least 700 short on numbers (900 if his epitaph is accurate). Herodotus 7.224 for the battlefield inscription which may have provided names; Pausanias 3.14.1 claimed a pillar at Sparta listed the names. In addition 1,000 Phocians and the entire fighting force of the Opuntian Locrians were summoned; we do not know whether they arrived, though the five epitaphic *stelae* mentioned by Strabo included them. Diodorus 11.8.5-11.10.3 for the Spartan night attack that almost killed Xerxes; discussed in Flower (1998).

96. See Herodotus 7.56-137 for a summary of the Persian troops and Xerxes' discussion with the exiled Spartan king, Demaratus. Plutarch *Laconian Sayings* 51.11 for *molon labe*. Herodotus 7.219.1-7.221 for Megistias and his son. Quoting Russell (1946) p 471 on Sparta.

97. The *Suda* stated that Tyrtaeus wrote a constitution for the Spartans (though probably not the *Eunomia* referred to in Aristotle *Politics* 5.6.1306b36) and encouraged them in war against the Messenians through his war songs. Jaeger (1939) pp 85-95 for discussion of Tyrtaeus and his influence. Plato *The Law* 629a for the hostile rumour that Tyrtaeus was a lame Athenian schoolmaster, likely Attic propaganda.

98. In contrast to the view we propose, Tarn (1939) p 128 was adamant that neither Alexander nor Aristotle were aware of the work of Herodotus.

99. For reference to Apple Bearers see Polyaenus 4.3.24. Scholars believe Alexander's historians used this term for the crack regiment, due to the counter-weights on their spear butts. An explanation of 'Apple Bearers' also appeared in Athenaeus 12.514b-c drawing from Heracleides of Cyme's *Persika*. Pausanias 10.19.9 ff gives one explanation of why they may have been known as 'Immortals' as casualty numbers were immediately replaced to keep the total number static.

100. Mark Twain (SL Clemens) *A Horse's Tale*, 1907, Preface.

101. Quote from Kimball (2000) p 4 for 'first slashing review'. Gibbon branded Herodotus a liar in his *Decline and Fall of the Roman Empire* suggesting he never visited Babylon. For Gibbon's quote see Grant (1995) p 61.

102. Grant (1995) p 57. Plutarch became a Priest of Apollo. Herodotus showed bias against the Boeotians, Corinthians and other Greek states.

103. Momigliano (1966) p 133.

104. Flower (1994) p 28 for the possible motives behind Theopompus' epitome of Herodotus.

105. Quoting Jaeger (1939) p 383 for Herodotus blending the scientist with the rhapsode. Herodotus 7.152 and echoed again at 2.123 and 4.5; compare to Curtius 9.1.34; see discussion in Baynham (1998) p 86.

106. Quoting Momigliano (1966) p 129 and p 134.
107. Plutarch 6-7. Chares, as recorded by Aulus Gellius 5.2.1, did record the sum paid for the horse (13 talents) and the derivation of the name (ox-head), due to the shape of its head, but nothing of its taming. Arrian 5.19.5 attributed the name to a brand mark or white mark on its head; the *Romance* 1.15 suggested its haunch. See full fragment in Robinson (1953) p 85. The *Romance* 3.33 made the comparisons of Alexander and Bucephalus to Bellerophon and Pegasus. See discussion of the taming of Bucephalus in Baynham *Romance* (1995). Plutarch 5.1-4 for Alexander's quizzing of Persian envoys. Quoting Green (1974) p 43.
108. Quoting Powell (1939) p 230; Samuel (1986) pp 433-435 for discussion of the letters in Plutarch's biography of Alexander.
109. Alexander spoke to Bucephalus at the point of his death and recognised that the horse had shared his fate, except in death, *Romance* 3.33. Whitmarsh (2002) p 180 draws the comparison to Plato's *Phaedra*.
110. Quoting Plutarch 42.1, translation by I Scott-Kilvert, Penguin Classics edition, 1973. Plutarch cited many letters unique to accounts of Alexander. He may have been quoting from other historians rather than the letters themselves but an intimacy with them is suggested that points to the latter. In Plutarch *Life of Alexander* the historian referred to personal letters of Alexander he had read or knew the contents of at 7.6, 8.1, 17.8, 19.5-8, 20.9, 22.2, 22.5, 27.8, 39.4, 39.7, 39.13, 42.1, 46.3, 47.3, 55.6, 55.7, 60.1, 60.11, 68.4. No other historian seems to have had access to them, and how genuine they were remains open to speculation. Arrian 7.12.5, Justin 12.14.3 mentioned slanders from Olympias in letter form.
111. The Hamburg and Florence papyri discussed in Pearson (1960) p 258 and Pearson (1955) p 448 for the Oxyrhynchus papyri. Quoting Powell (1939) p 230 for the earliest sign of the epistolary corpus. Cicero *De Officiis* 2.14.48 for the epistolary corpus; Marasco (2011) p 45 for other references.
112. Cicero *De Officiis,* Book 2, *Expediency*. Arrian 6.1.4 and 7.12.4-7 for examples of a letter from Alexander to Olympias and Antipater that Arrian believed to be genuine.
113. 'Impostures' is a term suggested by Rosenmayer in *Ancient Epistolary Fictions*, Cambridge University Press, 2001, and discussed in Ehrman (2014) p 44.
114. The epistolary collections are discussed in Gudeman *Greeks* (1894) pp 64-65.
115. Following the comments of Arthur-Montagne (2014) p 1 on the breadth of epistolary forms in the *Romance*; and p 3 for the reference to Pseudo-documentarism, a term emanating with William Hansen. For discussion of Mereklbach's 1954 work p 20. For full discussion of the epistolary corpus in the *Romance* see Arthur-Montagne (2014) pp 1-31.
116. Riedweg (2002) p 27. Also Teresi (2002) and Dalley (2013) p 58 for attributions to Pythagoras and the sources of his knowledge.
117. Porphyry *Life of Pythagoras*.
118. Diogenes Laertius *Plato* 1.
119. Plutarch *Symposiacs* Book VIII and Cicero *On the Nature of the Gods* 3.88 for the Pythagorean notes.
120. Petrarch found a corpus of unknown correspondence by Cicero in Verona in 1345; Highet (1949) p 83. Nepos *Atticus* 16.3 for the widespread publication of Cicero's work.
121. Gudeman *Romans* (1894) p 148 for a discussion on the Ciceronian forgeries, the *Epistola Ciceronis ad Octavianum,* for example.
122. Plutarch *Caesar* 2.3. Plutarch confirmed both men were pupils of the rhetorician. Highet (1949) p 84 for discussion of Petrarch's letter to Cicero. Momigliano (1977) p 80 for Petrarch's letter to Livy.
123. Discussed in Dalley-Oleson (2003). See Dalley (1994) pp 52-53 for references to the *Alammitu* palm that was used to depict a spiral screw device. Diodorus was ambiguous in his connecting the Egyptian screw with Archimedes; see Dalley (2013) pp 56-57 quoting Diodorus 1.34.2. Neither Strabo, Vitruvius nor Philo of Byzantium linked Archimedes to the screw device.
124. Aristotle *Meteorology* 1.14.25, Strabo 17.1.25, Pliny 6.33.165 for origins with Sesotris. Herodotus 2.158, Aristotle *Meteorology* 1.14 P 352b, Strabo 17.1.25, Pliny 6.33.166 ff for Darius I. Diodorus 1.33, Herodotus 2.158-159 for Necho II. The same authors (except Pliny) claim it was only completed by Ptolemy II *Philadelphos*.
125. Arrian 5.6.5 and Homer *Odyssey* 4.477 and 4.581 for the original name of the Nile and origins of Egypt.
126. Aristotle *Meteorology* 1.14.25.
127. For details of Ptolemaic irrigation in the region see DJ Thompson, *Irrigation and Drainage in the Early Ptolemaic Fayum*, in A Bowman and E Rogan (editors), *Agriculture in Egypt from Pharaonic to Modern Times*, Oxford University Press, (1999), pp 107-122.
128. Chugg (2002) p 8 for the population of Alexandria in Napoleonic times.
129. Plutarch *Coriolanus* 1.1. Most vividly described in Livy 2.33-35, Dionysius of Halicarnassus *Roman Antiquities* book 7, and Plutarch *Coriolanus*.

130. Livy 5.1.3 recorded that the Etruscan city of Veii fell to the Romans when the Etruscans abandoned her due to her continued kingships. Whether factual of a reflection of Roman opinion of monarchy is debatable. See Barker-Rasmussen (2000) for full discussion.

131. Virgil's *Aeneid* developed the story in Naevius' *Bellum Punicum* in which Aeneas journeyed from Troy to found Rome. Ennius' *Annales* followed (Fabius Pictor used the theme). Aeneas was supposedly the maternal grandfather of Romulus. Boardman (1964) p 207 for the tomb paintings. Herodotus 1.94 for Etruscan origins.

132. Herm (1975) p 191 for discussion of the Etruscan link. Recent gene tests suggest racial similarities between likely Etruscan descendants and Western Anatolian stock. This was originally thought a link to Lydia but linguistic evidence argues against it and against the claim at Herodotus 1.94 that Etruscans were migrated Lydians. Boardman (1964) p 199 for Greek opinion of Etruscan origins.

133. Quoting M Pallottino in his review of DH Lawrence's 1986 reprint of the 1927 *Etruscan Places*, Olive Press, London, pp 13-14.

134. Suetonius *Caligula* 52, Cassius Dio 59.17.3; there is however no evidence Caligula visited Egypt as an adult.

135. Strabo 13.1.27: 'This is not the site of ancient Ilium, if one considers the matter in accordance with Homer's account'; translated by HC Hamilton and W Falconer, published by Henry G Bohn, London, 1854.

136. Quoting D Feeney from Raeburn-Feeney (2004) Introduction xxix for 'compendium of myth'. Diogenes Laertius *Pythagoras* 4. It was Heracleides of Pontus who made the claim of reincarnation. Ovid *Metamorphoses* book 15 lines 160-175 for references to Pythagoras' reincarnation and recollections of the Trojan War.

137. Arrian 1.11.8, 6.9.3, 6.10.2 for Alexander taking the shield from the Trojan War from the temple of Trojan Athena. Homer 16.786-16.85. *Hoplon* is the route of Hoplite, and was the shield carried by Greek infantry. Otherwise called an *aspis*, a more generic term for a shield. The fall of Troy dated back past 1,100 BCE.

138. Suetonius *Nero* 19.

139. Suda α 1128= FGrH 618 T2.

140. Nero's career discussed in detail in chapter titled *Comets, Colophons and Curtius Rufus*.

141. Dio Crysostom *Discourses* 21: *On Beauty*, translation from the Loeb Classical Library edition, 1939.

142. Discussed in detail by Champlin (2003) pp 10-13.

143. Cassius Dio 80.18.1-3.

144. See Champlin (2003) 12-16 for relevant extracts from the *Sibylline Oracles*. St Augustine *City of God* 20.19.

145. Suetonius *Nero* 51, translation from the Loeb Classical Library edition, 1914.

146. Suetonius *Nero* 35 and the fragmentary *Lucan* in his partly extant *Illustrious Writers,* and from Statius' *Silvae* 2.7. Nero claimed they were both implicated in the conspiracy plot of Piso. Tacitus 15.60-64 for Seneca cutting his veins.

147. For the various accusations of matricide and reporting of Agrippina's death see see Tacitus 14.1-8, Suetonius *Nero* 34 and Cassius Dio 63.11-14. Seneca allegedly amassed a fortune according to Tacitus 13.42.4 and Cassius Dio 61.10.3 and 61.14.3 has 400,000,000; discussed in Finlay (1973) p 56. As a broad guide, one million *sestertii* at current gold prices (it was linked in value to the gold aureus) translates to over three million US dollars.

148. The *Pharsalia* was actually labelled *De Bello Civile, On the Civil War* in the manuscripts.

149. Tacitus 15.49 claimed Nero became jealous and banned Lucan's poems; according to Suetonius' *Lucan*, Nero lost interest in his poet friend who responded by insulting the emperor. Both Vacca's *Life of Lucan* and Statius' *Silvae* 2.7 refer to the contents of Lucan's *De Incendiis Urbis*. Lucan's treatment of Alexander discussed in chapter titled *Classicus Scriptor, Rhetoric and Rome* and his death in chapter titled *Comets, Colophons and Curtius Rufus*.

150. Plutarch 55-56 for the various reports of Callisthenes' death. The caging seems extreme but Curtius 7.1.5 did report that Alexander Lyncestis was caged for three years after his sentencing for treason; possibly also Vulgate fabrication. Justin 15.3 and Arrian 4.14.1-4 for other reports of chaining and torture. Athenaeus 434d, Plutarch *Moralia* 454e (*On Control of Anger*) for Callisthenes' refusal to drink; its authenticity is questionable; see discussion in Brunt (1974) p 67. The Loeb Classical Library edition, 1939, footnote on another interpretation reads: 'A jibe at Alexander's assumed divinity', Alexander taking the place of Dionysus, the wine god, until the physician god, Asclepius, would have to be called in; on the authenticity of the story see Macurdy, *Jour. Hell. Stud.* (1930), pp 294-297.

151. Preserved by Plutarch 14.1-6 and *Moralia* 331f or *Fortune* 10 and Diogenes Laertius 6.38 *Diogenes*, Cicero *Tusculan Disputations* 5.32.

152. See Brown (1949) pp 27-28 for the background to the dialogue between Alexander and Diogenes.

153. Diogenes Laertius *Diogenes* 40 and 60 for examples of publicly being called a 'dog'.
154. It remains unclear exactly what he was charged with. Diogenes Laertius *Diogenes* 74 for his life in slavery. *Diogenes* 6.20 suggested his father was a banker or moneychanger (*trapezites*) and he became involved in a scandal concerning the defacing of currency; possibly a political statement. A number of defaced currencies from Sinope and dating to the middle of the 4th century BCE had been discovered; discussion in Seltman 1938. Finlay (1973) pp 166-167 for the treatment of those charged with debasing currency.
155. Diogenes Laertius *Diogenes* 63 for *kosmopolites*. Various traditions given by Diogenes Laertius *Diogenes* 1.1 involved Diogenes with tampering with the currency of Sinope, which caused both him and his father to flee. Alternative versions blame his father and others still have Diogenes claiming he was persuaded to the act by artisans, when he was one of the curators. He apparently consulted Apollo at Delphi or Delos on whether he should undertake the scam.
156. Diogenes Laertius *Diogenes* 6 and 79 and Plutarch *Moralia* 717c for Diogenes' death.
157. Lucian *Menippus* 15 contained a scene depicting the piles of bones found in the underworld, where heroes and villains lay indistinguishable. Menippus appears to have provided much detail on Diogenes' life to later doxographers.
158. Diogenes Laertius *Diogenes* 6.54; Aelian 14.33 for the comparison to a 'mad' Socrates.
159. Plutarch 46.1-3 for Thalestris' meeting with Alexander; also Curtius 6.5.24-32, Justin 12.4.5-7, Diodorus 17.77.1-3. Justin provided an alternative name, Minithyha.
160. See discussion of the episode in Hammond (1993) pp 293-294.
161. *The Women Warriors – the Sarmatians,* The Circle of Ancient Iranian Studies and Archaeological and Cultural News: 'Amazon graves found in what is today known as Kazakhstan', 2001. More detail from the archeologist, Jeannine Kimball-Davis can be found at CSEN.org. Also Bosworth *A in the East* (1996) p 81 for the female warriors amongst Sacan nomads. Arrian 4.15.2-5 suggested this was close to Colchis on the Black Sea, where Curtius 6.5.24-26 for example suggested Hyrcania in the plains of the River Thermodon. Fully detailed in Mayor (2014) pp 34-52. It is also worth noting that over 112 weaponry-filled graves of Scythian women aged sixteen to thirty, previously identified as men, have been discovered at tombs between the Danube and River Don; see Antikas-Wynn Antikas (2014) p 7. Tarbell (1920) for the Amazonomachy in Greece. Hanson (1991) p 25 for Amazon light battle-axes.
162. Arrian 7.13.2-6 for the Amazon affair. Arrian 4.15.2-5 for the earlier encounter with the Scythians and offers of marriage with the daughter of the Scythian king or the regional chiefs. Following the observation in Heckel (2006) p 61 concerning Atropates. Arrian 7.13.1-4; 4.1-3,7.15.4 for further embassies from Scythians.
163. See chapter titled *The Reborn Wrath of Peleus' Son* for Alexander's emulation of Achilles. Quintus of Smyrna *Posthomerika* 18 ff for Penthesilea's arrival at Troy and Diodorus 2.46 for her legend; Pseudo-Apollodorus *Epitome of the Bibliotheke* 5.1 for her death at Achilles' hand. Pausanias 10.31.1 and 5.11.2 for the art that suggested Achilles repented the death of a woman he had fallen for.
164. Borza-Palagia (2007) p 114 for the decoration on the shield found in Tomb II.
165. Plutarch 46.4-5 for the episode involving Onesicritus and Lysimachus; more in chapter titled *Hierarchic Historians and Alexandrian Alchemy*. For Alexander's thirteen-day tryst with Thalestris, Justin 12.3.7, Curtius 6.5.32, Diodorus 17.77.3.
166. Aelian 16.39 for dragons; Strabo 15.1.43 for 300 and 500-year-old elephants; Strabo 15.1.28 for 180 cubit long snakes.
167. Curtius 8.10.32-36 for the whole Cleophis affair and siege of Massaga; *Metz Epitome* 45 for Cleophis' beauty, and Justin 12.7.9-11 for the further scandal. See Heckel (2006) pp 90-91 and the Curtius, Penguin Classics edition, 1984, p 294 footnote 68 for discussion of its authenticity. *Romance* 3.18-24 for the Candace episode. For the massacre of the mercenaries at Massaga see Diodorus 17.84.1-6 for the most damning version though it was captured by Plutarch 59.6-7; Arrian 4.28.7-4.30.4 claimed Alexander killed them as they planned to desert. Quoting Plutarch 59.6.
168. Lucian *How to write History* 7.
169. Strabo 11.6.4.
170. Suetonius *Julius Caesar* 7. De Polignac (1999) p 1 for the Arab tradition and the Straits of Gibraltar.
171. Quoting Macaulay (1828) Plutarch *Caesar* 15.5, Appian *Celtica* 1.2 for the one million slaves.
172. See Pitcher (2009) p 81 for discussion, taking Asinius Pollio's criticism cited in Suetonius *Julius Caesar* 56.4; and quoting Wilkes (1972) p 186.
173. Suetonius *Julius Caesar* 56.2-3; Suetonius was quoting from Cicero's *Brutus* 262.
174. Chrétien de Troyes was the author of *Perceval*.
175. The Arthurian origins discussed in Duggan (2001) p 48. *Perceval* was continued by four later writers, the later chapters known as the *Four Continuations*. The professional storytellers who

maintained the oral tradition were known as *jongleurs*. Fraser (1996) p 210 for 'pre-texts'. General discussion of what the pre-texts were in pp 211-227.

176. Pearson (1960) p 157.
177. Pearson (1960) p 262.
178. Brown (1949) p 54 contends Musicanus was a people, not a person or king.
179. The influences are well discussed in Stoneman (1994), Introduction. For Ctesias' tales from India see discussion in Pitcher (2009) p 155. Pearson (1955) p 446 for the letters suggesting Callisthenes had no accomplices in the conspiracy of the pages. Plutarch 55.6 for the letters to Craterus, Attalus and Alcetas in which the pages named no accomplices; thus suggesting Callisthenes' innocence.
180. Quoting K Dowden *Pseudo Callisthenes. The Alexander Romance* (2008) cited in and following the argument of Arthur-Montagne (2014) p 11.
181. *Romance* 3.34.106 for the oracles determining the fate of the body.
182. Discussion in Schmeling (1996) p 665.
183. In *Ayesha, The Return of She* Haggard developed the characters Khan Rassen and his wife, the Khania Atene, who claimed to be descendants of the generals of Alexander the Great.
184. The so-called 'golden age of automata' refers to the period broadly spanning 1860 to 1910 which itself followed the earlier 19th century automata exported in great quantities to China.
185. See Stoneman (1991) pp 14-17 for discussion. Recensions 'e' and 'g' of the *Romance* include this detail. For Alexander's visit to Jerusalem see Josephus 11.329-335 and 12.3-10 for Ptolemy's captives. The Jewish Quarter of Alexandria discussed in Vrettos (2001) pp 6-7.
186. Discussion of the numbers in *Philo of Alexandria, Philo's Flaccus, The first Pogrom,* PW van der Horst, Brill, 2003, p 136.
187. Quoting Spencer (2002).
188. Macaulay (1828).
189. The opinion of Himmelfarb (1986) p 163.
190. Braudel (1949) p 27.
191. See discussion on the works of Parsons and Jones in Mallory (1989) pp 13-14. Parsons' credibility was also undermined by his claim that the languages of the North American Indians were Japhetic too, in other words related to Japheth, one of the sons of Noah. Parsons additionally concluded the route language was Irish Magogian.
192. Discussed in Lincoln (2002) pp 1-18.
193. Quoting Pearson (1960) p 5.
194. The *Metz Epitome* is essentially Vulgate in style and hence probably Cleitarchus-derived though the source of the unique information it provides is problematic. See Heckel-Yardley (1997) XXII-XXIII for discussion.

5

CLASSICUS SCRIPTOR, RHETORIC AND ROME

Did the Roman-era historians faithfully preserve the detail they found in the accounts of Alexander's contemporaries?

The surviving biographies of Alexander and his successors are the output of the Roman-era. These are 'secondary' or even 'tertiary' sources whose testimony may have come to us through intermediary historians, some of them still anonymous. They were products of a no-less challenging environment than their Greek and Macedonian predecessors, as Rome's republic was transformed into an empire and free speech all but disappeared. Vulnerable to the censorship of warring dictators or a lengthening imperial shadow, these writers overlaid their own contemplations, biases and ideologies – and inevitably those of the state – on the story of Alexander.

We look at the effects of the prevailing doctrines and rhetoric to appreciate the extent to which Alexander was misrepresented, misinterpreted or simply mishandled by the Roman-era historians.

'It is hardly surprising if this material [the polished arrangement of words] has not yet been illustrated on this language, for not one of our people dedicated himself to eloquence, unless he could shine in court cases and in the forum. The most eloquent of the Greeks, however, removed from judicial cases, applied themselves first to other matters and then especially to writing history.'[1]

Quoting Marcus Antonius in Cicero *De Oratore*

'Eusebius, like any other educated man, knew what proper history was. He knew that it was a rhetorical work with a maximum of invented speeches and a minimum of authentic documents.'[2]

Arnaldo Momigliano *Essays in Ancient and Modern Historiography*

'This is not the site of ancient Ilium, if one considers the matter in accordance with Homer's account.'[3]

Strabo *Geography*

The city of Troy is still referred to as 'legendary'. Yet Thucydides, Arrian, and Alexander, who commenced his campaign with sacrifices at what were presented to him as the tombs of his Homeric heroes, were never in any doubt of its past glory.[4] Neither were the historians and geographers who dated the fall of the city anywhere from 1184 to 1334 BCE based upon the Dorian occupation of the Peloponnese supposedly two generations after.[5]

Modern excavations of the remains of the hill at Hissarlik in northwest Anatolia suggest some accuracy to Homeric geography, and this argues for Heinrich Schliemann's 1868 dissertation *Ithaka, der Peloponnes und Troja*, in which 'the father of Bronze Age archaeology' first claimed his Trojan find, though the diplomat-archaeologist, Frank Calvert, and before him the geologist, Charles Maclaren, had significantly pointed the way.[6] Yet the modest scale of the fortified mound, as Strabo's *Geography* noted, argues against its fabled size. Moreover, archaic references to Troy remain somewhat ambiguous.

Dardanus (a son of Zeus and Electra) was supposedly the founder of an eponymous settlement (Dardania) in the Troad and also a tribe, the Dardanoi, who were referred to interchangeably as Trojans in some sources. But the nearby city of Troy was known to the Greeks of the classical world as both Ilios and Troia (or Trosia) after two of Dardanus' descendants, Ilos and Tros. Wilusiya and Taruisa, two states comprising the Assuwan Confederacy listed in Hittite texts, remain contenders for the site whose origins were lost along with Greek knowledge of the Hittite Empire itself. References scattered through the texts of Herodotus and Strabo provide an interwoven genealogy of the tribes of Asia Minor, many with links to Crete as well as the legendary city, apparently justifying Homer's inclusion of Cretans, Lycians, Ionians and Paphlagonians among the diverse allies in the defence of Troy.

Schliemann himself was not good at differentiating fact from legend and he has since been termed a 'pathological liar'.[7] Nine distinct 'cities' have now been identified in the Hissarlik mound and none has turned up a definitive link to the citadel of Priam. The last settlement, Novum Ilium, was planted by Rome, no doubt to reinforce her own ancestral claims.[8] Rome was warned of rebuilding on the soil of Troy lest she suffer the same ill-fated fortune, and true to the prophecy, like its breached walls and the vaster empire of Alexander, her borders were to crumble and her temples were to fall.[9]

Alexander and Rome shared a common heritage and one symbolically apt for our claims. But if a homogenous metropolis had once existed in the Troad, does that mean the decade-long battle to bring its walls down was truly acted out? If the Epic Cycle is endemic to the recounting of Alexander's deeds, it is a historical fusion that raises many questions. We know the Macedonian conqueror lived, but just as with the crumbled ruins at Hissarlik, do we have the genuine article, or are we treading the literary foundations of later Roman construction?

A plate titled 'View of Hissarlik from the North. *Frontispiece*. After the Excavations. From the publication *Troy and Its Remains. A Narrative of Researches and discoveries made on the site of Ilium, and in the Trojan Plain*. By Dr. Henry Schliemann. Translated with the author's sanction. Edited by Philip Smith, B.A., Author of *History of the Ancient World* and of the *Student's Ancient History of the East*. With map, plans, views, and cuts, representing 500 objects of antiquity discovered on the site.' Printed 1875.

THE NON-PRESERVING ASPIC OF ROME

The early accounts of Alexander's contemporaries, and those sponsored by their courts, had to straddle the chaos of a Hellenistic world that saw the kingdoms of the *Diadokhoi* and their *epigonoi* absorbed by the expanding Roman super-state. The bloody process swallowed much of the literary output of the age so that the century before Polybius remains a 'twilight zone';[10] for almost seventy years after the Battle of Ipsus in 301 BCE there is no surviving continuous coherent account, Justin's severe epitome aside. Polybius himself stoically reflected in the opening of his book that the '... writings of the... "numerous historians"... whom the kings had engaged to recount their exploits have fallen into oblivion.'[11]

Diodorus, whose *Bibliotheke* unfortunately survives in tattered fragments for the post-Ipsus period and without the useful chapter *proektheses* (synopses or lists of the detail covered), also mourned the poorly documented years with a proem that underlined his own 'universal' efforts:

> And of those who have undertaken this account of all peoples, not one has continued his history beyond the Macedonian period. For while some have closed their accounts with the deeds of Philip, others with those of Alexander, and some with the *Diadokhoi* or the *Epigonoi*, yet, despite the number and importance of the events subsequent to these and extending even to our own lifetime which have been left neglected, no historian has essayed to treat of them within the compass of a single narrative, because of the magnitude of the undertaking.[12]

The literary wasteland gives the superficial impression that in Rome's sphere of influence, too, there was lack of interest in overseas history through this era, which, as McGing puts it, was neither 'proper Greek history, which lost its appeal after Alexander, nor yet the vital part of proper Roman history...'[13] But Rome had been establishing herself over the twelve-city confederation of the intensely pious Etruscans and other neighbouring tribes, which was clearly the early priority, and the war against Carthage (Qart-hadasht, 'New City' in Punic, Karthago to the Greeks) occupied its attention for the latter part of the period. Any trade delegations, government embassies, treaties and skirmishes that did take place between Rome and the Macedonian-dynasty-dominated Hellenic East in the post-Ipsus years were simply lost with intervening literature.

The narratives that did once knit the two worlds together once came from the now-lost works of Phylarchus (ca. 280-215 BCE), Aratus (ca. 271-213 BCE), Philochorus (ca. 340-261 BCE), Diyllus (ca. 340-280 BCE), and Demochares the nephew of Demosthenes, among a clutch of other names that have come to us through fragments. They included

Hieronymus' lost account which ended sometime soon after 272 BCE, and the non-extant history of Timaeus written in fifty years of exile in Athens (care of Agathocles the Sicilian tyrant) which closed at 264 BCE, the year Rome invaded his homeland, Sicily (he was from Tauromenium, modern Taormina). Diodorus' fragmentary *Bibliotheke* had hardly made any mention of Rome until this point, which, significantly, marked the beginning of its control of his place of birth in Sicily too.

But it was Polybius, whose own account commenced in 264 BCE with the First Punic War between Rome and Carthage, who saw first-hand the final fall of the former Macedonian-governed empire to the Roman legions, though he failed (in what text survives at least) to acknowledge Hieronymus as a source of the post-Alexander years, which, as one scholar notes, is remarkable given their parallel themes: the rapid expansion of superpowers that had risen from obscurity, and with the one subsuming the other.[14] Possibly influenced by his 'tour of duty' with Scipio, Polybius, who defined his work as *pragmatike historia*,[15] believed the recording of history meant subordinating 'the topics of genealogies and myths... the planting of colonies, foundations of cities and their ties of kinship' to the greater significance of the 'nations, cities and rulers'.[16] So imperial 5th century BCE Athens, for example, was, in Momigliano's view, 'a distant unattractively democratic world' to him, only salvaged, for a while, by enlightened leaders like Themistocles.[17]

Clearly familiar with (and influenced by) Herodotus, Thucydides and Xenophon, and highly opinioned on what 'history' should be, Polybius contended that monographs were inferior to his 'universal' approach. This was supposed to highlight that the earlier Greek accounts, especially those of the 4th century BCE, leaned to 'the great leader theory of history', focusing on single individuals and so revealing just dissected parts when the 'whole body' needed a post-mortem.[18] The Greek historians *had* placed war, with its victors, the vanquished, and the proponents of war, centre-stage in their perception of epochal change. His criticism of Theopompus' *Philippika*, now 'double abbreviated' through first Trogus and then his epitomiser Justin, brought the point home: 'It would have been much more dignified and more just to include Philip's achievements in the history of Greece, than to include the history of Greece in that of Philip.'[19]

Polybius began his main 'holistic' narrative of affairs in the Mediterranean Basin, in which he recorded Rome's contact with the *Diadokhoi* kingdoms to the East, in the 140th Olympiad, so 221/220 BCE,[20] the year Philip V ascended the throne of Macedonia and Hannibal Barca was appointed commander of Carthaginian forces in Spain. Unsurprisingly, he never actually named the Alexander-era historians at all, save Callisthenes and in a somewhat disparaging manner;[21] his fourteen digressions on Alexander's behaviour (besides five passing references), which offered little unique material, provided him little more than a somewhat stoical mixed review.[22] Nevertheless, these monographs, and Theopompus' unique character focus, provided Polybius with the anonymous essences he slotted into his 'entire network' with its many 'interdependences'.[23]

True to his polemical literary ancestral roots, Polybius didn't shy away from attacking 'competing' historians, Phylarchus, Philinus and Fabius Pictor, for example, who covered the wars with Carthage.[24] He was also highly critical of his forerunner, the long-lived Timaeus (Lucian claimed he lived to age 96), whose Olympiad reckoning system Polybius nevertheless adopted to calibrate his own chapters which commenced at the point at which Timaeus had closed his (the 129th Olympiad).[25] His loud invective against Timaeus, ironically, preserved much of the detail he had set out to destroy, and yet Polybius' charity 'was conspicuously lacking', for he also proposed: 'We should not find fault with writers for their omissions and mistakes, and should praise and admire them, considering the times they lived in, for having ascertained something on the subject and advanced our knowledge.'[26]

Timaeus' account, rich in detail of colonies, city foundations and genealogies (and highlighted coincidences – all the detail Polybius 'subordinated'), was probably worthy of a place on the shelves,[27] but the exiled Sicilian had himself famously criticised *everyone* and gained the title *epitimaeus*, 'slanderer', along the way; he must have invited additional criticism when he spuriously dated Rome's founding to 814/813 BCE (the thirty-eighth year before the first Olympiad) to synchronise it to Carthage's in order to imply the cities enjoyed twinned fates.[28] Possibly despising Timaeus for his self-declared lack of military experience, Polybius' summing up did elucidate the principal problem of the day: Timaeus '… was like a man in a school of rhetoric, attempting to speak on a given subject, and show off his rhetorical power, but gives no report of what was actually spoken.'[29]

But Polybius didn't remain faithful to his own critiques; he is branded a prejudiced eyewitness to the calamitous events of his day, and the frequent reconstituted speeches we read in Polybius were the product of his 'subjective operations'. His directionless last ten books read like personal memoirs 'focused on himself' in order to 'write himself into Roman history'.[30] In the opinion of one Greek scholar, Polybius could be '… as unreliable as the worst sensationalist scandalmonger historians of antiquity, provided that he is out of sympathy with his subject matter.'[31] If pragmatic his history *was*, at times holistic it was *not* in unravelling events. Yet within Polybius' focus on contemporary affairs, his assessment of constitutions articulated the notion of *anakyklosis*; this presented the theory, and even the prediction, of the evolution of governance through time.

Building on the discourses of Plato and Aristotle, as well as the sequence of empires described by Herodotus, his system of cyclical inevitability saw the rise and fall of city-states and their empires from 'primitive' monarchy through to (developed) monarchy, tyranny, aristocracy, oligarchy, democracy, ochlocracy (mob rule), and finally back to the beginning of the cycle with some form of monarchy.[32] Ironically, Polybius considered Athens at her prime as verging on ochlocracy (Plato might have agreed, for its *demokratia* had overseen the death of his friend and mentor, Socrates). He further believed that Rome's republican system of government, a 'mixed constitution' (a hybrid that contained elements of a monarchy, aristocracy and democracy), had broken the chain, and though he was not suggesting that this would prevent its natural decline, signs of which he pointed to even in his day, Rome was, in fact, to become a fine example of the *politeion anakyklosis*.[33]

As part of his perception of change, Polybius expressed an appreciation of what we might term 'globalism':

> Now in earlier times the world's history had consisted so to speak of a series of unrelated episodes, the origins and results of which being as widely separated as their localities, but from this point onwards history becomes an organic whole: the affairs of Italy and Africa are connected with those of Asia and of Greece, and all events bear a relationship and contribute to a single end.[34]

Whilst he credited Alexander's Asian empire with opening up the East, for him, this 'organic whole' now meant 'Rome' in her stellar fifty-three-year rise to rule the then-known world, 'Fortune's showpiece' as he described it.[35] Whether he was truly in awe of Rome and her conquests, or simply disdainful of her sway over Greece, we may never know, but (indirect) vexatious references we see in his books suggest the Romans were considered *barbaroi*, amongst the barbarian tribes.[36]

The pre-Polybian 'twilight zone' had its sequel, however, when 'an even more vexatious twilight descends' on Hellenistic history after Polybius passed.[37] Although homebred Roman historians were spurred into action after the Second Punic War (or 'Hannibalic War', 218-201 BCE), they focused on the progress of the mother city through the *Annales Maximi* and not on gathering in the detail of the broader Hellenistic story.[38] But Rome's early history commenced on shaky ground. The invasion by Gauls in 390 BCE and the fire that followed it left much of the city and its records in ruins. The vacuum let in falsehoods which made their way sometimes innocently, sometimes deliberately, into its founding story. Good examples of the latter are the formative speeches in Livy's *Ab Urbe Condita Libri*, literally *Chapters from the Founding of the City*, better known today as *The Early History of Rome*.[39]

In his *Lectures on The Philosophy of History*, first published in 1837, Georg Wilhelm Friedrich Hegel (1770-1831) termed this a 'reflective history' (as opposed to 'original' or 'philosophic' history), noting Livy '… puts into the mouths of the old Roman kings, consuls and generals, such orations as would be delivered by an accomplished advocate of the Livian era, and which strikingly contrast with the genuine traditions of Roman antiquity.'[40] It reminds us that narrative history is a personal philosophy of the past and will always be a 'child of its time'.[41] In an attempt to justify his dialogue with the past and even a republic he did not know, Livy, who 'praised and plundered' Polybius' books along the way, explained that: 'By intermingling human actions with divine they may confer a more august dignity on the origins of states.'[42] He nevertheless admitted the challenge he faced:

> The traditions of what happened prior to the foundation of the City or whilst it was being built, are more fitted to adorn the creations of the poet than the authentic records of the historian… The subject matter is enveloped in obscurity; partly from its great antiquity, like remote objects which are hardly discernible through the vastness of the distance; partly owing to the fact that written records, which form the only trustworthy memorials of events, were in those times few and scanty, and even what did exist in the pontifical commentaries and public and private archives nearly all perished in the conflagration of the City.[43]

Macaulay agreed that the chronicles to which Livy, amongst others, had access were filled with '… battles that were never fought, and Consuls that were never inaugurated… such, or nearly such, appears to have been the process by which the lost ballad-poetry of Rome was transformed into history. There was an earlier Latin literature, a literature truly Latin, which has wholly perished, which had indeed almost wholly perished long before those whom we are in the habit of regarding as the greatest Latin writers were born.'[44]

The earlier historians of Rome had more often than not appeared on the *fasti*, the list of city magistrates. These were the wealthy elite, a point that supports the contention by Malthus' 1798 *An Essay on the Principle of Population* that '… the histories of mankind that we possess are – in general – histories only of the higher classes', though the unfortunate woes of those below are inevitably exposed in passing.[45] If the accounts of the past do indeed revolve around the higher social strata, then historians have a dilemma, for: 'the upper current of society presents no criterion by which we can judge the direction in which the undercurrent flows.' So the perfect historian, according to Macaulay, is one who '… shows us the court, the camp, and the senate. But he shows us also the nation…' so that '… many truths, too, would be learned, which can be learned in no other manner.'[46] But they were few and far between. As far as Ammianus Marcellinus' retrospective view was concerned, the deeds of the Roman *plebeian* were in any case '… nothing except riots and taverns and other similar vulgarities… it prevents anything memorable or serious from being done in Rome.'[47] Perhaps Marcellinus, himself a soldier in imperial service, should have questioned why there were riots in the first place, for he might have revealed a cause of the empire's steady decline.[48]

These early republican historians, nevertheless, had advantages the later annalists did not: before imperial edicts closed them to public eyes, public records provided a first-hand account of events, for the *Annales Maximi* of the Pontifex Maximus, the *Commentarii* of the censors, and the *Libri Augurales* too had all been available to consult.[49] One of the outcomes was the avowed later use of the so-called *Libri Lintei, Linen Rolls* supposedly kept in the Temple of Juno Moneta, a doubtful documentary source supposedly consulted by the historian Licinius Macer (died 66 BCE) when nothing else was at hand.[50]

But Rome needed a heroic start in ink, and lacking the pedigree of the great cities of Greece, Augustus finally commissioned a founding epic from Virgil in the style of Ennius (who wrote in the hexameters of Homer) and Naevius (ca. 270-201 BCE). The result was the *Aeneid* which firmly root-grafted a Roman legendary past to Homer's heroes of Troy, a heritage reinforced in Dionysius of Halicarnassus' *Roman Antiquities*, also written in Augustus' reign.[51] According to Timaeus, the sacrifice of the October Horse at the Campus Martius in Rome was a commemoration of the Trojan Horse itself.[52]

The Mykonos Vase: a decorated storage container, *pithos*, and the earliest object known to depict the Trojan Horse from Homer's *Iliad* though the warriors wear the panoply of the later hoplite age. Found on the island of Mykonos in 1961 it dates to ca. 670 BCE and it resides today in the island's archaeological museum.

By the time the private Roman collectors who *were* interested in Greek and Macedonian affairs got their hands on the papyri containing the earlier accounts, much had already decrepitated. These antique seeds, rotting on a classical literary compost heap, did however fertilise new Roman rootstock, and in that grafted form the genes of some of them survived. *Classicus scriptor, non proletarius,* an expression first seen in Aulus Gellius' 2nd century *Attic Nights* (social standing was being linked to the quality of writing in the phrase) came to represent the works of a distinguished group of authors (writing in Greek or Latin) who were considered meritorious in Rome, and it was those that were destined to be copied, distributed and preserved; or, in the case of the Alexander biographies, given a Roman overhaul.[53]

In Macaulay's view, 'new' Roman output could not compare to Greek output of 'old' and he was scathing about what emerged after:

> The Latin literature which has come down to us... consists almost exclusively of works fashioned on Greek models. The Latin metres, heroic, elegiac, lyric, and dramatic, are of Greek origin. The best Latin epic poetry is the feeble echo of the *Iliad* and *Odyssey*. The best Latin eclogues are imitations of Theocritus. The plan of the most finished didactic poem in the Latin tongue was taken from Hesiod. The Latin tragedies are bad copies of the masterpieces of Sophocles and Euripides. The Latin philosophy was borrowed, without alteration, from the Portico and the Academy; and the great Latin orators constantly proposed to themselves as patterns the speeches of Demosthenes and Lysias.[54]

Macaulay additionally reminded us that for 'modern' scholars '... the centuries which separated Plutarch from Thucydides seemed as nothing to men who lived in an age so remote.'[55] Temporal gulfs aside, in the case of the Greeks and Romans it *was* their literary output, perhaps above anything else, that gave them the sense of self-identity that the barbarians pressing on their borders always lacked. So the wholesale loss of Greek and Hellenistic literature must have been incomprehensible to the scholars of the stalwart Roman Empire.

Rome did her fair share of literary damage; the Senate and Caesar had comprehensively inflamed the keepers and the contents of the libraries in Carthage and Alexandria. Although an unrepentant arsonist, Rome did become the most enduring beneficiary of Alexander's sweat, blood and *ichor,* his immortal blood.[56] Alexander's reception in the Eternal City, however, was something of a mixed one; whilst Rome displayed respect for the scale of the Macedonian conquests – they *had* after all paved the way for her own Eastern Empire – that appreciation was tainted by the 'filial forbearance, which educated Romans showed towards Greece in her childish and petulant decline'.[57]

A reconstruction of Carthage at the height of its power in the Punic Wars showing the circular Kothon, the military inner harbour in which up to 220 ships could be moored. The merchant harbour is in the foreground. The entrance could be entirely closed off with iron chains. Image from Rome II © The Creative Assembly Limited – under Licence by the Creative Assembly Limited.

'PERSUASION HAS NO SHRINE BUT ELOQUENT SPEECH' [58]

> … whence and how
> Found'st thou escape from servitude to sophists,
> Their dreams and vanities: how didst thou loose
> The bonds of trickery and specious craft?[59]

A damaging process had already been at work on the legacy of Alexander before Roman-era authors added their contemplations to the subject. Modern scholars bemoan, as did Polybius, that since the 4th century BCE, history had become the servant of rhetoric, the 'science of speaking well', according to Quintilian. The power of artful speech had been appreciated as a political tool as far back as Hesiod's *Theogonia* when a king's persuasiveness was portrayed as a gift of the Muses: 'Upon his tongue they shed sweet dew, and honeyed words flow from his mouth.'[60]

Hesiod had visited Delphi and had been shown the Omphalos, the sacred stone that assisted communication with the immortals. Possibly because of that he went on to receive posthumous good fortune, for in the *Certamen Homeri et Hesiodi* (*The Contest of Hesiod and Homer*, 'the poets who gave the Hellenes their gods'),[61] a narrative now traceable to the 4th century BCE and the Delian festival in honour of Apollo, it is Hesiod who takes the literary prize ahead of the father of the Trojan epics.[62] He might have believed that his victory was due to his instruction by the Muses in the pastures of Mount Helicon, but these were the same Muses that explained to him: 'We know how to tell many falsehoods which are like truths, but we know also how to utter the truth when we wish.'[63]

The pejoratives associated with 'artful speech', as the Muses hinted, remind us that it involved a less than clinical approach to capturing the facts. The writers of the period had a utilitarian view of history itself, considering their overriding responsibility to be the edification of the reader, or to eristic argument.[64]

> As for history – the witness of the ages, the light of truth, the life of memory, the teacher of life, the messenger of the past – with what voice other than the orator's can it be entrusted to immortality?[65]

As witnessed by this extract from *De Oratore*, Cicero believed orators alone should be entrusted with the past, and he outlined a series of noble tenets on how it should be recorded: 'The first is not daring to say anything false, and the second is not refraining from saying anything that is true. There should be no suggestion of suspicion of prejudice for, or bias against, when you write.'[66] Cicero was a trained rhetorician who assumed imperial posts, and he knew his noble tenet was asking too much of the day.[67] But, as pointed out to Cicero by his friend, Titus Pomponius Atticus, 'it is the privilege of rhetoricians to exceed the truth of history', a point of view the austere Brutus strongly objected to.[68] Cicero, no angel of method, further admitted that, 'unchanging consistency of standpoint has never been considered a virtue in great statesmen';[69] it was a damaging hypocrisy, if it was not espoused satirically, but presented so eloquently, who could object? And who can deny that the artistic *flumine orationis* of Demosthenes, Aeschines and Isocrates, or Cicero's powerful use of tricolons, framed some of history's greatest oils?[70]

Elsewhere, Cicero praised plain speaking and likened the rhetorical overlay to 'curling irons' (*calamistra*) on a narrative, further remarking that: 'All the great fourth century orators had attended Isocrates' school, the villain who ruined fourth century historiography.'[71] Unsurprisingly then, that when he branded Herodotus from Halicarnassus 'the father of history', he also bracketed him alongside Theopompus as one of the *innumerabiles fabulae,* the band of notorious liars.[72] Alexander *was* the century's greatest son, and his story was bound to come under the influence of the rhetorical 'whetstone', as Isocrates described himself.[73] So there emerged 'a sort of tragic history' that merged rhetorical narrative and tragic poetry together, a result that describes reasonably well the Roman Vulgate genre on Alexander.[74]

We can only touch lightly on a topic that is deep and without conclusion, for neither Cicero nor Marcus Antonius (died 87 BCE, grandfather of the Triumvir better known today as Mark Antony) finished their treatises on an art that encompassed what Ennius termed 'the marrow of persuasion', *suada*.[75] Rhetoric is embedded in the nature of a man and his desire to throw his persuasive cloak over another under 'the systemisation of natural eloquence'.[76] Diodorus even suggested that the Egyptians had long been fearful of the influence of such honey-coated speeches in legal proceedings so everything was conducted in writing in court; later papyri fragments suggest the Ptolemies maintained a sophisticated paper trail of written testimony through court clerks and scribes, as a legacy of that:

> For in that case there would be the least chance that gifted speakers would have an advantage over the slower, or the well-practised over the inexperienced... for they knew that the clever devices of orators, the cunning witchery of their delivery... at any rate they were aware that men who are highly respected as judges are often carried away by the eloquence of the advocates, either because they are deceived, or because they are won over by the speaker's charm...[77]

Timaeus claimed Syracuse in Sicily as the birthplace of rhetoric.[78] So its *floruit* in Athens was more of a 'categorisation awakening' than a beginning, and it brought with it a new appreciation of its method and application. There was never a *protos heuretes*, a single inventor of the art, as the wide corpus of recommended reading in Dionysius' *De Imitatione* suggests, for its development was firmly rooted in pre-history and Greece's Homeric past.[79] Homer provided us with a vivid image of Odysseus' skill with words: 'snowflakes in a blizzard', and Phoenix, the tutor to Achilles, encouraged him to '... be both a speaker of words as well as a doer of deeds.'[80] Here in the *Iliad* the power of discourse, *psychagogia*, was being recognised, and it was thought to persuade souls to take the direction of the truth.[81]

The etymology of *rhetorike* was formed from *rhetor* – typically describing a speaker in a court or assembly – and *ike*, linking it to art or skill, and the compound of the two was possibly first seen in Plato's *Gorgias*. Aristotle claimed Empedocles (ca. 490-430 BCE) had developed an 'art' that was already expressed in the Greek *logon technai*, the 'skills of speeches',[82] and, according to Cicero, the first manual *was* written by a Sicilian Greek, Corax of Syracuse, in the 5th century BCE.[83] Gorgias of Leontini (ca. 485-380 BCE), 'the father of sophistry' (the skilful use of false but persuasive arguments, often employed to present the merits of both sides of a case) of and *paradoxologia* ('nihilism' according to some commentators) ferried it to Athens where Tisias and Antiphon dragged rhetoric and sophistry into the Areopagus or the boule (citizen council) when pitting individual rights against the legal code. With them there did, indeed, appear *dissoi logoi*, the 'arguments on both sides'.[84]

The great Isocrates and Protagoras (ca. 490-420 BCE) 'clarified' truth in the streets as well as in the courts for fees previously unheard of, for logographers (speechwriters) were extremely well paid 'to make the weaker argument stronger', *ton hetto logon kreitto poiein*.[85] Protagoras is said to have charged 10,000 drachmas per pupil for a single course in his sophistry; its value was no doubt persuasively justified with 'man is the measure of all things'.[86] Ironically, at that time, *On Nature* by Anaxagoras (ca. 510-428 BCE), a revolutionary book full of groundbreaking cosmic theories (including the impiety that the sun was a ball of fire), could be purchased for just one drachma in the street.[87]

With no public prosecutor's office in Athens, individuals had to resort to private suits (*dike*) and self-funded public suits (*graphe*) to bring charges. Once their speeches had been written, gifted speakers were sought to deliver the desired result, for witnesses were not cross-examined, jurors were often ignorant of the law, and speakers were restricted in delivery time under the watch of a *klepsydra*, the judicial water clock. Paradoxically, whilst mendacity detected in speeches given at the boule or assembly was punishable by death, court case perjury remained risk-free, encouraging the subordination of 'fact' to *deimotes*, a 'forcefulness' of style.[88]

Isocrates protected the intellectual property of his teachings at his newly opened rhetorical school by penning *Against the Sophists* in which he claimed it is *impossible* to write a handbook on the subject,[89] and within two generations of its first public appearance in Athens, rhetoric was endemic to debate, whether legal or historical. Timon summed it up: 'Protagoras, all mankind's epitome, Cunning, I trow, to war with words.'[90] The 'cunning' was a verbal *mageia,* a word first recorded by Gorgias in his *Encomium of Helen*: 'The power of speech over the disposition of the soul is like the disposition of drugs… by means of some harmful persuasion, words can bewitch and thoroughly cast a spell…'[91]

By Alexander's day, the Akademia had been drawn in. Aristotle launched his *Gryllos* on Isocrates, prompting a riposte from Cephisodorus, and there followed detailed polemics from both sides: the *Protreptikos* and the *Antidosis*. Rhetoric was being vitiated by rhetoric to the detriment of literature in general, and as Aristotle argued, fine language was being disarmed by fine argument, skills that Demosthenes and Aeschines were to refine. Demosthenes had been aided by lessons from actors, by speaking with a mouth full of pebbles, from long nights rehearsing (his arguments were labelled as 'smelling of lamp wicks'),[92] and according to Aeschines, by fancy footwork as well.[93] When the great *logographos* was asked for the most important element in his craft, Demosthenes artfully replied 'only three things count, delivery, delivery and again, delivery', so Quintilian claimed.[94]

Isocrates and the Ten Attic Orators had much to answer for in Athens, because the political and forensic show-speeches, along with the declamations we encounter throughout classical works, were originally crafted here. Demosthenes, Aeschines, Hyperides, Lycurgus and

Deinarchus (ca. 361-291 BCE) all had something to say about Philip and Alexander, as well as their successors, and none of it was straight talk. Some of them called themselves 'philosophers', a term Pythagoras is said to have invented; it was a label described by Cicero as a 'lover of wisdom and spectator of the universe, with no motive or profit or gain.'[95] That popular claim appears spurious, however, and is challenged as an invention of the Platonist school; the origins of the compound word, 'philosopher', were perhaps inspired by Aristophanes' Thinkery in *Clouds*, with its farcical treatment of Socrates. In fact Herodotus suggested Croesus came close to the definition of a *philosophos* in his famous greeting to the Athenian sage and lawgiver, Solon, at Sardis ca. 560s BCE, if the episode is historic.[96]

Lucian said of street 'philosophers' in general that their 'argument is turned

upside down, they forget what they are trying to prove, and finally go off abusing one another and brushing the sweat from their brows; victory rests with him who can show the boldest front and the loudest voice, and hold his ground the longest'; the 'butcher's meat' of fact was being garnished 'with the sauce of their words'.[97] Their arguments, however, when preserved with an attached epistolary corpus, are useful indicators of the social currents of the day, but their influence on literature meant epideictic rhetoric fleshed out what might have once been leaner and untainted accounts, so that they now require bariatric surgery under *Quellenforschung*'s knife to get to the internal organ of fact.[98] Whichever way it is bottled, the tumult of rhetoric was drowning out the simpler tones of truth, as the Peripatetic school at Athens was soon vocally pointing out.[99]

A Roman marble herm of Demosthenes inspired by the bronze statue by Polyeuctus, ca. 280 BCE. Now in the Louvre in the Department of Greek, Etruscan and Roman Antiquities.

The Lyceum (unearthed in Athens in 1996) and later the Academy churned out manuals which loved to classify, a predisposition taken from Pythagoras. Aristotle quickly had rhetoric hung, drawn, and systematically quartered into a *sunagoge technon,* a collection of methods (in defiance of Isocrates' claim) and he then did the same to sophistry.[100] When he inherited the subject from Plato, who viewed it as the 'art of enchanting the soul',[101] he concluded: 'In the case of rhetoric, there was much old material to hand, but in the case of logic, we had absolutely nothing at all, until we had spent a long time in laborious investigation.'[102] Not to be outdone by Plato's six species, Aristotle saw four uses for the art (panegyric, encomium, funeral oration and invective), with three modes of persuasion and four lines of argument under five main headings for use in the seven courses of human action, discounting the subheadings. Plato didn't thank Aristotle for being 'out-classified' for the Platonists despised *kainotomia*, innovation; he soon termed him the 'the foal', presumably because, as Diogenes Laertius tells us, Plato said of his pupil's secession, 'Aristotle has kicked us off… '[103]

CETERUM CENSEO CARTHAGINEM ESSE DELENDAM

In Rome, the newly imported seductive oratorial arts, and the attendant new philosophies, were not universally accepted, and neither was Greece itself. The sapient Cato the Elder (234-149 BCE, also known as 'Cato the Censor'), who started life as a rigid Sabine farmer, warned his son:

> I shall explain what I found out in Athens about these *Graeci*, and demonstrate what advantage there may be in looking into their writings (while not taking them too seriously). They are a worthless and unruly tribe. Take this as a prophecy: when those folk give us their writings, they will corrupt everything.[104]

Cato did, nevertheless, appreciate the practical advantages of rhetoric; something of an antilogy.[105] In 181 BCE, newly unearthed Pythagorean manuscripts of Numa Pompilius, the legendary second king of Rome (who supposedly reigned 715-673 BCE), were burned in the forum (they were in any case frauds) for containing unsuitable Greek doctrine ('subversive of religion'), and Cato went on to warn of Greek doctors that they were 'sworn to kill all barbarians with medicine…'[106] In this censorious environment, the comedies of the home-grown playwright, Plautus (ca. 254-184 BCE), released between 205 and 184 BCE, stood little chance of being aired. There were no permanent theatres in Rome, possibly because drama was still considered a corrupting influence too (no doubt due to its Greek heritage), and it wasn't until 55 BCE that Pompey ('the Great') opened his theatre in the Campus Martius, inspired by a visit a few years earlier to Greek Mytilene.

Clearly xenophobic and a master of invective, Cato fought with distinction in the campaigns against Hannibal in the Second Punic War. It was an experience that furnished him with a call for a *rerum repetitio* when ending his senatorial orations: '*ceterum censeo Carthaginem esse delendam*' – 'furthermore, I maintain that Carthage should be destroyed'. Cato's rigid virtue would have gladly hurled a spear dipped in blood across the Carthaginian border, whilst the Hellenism of sophisticated and distinguished Roman families continued to offend him.[107] They included the *gens* of Scipio *Africanus* to whom he remained firmly opposed. Unsurprisingly, a collection of widely read pithy and conservative maxims, the *Disticha Catonis*, was falsely attached to the brooding censor.[108]

Cato supported the *Lex Oppia* (Oppian Law) which restricted women to wearing no more than half-an-ounce of gold adornment as an austerity measure in the troubled days following Hannibal's victory at Cannae (216 BCE). Rome itself was lucky to avoid an assault, and the two suffetes of Carthage and the Tribunal of One Hundred and Four must have demanded why the Carthaginian general failed to attack the city immediately after;[109] some 50,000 Roman soldiers had died in the battle and the path to the gates lay relatively undefended.[110] Cato additionally advocated the *Lex Orchai*, which limited guests at an entertainment, and the *Lex Voconia*, designed to check the amount of wealth falling in the hands of women. This inspired Livy to wholly construct a speech in which Cato entreated husbands to control their errant wives.[111] Though Cato's invective contributed to the eventual fall of Carthage, the result saw such great wealth arriving in Rome that it forced the repeal of the unpopular laws following street protests by women. The newly arriving funds did, however, justify Cato's adage, *bellum se ipsum alet*: 'war feeds itself'.

The Macedonian Alexander, an 'orientalist' who fell into the barbarian trappings of the Persian Great Kings, was not a figure to be rolled out at banquets in the presence of the censor. Cato had also fought at Thermopylae in 191 BCE thwarting the invasion of Antiochus III; it was a battle that ended Seleucid influence in Greece and suffocated the last gasps of Alexander's *Diadokhoi*. In the same year Cato gave a speech in Athens and he conspicuously delivered it in Latin although he spoke Greek.[112] He was a redoubt that for an influential time threw back many cultural imports, and it has even been proposed that his Latin works were instrumental in halting Greek from becoming the dominant language in Rome. Yet Cato's *Origines* (of Italian towns) in which Lucius Valerius had reminded him that he had emphasised the role of women in the founding of the city, and his rustic *De Agri Cultura* (*On Farming*) could not distract the populace from finally turning their heads to the more exotic and seductive themes of the Hellenistic Age.

GRAECIA CAPTA FERUM VICTOREM CEPIT ET ARTES INTULIT AGRESTI LATIO[113]

Cato blamed the campaign against Macedonia in 168 BCE for importing more Greek moral laxity into Rome, claiming, '... the surest sign of deterioration in the Republic [is] when pretty boys fetch more than fields, and jars of caviar more than ploughmen.'[114] His austerity continued to prevail, for a while, and in 161 BCE rhetoricians were expelled from the city. Some seven years earlier the still-circulating Alexander-styled currency had also been banned.[115] But in 155 BCE Athens impressed Rome with a 'philosophical embassy' sent to argue for the repeal of a 500 talent fine; it included the Stoic, Diogenes of Babylon (ca. 230-145 BCE), the Peripatetic, Critolaus (ca. 200-118 BCE), and the Sceptic, Carneades (214-129 BCE). Between them they disarmed all opposition by the magic of their eloquence so that the youth of the city flocked to hear them plead their case and became immediately 'possessed'.[116]

Although Cato, now almost eighty, arranged their speedy departure, the door to new ideas had been irreversibly opened and soon 'Rome went to school with the Greeks'.[117] When the official philosophical schools at Athens were closed in 88 BCE by edict of the Roman Senate,[118] Greece experienced a 'brain drain' as philosophers and rhetoricians journeyed west to become 'household philosophers' in Rome, though whether they too inscribed *Probis pateo* – 'I am open for honest people' (inscribed on city gates and on entrances to schools) – above the door is debatable.[119] And with them arrived the topic of Alexander on a tide of new philosophical doctrines and their associated 'wisdoms'.

The Attic style of epideictic flourished elsewhere, in Rhodes for example, where it perpetuated the tradition until Apollonius Molon settled on the island and taught Caesar and Cicero to orate.[120] As Lucian imagined it in the cultured centres, there were 'everywhere philosophers, long-bearded, book in hand... the public walks are filled with their contending hosts, and every man of them calls Virtue his nurse... these ready-made philosophers, carpenters once or cobblers.'[121] But 'Virtue lives very far off, and the way to her is long and steep and rough...',[122] and so we can only speculate on the quality and experience of the 'beards' arriving from Greece.

The Hellenistic era had witnessed the emergence of the philosophical schools of the *Kynikoi, Stoikoi, Skeptikoi* and the happier followers of Epicurus at the expense of the Academy and Lyceum of Plato and Aristotle, as thinkers tried to rationalise a radically changing world, or, as Epicurus espoused, withdraw from it, for he suffered from perennial bad health. Inevitably, Alexander became the perfect canvas on which to project their new ideas for Roman contemplation; the Macedonian king was used as an *exemplum* and his life a propaedeutic to a full-blown syllabus on rhetoric and in the process he became a punch-bag for a Roman conscience being newly tested by its own aggressive expansion in the East. As one scholar put it, Alexander was '... both a positive paradigm of military success and a negative paradigm of immoral excess, of *virtus* and *vitia* in a single classroom incantation.'[123]

Despite a further castigation of rhetoricians in Rome enacted in 92

BCE by the censors in an effort to stem their influence in the Senate,[124] a manual on rhetoric from the articulate politician Marcus Antonius had appeared sometime between in the decade before, though the still anonymous *Rhetorica ad Herennium* may have been the first Latin manual on the subject, a possible remodel the *Rhetorica ad Alexandrum* once attributed to Aristotle.[125] Cicero's *De Inventione Rhetorica* was published when he was still an adolescent (likely in 88-87 BCE), his *De Oratore* followed (55-46 BCE?), and soon after his *Partitione Oratoriae* and his *Brutus Or A History of Famous Orators*.

But by then free speech was dying in Rome; Cicero's manuals could

The bust of Cicero at the Capitoline Museum, Rome

not be fully exploited when civil wars threatened and proscription lists appeared, and his *De Optimo Genere Oratorum* was only published posthumously.[126] Some rhetors like Potamon of Mytilene, a renowned expert on Alexander, soon enjoyed the patronage of the Roman emperors, in this case Tiberius. Yet even for that notoriety, Potamon's works, including *On the Perfect Orator*, did not survive.[127] Finally, funded by a salary from the Privy Purse, Quintilian's twelve-book *Institute of Oratory* (written through 93-95 CE) and Tacitus' *Dialogue on Orators* emerged; Romans had finally 'submitted to the pretensions of a race they despised'.[128] So there

appeared the claim from Horace: '*Graecia capta ferum victorem cepit et artes intulit agresti Latio*' – 'Captive Greece conquered its fierce conqueror and civilised the peasant Latins.' Virgil had been right to warn of Greeks bearing gifts.[129]

THE RETURN OF THE RHETORICAL SON

When searching for the remains of the *original* Alexander, we have to deal with the realities of historians living within the literary *Pax Romana* ('absolutism as the price for peaceful order') for censorship *was* tangible and authors were fair game.[130] Precedents had been set and the sound of Praetorian Guards marching into the atrium was never difficult to imagine, and neither was the drifting stench of the Tullianum, Rome's notorious prison. If we detect Livy himself was attached to the idea of a Republic, he never quite told that to his emperor, Augustus, who had by then suppressed publication of the *Acta Senatus*, the official records of senatorial debates at the dawn of the Principate.[131] Livy, 'peculiarly Roman' with 'a hundred kings below him, and only the gods above him', had by now published much of his monumental 142-book *Ab Urbe Condita Libri*.[132] He was given the young Claudius to tutor and sweetened his history lessons by suggesting the Macedonians 'had degenerated into Syrians, Parthians and Egyptians' when referring to the Hellenistic kingdoms of Alexander's successors.[133]

It seems that there was still sensitivity to the lingering power of the *Diadokhoi*-founded dynasties in the wake of the self-serving propaganda of Octavian which held that 'the last of the Ptolemaic dynasty was threatening to hold sway in Rome itself'; that is, with the help of Mark Antony who fell under the spell of Cleopatra.[134] Livy, who commenced his long work when Diodorus (broadly) ended his, felt he needed to defend Rome from insinuations that she would have fallen to the Macedones:[135]

> Anyone who considers these factors either separately or in combination will easily see that as the Roman Empire proved invincible against other kings and nations, so it would have proved invincible against Alexander… The aspect of Italy would have struck him as very different from the India which he traversed in drunken revelry with an intoxicated army; he would have seen in the passes of Apulia and the mountains of Lucania the traces of the recent disaster which befell his house when his uncle Alexander, King of Epirus, perished.[136]

Livy, Lucan (39-65 CE), Cicero, and the stoical Seneca, managed to frame Alexander as an example of moral turpitude when highlighting the depravity of absolute power, and their *Epistulae Morales* and *Suasoriae* (persuasive speeches) flowed. Arrogance and false pride were the two principal vices of Stoic doctrine and the opening pages of Seneca's *On the Shortness of Life* could be an unfriendly dedication to Alexander, with its rejection of insatiable greed and political ambition, the squandering of wealth and the foolhardiness of inflicting dangers on others. In the case of Seneca, a tutor to young Nero, the Alexander-Aristotle relationship was clearly being relived. Lucan's *De Bello civili*, better known as *Pharsalia* and treading dangerous polemical ground under Nero, termed Alexander 'the madman offspring of Philip, the famed Pellan robber'; he was further described as nothing short of mankind's 'star of evil fate'. Lucan added: 'He rushed through the peoples of Asia leaving human carnage in his wake, and plunged the sword into the heart of every nation.'[137]

Seneca took at face value Trogus' claim (preserved by Justin) that Alexander caged Lysimachus with a lion as a punishment for his pitying Callisthenes; he had allegedly handed poison to the caged historian to end his suffering.[138] It was useful as a character defamation and yet Curtius clearly stated the report was nothing but a scandal; moreover, *this* Lysimachus was likely Alexander's Arcanian tutor and not the *Somatophylake* who inherited Thrace.[139] Seneca likewise accepted the ill-fated quip made by the Rhodian, Telesphorus, about Lysimachus' wife, Arsinoe (the daughter of Ptolemy by Berenice), along with his subsequent mutilation at Lysimachus' hand.[140] Athenaeus had read no evidence of mutilation and Plutarch credited the remark to Timagenes.[141] Neither episode was challenged, for each provided the perfect dish for a polemic on the corruption of kings and tyrants.

Alexander's deeds inspired the republican iconoclasts to vilify him publicly and the city's first men to emulate him privately; in Valerius Maximus' nine books of *Memorable Deeds and Sayings* (published sometime under Tiberius) the Macedonian king appears at the centre of the frequent *exempla* on behaviour encompassing *both* virtues and vices, suggesting a transition was in progress.[142] And despite their thunderous tirades and the continuous cloud-cover of the earlier Greek invective, the rays of grudging admiration managed to shine through.

As unbridled power manifested itself ever more comfortably through dictators in Rome, and as independent power was stripped from the *comitia*, the *concilium*, the plebeian tribune, and finally from the Senate, the diluted conscience of the Roman republic was more easily assuaged. When apotheosis was finally muttered and Eastern campaigns planned, Alexander emerged once more into the sunlight of imperial emulation when philhellenism returned to fashion, a somewhat ironic result in light of Macedonia's own suppression of Greek freedom.[143] Finally, emperors embraced Alexander in earnest, portraying him as a giant who turned the course of Hellenic history and ultimately that of Rome. They besieged his name, stormed his historical pages and inhabited the very footsteps he walked in.

Pompey, who shared the epithet *invictus* ('unconquered') with Scipio and Alexander,[144] and then Julius Caesar, Augustus, Caligula, Nero, Trajan, Marcus Aurelius (ruled 198-211 CE), Caracalla and Septimus Severus (145-211 CE) who locked up the Alexandrian tomb to deny anyone else a glimpse of Alexander's corpse, all felt the need to stylise themselves on the Macedonian conqueror in some way. Even Crassus believed he was treading in his footsteps *en route* to his disastrous invasion of Parthia, and probably Mark Antony did too, with similar calamitous results. Like Alexander, they managed to attach themselves to Heracles and Dionysus, but *unlike* the Macedonian, neither made it to India where the divine hero and god 'civilised' and procreated.[145]

Septimus Severus is even said (perhaps spuriously) to have reconstituted a Silver Shields brigade in emulation of the elite Macedonian hypaspist corps (mobile infantry, used on special missions). Caracalla, who named his officers after Alexander's generals, demanded the title 'Great', and he even took the name 'Alexander' after inspecting his body in its tomb in Alexandria; he deposited his own cloak, belt and jewellery, we are told, in return for Alexander's drinking cups and weapons.[146] Caracalla is said to have persecuted philosophers of the Aristotelian school based on the lingering Vulgate tradition that Aristotle had provided the poison that killed the Macedonian king (T9, T10).[147]

Alexander, with his unique *dunasteia* (broadly, his aristocratic house, thus 'dynasty'), was now being subsumed into the essence of Rome; Gore Vidal said of the emperors: '*The* unifying *Leitmotiv* in these lives is Alexander the Great.'[148] A century and a half ago Nietzsche encapsulated their historical perspective, reminding us why we need to reconstitute Alexander without the Roman-era additives:

> Should we not make new for ourselves what is old and find ourselves in it? Should we not have the right to breathe our own soul into this dead body? Being Roman they saw it is as an incentive for a Roman conquest. Not only did one omit what was historical; one also added allusions to the present and not with any sense of theft but with the very best conscience of the *imperium Romanum.*[149]

In this environment it was inevitable that a new wave of historians felt compelled to reconstruct the story of the Argead king.

A marble bust of Caracalla by Bartolomeo Cavaceppi (ca. 1750-70) based on a likeness in the Farnese collection in Rome and then Naples, believed to date from the 200s CE. In planning his invasion of the Parthian Empire, Caracalla equipped 16,000 Macedonians as a traditional phalanx despite the fact that it was by now an obsolete tactical formation. They were armed as 'in Alexander's day' with 'helmet of raw ox-hide, a three-ply linen breastplate, a bronze shield, long pike, short spear, high boots, and sword'. Unless this refers to other brigades outside the traditionally outfitted *pezhetairoi*, this description is challenging.[150]

THE EXTANT SOURCES – 'SECONDARY' AT BEST

The Roman-era writers who 'preserved' Alexander's history inevitably bemoaned the archaic unreliability of their *Graeci* literary ancestors, in the same way the historians of Hellas had been critical of their forerunners. Quintilian perhaps epitomised the Roman arrogance when he ranked Sallust beside Thucydides, comparing Livy with Herodotus and Cicero to Demosthenes, though he conceded in the process that the Greeks had provided the models for Rome's own literary achievements. Cicero himself had once hailed the orator Lucius Licinius Crassus (140-91 BCE) as the 'Roman-Demosthenes', yet that was a politically astute encomium for a mentor who became a powerfully wedded consul.[151]

But the biggest Roman-era historiographical disservice was not to name their sources at all. Even when considered worth preserving, the literary forerunners were, more often than not, publicly assassinated, quietly assimilated and destined to servitude as an anonymous section in voluminous *Bibliotheke* or a series of biographical *Vitae*. Moreover, any methodology for working with sources remained a highly personalised affair.

Arrian announced a basic and instinctive form of *Quellenforschung* with: 'Wherever Ptolemy and Aristobulus in their histories of Alexander, the son of Philip, have given the same account, I have followed it on the assumption of its accuracy; where their facts differ I have chosen what I feel to be the more probable and worthy of telling.'[152] But did Arrian appreciate the responsibility that came with the statement? For the version he selected stuck and all else has vanished for eternity, for: 'Every history written elbows out one which might have been.'[153] His approach was surely an emulation of Xenophon who voiced the same sentiment in his *Hellenika*, which, rather than a history of Greece, reads more like a book of prejudiced memoirs written for 'those in the know' (it was hostile to Thebes, in particular, for her ascendancy over Sparta).[154] If Arrian unconsciously let the nostalgia of the Second Sophistic slant his prose, and recalling that his *primary* sources had been politically intriguing, then both conscious and unconscious processes were at work on Alexander.

The result of these unconscious processes: 'All history is contemporary history, the re-enactment of past experience relevant to the present',[155] and as far as a historian, modern or from the classical past, '…time sticks to his thinking like soil to a gardener's spade'.[156] So 'a fully objective critique' of history is impossible, as a *Horizontverschmelzung*, a 'fused horizon', blinds interpretation with a 'historically effected consciousness'.[157] In other words, the Roman-era historians re-rendered Alexander in their own philosophies and words. Although individual ideology was not subject to state control (though clearly it was threatened by it), the wider biases of class, value, and culture were as prominent then as today. It is against this backdrop that the extant accounts of Diodorus, Justin, Curtius, Plutarch and Arrian were written under successive Roman dictators and emperors. Their information could not have been better than that they had inherited, though perhaps they thought otherwise, and at this point Rome was not devoid of primary and intermediary sources that had documented the era (in contrast to the period post-Ipsus), as evidenced by the many contributing historians named in Plutarch's accounts.[158]

Arrian explained *his* particular motivation for tackling the subject: no extant Alexander history appeared to be trustworthy, as a group they conflicted, and no single work captured the detail satisfactorily, to his taste at least: 'There are other accounts of Alexander's life – more of them, indeed, and more mutually conflicting than of any other historical character.' He added that the '… transmission of false stories will continue… unless I can put a stop to it in this history of mine.'[159] Pearson suggested Arrian's work was nothing less than a protest against the popularity of Cleitarchus' 'unsound history' which was circulating in Rome.[160]

But *Quellenforschung*'s forensic eye is revealing that what have been often termed 'good' sources – those behind the so-called 'court tradition' of Arrian, for example – include what are now considered deposits of highly dubious material. On the other hand, writers once deemed 'dubious' provide us, on occasion, with a core of credible information from genuine lost texts. But identifying where that core separates from the mantle and the crust remains a challenge, so as far as the value of these secondary sources to Alexander's story: 'The old custom of dividing their writings into "favourable" and "unfavourable" has now been abandoned for a more sceptical, cautious and nuanced approach.'[161] In Peter Green's opinion, 'The truth of the matter is that there has never been a "good" or a "bad" source-tradition concerning Alexander, simply *testimonia* contaminated to a greater or lesser degree, which invariably need evaluating, wherever possible, by external criteria of probability.' [162]

HISTORIA KATA MEROS

The earliest of the five extant writers dealing with the exploits of Alexander, the Greek Sicilian Diodorus, was constructing a 'universal' narrative along the lines of Polybius and Ephorus, and with no monographic pretensions towards the Macedonian king. Noting that events 'lie scattered about in numerous treatises and in divers authors', Diodorus echoed a rather Polybian case for his thirty years of research and compilation as part of the introduction we cited above:

> Most writers have recorded no more than isolated wars waged by a single nation or a single state, and but few have undertaken, beginning with the earliest times and coming down to their own day, to record the events connected with all peoples…[163]

With less space allocated to the extended didactic speeches we find in Thucydides, for example, and yet clearly influenced by what appears to be Ephorus' sentiment (derived from Isocrates) on 'moral utility', Diodorus once more focused on 'great men', and he seems to have scorned democracy with its 'vast numbers that ruin the work of the government' in the process.[164] Polybius had already commented on Athens' political system and perhaps set the tone: 'It naturally begins to be sick of present conditions and next looks out for a master, and having found one very soon hates him again, as the change is manifestly for the worse',[165] a statement that conveniently appears to back-up his anacyclotic model.

In his philosophical introduction, Diodorus informed us that his *Bibliotheke Historika* covered 1,138 years and was arranged into three distinct sections.[166] The first was the 'mythical' in which he introduced Greek and Egyptian creation theories and narrated events through to the Trojan War. The second was a compendium of accounts ending at Alexander's death, and he originally planned the third, the last twenty-three books, to run past the first 'unofficial' Roman Triumvirate of 60/59 BCE formed between Julius Caesar, Crassus and Pompey, and through to Caesar's Gallic Wars of 46/45 BCE. But he ceased at the earlier terminus, though later events *were* mentioned; the halt was probably prudent considering the danger of commenting on contemporary events during the bloody Second Triumvirate.[167] Of his original 'library', only books one to five, and eleven to twenty, survive anywhere near intact, though fragments from the remaining sections can be found in the 280 surviving epitomes of Photius.[168] Fortunately, Philip II, Alexander and the Successor Wars years under scrutiny, reside in books sixteen to twenty.

Diodorus' work has been a weapons testing ground for the deployment of *Quellenforschung* and yet we know little about his life beyond what he himself told us, along with one further reference by the Illyrian Eusebius Sophronius Hieronymus (ca. 347-420 CE), otherwise known as St Jerome: 'Diodorus of Sicily, a writer of Greek history, became illustrious.'[169] Diodorus hailed from one of the oldest and formerly wealthiest, and yet now (according to Cicero) one of the most impoverished, settlements in the interior of Sicily, Agyrium, where a surviving tombstone inscription is dedicated to a similar named 'son of Appollonius' – we assume the historian. In 36 BCE, in the decade in which Diodorus was likely publishing, Octavian stripped the Sicilians of their Roman citizen rights, *Latinitas*, previously granted to them by Sextus Pompey.[170]

Nevertheless, Diodorus afforded Agyrium – which may have suffered as a result of opposing Roman interests in the First Punic War – and its Heraclean cult (Heracles had supposedly visited the town) an importance out of context in the scale of his overall work (Timaeus was accused of much the same); he made 'events in Sicily finer and more illustrious than those in the rest of the world'.[171] Ephorus, too, had repeatedly assured his readers that the population of *his* home, Cyme in northwest Asia Minor, was 'at peace', possibly taking Euripides' words at face value: 'The first necessity of a happy life is to be born of a famous city', and apart from attachments to Homer and Hesiod, Ephorus inferred every Spartan or Persian military action had some strategic link with Cyme.[172] So when Diodorus digresses into a Cymian saga we can confidently pinpoint his source.[173]

Evidence suggests Diodorus' information gathering took place broadly between 59 BCE and the publication date somewhere between 36-30 BCE, a period in which Roman authority reached 'to the bounds of the inhabited world', a state of affairs that concerned him despite his admiration for Rome's earlier achievements.[174] But parts of his first books appear to have circulated earlier, released as a separate packet.[175] He seems to have spoken imperfect Latin (though living on Sicily gave him a 'considerable familiarity' with the language) and the jury remains out on whether he drew from Latin texts at *all* for detail on Roman affairs. Like Herodotus, he claimed to have travelled widely in the continents he would have termed 'Europa' and 'Asia', but at times his geography is just as shaky as Herodotus', in whose *Histories* we see the first references to those continental names. It is clear from his eyewitness testimony, however, that he did spend time in Egypt (from ca. 60/59 BCE) and he appears to have consulted the 'royal records' in Alexandria before basing himself in Rome (from ca. 46/45 BCE) for a 'lengthy' time, though no patrons nor reading circle associates were ever mentioned.[176]

Admitting he followed 'subject-system' subdivisions, Diodorus dealt with the fate of individuals sequentially, separating biographical threads rather than developing them in parallel, a method that complicates our understanding of the chronological progression; the result is at times akin to a 'kaleidoscopic disjunctiveness'.[177] Whilst dubbed 'universal' in approach, and indeed at times he *was* panoramic in his scope, Diodorus all too often provided us with a monographic narrative that Polybius would have termed *historia kata meros*, history 'bit by bit', a definition close to the criticism afforded to Thucydides (only mentioned once in the extant chapters of Polybius) by Dionysius of Halicarnassus, whose books, beside those of Polybius and Diodorus, represent the only surviving works of the Hellenistic era sufficiently intact to be of use to modern historians.[178]

Diodorus *was* cutting and pasting 'the numerous treatise from divers authors', squeezing them into a highly generalised timeframe, though he was not blind to the shortcomings of his method, as he himself explained:

> ... it is necessary, for those who record them, to interrupt the narrative and to parcel out different times to simultaneous events contrary to nature, with the result that, although the actual experience of the events contains the truth, yet the written record, deprived of such power, while presenting copies of the events, falls far short of arranging them as they really were.[179]

Polybius had encountered a similar problem, and Ephorus had preceded Diodorus with this approach: a balancing act of grouping related events together and yet fitting the whole into an annalistic (year by year) framework, earning the Cymian writer Polybius' praise as the 'first universal historian'.[180] In contrast, Seneca felt: 'It requires no great effort to strip Ephorus of his authority; he is a mere chronicler.'[181] Sempronius Asellio (ca. 198 to post-91 BCE) had already stated the flaw with the annalistic approach: 'Annals make only known what was done and in which year it was done, just as if someone were writing a diary, which the Greeks call *ephemeris*. I think that for us it is not enough to say what was done, but also to show for what purpose and for which reason things were done.'[182] A more modern interpretation: we get the 'gleam but no illumination: facts but no humanity'.[183]

In Diodorus' chronological progression, Alexander's achievement sat like a huge boulder – the greatest in history he believed – in the literary road from prehistory to the increasingly turbulent present, and one that could not be split this time with fire and sour wine.[184] In his opinion: 'Alexander accomplished greater deeds than any, not only of kings who lived before him but also of those who were to come later down to our time.'[185] And that would have been a slap in the face to the career of Julius Caesar had not Diodorus additionally and expediently stated that Caesar was the historical character he admired the most.[186]

The chapters focusing on Alexander in Diodorus' *Bibliotheke* are considered to be about one-tenth as long as Cleitarchus' narrative (estimated from scant evidence), whereas Curtius' biography roughly tracked Cleitarchus' original length; this uneven abridgement would explain many of the discrepancies within otherwise comparable Vulgate profiles.[187] And though a subject of intense debate, it remains easier (though less tantalising) to swallow the idea that the tones and nuances attachable to earlier Hellenistic historians that we see in the Roman-era Vulgate, also came from Cleitarchus, who, publishing in the 370s or 360s BCE, had himself incorporated these influences. The alternative requires us to accept that each Vulgate historian flitted between a number of earlier sources and yet still produced a markedly similar result. Any remaining variation in commentary we see simply reflects the ethnic backgrounds and social climates attachable to the latter-day authors and the varying degrees to which they compressed Cleitarchus' account.

For details of events that followed Alexander's death, scholars have reached a 'somewhat uneasy agreement' that Diodorus shifted sources to Hieronymus of Cardia, once again with a heavy compression of text.[188] Faced with the complete loss of Hieronymus' original account, the slant of Diodorus' chapter-opening *proemia* (prologues, which sometimes, however, conflict with his narrative) and the identification of unique diction may provide a valuable path back to his original sources.[189] As examples, *idiopragia* ('private power' rather than 'mutual gain') and the technical terms *katapeltaphetai* (literally 'catapultists') and *asthippoi* (elite cavalry units whose role is still debated) uniquely used by Diodorus to describe episodes we believe Hieronymus had eyewitnessed, act as tell-tales to his presence when we see them reused elsewhere.[190] Inevitably, in this shifting of sources at the point of Alexander's death, there was an overlap in information, and the result was untidy and conflicting with his later narrative.

In his opening proem, Diodorus expressed the fear that future compilers may copy or mutilate his work; perhaps this is suggestive of his own guilty conscience.[191] Classical writers frequently regurgitated their sources uncreatively, and Diodorus, the 'honest plodding Greek' who adopted a utilitarian and stoical approach, was no exception.[192] Termed an uncritical compiler, Diodorus took the path of least resistance in completing the 'immense labour' behind his interlocking volumes.[193] In 1865 Heinrich Nissen reasoned that Diodorus habitually followed single sources due to the practical difficulties of delving into multiple scrolls for alternative narratives.[194] As early as 1670 John Henry Boecler (and later Petrus Wesseling in 1746) determined he had been plagiarising Polybius to a scandalous degree and this was no better illustrated than in his digressions on Fortune.[195] It has even been suggested that Diodorus took his information through intermediaries, Agatharchides of Cnidus for example, in an already epitomised form. But there is little proof, and to what extent he did use *mittelquellen*, middle sources, or showed true independence of thought and opinion, remains *sub judice*.[196]

Diodorus' own declaration of method suggests he was not entirely mechanical and the title of his work, *Library of History*, was honest to the content, for it suggested nothing more than a collection of available texts,[197] which under Hegel's strict definition, would classify him as a 'compiler' not a 'historian'.[198] In a sense this is fortunate and we might thank him for lacking any great gift of originality, for a more personal interpretation might have rendered his Alexander sources unrecognisable, where instead (we believe) we receive a fair *impression* of Cleitarchus' underlying account of Alexander, and of Hieronymus' account of the years that followed. As it has been observed, some 'universal' historians were more 'universal' than others.[199]

THE *FLORUM CORPUSCULUM:* THE PETALS OF EPITOME

We would like to say much about Gnaeus Pompeius Trogus, a Romanised Vocontian Gaul writing 'in old fashioned elegance' in the rule of Augustus, and the least possible about Justin, in whose epitomised books Trogus' cremated ashes are compacted.[200] Unfortunately, little remains of

Trogus' original *Historiae Philippicae* (*et totius mundi origines et terrae situs*), 'the only world history written in Latin by a pagan.'[201] Justin did however provide useful *prologoi* or summaries of the contents of each chapter in his *Epitoma Historiarum Philippicarum libri XLIV* in a similar manner to Trogus himself and the anonymous 4th century *Periochae* compiler who summarised Livy's lost books. The problem with epitomes, as Brunt proposed, is that they '… reflect the interests of the authors who cite or summarise the lost works as much or more than the characteristics of the works concerned.'[202]

Within Justin's précis of Trogus there remains a clear bias in content towards Spain, Gaul (which reportedly sent envoys to Alexander in Babylon), Carthage, and the western provinces of the Roman Empire, understandable for an author born in Gallia Narbonensis, broadly modern Provence. Trogus' work stretched back to the dawn of time covering the successive great kingdoms in the style of Herodotus, but now extending further forward, through the empires of Assyria, Media, Persia, Macedonia and to Rome with its present Parthian challenge.[203] Trogus' family had made its mark in Rome; his grandfather and uncle served under Pompey the Great, and Trogus claimed his father was some kind of secretary-diplomat to Julius Caesar. This last detail suggests a switched allegiance, for Pompey and Caesar were opponents until the final decisive battle at Pharsalia in June 48 BCE, after which Pompey fled to Egypt and assassination by Pothinus, the eunuch of Ptolemy XIII *Theos Philopatros* (the 'father loving God').[204]

Of Trogus' forty-four books, those numbered seven to thirty-three focused on the rise and fall of Macedonia, and six of them on the deeds of first Philip II, and then Alexander. If Ptolemaic Egypt is considered an extension of their influence, then Macedonian dynasties dominated the texts through to book forty. All in all, Philip came off badly, a *sine qua non* of the late Roman republic: he was the terminator of Greek liberty, though both Polybius and Trogus credited him with laying the foundation stone of Alexander's success.[205]

Trogus' annalistic history did not pander to the audience in Rome whose imperialism is criticised through the device of rhetorical speeches, and Parthia is positioned as the moral heart of the Persian Empire, casting doubts on Roman incursions. Here Fortuna, the new incarnation of the Greek goddess Tyche, played her part in Alexander's quest to be named king of the world, *universum terranum orbem*.[206] Justin's epitome suggests Trogus' original work, though eloquent (sufficiently so for Trogus to have confidently criticised both Livy and Sallust),[207] appears to have reinforced the darker themes attached to Alexander, as well as other influences already embedded in Cleitarchus.[208] Of course, the closer-to-home exhortations of Roman republican polemic had their effect as well; corruption by wealth is blamed for the downfall of the Lydians, the Greeks, and ultimately, Alexander himself.[209]

How much of the vocabulary in Justin's epitome was his rather than Trogus' remains debatable, though scholars are now inclining to credit him with some originality and even linguistic creativity.[210] He was not naively epitomising, however; in his preface, which took the form of an epistle, Justin suggested he was arranging an anthology of instructive passages, omitting '… what did not make pleasant reading or serve to provide a moral.'[211] These selections were akin to the Greek classroom preparatory exercises, but now arranged as a history, and for all we know Justin might have simply been a student on such a syllabus. As Carol Thomas recently pointed out, Romans grew up with Alexander and: 'As a schoolroom staple he was a key figure in hortatory texts.'[212]

The petals of Justin's self-titled *florum corpusculum*, a little body of flowers, have sadly fallen too far from the original roots to tell us more about Trogus' pages.[213] Nonetheless, Justin's brief resume of his history is, sadly, the only surviving continuous narrative of events in the Eastern Mediterranean that spans the whole of the Hellenistic Age. Less optimistic is Tarn's conclusion of Justin's efforts: 'Is there any bread at all to this intolerable deal of sack?'[214]

OILS ON OIL AND PEARLS IN A PIG TROUGH

Tarn's 1948 source study also assaulted Curtius' *Historiae Alexandri Magni Macedonis*, if that indeed approximates the original title of our third extant book, and so enigmatic, though influential, is Curtius' work, that we dedicate a later chapter to his identification.[215]

Curtius was likely aboard the Roman *cursus honorum*, the senatorial career path, where training as a rhetorician was vital to success; it was not an uncommon twinning of abilities in the so-called Silver Age of Latin. But the dating of Curtius' work remains uncertain and there is no firm evidence it was widely known or ever used before the Middle Ages, after which interest was reignited.[216] The first two books of his monograph, in which Curtius might have identified himself more fully, have been lost. Judging by an encomium in his tenth chapter he would have prefaced his introduction with an imperial dedication that would have dated him nicely (T11). Frequent lacunae appear elsewhere and yet sufficient remains to propose both he, and Cleitarchus, shared a common bond: they placed the edification of their audience above purer historiographical pursuits, with the earlier production assimilated into Curtius' restaging of the play.

A 'gifted amateur', Curtius has been termed 'a Roman who wrote for Romans'.[217] He filled the gaps in the Cleitarchean masonry with his own colourful grouting and accessorised Alexander, and Darius III too for that matter, with speeches from his own rhetorical wardrobe; thus attired, the Macedonian king was paraded anew as digressions on *fortuna* and *regnum* – kingship – were readdressed. This was essentially the same story with a new editor and under a new literary censor, though studded with occasional unique and 'invaluable facts'.[218] Curtius justified his inclusion of less than credible episodes by explaining his journalistic dilemma: 'I report more than I believe, for while I cannot vouch for matters of which I am not certain, neither can I omit what I have heard.'[219] This was, as we now know, a familiar refrain from narrators rather than historians.

If we consider that Curtius embellished Cleitarchus, who had already embellished the agenda-laden works of Alexander's contemporaries, we appreciate how thick the sugar coating became on his bittersweet biography. Curtius' method has been described as one that frittered away priceless sources '... in the course of a tedious literary concept about the goddess Fortuna and many florid exercises in Roman rhetoric.'[220] Tarn and Syme summed him up as nothing more than a 'hasty irresponsible rhetorician' who was little more than a 'superior journalist', whilst Tarn's personal polemic is more colourful still: 'He can slough the rhetoric, as a snake sloughs a dead skin. And one neglects that rhetoric at one's peril, for scattered through it, like pearls in a pig-trough, are some quite valuable facts and strange pieces of insight; the book is both repellent and fascinating.'[221]

Once again, opinion is inclining towards a reinstatement of his credentials as a judicious historian; scholars including Seibert and Schachermeyr and more recently Errington and Baynham in particular, have done much to salvage him as worthy of respect.[222] His technical descriptions are at times superior to Arrian's even if his '... monograph remains something of a cliché of the Graeco-Roman rhetorical tradition.' Daniel Heinsius went as far as terming him *Venus Historicorum*.[223] A good summation comes from Olbrycht: 'Scholarly research has overestimated the rhetorical and artistic contribution of Curtius while neglecting its actual relation to historical events.'[224]

The monographs by Cleitarchus and Curtius may have been one-time bids for fame, for we are not aware they authored anything but a book on Alexander. Prising them apart is not an easy task as time firmly has laminated them together. But why did Curtius' work survive when Cleitarchus' account, once so popular in Rome, did not?[225] Although his had become the perfect pizza base for new moralistic toppings, Cleitarchus may have been disdained by the *literati* with pretensions. But the most significant answer to Curtius' survival is perhaps summed up with 'Latin'. Cleitarchus had published in Greek, the language later used by Roman intellectuals but not by the populace in general, and the effort required to translate a Greek work was greater than producing a new Latin text, so copies dwindled as Latin books proliferated in the later empire. That proliferation was especially true of books written by the politically connected, in which context it remains vexing why Curtius, likely himself a politician, is unreferenced before the Middle Ages.[226] The owners of the relatively few manuscripts most likely had no idea of their frailty and proximity to extinction, and when Rome's own borders finally broke and libraries were burned by barbarian torches, her own Latin productions followed the Greek tragedy into the flames.

Trogus and Curtius, at the heart of the Vulgate genre, were peddling their rhetoric just as the Athenian sophists and rhetors had honed their oratory skills in the courts, where, like ships 'before a veering wind, they lay their thoughts and words first on one tack then another...' And though Diodorus considered that 'history also contributes to the power of speech', we have reason to believe it was in fact the other way around.[227]

PORTENTS OF THE PRIEST AND EPIDEICTIC PREACHER

There is no doubting the eloquence of Plutarch, the author of the fourth surviving profiling of Alexander. He multi-sourced 'from the best to the very worst' with vigour to sculpt the character he wished to display, or rather its face, expression and eyes, for he mused 'our senses are not meant to pick out black rather than white' but to receive 'reflected impressions'.[228] Much of the detail that featured in his rendering of Alexander was derived from the oft-cited corpus of letters he believed to be authentic, though he also implied his access to books was limited in provincial Chaeronea, a town that still displayed the tree known as Alexander's Oak in his day. But, as we know, the composition of letters was a popular template in rhetorical training and sophists' lectures (*epideixeis,* 'digressions illustrative of character') with their harsh *suasoria* as part of learning *declamatio,* when deceit was not the aim but rather accomplished emulation.[229] In 1873 Hersher published his *Epistolographi Graeci* containing some 1,600 examples.[230]

Plutarch also indicated that his understanding of Latin was imperfect, and the appreciation of 'the beauty and quickness of the Roman style, the figures of speech, the rhythm, and the other embellishments of the language' did not come easy to him either.[231] In contrast to Diodorus' more monogamous method, Plutarch's frequent changing of source partners renders any attempt to identify the authors underpinning his biographical compendiums near impossible.[232]

Often labelled a 'Middle Platonist' for his philosophical stance (thus elements of Stoic and Peripatetic doctrine had been absorbed), Plutarch produced a number of 'educational' works; his *Moralia* (containing the possibly spuriously assigned *De Alexandri Magni Fortuna aut Virtute*) offers auxiliary insights from a complex commentator on the nature of men and their adherence to, or divergence from, the honour code and behavioural ideals of classical Greece. As a former pupil of Ammonius the Peripatetic (though he may have been a Platonist) in Athens, convictions from Aristotle's *Ethics* and *Politics* frequently raise their head. Whitmarsh has termed these essays 'virtual history', noting that the above collection, alongside *On the Fortune of the Romans* (also *Roman Questions* and *Greek Questions*), reflect Plutarch's political influence in both Greece and in Rome at its zenith.[233]

A senior Priest of Apollo at the oracle of Delphi, and employed to interpret the auguries of Delphic priestess Pythia, he maintained that gods never spoke but only gave signs, and that the divine escaped recognition if the belief was lacking.[234] Unsurprisingly, Alexander's death (like much of his life) became a chapter more sympathetic to mysterious portents, Chaldean prophecies, diviners and superstition, as well as the liberating of the soul to higher things, for Plutarch was also a firm believer in reincarnation.[235] Thanks to sources like Aristobulus, he, and Arrian a few decades after him, had all the materials they needed (T21, T22).[236]

Plutarch had no agenda of preserving history *per se*, as he himself freely admitted; he was hunting for vices and virtues 'from a chance remark or a jest that might reveal more of a man's character than the mere feat of winning battles', and he was plucking rhetorical leaves to flavour his biographical stews along the way.[237] But Plutarch was also dumping non-exploitable chapters, something of both Xenophon and Justin in his approach, and, moreover, he was inconsistent in his methodology too; where it suited his direction, Plutarch introduced *fabulae*, and where it didn't, he was quick to scorn exaggeration.[238]

The *Parallel Lives,* his cradle-to-grave biographies in which Greeks were paired with Roman counterparts – Alexander with Julius Caesar for example – illustrated his own political juxtaposition of citizenship in both Greece and Rome; perhaps his pairings were further inspired by Polybius' adjacent-chapter profiling of Hannibal and Scipio.[239] Outside of the requirement for skilled and artful comparison, Plutarch's was not an approach that fuelled his forensic curiosity. As for his biography of Alexander, Tarn suggested it was written late in life when 'the fire had burnt low and [he] was swamped by his much reading', though we know little of the relative chronology behind the production of his *Lives*.[240] The increasing tension between Alexander's self-control and his temper (disasters are always linked to excessive drinking in Plutarch's biography) is illustrated, as Mossman notes, by 'interweaving and contrasting epic and tragic elements throughout the *Life*' along with connections to the story of the god Dionysus, whence the call to drunkenness came.[241]

As far as Macaulay was concerned, Plutarch 'reminds us of the cookery of those continental inns… in which a certain nondescript broth is kept constantly boiling, and copiously poured, without distinction, over every dish…'[242] It was an unfair summation that belittles Plutarch's deep curiosity about human nature, and his 'pottage' contained ingredients we find nowhere else. Along with the Vulgate historians, and like the more recent restoration of Leonardo Da Vinci's *Last Supper*, the faded and flaking primary pigments were retouched in brighter oils and re-rendered in vivid tones that give us vivid moralistic portraits that are inevitably larger than the lives themselves.

THE STOIC NAIVETY OF A SOLDIER'S SOLDIER

The final extant narrative on the life and campaigns of Alexander is Arrian's *Anabasis*, which was the last one of them to be written. It was penned more than 400 years after the death of the Macedonian king, and some 550 years after Herodotus walked seemingly unawares past both the Hanging Gardens at Babylon and the Sphinx at Giza, for neither were mentioned in his parental *Histories*.[243] Arrian laid down his stylus some 670 years after Cyrus the Great was beheaded by the Massagetae,[244] 900 years after the first Greek Olympiad, and perhaps a millennium, or more, after the era of Homer, who was, in fact, a Babylonian hostage (a play on the Greek *homeros)* named Tigranes, jested Lucian.[245] The *Anabasis* appeared 1,300 years after Troy had supposedly burned to the ground, and some 2,000 years after King Hammurabi (or Khammurabi) had set down the social laws of the Babylonians on a stele.[246]

If Plutarch was adorning Alexander with epideictic passages, and Curtius was laying on rhetorical oils, then in contrast Arrian was applying paint-stripper 'to set the records straight', or so he would have us believe.[247] The conflict and vagueness he found in earlier works irked his precise military mind, as did the fame and choral odes afforded to lesser men than Alexander; the tyrants of Sicily and Xenophon's Ten Thousand for example, each of whom unfairly outshone his model Macedonian warrior.[248] This must explain why Arrian largely marginalised the deeds of Philip II which launched Alexander on his journey.[249]

Holding the positions of both Consul of Rome and archon of Athens through the decade of 130-140 CE, Arrian was a 'public intellectual' with *authoritas* in both peninsulas, like Plutarch and Polybius (from his association with Roman *nobiles*) before him.[250] He challenged the legends that frequented the Alexander accounts to show a judicial backbone, and Arrian appears to have been deeply religious with the requisite soldier's superstition. His *Anabasis* ended with 'I too, have had God's help in my work', implying a favoured client relationship with the divine, and if Alexander was a new Achilles then Arrian was to be his Homer.[251] Here he was employing a more subtle rhetoric than his forerunners: that of self-promotion through the façade of truth's envoy, whilst his personal reflections and pedantic, though shallow, autopsy of his sources at times betrays arrogance thinly disguised as investigative fervour.[252]

As a Romanised Greek from Nicomedia in Bithynia (northern Asia Minor) and the author of a *Bithynaika*,[253] we might conjecture Arrian credited Alexander's success with laying the foundation of Rome's Eastern Empire, thus furthering his own career. According to the *Suda*, Dio Chrysostom (ca. 40-post 112 CE, literally 'golden mouth'), a fellow Bithynian historian, had a generation earlier written *On Alexander's Virtues* in eight books and this must have set an influential encomiastic tone.[254] Close parallels between Arrian and Alexander certainly did exist: Arrian served in Trajan's war against Parthia (114-117 CE), a post that would have seen him marching south through Mesopotamia and eastern Babylonia, then down the Tigris to the Persian Gulf. And as with Alexander's reality check at the Hyphasis River in India, this hard-earned Roman territory was soon lost again to the Eastern barbarian kings.[255]

Arrian may have additionally likened himself to Alexander's secretary-soldier, Eumenes of Cardia, who became a central character in his sequel, *Events After Alexander* (*Ta Meta Alexandron*) which was based on Hieronymus' account, for both were Greeks operating under a foreign regime and each was tasked with pacifying Cappadocia. In Arrian's case this meant driving back the Alans; his treatise on the tactics used, *Deployment Against the Alans*, described his dispositions in classical Greek and Macedonian terms. He was literally walking in the footsteps of the Macedonian conquest, which had itself marched in the soleprints of Xenophon's leather *iphikratides*; appropriately Photius *did* term Arrian the 'young Xenophon'.[256] His eastern experiences may explain why Arrian's first chapters read as a hurried narrative of Alexander's consolidation of Greece and the Balkans, for he was impatient for his pages to land on the now familiar Asian soil.

When reviewing his list of sources, Arrian was drawn to Ptolemy, 'the soldier's soldier', and to Aristobulus, likely a supporting engineer, and he only drew from 'external sources' for missing detail and useful *legomena*. This did not stop him from being 'frequently warped by misunderstanding' in his narrative; geography, the sequence of events and names too, appear erroneously.[257] Whether Arrian was genuinely inspired to use Ptolemy 'as a king honour-bound to avoid untruth', or if he was simply being pragmatic in the face of limited sources, is debatable.[258] It is nevertheless difficult to fathom how, as an experienced field commander, Arrian could truly give credit to Persian troops numbers at the Battle of Gaugamela, stated at one million (five times larger than Curtius' estimation) with some 300,000 of them slaughtered. The Macedonians, he claimed, lost one hundred men.[259] Arrian did, however, mention that his tally related to Companions alone; he was not about to trivialise by recalling the death of the common soldier. But did he trust his source that far? Curtius has already taken (what appears) a sarcastic swipe at the figures recorded at Issus: 'so the Persians were driven like cattle by a handful of men', and '... whilst not more than 1,000 horsemen were with Alexander, huge numbers of the enemy were in retreat.'[260]

One observer notes that Arrian was 'engaging in a dialogue with the great historical masters' in the style of Tacitus, another orating product of the Roman *cursus honorum* with extensive military experience.[261] Influential with the Emperor Hadrian (76-138 CE), Arrian opened his story with 'I have no need to write my name, for it is not at all unknown among men',[262] a self-introduction that cannot help recalling Livy.[263] Arrian went on, not without self-confidence:

> ...let me say this: that this book of mine is, and has been from my youth, more precious than country and kin and public advancement – indeed, for me it *is* these things. And that is why I venture to claim the first place in Greek literature, since Alexander, about whom I write, held first place in the profession of arms.

The self-righteousness here is also somewhat reminiscent of the epilogue to Ovid's *Metamorphoses*, and it rings of Polybius who dedicated several chapters to the honour of the Scipios, which, nevertheless, read as his own *Curriculum Vitae*.

Scholarly debate is ever divided on Arrian's value as a historian. If, like Thucydides, he may have thought he was producing *ktema es aei*, 'a possession forever',[265] he was ultimately an 'apologist', and 'what emerges is a powerful portrait of Alexander... confident of the justice of his cause, careful of the legitimacy of his crusade, and pious at the moment of his triumph...'[266] But the need to combine the best qualities of a king, with the worst of a tyrant, would have produced a character portrait that could only have curdled on Arrian's pages, and he permitted no Vulgate agenda of moral decline to accommodate Alexander's transformation; even the king's drinking binges were, he accepted, 'a social courteousy to his friends'. So he exploited a lingering bigotry to legitimise the mass slaughter of 'barbarians', while praising the exceptional conquered tribes in condescending tones: 'Like the best of the Greeks, they claimed to know the distinction between right and wrong.'[267]

In the process, Arrian was forced to become a master of omission like Ptolemy before him,[268] and he dismissed what could *not* be erased with 'then there is a story – to me quite incredible'...'a thing one might have expected from an Oriental despot [Xerxes], but utterly uncharacteristic of Alexander.'[269] This last example was, paradoxically, expressing his disbelief in Alexander's destruction of the temple of Asclepius at Ecbatana, when he had earlier fulsomely reported his burning of the Achaemenid ceremonial capital at Persepolis.[270]

For all his posturing, Arrian's study of Alexander lacked creativity, as did its title, *Anabasis*, which once again emulated Xenophon's with its eight-book length. Tarn believed that of the seven surviving speeches in the book, most are once more, an 'allusion to Xenophon'; it was yet another example of 'subject matter fitting the moment'.[271] In fact, it has been argued that Arrian's own *agnomen*, Xenophon, which appeared in his full name, was likewise born of the nostalgia linking him to the pupil of Socrates.[272]

Arrian adopted the Ionic Greek dialect of Herodotus for his *Indike* in which Nearchus' log and elements of Eratosthenes and Megasthenes were being blended into a formless 'discussion of Indian affairs'.[273] And yet we must recall that the Second Sophistic, in which 'Greeks were Romans and Romans, it often seems, sought to be like Greeks', demanded nothing less.[274] It was a period that saw Cassius Dio pen a Roman history in Greek in a (poor) emulation of Thucydides, and the Cynic, Dio Chrysostom (most likely his grandfather), who was banished by the emperor Domitian, depart Rome with nothing more than the lessons and speeches of Plato and Demosthenes in his bags. The period inspired Quintus of Smyrna to finally bridge the Homeric gap between the end of the *Iliad* and the start of the *Odyssey* with an epic fourteen book *Ta meth' Homeron* (better known as the *Posthomerika*), literally 'things after Homer', and in one view, when the Roman Empire ceased to know Greek, its decline truly began.[275]

Arrian is himself credited with single-handedly preserving the teachings of his Greek-speaking Phrygian Stoic mentor, Epictetus (ca. 55-135 CE, the Greek name meant 'acquired'), in the form of the *Discourses* and *Enkheiridion Epiktetou*, a manual written, unsurprisingly, in the style of Xenophon's *Apomnemoneumata* (broadly, 'records') which preserved Socrates' recollections.[276] Inevitably, Epictetus' particular philosophical interpretations of kingship infiltrated his pupil's summation of the Macedonian king.[277]

If classical history was 'the circulated written works of a social elite', we have no better examples than these, for both Plutarch and Arrian enjoyed prominent political offices that provided wider publication capabilities, and thus we still read them today.[278] Although they were both educated far above the *plebeia* and the *hoi polloi*, Arrian and Plutarch were, nonetheless, shackled to the mind-set of the time. Arrian, hamstrung by a lifelong affection for his Pellan conqueror, rarely shone a torch into the undergrowth either side of his hero's well-trodden path, except where he saw thick clods sitting on an artificial-looking turf. He added nothing truly insightful to the detail found in the Vulgate, and Plutarch was satisfied to ponder, once again, fortune's tides and fate's inevitability in stoic fashion. Polybius had frequently deferred to *tyche* (not the deity Tyche, Rome's Fortuna, but broadly fate or providence, things beyond explanation), which 'steered almost all the affairs of the world', as a final explanation,[279] and a similarly stoical Arrian chose an easy route over 'wholehearted religious or philosophical commitment'.[280]

These five extant historians, representing the 'court' tradition and the 'Vulgate' genre (Plutarch arguably had a foot in each camp), represent the major part of what we have on Alexander today. The geographical treatise of Strabo and the forays into natural history by Pliny, make frequent references to the Macedonian campaign in the East, but little more than that. Supplementing them for detail on the Successor Wars we have Plutarch's biographies of the generals, kings and politicians who played their part in the fate of the *Diadokhoi*. We have fragments from anonymous epitomes and codices, such as the *Codex Palatinus Graecus 129*, known as the *Heidelberg Epitome* (so named for its discovery in the German city), with its four relevant excerpts, and whilst as vexatious as they are useful, they help us to build a picture of these dramatic war-torn years.[281]

The ironic result is that the *Historical Miscellany* of Aelian, a philhellene teaching rhetoric in Rome and whose accomplished florid Greek earned him the title *meliglossos* ('honey-tongued'), stands as an irreplaceable goldmine of diverse historical facts and fables, anecdotes, pithy maxims and moralising epithets that occasionally touched on Alexander's world. This, alongside Athenaeus' *Dinner Philosophers* (*Deipnosophistae*), in which some 1,250 authors and more than 2,500 works are referred to, takes on an incongruous weight in the preservation of the voices of the period.[282] Athenaeus' diversional by-product of the *Pax Romana* contains no fewer than sixteen of the thirty-six fragments we possess of Duris, the lost Samian historian, and thanks to the *Deipnosophistae* we have more lines of verbatim Theopompus, who 'claimed the first place in rhetorical education' and who ominously credited progress in the 'art of discourse' for the improving quality of historians,[283] than any other lost Greek historian.[284]

These cultural snapshots of the classical world, never intended to be histories themselves, beside Diogenes Laertius' *Lives and Deaths of the Eminent Philosophers* (whose detail occasionally overlapped statements found in the *Suda*), have been mined deeply for insights perhaps more thoroughly than their authors intended. Although Nietzsche held a dim view of compilers like Diogenes ('the dim witted watchman who guards treasures without having a clue about their value'),[285] we are faced with the fact that 'the somewhat greasy heap of a literary rag-and-bone-picker like Athenaeus' has nevertheless been 'turned to gold by time'.[286] Anthologies and compendiums like these, the productions of what Momigliano would have termed 'antiquarians' rather than 'historians',[287] caught the imagination of the reader, for anecdotal collections are usually accompanied by scandal, slanders and political intrigue: the sugar and spice that sells the bake more effectively than plain dough.

In the centuries between his campaigns in Asia and his refashioning in Roman literature, Alexander was immersed in the agar of philosophical doctrine and epideictic oratory, and preserved in the aspic of Graeco-Roman rhetoric, even if the authors were, at times, unconscious of the damaging effect. The reporting of his death provides us with a unique example of historical wind over tide, leaving us wallowing in uncertainty in the choppy waters of contradiction and romance, and from the Roman investigative viewpoint, logical currents appear to have been dominated by adverse intestate breezes. But if we strip away the additives that infuse his literary corpse, Alexander would become a blander tale attractive to no one. And if in the name of that colour and flavour we agree to leave them in, the health-conscious historian needs to label them with 'E numbers' denoting the misdirecting preservatives they are.

NOTES

1. Cicero *De Oratore* Book 2.13, translated by EW Sutton, Cambridge Harvard University Press, 1942, quoting Marcus Antonius.
2. Momigliano (1977) p 115.
3. Strabo 13.1.27, translated by HC Hamilton and W Falconer, published by Henry G Bohn, London, 1854. Strabo 13.1.1, and 13.1.38 additionally voiced the view that no trace remained.
4. For Alexander's arrival at Troy see Arrian 1.12.1-6, Diodorus 17.17.3 and ·Plutarch 15.7-9. Thucydides 1.10-11 is just one example of the historians Alexander would have read who clearly accepted the Trojan epics as fact.
5. For the dating of the fall of Troy see Robbins (2001) p 85. Early dates for the fall of Troy come from Duris at 1334 BCE and later estimates from Eratosthenes at 1184 BCE, for example. Most ancient historians inclined to dates between 1170 and 1250 (within the years proposed by Eratosthenes, Herodotus, Sosigenes, Timaeus and the *Parian Chronicle* for example). Apollodorus and the so-called *Canon of Ptolemy* also dated the fall of Troy. Fragments from ancient historians suggested the following dates BCE: Duris 1334, *Life of Homer* 1270, Herodotus ca. 1240, Cleitarchus 1234, Dicaearchus 1212, *Parian Chronicle* 1209, Thrasyllus 1193, Timaeus 1193, Eratosthenes and his disciples (Apollodorus, Castor, Diodorus, Apollonius, Eusebius) 1184/3; Sosibius 1171, Phanias ca. 1129, Ephorus ca. 1135; detail taken from Mylonas (1964) p 353. Robinson (1953) pp 60-61 for citations from Callisthenes' *Hellenica* and Plutarch's *Camillus* stating Callisthenes, Ephorus, Damastes and Phylarchus were in agreement on the month of its fall. See C Baikouzis, MO Marcelo, *Is an Eclipse Described in the Odyssey?* Proceedings of the National Academy of Sciences 105 (26): 8823, June 24, 2008, for the modern scientific dating of the fall of events said to have occurred at the fall of Troy. Modern archaeoastronomy places Troy's final fall at 1188 BCE, probably in the Greek month of Thargelion (May-June) – see Pearson (1960) pp 60-61 for ancient sources citing Thargelion; the method scientifically cross-references Homeric mention of Hermes (Mercury), Venus, the Pleiades and the 'new moon' along with the additional claim that 'the sun was blotted out of the sky', thus a total eclipse, on the day Odysseus' returned to Greece a decade later. An eclipse occurred on 16 April 1178 BCE, though suspiciously only the seer, Theoclymenus, witnessed the 'invading darkness'. Homeric discrepancies aside, and unlike most other disciplines for fathoming the past, archaeoastronomy is unique; its usefulness improves with time thanks to scientific advances in astronomical calculations that can be readily backdated.
6. A more extensive report of the finds made in excavations through 1871, 72, 73, 78, 79 was published in *Ilios, the city and country of the Trojans,* Harper & Brothers, New York, 1881; further discussions of recent works in J Sammer *The Identification of Troy* in *New Light on the Dark Age of Greece,* Immanuel Velikovsky Archive, March 1999. Frank Calvert had commenced excavations at Troy in 1865 finding the remains of Greek and Roman cities but lacked the funding to continue. The ruins are now labelled Troy VIIa in excavations.
7. The verdict on Schliemann came from D Easton *Schliemann's Mendacity – a False Trail?* Antiquity 58, 1984, p 198.
8. For Rome's claims to Trojan roots see Spencer (2002) pp 8-14 for full discussion citing Virgil's *Aeneid* and Ennius' *Annales.* Naevius' *Bellum Punicum* was the first *poem* to recognise the mythical connection of Aeneas (Latinised spelling) and his Trojans with the foundation of Rome. Also see Dionysius of Halicarnassus *Roman Antiquities* 1.14.1 ff.
9. Following Horace *Odes* 3.3.61-62; see discussion in Baynham (1998) p 11.
10. Quoting Hornblower (1981) p 3 for 'twilight zone'.
11. Polybius 8.10.11 for 'numerous historians', who probably included Duris, Diyllus and Demochares; see Bosworth-Baynham (2000) p 302. The oft-cited works of the pro-Athenian Diyllus (early 3rd century BCE, his history spanned 356 to 297 BCE, in twenty-six books), along with Timaeus' thirty-eight-book history of Sicily and then Pyrrhus of Epirus (which reached to the Punic War of 264 BCE), fell into that hole. As did the accounts of Phylarchus (3rd century BCE), the memoirs of Aratus of Sicyon (lived ca. 271-213 BCE) and Philochorus the Atthidographer (ca. 340-261 BCE), all of which are lost bar fragments. Extracts of Euphantus of Olynthus (whose *On Kingship* was likely dedicated to Antigonus *Gonatas*), Nymphis of Heraclea and Demochares the nephew of Demosthenes, whose history might have stretched back to Philip's reign ca. 350 BCE, suggest they also narrated the events of the early Hellenistic world. Discussion in Tarn (1948) p 63 and for Diodorus see Pearson (1960) p 239. Hammond (1994) p 16 for Diyllus and Diodorus 21.5 for Diyllus' twenty-six books.
12. Diodorus 1.3, translation from the Loeb Classical Library edition, 1933.
13. The lack of interest is an observation made in Shipley (2000) p 7; quoting McGing (2010) p 6.
14. A theme discussed in Hornblower (1981) p 236. Also see Bosworth-Baynham (2000) p 296.

15. Polybius 1.2.8 for *pragmatike historia*.
16. Polybius 9.1-2, translation by I Scott-Kilvert, Penguin Classics edition, 1979.
17. Momigliano (1977) p 69.
18. Quoting Billows (1990) p 2 and 'dissected parts' from Polybius 1.4.7-8. Flower (1994) p 148 ff for discussion of Theopompus exampling this. McGing (2010) p 51 ff for the works influencing Polybius.
19. Polybius 8.11.4. See discussion in Walbank (1962) p 2 ff for Theopompus' treatment. The criticism might be unfair as Philip V of Macedonia reduced the work to sixteen books when excerpting detail on only Philip II from it, so much of Theopompus' fifty-eight-book work must have dealt with other matters.
20. Polybius 1.3 stated that main narrative commenced at 220 BCE, the 140th Olympiad and at 1.5 he explained the Roman starting point as Rome's first overseas venture in the 129th Olympiad, so dovetailing with Timaeus' history. Discussed in McGing (2010) pp 21-22 and p 97 and in Hornblower (1981) pp 183-184.
21. Callisthenes is mentioned at Polybius 6.45.1 and 12.17-22 where he is termed 'ignorant' and unable to distinguish the impossible from the possible. See Robinson (1953) p 55 for the full entries.
22. Bosworth-Baynham (2000) pp 286-306 for a useful summary by R Billows of Polybius' view of Alexander; p 289 for the passages concerning Alexander. McGing (2010) p 130 ff for his dating and age.
23. Polybius 1.4 for 'entire network of events'. Hammond (1994) p 90 for 'double-abbreviated'.
24. Polybius' critique didn't deter him from extracting detail from their works; Philinus had lived through the First Punic War (264-241 BCE) adopting a pro-Carthaginian perspective, whilst Pictor fought for Rome in the Second Punic War against Hannibal (218-201 BCE); Polybius 1.14-15 for Philinus' role with Hannibal. Polybius also attacked Xenophon, Plato and Demosthenes, but Timaeus in particular, dedicating much of his twelfth book to a polemic on his methods.
25. Polybius 1.1.5; Polybius 12.11 described Timaeus' comprehensive cross-referencing of Olympiads with list of ephors, kings, Athenian archons and priestesses of Hera at Argos in the forms of tables; Momigliano (1977) pp 49-50. Lucian *Makrobioi* 22 for Timaeus' age.
26. Polybius 3.59.2; discussion and translation in Walbank (1962) p 1.
27. See discussion of Polybius' polemics against Timaeus in Walbank (1962) pp 8-11 and Momigliano (1977) pp 50-51. Pseudo-Lucian *Makrobioi* 22 claimed Timaeus lived to age ninety-six.
28. Strabo 14.1.22 for Timaeus' epithet. Also discussion in Walbank (1962) p 3. For Polemon's *Against Timaeus* see discussion in McGing (2010) p 65. Timaeus' invective spawned a twelve-book (or more) retaliatory work by the antiquarian Polemon, a contemporary of Polybius, suitably titled *Against Timaeus*. Momigliano (1977) pp 54-55 for the founding date of both cities, upheld by Timaeus.
29. Quoting Polybius 12.25a1-12.25b4 (Loeb) and 12.27.10-11 for his emphasis on the importance of military experience when writing about war.
30. Discussion in Pitcher (2009) pp 106-107 on Polybius' critiques and method. Also Green (1990) was particularly scathing about Polybius' partisan approach. For discussion of Polybius' speeches see Champion (2000) p 436 quoting FW Walbank for 'subjective operations'. Quoting Walbank and discussed in Momigliano (1977) p 71 on Polybius' final chapters. Following McGing (2010) p 15 for 'writing himself into Roman history'.
31. Quoting Hatzopoulos (1996) p 265.
32. Polybius provided his own explanation of *anakyklosis* at 6.3.5-6.4.13; following Bosworth-Baynham (2000) p 308 for Herodotus' empire progression.
33. Polybius 6.43.1, 6.44.9 and 6.10-18 for the 'mixed constitution' discussion. Polybius 6.9.12-14 for the prediction of Rome's decline and 6.9.10 for *politeion anakyklosis*.
34. Polybius 1.3.3-6, translation by I Scott-Kilvert, Penguin Classics edition, 1979.
35. Polybius 3.59.3 ff for credit to Alexander, quoting 1.1.3 and for 'Fortune's showpiece' 1.1.4. He was referring to the years 200 BCE, the beginning of Rome's war against Hannibal, down to 168/176 BCE and the defeat of King Perseus of Macedonia at the Battle of Pydna.
36. Polybius 12.4b.2-4; for his attitude to Rome and use of *barbaroi* discussed in Champion (2000) pp 425-444; more on the development of the Greek term *barbaroi* in chapter titled *The Rebirth of the Wrath of Peleus' Son*.
37. Quoting T Mommsen and cited by Walbank (1981) p 19.
38. The *Annales Maximi* were city records kept by the Pontifex Maximus; Cicero in his *De republica* 1.25 claimed they were legitimate until 400 BCE when an eclipse was mentioned. They were assembled into eighty books and finally published by Publius Mucius Scaevola in 130 BCE; for full discussion see Frier (1979) chapter 8 p 162 ff, and for their dating see Crake (1940) p 379.
39. Gudeman *Romans* (1894) p 145 for the unlikely speech, as an example, of Scipio *Africanus*

recorded by Livy, though Cicero informs us that Scipio left no written commentary on his activity.

40. Quoting Hegel (1837) II, *Reflective History, 1, Universal History.*

41. HG Gadamer *Wahrheit und Methode, Grundzüge einer philosophischen Hermeneutik*, Mohr-Siebeck, 1960 and quoting Braudel (1969) p 47 for the analogy to time and soil. Following Braudel (1969) p 4 and p 6 for liking narrative history to a personal philosophy and 'child of its time'.

42. Quoting Momigliano (1977) p 79 on Livy's use of Polybius.

43. Livy 1.1 and Livy Preface 1, translation by Rev. Canon Robert, EP Dutton and Co., 1912 and Livy 6.1 for his comments on the fire and loss of genuine public records.

44. Macaulay *The Lays of Ancient Rome*, Introduction.

45. Malthus (1798) 2.20.

46. Quoting from Macaulay (1828).

47. Quoting Gibbon (1776 to 1789) 26.5 on Marcellinus. For Tacitus' view of the lower classes and Ammianus Marcellinus, see Grant (1995) p 62.

48. Ammianus Marcellinus 15.5.22 and 31.16.9 for the declaration of his career and ethnicity.

49. Discussed in detail in Seeley (1881) pp 12-14.

50. The authenticity of the *Libri Lintei* has been questioned. Discussed in Gudeman *Romans* (1894) p 143. They appeared in the *Historia Augusta* 1.7-10 which is perhaps an endorsement of their doubtfulness.

51. Ennius' *Annals* was an epic poem in fifteen books, later expanded to eighteen covering Roman history from the fall of Troy (stated as 1184 BCE) down to the censorship of Cato the Elder in 184 BCE; see Brown (1959) p 5 for discussion. About 600 lines survive. Naevius' *Bellum Punicum* was the first *poem* to recognise the mythical connection of Aeneas and his Trojans with the foundation of Rome. Also Dionysius of Halicarnassus *Roman Antiquities* 1.14.1 ff. For Rome's claims to Trojan roots see Spencer (2002) pp 8-14 for full discussion citing Virgil's *Aeneid* and Ennius' *Annales.*

52. Discussed in Champion (2000) pp 431-432. It is an unlikely claim by Timaeus for horses were regularly sacrificed before battle by many barbarian tribes according to Polybius 12.4c.1.

53. Aulus Gellius 19.8.15.

54. Macaulay *The Lays of Ancient Rome*, Introduction.

55. Macaulay (1828).

56. Dioxippus is said by Aristobulus to have quoted Homer's lines on *ichor* the blood of the gods, after which Alexander snubbed him with a retort; see discussion in Tarn (1948) pp 358-359. The quote comes from Athenaeus 251a. Also Plutarch 28.3 has Alexander reminding his men that he was losing blood and not *ichor* from an arrow wound. The quote is also attributed to Callisthenes (Seneca *Suasoria* 1.5) and Anaxarchus (Diogenes Laertius *Anaxarchus* 9.60).

57. Quoting Dean (1918) p 41 on 'filial forbearance'.

58. Aristophanes *Frogs* 1391.

59. Diogenes Laertius *Pyrrho* 64-65 quoting Timon's *Silli*, translation from the Loeb Classical Library edition, 1925

60. Hesiod *Theogonia* 83-87, based on the translation by ML West, Oxford World Classics, 2008 edition p 5.

61. Herodotus 2.53 suggested Homer and Hesiod 'gave the Hellenes their gods'. Following Jaeger (1939) and the observation that Hesiod was uniquely speaking to men of his own time, about his own time.

62. The later date was first proposed by Neitsche *Die Florentinischer Tractat über Homer und Hesiod*, in Rhetorica (Rheinisches museum für philology) 25 (1870:528-40) and 28 (1873:211-49). For its link with the Delian festival see discussion in Shelmerdine (1995) p 8.

63. Hesiod *Theogonia* 22-34. Hesiod *Theogonia* 27 claimed the Muses instructed him as he tended his lambs in his mountain pastures. Translation from Jaeger (1939) p 75.

64. Following Barber (1993) p 103.

65. Cicero *De Oratore* 2.36, translation from Dominik (1997).

66. Cicero *De Oratore* 2.62-63, translation by AJ Woodman and appearing in Pitcher (2009) p 15. This was set after the death of Marcus Licinius Crassus (91 BCE) and shortly before the Social War and the war between Marius and Sulla commenced. Cicero's house had already been sacked and he himself had recently returned from exile.

67. For a summary of Lucian's career see the introduction by AM Harmon to *The Works of Lucian* in the Loeb Classical Library edition, 1913. Lucian, from Samosata on the banks of the Euphrates (in modern Turkey), entered imperial service late in life. Cicero's *De Oratore* was built around a fabricated dialogue in 91 BCE between L Licinius Crassus, Marcus Antonius the orator, P Salpicius Rufus and C Aurelius Cotta, plus others.

68. Cicero *Brutus* 11.42.

69. Discussed in Bailey (1978) p 104.

70. *Flumine orationis* – 'fluency of speech'.
71. Suetonius *Julius Caesar* 56.2, drawing from Cicero *Brutus* 262, for Cicero's likening rhetoric to curling irons; the analogy repeated in Quintilian 2.5.12, 5.12.18-120. Cicero *De Oratoria* 2.57-2.94 for the comment on Isocrates. For the dating of Cicero's treatises see Dominik (1997) pp 13-15 and *De Oratoria* 1.5 for Cicero's own description of his adolescence. The view that these historians (Flower (1994) p 46 for a list) attended Isocrates' school is rejected by Schwartz and Flower (1994) pp 44-62 and put down to Hellenistic-era invention or Cicero using the term 'school' in a metaphysical sense.
72. Discussed in Momigliano (1966) p 127 quoting Cicero *De Legibus* 1.1.5. for the 'father of history' label.
73. Cicero *De Oratoria* 2.57-2.94; Flower (1994) p 43 for the accreditation of the quote. Pseudo-Plutarch *Isocrates:* Isocrates was asked how, not being very eloquent himself, he could make others so? He answered: 'Just as a whetstone cannot cut, yet it will sharpen knives for that purpose.'
74. Quoting and following Grant (1995) pp 27-28. Polybius 2.56.10-12; discussed by TP Wiseman in Gill-Wiseman (1993) p 134.
75. Quintilian 3.1.19 recorded that neither Cicero nor the rhetor Marcus Antonius (died 87 BCE) completed their works on rhetoric. The Greek counterpart to *suada* was *peitho*, respectively stemming from 'sweet' and 'persuasion'; Dominik (1997) p 3 for discussion.
76. Quoting B Vickers *In Defence of Rhetoric*, Oxford University Press, 1988 and repeated in Flower (1994) p 185.
77. Diodorus 1.76.1. Bagnall-Derow (2004) pp 206-211 for Ptolemaic papyri detailing legal procedures.
78. Momigliano (1977) p 47 for Timaeus' view on rhetoric.
79. Following the discussion in Pernot (2000) p 10.
80. In the *Iliad* 9.442 Achilles' tutor, Phoenix, was appointed to teach him about the art of public speaking as well as fighting. At 3.212-223 there is a description of Odysseus' skill at public speaking.
81. Homer *Iliad* 9.343-344; *Psychagogia* was used by Plato in his *Phaedra* 261a and defined a positive aspect of rhetoric in persuading souls to see truth: *'techne psychagogia tis dia logon.'*
82. Diogenes Laertius *Empedocles* 3 also Diogenes Laertius *Zeno the Eleactic* 4. The origins of *rhetorike* in Pernot (2000) pp 21-23.
83. Cicero *Brutus* 46.
84. Guthrie (1971) p 270; for Gorgias' label see Wardy (1996) p 6. Antiphon's *On Truth* is preserved in *Oxyrhynchus Papyri*, xi, no. 1364, quoted in Kagan (1965) p 2965. In translation the Rock of Ares, also called Areopagus, situated northwest of the Acropolis, functioned as a Court of Appeal for criminal and civil cases in ancient times; discussed further in chapter titled *Wills and Covenants in the Classical Mind*.
85. Pliny 7.30 claimed Isocrates could charge 20 talents for a single oration.
86. Plato *Theatetus* 151e (and Sextus *Against the Mathematicians* VII.60) attributed the phrase to Protagoras' *Truth*. For the fees charged by the Sophists; see full discussion in Worthington (2007) pp 306-307. Aristotle *Rhetoric* 1402a23-5 recorded Protagoras' claim to 'make the weaker argument the stronger'.
87. For Anaxagoras *On Nature* see discussion in Boyer-Merzback pp 56-58. For Anaxagoras' imprisonment, see Plutarch *Moralia* 607f or *On Exile* 17 and *de Placitis Philosophorum, Anaxagoras*. Anaxagoras claimed the sun was a red-hot stone the size of the Peloponnese and not a deity.
88. See discussion of 5th century Athenian law court practice in Worthington (2000) p 161. The implication of lies at the Assembly and lack of punishment for court case perjury discussed in Worthington (2001) p 163 and p 224.
89. See discussion in Cahn (1990) p 128 and pp 147-149. Modern opinion is that Isocrates never wrote a treatise on the art of rhetoric.
90. Diogenes Laertius *Protagoras* 52, translation from the Loeb Classical Library edition, 1925.
91. Collins (2008) Introduction pp xiii for Gorgias' use of *mageia* and his *Encomium of Helen* 14 which related rhetoric to a drug or bewitchment; translation from Collins (2008).
92. Pytheas made the lamp wick slur in Lucian *Demosthenes: an Encomium* 15, recorded by Plutarch *Demosthenes* 8.3-4.
93. See the paired speeches in prosecution and defence discussed by Ryder (1975) pp 11-54. Aeschines went into voluntary exile to Rhodes when Demosthenes' speech *On The Crown* resulted in his victory over Aeschines' *Against Ctesiphon* in 336 BCE. For his help from actors and speaking with pebbles see Pernot (2000) pp 30-31. For the fancy footwork see Aeschines *Against Ctesiphon* 206.
94. Quintilian 11.3-6.
95. Cicero *Tusculan Disputations* 5.3.7. Riedweg (2002) p 91 citing Heracleides of Pontus' claim also recounted in Diogenes Laertius *Heracleides of Pontus* 1.12.

96. Riedweg (2002) pp 90-97 for full discussion, citing Croesus' dialogue with Solon in Herodotus 1.30.2.
97. Lucian *The Double Indictment* 6, translation by HW and FG Fowler, Clarendon Press, 1905. Quoting Lucian *Demosthenes, An Encomium* 10 for the meat sauce analogy.
98. Details preserved in Pseudo-Plutarch *Lives of the Ten Orators.*
99. See discussion on the Peripatetic objections to Demosthenes' style in Worthington (2000) pp 234-238. Demetrius of Phalerum and Theophrastus both attacked Demosthenes.
100. Aristotle *On Sophistical Refutations.* For Pythagoras' classifications see the anonymous *Life of Pythagoras* 10-19 preserved by Photius.
101. Aristotle *Rhetoric* translated by J Gillies, published by T Cadell, London, 1823, Book 3.1 and contents of Book 1.1-2.20. Also Diogenes Laertius *Plato* 93.
102. Cited and discussed in Barnes (2000) p 26.
103. Diogenes Laertius *Aristotle* 2 – 'Aristotle has kicked us off, just as chickens do their mother after they have been hatched.' Or perhaps the analogy is related to a quote by Diogenes the Cynic where he claimed 'men strive in digging and kicking to outdo one another': Diogenes Laertius *Diogenes* 6.27.
104. Cato *Praecepta ad Filium* (broadly *Maxims Addressed to his Son*), quoted by Pliny 29.13-14.
105. See discussion of Cato's familiarity with Greek rhetoric and educating his sons to its principles in Dominik (1997) p 6 quoting Quintilian 3.1.19 who stated Cato was the first he knew of to 'handle' the topic.
106. Pliny.29.13-14 for Cato's warning; Pliny 13.28, 13.84 and Livy 40.29 for the burning of the manuscripts.
107. The *rerum repetitio* was a Roman demand for reparations that usually led to war; the ceremony saw a blood-dipped spear hurled into the offenders' territory with a formal incantation, after which, and following a thirty-three day warning, war was declared. See Livy 1.24 and 1.32 for descriptions of the ceremony and procedures.
108. The *Disticha Catonis* discussed in Gudeman *Romans* (1894) p 149.
109. Hannibal was denied reinforcement by Hanno's political opposition in Carthage. See discussion in TA Dodge, *Hannibal*, Da Capo Press, New York, 1995 reprint of 1891 edition, pp 396-397, quoting Livy. The lack of reinforcements is blamed for his ultimate inability to subdue Italy. Hannibal's men wanted to march on Rome after Cannae. See Livy *Histories* 22.51. Even the Romans expected a siege of the city.
110. Losses at Cannae were variously recorded: Livy 22.49.8-25 gave 45,000 infantry and 2,700 cavalry. Polybius claimed 70,000 infantry killed with 10,000 captured. Appian *Hannibalic War* 4.25 claimed 50,000; Plutarch *Fabius Maximus* 16.8 claimed 50,000 infantry dead with a further 10,000 captured.
111. Livy 34.1.8-34.2.5.
112. For Cato's speech in Athens in Latin see Plutarch *Cato* 12.4. Whilst he spoke sufficient Greek, he gave the speech through an interpreter.
113. Horace *Epistles* 2.1.156-157, translation from *Epistles, and Ars Poetica,* Loeb Classical Library edition no. 194, edited and translated by HR Fairclough, 1929 p 408. In translation: 'Greece, the captive, made her savage victor captive, and brought the arts into rustic Latium.'
114. Polybius 31.25.5 quoting Cato.
115. Suetonius *Lives of Eminent Rhetoricians* 25 for the expulsion of rhetoricians from Rome. For the banning of coins see Atkinson (2009) p 39.
116. Plutarch *Cato* 22-23.
117. Quoting Highet (1949) p 105.
118. Athenaeus 213d. Athens had sided with Mithridates of Pontus in his revolt against Rome and the city felt the Senate's backlash. The so-called brain drain quote from Potter (2006) p 528.
119. *Probis pateo* was traditionally inscribed above the city gates or the doors of places of learning in the Roman world.
120. Plutarch *Cicero* 4.4-5; Quintilian 12.6.7; Valerius Maximus *Dictorum factomque memorabilium libri* (*Memorable deeds and sayings*) 2.2-3; Aelian *Varia Historia* 12.25; Pseudo-Aurelius Victor *De Viris Illustribus Urbis Romae* 81.2; Plutarch *Caesar* 3.1.
121. Lucian *The Double Indictment* 6, translation by HW and FG Fowler, Clarendon Press, 1905.
122. Quoting Hesiod from Lucian's *Hermotimos or on Philosophical Schools* 2.
123. Quoting Whitmarsh (2002) p 175 on paradigms.
124. The censorship of 92 BCE discussed in Dominik (1997) p 7.
125. Following the discussion in Dominik (1997) p 6. We inherit the *Rhetoric to Alexander* as part of the corpus of Aristotle's manuscripts but it is more likely attributable to Anaximenes of Lampsacus; see discussion in Pernot (2000) p 40. Dominik (1997) p 4 for Antonius' probable publication date.
126. The loss of the effectiveness of public speech causing change in Rome discussed in Dominik

(1997) p 224 following the observation of RW Cape; exampled by Seneca's *Suasoria* 6.1-27 and 26-7.

127. Following discussion in Pearson (1960) p 248 on Potamon of Mytilene. The *Suda* mentioned his link to Tiberius and Pseudo-Lucian's *Makrobioi* 23 for his age. The *On the Perfect Orator* was mentioned in the *Suda*. Plutarch 61 mentioned his expertise on Alexander.

128. Quoting Macaulay (1828); Pernot (2000) p 159 ff for Quintilian's career.

129. Horace *Epistle* 2.1.156-157: '*Graeci capta ferum victorem cepit et artis intulit agresti Latio.*' Virgil's line from the *Aeneid* book 2 was in fact 'fear the Danaans, even those bearing gifts!' In full, *Equo ne credite, Teucri! Quidquid id est, timeo Danaos et dona ferentis.* It referred to the wooden horse at Troy.

130. Quoting Pernot (2000) p 128.

131. Discussed in Pitcher (2009) p 53.

132. Excerpted from Macaulay (1828).

133. Livy 38.17.12.

134. As noted and proposed by Bosworth-Baynham (2000) Introduction pp 7-8.

135. Livy 38.17.12. The dating of Livy's work is uncertain; he commenced the *Ab Urbe Condita Libri* mid-life and completed it much later. He is thought to have been born ca. 60 BCE and to have died ca. 17/18, possibly the same year as Ovid, as claimed by St Jerome (Eusebius Sophronius Hieronymus ca. 347-420). Diodorus published sometime between 36 and 30 BCE.

136. Livy 9.17-18.

137. Quoting Lucan *De Bello civili* 10.20-52 and 10.1. Seneca *Epistles* 113.27-30, 83.18-25 and *Suasoria* 1.5-6 are good examples of vitriol hurled at Alexander; cited by Spencer (2002) p 89 and discussed at pp 140-143; Lucan 10.22-45 cited by Stewart (1993) p 14; for other polemics against Alexander see Livy 9.18.1-7, Cicero *Letters to Atticus* 12.40-13.28 also cited by Spencer (2002) pp 53-60.

138. The caging episode was retold in Justin 15.3.3-9, Plutarch *Demetrius* 27.3-4, Pausanias 1.9.5, Curtius 8.1.14-19, Valerius Maximus 9.3 etx.1, Seneca *de Ira* 3.17.2, 3.23.1, Pliny 54.

139. Heckel (2006) p 154 for the alternative identification of Lysimachus.

140. Seneca *Concerning Anger* 3.17.1-4 and *Concerning Clemency* 1.25.1. See citation in Curtius 8.1.17. The Lysimachus episode discussed in Heckel (1992) p 249.

141. Athenaeus 598b-c mentioned his being caged but does not mention the mutilation of the ears and nose that Seneca recounted. Plutarch *Symposiacs* 2.634f had the story almost identically transmitted about Timagenes making the fatal quip, but no punishment was mentioned.

142. Valerius Maximus' use of Alexander as an exemplum discussed in Wardle (2005).

143. See discussion in Spencer (2002) pp 15-21 for Rome's dictators and their emulation of Alexander; also p 37 for the Trajan-era admiration. Following discussion of I Worthington in Carney-Ogden (2010) p 167 for the return of philhellenism.

144. For the use of *inuictus* see Spencer (2002) p 168.

145. Atkinson (2009) p 245 for discussion on the last sighting of Alexander's body in Alexandria. Septimus Severus had the tomb locked according to Cassius Dio 7513.2 but Caracalla, who saw himself as a reincarnation of Alexander, allegedly saw the tomb in 215. De Polignac (1999) p 8 for discussion of the emperors emulating Alexander. For Crassus thinking he was following in Alexander's footsteps see Cassius Dio 40.17 and 68.29.1, 68.30-31 for Trajanus' emulation. Arrian 7.4-10 for a digression in Dionysus and Heracles in India.

146. *Historia Augusta, Alexander Severus* 50 for the Silver Shields. Further discussion in Roisman (2012) p 243. Stewart (1993) p 348 for Caracalla's title from the anonymous *Epitome de Caesaribus Sexti Aurelia Victoris* 21.4. Herodian 4.8.9 for Caracalla's deposits and Cassius Dio 78.7.1 for his withdrawals.

147. *Historia Augusta, Antoninus Caracalla* 2.1-3.

148. From Gore Vidal's 1959 review of Robert Graves' *The Twelve Caesars*.

149. F Nietzsche *The Gay Science,* Vintage Books, New York, 1974, pp 137-8, citing Nisetich (1980) p 73.

150. Herodian book 4.8-9 and Cassius Dio 78.7-8 for his emulation of Alexander and Cassius Dio 7-8 for his arming 16,000 Macedonians and mistreating followers of Aristotle's doctrine. See chapter titled *Sarissa Diplomacy: Macedonian Statecraft* for more on the *pezhetairoi*.

151. Quintilian 10.101-105. Cicero *De Officiis* 2.13. Crassus became consul in 95 BCE and married the daughter of Quintus Mucius Scaevola Augur who was an expert on Roman law and later defended Marius.

152. Arrian Preface 1.1-2 translation by A de Selincourt, Penguin Books edition, 1958.

153. Quoting Pitcher (2009) introduction p IX.

154. Compare the statement in Xenophon *Hellenika* 4.81: 'I shall pass over those actions that are not worth mentioning, dealing only with what deserves to be remembered.' For Xenophon's prejudices see Warner (1966) p 22 ff and for 'those in the know', p 34.

155. Quoting Benedetto Croce (1886-1952); discussed in Boardman-Griffin-Murray (1986) p 235.

156. Following the definition of Carr (1987) pp 29-30.

157. In 1960 Hans-George Gadamer published *Truth and Method* which refined earlier treatises on 'philosophical hermeneutics'; this was its central proposition.

158. Diodorus confirmed the wealth of literary materials when he arrived in Rome. Plutarch used at least twenty-four sources for his Alexander biography alone.

159. Arrian Preface 1.2 and 6.11.2, translation from Hammond-Atkinson (2013).

160. Pearson (1960) p 218.

161. Quoting Stewart (1993) p 10.

162. Green (1974) p 479.

163. Diodorus 1.3.

164. Diodorus 1.74.7 and 12.95.1 for his own comments on democracy. Quoting Sacks (1990) p 26 on 'moral utility'.

165. Polybius 8.24.1.

166. Diodorus 1.4.1.

167. Sacks (1990) p 171 ff for discussion of Diodorus' intended terminus.

168. See Goralski (1989) p 81 for reference to the 280 surviving works of Photius. Bosworth-Baynham (2000) p 311 for Diodorus' chronological scope.

169. St. Jerome *Kronikon*; the entry was cited under the Year of Abraham 1968 (49 BCE).

170. Diodorus complex attitude to Rome discussed in Sacks (1990) p 212 ff; p 129 for Sicilian loss of enfranchisement. Caesar has proposed *sine suffragio* for the whole island, though Mark Antony claimed he had requested *Latinitas* for Sicily, before Sextus Pompey; discussed in Sacks (1990) p 207 ff.

171. Diodorus 1.4.4 for Agyrium and 4.24 for its Heraclean cult. Diodorus 4.24 for Heracles' visit. Quoting Polybius 12.26 on Timaeus; discussed in Momigliano (1977) p 48. Diodorus 16.82.5 and 16.83.3 for hints of Agyrium's former importance; Sacks (1990) p 165 for discussion.

172. Plutarch attributed the *Ode* containing the line to Sosius in his *Demosthenes* 1.1 but to Euripides in his *Alcibiades* 11.

173. See discussion in Barber (1993) pp 84-90.

174. In his *Kronikon* St. Jerome stated Diodorus was in his prime in the year of Abraham 1968, which would suggest 49 BCE. His presence in Egypt in 59 BCE is suggested at 1.83.8 and further references to Egypt at 144.1-4 indicate he started composing as early as 56 BCE whereas at 16.7.1 his references to Tauromenium (modern Taormina) and Caesar's removal of the citizens relates to activity of 36 BCE. Diodorus 1.4.3 for the statement on Rome's expansion; Bosworth-Baynham (2000) pp 312-314 for a summary of Diodorus' attitude to Rome.

175. See Diodorus' comment at 40.8 on filching and earlier publishing by third-parties; his comment on 'before they were ready' rather than before the 'whole *Library* was completed' does, nevertheless, suggest he may have published packets himself.

176. 1.4.4 for Diodorus' claim to a 'considerable familiarity' with Latin. Herodotus 2.16 for Europe and Asia. Diodorus' geography of Mesopotamia put Nineveh on the Euphrates for example. He never mentioned the Acropolis at Athens. At 1.4.2 Diodorus mentioned Rome as the only other place he visited apart from Egypt. Diodorus 1.83.8-9 for his eyewitness account of an incident in Egypt and 3.381 for mention of the 'royal records' in Alexandria. Sacks (1990) p 189 for Diodorus' seeming lack of affiliations in Rome.

177. Discussion in Barber (1993) p 14 and p 17. See Green (2007) p IX for the term 'kaleidoscopic disjunctiveness', though applied to the earlier Hellenistic period.

178. See discussion in Pitcher (2009) p 115 for his method and p 127 quoting Dionysius of Halicarnassus *On Thucydides* 9.

179. Diodorus 20.43.7. Translation RM Greer from the Loeb Classical Library edition, 1954.

180. Polybius 15.24a and 5.31.3-5 for his recognition of the problem.

181. Polybius 33.2 and quoting Seneca *Quaestiones Naturales* 7.16, translation by J Clarke, 1910.

182. Sempronius Asellio *Rerum Gestarum Libri* fragment 1, translation from Dominik (1997) p 217.

183. Braudel (1969) p 11, commenting on Leopold von Ranke's adherence to contemporary documentary evidence.

184. Diodorus 17.117.5 commented that Alexander had accomplished greater deeds than any of the kings before or after his own time. Fire and sour wine – a technique Hannibal used to clear mountain paths when crossing the Alps; detailed in Livy 21.37.

185. Diodorus 17.117.5.

186. Diodorus 32.27.3 for his eulogizing Caesar; discussion in Sacks (1990) p 74 ff.

187. Discussed in Heckel (1984).

188. Quoting Hadley (2001) p 3 for the 'uneasy agreement'. Errington (1970) on the other hand sees the exclusive use of Hieronymus in books 18-20.

189. Sacks (1990) p 18 for the contradiction between *proemia* and narratives.

190. Discussed in Hornblower (1981) p 263. Diodorus 19.29.2 for the unique reference to *asthippoi*; discussed further in chapter titled *Sarissa Diplomacy: Macedonian Statecraft.*
191. Proposed and discussed by Hornblower (1981) p 26.
192. Tarn (1948) p 92 for his description of Diodorus as an 'honest plodding Greek'.
193. Diodorus 1.3.6 for 'immense labour'.
194. Discussed in Pitcher (2009) p 72.
195. Discussed in Hornblower (1981) p 19.
196. Examples are discussed at length by Simpson (1959) pp 370-379 and Hornblower (1981) pp 62-75. The degree to which Diodorus adhered to a single source and plagiarised its content is still debated, yet it seems clear he followed single authors where he could. Much of his history of Alexander closely correlates with Curtius' work suggesting Cleitarchus as a common link. For discussions see Anson (2004) pp 1-33, Hornblower (1981) pp 1-75 and also discussion in Baynham (1998) p 85. Following the views of Brown (1947) p 692 for the fortunate lack of creativity. Detailed discussion of Diodorus' methodology in Sacks (1990) p 21 ff citing Agatharchides.
197. 'Not entirely mechanical' following Hornblower (1981) p 63.
198. Referring to Hegel (1837) and its contention that only a recorder of contemporary events merits the title 'historian'. Recorders of events of the past are deemed 'compilers'. His *Lectures on The Philosophy of History* were originally delivered as lectures at the University of Berlin, 1821,1824,1827,1831. First published by Eduard Gans in 1837 and by Karl Hegel in 1840. 'Self evident' taken from the first line of III *Lectures on the Philosophic History.* They led to the concept of *Geistgeschichte* that unified the 'spirit' of the age.
199. Quoting Pitcher (2009) p 116.
200. Justin Preface 1 described Trogus as *vir priscae eloquentiae;* discussed in Baynham (1998) p 30.
201. Quoting Alonso-Núñez (1987) p 57.
202. Quoting PA Brunt (1980) p 494.
203. Justin 12.13.1 for the embassy from the Gauls; the succession of empires discussed in Alonso-Núñez (1987) pp 62-70.
204. Heckel-Yardley (1997) introduction p 2 quoting Justin 43.5.11-12.
205. Justin 11.6.3.
206. Justin 11.6.3, 12.13.1 and 12.16.9 for Alexander's quest to become king of the universe or the entire world.
207. See discussion in Heckel-Yardley (1997) Introduction pp 6-7.
208. Duris is reckoned to have been anti-Macedonian in his treatment of Alexander and his successors. See Shipley (2000) p 161 for discussion. Also Hornblower (1981) pp 68-70. This is largely disputed by Billows (1990) p 336.
209. See full discussion on Trogus' style and content in Alonso-Núñez (1987) pp 56-72.
210. The study by Yardley (2003) suggests Justin's creativity.
211. Discussed in Heckel-Yardley (1997) Introduction p 9. Also Baynham (1995) p 61.
212. Quoting C Thomas in Carney-Ogden (2010) p 178.
213. Horace described himself as a hard-working bee gathering sweetness from myriads of flowers, cited in Highet (1949) p 226.
214. Tarn (1948) p 125. Also see Tarn's summation of Justin in Watson-Miller (1992) pp 106-110.
215. Chapter titled *Comets, Colophons and Curtius Rufus.*
216. For arguments that a reference in Hegesippus' work (he died ca. 180 CE) might have been drawn from Curtius 9.4.30-31 see Fears (1976) p 217 footnote 18. Again they remain inconclusive and are refuted by Fears. Discussion in Baynham (1998) p 3 and in chapters titled *The Precarious Path of Pergamena and Papyrus* and *Comets, Colophons and Curtius Rufus.*
217. Discussion in Baynham (1995) p 15.
218. As an example see Curtius 4.14.9-26 for the speech provided before the battle at Gaugamela. Also Justin 11.9.9-10 for Darius' pre-battle rhetoric. Quoting Tarn (1948) p 92.
219. Curtius 9.1.34.
220. Renault (1972) p 412.
221. Tarn (1948) pp 91-92.
222. Curtius' relative merit discussed by Schachermeyr and Sibert and cited in McKechnie (1999) p 47, as well as in detail in Baynham (1998). For Errington's comments on Curtius see discussion in McKechnie (1999) p 47 and quoting Errington (1970) pp 49-77.
223. Summarising Baynham (1998) p 14. Romane (1987) observed Curtius' technical account of the siege of Tyre was superior to Arrian's. Heinsius' praise from WH Crosby's preface to the Cellarius edition published in 1854.
224. Quoting Olbrycht (2008) p 233.
225. For Cleitarchus' popularity see Pearson (1960) p 213; he was cited by Diodorus, Plutarch, Strabo, Cicero, Athenaeus, Pliny, Quintilian and Diogenes Laertius, to name a few, alongside references from many rhetoricians. The extant fragments can be read in Robinson (1953) pp 171-183.

226. Quoting Atkinson (2009) p 19. In the chapter titled *Comets, Colophons and Curtius Rufus* we argue that Curtius most likely published in the term of Nero; this preceded, or marked the very beginnings of the Second Sophistic when Greek writing and culture once again became popular.

227. Quoting Longinus *On Sublimity* 22.1 (full extract in Gray (1987) pp 470-471) and Diodorus 1.2.

228. In an analogy of his method Plutarch 1.3 explained he relied mostly on the face, the expression and the eyes and paid less attention to the other parts of the body. Quoting Tarn (1948) p 296 for 'best to worst'. Plutarch *Demetrius* 1.1 for the quote on senses.

229. The various themes of letters to and from Alexander discussed in Pearson (1955) p 449.

230. Discussed in Ehrman (2014) p 43.

231. In Plutarch *Alexander* he referred to personal letters of Alexander at 7.6, 8.1, 17.8, 19.5-8, 20.9, 22.2, 22.5, 27.8, 39.4, 39.7, 39.13, 42.1, 46.3, 47.3, 55.6, 55.7, 60.1, 60.11. No other historian seems to have had access to them and how genuine they were remains open to speculation. Plutarch *Demosthenes* 2.1.1-4 for his limited library.

232. See discussion on the unraveling of Plutarch sources in Hammond (1993) pp 1-2 citing Powell (1939) pp 229-240 and Tarn (1948) p 296.

233. Following Whitmarsh (2002) for 'virtual history' and noting the diptych comparisons.

234. Plutarch *Moralia* 404d or *De Pythiae Oraculis* 21, translated by Sir Thomas Browne, and Plutarch *Coriolanus* 75, cited in Clement *The Stomata (Miscellanies)* 5.88.4.

235. Plutarch 73-76. On reincarnation see *Moralia, Consolation to his wife (Consolatio ad Uxorem)*, Loeb Classical Library edition, vol. VII, 1959, pp 575-605 and J Rualdus *Life of Plutarch* 1624. In a letter to his wife concering the death of their daughter, Plutarch firmly suggested his belief in reincarnation or at least the survival of the soul.

236. Arrian 7.18 and 7.23. Aristobulus is cited several times as author of the mysterious portents.

237. Plutarch 1.2.

238. Compare his treatment of the meeting with the Amazon Queen and his account of Alexander's pre-death portents.

239. Polybius books 10 and 11 for the detail on Hannibal and Scipio. 'Cradle-to-grave' quoting SR Asirvatham in Carney-Ogden (2010) p 201.

240. Quoting Tarn (1948) p 297.

241. Quoting Mossman (1988) p 85.

242. Macaulay (1928).

243. 'Parental' as Herodotus has been termed the 'father of history'.

244. Arrian 4.11.9 and 5.4.5 for Cyrus' death at the hands of the Scythians and Herodotus 1.204-216.

245. Lucian *True History* 2.20.

246. Aristotle was demonstrably bigoted. Thus a social code written when Hellenes were learning to smelt iron would have undermined his own sense of superiority. Aristotle's proposal that Hellenes were born to rule over all other nations gave a moral underpinning to Alexander's invasion of the Persian Empire.

247. Hammond (1993) p 3 quoting JE Powell (1939) p 229.

248. Arrian 1.12.2-3 for a digression on the relative fame of Alexander and (in his opinion) lesser men that Rome favoured.

249. Discussion of Plutarch's relegation of Philip by SR Asirvatham in Carney-Ogden (2010) pp 202-204.

250. Quoting Atkinson from Hammond-Atkinson (2013) Introduction p xxxvi for 'public intellectual'. See Hamilton (1971) Introduction: Plutarch had been granted Roman citizenship with possibly an honorary Roman consulship and was also a Greek magistrate and archon in his municipality; also AH Clough *Plutarch's Lives,* Liberty Library of Constitutional Classics, 1864, Introduction. For Polybius see the Introduction to *The Rise of the Roman Empire*, Penguin Classics edition, 1979, pp 13-15 for his career in Achaean federal office and in Rome.

251. Quoting Arrian 7.30.3. As an example Arrian 4.28.2-3 and 5.1 and 5.3 for his doubt surrounding the legends of Heracles and Dionysus and India, and his doubt on the claimed geography of the Caucasus. Following SR Asirvatham in Carney-Ogden (2010) p 203 for the comparison of Arrian to Homer; Arrian 1.12.2 for his understanding of Alexander's self-comparison.

252. Arrian opened with a polemic against previous works, asking the reader to compare them against his own. See the introduction by Hamilton to the Penguin Books edition, 1971, p 9 for references to the style used in the *Indike* and Pearson (1960) p 112.

253. Photius' epitome 93 was a summary of Arrian *Bithynika*.

254. See Bosworth (1976) p 118 for discussion of Dio Chrysostom's earlier book.

255. Following Hammond-Atkinson (2013) Introduction p xv. For the Hyphasis River episode see chapter titled *The Rebirth of the Wrath of Peleus' Son*.

256. The Athenian general, Iphicrates, son of a shoemaker, is said to have started a trend in military leather sandals known as *iphikratids*; he and Xenophon were contemporaries; Diodorus 15.44.4. Photius epitome 58.4 for the 'young Xenophon'.

257. Quoting Bosworth (1976) p 137 on Arrian's errors.
258. Arrian Preface 2 for his accepting that 'as a king he would have been honour-bound to avoid untruth'.
259. Arrian 3.8.6 stated the total Persian numbers at Gaugamela as 40,000 cavalry with one million infantry whilst Curtius stated 200,000 infantry. Also Arrian 3.15.6 for Persian troop losses of 300,000, again far higher than Curtius at 40,000 and Diodorus at 90,000. For the one hundred men lost on the Macedonian side, Arrian 3.15.6.
260. Curtius 3.11.16-17.
261. Bosworth-Baynham (2000) Introduction p 4 for the quote. Tacitus had worked his way through to military tribute, questor, praetor and proconsul of Asia, serving with legions under Domitian, Nerva and Trajan; Pernot (2000) pp 128-129 for Tacitus' oratorical career.
262. Arrian 1.12.5.
263. Pliny's Preface to his *Natural History* included a Livian quote nowhere found in Livy's extant texts and must have come from a later work which read 'I have now obtained a sufficient reputation, so that I might put an end to my work, did not my restless mind require to be supported by employment.'
264. Ovid *Metamorphoses* Epilogue 875 ff. Polybius 31.22-25 is essentially an encomium to the Scipios in which Polybius stressed his own importance in his friendship and advice.
265. Thucydides 1.22.4.
266. For Arrian's deliberate omissions of the darker episodes see Baynham (1995) p 70. Quoting McInerney (2007) p 429.
267. Arrian 3.27.4-5 referring to the Ariaspians.
268. See discussion of Arrian's politics in the introduction by Hamilton (1971) Introduction.
269. Arrian 7.14.5-6.
270. Arrian 3.18.11-12. Arrian 7.29.4 for his acceptance of the reason, following Aristobulus, of Alexander's drinking.
271. Tarn (1948) p 286.
272. Arrian 1.12.1-3 for references to Homer and Xenophon. Arrian's use of the title Xenophon in his own name discussed in the 1958 Penguin edition of *The Campaigns of Alexander*, introduction p 1; refuted by Stadter (1967) p 155 ff who argued it was a genuine part of Arrian's name.
273. Quoting Pearson (1960) p 123 for the form and content of the *Indike*.
274. Quoting Porter (2006) p 4.
275. As proposed by Highet (1949) p 105.
276. Preface to the *Discourses of Epictetus* by Arrian headed *Arrian to Lucius Gellius, with wishes for his happiness*, translation by George Long from the 1890 edition published by George Bell and Sons. Arrian expressed (somewhat confusingly) his efforts with: 'I neither wrote these *Discourses of Epictetus* in the way in which a man might write such things; nor did I make them public myself, inasmuch as I declare that I did not even write them. But whatever I heard him say, the same I attempted to write down in his own words as nearly as possible, for the purpose of preserving them as memorials to myself afterwards of the thoughts and the freedom of speech of Epictetus.' Only four of the eight books are extant.
277. Arrian's stoic interpretations of kinship following Pearson (1960) Introduction p 7. The original title of the *Discourses* is unknown; it has been variously named the *Diatribai* and *Dialexis* amongst others.
278. Quoting Shipley (2000) p 236.
279. Polybius 1.4.
280. Quoting Grant (1995) p 53.
281. Discussion of the papyri in Bevan (1913) pp 22-25.
282. Pitcher (2009) p 171 for a discussion of Athenaeus' diversity.
283. Flower (1994) p 48 quoting Photius' *Life of Theopompus* F25 and p 157.
284. Billows (1990) p 333. Following Flower (1994) Introduction p 2 for Athenaeus' preservation of Theopompus; we have eighty-three verbatim quotations (598 lines of text) with 412 lines in Athenaeus. Flower (1994) p 156 for Photius paraphrasing Theopompus who claimed the 'first place in rhetorical education.'
285. Nietzsche, from an unpublished manuscript on Diogenes Laertius and his sources, a contribution of the history of ancient literary studies; quoted by Glenn W Most, Speech at the Israel Society for the Promotion of Classical Studies 42nd Annual Conference.
286. Quoting the comment of JR Lowell, 1867, see Loeb Classical Library edition, 1937, Prefatory Note p vii.
287. Momigliano (1966) pp 3-4 for the reference to antiquarians.

6

THE GUARDIANS AND THE GHOSTS OF THE CAMPAIGN *EPHEMERIDES*

Concerning events at Babylon, were the *Journal*, the *Pamphlet*, and the Vulgate accounts related in some way?

Alexander's last days in Babylon resulted in three differently reported outcomes stemming from at least three early influential sources. Two of them are potentially linked to the *Ephemerides*, official court diaries, or to their supposed author, with the third inspired by them both.

How genuine do they look, and can their claims be reconciled or linked in some way?

We take a closer look at the messages that underline each and at the possible identities of the authors, to reveal the architects of an early literary war that took place in the aftermath of Alexander's death.

'He [Alexander] recognised his officers when they entered his room but could no longer speak to them. From that moment until the end he uttered no word. That night and the following day, and for the next twenty-four hours, he remained in a high fever. These details are all to be found in the Diaries.'[1] (T3)

Arrian *Anabasis,* extract from the *Journal*

'When they asked to him to whom he left his kingdom, he [Alexander] replied, "to him who was the best man", but that he already foresaw that because of that contest great funeral games were in preparation for him. Again when Perdiccas asked when he wished divine honours to be paid to him, he said he wished it at the time when they themselves were happy. These were the king's last words, and shortly afterwards he died.'[2] (T7)

Curtius *The History of Alexander*

'When the Macedones had filed past, he called back those who were with Perdiccas. He took Holcias by the hand and ordered him to read out the Will. What follows is a copy of the Will dispositions, as taken down from Alexander by Holcias.'[3] (T2)

Greek Alexander Romance

There is a dictum that proposes 'many books are wrongly forgotten, but no book is wrongly remembered'. Yet one of the few absolutes we are presented with is that our central witnesses, who may be better termed our 'prime suspects', incriminate one another in their recounting of Alexander's death. Simply put, the *Journal* and the *Pamphlet* cannot exist together in history as factually based: if a Will was read as the *Pamphlet* claimed, the *Journal* hid the detail, and if the *Journal* is genuine, the *Pamphlet*'s fulsome testament, absorbed later by the *Romance*, was complete fabrication. And if either contained the truth, then Alexander's last words as portrayed in the Vulgate texts, cannot have been said in the context attached to them. So the dictum is surely flawed from the perspective of all their competing authors.

Having reviewed the primary historians who accompanied Alexander and those writing in the generation that followed, as well as the Roman-era authors who built their own interpretations from these earlier accounts, it becomes clear that each *did* adopt one, or elements of more than one, of these epitaphs. However, we also know that all of the mainstream accounts rejected, and so excluded, the reading of Alexander's Last Will and Testament in the unanimous belief that he failed to organise his estate and declined to nominate a successor (or successors) to govern the greatest empire the Graeco-Persian world had ever seen.

The archetypal documents behind these opposing endings have been reviewed only in isolation, when each is as undecipherable as the Phaistos Disk.[4] Their full potential becomes apparent when they are considered together, for the *Journal* and the *Pamphlet* bear witness to an ancient literary war. They were not the products of hair-splitting wordsmiths ridiculed for their sophistry in Aristophanes' *Clouds*,[5] nor were they ineffectual sponge-wielding fighters like those appearing in Commodus' gladiatorial games.[6] The *Journal* – despite its benign exterior – and the *Pamphlet*, were literary hoplites launched into the histories armed to the teeth with accusation, insinuation, strategic omission, and more dangerous still, a convincing reinsertion of detail. What becomes clear, when they are reviewed side by side, is that the one was born to end the allegations of the other. Their historic relationship was misunderstood and awkwardly dealt with by the classical historians who may have suspected, yet could not pinpoint, a subterfuge somewhere between Babylon and Alexandria some decades on when the first influential accounts appeared.

Each production has at least one enigmatic individual attached to its story. Thanks to a reference in Athenaeus' *Deipnosophistae* relating to the *Journal* extract (T3, T4), we have Diodotus of Erythrae who was cited as one of the compilers of the official court diaries, the *Ephemerides*, working we assume under Alexander's *archigrammateus* (chief clerk), Eumenes of Cardia, who was also cited as its compiler.[7] Diodotus was never mentioned again; he is a human *hapax legomenon,* a single textual occurrence (as was Evagoras who was named as secretary of the huge Indus-Hydaspes fleet) – it seems the histories bypassed intelligence, surveying and clerical staff unless they appeared in a military capacity.[8] But if Athenaeus' text came down to us from the single corrupted manuscript that was transferred from Constantinople to Vienna in 1423 by the Italian historian, Giovanni Aurispa, then rather than 'Diodotus', a 'Diognetus' of Ethyrae, one of the known *bematistes* (map makers) on campaign, may well be our man.[9]

In support of the existence of the *Pamphlet* and its circulation in the Successor Wars – a scholar-backed theory born of its clear political designs and dissimilarity to the rest of the *Romance* – Plutarch gave us Hagnothemis who apparently first heard of its detail and Aristotle's alleged involvement in the conspiracy to poison Alexander (T9, T10).[10] Additionally, we have Holcias who allegedly read the Will aloud to the gathered *megistoi,* the most powerful generals at Alexander's bedside at the morning of his death. Never previously mentioned in the campaign histories, Holcias was sufficiently important to the *Pamphlet* author to be cited as inheriting the governorship of Illyria (T1, T2).[11]

The obscurity of these individuals has cast doubts over the authenticity of both productions, for surely these notable men, here briefly illuminated like motes caught in a sunbeam, ought to have appeared more frequently in the campaign accounts. But we have noted the pernicious power of the pen: able to ink in an ally to the pantheon of history or whiteout an opponent to the exile of anonymity.

THE BOOK OF DEATH: *PAMPHLET* PARTISAN PINPOINTING

The content of the enigmatic Will-citing *Pamphlet* is believed to be best preserved (in the final chapter of the third book) in Recension A (the oldest) of the *Greek Alexander Romance* (T2) as well as its later redactions, but it is also fulsomely detailed at the conclusion to the *Metz Epitome* to which it did not originally belong (T1).[12] A later corrupted and even briefer reference to the Will (likely sourced from the *Romance*) remains in the *Excerpta Latina Barbari*, an 8th century poor Latin translation of the earlier anonymous 5th century Greek *Kronika Alexandrina*; it stated: 'When he was close to death, Alexander left a testament, that each of his officers should rule in their individual provinces, as Alexander had instructed, as follows…'[13]

We do not know when the first edition of what is otherwise known as a Pseudo-Callisthenes production entered circulation; the more historical and less fabulous parent of *Romance* archetype 'α' was possibly written some fifty years to one hundred years after Alexander's death when all the necessary ingredients had been established.[14] Neither do we know exactly when the detail from the *Pamphlet* first entered the *Romance* – whether soon after its genesis, as the so-called *Liber de Urbibus Alexandri* appears to have done with its pro-Ptolemaic list of cities – or if it was swept up much later, as it was into the 3rd century *Metz Epitome*.[15] A *possible* clue is a papyrus dating to the Ptolemaic period (ca. 100 BCE) and it houses a further fragment of the Will *without* any *Romance* attachments.[16] But once the *Romance* did absorb the earlier political document, much didactic filler was inevitably built around its original content. But the key elements comprising the archetypal *Pamphlet* are not difficult to pinpoint, for any obvious *thaumata*, marvels, would have hamstrung its focused political and military aims in the Successor Wars.

One 'marvel' attached to the description of Alexander's death we see in the *Romance may* have existed in the original political *Pamphlet*. Taking the form of a gruesome prodigy – which may have served to represent the imminent treachery of Alexander's men – a half-child, half-beast, was brought to the king. Its description recalls the monstrous sea-goddess Scylla from Greek mythology, a composite animal resonant of the cheetah-serpent-eagle-like *sirrush* symbolising Babylonian Marduk. Here the top human part of the body was dead but the limbs of the animals were still alive, thus it was potentially meant to imply that Alexander's men had killed their host.[17] And though this detail looks more convincingly like a later intruder, we will soon discover (below) that superstition and the portentous played a significant role in the psyche of the time, concerning soldiers in particular.

Whether original or not, what comes next is the clear central intent of the *Pamphlet* author, or authors: a description of the plot to poison Alexander in Babylon, with an outline of the political background as well as the means and the motive. It was Alexander's chief cupbearer (*archioinochooi*) Iolaos, the son of the presiding Macedonian regent, Antipater, who handed him the poisoned wine at the impromptu party (or banquet) hosted by Medius of Larissa. The *Pamphlet* named those complicit in the regicide: alongside some fourteen attendees who were 'in the know' at Medius' banquet, though the central architects of the crime were clearly named as the Macedonian regent and his sons (so Aristotle's part appears to be a later claim).

This was a heavyweight line-up that was afforded a modicum of credibility by Antipater's alleged summons to Babylon by Alexander before his death; he was, it is said, fearful that Alexander was planning to execute him, and so he took the initiative.[18] As significant as the guilty were the few guests named as ignorant of the plot: Perdiccas, Ptolemy, Lysimachus, Eumenes, Asander and Holcias (T1, T2).

Following a description of the king's sudden pain after drinking from the cup and his worsening condition, as well as Roxane's tender intervention when Alexander attempted to throw himself into the Euphrates, the surviving texts detailed a private reading of the testament by Holcias to a small select group of the king's most trusted men. Besides Holcias himself, three more of the 'innocent' group were listed as present when Alexander drafted his Will, and we are no doubt expected to imagine that Eumenes, royal secretary and keeper of the *Ephemerides*, would have overseen the scribes who recorded Alexander's final wishes in the form of a testament.

Strikingly prominent in the *Pamphlet* is the favourable treatment of Rhodes, both within the main Will narrative and in Alexander's so-called 'Letter to the Rhodians' which preceded its bequests. The florid letter, in 'clotted officialese' and supposedly written to the island's boule and demos (broadly the council and people), is widely considered a later interpolation, though contiguous references in the earliest surviving version of the *Romance* suggest that embellishment, not complete invention, gives us its now extended form.[19]

The *Metz Epitome* preserved additional detail of Alexander's final utterances in which he pledged his friends to recognise the Will and urged the new acting chiliarch, Perdiccas, along with his absent regent (the king being unaware of Antipater's part in the plot), to see that its terms were carried out.[20] Finally, as Alexander's energy was spent, he beseeched the gods to accept him and passed his ring to Perdiccas to whom he had pledged his wife in marriage, and placed his and Roxane's hands together in public affirmation. As in the Vulgate accounts of Curtius, Diodorus and Justin (T6, T7, T8), the king remained vocal to the end, but here giving instruction to his men about his estate and burial wishes.

Also uniting the claims of the *Pamphlet* and the Vulgate genre is the common agreement that Alexander was finally proclaimed dead perhaps five days after the first dose of poison, after which Perdiccas had the body laid in a coffin and dressed in his regal robes, whereupon he announced the king's passing and then read his Will to the larger gathering of men.[21] This lucid and coherent reporting *does* contrast in every way to the general tone of the rest of the 'fabulous' *Romance*; even Roxane is, for example, correctly referred to as Alexander's Bactrian wife whereas she is referred to as the daughter of Darius III in the preceding *Romance* text.[22]

The whole construction – the prodigy, the background to the conspiracy, the writing and then reading of the Will with Alexander's final instructions – was dubbed the *Liber de Morte Testamentumque Alexandri Magni – The Book of the Death and Testament of Alexander the Great* – by Reinhold Merkelbach in 1954, following the title of a manuscript from the Escorial Monastery in Spain (*Codex Scorialensis* b III 14 E), though the simplicity of the title '*Pamphlet*' seems to better suit the political origins that Adolf Ausfeld pointed to some sixty years before.[23] The *Pamphlet* has been termed 'neither romance, nor history, but rather a political propaganda', a conclusion not too distant from the verdict on the *Journal* (below).[24] Whilst the identity of its authorship divides the community of scholars, the *Pamphlet*, which (prodigy aside) provided a more rational conclusion to Alexander's final days than any 'serious' account, still sits in a rejected corner, where the *Journal* still enjoys more legitimate attachments in the final pages of the biographies of Arrian and Plutarch (T3, T4).

Many commentators are united in the belief that the *Pamphlet was* circulated for political effect in the first decade (or so) of the Successor Wars following Alexander's death. Their studies have focused on the identification of its publisher, with the divining rod being the political slant of the Will along with the guilt, or exoneration, attached to those at Medius' banquet. With some justification, then, we could say that a *genuine* Will has never been the subject of an investigation, only an assumed *fabrication* has come under scrutiny. Bosworth came as close as anyone to the genuine article when stating that 'the production of Wills, *post mortem,* was a feature of Attic Inheritance cases…', and therefore, '… it would not have seemed beyond belief that the Will of Alexander had been suppressed.'[25]

Perplexing then is the unchanging conclusion that the *Pamphlet* Will *is* pure propaganda. Neither have historians satisfactorily questioned *why*

Alexander 'decided' to die intestate, for the nature of his death was far from sudden; his decline incontrovertibly took place over a number of days in *all* extant accounts, providing him an opportunity to designate heirs and successors, and to disseminate the power in a manner that would have truly prolonged his legacy.

So what of the *Pamphlet*'s authorship? Since Ausfeld's 1894 critique separated it from the clearly unhistoric elements of the *Romance,* so providing the credibility for its political birth in the *Diadokhoi* years, a number of studies have summarised the conflicting datum lines.[26] What *is* unanimously agreed upon is that the *Pamphlet* was partisan in its construction: 'It is replete with details, tendentious and misleading, anchored to historical personages.'[27] In which case we may conclude that its construction and design coincided with the political agenda of at least one of those cited as 'innocent': 'No one was unaware of what was afoot, with the exception of Eumenes, Perdiccas, Ptolemy, Lysimachus, Asander and Holcias.'[28]

The conspicuous salvation of Ptolemy and Perdiccas led to deductions that one or the other was the author – wholly logical proposals at first glance. Perdiccas died three years after Alexander, and yet hostility between him and Ptolemy was evident from the settlement at Babylon onwards, and perhaps even *at* Babylon, eventually culminating in war.[29] This is troubling, for it would have been 'remarkably counter-productive' for Perdiccas to extricate Ptolemy from guilt if the chiliarch was the author.[30] This alone ought to rule out Perdiccas who was killed in the summer of 320 BCE (according to the 'low' chronology, which we follow); even Tarn's 1921 case for its *termini ante* and *post quem*, and which did hinge on Perdiccan origins, conceded that it *may* have been a somewhat later publication (specifically, from the years that saw the new regent, Polyperchon, in opposition to Cassander commencing late 319 BCE).[31] We suggest the latter dating is broadly correct but the identification of the author (or co-authors) still needs to be resolved.

Bosworth (and others) argue for a Ptolemaic *Pamphlet* and for a publication period following the so-called Peace of the Dynasts of 311 BCE; military successes in Asia Minor and Greece saw the Egyptian satrap facing his rivals with a new confidence that led him to intrigue for the hand of Cleopatra, Alexander's sister. Bosworth argues that in this context, and courting Rhodian naval power, the *Pamphlet* was issued at the expense of Ptolemy's rivals. The Will *does* indeed pair Ptolemy with Cleopatra. But the same reasoning that discounts Perdiccan authorship can be applied here: there was no logic in Ptolemy absolving his arch rival Perdiccas, or *his* chief supporter, Eumenes, from conspiratorial guilt. Both had been dead some years by 311 BCE and Ptolemy could have easily slandered them, despite their former affiliations to Cleopatra.[32] But, above all other arguments, we know from Arrian's statement that the conclusion to Ptolemy's book either corroborated, or itself invented, the *Journal* entry, with its speechless and intestate conspiracy-free death, and this was the antithesis of the claims made by the author of the *Pamphlet*.[33]

An alternative publication date has been proposed in a more recent study of Alexander's mother, Olympias, in which the *Pamphlet* is indeed referred to as a 'scrap of partisan literature'. Its origins are pinned on the decade after her death in 315 BCE, when Olympias' 'airbrushed' image fitted the sentiment of that time as nostalgia for the murdered queen mother newly surfaced.[34] Yet the term 'scrap' may understate its virulence; its survival through the wars of the *Diadokhoi,* and in one form or another through the 2,300 years since, speaks for its historical stamina. Nevertheless, Olympias may well have been involved in the *Pamphlet's* provenance, as we shall discover in later chapters.[35]

Heckel built on earlier theories that also positioned the *Pamphlet* as a product of Polyperchon and his regency ca. 317 BCE (Polyperchon held the regency until ca. late 316 or early 315 BCE when Cassander attained power).[36] The seeming flaw is that Polyperchon was never himself mentioned in the document when he had every chance to grant himself Will-sanctioned authority, hardly an effective strategy if he sought approbation from its circulation. When developing his case, which proposed Holcias was working in league with Polyperchon, Heckel saw this as 'subtle and ingenious'. But that subtlety verges on self-incrimination; as Bosworth points out, Polyperchon owed his own regency to the dying wish of Antipater, and to damn the former regent with regicide was to call into question his association and the resulting appointment.[37]

Polyperchon finally came to terms with Cassander in 309 BCE and received grants and troops in return for the murder of Heracles, Alexander's eldest son.[38] Bearing in mind the vitriol with which the *Pamphlet* treated Cassander and his family, it seems implausible that he would have entertained any strategic alliance (which lasted almost a decade) with the by-then vulnerable Polyperchon if he was known to be, or suspected as, the author. Moreover, it is unlikely that Polyperchon would have promoted a son he had written out of the *Pamphlet*, for Heracles was never recognised in the reissued Will.

Hammond suggested that Antigonus, not present at Babylon and so not on Medius' guest list, may have been behind the design of the conspiracy theory, and yet Heckel summarised why the influential veteran has never been proposed as its author: of all the major coalition players, he alone has no significant role.[39] Additionally, he fought against those named innocent in the Successor Wars. We propose, nevertheless, that Antigonus *did* indeed have an *influence* on the birth of the *Pamphlet*, though its delivery and the midwife were not what he had in mind.[40]

The shifting sands of proposed authorship clearly illustrate that none of the aforementioned proposed authors is a comfortable match to its content, and for each candidate there remains an indigestible logic and a very 'nasty conundrum'.[41]

Having ruled out the more prominent candidates, the innocent list is whittled down to the king's Bodyguard Lysimachus, the Carian satrap Asander, the king's secretary Eumenes and the elusive Holcias. Lysimachus' initial participation in the Successor Wars fell in line with Antigonus, as did the early actions of Ptolemy, each related by marriage through daughters of Antipater, and both were to demand their just rewards for their part in Antigonus' eventual victory over Eumenes. So Lysimachus had no reason to salvage the former royal secretary from guilt either.[42] Asander was most likely a relative of Antigonus *Monophthalmos*; he appears to have defected from Perdiccas in 321/320 BCE and we believe he supported Antigonus until 315 BCE, after which he switched allegiance to Ptolemy.[43] Asander would have harboured no desire to put the former chiliarch he betrayed on the innocent list, and neither his supporter Eumenes, nor the opposition rebel Holcias who was eventually captured by Antigonus. So they too can be discounted as credible *Pamphlet* authors.[44]

Putting Holcias aside for the time being, this leaves us with Eumenes of Cardia, who did enjoy the support and trust of Olympias, and reportedly, Polyperchon too, from late 319-316 BCE. Following Perdiccas' defeat in Egypt, and again at a strategic reconvening of generals at Triparadeisus later in 320 BCE (some argue that was 321 BCE, following the 'high chronology'), Eumenes was proscribed with the surviving Perdiccan remnants.[45] History has never handed Eumenes the pen because Lysimachus, Ptolemy and Asander, named innocent of guilt, appear to have opposed him through the First and Second *Diadokhoi* Wars. However, as we will show, there were two, or possibly three, periods between his release from a siege at Nora in 319 BCE, and his execution at the end of 316 BCE (or early 315 BCE), when the line-up in the *Pamphlet* would have suited his, and significantly Olympias', desperate position – and by association, Polyperchon's too. For Eumenes needed Ptolemy and Lysimachus in a coalition against the by then powerful Antigonus *Monophthalmos*, although as events were to show, they believed they did not need *him*; and in that they were quite mistaken, as the next fifteen years would prove.[46]

THE WILL: ORIGINATION AND CONTAMINATION

Tarn was correct in stating that the *Pamphlet* Will – in the form we inherited it – has been contaminated to some degree. Unsurprisingly, in the Latin *Metz Epitome* it is the Roman gods who are called to witness the content of the Will: Jupiter, Hercules, Minerva and Mars, rather than the Olympian

Zeus, Heracles, Athena and Ares, the deities beseeched to punish any who acted in contravention of its dictates. Obviously the 'senate' at Rhodes is Roman overlay too.[47] In the *Romance* equivalent there appear to be later textual additions and even some omissions, again possibly politically motivated. It has, for example, been proposed that Julius Valerius' first Latin translation of the original Greek *Romance* text deliberately omitted the prediction – reportedly emanating from Serapis, the new deity conceived in Ptolemaic Egypt – that Alexandria would surpass 'the more ancient cities', for Rome had by then supplanted the Egyptian city as the universal metropolis.[48]

Of course Wills could be updated and amended during the testator's life. Alexander is portrayed as penning or, we suggest *revising*, his Will throughout the night, when a slave boy, Hermogenes, recorded the words, and another, Combaphes, held a lamp. Those named as present with them were Ptolemy, Lysimachus and Perdiccas, while Holcias read out the finished document.[49] Along with Eumenes, not specifically mentioned in this scene (his presence as royal secretary may have been implied), these comprised five of the six innocents, and so there can be no doubt that the allegations of conspiracy, and the setting of the Will, were penned by the same hand as a cohesive packaged product.

If Eumenes *was* behind the authorship of the *Pamphlet*, why did he absent himself from his description of the Will's drafting? Was that not as self-defeating as Polyperchon's absence if *he* had written it? Well, as a jealous Neoptolemus once reminded the men gathered in post-Alexander Babylon, Eumenes' fame with the royal pen was well known empire-wide; it would have naturally been assumed that it was he who turned the papyrus draft into an officially sealed vellum testament, just as Aelian assumed Eumenes prepared the *Ephemerides* (T5).[50] By citing himself (and Perdiccas whose orders he followed) as 'innocent', as well as re-broadcasting his own significant satrapal inheritance (Cappadocia and Paphlagonia), Eumenes achieved all he needed to without the suggestion of overt manipulation. And this is exactly why, as we shall argue, Ptolemy did not include himself more prominently in the *Journal*.

HOLCIAS THE *TAXIARCHOS* AND HAGNOTHEMIS THE LOST TEAN

So who was Holcias, the man who features so prominently in the *Pamphlet* and who read Alexander's Will at the initial private gathering? Did he perhaps have some significance to the pamphleteer(s)? The answer is yes, if Eumenes, in league with Olympias, was author.[51] Care of a passage in Polyaenus' *Strategemata* (*Stratagems of War*), we find Holcias who was apparently sympathetic to the Perdiccan cause, and thus to Eumenes. He defected, or escaped, from the army of Antigonus; Holcias and his 3,000 heavy-armed Macedonian renegades were finally rounded up when Eumenes was under siege at the fortress of Nora in late 319 BCE.[52] So it appears he was a prominent and trusted commander despite Tarn's conclusion that Holcias was nothing but a 'ringleader of some mutinous soldiery'; but then Tarn believed: 'Alexander's fictitious Testament is not historical evidence for anything.'[53] Curiously, Holcias was offered a pardon and paroled to Macedonia on the promise of inactivity. His subsequent disappearance suggests he was either disposed of in Macedonia when Cassander came to power, or that contemporary historians decided to 'write him out of Hellenistic history', in the same way, Bosworth suggests, he may have written himself in.[54]

The same identity questions may be asked of the otherwise unreferenced Hagnothemis (or Agnothemis); could this be a corruption of 'Hagnon (or Agnon) of Teos', as both characters appear in Plutarch's *Life of Alexander*?[55] Hagnon was a flamboyant flatterer and influential figure at the campaign court and he was apparently hostile to Callisthenes.[56] An extract from Plutarch's *How One May Discern a Flatterer from a Friend* suggested Hagnon managed to deceive Alexander with his fawning.[57] Arrian's *Indika* captured his role as a *trierarchos* selected to fund and equip a barge in the mammoth Hydaspes-Indus fleet, a clear indicator of his wealth.[58] Further, Plutarch and Athenaeus claimed a Companion named Agnon wore golden studs in his sandals (or boots) at the court banquets, and this is surely the same man (Arrian appears to have named him Andron, or more likely, a manuscript corruption did).[59]

A surviving Greek inscription suggests that at some point in the Successor Wars Hagnon joined Antigonus, possibly upon the death of Craterus (arguably the most influential of Alexander generals in Asia when Alexander died), for we find Hagnon operating in Caria in the region of Ephesus in the period 320-315 BCE (he was granted citizenship of the city in 321/320 BCE), an understandable location if he hailed from nearby Teos. Plutarch claimed that 'Hagnothemis' was the first to hear and rebroadcast Aristotle's part in the *Pamphlet* allegations; he in turn had garnered the detail from Antigonus at a time, we suggest, when he was on his way to becoming the most powerful man in Asia, a position he achieved with his eventual defeat and execution of Eumenes at the close of 316 BCE.[60]

THE EPHEMERAL *EPHEMERIS* AND THE *JOURNAL* JURY

We know that everything claimed by the *Pamphlet* was thoroughly undermined by the content of what we term, for simplicity, the *Journal*. Cited by Plutarch and Arrian at the close of their books (T3, T4), this was presented as a fragment extracted from *hai basilikoi Ephemerides*, the king's official campaign journal or diaries. Arrian stated that *both* Aristobulus and Ptolemy either ended their accounts at this point, or that they had no more detail to add on Alexander's death other than that claimed in this *Ephemerides* extract.[61]

It is tempting to visualise this entry as part of a log of the king's daily orders and movements, as Arrian and Plutarch probably did. More likely there existed, for a time, a vast corpus of campaign correspondence covering ordinances, requisitions and ledgers that comprised of a record of the camp and army activity, and the king's movements would have been an integral part. Some commentators argue the Macedonian kings had enjoyed a long tradition of journal keeping, and certainly Lucian later referenced the *Makedonika hypomnemata tes basilikes oikias*, which covered the movements of the Macedonian regent, Antipater, through 322-319 BCE. Although this may be no more genuine than the epistolary corpus cited by Plutarch as emanating from the Macedonian court, it was, nevertheless, conceived from a well-known practice, and one that was continued by the Antigonid kings.[62] Polybius referenced the *basilika grammata* that the Antigonids tried to keep from Roman hands, and Hieronymus would later extract from Pyrrhus' own *hypomnemata*, his official memoirs (*hypomnemata* can additionally be translated as 'drafts', 'accompanying notes', or even 'inventories').[63]

According to some commentators, the practice of maintaining court journals commenced with Alexander himself, following the Persian archive tradition.[64] If the tradition went back further, we could imagine Eumenes had maintained records for Philip II in Pella when employed at the royal court from aged twenty, and if the former conclusion is correct, he maintained a similar role as the campaign advanced through Asia.[65] Lucian did refer to (perhaps tongue in cheek) a letter sent from Eumenes to Antipater in Pellan detailing Hephaestion's embarrassing slip of the tongue before battle at Issus in 333 BCE, a probable by-product of Eumenes' secretarial role.[66]

Adding to the breadth of arguments is the idea that the *Ephemerides* actually existed in the form of cuneiform clay tablets at Babylon and only concerned Alexander when he was in residence.[67] But such tablets only had room for the briefest of detail; we actually have the inscription relating to the very day that Alexander expired: it simply related: 'The king died, clouds made it impossible to observe the skies.'[68]

The Babylonians were hoarders of inscribed cuneiform tablets;[69] Callisthenes encountered thousands of years of astronomical diaries (said to date back 31,000 years) in this format and he set about sending them back to Greece; the oldest extant diary we know of, however, dates to 651 BCE, though records for the 8th century BCE are referenced elsewhere: Berossus, the resident Chaldean priest of Bel-Marduk, did claim they dated back far further into antiquity, but any explanation of events or causal links we might have hoped to find in them was, it seems, subordinated to temporal precision by celestial observation.[70] As one scholar points out, clay is far more durable than papyrus; a city set ablaze only hardens the material; as a result, the surviving corpus of Babylonian and Assyrian clay inscriptions exceeds the entire library of extant Latin texts, on a word count basis.[71]

Whatever were the origins of the king's *Ephemerides*, by the time the army finally returned to Babylon from the eastern satrapies, and when

This clay cuneiform tablet records what we now term Haley's Comet sometime between 22nd and 28th of September 164 BCE. British Museum, London. BM 41462.

considering the logistical challenge of running a vast empire, Eumenes, who by now had a cavalry command of his own, would have required a whole secretariat dealing with court records, and that would have been the information nerve centre of the expanded Macedonian-governed world.[72] Diodotus (or Diognetus) may well have been involved in its management, no doubt supported by others; Myllenas, for example, was additionally referenced by Curtius as a *scriba regis*, a royal secretary, who, like Eumenes, saw active military service.[73]

We have already challenged assumptions that these official records survived the Successor Wars, for the conflicts within the extant accounts clearly suggest otherwise. Suspiciously, the *only* alleged survivor of the once-vast *Ephemerides* is the *Journal* entry cited by Plutarch and Arrian which dealt with Alexander's death. Their two versions are remarkably similar, and the divergences are easily explained. Plutarch claimed to be reciting the *Journal* entries almost 'word for word' and yet he précised his source more aggressively than Arrian, so what *was* cited by him *was* almost verbatim. Still, the style, pace, and daily references undeniably parallel one another so that we cannot doubt they were virtually metaphrasing a single source.[74]

The *Journal* presented a dry and pedestrian account of Alexander's twelve-day illness at Babylon (a far longer journey to death than the five or so days suggested by the *Pamphlet* and Vulgate texts), and though short on detail and prosaic in style, the reporting is punctuated by references to the king's nightly drinking at the Macedonian-style *symposia* that preceded his decline.[75] These gatherings – like the final party at Medius' residence – more often than not degenerated into *komoi*, the drinking binges documented at *both* ends of Alexander's campaign, though his darkest moments in between were frequently accompanied by alcoholic excess.[76]

According to the *Journal*, at the conclusion of Medius' party, Alexander experienced a fever after which he bathed and slept with no dramatic decline in health; Aristobulus, ever watchful over his dead king's reputation, justified the alcoholic consumption by claiming the raging fever moved him to quench a voracious thirst with more wine.[77] In fact the *Journal* depicts Alexander in firm organisation mode for days thereafter, bathing and attending to religious rites (the Macedonian king's role was to mediate between the men and their gods), fleet logistics and the continued organisation of the army for the forthcoming Arabian campaign, all of it reported in an unemotional and almost sepulchral style.[78] Towards the end, the *Journal* entries become briefer still as Alexander slid into a coma and towards his speechless silent death.

That silence remains deafening, and, moreover, stylistically the *Journal* stands out like a torn sepia photo stapled unconvincingly to the end of a Technicolor film, a production that had paused for a moment and then resumed with a personality-changed cast that had been furnished with newly authored scripts. The meek bedside Companions who acquiesced to Alexander's failure to nominate a successor became lions of ambition in the dangerous days that followed, when the monochrome entries found their colour once again.

We contended that no matter how comprehensive a cover-up, clues always remain. The *Journal* entry, silent on the testament and recording no instructions from the king, may have, nonetheless, unintentionally preserved the silhouette of a reading of the Will, for the entry reads:

> On the next day, his condition now worsened, he [Alexander] just managed to make the required sacrifices, and then sent instructions to the generals to wait for him in the palace courtyard and the battalion and company commanders to wait outside his door.[79]

At this point, Alexander was only just able to speak, making sacrifices with difficulty and finally commanding his chief officers (down to *pentakosiarchai* and *chiliarchai*, commanders of 500 and 1,000 men) to be on close call; so he, and those closest to him, must have appreciated how gravely ill he was.[80] In these circumstances the summons was unlikely to have been to provide them with further orders concerning the forthcoming expedition to Arabia. If, as the Vulgate texts claimed, Perdiccas, or Ptolemy, had to prise out of Alexander a decision on succession, and if, as the *Journal* claimed, he was speechless for his final two days, then here, with the commanders assembled immediately outside his bedchamber, something momentous was being written or being said inside.

The *Journal* entry in Arrian and Plutarch included two further significant episodes that perhaps tell us, once again, more than the original author may have supposed or intended. The first concerns the Macedonian infantry, which forced its way into the king's bedchamber where the Bodyguards and select Companions had their king closely quarantined. Fearing his death was being kept from them, the infantry officers smelled intrigue: '… others wished to see his body, for a report had gone around that he was already dead, and they suspected, I fancy, that his death was being concealed by his guards.'[81] The forced entry, or as Arrian more tactfully put it, 'insistence' on seeing the king, suggests there was a huge lack of trust in the senior command whose cavalry status still resonated of the old aristocratic landowner-serf divide that underpinned the Macedonian tribal structure.

This episode of near mutiny became a permanent fixture in all accounts, and as it closely paralleled what was claimed in the *Pamphlet*, we would be justified in concluding that this was a genuine state of affairs. At this point, however, the king was still conscious, though conspicuously speechless, as the officers filed past him. According to the *Journal*, sometime after the intrusion and when all the soldiers had departed the bedchamber, Alexander was pronounced dead. Plutarch was clear that Aristobulus pinpointed that to the 30th of the Macedonian month of Daisios, which corresponded to the 'moon of May' (spanning May-June in the modern calendar), some two days after the *Journal* statement that it occurred on the 28th; Plutarch was obviously drawing from *both* sources in parallel here.[82]

Daisios was a hollow month of twenty-nine days and any reference to 'month end', and whether that meant the 29th or 30th, could have caused additional slippage between accounts.[83] The latter date for the pronouncement of Alexander's death – which was two full two weeks after Medius' party on the 16th – may capture what Ptolemy's sanitary affair chose not to: two days of confusion as the tenuous life-signs ebbed and flowed, certainly not a fitting epitaph for the Macedonian king. The timing of Alexander's medical death has often been disputed, for his body professedly stayed fresh for days thereafter. If not more Vulgate *thauma*, this hints at a huge blunder in the prognosis when a deep coma may indeed have fooled the audience for some time.[84]

Considering the ubiquity of these episodes, we are not accusing Ptolemy of *complete* journalistic invention with what we propose was his brilliant example of pseudo-documentarism, for much we read in the *Journal* probably did take place; the nightly drinking and frequent celebrations that paint a month of irresponsibility may well be factual, even if it was an already developed Greek *topos* in Philip II's day: Demosthenes, and more recently Theopompus, had certainly implicated the Argead court in bouts of extended insobriety.[85] Conversely, when upholding the historicity of the *Pamphlet* Will, we are not claiming *all* the detail as genuine. Both authors needed to interweave their fictions with verisimilitude if they were to pass them off as genuine to have the desired effect, and so a rather appropriate symmetry existed in the ranks of this literary confrontation.

The second contentious episode was a visit by other Bodyguards and court intimates to the Temple of Serapis to ask for divine guidance, and this does appear to be an overtly Ptolemaic device.[86]

THE LOST HALF-MONTH: AELIAN'S ORPHANED *JOURNAL*

Before we discuss Serapis and its importance in Hellenistic Egypt we need to mention other briefer references to the *Ephemerides* that have survived, though they provide no additional detail and none of them contradicts the contention that only one event was being recorded. We find the first in Plutarch's *Moralia*, in which Philinus, a close friend of the historian, rebutted claims that Alexander drank moderately by citing the drink-laden entries as his witness to excess.[87] A second is an *earlier* reference in Plutarch's *Life of Alexander* detailing the king's daily routine of hunting, bathing and dining, but once more the emphasis is on frequent drinking sessions (Plutarch commented apologetically: 'but over the wine, as I have said, he would sit long, for conversation's sake'). Similar is the *Ephemerides* extract that can be found in Athenaeus' *Deipnosophistae*, which additionally claimed Alexander slept two days and nights consecutively following a night of carousing.[88]

The water is supposedly muddied by the fragment found in the *Historical Miscellany* of Aelian (T5):

> The following behaviour of Alexander was not commendable. On the fifth of the month of Dios he was drinking with Eumaeus, they say; then on the sixth he slept because of the excesses. During the day he got up only long enough to discuss with his generals the following day's

march, saying it would commence early. On the seventh he feasted with Perdiccas and drank freely again. On the eighth he slept. On the fifteenth of the same month he drank to excess once more, and on the following day he did what he would usually do after a party. On the twenty-seventh he dined with Bagoas – the distance from the palace to Bagoas' house was ten stades – and on the twenty-eighth he slept.[89]

This text is possibly incomplete, for though it is clear the *Ephemerides* was being referred to, the source was never formally introduced. Like much else in Aelian's compendium of historical titbits, the detail was tersely thrown in beside other non-relevant text. But here again alcohol abuse served to illustrate the decline in Alexander's behaviour against a background of earlier finer Homeric qualities and restraint. However, Aelian's excerpt made calendar references that contradicted Arrian and Plutarch, and thus, some scholars have argued, it was referring to a totally different event. One proposal for that is Alexander's previous visit to Babylon in 331 BCE, or his stay in Ecbatana, the summer residence of the Great Kings, in the autumn of 324 BCE, the year before his death.[90]

This last interpretation is linked to the decline in health of Hephaestion, the king's closest friend and first *chiliarchos*, perhaps prompted by a fragment of Ephippus' *scandeleuse* which claimed this too was preceded by prodigious drinking bouts.[91] Moreover, an enmity had existed between the alleged *Ephemerides* author, Eumenes, and Hephaestion (whose above reported slip of the tongue may be evidence of that),[92] so the alcoholic slant supposedly deflected blame away from Eumenes, for Alexander suspected his friend's death was due to deliberate poisoning. Attaching this *Ephemerides* extract to a different campaign episode would, of course, back up Hammond's contention that various portions of the official campaign log were in circulation.[93] But that is a vexing conclusion, for Aelian's chapter is headed *Of Alexander*, and Hephaestion was never mentioned at all.[94] And if taken together as *two* distinct episodes, these extracts would suspiciously confirm that any surviving *Ephemerides* fragments recorded little more than a string of decadent *symposia* and fatal illnesses.

Aelian's text is deemed to conflict with that of Plutarch and Arrian because it commenced on the 5th of the Macedonian month of Dios, the month of Zeus linked to the moon of October, with the main narrative focusing on drinking bouts that followed on the 6th, 7th and 8th, then to the 15th and 16th, after which it jumped to the king's dining on the 27th, and sleeping on the 28th. Yet here no sign of illness or fever had taken hold of Alexander and Medius' party is not mentioned at all.[95] But a little lateral thinking offers some reconciliation, and the clues lay in the opening statements of Plutarch and Arrian. Plutarch told us that *previously* (that is before the commencement of Alexander's two-week decline) and upon hearing the news of Hephaestion's posthumous elevation to hero (or god) as approved by the oracle at Siwa, Alexander had allowed himself to indulge in a number of sacrifices and drinking bouts.[96] Arrian also mentioned that Alexander had *previously* celebrated the customary sacrificial rites with a view to his success. Diodorus also commented on these earlier events claiming that following Hephaestion's funeral, the king turned to amusements and festivals.[97] How then can this help unite the texts?

The answer is to assume Aelian's 'Dios' (Δίος in Greek) was a corruption of 'Daisios' (Δαίσιος) and then to insert Aelian's detail of banquets from the 5th to the 15th into the narrative *before* Medius' *komos* which took place on the 15th/16th whence Plutarch and Arrian began *their Journal* entry (as implied by the date references in Plutarch's text). The result is a neatly dovetailed account of a full month's activity including the 'previous' celebrations Plutarch and Arrian referred to, and this is where Plutarch's references to hunting would have originated. A corruption of names in Aelian's text appears an inherent part of the confusion, for we would expect his reference to Alexander's drinking at the residence of 'Eumaeus' (Eumaios) on the 5th should read either 'Eumenes', or perhaps 'Ptolemaios' – so Ptolemy.[98]

To finally resolve the conflict, the banquets described by Aelian on the 24th, 27th and 28th would have taken place at the end of the *previous* month, erroneously repositioned by a manuscript copyist trying to make chronological sense, possibly due to the lack of any introduction in Aelian's account; as we will discover, the extant manuscripts are studded with scribal errors. Repositioning the activities of the 24th, 27th and 28th to the previous month makes better sense considering the gathering took place at the residence of Bagoas 10 *stadia* (1.25 miles) from the royal palace, an unlikely journey if Alexander was already at death's door. Considered this way, the middle-month date references finger-join too well for us to dismiss any coincidence out of hand.

Further evidence that Aelian's passage preceded the other *Journal* entries comes in the form of his statement that on the 6th of the month Alexander discussed a 'march' with his generals, which was supposed to commence early the following morning. Alexander was preparing to *follow* the progress of the land army into Arabia with the fleet, so the army's departure was indeed due to commence in advance.[99] Arrian discussed how, in the days before his own *Journal* narrative commenced, fleet exercises were taking place 'constantly'; troop manoeuvres and army reorganisation was well underway and it seems this new campaign, or as Tarn suggests 'a voyage of discovery', was postponed because of the king's unrelenting fever.[100]

If we are correct, it appears the archetypal *Journal* entry cited (a little over) a *full* month's activity. So why did the entry of Arrian and Plutarch not cover the whole period? The reason for their brevity is clear: the king's illness commenced halfway through, at Medius' *komos*, and they were simply reporting on how Alexander died. This late start-point is supported by Plutarch's words: 'according to the *Journal* his *sickness* was as follows...'.[101]

Aelian's agenda was different: for didactic purposes he was focusing on serial alcoholism and not the aftermath. He closed his entry with a revealing accusation:

> ... one of two alternatives follows: either Alexander damaged himself with wine by drinking so often within the month, or the authors of these stories are telling lies: from them one can infer that such writers, who include Eumenes of Cardia, tell similar tales on other occasions.[102]

The 'other occasions' could, of course, include the aforementioned letter to Antipater concerning Hephaestion, or even later invents which established Eumenes' reputation for brilliant documentary subterfuges in the Successor Wars.[103] Aelian's conclusion, which clearly referred to a *whole* month, was that 'a drinking marathon unique in history' was an impossibility, or suggestive of an author who wished the king's death to seem it attributable to such.[104] Whilst it seems that Aelian believed he was reading a *genuine* fragment of the royal diaries, he was perhaps the first classical author to (obliquely) question the authenticity of its content. As we know, Athenaeus' *Deipnosophistae,* written as a dialogue within a dialogue in the style of Plato, credited Eumenes with exactly the same secretarial role.[105] His work is uncertainly dated but its contempt for Commodus (emperor 180-192 CE), the son of the emperor Marcus Aurelius, provides a clear *termini post quem*, and from that we can conclude that these authors were potentially contemporaries living in Rome.

Aelian's cynicism raises a fundamental question: could, or would, Eumenes or any other court secretary, have been allowed the latitude to capture such degenerative behaviour in the real-time official *Ephemerides*? Surely not. Instead we are proffering Ptolemy as the architect of this specific entry, and his penchant for subterfuge may have been more developed than we first suspected; he fabricated a sufficiently convincing extract from the official campaign diary to wind up his authoritative history, whilst heaping responsibility for its content on the royal secretaries. As Eumenes had died some years before Ptolemy came to publish, there was not much he could do about it. Additionally, Ptolemy's association with the *Journal* is completely plausible; he was after all behind the foundation of the Alexandrian Library that rapaciously collected documents of all kinds.

Certainly his son, Ptolemy II *Philadelphos*, left extensive *basilikai anagraphai* and *hypomnemata*, the 'royal records' that Diodorus was aware of, and which Appian of Alexandria later drew from. An extract from a later royal journal appears in the 'propagandistic' *Gaurob Papyrus* describing events in the reign of Ptolemy III *Euergetes*, whose twenty-four-volume collection of *hypomnemata* provided Athenaeus with material. This was possibly part of an epistolary tradition that inspired parallels in the *Romance*.[106] It seems Arrian and Plutarch were satisfied that Ptolemy was guardian of Alexander's royal *Ephemerides* too.

To add muscle to our argument for a common *Journal* fragment, we have a literary 'gene-marker' to guide us. Both Plutarch and Arrian noticeably sandwiched their extracts between remarks which inform us when they opened and closed their metaphrasing (T3, T4).[107] Uniquely in his final chapter, Plutarch employed the term *kata lexin*, 'almost word for word', to describe his entry, and Arrian added 'all these details are to be found in the *Journals*'.[108] This is rare evidence of *ipsissima verba* and logically suggests that Ptolemy had been quite precise on the entry and exit points. The stress Arrian and Plutarch placed on informing us that this was uniquely sourced material rules out any speculation that other parts of their books were *Journal* derived; Arrian conspicuously omitted any reference to it when detailing his sources on his opening page.[109]

Could Ptolemy have credibly accessed the original campaign diaries? In 1894 Wilken first proposed he did and later scholars endorsed him.[110] Pearson proposed an alternative explanation: the *Journal* entry *was* a fake, and yet because it corroborated Ptolemy's detail, its author was familiar with Ptolemy's book, and thus a verisimilitude was achieved. Pearson did not contemplate that the authors were one and the same, though he did conclude that its style was Alexandrian by comparison with a papyrus found there in the Roman era.[111] If Ptolemy did have the complete campaign corpus, what happened to it and why did he not strengthen the veracity, authority and uniqueness of his history with *more* frequent references to the campaign logs, most relevantly for events he could not himself have witnessed? The answer is probably straightforward: if he did have the *Ephemerides*, it would have been foolhardy to broadcast its whereabouts to those who would undermine him by accessing it themselves, for it appears he greatly inflated his own role in the Asian campaign. Like much else surrounding the death of Alexander, the official records, in whatever condition they survived, remained a closely guarded affair.

If any campaign documentation *did* survive the Successor Wars, which saw Antigonus plundering Babylon (310/309 BCE), then Ptolemy *would* surely have coveted what remained. Strabo implied that he knew of Babylonian records from which he concluded the campaign historians had provided only cursory *geographic* detail compared to expert data he found.[112] This material may have included the topographical records of Baeton and Diognetus (termed *itinerum mensores*, 'measurers of roads'), Philonides and Amyntas, whose names appeared in the texts of Athenaeus,

Aelian and Pliny, though these eyewitness accounts seem, once again, to have included the marvels of India, thus we may question their intent.

The polymath Eratosthenes (ca. 276-194 BCE), however, who became chief librarian at the Library of Alexandria around a century later, stated that no copies of such records, the *stathmoi* (measurements or stages), were available for him to consult, and we would have expected Arrian to use them, or at least reference them, if only to follow the example set by Xenophon who referred to these types of precise records in his *Anabasis*. This upholds the contention that the campaign *Ephemerides*, Strabo's Babylon-originating data aside, disappeared in the Successor Wars.

It is not difficult to imagine how Ptolemy first came into possession of any archival material from Babylon following Alexander's death. War with Perdiccas commenced in earnest when Ptolemy hijacked, or rescued (depending upon the interpretation), Alexander's funeral cortège somewhere near Damascus in Syria and 'escorted' it to Egypt against Perdiccas' wishes.[113] Aelian provided a colourful addition to the episode in which the bier carrying the coffin of hammered gold and pulled by sixty-four mules, was a decoy that included a replica of the dead king's corpse; the real body was sped to Egypt by a different route.[114]

Aelian's account went on to report that Aristander of Termessus, the by-now famous seer, had predicted at Babylon that whichever land received the body would remain prosperous and forever unvanquished. Whilst this too has the air of a later Ptolemaic device, no one (after Perdiccas) demanded the return of Alexander's mummified remains, and this suggests some legitimacy to Ptolemy's action, though it must be said that no one was ever able to cross the Nile to remove him from power. In the Vulgate texts the final destination of the bier does appear to have been the oracular Ammonium at Siwa in the Egyptian desert, the home of the Zeus-Ammon and Alexander's 'immortality', and the extant Wills additionally claim that Alexander chose to be entombed in Egypt, though this may have been politically opportune if Ptolemy was being courted.[115]

Pausanias concluded that Perdiccas planned to escort the bier to Aegae, the traditional burial ground of the Macedonian royalty. Whether endorsed by the Common Assembly at Babylon, or stemming from Perdiccas' later opportunism, Pausanias' interpretation is possibly supported by either of two noteworthy turns of events: the first is the Macedonian regent's proffering his daughter (Nicaea) to the chiliarch, in which case Perdiccas was probably on safe ground when taking the body 'home', for who except Ptolemy's supporters could object? Aegae, 'the city of goats', became the spiritual home of the Argeads when Caranus renamed the Phrygian settlement of Edessa (meaning 'water', one of two cities so-named) some four centuries before. Moreover, King Perdiccas I had prophesised the end of the Argead line should any king be buried anywhere else.[116]

The second event that might have helped Pausanias' conclusion was the collapse of that initiative with Antipater, following which we read Perdiccas and his generals voted in favour of defeating Ptolemy in Egypt 'in order that there might be no obstacle in the way of their Macedonian campaign'.[117] Perdiccas most likely planned to keep the bier close (in Syria we propose) until events developed sufficiently to escort it to its permanent home in his bid for control of Pella.[118]

So it is likely that royal archives and campaign correspondence departed Babylon with Perdiccas and remained with him as he planned his attack on the Nile.[119] Letters between he and Demades in Athens were reportedly retrieved from the archives immediately after his death, suggesting Perdiccas had indeed journeyed with the tools of bureaucracy about him.[120] His initial attack on the Ptolemaic defences at Pelusium, a necessary entry point into Egypt to avoid the marshes of Typhon's Breathing Hole, and again near Heliopolis further up the Nile, failed, and cost him his life; thereafter, deals were brokered, promises exchanged and possibly court correspondence too. Ptolemy even acquired Perdiccas' surviving elephants – those his men had not managed to blind with pikes at the battle of the Fort of Camels. Ptolemy was most likely already in league with Seleucus (possibly one of Perdiccas' assassins) who, we will argue, had already inherited the governorship of Babylonia, in which case further exchanges of court correspondence would have taken place.[121]

THE CULT OF SERAPIS: A CASE OF ANTHROPOMORPHIC EDITING?

Here we expand on the *Journal* references to the cult of Serapis through which its author might have made his biggest blunder. Some scholars find this problematic and so the topic has already been discussed, but not quite with the significance it might merit to our particular case.

> The Diaries [*Ephemerides*] say that Peithon, Attalus, Demophon and Peucestas, together with Cleomenes, Menidas and Seleucus spent the night in the temple of Serapis and asked the God if it would be better for Alexander to be carried into the temple himself, in order to pray there and perhaps recover; but the God forbade it, and declared it would be better for him if he stayed where he was. The God's command was made public, and soon afterwards Alexander died – this, after all, being the better thing.[122] (T3, T4 abbreviated)

The *Journal* clearly named the individuals who spent the night in the temple of the healing god to ask divine guidance on Alexander's worsening condition. The group appears to have included two of Alexander's leading seers, Demophon and Cleomenes; it was Demophon who had warned Alexander not to enter the Mallian city in India where he was nearly killed.[123] More intriguing is the presence of Peithon, Peucestas, and Seleucus, the men either complicit in Perdiccas' murder, or the most prominent of those named guilty at Medius' *komos*.[124] The list also looks to have included Attalus (initially hostile to Perdiccas but who became his brother-in-law as part of the settlement at Babylon), and Menidas who had recently arrived in Babylon from recruiting in Macedonia, which suggests he could have arrived with Cassander the scheming son of the allegedly scheming Macedonian regent.[125] It is a line up which has the distinct air of a *Pamphlet* riposte.

It is generally accepted by modern historians, and supported by a story in Plutarch's *Isis and Osiris*, that the cult of Serapis was started in Egypt by Ptolemy I *Soter* at least a decade after Alexander's death, and probably later still;[126] the earliest known cult statue in Alexandria was initially thought to have been sculpted by Bryaxis around 286-278 BCE, but this appears to have been a colossal likeness of Pluto (evidenced by its inclusion of Cerberus and a serpent) dating back to 350 BCE that was later shipped to Alexandria from Sinope on the Black Sea to be renamed in its new home by Ptolemy I *Soter*.[127] Plutarch further asserted that Serapis *was* the Egyptian name for the equivalent of Pluto, either correctly, or guided by this episode. All in all, some forty-two temples to the new god appeared across Egypt with the intention of uniting the Graeco-Macedonian ruling classes with their Egyptian subjects; the most prominent was perhaps in the Egyptian Quarter of Alexandria itself.[128] A reference to the Serapeum in Alexandria and to the 'great Serapis, ruler of all' appeared in the *Romance* version of the Will (as well as other chapters), which does rather point to Egyptian influence in the book's provenance.[129]

The integrity of the *Journal* entry as an *unedited* source rests on the existence of a Serapis cult in Babylon earlier than 323 BCE.[130] This appears to counter the evidence (so some studies believe), yet the notion may be challenged by the wording in the Curse of Artemisia which mentions an 'Oserapis' who was possibly worshipped at Memphis before Alexander's Egyptian invasion. But *this* deity, whilst similarly linked to death and the afterlife, was usually depicted as a mummified human male with the head of a bull, with a solar disk between its horns, and this bears little resemblance to the statues and depictions of the familiar Ptolemaic Serapis.[131]

Egyptian residents of Babylonia could have twinned its temple of Bel-Marduk with that of Oserapis if they saw a religious overlap; moreover, it was not uncommon for authors to employ contemporary names and terms to describe an earlier equivalent for the sake of clarity for the reader;[132] Herodotus equated Egyptian gods with Greek gods, and vice versa, long before Alexander's day.[133] We also know the new syncretised

'Serapis' *was* in effect the cult of Asclepius reinvented with a twist: it fused the Memphite cult of the bull Osiris-Apis with elements of Zeus and indeed Pluto.[134] Alexander is specifically cited as having destroyed the temple of Asclepius in Ecbatana following Hephaestion's death, and so the healing god, at least, was an Eastern resident by then, if not another divine approximation.[135] As a further parallel, Zeus-Ammon was itself a Hellenisation of Egypt's Ammon-Ra. Why then all the fuss?

The theonymic hubris may be necessary because the reference to Serapis seems, nevertheless, self-damning if scholars upholding the 'late' emergence of the god in Egyptian are correct on the dating and naming conventions; the *Journal* may have been promoting a new anthropomorphic god, but an original secretarial entry compiled in 323 BCE would have used the Eastern title of the deity, or specifically 'Oserapis', if there *were* 'striking similarities'. But after Ptolemy's reshaping of the god with elements of Greek religion, *that* identification no longer held. If it was the *new* Hellenistic god that was being referred in the *Journal*, as the name we read implies, that would have been back-formation by the *Journal* author, and at best, the *Ephemerides* entry was edited, with Serapis' development in Egypt again pointing to Ptolemaic *Pamphlet* origins.[136]

A statue of Asclepius with a sacred snake, exhibited in the Archaeological Museum of Epidaurus, Argolis, Greece. This is a copy of the unearthed original now in the National Archaeological Museum of Athens.

There is a further reference to Serapis in Plutarch's narrative of Babylon, linked to an imposter who fatally adorned himself with the royal robes and irreverently took the throne while Alexander was exercising. When questioned on his treasonous behaviour, he claimed Serapis' divine will had unchained him and he blamed his otherwise inexplicable actions on the god's command[137] (T21, see T22 also). This account *was* obviously complied many years later, so the use of a familiar deity to approximate an eastern god is less troubling. We know Arrian cited Aristobulus as his source on similar episodes such as the Chaldean prophecies, but not specifically for *this* epoptic event. So here the Serapic reference could be further evidence of Ptolemy's own strategic interweaving of 'his' god and the portentous into the end of his book to signal the king's imminent, inevitable and fate-determined end, though one clearly hastened by his unrelenting alcoholism, as the *Journal* made clear.[138]

If the cult of Serapis was connected to the snake, as some scholars suppose, then Ptolemy's claim that two talking serpents (Aristobulus mentioned ravens, Strabo stated crows) guided Alexander and his entourage to the Egyptian oracle at Siwa in the Libyan desert,[139] alongside Alexander's dream vision of an antidote-bearing serpent in India used to cure Ptolemy's own wound, suggest he *was* introducing his new deity more insidiously through his work.[140] The snake-god, Glycon, was after all the alleged reincarnation of the healing god Asclepius, Serapis' forerunner, and the *Romance* wove in the legend of the 'good fortunate' serpents (representing Agathos Daimon, the good fortune spirit) that appeared at the founding of Ptolemaic Alexandria.

Statuettes recovered from the city appear to show Alexander in a snake-fringed aegis (an animal-skin throw) and we should recall the claims that Olympias was seen with snakes in her bed; she was reportedly entwined by a huge serpent when she conceived her son, though this may be a product of Plutarch's hostility to her involvement in the Orphic rites and cults of 'magic'.[141] But in this tradition, Alexander's alleged father was Nectanebo II (ruled 360-342 BCE) of the Thirtieth Dynasty, the last pharaoh of Egyptian stock; if Alexandria was the birthplace of this *Romance* claim, then the Ptolemies were truly immersing themselves in a realm of demi-gods. It was the perfect amalgam for a dynasty that had assisted Alexander in his deeds and which was nevertheless conscious of its 'new' ancient subject population.[142]

Demetrius of Phalerum, Ptolemy's learned court philosopher who had been expelled from Athens in 307 BCE by Demetrius *Poliorketes*, the son of Antigonus *Monophthalmos*, is said to have written five books focusing on 'true dreams' surrounding cures deriving from Serapis, composing paeans in the god's honour after his own blindness had been healed.[143] Demetrius appears to have been a major part of Ptolemy's fast-developing PR machine in the post-Ipsus years, which culminated in Alexander's prayer to Serapis, a section of which was discovered in fragmentary form on a papyrus dating to the 1st century BCE.[144] Demetrius' *Peri Tyches* (*On Fortune*), published around 310 BCE, which gave fortune the lead role over virtue in Alexander's success, may well have stirred Ptolemy to remind the world of his *own* part in the campaign.[145]

Under the sanctuary of Ptolemy I *Soter*, after a term in Thebes (in Boeotia), Demetrius of Phalerum shepherded the expansion of the

Alexandrian Library from the Palaces in the Brucheion, otherwise referred to as the Royal Quarter and which would soon house the Mausoleum where Alexander was buried. Demetrius' initial good fortune did not last forever; he was exiled once again by *Soter's* son, Ptolemy II *Philadelphos*, most likely for backing his half-brother, Ptolemy *Keraunos*, upon his father's death; Demetrius' was an unsurprising stance since *Keraunos* was the son of Eurydice, the sister of Cassander who had initially installed Demetrius in Athens. The learned and experienced philosopher from Phalerum, who reportedly died of a snakebite in Upper Egypt where he was continuing his literary pursuits,[146] is said to have once advised Ptolemy I 'to acquire the books dealing with kingship and leadership' and to read them 'for the things their friends do not dare to offer to kings as advice, are written in these books'.[147] It seems that Ptolemy quickly learned his lessons on kingship and subterfuge.

A bust of Serapis wearing a *kalathos*, a ceremonial basket used in religious processions and a symbol for the land of the dead. Statues of Serapis depicted a figure resembling Hades or Pluto, gods associated with the underworld, often with a sceptre and the hellhound Cerberus at his feet along with a serpent. Graeco-Roman Museum, Alexandria.

POLITICS OF THE PORTENTOUS

Serapic involvement with the *Journal* brought divine judgement into the picture, and this, in turn, worked well beside the biographical elements questioning Alexander's sanity, for the picture painted by Plutarch is one of a king losing his reason:

His confidence now deserted him, he began to believe that he had lost the favour of the gods, and he became increasingly suspicious of his friends... Meanwhile Alexander had become so obsessed by his fears of the supernatural and so overwrought and apprehensive in his own mind, that he interpreted every strange or unusual occurrence, no matter how trivial, as a prodigy or a portent...[148] (T21)

The message is clear: the king had become 'a slave to his fears'. Did eyewitness historians dare to go this far, or was this *fabula* scooped up later? For death-heralding omens do, as we know, proliferate Alexander's final chapter (T21, T22, T23, T24), in both the Vulgate accounts and the court genre. Arrian's account corroborates this in a more sanitised way, but we know he demonstrably 'whitewashed' Alexander where necessary.[149] Nevertheless, this suggests a court source (or sources) may indeed have allowed this degenerate image to creep in.

The Roman emperor Domitian (ruled 81-96 CE) once quipped that no one believes there has been a conspiracy unless a ruler is actually killed.[150] But here we contend with the opposite, for Plutarch reported that no foul play was suspected in Babylon *at the time*. This is surprising in light of the regicidal history of the Argead kings and something of a contradiction to his claim that Alexander feared assassination from the agents of Antipater, his regent in Macedonia. Plutarch, who earlier described the portents heralding in Alexander's end, appears to have immanentised the eschaton, for this was an environment in which suspicion was unlikely to have ever been absent.[151]

The inclusion of portents, going back, in fact, to the death of the Indian gymnosophist Calanus a year before,[152] would, as Peter Green observed, '... certainly suggest that the king's death was due to natural or divine causes, rather than to human agency.'[153] And surely achieving that was the very purpose. Today, at least, this appears a rather obvious misdirection, but in Alexander's time the gods were not to be dismissed; the naming of Demophon and Cleomenes at the Serapic temple anchored down the legitimacy of its reply: 'Leave Alexander where he is, for it would be the better thing.' This, and the collection of divinations that preceded the king's final decline, had the desired effect; the superstitious and stoical Arrian concluded: 'The truth was that divine power was leading him on to the point, which once reached, would seal his imminent death.'[154]

The Chaldean Magi had doubtlessly exploited the portent-gullible Macedonians to their advantage in Babylon when competing with Alexander's Greek 'philosophical corps' for control of his soul, and Diodorus captured something of the mystery that surrounded them: 'For they are reputed to possess a great deal of experience and to make most exact observations of the stars. Indeed they declare that for many myriads of years the study of these matters has been pursued among them.'[155] Numerical cryptograms were even used in haruspicy 'to mystify the profane'; some Assyrian and Babylonian inscriptions remain undeciphered today; Herodotus referred to the Magi as *pharmadeukantes*, 'having performed magical rites'.[156]

The weight of superstition ('the mad daughter of a wise mother', according to Voltaire) in the classical period has probably been underestimated in modern interpretations of events. The huge number (over 1,700) of excavated lead curse-tablets (*tabellae defixiones* in Latin) housing a spell, *katadesmos*, with their Homeric verse incantations (*epoidai*), attests to the wide-held belief in *mageia* and the *daimones* of the underworld (commonly Hermes, Charon, Hecate, Pluto, Kore or Persephone), as well as to the belief in bewitchment, *pepharmakeusthai*.[157] These tablets were often folded and pierced with nails, buried in graves, tombs and temples, or thrown down wells accompanied by figurines and invocations in an indecipherable language, supposedly that of demons. This provoked the accursed to wear amulets in defence. Apparently, and as later depicted in Lucan's *De Bello civili*, Thessaly was the commercial centre of witches (*pharmakes*) whose services could be readily hired to send enemies down to Hades 'where the bloodless, bodiless and boneless endlessly wandered' around the palace of Pluto.[158] Ephesus was the centre of magic and magicians, *mystagogos*, whose *Ephesia grammata*, mystical words, were arranged in formulas and incantations hissed in chthonic temples.

Epileptics were thought to have the Sacred Disease and to be possessed by the gods;[159] magnetic lode stones were thought to contain souls, and those who died without funeral rites (the *ataphoi*) were considered condemned to a less than idyllic underworld community. Athens even had a separate court for trials of inanimate objects, including figurines that were held responsible for murder.[160]

In Greece, four locations had become renowned for their *nekyomanteia*, prophecy places of the dead, often located in caves and staffed by Sybils, the *psychagogoi* or 'evocators' of the spirits. Here, as at the *psychomanteia*, the drawing places of ghosts, necromancy was practised, sacrifices made, and the spirits recalled from the underworld for cults, rituals and other chthonic requests.[161] The ever-rationalising Aristotle even let *daimones* feature in his treatise on animals, that is if the work can be truly credited to him; but precedents had been set, for Plato's *Laws* referred to prophets, sorcerers and divinely guided healers in a matter of fact way.[162]

Theocritus, based in Alexandria, was to publish a poem *Pharmakeutria*, the *Sorceress*, that was steeped in magical rites. The protagonist, a young Greek girl, consulted experts on drugs to bring back her lover's affections; the recommended potion included coltsfoot and pounded lizard, as spells and incantations to Hecate and the Moon were to be recited whilst pounding on a bronze gong. We have evidence that some formulas for the *kykeon*, the Greek mix of wine, barley and other potentially psychoactive substances, provided hallucinatory results that added to the drama.

The Romans were no less superstitious; a read of Valerius Maximus' *Nine Books of Memorable Deeds and Sayings* illustrates the fear of omens and auspices (in Latin literally a 'bird sighting' – from *avis* and *spicere*) embedded in the belief code of the time. In Rome the *Twelve Tables* (451-450 BCE) described by Pliny, limited anyone from incanting a *malum carmen,* an evil charm.[163] It did little to deter Gnaeus Calpurnius Piso (ca. 44 BCE-20 CE) from leaving '… spells, curses and lead tablets engraved with the name Germanicus, with half-burnt ashes smeared with blood and other magic by which it is believed that living souls are dedicated to the infernal powers.' Ammianus Marcellinus' (ca. 325-post 391 CE) retrospective look at Rome (his *Res Gestae* – broadly, 'things done' – continued chronologically where Tacitus' *Histories* had ceased) contained repeated references to the menace of the blacker arts of magic.[164]

A lead curse tablet found in a graveyard in the area of the Agora at the Macedonian capital of Pella. The *daimones* were being invoked and a curse was being cast upon the marriage of Thetima and Dionysophon by a jilted lover or an existing wife. The language is harsh Doric of northwest Greece, suggesting a unique dialect may have been used in Pella before the 4th century BCE. Found in 1986 it was published in the Hellenic Dialectology Journal in 1993. Now on display in the Archaeological Museum of Pella.

But here, preceding Alexander's death in Babylon, superstition, *deisidaimonia,* was being harnessed well. The healing god had spoken and Asclepius had finally turned his back on the troubled Macedonian king. The *Journal* recorded that Alexander was speechless for his final two days. If so, he had by definition spoken the day before. What orders did he give to the officers told to remain on call right outside his quarters?[165] What discussions took place with his intimates, his wife, secretary and Bodyguards? No doctor or physician is mentioned in the *Journal,* and not a purge, poultice, or prayer. There is a troubling lack of zeal to save Alexander after Serapis had spoken. Whatever *was* said in the dying king's chamber was truly sanitised, muted and dried by Ptolemy to the brevity of a cuneiform tablet.

One final *Journal* detail is, however, noteworthy, for its author appears to have provided some valuable PR to both Nearchus and Medius. Alexander is portrayed listening to his navarch's account of his sea voyage and instructing him on the forthcoming campaign, presumably as admiral of the fleet heading to Arabia, whilst Medius' intimacy with the king is highlighted by the drinking party he hosted and his playing private games of dice with the king (T3, T4). Both men had become valuable naval commanders, each supporting Antigonus at a time when Ptolemy needed as much sea power as he could muster; moreover, the somewhat negative image of Alexander depicted in the *Journal* would have sat rather well with the *Pamphlet*-vilified Cassander, who was now Ptolemy's ally. So, was the high profile of Nearchus and Medius an overture designed to swing their loyalty Ptolemy's way?

With this in mind, the most relevant period for its release would have been between late 313 and 307/6 BCE, when both nautical men were known to be active, Nearchus advising Demetrius at the battle at Gaza, and Medius seeing naval action at the battle off Salamis; this was a period in which Antigonus was threatening to invade Egypt itself (he tried unsuccessfully in 306 BCE).[166] It raises the question whether Ptolemy might have commenced distributing the home-baked *Ephemerides* fragment to counter the claims in the *Pamphlet* (most likely issued sometime between 318 and the end of 316 BCE) ahead of inserting it into the final pages of his book. Of course the uniqueness of the *Journal* may have also led to it being extracted from Ptolemy's book and circulated independently some decades on.

So what do modern scholars conclude of the *Journal*? Generally, though not universally, it is branded a fraud; its historicity appears as valid as the *Ephemeris* of Dictys of Crete with its claims to be an eyewitness account of the siege of Troy.[167] One theory concludes, ironically, that the *Journal* was a production of Eumenes and circulated within two years of Alexander's death, when he was supposedly under instruction from the Macedonian generals to counter any rumours of regicide. Interestingly, a 1986 study saw the hand of Ptolemy in its fabrication.[168] It is worth repeating Heckel's contention, '… that there is no evidence whatsoever that the *Journal* contained anything of a military or political nature.' Heckel follows with, 'given the suspicious nature of the portions cited, there is a strong possibility that the *Journal* is a fabrication, an attempt to disguise the truth about the king's last days, with the false claim that details given were extracted verbatim from an official journal'.[169] Bosworth rather appropriately rounded-off his detailed appraisal with: 'paradoxically' the Alexander *Romance* 'is nearer to the truth than the Royal *Ephemerides*'.[170]

THE VULGATE: THE HYBRID 'MUDDY STREAM'

What is the relationship of the Vulgate portrayal of Alexander's death – represented by the accounts of Diodorus, Curtius and Justin (T6, T7, T8) – to the *Journal* and the *Pamphlet*, for the Vulgate stance on Alexander's last words – which left the kingdom 'to the strongest' – contradicts them both? As Lane Fox neatly summed it up for the *Journal*, if '… speechless for two days on his death bed, he can hardly have been so articulate in his utterances to his troops.'[171] Furthermore, the clarity of the *Pamphlet* Will left no room for ambiguity: if the historian at the root of the Vulgate was aware of the claim of conspiracy, he was surely aware of Alexander's lucid testament that sat beside it. Assuming Cleitarchus was the source from which the Vulgate genre drew, as is widely accepted, the Will's omission from his final pages was deliberate and clinical; it was an early literary keyhole-surgery that separated out the episodes to create the wrap to the genre Tarn termed a 'muddy stream… full of flotsam'. [172]

The 'late' publishing Cleitarchus would, as we have argued, have been on safe ground when dispensing with the Will and probably the detail of the partition of the empire with it; when he came to publish (we suggested the late-280s through the 270s BCE), the first generation of the *Diadokhoi*, the testament inheritors who fought for control of far larger domains than any granted to them by Alexander, were dead, and *their* offspring were embroiled in internecine strife. But to reinsure his position, we propose Cleitarchus highlighted Ptolemy's noteworthy grant of Egypt and he provided an encomiastic description of his honouring Alexander's newly interred corpse at Memphis.[173] The task facing Cleitarchus was daunting. The *Journal* and the *Pamphlet* were essentially the two outer-limit posts between which he could build his syncretic account of events at Babylon; he needed to accommodate 'silent' intestacy alongside rumours of a clearly vocal king, and incorporate claims of conspiracy (aware it had exonerated Ptolemy) with reports of death-heralding portents and alcohol excess.

Finally, Cleitarchus had to maintain the notion that it was Perdiccas who orchestrated the division of the empire, when the *Pamphlet* made it clear that the appointments came from Alexander's Will (T1, T2). All this had to be achieved from a desk in Ptolemaic Alexandria at a time, if he published sufficiently late, when competing claims from Hieronymus were entering circulation. The city was full of veterans, or by now their offspring, and so Cleitarchus' final result needed to incorporate additional detail he had garnered from them: the infighting, the challenge to Perdiccas, the executions and the proclamation of the new half-wit king, Arrhidaeus, who became Philip III. It was a construction that required deft hands, lateral thinking and the sacrifice and subordination of parts of one account to another.

So, finally, what do scholars, old and new, make of the Vulgate claims? Arrian and Plutarch, adherents to the *Journal*, adopted a dismissive stance on the allegations of the conspiracy that led to Alexander's poisoning: 'I do not expect them to be believed' and they are 'pure fabrication'.[174] As far as the lingering hearsay of the Will, Cleitarchus' erasure of its presence, alongside his epitaphic 'to the strongest' and the reference to Homeric 'funeral games', were the nails in the testate coffin for the Roman-era historians.[175] But it was Curtius who made the most vocal assault on the Will (T11):

> … some have believed that the provinces were distributed by Alexander's Will, but we have learned that the report of such action was false, although handed down by some authorities.[176]

The repeated plurality of the 'some' (the plural has been challenged) and 'sources' suggest Curtius knew of more than one Will-adhering account.[177] Although he would have been undermining his own credibility if he was referring above to the *Romance* as we read it today, we must again accommodate the possibility (or probability) that the archetypal text 'α', then named something along the lines of *The Life of Alexander of Macedon*, had not yet become so blatantly 'romanced'. Because if Curtius was echoing Cleitarchus' own testate denial, we would expect to see it reappear in other Vulgate verdicts; moreover, as Cleitarchus' book was so popular in Rome, Curtius' statement would have been a ridiculous plagiarism when he presented it, as he did, as investigative skill. Curtius' short *melete*, or forensic speech (written mid-1st century CE we propose), is quite out of character with his final chapter narrative, and we will argue for its political significance to him at the political heart of Rome's imperium.[178]

Apart from Curtius' Will dismissal, we additionally have an earlier comment from Diodorus (written before ca. 30 BCE) which appeared in the prelude to his account of the siege of Rhodes (his narrative commencing with events in 305 BCE); it confirmed Alexander's testament had resided with the islanders: '… honouring Rhodes above all cities [Alexander] both deposited there the testament disposing of his whole realm and in other ways showed admiration…'[179] Once again, it is highly unlikely that Diodorus would have included this detail in his *Library of World History* if extracted from the *Romance* (the *Metz Epitome* post-dated both Curtius and Diodorus). Arrian did refer to one 'brazen' writer who recorded that the dying Alexander attempted to throw himself into the Euphrates and yet he stopped short of branding this source a book of ridiculous fables, so he, perhaps like Curtius and Diodorus before him, was either dealing with an early 'α' text *Romance*, or the still free-floating *Pamphlet*.[180]

It is not impossible that other *bona fide* historians we are unaware of, or those we know of but whose accounts are lost, accepted the Will as factual.

One of them was potentially Hieronymus, an eyewitness to the events of the Successor Wars and Diodorus' principal source, and we explain in later chapters how his reference to a testament could have been overlooked, or simply dismissed by historians epitomising his account.[181]

We have already speculated when the *Pamphlet* first entered circulation and we have proposed a link to the scheming of the king's former secretary, Eumenes. We do have additional corroborating reports from Plutarch, Diodorus and Curtius that the detail of its conspiracy hit Greece a few years after Alexander's death (T10, T6, T11).[182] The allegations, we are told, spurred Olympias into a bloody pogrom of revenge against the house of Antipater, the architect of the plot.

A further (though more dubious) corroboration is found in the *Lives of the Ten Orators*, erroneously attributed to Plutarch, but now considered pseudepigrapha (literally those 'inscribed with a lie');[183] it alleged that in the Lamian War, Hyperides, the Athenian logographer, gave a speech just a year after Alexander's death proposing honours to Iolaos for his serving the poisoned wine. The source of this detail is unreliable and it seems to conflict with Plutarch's statement that it took five years for rumours of regicide to filter back to Olympias in Epirus. That would make it 318 BCE, the year Eumenes was freed from captivity at Nora, though the allegations would have taken time to travel and percolate.[184] Moreover, Olympias' revenge killings of ca. 317 BCE do appear historical, even if the claims that justified them were not.

A fragment of Arrian's *Events After Alexander* somewhat dispels the earlier *Pamphlet* release date as well, for it claimed Iolaos met with Perdiccas to broker a marriage to his sister, Nicaea; Perdiccas was not murdered until 321/320 BCE, and if Iolaos was already a publicised assassin (whether true or false), it seems unlikely that he would travel back to Asia to discuss a marriage with the dead king's *chiliarchos*, for Perdiccas, like Eumenes, was a clear ally of Olympias.[185] Ominously, Iolaos was said to have been accompanied by Archias; this may have been Antipater's 'unconvincing' actor-turned-assassin from Thurii who became infamous for his hunting down of Hyperides, Aristonicus, Himeraeus (the brother of Demetrius of Phalerum) and Demosthenes who had made a career out of anti-Macedonian speeches.[186]

CONSPIRACIES WITHIN TESTATE CONSPIRACY

The acolytes to intestacy are surely correct on one point: the *Pamphlet*-based Will, in the form we have it today, was published by a person (or people) at the centre of the Successor Wars to further his, or their, political ends. However, it appears that all theorising to date has overlooked a very basic logic: recirculating a Will that had never existed would have been dangerous and self-defeating for any one of the six innocents (or anyone in their employ), for all were notable figures; even Holcias had a *taxiarches* command at the very least, and he *may* even have hailed from a prominent Illyrian family.[187] A reissued Will would only have been an effective tool if it played on the knowledge, or the suspicion, that a real Will had been read at Babylon. The author of the *Pamphlet* was appealing to those who knew full well what had taken place in June 323 BCE, and he, or they, positioned their reproduction with such effective verisimilitude that nothing short of a full-scale campaign to eradicate it had to be undertaken.

As we will discover, Eumenes' actions in the Successor Wars, and his alliance with Olympias, strengthen his candidacy for *Pamphlet* authorship to the point where a partisan document of this nature appears an inevitable production from his campaign tent. Linking Ptolemy and Lysimachus to its genesis by proposing they witnessed the Will's drafting was a stroke of genius that provoked an equally deceptive retort: Ptolemy's *Journal* extract with its implication that Eumenes and Diodotus of Ethyrae were the royal secretaries who compiled it.

In 309 BCE, fourteen years after the settlement at Babylon and while based on the island of Kos overseeing the birth of a son who would eventually be epitheted *Philadelphos*, Ptolemy I, now satrap of Egypt and soon to name himself king (and soon to gain the epithet *Soter* for his part assisting the Rhodians under siege), compelled Polemaeus, a talented though 'presumptuous' defecting nephew of Antigonus, to drink hemlock.[188] Following this Cassander, via Polyperchon, arranged for Alexander's oldest son, Heracles, to be executed, having already disposed of Roxane and the young Alexander IV, so exterminating Alexander's direct branch of the Argead line.[189] Diodorus reported that Ptolemy was 'relieved', as were Cassander, Lysimachus and Antigonus.[190] Ptolemy was now in league with Cassander and so rumours of the *Pamphlet*-based conspiracy were indeed 'extinguished by the power of the people defamed by the gossip', a comment no doubt recalling Olympias' execution by Cassander in 316/315 BCE.[191] With allegations of treason at Babylon buried, the Will soon succumbed to a similar acid bath in Ptolemy's book.

Although Alexander's Will had been the legitimising agent for kingdoms that emerged from the governorships of Antigonus, Ptolemy, Lysimachus and Seleucus, built around their 'rightfully' inherited satrapies and regional *strategoi* roles, once they had established themselves the Will became redundant, and its memory fell into the hands of men who neither wanted it, nor could afford it, to resurface.

As far as the reporting of Alexander's death, it seems that little, save Cleitarchus, squeezed in between the Heraclean *stelae* of the silent *Journal* on one hand, and the vociferous *Pamphlet* on the other, except perhaps the teenage Heracles himself for a moment, care of Polyperchon, care of Antigonus;[192] and of course Ephippus' *On the Death* (or *Funeral*) *of Alexander and Hephaestion* with its tales of hard drinking, which linked the deaths of the king and his closest Companion to alcohol abuse. Arrian cited an 'Ephippus of Chalcidice' as overseeing the garrisoning of Egypt; did he stay on and become a tool that Ptolemy put to work?[193]

'Absence of evidence is not evidence of absence' is an adage often applied when sources are thin, and it is particularly apt for the *Journal* and the *Pamphlet*, for their origins have stonewalled historians, the *Journal* dividing the community into believers and atheists, while the *Pamphlet* has no disciples at all. Fighting their cases in different arenas, they have done nothing but stare each other down since the Successor Wars, for the genesis of both lay there. As for the final outcome, Ptolemy's *Journal* entry became something of a glacis at the foot of Alexander's intestate walls, and no subsequent historian's inquisitive scaling ladders have quite reached to the top.

NOTES

1. Arrian 7.25.6, translation by A de Selincourt, Penguin Classics edition, 1958.
2. Curtius 10.5.5-6, based on the translation in the Loeb Classical Library edition, 1946.
3. Based on the translation in Stoneman (1991) p 32.
4. The Phaistos Disk from Crete is covered in a number of symbols whose meaning remains unknown. It dates to the Minoan Age ca. second millennium BCE. Its authenticity is nevertheless debated and even if genuine, the symbols might not represent words.
5. Aristophanes *Clouds*. Originally produced for the Dionysia of 423 BCE and targeting the intellectual trends within the city; the ridicule of the Sophists and their methods of arguing is a theme running throughout the play.
6. *Historia Augusta, Life of Commodus* 9.6 and Cassius Dio 73.20.3 reported Commodus rounded up those with diseases of the feet and armed them with sponges alone whilst he clubbed them to death himself in the arena imagining they were giants.
7. For Diodotus, see Athenaeus 10.434b for Diodotus and Eumenes, and Aelian 3.23 additionally for Eumenes. *Archigrammateus* may well be a Hellenistic term that would not have been used before; Sekunda (1984) p 12.
8. Arrian *Indike* 18.8 for Evagoras.
9. The manuscript is referred to as the *St Mark Codex A*. Recently Chugg (2007) pp 226-229 suggested Diodotus was a *bematistes* (map maker) and thus, an author of the *Stathmoi, the Stages* correcting the name to Diognetus of Ethyrae mentioned as a bematist at Pliny 6.61. This has no bearing on our argument except to illustrate how misidentification has crept into extant texts. Further identification suggestions from Heckel (2006) p 308 footnote 301.
10. Plutarch 77.3-4. By then Antigonus was referred to as 'king' but this does not necessarily mean the rumours circulated after 306 BCE when he was formally crowned. Plutarch may well have not been clinical in the differentiation between when Antigonus was considered a dynast and king.
11. Holcias' role in the Will reading and his satrapal inheritance of Illyria is mentioned at *Metz Epitome* 97-98,103,106,109, 111-112, 114-116, 122, and also *Romance* 3.31-23. Heckel (2006) p 314 footnote 373 for citations. Polyaenus 4.6.6 mentioned he was pardoned for his opposition to Antigonus on the proviso that he retired to non-activity; his role discussed in greater detail in the last three chapters.
12. Fraser (1996) p 41 for the correct title of what we now term the *Liber de Morte*. The oldest manuscript of recension A of the *Romance* is the MS Parisinus 1711, a descendant of the original *Romance* from some 700 to 800 years earlier; fuller discussion in chapter titled *Mythoi, Muthodes and the Birth of Romance*.
13. Discussion of the *Excerpta Latina Barbari* (so-named *barbari* after Scaliger's description of the translator's poor skills: '*homo barbarus ineptus Hellenismi et Latinitatis imperitissimus*' in Fraser (1996) pp 14-15. Other similarities with the *Romance* suggest this was its source.
14. See discussion in Stoneman (1991) p 14. The oldest fragment containing the Will is considered to be Pap. Gr. Vindobonesis 31954, see Pearson (1960) p 261 and footnote 96 for details. See chapter titled *Mythoi, Muthodes and the Birth of Romance* for dating discussion of the earliest texts.
15. For its preservation in other *Romance* recensions, see Bosworth-Baynham (2000) pp 207-208; Heckel (1988) p1 footnote 1; Stoneman (1991) pp 8-11. For further discussion on dating of the first Alexander *Romance* and *Metz Epitome* see Stoneman (1991) pp 8-9. Fraser (1996) pp 41-46 for discussion of the *Liber de Urbibus Alexandri*.
16. Fraser (1996) p 213 for discussion of the Egyptian papyrus containing a fragment of the Will. Of course the Will could have been extracted from the *Romance* and reproduced as a stand-alone document, but it remains more likely that it *came* from a stand-alone document.
17. *Romance* 3.30, *Metz Epitome* 90-94. Scylla was a part-human, part-beast monster from Greek mythology; here a baby born as a human boy from the belly up, below which it was part lion, panther, dog and boar. As Merkelbach and Heckel (1988) p 9 agrees, the beast represented Alexander's own men and their betrayal and not his subject nations as translations suggest. See *A Baleful Birth in Babylon* by EC Carney in Bosworth-Baynham (2000) p 242 ff for the context of the Scylla and its possible historicity. Spargue de Camp (1972) p 140 for the *sirrush*.
18. Antipater's fear of assassination by Alexander expressed or implied at Justin 12.14.3, Curtius 10.10.5, Arrian 7.12.4-7 who alone reported that Alexander had summoned Antipater to Babylon; this may well have been a hangover of the whole conspiracy rumour. Arrian nevertheless attempted to defend what he believed was an actual summons.
19. Quoting Stoneman (1991) Introduction p 12 for 'clotted officialese'. *Metz Epitome* 110 for the roles of Perdiccas and Antipater. Heckel (1988) pp 12-14 for full discussion referring to Recension A of Pseudo-Callisthenes and Heckel-Yardley (2004) p 285 for a full translation of

the *Metz Epitome* version of the Rhodian 'interpolation'. Bosworth-Baynham (2000) p 213 agrees the Rhodian issue could have formed part of the original *Pamphlet* Will. See Stoneman (199) pp 152-153 for a translation of the *Romance* version of the Letter to the Rhodians. The Letter to the Rhodians is concurrent in Pseudo-Callisthenes. A. Fraser (1996) p 212 for the Boule and demos and discussion on the Latin manuscript in which the letter appeared separately. Discussed in further detail in chapter titled *The Silent Siegecraft of the Pamphleteers*.

20. Heckel (1988) p 14 for translation and discussion. Chapter titled *The Reborn Wrath of Peleus' Son* for more on the chiliarchy. Atkinson (2009) p 178 proposed *chiliarchos* was the equivalent post of the Achaemenid *hazarapati*, the king's second in command. The term traditionally meant commander of a thousand men, but the Persian usage was adopted, meaning the king's second in command. Also Collins (2001) for the development of the chiliarch role.

21. For the five days citation see discussion in Heckel (1988) p 13.

22. *Metz Epitome* 118, *Romance* 32 for confirmation of Roxane's Bactrian (or Sogdian) father whereas *Romance* 20; Stoneman (1991) p 110, 113, 114 – she became the daughter of Darius. Discussed in Tarn (1948) p 335 footnote 2, thus Tarn concluded the Will is far older than the rest of the *Romance*.

23. Merkelback (1954); Ausfeld (1894) pp 357-366; discussed in Baynham p 74. The detail describing pre-death portents was not part of the original *Pamphlet* but a later addition. Fraser (1996) p 213 for the Escorial manuscript attachment.

24. Quoting Heckel (1988) p 1.

25. Quoting Bosworth-Baynham (2000) p 240.

26. As examples, Heckel (1988) pp 1-5, Bosworth-Baynham (2000) pp 207-241, Atkinson (2009) pp 229-230. Ausfeld (1901) proposed a dating of 319 BCE. He and later Merkelbach (1954) concluded Holcias might have been the self-promoting author. These first conclusions were clouded by the views of Wagner (1900), Reitzenstein (1904) and Nietzold (1904).

27. Quoting Bosworth-Baynham (2000) p 241.

28. *Metz Epitome* 97-98 for the full list given in Heckel-Yardley (2004) p 283.

29. Pausanias 1.6.3. Ptolemy murdered Cleomenes, whom Perdiccas had reappointed in Egypt and Ptolemy's speech at Babylon in Curtius 10.6.13-16 clearly undermined Perdiccas' position; see chapter titled *Babylon: the Cipher and Rosetta Stone*. The date of Perdiccas' death, May/June 320 BCE, is backed up by the *Babylonian Chronicle* extract BM 34, 660 Vs 4, also known as *The Diadokhoi Chronicle* or *Chronicle of the Successors*.

30. Citing Bosworth in Bosworth-Baynham (2000) p 209.

31. Others, notably Siebert and Samuel dismiss the idea of the *Pamphlet* altogether as a propaganda piece emanating from the Successor Wars; see Heckel (1988) pp 4-5 and footnotes for full citations. For explanation of the so-called 'high' and 'low' chronologies see chapter titled *The Silent Siegecraft of the Pamphleteers*.

32. Bosworth (1971) noted this 'anomaly' and salvaged Ptolemaic authorship by suggesting the Will be unyoked from the conspiracy detail in the *Pamphlet* (thus inconsistencies stemming from those named guilty and innocent in the plot disappear); he was alternatively proposing that there might be substance to the spurious story which appears to be a later *Romance* 3.32.9-10 addition. Here Perdiccas initially tried to share power with Ptolemy; a plan that backfired when he himself was unexpectedly passed the ring by the dying king. Yet this episode has been 'long recognised' as Ptolemy's own propaganda, and one that in fact *reconfirmed* Perdiccas' inheritance of power. Would it not have been far simpler for Ptolemy to simply claim Perdiccas was guilty?

33. Arrian's statement that 'neither Aristobulus nor Ptolemy had anything to add' is much debated and does not necessarily mean the book was ended here, only that account of Alexander's death did. There is equally no evidence that either extended their books past this point.

34. Quoting Carney (2006) p 110 for 'scrap of partisan literature'.

35. The alliance of Olympias and Eumenes and the circumstances behind the *Pamphlet* discussed in chapters titled *The Tragic Triumvirate of Treachery and Oaths* and *The Silent Siegecraft of the Pamphleteers*.

36. Heckel (1988) with a good summary of previous work on pp 1-5.

37. Following the reasoning in Bosworth-Baynham (2000) p 212. If Polyperchon wished to damn Cassander, his new opponent, he could have achieved this without implicating Antipater.

38. Diodorus 20.20 for Polyperchon's return to affairs; 20.28.1-3 for his alliance with Cassander and troops and grants.

39. Hammond (1993) pp 145-146. He suggested Antigonus shifted blame to Aristotle (implicated in the Vulgate tradition) to counter Olympias' accusations against Antipater and his sons, before providing Hagnothemis with the story. Quoting Heckel (1988) p 5 on Antigonus' insignificance.

40. See chapter titled *The Silent Siegecraft of the Pamphleteers* for Antigonus' possible influence.

41. Quoting Bosworth in Bosworth-Baynham (2000) p 210.

42. Diodorus 19.57.1-3 for the demands of Lysimachus, Ptolemy and Cassander for their role in Eumenes' defeat. Lysimachus' men had captured and executed White Cleitus on behalf of

Antigonus; Justin 13.6.16 for Cleitus' operation under Perdiccan forces. For his operations under Polyperchon, see Plutarch *Phocion* 34.2-4 and 35.2.

43. Arrian *Events After Alexander* 25.1 and Bosworth-Baynham (2000) pp 210-211 for Asander's relationship with Antigonus. Contra Heckel (2006) p 57 there is actually little evidence Asander supported Perdiccas and then defected to Antigonus. His grant of Caria is as we pose, an original Will appointment and not a result of his pro-Perdiccan politics.

44. Heckel (1988) pp 64-65 suggests Asander was opposed to Antigonus, yet Heckel (2006) p 57 clarifies he was aligned with Antigonus at least until 315 BCE, after Eumenes' death. Thus he opposed Eumenes before. For his defection to Antigonus see Arrian *Events After Alexander* 25.1 and Diodorus 19.62.2 for his later defection to Ptolemy. Detailed discussion of the alliance between Polyperchon, Eumenes and Olympias in chapter titled *The Silent Siegecraft of the Pamphleteers*.

45. Eumenes and 50 Perdiccans were first outlawed and sentenced to death in Egypt by the troops upon hearing of the death of Craterus: Diodorus 18.37.1-3, Plutarch *Eumenes* 8.2, Arrian *Events After Alexander* 1.39, Justin 13.8.10-13.8.14.1.1, Appian *Syrian Wars* 53. For the dating of Triparadeisus and the 'high' and 'low' chronologies of the years 323/319 BCE see Wheatley (1995) and chapter titled *The Silent Siegecraft of the Pamphleteers*.

46. The alliances and political intrigues of the two factions led by Eumenes and Antigonus covered in detail in chapters titled *The Tragic Triumvirate of Treachery and Oaths* and *The Silent Siegecraft of the Pamphleteers*.

47. Tarn (1948) pp 378-388. *Metz Epitome* 123 for the gods and 97 for the reference to the 'senate' at Rhodes.

48. Following and quoting de Polignac (1999) p 8; the emergence of Serapis discussed in detail below.

49. For the penning and private reading of the Will by Holcias to Ptolemy, Lysimachus, Perdiccas and Roxane see *Metz Epitome* 106, *Romance* 3.33.1.

50. Plutarch *Eumenes* 1.2 for Neoptolemus deriding Eumenes' position as secretary. See below for Aelian linking the *Ephemerides* to Eumenes.

51. Holcias' full significance to the *Pamphlet* discussed in chapter titled *The Silent Siegecraft of the Pamphleteers*.

52. Polyaenus 4.6.6 for Holcias' defection, capture, and repatriation to Macedonia. Holcias' activity discussed in further detail in chapter titled *The Silent Siegecraft of the Pamphleteers*.

53. Quoting Tarn (1948) p 317.

54. Taking the observation from Bosworth-Baynham (2000) p 240.

55. For Hagnothemis see Plutarch 77.3 and for Hagnon of Teos see Plutarch 40.1.

56. Discussion of sources for Hagnon in Heckel (2006) p 128 and also Billows (1990) pp 386-388. For Hagnon's hostility to Callisthenes see Plutarch 55.2.

57. Plutarch *Moralia* 65d or *How One May Discern A Flatterer from A Friend* 442.

58. Arrian *Indika* 18.8 for Hagnon's *trierarchos* role. Trierarchies were expensive and often didn't return capital to those obliged under the Athenian system of 'liturgy'. It came with the obligation to fit out and provision a naval ship.

59. Athenaeus 12.539c, Plutarch 40.1, Aelian 9.3 for his extravagance. Arrian *Indike* 18.8 for example called the Tean 'Andron' suggesting how easily names can be eroded in transmission. Nepos additionally erroneously named Hagnonides as Hagnon; Heckel (2006) pp 128-129 for references.

60. Heckel (2006) p 310 footnote 300 for discussion of Hagnon's whereabouts in 315/314 BCE. Plutarch 77.2-3 for Hagnothemis hearing of the plot from Antigonus who here is called a 'king' but this does not suggest he had been formally crowned yet. It is more likely the title represented Antigonus' supremacy in Asia.

61. Plutarch 76-77; Arrian 7.25-26. The Greek translation of Arrian's claims that Aristobulus and Ptolemy had nothing more to say is much debated; see Arrian 7.26.3 *Alexander the Great, The Anabasis and the Indica*, Oxford World Classics 2013 edition, footnote to 7.26.3 on page 324 for discussion.

62. Lucian *Encomium of Demosthenes* 26 for reference to the Macedonian royal archives. Polyaenus 4.6.2 for the Antigonid *hypomnemata*. Discussed in Marasco (2011) p 57.

63. Discussed in Marasco (2011) pp 57-65; see chapter titled *Babylon: Cipher and Rosetta Stone* for further discussion of *hypomnemata*.

64. Persian archive tradition suggested at Hellanicus fr. 178, Herodotus 1.99, 3.128, 8.85.4, 8.90.4, *Old Testament, Ezra* 4, *Old Testament, Esther* 6.1, 10.2; Anson (2013) p 57 and Momigliano (1977) p 31 for discussion. Hammond (1988) pp 129-150 is the most vocal on the existence of a complete campaign journal. Also see Anson (1996) pp 501-504 for discussion. Robinson (1953), Preface, believed the journals entered the 'general stream' of histories early on.

65. Nepos *Eumenes* 1.4-6 and 13.1 (aged twenty), also Plutarch *Eumenes* 1.1-3 for his background;

more in chapter titled *The Tragic Triumvirate of Treachery and Oaths*.

66. Lucian *A Slip of the Tongue in Greeting* 8.
67. The *Journal* format in cuneiform tablets was proposed by Cartledge (2005) p 278.
68. Citing Van der Spek (2003) pp 289-346.
69. As pointed out by Casson (2001) p 1.
70. An attested greater antiquity of the astronomical observations came from Porphyry through Simplicius, so may be an exaggeration; discussion in Neugebauer (1957) p151 and Robinson (1953) p 45 for citation. Polcaro-Valsecchi-Verderame (2008) p 5 for the oldest extant diary. For Berossus' claim of antiquity see Drews (1975) p 54.
71. Quoting Dalley (2013) p 1 for the extent of Babylonian and Assyrian writings.
72. 'Nerve centre' following the comment by Anson (2004) p 233.
73. Curtius 8.11.5 for Mullinas, but possibly identifiable with Myllenas son of Asander; see Bosworth *A in the East* (1996) p 51 for discussion on identity and Heckel (2006) p 120. He was placed in command of lightly armed troops.
74. See discussion in Robinson (1953) The *Ephemerides* p 69 in agreement with 'metaphrasing'. Not all historians agree with the similarity; see discussion in Bosworth *A to A* (1988) chapter 7 and Anson (1996) p 503 footnote 6. Nevertheless Bosworth p 506 did concede that a single source was being followed.
75. See the version from Aelian below, which reported the binges leading up to Alexander's illness.
76. Baynham (1998) p 96 for a list of tragic episodes linked to *komoi*. Borza (1995) pp 159-169 for discussion on the Macedonian banquets and drinking parties. The most famous was given by Medius heralding in Alexander's death, and a nine-day festival was given on the eve of Alexander's departure for Asia; see p 160.
77. Plutarch *Alexander* 75.6.
78. Following the definition of Briant (1974) p 138 for the king mediating between the gods and men.
79. Arrian 7.25.6.
80. The presence of these commanders discussed by B Bosworth in Carney-Ogden (2010) p 92.
81. Arrian 7.26.1; this is also related at Plutarch 76.8 and Justin 12.15. There is a lacuna in Curtius where we expect this to feature. Diodorus' brevity appears to have passed over this detail.
82. Plutarch 75.6 stated 30th and at 76.9 the 28th.
83. See Atkinson (2009) p148 for discussion of the hollow month of Daisios and possible confusion that it caused.
84. Curtius 10.10.9-14 stated seven days and Aelian 12.64 referred to a thirty-day period; it is highly unlikely that a body could remain unattended that long in the climate of Babylon in June. Plutarch 77.5 follows the 'fresh corpse' tradition without being specific on duration apart from 'many days'. Hammond and Engels argued that malaria brought on a deep coma that fooled the audience; see discussion in Atkinson (2009) p 232. More detailed discussion on the cause of death in chapter titled *The Damaging Didactic of the Classical Death*.
85. Arthur-Montagne (2014) p 3 for the explanation and origins of pseudo-documentarism. Discussion of the Macedonian symposia and its rhetorical treatment in Greece by F Pownall in Carney-Ogden (2010) pp 55-65.
86. Serapis dealt with in more detail below.
87. See fragment in Robinson (1953) pp 31-32 from Plutarch's *Moralia* 623e or *Quaestiones Conviviales* 1.6.1 .
88. Plutarch 23-24 and Athenaeus 434b. Whilst Plutarch's earlier *Journal* reference does not mention Babylon, the grandeur of the dinner arrangements and the king's sleeping habits hardly suggest an 'on campaign' occasion. Athenaeus may have followed Plutarch's detail; we cannot in fact be sure where Plutarch's *Journal* detail begins and ends in this passage.
89. Aelian 3.23.
90. Bosworth *A to A* (1988) pp 158-167 for these proposals and Hammond (1988) pp 170-171. Also Anson (1996) pp 501-504 Robinson (1953) Preface p x suggested the *Journal* extract dealing with Alexander's death could be a surviving extract from Strattis' *On the Deaths of Alexander*. Discussion summarised well in Atkinson (2009) pp 142-143.
91. Athenaeus 120c-d, 146c-d, 434a-b, each extracting from Ephippus' *On the Funerals of Alexander and Hephaestion* and each is suggestive that drinking bouts took place before Hephaestion's death.
92. Hammond (1988) pp 177-180 for the identification with Hephaestion. Athenaeus 120c-d for the fragment of Ephippus; full text in Robinson (1953) p 86. That Eumenes reported Hephaestion's slip of the tongue, an embarrassment, suggests he might have been subtly undermining him; Lucian *A Slip of the Tongue in Greeting* 8, and see above.
93. Hammond (1988) pp 129-150 is the most vocal on the existence of a complete campaign journal. Also see Anson (1996) pp 501-504 for discussion. Robinson (1953), Preface, believed the journals entered the 'general stream' of histories early on.

94. Aelian 3.23. It is quite clear that Alexander is being referred to, as the drinking bouts formed a part of Aelian's overall treatment of him.
95. The paralleled and columned comparisons of the *Journal* entries from Plutarch, Arrian and Aelian are provided in Robinson (1953) The Ephemerides pp 64-68. Some confusion still exists as to the modern month equivalent to the Macedonian calendar. Josephus' commentary in which he juxtaposed the Macedonian calendar against the Hebrew, Athenian and Roman months is useful though. Also details in Hannah (2005) p 95 for reference to 29th Daisios.
96. Plutarch 75.3, Diodorus 17.115.6, Arrian 7.23.8 for Hephaestion's elevation. Diodorus claimed this was to a 'god' whilst Arrian claimed the oracle permitted 'hero' only.
97. Diodorus 17.116.1.
98. At Aelian 3.23 Alexander is cited as drinking with Eumaios (or Eumaeus) on the 5th and with Perdiccas on the 7th. See Heckel-Yardley (2004) p 43 footnote 14 for detail of the possible mistransmission of the name.
99. Arrian 7.25.2.
100. Arrian 7.23-24. Tarn (1948) p 395 questioned whether it was a military campaign, likening it to the crossing of the Gedrosian Desert.
101. Plutarch 76.1.
102. Aelian 3.23.
103. See chapters titled *The Tragic Triumvirate of Treachery and Oaths* and *The Silent Siegecraft of the Pamphleteers* for Eumenes' subterfuges.
104. Quoting Bosworth (1971) p 467 on the drinking marathon.
105. Athenaeus 10.434b.
106. Appian *Proem* 10 and Diodorus 3.38.1 for the royal archives in Alexandria; discussed in Murray (2012) p 189 and Marasco (2011) pp 54-55 and quoting C Bearzot from Marasco (2011) for 'propagandistic' and pp 67-68 for *Euergetes'* collection of *hypomnemata*.
107. Arrian 7.25-26.
108. Plutarch 77.1.
109. Arrian Preface 1.1-4.
110. Well covered by Bosworth *A to A* (1988) chapter 7 and Pearson (196) pp 260-261.
111. Pearson (1960) p 261.
112. Strabo 2.1.6, discussed in Pearson (1955) pp 440-443.
113. Diodorus 18.3.5, Justin 13.4.6 for Arrhidaeus' instructions to build and deliver the funeral bier. No author linked its final destination to Alexander's own wishes, but rather to the opposing wishes of Perdiccas and Ptolemy. Also Stewart (1993) p 221 for discussion of Alexander's intent. See chapter titled *Lifting the Shroud of Parrhasius* for alternative theory on its destination: Perdiccan-held Syria. The suggestion that Ptolemy 'hijacked' the funeral bier is found in Arrian *Events After Alexander* 1.25 Pausanias 1.6.3 (stated Perdiccas planned to take the body to Aegae), Strabo 17.8, Aelian 12.64. We propose this is Hieronymus-derived propaganda against Ptolemy. Diodorus 18.28.2 suggested its intended destination was the sanctuary of Ammon at Siwa whilst Ptolemy decided to entomb it in the city Alexander had founded himself.
114. Aelian 12.64 for the alternative version of the hijacking of Alexander's body. Diodorus 26.2-28.2 for a description of the funeral bier.
115. Aelian 12.64 for Aristanders' prediction. *Romance* 3.32, *Metz Epitome* 119 for Alexander's wish to be entombed in Egypt. For Alexander's previous journey to Siwa see Diodorus 17.49.2-52.7, Arrian 3.4-5, Curtius 4.7.8-4.89, Plutarch 26.3-27.11, Justin 11.11.1-13, Strabo 17.1.43, *Itinerarium Alexandri* 48-50.
116. Justin 7.1.7-10 for the etymology of Aegae and Justin 7.2.4-6 for King Perdiccas I's prophecy. Hammond (1991) p 12 for the Phrygian cities of Edessa. Herodotus 5.22 for the line of Perdiccas I.
117. Diodorus 18.25.2-3.
118. Syria discussed further in chapter titled *Lifting the Shroud of Parrhasius*.
119. Arrian *Events After Alexander* 24.1-8 for the statement that part of the motivation for Perdiccas' invasion of Egypt was to gain control of Alexander's body. Discussed in Erskine (2002) p 171. For Typhon's Breathing Hole see Plutarch *Antony* 3. The Egyptians referred to the region inland of Pelusium at the Acregma and Serbonian marshes as Typhon's Breathing Hole. Perdiccas was in fact murdered further up the Nile near Heliopolis.
120. Diodorus 18.48.1-4, Plutarch *Phocion* 30.5-6, Plutarch *Demosthenes* 31.34-6, Arrian *Events After Alexander* 1.13-15 for the tradition of letters between Perdiccas and Demades undermining Antipater.
121. See chapter titled *Lifting the Shroud of Parrhasius* for arguments for Seleucus' satrapal appointment of Babylonia. Ptolemy's men used their pikes to blind Perdiccas' elephants in the battle on the Nile; Diodorus 18.34.2. Chapter titled *The Silent Siegecraft of the Pamphleteers* for Seleucus' possible participation in Perdiccas' murder.

122. Arrian 7.26.2-3.
123. Following the identifications of Heckel (2006) pp 109 and 89; for Demophon in Mallia see Diodorus 17.98.3-4, Curtius 9.4.27-29.
124. Seleucus may have been mentioned as a guest: the corrupted 'Europios' was possibly a reference to Seleucus' *ethne*. Menidas had a history of serving alongside Ptolemy and Attalus; detail in Heckel (2006) p 165. For his service with Ptolemy see Arrian 4.7.2, Curtius 7.10.11. The identification of Attalus cannot be confirmed; the most prominent individual would have been the commander who became Perdiccas' brother-in-law; Heckel (2006) pp 62-63 for his career. For Peithon's prominence and standing at Perdiccas' death, Nepos 5.1 Diodorus 18.39.6, Arrian *Events After Alexander* 1.35, *Heidelberg Epitome* 1.3. For discussion of Seleucus' presence in Egypt at Perdiccas' death; discussed further in chapter titled *The Silent Siegecraft of the Pamphleteers.*
125. Arrian 4.18.4 for Menidas' recruiting campaign in Macedonia and 7.23.1 for his return. Attalus was never heard of after his capture from a siege of the last Perdiccans lasting sixteen months; see Diodorus 19.16.5. His death is not specifically attested. He had already married Perdiccas' sister Atalante; Diodorus 18.37.2. Asander was present in Babylon and at Medius' party according to the *Pamphlet*; detailed discussion in chapter titled *The Silent Siegecraft of the Pamphleteers.*
126. See Stoneman (1991) p 12 for discussion and *Romance* 1.32 for Alexander's relationship with Serapis. Also Atkinson (2009) p 233 for a discussion and opinion on the dating and origination of Serapis. Diogenes Laertius *Diogenes* 63 claimed that Diogenes the Cynic referred to Serapis yet this is a late composition and does not prove the early use of the name or its existence in Babylonia.
127. Plutarch *Isis and Osiris* 27-28 (361f-362e) for the shipping of the statue from Sinope to Alexandria, and footnote 7 from the Loeb Classical Library edition, 1940, for discussion on its origins. The sculptor *may* have been the celebrated Bryaxis of Athens. Ptolemy allegedly had a dream vision of the statue which sounds like a veiled mandate for its theft.
128. Vrettos (2001) p 34 for the temple in the Egyptian quarter.
129. *Romance* 3.32 for the reference to Great Serapis and its link with Alexandria. Also mentioned at 1.21; see Stoneman (1991) p 110.
130. See Anson (1996) pp 501-504 for discussion.
131. For Oserapis see Bosworth *A to A* (1988) pp 168-170 and Atkinson (2009) citing Goukowski (1978). Following the text in Eidinow-Kindt (2015) p 319 for the description of Oserapis.
132. See chapter titled *The Precarious Path of Pergamena and Papyrus* for examples. Following Bosworth (1971) p 120 for 'strikingly similar' in resemblance. As an example of the use of contemporary terminology, Curtius used *testudo* at 5.3.9 and implied its shield formation again at 5.3.21 and 7.9.3
133. See Plutarch's *Isis and Osiris* 27-28 for examples of other gods the Greeks claimed were identical to Egyptian deities. In fact Serapis was claimed to be none other than Pluto.
134. Discussed in De Polignac (1999) p 6. A tradition circulates that the Sumerian deity Enki (Babylonian Ea) was titled 'Serapsi' ('king of the deep') but there is little, it seems, to substantiate this.
135. However evidence has been found to prove that Ea, alternatively the Chaldean-named Sarm-Apsi, 'king of the deep (sea)', who was also great in learning and magic, had a temple in the city. For the Chaldean god see Cumont (1911) p 73. Also Bosworth (1971) pp 120-121. Arrian 7.14.5 for the references to the temple of Asclepius in Ecbatana.
136. Following Bosworth (1971) p 120 for the incorporation of elements of Greek religion and the argument that the new Serapis would have lost is resemblance to Bel-Marduk; Bosworth, however, sees this as an argument that the *Journal* entry is 'early' for any comparison to have been made.
137. Plutarch 73.8.
138. Plutarch 73.7-9 and more briefly Arrian 7.24-25 described that Alexander and his friend, whilst playing ball (possibly the game of *sphaira*), beheld a man seated on the king's throne, in silence, wearing the royal diadem and robes. He claimed the god Serapis had come to him and bid him sit on the throne. Alexander had him 'put out of the way' as advised by his seers. Arrian 7.17.5 and 7.18.1-3 for reference to Aristobulus' reporting of portents and seers.
139. Arrian 3.3.6 reported that Aristobulus claimed they were guided by two ravens; see discussion in Robinson (1953) Preface p xiii. Strabo 17.1.43 for crows.
140. Diodorus 17.103.7-8 for Ptolemy's poisonous wound in India. Further discussion in Heckel (1992) p 26.
141. Plutarch 2.5-6; Olympias' Bacchic behaviour also implied at Athenaeus 13.560 (from Duris); discussed in Carney (2006) p 96 ff.
142. See the references to Glycon in Lucian's *Alexander or the False Prophet,* discussed in Costa (2005) p 129. For the Alexandrian serpents see Carney-Ogden (2010) p 126. Carney-Ogden (2010) pp 126-127 for the snake-fringed aegis. Plutarch 2.6 and Justin 12.16.1-4 for Olympias and the

serpent and Alexander's more than human conception. Here the Pharaoh Nectanebo was the true father of Alexander and visited Olympias disguised as Ammon; *Romance* 1.1-12 for the full account of Nectanebo. Carney (2006) p 97 for Plutarch's treatment of Olympias though he himself was an initiate of the cult of Dionysus (*Moralia* 611d-e).

143. Diogenes Laertius *Demetrius* 76 for the curing of Demetrius' blindness; the reference to five books comes from Artemidorus *Oneirokritikon* 2.44 9 (*On the Interpretation of Dreams*), though these books are not mentioned by Diogenes Laertius. Harris (2009) p 155 footnotes 186 for discussion on sources behind Demetrius of Phalerum's association with Serapis.

144. Demetrius of Phalerum was ousted from Athens in 307 BCE by Demetrius *Poliorketes*; he headed first to Thebes and around 297 BCE to Egypt. Pearson (1960) p 260 for discussion on the prayer to Serapis.

145. For the dating of Demetrius' *Peri Tyches* see discussion in Bosworth-Baynham (2000) p 299; Demetrius stated the fifty-year rise of Macedon, which would logically date from Philip II's reign from ca. 360 BCE, suggesting it was written around 310 BCE. Polybius gave further guidance stating that Demetrius published some 150 years before the end of the Third Macedonian War culminating in the battle at Pydna in 168 BCE. It is a very loose triangulation but suggests Demetrius' work was one of the first treatises to deal with Alexander in a meaningful philosophic way.

146. For the fatal snakebite see Diogenes Laertius *Demetrius of Phalerum* 78, Cicero *In Defence of Rabirius Postumus* 9.23. Plutarch *Moralia* 48e-74f (*How to tell a Flatterer from a Friend* 28 69c-d) for the reference to 'near Thebes'; full text in Fortenbaugh-Schütrumpf (2000) pp 75-77.

147. Plutarch *Sayings of Kings and Commanders* 189D, full text from Fortenbaugh-Schütrumpf (2000) pp 81-82.

148. Plutarch 74.1-2 and 75.1, translation by I Scott-Kilvert, Penguin Classics edition, 1973. The portentous signs are scattered through Plutarch 73-76 and appear less vividly in the accounts of Arrian 7.16-17, Diodorus 17.116-117, Justin 12.8.3-6. A lacuna in Curtius' final chapter has swallowed his detail.

149. 'Whitewashed' quoting Heckel-Yardley (2004) Introduction p XXIII.

150. Suetonius *Domitian* 21.1.

151. Plutarch 74.2 for the fear of assassination, 77.2 for the lack of suspicion at Babylon. The portentous signs are scattered through Plutarch 73-76 and appear less vividly in the accounts of Arrian 7.16-17, Diodorus 17.116-117 and Justin 12.8.3-6. A lacuna in Curtius' final chapter has swallowed any comparable detail.

152. Plutarch 69.7 reported that Calanus, before climbing onto his funeral pyre, told Alexander he would soon meet him again in Babylon.

153. Green (1970) p 258.

154. The detail of pre-death portents straddles all traditions: Arrian 7.16.7 for the divine hand in Alexander's death and 7.18.2 and 7.18.5 for Pythagoras' diving to reveal livers with no lobes. Also 7.24-25, and Aristobulus was mentioned five times as a source for superstitious episodes. More portentous episodes at Diodorus 17.115.5, Plutarch 73-74, Justin, 12.13. Curtius' account surely contained the detail too, but a lacuna exists in the opening of his final chapter. The half-child half-beast Scylla-like creature appears at *Metz Epitome* 90-95 and the *Romance* 3.30; the seer Philip saw this as an ill omen for Alexander.

155. Diodorus 19.55.8, translation from the Loeb Classical Library edition, 1947. Quoting McKechnie (1995) p 418 on 'philosophical corps'. Diodorus 17.112.5 for allusions to his soul.

156. Citation from Ifrah (2000) pp 158-161. Herodotus 7.113-114.

157. Collins (2008) for full discussion of magic in the ancient Greek world, Introduction p xiii for *defixiones* and *epoidai*.

158. From Ovid's *Metamorphoses* book 5, *Ino and Athamas*, line 444. Hades was later referred to as Plouton (the Roman Pluto) and Hades came to denote the place, rather than the person who ruled the underworld. Lucan *De Bello civili* book 6 has a son of Pompey consulting a witch on the outcome of the forthcoming battle against Caesar.

159. Collins (2008) Introduction p xiii for discussion of *On the Sacred Disease* from the Hippocratic corpus and p 53 for the commercial centre of witchcraft, following Aristophanes' *Clouds*.

160. For magnetic stones and Thales of Miletus see Collins (2008) pp 8-9 and p 46 for the Athenian court for inanimate objects.

161. Detail of the *nekyomanteia* in Ogden (2001) pp 167-195.

162. Aristotle *History of Animals* books 7-10 feature demons working in conjunction with the influence of stars. Plato *Laws* 933a-e as an example.

163. Collins (2008) p 143 for the *Twelve Tables* described in Pliny 28.10. The 'evil charm' could also mean a slander or abusive curse.

164. Discussed in Collins (2008) p 148, and Tacitus 2.69.3, translation from Collins (2008). Momigliano (1977) p 136 for Ammianus' references to magic.

165. Arrian 7.25.6, Plutarch 76.

166. Nearchus was an advisor to the young Demetrius at Gaza in 312/2 BCE according to Diodorus 19.69.1 and Medius served at Salamis in 307/6 BCE; see Diodorus 20.50.3 and Plutarch *Demetrius* 19.1-2.

167. Notable exceptions being Hammond (1988) and (1993), and Robinson (1953) Preface p x which ingeniously regarded the *Journal* extract as a surviving fragment of Strattis' *On the Deaths of Alexander*. The comparison with Dictys encouraged by Bosworth *A to A* (1988) p 181.

168. Discussed in Bosworth (1971). A useful summary of arguments is given in Atkinson (2009) p 143. The Ptolemaic link came from Wirth in 1986; see Atkinson (2009) p 143 for detail.

169. Heckel (1993) summarises the *Journal* arguments well and the quotations from Heckel are drawn from here. In this review of Hammond's work on sources, Heckel pointed out that the pre-eminent modern Alexander scholars: Badian, Bosworth, Samuel and Pearson, had discredited the *Journal* convincingly.

170. Quoting Bosworth (1971) p 136; author's italics.

171. Lane Fox (1980) p 410.

172. Tarn (1948) p 43.

173. The corpse was likely moved from Memphis to Alexandria in Cleitarchus' day once the Sema was built; Pausanias 1.7.1 claimed Ptolemy II *Philadelphos* brought the body from Memphis to Alexandria. Cleitarchus' wrap-up discussed in detail in chapter titled *Babylon: the Cipher and Rosetta Stone*.

174. Arrian 7.27.3 and Plutarch 77.5 respectively.

175. Curtius 10.5.5, Arrian 7.26.3, Diodorus 17.117.4.

176. Curtius 10.10.5-6.

177. Chugg (2009) p 5 refutes the use of the first personal singular in favour of the first person plural, and in other translations 'we' is used; as an example the translation by John C Rolfe of 1946 published by the University of Michigan. Nevertheless it was not unusual for an author to use the plural 'we' when referring to his own efforts and this does not convincingly argue that Curtius was paraphrasing Cleitarchus, for example. Polybius in particular switched between singular and plural where emphasis demanded it and in particular to stress the veracity of either eyewitness reporting or personal vouching for facts; discussion in Marmodoro-Hill (2013) pp 199-204.

178. Discussed in the chapter titled *Comets, Colophons and Curtius Rufus*.

179. Diodorus 20.81.3 based on the translation from the Loeb Classical Library edition, 1954. See Tarn (1939) p 132 for a discussion on whether Diodorus 20.81.3 drew from the *Romance* and *Letter to the Rhodians*, as proposed by Ausfeld. Heckel (1988) p 2 suggested Hieronymus was the source.

180. *Romance* 3.32.5-7 and *Metz Epitome* 101-102. Arrian 7.27.3 for his recounting the tradition of Alexander's attempt to disappear into the Euphrates.

181. Hieronymus as a source of Will references is discussed in chapter titled *Wills and Testaments in the Classical Mind, Babylon: the Cipher and Rosetta Stone* and Rhodian rhetoric in *The Silent Siegecraft of the Pamphleteers*.

182. For Olympias' pogrom see Diodorus 19.11.8 and 19.35.1, Justin 14.6 (slaughter of nobility but no revenge for conspiracy mentioned); Curtius 10.10.18 suggested rumours were 'soon suppressed by the power of people implicated by the gossip'. Thus rumours abounded early and before Cassander had the last of Alexander's family murdered.

183. Plutarch *Demosthenes* 28.4 and *Moralia* 849b (*Life of Hyperides*) for Hyperides having his tongue cut out, 849f for his proposing honours for Iolaos. Some editions of the *Moralia* contained the spuriously assigned *Lives of the Ten Orators*.

184. Plutarch 77.1-2 and reinforced by Curtius 10.10.18-19. Olympias' pogrom is also recorded in detail by Diodorus 19.11.809 and 19.51.5. If we give six months either way in latitude to Plutarch's 'five years' from June 323 BCE then the whole of 318 BCE becomes a candidate for rumours reaching Greece.

185. Arrian *Events After Alexander* 1.21.

186. Demosthenes termed Archias' acting 'unconvincing' when confronted by him at his death. Plutarch *Demosthenes* 29, Plutarch *Moralia* 846f, 849d. Arrian *Events After Alexander* 1.13-14 for his role hunting down 'exiles'.

187. Heckel (2006) p 140 for Holcias' possible background.

188. Diodorus 20.27.3.

189. Diodorus 19.51; Justin 14.6.6-12.

190. Diodorus 20.27.1-20.28.29 and 19.105 for the relief.

191. Curtius 10.18-19, reiterated in Diodorus 17.118.2 and Justin 12.13.10.

192. Heracles' reemergence under Polyperchon discussed in chapter titled *The Tragic Triumvirate of Treachery and Oaths* and *Lifting the Shroud of Parrhasius*.

193. Full discussion of Heracles' identity and Polyperchon's role in promoting him in chapter titled *Lifting the Shroud of Parrhasius*. Arrian 3.5.2-3 for the identification of Ephippus in Egypt and Athenaeus 3.120c-d and 4.146c-d for the drinking references.

7

THE DAMAGING DIDACTIC OF
CLASSICAL DEATHS

Were 'deaths' accurately chronicled in the ancient world?

Nothing was more colourfully narrated in Greek, Hellenistic, and Roman-era histories than the deaths of tyrants, kings, emperors, and their nemeses: recalcitrant politicians.

The epitaphic allegations attached to them, being posthumous commentaries by nature and often linked to rumours of political intrigue and assassination, were all the more easily manipulated for didactic effect.

We take a look at the most notorious of cases to help us appreciate how conflicting claims attached to Alexander's death were able to exist side-by-side in the mainstream accounts, and why his alleged intestacy was so readily accepted.

'I, who crossed all the inhabited earth,
And the uninhabited places, and the places of darkness,
Was unable to evade fate.
A small cup can yield a man to death,
And send him down among the dead with a drop of poison.'[1]

Greek Alexander Romance

'I shall make just as pretty a cupbearer as you – and not drink the wine myself.
For it is the fact that the king's butler when he offers the wine is bound to dip
a ladle in the cup first, and pour a little in the hollow of his hand and sip it, so
that if he has mixed poison in the bowl it will do him no good himself.'[2]

Xenophon *Cyropaedia*

'It is possible to provide security against other ills,
but as far as death is concerned,
we men live in a city without walls.'[3]

Epicurus *Vatican Sayings*

The sacred medical oath of Hippocrates of Kos commenced with: 'I swear
by Apollo the physician, and Asclepius, and Hygeia, and Panacea, and all
the gods and goddesses…', and its fourth paragraph pledged: 'I will neither
give a deadly drug to anybody if asked for it, nor will I make a suggestion
to this effect.' The deities must have been mortified, for Persia, Greece,
and then imperial Rome, saw the oath abandoned to aconite, arsenic and
antimony, the toxic salt and pepper (and eyebrow cosmetic) of emperors,
tyrants and kings.[4]

Although it is ascribed to Hippocrates, the oath likely has its roots
with the Pythagoreans' own moral code, the so-called Golden Verses,
whose original and less poetic geometric pledge put great store in a
numerical triangle, the *Tetraktys*.[5] The 'father of medicine' and the 'father
of numbers' had a fascination with death, Hippocrates with its prevention,
and Pythagoras with its mitigation through the transmigration of the
soul. Both sought harmony, whether in the four humours of the body
or with the number four itself; for Hippocrates imbalance was *dyskrasia*,
and for Pythagoras it was simply discordant, for he was the first music
therapist and master of the quadrivium.[6] Each had influential or even
mystical associations by Alexander's day, and more significantly to our
investigation, they both shared uncertain, though legendary, deaths.

If Wills were manipulable, so was death itself, and so we need to
contemplate how the closing pages of traditional biographies were
crafted. Death has mutated into a didactic digression too many times for

us to question its penchant for doing so. Sometimes deliberate, at other times accidental, the metamorphosis is only magnified with time and fame. Alexander was born into an era when death was a lesson on life, or according to Seneca, life was a lesson on death: 'It takes a whole life to learn how to die.'[7] And when Alexander departed, he bequeathed the class one more exploitable episode.

THE MANY-FRAYED STRANDS OF LEGENDARY EPITAPHS

Many legendary figures suffered posthumous reconstructions, and from the Homeric past through to Athens' Golden Age, colourful examples are not difficult to find. Empedocles the 'purifier', a cosmogenic philosopher from Sicily who put his ideas into verse and became known as the 'wind-forbidder', is said to have jumped into the fire of Mount Etna to ensure his apotheosis. Once charged for stealing the discourses of Pythagoras, who clearly influenced his ideas, Empedocles was trying to arrange a heavenly disappearance after a banquet but was apparently betrayed by one of his distinctive brass-soled slippers he misplaced on the climb up. This was not the finite conclusion it suggests, for he, like Pythagoras, believed in reincarnation.[8] With no volcano at hand, the *Romance* captured Alexander's attempt at a similar vanishing act by using the River Euphrates (T1, T2). Where Empedocles gained a cult, Alexander gained the ill-timed intervention of Roxane, his pregnant wife. The *Romance* compilers (though this particular detail *may* be *Pamphlet*-derived) were not so original in their imagery and most elements can be found in earlier tales whilst much was regurgitated later, in Suetonius' biographies of the Roman Caesars, for example, or more pertinently, in the *Scriptores Historiae Augustae*.[9]

These vivid and influential Greek characters were already associated with magic by Aristotle's day; Empedocles, the founder of the Italian school of medicine, raised the dead and was said to be able to manipulate the weather; he was possibly the first philosopher to propose the existence of four divine primordial cosmic elements: earth, wind, fire and water, and his passing provides us with an early example of the 'multiple death tradition'.[10] Pythagoras was in two places at once, sported a golden thigh and reportedly once turned a wild bear to vegetarianism, so the legends go,[11] and after his death, honey growing on Hippocrates' grave was, unsurprisingly, said to have medicinal powers.[12]

Hippocrates, already epitheted 'the great', according to Aristotle, had several deaths too – at the ages of 80, 90, 104, and 109. The latter numbers were apparently shared with his friend, Democritus of Abdera, so meriting a place in Pseudo-Lucian's *Makrobioi*, a compendium of the 'long lived',[13] Pythagoras' own numerical preoccupation concluded with the statement '*all* things are numbers' and he is oddly said to have lived to 104 as well, sharing the illustrious age with Hieronymus the Cardian historian.[14] That may not be coincidence: as pointed out by the historian Truesdell Brown, 104 – thus the 105th year – is a mystical numerical combination and the sum of the first fourteen integers.[15]

Competing stories in circulation would have us believe that Pythagoras was slain twice: he was either foiled by a bean field he refused to enter leading to his capture and burning at the stake; alternatively, he withered away from a self-imposed starvation when philosophically pondering a world that had rejected him.[16] Yet 'any chronology constructed for his life is a fabric of the loosest possible weave',[17] a conundrum facing Hermman Diels when attempting to separate direct quotations ('B' fragments) from the later *testimonia* ('A' fragments) related to the Samian polymath and other pre-Socratic thinkers in his 1903 *Die Fragmente der Vorsokratiker*.

Doxographies, as we have noted, *were* apparently highly exploitable and early doxographical material was particularly susceptible to becoming pseudepigrapha, for so little was known about the lives and writings of Neo-Platonist philosophers, who, by then, were already wrapped in the climbing ivy of myth. The Neo-Pythagorean scholars, for example, tended to attribute their own written treatises back to Pythagoras himself. Prizing apart the originals from the latter-day treatises demands every weapon *Quellenforschung* and the ancillary disciplines of historiography can muster in stripping away the accretion. Diels, the originator of the term 'doxography' which was originally linked to philosophical opinions (*doxai*) on theology, cosmology, metaphysics and other sciences, attempted to narrow down their tenets to the original sources in his monumental 1879 *Doxographi Graeci*.

And here we encounter the first of many of history's many ironies, as none of the influential philosophers, including Pythagoras himself, preserved their own doctrines in writing either. Anaximenes, Socrates, Thales (ca. 624-546 BCE), Arcesilaus (ca. 316-241 BCE), Carneades and Pyrrho of Elis (ca. 360-270 BCE) each relied on oral tradition, and yet their ideas are better preserved than written works of 'Philippic' proportion, Theopompus' fifty-eight-book *Philippika* amongst them.[18] But do the doxographies we have truly preserve 'their' ideas? Or are they the oversimplifications, or later interpretations of the students and disciples that were neatly systemised by Theophrastus in his *Physikon doxai*, often translated as *Tenets of the natural philosophers*?

Chrysippus (ca. 279-204 BCE), the Stoic sophist who taught 'divine logic' and supposedly authored some 705 books, gave wine to his donkey and finally died of laughter as he watched its ungainly attempts to eat figs.[19] A different end comes from Hermippus who reported that he expired from the effects of unmixed wine at a sacrificial feast.[20] Zeno of Citium, the founder of Stoicism, was an austere character who nevertheless enjoyed drinking at *symposia* too; his experiences prompted his sober advice: 'Better to trip with the feet than with the tongue.' Diogenes Laertius reported the irony: 'When he was going out of his school, he tripped, and broke one of his toes, and striking the ground with his hand, he repeated the line out of the *Niobe*, "I come: why call me so?"… he immediately strangled himself, and thus he died.'[21] Lucian, on the other hand, suggested that after his famous stumble (when entering the assembly) he starved himself to death at home alone.[22] So it seems Plato was insightful when composing *his* *Symposium* in which it was successfully argued that tragedy and comedy may reside together in the composer's pen.[23]

Diogenes the Cynic had an assortment of conflicting demises that spawned a whole literary genre, with none of them taking place in his famous Corinthian barrel. One version claimed he was seized with colic after eating a raw octopus, and another beleived he was actually feeding the octopus to a group of dogs, one of which fatally bit the sinew of his foot. A variation proposed his last wish was to be thrown naked to the hungry pack; the canine attachment is surely an allusion Diogenes' dog-like behaviour, his epithet *kynikos*, and possibly to his consent of cannibalism.[24] A further tradition claimed he died by voluntarily holding his breath for two days; his friends found him wrapped in his cloak intact whereafter they quarrelled over the honours to bury him, despite his wish to be thrown in a ditch for nature to consume him.[25] He was reportedly aged eighty-one, or perhaps ninety.[26] Ironically, for all his cynical attributes, he was 'canonised' by the Stoics, though both philosophical sects must have found some personal harmony in his ideas, for many of them lived long as well and qualified for inclusion in the *Makrobioi*, a point its author duly noted.[27]

THEATRICAL LINES FOR A CLASSICAL STAGE

Portentous births and mysterious deaths – life's beginning and end – were fully exploited for their didactic contents and for the symmetry that the Epicurean Lucretius (ca. 99-55 BCE) philosophically likened to 'nature's mirror'; after all, 'the art of living well and the art of dying well are one.'[28] Do dying men speak, even those who have been poisoned? Well, apparently Socrates did after a shock dose of hemlock; his last recorded words were: 'Crito, I owe a cock to Asclepius; will you remember to pay the debt?'[29] It was the perfect utterance from a man at peace with himself and possibly an allusion to life's debt to the healing god.[30] The words were immortalised by Plato (whose real name was Aristocles) in his *Phaedo*, a notable yet unlikely absentee from Socrates' final hour. Plutarch added that after Socrates had downed the fatal draught, 'he engaged in philosophy and invited his companions to do the same.'[31]

As one scholar points out, Socrates had 'spent his entire life trying to fathom the mysteries of life: what is virtue? what is justice? what is beauty? what is the best form of government? what is the good life?... What Socrates found was that no Athenian citizen could give him a definition of any moral or intellectual virtue that would survive ten minutes of his questioning.'[32] Hemlock was his reward, and it made Plato reconsider the ideal state; his *Seventh Letter* betrayed his disenchantment with Athenian politics, a state of affairs that would only change, he proposed, when its leaders philosophised once again. Plato's account of Socrates' death so affected the stoical Cato the Younger that he read the *Phaedo* twice the night of his own suicide in 46 BCE.[33] On hearing of Cato's self-murder, Caesar reportedly lamented: 'Cato, I grudge you your death, as you would have grudged me the preservation of your life.'[34]

The great speaker Demosthenes was, as we might imagine, credited with rather immortal lines for his epitaph, when Archias, the thespian-turned-assassin, had him surrounded in the (supposedly sacred) Temple of Poseidon on the island of Calauria (Poros). Contemplating the pledges of fair treatment Antipater was delivering via his 'exile hunter', Demosthenes replied with, 'Archias, I was never convinced by your acting, and I am no more convinced by your promises', whereupon he sucked poison from his reed pen and rounded off with a speech from Sophocles' *Antigone* as the effects took hold.[35]

Tradition was not content with the one recital (which may have originated with Duris' allusion to tragic drama) and Plutarch dedicated the next chapter to recording its many pluralities. The wording on the bronze statue supposedly erected by the Athenians to his memory is even questioned and it was rumoured that Demosthenes composed the eulogy himself.[36] Lucian took up the mantle in his usual satirical style, claiming Antipater did indeed lament the death of the anti-Macedonian orator:

> Archias! methinks you comprehend neither the nature of Demosthenes, nor my mind. No man that ever lived do I admire more than Demosthenes... the Attic orators are but babes in comparison with his finish and intensity, the music of his words, the clearness of his thoughts, his chains of proof, his cumulative blows...[37]

Aristotle was to follow Demosthenes to the Elysian Fields soon after: 'Eurymedon, the priest of Deo's mysteries, was once about to indict Aristotle for impiety, but he, by a draught of poison, escaped prosecution. This then was an easy way of vanquishing unjust calumnies.' The charge of impiety (*asebeia*) was difficult to counter; Aristotle ended his life by taking aconite at the age of seventy at Chalcis in 322 BCE. Of course, a host of other sources simply claimed he died of a stomach ailment after placing 'a skin of warm oil on his stomach' to alleviate the pain.[38]

Rome was no less creative with its renderings of famous deaths. On the Ides

The Death of Demosthenes. Litho illustration from *Hutchinson's History of the Nations*, ca. 1910, after a picture by Bramtott. He reportedly took poison in the Temple of Poseidon on the island of Calauria.

of March (15th) 44 BCE Julius Caesar, *dictator perpetuo,* managed to utter (in Greek no less) '*Kai su, teknon?*' – popularly translated as 'you too, child?' – upon seeing Brutus amongst those who delivered the twenty-three stab wounds that came in thick and fast. Inevitably, portents foretold Caesar's end, just as they had Alexander's, for livers with no lobes were 'tokens of mighty upheavals'.[39] Suetonius gave us the tradition, though Plutarch was more dubious about any such lines, and *Kai su* may have carried a more accusatory and threatening tone towards Caesar's young protégé, and that is what we might expect to have come from the dictator's mouth.

The classical portrayal failed to deter Shakespeare from giving us the immortal epitome of betrayal, the macaronic line, '*et tu Brute? Then fall, Caesar*'; it was a pastiche already popular in the bard's day.[40] In the six of his plays that were constructed around Greek and Roman historical themes, Shakespeare gave new lives, deaths and voices to characters from the past, and he didn't get away scot-free himself; his tomb at Holy Trinity Church, Stratford, bears a highly inauthentic sounding god-fearing curse that was supposedly the bard's very own.[41]

It is not Caesar, however, but Cicero who has a special bearing on our case, for the conclusion to his story was reported by a corpus of heavyweight historians: Plutarch, Appian, Cassius Dio, Seneca, Asinius Pollio (a successful defence lawyer in accusations of poisoning) and Livy.[42] Cicero's departure has been described as 'the most widely-evidenced of "famous deaths" in the ancient world', in which 'obfuscation, anomalies and contradictions exist, suggesting blatant manipulation of his story'.[43] Cicero had pointed out that all who wish death upon a man, whether they clutch the knife or not, are as guilty as one another; this was a dangerous premise to make considering Brutus, who was in fact rumoured to be Caesar's son (from the dictator's affair with Servilia), had called for *him* to restore the republic when plunging his dagger into Caesar.[44] In a later letter to Scribonius, one of the conspirators, Cicero, who already enjoyed the honorific *Pater Patriae* for his part in suppressing the Cataline conspiracy, began with: 'How I could wish that you had invited me to that most glorious banquet on the Ides of March.'[45]

Cicero labelled his subsequent attacks on Mark Antony in the Senate '*Philippics*' in emulation and admiration of Demosthenes' earlier verbal assaults on Alexander's father. An unsurprising victim of the proscriptions of Antony and Octavian, Cicero is credited with six deaths, just ahead of Callisthenes' five and the four attached to Pyrrhus of Epirus.[46] Cicero was beheaded and had his hands chopped off, for they were the damning instruments that penned his scathing polemics against the wayward triumvir. They were nailed to the rostra, either one, or both.[47] His last words are recorded as, 'There is nothing proper about what you are doing soldier, but do try to kill me properly.' In yet another version, Fulvia, Antony's wife, pulled out his tongue and repeatedly stabbed it with a hairpin.[48] The popularity for oratorical declamation against Cicero's killers seems to have added new wood to the allegorical fire and his death soon frayed into many competing strands.[49] Octavian is said to have hesitated for two days before adding Cicero to those sentenced, and so regretted the act in later years that he assisted Cicero's son to a co-consulship.[50]

Roman deaths *were* brutal and just as vividly reported. The emperor Valerian (ca. 190s-260s CE) was skinned and stuffed with straw, whereas the decapitated head of Gaius Gracchus was filled with molten lead to a weight of 'seventeen and two-third pounds' to exploit the promise that it would be worth its weight in gold once handed to his enemies.[51] Of course, less dramatic versions existed, and there are claims Valerian's death was simply the stuff of Christian propaganda. Others were 'cleaned-up' before sale in their endeavour to instruct. No one mentioned the real effects of hemlock, the 'sin of Athens': choking, nausea, bile and convulsions, for none wished to imagine Phocion or Socrates writhing on the floor in their own vomit.

Aristophanes had described the drug's more benign symptoms in his *Frogs* written six years earlier,[52] and, in fact, Plato's *Phaedo*, which described Socrates' final hours in 399 BCE, has led to the question of whether hemlock was used at all, for it was never specifically named.[53] Theophrastus helps us out with his suggestion that a cocktail of hemlock, poppy and herbs would render death more peaceful.[54] Phocion, once a pupil of Plato and who had been elected city *strategos* forty-five times (once turning down a 100-talent gift from Alexander), was to suffer for his pro-Macedonian policy; condemned to die on the day of the Athenian festival of Olympia, he had to pay 12 drachmas to his executioner for more hemlock to be bruised.[55]

Although Plato gave Socrates some dignity, hemlock *was* unpredictable. When Nero ordered Seneca's death, his stoic teacher severed the arteries of his own arms, legs and knees, but his frail body lingered on, and so he resorted to asking a friend to provide the poison of 'those condemned in Athens'. It failed to take hold because his limbs were too cold for the blood to circulate and he had to be content with suffocating from the steam of the bathhouse, according to Tacitus' account.[56]

TOXIKON PHARMAKON: POISON ARROWS FROM AN AUTHOR'S BOW

The use of hemlock and other poisons was widespread; when laying out the basis of his ideal state, Plato had divided magic into two categories, and the first focused on harm to the body caused by food, drinks and unguents – *pharmaka deleteria*, thus by poisons.[57] A 5th century BCE Athenian law prohibited their use, as did the *Tean Curses*, read each year by city officials and banning production of harmful drugs.[58] Hippocrates had reported on the use of arsenics for skin ulcers and the methods to control the absorption of poisons a century and a half before Alexander's day.

Strabo claimed that more than sixty citizens of the island of Kea were ordered to take the poison in the 4th century BCE during a food shortage to ensure the survival of others.[59] Theophrastus (and later Juvenal) described the skills behind aconite poisoning along with masking techniques, recommending strychnine for practical purposes since the poison's taste, pertinently, could be disguised in wine.[60] Ovid dated the use of aconite (also named wolfsbane) back to the Bronze Age, terming the plant the 'stepmother's favourite brew'.[61] In legend its effect commenced when Heracles dragged the hellhound, Cerberus, from the underworld to the daylight; the beast was so terrified that foam from its slavering mouth took root in the soil and spontaneously grew into the plant.[62] Perhaps Ovid even contemplated taking it himself after his life banishment by Augustus to Tomis on the Black Sea at the fringe of the Roman Empire; now a *relegates*, he published his *Tristia*, a sorrowful 'exile poetry' that was in fact a veiled *suasoria* ('persuasion') in pleading his case to the emperor against the still unknown charges.[63]

There can be no doubt then, that the art of poison was highly developed by Alexander's day. The craft was truly ancient and spears and arrowheads are a good place to start. Deadly nightshade (possibly Pliny's *strychnos*) is one candidate for the ingredient in Latin *dorycnium*, 'spear poison', suggesting a widespread use of the sap that would have been smeared on a blade.[64] The Greek word for bow was *toxon*, the arrow was *toxeuma* (also *oistos*), and poison was *pharmakon*, thus arrow poison was known as *toxikon pharmakon*. The Roman derivative was *toxicum* when referring to poison alone, though it still originally implied an archer's toxin.[65] The weapons wielded by *toxotai*, the formidable horseback archers, were renowned for their poison tips in Scythia; the viper-extracted *scythicon* they used on arrowheads was lethal and so were the circling cavalry that could unleash 200 to 300 arrows per *gorytos*, the two-compartmented quiver that accompanied their compact 'cupid' bows.[66] Toxic plants would have been collected by *rhizotomoi*, skilled 'root-cutters' who used knives to dig out what they dared not touch themselves.[67]

In the *Odyssey* Homer related that Odysseus made a special voyage to obtain supplies of a deadly poison to coat the bronze tips of his arrows, and he further described the 'drugs mixed together, many good and many harmful' that were used when Helen spiked the drinks of Telemachus and Menelaus.[68] Heracles famously dipped his arrows in the poison of the slain Lernean Hydra and Alexander's troops suffered the consequences of malevolent archery in India when both the enemy arrows and sword blades were coated with viper and cobra venom; this was in contravention to the Hindu *Laws of Manu*, for Brahmins and the higher castes prohibited their use. Local Indian physicians had to be employed by the Macedonians to neutralise the effects and in the Vulgate texts Ptolemy almost succumbed before Alexander reportedly found an antidote, though this sounds suspiciously like Cleitarchean propaganda.[69]

Diodorus described the snakes behind the various venoms used and the Indian custom of burning wives on the dead husband's funeral pyre; supposedly it was to discourage them from poisoning their spouses:

> The country, indeed, furnished no few means for this, since it produced many and varied deadly poisons, some of which when merely spread upon the food or the wine cups cause death. But when this evil became fashionable and many were murdered in this way, the Indians, although they punished those guilty of the crime, since they were not able to deter the others from wrongdoing, established a law that wives, except such as were pregnant or had children, should be cremated along with their deceased husbands...[70]

Ancient Persian texts described further toxins and their methods of fabrication. The Great Kings took precautions and kept a calculus, the stone from the kidney or gall bladder of the mountain goat, at the bottom of their wine cups, for the nobility dished out poisons at dinner; the chapter heading extract from Xenophon's *Cyropaedia* confirmed the ubiquity of the crime. The porous structure of the calculus was credited with counteractive powers and was called a *padzahr*, which broadly translates as 'against poison'.[71] Diodorus related how Darius III thwarted the assassination attempt by the grand vizier, Bagoas the 'kingmaker', finally forcing the captured eunuch to drink his own brew.[72]

Plutarch and Ctesias reported that Queen Parysatis, mother of Artaxerxes II, fatally intoxicated her daughter-in-law by means of a carefully prepared knife; venom was administered by her maidservant to the side of a blade used to cut a bird in half. Taking the untainted meat, Parysatis chewed in pleasure while her daughter-in-law choked on her inheritance; Hesiod's advice was never more relevant: 'Invite your friend to supper, not your enemy.' Revenge can, however, be a double-edged sword, for Plutarch went on to explain that: 'The legal mode of death for poisoners in Persia is as follows. There is a broad stone, and on this the head of the culprit is placed; and then with another stone they smite and pound until they crush the face and head to pulp.' That was the fate of the maidservant, while Parysatis was packed off to Babylon in shame.[73]

THE BREW IN THE ASS'S HOOF

Prolific as poisoning was, there can equally be no doubt that assassination was an integral part of Macedonian machinations; Badian noted: 'Only two of Alexander's predecessors in the 4th century BCE had not died by assassination... and only three among all the successors of Darius I.'[74] Alexander and his father, Philip II, had contributed generously to the death toll of candidates (and their supporters) for the throne, and Pausanias alleged Cassander used poison when murdering both of Alexander's sons: Alexander IV and Heracles.[75]

Analysing the *cause* of Alexander's death is not our central aim, but it is worth taking a look at recent autopsies of the claims. Peter Green's portrayal of Alexander reminds us that 'our ancient sources all record a tradition that Alexander was poisoned', recalling that even Arrian and Plutarch referenced the conspiracy adjacent to their *Journal* extracts (T9, T10).[76] Green's influential portrait concluded, 'this, rather, suggests poison, of a king who was unbearable and murderous', and yet he added: 'The illness had been long. On this one fact alone, all stories of poison founder... If, on the other hand, the King was not poisoned, the chances are that he was suffering from either raging pleurisy or, more probably, malaria.'[77] These apparent volte-faces reemphasise the lack of evidence, or rather an investigative fog. Others too have argued for natural causes of death, with typhoid fever, West Nile encephalitis, methanol toxicity, acute pancreatitis and perforated peptic ulcers being promoted. Mary Renault quite plausibly suggested a water-borne disease, acquired from drinking the contaminated and excrement-filled Euphrates, had developed into pneumonia and then to pleurisy.[78]

Plutarch and Arrian knew of a tradition – an offshoot of the *Pamphlet*'s finger pointing (T1, T2) – that claimed Aristotle gathered the poison from the River Styx by the cliffs of Nonacris (in the northern central Peloponnese) and he had it ferried to Babylon in a mule's hoof, for this was the only vessel capable of holding the ferment.[79] The only cure, proposed Lucian in his satirical *Dialogues of the Dead*, was repeated draughts of Lethe water from the river of oblivion, defying the mantra of Orphic mythology.[80] Plutarch claimed that three days after Alexander had been pronounced dead, his body, which had been left untreated in the stifling June heat, remained in perfect condition.[81] Curtius incorporated typical Vulgate *thauma* – the king kept his vital look for a full six days, to the extent that the embalmers dared not touch him fearing he may still be alive; Aelian mentioned an even more discreditable thirty days, unless this is a later manuscript corruption.[82]

This condition, as many toxicologists would confirm, is an argument *for*, not *against*, the presence of chemical poison (if not methanol toxicity): 'a remarkable preservation of the body is commonly, but not constantly, observed', concluded one authoritative publication on arsenic use.[83] Milne has argued for strychnine use at Babylon, though Engels proposed malaria to explain the preservation; both conditions, when resulting in either cyanosis or deep coma, could have led to the delayed putrefaction of the body.[84]

However, a recent study of the episode in New Zealand by the National Poisons Centre in the Department of Preventive and Social Medicine at the University of Otago, perhaps the most detailed literary autopsy since the 1996 clinicopathological report prepared for the *New England Journal of Medicine*, argues against the above conclusions. It states that 'lethal doses of strychnine' would 'typically cause death within 3-5 hours', not longer. Moreover, in cases of arsenic poisoning 'death occurs within 24h to 4 days'; 'these symptoms do not match those displayed' by Alexander 'and can therefore also be discarded.'[85] Although the Greeks would have had access to a wide range of attested toxic plants such as (using today's scientific botanical labels) *aconitum* (aconite), *conium maculatum* (hemlock), *artemisia* (wormwood), *hyoscyamus niger* (henbane), and *colchicum autumnale* (autumn crocus), a better fit to Alexander's relatively long decline would be the alkaloids present in *veratrum*, notably *veratrum album*: white hellebore.

Plutarch recorded that Alexander had earlier written to Pausanias, the physician treating Craterus, to remind his veteran general to be vigilant in his use of hellebore, widely used as a self-induced purge, as was antimony.[86] 'Its emetic properties were well known to the Hellenes and it was readily available from Alpine pastures of Europe and Asia.'[87] A key symptom of *veratrum* poisoning is the onset of epigastric pain that may also be accompanied with nausea and vomiting, and though victims can become completely incapacitated and even unable to move or speak, they do remain conscious. The National Poisons Centre report concluded that '*veratrum* alkaloids are readily extracted into alcohol by fermentation, and it is therefore possible' that Iolaos spiked Alexander's wine 'with a volume of fermented *veratrum* extract.'[88]

'THY SECRET FIRE BREATHE O'ER HER HEART, TO POISON AND BETRAY': THE TALE OF TOXIC ROME[89]

We may never know what truly killed the Macedonian king at Babylon, but reports of poisoning in Roman and Hellenistic history suggest the ancient art of toxicology was long established in the West. Archagathus, the grandson of Agathocles the tyrant of Syracuse, arranged for his grandfather's *eromenos* (a younger male lover), Menon, to load his king's tooth-cleaning quill with a putrefactive drug. As a result, Agathocles was unable to utter a sound, even when being burned alive by Oxythemis, the envoy of Demetrius *Poliorketes*, the patron of the Cardian historian Hieronymus.[90] Once again, this is just one tradition and alternative endings exist. Inevitably the art of poison arrived in Rome; her ever-practical hand was employed in its development and it was to become big business across the empire.

As early as the drafting of the laws of *Twelve Tables* (ca. 450 BCE) special dispositions were put in place for cases of murder from drugs.[91] The first recorded Roman crime involving accusations of poisoning dates back to 331 BCE (the same year Alexander defeated Darius III at Gaugamela) when a suspiciously high mortality rate pointed to the guilt of 190 Roman matrons who were then forced to drink their own cocktails.[92] Similar cases in 186 BCE and 182 BCE resulted in the implication and death of over 5,000 alleged conspirators, again many of them women, when illustrious magistrates, consuls and men of rank mysteriously died. In 154 BCE two more ex-consuls were poisoned by their spouses and so prevalent was the use of poison by disgruntled wives that by Quintilian's day the term 'adulteress' was apparently synonymous with the term 'poisoner'.[93] Cicero, Juvenal, and Tacitus reported various cases of patricide, matricide and even filicide using toxic substances, and they also named the women who provided the tools for a fee.[94]

Pliny was particularly lucid on the sources and types used, including a vivid description of hemlock, *cicuta* in Latin, now so widespread that in 82

BCE the dictator Sulla (ca. 138-78 BCE) promulgated a strict law against its use.[95] The *Lex Cornelia de sicariis et veneficis* at this point categorised poisoners, assassins and magicians together.[96] The term *scelus,* a crime, was employed by historians like Tacitus to indicate murder by poison, and the *pigmentarii,* the druggists behind them, were similarly restrained by law.[97]

Mithridates VI of Pontus (ruled ca. 120-63 BCE), himself an adept in the art of poisons, had Crateus, his talented *polypharmakos* (broadly a 'herbalist'), ever by his side.[98] He was perhaps following Attalus III of Pergamum (ca. 170-133 BCE) who, according to Plutarch, '... used to grow poisonous plants, not only henbane and hellebore, but also hemlock, aconite, and *dorycnium*, sowing and planting them himself in the royal gardens, and making it his business to know their juice and fruits, and to collect these at the proper season.'[99]

The redoubtable Mithridates, who claimed descent from both Alexander and Darius I, and who reintroduced a Macedonian-styled phalanx formation when facing Sulla in battle, was so fearful of assassination that he self-vaccinated with a daily dose of a wide range of known toxins in search of the universal antidote, the *theriac,* an illusive mix that became known as *antidotum mithridatium.*[100] Rome granted Gnaeus Pompey wide-ranging powers to capture the Pontic king through the *Lex Manilia.* Pompey initially delayed any action, preferring first to establish useful alliances with the dynasts of the East in his own *imitatio Alexandri.* When finally caught, Mithridates had apparently built up such a constitution that he was unable to commit suicide by taking poison and had to resort to falling on the sword of a Celtic bodyguard, Bituitus, taking the knowledge of twenty-one languages with him.[101] A less romantic tradition had him dying at the hand of the troops deserting to his son, Pharnaces; ambivalent on how he died, Rome granted Pompey honours for terminating the Pontic threat.[102]

The Julio-Claudians used poison as liberally as garlic in defiance of Sulla's decree.[103] Germanicus, Nero's grandfather, was rumoured to have fallen foul of the famous *venefica*, Martina, an accomplished maker of drugs and invocator of curse tablets.[104] Tacitus dedicated considerable space to the intrigues and suspicions that fell upon Gnaeus Calpurnius Piso, Munatia Plancina, and ultimately their employer, the emperor Tiberius, in the wake of Germanicus' death; the toxic term *venenum* (possibly derived from 'Venus' and originally meaning a love potion) appears on forty-four occasions in Tacitus' *Annals.*[105] Nero and Agrippina had the infamous Locusta in their service and they both kept the *venefica* gainfully employed after she (allegedly) assisted in the deaths of Claudius and his son; Locusta later opened an academy of poisons and tested her arts on convicted criminals. Agrippina went on to accuse Lollia Paulina, a rival for the position as fourth wife to Claudius, of black magic, and confiscated her property without trial.[106]

Wealthy Romans, like the Persian nobility, had become so fearful of being targeted that *praegustatores* were indeed widely employed. These professional tasters, commonly slaves or freedmen, eventually formed a *collegium* and with good cause, for the emperors (or families of) Augustus, Caligula, Claudius, Nero, Vitellius (emperor 69 CE), Domitian, Hadrian, Commodus, Caracalla, Elagabalus (emperor 218-222 CE) and Alexander Severus, were all associated with some form of scandal involving poison.[107] As in much else, Rome may have learned from Greek and Persian experience, but she was to have the last word on its sophistication.

It is the emperor Claudius once again who interests us the most in any comparison to the reporting of Alexander's illness. Suetonius recorded that 'most people thought he had been poisoned' and by his official taster no less.[108] Suetonius followed with, '… an equal discrepancy exists between the accounts of what happened next. According to many, he lost his power of speech.'[109] Suetonius described a painful night and brief recovery, followed by a second dose of poison and then a coma. Tacitus reported that the second dose was administered to Claudius on a feather, a technique used to induce vomiting and a standard part of the physician's purge.[110] Compare this to the *Metz Epitome* and the *Romance* texts (T1, T2), which extend the Vulgate recounting of the conspiracy in Babylon. Here we have the description of the second poisoning from a feather by Alexander's cupbearer, Iolaos (Chares interestingly claimed Ptolemy had been Alexander's taster), along with the king's final night of agony and speechless condition, juxtaposed beside the *Journal's* claim that Alexander was speechless for the final two days and nights (T3, T4):[111]

> In the meantime, Alexander was in a sorry state. He wanted to vomit and so asked for a feather: Iolaos gave the king a feather smeared with poison. When he put this down his throat… he was continuously racked with renewed and ever more excruciating pains. In this condition, he passed the night.[112]

Had Roman biographers taken their lead from Pseudo-Callisthenes, or was the *Romance* itself a hydroscopic palimpsest (it had already absorbed the *Pamphlet*) that continued to absorb Roman biographical trends before adopting its final form in which less-colourful *Pamphlet* claims had been embellished? Perhaps, like the ever-present storms at sea in Greek plays (replayed in Virgil's *Aeneid*), the central themes of the classical world simply infected and inhabited any biography with a low immune system. In which case Marcus Aurelius' philosophical reflection comes readily to mind: 'Constantly reflect on how all that comes about at present, came about just the same in days gone by…. [at] the whole court of Philip, or Alexander, or Croesus, for in every case the play was the same, and only the actors were different.'[113]

'QUALIS ARTIFEX PEREO' – MUSHROOMS: THE FOOD OF THE GODS[114]

Claudius had reportedly dined on fatally seasoned mushrooms, a last meal Nero termed 'the food of the gods',[115] and tradition gives us a death that implicated three assassins.[116] Nero, whose name theatrically stood for 'strong' or 'valiant' in the Sabine tongue, had his personal guard, the Phalanx of Alexander, to call upon, so any rumour of Agrippina's hand in the murder was surely 'suppressed by the power of the people implicated by the rumour', to repeat Curtius on Cassander's suppression of the *Pamphlet* rumours.[117]

Having murdered his mother, possibly two wives, as well as two literary intellectuals, along with countless other prominent citizens who were sacrificed to divert the wrath of an approaching comet, Nero finally went mad and planned to poison the entire Senate.[118] Deserted by his bodyguard, Nero discovered that the golden box containing Locusta's poison had abandoned him too. After a dramatic earthquake and a lightning storm accompanied his hurried flight from Rome, he had a grave dug, exclaiming: '*Qualis artifex pereo!*' – 'What an artist dies in me!' As horsemen could be heard fast approaching, Nero recalled the *Iliad*: 'The thunder of galloping horses is beating against my ears', and when his pursuers finally closed in, he is said to have stabbed himself in the throat, and yet managed to utter: 'Too late! But ah, what loyalty!' It was a thanks to the centurion attending him.[119] His death fell on June 9th, or more curiously, *possibly* on the 11th of the month (in the year 68 CE), for the latter day of the year was portentously shared with Alexander.[120]

But the artist in Nero never died; his death inspired ongoing rumours that captured the imaginations of his biographers and the artistry began in earnest. More in keeping with Nero's reputation, an alternative version has him smashing two invaluable Homeric crystal goblets to deny his successors their use upon hearing of the defecting legions.[121] Nero had intended to throw himself into the Tiber, and history really ought to have granted the self-proclaimed 'great tragic actor' a more extended soliloquy. Alas that would not do, as it was well known Agrippina had forbidden philosophy from his classes, just as Seneca had hidden all rhetorical works from his avowed pyromaniac pupil.[122]

Nero had, in fact, attempted a more practical immortality by slotting his name into the Roman calendar, following in the footsteps of Julius Caesar and Augustus.[123] Luckily, the suggested spring month, Neroneus, became nothing more than an April folly, whereas Commodus later attempted to rename *all* twelve months after his own by-now twelve adopted names;[124] Rome declared a *de facto damnatio memoriae* naming him a public enemy, restoring all nomenclatures to their rightful places.[125] Commodus was strangled in his bath after another bungled attempt at poison. As Nietzsche warned, the conscience of the *Imperium Romanum* was not prickled by wholesale linguistic, literary, or intercalary, reinvention.[126]

ALLEGORICAL PICTURE FRAMING

Death in itself does not sell scrolls unless the literary taxidermist has stuffed the corpse with a didactical potpourri, for the final pages of a parchment had to justify the price; and whether to eulogise or to condemn, the classical era demanded that the death suitably picture-framed the life. So underlying all great exits were fitting allegorical stories that alluded to deeper meanings, sometimes subtle and oft-times blatant. The bean field was a foil to ridicule Pythagoras' strict vegetarian doctrine, a stance summed up by Ovid with 'what a heinous crime is committed when guts disappear inside a fellow-creature's guts';[127] Pythagoras had warned against the *kuanos*, kidney pulses or broad beans, after he noted its organ-like shape, providing Plutarch much to ponder in his treatise *On the Eating of Flesh*.[128]

Socrates' nobility in the face of hemlock magnified Athens' sin against philosophy, though somewhat more satirical was Lucian's summation:

> Yes; and very serviceable his dissertations on Justice were to him, were they not, when he was handed over to the Eleven, and thrown into prison, and drank the hemlock? Poor man, he had not even time to sacrifice the cock he owed to Asclepius. His accusers were too much for him altogether, and *their* philosophy had Injustice for its object.[129]

Cicero's humble courage sat beside a warning on political meddling, and Nero's poor theatrics recalled his destructive self-deluded life on both the political and thespian stages. As far as his final exclamations, it has been pointed out that they were 'self-consciously bathetic' and doused in a sarcasm to highlight how far he had tumbled. *Qualis artifex pereo,* alluding to his dying artistic talent, was, according to Cassius Dio, oft-quoted and in general use. And quite in contrast, Demosthenes' clever and pithy riposte to Archias recalled the opening of a prosecutor's speech worthy of the formidable *logographos*.[130]

Because Aeschylus was the 'father' of the tragedians (Callisthenes thought he 'wrote his tragedy in wine which lent vigour and warmth to his work') a sense of the calamitous was required to frame his final day.[131] Both Pliny and Aelian recorded that he perished when an eagle dropped a tortoise from a height, mistaking his bald head for a stone, a suitably sorrowful conclusion for the man who had fought bravely at Salamis and Marathon, and who humbly termed his plays 'nothing but crumbs from the rich-laden banquet of Homer'.[132] Equally tragic, though from a different angle, was the death of Archimedes the geometer; he was reportedly stabbed by a common Roman soldier after resisting arrest with '*noli turbare circulos meos*', 'do not disturb my circles', a perfect geometric epitaph. The attacking general, Marcellus, had ordered that he was taken alive, so impressed were the Romans with his defensive techniques at the siege of Syracuse that ended in 212 BCE; his tomb, constructed on the orders of Marcellus, was nevertheless left unattended and overgrown until Cicero rediscovered it in 75 BCE.[133]

Pyrrhus, who fought at the Battle of Ipsus in 301 BCE at the tender age of eighteen beside his new patron and brother-in-law, Demetrius *Poliorketes*, was to become one of history's greatest commanders. He resembled Alexander 'in appearance swiftness and vigorous movement' as well as in his descent from the heroes Achilles and Heracles. 'The other kings, they said, represented Alexander with their purple robes, their body-guards, the inclination of their necks, and their louder tones in conversation; but Pyrrhus, and Pyrrhus alone, in arms and action.'[134] He went on to gain a reputation for unsustainable 'Cadmean' (today we use 'Pyrrhic') victories in Italy.[135]

Having himself skirted with death by poison at the hand of his cupbearer (who in fact betrayed the plot arranged by his co-king, Neoptolemus, the son of Cleopatra, Alexander's sister), and in return for all his hubris and unrelenting hostility, Pyrrhus was finally felled by a roof tile that defied the stoutness of his iconic goat-horned helmet; it was thrown down by an old woman defending her son when Pyrrhus was trapped in the narrow streets of Argos after his famous elephants had fallen and blocked the escape route out of the city's main gate.[136] Pyrrhus finally collapsed and fell from his horse by the tomb of the Homeric Licymnius, an Argive warrior killed by Heracles son, Tlepolemus, who was then banned from the *polis* for the homicide.[137] Pyrrhus' own instruments of war finally had sealed his fate and the grave on which he crumpled sang of his own sin against the city.

The Successor Wars in which Pyrrhus and Demetrius *Poliorketes* immortalised themselves were brutal, and the penalty for speaking out inappropriately was just as harsh: we recall that Hyperides, who is said to have proposed honours for Alexander's poisoner, reputedly lost his tongue on Antipater's orders; if anecdotal it surely captured the danger of the day.[138] Anaxarchus, a campaign philosopher who had accumulated great wealth, supposedly suffered the same fate when Nicocreon the Cypriot tyrant ordered him crushed by mortar and pestle after his tongue had been non-surgically removed; it was all for an indiscretion in which he had earlier suggested to Alexander at Tyre that he should serve up Nicocreon's head on a platter.[139] Diogenes Laertius recorded Anaxarchus' bold, but unlikely, retort: he bit off his own tongue and spat it at his tormentor. This too was a less than original epitaph for it was one he shared with Zeno of Elea.[140] Known in life as *eudaimonikos*, 'a happy one', the rendering of Anaxarchus' execution was, no doubt, a contrived lesson on careless talk and perhaps on the false tenets of eudaimonic philosophy.[141]

Ultimately death does not belong to the deceased but to those recording it, whether accompanied by a 'do kill me properly', 'a cock to Asclepius', or an empire 'to the strongest'. In Alexander's case, the reply (to the question on succession) was something of an *hysteron proteron*, a rhetorical device that places the later event first, for his vision of posthumous 'funeral games' had already been uttered. Those words, if ever said, would have been an act of 'consummate irresponsibility', as one scholar points out.[142] But these details, in Plutarch's opinion, graced the scrolls because '… certain historians felt obliged to embellish the occasion, and thus invent a tragic and moving finale to a great action.'[143] The real deaths, and the actual last words, are lost from biographies; they were most likely panic-stricken, god-fearing, bile and blood-spitting utterances that served no rhetorical purpose. A quick read of Ovid's depiction of Heracles' agony from the poisoning of the Learnean Hydra would well illustrate the point.[144]

So what of Cyrus the Great and his tranquil deathbed meditations on a fulsome life, as presented in Xenophon's eulogy of the Achaemenid king? Well, other accounts corroborate a blood-soaked death at the hands of Tomyris, queen of the promiscuous, carnivorous and bronze-bladed Massagetae; his severed head was pushed into a skin filled with human blood, after which the queen proceeded to harangue him.[145] Another version, captured in Ctesias' *Persika*, saw Cyrus perish when fighting the Hyrcanian Derbices in the Upper Provinces, whilst Berossus claimed the kill came from Dahae archers near the Caspian Sea. Both Ctesias and Xenophon were present at, or fought in, the formative battle at Cunaxa, but with opposing armies, Xenophon fighting for the later pretender to the throne – Cyrus the Younger – and Ctesias allied to his throned brother, King Artaxerxes II. Ctesias' report of Cyrus' death in the battle was so drawn-out that Plutarch quipped: 'As with a blunt sword, he is long in killing Cyrus, but kills him at last.' So it is unsurprising that their history of Cyrus the Great maintained a similar conflict to the end.[146] Ctesias claimed the Susa archives as his source for detail – spuriously so. Xenophon claimed nothing except a heightened sense of theatre; nevertheless, it is his account that has gained the greater literary following.[147]

The Athenian-born Xenophon, almost 'immortalised' in his capacity as the only 4th century historian whose accounts survive, also chose epitaphs that suited his pro-Spartan biographies. In his *Agesilaus* he omitted his patron's death altogether so as not to detract from the impact of his life, just as he did for Alcibiades in his *Hellenika*.[148] Even Xenophon's *Anabasis* is missing three months; a gap that suggests it was a 'black period' for the 10,000 stranded Greeks.[149]

The Death of Archimedes. **Engraving by the French painter Gustave Courtois (1853-1923). His alleged last words to an approaching soldier were: 'Do not disturb my circles'.**

THE WARPED REFLECTIONS OF NATURE'S MIRROR

Birth was just as exploitable as death, both its timing and genealogy. But the dating of birth and death was not determined by science and was often guided by the author's *floruit,* literally his 'flowering'. For without an attested date, standard procedure was to deduct fifty years from the production of a first masterpiece to arrive at the author's birth, and then to add on the attested lifespan to arrive at his date of death. Thus we arrive at the tenuously approximated arrivals, alongside the spurious expirations, of Thucydides, Aristophanes and Aeschylus.[150] Suspiciously, Socrates' birth was said to have been on the 6th of the month of Thargelion, and the Persians were defeated at Marathon on the 6th of Beodromion, the day of the month that Alexander reportedly faced Darius at the Granicus River, and the day (the 6th) the Macedonian king was said to have been born.[151] But where the former events brought luck to Athens, the last date did not. As conspicuously dubious was the birth of Euripides, allegedly born on Salamis the very day of the epic sea battle against Xerxes on 23rd September 480 BCE in the Euripus Strait (hence his patronymic); though the coincidence may have been propitious in the psyche of the Macedonian king, the *Parian Chronicle* records that Euripides arrived some years before.

Hippocrates' legendary genealogy traced his heritage directly back to the healing god, Asclepius, whilst his maternal ancestry found its way to Heracles. Genealogical engineering was a popular pastime in Greece and Rome for those in search of a personal *theogonia*. Mark Antony invented 'Anton', a son of Roman Hercules, and the emperor Commodus wielded his Herculean gladiatorial clubs with lion skins draped over his shoulders to certify similar heroic links.[152] He then refashioned the head of the Neronian Colossus, later Sol Invictus, to represent himself as the hero.[153] Sparta claimed descent from the sons of Heracles, and not to be left out, the Attalid dynasts later carved a frieze of Telesphorus, Heracles' son, on the altar at Pergamum, so staking their own claims to the mythical past.[154]

Birth, death and genealogy: the malleable clays pinched, kneaded, spun, and finally fired into the legendary earthenware in which colourful lives, deaths, and the posthumous philosophical debates on them, were finally served up. The Pythagorean Golden Verses were almost certainly a later syncretic compilation; Pythagoras most likely took the ideas of a 'numerological harmonious' celestial world from Mesopotamia, transposing them into his 'music of the spheres'.[155] Plato then absorbed his teachings into his own metaphysical concepts, culminating with his declaration that 'God forever geometrises'.[156] And for all Pythagoras' 'greatness', anti-Pythagorean rebellions expelled their communities from southern Italy, sick of their secret elitist cliques with oligarchic aspirations, a picture which rather undermines the tradition of their ascetic vegetarian advice. Pythagoras was, as Bertrand Russell once termed him, a '… mixture of philosopher, prophet, man of science and charlatan.'[157]

Hippocrates' revered medical teachings were far from universally accepted; his school on Kos, and the rival school at Cnidus, vied for credibility over the merits of 'prognosis' and 'diagnosis', though neither could perform an autopsy on one another's opinions for the code was strictly opposed to post-mortems. The penultimate verse of the Hippocratic Oath reads (broadly) in translations: 'All that I may see or hear (even if not invited)… I will keep secret and will never reveal.' And he was true to his pledge, for whilst medicine and Hippocrates are inseparable today, very little is actually known about what he truly advocated in his lifetime, and none of the Hippocratic Canon can be attributed to him for certain. As with the corpus of Aristotle's extant treatises, much material is surely the product of 'disciple' notes and not his original ink.[158]

Hippocrates supposedly espoused: 'Life is short, opportunity fleeting, judgement difficult, treatment easy, but treatment after thought is proper and profitable'; this is not a surprising conclusion considering that he charged for his work. He also determined: 'If the eyes move rapidly, it is highly probably the patient is mad', and further, 'chilling combined with stiffening is fatal.'[159] No wonder that the physician Asclepiades (ca. 120s-

40 BCE) ridiculed Hippocrates' work as nothing more than 'a meditation on death', that is until we recall that Asclepiades was himself termed a penniless professor of rhetoric who talked his way to medical fame.[160]

The attested 'lives' of Hippocrates, Asclepiades and Pythagoras the meta-physicist who dreamed up the *kosmos*, were proto-romances, and if not as fulsome as Alexander's, they were sufficiently developed for their deaths to take on an air of mystery. But our attempts at classical myth-busting are certainly not new. True to his iconoclastic style, Timaeus rejected Empedocles' volcanic end by claiming he simply went to the Peloponnese,[161] whilst a notebook with the formula to Mithridates' mysterious *mithridatium*, the supposed super antidote of legendary efficacy, was unearthed by Pompey and found to be a simple mix of rue, salt, nuts and figs which suggests it was no more effective than a cup of *Hyppokras*.[162] Mithridates most likely had a duck do his toxic ingesting for him, but not to be outdone, according to Celsus' *De Medicina,* the Romans added new ingredients to his recipe to bring them up to thirty-six in total; Galen (ca. 130-200 CE), whose own medical treatises remained in use for over 1,300 years, signed it off, and Agrippina supposedly enjoyed its benefits, vexing Nero's attempts at matricide, and no doubt Locusta's efforts too.[163]

Pliny asked: 'Which of the gods, in the name of Truth, fixed these absurd proportions?' It could have been a statement about the empirical weight of dubious deaths, but in fact he was referring to *mithridatium* itself. Somewhat appropriately, when Pliny recorded the ingredients of the Pontic formula, he included the phrase 'to be taken with a grain of salt', Rome's *cum grano salis*, from which we derive our sceptical expression. And that is surely how we should read the description of Mithridates' own toxin resistance when finally captured, for Rome was rather good with poison by then.[164]

When describing the source of the drug that professedly felled Alexander, it appears that the obviously educated originator of this story (which now implicated Aristotle) was exploiting a well-known legend. In Greek mythology the gods swore their oaths upon the dark waters of the Styx (possibly the modern Mavroneri River) at Nonacris; if their word was broken, Zeus forced them to drink a cup of the icy cold flow causing coma and loss of speech.[165] Pliny, Aelian and Strabo all report the tradition of deadly sulphurous streams trickling from the mountains; Pausanias commented the 'lethal power' of the Styx, 'seemingly invented for the destruction of human beings', was first recognised after goats drank from the watercourse and subsequently perished.[166] Through time the locals renamed it the 'Black' or 'Terrible Waters' in support of its deleterious effects on metals and clay containers.[167] If there is any truth to this, there must have been many who would have suffered the consequences.

But history doesn't recognise the 'middle men', the 'un-dead'. There are, for example, scant references to the fate of the wounded on Alexander's campaign; the snow-blinded, frostbitten, the leprosy-afflicted, or the malaria-ridden who languished forever in a mud-brick Alexandria rather than returning to families across the Hellespont.[168] None of the *opomachoi*, those unfit for battle, the bone-shattered, limb-lost and dysentery-emaciated infantrymen, were feted by fanfare or captured by Lysippus and Apelles in bronze or paint. Nor were the vulnerable *skeuophorio*, the baggage handlers targeted in the thick of the fight when possession of booty could decide a battle's outcome. For there was no epideictic value in those whom fame had bypassed and Tyche had neglected. The Macedonian conqueror was indeed fortunate to have died so thoroughly, for a partial recovery, or even maiming, might have taken the 'Great' out of his name.

But Alexander did not endure completely unscathed. Plutarch's sources claimed the king became excessively paranoid, assuaging his fears with drinking and sacrifices and with 'foolish misgivings' concerning his *hetairoi*, and it has also been suggested that this was the direct effect of mind-altering drugs covertly administered by those planning his death. Alexander filled the palace at Babylon with soothsayers of every description, and 'now distrustful of the favour of Heaven and suspicious of his friends' he became a 'slave to his fears'; an intruder in the throne room was 'put out of the way' when possibly doing nothing more than enacting the ancient ritual of the 'substitute king' in the Babylonian New Year festival.[169] We have, it seems, been passed the description of a man losing his sanity; it captured something of the excess and paranoia of Caligula (who reportedly died leaving a trunk filled with poisons behind) and Nero rolled into one.[170] And in Alexander's case, the poison, the intrigue and his famous last words were all stirred together in a rhetorical mortar and pestle and ground into a textual *mithridatium* that inoculated history against the truth in an era of stoic reflection.

TESTAMENTAL SUICIDE AND THE STOIC OVERLAY

Stoicism has been termed 'a system put together hastily, violently, to meet a bewildered world'; it was more of a therapy than a philosophy, and that was certainly needed, for following Alexander's death, the world was thrown into turmoil by the early unsettled Hellenistic monarchies, 'when political freedom became a simple political catchword, rather than a battle cry'; the *polis*, the Greek city state, became subordinated to new and revived leagues, kingdoms and the ever eastward-lengthening shadow of Rome.[171]

Zeno of Citium (in Cyprus) established the school of the *Stoikoi* in 301 BCE from his *Stoa Poikile*, the painted arch in the Athenian Agora, directly after the Battle of Ipsus. Thereafter almost all of the successors of Alexander professed to be Stoics who believed *logos* could explain the order and coherence of the universe in which a man could plan and rationalise against overwhelming odds.[172] Stoicism became the dominant philosophy for the Roman era *literati* once Panaetius arrived from Athens for a tour of indoctrination, despite the century and a half of attempts by the Sceptics (and Cato) to combat the spreading doctrine. The Stoa managed to maintain its existence until 529 CE when Justinian (ca. 482-565 CE) closed the philosophical schools at Athens to prevent 'paganism' undermining the purity of the Christian Church; it was an event that was to usher in the Dark Ages of Europe.[173]

Panaetius befriended Scipio Aemilianus, whose Scipionic Circle of intellectuals included the poet Terence (ca. 195/185-159 BCE, collected as a slave on the campaign against Carthage), Sempronius Asellio, and the once-hostaged Polybius. Polybius' own outlook, and his frequent use of *tyche*, appears to have stemmed from here.[174] Panaetius' wisdom later found fertile ground in Cicero, in whose *Paradoxa Stoicorum* we find a plain-language explanation of the doctrine.[175] Cicero claimed 'some Stoics are practically Cynics'.[176] The schools had indeed been connected through Crates of Thebes, a follower of Diogenes the Cynic and teacher to Zeno.[177]

Stoicism helped shape the *suasoria* of Seneca, who used Cato the Younger (grandson of the elder paladin of the republic) and his 'heroic suicide' as a righteous example of the opposition to tyranny. The imperial tendrils of Stoic *prohairesis* (moral choices) crept in through Augustus' teacher, Athenodorus of Tarsus, and ultimately it laid the foundations for the *Meditations* of Marcus Aurelius, the last of the 'five good emperors', nostalgically written in Greek and housing reflections on a life that witnessed an empire at its peak.

Ataraxia (tranquillity), *autarkeia* (self-sufficiency) and *eudaimonia* (loosely, 'happiness') all took on new relative weights in their associations to Tyche, now Fortuna, and *moirai*, now *fatum,* but their roles remained essentially the same. The vocabulary encompassing new doctrines (*areskontai*) was certainly not new, but only its emphasis, for no radical new philosophies emerged in the Hellenistic era; Pythagoras had already made the distinction that: 'Fate is determined, orderly and consequent, while fortune is spontaneous and casual.'[178] What we classify today as Cyrenaicism, Pyrrhonism, Peripateticism, Epicureanism and Stoicism developed like a palimpsest of derivative anecdotes piled on one another and subtly realigned with the metaphysical inclinations of each new sage. 'Slight changes were made… in the superstructure. But nobody thought of examining the foundations.'[179]

The Megarian school of Stilpo, personally known to Ptolemy and attended by Demetrius *Poliorketes,* Zeno and Cleitarchus, has, for example, been described as 'a hybrid produced by grafting 'Socratic ideas on the Eleatic trunk'; Stilpo himself 'attempted to fuse Megarian dialectic with the Cynic way of life'.[180] What we term Middle Platonism, which absorbed Stoic and Peripatetic doctrine, was another hybrid result, and though 'men give more renown to that song which comes newest to their ears', the development of Western philosophy has been described as consisting of nothing more than a 'series of footnotes to Plato', who most likely borrowed ideas from Zoroastrianism.[181]

Despite the philosophical background noise and their elitist pretensions, Arrian and Plutarch, for example, ought to have raised their heads above the epideictic din to question why Alexander made no attempt to formally arrange his far-reaching estate, and neither of them considered that the king's *Journal* they cited is by definition a propaganda document of a royal court. But Ptolemy's pedestrian treatise appealed to Arrian's military palate so that he mistook platitudinous competency for historical fidelity. As has been neatly pointed out, what Ptolemy had not written, Arrian could not have read, so he and Plutarch fell into the same *Journal*-baited trap.[182]

Arrian's misplaced faith took the form of a liturgy to the fidelity of *basileia*:

> …but my view is that Ptolemy and Aristobulus are more trustworthy on their narrative. Aristobulus accompanied Alexander on his campaigns. Ptolemy not only campaigned with Alexander, but as a king himself, it would have been more dishonourable for him than for anyone else to provide untruths; moreover both wrote when Alexander was dead and so there was no compulsion nor anything to gain from writing anything but what actually happened…[183]

The sentiment from Arrian recurs in the speech given by Alexander to his untrusting and debt-burdened men after mass weddings at Susa.[184] In his *How to Write History* Lucian wryly noted: 'The impossible was believed of Achilles because Homer, preserving his deeds posthumously, would therefore have no motive for lying.'[185] Lucian had identified an Achilles' heel in historical method, and it sounds remarkably similar to Arrian's *prolalia*. Had Ptolemy himself opened with a similar self-declaration on his content? We might try and approximate it:

> I write as a King whose word and honour counts above all things, and as a Companion and Bodyguard of King Alexander III of Macedonia, privileged myself to be present at and a part of great events; and just as Homer recorded the deeds of Achilles with no agenda – for his subject was then long dead – I write an account only of things that truly took place, as I witnessed them.

Could Arrian's *Anabasis,* which ended with the notorious *Journal* extract (T3), have been metaphrasing Ptolemy at *both* ends of the book?[186]

In stark contrast to the views of Plato and Pythagoras, the Stoics (and Epicureans) were tolerant of suicide in extreme circumstances, considering it an appropriate escape from the frustrations of the world.[187] Not only was suicide the man's right, it was also considered a rational means of achieving *ataraxia,* freeing the soul from the suffering body, if *moira* or *fatum,* the Greek and Roman embodiments of 'inevitability' and the twist of fate, had decreed an impossible position.[188] Although Tacitus, as one example, placed little value on 'self-murder', which he considered politically useless, he did incorporate its detail to add dramatic tones to his chapters. He also reported on more widespread suicides which were prompted by the fact that Wills remained valid (and so bequeathed assets) for those who killed themselves, whereas those condemned to death by execution forfeited their estates if they did not.[189]

Pliny came to regard suicide as the greatest gift amid life's hardships.[190] Livy recorded that the residents of Marseilles (excluding soldiers and slaves for whom suicide was illegal) had petitioned the Senate and were given permission to end their life by taking hemlock that was provided to them by the state free of charge. At home 'patriotic suicide' became widespread; a high proportion of well-known philosophers ended their lives this way (some forced to) including Seneca and Lucretius whose poem *On the Nature of Things* introduced Epicureanism to Roman culture.[191]

The Roman intellect was therefore receptive to what we might term Alexander's 'succession suicide' and his vision on posthumous chaos; his last words, more cynical than useful, somehow became a demonstration of *katheikon,* moral duty, stoic behaviour espoused by Cicero in his posthumously published *De Officiis*, encapsulating his own moral code and definitions of moral duty. Moreover, Alexander's words suggested he was dying content, as Epictetus proposed everybody should.[192] Plato had proposed: 'If a man has trained himself throughout his life to live in a state as close as possible to death, would it not be ridiculous for him to be distressed when death comes to him?'[193]

But where did the Vulgate allusion to 'funeral games' originate? If Onesicritus *had* provided a fearful and guarded narrative on Alexander's passing, as the *Pamphlet* detail from the *Metz Epitome* claimed,[194] and if the title of his book, *On the Education of Alexander*, did indeed set out to emulate Xenophon's account of Cyrus, then Cleitarchus might have been able to extract useful reflections from there.[195] For Cyrus, on his deathbed, demanded his sons to throw 'entertainment that is fitting in honour of a man'. The narrative concluded with: 'But no sooner was he dead than his sons were at strife, cities and nations revolted, and all things began to decay.'[196] It required the lightest touch of the stylus by a historian schooled by the Cynics (as he was) and with a good knowledge of Xenophon to conjure up the now-famous premonition of posthumous chaos.

Lucian claimed he found the following reflection from Alexander in Onesicritus' work:

> Dying, I should willingly come back to life again for a little while, Onesicritus, that I might learn how men read these things then. If they praise them and admire them now, you need not be surprised; each imagines he will gain our good will by great deceit.[197]

It is perhaps a Homeric allusion to the brief return of Protesilaus from the dead and it might have been another product of Lucian's satirical imagination.[198] But it hints that Onesicritus *was* somehow associated with the coverage of Alexander's death and perhaps he truly did steer clear of revealing too much; was Onesicritus' closing chapter longer than we suppose? For though Thucydides noted that: 'fear drives out memory', Plutarch added, 'unless philosophy has drawn her chords about them'.[199]

We might similarly question who, or what, inspired Cleitarchus to equip Alexander with the now immortal Vulgate reply – 'to the strongest' – when questioned on succession (T6, T7, T8, T9). These words may indeed have actually been said, or rumour had it they were uttered, though in a very different context. But if Cleitarchus had been obliged to erase the testament from his account, the vacuum at Babylon needed filling with another epitaphic construction. What further inspiration did Cleitarchus have before him?

Onesicritus' sixth question to the wisdom-laden gymnosophists in India – how might a man most endear himself to mankind? – carried the reply, 'if he were the strongest, and yet an object of fear to no one'.[200] In addition, he had the immortal lines originating with Euripides, but possibly recirculating in Cleitarchus' day with a story now relating to Pyrrhus: for the Epirote king had three sons, named Ptolemy, Alexander and Helenus, by three different wives, and as a boy one of them is said to have asked his father which son would eventually inherit his kingdom. Pyrrhus replied: 'To that one of you who keeps his sword the sharpest.' Plutarch revealed: 'This, however, meant nothing less than the famous curse of Oedipus in the tragedy: "with whetted sword", and not by lot, the brothers should divide the house. So savage and ferocious is the nature of rapacity.'

The line came from *The Phoenician Women* of Euripides, the tragedian Alexander seems to have been most attached to. The play continued with: 'So they [his sons] were afraid that the gods might fulfil his prayers if they dwell together.'[201] It is noteworthy that Cassander, at the centre of the conspiracy, and who *did* wipe out Alexander's Argead line, had offered a reward of 200 talents for the infant Pyrrhus so that he could terminate the

Pyrrhidae too.[202] So was Cleitarchus' syncretic conclusion a classic *oratio oblique* built on indirect inferences to already 'classic' but well-worn tragic endings, with an outcome that would have freed him from attempting to capture an unspeakable truth? If a part of his intent was to portray a death resonating of selfishness in the face of impending chaos, then Stoicism simply re-rendered that as 'selflessness' and that interpretation stuck.

Alexander's death scene is of course a didactic pastiche, and yet Justin's summation provided a perfect example of the Stoic interpretation:

> While they (the soldiers) all wept, he not only did not shed a tear, but showed not the least token of sorrow; so that he even comforted some who grieved immoderately, and gave others messages to their parents; and his soul was as undaunted at meeting death, as it had formerly been at meeting an enemy.[203]

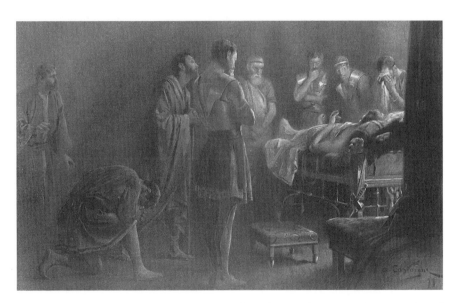

The Dying Alexander Receiving his Soldiers by **Andre Castaigne, painted 1898-1899.**

Arrian's mentor, the Stoic Epictetus, is alleged to have taught him:

> Actions do not disturb people,
> but opinions about actions;
> for example, death is nothing terrible,
> or else it would have appeared so to Socrates also,
> but the opinion about death, that it is terrible,
> that is what is terrible.[204]

This was a philosophical approach that hardly fostered enquiry, and so Alexander's end was ultimately chewed over with an *apatheia* (removed dispassion) that would have made even Zeno proud. As Lucian observed in his *True History*, the Stoics were still climbing the steep hill of virtue and had little energy left.[205] The *vita activa* of the Roman Republic had given way to the *vita contemplativa* of philosophical reflection that glanced off the surface of unexplained and troubling events beneath, and inevitably Alexander's biography fell into its clutches.

The liberally sprinkled Hellenistic attributions to *pothos,* an inner yearning that attached itself to Alexander, and to *tyche* that was first showcased in Demetrius of Phalerum's *Peri Tyches* which so impressed Polybius, took on the new mantle of stoic vocabulary and digressions on divine Fate, Providence and Destiny, uniting the various philosophical loose ends.[206] Alexander's campaign historians were not alone in introducing *pothos* to a tale longing to be told;[207] Thucydides, Herodotus and Pindar had all employed it before them.[208] However *pothos* is a misleadingly gentle word for that age of destruction, when *pleonexia* and *philochrematia*, greed and the love of money, might have been used instead.

If the 'yearning for more' became the stock rationale for Alexander's otherwise unacceptable behaviour, then the Greek term *pothos*, and the Roman equivalent, *ingens cupido,* have much to answer for. In Greek mythology, Pothos was the son of Zephyr the Westerly Wind, though somewhat more relevantly, it was also the name of the Delphinium flower that Greeks placed on an ancestor's tomb.[209] Its stoical overtones seem to have given off a fragrance that sidetracked investigative minds, leaving Alexander with an unmarked grave and a makeshift headstone with the indelible intestate graffiti, 'to the strongest', scrawled awkwardly across it (T6, T7, T8, T9).

NOTES

1. Translation from Stoneman (1991) p 33.
2. Xenophon *Cyropaedia* Book 1.3.8-10, translated by HG Dakyns, Project Gutenberg.
3. Epicurus, *Vatican Sayings* 31.
4. According to Pliny 33.33-34 antimony found in silver was used as eyebrow cosmetic.
5. Guthrie-Fideler (1987) p 28. The oath was sworn to the discoverer of the *Tetraktys*, the triangular formation of the first ten numbers. See also Riedweg (2002) p 29. It was also known as the *Mystike Tetras*.
6. *Dyskrasia* is a term attributed to the Hippocratic imbalance of The Four Humours of the body. Iamblichus *Life of Pythagoras* 15 and 25. The quadrivium disciplines were: arithmetic, geometry, music and astronomy.
7. Seneca *On the Shortness of Life*, translation by CND Costa, Penguin edition, London, 1997, p 10.
8. Diogenes Laertius *Empedocles*. See discussion in Gottschalk (1980) pp 14-20. Heracleides reported Empedocles' death in his treatise *On Diseases*.
9. Much of the *Scriptores Historiae Augustae* tends towards romance: examples of pre-death portents can be seen at *The Two Maximini* 31, *Severus Alexander* 60, *Caracalla* 11 and *Commodus* 16.
10. Empedocles is considered the first philosopher to bring all four basic elements in a creation theory; see discussion in Collins (2008) p 32.
11. Aelian 2.26 citing Aristotle's lost work, *On the Pythagoreans* (Fr. 191 R). Russell (1946) p 60 ff for Empedocles' career.
12. Felix Martí-Ibanez *A Prelude to Medical History*, MD Publications Inc, New York, 1961, Library of Congress ID: 61-11617.
13. For Democritus' age at death see Pseudo-Lucian *Makrobioi* 18 citing 104 and Diogenes Laertius 9.43 for age 109. The 'pseudo' attached to Lucian here denoting that the prosopography is possibly another spuriously assigned work. For reference to Aristotle's claim see Jones (1886). For several deaths see Margotta (1968) p 66. Soranus penned a doxography and the *Suda* has further conflicting detail.
14. Photius *Life of Pythagoras* 1 and Pseudo-Lucian *Makrobioi* 22 for Hieronymus' age.
15. Brown (1947) pp 685-686.
16. Diogenes Laertius *Pythagoras*.
17. Quoting Huffman (1993) pp 1-16.
18. Diodorus 16.3.8 for the length of Theopompus' *Philippica*; discussion in Plutarch *Moralia* 328a-b or *Fortune* 4 for the philosophers who did not write anything of their doctrine down.
19. Diogenes Laertius *Chrysippus* 3.
20. Diogenes Laertius *Chrysippus* 7.
21. Diogenes Laertius *Zeno* 7.28.
22. Lucian *Makrobioi* 19.
23. Plato *Symposium* 223d: 'Socrates was driving them to the admission that the same man could have the knowledge required for writing comedy and tragedy – that the fully skilled tragedian could be a comedian as well.' Translation by NH Fowler, Harvard University Press, 1925.
24. Brown (1949) p 52 for Diogenes' approval of cannibalism.
25. The various deaths outlined through Diogenes Laertius *Diogenes*.
26. Censorinus *De Die Natali* 15.2 stated age eighty-one and Diogenes Laertius *Diogenes* claimed 'nearly ninety'.
27. See discussion in Brown (1949) p 29 and p 31 for 'canonised'. The Academy's rejection of Diogenes is credited for his elevation by the Stoics. Pseudo-Lucian *Makrobioi* 2.18-22.
28. Epicurus *Letter to Menoeceus* for nature's mirror. Lucretius preserved much of Epicurus' doctrine in his epic poem *On the Nature of Things*. The 'symmetry' argument was supposed to take away the fear of death.
29. Plato *Phaedo* 117e-118a.
30. See discussion in Griffin (1986) p 199 for reference to Socrates' alleged last words in Plato's *Phaedo*.
31. Plutarch *Moralia* 607f or *On Exile* 17, translation from the Loeb Classical Library edition, Vol. VII, 1959.
32. Quoting S Kreis (2000) *Lectures on Ancient and Medieval European History, Lecture 9, From Polis to Cosmopolis: Alexander the Great and the Hellenistic World, 323-30 B.C.*, updated 2010.
33. Plutarch *The Younger Cato* 68.2 and 70.1 for Cato's reading of Plato's *Phaedo*.
34. Plutarch *Cato* 72.2.
35. Plutarch *Demosthenes* 29.3 translation from the Loeb Classical Library edition Vol. VII, 1919.
36. Plutarch *Demosthenes* 30.5-6. Kebric (1977) p 23 footnote 30 for possible origins with Duris.
37. Lucian *Demosthenes: An Encomium* 31-32 translation by HW and FG Fowler, Clarendon Press, 1905.

38. Diogenes Laertius *Aristotle* 8, translation from the Loeb Classical Library edition, 1925, and *Aristotle* 7 for his death by aconite. Chroust (1970) p 650 footnote 90 for the alternative traditions. Eurymedon (or Demophilus) had tried to associate Aristotle's encomium (or hymn) to Hermias with impiety for casting Virtue as a goddess and for the inscription on his statue at Delphi; Diogenes Laertius *Aristotle* 5-6.

39. Suetonius *Caesar* 82.2 and Plutarch *Caesar* 66.9. *Kai su* is more convincingly a threatening accusation than a philosophical lament. Ovid *Metamorphoses* book 15 lines 794-797 for 'upheavals'.

40. The existing popular line of Shakespeare appeared in Richard Fede's Latin play *Caesar Interfectus* of 1582 and *The True Tragedie of Richard Duke of Yorke & co* of 1595, a source work for *Henry VI, Part 3*. See discussion in Malone *The Works of William Shakespeare,* Chapman and Hall, London, 1866, p 648.

41. The words read 'Good friend for Jesus' sake forbeare, To dig the dust enclosed here. Blessed be the man that spares these stones, And cursed be he that moves my bones.'

42. Kaufman (1932) p 165 for Asinius Pollio's role as a defence lawyer in accusations of poisoning.

43. Discussion in Wright (1995) and also Roller (1997) pp 109-130. A fulsome account of the death is Plutarch *Cicero* 46.3-5. For the proscriptions see Cassius Dio 47.8.4.

44. Cicero *Second Philippic* 12.

45. Cicero *Ad Familiares* 10.28.

46. For Callisthenes' death see Lane Fox (1980) chapter 3, footnote 15. For Pyrrhus' death see Hornblower (1981) citations p 248, Plutarch *Pyrrhus* 34, Pausanias 1.13.8 gave two accounts; Hieronymus provided another derivative.

47. Livy claimed both hands were cut off. Appian, Cassius Dio and Valerius Maximus claimed just one.

48. Cassius Dio 47.8.4.

49. Seneca the Elder recorded that Cicero's death was a popular oratory topic.

50. Plutarch *Cicero* 46.3-5.

51. For Valerian's death see Lactantius *De Mortibus Persecutorum* 5; Plutarch *Gaius Gracchus* 17 for reports of Gracchus' death.

52. Aristophanes *Frogs* 116-26.

53. The nature of Socrates' poison has been disputed since the publication of Johannes Weepers' treatise *Cicutae aquaticae historia et noxae,* Basel, 1679. See full discussion in Brickhouse-Smith (2001). Full paper of the authors titled *Hemlock Poisoning and the Death of Socrates: Did Plato Tell the Truth?* can be read in the *Journal of the International Plato Society,* State University of New York at Buffalo.

54. Theophrastus *Enquiry into Plants* 9.16.8.

55. Plutarch *Phocion* 36.3-4. The executioner refused to 'bruise' more hemlock unless he paid 12 drachmas. Blackwell (1999) p 63 for discussion of Phocion's career. Aelian 11.9 for Phocion's gift from Alexander.

56. Tacitus 15.60-62.

57. Following Collins (2008) p 43 using Plato *Laws* 11.933a as examples.

58. Collins (2008) p 134.

59. Strabo 10.5.6, see full discussion in Griffin (1986) p 192.

60. Theophrastus *Enquiry into Plants* 9.16.2 for aconite and 9.11.5-6 for strychnine, referenced in Engels (1978) pp 224-228 although this apparently refers to the non-lethal and less bitter variety. See Kaufman (1932) p 164 for discussion about masking poison in wine and Juvenal 1.69-70 and 6.663

61. Ovid *Metamorphoses* 7:404-424 where Medea attempted to poison Theseus with an aconite mix.

62. Full story in Ogden (2001) p 169; Ovid *Metamorphoses* 7.406 ff and Pliny 27.4 for the link to Cerberus and Heracles.

63. Quoting D Feeny in the Introduction XIX to Ovid's *Metamorphoses,* Penguin Classics edition, 2004. Whilst the charge against Ovid is unknown, it seems his *Ars Amatoria, The Art of Love,* offended the conservative Augustus.

64. Mayor (2003) p 72 for 'spear poison'. In Latin *strychnos* (the root of strychnine) – 'a king of nightshade' – became the generic word for plants with similar effects. Pliny 21.177-182 and Celsus stated that what the Greeks knew as *strychnos* (acrid) was known as *solanum* by the Romans.

65. Hutchinson (1997) p 314, Mayor (2003) p 41 and Luch (2009) p 2.

66. The compact Scythian bow was so-called due to its double-curved shape, reminiscent of a heart. Discussion of its effectiveness in Snodgrass (1967) p 82. The arrows were most likely held in the draw-hand for rapid horseback firing.

67. Collins (2008) p 30 and Cilliers-Retief (2000) p 90 for the *rhizomotoi*.

68. Homer *Odyssey* 1.300-310. Helen's actions discussed in Collins (2008) p 144 quoting Homer *Odyssey* 4.230.

69. Diodorus 17.103.7-8 and Curtius 9.8.22. Ptolemy suffered the consequences and allegedly

nearly died before an antidote was found. Discussion of the *Laws of Manu* in Mayor (2003) p 91. Strabo 15.2.5-7 for a description of the snakes and their effects in India.

70. Diodorus 17.90.5-6 and 17.103.5 for the venomous snakes and the preparation of poison, and quoting 19.33.2-4.
71. Blyth (1906) p 573.
72. Diodorus 17.5.6.
73. Hesiod *Work and Days* 342, Photius *Epitome* 72 of Ctesias' *Persica,* 29; Plutarch *Artaxerxes* 19 for Parysatis' poisoning of Stateira.
74. The list of assassinations discussed in Bosworth-Baynham (2000) p 53; Anson (2013) pp 80-81 for a list of the Argead kings who died in court intrigues.
75. Pausanias 9.7.2 for the allegation of poison at the death of Alexander IV and Heracles.
76. Green (1970) p 259.
77. Green (1970) p 260.
78. See Atkinson-Yardley (2009) pp 148-149 and Atkinson (2009) pp 28-46 for a useful summary of the theories propounded to date on a natural death. Renault (1975) pp 228-230.
79. A mule or ass's hoof according to Plutarch 77.4, Pliny 30.149, Vitruvius 8.3.16; Justin 12.14; Pausanias 8.17-18; the *Romance* 3.31 on the other hand claimed lead inside an iron container was used; it made no mention of Aristotle. The *Metz Epitome* stated that Antipater 'prepared some poison in a small iron box. This he locked within an ass's hoof with an iron clasp, that the virulence of the poison might be contained.'
80. Lucian *Dialogues of the Dead* 13. The Lethe was one of the five rivers of Hades, also referred to as *Ameles potamos*, the river of oblivion (the broad translation of *lethe*). Orphic mythology demanded the dead drink not from Lethe (Forgetfulness) but from the pool of Mnemosyne (Memory). Author's interpretation – Lethe water as a cure for Aristotelian 'Goods' (plural) rather than 'Good' and here seen as a sarcastic play upon the poison Aristotle allegedly furnished to Cassander from the Styx...thus he refers to hellebore in the previous sentence as it was a known purge and assisted in vomiting to empty the stomach of poison.
81. Plutarch 77.5, Aelian 12.64 claimed thirty days unburied; Aelian 13.30 for Olympias' grief upon hearing it.
82. Curtius 10.9-13; Aelian 12.64.
83. Blyth (1906) p 573.
84. Milne (1968) pp 256-6 argued for strychnine poisoning; Engels (1978) pp 224-228. See Atkinson-Yardley (2009) pp 232-233 and Atkinson (2009) p 26 for the coma theory. Curtius 10.9.1, Plutarch 77.5 and Aelian 12.64 for references to the corpse remaining fresh for days (or a month – Aelian) after being pronounced dead. The clinicopathological protocol was established by Dr DW Oldach in the *New England Journal of Medicine* 338, no. 24 (11 June 1998), pp 1764-1769.
85. Schep-Slaughter-Vale-Wheatley (2013) p 4.
86. Plutarch 41.7. For antimony use see U Arndt *The Philosopher's Magnet – Alchemic Transmutation of Antimony*, first published in the magazine *Paracelsus*, November 2005, pp 12-17.
87. Schep-Slaughter-Vale-Wheatley (2013) p 5.
88. Schep-Slaughter-Vale-Wheatley (2013) p 4.
89. Virgil *Aeneid* 1.657-694, translation by Theodore C Williams, Houghton Mifflin Co. Boston, 1910.
90. Diodorus 21.16.4-6.
91. Kaufman (1932) p 166 for the *Twelve Tables*.
92. Full discussion of the early tradition of poison in Kaufman (1932) pp 156-157.
93. See Kaufman (1932) pp 157-158 for full discussion.
94. Kaufman (1932) pp 158-159 for examples.
95. Many references appeared in Pliny 2.197; at 20.197-199 he recorded suicide by opium; 21.177-182, the use of deadly nightshade; 25.35-27 henbane, 25.47-61 hellebore; 16.50-51 and the effects of yew; 22.92-99 toxic mushrooms; 24.93-96 Spanish fly; 29.66-68 snake venom; various other references are made to spiders and other venomous animals, see Kaufman (1932) pp 161-164 for full details. Pliny's vivid description of hemlock can be found at 25.151-154.
96. Discussed in Cillers-Retief (2000) p 89.
97. See Kaufman (1932) p 166 for Sulla's law and its ramifications and also Cilliers-Retief (2000) p 89 referring to Tacitus 1.5.2, 4.10.2, 6.33.1, 12.66.3.
98. Appian *Mithridatic Wars* 16.3. For Crateus see Cillers-Retief (2000) p 90.
99. Plutarch *Demetrius* 20.3-4. Translation from the Loeb Classical Library edition, 1920.
100. Hojte (2009) pp 121-130. Snodgrass (1967) p 129 for Mithridates' battle technique involving the Macedonian *sarissa*-type phalanx. The antidote was also referred to as *mithridatacum*.
101. Cassius Dio 37.13, also Appian *Civil Wars* 16.111. Full discussion of Pompey's *imitatio Alexandri* in Hojte (2009) pp 121-130.

102. For his alternative death Cassius Dio 37.13.

103. See Cilliers-Retief (2000) p 89.

104. See Kaufman (1932) p 156 for discussion on drug manufacture in Rome.

105. Tacitus 12.66 and 13.15 recorded that Martina was suspected of poisoning Germanicus. Citing the observation made in Atkinson (2009) p 239 on *venenum*. Cilliers-Retief (2000) p 89 for the possible roots of *venenum*.

106. Suetonius *Nero* 33.3-34. For Locusta, Suetonius *Nero* 33 and 47.

107. Discussion of the tasters' roles in Kaufman (1932) p 160.

108. Suetonius *Claudius* 44.

109. Suetonius *Claudius* 44.3.

110. Tacitus 12.66-67.

111. For Iolaos as official cupbearer see *Romance* 3.31.4, *Metz Epitome* 96, Arrian, 7.27.2 and Plutarch 74.2. For Ptolemy's role as 'taster' see Robinson (1953) p 78 for full citation from Chares.

112. *Metz Epitome* 99, translated from Heckel-Yardley (2004) pp 218-289; also *Romance* 3.32.

113. Aurelius *Meditations* 10.27.

114. Translates loosely as 'what an artist dies in me'; Nero's alleged last words.

115. Suetonius *Nero* 33, confirmed by Cassius Dio 60.35 who stated Nero's quip meant that once Claudius had eaten the mushrooms he joined the gods.

116. Suetonius *Claudius* 44 claimed he was in Rome whereas Tacitus 12.66 stated he was in Sinuessa. His death is additionally recorded by Josephus 20.148 and 151, Cassius Dio 60.34, Pliny 2.92, 11.189, 22.92 citing Halotus, his taster, Xenophon, his doctor and Locusta as the assassins.

117. Suetonius *Nero* 1 for the origins of Nero's name. Suetonius *Nero* 19 for his personal phalanx. Curtius 10.10.18-19.

118. Suetonius *Nero* 35-39 and for his planned poisoning of the Senate, Suetonius *Nero* 43.

119. Suetonius *Nero* 49.1.

120. Alexander died either on June 10th or 11th. If the 10th, it is likely, from the body's continued state of preservation, that physical death took place hours after it was announced. Modern astronomical calculations suggest the 11th rather than the 10th; full chronological discussion in Depuydt (1997) pp 117-135, Hannah (2005) p 95, Stoneman (1991) p 159. For Nero's death on the 11th see C Murison, *Galba, Otho and Vitellius: Careers and Controversies*. Spudasmata 52. Hildesheim: Georg Olms, 1993, p 6.

121. The goblets were smashed in a rage when Nero heard of the defection of his northern Italian legions. The goblets were termed 'Homeric' as they were engraved with scenes from Homer's poems. For recent reinterpretations of Nero's exclamations see Pitcher (2009) pp 50-51.

122. Suetonius *Nero* 47. For Seneca and Agrippina, *Nero* 52 and 38.

123. July and August, after Julius Caesar and Caesar Augustus.

124. Suetonius *Nero* 55.

125. *Historia Augusta, Life of Commodus* 10.8.

126. Nietzsche (1974) pp 137-8.

127. Ovid *Metamorphoses* book 15 lines 87-90.

128. Pythagoras allegedly forbade the consumption of kidney beans. The Egyptians did the same relating its shape to the male testicle. In fact there may have been sound medical grounds for the advice or it may have been religious and to do with transmigration: 'eating broad beans and gnawing on the head of one's parents are one and the same'; Grmek (1989) p 218 and pp 210-244. *On the Eating of Flesh* appears in Plutarch *Moralia*.

129. Lucian *The Double Indictment* 5.

130. Plutarch *Demosthenes* 29-30.

131. Lucian *Demosthenes: an Encomium* 15.

132. Pliny 10.3.6-8; Aelian *De Natura Animalium* 7.16, Valerius Maximus *Factorum et Dictorum Memorabilium* 9.12.2 also has a version in which blinded by the sun's reflection from Aeschylus' bald head, the eagle was dazzled into dropping the tortoise. For his part at Marathon, see Lattimore (1953) pp 1-3. Aeschylus' reference to Homer is at Athenaeus 8.347e.

133. Plutarch *Marcellus* 19.4-6. The text describes how Archimedes defied arrest telling the soldier he was in the middle of a mathematical problem. These were Archimedes' last words. The reply has since evolved.

134. Plutarch *Pyrrhus* 8.1. Translation from the Loeb Classical Library edition, 1920. Plutarch *Pyrrhus* 1.4 and Justin 17.3.4 for Pyrrhus' descent.

135. See discussion in Green (2007) pp 46-48. Pyrrhus allegedly exclaimed 'another such victory over the Romans and we are ruined!' after the battle at Asculum; Plutarch *Pyrrhus* 17.4 and 21.4 ff. The ancient Greeks would have termed a self-defeating victory 'Cadmean' after Cadmus' loss of all his companions when trying to slay the water-dragon.

136. Plutarch *Pyrrhus* 5.3-7. Pyrrhus always wore a helmet with goat horns protruding.

137. Plutarch *Pyrrhus* 34 for Pyrrhus' death in Argos and Pausanias 2.22.8-25.8 for the Homeric story

attached to the tomb of Licymnius. He was the illegitimate son of Electryon, the son of Perseus and Andromeda.

138. Plutarch *Demosthenes* 28.4, Arrian *Events After Alexander* 1.13 for the cutting out of Hyperides' tongue and Plutarch *Moralia* 849f or *Life of the Ten Attic Orators* 9, *Hyperides*, for linking that to his proposing honours for Iolaos.

139. A claim possibly inspired by or backed up by Plutarch 28.4 in which Alexander claimed Anaxarchus wanted to see a row of satrap heads on the dinner table, rather than humble fare. Diogenes Laertius 9.59 and Valerius Maximus 3.3.ext 4 for the 'tale' of his biting off his own tongue.

140. Diogenes Laertius *Anaxarchus* 9.2-3. Also *Zeno* 9.5. According to Hermippus he was crushed with mortar and pestle but the common tradition was that Zeno bit off his own tongue and spat it at 'the tyrant'.

141. Borza (1995) pp 175-176 for discussion of the Eudaimonic school of philosophy.

142. Quoting Borza-Palagia (2007) p 108.

143. Plutarch 75.5.

144. Ovid *Metamorphoses* 9:159-210.

145. Herodotus 1.204-216. The Massagetae was a tribe with close links to the Scythians. See Arrian 4.11.9 and 5.4.5 for Cyrus' death at the hands of the Scythians. Also referred to in Lucian's *Charon of the Observers* 13.

146. Xenophon *Cyropaedia* 1.7.9. For Ctesias see Photius *Epitome* 72 of Ctesias' *Persika*, in which Cyrus dies in battle against the Derbices of Hyrcania. Also Cook (1983) p 21 for the Cunaxa references.

147. Diodorus 2.32.4, discussed in Grafton (1990) p 9. Herodotus 1.214 for Cyrus' death.

148. Xenophon *Agesilaus* as proposed by Brown (1949) p16. For Alcibiades see Xenophon *Hellenika* 11.1.25.

149. As suggested by Pitcher (2009) p 123.

150. Pausanias 1.23.9 claimed Thucydides was murdered on his return to Athens, which, due to his exile, must have been after the city's surrender in 404 BCE. However evidence exists that he lived past 397 BCE. Plutarch claimed he was interred in Cimon's family vault; Plutarch *Cimon* 4.1.

151. Plutarch *Camillus* 19 for the date of Marathon; Plutarch dedicated the paragraph to how unlucky the month of Thargelion was for 'barbarians'.

152. Plutarch *Antony* 4 for his emulation of Heracles, and for Commodus see Cassius Dio 72.15.5 and *Historia Augusta, Commodus* 9. For a summary of the Roman emulation of Alexander, see discussion in De Polignac (1999) p 8.

153. *Historia Augusta, Commodus* 17; Cassius Dio 72.22.

154. The Return of the Heracleidae is also known as the Dorian invasion, when the scattered sons of Heracles come home to claim their rightful ancestral lands, including Sparta; see Herodotus 8.73, Pausanias book 1.32, 1.41, 2.13 , 2.18, 3.1, 4.3.3, 4.30.1; Euripides *Herakleidai* 6.52 and 9.27.

155. Riedweg (2002) p 161.

156. The Plato reference from Plutarch *Moralia* 718b-720c.

157. Theopompus proposed Pythagorean philosophy was not more than an attempt at tyranny, FGrHist 115 F73, also Diogenes Laertius *Pythagoras* 8.39, discussed in Riedweg (2002) pp 101-108. See further discussion in Riedweg (2002) Preface, p X, quoting Russell (1946) p 60.

158. See discussion in J Chadwick and WN Mann *The Medical Works of Hippocrates*, Blackwell Scientific Publications, Oxford, 1950 pp 1-3.

159. Hippocrates *Aphorismoi* 1.1 and *Prognosis* 7.

160. Pliny 26.7. Discussion of Asclepiades rhetorical career in E Rawlinson *The Life and Death of Asclepiades of Bithynia, Classical Quarterly* 32 (ii), 1982, pp 358-370. Plato described Hippocrates as an Asclepiad in his *Protagoras* suggesting he was a priest of the Asclepion of Kos.

161. Diogenes Laertius *Empedocles* 5 and 8.69-71. See discussion in Gottschalk (1980) pp 14-20.

162. Suetonius *Nero* 33-34. For *mithridatium* see Cilliers-Retief (2000) p 90 and Mayor (2003) p 150 ff. *Hyppokras* was a spiced wine traditionally credited to Hippocrates.

163. Pliny described how *mithridatium* actually contained the blood of ducks that had been fed multiple poisons, also cited by Aulus Gellius 17.16. Agrippina took antidotes and Nero, despite repeated attempts, was unable to poison her; see Suetonius *Nero* 33-34. For the Roman-expanded recipe for *mithridatium* see Celsus *De Medicina* V.23.3, Cassius Dio 37.13. Galen prepared *mithridatium* for Nero and Marcus Aurelius too.

164. Two versions of the origination of the expression exist. The etymologist C Ammer traced it back to the Latin expression *cum grano salis*, citing Pliny's description of *mithridatium* in *Natural History*, 29.24-25, which first used the expression; the alternative tradition traces its first use in the English language back to 1647, see *Oxford English Dictionary*, as simply the flavouring for bland dishes.

165. For the punishment of the gods at the Styx see Hesiod *Theogonia* 775-819.
166. Pausanias 8.17-19 and quoting from Mayor (2010) p 4.
167. Full discussion of the waters of the Styx at Nonacris in Mayor (2010) pp 1-29. Modern theory suggests that if indeed this was its source, the effects came from naturally occurring corrosive acids, lethal minerals from (non-evident) ancient mining close by, toxic salts from the venting of a thermo-active fault-line, or the seasonal flooding and washing-in of local toxic plants. A case has also been made for the presence of the killer bacteria Calicheamicin occurring in *Micromonospora echinospor* thought to be present in adjacent limestone and soils. Discussed in Mayor (2010) pp 9-13.
168. Borza (1987) for discussion of malaria in Alexander's army.
169. Atkinson (2009) pp 35-36 for discussion of mind-altering drugs. For his paranoia and fears Plutarch 74.2-5, translation from the Loeb Classical Library edition, 1919 and Plutarch 73.7-9. Arrian 7.24-25 described that Alexander and his friend, whilst playing ball, beheld a man seated on the king's throne, in silence, wearing the royal diadem and robes. He claimed the god Serapis had come to him and bid him sit on the throne. Alexander had him 'put out of the way' as advised by his seers. The whole episode sounds remarkably like the Babylonian ritual of the substitute king; following Oates (1979) p 140, Green (1974) p 472.
170. For paranoia see Suetonius *Caligula* 56-57 and on his excesses 52,54,58; for paranoia, see Suetonius *Nero* 46 and for excesses *Nero* 42.
171. Bevan (1913) p 32 and quoting Adams (1996) p 33 on 'political freedom'.
172. See discussion Bury-Barber-Bevan-Tarn (1923) p 26. The name Stoicism comes from the *Stoa Poikile* or 'painted arch' from where Zeno commenced teaching in the Agora at Athens. That the early successors declared themselves Stoics was observed by Murray (1915) p 47. Long (1986) p 18 for explanation of *logos*.
173. Following Tarn (1927) p 325 and the comment that the school of Plato (after 266 BCE when Arcesilaus centred Platonism on Scepticism) became a 'parasite upon the Stoa'. Long (1986) p 235 for the fate of the Stoa.
174. See discussion on Polybius' use of *tyche* in Brouwer (2011) pp 111-132 and McGing (2010) pp 195-201.
175. Cicero's references to Panaetius can be found in his *De Finibus* 4.9 in the *De Officiis* 1.26, *Laelius De Amicitia* 27; *Pro Murena* 31; *De Natura Deorum-Velleius* 1.13.3.
176. Cicero *De Officiis* 1.35 for his thoughts on moral duty.
177. Brown (1949) for the career of Crates and his links to both philosophical schools.
178. Photius (anonymous) *Life of Pythagoras* 11.
179. Macaulay (1828).
180. Quoting from Brown (1950) p 136.
181. Quoting Whitehead (1929) p 63 and Homer *Odyssey* 1.351-2. Plato's borrowings from Zoroaster were parodied by the Epicurean Colotes; discussed in Momigliano (1977) pp 18-19.
182. Pitcher (2009) p vii.
183. Arrian excerpts from 1.1.1-3. Here *basileia* meaning 'kingship' not queen, differentiated in Greek by a diacritic (not used here).
184. Arrian 7.5.2-3.
185. Lucian *How to Write History* 2.40-41 noted that many people believed Homer's account of Achilles' deeds as he wrote long after the hero's death and hence had no agenda as a historian. Arrian stated something similar in his opening page of his Alexander biography.
186. Lucian and Arrian were broadly contemporaries. However Lucian outlived him and made reference to Arrian's works with which he was undoubtedly familiar. We propose Arrian's opening statement about Ptolemy's may in fact mirror Ptolemy's opening, which Lucian may also have read.
187. Both Plato and Pythagoras objected to suicide except in *exceptional* circumstances. See Plato *Phaedo* 61d-e; Pythagoras prohibited suicide; see discussion in Riedweg (2005) p 110.
188. Discussed in Long (1986) p 206. Also see Cicero *De Finibus* 3.60-61. The Moirae were the three parthenogenous daughters of the Goddess of Necessity: Clotho, Lacheis and Atropus. Under the Roman Stoic doctrine, the meanings of fate and fortune became hardly discernible. See discussion in Levene (1993) p 13.
189. Tacitus 6.29; see Griffin (1986) p 193 for full discussion on Tiberian treatment of suicide.
190. Following Griffin (1986) p 193 and Pliny 2.5.27 and 7.5.190.
191. Discussed in Magee (1998) p 45.
192. From the Stoic term *kathekon*; Cicero ambiguously translated it as *officium*. For discussion see Shipley (2000) pp 188-190. Zeno first developed the term along with *apatheia*, from which we derive 'apathy'. The teachings of Epictetus were preserved by Arrian in the *Discourses* and *Encheiridion Epictetou*.
193. Plato *Phaedo* 67a-68b.

194. *Metz Epitome* 97 for the allegation that Onesicritus avoided naming guests at Medius' party. This might be a later addition or it might have originated with the author of the *Pamphlet*.

195. Justin replaced the allusion to 'games' with a wholly darker premonition on the bloodshed and slaughter that would follow, but this could have originated with Trogus, not Cleitarchus.

196. Xenophon *Cyropaedia*, translation by HG Dakyns, Epilogue, section 2.

197. Lucian *How to Write History* 40-41, translation from Brown (1949) p 5. See discussion of the authenticity of this extract in Brown (1949) p 2.

198. Homer *Iliad* 2.705 for his slaying by Hector. Protesilaus was Thessalian and the first Greek to step ashore at Troy. His wife negotiated his leave to visit her from Hades for a few hours. This was referred to in many later works, for example Lucian's *Charon of the Observers* 1 and Ovid's *Heroides* 13.

199. Thucydides 2.87 and Plutarch *Moralia* 333c (*On the Fortune or Virtue of Alexander*).

200. Onesicritus' dialogue with the Indian sages preserved in Strabo 15.1.63-65; discussion of question 6 in Brown (1949) p 47.

201. Plutarch *Pyrrhus* 9-10 for the story of Oedipus and his advice to his sons. Taken from Euripides' *Phoenissea* line 68. Translation from the Loeb Classical Library edition, 1920. Oedipus had invited his sons, unwittingly fathered with his own mother, to fight for the kingdom to the death, which they were to do.

202. Plutarch *Pyrrhus* 3.3.

203. Justin 12.15-16.

204. Arrian *Enkheiridion Epiktetou* 5, *Opinions Disturb*.

205. Lucian *A True History* 2.18.

206. See Baynham (1995) p 105 for a discussion of *tyche* important in Hellenistic biography. Demetrius of Phalerum *Peri Tyches* 29.21 1-7 discussed in Bosworth-Baynham (2000) p 295. Also Billows' discussion on Polybius and *tyche* referenced in Bosworth-Baynham (2000) pp 294-295.

207. See Atkinson (2009) pp 161-162 for a useful summary of Curtius' use of *pothos* and other motifs of 'common desire'.

208. Thucydides 6.24.3, Pindar *Pythian* 4.184-5. *Pothos* is a *hapax* in Thucydides and certainly conspicuous. The term appeared often in Herodotus. See discussion in Hornblower (2004) p xv, and p 454.

209. Theophrastus *Enquiry into Plants* 6.8.3.

8

WILLS AND COVENANTS IN THE CLASSICAL MIND

Would kings, dictators and statesmen have used Wills in the classical world to assure successions, pass down estates and document their last wishes?

Is the claim that Alexander made a Will at Babylon supportable in the context of the social practice, succession precedents and legislation of the time?

We review the development of what we now refer to as the Last Will and Testament, and look at infamous examples of their manipulations, implementations and the world-changing repercussions in the classical world.

'Thus it is an error of men who are not strictly upright to seize upon something that seems to be expedient and straightaway to dissociate that from the question of moral right. To this error the assassin's dagger, the poisoned cup, the forged Wills owe their origin; this gives rise to theft, embezzlement of public funds, exploitation and plundering of officials and citizens; this engenders also lust for excessive wealth, for despotic power and finally for making oneself king even in the midst of a free people.'[1]

Cicero *De Officiis*

'All will be well but in case anything should happen, I make these dispositions'; thus began typical Greek Wills in the age of Alexander, and so opened the Wills of both Aristotle and Theophrastus, legends of the Lyceum in Athens and contemporaries of the campaigning king.[2] These were not the hastily penned bequests of men dying unexpectedly, but highlighted a judicious respect for mortality in a legal system that recognised trusts, inheritances and estate planning.

Aristotle's Will was substantial enough to provide Anton Chroust with sufficient detail for a treatise on Greek estate law.[3] A product of the Peripatetic School, Aristotle's *diatheke* (Greek: διαθηκη), more literally a 'covenant' denoting a formal and legally binding declaration of benefits given by one party to another, did not have room for rhetoric; the testament was precise, practical, and provided for multiple scenarios. We have many other examples that demonstrate the intricacy, ceremony and sophistication that Wills had attained by the 4th century BCE, along with the challenges and frauds that accompanied them.

Hipponax, an Athenian doctor, noted the arrangements of his patient, Lycophron, as his death approached: 'He made his Will and called in his friends to witness it, and one must hope there can be no doubt about the validity, the signets attached etc, for otherwise the heirs may find themselves in a pretty lawsuit.'[4] Lycophron's Will pledged his young wife and the guardianship of his daughter to a trusted bachelor friend, and it included instructions for his tomb with financial legacies to other named associates; lastly, three reliable friends were appointed as the executors. The full title of the testator – the person making the Will – was Lycophron the Marathonian, for Athenian legal documents recorded the *demos* – the residential district of the interested parties (each *deme* had its own sanctuary and founding deity) – alongside the *onoma*, a personal name, and the father's name, the *patronymikon*.[5] Good examples would be Alcibiades Cleiniou Scambonides – Alcibiades, son of Cleinias from the *deme* of Scambonidai – and Demosthenes, son of Demosthenes, of the deme Paiania.[6] In the case of a *metoikos,* a foreign resident, the place of birth was required.

The description of Lycophron's funeral rites made it clear that the formalities demanded were part of a highly ritualised event. The Will was replete with litigious connotations suggesting an attention to detail in accordance with the demands of (the still not fully deciphered) Athenian legislation.[7] By the time the Athenian Constitution had been drafted, the mechanism of passing an estate had been formalised into what we term today the Last Will and Testament, derived from the Roman *testamentum*. Not *all* Greek states permitted the individual such latitude, yet the use of Wills was undeniably widespread in the developing Hellenic world.

So, would the type of Will that survives in the various redactions of Alexander's *Romance* and in the *Metz Epitome* have truly been the mechanism Alexander would have used to assure a clean succession? The answer lies in part in our analysis of the Macedonian king and in our interpretation of the authority a Will could have carried in the unique position Alexander found himself at Babylon in June 323 BCE.[8] But how much of the original was transmitted faithfully by the author of the *Pamphlet* is another question altogether.[9]

THE DEVELOPMENT OF THE GREEK *DIATHEKE*

Wills did not originate in Classical Greece. Bronze Age texts preserve the death-covenants of northern Mesopotamia preceding the neo-Babylonian period (626-539 BCE), where tablets and other inscriptions reveal the double estate share due to the eldest sons.[10] Older still are the written testaments of Egypt. Sir Flinders Petrie, the 'father of Egyptology' who excavated at Oxyrhynchus, Tanis, Hawara and Abydus and into mummy cases at Gurob, discovered their oldest recorded forerunners dating back 4,500 years; they have been described as 'so curiously modern in form that it might almost be granted probate today'.[11] The Greeks adopted much from Egypt and that may well include the architecture of legal inheritance, and its development in Hellas is evidenced.

Hesiod composed his highly valued *Works and Days* sometime around 700 BCE (though dating is speculative); it was a didactic poem that captured a dispute with his brother, Perses, over his squandering of a disproportionate share of their father's estate that had avowedly been left to them equally in his Will, and the bribed judges who ruled against Hesiod were attacked through his book. The 800 lines of agricultural instruction, the 'first that spoke to men of his own time' (poetry usually recalled ages past), no doubt boosted Hesiod's career as a professional rhapsode, and may have prompted, in the circumstances, his aphorism, 'the half is greater than the whole'.[12]

According to Plutarch, a Spartan ephor, Epitadeus, proposed the Lycurgan law, *rhetra* (legend dates it to 885 BCE), of leaving all possessions to one's son were outdated so that new Will bequests were needed as well as lifetime gifts; Lacedaemonian inheritance was further complicated by land lots that could not be bought or sold in life or passed from father to son, but which could be bequeathed at death to *anyone*, claimed Aristotle in a hostile appraisal of its constitution which claimed that two-fifths of the state was owned by women as a result.[13] In Athens, Solon began the articulation of estate planning in his set of laws constituting the *seisachtheia* (literally: 'shaking off the burdens'), enacted in 594/3 BCE once he had been appointed archon and *diallaktes* (arbiter on social issues).

Although Solon was praised for introducing Wills, the law under the Draconian Statutes still firmly favoured the Athenian nobility, a class that dominated in Attica longer than in other regions of Greece. Solon's own father had 'impaired his estate in sundry benevolent charities', prompting him to apparently declare: 'Wealth I desire to have; but wrongfully to get it, I do not wish. Justice, even if slow, is sure.'[14] However, by 500 BCE, in line with Cleisthenes' transformation of the Areopagus – the aristocratic judicial court – into a more citizen-represented boule (council), laws on intestacy evolved: inheritance rules relating to orphans and heiresses, property settlement, donations and adoption (*eispoiesis*) were debated, refined, and inevitably, contested.[15]

And here, most relevantly, there is plentiful evidence that testators were fearful their Wills could be hidden, manipulated, or subverted in some way, and this was illustrated by the efforts they made to have them recorded and authenticated. One example is Callias, who, returning from his questionably successful mission to Susa to broker a peace with Persia (sometime in the 440s BCE) and fearing he would be cut off by a 'wicked conspiracy' in his absence, is said to have made an open declaration of his Will before the popular assembly at Athens.[16] Subversions were facilitated when the testator declared a Will before witnesses as a *memorium,* a verbal recitation without committing it into writing. This required something of an honour-based code, like the timeworn tradition of vocal *inter vivos,* or the auricular living covenants and the *nuncupative* testaments of Rome. Confusingly, a commercial covenant was also referred to as a *diatheke,* thus an assignment or contract, the very word used to denote what we now term a Will.

The latitude for challenging estate-related bequests narrowed when Solon introduced documented testaments that would be pronounced before several *ephetai* (judges) and members of the *dikasteria,* jurors of the popular court; according to Diogenes Laertius, Solon's own Will ('injunctions to his relations') requested that his ashes be scattered around his birthplace at Salamis.[17] In Athens the practice of authentication involved depositing Wills at public offices, signed and sealed in the presence of magistrates who were very often at their original drafting; in more notable cases, the city archons were present too. The procedures epitomise Athens' more general shift from orality to the increasing use of writing.[18]

This development unfortunately also locked in Solon's less attractive legislation, some of it termed 'peculiar' by Plutarch, the *epidikasi*, for example, a procedure that oversaw the law of the *epikleroi*. These Athenian heiresses, daughters of fathers with no male heirs, were required to marry their father's closest male relative (agnate) to keep property within the family, with sex provided to her thrice per month as a show of esteem. The ruling often led to the *epikleros* residing in a household with an existing wife, and it led to further conflict where the heiress daughter was already married herself.[19] Married daughters had no claims against an estate if not named in the Will; in the event of the father's intestacy, unmarried daughters had no claim against their father's estate except for dowry and maintenance until they wed, at which point their estate went with them to the new male husband. If a daughter subsequently gave birth to a son by the agnate male relative, he would ultimately acquire that part of the estate.[20]

Diogenes Laertius stated that it was Ariston of Kea who penned the *Wills of the Peripatetic Scholars*, testaments whose legal structure was motivated by the desire to maintain the private ownership of the philosophical school itself, including its all-important library. It is likely that all recensions of the Peripatetics' Wills come from this collection. Apart from those of Aristotle and Theophrastus, the list included the testaments of their successors: Strato of Lampsacus (ca. 335-269 BCE), Arcesilaus (ca. 316/5-241 BCE), Lyco (ca. 299-225 BCE) and Epicurus (ca. 341-270 BCE).[21]

Epicurus was born just fifteen years after Alexander and he founded the eponymously named philosophical movement following the Macedonian king's death. Although only a few fragments of his treatises survived, we know his family was dislodged by the Successor Wars and moved from Samos to Colophon, a city eventually destroyed by Lysimachus. Epicurus, for whom 'pleasure was the beginning and end of a blessed life', finally died in Athens aged seventy-two and his sophisticated Will is another lesson in estate planning: he set up a Lifetime Trust and included a Deed of Gift within it so that his Epicurean school and its iconic 'Garden' would continue to flourish. The Will provided for the future funeral costs of his family and it contained annuities and marriage directions for children of the prominent members of his school.[22]

Arcesilaus, a former pupil of Theophrastus and founder of the Middle Academy which brought scepticism into philosophical debate, attacked the doctrine of the Stoics which claimed that truth is defined by perception alone: *kataleptike phantasis*. In pure Sceptic fashion, Arcesilaus claimed 'to know nothing, not even his own ignorance', and yet he knew how to prepare for death.[23] Three copies of his Will were prepared, one deposited at Athens with friends, another at Eretria, and a third was sent home to a relative, Thaumasias, with a covering letter explaining his rationale:

> I have given Diogenes a copy of my Will to convey to you. For, because I am frequently unwell and have become very infirm, I have thought it right to make a Will, that if anything should happen to me I might not depart with feelings of having done you any injury, who have been so constantly in affection to me.[24]

He died, according to Hermippus, after delirium caused by an excess of wine, an end he purportedly shared with the great Stoic, Chrysippus (ca. 279-204 BCE).[25]

ROME – A TESTAMENT TO THE VULNERABLE *TESTAMENTUM*

Wills played a heavyweight role in the subterfuges of Rome, in some cases directing, or misdirecting, the fate of the empire. In his *Romulus* Plutarch referenced the dying wish of the semi-mythical Larentia (supposedly 7th century BCE) who bequeathed to the people of the city the substantial estate she had herself inherited from a wealthy citizen.[26] Not all were so generous in their dealings; in his voluminous account of the city's rise and fall, Edward Gibbon penned a whole chapter on the intricacies of the Roman testament and one particular extract is worth quoting:

> ... the order of succession is regulated by nature, or at least by the general and permanent reason of the lawgiver: but this order is frequently violated by the arbitrary and partial *wills*, which prolong the dominion of the testator beyond the grave.[27]

Wills existed, then, not only to organise the wealth of a past life, but to direct the path of the future; in the case of Roman law, this ability applied solely to those with *testamentifactio*, the legal capacity to do so, and that meant citizens who were *patresfamilias*, the male family heads. Only women who were widowed and not in the power of a father, or who remained unmarried after the death of their father, could make a Will, and only then with the consent of her *Tutores* (broadly, a Will executor).[28]

Cicero, whose wisdom and warnings to his son heads the chapter, went on to detail a forged Will brought from Greece which purported to be the dying testament of the wealthy Lucius Minucius Basilus (died 43 BCE). The forgers made themselves joint heirs and 'the more easily to procure validity for it' they included as beneficiaries the influential Crassus and the orator Quintus Hortensius (114-50 BCE) who gladly accepted the windfall; this subterfuge took place despite the fact that those who did sign forged testaments were now liable to punishment by the Cornelian Law (*Lex Cornelia testamentaria*) resulting in *deportatio in insulam*, the loss of property and citizenship.[29] Tacitus recorded a similar 'remarkable crime' involving the forged Will of Domitius Balbus: being old, childless and wealthy, his kinsman Valerius Fabianus, along with distinguished accomplices, saw an opportunity to execute his estate in their favour.[30]

In his *Letter to Cornelianus* Pliny mentioned the emperor's injunction to senators then in consultation on a case presiding over a testament in which some of the codicils appeared fraudulent,[31] and Suetonius recorded that Augustus vetoed the law designed to check freedom of speech in Wills, which suggests a tradition of posthumous polemic may have made its way into them.[32] Suetonius also gave us the Wills of Julius Caesar (which reappeared in Pierre Hamon's 16th century adaptation of a genuine Ravenna papyrus),[33] Augustus himself, and more relevantly, the blocked testament of Claudius. Suetonius stated that during Nero's imperium, reforms to Wills were made and 'it was provided that the first two leaves should be presented to the signatories with only the name of the testator written upon them, and that no one who wrote a Will for another should put down a legacy for himself.'[34]

Nevertheless, to fund his megalomania and his new construction projects, Nero incentivised the advocates to pressure individuals 'ungrateful to the emperor' to bequeath their estate to the Privy Purse, often demanding their immediate suicide to set it in motion; even Seneca, his teacher, was implicated in estate-rigging: 'In Rome, he spread his nets to catch the Wills of childless men.'[35] Nero's targets were given proper burials in the *Exitus Illustrium Virorum*, the list of illustrious 'exits', which became popular reading in post-Nero Rome, and one of them, unsurprisingly, was Seneca himself.

The young Octavian, the adopted son of Julius Caesar (after which he assumed the name Gaius Julius Caesar Octavianus, later titled 'Augustus'), exposed the Will of Mark Antony, having impiously extracted it from the Temple of the Vestal Virgins to show a conservative Rome the extent of the triumvir's orientalisation, for Antony had requested burial in Egypt, as Alexander's extant Will demands; in fact Antony was to be buried alongside Alexander in the Mausoleum of Alexandria. His Will was deemed a *testamentum inofficiosum* and Octavian later learned of codicils and the means to amend a testator's last wishes while governing 'a restored republic' that was 'in practice a disguised autocracy', or, in Herodian's view, an aristocracy.[36] Soon to be hailed as 'Augustus', his own Will occupied three scrolls: the first contained funeral directions, another a record of his administration, and the third a troop and treasury summary with directions for future governance. Judging by his *Deeds of the Divine Augustus*, compiled just before he died in the year 14 CE, and which reads like an Achaemenid commemorative inscription, Augustus was obsessed with numbers and accounts.

In its breadth the empire Augustus governed was equal to Alexander's, though the parallel stops there, for the authenticity of his testament has never been called into question. Suetonius described its preparation:

> … he [Augustus] had made a Will in the consulship of Lucius Plancus and Gaius Silius on the third day before the Nones of April, a year and four months before he died, in two note-books, written in part in his own hand and in part in that of his freedmen Polybius and Hilarion. These the Vestal Virgins, with whom they had been deposited, now produced, together with three rolls, which were sealed in the same way. All these were opened and read in the Senate.[37]

The foremost of Augustus' propagandists, Virgil, requested that his *Aeneid* be burned at his own death and he took the precaution of leaving his emperor a quarter of his estate, no doubt having witnessed Augustus' early interest in Mark Antony's last wishes.[38] Luckily, his executors impressed upon the author the importance of changing that literary request, and we are fortunate to inherit Virgil's work.[39]

Herod the Great, the Rome-befriending client-king of Judea (later Syria Palestina) died of natural causes in 4 BCE, and his Will directed that his kingdom be divided amongst his three sons, Archelaus, Herod Antipas and Philip. The three heirs travelled to Rome to petition Augustus to ratify their father's wish. A majority of Jerusalem Jews, however, sent a delegation of their own, asking the emperor to abolish the Herodian dynasty and place the region under direct Roman rule. Their plea was denied; Augustus upheld the dead king's bequest and so there emerged three smaller territories.

The arms of Rome stretched far and wide, and even Britain submitted to its authority on succession. Prasutagus, husband of the rebellious Boudicea of the Iceni (died ca. 61 CE), and who had submitted to (or had been reinstated by) Claudius upon his reinvasion, named the Roman emperor, alongside his own daughters, as a co-inheritor of his kingdom to ensure nominal autonomy. According to Tacitus, although he lived long and prospered under the arrangement, the Will was later ignored, allowing Roman plundering of the kingdom and displacement of the Iceni nobles.[40]

Similarly, the curious Will of Ptolemy VIII *Euergetes* II gifted Cyrenaica to the Roman Republic in the event that he should die without issue; the territory had essentially been placed in a *fidei-commissa*, a Roman trust fund.[41] No doubt this was a deterrent against assassination for an 'unholy' attempt had (allegedly) been made by his brother, prompting *Euergetes* to solicit support from the Senate.[42] On his deathbed his son,

Ptolemy Apion, himself childless, enacted the Will provision which is still preserved in an inscription today, and the province was duly ceded to the Roman Republic.[43] It was somewhat inevitable that the Ptolemies, who followed the Argead tradition of polygamy and the Pharaonic tradition of consanguineous marriage, would be in trouble with internecine dynastic intrigue.

Attalus III of Pergamum followed a similar path with his kingdom in 133 BCE to avert a succession crisis; the Roman *popularis*, Tiberius Gracchus (ca. 160s-133 BCE), gladly accepted the bequest to fund his grain laws. Hellenistic dynasts were choosing Rome as their favourite heir, but altruism was never the motive. The trend of seeking powerful guardians to deter assassination of the royal line was most vividly expressed in the Will of Nicomedes I of Bithynia who had previously named Antigonus II *Gonatas* of Macedonia, and Ptolemy II *Philadelphos* of Egypt, as well as the cities of Heraclea Pontica, Chios and Byzantium, as an illustrious melee of guardians for his children. We also have numerous papyri detailing the Wills of military settlers which followed Greek legal formulae in the era of the Ptolemies, including dowries and the passing down of slaves; typically, the opening lines once again followed the format of Aristotle's testament.[44]

We touched on the corrupting of the Will of the Roman emperor Claudius, and its relevance to our investigation *is* striking. Suetonius reported that when Claudius composed his testament he had the magistrates witness it, but it was blocked by Agrippina (the Younger), his niece and fourth wife, who was also the sister of Caligula, and fatally for him, the mother of Nero who was by now Claudius' adopted son (as well as grand-nephew). We may assume Agrippina destroyed the Will when she burned Claudius' notes and killed his secretary. Suetonius captured the detail:

> Towards the end of his life, he [Claudius] had shown some plain signs of repentance for his marriage with Agrippina and his adoption of Nero... Not long after he made his Will and sealed it with the seals of all the magistrates. But before he could go any further, he was cut short by Agrippina... That Claudius was poisoned is the general belief... His death was kept quiet until all the arrangements were made about the succession... The principal omens of his death were the following: the rise of a longhaired star, commonly called a comet...[45]

The conspicuous comet has some bearing on our quest for the identity of Curtius, the intriguing historian behind the most vivid renderings of events on Alexander's campaigns.[46]

Claudius did openly regret adopting Nero, and his Will was certainly drafted to nominate Britannicus, his natural son by a former wife, as his successor. Claudius' death was not revealed until all arrangements for Nero's succession had been finalised; the vanished *testamentum* and the suspicion of poisoning soon fell on Agrippina.[47] Later, with Nero in power and with her influence over him waning, Agrippina, ironically, tried to elevate Britannicus once more. However, on the 12th February 55 CE, Britannicus mysteriously died the day before his fourteenth birthday and before the official proclamation of his adulthood. Tradition blamed Nero and poison; Nero blamed it on an epileptic fit but he soon devised methods to do away with Agrippina.[48]

No less relevant to the fate of the Roman *testamentum* are the manipulations of Caligula, whose ancestry could be traced to both the winner (Octavian), and the loser (Mark Antony), of the battle at Actium, and who himself greatly admired Alexander. Concerning the death of Tiberius (in 37 CE), Cassius Dio wrote:

> Tiberius, to be sure, had left the empire to his grandson [named] Tiberius as well; but Gaius [Caligula] sent his Will to the senate by Macro and caused it to be declared null and void by the consuls and the others with whom he had arranged matters beforehand, on the ground that the testator had not been of sound mind as shown by the fact that he had permitted a mere boy to rule over them...[49]

Rumour abounded that Caligula, 'the viper to the Roman people', had murdered Tiberius to hasten an inheritance that also saw him reinterpreting any Wills that bequeathed estates to his forerunner in order to redirect funds to himself; he is said to have squandered the 2,700,000,000 sesterces amassed, deifying himself in the process.[50] Although Caligula's death, less than four years later, lacked the colour of his short life (he died in his twenty-ninth year), it was, inevitably, just as controversial. Reports of his assassination – professedly condoned by the Praetorian Guard, the Senate, army and equestrian order – vary through Josephus and Suetonius.[51] It appeared very 'Julian' with thirty or so reported stab wounds in the Palatine Hill Cryptoporticus, an underground corridor (unearthed by archaeologists in 2008), with a complicit senator named Cluvius Rufus.[52] Caligula was reportedly entombed in either Augustus' family mausoleum, or at Lake Nemi where, in 2011, police claimed to have unearthed his remains.

PELLAN INHERITANCE AND THE REGENT EXECUTOR

If we have successfully illustrated the ubiquity of Wills in Greece and Rome and their place in the legal mechanism for transferring power before, during, and after, Alexander's reign, we need to ask whether Macedonia adopted the same tradition. On one hand it may be irrelevant, as Alexander was more Greek in education, 'Homeric' in spirit, and Macedonian in arms alone. But we have examples of noteworthy testaments attached to

A 1ˢᵗ century marble of Claudius. Naples National Archaeological Museum, Farnese Collection. Following his death rumour circulated that his Will had been blocked by Agrippina despite it having been sealed by the magistrates, to enable his adopted son, Nero, to become emperor.

men who featured in Alexander's story, and evidence that Macedonian law recognised their structure.

Aristotle prepared for his own death by appointing Antipater, the Macedonian regent, as the general executor of his Will, and this is significant to us for several reasons. Firstly, it confirms that a bond and a trust existed between the two men, a fact exploited by a tradition which linked them, working in unison, to the plot to murder Alexander; Aristotle supposedly provided the poison ferried to Babylon by Antipater's sons, a garnish to the claims made in the Vulgate genre (T9, T10).[53] Diogenes Laertius knew of nine letters sent from Aristotle to the regent (compared with four to Alexander), and though a tight relationship does not necessarily point at covert activity, it does suggest mutual interests, and 'ample traces' of correspondence between them still exist.[54]

A Nicanor was named as Cassander's garrison commander at Athens; if, as many commentators believe, he was Aristotle's nephew (who married Aristotle's daughter under the terms of his aforementioned Will), we have further evidence of those close relations.[55] But above all, Aristotle's testament indicates that the Macedonian nobles, at any rate, were familiar with the Will as a mechanism of estate planning, for it is hardly likely

Antipater would have been enrolled in such a pivotal role if not willing to recognise and uphold its legality. Aristotle may himself have been granted full Macedonian citizenship by the time he died, either for his services to the monarchy, or simply because Stagira where he was born was now part of a greater Macedonia.

The appointment of Antipater as the executor may additionally suggest Aristotle was seeking the regent's protection, for it appears he fled Athens after Alexander's death, fearing reprisals for his long career supporting (and supported by) the Macedonian monarchy. Yet the city-state of Chalcis was not significantly safer or much further from assassins' reach. A well-documented enmity had existed between Olympias, the queen mother, and Antipater;[56] if Hyperides had indeed already lost his tongue for proposing honours to Iolaos for his part in the Babylonian plot (and even if not) we wonder if Aristotle feared the agents of Olympias rather more than those of Athens.[57] A few years on, Olympias did wreak vengeance on Antipater's sons, no doubt guided by, or at least legitimised by, the plot 'revealed' in the *Pamphlet*. So it may have been Olympias who dislodged Aristotle's honour plaque (he was feted along with Callisthenes) that was recovered from the bottom of a Delphian well.[58]

In his own Will Aristotle, notably, asked that life-size stone statues to Zeus and Athena the Saviour be erected, just as Alexander's extant Will requested statues of himself, the gods and his parents to be set up in the most noteworthy of cities.[59] As neither Alexander nor Athens was mentioned in Aristotle's Will, Chroust suggests that it was probably penned in Chalcis in 322 BCE after the king's death (his birthplace, Stagira, may have formerly been a colony of Chalcis).[60] For Aristotle *was* a *metoikos,* a guest-resident of Athens who would usually pay the non-resident tax (*metoikion*) of 1 drachma per month for males (half for females, unless they or the males had exemption by equalisation, *isotelia),* and as such the Will would traditionally have carried no authority in the city, though as a possible former colony of Athens and member of the Delian League, Athenian law may have been observed in Chalcis.[61] Obtaining Athenian citizenship was not a formality; we read of just fifty grants of citizenship between 368 and 322 BCE, and as a resident alien Aristotle would have been banned from owning property in the city-state and, in fact, in Attica too.[62]

If Peripatetic-era Wills were rhetoric free, they were not necessarily safe *from* rhetoric. Demosthenes' father's Will had been exploited by his guardians and that prompted his first judicial speech at the age of twenty to reclaim what was left of the estate, thus setting in motion his oratorical career. His inheritance included over thirty sword-making slaves, and twenty slaves engaged in the manufacture of furniture, bringing in a total of 4,200 drachmas annually; there were also interest-bearing loans out at twelve per cent besides property and chattels.[63]

Many were maritime credits set up between the *emporos* (merchant) and *naukleros* (shipowner) in a sophisticated contract and cargo obligation system outlined in Demosthenes' cases against Aphobus, Lacritus, Zenothemis, Phormio and Apaturius, in which he claimed he had been swindled. A new law for commercial action, *dike emporike*, allowed for the speedy settlement of disputes, though, interestingly, loans were dissolved in the case of a shipwreck; this led to many false claims of cargoes being lost at sea, a loophole widened by the fact that maritime-loan interest was only payable at the expiration of the contract period (unlike monthly interest on land mortgages).[64]

But we do have one later example that clearly testifies to the existence of Macedonian royal Wills: that of Antigonus III *Doson* (ca. 263-221 BCE), the grandson of Demetrius *Poliorketes* (and great-grandson of Ptolemy I *Soter*); Polybius knew the details and he stated that *Doson* nominated to power a loyal top echelon 'in order to avoid conflicts'; the testament further demanded that its content be read in public, though whether that meant to a convened Assembly of Macedones (the *Pamphlet* claimed Alexander's Will had been similarly read out at such a gathering) or to a wider audience is not clear.[65]

We are not proposing that the typical tribesmen who made up the Macedonian infantry ranks would have been adept in the subtleties of inheritance; nevertheless, Alexander's veteran campaigners had possessions, booty and possibly land grants too with relatives still at home and now in Asia by virtue of wives and sons accumulated over the years. Death on campaign was only ever a spear point away and mobile bank deposits took a primitive form: pursers in charge of heavily guarded waggons. Some form of written covenant must have existed to ensure the wealth was distributed as the campaigners would have wished, should they perish in the phalanx or from a snakebite in India.[66] Further, we contend that the Macedonian monarchs required more than the Common Assembly's traditional beating of spear on shield to shepherd through the intricacies behind succession, for the 'back office' of regal power would have required that the dissemination of inheritances, appointments and bequests be honoured and documented.

More specifically, we contend that Alexander, in the never-before-witnessed 'impious' position as Great King of Persia, ruler (if not the formalised pharaoh) of Egypt, 'King of Lands' in Babylonia, tribal King of Macedonia as well as *hegemon* of the League of Corinth, would have needed a particularly well-constructed and clear legal document to pass on the expanded reins of power in a meaningful way. For the territory now nominally under Argead rule was immense, and at the point of Alexander's death there still existed his own sons in Asia and sisters (and half-sisters) in Epirus and Pella who could maintain the Macedonian royal line.

The lion hunt floor mosaic found in the so-called House of Dionysus in Pella, dating to ca. 325-300 BCE. Some scholars believe it depicts Alexander being assisted by his veteran general, Craterus, in a game park in Syria, based on similar bronze figures at Delphi, dedicated by Craterus or his son. The design could suggest that Alexander's left foot had been trapped by the lion's paw, but the identifications remain unsubstantiated. Archaeological Museum, Pella.

The fresco on the northern wall inside Tomb I at ancient Aegae depicting the mythical Abduction of Persephone by Hades. This remarkable decoration in what is known as The Tomb of Persephone is possibly the 'restrained palette' of Nicomachus of Thebes, and points to the importance of its inhabitant, once thought to be King Amyntas III or King Alexander II. Discussed in *Postcript. Of Bones, Insignia* and *Warrior Women: The Return to Aegae.*

The entrance of Tomb II at of ancient Aegae, widely held to be the tomb of Philip II, Alexander's father. The iron and gold-encrusted breastplate, along with the gold larnax below that contained the cremated bones of a male thought to be in his forties when he died, were found in the main chamber.

The Scythian *gorytos* (quiver) and a pair of ornate greaves were photographed as the were found lying in the antechamber. One of the greaves is shorter and narrower tha the other; recent analysis of the bones confirm the female, estimated to have been in h early or mid-thirties at death, had experienced a major fracture to her left tibia. See *Pre Report: The Tomb of Philip II Confirmed* and *Postcript. Of Bones, Insignia and Warrior Wome The Return to Aegae.*

The so-called 'Alexander Sarcophagus' which takes pride of place in the Istanbul Archaeology Museum. Made from Pentelic marble, it was discovered with three others in a necropolis near Sidon in 1887 and has been linked to Abdalonymus, appointed king of Sidon by Alexander in 333 BCE, or Darius' former satrap, Mazaeus. It is noteworthy that within the Greek workmanship and carved on one pediment is a relief thought by some to depict the murder of Alexander's former chiliarch, Perdiccas. Its background and history discussed in chapter titled *Lifting the Shroud of Parrhasius.*

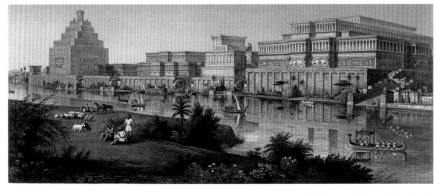

The Palaces of Nimrud Restored, a reconstruction of the palaces built by Assurbanipal on the banks of the Tigris, from Discoveries in the Ruins of Nineveh and Babylon by Austen Henry Layard, 1853, colour litho. At the ancient Assyrian capital of Nineveh clear signs of horticulture and an irrigation system exist, with descriptions confirmed by tablets and in panel sculptures. These intricate gardens also existed at Kalhu, later named Nimrud, and Dur-Sharrukin, the 'Fortress of Sargon', modern Khorsabad. The 'Hanging Gardens' of Babylon may have been located at Nineveh, known as 'Old Babylon' in antiquity. Discussed in chapter titled *Babylon: Cipher and Rosetta Stone.*

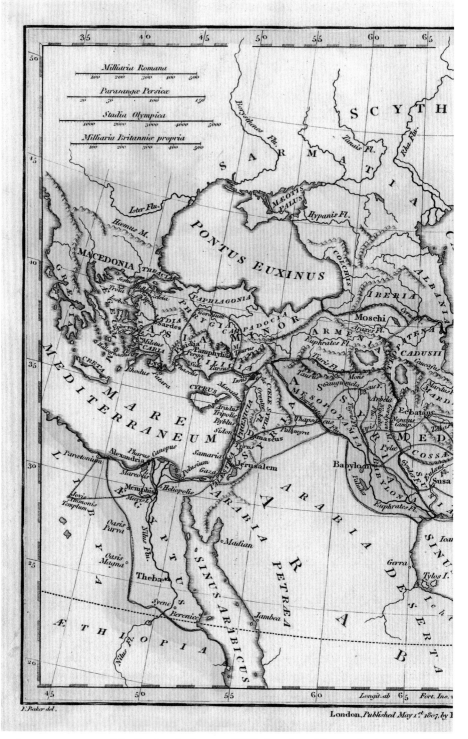

A map annotated in Latin dating to 1807 showing Alexander's route (in red) through the Persian Empire. Nearchus' naval voyage from the Indus delta to the Persian Gulf is also shown (in black).

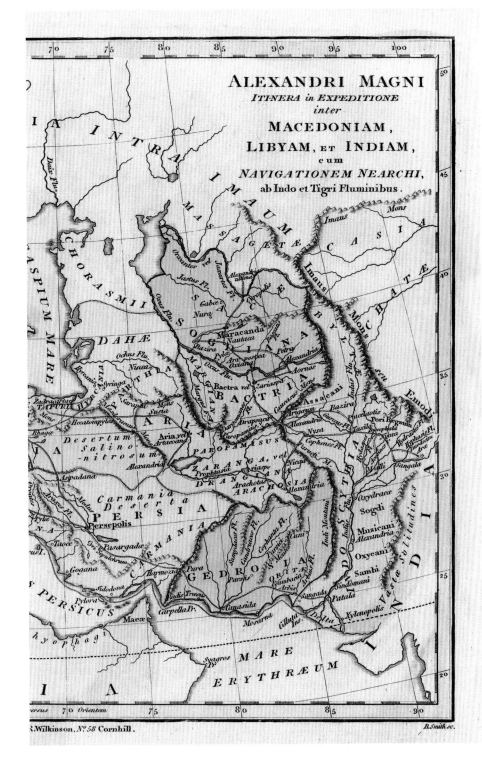

A page from the *Greek Alexander Romance* manuscript MS Bodleian 264, folio 218, recto, in the Bodleian Library, Oxford University. The manuscript illuminations in gold (gilding), silver and vibrant inks, were produced by the workshop of the Flemish illuminator, Jehan de Grise, between 1338 and 1344, and were ubiquitous through the Gothic period. By kind permission of Oxford University Press. See detail in chapters titled *Mythoi Muthodes and the Birth of Romance* and *The Precarious Path of Pergamena and Papyrus*.

An *ekphrasis* in late-medieval art was reasserted throughout the Renaissance merging contemporary and classical themes. One example is Albrecht Altdorfer's *The Battle of Alexander at Issus* painted in 1529 and commissioned by Duke Wilhelm of Bavaria. Soldiers wear turbans in Turkish style and women wear feathered toques in the fashion of the German court. Painted when the Turkish push towards Vienna threatened apocalyptic events, Altdorfer's canvas has been described as capturing a 'cosmic Armageddon'. More in chapter titled *The Reborn Wrath of Peleus' Son*.

The kingdoms of Alexander's successors after the Battle of Ipsus in 301 BCE. The map is reproduced from the *Historical Atlas* by William Shepherd (1923-26). For the background to the successor kingdoms see chapter titled *Sarissa Diplomacy: Macedonian Statecraft.*

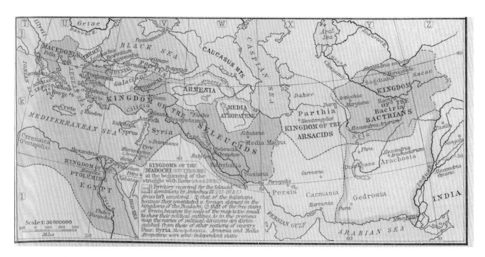

A map of the Macedonian-governed empire ca. 200 BCE at the beginning of the struggle with Rome. Both maps provided by the kind permission of University of Texas at Austin.

THE SEV'NFOLD, VAST, IMPENETRABLE SHIELD

There can be no doubt that Alexander, along with those of his higher echelons at the Macedonian court, would have been well acquainted with the construction and legal basis of the Will, a far surer mandate for influencing the future than fate, fortune, friends, and the fickle will of the gods. If he was as attached to Homer and the heroic past as sources suggest, then he would have been familiar with the pre-suicide speech of Ajax in the Sophocles tragedy that had the airs and form of an oral testament in which, and against the norms of a warrior protocol which requested burial with armour, Ajax left his 'vast sev'nfold shield' to his son, Eursaces.[67] The *Iliad* made references to the oral disposition of estates linked to Agamemnon and Hector, whilst Sophocles' *Trachiniae* (*Women of Trachis*) described the hero uttering an oral Will in the madness of dying.[68]

As for Alexander's generals, they would have demanded clarity on succession long before their eventual return to Babylon in 323 BCE, and probably before the Macedonian war machine headed into Asia. Alexander may indeed have satisfied their early demands by penning a fulsome testament that dedicated his own panoply to temples and shrines as we read in the *Pamphlet*.[69] We must not forget that Alexander had borrowed handsomely from his nobles to fund the crossing to Asia, no doubt on the promise of land grants and commercial concessions, repayments that would have needed documenting and underwriting in some way should he die.[70]

Perhaps a Will was first drafted when Antipater and Parmenio pleaded with their king to take a wife and produce an heir before crossing the Hellespont.[71] It may have been updated at various stages as influential *strategoi* were killed, executed or elevated, following the murder of Parmenio, for example, or the running through of Black Cleitus, or perhaps after Alexander's near-death experience in India when Craterus and Ptolemy echoed the common fear that: 'He should set a limit to the pursuit of glory and have regard for his safety, that is, the safety of the state.'[72]

We could imagine that the new marriages at Susa would have prompted the discussion of a succession document as a new military and administrative order was clearly then emerging. Surely additional provisions would have been added when his wife fell pregnant and his closest friend and *chiliarchos*, Hephaestion, died at Ecbatana in 324 BCE. If the future of empire administration had been planned and documented by Alexander in some form of covenant, beside the contingency for a world without him, then the most influential of Alexander's Bodyguards and Companions were probably privy to its content. In which case we should not visualise a last-minute and hastily drafted *diatheke* or oral whisper as

Alexander approached death, for that could have come at any time on the decade-long campaign. Wills are about planning ahead, and about catering for all possible scenarios.

Aristotle had already laid out his *Nicomachean Ethics* when Alexander was a child. In it he had proposed 'we should as far as possible immortalise ourselves'.[73] In life and deeds Alexander followed his advice and attempted *homoiosis theoi*, a likeness to the gods. Yet historians believe he failed at the final hurdle in prolonging the influence of all he had achieved. Why, having seen the Mausoleum at Halicarnassus, and having admired and repaired the humbling tomb of Cyrus, having marched past the Pharaonic pyramids at Cheops and after demanding a funeral pyre of Babylonian proportion for Hephaestion, would Alexander have not planned such a monument for himself?[74] We will make a case that the rejected so-called last plans found at Babylon are a missing piece of this intestate puzzle (T25).

Who in Alexander's retinue would have been the likely candidate to draft the king's Will? Eumenes' *Curriculum Vitae* needed no explanation then and needs none today; Hieronymus, Plutarch and Cornelius Nepos saw to that with their biographing of the Cardian royal secretary. Eumenes knew the intimacies of the treasury, the politics in Pella and the administrative shape of the empire, and this neatly leads us to one significant piece of evidence that points towards the use of Wills on campaign: the testament of Eumenes himself. Plutarch tells us that he wrote, or amended, his own Will on the eve of his final battle at Gabiene at the close of 316 BCE. Learning of the coming treachery of his men, Eumenes retired to his tent and drafted his last wishes, in the process tearing up and destroying his papers so that none of the secrets they contained would be known.[75]

Plutarch compared Eumenes to the Roman general Quintus Sertorius, and he found an obvious corollary for Alexander in Julius Caesar.[76] Like Eumenes who had helped avert civil war at Babylon, following Caesar's death it was Mark Antony who presented the compromise that temporarily reconciled the Caesarean faction – along with the Senate and the army – with the Caesaricides (who believed they were *liberatores*) led by Cassius (ca. 85-42 BCE) and Brutus (85-42 BCE). On 19th March 44 BCE Caesar's Will was opened and read, and it appointed as his principal heir the nineteen-year-old Gaius Octavius Thurinus ('Octavian' after his adoption through the Will), who was then stationed with the Roman legions in Macedonia (though in Apollonia in Illyria when he heard the news).

A decade later, in the autumn of 34 BCE, Antony, Cleopatra and Ptolemaic Egypt issued the Donation of Alexandria, which distributed Rome's Eastern Empire (brazenly including the undefeated Parthia)

The tomb of the Carian satrap Mausolus and Artemisia II at Halicarnassus, modern Bodrum, Turkey and built between ca. 353-350 BCE. Some 148 feet high and with reliefs carved by four celebrated Greek sculptors, Leochares, Bryaxis, Scopas and Timotheus, Antipater of Sidon considered it among the Seven Wonders of the World. Alexander surely visited the tomb after taking the city. Earthquakes destroyed it between the 12th and 15th centuries after which many of the marble blocks were used by the Knights of Saint John to fortify Bodrum Castle. Image from Vitruvius' *Ten Books on Architecture*, e-text made available by the Gutenberg Project.

between their children. The young Alexander Helios was appointed king of Armenia, Parthia and Media (also unconquered); his fraternal twin, Cleopatra Selene II, was to rule Cyrenaica and Libya, whilst their third child, the infant Ptolemy II *Philadelphos*, was given Syria and Cilicia, and he was dressed for the occasion in Macedonian garb. Caesarion ('Little Caesar', formally Ptolemy XV *Philopator Philometor* Caesar), Julius Caesar's son by Cleopatra, became 'king of kings' and the co-ruler of Egypt. A festival imitating a Roman triumph was held in which Antony was dressed as Dionysus-Osiris with Cleopatra garbed as Isis-Aphrodite.

The legitimisation of the half-Roman Caesarion as Julius' bloodline heir undermined Octavian, just as Alexander's own half-barbarian sons threatened the potential power of his *Somatophylakes*. Antony claimed Octavian had earned his adoption through unnatural relations with Caesar (further rumours suggested Caesar's *last* Will did not recognise Octavian as his heir, but Caesarion instead), and allegations had already surfaced (through Cicero) that Antony had a part in Caesar's murder; the rift with Rome was complete.[77] Octavian and his innovative general, Agrippa (ca. 63-12 BCE), now with his naval crown and bronze-plated heavy ramming quinqueremes ('fives', referring to the rowing configuration) with their new grappling irons, would soon meet the threat from Egypt off the coast of Actium in western Greece.[78]

Antony and Cleopatra, who had herself inherited power with her brother (Ptolemy XIII) under the Will of her father, Ptolemy XII *Auletes* ('piper' or 'flute player', or alternatively, *Nothos*, 'bastard', ca. 117-51 BCE) had come within a battle of making Rome a tributary ('Capitol Hill would bow to her isle of Canopus') or dividing her empire. So the horror at Antony's exposed 'oriental' testament was understandable in Rome.[79] Appreciating that Egypt had the financial resources to outfit a significant army, Rome never allowed a senator to become proconsul of the region and filled influential posts there from the lower equestrian ranks.[80]

The promises of the Donation of Alexandria were short-lived, and within four years the orphans of the Egyptian dynasts were paraded at Octavian's triumph in Rome.[81] Yet Egypt, the fertile land of romance, hadn't disappointed in developing their legendary lives. After failed negotiations and inconclusive skirmishes, Antony and Cleopatra met their oft-misconstrued ends in Alexandria. But contrary to the popular imagery, Plutarch informed us that no writhing asp was ever found in the monument in which Cleopatra had interned herself; on the contrary, a hollow comb was retrieved that might have contained the poison that vexed the Psyllian snake charmers who were sent in to find the serpent.[82]

Their story has a further twist, for Pliny reported that so suspicious had Antony and Cleopatra become of one another *before* the battle at Actium on 2nd September 31 BCE, he had a *praegustatore* (a professional taster) sample the food she served him on her royal barge. In response, she dared Antony to drink the wine in which her garlanded flowers (secretly poisoned at the extremities) had been dipped, and laughingly restrained him at the last moment, poisoning a slave instead, as a demonstration of her cunning.[83] Whilst the attested malaria attack was, no doubt, debilitating on Antony's crew,[84] we should question why Quintus Dellius defected with the triumvir's battle plans, for this appears to have coincided with Cleopatra's sailing over the horizon in the direction of Egypt.[85]

The earlier communications between the ill-starred lovers appears to have been bitter too. At some point Cleopatra sent Octavian, who had been wintering on Samos, a gold crown and throne with an offer to defect in favour of her sons. In parallel, Antony offered Octavian *his* capitulation with an agreement to live as a private citizen in Athens. Only the rejection of both offers, from one side or the other (Octavian demanded Cleopatra kill or expel Antony as part of his amnesty, and he never replied to Antony), saw them reunited in Alexandria, a somewhat less than romantic path to their final tragedy than is commonly envisaged.

'I FOUND IT OF BRICK, I SHALL LEAVE IT OF MARBLE'

Upon entering Alexandria when the final resistance of Cleopatra and Antony had collapsed, Octavian, who later used a signet ring with a gem-engraved likeness of Alexander to seal official documents, requested that the Macedonian king's incarcerated body be exhumed from its shrine in the Sema; like Julius Caesar before him, he was interested in seeing little else in the city. When asked if he wished to see the tombs of the Ptolemies, Octavian is said to have replied: 'I came to see a king, not a row of corpses.' Perhaps the words of his then-present philosopher friend, Areius, had been influential: 'Not a good thing were a Caesar too many.'[86]

In Cassius Dio's coverage of the episode the emperor irreverently fingered Alexander's head and broke off a part of his nose, though this might have been a story propagated by the Alexandrians themselves.[87] Octavian's visit was not just cultural; he ferried its wealth back to Rome whereupon interest rates dropped by two-thirds, and he further laid claim to the 12,500 talents annual income that Egypt was still able to amass.[88] Alexandria flourished in the wake of the Battle of Ipsus in 301 BCE and only began its decline after Octavian's sacking of the city; both are the most widely accepted termini of the Hellenistic era.

The Prima Porta Augustus in the Braccio Nuovo of the Vatican Museums, discovered in 1863 in the so-called Villa of Livia. It is believed to be a copy of a bronze original dating to ca. 20 CE.

The once frail Octavian became the long-lived Augustus who survived to see the birth of the grandson of his granddaughter.[89] He was the precursor of the Principate (still clothed as a republic), founder of the Praetorian Guard and *Consilium Principis,* and he turned the *mos maiorum* into Constitutional Settlements and a new legal order; he was in every sense a true empire administrator. His alleged deathbed comment, 'I found Rome made of brick and I leave her clad in marble', summed up his tangible achievement; he had spent some 2,400,000,000 *sestertii* on the city.[90] And Augustus may have sensed historic foul play, for as the author of a fulsome Will, he apparently remained vexed at why Alexander, who was no less endowed with titles conferring the absolute power of *imperium*, ultimately failed to 'set his empire in order'.[91] But Alexander's long lost Will, suppressed at Babylon we venture, *had* essentially been an imperial edict; it was the legal mandate that was to indelibly stamp his ambition, vision, and bloodline across the face of his now vast empire. It beckoned in the Hellenistic era in which the former veneer of independent city-states, island federations, client kingdoms and semi-autonomous satraps acting as 'royal landlords', vanished in an instant.[92]

Napoleon Bonaparte penned a fulsome Will on April 15th 1821 at Longwood on the island of St Helena. It dealt with his wife, his son, his veterans and his generals, those who were loyal and those who calumniated against him. The document contained directions for his burial and its religious observances, and it dealt with his fortune; annexed to the last page was an inventory of his chattels should any confusion arise. The greatest conqueror of his age may even have read Suetonius' account of the Will of Augustus, for there appear to be many similarities.[93] Some years earlier, in 1806, Napoleon had commissioned what is now known as the Table des Grands Capitaines in porcelain and gilded bronze. Inlaid around the table were cameos of twelve of antiquity's greatest commanders, with the centre reserved for a likeness of Alexander III of Macedonia.[94] Recalling Augustus' dismay at Alexander's maladministration, and to quote the utilitarian view of truth once espoused by Napoleon, we wonder if they too concluded that his intestate end was 'nothing more than a fable agreed on'.[95]

NOTES

1. Cicero *De Officiis* 3.8.36.
2. Diogenes Laertius *Aristotle* and *Theophrastus*.
3. Chroust (1967) pp 90-114 and Chroust (1970) p 629.
4. Davis (1914) Part 2, Ch. XI, *The Funerals,* section 69.
5. Suetonius *Nero* 17 for an example of the use of 'testator'.
6. Example provided by Hansen (1999) p 96.
7. Davis (1914) Part 2, Ch. XI, *The Funerals,* section 69. How Solonian law translated into Will structures is not fully clear as the speeches we draw inspiration from may be abiding by, challenging, reinterpreting, or suggesting new avenues of law.
8. See chapter titled *Babylon: the Cipher and Rosetta Stone.*
9. A discussion of the deviation from the original Will can be found in chapters titled *The Silent Siegecraft of the Pamphleteers* and *Lifting the shroud of Parrhasius.*
10. Keyser (2011) p 111 for the Mesopotamian and neo-Babylonian Wills.
11. Harris (1911) pp 12-13 and Kenyon (1899) p 58 for the mummy cases at Gurob.
12. Hesiod *Theogonia* 22-34.
13. Plutarch *Agis* 5.1-4 and for general attributions to the *rhetra* of Sparta see Plutarch *Lycurgus.* Detailed discussion of Spartan law and estate planning in Avramović (2006). Russell (1946) p 99 for Spartan land law and Aristotle *Politics* 1270a ff.
14. Plutarch *Solon* 2.1-3, translation from the Loeb Classical Library edition, 1914.
15. In translation the 'Rock of Ares', also called Areopagus, situated northwest of the Acropolis, functioned as Court of Appeal for criminal and civil cases in ancient times. Discussed in Arnaoutoglou (1998) pp 1-5.
16. Callias was fined 50 talents upon his return, but seems to have brokered a peace known as the Peace of Callias, see Herodotus 7.151, Diodorus 12.4, Demosthenes *De Falsa Legatione* in Shilleto (1874) p 428. Neither Thucydides nor Herodotus mentioned the peace treaty.
17. Diogenes Laertius *Solon* 1.62.
18. Chroust (1970) p 635.
19. Plutarch *Solon* 20.1-4 for the laws relating to women. Sparta had a similar rule for its *petrouchoi.* If an *epikleros* was already married but childless, she might have been forced to divorce under this arrangement.
20. Chroust (1970) p 636.
21. Chroust (1970) p 629.
22. Diogenes Laertius *Epicurus* 10.
23. Quoting Cicero *Academica* 1.12. For a fuller discussion on the meaning of *kataleptike phantasis* see Striker (1996) pp 106-107.
24. Diogenes Laertius *Arcesilaus* 4.19.
25. See chapter titled *The Damaging Didactic of the Classical Death* for discussion on Chrysippus' purported death.
26. Plutarch *Romulus* 5.3. Larentia may better be termed 'mythical' for her associations to Heracles but other traditions see her marriage to a wealthy citizen, Roman or Etruscan, as historic.
27. Gibbon (1776 to 1789) Chapter XLIV: *Idea Of The Roman Jurisprudence*, Part V.
28. Cicero *Topica* 4 for women's right to Wills.
29. Cicero *De Officiis* 3.73. Suetonius *Augustus* 33.2 for the Cornelian Law; this applied to anyone who '*testamentum malo scripserit, recitaverit, subjecerit, suppresserit, amoverit, resignaverit, deleverit…*', according to Julius Paulus *Sententiarum receptarum ad filium libri quinque* 5.25.
30. Tacitus 14.40.
31. Pliny *Epistles, Letter To Cornelianus.*
32. Suetonius *Augustus* 56.1.
33. Grafton (1990) p 28 for the Ravenna papyrus. Quoting Pearson (1960) p 262.
34. Suetonius *Nero* 17.
35. Following Suetonius *Nero* 32.2 and quoting Tacitus 13.42.4 on Seneca, though the accuser, Publius Suillius, may have been seeking revenge with spurious claims.
36. Quoting Wiseman (1991) Introduction p vii. Herodian 1.1.4.
37. Suetonius *Augustus,* from the Loeb Classical Library edition, 1914.
38. Discussed in Arnaoutoglou (1988) p 118.
39. See reference to Vegio in the chapter titled *The Precarious Path of Pergamena and Papyrus.*
40. Tacitus 12.31 for Prasutagus' installation by Claudius, and 14.31 for the Will.
41. This is recorded by an inscription but does not appear in literary sources.
42. A 'detersent against assassination' proposed by Shipley (2000) p 210.
43. According to Justin 39.5. Ptolemy Apion was the son of the king and a concubine. The sources

are the *Periochae* to Livy's *Ab Urbe Condita Libri* 70.5 for the dating of 96 BCE. Confusion exists on the Will's claims. Appian *Mithridatic Wars* 121 stated that Apion left Cyrene to Rome. Ammianus Marcellinus 22.16.24 corrected this to 'the dry part of Libya', whereas Cyrene and the other cities of the Pentapolis were handed over 'by the generosity of King Ptolemy XII'. Bagnall-Derow (2004) pp 92-93 for the Will inscription at Cyrene and its 'unholy' allegation.

44. Bagnall-Derow (2004) pp 241-244 for Greek-style Wills of settlers in Egypt.
45. Suetonius *Claudius* 43-46, translation from the Loeb Classical Library edition, 1914.
46. Discussed in chapter titled *Comets, Colophons and Curtius Rufus*.
47. Suetonius *Nero* 43-46.
48. Tacitus 13.16 for Britannicus' coming of age and death; also Josephus 20.8.2; Suetonius *Nero* 33; Cassius Dio 61.7. For the various traditions of Agrippina's death, see Tacitus 14.1-8, Suetonius *Nero* 34, Cassius Dio 63.11-14.
49. Cassius Dio 59.1 translation from the Loeb Classical Library edition, 1914-1927.
50. Suetonius *Caligula* 11 for 'viper'. Suetonius *Caligula* 12; Tacitus 6.50 suggest the Praetorian Prefect, Macro, smothered Tiberius with a pillow, whereas Suetonius suggested Caligula did the killing himself. Suetonius *Caligula* 37 for his profligacy and 22.3, 52.1 for the suggestion of his self-deification.
51. Suetonius *Caligula* 57-58, Josephus 19.1.14.
52. Suetonius *Caligula* 56-58 and Josephus 19.1.13. More on Cluvius Rufus and his significance to the study in chapter titled *Comets, Colophons and Curtius Rufus*.
53. Arrian 7.28, Plutarch 77 for Aristotle's involvement.
54. Quoting Chroust (1973) p 195 on 'ample correspondence'.
55. Diogenes Laertius *Aristotle* 12 for the letters. Quoting Chroust (1970) p 12 for the correspondence with Antipater and pp 9-11 for Aristotle's citizenship. See chapter titled *The Silent Siegecraft of the Pamphleteers* for more on Nicanor. At the time of Aristotle's death, Nicanor was said to be away on a 'dangerous mission' which further suggests a role under Cassander; discussed in Chroust (1970) p 640; the known danger may explain why Theophrastus was named as 'interim heir designate' in Aristotle's Will. Also Pausanias 6.4.8 for Aristotle's influence with Antipater; discussed in Bosworth (1971) p 114.
56. Olympias and Antipater quarrelled and she departed Macedonia for Epirus: Diodorus 18.49.4, Pausanias 1.11.3, Arrian 7.12.6-7, Plutarch 68.4-5, Justin 12.14.3.
57. Plutarch *Demosthenes* 28.4 for the cutting out of Hyperides' tongue, and Plutarch *Moralia* 849f (*Life of Hyperides*) for linking that to his proposing honours to Iolaos.
58. See discussion in Barnes (1995) p 6. Aristotle allegedly wrote to Antipater informing him the honours bestowed on him had been stripped. An inscription honouring him and Callisthenes and dating to 330 BCE has been found in pieces down the bottom of a well at Delphi. Marasco (2011) p 45 for Aristotle's letter to Antipater concerning the withdrawn Delphic honours, cited in Aelian 14.1; an inscription by Aristotle was mentioned in Diogenes Laertius *Aristotle* 5-6.
59. In the *Romance* 3.33 and *Metz Epitome* 122, Alexander requested gilded statues to be erected in Delphi and Athens; and statues of his mother, father and select gods in Egypt. See Heckel (1988) p 17 for *Metz Epitome* translation and Stoneman (1991) p 155 for the *Romance*.
60. Chroust (1979) p 637; Stagira was a colony of either Chalcis or Andros.
61. A visitor to the city (*parepidemos*) would have had some days' exemption before taxes became payable ahead of becoming a metic.
62. Hansen (1999) p 130 for the fifty grants of citizenship.
63. Finlay (1973) p 116 for the breakdown of Demosthenes' father's estate. Aeschines *On the False Embassy* 93 claimed Demosthenes was called the 'son of a sword-maker'.
64. Demosthenes *Against Aphobus* 1.9-11, *Against Apaturius* 4-5, *Against Phormio* 9 for details of Demosthenes' commercial activity. Finlay (1973) p 162 for the *dike emporike*. Archibald-Davies-Gabrielson (2005) p 138 for loan payments.
65. Polybius 4.87.7-8; discussed in Marasco (2011) pp 57-58 and following the observations of C Bearzot p 58.
66. See discussion of the importance of waggons and wealth in Billows (1990) pp 102-103 citing Diodorus 19.42.4-43; and evidence of their vulnerability in battle in Plutarch *Eumenes* 16.5-6, Polyaenus 4.6.13. Also Anson (2004) pp 187-9. More details of the baggage trains that followed the campaigning *Diadokhoi* in chapter titled *The Tragic Triumvirate of Treachery and Oaths*.
67. Sophocles *Ajax* lines 565-577.
68. Discussed in Keyser (2011) pp 115-117. Details found in the *Iliad* 2.100-108, 6.476-481. Heracles' oral Will as interpreted from lines 161-163 in Sophocles *Trachiniae*; discussion in Keyser (2011) pp 117-118 also referring to Euripides *Heracles* lines 460-473.
69. The *Metz Epitome* 120 and *Romance* 3.33 has Alexander leaving his arms and insignia to the temple of Hera at Argos.
70. For Alexander's financial position and borrowing of 800 talents see Plutarch 15.1-3, Curtius

10.2.24 and Arrian 7.9.6 for his borrowing 800; discussed in chapter titled *Sarissa Diplomacy: Macedonian Statecraft*.

71. Diodorus 17.16.2.
72. Curtius 9.6.6-14 and 9.6.15 for Craterus' and Ptolemy's speeches and concerns.
73. Aristotle *Nicomachean Ethics* book 10 1177b32-1178a but a theme recurring through books 9 and 10.
74. Arrian 1.12.1 and Aelian 12.7 confirmed Hephaestion crowned, or wreathed, Patroclus' tomb at Troy whilst Alexander did the same to the tomb of Achilles, suggesting their parallel relationship.
75. Plutarch *Eumenes* 16.2-4; see chapters titled *The Tragic Triumvirate of Treachery and Oaths* and *The Silent Siegecraft of the Pamphleteers* for more on Eumenes' death.
76. Plutarch *Sertorius* 1.4 for comparisons with Philip, Antigonus and Hannibal.
77. Suetonius *Augustus* 68 for Antony's accusation and Cicero *Second Philippic* 14 for accusations of Antony's part in Caesar's murder.
78. The rowing configuration of the larger Greek and Roman ships is uncertain; see chapter titled *Sarissa Diplomacy: Macedonian Statecraft* for further discussion.
79. Ovid *Metamorphoses* book 15 line 825.
80. Arrian 3.5.7 explained that Rome always kept Egypt under surveillance and never allowed senators to become proconsuls lest they raise an army.
81. Cassius Dio 51.21.8 for the orphans being paraded in Rome.
82. Plutarch *Antony* 86. According to Suetonius *Augustus* 17, Octavian had Psyllian snake charmers brought in to try and suck the poison from Cleopatra's bite. Antony stabbed himself thinking Cleopatra was already dead.
83. Pliny 21.10.
84. For the malaria attack on the Egyptian crews, Cassius Dio 50.1.15, 50.12, 50.15.
85. For the defection of Quintus Dellius see Cassius Dio 50.23.1-3.
86. Suetonius *Augustus* 18, Cassius Dio 51.16.5 for Augustus' comment and treatment of Alexander's corpse. Plutarch *Antony* 81-82 for 'not a good thing were a Caesar too many' and also in Plutarch *Sayings of Kings and Commanders* 207D8. Lucan *On the Civil War* (*Pharsalia*) 10.14-52 for Caesar's ignoring all the sites of Alexandria, intent on seeing the tomb of Alexander.
87. Following Erskine (2002) p 163 for the possible birth of the Alexandrian tradition.
88. Strabo 17.13 quoting Cicero for the 12,500 talents income.
89. Discussed in Pitcher (2009) p 59 quoting Syme (1939) p 1; as Syme explains, M. Junius Silanus, the grandson of Augustus' granddaughter Julia, was born in 14 CE, the year Augustus died; Pliny 7.58.
90. For Augustus' comment about Rome on his deathbed see Cassius Dio 56.30.3 Suetonius *Augustus* 28. *Deeds of the Divine Augustus* appendix 1 for the total expenditure during his office.
91. Suetonius *Augustus* 18.1 for 'brick and marble' and Plutarch *Sayings of Kings and Commanders* 207D8 for Augustus' comment on Alexander's lack of empire administration.
92. 'Royal landlords' following Anson (1994) p 233.
93. Both Wills bequeathed funds to their veteran soldiers, as well as the state, and both provided a detailed breakdown of financial summary. For Augustus' Will see Suetonius *Augustus* 101.
94. The table, which took six years to complete, now resides in Buckingham Palace.
95. Referring to 'What then is, generally speaking, the truth of history? Nothing more than a fable agreed upon', *Memoirs of Napoleon*. Also attributed to Voltaire.

9

BABYLON: THE CIPHER AND ROSETTA STONE

What truly happened at Alexander's death in Babylon and can events be reinterpreted in the presence of a Will?

The conflicting reports of what came to pass in the days either side of Alexander's death raise more questions than they answer; Babylon was itself a city shrouded in myth.

The circumstances embodied in the claims of the Vulgate, the *Journal* and the *Pamphlet* texts were born here, and so was a mysterious list of projects known as the king's 'last plans'. What was really said at the gathering of men-at-arms, and by whom, and to what end? And could the dialogues have been related to a Will? Crucially, how were events at Babylon portrayed by the eyewitness writers who had a vested interest in the outcome?

We return to June 323 BCE and to the infighting that was a precursor to Macedonian civil war, and we overlay the testament on the confused narratives we have.

Diogenes to Alexander:
'But now, whom did you leave your great empire to?'
Alexander to Diogenes:
'Diogenes, I cannot tell you. I had no time to leave any directions about it,
beyond just giving Perdiccas my ring as I died. Why are you laughing?'[1]

Lucian *Dialogues of the Dead*

[At Babylon] 'the chiefs, moreover, were looking to sovereignty and offices of
command; the common soldiers to the treasury and heaps of gold, as a prize
unexpectedly presented to their grasp; the one meditating on the possibility
of seizing the throne, the other on the means of securing wealth and plenty.'[2]
(T12)

Justin *Epitome of the Philippic History of Pompeius Trogus*

'Babylon' is the Hellenic variant of the Akkadian *Bab-ili* meaning 'gateway
of the gods', though the origins of the name, from an unknown language,
are otherwise obscure.[3] In the *Old Testament* the Hebrew name for the city
of the immortalised gardens appears as 'Babel' (or Bavel) derived from the
verb *bilbél*, and its meaning was 'confusion'.[4]

The emblematic Hanging Gardens of Babylon, once credited to
Queen Semiramis, still elude us, however, and no cuneiform tablet found
in the myriad excavated from the city ruins suggested their existence.[5]
In his three-book *Babylonaika* (known in antiquity as the *Chaldaika*),
Berossus, wisely it seems, criticised the Greeks for too many attributions
to Semiramis, including the founding of the city.[6] Following the creation
tale laid out in the *Enûma Elis,* many credited Babylon's origins to the
god Bel-Marduk, though Josephus named Nabonidus as the constructor
of its burnt-brick and bitumen walls, whilst Pliny preserved a tradition
that Cyrus was an alternative founder of the gardens, though here he was
termed 'king of Assyria', possibly because of a manuscript confusion of
Σύρος (Assyrian) with Κῦρος (Cyrus).[7]

Two further fragments that cite Berossus are preserved in Josephus'
Jewish Antiquities and his *Against Apion*, and they proposed Nebuchadnezzar
II as the creator of the gardens for his Median wife, Amyhia (or Amyitis),
but without specifically saying where they were. Josephus, who was
drawing from the compilation of Alexander *Polyhistor* (1st century BCE,
literally the 'much learned'), was himself chronically unreliable and
ambivalent on their origins,[8] for he credited Megasthenes (ca. 350-290
BCE) with a second and identical reference to them, rendering Eusebius
and his *Kronographia*, which epitomised these earlier opinions, just as
vexatious a source.[9] Curtius, who claimed the gardens were still visible
in his day, and Diodorus, following either Ctesias or Cleitarchus (or

the one through the other), proposed an *unnamed* Assyrian king as their founder, whereas Strabo and Pseudo-Philo of Byzantium steered clear of nominating anyone at all.[10]

The Greek historian Abydenus, in his *History of the Chaldeans and Assyrians* (date unknown, probably Hellenistic era) now preserved in Eusebius' *Praeparatio Evangelica*, stated that Megasthenes also attributed gardens to Nebuchadnezzar II, and yet these were in Teredon some 200 miles to the south. One fragment recounting the deeds of the Assyrian king reads: '… and [he] built the city of Teredon to check the incursions of the Arabs; and he adorned the palaces with trees, calling them hanging gardens.'[11] And certainly the poem by the Greek epigrammatist, Antipater of Sidon, in which he voted them to the Seven Wonders of the Ancient World, never specifically linked the Hanging Gardens to the 'lofty walls' of Babylon, which were reportedly wide enough for two chariots to pass and with a higher (but narrower) inner wall built of mud brick.[12] To further confuse us, Diodorus included the 130 feet-long by 25 feet-wide (and just as thick) Obelisk of Semiramis at Babylon amongst the Seven Wonders of the World (originally *theamata*, 'sights', changed to *thaumata*, 'wonders' by Diodorus and Strabo), possibly following Callimachus, but the gardens, mentioned by Diodorus a paragraph earlier, were absent from the list.[13]

A cuneiform tablet known today as the *East India House Inscription* by Nebuchadnezzar II sits in the British Museum. It recorded the Great King's reconstruction of Babylon, including the Esagila Temple and shrines in the city.[14] This inscription *also* failed to mention gardens, as did the collection of tablets listing the topographical make-up of the city known as *Tintir*, copies of which were kept in Nineveh.[15] Herodotus' *Histories* bypassed them completely and Xenophon's *Cyropaedia* described the great walls but conspicuously he saw no hanging vegetation either, and for all its alluring *fabula*, the marvel-hungry *Greek Alexander Romance* is devoid of gardens at Babylon.[16]

But at the ancient Assyrian capital of Nineveh, supposedly destroyed in 612 BCE (though it may have seen a resurgence under the Seleucids), clear signs of horticulture and an irrigation system exist, with descriptions confirmed by tablets and in panel sculptures. These intricate gardens, which also existed at Kalhu (later named Nimrud) and Dur-Sharrukin ('Fortress of Sargon', modern Khorsabad) called upon Assyrian knowledge of dams, weirs, aqueducts, canals, sluices and bronze casting techniques that could manufacture large irrigation screws, technology that had already been employed by Ashurnasirpal II in the 9th century BCE.[17] Alexander's army would have passed the Jerwan aqueduct in the proximity of Gaugamela in 331 BCE, the ruins of which suggest concrete was in use centuries before Rome 'developed' it.[18]

Interestingly, Berossus, the inventor of the sundial according to Vitruvius (ca. 80/70-post 15 BCE), produced a work on Assyria besides the *Babylonaika* penned in Hellenistic *koine*.[19] Sennacherib (ca. 705-681 BCE), son of Sargon II and the most prominent of the kings of the Assyrian Empire centred at Nineveh, left detailed botanical inscriptions with mature gardens clearly depicted on the sculptures of his grandson, Assurbanipal.[20] On the octagonal stone Sennacherib Prism he described a construction that was fed by the River Khosr and he referred to his irrigation device in intriguingly familiar terms:

> … in order to draw water all day long, I had ropes, bronze wires and bronze chains made; and instead of a *shaduf* I set up great cylinders and *alamittu-*screws over cisterns… I raised the height of the surroundings of the palace. A park imitating the Amanus mountains I laid out next to it…[21]

The description is familiar because Robert Koldewey's 1898-1917 Babylonian excavations claimed to have unearthed a hydraulic machine with 'buckets attached to a chain on a wheel', though archaeologists now suggest this was nothing more than his overactive imagination.[22] Sennacherib rebuilt the ancient Assyrian city at Nineveh and he named it as his new capital. He was later murdered by his own sons, not necessarily there however, but possibly at Babylon.[23] And yet the *Book of Judith* in the biblical Apocrypha commenced with the statement that Nebuchadnezzar II, the Chaldean king of the Neo-Babylonian Empire, was in fact the king of the Assyrians who ruled in Nineveh, with rabbinical literature that detailed the invasions of Jerusalem placing him as the son-in-law of Sennacherib. Here it claimed the latter was 'king of Babylon'; Jewish texts, it appears, frequently confused either the two kings or the cities.[24]

'Confusion' then is the better etymology for 'Babylon', and it is a wholly appropriate reminder of the poor soil in which traditions may have sunk their roots. This fusion of fable and hanging flora remains relevant to the 'legend' of Alexander's death, for that too was born in the ancient campaign capital that straddled the Euphrates River.

At the heart of our debate lies the 'Babylon settlement' whose calamitous conclusion narrowly avoided a full-scale confrontation between the cavalry command led by the aristocratic Bodyguards, and the peasant-recruited infantry under their veteran commanders. Just as cultures and armies clashed here, so did our sources. The textual result sits like a badly erected bridge between the closing pages of the Alexander biographies and the opening chapters of the follow-on accounts that marched into the calamitous years of the Successor Wars. We sense the Roman-era historians were not entirely comfortable with what they saw in the earlier sources, particularly in the eyewitness testimony, but true to their reputation as engineers, they soon shored-up the span with their own rhetorical timbers, just as Nietzsche warned they were apt to.[26]

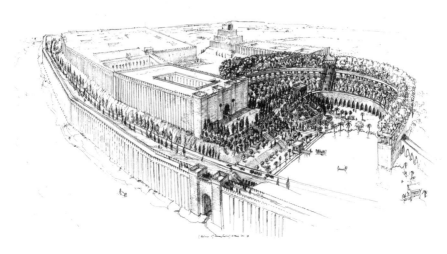

A reconstruction of the palace of Sennacherib at Nineveh by artist Terry Ball. It follows Sennacherib's own description and Josephus' account of gardens set outside the palace on a high citadel and 'to be a Wonder for all peoples', 'employing aqueducts, screws, lake and drainage'. Much evidence suggests the Hanging Gardens of Babylon were actually at Nineveh. The ziggurat of the Temple of Ishtar is shown in the background. Provided with the kind permission of Stephanie Dalley, Assyriologist, Oriental Institute and Wolfson College Honorary Senior Research Fellow, Somerville College, University of Oxford.[25]

REFOCUSING THE BLIND CYCLOPS

Unravelling the events that took place between Alexander's death on the 10th or 11th of June 323 BCE, and the fragile accord that was reached some indeterminate days later, becomes essential if we are to understand how, and why, the Will was whitewashed from the mainstream accounts. In the process we reveal an unsung hero, Eumenes, who helped make the settlement possible. Two early narratives of the conflict that ensued survived through later intermediaries: Cleitarchus' syncretic account that lives through Curtius' closing pages (T11), and the opening chapter of Hieronymus' history of the fifty years that followed, preserved most completely in Diodorus' eighteenth book (T13). Further pixels from the picture are visible, thanks to Photius, the Patriarch of Constantinople (ca. 810-893 CE), in the epitomised fragments of Arrian's *Events After Alexander* and Dexippus' derivatives of that, which, once again, originate with Hieronymus' *History of the Diadokhoi* or *Epigonoi* (T14, T15).[27] Alongside them we have Justin's thirteenth book in which précised elements of both Cleitarchus' and Hieronymus' accounts appear to be bound together (T12).

The accounts of these two historians conflict; this is unsurprising as they lived and worked under opposing political regimes: Cleitarchus under the Ptolemies, and Hieronymus at the Antigonid court. Cleitarchus provided the pre-packaged drama that filled the final chapter of the Vulgate biographies, whilst Hieronymus' summation was attractive to any writer extending their work into the Successor Wars, for it set the scenery for the follow-on events; thus Arrian, Diodorus and Trogus (visible through Justin) used it to open their own accounts of those post-Alexander years.

Judging from Diodorus' text, Hieronymus commenced with a summation of the fallout from the king's death: he listed the 'chief and most influential commanders' and he went on to describe the embassies between the rival factions, the compromise reached, the punishment of the dissenters, the crowning of Alexander's half-brother, Arrhidaeus, and Perdiccas' precarious retention of overall command which was aided by Eumenes who remained inside the city walls to broker a compromise.[28]

In this environment, Perdiccas, the king's former acting *chiliarchos*, now represented something of an uncomfortable hybrid authority that arguably encompassed the regency of a kingdom, the guardianship of new kings, and a mandate to oversee the empire, under one, or all, of the contentious titles of *epimeletes, prostates* and *strategos* (though now he was effectively *strategos autokrator*). Therein lay the dilemma and the source of the hostility towards the senior *custodis corporis*, the Latin rendering of 'Bodyguard', for whatever authority Macedonian tradition attached to these titles, here, emerging from a series of unique events at Babylon, their boundaries were being self-determined. It was in this new post-Alexander world that the term *chiliarchos*, used to denote the king's second-in-command (and possibly only meant for Hephaestion, initially), was contested and appears to have fallen out of use after Antipater died (late 319 BCE), though others would certainly act as if they had inherited the title.[29]

Greek historians of the age of Philip and Alexander were accustomed to opening their accounts with a geographical digression to establish the terrain for the reader; Thucydides had established the style for the later chroniclers, and evidence suggests the openings of Hecataeus, Timaeus and Ephorus followed suit.[30] Hieronymus was not atypical; he explained the shape and extent of Asia, and this provided a framework on which he could pin his list of the newly appointed (and reconfirmed) provincial governors in what amounted to informal *prokataskeue* (introductions) to place characters in context. All this detail, from the truce between the army factions to the governorship of the empire, is preserved well enough in the Hieronymus-derived summaries, though compressed to varying degrees. But what might once have been a vibrant excursion into the origins and *ethnoi* of the Persian Empire has since (possibly) crumpled to a 'tired, perfunctory catalogue of satrapies' in the condensing.[31]

Diodorus' attempt at conjoining what he saw in the scrolls of Cleitarchus and Hieronymus was not wholly successful, and it resulted in an untidy and inaccurate syncretised abbreviation.[32] This stemmed in part from Cleitarchus' own earlier dilemma of blending the claims in the *Journal* and *Pamphlet* with non-corroborating eyewitness testimony from veterans in Alexandria, and now with potential contradictory claims from Hieronymus as well. Diodorus additionally opened his follow-on (eighteenth) book with one hugely misleading statement: 'Alexander the king had died without issue, and a great contention arose over the leadership' (T13).[33] Here he failed to mention the pregnancy of Roxane, though his later books featured her and her son who became King Alexander IV, and he also bypassed any mention of Heracles, Alexander's existing son when, once again, the boy appeared in his later chapters. Furthermore, no reference was made to a Will at this point, though Diodorus clearly referred to Alexander's testament when recounting events at Rhodes that took place some eighteen years on, so he was clearly aware of a source that cited its existence.[34]

The motivation for compression is only so strong and it is usually dispensed when momentous detail is afoot; events at Babylon *were* momentous. So we may conclude that, like Cleitarchus, some two centuries before him, Diodorus was faced with the irreconcilable, though he chose to sidestep controversy and move speedily on. After all, *unlike* Cleitarchus' monograph, his library of world history spanning 1,138 years still lacked the twenty-three books that would cover the next 280 years down to the Roman dictators. Fatally for the Will, the common link preserved in all the conjoined accounts was the distribution of the empire by Perdiccas at the conclusion of the Babylonian settlement, for this suggested the action was necessary because Alexander had failed to transfer power and designate successors himself.

The account of the Roman Curtius, who was most probably a professional rhetorician with political clout, is the most detailed extant narrative of the infighting that led up to that final settlement, and is punctuated by vivid dialogues (T11).[35] The themes Curtius overlaid on events do look to be choice Roman reincarnations that were 'fitted to the occasion'. Considering the trend of his day – the use of *comparatio* (Greek *synkrisis*) and declamation for comparative and didactic effect – it is likely Curtius elongated Cleitarchus' speeches and suitably paired them with counter-speeches in his own sculpting of the dialogue. His use of *oratio recta* and *oratio obliqua* (direct and indirect speech modes), employed, for example, when earlier recounting each pre-battle speech (*epipolesis*) Alexander delivered, kept a momentum-filled hold on his audience.[36] Rome's *cursus honorum* influenced Curtius' retrospective view of history and so we must appreciate the Babylonian dialogues for what they really are: thematic echoes of the originals that had been first sterilised of anti-Ptolemaic toxins by Cleitarchus, and which were now reworked by a Roman *nobilis* to please the Roman *populus* serving an unpredictable *imperium*.[37] As a result, the occasion was 1st century CE Rome as much as 4th century BCE Babylon, a poetic *mimesis* that re-rendered 'Cleitarchean Babylon' through the Roman Principate.

Seneca is said to have warned that we 'should not be surprised, that each man selects the things fit for his pursuits from the same material', and noting that 'the dramatist creates' whereas 'the historian only disposes', here, at Babylon, Curtius' outcome appears 'pure theatre'.[38] We have an uncomfortable melee of anti-barbarian voices that rejected both of Alexander's sons (one *in utero*), highly treasonous accusations hurled at Perdiccas, a suddenly articulate halfwit royal, and the contentious suggestion of group rule by other Bodyguards.[39] It is worth quoting Ernst Badian at this point, for he captured the shortcomings of reconstructions that adhere too literally to the texts: 'It is the frequent penalty of excessive concentration of *Quellenforschung*... that it can become the aim of scholarship to find out what was said by whom rather than what in fact happened.'[40]

Curtius' recounting of events at Babylon may have reconstructed 'constitutional procedures' on the basis of the few previous examples he saw of the army's intervention into 'state' affairs: the trial of Philotas, for example, an episode he most likely heavily embellished as well.[41] Nevertheless, the original deeper Cleitarchean currents can still be felt beneath the rhetorical eddies and riptides that pushed Curtius' metarepresentations along. For there remains clarity to the emotions emanating from the Assembly gathering that was convened to hear the fate of the empire: the ambition, distrust, uncertainty, divided loyalty and outright jealousy of the gathered generals, 'lightened only by adventurous hopes and shadowy ambition'. This was all neatly summed up by Justin in the chapter-heading text.[42]

'Demades, after the death of Alexander, compared the Macedonian army to the Cyclops after his one eye was out, seeing their many disorderly and unsteady motions.'[43] And much work has been done attempting to unravel those 'unsteady motions' using the prevailing 'standard intestate model'. But a reinterpretation of the events at Babylon can be explained equally well, or in fact, better, in an environment with a Will, as we will try to demonstrate.

The claims within the *Pamphlet*, preserved in the *Romance* and *Metz Epitome* (T1, T2), stated that a Will was drafted, or more logically revised, through the day and night when Alexander's hopes of recovery were fading, though he was still sufficiently lucid to dictate his wishes to his most trusted men.[44] Although the content of the testament would have held no big surprises for the top echelons, no one could have been completely satisfied with the result. As we might expect, the first reading was a private Bodyguard affair, but word inevitably got out. But what spread was probably the rumour of a *posthumous* Will recital, at which point the excluded higher-ranking infantry officers – those already told to wait outside the bedchamber doors – forced their way in 'suspecting intrigue' or believing that their king was at death's door.[45]

Their right of entry could not be denied under Macedonian court custom; they were acknowledged by a barely conscious Alexander and withdrew to brood on the implications of what the testament might contain, and to ponder whether his wishes would be accurately transmitted, or respected, by those who *were* destined to inherit power. Though constitutional, the intrusion breached Macedonian *military* protocol under which the Bodyguards and royal pages restricted entry to the king; it was an episode that foreshadowed the divided loyalties that would manifest themselves so clearly in the troubled days ahead.

Alexander then passed into a deep coma. Once life signs were beyond detection, Perdiccas summoned the Companions and most eminent infantry officers and publically pronounced the king 'dead'. At this point Curtius provided a two-and-a-half-page digression on the mourning that followed, when 'conqueror and conquered were indistinguishable' in their grief. He detailed the regrets of the army at denying their king the divine honours he sought (we recall they derided his attachments to his new 'father' Zeus-Ammon at Opis), and he listed Alexander's qualities and their attachments to fate and fortune.[46] Justin's précis suggests Trogus followed a similar rhetorical template, but here the Macedonians '… rejoiced at his death as at that of an enemy, execrating his excessive severity and the perpetual hardships of war to which he exposed them.'[47] Whilst these sentiments appear polarised, both the feelings of grief *and* relief were doubtlessly present at Babylon, and a complex conjoining of both emotions likely existed in many of those then present.

But to understand the framework of the severe discord, we need to unravel the mechanism that drew those colliding parts – the infantry officers, cavalry command, Bodyguards and chiliarch – together, and then summarily sundered them. An insightful comment in Bosworth's study on the legacy of the Asian campaign captures the challenge of analysing what we have:

> … the situation then was constitutionally unique and politically complex. In that light, it comes as quite a shock to read much of the traditional literature on the Settlement. It presupposes that there was something akin to statute law, with fixed positions and procedures for a regency, and deals with a single definitive settlement, which was reached at Babylon and agreed by all the diverse players in the dynastic game.[48]

Of course, a Will would have provided those missing ingredients: a form of statute law, fixed positions and procedures; a defined mandate yet open to ambiguity, abuse, and inevitably, to challenge. For here in foreign lands 'the king's power was not institutional but situational', and so too was the Common Assembly of Macedones, the *koinon Makedonon*.[49]

THE CONCLAVE OF THE *KOINON MAKEDONON*

The origins of the Common Assembly are obscure, as is the extent of its constitutional authority at home and more so overseas in Babylon in 323 BCE; arguments on Macedonian constitutionalism have, as one scholar recently noted, generated a 'cottage industry'.[50] On one extreme, commentators on the issue see the Assembly representing formalised state law, and on the other it was nothing but a *nomos* (here an established 'characteristic of a free society' or a tradition) that enabled traditional *isegoria*, freedom of speech, with a dominant warlord.

The debate on whether the Macedonians had even formalised the national title 'king', *basileus Makedonon*, remains just as vigorous, though Herodotus and Thucydides believed that they had.[51] Nevertheless, *basileus* was never minted on Philip's coins, which suggests in Macedonia the warlord status may have eclipsed any regal recognition; he simply remained 'Philippos Amyntou Makedonios' to his men. Only towards the end of Alexander's reign were coins struck with *Alexandrou basileus*;[52] again this suggests the unique army-commander bond was not supplanted by the formalities of *regnum* until the campaign was well advanced; symbolically this correlates with Alexander's character metamorphosis in the Vulgate biographies.

With probable roots in a conclave that supported the sovereign power of a warrior-elected leader, the Assembly continued to evolve as equestrian aristocratic landowners emerged in the military state; they acted as a balance, or conduit of authority, between the king and the growing power of the nobility on whom mineral extraction, harbour levies, timber felling, and other commercial leases had been bestowed. The king was deemed to *control* all the state assets, the judicious distribution and gifting of which assured him their support; this does not undermine the notion that the 'people' considered that the treasury was to be used for their wellbeing and protection.[53]

In turn, the Assembly guarded against a coup by nobility, who, for their privileged positions, were doubtless expected to furnish troops on demand and organise local defence. Whilst in the reign of Philip II 'hardly more than a hundred chiefs of aristocratic families formed the King's Companions', he could have easily become a hostage if he abused their support, which is perhaps why he instituted his own private royal guards brigade.[54] Under Philip, the northern and western cantons, which had previously enjoyed a degree of autonomy, were eventually folded into a more centralised state; their nobles and their sons were enrolled into the elite Companion Cavalry.

It was probably at this point that a more formalised Assembly was convened to represent wider national interests, perhaps held in an amphitheatre to house its larger diverse audience; at *less* formal occasions, ad hoc *ekklesiai* were called to discuss a broader range of issues.[55] This public forum of expression would have provided the veneer of checks, balances and regional representation, even if the Macedonian 'king' could ultimately sway its vote, whether by charm or execution, or by the threat of his personal pike battalions.[56] We should note the tradition in close-by Epirus of swearing 'solemn oaths' to Zeus Areius at Passaro each year in which the people and king agreed to abide by the laws.[57] But when it came to voting on matters of state during a military campaign, inevitably the common 'people' *were* the Macedonian 'army'. More often than not, under these circumstances – war – the 'Assembly' became a hastily convened *synedrion,* for the army was in fact a far easier body to assemble; it was also easier to manipulate and manage than scattered peasants and the landlord nobility of peacetime.

Where a *synedrion* represented a more frequently assembled privy council of the king and his *philoi* – his close friends and advisers (the 'companionate') – an Assembly was a more formal and far less frequent gathering of *all* the leading men-at-arms, perhaps convened twice a year: at the beginning of the campaign season (the *panaitolika* or *Xandika* in the month of Xandikos, broadly March) and at its end (the *panegyris* in Dios, broadly October).[58] At an Assembly, the *hetairoi* who had become the king's Companions, and the peasant-stocked infantry (many of whom started life as pastoral herders: 'milk-drinkers', Euripides would have labelled them) represented by senior battalion commanders, came together to vote on critical state decisions;[59] if the idea of some quasi-democratic process is suggested by such a conclave, it remains unlikely that representation ever saw uneducated tenant farmers in the king's hall. In fact, it may have been *only* military men, perhaps one-tenth of the national male population, who were *ever* enfranchised in any way.[60]

The Assembly was, in effect, an extension of the king's own personality in what may still have been the absence of wider constitutional laws in Macedonia; when the court gatherings ended in *komoi*, the traditional drinking parties with their distinct Homeric origins, bonds were galvanised between officers and their commander-in-chief – the national *strategos autokrator* – whose office now represented the foremost religious official, a role in which he became their intermediary with the national gods.[61] It was a relationship that permitted the nobles and army officers access without the formalities of rank, ceremony, and formalised obeisance, and though they were still subjects of a monarchy, this explains the Macedonian abhorrence of Achaemenid-style *proskynesis*.[62]

The king was effectively inviting select guests into his *oikos* (household), and that, in turn, provided him the opportunity to monitor revellers who would have been watched, probed and eavesdropped upon for any signs of dissent. Attending the guests were the corps of royal pages, *paides basilikoi*, aged fourteen to eighteen, the sons of the nobles prudently retained as behavioural security. Alexander continued the custom of maintaining these unofficial 'hostages', though it almost led to his undoing in Asia.[63]

The principal functions of the *koinon Makedonon* appear clearer than its origins. The common Assembly retained the ability to elect a new state leader and it became judge and jury in cases of treason. Although it had been invoked, for example, at the trial of Philotas (and his father, Parmenio, *in absentia*), and at Cassander's revenge-fuelled trial of Olympias some eight years on, quicker executions appear to have taken place on the king's direct command; Alexander did not wait for common opinion to execute the thirteen ringleaders of the dissent at Opis.[64] But to what extent, as *basileus*, he could act independent of the Assembly, remains conjecture; Curtius stated that in capital cases, '... the position of the king counted for nothing unless his influence had been substantiated before the trial.'

If, on the other hand, the king's power was absolute (as some scholars see it), how far that could extend probably depended, once again, on his personal charisma, his diplomatic skills, the weight of support he enjoyed from his nobles (as a result), and the nature of the immediate danger being faced; a popular leader would get his way with a minimum of formality, where an unpopular figurehead (or a popular king making an unpopular decision) would need formal Common Assembly approval to avoid revolt.[65]

This would explain why the dividing line between constitutionalism and autocracy is blurred in the evidence we have; we can see the Assembly's 'meteoric' appearance when Philip ascended the throne, and its complete disappearance once he had established himself. Similarly, we see the same trend in Alexander's reign: an Assembly was convened for the trial and executions of his father's (alleged) assassins, when he himself had little *established* support, and we have scant references of its convening in the spectacular successes of Alexander's early campaign years in which his leadership was unchallenged. Only when storm clouds gathered did the Assembly feature once more – at the trials of Philotas and then Alexander Lyncestis, and for Cleitus' posthumous condemnation.

The Assembly featured even more loudly in the army mutinies that followed.[66] Consider this phenomenon in light of the timing of

Cassander's later appeal to the people to justify Olympias' execution (the point at which his own rule commenced, probably 316 BCE), and Demetrius *Poliorketes'* speech in 294 BCE which undermined Cassander's reign.[67] Notably, Perdiccas did *not* gain (though he sought) Assembly approval when attacking Ptolemy in Egypt (a sham trial appears to have backfired), and that may well have cost him his life.[68]

The Assembly also had to deal with the rules of succession, which are not wholly clear. Primogeniture was not the *absolute* requirement in Macedonia, although elder brothers (or uncles) often prevailed for purely practical reasons, often on the pretext of guardianship of the young; Philip II's *epimeletia* for his brother's son, Amyntas Perdicca, is just one example.[69] But as suggested in a speech recorded by Livy, in which the Macedonian prince Perseus was berating his younger brother (Demetrius), primogeniture *was* an established *tradition*.[70]

Alexander's ancestors had often produced several male heirs who were proclaimed joint kings: Alexander I left five sons behind him who, in turn, produced ten (known) grandsons from five collateral branches of the royal line. The period 399-391 BCE saw six kings in eight years from three competing lines,[71] and six sons and a daughter were born to Amyntas III (died ca. 370 BCE), including Philip II. In practice, the conflicts engendered by this 'oversupply of kings' often led to pretenders to the throne (often backed by interested neighbouring states) and, inevitably, to fratricide, a result the Successor Wars were to amplify.[72] At other times kings were elected *in utero* or brothers shared the rule, and if still immature, more formalised guardians would be appointed; here again the Assembly could play its part, though whether this represented a succession *requirement* is again unclear.[73]

Considered against the background of the Assembly's traditional function, the situation in Babylon in 323 BCE was unique, and it would inevitably challenge the judicial boundaries and the authority of those presiding. Alexander's early 'security measures' – the execution of conspirators, pretenders and their relatives upon his own accession (including Amyntas Perdicca) – 'had ensured the Argead house was virtually extinct', and of course that had suited his immediate cause.[74] But Alexander had filled the void by unsatisfactory means, as far as the rank and file picking up the pieces at Babylon were concerned.

The Macedonian army was, we propose, now being subordinated in a king's Will to what were deemed defective options: an as yet unborn half-Asiatic child, a further juvenile half-Asiatic son, and a mentally defective Argead, while a distrusted chiliarch was acting as *de facto* head of state. Moreover, the endowments of the Will failed to recognise, or even mention, the common foot soldiers who had played a major part in transforming a kingdom into an empire. If we assume that the attendance by the infantry officers was a requisite part of the Assembly vote, at Babylon they were hamstrung, for they lacked the voice of the influential veterans, Craterus, Antipater and Antigonus. For these were the men who commanded their true respect and they were generals who could have overshadowed the presiding and now hugely wealthy Persian nobility-married *Somatophylakes*.

In his earlier coverage of events, Cleitarchus might have envisioned a gathering in the great throne room of the palace, and though it is tempting to visualise a sea of men, the Bodyguards most likely orchestrated a quarantined affair; three courtyards are thought to have led to the throne room of the Summer Palace and they presented a practical means of separation.[75] Indeed a herald called the officers by name; although 'many were unable to enter the royal quarters', the select summons was widely disregarded and others squeezed through the cordon. Wherever the gathering took place, waiting outside of the palace grounds *was* surely a sea of anxious and impatient men.[76]

Perdiccas, now something of a 'grand vizier' in the temporary absence of a king, chaired the meeting and the salient points of the king's Will were read aloud. Curtius described how 'a crowd of the rank and file was anxious to know to whom the fortune of Alexander would pass' (*scire in quem Alexandri fortuna esset transitura*).[77] But before we jump into the boiling caldron of disquiet that followed, we should take a look at Perdiccas' first course of action on which the parties *were* all agreed: the cancelling of the ruinously costly and unrealistically ambitious 'last plans'. For embedded within them may be the remains of the bequests from an equally extravagant and ruinous Will.

HIDDEN *HYPOMNEMATA* AND A MISSING FUNERAL PYRE

> For when Perdiccas found in the memoranda of the king orders for the completion of the pyre of Hephaestion, which required a great deal of money, and also for the other designs of Alexander, which were many and great and called for an unprecedented outlay, he decided that it was inexpedient to carry them out. But that he might not appear to be arbitrarily detracting anything from the glory of Alexander, he laid these matters before the common assembly of the Macedonians for consideration.[78] (T25)

Historians appear to accept that although Alexander declined to write a Will, he *had* kept personal *hypomnemata* in which his grandiose plans were outlined in detail. Immediately after his death Perdiccas apparently 'found' in the king's memoranda, *en tois hypomnemasi tou basileos* (we might suppose in the Eumenes-managed secretariat), a number of incomplete projects and wishes. The most prominent of them included a funeral pyre for Hephaestion, fleet building on an unheard of scale, harbour constructions that could dock 1,000 warships, population transfers and racial *synoikismoi* through the establishment of new mixed cities, as well as plans to campaign in Arabia and the West, supported by an ambitious new network of roads.

Some are credible as part of the projects that featured in the main narrative of ongoing military preparations with the associated harbours, canals and dredging improvements at Babylon, though the reported scale, if anywhere near accurate, is extraordinary.[79] As far as the remainder, reaction amongst scholars ranges from wholehearted acceptance to wholesale disbelief,[80] but obvious Hellenistic and Roman embroidery has been spotlighted and some non-authentic-looking embassies appeared from far-off supplicants seeking Macedonian 'friendship' at the same time.[81]

What remain notably out of tune in Diodorus' list of scuppered projects were the king's requests for tombs, temples and monuments, for these have a distinctly 'testamental' aroma:

> … to erect six most costly temples, each at an expense of 1,500 talents… The temples mentioned were to be built at Delos, Delphi, and Dodona, and in Macedonia a temple to Zeus at Dion, to Artemis Tauropolus at Amphipolis, and to Athena at Cyrnus. Likewise at Ilium in honour of this goddess there was to be built a temple that could never be surpassed by any other. A tomb for his father Philip was to be constructed to match the greatest pyramids of Egypt…[82] (T25)

This detail should be compared with the donatives and memorials demanded in the *Metz Epitome* and *Romance* Wills, in which we read of a tomb for Philip to 'rival the pyramids'; this was, more credibly, to be a great earthwork tumulus in the established Macedonian tradition.[83] The label *hypomnemata* could credibly have *accompanied* a lifetime covenant or a written testament as well, and it can be equally translated as 'drafts', 'accompanying notes', or even 'inventories', such as the list of names, deeds and events that once featured in Strabo's *Historika hypomnemata* and in the *Hypomnemata* of Aristoxenus and Hegesander which we do now refer to as 'memoirs' or 'commentaries'.[84]

Texts are ambiguous on whether these so-called 'last plans' were discussed at the first, or possibly a second, Assembly; it seems the degeneration of the initial gathering required a further conclave once the infighting that followed Alexander's death had died down, and it was here that decisions were finally ratified. Claims that Alexander's body was left untreated for some three, six, or even (an impossible) thirty days, before the seer Aristander addressed the Assembly, add to the confusion.[85] When he did finally broach the issue of the *hypomnemata*, Perdiccas' arguments would have focused on treasury limitations and the impracticalities of implementing such heady schemes; he would surely have used the opportunity, now that the Will had been broadcast aloud, to solicit the cancelling of *both* the ongoing campaign plans *and* the Will-demanded monuments in a single breath, thus they were fused together in the recounting of the session.

Making the Will contents public, as Hatzopoulos has pointed out, would have reflected contemporary Macedonian practice, and according to Polybius, a century later Antigonus III *Doson* left a Will in which 'he gave account of his administration to the Macedonians' and he notably appointed an *epitou grammateiou*, who Hammond believed was a secretary in charge of the royal archives; this surely paralleled the role of Eumenes.[86] And here at Babylon, rather than sounding controversial, the project abandonments proposed by Perdiccas likely brought a sense of relief to the soldiers who must have been thinking of heading home with booty and back-pay; it would have been additionally supported by the Bodyguards who planned to journey to their new satrapies with the treasuries still intact.

Also annulled was the pending change of command in Macedonia, in which Antipater was supposed to step down in favour of the returning Craterus who would have then enjoyed the support of the 10,000 veterans discharged at Opis.[87] On this issue, Perdiccas may have disguised his true intent by arguing for a 'respectful' *status quo* – in terms of both Craterus' location (Cilicia) and Antipater's regency – as he is unlikely to have relished the prospect of such a sizeable and experienced force congregating in Macedonia under a potentially hostile regent (old or new). Perdiccas would have wanted to assimilate Craterus' veterans into his own ranks when considering that as few as 13,000 Macedonian infantry and 2,000 cavalry are thought to have remained at Babylon in the royal army; the rest were Asiatic troops, though newly arrived recruits make calculations uncertain. This annulment *may* have been contentious as Craterus had supporters in Babylon; many infantry officers present would have served under him, including the vocal battalion commander, Meleager, the most important infantry officer then present and the man at the centre of what would next take place.[88]

Craterus and his veterans (including the commanders White Cleitus, Polyperchon, Antigenes and Gorgias) *were* still camped in Cilicia when Alexander died, though why they had delayed there remains unexplained. News of the king's death could conceivably have reached Cilicia in ten to twelve days by royal relay and faster by crier, and yet there is no record of Craterus immediately stirring to action.[89] He may well have been watching events at Babylon unfold, and he may even have considered making a bid for Perdiccas' post if the winds blew favourably, possibly soliciting reaction first from Antigonus in Phrygia; he, in turn, was no doubt making contact with Antipater in Pella. Craterus and Antigonus might between them have discussed a united front against the Perdiccan royal army in Asia Minor on the expectation of defections, as they did later.[90] Even when news of the Lamian War reached them, they may have contemplated letting Antipater embroil himself in trouble in Greece; having dealt with Perdiccas, they would then cross the Hellespont to save the day and re-administer Hellas and Asia on their own terms.

Many were the permutations (and unhatched schemes we may never know of) and many were the risks; in the end, both Craterus and Antigonus decided to cross to Macedonia, but not until clear threats on both sides of the Aegean had emerged.[91] As it turned out, the Lamian War in Greece, which commenced soon after news of Alexander's death reached Athens, initially benefited Perdiccas (it is not beyond reason that he was in touch with the Greek uprising) – as it prevented any concerted action being taken against him for a year or more (and it vacated their satrapies) – but it ultimately played a major part in uniting the veteran generals against him.

The textual positioning of the 'last plans' in the extant manuscripts of Diodorus' *Bibliotheke Historika* has led historians to link Craterus to certain other of these cancelled projects, for the *hypomnemata* entry began (immediately after the allocation of satrapies):

> It happened that Craterus, who was one of the most prominent men, had previously been sent away by Alexander to Cilicia with those men who had been discharged from the army, 10,000 in number. At the same time, he had received written instructions that the king had given him for execution; nevertheless, after the death of Alexander, it seemed best to the successors not to carry out these plans.[92] (T25)

A description of each project immediately followed. Quite credibly, Craterus could have been given a shipbuilding task by Alexander, for Cilicia was rich in timber from the Taurus ranges and in high-grade iron. Pitch, tow, copper, cloth, shipwrights, carpenters, sawyers and smiths would have been additionally required; canvas, goat hair, flax and papyrus for ropes and sailcloth, bitumen, bailing buckets, anchors, anchor chains and other tools and accessories needed procuring, and that would have taken time. We are told copper, hemp and sails *had* been requisitioned from Cyprus, and cedar wood from Mount Libanus (Lebanon) whose forests were made famous by the *Epic of Gilgamesh* and eulogised by Diodorus; sailors and pilots from all parts of the world *were* already collecting at nearby Thapsacus on the Upper Euphrates some 700 km from Babylon for the planned Arabian-African circumnavigation.[93]

As part of this grand expedition, Cilicia might have been a recruiting point for deck soldiers (*epibatai*), oarsmen (*nautai*) under a rowing master (*keleustes*) and helmsman (*kybernetes*), with naval officers (*hyperesia*) operating under fleet trierarchs.[94] The royal treasury at Cyinda would have been called upon to fund it, assuming the Eastern treasury hauls had already been deposited there; possibly the movement of gold and silver was a part of Craterus' brief, aided by the Silver Shields brigade – the *Argyraspides* – on their journey westward from Opis, and that would explain their slow progress as well as their continued presence in Cilicia.[95]

Craterus' brief may have additionally tasked him with transporting his veterans in part of the new fleet back to Macedonia, and then sending Antipater back with new recruits, that is if claims that the aged regent had been summoned are genuine; certainly Alexander would not have left Macedonia devoid of a regent and an army.[96] 'White' Cleitus did construct (or inherit) a navy in Cilicia that was to clear the path for Craterus' *re-crossing* the Hellespont two years on; using part of a 240-strong Macedonian fleet Cleitus successfully engaged the Athenians in two battles off Amorgas and the Echinades in the Lamian War.[97] A sea voyage home by Craterus could have even included a punitive action against Athens, for Alexander must have been aware of the mercenary concentrations at Cape Taenarum and the polemical noises filtering out of Greece in the months before his death.[98]

But the overriding instruction to Craterus was clearly to relieve Antipater of his regency, and the link-line in Diodorus' paragraphs dealing with the conglomerated plans – 'at the same time, he had received written instructions' – could equally have referred to Alexander's orders to Perdiccas.[99] Moreover, Diodorus' *previous* paragraph closed with an account of the preparations for Alexander's sarcophagus and its journey to Egypt: 'The transportation of the body of the deceased king and the preparation of the vehicle that was to carry the body to Ammon they assigned to Arrhidaeus.'[100] The whole passage is badly constructed and the true division of the historian's original intent has been lost.

This may have been due to Diodorus' own confusion on a Will that appeared nowhere in Cleitarchus' account of Babylon, but which might have featured in Hieronymus' summation of events in which the testament wishes were, nevertheless, ambiguously distinguished from expedition *hypomnemata* – cloudy water made murkier by Diodorus' own précising. Or it was because we are reading incompetent transmissions by scribes who were themselves unclear on the separation.

We know that in classical Greece the word *diatheke* would have most commonly been used when referencing a Will, yet it was more specifically a covenant in the legal sense of a contract. Derived from *diatithesthai* – 'putting aside' – the structure *katalipein diatithemenon* – 'to leave by testament' or by 'covenant' – *may* indeed have been used by

Hieronymus somewhere in this narrative.[101] And unless the immediate text was accompanied by clear Will-invoking dialogue (Aristotle's Will, for example, quoted in full by Diogenes Laertius), the 'contract' was easily shadowed in ambiguity for later historians. If Hieronymus had simply stated 'as the king had covenanted' against these projects, there was little to support a Will further in the context of Perdiccas' speech. This would explain the military nature of some of the 'last plans' and the commemorative nature of others.

As a result, the references to Craterus were sandwiched confusingly between the division of the empire, and Perdiccas' dilemma with the 'last plans', potentially with the Will bequests within them.[102] But the final instruction, which concerned Alexander's funeral hearse, would have been one Will-demanded project that Perdiccas and the Assembly dared not reject; they may simply have acquiesced to it as posthumous compensation to their king.

What Diodorus *did* make clear was that he was openly excerpting from a fuller list – 'the following were the largest and most remarkable items of the memoranda' – while he added that others 'were many and great' (T25).[103] We would imagine that the list included journal entries from the Eumenes-supervised *Ephemerides* that detailed still more demands and projects with their scheduling and costs.[104] It takes no great leap of faith to appreciate how a 'journal' – generically *ephemerides* to Plutarch and Arrian – became *hypomnemata*. Neither is it difficult to appreciate how a reference to 'last wishes', a term often associated with a Will, became part of 'last plans' by a historian merging detail from conflicting sources.

Hieronymus was not looking to delve into the campaign past too deeply as his own forty-plus years of active service were begging their space on parchment. He may not have been a dispassionate Thucydides but neither was he a sensationalist; we recall Dionysius described his book as 'longwinded and boring'.[105] Judging from Arrian's précis of it, his *Events After Alexander*, Hieronymus' summation of Babylon appears to have been 'matter of fact', not plumped up with rhetoric. Moreover, he would not have spent time dissecting a Will whose boundaries and bequests were challenged by his patrons from the outset, and his narrative was dull testate ash when compared to Cleitarchus' intestate flames. It could have conceivably looked something like this:

> Perdiccas dispensed the regional governorships as the king had covenanted and arrangements were made for the transport of the king's body to its final resting place; the task of preparing the funeral bier given to Arrhidaeus. Perdiccas brought before the Assembly the king's list [*hypomnemata*] of last wishes which included... [here followed the list Diodorus précised]... At the same time he cancelled the other projects found listed in the royal diaries [*Ephemerides*] for the completion of a

funeral pyre for Hephaestion, and the plans Craterus had been given
for the repatriation of 10,000 veterans to Macedonia, as well as for his
construction of 1,000 warships larger than triremes for a campaign
West, and a road to run through Libya to support the campaign; the
construction of new cities with population transfers between them
were also cancelled due to the financial situation and uncertainties
that faced them... All these final plans were then presented before the
Assembly...

But did the overt grandeur of the projects originate with Hieronymus?
Communis opinio holds that their descriptions are more in keeping with
Cleitarchus' sensational style and thus more Vulgate exaggeration that
approached *thauma* with their scale.[106] If so, how did the detail end up in
Diodorus' *follow-on* book, which leaned principally on Hieronymus? The
answer is straightforward enough: Curtius made it clear that Alexander
had already announced many of the projects, along with his desire to
campaign westwards, the *previous year*, and they remained at the planning
stage, or were at least incomplete, with Arrian providing corroborating
detail.[107] When switching sources at the point of Alexander's death,
Diodorus embellished what he found presented blandly by Hieronymus
with this earlier material that was painted in Cleitarchean colour. As one
historian has commented: 'The more austere history of Hieronymus was
enriched by supplements from the Alexander Vulgate.'[108] Hellenistic, and
then Roman imaginations, may have later inflated the scale of the projects.
'Fascinated by the King's personality, historians have failed to see that the
story of the *hypomnemata* belongs not to the history of Alexander, but to
the history of the Successors', so concluded Badian, and so we *partially*
conclude too.[109]

Wrapping up the mystery behind the last plans is the aforementioned
reference to Hephaestion's funeral pyre.[110] Debate continues on whether
the pyre, supposedly costing 12,000 talents and described by Diodorus
in the same detail he afforded Alexander's funeral carriage,[111] was to be
burned as a *pyra* as part of a ritualised funeral ceremony which '... not
only surpassed all those previously celebrated on earth but also left no
possibility for anything greater in later ages', or whether it was built as
a permanent monument, a *heroon* or hero shrine, as its alleged position
(according to Koldewey) inside the Babylonian city walls might suggest.[112]

Texts, including episodes recorded by Plutarch, Justin and Lucian, are
also somewhat ambiguous as to what funerary ceremonies took place at
Ecbatana and Babylon, and also when they took place; Aelian certainly
included the description of Alexander throwing armour, gold and silver
onto Hephaestion's pyre in his retribution on the acropolis at Ecbatana,
but he added that the pyre was actually burned at *Alexander's* death – thus
at Babylon – the latter backed up by Alexander's appointing Perdiccas to

transport Hephaestion's body there.[113] Backing up the latter part of Aelian's claim is the suggestion the lavish pyre, or tomb, remained incomplete, possibly because Alexander 'longed for' the Rhodian architect, Deinocrates (or Stasicrates, responsible for the building of Alexandria), to construct it and he was not immediately available.[114] Yet Diodorus suggested the funeral took place before Alexander 'turned to amusements and festivals' following Hephaestions' elevation to god (or 'associate god').[115]

Hieronymus would not have bypassed a construction as significant as that Diodorus described, with its thirty compartments forming furlong-length sides, with foundations formed from the golden prows of 240 quinqueremes (which must have depleted the fleet) supporting seven ornate tiers soaring to 140 cubits (perhaps 210 feet).[116] Unfortunately, a lacuna in Curtius' final chapter deprives us from seeing what we might then have concluded were clear Cleitarchean origins and Plutarch's brevity reveals little more.[117] An obvious alternative source for the detail is Ephippus the Olynthian, whose alleged work was titled *On the Death* [or *Funeral*] *of Alexander and Hephaestion*; the description certainly fits the extravagances he attributed to the king's court, though that additionally suggests unreliability.

Curious *is* Koldewey's claim that he found remnants of the rubble from the Esagila Temple beside evidence of Hephaestion's commemorative located *inside* the city walls, east of one of the palaces (there were three inside Babylon's outer wall) and north of the (probably Hellenistic-era) Greek theatre; sources relate that it had taken 10,000 men two months to move the temple debris when Alexander rekindled his plan to rebuild the shrine to Bel-Marduk after his return from the East.[118] But according to Diodorus, Hephaestion's pyre was being constructed from a 10-furlong demolition of the outer city wall. Was the material, in fact, to come from that inner temple rubble? Because demolishing Babylon's famous defences would have been extremely counterproductive from both a military and public relations perspective, though it is unclear how much of the outer fortifications were still in place in Alexander's day; Mazaeus' hasty capitulation soon after defeat at Gaugamela might suggest the city was already far from impregnable.[119]

What *is* clear is that before Alexander's death each of his generals and 'friends' provided gold and ivory likenesses (*eidola*, like those found in Tomb II at Vergina) of Hephaestion and they surely did this to please a by-then unstable Alexander, and likely at his request.[120] At the Assembly in June 323 BCE, however, and with the king dead, the inheritors of power would not permit the treasury to be squandered further on Hephaestion, for Alexander's former *chiliarchos* was far from unanimously liked.[121]

When debating the permanence of the extraordinary memorial we should recall that other monuments to Hephaestion were planned in

Alexandria. In a letter to Cleomenes, Alexander had allegedly warned his wayward *arabarchos* that Hephaestion's two 'shrines', the first on the Island of Pharos, and the second in the heart of the new city, needed to be splendid to exonerate him from the repercussions of his financial mismanagement.[122] If shrines were in fact mausoleums, or if one of them had been designed to house his mummified corpse, and recalling Homer's 'don't bury my bones separately from yours, Achilles, but together, just as we were raised in your house', should we not expect that Alexander planned to inter his former intimate in his new city as a symbolic reuniting with *his* Patroclus?[123]

Again there is no evidence that the Alexandrian commemoratives were completed; Ptolemy apparently stopped construction when he decided to terminate Cleomenes for his alleged Perdiccan sympathies, though the more likely motivation was Ptolemy's desire for treasury control at a time when Egypt was still nominally raising tribute for the kings at Pella.[124]

A reconstruction of the funeral pyre of Hephaestion based upon the description given by Diodorus. A woodcut by Franz Jaffe ca. 1900.

STORMY SEAS AND THE FIRST FLUSH OF FREEDOM

When addressing the Assembly, it comes as no surprise to read that Perdiccas broached the succession issue by placing Alexander's ring, crown and robes in front of him for the crowd to see.[125] If the king's Will was known to have been drafted and first read in the presence of the Bodyguards, then Perdiccas was re-emphasising the authority that stemmed from the bequests within the testament. Yet this brought with it the suspicion that he might have unduly influenced the king or the shape of the document itself.

What we consider as an ongoing *chiliarchia* implied Perdiccas' authority filtered down through the *Somatophylakes* to the cavalry officers (*ilarchoi*), then to the infantry commanders (*taxiarchoi*) and down to the troops below them. Perdiccas was himself of royal stock from the house of Orestis, the westernmost Upper Macedonian canton that lay closest to Epirus, as was Leonnatus. By now, however, the common soldier, whether *pezhetairoi*, esteemed *asthetairoi* or other *hypaspistai* regiments, and the veterans amongst them, found the true source of authority in their immediate commander.[126] A later parallel would be the Roman army, whose legionnaires put faith in their centurion ahead of the tribunes or legates – the equestrian classes above. For rather than galvanising an army far from home into a homogenous national unit, Alexander's campaign had seen the social, political, and even the financial gaps, widen.

So the untested fabric of the Assembly on foreign soil was being stretched further by an army behaving ever more like a mercenary unit than an imperial force.[127] The description of the mindset of the Macedonians that the exiled Charidemus provided to Darius III before the battle at Issus – soldiers motivated by 'poverty's schooling' – was by now long redundant.[128] Since the mutinies in India and at Opis, their willingness to be swayed by their king – the single tenuous thread that had held the authority chain together – had been tested too.

In Curtius' portrayal, Perdiccas handed back the ring of authority he had received from Alexander and then begged the Assembly to choose a new leader, adding that he hoped Roxane's child, due within three months (or sooner), would be a boy (T11).[129] Though the Macedonian army had rallied behind royal infants before, the cradled King Aeropus I, for example, who was once carried into battle (reigned ca. 602-576 BCE),[130] here, in contrast to Perdiccas' seeming humility, this final wish appeared to broadcast several tendentious messages. The first was his own vested interest in that outcome, and thus his personal ambition, for he had either been given Roxane's hand in marriage (as the *Pamphlet* Will claimed) or he had become Roxane's *de facto* protector, which amounted to much the same thing.

Perdiccas' words further implied that the claims of other contenders – the existing son, Heracles, and even the king's half-brother, Arrhidaeus – might be undermined by his supremacy, despite any wishes in their direction Alexander had articulated in the Will. The chiliarch is reported to have rounded-off his speech with, '... meanwhile, nominate those you want as your leaders.'[131] Perdiccas would not have handed back the emblem of power, when, as events were to show, he did all he could to wrest that power from those who would oppose him. The conclusion to Perdiccas' speech has the hallmark of a Cleitarchean device, and one that legitimised Ptolemy's role in the power play that followed – if it was not Curtius' own overlay.[132]

The Will demands themselves were sufficiently contentious to cause Assembly uproar. In the thick of the clamour we hear that Nearchus upheld the claims of *both* of Alexander's potential sons to the throne, but with a sensible reminder that Roxane may birth a girl, a situation that demanded the recognition of the absent three- or four-year-old Heracles.[133] Nearchus had married into the family of the boy's mother at Susa, a fact that has encouraged speculation that it was his account – which must have therefore been published before ca. 310 BCE (when the boy was murdered on Cassander's instigation) – which brought Heracles out of obscurity as a prelude to his promotion.[134] But at Babylon, Nearchus was pushing his case a little too vigorously, and the crowd saw through another nepotistic promotion that was summarily rejected. If Nearchus *did* subsequently advance the boy's claim through the medium of his book, it is unlikely he would have mentioned that humiliating Assembly rejection.

At this juncture, Ptolemy was introduced into the Assembly in a pivotal role: he gave a speech that amounted to a total rejection of *both* of the 'half-barbarian' princes mothered by a 'conquered race'.[135] In a sense, this was a rejection of Nearchus too; already famous for his sea voyage, Nearchus did indeed steadfastly oppose the Ptolemaic regime in his service under Antigonus in the years to come. But the clearly treasonous words credited to Ptolemy could never have been *publicly* delivered by a *Somatophylax* or one of the *hetairoi* so soon after the king's death, intestate or otherwise.[136]

No doubt *private* utterances proffered exactly this view, especially amongst the infantry for whom the Persians were still the 'enemy'; the notion of a half-Asiatic on the Macedonian throne was, at that time, a wholly abhorrent concept. However, as with the alleged burning of Persepolis by Ptolemy's courtesan Thais, the moral message emanating from this rework, if Cleitarchean, would have suited the tone of the day some thirty-plus years on in Ptolemaic Alexandria in which even Egyptians recalled the heavy hand of the Persian yoke. Ptolemy, who declined to cover the Babylonian aftermath in his own book, notably never took a wife of Asiatic or Egyptian stock, marrying and fathering children with sisters and daughters of the Macedonian *Diadokhoi*.[137]

Curtius' own idea of Roman superiority, *if* overlaid on Cleitarchus' words, would have permitted the reinforcing of such a prejudice against the conquered races; Curtius left us in no doubt of his attitude to barbarians when describing the 'best' of them: 'However, the comprehension of the Scythians is not so primitive and untrained… in fact, some of them are even said to be capable of philosophy.' But this was hardly original; as Baynham has pointed out: 'The idea of certain Scythians as "virtuous savages" (recalling that "Scythians" was a general Greek and Roman term for northeastern "barbarians") was also a well-known literary *topos*.'[138]

What followed from Ptolemy appears couched in *koinopragia*, the suggestion of a working together for a 'common interest' – in this case 'group rule' – as this undermined Perdiccas' *hegemonia ton holon,* his absolute supremacy.[139] In fact, Arrian had earlier stated that Alexander 'made no fresh appointment to the command of the Companion cavalry' after Hephaestion's death; this sounds like a regurgitation of Ptolemy's attempt to suggest that the chiliarch post – the equestrian command but perhaps here meant to imply the second-in-command – had disappeared,[140] a statement which contradicts Arrian's *Events After Alexander* (taking its detail from Hieronymus) in which Perdiccas had clearly assumed Hephaestion's role. Regardless of 'official' titles held at this point, Cleitarchus appears to have prudently made it clear that where 'some agreed with Ptolemy, fewer followed Perdiccas' (T11).[141]

Although the Macedonians 'had no use for republicanism' this recommendation might have had more legitimate origins. For group rule, by what would be akin to a privy council, would have been credible and workable on the basis that a Bodyguard-dominated *synedrion* of a few 'super-governors' *had* been selected by Alexander to bind the empire together cohesively. Whilst we propose his Will implemented just that, it also required them to operate under a centralised authority: Perdiccas, who retained control of the royal army in the name of the king(s).[142] Watching the rising hostility towards the chiliarch with some satisfaction, the Bodyguards had thought it the right moment to tender their own claim for that power *without* central handcuffing. This proposal was nevertheless rejected by the throng of men, which now firmly inclined away from the aristocratic *megistoi* in favour of more traditional roots in the heat of the indignant moment. Additionally, group rule implied the Assembly itself was being subordinated to an aristocratic collective.

As a countermeasure to that dissent, Aristonus, a *Somatophylax* who featured less frequently in the extant texts, reminded the assembly that the Will vested power in Perdiccas above all others, a position confirmed by Alexander's emblematically passing him the royal seal (T11).[143] This endorsement is indeed consistent with Aristonus' later Perdiccan support, and whilst it is counterintuitive to accept that Cleitarchus would have wished to reinforce knowledge of Perdiccas' primacy (which could, nevertheless, hardly be hidden against the background of his actions in the next three years), the greater message that emerged in the narrative is the flaw in the man, and thus the flaw in Alexander's choice.[144] Aristonus' timely reminder could not be denied, but Perdiccas '… wavered between inclination and shame, and believed that the more modestly he sought what he coveted the more persistently they would press it upon him. So, after delaying and being for a time uncertain what to do, he finally retired to the back part of the Assembly, and stood behind those who were nearest to the throne' (T11).[145]

This paragraph has been long discussed, and is viewed by some scholars as Curtius' re-rendering of the 'Tiberian farce', for Tiberius had initially declined the emperorship, 'a wretched and burdensome slavery' that held what he had termed a 'wolf by the ears'.[146] And it is noteworthy, too, that Tiberius' hesitation followed the reading of Augustus' Will, which reportedly began with 'since a cruel fate has bereft me of my sons…'[147] Curtius was possibly embellishing Cleitarchus' portrayal of a devious chiliarch milking the moment at the expense of the other *Somatophylakes*, and presenting it as a familiar episode his Roman audience could readily relate to, though here without any attachment to a Will.[148]

There followed a contentious voice from the infantry credited to the infantry brigade commander Meleager, here portrayed as a demagogue articulating a common resentment (Curtius implied 'hatred', *invisusque*) of the haughty Perdiccas who had probably failed to integrate with the common soldier on campaign. Yet it might have been that very aloofness and distance from any faction that had made him effective as Alexander's second-in-command; Hephaestion may well have represented this dispassionate authority before him. It appears Cleitarchus was using Meleager as the sacrificial anode through which his negatively charged portrayal of the chiliarch was passed, and the officer's accusation was clear: Perdiccas *would* use Alexander's wife and son, the future king of Macedonia, to exploit his own position.[149]

The theme of unchecked ambition captured the dark mood of the Assembly. In contrast to the 'Cleitarchean-Curtiana', we have Justin's alternative précis: Meleager argued that their proceedings should not be suspended for the result of an uncertain birth, for residing at Pergamum *was* Alexander's son Heracles – as Nearchus had already reminded them – and better still, already at Babylon was Arrhidaeus, Alexander's half-brother; both of whom *were*, we propose, recognised in the Will. Alexander's appointing his mentally deficient half-brother as a figurehead king, in the absence of other options, was to provide Argead continuity until his sons came of age, and potentially after the 'strongest' or 'most worthy of them' – *toi kratistoi* in Greek (τῷ κρατίστῳ) and transmitted as *qui esset optimus* or *dignissimus* in Latin[150] – was chosen to wear the crown. To reinforce his case Meleager reminded the Assembly that Arrhidaeus was begotten by Philip (*Philippo genitus*) and so part of his line (or kin, *stirpem Philippi*).[151]

Yet what follows suggests Justin conflated the previous sentiment of Nearchus and Ptolemy with Meleager's own dissent into a senseless contradiction; for here again Roxane's Asian origins were rejected with: 'It was unlawful that kings should be chosen for the Macedonians from the blood of those whose kingdoms they had overthrown'. This is senseless if it came from Meleager (rather then Ptolemy, but Justin's text is garbled at this point) because Heracles was also half-Asiatic. Justin later confused the Arrhidaeus Meleager was promoting (Alexander's half-brother) with the same-named constructer of the funeral hearse, and so his accuracy can hardly be relied upon.[152] Justin finished by incorporating the claim that Alexander made no mention of Roxane's issue; we may presume that this, once again, alluded to the brevity of his last words in the Vulgate genre texts.[153]

Meleager was a notable *taxiarchos* with prominent military posts stretching back twelve years, and he had been amongst the six elite phalanx leaders at the Battle of Gaugamela alongside Craterus, Perdiccas, Coenus, Amyntas and Polyperchon.[154] Although he was the highest-ranking *infantry* officer in Babylon, and the only one mentioned in Arrian's list of the *megistoi*, other recorded incidents on campaign suggest Meleager was indeed opinionated with a voice that at times had bordered on insubordination.[155] At the Babylon Assembly, and understandably angry if he had been passed over in the Will – possibly for exactly that reason – Meleager next proposed that Alexander's half-brother, Arrhidaeus, carry the name 'King Philip III' for political poignancy. It was effective; as Justin put it, he was exploiting an 'indignant infantry' that had been given no share in deliberations.[156]

How incendiary Meleager's speech really was (if indeed it came from him) remains conjecture; if Alexander's Will did recognise Arrhidaeus in some ceremonial and figurehead role, the speech was not treasonous at all. If properly managed under a *basileon prostasian*, a formal court guardianship, Arrhidaeus was in fact the perfect 'safe' choice as an interim Argead figurehead, as Alexander may have reasoned, and Meleager could have been reminding the Assembly of just that.[157] Yet the speech also captured a significant reality: although the Macedonians were prepared to maintain their loyalty to the Argead house, Alexander's sons, born, unborn and bred of Asiatic wives, were simply not acceptable as immediate choices, and neither were the highborn *hetairoi* to whom the empire was being conspicuously distributed. Curtius recorded that Alexander's 'friends had been shamed' when he chose to marry Roxane, a girl from the 'subject people'.[158] Of course none could have voiced this in Bactria or at the Susa weddings. Cleitus, who headed the elite king's cavalry bodyguard, the *ile basilike*, was run through for his straight talking, and the executions at Opis provided an instructive example of what befell dissenters. But here in Babylon, with Alexander dead, these sentiments were emerging at last.

Intriguingly, a fragment of the cuneiform tablet *Babylonian Chronicle* recorded the reign of Arrhidaeus (indeed titled 'King Philip III' on it) as eight years long, where Diodorus claimed six years and four months (Justin simply stated six years). If the *Chronicle* is accurate, it suggests Alexander *had* elevated his half-brother to 'ceremonial king' (in Babylon at least) in 324 BCE, as Bosworth has proposed. This possibility may also be implied by a speech in which 'a man unknown to most of the Macedonians' and apparently of lowly birth claimed Arrhidaeus was recently made the king's 'associate in sacrifices and ceremonies'.[159] Indeed, a bond may have been established between him and Alexander who conspicuously exempted Arrhidaeus from execution at Philip's murder some thirteen years before, when we imagine Olympias must have pushed for his immediate death.

Arrhidaeus may well have been capable of basic regal functions despite his impaired condition and the rumours that Olympias gave him mind-destroying drugs as a boy.[160] He was possibly epileptic (as the *Heidelberg Epitome* stated), or perhaps more plausibly, autistic, for epilepsy did not stop Socrates, Caesar or Caligula, each inflicted with what the Romans termed *morbus commitialis*, from making their indelible marks.[161]

Historians (old and new) are generally in agreement that the speech which followed from the prominent Bodyguard, Peithon son of Crateuas, was a further show of support for Perdiccas, for in 'plain language' he gave an assessment of Arrhidaeus (though this opinion was attached to Ptolemy in Justin's précis); we assume that means he highlighted his mental limitations. 'Peithon began to follow the plan of Perdiccas, and named Perdiccas and Leonnatus, both of royal birth, as guardians (*epitropoi, tutores* in Latin) of the son to be born to Roxane'; in fact Macedonian tradition held that *only* a member of the royal house could in fact be regent. Roxane's potential son was now *symbasileos* alongside Arrhidaeus, just as we propose the Will demanded.[162] But Peithon subjoined that Craterus and Antipater should direct affairs in Europe, with Justin reiterating this expanded line-up of guardians. Hidden below the Cleitarchean intestate *scandaleuse* it appears Peithon was presenting a credible counter-suggestion that maintained the basic fabric of the Will.[163]

Here the hermeneutical debate thickens, for to conclude that Peithon was upholding Perdiccas' position is not consistent with their relations immediately after the settlement. Neither are Peithon's actions that came to justify Perdiccas' suspicion, for he was one of his assassins in Egypt some three years on.[164] If the Will had indeed granted Perdiccas overall command, Peithon's speech was anything but supportive; rather it was designed to neutralise his sole possession of the boy and made to counter Aristonus' speech. In line with the mood of the gathering, Peithon sweetened the suggestion by bringing the popular but absent Craterus and Antipater into the frame.

What becomes apparent here is Leonnatus' high standing amidst the Macedones; previously described by Curtius as *ex purpuratis* ('from the purple'), he was clearly now the 'second man' then present beside the chiliarch, perhaps due to those regal roots (T11, T12).[165] Peithon's proposal held; the ageing regent, Antipater, was reconfirmed in his role, and the popular Craterus, arguably the most senior infantry commander still in Asia, and who had been given supreme control of the entire army when campaigning the eastern satrapies, was given *prostasia* (a protector's role) alongside him, and 'charge of royal property'. The exact division between his military and civil duties remains speculation, but for Craterus it was something of a compensation for his own regency now on hold. But whether this would emerge as an 'honorific without power', or arguably the top role in the empire that eclipsed even a *chiliarchos*, only time would tell.[166] Did Craterus have agents in Babylon, and was Peithon effectively one of his men?

We might speculate that not all of the infantry officers present cared who governed the lands outside Macedonia, or perhaps the lands east of the Greek coastal cities of Asia Minor, for the army had seen its fill of India and the upper satrapies. They did, however, care about the fate of the Macedonian throne and their right to participate in its destiny. Moreover, the convocation in Babylon *was* unique and perhaps a once-in-a-lifetime opportunity to decide on something truly hard-earned and of real value to returning veterans. Antipater's regime in Pella had already been instructed by Alexander to endow the repatriated campaigners with garlands and *prohedria*, the privilege of front row seats at public performances.[167] But those picking up the pieces at Alexander's death – the men who were forced to remain in Asia – had not yet enjoyed the fruits of their labour, and now, under the new regime unfolding before them, they wondered if they ever would.

But there were likely to have been quite different mindsets coalescing within the infantry ranks that now included men intent on getting home, those ambivalent as they had little to return to, and those who could not return. Within these last two groups were genuine settlers with wives, concubines, children and waggons laden with booty, and career fighters looking for the next chance to plunder or obtain a land grant as a reward. Finally, there were auxiliary mercenaries and exiles, principally Greeks.

Arrian claimed 10,000 Macedones were registered at Susa as having married Asiatic wives, and though the figure is more than suspiciously high, it is likely that a good number of those then in Babylon had good reason to stay.[168] For them the future was in the 'empire' under the wing of the generals who controlled the wealth and vast resources of the newly opened lands they had seen first-hand. As far as *these* soldiers were concerned, the stature of the immediate commander or satrap of the provinces *did* matter. Some ninety per cent or more of the governors appointed by the prominent *Diadokhoi* remained Macedonian or Greek; opportunity abounded for a talented officer, moreover evidence suggests a further 15,000 to 20,000 settlers arrived in the next two decades when new 'Pellas' were founded in Asia.[169]

With this in mind, the surviving texts most likely provide an oversimplified interpretation of the position of the Macedonian soldiers that remained in Babylon, for they are treated as 'state conscripts' billeted where directed. If an accurate picture when Alexander was alive, judging by the tone of the Assembly, this was hardly the case now. Many veterans surely attempted to attach themselves to a province and a new patron under the cleruch system that most suited their situation, if not immediately and upon departing Babylon, then over the next several years once the outcome of the early conflict and Lamian War had been decided. So Ptolemy, Peucestas, Lysimachus, Seleucus, and Peithon, once free from central command (and probably even before), would each have been making financial offers, pledges for the future and offers of land grants, to secure a solid core of Macedonians and Greeks in their own satrapal armies. Justin did claim that Alexander's 'friends' had already been secretly paying court to the common soldier to win the favour of the army before the king had died.[170]

Although the infantry officers at the Assembly were arguing the fate of the old kingdom – excluded as they were from wider decisions and from Will bequests – the Bodyguards were gathered in the spirit of 'empire' and for their Will-inherited chunk. So we might surmise that without the confrontational overlaps – Perdiccas' role that would oversee *both* kingdom and empire, the future of Alexander's half-caste sons, and the fate of the Asian treasuries (and its impact on back-pay and any promised bonuses) – the Assembly could have separated the Macedonian cake from its new Asian icing rather less contentiously.

Up to this point, the *immediate* demands of Alexander's Will superficially remained intact, if stretched a little at the edges by wider guardianships. Perdiccas' position was not specifically cancelled, Roxane's unborn son remained a *potential* king, and the most prominent Bodyguards now had a hand in his protection as well as the management of Arrhidaeus' temporary *basileia*. Craterus had been finally recognised in office and the *Somatophylakes* would get their testament-confirmed regional rewards and ceremoniously erect a statue or two to Alexander, as the Will demanded.

Additionally, Alexander would be buried with suitable splendour in Alexandria, and at this stage, no Will-demanded marriage match to Argead women (those visible, for example, in the *Romance* and *Metz*

Epitome testaments) had been openly repudiated.[171] But just when further conflict looked to have been avoided, Meleager dragged the unwitting halfwit Arrhidaeus into the thick of the confrontation. If theatrical, it is not impossible that he was physically presented, and the crowd once again began to slide towards the wholesale rejection of Alexander's sons in favour of a more permanent elevation of a purer Argead heir – beyond the Will's design.[172] It was at this point that the subtle dividing line between tradition and treason *was* being tested.

To quote Curtius who was clearly recalling (and adding to) lines from the *Iliad*: 'No deep sea, no vast and storm-swept ocean rouses such great billows as the emotions of a multitude, especially if it is exulting in a liberty which is new and destined to be short-lived.'[173] The 'funeral games' predicted by the Vulgate dying king now began. Donning arms and cuirass, and adorning Arrhidaeus with Alexander's robes, Meleager led a rebellious procession out to claim the dead king's body, with a phalanx '… ready to glut themselves with the blood of those who had aspired to a throne to which they had no claim.'[174]

Assemblies did (we believe) gather 'under arms' and so soldiers were permitted to attend with their weapons, though tradition required them to remove their helmets when addressing the king.[175] 'In terror, Perdiccas ordered the locking of the chamber in which Alexander's body lay. With him were 600 men of proven valour; he had also been joined by Ptolemy and the company of the Royal Pages.'[176] There followed a skirmish – in which the excited Arrhidaeus was featured – over possession of the corpse that had become a prize and an emblem of authority; this was hardly the action of men who had been abandoned by Alexander with a quip about the bloodshed he knew would soon follow. Whether this took place exactly as we read it, or whether it is, once more, a Homeric comparison, is open to speculation, but Aelian recognised that the struggle was '… in some ways akin to the one over the phantom at Troy, which Homer celebrates in his tale, where Apollo laid it down among the heroes to protect Aeneas.'[177]

A valiant defence reportedly ensued, though Perdiccas is not specifically credited with any heroics, but rather with early submission: 'After many had been wounded, the older soldiers… began to beg the men with Perdiccas to stop fighting and to surrender to the king and his superior numbers. Perdiccas was the first to lay down his arms, and the others followed his example.'[178] Actually, the text more convincingly placed Ptolemy as one of the more effective 'protectors'. If we reiterate that Curtius, writing as he was some three and a half centuries after events, had no obvious political pretensions towards the *Diadokhoi* except to add sizzle to an already well-seasoned biographical steak, then Cleitarchus remained consistent in his overall treatment of both Perdiccas and Ptolemy. We may assume he took his lead from the Egyptian dynast's *own* treatment of the chiliarch which had been published some years before.[179]

The outnumbered senior command was forced to retire, though Perdiccas did initially attempt to remain in the city to keep the veneer of unity intact. Meleager warned that Perdiccas' 'undisciplined spirit' would result in a coup, and he urged Arrhidaeus to call for his death. He added: 'Perdiccas well remembered how he had treated the king', and 'no one could be truly loyal to someone he feared'; this clearly called into question Perdiccas' earlier behaviour.[180] Arrhidaeus acquiesced and Perdiccas was summoned; according to Justin, the prominent phalanx commander, Attalus, dispatched some of his men to assassinate the chiliarch.

The plan failed; protected by sixteen royal pages, the chiliarch faced-off the would-be assassins, 'Meleager's lackeys', who summarily fled in terror, whereupon Perdiccas joined Leonnatus with the cavalry on the plains outside the city. Justin (who was clearly blending the narratives of Cleitarchus and Hieronymus) credited Perdiccas with delivering an effective speech calling for national unity with 'eloquence particular to himself' (T12).[181] A blockade was initiated and this led to a famine inside the walls after only a few days, though this was possibly a rhetorical device inserted to heighten the tension; Curtius himself had already stated significant tracts of land remained under cultivation in Babylon to feed the population in case of such a siege, unless Xerxes' earlier diversion of the Euphrates had ruined the initiative.[182]

When considering Macedonian army numbers at Babylon in the summer of 323 BCE, and with the addition of Asiatic auxiliaries, it is possible that the main body of the cavalry, with their mounts and equipment, were already billeted along the river outside the city which is estimated to have contained no fewer than 300,000 to 400,000 inhabitants.[183] The elephant corps, at least, would have been more safely attended outside the inner wall, and keeping Macedonians and Asian levies billeted apart was probably a prudent move. Some 20,000 Persian troops had recently arrived under the command of Peucestas along with 'a good number of Cossaeans and Tapurians' besides recruits from Caria and Lydia under Philoxenus and Menander.

We do not know how many of the armed Asiatic *epigonoi* from Susa were present, or what percentage remained of the 30,000 Greek mercenary infantry and 6,000 cavalry that had survived the march through Gedrosia and forced settlements and garrison duty along the way.[184] Although the Summer or Outer Palace of Nebuchadnezzar II in the Babil suburb of Babylon was constructed with defence in mind and as a military headquarters (as were the structures referred to as either the Northern and Southern Fortresses or Palaces, close to the Ishtar Gate), it could not have accommodated anywhere near these numbers.[185] And recalling that new campaigning West was being planned, the city would have swelled significantly if housing the whole army inside its eight fortified gates, or perhaps its inner wall.[186]

Artist's rendition of the ancient city of Babylon

10

An artist's impression of Babylon at its height with walls and moats intact; the condition they were in by Alexander's day in questionable. Cultivated tracts of land inside the walls, to feed the population in case of a siege, are shown, in line with Curtius' description. The old city is on the right of the Euphrates looking north, and the new on the left. Herodotus' description: 'The city stands on a broad plain, and is an exact square, a hundred and twenty furlongs in length each way, so that the entire circuit is 480 furlongs. While such is its size, in magnificence there is no other city that approaches to it. It is surrounded, in the first place, by a broad and deep moat, full of water, behind which rises a wall 50 royal cubits in width, and 200 in height.'[187]

With food reputedly short, with significant hostile troop numbers amassed on the surrounding plains, and when reflecting further upon their insubordination to both the higher command *and* the demands of Alexander's Will (we imagine), the infantry officers began to contemplate their fate. Sources drawing from Hieronymus' summation cited Meleager as one of the emissaries sent *from* the cavalry command *to* the infantry to negotiate a truce, whereupon he defected to their cause and became its *de facto* leader; if so, Perdiccas clearly misread where Meleager's true allegiances lay (T13, T14). This was an unlikely appointment if he had already attacked Perdiccas so vehemently at the Assembly, so we must treat the vitriol within his Curtian speech with care.[188] The envoy role (possibly after he was promised a share of command) *is*, however, sound if we consider his campaign career in which he served under both Perdiccas and Craterus and which spanned the authority of both infantry phalanx and Companion Cavalry command, though this appointment does upset Curtius' chronology of events.[189] Whether royal traitor or peoples' hero we may never know, but at some point Meleager crossed the line.

Curtius next narrated what appears to be a rather genuine and unadorned picture (he 'sloughed his snake skin of rhetoric', using Tarn's words) of the state of affairs in the palace: 'In fact, the royal quarters still looked as they had before: ambassadors of the nations came to seek audiences with the king, generals presented themselves and armed men and attendants filled the vestibule.' Envoys were arriving from across the known world with new pledges of fealty to the new Great King, and this was undoubtedly to avert the Macedonian war machine from landing on *their* shores. This short and rhetoric-free digression paints a poignant picture of the confusion that must have terrified both Macedonian and foreign statesman alike, when 'mutual suspicion' prevailed so they 'dared not converse with anyone but turned over secret thoughts each in their own minds...'[190]

Following Meleager's defection, the infantry faction now *formally* proclaimed Arrhidaeus 'King Philip III of Macedonia' (perhaps enacted through a hastily convened 'infantry' Assembly) and to quote Plutarch more fully: 'A mute diadem, so to speak, passed across the inhabited world.'[191] In response, Perdiccas sent the infantry officers his new terms: a truce would require them handing over the troublemakers. Meleager, sensing a backing wind, had already spent three days 'brooding over plans he kept changing'. The trapped infantry now fully appreciated the gravity of their position, for they had now been branded 'traitors'. Many surely reflected on the vast distance home and on Arrhidaeus' capacity to lead them there, for they were 'in the midst of foes dissatisfied with the new rule', which rather summed up the state of the Macedonian-governed empire. When the terms of the truce were announced, uproar ensued and soldiers armed themselves once more.[192]

The clamour brought the newly crowned Arrhidaeus out of his tent. The halfwit king was not so mute after all, and though up to this point he had been 'cowed by the authority of the generals', he made an impassioned plea for peace and reconciliation and for a funeral that had yet been denied Alexander.[193] He reportedly ended with: 'So far as I am concerned, I prefer to relinquish this authority of mine rather than to see the blood of fellow citizens flow because of it, and if there is no other hope of accord, I beg and entreat you to choose a better man (or more 'valued'– *potiorem*).'[194]

If Cleitarchus had heard reports that Arrhidaeus had been associated with performing sacrifices and ceremonies at Babylon, he could have drawn a number of conclusions, as could we.[195] The first: Alexander did indeed have plans for him, perhaps as a figurehead in Pella, when Alexander headed to Arabia and to the West along the southern Mediterranean shores; Craterus' installation at Pella might have been to facilitate and oversee just that. New mention of his name in the ceremonial role could also suggest that Arrhidaeus may have *recently* arrived from Macedonia for he was never previously mentioned in any campaign account (he could have arrived with Cassander, for example). So as far as Cleitarchus and Curtius after him were concerned, Arrhidaeus *was* capable of some articulation; it was that perception which led to the construction of the impossibly noble speech from the half-witted Assembly pawn who apparently never uttered a coherent word again until his death some six years, or so, later.[196]

Curtius' overlay developed what was essentially a *contio*, a Roman-style public debate, with the author presiding as the literary magistrate; in fact *contiones* appear throughout his monograph as informal debates in the presence of varied audiences: advisers, commanders, or in front of the entire army in the manner of those attached to Scipio Africanus.[197] Arrhidaeus' speech appears, once again, to be sautéed in Roman seasoning, here capturing elements of the cowed Claudius who was found hiding behind curtains upon the assassination of Caligula, for Claudius also surprised Rome later with his own (though genuine) eloquence.[198] And as it has been noted, Arrhidaeus' olive branch captured something of the Roman struggle between *optimates* against *populares* in its attempt to please the 'people'.[199]

If the manipulative hand of Curtius is undoubtedly at work, it seems unlikely he would have placed such vocal articulation upon an otherwise completely dumb character unless Cleitarchus had recorded *some* communication, as Curtius would have been risking his credibility at a crucial juncture in his book. Ultimately, the voice provided to Arrhidaeus was one that reinforced his inability, or refusal, to govern the state, let alone the empire, and this provides further justification to Ptolemy's proposal of group rule by those who *could*; that is more suggestive of Cleitarchus' agenda. The infantry commanders had made fools of themselves elevating Arrhidaeus beyond the Will's design, and they were about to atone in blood.

The envoys sent out from the Cavalry camp now returned; those chosen had been Greeks including mercenaries, not Macedonians, and it seems they provided Perdiccas with a list of troublemakers.[200] Eumenes may well have had an active hand in that, for he '… remained behind in the city and mollified many of the men at war and made them more disposed towards a settlement of the quarrel.' Plutarch suggested Eumenes sided with Alexander's 'principal officers, or companions, in his opinions', but he further stated that Eumenes had remained silent in the Assembly as he '… was a kind of common friend to both and held himself aloof from the quarrel, on the ground that it was no business of his, since he was a stranger, to meddle in disputes of Macedonians.'[201] Moreover, if Eumenes *had* been instrumental in drafting Alexander's Will, he needed to maintain the veneer of neutrality lest any suspicion of manipulation fall on him.

A brief calm and fragile concord emerged, and one that superficially accepted Meleager as a 'third' general (*hyparchos*) alongside Perdiccas himself (and, we assume, Leonnatus, if absentees were not being referred to). Justin interpreted the outcome: 'Such an arrangement being made, Antipater was appointed governor of Macedonia and Greece; the charge of the royal treasure was given to Craterus; the management of the camp, the army, and the war, to Meleager and Perdiccas' (T20). Both armies exchanged salutations and were finally reconciled, or so they thought.[202]

THE HEADLESS *SYNEDRION*

With the complicity of an unwitting Meleager, Perdiccas (probably with the help of the previously hostile Attalus, now promised the hand of his sister) called for a lustration of the 'united' army.[203] This was a ritual of purification linked to pastoral migration and the springtime cleansing of men in arms, and it was usually held in the month of Xanthikos, shortly before the vernal equinox in March. The religious observance should have signified reconciliation and it may have been invoked at the accession of new kings.[204] Protocol called for a bitch to be cut in two (fore part placed to the right, hind part and entrails to the left) and for the army to march between the disembowelled flesh, with royal insignia and the king's weapons carried before it. Possibly because the infighting at Babylon had commenced in the last days of Daisios, when superstition held no battle should take place, the importance of the delayed ceremony was heightened.[205]

The cavalry and war elephants were arranged opposite the phalanx, and the infantry soon sensed a trap. Perdiccas 'in his treachery' had the new king call for the execution of the dissenters. The infantrymen were 'stunned', the insurgents singled out, and the elephants urged forward by their Indian *mahouts*. Some three hundred men (thirty according to Diodorus) were trampled at the foot of the city walls and an outmanoeuvred Meleager took refuge in a nearby shrine where he was hunted down and 'not even protected by the sanctuary of the temple', a further slur on Perdiccas' impiety (T11, T14, T20).[206] Despite the inference that Perdiccas was operating alone, which may again serve to illustrate his manipulation of affairs, the Bodyguards and influential Companions, now acting as a kingless *synedrion,* were probably united in the action to protect their combined inheritances. If so, it was the only unity they would ever know and the 'first flush of freedom' was indeed short-lived. Compromise is never sweet but as Aristotle's *Politics* reasoned, 'a common danger unites even the bitterest of enemies'.[207]

The sedition had been quelled and yet a dilemma remained: the distant Heracles in Pergamum had been vocally rejected, and the pregnant Roxane could still bear a girl. King Philip III *had* to be recognised as the new king simply to avoid further bloodshed. So the Babylonian settlement was concluded; like the Will itself, it was an uneasy and unworkable state of affairs that fully satisfied no one, whilst dissatisfying many.

It was at this point, we propose, that Perdiccas allotted the satrapies as Alexander had detailed in his testament, and not in accordance with his own machinations, as has always been unanimously believed (T16, T17, T18, T20). The most influential generals must have had their say in 'who fitted where' for it would be naive in the extreme to assume no discussions had ever taken place between Alexander and his *Somatophylakes* about empire 'administration'.[208] The appetite and territorial ambition of each manifested itself throughout the Successor Wars and was unlikely to have been absent before. Perhaps at Susa when gold crowns were bestowed on the court favourites, requests were tendered, promises made, and a broad shape of 'who would govern where' was in place long before the return to Babylon, if not before, following Alexander's earlier brushes with death.[209]

Even if the king had survived his last illness, the new campaigns westward would have necessitated the installation of loyal satraps behind him; Plutarch was specific that the already feverish king '… conversed with his officers about the vacant posts in the army, and how they might be filled with experienced men.' This shortfall is most readily explained by the appointment of *Somatophylakes* and other prominent officers as governors in Asia.[210] If Alexander's Will did reflect these pre-agreed divisions, it did not preclude last-minute amendments, explaining the overnight drafting we read of in the *Pamphlet*-derived texts. If the principal men were to become regional overlords, Perdiccas may, nevertheless, have been influential in selecting their under-governors and perhaps in surrounding his own provincial base of operations with men loyal to him.[211]

Curtius made it clear that Perdiccas 'exposed the royal throne to public view' at each Assembly gathering (T11).[212] Justin, who reported that a second conclave took place after the lustration, corroborated that: 'These proceedings they conducted with the body of Alexander placed in the midst of them, that his majesty might be witness to their resolutions' (T20).[213] Arrian's *Events After Alexander* added: 'nevertheless, he [Perdiccas] proclaimed for the satrapies those who were suspected [to receive them], as if under the orders of Arrhidaeus' (T14).[214] Here the reference to 'Arrhidaeus' could be interpreted differently if Arrian, or his epitomiser, Photius, misconstrued the phrase 'in the presence of the king', or 'as the king had wished'.

We suggest that each text preserved a key ingredient: Perdiccas, and surely the Bodyguards too when considering the audience they faced, were making it absolutely clear that the regional distribution of power being made came from Alexander's testament. Perdiccas may have even read aloud something approximating the final lines we see in the *Metz Epitome* Will: 'Should any of these named act in contravention of my Testament, I beseech the Olympian Gods to see that he not go unpunished',[215] not an unlikely insertion by a suspicious dying king. Thereafter, Perdiccas took steps to ensure all formal proceedings continued in the same manner, with the king's insignia making it quite clear whence his own, and inconveniently King Philip III's, elevations stemmed from. As Atkinson put it, Alexander was never so revered as when he was newly dead.[216]

When constructing the 'life' (and its legacy) of Alexander, Plutarch mined for information outside the texts of Cleitarchus, Hieronymus, and the eyewitness historians, and so he alone tantalised his audience with a unique and politically explosive snippet: following his own claim that 'nobody had any suspicions [of conspiracy] at the time', he concluded his Babylon narrative by alleging that Roxane conspired to kill Stateira, Alexander's Persian wife, and her sister, Drypetis, the widow of Hephaestion. Both were daughters of the deposed Great King Darius III; captured after the battle at Issus in 333 BCE, they were later installed at Susa. Plutarch further claimed that the sisters had been lured to Babylon with a forged royal letter, whereupon they were murdered and their bodies were concealed down a backfilled well.[217] Apparently Roxane had Perdiccas' consent; if the episode has any substance, we might again implicate the royal secretary, Eumenes, a clear Perdiccan, for his secretarial seal would have rendered the correspondence genuine.[218] The royal women were, alas, more collateral damage of yet more cancelled plans; Hephaestion's heroic legacy was already in trouble and so were the members of Alexander's Persian family.

What finally departed Babylon was an army held together by resented compromises and badly veiled accords. Even Eumenes' role in brokering peace has been described as a necessary deal at Perdiccas' expense, though the intent must have been otherwise.[219] Essentially, three factions had emerged: firstly the Perdiccans, the most prominent of whom were Aristonus and Eumenes, along with Alcetas (Perdiccas' younger brother), Attalus the son of Andromenes (soon to be Perdiccas' brother-in-law) and *his* brother Polemon, alongside the resourceful Docimus whose future allegiances with Antigonus and finally with Lysimachus (at least to the conclusion of the battle at Ipsus) were punctuated by reported acts of treachery. The soon-to-be-famed Medius briefly joined Perdiccas' ranks too.[220] Apart from a reference by Justin to his command of the guards (again possibly confusing his *future* post in the post-Perdiccas world) there was no mention of Cassander who had recently arrived in Babylon, and who may, indeed, have departed rather quickly following Alexander's death to inform his father in Pella and potentially other generals on the way, a state of affairs the *Pamphlet* later capitalised on.

Opposing them there coalesced an anti-Perdiccan Bodyguard faction that closed ranks in a compact *synaspismos* that proposed group rule on empire matters to undermine his chiliarchy, at the heart of which were Peithon, Ptolemy and Seleucus (neither Peucestas not Lysimachus were mentioned at the Assembly). The third group, the throng of men-at-arms and their infantry officers, had now empowered themselves under 'their' King Philip III, and they called for the voices of Antipater and Craterus to protect their interests. The rejected Heracles featured no more and his backers had to fall in line elsewhere; Nearchus, who likely inherited a satrapy himself and who disappeared from texts for the next few years, *appears* to have kept his head low.[221]

The *Somatophylakes* were dispatched to their satrapies and Eumenes finalised plans to pacify Cappadocia, as his Will grant required. It is unlikely Perdiccas could have departed Babylon until after Roxane had given birth; a boy *was* born and the result underpinned Perdiccas' primacy through his immediate guardianship and, not impossibly, through his marriage to Roxane, the terms of the Will that gave Meleager his suspicions. But this was not a time for reflection, it was a time for moving on before any further challenges emerged. Events that followed indicate the anti-Perdiccan league did communicate with Antipater in Macedonia, and its members probably pledged their support for his ongoing regency. Antipater, meanwhile, was offering his daughter, Nicaea, to Perdiccas to leverage his own position (or buy time), an arrangement Perdiccas milked while developing further options.[222]

To counter the regent's long-established influence in Greece, Perdiccas is said to have opened a dialogue with Demades, the Athenian demagogue, who invited him 'to cross over swiftly into Europe to oppose the oligarchs of Antipater' whom he likened to a 'rotten thread'. Perdiccas was likely bartering with Athenian 'freedom' to undermine Antipater's regime (the ultimate aim of Greek forces in the Lamian War), and he secretly planned to reject Nicaea in favour of marriage to Cleopatra, Alexander's full-sister, which suggests further correspondence was taking place with Olympias, likely brokered through Eumenes.[223] Perdiccas next installed Docimus in Babylon, removing the previous governor, Archon, who might have assisted Ptolemy's preparations for capturing Alexander's funeral hearse, and he supported Cleomenes in his ongoing administrative role in Egypt, so undermining Ptolemy's administrative control.[224]

Perdiccas (or Alexander through his Will) had already ordered Leonnatus and Antigonus to assist Eumenes in the invasion of Cappadocia; both refused and ended up crossing over to Greece and Macedonia and linking up with Antipater.[225] The first 'domestic' clash of arms (outside of the trouble at Babylon) came about with Ptolemy's hijacking (or 'rescuing') Alexander's funeral hearse, following which Medius and Aristonus were put to use by Perdiccas in an invasion of Cyprus, whose kings were now supporting the Ptolemaic regime. The responses were inevitable, and so commenced the '... greatest armed conflict between fellow Macedonians in more than a generation.'[226]

Peithon, along with Antigenes who commanded the Silver Shields brigade, grudgingly operated under Perdiccas until his (officially, King Philip III's) failed retaliatory invasion of Egypt, whereupon they (and possibly Seleucus) murdered him in his tent in May/June 320 BCE.[227] Perdiccas' disastrous attempts at canal dredging when attempting to cross the Nile, and his failed attacks at the Fort of Camels at Pelusium and above the delta near Heliopolis on the route to Memphis, may well have been in part due to the lack of army enthusiasm and this treachery in the planning; Perdiccas had been forced to grant gifts and promises just to keep the officers from defecting to Ptolemy.[228]

Photius' epitome of Arrian's *Events After Alexander* (uniquely) recorded that Perdiccas aired in front of the army (thus an impromptu Assembly) 'many charges' against Ptolemy, who successfully defended himself. It is hardly credible that Ptolemy attended a 'show trial'. Any speech at *this* point was simply Perdiccas attempting to prop up morale with accusations before the attack, and, as Diodorus recorded, Ptolemy defended his actions in person when he crossed the Nile to greet the Macedonians the day *after* Perdiccas' death.[229]

The highborn Leonnatus had previously defected to Greece with his own plans for Macedonia, and Peucestas must have been content in being safely installed in Persis (broadly today's Fars Province of Iran centred at Shiraz) away from the crisis. Lysimachus would have been equally relieved to be governing a satrapy across the Hellespont removed from the initial strife, though Seuthes III, who married a Macedonian bride and tried to re-establish the Odrysian Kingdom, gave him a run for his money in Thrace. Neither Lysimachus, nor Peucestas, had anything to lose from watching those embroiled in the emerging factions begin to self-destruct. 'Centrifugal forces were at work', and the fabric of the Will was not resilient enough to hold them together.[230] The Babylonian settlement, finalised on the plains outside the 'gateway of the gods', had simply been the early sparks of the pyrotechnics of the *Diadokhoi* Wars.

CLEITARCHUS' *CORONA GRAMINEA*

Throughout his portrayal of the Babylon settlement, Cleitarchus appears to have endowed Ptolemy with a 'patriotic' anti-barbarian voice, and to have burdened Perdiccas with a treacherous usurper's role. Ptolemy was, in addition, presented as the rational, legitimate and even 'democratic' voice of the Bodyguards with his proposal of group rule. But Cleitarchus' reshaping of events fulfilled further aims: Alexander's leaving an empire 'to the strongest' (T6, T7, T8, T9) nullified the significance of Perdiccas receiving the king's ring, while the Will was neatly removed from the centre of events. It was a literary triumph capitalised on by Curtius and deserving of a Roman *corona graminea*, a grass-crown, for its influence on later interpretations, and for its challenging the boundaries established by the *Pamphlet* and the *Journal*.[231]

So where did Cleitarchus end his account? Well, as far back as 1874 Rosiger noted the pro-Ptolemaic slant in the post-Babylon narratives of Diodorus (and Justin's epitome of Trogus), whose detail ought to have been sourced from Hieronymus.[232] But that slant makes little sense when considering the Cardian historian served first under Eumenes (a Perdiccan) and then the Antigonid dynasty, both demonstrably hostile to the Ptolemaic regime. And it seems doubtful that Diodorus, based in Romanised Sicily, had such personal inclinations in favour of Ptolemy I *Soter*, unless it was to highlight Rome's recent crime of annexing Egypt.[233]

The first of Diodorus' uncharacteristic encomia dealt with the transport of Alexander's body: 'Ptolemy, moreover, doing honour to Alexander, went to meet it with an army as far as Syria, and, receiving the body, deemed it worthy of the greatest consideration.'[234] Diodorus followed with a description of Alexandria 'lacking little of being the most renowned of the cities of the inhabited earth', which neatly supported an earlier laudatory reference to the city. This statement *may* include some personal admiration, as Diodorus had himself spent time researching in Alexandria and Strabo certainly lauded the city following his stay a few years on (perhaps through 25/24-20 BCE).[235] After describing the tomb Ptolemy had prepared for the sarcophagus, along with sacrifices and magnificent games that perhaps still included the Archaic *hoplitodromos*, the race in full hoplite panoply, Diodorus continued:

> For men, because of his graciousness and nobility of heart, came together eagerly from all sides of Alexandria and gladly enrolled for the campaign... all of them willingly took upon themselves at their personal risk the preservation of Ptolemy's safety. The gods also saved him unexpectedly from the greatest dangers on account of his courage and his honest treatment of all his friends.'[236]

Diodorus' eulogistic tone dovetailed with Curtius' concluding paragraph which is backed up by the *Parian Chronicle*: '... but Ptolemy, under whose control Egypt had come, transported the king's body to Memphis, and from there a few years later to Alexandria, where every honour was paid to his memory and his name.'[237] Further, we have Diodorus' polemic against Perdiccas' Egyptian invasion which framed Ptolemy's higher qualities: 'Perdiccas, indeed, was a man of blood, one who usurped the authority of the other commanders, and in general, wished to rule by force; but Ptolemy, on the contrary, was generous and fair and granted to all commanders the right to speak frankly.'[238]

The overtly favourable treatment of Ptolemy *does* look Cleitarchean, and yet that would indicate his account extended past Alexander's death and even some two or more years into the Successor Wars. What seems more likely is Cleitarchus summed up his book with forward-looking laudations but only extended his main narrative to the logical conclusion for an Alexandrian historian: Alexander's interment in Egypt.[239] And within this wrap-up, Cleitarchus constructed his account of the funeral hearse arriving along the lines: 'Alexander's body remains in Egypt where Ptolemy paid it the greatest of respect, despite the hostile attempts of Perdiccas, a man of blood and violence, to cross the Nile and acquire it for his own glory'; this was a sentiment that was dragged into the Successor War accounts by the Vulgate authors writing follow-on books, and so by Diodorus, and Justin. Perdiccas' failed invasion must still have been a vivid memory in Cleitarchus' day. Of course, it is not impossible that Cleitarchus was regurgitating Ptolemy's own self-promoting ending, though neither Arrian nor Plutarch captured any hint of that.

Diodorus followed with: 'Egypt was now held as if a prize of war.' A prize it was, 'due to Ptolemy's prowess'; its annual income grew to 14,800 talents with an export income from 1,500,000 *artabae* of grain under his son, Ptolemy II *Philadelphos*;[240] no wonder he could afford to have his 'enlightened reign', nurtured by Strato from the school of Aristotle, eulogised in the *Encomium* by the poet Theocritus.[241]

Pharaonic Egypt had been divided into forty-two nomes, or provinces, in three major regions: the Nile Delta, the Fayyum (being rapidly drained and reclaimed), and the Nile valley. These in turn were divided into *toparchies* under a *topogrammateis* with a sophisticated tax and administration system. We have a papyrus detailing Egypt's complex revenue laws and it reported on farmed goods and their regional taxation that was overseen by an *antigrapheis* (checking clerk) appointed by an *oikonomos* (manager of financial affairs), who in turn reported to a *grammataios basilikos*, the head of record-keeping in the nome.[242] In the delta, inhabited by Greek traders since at least the reign of Pharaoh Psammetichus (664-610 BCE), the centres of business – Pithom (Heroonpolis), Naucratis with its Hellenion (a religious sanctuary for all

Greek tribes mentioned by Herodotus) on the east bank of the Canopic branch of the Nile, and even Heraclion (Thonis), if not yet inundated – would have likely fallen under Cleomenes' revenue net. Alexander had left other administrators, military and civilian, about him, including *komarchoi* (village headmen) and *myriarouroi* (new land cultivators).[243]

The fate of Heraclion, which sunk into the wash of the Nile Delta most likely following seismic tremors (now some 4 miles further offshore and only recently rediscovered) highlights the sound planning of establishing Alexandria in a location protected by a limestone outcrop. The growing city, with its typically Hellenistic grid plan which saw a 100-foot-wide Street of the Soma and Canopic Way dissect its heart, and a new direct canal to a branch of the Canopic Nile, was no doubt established to eclipse its Greek forerunners. We do have some evidence that Alexander adopted a policy of forced resettlement to populate it; Pseudo-Aristotle's *Oikonomika* detailed his closure of a town and its established market at nearby Canopus.[244]

Ptolemy had initially, and expediently, interred Alexander's body out of harm's way at Memphis, possibly in the Imensthotieion – the Temple of Ammon and Thoth – or in the necropolis of the Nectanebo II Temple at Saqqara. The sources that claimed Alexander wished to be buried in Egypt do look to be Hieronymus-derived, and this lends them authenticity.[245] Here the sarcophagus may have originally been surrounded by the life-sized semi-circle of statues of the Greek poets and philosophers most influential to Alexander, and found by excavations in the Avenue of Sphinxes in 1850/51.[246] So Diodorus' stating that 'he [Ptolemy] decided for the present not to send it [the body] to Ammon, but to entomb it in the city that had been founded by Alexander himself', appears contradictory, though it was probably the result of his usual compression; it seems Ptolemy I *Soter*, or his son Ptolemy II *Philadelphos* (or according to Zenobius, Ptolemy IV *Philopatros* even later) finally transferred Alexander's corpse to the Sema at Alexandria sometime after the battle at Ipsus in 301 BCE when borders were under less of a threat.[247] The Alexandrian Sema resonated with the heroic connotations found in the *Iliad* and *Odyssey* and the bodies of the Ptolemies were now inseparable from that of Alexander;[248] the arrival of his corpse may have coincided with Cleitarchus' own residence in the city, thus again explaining why it featured prominently in his closing paragraphs.

With origins in Egypt it was somewhat inevitable that the relocation was foretold by portents in the *Romance* texts: contrary to earlier predictions of Alexander's seers, the chief priest of Memphis predicted that wherever the body rested would be 'constantly troubled and shaken with wars and battles'.[249] A myth emerged which held that the empty green breccia (granite) sarcophagus of Pharaoh Nectanebo II, never used by him and so ferried to Alexandria from Memphis, was its possible first resting place. If

Alexander's mummified body *was* placed in Nectanebo's coffin it would help explain why the latter featured so prominently in the *Romance*, which claimed the last Egyptian-born pharaoh had impregnated Olympias.[250] In a later age, this stone sarcophagus was used as a ritual bath in the Attarin Mosque, as suggested by the twelve drainage holes drilled around the base. Ptolemy's alleged reuse of the pharaonic granite casket which now resides in the British Museum, does paradoxically support Aelian's contention that the hearse with the original gilded sarcophagus was just a decoy while Alexander's casketless remains were sped to Egypt by a secret route.[251] But there is scant evidence to support these alluring ideas.

What was an original sarcophagus of gold did become a tempting prize; Strabo reported that it was plundered by Ptolemy *Pareisaktos* of Syria (the 'Usurper', alternatively known as *Kokkes*, 'scarlet', possibly identifiable with Ptolemy XI, installed by Sulla ca. 80 BCE). Strabo added that by his day, however, Alexander's body resided in another coffin of alabaster (some translations say 'glass').[252] How or when it lost its illustrious inhabitant, remains one of history's great mysteries. But as Erskine has pointed out: one way or another, Alexander had travelled further *after* his death than most Greeks travelled in a lifetime.[253]

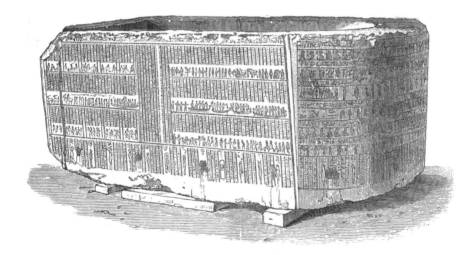

A drawing of the sarcophagus of Nectanebo II found in the Attarin Mosque at Alexandria. The idea that it once contained the body of Alexander is still widely propagated; an engraving, for example, by Thomas Medland and William Alexander was featured on the cover of *The Tomb of Alexander the Great, a dissertation on the sarcophagus brought from Alexandria and now in the British Museum* **by ED Clarke published in 1805. The decorative carving on the sides, however, narrates the Egyptian** *Book of the Underworld* **without reference to Alexander. The sarcophagus was obtained by the Napoleonic Expedition to Egypt, and arrived in the British Museum in 1802 under the Treaty of Alexandria.**

Diodorus provided an extremely detailed description of the funeral cortège and the hearse that departed Babylon, most likely in late spring 321 BCE, in which Alexander travelled many of those miles. Some historians believe this detail could be of Cleitarchean origin too (perhaps originating with Duris) despite Athenaeus' statement that it came from Hieronymus.[254] If Cleitarchean, we would have expected the Vulgate wrap-ups to have been lured a page or two further to capture the fulsome colour of the 'Ionic temple on wheels'.[255] The description of its friezes, carvings and adornments is long, precise and rhetoric-free in line with Hieronymus' style. It has been insightfully noted that 'not a single image of peace was included among these awesome tableaux of Macedonian military might', and further, that the description failed to feature the regular phalanx at all, a punishment perhaps for the infantry dissent at Babylon.[256] But the clue to the original source of the description comes from Diodorus' concluding words: 'and it appeared more magnificent when seen than when described', because 'seen' is the regurgitation of a statement that could have only been made by an eyewitness historian.

The construction of the bier required almost two years.[257] Hieronymus *may* have returned to Babylon with Eumenes following the unsuccessful Cappadocian invasion, or more likely, he witnessed the bier on its journey to (or in) Syria (where we propose Perdiccas was based) before it was seized.[258] An intimate description would have reinforced Hieronymus' credentials and acted as the perfect badge of authenticity for the opening of his book. For similar reasons we should not discount the Cardian historian as the source of the lengthy detail on Hephaestion's funeral pyre; he was after all campaigning with Eumenes in the six and a half years of war that followed Alexander's death, when much information would have been passed between them. So the last pages of Diodorus' seventeenth book, and the early pages of his eighteenth, were indeed a 'patchwork' of the interweaving of Cleitarchus and Hieronymus with confusing repercussions.[259]

A mid-19th century artist's impression of Alexander's funeral hearse, an 'Ionic temple on wheels', on its way from Babylon towards Damascus, pulled by sixty-four mules following the description by Diodorus.

THE ARCHETYPE OF THE SATRAPAL LIST

There remains some uncertainty as to the identity of the archetypal source behind the lists of governors and satrapies in the division of the empire at Babylon (T16, T17, T18, T19, T20). Yet, again, there really is no need to look any further than Hieronymus; many of the governorships were short-lived, providing a tight temporal triangulation. But lest we be accused of textual goropism, we should take a closer look at the evidence.[260]

As Diodorus and Trogus *were* writing continuous world histories, and not simply monographs on Alexander, their rundown of the satrapal list sat in the logical position: at the *opening* of their books heralding in the Successor Wars, consistent, we suggest, with its position in Hieronymus' own account. As expected, their texts, alongside Photius' epitomes and Arrian *Events After Alexander*, are remarkably similar in content, pace and non-florid style, with the inevitable compression scars epitomisers leave.[261]

Curtius, on the other hand, did not have the luxury of extended spacing, for he was *not* writing a follow-on account. So to retrieve the detail he needed, he alone delved ahead into Hieronymus' first chapter to retrieve the satrapal list for his biographical summation. This is exactly where he *may* have seen Hieronymus' reference to the Will he so vocally rejected. In that interpolating process, Curtius shunted Cleitarchus' conspiracy detail back to his final page to give it the dramatic Vulgate wrap-up position.

Curtius wound up his book with a reference to Cassander's murder of the remaining Argead line in 310/309 BCE.[262] Doubting Cleitarchus' book reached forward this far, it once more backs up our contention that Curtius extracted detail from Hieronymus. Plutarch also extracted his own concluding lines on Olympias' revenge (and much detail for his *Parallel Lives*) from Hieronymus, and for similar reasons: biographies required suitably rounded-off epitaphs where ongoing universal histories did not. Of course, Curtius could have extracted this detail on Cassander's retribution 'second-hand' from an earlier Hieronymus-derived source, so Diodorus or even Trogus,[263] but this would still leave the origin of his polemic on the Will unexplained (unless he was referring to Diodorus' *later* reference to it); but as Pearson pointed out, no Latin author seems to have respected Diodorus or used him extensively.[264]

Could Cleitarchus have detailed the divisions of the empire? The positioning of this tight and specific detail in the *follow-on* histories (including that of Arrian, who was not a Cleitarchean adherent) argues against that. Moreover, the list dovetails too neatly with the direction of Hieronymus' geographical treatise and the detail does suggest a single source. With some minor discrepancies aside (which can largely be blamed on lacunae and brevity), the surviving satrapal lists agree on the *core* territorial claims, or roles of, Ptolemy, Peithon, Lysimachus, Peucestas, Eumenes, Antigonus, Leonnatus, Laomedon, Antipater and Craterus.[265] The first three named Bodyguards, and the order of their names, remain identical in all accounts, as broadly do the Asia Minor divisions.[266]

Additionally, if we take each account up to this point, we see striking concord markers; any variation in expansiveness of some provincial detail would have occurred when the list was alternatively sourced from Hieronymus' original (Diodorus, for example, T16) or from epitomes (or summaries) of them (so Justin, Photius' précis of Arrian and Dexippus, T17, T18, T20). Clear stemma clues begin with a short digression mentioning Cleomenes in Egypt, thus linking Photius' précises with Justin's (T17, T18, T20). We have references to Antigonus almost identically transmitted in Curtius, Diodorus and Arrian's précis by Photius (T19, T16, T17) as far as the specificity of his domain: 'Pamphylia, Lycia, and what is called Great Phrygia', while the eastern border of Eumenes' territorial boundary is uniformly marked with 'as far as Trapezus' in Curtius and Photius' epitomes. Diodorus additionally referred to Eumenes' task of pacifying his domain with 'all the lands bordering these, which Alexander did not invade'; this concurs (though less closely) with Curtius' reference to Eumenes 'conducting hostilities' with Ariarathes, king of the still-independent portion of Cappadocia.[267]

Photius and Dexippus were both epitomising Arrian's *Events after Alexander*, itself a *long* summary of Hieronymus' successor history.[268] If the lists of Justin and Curtius can be linked to these accounts by what cannot be casual coincidences, and if Curtius is linked to Diodorus by a similar territorial digression, then the conclusion starts to appear axiomatic. There is, however, some divergence in the second part of the roll call of satraps in the eastern and upper provinces where governorships were to remain largely unchanged, and in particular with the roles linked to Seleucus, Craterus and Perdiccas.[269] But these were the most difficult appointments to decipher due to what we propose were overarching authorities or pan-provincial mandates with regional satraps under them. The relative authorities of what were once the *chiliarchos* of the empire, the *epimeletes* to the new kings, and the *prostasia* of the remaining *strategoi*, as well as Seleucus' first hipparchy cavalry command, were easily misinterpreted; Hieronymus himself may have transmitted them ambiguously, or misrepresented them deliberately as a client of the Antigonids.[270]

The various terminologies associating satrap with satrapy should not necessarily be considered a source 'variance'; these are as much the product of modern translation as they were early scribal interpretation. To 'rule', to 'govern' and 'take charge of'; and 'received', 'fell to', or 'were allotted to', with the geographical tags 'adjacent', 'close to' and 'bordering', do not require more than a single source. What *is* surprising is the lack of bandwidth these early historians used in their regurgitations, for they must have been tempted to season the list with additional commentary. Yet they did not, and neither did they significantly rework the order of its presentation. It seems they appreciated the logical geographical progression being made through Asia, from South to North (Egypt to Thrace) in the first part of the list, and perhaps this formative detail was simply too unique to be adorned with rhetoric, even if some original background colour (satrapal history, for example) was stripped away in the process.

So what is the significance of establishing Hieronymus as the historian behind this detail? In short, it helps to explain the Will's disappearance, as he alone could have referred to it when recounting events at Babylon and linked it to the handing out of satrapies, and yet the following circumstances would have combined to bypass that claim: although Arrian used Hieronymus for his *Events After Alexander*, he and Plutarch were ultimately adherents to the intestate *Journal*. If Arrian sidestepped the testament in his Babylon summation, then Photius and Dexippus would not have seen it either. As Diodorus and Trogus were drawing from Cleitarchus for detail of Alexander's death, a Will could hardly feature in their account of the settlement at Babylon.

And so the Will was crowded out – of accounts we know about, at least – leaving Curtius to remind us that it once existed in an unnamed source (or sources) *he* was reading. If that did *not* include Hieronymus, or an early less embellished copy of the *Pamphlet*, and if he was not making reference to a more sober forerunner of the *Romance* (still reputationally unlikely), then the Will had found new friends elsewhere; the late-Roman-era *Metz Epitome* indicates that the detail that we now call the *Liber de Morte Testamentumque Alexandri Magni* was independently, and still anonymously it seems, floating around the Roman literary world for centuries thereafter, for when Arrian and Plutarch dismissively summarised the conspiracy rumours, neither mentioned the author's name (T9, T10).[271]

THE LOST *EPITAPHIOS AGON*

> You must have been present at the funeral of many a hero, when the young men gird themselves and make ready to contend for prizes on the death of some great chieftain, but you never saw such prizes as silver-footed Thetis offered in your honour; for the gods loved you well. Thus even in death your fame, Achilles, has not been lost, and your name lives evermore among all mankind.[272]

Since Homeric times, funeral games and orations had been a requisite *patros nomos,* an ancestral custom, at the death of a king, hero or dignitary.

Why was no *epitaphios logos* recorded for Alexander at Babylon, the funerary oration Demosthenes so praised and which was indispensable to the Greeks?[273] Hesiod recited a poem at the death of the 'warlike' King Amphidamas in Chalcis and won a prize for his delivery, and Pericles reportedly delivered his eulogy for the Athenian dead a century before at the Kerameikos, the city cemetery; it was an oration that appears more a tribute to his own urban reforms rather than to the men who faced Sparta.[274] Isocrates' *Panegyric to Evagoras*, the Cypriot 'model' king who opposed Persian might, would have been the perfect template, for it too avoided detail of an unfortunate death; that encomium earned Isocrates 20 talents.[275] Theopompus, famous throughout Greece for his public speeches and 20,000 lines of written epideictic orations, had delivered another at Mausolus' funeral at Halicarnassus in 353 BCE, three years after Alexander was born.[276] More relevant still, we have Demosthenes' epitaph from the pro-Athenian allies who died at Chaeronea in September 338 BCE facing the new Macedonian *sarissa* and cavalry wedges.[277]

When summing up Thucydides' rendition of Pericles' speech, Cicero commented: 'You do not know whether this matter is being illuminated by the diction of his words, or by his thoughts'; he was in fact being complimentary to the exiled Attic historian.[278] Yet it remains highly unlikely, as Cicero knew, that Thucydides captured Pericles' original wording, for he was acutely aware that *laudationes funebres* sanctioned embellishment and exaggeration on sentimental grounds; little damaging for non-influential dialogues, but when bestowed on the movers of history, the detail behind weighty historiographical judgements on them becomes questionable.

So where *were* the *Homeridai* and the orators to deliver the encomia at Babylon? They were, it seems, as speechless as Alexander had become. The dual silence is undecipherable, or taking our suspicions aboard, perhaps wholly comprehensible. Apart from a brief and unlikely reference in Arrian in the wake of the festivities dedicated to Dionysus at Ecbatana,[279] any details of Alexander's funeral games were, as it turned out, reserved for his father Philip, his brother-in-law (and uncle) Alexander Molossus, and for the burial of *his* 'Patroclus', Hephaestion.[280] Alexander had to wait until Ptolemy secured the sarcophagus and threw 'magnificent games' to honour his king, thereby honouring his city, and to no lesser degree, himself.[281]

What we read today of events at Babylon is an episodic palimpsest of settlements within settlements, by both men-at-arms and by historians in conflict, and it remains as misunderstood as any momentous juncture in history. The tectonic plates of Ptolemy's *Journal*, Cleitarchus' syncretic theatre, Hieronymus' possibly Will-derived satrapal list and the enigmatic *Pamphlet*, collided at the point of Alexander's death. As with all tectonic activity, fault lines open up and something of the substrata is fortuitously revealed.

But the legendary 'wonder' linked to Semiramis that made the city famous is still shrouded in fog. 'Semiramis' is actually a Greek derivative of the Sumerian *Sammuramat*, 'woman of the palace', perhaps the official consort of the Great King and a title variously attributed to Assyrian queens of repute.[282] And 'wonders of the world' did not begin in classical antiquity with Antipater of Sidon, as such expressions were used by the Assyrians long before; Sargon used similar eulogistic terms for his gigantic copper sculptures, and in fact Sennacherib used the term 'wonder for all peoples' to describe his own palace and gardens in Assyria. The terminology became commonplace and identical phraseology attached itself to Nebuchadnezzar's new Babylonian walls, gates and palaces.[283]

As for Babylon's eponymous gardens actually 'hanging' – *kremastos* in Greek, *pensilis* in Latin – the expressions 'balconied', 'suspended' or 'overhanging' translate equally well.[284] And though Curtius *did* claim they were still in evidence in his day, with descriptions of the ornate irrigation devices provided by Strabo, Diodorus and Philo of Byzantium, the Persian diversion of the Euphrates just twenty-three years after Nebuchadnezzar's death, would have likely rendered them arid, for a while if not permanently, along with the canals that formed a moat around the city. Ruins may have remained, if indeed such gardens ever existed in Babylon, for none of the above historians seems to have provided, or even drawn from, a recent eyewitness account.[285]

Nineveh *is* the more convincing location for the gardens, and Ctesias and Diodorus did place Nineveh, like Babylon, on the Euphrates instead of the Tigris.[286] Moreover, the ancient Assyrian capital *was* referred to as 'Old Babylon' in local sources, and numerous examples exist in which one was mistaken for the other; stolen idols were ferried back and forth, and the pugnacious rhetoric of one is remarkably similar to the other right down to the pulling down of walls and the flooding of the city.[287] In fact three cities were variously known as 'Nineveh' or 'Old Nineveh' in antiquity, whilst a further 'Babylon the second' was located both at Borsippa (close by), and another south of Cairo in Roman times. Astronomical observations suggest that the Assyrian cities of Nimrud and Sippar were referred to as 'Old Babylon' or as the 'Other' or 'Second Babylon' too, each of them claiming to be the 'gateways of the gods'; Nineveh had eighteen gates specifically dedicated to the deities.[288]

How do we read all this babble from antiquity? The answer is with care, for even 'babble' is supposedly derived from the same roots as Babylon, but like much else associated with it, this is a false cognate supported only by biblically dated vagaries of linguistic coincidence.[289] And yet without Jean-François Champollion at hand, one of the heroes of hieroglyphic deciphering, the Babylonian settlement does appear a 'Rosetta Stone' that helps us to compare and decode the source-divergence at the point of Alexander's death, essential when the Bodyguards departed the city with the cipher keys in their pockets.

Alexander's final wishes at Babylon were eventually manipulated away from him by his men and by historians in a flanking manoeuvre he had never witnessed on the battlefield. Dried in embalmer's natron and bound in Ariadne's linen following the Eastern practice, his body was finally mummified to preserve his corpse from the summer heat.[290] But before Alexander's organs were replaced and protected by Canopic jars, the truth behind his death was being ignominiously buried elsewhere.[291] He had no choice in the matter; even the Olympian Gods charged with overseeing his testament could not change the course of what took place next. For despite the giants of the age it empowered, Alexander's Will was just a frail document after all, and one not destined for the Alexandrian archives. It had no Solon to defend it and no Senate to enact it. His testament was as vulnerable as the material on which it was penned, and as flammable as its own short-lived content. Alexander 'died untimely', and like the truth behind events at Babylon, his Will was soon 'hidden, like a brilliant light beneath a bushel', to quote from the final line of *Greek Alexander Romance*.[292]

Front face of the trilingual Rosetta Stone, the 'foundation' of modern Egyptology, erected during the reign of Ptolemy V *Epiphanes* and found at Rosetta (modern Raschid) in the Nile Delta in 1799 by the Napoleonic expedition to Egypt. The decree, issued at Memphis, is inscribed on the granodiorite stele in three scripts: Egyptian hieroglyphs, demotic and Greek, assisting translators, most notably Jean-François Champollion in 1824, in their race to decipher hieroglyphs. Nevertheless it took twenty years for any comprehensive understanding of the pictographic symbols to emerge. The inscription mentioned the Macedonian 4th of the month of Xandikos dating it to March 27th 196 BCE. The Rosetta Stone has resided at the British Museum since 1802.[293]

NOTES

1. Lucian *Dialogues of the Dead* 13.
2. Justin 13.1, translation by Rev. JS Watson, Henry G Bohn, London, 1853.
3. Gelb (1955) pp 1-4. Babylon is a Greek adaptation of *Babili* (*bāb-ili,* gateway of the gods).
4. The *Old Testament,* Genesis 11.7-9 for the myth of the Confusion of Tongues and Tower of Babel.
5. Oates (1979) p 151. The excavations of the site by Koldewey, which purportedly unearthed a bucket and chain system of irrigation, have now turned up lists of rations for the Jewish exiles suggesting a warehouse instead. Herodotus 1.184-191 for references to Semiramis.
6. Berossus Book 1 detailed the origins of the world and civilisation, book 2 the history of the antediluvian kings, the flood and rulers to 747 BCE (Nabonassar's accession), book 3 the recent history down to the accession of Antiochus I; Beaulieu (2006) p 117 for detail. Diodorus went on to describe decorations he attributed to Semiramis, his supposed founder of Babylon who was mentioned fifty-eight times in his second book. And yet she was a queen he associated with the mythical King Ninus of Assyria who never appeared in the cuneiform tablet *Assyrian King List.*
7. Curtius 5.1.25 stated 'most people have believed it was found by Bel'. Discussion at Pliny 19.19.4, and for his confusion see Reade (2000) p 200. Josephus *Against Apion* 1.20 for Nabonidus as builder of the walls. Curtius 5.1.16 described the Babylonian walls as bitumen-cemented, using the bitumen stream that poured from a cavern at nearby Mennis.
8. For Polyhistor's unreliability see Dalley (1994) p 55.
9. Berossus' *Babylonaika* is transmitted through the opening chapter of Josephus' *Jewish Antiquities* 1.92-95, *Against Apion* 1.128-13 and by Alexander Polyhistor through his forty-two books on world history and geography. Megasthenes' references are preserved by Abydenus in his *History of the Chaldeans and Assyrians,* which in turn is preserved in Eusebius' *Kronographia.*
10. Curtius 5.1.35. Diodorus, like Cleitarchus, used 'Syrian' for 'Assyrian'; see Pearson (1960) p 230.
11. Eusebius *Praeparatio Evangelica* book 10 and *Kronographia* 49, translation from the Internet Sacred Text Archive.
12. There is confusion on the identity of either Antipater of Sidon or Antipater of Thessalonica; his poem appeared in the *Greek Anthology* 9.58. Curtius 5.1.25 for the width of the walls being wide enough for two chariots to pass. Sprague de Camp (1972) p 137 for detail of the inner wall.
13. Diodorus 2.11.5 for the obelisk of Semiramis and 2.10.1 ff for the Hanging Gardens; discussed in Dalley (2013) p 4. Following Dalley (2013) p 30 for references to *thaumata* by Diodorus and Strabo. 'Wonders of the world' did not begin in classical antiquity with Antipater of Sidon; such expressions were used by the Assyrians long before; Sargon used similar terminology for his gigantic copper sculptures, and in fact Sennacherib used the term 'wonder for all peoples' to describe his own palace and gardens in Assyria. The terminology became commonplace and identical phraseology attached itself to Nebuchadnezzar's new Babylonian walls, gates and palaces; discussed in Dalley (1994) p 54.
14. *The Indian House Inscription of Nebuchadnezzar* cuneiform tablet was presented to representatives of the East India Company in 1801 in Baghdad.
15. Full details of *Tintir* can be found in George (1992). Copies of the *Tintir* tablets were kept at Nineveh; see discussion in Dalley (1994) p 50.
16. Dalley (2013) p 26 and her observation that the *Romance* failed to mention the gardens.
17. Dalley (2013) p 43 for the panel sculpture discovered in 1854 showing gardens at Nineveh. Also pp 83-105 for the engineering feats and water management systems. Evidence has now come to light that Nineveh resurged under the Seleucids; see Dalley (2013) pp 179-2002 for Nineveh's revival.
18. Dalley (2013) p 97 for the observation that Alexander would have come across the Jerwan aqueduct and p 98 for the Assyrian use of concrete. Diodorus 2.10.5 did mention the use of 'cement' in the base of the Hanging Gardens.
19. Vitruvius *The Ten Books on Architecture* book 9, chapter 8, *Sundials and Waterclocks.* Clayton-Price (1989) p 43 for discussion of Berossus' other work.
20. For the sculptures of Assurbanipal see Dalley (1994) p 50.
21. Updated translation taken from Dalley (2013) p 212. The *alamittu* is the male date palm, which has a natural spiral pattern on its trunk. A *shaduf* is a traditional bucket, pole and cantilever water-raising device. The screw represents an Archimedes Screw comprising a carved palm trunk inside a brass cylinder.
22. Discussion in Saggs (1984) pp 163-164. Koldewey wrote of his machine 'where buckets attached to a chain work on a wheel'; his full text in Sprague de Camp (1972) p 143. For Sennacherib's wording see Dalley (1994) p 52.

23. *The Old Testament* II Kings 19.36-37; the passage cited has him staying at Nineveh before he was killed. *The Indian House Inscription of Nebuchadnezzar* p 127.

24. See Dalley (1994) p 47 for discussion on the confusion between Nebuchadnezzar and Sennacherib and p 108, for example, in the *Book of Judith*.

25. Quotes from Dalley (2013) p 147.

26. See chapter titled *Classicus Scriptor, Rhetoric and Rome* for Nietzsche's full quote from Nietzsche (1974) pp 137-8.

27. Billows (1990) p 331 for discussion of the name of Hieronymus' book or books.

28. As detailed at Arrian *Events After Alexander* 1.2; Eumenes' role at Plutarch *Eumenes* 3.1; discussed in more detail below.

29. Anson (1992) pp 39-41 and Blackwell (1999) p 88 for discussion of the various titles afforded to Perdiccas; Diodorus 18.23.2, Appian *Syrian Wars* 52 for *prostates;* Diodorus 18.2.4 for *epimeletes;* Arrian *Events After Alexander* 1a.3 for *epitropos,* Plutarch *Eumenes* 3.6 for *strategos.* Also Collins (2001) for the development of the chiliarch role. Livy 40.6.3 for an example of *custodes corporis* being employed; Roisman-Worthington (2010) p 459 for discussion. Full discussion of titles and relative authorities in Anson (1992) and Hammond (1985) p 157 for the disappearance of *chiliarchos*. Cassander was appointed chiliarch by Antipater following Triparadeisus, *Arrian Events After Alexander* 1.38, though this was arguably just command of the Companion Cavalry previously under Seleucus as suggested by the *Heidelberg Epitome*; see Collins (2001) p 279. Cassander may have retained the position under Polyperchon implied by his being second-in-command; Diodorus 18.48-4-5, Plutarch *Phocion* 31.1; Collins (2001) p 279.

30. Hieronymus' geographical excursions discussed in Hornblower (1981) p 86. Hieronymus may have added further background detail on the history of Macedon and events leading up to Alexander's campaign; see Hornblower (1981) p 80 and Bosworth-Baynham (2000) p 304 for the suggested detail that might have been included. Polybius 12.26.4 for the suggestion of Timaeus' geographical width.

31. Quoting Bosworth (2002) p 170 on Diodorus' preservation of Hieronymus' geographical digression.

32. See Hornblower (1981) pp 90-96 for full discussion on Diodorus' sources and use of Cleitarchus and Hieronymus.

33. Diodorus 18.2.1, translation from the Loeb Classical Library edition, 1947.

34. Barsine's identity discussed further in the final chapter titled *Lifting the Shroud of Parrhasius*. Diodorus 20.20.1, 20.28.1 for Heracles; 20.81.3 for the Will; discussed in chapters titled *Guardians and Ghosts of the Ephemerides* and *The Silent Siegecraft of the Pamphleteers*.

35. See chapter titled *Comets, Colophons and Curtius Rufus* for discussion of Curtius' identity and career.

36. An *epipolesis* was a troop review, typically pre-battle in which a rousing speech was given to boost morale. For full discussion of the themes in Alexander's speeches to his troops see Inglesias-Zoido (2010).

37. Thorough treatment has been given to Roman themes in Curtius' final chapter in Atkinson (2009). Also a discussion of Curtius' independence of thought in Errington (1970) pp 72-75. Curtius' approach discussed in chapter titled *Comets, Colophons and Curtius Rufus*.

38. Digory Whear *On the Plan and Method of Reading Histories*, 1623, chapter 3.3 quoting Seneca. Quoting Macaulay (1828) for the dramatist and historian comparison. Quoting McKechnie (1999) p 52 on 'pure theatre'.

39. Curtius 10.8.16 and 10.7.8 for Arrhidaeus' speech. Perdiccas and Leonnatus were appointed as joint guardians at the Assembly and the compromise included Antipater and Craterus; see Justin 13.2. Also Ptolemy supposedly proposed group rule; Curtius 10.6.15. Justin 13.2 captured the same undertones, suggesting the framework was indeed from Cleitarchus, unless we are prepared to accept Curtius was following Trogus' lead.

40. Badian (1968) p 189.

41. Lock (1977) p 96 for discussion of the reconstructed constitutional procedures. And for Curtius' embellishment p 104 referring to a law that demanded all relatives of those condemned to death were destined to die also. Baynham (1998) pp 171-180 for Roman themes in Curtius' account of the Philotas affair.

42. Justin 13.1, translation by Rev. JS Watson, Henry G Bohn, London, 1853. Quoting Bevan (1902) p 28 on ambition at Babylon.

43. Plutarch *Galba* 1, translation by J Dryden, 1683; repeated at Plutarch *Moralia 336e-f.*

44. *Romance* 3.32, *Metz Epitome* 103.

45. Arrian 7.25.6 for the officer waiting outside the door. Arrian 7.26.1, Justin 12.15.2-4, Plutarch 76-77 for the forced entry.

46. Curtius 10.5.9-10.6. For the mutiny at Opis and alleged rejection at (or derision of) his attachment to Zeus-Ammon; Plutarch 71.1, Diodorus 17.109.2. More in chapter titled *The Reborn Wrath of Peleus' Son*.

47. Justin 13.1, translation based on Rev. JS Watson, published by Henry G Bohn, London, 1853.
48. Quoting Bosworth (2002) p 32, by permission of Oxford University Press, www.uop.com.
49. Quoting Mitchell (2007) and discussed in Atkinson (2009) p 181.
50. Following the discussion in Anson (1991) pp 230-247 and quoting WS Greenwalt in Carney-Ogden (2010) p 152.
51. A good summary of arguments in Lock (1977); Hammond (1991) for Herodotus' and Thucydides' confirmations.
52. Following the argument in Thomas (2007) p 59. Amyntou, the son of Amyntas.
53. See chapter titled *Sarissa Diplomacy: Macedonian Statecraft* for more on the people and state assets.
54. This explanation of the origins of the Assembly is supported by Lock (1977) and Anson (1991) and reproduces the earlier study of Granier (1931). See further discussions in Lock (1977) pp 91-107. Also see Thomas (2007) p 59 and citing Herodotus 9.44 who outlined the dual role of king and commander. Anson (2013) pp 26-42 sees a less formal structure, suggesting there were no fixed rules for bringing the Assembly together. Quoting Hatzopoulos (1996) p 267 for hardly one hundred aristocratic families.
55. Anson pp 24-42 for discussion of the Assembly role.
56. Hammond (1994) pp 38-39 for the naming convention. Flower (1994) pp 110-111 for Theopompus' stating 800 Companions. For the theatre location see discussion in E Carney in Carney-Ogden (2010) p 45.
57. Plutarch *Pyrrhus* 5.2 for the Epirote tradition.
58. The twice per year formal meetings as proposed by Hatzopoulos (1996) p 270; Hammond (1989) p 218 for the *Xandika*.
59. Wilkins-Hill (2006) for the pastoral industry in classical Greece and Euripides *Elektra* for the epithet 'milk drinker'.
60. Billows (1990) p 246 for discussion of the synedrion and its function. Anson (2013) p 41 for doubts about a 'people's assembly'. Hatzopoulos (1996) p 264 ff for the contention that it was not always represented by the army but by a broader 'commonwealth, especially in the Hellenistic era' and p 286 for the observation of the ease of assembling the army at war rather than a population in peace. Diodorus 19.46.4; Polyaenus 4.6.14 saw it as a *synedrion*. Hammond (1991) p 42 believed only serving men could attend the Assembly.
61. For discussion on the religious position of the Macedonian king see Roisman-Worthington (2010) p 10.
62. First described in Herodotus 1.134.
63. Arrian 4.13.1 for Philip's formation of the corps of the royal pages.
64. Quoting Borza (1990) pp 245-246. Hammond (1978) pp 340-342 for Macedonian trial procedure. For the Assembly's role in treason, see the coverage of the Philotas affair, especially Curtius 6.7-11, which gave additional detail that all Macedonians present were invited to the trial. Also covered in Diodorus 17.79, Plutarch 49.3-12, Arrian 3.26.1, Justin 12.5.1-3 and the text that follows in each for this subsequent execution. Also Diodorus 19.12.2 made it clear that it was an Assembly decision that levied a death sentence on Eumenes; presumably his action against Craterus was deemed treasonous. For Olympias' death after an Assembly gathering, Diodorus 19.51.1-4 and Justin 14.6.6; both recorded a judicial proceeding in the form of an Assembly gathering. Arrian 7.8.3 provided the most negative coverage of the hasty execution of ringleaders at Opis.
65. Anson (1991) as an example of the interpretation of absolute power. Curtius 6.8.25 suggested in peacetime royal power was not effective in Assembly trials, 'except in as far as a king's personal prestige had been of influence before the verdict'; translation from Hammond (1978) p 341.
66. As observed by Hatzopoulos (1994) pp 265-266; Diodorus 16.3.3 and Justin 7.5.10 for Philip's early use of the Assembly and Curtius 8.2.12. Anson (1991) p 231 ff for list of Assembly gatherings. Hammond (1978) pp 340-343 for the Assembly and trials following Philip's death. Curtius 9.4.15 for the Assembly in Mallia.
67. Curtius 6.8.25. For Demetrius' speech see Plutarch *Demetrius* 37.2-4, Justin 16.1.10-18; Cassander had addressed the Assembly at (or most likely after) Olympias' death: Diodorus 19.51.1-2, Justin 14.6.6-13. Discussed in detail in Hatzopoulos (1996) pp 274-275.
68. The text of Arrian *Events After Alexander* 1.28 which suggested Perdiccas publicly brought charges against Ptolemy, is unclear; Ptolemy allegedly cleared his name such that the royal army was against the attack.
69. See chapter titled *The Reborn Wrath of Peleus' Son* for more on Amyntas' execution.
70. Livy 40.9.8 for Perseus' claims to the right of primogeniture; though this is a later event, it is unlikely the rules of succession had changed.
71. Hammond (1991) pp 35-38 for the grandsons of Alexander I, polygamy and succession traditions.
72. Hammond (1991) p 34-35 for the equal rights of Macedonian princes. Justin 8.4.4-6 for the offspring of Amyntas III. 'Oversupply' quoting Bosworth (1992) p 29.

73. See discussion in Lock (1977) p 92 for the dominance of primogeniture. Hammond (1994) p 18 for the joint rule discussion; this occurred after the death of Alexander I of Macedonia.
74. Following and quoting Bosworth (1971) p 128.
75. Schachermeyr (1970) pp 81-84 cited in McKechnie (1999) p 47; Justin 13.2 mentioned the meeting took place in the palace.
76. Curtius 10.6.2.
77. Curtius 10.6.1.
78. Diodorus 18.4.1-4, based on the translation from the Loeb Classical Library edition, 1947.
79. Arrian 7.1.1-3 and Curtius 10.1.17 for the proposed voyages around Arabia, Africa and the conquest of Carthage and the Scythians via the Black Sea; Arrian 7.19.3-5 for the Babylonian projects.
80. Quoting Bosworth *A to A* (1988) p 186. A good summary of the views up to his time can be found in Badian (1968) rejecting Tarn's cynicism and supporting Wilken and Schachermeyr in their belief in the detail.
81. Full discussion of views and Hellenistic and Roman contamination in Tarn (1948) pp 378-399. Also Tarn (1939) pp 124-135. 'Embroidery' quotes Badian (1968). See Tarn (1948) pp 374-378 for discussion of the invented embassies and chapter titled *Hierarchic Historians and Alexandrian Alchemy*.
82. Diodorus 18.4.4-6 based on the translation from the Loeb Classical Library edition, 1947. The footnote reads 'Cyrnus in Macedon is otherwise unknown, but the name is found elsewhere in Greece (Herodotus 9.105, Pliny 4.53)…'
83. Alexander had already constructed a large tumulus some 125 feet high and 'great in circumference' for Demaratus of Corinth; Plutarch 56.2; a tumulus for Hephaestion; Plutarch 72.5; and a first modest tumulus for Philip upon his death; Plutarch 11.2.1.
84. See discussion in Behrwald (1999). The *Historika Hypomnemata* was used and quoted by Timagenes through Josephus 13.3.9. Strabo also associated the term *hypomnemata* with his *Geography*. Others such as Hegesippus titled their memoirs *hypomnemata*. Athenaeus 4.162a for reference to Hegesander's work. Plutarch 4.4 for Arostoxenus' title.
85. Curtius 10.10.1 for the re-entry into the city. Plutarch 77.5 for three days, Curtius 10.9.13 for six days, Aelian 12.64 for thirty days, following which Aristander the seer entered the Assembly.
86. Hatzopoulos (1996) p 295 and Polybius 4.87.7-8 for Antigonus *Doson*'s Will; translation from Marasco (2011) p 57 and following the observations of C Bearzot in Marasco (2011) p 58.
87. Arrian 7.12.3-4, Diodorus 18.4.1, Justin 12.12.7-9 for Craterus replacing Antipater.
88. For Meleager's career see Heckel (2006) pp 159-161; for his service with or under Craterus, see Arrian 3.18.4, 6.17.3 and Curtius 5.4.14. Heckel (1988) p 20 sees Meleager as looking after Craterus' interests in Babylon. Curtius 10.2.8 ff for the remaining Macedonian troop numbers after the demobilisation of the veterans at Opis.
89. Chapter titled *The Tragic Triumvirate of Treachery and Oaths* for more on communication systems.
90. Bosworth (1992) p 32 for Craterus' resources.
91. Diodorus 18.12.1 for Antipater's call for help. Bosworth (1971) p 125 and Atkinson (2009) pp 238-239, for discussion on Craterus' delay in Cilicia and the rumours that Craterus had been sent to assassinate Antipater. Heckel (1988) p 21 footnote 8 suggested Craterus' delay might have been due to unrest in Cilicia, where the Satrap, Balacrus, had been killed by the Pisidians. Anson (2014) p 39 for the ten days of travel from Babylon to Cilicia. Diodorus 18.25.3 for Antigonus reporting Perdiccas' design on the Macedonian throne.
92. Diodorus 18.4.1 based on the translation from the Loeb Classical Library edition, 1954.
93. Curtius 10.1.19 for the commodities requisitioned from Cyprus and Mount Libanos, Lebanon. Meiggs (1982) p 49 for the *Epic of Gilgamesh* and Diodorus 19.58.3.
94. Plutarch 68 and Curtius 10.1.19 for Thapsacus and the planned navigation of Africa. Morrison-Coates-Rankov (2000) pp 109-111 for naval crews.
95. Murray (2012) p 96 and p 190 for discussion of the equipment needed to build and fit out a ship. For the implied journey west by Craterus and his veterans including Antigenes, the commander of the Silver Shields, see Justin 12.12.8 implied in Arrian 7.12.4, Curtius 10.10.15. As Antigenes was later found in Egypt, it is reasonable to assume he remained in Cilicia and was collected by Perdiccas on his journey to invade Egypt in 321/320 BCE; Arrian *Events After Alexander* 1.35 and Diodorus 18.39.6 for his part in Perdiccas' assassination.
96. Justin 12.12.9, Arrian 7.12.4 for confirmation that upon Alexander's death the replacement troops remained in Macedonia.
97. 'White Cleitus': so-named to distinguish him from 'Black' (*Melas*) Cleitus, son of Dropidas. Diodorus 18.15.8-9, Plutarch *Moralia* 338a, Plutarch *Demetrius* 11.3 for the actions off Amorgas. Diodorus 18.15.8 for 240 ships. The *Parian Chronicle* also referred to the battles. Heckel (2006) p 88 for the 130 ships and Echinades; after victory Cleitus' fleet swelled. Cleitus was given charge of Perdiccas' fleet before his invasion of Egypt; Justin 13.6.16

98. Diodorus 18.15.8-9 for the fleet assembled by White Cleitus who accompanied Craterus as far as Cilicia; Arrian 7.12.4, Justin 12.12.8. This is a highly compressed account and possibly compresses two naval actions into one. See footnote 51 to the Loeb Classical Library edition, 1947, of Diodorus 18.15.8 for discussion. Bing (1973) p 347 for discussion of Cilician natural resources including high-grade iron. Anson (2014) for the observation that Craterus might have been required to suppress a revolt in Greece.

99. Diodorus 18.3.4 with earlier confirmation in Diodorus 17.109.1 and Arrian 7.12-13.

100. Diodorus 18.3.5, Justin 13.4.6 for Arrhidaeus' instructions to build and deliver the funeral bier.

101. Avramović (2006) p 4 for discussion of the Greek terms relating to Wills. Also see discussion on the ancient Greek term *diatheke*, which was used for both lifetime covenants and Wills, in chapter titled *Wills and Covenants in the Classical Mind*.

102. Badian (1968) p 203 agrees that Diodorus was unclear on the relationship of the orders of Craterus to the document produced by Perdiccas encapsulating the last plans. Also Hornblower (1980) pp 94-95 for discussion on Diodorus' clumsiness with linking Craterus' instructions to the last plans.

103. Diodorus 18.4.2 and 18.4.4.

104. Badian (1969) p 204 supports the case for Eumenes' hand in the extracting of the last plans from the campaign paperwork.

105. Dionysius of Halicarnassus suggested Hieronymus' style was boring, see Hornblower (1981) p 1 and Bosworth-Baynham (2000) p 304, the historian Psaon was also listed.

106. As proposed by Hornblower (1981) pp 50-51 and pp 94-97 for examples of *thauma*.

107. Curtius 10.1.16-19, Arrian 5.26.1-3, 5.27.7, 7.1-5. Also see discussion in Green (2007) pp 6-7.

108. Quoting Hornblower (1981) p 94.

109. Badian (1968) p 204.

110. A good summary of the opinions, uncertainties, and the reporting of Hephaestion's funeral pyre can be found in McKechnie (1995).

111. Diodorus 17.114.4-17.116 also Arrian 7.14.7, 7.23.6 for the magnificence of the funeral.

112. As suggested by E Carney in Bosworth-Baynham (2000) pp 173-176, assuming Koldewey was correct in identifying the pyre's remains inside the walls. Diodorus 18.4.2 used *pyra* rather than a tomb or more permanent structure; McKechnie (1995) p 421. Quoting Diodorus 17.114.1. Diodorus 17.114-17.116 for the full episode.

113. Diodorus 17.110 and Arrian 7.14.8 located the funeral pyre with their Babylonian narrative, whereas Plutarch 72.5, Justin 12.12.12 and a reference from Lucan contain references against events in Ecbatana. Aelian 7.8 for the armour and destruction of the acropolis of Ecbatana. Diodorus 17.110.8 for Perdiccas being charged to take Hephaestion's body to Babylon.

114. See Heckel (2006) p 106 for his identification and projects, artistic or architectural. Plutarch 72.5 for the name Stasicrates. He is otherwise referred to as Deinochares, Diocles, and Cheirocrates. He may have been in Babylon overseeing the city's reconstruction projects, or in Ephesus overseeing the reconstruction of the Temple of Artemis, for Plutarch's use of 'longing' suggests he was not immediately available.

115. Diodorus 15.115.6. Anson (2013) p 114 for discussion of 'associate god' as indicated by Diodorus 17.115.2-116.1. Plutarch 72.1-3, Arrian 7.14.7, 7.23.6 for Hephaestion's elevation. Arrian claimed the oracle permitted 'hero' only. Discussed in McKechnie (1995) p 420.

116. Diodorus 17.115.1-5.

117. Plutarch 72-73.

118. Koldewey (1913) pp 310-311. Strabo 16.1.5 for the clearing away of the foundation rubble from the Esagila Temple; cf Arrian 7.21.5 who attributed the work to a sluice project. Koldewey claimed to have found its remains along with the rubble from the clearing of the Esagila Temple dumped close by. For Strabo's testimony on the rubble from Esagila see Oates (1979) p 140 and Pearson (1960) p 181. Arrian 7.17.1.2 for Alexander's plans to rebuild the temple on his return to Babylon; the Chaldeans attempted to talk him out of it although Diodorus 17.112.3 claimed they predicted safe passage for Alexander into the city if he did immediately set about repairing the temple.

119. Diodorus 17.115.1 for the tearing down of 10 furlongs of the city walls. The Attic stade (furlong) was equivalent to 185 metres or 220 yards, whereas the Olympic stade to 176 metres or approximately 209 yards. Herodotus 2.6 has a stade at 600 feet (a *parasang* was equal to 30 stades) discussed in Gershevitch-Fisher-Boyle (1968) p 628. Mazaeus capitulated after Gaugamela; Curtius 5.1.17-19, suggested at Diodorus 17.64.4, Arrian 3.16.3.

120. Diodorus 17.115.1 for the likenesses (he stated the *eidola* they made were to fulfil Alexander's 'desires', but again it doesn't explicitly say that he had requested them to be made. Diodorus 17.115.5 for the covering of expenses. Nearby cities were to contribute too. Hammond (1998) p 337 for *eidola* discussion.

121. Arrian 7.23.6-7 for the plans for Hephaestion's hero shrines. Plutarch 47.9-12 and *Eumenes* 2.4 for an indication of those who disliked Hephaestion; it included Craterus and Eumenes.
122. Arrian 7.23.8 for the letter to Cleomenes. For *Arabarchos* see Heckel (2006) p 88; it was a financial administration position akin to revenue collector. For his death see Pausanias 1.6.3.
123. Homer *Iliad* 23.83-84.
124. For Ptolemy's execution of Cleomenes for his support of Perdiccas see Pausanias 1.6.3.
125. Curtius 10.6.4.
126. Tarn (1948) p 148 for hypaspist discussion. There is some confusion as to whether *pezhetairoi* also referred to heavier infantry but not pike-bearers. See also Anson 1985 for further discussion of the origins of the *pezhetairoi*.
127. Following the mercenary comparison discussed by Anson (1991) pp 230-247.
128. Curtius 3.2.13-16 for Charidemus' description of the Macedonian army. His honesty cost him his life. Arrian 1.10.4 for Charidemus' exile from Athens. Charidemus (alone of the Athenian orators) had been banished by Alexander after Thebes fell.
129. Curtius 10.6.4-10.9.21. See Atkinson (2009) p 180 for discussion on the pregnancy; Roxane was either six months pregnant according to Curtius 10.6.9 or eight months according to Justin 13.2.5. See Errington (1970) p 56 for discussion on Perdiccan hopes for Roxane and a son.
130. Justin 7.2.6-13. The Macedonians had carried the cradled Aeropus to the battle and positioned him behind their lines to spur them on against the Illyrians. The chronology of his reign is uncertain.
131. Curtius 10.6.8.
132. See references to the 'Tiberian farce' below.
133. Curtius 10.6.10-11. Justin 13.2 attributed the same suggestion to Meleager, the notable infantry officer, who informed the Assembly that Heracles was then based at Pergamum. Further, Justin credited Meleager with reminding the gathering that Arrhidaeus was present in Babylon, and so *immediately* available. It appears that Justin carelessly, or even consciously, merged both speeches into one, something of an over 'efficiency' in his epitomising efforts. Justin may in fact have merged three speeches together, for Meleager supposedly rounded off with a rejection of both of Alexander's Asiatic sons, a blatantly contradictory declaration.
134. See final chapter titled *Lifting the Shroud of Parrhasius* for full discussion of the identification, or misidentifications, of Heracles' mother and her sisters.
135. Curtius 10.6.13-16.
136. Reiterated by Brunt (1975) p 33.
137. Ptolemy's marriage policy discussed in Ellis (1994) pp 41-43.
138. A view argued by McKechnie (1999) pp 44-60. Quoting Curtius 7.8.10, translation from the Lobe Classical Library edition, 1946. Quoting Baynham (1998) p 88 on Scythians.
139. Curtius 10.6.15 for the group rule suggestion, reiterated at Justin 13.2.
140. Arrian 7.14.10.
141. Curtius 10.6.15-16. Following the observation of Stewart (1993) p 214 for *koinopragia*. Arrian *Events After Alexander* 1.3 Perdiccas' chiliarchy.
142. Discussion of the mechanism behind the suggestion of group rule in chapter titled *Lifting the Shroud of Parrhasius*. Quoting Hammond-Walbank (1988) p 145 on republicanism.
143. Curtius 10.6.16-18.
144. See Heckel (2006) p 50 for discussion and Diodorus 19.35.4 for Aristonus' role under Polyperchon who was guardian to the kings, thus suggesting a real fealty to Alexander's wishes and sons.
145. Curtius 10.6.18-20 based on the translation in the Loeb Classical Library edition, 1946.
146. See Atkinson (2009) p 179 for discussion of Perdiccas' returning of the ring at Curtius 10.6.5.1 and other Roman examples, most prominently Tiberius, described in Tacitus 1.11.1 and 12, Suetonius *Tiberius* 24.1-2, Cassius Dio 57.2.3, Velleius Patreculus *Compendium of Roman History* 2.124. Errington (1970) pp 50-51 for comparisons between Arrhidaeus and Claudius. Suetonius *Tiberius* 25.1 for the 'wolf by the ears'.
147. Suetonius *Tiberius* 23-25 for references to 'slavery' and his 'cruel fate'.
148. See chapter titled *Comets, Colophons and Curtius Rufus* for Curtius' possible reasons for bypassing any Will reference.
149. Curtius 10.7.7 for Meleager's hatred of Perdiccas. Curtius 10.6.20-24, based on the translation from the Loeb Classical Library edition, 1946.
150. Diodorus 17.117.4 and Arrian 7.26.3 for *toi kratistoi* from *kratistos*: 'the strongest or noblest'. Latin interpretation of that from Curtius 10.4.5 *qui esset optimus* (the 'best') and *dignissimus* (broadly the 'most worthy') from Justin 12.15.
151. Curtius 10.7.2, 10.7.10; reiterated in Hatzopoulos (1996) p 270.
152. Justin 13.2. The broad term 'Persian' was being employed; Roxane was Bactrian or Sogdian. At Justin 13.4.6 he later proposed 'King Arrhidaeus' was charged with the task of conveying

Alexander's body to Egypt. He also later termed Amphimachus, satrap of Mesopotamia the 'brother of the kings' though again he was more likely the brother of the Arrhidaeus who later became the satrap of Hellespontine Phrygia.

153. Diodorus 17.117.4 and Arrian 7.26.3 for *toi kratistoi*: 'the strongest or noblest'. Latin interpretation of that from Curtius 10.4.5 *qui esset optimus* (the 'best') and *dignissimus* (broadly the 'most worthy') from Justin 12.15.

154. Arrian 3.11.9 for the phalanx leaders, see discussion in Tarn (1948) p 142.

155. See Curtius 8.12.17-18 for Meleager's dangerous quip at the banquet at which Alexander gave Omphis, dynast of Taxila 1,000 talents; the same is suggested by Plutarch 59.5 in abbreviated form without names being mentioned. Alexander suppressed his anger recalling the Cleitus episode. Arrian *Events After Alexander* 1.2 lists Meleager amongst the *megistoi*.

156. Curtius 10.7.7 for Meleager's proposal that Arrhidaeus be crowned King Philip III. Justin 13.3.

157. Curtius 10.7.1-3. Justin 13.2 credited this speech to Meleager. See discussion in Atkinson (2009) on Arrhidaeus' mental state. Rather than an affirmation that he was able to function in some titular capacity, the cited excerpt from Plutarch *Phocion* 33 5-7 confirmed Arrhidaeus' retarded state and mental simplicity.

158. Curtius 8.4.30 for the Macedonian reaction to the marriage with Roxane. For the Macedonian tradition of the symposium see Borza (1995) pp 159-168.

159. Diodorus 19.11.5 and Justin 14.5.10 for the regnal term. Discussed in Anson (2003) p 377 and following the proposal of Bosworth (1992). Curtius 10.7.2 for Arrhidaeus becoming the king's associate in ceremonies and sacrifices.

160. Athenaeus 13.557d, Justin 9.7.3, Plutarch 77.8.

161. Porphyry of Tyre FGrH 260 F2, *Heidelberg Epitome* 1 called him epileptic. Socrates *daimonion* was described in Plato's *Apology* 31c–d, 40a which has been postulated as epilepsy. Caesar's fits have likewise been posthumously attributed to epilepsy; see Plutarch *Caesar* 17, 45, 60, and Suetonius *Julius* 45. The symptoms exhibited by Caligula and described in Suetonius *Gaius* are likewise suggestive of epilepsy.

162. The qualifications for regent discussed in Miller (1991) p 51, quoting Hammond-Griffiths (1979) p 182. Hammond (1985) p 157 and Justin 13.2.13 for the use of *tutores*. Justin 13.2 for Ptolemy's wording.

163. For Peithon's speech see Curtius 10.7.8-9. Curtius himself stated Peithon was following Perdiccas' cause. Justin 13.13-14 for the guardian line-up.

164. Peithon was one of Perdiccas' assassins in Egypt; Diodorus 18.36.5. Perdiccas is said to have suspected intrigue immediately after Babylon when Peithon left to quell the mercenary revolt; Diodorus 18.7.4-6.

165. Curtius 10.7.8, 10.7.20, 10.8.4 and Justin 13.2 for Leonnatus' prominence. Curtius 10.7.8 for confirmation that Perdiccas and Leonnatus were of royal stock. Curtis 3.12.7 for *ex purpuratis*, thus wearing the purple, suggestive of a highborn courtier.

166. For the *prostasia* discussion see Errington (1970) p 56 and also Goralski (1989) p 87. Heckel (2006) p 96 for discussion of Craterus' supreme commands. He was clearly at that stage the second-in-command. Quoting and following Anson (1992) p 39 for the 'honorific' role or a more powerful position. Hammond (1985) p 156 for the relative roles of Craterus and Antipater. Arrian *Events After Alexander* for Craterus as *prostates* of the kingdom of Arrhidaeus and Justin 13.4.5 for 'royal property'.

167. Alexander instructed Antipater to ensure the veterans were provided with garlands and front seats at performances; Plutarch 71.8, Diodorus 18.18.7.

168. Arrian 7.4.8 for the 10,000 alleged marriages to Asian wives; each was given a wedding dowry. Billows (1990) p 306 for the governing ethnicity.

169. Billows (1990) p 355 for total Macedonian numbers in Asia up to 203 BCE. Pliny 6.31.139 mentions a Pella in the district of Alexandria on Tigris. Anson (2013) pp 138-139 for city-founding discussion. Billows (1990) p 299 for 'Pella' being used as a name for new settlements, specifically what was to become Seleucid Apamea.

170. Justin 12.15, relating the activity to the last days of Alexander's illness.

171. See chapter titled *Lifting the Shroud of Parrhasius* for discussion of the marriages.

172. Whilst Arrhidaeus was a son of Philip II, his mother was in fact Thessalian, though likely of aristocratic heritage; see Athenaeus 13.557c and Arrian *Events After Alexander* 1.1. Discussion in Heckel (2006) p 52.

173. Curtius 10.7.11-12, following Homer's *Iliad* 2.142-146.

174. Curtius 10.7.14-15.

175. Hammond (1991) p 41 for Assembly protocol.

176. Curtius 10.7.16.

177. Aelian 12.64, referring to the *Iliad* 5.449.

178. Curtius 10.7.16-20.

179. For Ptolemy's treatment of Perdiccas in the campaign, see Errington (1969) pp 238-239. For the relative dates of Cleitarchus and Ptolemy publishing their accounts, see chapter titled, *Hierarchic Historians and Alexandrian Alchemy*.
180. Curtius 10.8.1.
181. Justin 13.3.1-13.4.1.
182. Curtius 10.8.1-12 for the face-off, departure from the city, and famine and 5.1.27 for the cultivated areas to provide for the population in case of a siege. See below for Xerxes diverting the Euphrates when besieging the city.
183. Curtius 10.2.8 stated 13,000 Macedonian infantry and 2,000 cavalry. Bosworth (2002) pp 64-97 for estimates of total troop numbers. Sprague de Camp (1972) p 136 for the 300,000 to 400,000 estimate. A higher estimate of 600,000 is from Kloft (1992) p 10 though no dating is specified and the number is likely based on the later population of Seleucia on Tigris. See population discussion in Boiy (2004) pp 229-232. Further city size discussion in Archibald-Davies-Gabrielson (2005) p 29 ff.
184. Arrian 7.23.1, Curtius 8.5.1, Diodorus 17.108.1-2, Plutarch 47.3 and 71.1 for the arrival of new recruits. Diodorus 17.95.4 for the mercenary contingent that arrived in India before the voyage down the Hydaspes-Indus.
185. See Reade (2000) p 203 and p 215 for discussion of the Summer or Outer Palace and its military construction and purpose.
186. Curtius 10.7.1-3 and 10.9.20 used the term *bellorum civilium Macedonibus* when describing the fighting at Babylon following Alexander's death.
187. Herodotus 1.178. Also Aristotle *Politics* 1.3 for the great spaces enclosed by the walls.
188. See Diodorus 18.2.2-4 and Justin 13.3.2 closely track. The same is implied, but not expressly stated in Arrian *Events After Alexander* 1.2-4.
189. Heckel (2006) pp 159-161 for Meleager's various commands. See below for Meleager's temporary elevation to third-in-command.
190. Curtius 10.8.8-11.
191. Plutarch *Moralia* 337d-e. See Heckel-Yardley (2004) p 34 for translation.
192. As suggested at Curtius 10.5.12 (quoted) and 10.8.10. 10.8.7 for Meleager's three-day deliberations over uncertain plans.
193. Curtius 10.7.13.
194. Curtius 10.8.16-20.
195. Curtius 10.7.2 for Arrhidaeus taking part in sacrifices and ceremonies.
196. Diodorus 19.11.5 stated six years four months and Justin simply six years. However the date of the formal commencement of his reign is not specified. Arrhidaeus is later attested to have 'received Phocion', but this was in essence an embassy to Polyperchon, Arrhidaeus' regent and his *epimeletes*. In an outburst of anger he almost ran Hegemon through with a spear; again this suggests he was neither self-controlled nor predictable; Nepos *Phocion* 3.3, Plutarch *Phocion* 33.8-12
197. McKechnie (1999) pp 59-60. A *contio* was a Latin term for a public gathering though Livy for example used the term for a meeting, its audience and its speeches. Historians have reconstructed speeches given at public ceremonies when, inevitably, little real-time recording took place. Thus *contio* speeches are often nothing more than approximations, at best, of the spirit behind the original. See discussion in Frolov (2013). Hammond (1978) p 341 for the *contio* in the manner of Scipio.
198. McKechnie (1999) p 59 and see full article for discussion on Roman themes in Curtius' portrayal of Arrhidaeus.
199. Following the observation in McKechnie (1999) p 59 of the allusion to the Roman struggle of the common man and aristocrat.
200. Curtius 10.8.15 mentioned Damyllus (or Amissus) as one of the envoys; this might be a corruption of 'Damis' who defended Megalopolis against elephants in 318 BCE (Diodorus 18.71.2-3); see identity discussion in Heckel (2006) p 102. The other envoys were named as Pasas (or Pasias) a Thessalian and Pertilaus (or Perilaus); Heckel (2006) p 202 for identity discussion.
201. Plutarch *Eumenes* 3.1 for his neutrality and continued presence inside the city. Translations from the Loeb Classical Library edition, 1919.
202. Curtius 10.8.22-23; the infantry 'thought' the armies were reconciled. Arrian *Events After Alexander* termed Meleager Perdiccas' *hyparchos* whereas Justin 13.4-5 implied they were equals; see discussion by Heckel in *Quintus Curtius Rufus, The History of Alexander*, Penguin edition 1984, p 301 footnote 44.
203. Attalus, son of Andromenes, was probably enrolled by Perdiccas into his plan with the promise of marriage to his sister, Atalante; he had served with Meleager on campaign. Justin 13.3.2-7 has Attalus backing up Meleager at the Assembly, more below.
204. Anson (2013) suggests the lustration was linked to the death of the kings. Hammond (1991) p 32 for more detail on weapons and insignia.

205. Curtius 10.9.12, Justin 13.4.7. See discussion on the chronology of the mutiny and lustration in Bosworth (2002) p 55. Polybius 23.10.17 for the sacrifice to Xanthus in the eponymous month, though here horses are referred to, not dogs. Tarn (1948) p 107 for Macedonian superstition related to fighting in Daisios, based upon Plutarch 16 claiming that Alexander doubled the length of April to justify the River Granicus battle.

206. Curtius 10.9.20 for the use of 'treachery' to describe Perdiccas' actions. Curtius 19.9.20-21, Justin 13.4.7-8, Arrian *Events After Alexander* 1a.4 Diodorus 18.4.7 placed Meleager's death after the division of empire. Curtius' account suggests Perdiccas arranged the lustration with the unwitting Meleager himself; Justin claimed Perdiccas acted without the knowledge of his colleagues.

207. Aristotle *Politics* 5.5 translated by B Jovett, published by The Internet Classic Archive.

208. See Anson (1988) p 476 for discussion on the view of Briant and Errington that Perdiccas was acting in consultation with the other influential generals, as echoed by Diodorus 18.3.1, though these arguments exclude a Will.

209. See chapter titled *Wills and Covenants in the Classical Mind* for arguments relating to the call for Alexander to write a Will.

210. Plutarch 76.4.

211. Perdiccas' inheritance and his attempt to install allied governors discussed in the final chapter titled *Lifting the Shroud of Parrhasius*.

212. Curtius 10.6.4.

213. Justin 13.4.4, translation based on Rev. JS Watson, published by Henry G Bohn, London, 1853.

214. Arrian *Events After Alexander* 1.5 based on the translation in Goralsky (1989) p 86.

215. *Metz Epitome* 123, translation from Heckel-Yardley (2004) p 289.

216. Curtius 10.6.1-4. Quoting Atkinson (2009) p 26.

217. For their capture at Issus see Curtius 3.11.25, Diodorus 17.36.2, Arrian 2.11.9, Justin 11.9.12, Plutarch 21.1. For their installation in Susa, Curtius 5.2.17 ff, Diodorus 17.67.1, and death at Babylon see Plutarch 77.6.

218. Badian (1968) p 203 suggested Eumenes did indeed have the king's papers or *hypomnemata* that outlined the last plans. We propose that position would have been used for faked correspondence too.

219. Siebert (1969) pp 27-28.

220. See discussion in Heckel (2006) p 115. The final mention of Docimus is after Ipsus at which he had defected to Lysimachus. He most likely betrayed the Perdiccans when besieged following the battle with Antigonus in Pisidia; see Simpson (1957) pp 504-505. See Heckel *A and A* (1978) for the argument for Attalus' marriage to Atalante *after* Babylon to secure his support. Justin 13.3.2-7 suggested Attalus had sided with Meleager and sent assassins to kill Perdiccas. Arrian *Events after Alexander* 24.6 for Medius serving in the invasion of Cyprus in 321/210 BCE.

221. Nearchus' initial whereabouts after Babylon are not recorded. He next emerged supporting Antigonus against Eumenes in 319/318 BCE. As there was no initial hostility with Antigonus until Perdiccas' plans to repudiate Nicaea were revealed, he may well have assumed the governorship of his satrapy, or served the royal army until Perdiccas' death. Full discussion in the final chapter titled *Lifting the Shroud of Parrhasius*. For Nearchus' marriage at Susa Arrian 7.4.6. Nearchus was married to the daughter of Barsine and Mentor; see discussion in chapter titled *Lifting the Shroud of Parrhasius*.

222. See discussion of Ptolemy's ongoing communications with Antipater in Errington (1970) pp 65-67. Leonnatus also defected to Greece, assisting Antipater in the Lamian War, and it appears he tried to turn Eumenes against Perdiccas too. Perdiccas' eventual murder by Peithon and the Silver Shield commanders (and possibly Seleucus) suggests a broad early coalition against him; for Seleucus' possible presence in Egypt see chapter titled *The Silent Siegecraft of the Pamphleteers*. Arrian *Events after Alexander* 1.21 for Antipater's offer of Nicaea in marriage, Diodorus 18.23.1 for Perdiccas seeking her hand.

223. Perdiccas' dialogue with Demades discussed in Errington (1970) p 62; Diodorus 18.48.2, Plutarch *Phocion* 30.5-6, Plutarch *Demosthenes* 31.4-6, Arrian *Events After Alexander* 1.14-15 each described, with some variations, how letters from Demades to Perdiccas were later discovered, requesting Perdiccas' intervention in Greece. If genuine, their earlier concealment suggested to Antipater that Perdiccas was planning trouble. The correspondence may have been fabricated to enable Antipater to remove him; Goralski (1989) p 106 for discussion. Arrian *Events After Alexander* 1.14 for the 'rotten thread' analogy.

224. For Docimus' activity see Arrian *Events After Alexander* 24, 3-5 and Plutarch *Eumenes* 8.4. Pausanias 1.6.3 for Cleomenes' support from Perdiccas.

225. Antigonus was ordered by Perdiccas to support Eumenes' invasion of Cappadocia; he defected to Antipater and Craterus Macedonia instead; Plutarch *Eumenes* 3-4, Diodorus 18.23.3-4, Arrian *Events After Alexander* 1.20.

226. For the failed invasion of Cyprus involving Medius and Aristonus see Arrian *Events After*

Alexander 24.6. Quoting Roisman (2010) p 118.

227. The date of Perdiccas' death, May/June 320 BCE, is backed up by the *Babylonian Chronicle* extract BM 34, 660 Vs 4 though still disputed; see Anson (2003) for discussion on 'high' and 'low' chronologies. For Seleucus' possible participation in Perdiccas' murder see chapter titled *The Silent Siegecraft of the Pamphleteers.*

228. For Perdiccas' murder see Arrian *Events After Alexander* 1.35, Diodorus 18.39.6, Nepos 5.1, Diodorus 18.36.5. For the canal project Diodorus 18.33.2-3, possibly to allow Attalus to bring the fleet in tow as Perdiccas advanced. Detailed discussion of the attack in Roisman (2012) pp 97-103. Diodorus 18.33.5 for Perdiccas' promises and gifts.

229. Arrian *Events After Alexander* 1.28; this could be the epitomiser's confusion of Diodorus 18.36.6, a speech Ptolemy gave after Perdiccas' death. Diodorus 18.36.6 for Ptolemy addressing the Macedonians after Perdiccas' death.

230. Quoting Hornblower (1981) p 103 on 'centrifugal forces'.

231. In Rome the Grass Crown was the highest and rarest of military decorations, associated with breaking a blockade to save the day.

232. AF Rosiger, *De Duride Samio, Diodori Siculi et Plutarchi auctore*, Gottingen, 1874. See Justin 13.6 for his favourable treatment of Ptolemy. Trogus' treatment is epitomised at Justin 13.6 to 'Ptolemy, by his wise exertions in Egypt, was acquiring great power; he had secured the favour of the Egyptians by his extraordinary prudence.'

233. The Battle of Actium took place in 31 BCE, probably when Diodorus finished his work but Caesar had by then already caused damage in the city, see chapter titled *The Precarious Path of Pergamena and Papyrus* for more detail.

234. Diodorus 18.28.3 based on the translation from the Loeb Classical Library edition, 1954; also recorded by Strabo 17.8 and the *Romance* 3.34.6 though dates of the transfer from Memphis to Alexandria are not given. Pausanias 1.7.1 stated Ptolemy II *Philadelphos* brought the body to Alexandria from Memphis. An alternative fate for the sarcophagus discussed in the final chapter titled *Lifting the Shroud of Parrhasius*. Also see Aelian 12.64 for an alternative tradition.

235. Diodorus 18.28.3 and the earlier references to Alexandria at 17.52.1-6; Strabo 17.8 for his description of Alexandria.

236. Diodorus 18.28.5-6, based on the translation from the Loeb Classical Library edition, 1954.

237. Curtius 10.10.20, based on the translation from the Loeb Classical Library edition, 1946; Pausanias 1.7.1 stated Ptolemy II *Philadelphos* brought the body from Memphis to Alexandria.

238. Diodorus 18.33.3, based on the translation in the Loeb Classical Library edition, 1954 and reiterated at Justin 13.4.

239. Hornblower (1981) for discussion of Cleitarchus' extending of his account to the burial in Egypt. For a good discussion of Diodorus' change of source for these episodes see Anson (2004) pp 23-25.

240. For the 'prize of war', Diodorus 18.39.5 and repeated at 18.43.1, so suggesting Hieronymus' own sentiment. Archibald-Davies-Gabrielson (2005); 14,800 talents plus 1,500,000 *artabae* of grain by the reign of Ptolemy II *Philadelphos*. An *artaba* was originally a Persian unit which spread west and was adopted by Rome; the Egyptian dry capacity was around 36.18 litres.

241. St Jerome *Commentariorum in Danielum* 3.11.5 for Egyptian income under *Philadelphos*.

242. Bagnall-Derow (2004) pp 181-195 for the Egyptian Revenue Laws and pp 285-288 for Egyptian administration.

243. Herodotus 2.180-182, 3.47 for the early Greek presence in Egypt and 2.178 for the Hellenion; discussed in Boardman (1964) p 113 ff and Anson (2004) p 197 (Hellenion). For Cleomenes' *hyparchos* role in Egypt, see Justin 13.4.11, *Arrian Events After Alexander* 1.5 Dexippus FGrH 100 F8 2. For his governorship of Pithom see Arrian 3.5.4 and for his financial mandate see Arrian 3.5.4, Curtius 4.8.5. For his maladministration, Arrian 7.23.6, 7.23.8. Diodorus 18.14.1 claimed Ptolemy found 8,000 talents in the Egyptian treasury. Pausanias 1.6.3 for his support and friendship with Perdiccas and his death at the hands of Ptolemy. Pharaonic Egypt comprised forty-two nomes and the designation survived into Roman times, with nomarchs often minting their own currency. Manning (2005) p 2 for the major Egyptian regions. Anson (2013) pp 148-149 for Alexander's administrators in Egypt.

244. Pseudo-Aristotle *Oikonomika* 2.1352.

245. Arrian *Events After Alexander* 1.25 for Arrhidaeus' complicity. Diodorus 18.3.5, Justin 13.4.6 for Arrhidaeus' instructions to build and deliver the funeral bier. Curtius 10.5.4, 18.3.5, Justin 12.15.7, Arrian *Events After Alexander* 1.25, Pausanias 1.6.3, Strabo 17.8. for Alexander's desire to be buried at Ammon. Justin 13.4.6 reported the body was supposed to be destined for Egypt as did Arrian *Events After Alexander* 1.25; assuming this was Hieronymus-derived then this argues strongly for Egypt as the legitimate destination. For accounts of the hearse's fate and Ptolemy's interception, see Diodorus 18.28.2, Strabo 17.8, Arrian *Events After Alexander* 1.25, Pausanias 1.6.3, Aelian 12.64. Pausanias 1.6.3 stated Perdiccas planned to take the body to Aegae,

and Arrian *Events After Alexander* 1.25 suggested similar, both possibly following Antigonus' warning to Antipater, which may have been propaganda. No author linked its final destination to Alexander's own wishes, but rather to the opposing wishes of Perdiccas and Ptolemy. The Will stated the destination was Egypt. Also Stewart (1993) p 221 for discussion of Alexander's intent. See chapter titled *Lifting the Shroud of Parrhasius* for alternative theory on its destination: Perdiccan held Syria.

246. See discussion of the statues in Chugg (2009) p 44 and Chugg (2002) p 17.

247. Diodorus 18.28.3.

248. See full discussion and research in Chugg (2002) and for the location in Atkinson (2009) pp 242-245. Strabo 17.8 for confirmation of the Sema being part of the royal palaces and housing the tombs of Alexander and the Ptolemies; also Erskine (2002) for discussion and p 165 for the comment on inseparability. The *Proverbs of Zenobius* 3.94 (now available in the *Corpus paroemiographorum graecorum* I, p 81) reported that Ptolemy IV *Philopatros* built a burial complex, the Mnema, later called the Sema, to house all the royal corpses; discussed in Erskine (2002) pp 165-166. The *Romance* 34.6 also confirmed the existence of the Sema (named the Soma of Alexander).

249. *Romance* 3.34.1-6 for the oracular predictions.

250. *Romance* 1.1-12, discussed in chapter titled *Guardians and Ghosts of the Ephemerides*.

251. Aelian 12.64 for the alternative version of the hijacking of Alexander's body.

252. Also known as Ptolemy '*kokkes*' or 'scarlet'; see Strabo 17.8 who also mentioned its location in the Sema, the burial place of kings.

253. Discussed in detail in Chugg (2004) and (2007) and following Erskine (2002) p 167.

254. Diodorus 18.26-28. For accounts of the hearse's fate see Diodorus 18.28.2, Strabo 17.8, Arrian *Events After Alexander* 1.25, Pausanias 1.6.3. For the dating see discussion in Atkinson (2009) p 242. Athenaeus 5.206e confirmed Hieronymus provided the funeral bier detail. Kebric (1977) p 66 for its Durian style.

255. 'Ionic temple on wheels' quoting Stewart (1993) p 216.

256. Quoting Stewart (1993) p 220 for the observation that 'no image of peace' was included in the description and p 221 for the absence of the phalanx.

257. Diodorus 18.26.1-3. The exact chronology according the Roman consulships is open to debate; see discussion in Loeb edition, 1947, footnotes on pp 86-87. However Diodorus closed a previous paragraph with 'such then were the events of this year', generally attributable to 322 BCE. And Diodorus stated at 18.28.2 that the engineer, Arrhidaeus, took almost two years completing his work.

258. For the timing of Eumenes' flight to Perdiccas in the face of Leonnatus' intriguing see Anson (1986) p 214. However Perdiccas' whereabouts are not attested; the assumption that Eumenes returned to Babylon does not need to be made. Perdiccas might have been closer, in Syria for example, where he meant the hearse to reside; see chapter titled *Lifting the Shroud of Parrhasius* for discussion.

259. 'Patchwork' quoting Hornblower (1981) p 94.

260. Diodorus 18.5 1-7. See Tarn (1948) pp 6-7 for chronological arguments and p 33 for name-related arguments and Hornblower pp 80-82 for Tarn's dating of the satrapal list in Diodorus' geographical digression. Goropism or a goropianism stems from Goropius Becanus who proposed all Indo-European languages were traceable to Dutch (Antwerpian Brabantic) just as Parsons similarly traced them to Irish. Thus a goropism refers to an absurd etymology claimed to stem from a single root.

261. A position supported by Hornblower (1981) p 80.

262. Curtius 10.10.19.

263. See dating discussion for Curtius in chapter titled *Comets, Colophons and Curtius Rufus*. Curtius might also have been able to draw from Trogus, assuming he published earlier.

264. Pearson (1960) p 217 reinforced by MCJ Miller in Watson-Miller (1992) p 108. Curtius' Will dismissal could refer to Diodorus' later Will reference at 20.81.3 but Diodorus never specifically linked the division of the empire with the Will. And neither did Justin and so Trogus.

265. There are some discrepancies: in Curtius' account, the text dealing with Macedonia failed to mention either Craterus or Antipater, and simply mentioned 'the king' holding supreme power: Curtius 10.10.1-5. Here Asander has been mistaken with, or corrupted to, Cassander. There is another lacuna in Photius' epitome of Arrian's *Events After Alexander* 1.7 dealing with the eastern provinces. And Justin's précis of Trogus work is corrupted the most, containing several otherwise unattested appointments, suggesting he clumsily merged the satrapal allocations at Babylon with those made later at Triparadeisus; Nearchus appeared in Lycia and Pamphylia, and Cassander appointed to the king's guard, as he was at Triparadeisus.

266. Ptolemy, Laomedon and Philotas are the first three names in all versions. Antigonus, Asander, Menander and Leonnatus likewise appear in the same order in all. Eumenes and Peithon always

appear side by side although their relative positions in the overall list change. A reference to Illyria in Justin's epitome is a corruption of either Pamphylia or Lycia, each assigned to Antigonus.

267. Diodorus 18.3.1-2; Curtius 10.10.3; Arrian 1.5-6 and Dexippus all echo a similar sentiment. Justin 13.4 does not, yet was epitomising radically. A useful table of the comparative allocation appears in Goralski (1989) pp 104-105. Curtius 10.10.3-4 suggested Eumenes declined his 'assignment'. None of the Hieronymus-derived satrapal breakdowns mentioned Eumenes declining his task. This is better translated as 'he alone failed to complete his assignment', for once Antigonus and Leonnatus refused to aid him, Eumenes needed the royal army under Perdiccas to complete the job.

268. For the relative length of Hieronymus' books and Arrian's *Events After Alexander* see Hornblower (1981) pp 97-99.

269. The extant Will texts also state 'the satraps should retain what they variously govern.' See Heckel (1988) p 16. It is a sentiment echoed in Curtius 10.10.3-5 Arrian *Events After Alexander* 1.7; Diodorus 18.3.2 and Justin 13.4.

270. For a full discussion of the misunderstood references to the Seleucus' inheritance and in fact the relative authority of the eastern satraps, see final chapter titled *Lifting the Shroud of Parrhasius*.

271. Arrian 7.27.1-3, Plutarch 77.5.

272. Homer *Odyssey* 24.57-97, translation by S Butler, 1900.

273. Demosthenes *Against Leptines* 141, in which he praised the Athenians' funeral orations.

274. Hesiod *Works and Days* 650-660. Thucydides 2.34.1-3 for Pericles' speech, however the authenticity of its content is questionable. See Grant (1995) p 47 footnote 19 for discussion. The speech was given in the first year of the Peloponnesian War 431/430 BCE. See discussion in Grant (1995) p 47 and Hansen (1999) p 73 for the digression on the Athenian constitution.

275. Pseudo-Plutarch *Isocrates*; Evargoras' son, Nicocles, paid him 20 talents for the encomium.

276. Flower (1994) pp 26-27 for Theopompus' oratorical fame.

277. Recorded by Demosthenes *On the Crown* 285 and Plutarch *Demosthenes* 21, discussed in Worthington (2000) p 91.

278. Cicero *De Oratore* 2.56.

279. Arrian 7.14.10 claimed funeral games were held for Hephaestion and that the same 3,000 artists 'were said to have' taken part in Alexander's funeral games (7.14.1). His wording is cautious or shows doubt ('it is said'). The funeral games seem highly unlikely against the background of infighting at Babylon and the general tone of fear and hostility and lack of mention in other sources.

280. Homer *Iliad* 23.257-897 for Patroclus' funeral. For details of Philip II's funeral see Antikas (1995) pp 86-97. Philip II of Macedonia was buried in 336 BCE, and following Hephaestion's funeral in Ecbatana in 323 BCE, Alexander threw extravagant games with participants described. Justin 12.3.1 for the funeral games and three-day mourning for Alexander Molossus.

281. Diodorus 18.28-4-5.

282. Dalley (2013) pp 121-124 for discussion of the widespread use of Semiramis. The title 'Semiramis' potentially included the second wife of Sennacherib, Naqia. Herodotus 1.184-191 for additional references to Semiramis.

283. Following Dalley (1994) p 54.

284. Dalley (2013) p 20 for discussion of the Greek *kremastos*. Pliny 19.194 for an example of *hortos pensilis*.

285. Strabo 16.1.5, Diodorus 2.10.1-6 for the irrigation devices. Following discussion by Dalley (1994) p 46. How permanent the river diversion was is debatable.

286. Diodorus 2.7.1, also discussed in Dalley (1994) pp 45-58 and for Ctesias see Van der Mieroop (2004) p 1.

287. Discussed in detail in Van der Mieroop (2004) pp1-5.

288. Dalley (2013) p 112 for the gates at Nineveh and p 117 for the Borsippa references. Dalley (2013) p 119 for references to Nimrud and Sippar. Herodotus' geography quite clearly argues that he was not aware of the two distinct dynasties of Babylonia and Assyria when he termed Babylon the 'new Assyrian capital' after Nineveh's destruction; Strabo seems to have followed suit. Dalley (1994) pp 47-48 quoting Herodotus 1.179 and Strabo 16.1.16. An inscription depicting the sacking of Babylon by Sennacherib in 689 BCE is closely paralleled by Nabopolassar's revenge sacking of Nineveh in 612 BCE, heralding in the Neo-Babylonian period (612-539 BCE).

289. For the etymology 'gate of the gods' see Dalley (1994) p 50.

290. Linen was made from Nile flax although attributed to the Lydian Ariadne.

291. Egyptian embalmers placed the organs of the deceased in four Canopic jars before mummification. See Casson (2001) p 122.

292. *Romance*, final line of the poem on the concluding page.

293. Quoting Bevan (1927) p 262 for 'foundation' of modern Egyptology.

10

THE TRAGIC TRIUMVIRATE OF TREACHERY AND OATHS

Did Eumenes of Cardia have the credentials to be the chief architect of the *Pamphlet* and *was* it he who broadcast the existence of Alexander's Will?

The first eight years of the Successor Wars in Asia were dominated by the rivalry between the supporters of Perdiccas and the opposing Macedonian coalition, out of which emerged a remarkable conflict between Eumenes and Antigonus *Monophthalmos*.

We review the unique, tragic and mercurial relationship between these former generals of Alexander and their respective patronage of the eyewitness historian who recorded their careers. For in these years emerged the tensions, battles, treacheries and alliances of desperation that led to the drafting of the *Pamphlet* and to its subsequent eradication.

'Antigonus paid no heed to the edicts of Perdiccas, being already lifted up in his ambitions and scorning all his associates.'[1]

Plutarch *Life of Eumenes*

'If Eumenes could have contented himself with the second place, Antigonus, freed from his competition for the first, would have used him well, and shown him favour.'[2]

Plutarch *The Comparison of Sertorius with Eumenes*

'I regard no man as my superior, so long as I am master of my sword.'[3]

Plutarch *Life of Eumenes*

'The account given by Hieronymus is different... for a man who associates with royalty cannot help being a partial historian.'[4]

Pausanias *Guide to Ancient Greece*

Like much of Greek culture, the concept of mediation was rooted in mythology. Negotiations were best conducted in a neutral location, ideally Themis' home, Delphi, where Heaven and Earth were thought to meet.[5] Mediation demanded the qualities of *ethos*, *pathos* and *logos* from a presiding *proxenetas* who performed his sacred role though the presence of Rhea, 'the mother of gods', who bore the law-giving Demeter, and through her, to the adjudication of Themis, the ancient goddess of justice. Its Latin evolution encompassed the names *intercessor, interpolator, conciliator, interlocutor* and *interpres*, the roots of many of our modern words associated with a brokered settlement. Clearly, in the Greek and Roman worlds, the mediator role was already valued and much employed.

Eumenes of Cardia was without doubt the mediator of Alexander's generation, and here we explain his impact on the early Successor Wars when his coercive genius heralded in a remarkable solo career. For an influential time, the son of a 'man whom poverty drove to be a waggoner', according to Duris of Samos, or the son of an impoverished funeral musician, in Aelian's text, innovated something of a political sensation in his bid for survival in Alexander's fragmenting empire.[6]

Eumenes was first employed for seven years as Philip II's secretary from the age of twenty (ca. 342 BCE) at the royal court at Pella.[7] Long before Alexander set off on his Asian campaign, Eumenes had successfully straddled the growing divide between Philip and Olympias, as well as Alexander's own rift with his father.[8] The decade-long Asian campaign saw him reconcile his additional administrative duties under Alexander (he was now termed a *hypomnematographos*, broadly an 'archivist') with a cavalry command, while integrating his Greek origins into the Macedonian war machine.[9] And he remained a friend, confidante, and finally, an accomplice, of Olympias until his death, a relationship, we argue, that played a significant factor in the birth of the *Pamphlet*.[10]

As his prominence grew, Eumenes engendered and sidestepped the jealousy that stemmed from his proximity to, and rapport with, Alexander; it was an intimacy that rankled with Hephaestion, the king's first chiliarch.[11] After Hephaestion's death in Ecbatana in 324 BCE, Eumenes was entrusted with Perdiccas' cavalry command once he assumed Hephaestion's hipparchy of the Companion Cavalry.[12] The increased responsibilities saw the Cardian royal secretary become a court *hetairos* and the status brought him wealth, and that qualified him as a *trierarchos* of the Hydaspes-Indus River fleet; a melted mass of gold and silver totalling (the suspiciously high sum of) 1,000 talents was reportedly retrieved from his burned tent in India.[13] Moreover, Eumenes was one of the few men Alexander selected to marry into the Persian nobility at Susa, where he, along with Ptolemy and Nearchus, became a relative of the king's mistress, Barsine, who had a son, Heracles, with Alexander.[14]

Crucially at Babylon in the days after Alexander's death, Eumenes managed to bridge the divide between the senior infantry officers and the aristocratic cavalry Companions when brokering a settlement which averted Macedonian 'civil war'.[15] At the opening of his account of the Successor Wars, Arrian gave a summary of the leading commanders at Babylon and it included all of the surviving *Somatophylakes*:

> The most eminent of the cavalry and leaders were Perdiccas the son of Orontes, Leonnatus the son of Anteas, and Ptolemy, son of Lagus. The ones after them were Lysimachus the son of Agathocles, Aristonus the son of Peisaeus, Peithon the son of Crateuas, Seleucus the son of Antiochus, and Eumenes of Cardia. These were the leaders of the cavalry; Meleager led the infantry.[16]

As many as fourteen names have been associated with the position of *Somatophylax* in the campaign accounts; some died and one was executed, whilst others were retired (those originally appointed by Philip II) or they simply faded out of the story.[17] After Hephaestion's death, a vacancy presented itself and Peucestas was already absent in the East; possibly an established royal hypaspist (or a *hyperaspisantes*), Peucestas had become an 'eighth' addition to a fellowship traditionally seven in number, which might have upset the Pythagorean association of 'seven' with 'opportunity'. Peucestas had been appointed governor of Persis and the Bodyguard role was only bestowed on those operating in the king's immediate presence (as the title suggests).[18] In which case – and perhaps alongside a recently promoted Seleucus – Eumenes was being cited in his place, an elevation that might have come with the acquisition of Perdiccas' hipparchy.[19]

Eumenes' significance to Alexander and the campaign is unquestionable. Recalling the politics that shaped the early eyewitness accounts, we should not be alarmed or even surprised that neither Ptolemy, Aristobulus nor Cleitarchus mentioned Eumenes' military prominence more frequently. But it was in the Successor Wars that Eumenes demonstrated the abilities that argue so strongly for his candidacy as author (or co-author) of the *Pamphlet*. For we are presented with a string of brilliant intrigues borne out of his precarious position as a prominent Greek satrap in a Macedonian-controlled empire.

THE SUCCESSFUL *SYNEDRION* AND THE FAILED *SYNASPISMOS*

Eumenes' solo career commenced the minute he departed Babylon to take up his satrapal inheritance; Cappadocia. Hieronymus appears to have given the impression that Alexander bypassed much of Cappadocia, so leaving it *aporthetos*, wholly unconquered, due to his preoccupation with facing Darius III.[20] This was perhaps to emphasise the task Eumenes now faced, though clearly no Macedonian had been governing the province since. Eumenes' expansive grant included Paphlagonia as far eastwards as Trapezus (modern Trabzon in Turkey), the influential Black Sea port found by Milesians (T16, T17, T18, T19, T20). It was the city Xenophon and his Greeks (by now 6,000 according to Isocrates, most unable to return home because of their 'faults') finally reached as somewhat unwelcome arrivals, but had circumstances been different, Xenophon would have founded his own colony there.[21]

Paphlagonia had previously been associated with Hellespontine Phrygia,[22] and according to Strabo, Cappadocia had since been divided into two: Cappadocia Pontica in the north, and Cappadocia Proper (or Cappadocia near Taurus) in the south where Sabictas was governor.[23] Under Persian rule the northern region *had* extended to the Black Sea coast past Amisus and Trapezus, effectively absorbing the kingdom of Pontus. Lycaonia, too, had formerly been part of the southern Cappadocian satrapy.[24]

Ariarathes, the first 'king', had retained independence in the northern region, which was nominally under Achaemenid rule, and although he is not attested as fighting for Darius at Issus, he *may* have been present at Gaugamela. Alexander had annexed the south, but Ariarathes seems to have regained control of the southern region soon after, possibly through an accord struck with Antigonus for the king's neutrality in the interest of keeping the Royal Road open.[25] Ariarathes was eighty-two, wealthy, and a figure of much historical confusion, but he appears to have had at his disposal some 30,000 infantry (many of them mercenaries) and 15,000 cavalry to defend his still ungarrisoned kingdom.[26] Eumenes' expansive inheritance and the trust placed in him by Perdiccas in the First *Diadokhoi* War made it abundantly clear that he had already proven himself as a commander of men.

After two decisive battles the sidetracked Perdiccas was in no mood for leniency. Ariarathes was tortured and crucified and all his followers impaled, or, according to Justin, Ariarathes killed his wife and children himself to stop them falling into Macedonian hands.[27] A rebellious Lycaonia and Pisidia soon felt Perdiccas' wrath; the city of Laranda was stormed, all men of fighting age put to the sword with the population sold into slavery. A defiant Isauria put up a fight and its defenders self-immolated in despair, but Antigonus' Phrygia was never touched at this time.[28] Perdiccas' iron fist set the tone for Diodorus' description of the next campaign against Egypt, led by a chiliarch now described (possibly following the sentiment in Cleitarchus' final pages) as a 'man of blood' and a 'usurper of power'.[29]

The rising tensions between Perdiccas and the 'anti-royalist' faction through the next two years saw the repudiation of Antipater's daughter, Nicaea (Perdiccas had recently married her, or was pledged in marriage, texts are ambiguous), in favour of a union with Alexander's sister Cleopatra, who probably arrived at Sardis at about the same time.[30] Indeed, Perdiccas had initially planned to 'work in harmony' with Antipater, but Eumenes' advocating the marriage to Cleopatra put an end to that. The implication here is that only after success in Cappadocia (and the death of Leonnatus), and underpinned by Eumenes' friendship with Olympias, did Perdiccas seek what was reportedly an independent path to supreme power in Macedonia. But these two years also saw Antigonus and Leonnatus abandon their satrapies and cross to Thessaly and Macedonia in support of Antipater, or to further their own designs; both had refused to assist Eumenes in his pacification of Cappadocia, and both probably underestimated the extent of his military acumen.[31]

Upon their return to Asia following victory in the Lamian War, a *synedrion* was convened by Antipater and Craterus (Antigonus *may* have been present). It appears the former Perdiccan fleet commander, White Cleitus, was now supporting their cause. After naval victories off Greece, Cleitus was said to have been sporting a trident and playing the part of Poseidon while walking on purple carpet, and his newly expanded fleet had facilitated the regent's re-crossing to Hellespontine Phrygia in the spring of 320 BCE.[32] The gathering of generals close by signalled the opening of what is referred to as the First *Diadokhoi* War, and here it was decided that Craterus would confront Eumenes, or turn him to their cause. The regent and Antigonus would face the remainder of the royal army under Perdiccas.

At an earlier Perdiccan war council convened after instating Eumenes in Cappadocia, and following further campaigning to install Perdiccas' younger brother, Alcetas, in Pisidia, it had been decided that the bulk of the royal army would invade Egypt in response to Ptolemy's capture of Alexander's funeral bier, for that action (justified or otherwise) amounted to a 'declaration of independence' from the central authority the acting chiliarch represented. Perdiccas additionally ordered the invasion of Cyprus; a fleet of merchant ships procured from Phoenicia set off from Cilicia led by the Rhodian admiral Sosigenes, though the *Somatophylax* Aristonus was in overall command.[33] Along with other Cypriot kings, Nicocles, who was already minting independent coinage, had recently aligned with Ptolemy who needed the island's timber resources and strategic location for his own naval plans; they were now besieging the city of Marium with almost 200 ships, a state of affairs which suggest a pro-Perdiccas initiative in governance must have been formerly in place.[34]

In response to the threat of hostile forces crossing from Macedonia, Eumenes, along with Alcetas and Neoptolemus, were to delay for as long as possible any bridgehead being formed near the Hellespont. If too late, they were to hinder the regent's southwards progress until the royal army could unite with them once more. Eumenes was now commander-in-chief west of Mount Taurus as well as 'commander of the forces in Armenia and Cappadocia with plenary powers'.[35] His military mandate now encompassed Paphlagonia, Caria, Lycia, and Phrygia, in other words, Antigonus' abandoned satrapies, 'in addition to the provinces that he had already received'.[36]

But it was here that Eumenes' ethnic dilemma as a Greek commanding Macedonians began to manifest itself: Alcetas '… flatly refused to serve in the campaign on the ground that the Macedonians under him were ashamed to fight Antipater, and were so well disposed to Craterus that they were ready to receive him with open arms.' The rift with Alcetas had widened over Eumenes' advising Perdiccas to seek Cleopatra's hand (Alcetas argued for the marriage to Nicaea) and it was unlikely to heal now. In addition, Neoptolemus was already hatching plans to undermine Eumenes' new command because it subordinated his own authority in Armenia.[37] Eumenes summoned him on suspicion of treachery and drew up his forces for a confrontation; his cavalry routed Neoptolemus' infantry though he managed to flee with three hundred horsemen to the fast approaching regent and Craterus.[38]

Envy, it is said, slays itself by its own arrows. Neoptolemus, a notable *archihypaspistes* – a commander of the mobile infantry – and possibly a scion of the royal house of Epirus, had famously mocked the Cardian after Alexander's death: he proposed that where 'he had followed the king with shield and spear, Eumenes had followed with stylus and tablet'.[39] But the pen he slighted was to become Eumenes' most effective weapon, and it helped him survive these few remarkable years in which the *Pamphlet* was launched.

A head-on clash with Craterus was now inevitable, and it came in May 320 BCE (perhaps ten days after the initial confrontation with Neoptolemus) somewhere close to Cappadocia.[40] Prior to the battle and to raise the spirits of his men, Eumenes exploited his former intimacy with Alexander; he described his portentous dream vision in which two images of the king had confronted one another, one helped by Athena and the other by Demeter. Demeter prevailed, and '... culling ears of grain, she wove them into a victory wreath.' Having learned that the enemy's *synthematon,* its watchword, was 'Athena and Alexander', and, moreover, since they were fighting for grain-planted land, Eumenes spurred his army on towards a god-augured mission, ordering '... all his men to crown themselves and wreath their arms with ears of grain.'

It is probably no coincidence that this appears an emulation of Philip II, for he had once played a similar laurel-wreathed card when 'marching his soldiers to battle as if under the leadership of a god' (Apollo) before the Battle of the Crocus Field in 353/2 BCE in the Third Sacred War; Alexander himself had also declared a 'victory dream' when besieging Tyre.[41] And here on the plains that favoured cavalry manoeuvrability, and to guard against any drop in morale, Eumenes made sure his men were still unaware that it was the much-loved Craterus who his Macedonian contingent would be riding out to fight.

Neoptolemus and Eumenes spotted one another and 'their horses dashed together like colliding triremes'; 'carried away by their anger and their mutual hatred', they let the reins fall from their left hands and grappled each other to the ground.[42] Although he sustained wounds in his arms and the thigh, Eumenes dealt a deathblow to the neck and reportedly stripped his dying opponent of his armour in the style of the Homeric heroes (Ptolemy appears to have provided himself similar Iliadic honours in India).[43] Neoptolemus had simply failed to appreciate that 'to hold a pen is to be at war'; he preferred the oils of Apelles to paint him on horseback when commemorating his part in Alexander's campaign.[44]

Eumenes had wisely deployed his Asiatic squadrons against Craterus, who was dumbfounded as to why Eumenes' 'Macedonians' did not desert; Craterus and his purple *kausia* fell *en homiloi*, 'in the crowd', and his wounded body, trampled by his own horse, was not immediately recognised, though he ended up dying in Eumenes' arms.[45] Despite this resounding and unexpected victory, the Perdiccan alliance was fractured with the chiliarch's death in Egypt just a few days later, following which the reconciled Macedonian factions by the Nile levied a death sentence on Eumenes as soon as they learned of Craterus' death.[46] For it was alleged that in Egypt some fifty of Perdiccas' supporters had been condemned to die.[47] The list included Perdiccas' sister, Atalante, fatally then in camp and by now married to the newly pro-Perdiccas Attalus, and the proscriptions list targeted Eumenes too.[48] It was a wholesale effort to wipe out any support for the royalist faction.

The next *synedrion* of the anti-Perdiccan coalition, in late summer of 320 BCE (adhering to the 'low' chronology), took place at Triparadeisus, a convergence of a trio of ancient game parks probably close to the source of the Orontes River in northern Syria. Old acquaintances were reunited, the most prominent being those of Peithon, Antigenes and Seleucus who greeted Antipater for the first time in some fourteen years. Almost as many years had passed since the campaign train had marched south out of Asia Minor leaving Antigonus in command of a region centred on Phrygia. Some veterans of the united phalanx must have met young sons they had left behind in Macedonia, but now as grown men in arms.

Antipater, approaching eighty years old, appointed a younger generation of personal Bodyguards to the kings (Arrhidaeus, now Philip III, and Roxane's son, Alexander IV) who had been taken to Egypt in Perdiccas' campaign entourage; the new *Somatophylakes* included Lysimachus' youngest brother, the brother of the absent Peucestas, Antigonus' nephew and Polyperchon's son.[49] The royal roles once united in Perdiccas – chief guardian of the kings, overseer of the realm and commander-in-chief of the royal army in Asia – were now divided between Antipater and Antigonus *Monophthalmos*. It was here that the one-eyed veteran was, in fact, provided with plenipotentiary powers that would result in him founding his own dynasty, a somewhat ironic outcome if the regent already suspected his expansionist ambition:

> As general of the royal army he appointed Antigonus, assigning him the task of finishing the war against Eumenes and Alcetas; but he attached his own son Cassander to Antigonus as chiliarch, so that the latter might not be able to pursue his own ambitions undetected.[50]

Antigonus was, as Diodorus put it, '... chosen supreme commander of Asia...and at the same time he had been appointed general of a great army.' In fact Diodorus later referred back to this appointment as 'regent (*epimeletes*) of the kingdom'.[51] Antigonus assumed the role with enthusiasm and there soon began a number of skirmishes and set-piece battles with Eumenes that extracted the best, and arguably the worst, from the former Pellan court associates. Our extant sources severely compressed the eyewitness testimony of Hieronymus of Cardia, then serving Eumenes; nonetheless, what we do have suggests he must have originally given vivid descriptions of these complex battles, the detail and tactical observations perhaps only rivalled by the accounts of the civil war between Caesar and Pompey.

The more subtle part of the *machtpolitik* that saw Eumenes and Antigonus searching for 'royal legitimacy', as well as military supremacy on the plains of Asia, employed magnanimous gestures that gave the illusion of official sanction to their respective campaigns; each was presenting himself as a constitutionalist legitimised by the kings.[52] Typifying the charade, Eumenes requisitioned new cavalry in the Troad to equip his *hipparchos*, the cavalry officer Apollonides:

> When Eumenes fell in with the royal herds of horse that were pasturing about Mount Ida, he took as many horses as he wanted and sent a written statement of the number to the overseers; at this, we are told, Antipater laughed and said that he admired Eumenes for his forethought, since he evidently expected to give an account of the royal properties to them, or to receive one from them.[53]

Having narrowly avoided an earlier ambush by Antigonus, Eumenes journeyed once more to meet Alexander's sister, Cleopatra, still based at Sardis.[54] The meeting was brief; Cleopatra warned him off fearing it would further antagonise the regent who was fast approaching with his army on its way northward from Syria. A battle on the plains outside the city was averted but she and Antipater, nevertheless, clashed, though she 'defended herself vigorously' and 'brought counter-charges against him'. He may have upbraided her for her attempted liaisons with Leonnatus and then Perdiccas; she would have reminded him that she was royalty where he was not. She would have likely said more besides: her wish to enter into a union with Alexander's chosen *epitropos* and parley with her brother's former secretary, Eumenes – now unlawfully proscribed in her opinion – was her decision to make. Furthermore, Antipater's proffering his daughters to the leading *Diadokhoi* was threatening her dead brother's wishes and his last instruction which had demanded he step down as regent in Macedonia in favour of Craterus.[55]

We may imagine them storming at one another about much else, and what was reportedly an amicable-enough parting would be their last meeting ever. Had the infantry not already revolted over the death of Philip's other daughter, Cynnane (killed recently by Perdiccas' brother Alcetas), and if the Perdiccans had already been fully rounded up, who knows what measures the regent might have taken right there to silence Cleopatra for good.[56]

With the newly united royal army seeking him out, Eumenes occupied Antigonus' winter base at Celaenae in Phrygia, 'a landscape more of villages than cities', in late 320 BCE. The surrounding plains were fertile and the city stood on the crossroads of the ancient highways to Ephesus to the west, and to the narrow defile of the Cilician Gates to the east, and to Synnada and Telmessus on the north-south route. Alexander had first taken Celaenae (broadly occupied by modern Dinar in southwest Turkey) in 333 BCE after a sixty-day 'truce' in which the citizens put their faith in the strength of the walls and in military aid they were expecting.[57] Antigonus was given 1,500 troops to see out the siege and the city had been a Macedonian stronghold, as well as Antigonus' winter quarters, ever since.[58]

A map of Asia Minor showing Antigonus' sphere of influence under Alexander. Image from *Antigonos the One-Eyed and the Creation of the Hellenistic State* by Richard Billows (1990). Provided with the kind permission of The University of California Press.

Celaenae had both a legendary and a historic legacy; it was here that Apollo flayed the satyr Marsyas after their ill-fated musical contest, and the city was once the mustering place of the Greek mercenaries (mostly Peloponnesians) fighting for Cyrus the Younger. The famous '10,000' included a then little-known Xenophon whose *Anabasis* remains the only eyewitness account of a mercenary army at war.[59] The city was also renowned for its enormous game park fed by the River Meander (today's Buyuk Menderes) and the River Marsyas which flowed through the middle of its fortifications.[60] Eumenes' occupation of Celaenae was undoing a decade of Antigonid control. It was as symbolic a gain as it was practical, and he set about rewarding his troops with homesteads and castles from the spoils, and distributing 'purple caps [the Macedonian *kausiai*] and military cloaks'; these were 'a special gift of loyalty among

Macedonians' which signified the bearers as *philoi* and *hetairoi* of the king or their leader.[61]

To spike the gathering of 'outlaws', Antigonus is said to have smuggled letters into the camp offering 100 talents for Eumenes' death, though Plutarch is vague on exactly where this occurred and we don't know where he sourced it. The move apparently backfired as spectacularly as if it had been a ruse of Eumenes himself: once the letters were found, 'his Macedonians were highly incensed and made a decree that a thousand of the leading soldiers should serve him continually as a body-guard, watching over him when he went abroad and spending the night at his door…'[62] If the textual recovery of the *Gothenburg Palimpsest* is correct, he, or perhaps Antipater, had good reason for the assassination attempt; either *en route* from Lydian Sardis to Phrygia, or in the environs of Celaenae itself, Eumenes made a mockery of Antipater's forces (if this is *not* a misspelling of 'Antigonus'); his army was too fast and too mobile and it eluded the regent's greater numbers, taking 800 talents in booty leaving Antipater as 'nothing but a spectator' to the suffering of his outmanoeuvred men.[63]

With success under his belt, Eumenes had called together the scattered Perdiccan remnants to Celaenae: Alcetas, Perdiccas' brother-in-law Attalus (who had briefly held Tyre with the remnants of the Perdiccan fleet in the wake of Perdiccas' death), *his* brother Polemon, and Docimus the deposed governor of Babylonia; they either arrived in person or communicated through envoys.[64] Despite Alcetas' initial enthusiasm (which may simply have been a ruse to commandeer command), the Perdiccan generals refused to unite under Eumenes and they moved southwest into Caria, leaving him without the benefit of their combined numbers. The chance for a 'royal *synaspismos*' was gone, and closing in was Antigonus now strengthened by a further 8,500 of Antipater's infantry (the regent himself was heading to Macedonia with the kings) along with a mounted contingent. Eumenes had no choice but to head to the plains of Cappadocia where his own superior cavalry could operate at full potential and perhaps exert what influence he wielded in his expansive 'home' satrapy.[65]

As Alexander had demonstrated in the set-piece confrontations with Darius, accomplished horsemanship could turn battles, despite huge disparities in infantry numbers. Yet even mounting a horse with traditional cavalry weapons – a bow, short sword (the *xiphos* or curved *kopis* and *machaera* favoured by Xenophon who *Hipparchicus* menacingly advised charging at the enemy with lances pointed forward between the horses' ears), spear (*hasta*) and javelins (*akon* or *palton*, often two) or the longer lance (*xyston*) carried by *sarissophoroi* – required skill and experience.[66] Although Alexander's Companion Cavalry and perhaps other 'heavy' regiments had worn metal corselets (Thucydides had mentioned the breastplates on the horsemen of two generations before), the king is himself portrayed as wearing what appears to be a *linothorax* of linen (metal plates may have been hidden inside) painted with the head of Medusa and with shoulder pieces (*epomides*) extending above; Curtius claimed Alexander *rarely* wore a cuirass and only then on the insistence of his friends.[67]

But here in the heat of Asia, any armour worn by local levies beneath a *clamys* or *chiton* was probably no more than that or a *spolas*, a leather jerkin often with hanging pinions of metal; certainly the lightly armed cavalry, the *prodromoi*, valued speed and agility over defensive panoply. The burning of old armour when Alexander had entered India suggests the army was predominantly outfitted in combustible material rather than metal.[68] A broader-rimmed Boeotian-style bronze cavalry helmet sometimes replaced the taller Phrygian type and it gave better visibility as well as reasonable protection against sword-slashes to the face, though the broader-rimmed soft hat, the *petasos*, was reportedly worn as often (perhaps in scouting rather than battle).[69] To provide some degree of lower protection, leather riding boots (or high strapped and socked sandals) were preferred because protective bronze grieves were impractical as lower leg movement was needed to control the horse when thighs kept a tight grip on its flanks. So these body parts also remained unprotected by a *parameridion*, a thigh guard often seen in 6th century art, due to the need for flexibility.

Mounted skirmishers, *hippakontistai*, wore little more than padded cloth and there is no mention at all of protection for their mounts – the apron-like *parapleuridia* that Xenophon described on Persian heavy cavalry, for example, and also described by Curtius at the battle of Issus. They were so heavily clad that the Thessalian cavalry were able to outmanoeuvre them, an image that conjures up the heavily protected cataphract-like cavalry of the Roman era.[70] Saddles and stirrups had not yet been developed; riders sat on skin shabraques or lined cloths and relied on reins attached to the sidebars of snaffle-bits and harsher spiked rollers, along with prick-spurs attached to boots, to control the horse.[71] So accurate javelin throwing in a rising position required balance and coordination, and so did lance thrusting sideways and over the head. Pulling off wheeling tactics and keeping in tight formation was critical to survival, as were well-trained horses responsive to aids (the rider's commands). Asian bloodstock and experienced riders were invaluable to both armies as a new generation of multi-tasked *xystophoroi*, mounted spearmen, emerged in the battles across the Hellenistic world.

Eumenes' cavalry command in India and his acquisition of Perdiccas' hipparchy make it clear that he was obviously a seasoned campaigner on horseback who must have mastered the techniques of the flying wedge and the oblique order flank-guard introduced by Philip and Alexander.[72] Eumenes would now need to call on that experience; it was early 319

A carved figure of a Macedonian or perhaps a Thessalian cavalryman in Boeotian helmet on the Alexander Sarcophagus. The shape of the helmet was formed by hammering out sheets of bronze on a carved stone former. Apart from that the rider is unprotected. The infantryman, possibly a hypaspist, wears a Phrygian helmet more typical of the *sarissa*-bearing phalangites. The spears they once wielded have broken off the carving. Istanbul Archaeological Museum.

BCE and he wisely prepared his forces on favourable Cappadocian ground where his mounted brigades could be effectively deployed. It became clear that battle was inevitable once scouts confirmed Antigonus' approach, and Plutarch displayed his open admiration of, or sympathy for, Eumenes in what occurred next:

> Now, prosperity lifts even men of inferior natures to higher thoughts, so that they appear to be invested with a certain greatness and majesty as they look down from their lofty state; but the truly magnanimous and constant soul reveals itself rather in its behaviour under disasters and misfortunes. And so it was with Eumenes. For, to begin with, he was defeated by Antigonus at Orcynia in Cappadocia through treachery.[73]

That treachery, according to Justin, included more bribes for Eumenes' head. Finding the covert correspondence, Eumenes claimed these were *his* own forged tell-tales to gauge the strength of loyalty in the ranks, which somewhat casts some suspicion on the veracity of the other reported rewards for his death.[74] Loyalty proved thin: shortly before battle Eumenes witnessed the defection of an officer with 3,000 infantry and 500 mounted men, whilst Antigonus corrupted Apollonides with 'great promises' and 'secret persuasion' to defect once fighting had commenced.[75]

But before leaving the field in the face of these setbacks, Eumenes had the opportunity to seize the enemy baggage train. Knowing the booty would only slow down his own retreat, he sent a secret communication to its defender, Menander, a high-ranking Companion serving Antigonus, imploring him for the sake of 'old friendships' to move himself to higher ground to better defend it. The false magnanimity impressed the enemy troops but Antigonus saw through the misdirection: 'Nay my good men, that fellow did not let them go out of regard for you, but because he was afraid to put such fetters on himself in his flight.'[76] Luxury and distractions, a condition Plutarch described as *malakoteroi*, getting 'softer', would have encumbered the mobility of any army. This was vintage Eumenes playing vintage Alexander, who had in fact been following Xenophon when he burned the army's accumulated wealth before entering India: 'thus deprived of their treasures, [they] immediately became anxious for more; and, in order to obtain it, of course ready for new enterprises.' And that meant booty from victory in future battles and plundering the surrounding area meanwhile.[77]

Eumenes reportedly 'lost' 8,000 men at Orcynia in spring 319 BCE from of a total of 20,000 infantry and 5,000 cavalry; it is a huge number that must have comprised the dead, wounded, captured *and* probably the deserters too, and he was left with no option but flight.[78] The flattering version of events painted his departure as an *anaklesis,* a tactical feint, in this case to double-back to the battlefield to burn the dead on pyres made from wooden village doors – that is if Plutarch was not confusing the occasion with the 'magnificent burial' mentioned by Diodorus after the later clash at Paraetacene.[79] What is revealing for any analysis of camp practice and the distinctions of hierarchy is the report that officers were burned on separate pyres from those of the common soldier.

A more sober narrative from Diodorus suggested Eumenes was overtaken in his flight and had little directional choice. The best hope of immediate survival lay in the mountain fortress of Nora, but before entering that 'lofty crag', Eumenes '... persuaded most of his soldiers to leave him, either out of regard for them, or because he was unwilling to trail after him a body of men too small to give battle, and too large to escape the enemy's notice.'[80] The First *Diadokhoi* War was all but over.

THE SIEGE, THE HOSTAGE AND THE MASTER OF HIS SWORD

Following Eumenes' incarceration at Nora, Antigonus found himself in a formidable position, potentially dominating the empire from the Mediterranean shores of Asia Minor to the eastern borders of Armenia. He was, of course, still acting for the Pellan court, or so his official dispatches would have claimed. But secretly he aspired to '... greater things... and decided... he would no longer take orders from Antipater, while maintaining the pretence of being well disposed to the aged regent.'[81]

Antigonus invested the stone stronghold with 'double walls, ditches and amazing palisades' so there was no hope of escape for Eumenes and his 600 loyal confederates. The fortress of Nora was termed 'impregnable' and 'marvellously fortified, partly by nature, partly by the work of men's hands'; presumably this explains why we read of no storming attempts.[82] The beseiger instigated a hostage exchange and invited Eumenes to parley, sending in his own talented nephew, Polemaeus (who would later try and subdue Eumenes' satrapies), for goodwill. Eumenes exposed himself for negotiation and Hieronymus was offered in exchange;[83] this achieved hostage symmetry for the historian was possibly Eumenes' own nephew.[84]

The commencement of the siege was a fulcrum point for Hieronymus and his history; it was (we beleive) the moment his two patrons – present and future – first met in his presence. Yet it was Plutarch, and not Diodorus (who appears to have more rigidly followed Hieronymus), who most effectively captured the poignancy of the face-off between the veteran general and his captive who was now demanding full satrapal reinstatement and the return of his possessions:[85]

> ... the bystanders were amazed and they admired his [Eumenes'] lofty spirit and confidence. But meanwhile, many of the Macedonians came running together in their eagerness to see what sort of a man Eumenes was; for no one else had been so talked about in the army since the death of Craterus. Then Antigonus, afraid that Eumenes might suffer some violence, first loudly forbade the soldiers to approach, and pelted with stones those who were hurrying up, but finally threw his arms about Eumenes and, keeping off the throng with his bodyguards, with much ado removed him to a place of safety.[86]

Despite the alleged warmth, Antigonus demanded that Eumenes address him as 'his better' and received as a result the following alleged response: 'I regard no man as my superior, as long as I am master of my sword.'[87] We imagine that exchange was the end of any chance of progress through immediate negotiations.

Some six months or more into the siege, and soon after the death of Antipater in Macedonia in autumn 319 BCE, Antigonus invited Eumenes to 'share in his own undertakings'.[88] According to Plutarch, before Eumenes was released in early 318 BCE, Antigonus demanded he sign an oath of loyalty. Eumenes allegedly amended the wording, cunningly adding the words 'Olympias and the Kings' to those he pledged his fealty. Both the original and the extended oaths were shown to the Macedonian siege captains, who agreed that Eumenes' version was the fairer, whereupon they let him loose.[89] The inference here is that the amendment embedded the latitude for Eumenes to oppose Antigonus if his actions were deemed hostile to the Argead royal house. If this episode genuinely took place, this was a strategic *hypotaxis*, a hidden formation behind Eumenes' visible ranks, and as Green pointed out, the oath-taking was in the spirit of Euripides' *Hippolytus*: 'My tongue swore, but my mind remained unsworn.'[90]

When eventually informed of Eumenes' dissimulation, Antigonus ordered the siege to be reinstated, no doubt pondering the consequences of the amendment and possibly Achilles' response to Odysseus' speech: 'As hateful to me as the gates of Hades is the man who hides one thing in his thoughts, but says another.'[91] It was too late; Eumenes had fled the vicinity and was heading to Cilicia. This episode is absent from Diodorus' text, either due to aggressive précising or because Hieronymus thought it cast a shadow on Eumenes' volte-face.[92] Of course the rerendering of the oath may simply be a device of a later historian, which might, nevertheless, be a subtle embellishment of a less attractive truth: Eumenes simply did not honour his word to Antigonus and claimed a higher loyalty when justifying it.[93]

What *does* appear to be clear is that once he departed Nora, Eumenes initially tarried in Cappadocia, apparently provisioning for campaigning and returning his Cappadocian hostages for 'horses, beasts of burden and tents'.[94] The delay, potentially several months, suggests that Eumenes was either using the time he had to physically recover from the siege and raise troops before Antigonus' inevitably hostile reply came back to Nora. But in an oathless scenario, it suggests that Eumenes may not have immediately abandoned an alliance with Antigonus at all; he may have been waiting for word from across the Hellespont from former Perdiccans still on the loose before declaring his hand.[95] Eumenes was most likely rounding up any men he had dismissed before entering the fortress, and he managed to rather quickly assemble a corps of 1,000 cavalry and some 2,000 soldiers in total, including those who had been freed with him.[96] Having lost his waggons at Orcynia, the only way his supporters were going to retrieve their possessions would be to fight alongside him again, for defection to Antigonus was unlikely to yield the same tangible reward, his promises aside.[97]

With Menander hot on his heels once his direction was known, Eumenes traversed the Taurus Mountains and descended into Cilicia. His immediate goal was Cyinda, a fortified treasury in a still-debated location that held nearly 20,000 royal talents; it was possibly the ancient Kundi that served a similar purpose for the Assyrian kings.[98] The Second War of the *Diadokhoi* was about to begin.

En route, or in fact before his departure from Cappadocia (and perhaps precipitating it), Eumenes received two remarkable missives that regally empowered him once more.[99] They were, it is claimed, from Polyperchon, Antipater's successor as regent in Pella; the first offered him either co-guardianship of the kings in Macedonia, or, should Eumenes prefer, money and an army to fight Antigonus in Asia. Polyperchon additionally offered to journey across the Hellespont himself if Eumenes needed further support, presumably with the elephants Antipater had taken to Macedonia.[100] The second letter compensated Eumenes with 500 talents for his personal losses, it authorised further funds for the raising of an army, and it assured him the crack Silver Shields brigade had been summoned to operate under him.[101]

Eumenes was transformed from prisoner to royal commander-in-chief in a matter of weeks. Diodorus recorded the general dismay: 'All wondered at the fickleness of Fortune (Tyche)... for who, taking thought of the inconstancies of human life, would not be astonished at the alternating ebb and flow of fortune?'[102] In fact we see a full page of epeidectic reflections on that Polybius would have termed *ekplektikai peripeteiai,* 'sensational reversals'. Eumenes would now command the 3,000 strong *Argyraspides*; we can only speculate if they constituted, or incorporated, some of the 3,000 'most rebellious Macedonians' (a description which recalls the *ataktoi* 'unruly' brigade) that Antigenes, now the satrap of Susiane and Silver Shields commander, had been given when tasked with collecting treasure (or revenues) from Susa. Whether the *Argyraspides* were still on treasury duty there, or had already returned to Cyinda in Cilicia, remains *sub judice*, but they reportedly journeyed a 'considerable distance to meet Eumenes and his friends',[103] and fast approaching was the winter of 318 BCE.

The treasuries across the empire held immeasurable wealth and crack squads would have been required to defend them, overseen by a local trusted *phrourarchos*, or more specifically a *gazophylax*, a treasury officer. Located in natural fortresses – *phrouria* – these treasuries had to be defensible; the 'lofty crag' of Nora itself later became a depository for Sisines (ruled 36 BCE-17 CE), Rome's client king of Cappadocia in Strabo's day.[104] The consistent nature of the roles of the allegedly aged Silver Shields (though surely not as advanced in age as Diodorus claimed: the youngest sixty) raises the question of whether their role as roving treasury guards, or porters of treasure from one citadel to another, was the true inspiration behind the brigade's name.[105] Possibly with this crucial 'state' duty came expensive silver adornment for their armour and shields, for heavy and soft semi-precious metal was not a practical accessory in battle; and yet what better way to recognise and secure the loyalty of the defenders of the royal deposits?

Although Eumenes had been provided with a suspicious-sounding *carte blanche* to dig into state funds and campaign against the extremely powerful Antigonus – who had in fact never *directly* challenged Polyperchon's authority in Pella – Eumenes declined his new military mandate and the 'donation from the kings'. This was quite brilliant: he was shunning a royal promotion he may (as we will argue) himself have birthed: '...he said, it was not of his own will that he had yielded with respect to his present office, but he had been compelled by the kings to undertake this great task.'[106] The feigned reluctance was a showpiece designed to eventually bank the silver in a more loyal purse, for the Silver Shields were always unpredictable.[107] Appreciating that 'the fickleness of fortune tests the reliability of friends', Eumenes 'prudently made his own position secure':[108]

> These men, on receiving their letters, ostensibly treated Eumenes with friendliness, but were plainly full of envy and contentiousness, disdaining to be second to him. Eumenes therefore allayed their envy by not taking the money, alleging that he had no need of it; while upon their love of contention and love of command, seeing that they were as unable to lead as they were unwilling to follow, he brought superstition to bear.[109]

That new play on superstition saw Eumenes declare another dream vision of Alexander; the Cardian commander was acting out the role of a *theios aner*, a divine man, who now saw an *eidolon*, a ghostly apparition, though whether Eumenes emerged Pythia-pale and still trancelike from his commander's tent (*strategion*) we can only ponder.

Eumenes had certainly learned what moved and mystified soldiers through a decade on the march, and that included *phantasmata*. Here, in the fragile, suspicious and intriguing air of Eumenes' camp, the soldiers' natural *deisidaimonia* was being artfully employed once more. The campaign headquarters became a mobile *nekyomanteion*, a chthonic prophecy place, with Eumenes a self-proclaimed *hieromnemon*, a sacred deputy. He required the troops and the *hegemones* that led them to 'make ready' a gold throne in a magnificent tent, and arranged alongside it the diadem, sceptre, crown and armour of Alexander, and here he would conduct his councils of war. This, we recall, is reminiscent of Perdiccas' actions at Babylon and of Ptolemy's speech that suggested 'group rule' by council in the presence of the symbols of royal office.[110] The rundown of insignia sounds familiar too: it is reminiscent (though not perfectly matching) of the finds in Tomb II at Vergina.[111]

What was transmitted as a 'tent' in Cilicia was more realistically a royal pavilion formed from multiple open canopies.[112] Incense was burned upon an altar to invoke the presence of 'Alexander the God' and to raise the *esprit de corps*; it was a charade through which Eumenes reinforced his own unique relationship with their dead king and to the Argead house in the frequent *synedria* that were to follow.[113]

Just how Eumenes, or the vaults at Cyinda, came into possession of this unique royal insignia needs some thought. Perdiccas could have housed them there when (we propose) he was based close by in Syria, and he may have passed the items, including the tent, to Eumenes (perhaps anticipating Macedonians would resent his command without them) before he marched on Egypt; if these were the very same royal symbols that had been placed in Alexander's funeral bier as it departed Babylon, then Attalus and Polemon and their men had managed to salvage the portable regalia before Ptolemy took control of the sarcophagus; there was, significantly, no further mention of Alexander's insignia in relation to Ptolemy's burial of his body in Egypt, though his weapons and armour *were* later mentioned when Roman emperors liberated them from the tomb.[114] Eumenes could not have held onto them in his flight to Nora, and so it is more likely that several ceremonial 'sets' were in circulation; Diodorus' reference to '*a* throne from the royal treasure' has the ring of a generic item. The Persian treasuries had been raided and could have yielded diadems, sceptres and thrones and they could have been ferried west by the Silver Shields on their march from Susa, along with darics and uncoined precious metal.

In these convocations, Eumenes no doubt reminded his officers of Alexander's Will, and of the rightful inheritances of his sons and mother whose legacy they were defending, for the Silver Shields, once destined for Macedonia with Craterus, had not been present in Babylon when the king died. No doubt somewhere in his speech Eumenes would have slipped in his own rightful inheritance while pointing out to them that Antigonus' lands would be available to them as prizes of war. His thaumaturgy worked; the officers were '… filled with happy expectations, as if some god were leading them.' The dream vision produced the cult of Alexander and with it the acceptance of his supreme command. Curiously, a similar cult appeared on the island of Rhodes, which was so prominently favoured in the *Pamphlet* Will.[115]

The army wintered near Cyinda and Eumenes sent out recruitment agents who '… travelled through Cilicia, others through Coele-Syria and Phoenicia, and some through the cities in Cyprus.'[116] He was clearly blocked from mustering support from further north by Antigonus' dominence in Asia Minor, and mustering in Cyprus must have been a calculated risk after the recent Perdiccan defeat there. But the initiative added 10,000 infantry and 2,000 cavalry to his ranks, though we wonder whether Eumenes concealed the identity of his opponent, as Cyrus had when sending out scouts to the Peloponnese for the war against Artaxerxes II; he had claimed they would be facing Tissaphernes and the Pisidians rather than the Persian Great King. Similarly, and with the recent turn of events, facing Antigonus would have been a daunting prospect for any mercenary to contemplate, even at Cyrus' rate of a gold Persian daric per month.[117]

Arms and armour were expensive if not provided by the state; in the previous century Aristophanes recorded a price of 1,000 drachmas for a corselet and 100 for a helmet which meant that many mercenaries could not afford to present themselves as hoplites but rather as light skirmishers, or peltasts who had become increasingly important in engagements in the Peloponnesian War.[118] A good deal of them *were* impoverished: the litany of their possessions given by the poets included (apart from haversacked cheese and onions) armour, a wallet, a blanket and a wine cup, possessions handed down from father to son, including the indestructible *hoplon* and more practical descendants of the Corinthian helmet.[119] That would have been customarily hung on the wall of the owner's house during his lifetime and possibly buried with him after being 'killed' or rendered unusable by bending the cheekpieces outward; if a helmet fitted a son, it could be passed down. In harder times mercenaries appeared in an array of different helmets, many of them taken, inevitably, from the dead.

What Macedonian state regulars had once been paid under Philip and Alexander remains a vexatious question; many scholars assume that if the state fed, outfitted and housed them, then in Philip's day at least, booty was the only remuneration they saw. Although Curtius and Diodorus gave us bonus figures in Asia, their relation to any set pay is never explained; Macedonian officers were reportedly on double, or even triple, pay (for example the *dekastateroi*, 10-stater men and the *dimoirites*), a comparison only possible if regulars were paid too. So an equalisation between mercenary and state conscript must have taken place at some point in Alexander's campaign in Asia (if not from the outset), especially when mutinies were appearing.[120] Conditions were just as challenging here in the post-Alexander world, and the ever-threatening Silver Shields would, no doubt, have demanded special treatment despite the fact that they were still ostensibly national conscripts doing the king's biddings.[121]

Having weathered new attempts to solicit the Silver Shields' defection, this time by Ptolemy who had anchored at Zephyrium in Cilicia (modern Mersin, and surely with an eye on the riches in Cyinda), and with Antigonus now fast on his heels and attempting to subvert the crack brigade again, Eumenes marched south with the new recruits to Phoenicia in early spring 317 BCE.[122] He planned to '… assemble a considerable fleet, so that Polyperchon, by the addition of the Phoenician ships, might have control of the sea and be able to transport the Macedonian armies safely to Asia against Antigonus whenever he wished.' A new fleet could, vitally, oust Cassander's garrison from Piraeus. But the outcome was disastrous: laden with 'great sums of money', the ships' captains defected to Antigonus' approaching fleet 'splendidy adorned' from its recent victory over Cleitus who, along with Arrhidaeus the new satrap of Hellespontine Phrygia, had defected in the face of Antigonus' aggression – helped on (we suggest) by Olympias' pleas for support. Eumenes and the ill-fated Rhodian fleet admiral, Sosigenes, watched on powerless to intervene as his working capital (whether destined for Polyperchon or use rather closer to the Hellespont) was rowed away.[123]

Eumenes had clearly dug deep into the reserves at Cyinda using the royal mandate, despite his earlier feigned reluctance. To rebuild and equip something like 20,000 infantry and 5,000 cavalry, the numbers Eumenes had under him at Orcynia and the minimum force he could expect to face Antigonus with again, would have required something approaching 2,000 talents per year, accounting for infantry basic pay (*misthos*) and the ration allowance (*siteresion*). Mercenary infantry were paid a minimum of 4 obols per day and as much as 6 (a drachma), and cavalry twice this sum, or more, when accounting for the extra provisioning of their mounts.[124] Treasury coffers had to additionally cover the cost of winter billeting, the requisitioning of consumables, and the manufacture of *new* weapons and armour.

With the nucleus of a new land army still about him, but with his paths back to Cilicia and into Asia Minor blocked, and with an Antigonid army of 20,000 infantry and 4,000 cavalry heading his way, Eumenes was once again left with little choice in the matter of direction. He headed east through Coele-Syria and into Mesopotamia on his way to the further eastern satrapies, for they held more promise and less prejudice against his own Greek origins. Eumenes must have already heard rumours of eastern satrapal unrest, and this was a situation he could potentially exploit.[125]

WAR IN THE EAST: FIGHTING FOR THE *APOSKEUE*

Eumenes' army, still insufficiently large for a set piece battle, arrived in Mesopotamia, or northern Babylonia, sometime in late 317 BCE and wintered in the 'villages of the Carians'.[126] More letters had conveniently 'appeared' from the kings to assist his passage:

> He [Polyperchon] had already sent to the commanders of the upper satrapies the letter from the kings in which it was written that they should obey Eumenes in every way; and at this time he again sent couriers bidding the satraps all to assemble in Susiane each with his own army... for it was to him alone that the kings in their letter had ordered the treasurers to give whatever sum he should ask.[127]

The Mesopotamian governor, Amphimachus, must have joined Eumenes at this point for he is later found in the allied ranks; this is an unsurprising realignment if he can be identified as the brother of Arrhidaeus the satrap of Hellespontine Phrygia who had already turned against Antigonus.[128]

Eumenes narrowly avoided disaster when Seleucus diverted an old canal to inundate his camp some 300 stades (approximately 34 miles) from Babylon. Overtures to the prominent *Somatophylax*, the governor of Babylonia, had failed; Seleucus replied that: 'He was willing to be of service to the kings, but that he would nevertheless never consent to carrying out the orders of Eumenes, whom the Macedonians in assembly had condemned to death.'[129] Rather predictably, Seleucus, along with the now-present Peithon son of Crateuas, once more attempted to seduce the Silver Shields by reminding them Eumenes was a 'foreigner' responsible for the deaths of many Macedonians; he and Peithon simultaneously sent dispatch riders to Antigonus to solicit his support in the East in a combined front.

Tarn proposed that Eumenes may have initially held the citadel in Babylon with his 15,000 infantry and *agema* of 300 cavalry, but this seems unlikely and he was harried further east into the Persian heartland when Seleucus, under truce, conceded Eumenes a river crossing, only too glad to see him head out of his province.[130] Nevertheless, with the Susa royal treasury now open to him under the 'kings' decree', and guided by Alexander's continually invoked spirit, Eumenes would soon be in command of a force to be reckoned with, and it would soon significantly include war elephants from India.[131]

A roman copy of a Greek bust of Seleucus found at Herculaneum and now at the Museo Archeologico Nazionale di Napoli. Photo by Massimo Finizio.

The eastern satraps and some 18,700 infantry and 4,600 cavalry with 120 elephants had already assembled at Susiane (ancient Elam, the region centred on Susa and extending to the south) under the command of Peucestas, a fortuitous gathering if Eumenes could exploit it. The alliance was precipitated by the mutual threat from Peithon, who had killed the Parthian satrap and installed his own brother, Eudamus, in his place, whereupon those fearing his further expansion combined to force him back to Media; this was the precursor to his presence with Seleucus in Babylonia.[132]

News of this unrest (if not its immediate outcome) *would* have reached Eumenes long before; the Achaemenid kings (and possibly the Assyrians before them) had established an elaborate system of lookout posts (*skopai*) and relay stations (*stathmoi*) located every 12 to 17 miles along the network of Persian Royal Roads from Sardis in Lydia to Ecbatana in Media, and onto Susa. Couriers, signal-fires and specially trained 'criers' made for same-day communications empire-wide; though mounted royal messengers could physically traverse the 1,600-mile Royal Road from Sardis to Susa in some seven days (conventional travel required ninety days) the Persian messaging system could avowedly send a basic voice communication from Susa to Greece in two days and nights.

Dispatch riders carried more detailed missives along the well-developed routes and there is evidence that homing pigeons were already in use; in his later sphere of influence, Antigonus would maintain the infrastructure 'to have quick service in all his business'.[133] And Peucestas, on Eumenes' urging, put it to good use here when summoning by messenger in a single day a further 10,000 archers who were nevertheless a month's march away.[134]

A map showing the most famous section of the network of Persian Royal Roads, here extending from Susa to Sardis.

Coded messages must have been used as a precaution against interception when seals alone provided insufficient protection. Plutarch first described the method of the coded message scroll, the *skytale* ('stick');[135] he may have taken the explanation from Apollonius of Rhodes (3rd century BCE) in his treaty *On Archilochus* which would date its use as far back as the 7th century BCE (the time of Archilochus, the controversial poet-warrior).[136] Thucydides, Xenophon, Aristophanes and Pindar all record the *skytale's* use; it was known as a Spartan device which perhaps accounts for their laconic prose, for the message strip didn't have room for more than the most rudimentary of text.[137] No doubt something similar was employed in the Successor Wars: and a coded message was allegedly sent by Cassander to his father after Alexander's death, so the conspiracy claims in the *Pamphlet* appear to have stated, and Eumenes, who had operated at the nerve centre of Alexander's administration, would have been well placed to have developed a network of agents and informants across the troubled empire.[138]

Antigonus' now even more formidable army was advancing on the treasury at Susa after successfully concluding a self-serving alliance with Seleucus and Peithon.[139] He attempted to force a river crossing to establish a bridgehead close to where the 4-*plethra*-wide (approximately 400 feet) Coprates River flowed into the Pasitigris (the modern Karun), apparently unaware of the proximity of Eumenes, who, alone from the gathered commanders, led a repelling action that led to the capture of 4,000 of Antigonus' men.[140] It was a disaster and Antigonus was forced to march north into Media after reviewing local options. He made a similarly costly decision by taking the short route (nine days) through the mountainous territory of the never-subdued Cossaeans, the unruly tribe that guarded the passes; this was the same tribe Alexander had butchered after the death of Hephaestion some seven years before. Their lingering hatred was poured down on the Macedonians in the form of rocks and arrows; Nearchus barely made it out alive with his advance brigade of lightly armed troops.[141]

While Antigonus retreated to Ecbatana, Eumenes and the Silver Shields commanders advocated returning to the Mediterranean coast with the eastern army, no doubt to exploit the vacuum created by Antigonus' absence. The eastern satraps disagreed; fearing a split in the new coalition, Eumenes led the gathered forces on a twenty-four-day march to Persepolis though arid valleys, elevated plains, and finally hospitable parks in the densely populated country. When they arrived in the capital of Peucestas' sphere of influence the army was fêted. The men were arranged in a remarkable series of concentric circles for a feast, which recalled the format of Alexander's Susa wedding celebrations, and Peucestas was no doubt playing on just that.

But this would be no marriage. At Persepolis Peucestas prudently offered sacrifices to the memories of Alexander and his father, so perhaps more than we might suppose of the royal palace, or surrounding buildings at least, must have survived Alexander's firing of the former Achaemenid capital some thirteen years before. Eumenes, here termed Peucestas' former 'friend' (though 'colleague' may once again be implied), sensed the eastern satraps were attempting to beguile his men.[142] Plutarch captured the scene:

> Moreover, by flattering the Macedonian soldiery extravagantly and lavishing money upon them for banquets and sacrifices, in a short time they made the camp a hostelry of festal prodigality, and the army a mob to be cajoled into the election of its generals, as in a democracy.[143]

Uniquely popular with the Persians for his adoption of their language and customs, Peucestas controlled the wealth of Persis and Pasargadae and what remained of Persepolis itself, though much of the treasury had already been ferried to Susa, a clear target for all.[144] The question of supreme command inevitably arose.

To counter the seduction, Eumenes drafted a fake letter written in Assyrian and claimed it had arrived from Orontes, the Persian satrap of Armenia, a known friend of Peucestas and one who had previously fought for Darius at Gaugamela. Its contents falsely claimed the hostile Cassander was dead, Olympias was in control of Macedonia, and Polyperchon was making good on his earlier offer to march through Asia with the royal army from Macedonia.[145] If true, it would have signified a tide turned, and Eumenes' influence as Pella's favourite son would have been unquestioned. The gambit worked: Eumenes was voted in '… with the prospects that he would be able by help of the kings to promote whomever he wishes and exact punishment from those who had wronged him.' As part of his plan to further undermine his host, and using his new authority, Eumenes brought false charges against Sibyrtius, the Greek satrap of Arachosia and another close friend of Peucestas; Eumenes seized his baggage '… to overawe those who did not obey him or who craved command', and Sibyrtius may have immediately fled to join Antigonus.[146]

There followed a financial manipulation intended as an insurance policy; Eumenes extorted 400 talents from those whose loyalty he questioned calculating that they would prefer him alive to receive repayment in full.[147] 'The consequence was that the wealth of others was his body-guard, and that, whereas men generally preserve their lives by giving, he alone won safety by receiving.'[148] The continued fragility of Eumenes' position was evident: his Macedonian campaign veterans were now serving an outlaw while being hounded around an empire they had themselves fought to secure; furthermore, they were being hunted by *strategoi* and *Somatophylakes* they had previously served under. The cost of fealty to the new kings in Pella was beginning to take its toll, and the promised treasury silver was fading to the duller and unpredictable tincture of argent.

Eumenes' subterfuges, by now a wholly necessary and integral part of his arsenal, could only have ever been shortlived, and, somewhat suspiciously when considered beside the central allegations of regicide in the *Pamphlet*, Eumenes fell seriously ill a few days after the banquet Peucestas and his friends had thrown.[149] We have no idea whether he took the precautions of employing an *edeatros*, a court food taster to guard against poisoning, but Eumenes was so weak that he had to be carried around in a litter 'outside the ranks where it was quiet and his sleep would not be broken'. Assassination was only ever a wine cup or bribed bodyguard away, and so each of the *Diadokhoi* appears to have created a personal cavalry guard unit for protection; Eumenes and Antigonus, whose repaired army was heading his way, both retained a handpicked *agema* of some 300 mounted men in the style of the late Argead kings.[150]

When Antigonus' formation of 'golden flashing armour and purple-towered elephants' was spotted descending the nearby hills, the Macedonians called for Eumenes to lead them and refused to deploy without him, beating spear on shield in acknowledgement when he finally appeared. The description of him greeting his men from his litter recalls Alexander's plight in India when he too was recovering from the near mortal wound suffered at Mallia.[151] Aware of his incapacity, Antigonus prepared to attack but noting the impressive discipline and organised battle order that was unravelling on the plain below, he hesitated and laughed off Eumenes' plight: 'This litter, it would seem, is what is arrayed against us', whereupon he retired his ranks and set about pitching camp.[152]

The two armies settled just 3 stades apart (approximately 660 yards) in the region of Paraetacene in Media (near modern Isfahan), with a river and ravines separating the two camps; the unsuitable terrain was likely the reason battle did not immediately commence. It was summer 316 BCE, and the generals pondered their next move for a further four days whilst pillaging the countryside to keep the troops fed, so skirmishing likely took place between the foraging parties vying for precious provisions.[153] Once again, Antigonus sent envoys into Eumenes' ranks to solicit desertions from the eastern satraps and to lure the *Argyraspides* with promises of land grants, honours, gifts and employment within his army. Eumenes deflected the temptation with Aesop's fable of the lion and the maiden to illustrate the covert intent; it was a story that warned against succumbing to false promises.[154] Here the divergence between the accounts of Diodorus and Plutarch widens in both detail and chronology, and yet each captured something of the manoeuvring ahead of the approaching need to winter their forces in the well-provisioned town of Gabiene.

Well-paid 'deserters' were employed on both sides to carry disinformation to the enemy camp in attempts to steal a march. Eumenes sent his baggage train ahead during the night; Antigonus countered with a cavalry push. Spies were sent out, false battle lines were exposed, and the opponents finally came to a halt and arrayed for a confrontation.[155] In Diodorus' words, 'The two armies each outwitted the other as if they were taking part in a preliminary contest of skill and showing that each placed his hope of victory in himself.'[156]

Aposkeue, the 'baggage', is an insufficiently weighty and rather dismissive terminology for a waggon train housing 'wives, and children, mistresses, slaves, gold, and silver', the accumulated possessions and wealth of a decade or more of campaigning.[157] When families, chattels and weapons were captured it left veterans 'dismayed and despondent at the loss of their supplies'.[158] Engels has argued that there would have been one camp follower for every two combatants in Alexander's train from the victory of Gaugamela onwards, and in addition, each *dekas* of infantrymen would have had a servant in charge of a mule or a camel laden with their goods, including tents.[159] 'Baggage' also changed the face of warfare and mobility; Philip, and Alexander too in the early campaign, had resisted using waggons (only mentioned from the actions in Iran onwards), preferring an agile army that carried its own panoply (helmet, shield, breastplate/cuirass, fabric-lined greaves, spear) and even hand mills for grinding grain, in backpacks possibly weighing as much as 80 lb.[160] Now waggons *were* needed to carry pay, prizes of war and consumable provisions in the regions immediately devoid of forage and livestock. Plutarch's description of Antigonus' train at Orcynia included 'many freemen, many slaves, and wealth amassed from so many wars and plunderings'.[161]

Baggage was booty for the victor, and it acted as hostage for the good behaviour of the vanquished, who, more often than not, were enrolled in the victor's ranks. Craterus had motivated his men before battle with the promise of Eumenes' possessions, just as Eumenes had coveted and exploited Neoptolemus' waggons some ten days or so before; his securing them had been instrumental in compelling the captives to enter his service, along with his threat to harry the leaderless forces to starvation should they not.[162] Clearly, the loyalty of an army of 'detainees' was questionable when its cause was muddied by deceits and bribes, and it helps explain the frequent turncoating we see in the Successor Wars. The lack of mobility of these heavily laden waggons explains why no mercenary squad, or private army, raided the treasuries scattered across the empire, for talents of gold and silver were not easily moved, minted, or shipped, unless huge manpower was available.

The soldiers now risking their lives in the malaria-ridden regions of Asia Minor, Mesopotamia, and on the Iranian Plateau in freezing forced marches north of the Zagros Mountains, cannot by this stage have been fighting for a figurehead in Pella, despite Eumenes' dream visions and the royal letters of empowerment.[163] The promises of land grants in Asia with cultivation leases and earnable tax immunity, a *philanthropon*, were now more valuable weapons, as Antigonus knew.[164] Satrapal tribute, which Pseudo-Aristotle's *Oikonomika* (possibly written by Theophrastus) divided into six categories, was set at something like one-tenth of agricultural production (from both land and animals) and was considered state or satrapal property, whilst mining remained a royal monopoly. So exemption from excise *was* precious; Alexander had himself once granted tax exemption to the families of fallen cavalry officers at the Granicus

River battle.[165] But these early Hellenistic armies, operating far from home and fighting for a cause they must have questioned nightly before the satrapies had coalesced into any kingdoms they might call home, were volatile, disgruntled and lacked any national cohesion. But what other choices did they have? War affected everyone: those involved and those watching on, and any claims to impartiality were unlikely to have been heeded.

Diodorus' description of the battle that ensued at Paraetacene was remarkably detailed; it obviously tapped into an ore-laden seam from Hieronymus that captured a formative day of war.[166] He described the intricate battle lines, the manoeuvres and counter-manoeuvres, oblique fronts, wheeling tactics and flanking movements that pitted Antigonus' 28,000 infantry (including new reinforcements under Seleucus and Peithon), 8,500 cavalry and sixty-five elephants, against Eumenes' allied total of 35,000 foot soldiers, 6,100 horsemen and 114 elephants. These beasts, the 'tanks' of the ancient battleground, had been delivered by Eudamus for a reward of 200 talents from the Indian kingdom of Porus who had been 'treacherously murdered' in the process,[167] and whose lands now extended over '… all the Indian territory he had by then conquered – seven tribal nations and over 2,000 towns.'[168]

Alexander's example of delivering a pre-battle *epipolesis*, a troop review incorporating a morale-raising speech in which commanders had been called out by name, was now impossible, though Eumenes may himself at this stage have been multi-lingual and speaking the Aramaic that bound the officialdom of the Achaemenid Empire together. These were diverse coalition armies; only 6,000 of the infantry that fought under Eumenes were specifically referred to as Macedonians, and the 8,000 provided to Antigonus by Antipater were probably a generation younger than the veteran campaigners.[169]

The exotic line-ups within the ranks of each general included specialist troops from across the Graeco-Persian world: mounted lancers (*sarissophoroi*) and lighter mounted skirmishers (*hippakontistai*), heavy shock cavalry under their *ilarches*, swift light mounts (*hippeis prodromoi*), possibly double-mounts (*amphippoi*), *sarissa* bearers (*pezhetairoi*), mobile hoplite infantry (*hypaspistai*), bowmen (*toxotai*), javelin-throwers (*lonchophoroi* and *akontistai*), slingers (*sphendonetes*) with their favoured long-range elliptical lead pellets, scouts (*skopoi*), skirmishers (*pezakontistes* or *hamippoi* who linked up with the cavalry), mercenary units (*archaioi xenoi*), ambushers and even armed slaves, all variously positioned under Greek, Macedonian and Asiatic commanders.[170] And doubtless there were hardened officers at their backs watching for signs of reluctance, cowardice and desertion, for many men on both sides *were* captives from previous encounters, now being ordered to attack their former comrades-in-arms.

A further 8,000 of Antigonus' numbers consisted of *pantodapoi,* the Asiatics equipped in Macedonian style. They appear to be a legacy of Alexander's Susa *epigonoi* and no doubt a corps of *paides basilikai,* 'royal' pages, existed, though they may now have included sons of Asiatic nobles as good behaviour hostages.[171] In front of the armies and at the wings stood armoured elephants ridden by their *mahouts,* with each general praying to the gods that once feathered with arrows and spears they did not turn and stampede through their own lines.

Both Eumenes and Antigonus would probably have employed *ektaktoi,* supernumeraries including messengers, to distribute their orders through the ranks.[172] Dispatch riders would have been galloping behind the lines with tactical revisions as the opening gambits developed and as formations advanced and collapsed, revealing opportunistic or vulnerable gaps in the line. Flags would have been waved to signal the orders and units were given instruction through the *chiliarches, taxiarches, hyparchoi* and the mercenary *xenagoi;* some would have been understood and others potentially confused as Greek, rural Macedonian, Aramaic, and the languages of the Asian satrapies were passed through the ranks. Above the dust and the clamour, the stench of horses, elephants, leather, and sweat beneath leather would have drifted across the battlefield, along with the smell of fear from those terrified by the reputation of the Macedonian killing machine they had not yet participated in themselves.

Strategically placed throughout each army were buglers (*salpinktes*) who heralded the *polemikon,* the order to join battle, and the set-piece moves of the *ektaxis,* the intricate battle order, on the bronze and reeded *salpinx.*[173] The sheer numbers amassed for battle were a challenge to communication so that besides buglers, a herald (*stratokerux*), a signalman (*semeiophoros*), an aide (*hyperetes*) and a file closer (*ouragos*) had been added to each sixteen-by-sixteen-man phalanx formation (*syntagma*) by Alexander.[174] Whether, in the Spartan model, each man placed a small wooden stick (*skytalis*) carved with his name in a bowl to be retrieved after battle (thus an early form of 'dogtag') to signify his survival, is unknown, as is the use of a *katalogos,* a pre-engagement muster roll.[175] But the stage was now set for what could be the decisive battle for an empire, for few regional satraps had managed to remain out of the confrontation; even the absent Ptolemy in Egypt and Lysimachus in Thrace, notionally aligned with Antigonus, must each have been wondering when the eventual victor would head their way.

This was highly developed high-stakes warfare of *logismos* (calculation) and spearheading Eumenes' attack were the inimitable 3,000 Silver Shields, whose campaign *empeiria,* their artful battle experience, saw them smash through the opposing phalanx with few casualties; the result suggests their hypaspist training saw them either hit the opposing rigid *sarissa* phalanx in the vulnerable flanks, or they targeted other lighter troops; the crack brigade may have even rolled up the younger and inexperienced Macedonians provided by Antipater. It was a spectacular penetration that nevertheless left the units on their own left flanks exposed.

The light manoeuvrable cavalry under Peithon which faced Eumenes' right wing was pushed back to nearby foothills by a reinforcement of horsemen; they were backed up by the elephants Peithon had attempted to intimidate with spears and arrows. To counter the setback on his left, Antigonus' own cavalry unit charged through the gap in the phalanx, threatening Eumenes' left wing where Eudamus' mounted men were stationed. Both generals tried to rally their men and reorganise their ranks, and by lamp-lighting time the armies were still arrayed on the field for a new confrontation in what now appeared an eerie stalemate silhouetted by a full moon. By midnight, the armies retired to their camps bloodied, exhausted and no doubt dehydrated and famished. The result was inconclusive and once again the defence of their respective baggage trains played a significant role in that outcome.

Antigonus reportedly lost 3,700 foot soldiers and fifty-four horsemen with a further 4,000 men wounded, where Eumenes lost 540 infantry and 'very few cavalry', with some 900 injured.[176] The losses were to some extent irrelevant, for Antigonus managed to occupy the ground of the fallen and thus had first rights to the burial – a key component in claiming victory – when Eumenes' men refused to abandon their waggons.[177] There is no mention, however, of the penetrating lament of the *aulos*, the reed pipe played at death, or of a *tropaion*, the symbolic victory 'tree' on which the panoply of the fallen was hung with shields about the base and erected at the spot at which the tide of the battle was turned.[178] This might suggest Antigonus knew his claim to the ground was dubious considering his far greater losses; according to Polyaenus, Antigonus detained the herald Eumenes sent to agree the terms of cremation and burial until all his own dead had been burned on a pyre.[179]

Eumenes countered with his own 'magnificent funeral' once the enemy had departed; he *had* erected a *tropaion* previously after battle with Craterus. The aftermath of Paraetacene was also the occasion that saw the fallen Indian general, Ceteus, burned on a pyre, as his two wives vied for the honour of being torched alive beside him in the tradition of *sati*, as the Macedonians watched on with a morbid fascination.[180]

It was Eumenes' army that, nevertheless, managed to gain entry into the environs of Gabiene, while Antigonus, smarting from his deeper wounds, retired again to Gamarga in Peithon's home satrapy of the still-unplundered Media to re-provision as winter closed in. The armies were separated by a nine-day march through a bitterly cold and waterless desert '… that contained nothing but sulphur mines, and stinking bogs, barren and uninhabited.' The alternative route involved a twenty-five-day march through a more hospitable landscape.[181]

It was close to the winter solstice and Antigonus had his men prepare ten days' food that did not require cooking, and fearing he had spies in his camp, he let it be known that he was marching to Armenia. He struck out across the desert instead and issued orders that no fires were to be lit at night, a plan that was soon challenged by winds and bitter cold, forcing his men to heat themselves after five days on the march. The flames alerted local inhabitants to his presence; fast camels were sent to Peucestas, who, noting the abundance of the enemy lights, prepared to make off with his eastern command. Fearing a wholesale *rhipsaspia*, a dropping of shields in flight, Eumenes 'calmed their fears' by promising a delaying action, and he quickly roused his troops from their scattered billeting. Riding to a position clearly visible to Antigonus' forces, he likewise ordered a string of fires to be lit as if a consolidated battlefront faced his advancing army. Antigonus abandoned his frontal assault and headed to provision.[182]

The one-eyed veteran general was initially 'filled with rage and mortification, imagining that the enemy must long ago have known his plans'. Realising 'that he had been out-manoeuvred' by a ruse straight from Xenophon's *Hipparchikos*, Antigonus nevertheless determined to settle their disputes by an immediate pitched battle.[183] He was informed that Eumenes' forces were still strung out, with some detachments stationed a six-day march from others; Plutarch claimed Eumenes' unruly Macedonians had distributed themselves where they liked.[184] Keen to exploit the opportunity, Antigonus marched on Gabiene. Eumenes gathered his dispersed forces into a palisaded fort but the elephant contingent was slow to arrive; a cavalry clash ensued that saw Eumenes narrowly avert the capture of the entire corps of Indian beasts.[185]

That would have been a decisive loss; as well as being deployed to trample infantry ranks, elephants were used to deflect cavalry charges, for horses detested their smell and were reduced to wheeling around them. Elephants were notoriously difficult to bring down, though they needed careful managing even in front of friendly ranks; at the battle at Gaza some four years on a total of fifty archers, javelineers and peltasts would be positioned between each of them. Directing them was even more precarious when they clashed head on when they would attempt to gore one another in the flanks; moreover, 'leading' elephants are repeatedly mentioned, suggesting the hierarchy behaviour of the fighting herd hinged on the alpha males, the largest bulls, which were even less predictable and more aggressive when mature bulls were in musth.[186]

The logistics involved in provisioning these armies were intricate and daunting, and the quantity of food needed to support them was enormous. Asian elephants could consume up to five per cent of their 11,000-plus-lb

(5,000-kilogram) bodyweight per day, and they regularly consumed 330 lb (150 kilograms) of plant material while drinking 70 pints (40 litres) of water. This made them a hindrance to both sides in siege warfare, as Polyperchon found out when enveloping Athens, and as Olympias would witness when bottled up at Pydna.[187] And yet a daily elephant march might only cover 10 miles where the rest of the army could average 15.[188] The 6,000-8,000 warhorses required high-starch fodder and the 30,000 men needed victualing with at least 3,600 calories and food containing 2.5 ounces (70 grams) of protein; the traditional daily ration in Persia had been 1 *choenix* of grain per day.[189] Packhorses and mules, able to carry some 200 lb (camels could porter 300 lb) also needed 10 lb of grain and 8 gallons of water per day, though they (camels in particular) could be eaten on the march once their loads were expended.[190] Hundreds of transport animals were needed to carry just a few days' rations for armies of this size.

According to Polyaenus, 10,000 water casks had to be readied for Antigonus' ten-day march to confront Eumenes through the desert that provided 'neither water, nor grass, nor wood, nor plant'.[191] As Briant has pointed out, the Achaemenid administration did have a system of well-stocked official storehouses that would have been raided when possible, but we have no idea whether the Macedonians replenished them. So the strategic value and the scarcity of well-provisioned quarters, especially in winter on the Iranian Plateau, was illustrated by the dispersed nature of Eumenes' men (ill discipline was probably not the sole reason) in even the well-provisioned region of Gabiene.

The path of the Macedonian war machine, both campaigning with Alexander and now when total numbers were hardly diminished, must have been one of devastation from aggressive foraging and forced requisitioning. Engels calculated that passing armies of the broad sizes recorded would have devoured a 25-square-mile wheat crop and drained 100,000 gallons of water. Foragers could collect supplies from a 60- to 80-mile radius or a four-day journey from a stationary camp; this was reduced to 15 to 17 miles when on the move.[192]

Besides troop numbers, many non-combatant camp followers were retained in some capacity: the interpreters, metalsmiths, cooks, herders, tanners, porters, waggon-drivers, hunters, slave traders, clerks, doctors, paymasters, guides, map-makers and engineers; most of a soldier's pay would in fact have been 'reinvested' in the camp economy as evidenced by the debts run up by the army under Alexander in the East.[193] This extravagant early Hellenistic warfare was heavy on cost and consequences, and it was only made possible by depleting the treasuries accumulated by the Achaemenid kings under a complex network of tax levies they had established over centuries. Such expenditure could not be sustained for long in the absence of the administrative stability needed to replenish those coffers.

The pre-battle manoeuvres and continued chicanery, the double deceits and the realities of the brutal climate in this seasonal campaigning set the scene for the forthcoming final confrontation at Gabiene at the close of 316 BCE. Eumenes had employed his Cappadocian levies effectively, and by now, Antigonus had also harnessed the skills of *xenagoi*, foreign auxiliaries: Lycian, Pamphylian, Phrygian and Lydian troops were supporting the Macedonian ranks, no doubt supplied by Nearchus and Menander, governors of these regions; Antigonus' long tenure of Asia Minor was being well exploited.[194] They were supported by local Medians, care of Peithon, and alongside them Tarentine cavalry, local conscripts and mercenaries had been gathered from Alexander's settlements along the way. Apart from harnessing their unique skills, fresh recruits arrived with little or no accumulated baggage, reducing their weighty vulnerability.[195]

'Not out of goodwill or kindness, but to protect the money they had lent him [Eumenes]', Phaedimus and Eudamus, who was now master of the elephants and who was possibly *strategos* of a region of India, brought word of the planned treachery of Teutamus, the Silver Shields commander.[196] Eumenes may have already suspected intrigue; Teutamus had almost been turned by Antigonus' promises before they departed Cilicia. Before the final scene played out, however, Eumenes might have dealt one more effective theatrical card. Facing opponents a generation younger, Antigenes of the Silver Shields sent out a horseman to the opposing phalanx; he proclaimed: 'Oh wicked men, you are sinning against your fathers, who conquered the world under Philip and Alexander!' This recalls the vocal threats from Xennias 'in the Macedonian tongue' when he attempted to dissuade the opposing Macedonians from fighting Eumenes' veterans before the battle with Neoptolemus. Here, at Gabiene, it was a masterstroke of mental warfare and more effective than the traditional Macedonian battle cry of '*Alalalalai*' to Enyalius, an epithet for Ares, the god of war.[197]

Antigonus had strengthened his right wing; screened by the strongest elephants, Eumenes took position directly opposite on his own left as they prepared for the final face-off. As trumpets blasted and ranks engaged once more, Antigonus' infantry ranks again collapsed under the Silver Shields' charge. But the advancing elephants trampled dust from the uncultivated salt flat into a confusing haze, enabling the Median cavalry under Peithon and the Tarentines to seize Eumenes' baggage train, while father and son – Antigonus and the young Demetrius – flanked the cavalry wing under Eudamus' command. Although the *Argyraspides* killed 5,000 of those facing them without a single casualty (so propaganda claimed), the loss of the baggage train, along with Peucestas' 'lax and ignoble' withdrawal from the battlefield, handed the day to Antigonus.[198] It was Peucestas' non-performance that the Silver Shields ultimately blamed on their final defeat; perhaps it was a bittersweet *on* the battlefield revenge coordinated with *Monopthalmos* for his having been out-generalled by Eumenes *off* the battlefield at Persepolis. Or Hieronymus may have simply saddled Peucestas with a legacy of betrayal for his earlier attempt to wrest control from Eumenes.

Eumenes' repeated cavalry charges had not turned the tide. The now cut-off veteran infantry commanders were forced to form a defensive hollow square, as recommended by Xenophon in his *Anabasis*, a formation Homer might have termed a *purgoi* (literally 'tower'); they retreated to safety by the bank of a river spitting accusations at Peucestas as they went.[199] His Asian satraps advised flight; Eumenes proposed fighting as their overall casualties were few.[200] But the capture of their baggage, and the loss of '2,000 women and a few children', decided the outcome for the influential hypaspist brigade who now asked themselves why the '... best of the soldiers of Philip and Alexander, after all their toils, in their old age be robbed of their rewards.'

Teutamus soon opened covert negotiations with Antigonus.[201] Promises were exchanged, Eumenes was seized and handed over, and Plutarch recorded a scathing speech in which Eumenes upbraided the traitors. He and Justin, possibly drawing from Duris of Samos if he *did* display any hostility towards the Cardian (that *would* be consistent with his apparent iconoclastic treatment of the reputations of other 'great men', especially those working on behalf of the Macedonian regime), presented the allegation that Eumenes attempted to flee.[202] So guarded as if he was 'a furious lion or a savage elephant', Eumenes was eventually executed when a *synedrion* of Macedonians voted for his death despite the reported pleas from Demetrius and Nearchus for his life to be spared.[203] He was aged forty-five.[204]

Antigonus slew Eudamus; Antigenes, the long-time career soldier honoured by Alexander in a military contest some fifteen years before and more recently rewarded for slaying Perdiccas in Egypt, was reportedly thrown into a pit and burned alive. Teutamus' earlier intrigues might have saved his life, though his fate is unattested. Amphimachus the governor of Mesopotamia, and Stasander, a supporting satrap from Areia-Drangiana, were most likely executed too. A further 1,000 of the *Argyraspides* were sent off to Arachosia, broadly modern Afghanistan; Diodorus claimed the region's satrap, the previously humiliated Sibyrtius who subsequently enjoyed a long tenure there, was given orders to send them on dangerous missions to annihilate the unit. The rest were forced into garrison duty '... that not a man of them might ever return to Macedonia or behold the Grecian sea.'[205] The Silver Shields brigade was never heard of again, though Seleucus might have later managed to recruit survivors into his ranks.[206]

Meanwhile, in Macedonia the fate of Olympias, Roxane, Alexander IV, his fiancée Deidameia the Epirote princess and Thessalonice with them, was in the balance, as they were besieged by Cassander at Pydna.[207] Although Aristonus still held Amphipolis and Monimus controlled Pella, neither they nor Olympias' nephew, Aeacides of the Molossian royal house, nor Polyperchon who was himself under siege in Azorus in northern Thessaly, were able to come to her aid by land or sea. After holding out for months by eating the rotting flesh from the corpses, and while watching her followers (and elephants) die of starvation, Olympias' soldiers asked her to release them from her service. Following her own failed escape by ship she sued for terms with Cassander who agreed to nothing but her personal safety; she ordered Aristonus to submit and hand over Amphipolis on similar pledges of safety.

Cassander had Aristonus, Alexander's former Bodyguard, murdered immediately, and he called for a similar end to Olympias who was condemned in absentia by a hastily convened Assembly, as any wider forum might have voted more sympathetically. After failing to lure her into a further sham escape attempt, some 200 of Cassander's best soldiers were sent in for the kill, but they were 'overawed by her exulted rank'. It was left to relatives of Olympias' victims to finally slay her. She was either run through with a blade or summarily stoned to death, though she 'uttered no ignoble or womanish plea' so that 'you might have perceived the soul of Alexander in his dying mother'. Clearly recalling her treatment of the grave of his brother Iolaos, Olympias' body was left unburied by Cassander, though her clan, the Aeacids, possibly under Pyrrhus (who named his daughter Olympias), may have interred her nearby with honours some years later.[208] The 'royal alliance' perpetuated by Olympias and Eumenes, which saw them both under siege, had finally been wiped out.

Eumenes' portfolio of subterfuges had ensured his survival for a time, but there remains an inevitability to the fate of 'the pest from the Chersonese' as the Macedonians lately called him.[209] His credentials, though impressive, were ultimately non-Macedonian in *origin*. Despite his intimacy with the dead king and his last acting chiliarch who both sheltered him from the full force of prejudice, he remained an ineligible candidate for either the throne at Pella, or as *strategos* of the Asian Empire; we recall that Eumenes had himself refrained from voting at the Common Assembly at Babylon (an enfranchisement only possible if he *had* been nationalised as a citizen by Philip or Alexander). He was ultimately impotent with anyone but his own Asian levies, a handicap he himself is said to have openly voiced.[210] It is a testament to Eumenes' charisma and powers of persuasion that he managed to hold the Macedonian core of his coalition together to fight three major pitched battles when veteran home-grown generals of repute lay across the plain.

Alexander's *hetairoi* appear to have discarded their Asiatic wives at, or soon after, his death, with the notable exception of Seleucus who remained married to Apame the daughter of Spitamenes, and possibly with the exception of Eumenes too.[211] For Plutarch and Nepos reported that at his death Eumenes' bones were conveyed to his mother, wife, and children in Cappadocia in a silver urn following a 'magnificent funeral'.[212] We have no evidence that Eumenes was married to anyone other than a daughter (or granddaughter) of Artabazus, which explains the presence in his ranks of Artabazus' son, Pharnabazus.[213] This suggests that far from abandoning his wife, Eumenes saw the value in maintaining his marriage with Persian nobility.

'Children have to be deceived with knucklebones, men with oaths.' The aphorism has been variously attributed to Philip II and the Spartan, Lysander.[214] Oaths, Wills, royal mandates, faked letters, dream visions, guile and brilliant deceits, and we suggest the *Pamphlet* too, had become part of Eumenes' repertoire. If he *had* departed Babylon with any notion that he might enjoy a quiet governorship once installed in Cappadocia, he miscalculated badly. For one man above any other harboured a very different design.

'ALEXANDER REAPED ASIA, AND I BUT GLEAN AFTER HIM.'[215]

> Eumenes went down to meet him [Antigonus] and they embraced one another with greetings of friendship and affection, since they had formerly been close associates and intimate companions.[216]

The relationship between Eumenes and Antigonus is truly intriguing. The poignant moment highlighted here, which took place early in the siege at Nora, implied Antigonus felt some kind of 'guardianship' as well as affection for the gifted young former court secretary, a bond that must have been established during Eumenes' years under Philip at Pella.[217]

Eumenes had a worthy adversary in Antigonus son of Philip from Elimea in Upper Macedonia, who was some twenty years his senior. Already honoured as a benefactor to the Ionian League city of Priene (Caria) in 334 BCE – the very first year of Alexander's Asian campaign – little is heard about Antigonus' offstage services in the decade that followed his mopping-up duties after the battle at Issus, from which as many as 8,000 Greeks, besides Asiatic soldiers, had managed to escape. It was a significant mandate fulfilled with extremely limited troops, and in the face of the Persian successes of Pharnabazus who was retaking the coastal cities of Asia Minor, for this clearly constituted a threat to the entire Macedonian rear.[218]

Throughout Alexander's *anabasis* into the Persian interior, Antigonus operated as his regional *strategos* in central Asia Minor. He may have even struck an accord that kept Ariarathes, king of the still-unconquered Cappadocia, from causing trouble, a stable relationship that could explain the reason, or the excuse, for Antigonus' refusal to assist Eumenes' in taking control of the region. Justifiably then, he had more cause to resent Eumenes' inheritance than anyone. But we sense Antigonus' responsibility was wider still, maintaining communications and safe passage from the Mediterranean coast through Asia Minor into Mesopotamia, whence Parmenio's own regional command protected Alexander's back when he was in the further eastern provinces.[219]

The years 320 BCE to the close of 316 BCE, in which he battled with Eumenes, are studded with military intrigues that appealed to Polyaenus (who claimed to be of Macedonian descent) and many were attributed to Antigonus *Monopthalmos*.[220] From the Battle of Paraetacene to Eumenes' death at the beginning of 315 BCE, through the Third *Diadokhoi* War (which lasted to the Peace of the Dynasts in 311 BCE) and on down to the battle at Ipsus in 301 BCE, Antigonus dominated the literary sources. He reportedly summed up his fate (and his own harsh money-raising tactics) with: 'Alexander reaped Asia, and I but glean after him.'[221]

When Antipater promoted him at Triparadeisus to his *strategos* in Asia, Antigonus had two ambitious and capable sons fast maturing, with a brother, a half-brother and two talented nephews entering his ranks; it was a dynasty evolving to match any that might make a challenge for power.[222] The charismatic general, with his intimidating physique and booming voice, must have been a mighty personality to overshadow Alexander's *strategoi* and former *Somatophylakes* as he did in the intervening years; he stopped Ptolemy from (permanently) expanding north from Egypt, he kept Lysimachus west of the Hellespont and Seleucus east of the Euphrates until the year before his death.[223] Moreover, his politicking in Greece through his capable son, Demetrius, ensured Cassander never quite dominated the peninsula with the result that no hostile coalition could attack his interests from there.

Though blind in one eye, Antigonus never lost sight of opportunity. He appreciated the value of Asiatic cavalry, neutralising the effect of Eumenes' own locally recruited mounted troops so that the manoeuvres at Orcynia, Paraetacene and Gabiene were matched by a dexterity that rendered total victory impossible.[224] Although at times stubborn and failing to heed the advice of subordinates, Antigonus was also an innovator who adopted field fortifications such as the palisade and ditch castrametation developed by Chabrias and Iphicrates a century before.[225] Both he and Eumenes were clearly masters of psychological warfare; Antigonus' attempts to lure the Silver Shields to his cause with barbed accusatory letters, requiring Eumenes to deliver counter-speeches to stifle the defections, was part of a game being waged both ways.[226] But after the capture and execution of White Cleitus in 318 BCE, it was the one-eyed general who 'gained a great reputation for military genius'.[227]

Tarn noted that Antigonus (and surely Eumenes too) often took himself out of the battle to direct the developing set pieces from a withdrawn or elevated position, so complex had the formations, gambits and counter-moves become.[228] Understanding and studying the enemy was essential, for both were duping the other into believing their ranks were swelled by arriving allies or ready for battle when in fact they were not.[229] The description of Antigonus' analysis of the opposing troops' disposition at Paraetacenae bears out Tarn's observation:

> As Antigonus looked down from a high position, he saw the battle lines of his enemy and disposed his own army accordingly. Seeing that the right wing of the enemy had been strengthened with the elephants and the strongest of the cavalry, he arrayed against it the lightest of his horsemen, who, drawn up in open order, were to avoid a frontal action but maintain a battle of wheeling tactics and in this way thwart that part of the enemies' forces in which they had the greatest confidence.[230]

The battle at Gabiene just a few months later would have developed in just as intricate a fashion had not the plain been completely shrouded in dust.[231] With the Silver Shields encircled and Eumenes in chains, Antigonus had strengthened his position in Asia to the point where he was unassailable, with a multi-province income of 11,000 talents per annum via his network of *dioiketai*, the revenue-collecting financial officials; he was on his way to becoming 'the mightiest king of his day'.[232] And by 315 BCE any power balances that Alexander's testament had attempted to put in place were truly being tested; the tectonic plates were shifting and tremors were afoot.

Emboldened by his defeat of Eumenes, Antigonus soon deepened the groans of a fracturing empire to a full earthquake. He removed Peucestas from his Persian domains after winning over Xenophilus, the *phrourarchos* of the citadel at Susa who capitulated soon after Gabiene.[233] Antigonus availed himself of its 15,000 talents with Seleucus' blessing, having extended *his* authority over Susiane, for together they now planned to rule the East, or so Seleucus initially believed.[234] The haul included the Persian king's golden jewel-encrusted climbing vine (possibly symbolising fecundity and strength) mentioned by Herodotus a century before.[235]

Antigonus had already stripped Ecbatana of 5,000 talents in uncoined silver, and following his execution of Peithon, whom he suspected of plotting against him (the charges may well have been fabricated), he raided 'Persia', collecting further gifts and spoils, some 25,000 talents in all.[236] It took twenty-two days for the pack camels and waggon train loaded with treasure to reach Babylon, a westward transfer of wealth that might suggest Antigonus' lack of faith in his ability to control the eastern satrapies indefinitely. Much of the gold and silver would have ended up in the treasury at Cyinda and the other easily defended citadels of Pergamum and at Sardis on the steep rocky spur that extends out from Mount Tmolus.[237]

Upon his arrival in Babylon in late 315 BCE, Seleucus honoured Antigonus with gifts 'suitable for a king'. Whilst the generosity proved somewhat prophetic, Seleucus had miscalculated Antigonus' intent; for in the self-appointed guise of *chiliarchos* to the kings – effectively Perdiccas' previous role as the empire overseer – Antigonus demanded accounts for the provincial revenues. Seleucus repudiated what amounted to a challenge to his authority and upheld his claim to the region that had been 'given him in recognition of his services rendered while Alexander was alive', whereafter he fled to Egypt with nothing more than fifty horsemen fearing he would be 'seized' and 'destroyed' as Peithon had been before him. But 'by condemning himself to exile', he had surrendered his own satrapy, even if he emerged as a successful fleet commander working in league with Ptolemy, who now saw the writing on the wall.[238]

The year that spanned late 316-315 BCE, in which Antigonus swung the former regent, Polyperchon, to his cause (though in a toothless role in the Peloponnese), was an extraordinary period for the one-eyed general, and it laid the foundations for an invasion of Phoenicia and Syria. Antigonus' successes were only overshadowed by Ptolemy's acquisition of Cyprus and the continued defiance of Tyre which would eventually lead to a siege lasting fifteen months (ending late 314 BCE).[239] For not only did Antigonus finally have a navy of some 240 fully equipped warships (construction of which employed 8,000 men) and full control of the treasuries, he gained essential new minting facilities; within his original sphere of influence over Pamphylia, Lycia and Greater Phrygia, only Side on the Pamphylian coast had any history of striking coins.[240]

But Antigonus' unwillingness to share the Asian soil and his combat spoils heralded in the Fourth *Diadokhoi* War (commenced 308 BCE) which resulted in successes in Athens (307 BCE) and Cyprus (306 BCE) but disastrous assaults on Rhodes (305-304 BCE) and Egypt (306 BCE). His bid for outright supremacy finally rallied the new self-proclaimed kings – Lysimachus, Seleucus, Cassander and Ptolemy – into a determined *koinonia*, a commonality of purpose, that culminated in the confrontation at Ipsus in 301 BCE: 'Prompted not so much by goodwill towards one another as compelled by the fears each had for himself, they moved readily to make common cause in the supreme struggle.'[241]

Their motivation was simple: combining numbers prevented Antigonus from dealing with them piecemeal. Cassander was absent from the battle though he sent two contingents of men: a modest force under Prepelaus, and one of 12,500 soldiers under his brother, Pleistarchus (many were lost in the sea crossing), while Ptolemy ventured north only as far as Sidon. The ruse Antigonus used to stop the Egyptian dynast in his tracks looks somewhat familiar: he dispatched men with false reports of his victory over Seleucus and Lysimachus, along with his plan for the invasion of Syria; Ptolemy retired to Egypt fearing the worst.[242] The deceit was vintage Eumenes reincarnated, but the rest of the coalition army was regrouping in northern Asia Minor for the eventual clash on the Phrygian plain.

Stumbling out of his tent and apparently falling flat on his face, Antigonus is said to have approached the battlefield at Ipsus without his usual infective bonhomie.[243] Perhaps he still had the dark Magi prophecy on his mind which harked back to Seleucus' escape at Babylon some fourteen years before:

> ... then, the Chaldean astrologers came to him and foretold that, if ever he let Seleucus escape from his hands, the consequence would be that all Asia would become subject to Seleucus, and that Antigonus himself would lose his life in a battle against him.[244]

Or, after decades of indecisive campaigning, a sepulchral father and son may have recalled the words now attributed to Plato: 'Only the dead have seen the end of war.'[245] Antigonus may have simply foreseen the carnage that would result from 150,000 armed men fighting under the lethal command of the Macedonian kings whose pike-bearers were potentially now armed with the longest *sarissai* ever seen.[246] Some 475 war elephants were arrayed alongside scythed chariots, the *drepanephoroi*, ready to be let loose on the amassed *phalanges*, for Hellenistic warfare now harnessed the most ruthless devices ever witnessed on the battlefield.[247]

The picture of the battle itself and the campaign leading up to it is ill-defined because Diodorus' twenty-first book survives in tatters.[248] However, Plutarch's *Life of Demetrius* captured something of the tension. Summoning Demetrius from Greece (where he almost fought a major battle with Cassander in Thessaly), and apparently surprised by Lysimachus' incursion into Asia Minor while he himself was paying more attention to games and festivals in his new Syrian capital, Antigonea, Antigonus predicted his enemies would be 'scattered asunder with a single stone and a single shout, as if they were a flock of granivorous birds'.[249] And yet signs augured otherwise:

At that time, moreover, bad omens also subdued their spirits. For Demetrius dreamed that Alexander, in brilliant array of armour, asked him what watchword they were going to give for the battle: and when he replied 'Zeus and Victory', Alexander said: 'Then, I will go away and join your adversaries: they surely will receive me.'[250]

If Gaugamela had been a 'Panhellenic set-piece', then Ipsus was the Hellenistic equivalent: a multi-national tableau with mercenaries and Asiatic troops featuring prominently on both sides. The battle lines would once again have been arrayed with great *empeiria*, for the *Diadokhoi* each by now had thirty years, or more, of campaigning under their belts. But what initially appeared a 'brilliant' cavalry action by Demetrius was not so impressive after all, for the 'flight' of Antiochus, the son of Seleucus, looks familiar and contrived. Demetrius was isolated behind a wall of elephants and could not ride to the aid of his father who was being overwhelmed; Demetrius barely managed to escape with some 9,000 men.[251]

Warned of the direction of the enemy's approach, Antigonus simply retorted with: 'But who but me would be their mark?' He fell at the 'battle of the kings' in a shower of javelins, by now in his mid-eighties. It was an age that Ptolemy himself attained, and Seleucus and Lysimachus almost, remarkable achievements in such violent times (and when the average lifespan of the period was thirty-eight years, due to various causes).[252] Antigonus' corpse was abandoned by all but the faithful Thorax of Larissa, though it was later afforded the courtesy of a burial with royal honours.[253] Ipsus indeed proved *kakodaimones,* an ill-starred day, and as it has been pointed out, it was a propaganda failure too.[254] Despite all Antigonus' positive work and progress in Asia – the sophisticated and largely successful administrations, colonisations and new city foundations – the results were once again reaped by the victors; he is remembered as an ambitious warlord rather than a cultured empire administrator, when the reality surely lay somewhere in-between.

The 'centripetal leaders', Perdiccas and Antigonus (and arguably Eumenes too), who attempted to maintain the unity of Alexander's empire under central authority (ultimately their own, with their accomplices), were finally eclipsed by the 'centrifugal forces' vying for a chunk of the 'great carcass'.[255] The commonality of purpose that had brought the victors together was nothing more than a veneer and the spoils of Asia were once again divided.

Pliny stated that Antigonus had once commissioned the celebrated artist, Protogenes, and his own friend Apelles, to paint him in profile to avoid the complication of his disfigured eye, for Antigonus is said to have often joked at his cyclopean nickname, *heterophthalmos.*[256] Yet when it came to immortality in oils he was more perspicacious, defying Cicero's assertion that: 'Things perfected by nature are better than those finished by art.'[257] Also present at the 'battle of the kings' was the historian Hieronymus, and this too provides a tutorial reminder that a historian's profiling rarely mirrored the true face of events. So we must ask: *did* Hieronymus give us portraits with true likenesses, or simpler and more attractive profiles of his patrons? Those closer to events remained just as curious; Plutarch reported that a peasant was found digging at Ipsus some years after the formative battle. When questioned on his activity, he replied: 'I am looking for Antigonus.'[258]

The Battle of Zama by Henri-Paul Motte, 1890. Although the battle at Zama between Hannibal and Scipio took place a century after Ipsus, this engraving captures the terror of facing war elephants, the 'tanks of the ancient battleground'. According to Polybius, in earlier wars the Romans hamstrung captured Seleucid elephants.[259]

BENE QUI LATUIT BENE VIXIT – 'TO LIVE WELL IS TO LIVE CONCEALED': HIERONYMUS THE TRAPEZE ARTIST[260]

The narrating of the years in which Eumenes and Antigonus faced off in many ways constituted Hieronymus' own 'Babylonian compromise', an equivalent to the dilemma Cleitarchus faced when narrating events surrounding Alexander's death. Serving both of the protagonists, Hieronymus co-joined their stories in person and in ink and so his history of the Successor Wars was always destined to be a compromised narrative.

For reasons we can only speculate, Hieronymus was spared execution when captured at Gabiene; he was employed by the victor and served three generations of Antigonids.[261] Neither yet a historian and never a general, his exact role under Eumenes remains unclear, though on later occasion he was titled *epimeletes,* suggesting a guardianship of affairs. Yet his wounds at Gabiene suggest that as a *philos* of Eumenes (here more representative of personal or technical staff) he did see action in the ranks.[262]

Hieronymus was later cited as 'overseer of revenue' from the extraction of naturally occurring bitumen (*asphaltum*) at the Dead Sea, a valuable resource used in mummification and shipbuilding. He was likely installed in the region as part of Demetrius *Poliorketes*' flawed expedition against the Nabateans, as Diodorus' detailed narrative suggests we have a somewhat disgruntled eyewitness account; Antigonus had failed here before him and Hieronymus apparently saw little value in a second unprovoked attack. The Nabateans also had a monopoly on the highly profitable frankincense trade and Hieronymus might have visited an early settlement at Petra, the rock-carved city rediscovered by the Western world some 2,100 years on.[263]

His defeat at the hands of the Arabs did not deter Demetrius from appointing Hieronymus governor, *epimeletes kai harmostes,* of Boeotia, centred at Thebes; once again it was a post that ended in expulsion.[264] So we may speculate that Hieronymus' most successful role on a campaign had been as an envoy, or perhaps *parakletos,* advocate, travelling between Eumenes and Antigonus through the siege at Nora and which ultimately resulted in Eumenes' release.[265]

Hieronymus was to have a far more significant part to play through the age of the *Diadokhoi* in something of a 'Polybian role', when the captive came to admire his captor (if not necessarily the country that bred him) in the role of an influential client historian. Antigonus, his son Demetrius, and *his* son Antigonus II *Gonatas*, especially, appear to have been tolerant of writers and historians at their courts, perhaps due to the time the latter generations spent 'governing' over 'educated' Athens. *Gonatas*, who claimed Heraclid origins and a more useful political descent from the Argead house, invited the Stoic Zeno of Citium to complete his royal 'reason and education', for like Philip II, he knew the Macedones needed 'enlightening'; he even appointed Zeno's student, the philosopher Persaeus of Citium, to govern a newly recovered Corinth.[266] It may well have been Antigonus II *Gonatas* who constructed the Great Tumulus at Vergina, which protected the Argead necropolis from further plundering in the wake of the Celtic Gauls (Galatai); and he, or his father, may have been responsible for the tomb (Tomb III) that is thought to house the remains of Alexander IV, the son of the Alexander and Roxane. Both posthumous reverences would have reinforced a useful association with the Argead line.[267]

In his career with *Monophthalmos* after Eumenes' death, Hieronymus would have become associated with Nearchus who was appointed as an adviser to Demetrius in Syria in late 313/312 BCE.[268] Dismissing his advice, Demetrius attacked Ptolemy at Gaza with disastrous results.[269] And yet it appears that unless Diodorus (and Trogus) was drawing from a new source, Hieronymus curiously underlined the chivalry stemming from these confrontations after which captured officers, personal effects, and even generals, were returned unharmed. The portrayal of Ptolemy's generosity was perhaps simply the mechanism by which Demetrius' reciprocal honour, following a later reversed outcome, could be fully displayed; similar sentiment *is* evident in Diodorus' account of the aftermath of Antigonus' siege of Tyre.[270] Possibly, having witnessed the futile attempts of the *Diadokhoi* to forge a greater empire, Hieronymus was simply praising Ptolemy and his own final patron for a policy that resisted such a self-destructive path.

We cannot underestimate the complexity of the task facing the Cardian historian when he finally laid out his scrolls. The consecutive years captured by his history outspanned the chronological breadth of Thucydides' *Peloponnesian War*, Xenophon's *Anabasis* and Alexander's campaign histories combined. Hieronymus' career had witnessed Eumenes' execution, the early death of Antigonus' younger son, Philip, in 306 BCE, the disastrous invasion of Egypt in the same year when 80,000 infantry, 8,000 cavalry and eighty-three elephants supported by a fleet of 150 warships and 100 transports faired no better than Perdiccas' attempt seventeen years before.[271] In fact, Ptolemy, who might himself have had no more than a core of 5,000 Macedonians in an army of some 30,000 men, used similar tactics again; he offered rich sums of money for enemy troop defection so that Antigonus had to post slingers to deter the deserters from leaving his ranks.[272]

After the failed year-long siege of Rhodes by Demetrius *Poliorketes* in 305 BCE, came the collapse of Antigonus' Asian empire, where Hieronymus would have seen his by-now corpulent patron lying on the Phrygian plain at Ipsus.[273] He would have watched on as the once charismatic Demetrius *Poliorketes* was reduced to drinking himself to death by 283 BCE without the twang of a Scythian bowstring to bring him to his senses, and he would have recalled that Demetrius' wife, the thrice-widowed Phila the daughter of Antipater, had committed suicide by drinking poison five years earlier when Demetrius lost control of Macedonia (288 BCE).[274] Hieronymus would have additionally heard reports arriving from his native city, Cardia, as it was ruined by Lysimachus in 309 BCE, with his own eponymous city of Lysimachia rising in its place. This might have inspired him to claim it was Lysimachus who desecrated the royal graves at Aegae when warring against Pyrrhus (rather then the opposite) who had briefly ruled in the western part of Macedonia.[275]

Under Antigonus II *Gonatas*, the 'enlightened despot' who finally defeated the Gallic Celts near Lysimachia in 277 BCE, and who surrounded himself with philosophers, poets, writers, and the god Pan in no small way (though undertaking the occasional execution of hostile historians, Medius of Larissa amongst them), Hieronymus was provided with a modicum of *homonoia* in which he afforded his final patron's grandfather with some biographical payback for the years he campaigned for the Pellan court.[277] After the early turbulent years of *Gonatas'* reign, this may have been the environment in which Marsyas of Pella was able to publish his account.[278] Athens, on the other hand, was less fortunate; after its attempted bid for freedom in the Chremonidean War stirred up by Ptolemy II *Philadelphos*, and following *Gonatas'* victory over the Greek coalition at Corinth in 265 BCE, the city was again starved to submission and garrisoned until 229 BCE.

By the time Hieronymus' final patron finally attained the throne, a threadbare Macedonia was now a shadow of its former self, reflecting upon which Antigonus II *Gonatas* became 'the first Stoic king'.[279] Hieronymus lived through the death of one of *Gonatas'* sons, Alcyoneus, whose passing *was* stoically accepted by his father, and he witnessed the self-destruction of the once brilliant Pyrrhus (whose memoirs he used). Ultimately, he bore witness to the last of the sons and daughters of Alexander's *Diadokhoi* relentlessly tearing each other's kingdoms apart. The 'heroic' part of the Hellenistic period had drawn to a close; 'few people still believed in either the possible unity of Alexander's empire or in the "freedom" of the Greeks'. So it comes as no surprise that 'a dark thread' ran through the whole of Hieronymus' history.[280]

But there remain loose threads, missing strands and twisted fibres too in the accounts of those who extracted their detail from Hieronymus, and these have a direct bearing on our

A bust of Lysimachus at the Museo Archeologico Nazionale di Napoli. He had reportedly lost fifteen children by the time he died at age seventy-four at the Battle of Curopedion in 281 BCE.

case. As the Second War of the *Diadokhoi* drew to a close with Eumenes' capture at Gabiene, it appears Hieronymus' reporting was still steeped in a reflective anger that went back to his compatriot's death. It is, for example, difficult to imagine Antigonus' rationale for destroying the crack, if unruly, Silver Shields unit that was now ostensibly his to use. It seems more likely that Antigonus' (as well as Hieronymus') own complex nature was being exposed; the result was an awkward and not wholly convincing fusion of retribution and *pathos* that positioned the captor as despising the *Argyraspides'* treachery more than Eumenes himself. So Antigonus' alleged regret at the execution of his former Pellan court friend and a still truculent foe, and his harsh retribution, was most likely in part the historian's reflection of his own complex emotions on the episode.[281] In Plutarch's expanded account of the aftermath of Gabiene, similar sentiments can be found; Antigonus 'could not endure to see Eumenes, by reason of their former intimate friendship'. After deliberating for some days on his dilemma, Eumenes was deprived of food before being dispatched.[282]

Any hesitation Antigonus *had* shown to his men was surely contrived and politically expedient, for his army now swelled with ranks of angry captured soldiers, and this was most likely why Peucestas was not immediately executed, for his eastern coalition was significantly present.[283] Yet the 'victor weeping over the vanquished is a motif of Hellenistic historiography'; it was a lamentation Antigonus II *Gonatas* was to later afford to Pyrrhus, and one Eumenes himself had lavished on the fallen Craterus. This tragic emphasis appears to have been at the heart of the writings of Duris, a strong candidate for detail of the period and a source Plutarch seems to have frequently used.[284] But who could blame the one-eyed general for Eumenes' final execution? The Cardian was simply too unpredictable an adversary to trust in any future coalition, as Antigonus' men appear to have vocally pointed out.[285]

The moment that Eumenes died was, as Hornblower points out, the event that emancipated Hieronymus as a historian, for thereafter he joined the hunter rather than the hunted, with no offers or mediations now tugging at his loyalties.[286] But when faced with the task of biographing these two opponents years later, Hieronymus attempted to preserve the *andreia*, the warrior virtue, of each, while permitting the deceptions that hallmarked a great general: the hero Odysseus, for example, and the Spartan cunning that Xenophon had espoused and Polybius seems to have admired. Even the laudatory *Cyropaedia* permitted a lesson on chicanery.[287] Hieronymus' early pages had additionally needed to salvage Eumenes from the Perdiccan wreckage (the chiliarch's charges against Antigonus were termed 'false and unjust') and then carefully preserve the *arete* of those he subsequently served, whilst maintaining a sense of *isothenes*, balance, in their competing skills.[288]

As one example, the 100-talent bribe Antigonus offered for non-lethal defection at Orcynia appears to have been recorded by Hieronymus; it was an offer that the cavalry officer, Apollonides, readily accepted, though he was captured by Eumenes and summarily hanged.[289] But to balance the books and throw some legitimacy Antigonus' way, Hieronymus made it clear he was heavily outnumbered, thus justifying the clandestine necessity.[290] And though Eumenes and Antigonus were undoubtedly prepared to destroy one another's army, a complete absence of personal hatred is implied by Hieronymus' account; differences were purely political and battle was the unfortunate consequence of that.

So there remained an overall *dikaiosune*, 'justness', to the confrontations and once again this might have represented an autobiographical perspective. The detail of Antigonus' attempts to bribe Eumenes' men to deliver up his head come from Justin and Plutarch, not Diodorus (thus probably not from Hieronymus); it may be another anti-Macedonian device of Duris whose life was pulled apart by the *Diadokhoi* feuding over his home at Samos, even if they had managed to keep the island out of Athenian hands.[291]

Inevitably, there must have been occasions when Hieronymus, like Arrian, was not able to reconcile the deeds of his masters to the realities of war and the more nefarious tactics of battle. The potential use of caltrops or *abatis* (akin to wooden crisscrossed 'barbed wire') to slow the advance of cavalry and elephants was never mentioned. Such tactics were reserved for later confrontations, when Ptolemy employed 'a studded chained boom' against Demetrius' war elephants at Gaza, for example, and when 'tormented by their wounds' the beasts ground to a halt and were captured. Damis, a veteran who fought in Alexander's elephant corps in India, had shown the way at the siege of Megalopolis in 318 BCE when he himself 'studded many great frames with sharp nails and buried them in shallow trenches, concealing the projecting points' to stop the elephants that had returned to Arcadia for the first time in perhaps 300,000 years.[292] Damis' effective defence contributed to Polyperchon's failure to take the city, after which he was regarded with contempt by Greek and Macedonian alike.[293] Would Eumenes and Antigonus, who exploited all the weapons, strategies, and cunning at their disposal, have neglected the havoc of what amounted to 'anti-tank mines' in their broad *strategemata*?

Diodorus' texts are strikingly light on the detail surrounding what may have been a planned, and then delayed, invasion of Macedonia in late 313 BCE by Antigonus, when Cassander sent reinforcements into Caria to distract him from crossing to Europe, for Antigonus was next reported heading to Phrygia into winter quarters.[294] Similarly, a two-year campaign against Seleucus in Babylonia spanning the years 311/310-309/308 BCE appears to have been almost passed over by Hieronymus.[295] Diodorus' annalistic framework once again confused chronology by running the archon years of 313/312 and 312/311 together, but as Plutarch captured the conflict in greater detail, the full extent of the campaign appears misrepresented.[296] The reliable and (we assume) agenda-free Babylonian astronomical diaries, alongside the (less impartial) *Babylonian Chronicle* (*Babylonaika*) dating to ca. 280 BCE (possibly housing detail compiled by Berossus) confirmed the confrontation too.[297]

With Antigonus wintering at Celaenae, and Demetrius in Cilicia still smarting from his defeat at Gaza in spring 312 BCE, Seleucus took the opportunity to reclaim Babylon and invade the upper satrapies, while Ptolemy raped Phoenician Syria and the coastal cities of Palestine.[298] In Seleucus' absence in the East, Demetrius opportunistically seized the Babylon citadel in spring 311 BCE in a 'lightning raid', only to be ousted upon Seleucus' return; this set the scene for the full Antigonid invasion the following year.[299]

But as Plutarch revealingly commented: 'By ravaging the country Demetrius was thought to admit that it no longer belonged to his father.'[300] The fragmentary *Babylonian Chronicle*, whilst difficult to decipher, appears to focus on the chaos caused by Antigonus' invasion. If the destruction of the city was as extensive as archives suggest, then its compiler had every reason to adopt what we might conclude was a pro-Seleucus stance, and more so if Seleucus *was* the rightful inheritor of Babylonia, as we will propose.[301] The *Chronicle* and astronomical diaries recorded 'panic was present in the country' and 'weeping and mourning in the land' with further fragments suggesting food stores and treasuries were raided through 310/309 BCE (possibly from September 310 BCE to the following August). It ended with a final head-on clash in which Seleucus caught the army of Antigonus unawares at early dawn. He had partly razed Babylon and it was now full of rubble forcing Seleucus to found a new capital, Seleucia-on-Tigris, some 40 miles to the north. The new city covered 550 hectares and the populations of Borsippa, Babylon and Kytha were transported there to populate it.[302]

Finally, bested by Seleucus and with his own forces stretched across Asia Minor and the Levant, Antigonus extracted what remained of his army from Babylon in late 309 BCE; it was his return west that probably put a halt to Ptolemy's own successful campaign in Greece.[303] And with that withdrawal Antigonus lost hope of seeing any revenue from the lands to the east; in fact Demetrius' short incursion the year before marked the beginning of the 'official' Seleucid era and the arrival of Seleucus' epithet, *Nikator*, 'bringer of victory'.[304]

Diodorus' brevity may of course be due to an undetected lacuna, but it seems more likely it was Hieronymus sanitising detail of the unhappy campaigns. A year or so earlier, the treaty that followed the 'Peace of the Dynasts' in 311 BCE between Antigonus, Cassander and Lysimachus (and only later Ptolemy, who lost his claims to Syria and Phoenicia) and under which the empire was redistributed ostensibly in the name of the now teenaged King Alexander IV, omitted Seleucus completely. Diodorus' text implied the parties had agreed Babylonia was to be absorbed by Antigonus himself as part of his 'first place in Asia', and this was possibly Hieronymus' means of justifying the failed campaign that followed. But ceding Antigonus Babylonia was unlikely to have been tolerated by Ptolemy who had been operating with Seleucus, for at that stage Antigonus remained powerful enough to absorb them both, a prospect less likely if they led two satrapal armies.[305]

Other counterproductive episodes never featured in Diodorus' texts, Demetrius' cold blooded execution of Cassander's garrison commander, Dionysius, at Munychia in 307 BC, for example, and there is one further explanation for that: Hieronymus was less inclined to expand on events he did not himself witness.[306] As he initially campaigned with Eumenes after Alexander's death this would explain Seleucus' absence from the extant accounts for almost three years between his role at Triparadeisus and his hostility to Eumenes in Babylonia in 317 BCE; this was itself an event which followed Eumenes' failures in Phoenicia which were once again reported in greater detail elsewhere.[307] And yet Diodorus' later description of Seleucus' behaviour in the eastern satrapies as 'generous and gracious'[308] suggests Hieronymus (unless we are crediting him with too much influence on Diodorus) was not attempting a complete character whitewash of his patron's eastern foe, despite the treatment he afforded him in his dealings with Demetrius in the wake of defeat at Ipsus:

> It seemed a violent and outrageous proceeding that one [Seleucus] who had possessed himself of the whole domain from India to the Syrian sea should be so needy still and so beggarly in spirit as for the sake of two cities to harass a man [Demetrius] who was his relative by marriage and had suffered a reverse of fortune.[309]

When he finally settled down to put memories on scrolls, Hieronymus would have been looking out on a Seleucid Empire that encompassed almost all of the Asian satrapies his masters had fought to acquire, a bitter reflection perhaps assuaged by the knowledge that Seleucus' son, Antiochus I, was besotted with Antigonus II *Gonatas*' sister, Stratonice, who thus became queen of the eastern Seleucid realm.

Although Seleucus had once rejected Eumenes' overtures, he must have watched his duplicities with a developing interest, for he appears to have taken a leaf from the Cardian book of war, as Pyrrhus may have after him. For some three years after the battle at Gabiene, and when heading through Mesopotamia on his way to reclaiming Babylon, Seleucus motivated his own outnumbered and terror-stricken troops by relating his previous 'dream-sleep' vision of Alexander:

… when he had consulted the oracle in Branchidae, the god had greeted him as King Seleucus, and Alexander standing beside him in a dream had given him a clear sign of the leadership that was destined to fall to him in the course of time.[310]

Appian's *Syriaka* claimed the oracle at Didyma had foretold Seleucus' ascendancy in Asia when he was still serving under Alexander. So if Hieronymus' history appears free from much of the didactic digression that infected later Hellenistic-era reporting, he did see the literary value of *tyche*, the epoptic, proto-cults and *logoi* as military ruses in what was otherwise a secular history; the predictions of Seleucus' kingship may have been Hieronymus' means of accounting for such great 'enemy' success in the face of his own patrons' failures, if it was not later Seleucid propaganda.[311]

Portentous episodes do frequently appear in the *Diadokhoi* accounts of Diodorus, Arrian, Appian and Plutarch who claimed that even the *Pamphlet*-damned Medius was granted a dream vision.[312] When we consider the immense task Diodorus had set himself, it seems unlikely that the philosophical reflections that often accompanied these events originated with him, because his *Bibliotheke* otherwise exhibited little interest in such 'proto-stoic' reflectivity. Then again, we must recall his attachment to Polybius, and in turn, *his* quoting of Demetrius of Phalerum who embraced Tyche in no small way.[313] But for Hieronymus the *real* gods were the generals he served, and in the absence of a wider debate on *aition*, causality, his deference to fate and omens was perhaps simply a neat means of cauterising its strands. His 'legitimisation and delegitimisation of actions and agendas', was, as Roisman commented, 'a broadly elitist approach towards actors and history, with little credit given to their followers'.[314]

Hieronymus, purportedly long-lived and with his faculties about him to the end, was essentially a captive of his times, swept along on a Macedonian storm he could neither shelter from nor outrun.[315] His history was demonstrably, and yet understandably, partisan. An omitted campaign here, a swerved satrapy there, a character painted as capricious in-between; all grist to the mill for a 'court' historian with the power of 'judicious selection, rejection, and arrangement'.[316] In negotiating the political tides washing over him Hieronymus knew exactly which subterfuges would stick; he was after all the only (attested) person still alive in the 270s BCE who had enjoyed such an influential eyewitness position in the *Diadokhoi* intrigues. Of the hostile dynasties, only the Ptolemies and Seleucids remained powerful enough to dispute any content that unduly promoted the claims of his patrons. But, by now, these warring *epigonoi* were intermarried and they were unlikely to have cared less how the original satrapies were portioned out at Babylon, or won by the spear by their *progonoi* a half century before.

Alexander, however, did *not* reside within Hieronymus' pantheon of gods, and his legacy was manipulable for political effect. So when viewing the list of satraps and satrapies that sit within the distribution of power at Babylon, and then those within the *Pamphlet* Will, we may well be looking at the outcome through *two* distorted lenses. This is why historians need to beware when analysing the slant of the testament against what they consider the 'real historical situation' in 323 BCE, and even at Triparadeisus two or three years on, for Hieronymus was formative in the construction of each: he provided both the benchmarks *and* the comparison data.[317]

Pausanias the Greek travelographer-cum-antiquarian was a realist who understood Hieronymus' bias: 'For a man who associates with royalty cannot help being a partial historian.'[318] If Pausanias' declaration was in fact a veiled character slur, its denunciation of regal association would have encompassed all of the 'primary' Alexander historians including the Pellan Marsyas, half-brother we believe to Antigonus himself.[319] Marsyas' position must have been a very delicate one and it may explain why his history appears to have tailed off in Egypt before, or soon after, the *Diadokhoi* became the ruthless giants who surrounded him in adulthood.[320]

If Hieronymus' pages were slanted towards his patrons, encomia they were not, and neither did they encroach upon Lucian's narrow isthmus that divided history from panegyric. His admiration was anything but monotone; as Billows points out, the sibling works of Diodorus and Plutarch include some twenty-one passages that illustrated Antigonus' excessive ambition, if that latter was not Duris sourced once more. We can, in fact, see a subtle dimming in the image of the father to the brightening of his son's, in which condemnation of Antigonus' lust for power was merely an abrasion that polished the story of Demetrius' extraordinary bid for survival.[321] Pausanias concluded that Hieronymus was ultimately hostile to *all* kings except Antigonus II *Gonatas*, who was, ironically, the grandson of Antipater and so the nephew of Cassander.[322] Modern studies go further still and even propose an *anti*-Macedonian element underpinned Hieronymus' elitist narrative.[323]

Although Seleucus, Peucestas and Lysimachus faired badly in Hieronymus' pages, as did Pyrrhus in the historian's desire to please his last king, Polyperchon was afforded more mercurial treatment.[324] Hieronymus' agenda was clear: his portrait reflected Polyperchon's alignment with, or opposition to, his own patrons, firstly his support for Olympias and (it is claimed) Eumenes, and then Antigonus from 315 BCE, and finally his alliance with Cassander who arranged the termination of Alexander's Argead line. The historian's tone towards Polyperchon changes at, or soon after, Eumenes' final capture in late 316 BCE, when the previously loyal (if not dominant) *epimeletes* and regent was painted as ever more ineffectual. The final character assassination came when Alexander's son,

Heracles, faced his. The last episode may have genuinely disgusted the historian, for Polyperchon's submissive surrendering up of the teenage Heracles in 309/8 BCE in Cassander's interest for 100 talents and a share of power ended a scheme that may well have been crafted at Celaenae, for Polyperchon's survival in the Peloponnese in the years leading up to Heracles' re-emergence must have been down to Antigonus' sponsorship; this suggests a common agenda for the boy and a plan in the making.[325]

The greatest beneficiary of Hieronymus' pen remains Eumenes, and were it not for his fellow literary Cardian, the former royal secretary might have been portrayed as an undeserving Greek pawn hounded around a hostile Macedonian chessboard. On the contrary, Hieronymus made sure he was remembered as a master strategist, consummate general, friend of the queen mother, and, for a time, the most 'legitimately' backed successor east of Macedonia. This was something of a 'cleaning symbiosis' between the historian and his patron for mutual historical gain.[326] 'It is not the strongest that survive, nor the most intelligent, but those most responsive to change'; and this sums up the careers of both of famous Cardians.[327]

Aside from Alexander himself, no one of the age attracted more biographers than Eumenes. None of the long-lived dynasts, Antigonus, Ptolemy, Seleucus, nor Lysimachus, merited Plutarch's biographical attention, and it has been insightfully suggested that as Macedonians who had oppressed Greeks they presented negative models.[328] Unsurprisingly, the portrait of Eumenes embodied in the extant texts is one of outright admiration, and yet no biographer has ever proposed him as author of the *Pamphlet*.[329]

Although Eumenes left us no history 'book', if he was indeed the keeper of the royal *Ephemerides* as Aelian and Athenaeus supposed, then his entries were a truly unimpeachable account of the campaign years.[330] In which case, we should add him to our illustrious list of exiled 'historians', for in the summation of his biography of Quintus Sertorius, Plutarch stated that Eumenes had been alienated from Cardia, and in earlier corroborating text from Plutarch's *Life of Eumenes* it is clear this was courtesy of the tyrant Hecataeus.

But exile suggests his humble beginnings as a waggoner's son, so a *kakopatrides* from a lowborn father, are highly unlikely, as Plutarch surmised.[331] Yet this, like much else, was propaganda of the *Diadokhoi* type, for even Antigonus was termed a simple 'common labourer'; the same passage in Aelian reported that both Darius III and Demetrius of Phalerum were born as slaves, and it further termed Polyperchon a 'bandit'.[332] Unable to challenge his obviously important roots, someone even released a disparaging character portrayal in which Antipater denied Cassander, then aged thirty-five, the right to recline at *symposia* because he had not speared a wild boar without a net.[333] It is impossible to say just how early this material emerged but it was designed to suggest Cassander had not advanced beyond the status of the *basilikoi kynegoi*, the hunting corps of royal pages.

If Duris was the source behind claims of Eumenes' humble parentage, he may have drawn inspiration from his brother, Lynceus, for he was an author of comedies and light-hearted anecdotes. Furthermore, Duris is alleged to have studied under Theophrastus,[334] whose mentor, Aristotle, was much maligned by his association with the conspiracy to poison Alexander, claims that may (is his time) have been pinned on Eumenes.[335] With a son (or father) who won a title as an Olympian boxer, Duris may have admired Eumenes' reported talent as a wrestler, but that seems as far as his admiration went, for ultimately Eumenes was a supporter of one faction of the Macedonian regime, which, as we know, overshadowed Duris' own authority on Samos.[336]

The melded careers of Hieronymus, Eumenes and Antigonus who could have once joined forces as the outcome at Nora, were formative in the shaping of events of the early Successor Wars, and one of the most significant first publications to emerge from the era, we believe, *was* the still anonymous *Pamphlet*. Taking into account everything we know about Eumenes' brief career, between his incarceration at Nora and his death after battle at Gabiene some three years later, he alone ought to be proposed as the architect of the 'partisan scrap'.[337] It fits his behavioural patterns perfectly: he was demonstrably a born pamphleteer. From whatever angle we inspect the *Pamphlet* Will alongside the conspiracy allegations, there was only ever one man and one woman who in those years had cause to line up the names with the peculiar associations we see them in the *Liber de Morte Testamentumque Alexandri Magni*: Eumenes and Olympias.

If the three Alexandrian-influenced historians – Ptolemy, Aristobulus and Cleitarchus – had a monopoly on the recording of events up to the point of Alexander's death, the 'tragic triumvirate' of Hieronymus, Eumenes and Antigonus, dominated the shaping and the recording of the history of the next twenty years and beyond; it seems things had a way of evening out under the unique and exigent demands of the day.

NOTES

1. Plutarch *Eumenes* 3.3.
2. Plutarch *Eumenes, The Comparison of Sertorius with Eumenes* 2, translation by John Dryden 1683.
3. Plutarch *Eumenes* 10.2, translation from the Loeb Classical Library edition, 1919.
4. Pausanias 1.13.9.
5. The evolving role of the mediator in Ancient Greece discussed in Gutierrez (2012). Demeter was associated with the epithet *thesmosphoros*, 'giver of laws', and through her to Themis.
6. Plutarch *Eumenes* 1.1. For other examples of Plutarch's use of Duris see *Alcibiades* 32, *Demosthenes* 19.3. Anson (2004) p 35 cites Aelian 12.43 for the alternative background of Eumenes' father.
7. Nepos *Eumenes* 1.4-6 and 13.1 (aged twenty), also Plutarch *Eumenes* 1.1-3 for his background.
8. The most notable rift being the Pixodarus affair; see Plutarch 10.1-2 and Alexander's fleeing to Epirus following his outburst following Attalus' drunken toast; Plutarch 9.7.10, Athenaeus 13.557d, Justin 9.7.3-4.
9. *Metz Epitome* 116; see discussion in Heckel (1992) p 346. The title *hypomnematographos* is also discussed in Shipley (2000) p 264. For Eumenes' first attested cavalry command, Arrian 5.24.6.
10. Diodorus 18.58-3, Plutarch *Eumenes* 13.1, Nepos 6.3 for examples of the trust placed in Eumenes by Olympias.
11. Arrian 7.12.7 and 7.14.9-10 as an example of the tension that existed between Eumenes and Hephaestion.
12. Arrian 7.14.10. The hipparchy retained Hephaestion's name out of respect.
13. Plutarch *Eumenes* 2.3 for the wealth found in Eumenes' tent. Discussed in Anson (2004) p 42 and Berve (1926). He was awarded a golden crown at Susa, see Arrian 7.5.6. Arrian *Indike* 18.7 for the trierarch role.
14. Plutarch *Eumenes* 1.3 and Arrian 7.4.6 for Eumenes' bride; Ptolemy and Nearchus, along with Eumenes, allegedly married into the line of Artabazus; his daughter, Barsine, was the mother of Heracles, Alexander's older son; discussed further in chapter titled *Lifting the Shroud of Parrhasius*.
15. Plutarch *Eumenes* 3.2 for details of Eumenes' role in the Babylonian Settlement. Curtius 10.7.1-3 and 10.9.20 used the term *bellorum civilium Macedonibus* when describing the fighting at Babylon following Alexander's death.
16. Arrian *Events After Alexander* 1.1-3 based on the translation in Goralski (1989) p 84. Seleucus was not listed in Arrian's earlier list of the *Somatophylakes* but he may well have been elevated by 323 BCE. If the number had risen to eight and considering Hephaestion had died and Peucestas was governing Persis and the surrounding regions, then both Seleucus and Eumenes might have been enrolled. Further discussion in chapter titled *Lifting the Shroud of Parrhasius*.
17. Full discussion of the *Somatophylakes*, their numbers and background in Heckel *Somatophylakes* (1978). It was Berve who identified 14 individuals that could have qualified for inclusion. Tarn 1 (1948) p 12 identified 13 individuals with the role.
18. Arrian 6.30.2 for Peucestas' governorship of Persis.
19. Arrian 1.11.7-8 suggested the hypaspists carried the king's weapons, taken from Troy, into battle; as Peucestas allegedly carried the shield from Troy at Mallia, then he is credibly a former royal hypaspist of perhaps 200 elites. Arrian 6.28.3-4 for the seven becoming eight. The Pythagoreans associated the number seven with 'opportunity', according to Aristotle, whose lost treatise on the Pythagoreans is preserved in fragments by Alexander of Aphrodisias. See discussion in Riedweg (2002) p 194. The number seven was also associated with the wisdom of the Seven Sages of the *Epic of Gilgamesh* and Mesopotamian and Assyrian Seven Gods (the Pleiades) as well as the seven heavens and earths; Dalley (2013) p 6 for the associations of 'seven' in Mesopotamia. Arrian 6.28.4 did not include Seleucus in his line of Bodyguards but this was referring to the *Somatophylakes* at Carmania in 325/4 BCE. Seleucus was apparently later singled out for marriage honours at Susa; Arrian 7.4.6. Hephaestion died in 324 BCE requiring a further replacement. With Peucestas governing Persis, both Seleucus and Eumenes might have been enrolled as *Somatophylakes*. Further discussion earlier in the chapter.
20. Alexander's failure to conquer Cappadocia at Diodorus 18.3.1-2,18.16.1 and implied at Curtius 10.10.3.
21. Dexippus FGrH 100 F8.6; Plutarch *Eumenes* 3.2 for the extent of Eumenes' grant. Xenophon proposed the idea of founding a mercenary-based colony on the Black Sea coast but met with local opposition. Parke (1933) p 29 for discussion of Xenophon's numbers, quoting Isocrates *Panegyrikos* 4.146.
22. Arrian 2.4.2, Curtius 3.1.22-24 and 4.5.13 for the previous association of Paphlagonia with Hellespontine Phrygia.
23. Arrian 2.4.2 for Sabictas. Plutarch *Eumenes* 3.6 for Ariarathes' control of all Cappadocia. See

the discussion by Hornblower (1981) pp 240-243. Arrian 2.4.1-2 suggested Alexander had conquered the whole region. However Strabo 12.534 suggested there were two distinct Cappadocian satrapies.

24. Xenophon 7.8.25 for the inclusion of Lycaonia.
25. Ariarathes' position under Persian authority is discussed in Anson (1988) pp 471-473 footnote 4. Anson noted that Curtius did not mention a Cappadocian contingent at Issus, citing Curtius 3.2.6. Also Anson noted that Bosworth concluded the Ariaces cited by Arrian 3.8.5 might have been a mistransmission of 'Ariarathes' at the battle of Gaugamela.
26. As proposed in Anson (1988) p 474. Diodorus 18.16.2 for the mercenary contingent.
27. Lucian *How to Write History* 2.13. Diodorus 18.16.2-4 and 18.22.1 and Appian *Mithridatic Wars* 2.8 reported Ariarathes himself was tortured and impaled. Justin 13.6.1 agreed.
28. Diodorus 18.22.1-8 for Perdiccas' campaign in Pisidia.
29. Diodorus 18.33.3 for 'man of blood'; discussion of the source of the sentiment in chapter titled *Babylon: the Cipher and Rosetta Stone.*
30. Diodorus 18.23.1 for the arrival of both women. Diodorus 18.23.1, Arrian *Events After Alexander* 1.21, Justin 13.6.4 for Perdiccas' seeking the hand of Cleopatra. Only the *Heidelberg Epitome* FGrH 155F-4 suggested the marriage took place.
31. Further detail on Antigonus 'defection' to Antipater below and for Leonnatus' refusal to assist Eumenes in chapter titled *Lifting the Shroud of Parrhasius.*
32. Diodorus 18.29.6 for the convening of the council of war. Errington (1970) p 61 for discussion of Cleitus' association with Craterus. He was victorious at sea assisting Antipater in the Lamian War, receiving Lydia at Triparadeisus as a result, Diodorus 18.39.6, Arrian *Events After Alexander* 1.37. Yet Cleitus had assisted Perdiccas before his failed invasion of Egypt, see Justin 13.6.16. His new alignment with Craterus and Antipater is implied at Arrian *Events After Alexander* 1.26 with their re-crossing the Hellespont, but a change of allegiance was never specifically stated. For Cleitus' behaviour following naval victories in the Lamian War see Plutarch *Moralia* 338a. Athenaeus 12.539b-c for his walking on purple robes, and this suggesting royalty. For his victory in three naval battles see Diodorus 18.15.8-9.
33. Arrian *Events After Alexander* 24.6 for the Cyprus affair.
34. For Nicocles issuing his own coinage immediately after Alexander's death, see Bellinger (1979) p 88.
35. 'West of the Taurus' suggested by Nepos 3.2, Justin 13.6.14-15 and following the observation in Heckel (2006) p 121. Plutarch *Eumenes* 5.1 for Eumenes' wide-ranging powers.
36. Following Justin 13.6 who mentioned Antipater too, though it appears he headed south with Antigonus.
37. Arrian 2.27.6 for Neoptolemus' dissent; the havoc he caused in Armenia (Plutarch *Eumenes* 4.1) suggests he was already disdainful of central authority. Plutarch *Eumenes* 5.2-6, Diodorus 18.29.2-6, Justin 13.6.15-13.8.5, Arrian *Events After Alexander* 1.27 for his subordination to Eumenes' command and intriguing with and defection to Craterus.
38. Plutarch *Eumenes* 5.2-4, translation from the Loeb Classical Library edition, 1919.
39. Plutarch *Eumenes* 1.2.
40. Diodorus 18.29.4 and 37.1. Plutarch *Eumenes* 8.1 for the timing: '10 days after the former'. Also see Billows (1990) p 65 for the May dating.
41. Diodorus 16.35, Justin 8.2.3-5 for Philip leading a coalition of Macedonians, Thessalians and Thebans wreathed like gods. This was the so-called Battle of the Crocus Field in Thessaly. For Alexander at Tyre see Curtius 4.2.17, Arrian 2.18.1-2, Plutarch 24.3.
42. Plutarch *Eumenes* 7.4-6 for 'dashing together like triremes' and the fight, and Diodorus 18.31.1-5 for their grappling together. Also covered at Arrian *Events After Alexander* 1.27 and Justin 13.8.4.
43. Arrian 4.24.3-5 for Ptolemy's slaying and stripping the Indian leader of his armour; presumably Ptolemy provided the detail.
44. Voltaire, *Letter to Jeanne-Grâce Bosc du Bouchet, comtesse d'Argental*, 1748. It appeared in a letter to Marie-Louise, 1752: 'To hold a pen is to be at war. This world is one vast temple consecrated to discord.' Pliny 35.96 claimed Neoptolemus commissioned Apelles to paint him in a cavalry battle. Achilles had lent his armour to Patroclus who was killed by Hector who stripped the armour from him. Achilles then stripped Hector's armour from his shoulders. This appears a humiliation. Achilles' son was named Neoptolemus; *Iliad* 22.247-366 and 367 ff.
45. Plutarch *Eumenes* 6.3-6. For varying reports on how Craterus died see Plutarch *Eumenes* 7.5-6, Arrian *Events After Alexander* 1.27 Nepos 4.3-4, Diodorus 18.30.5. Pharnabazus and Phoenix commanded the cavalry against Craterus' wing; Eumenes claimed they were facing Neoptolemus and Pigres.
46. Diodorus 18.37.1-3, Arrian *Events After Alexander* 1.39, Justin 13.8.10-14.1.1, Appian *Syrian Wars* 53 for the death sentence levied on Eumenes and his outlaw status. Plutarch *Eumenes* 8.2, Diodorus 18.41.6-8 and 19.12.2 also made it clear that an assembly gathering in Egypt resulted in a death sentence.

47. For the sentence of death placed on Eumenes and fifty Perdiccans see Diodorus 18.37.1-3, Plutarch *Eumenes* 8.2, Arrian *Events After Alexander* 1.39, Justin 13.8.10-14.1.1 Appian *Syrian Wars* 53, Atalante's two daughters by Attalus apparently survived her and were later murdered with Olympias at Pydna.

48. Diodorus 18.37.2 for Attalus' marriage to Atalante; Heckel (2006) p 62 (Attalus 2) for the underlying motives.

49. Arrian *Events After Alexander* 1.38. This assumes that the Ptolemy being referenced should read 'Polemaeus' in which case he was son of Ptolemy, Antigonus' brother; Billows agrees, see Heckel (2006) p 224 for discussion.

50. Diodorus 18.39.6-7, derived from translation from the Loeb Classical Library edition, 1947 and reiterated by Arrian *Events After Alexander* 1.38.

51. Diodorus 18.50.1-2 for Antigonus' role as *strategos* of Asia Minor. For his *hegemon* or supreme commander, Diodorus 18.39.7, Arrian *Events After Alexander* 1.38. Diodorus 19.29.3 referred to Antigonus' role as 'regency'. Discussed in Anson (1992).

52. 'Constitutionalist' summarising the comment and observation in Billows (1990) p 316.

53. Plutarch *Eumenes* 8.3, translation from the Loeb Classical Library edition, 1919.

54. Arrian *Events after Alexander* 24.8 for the narrowly avoided ambush.

55. Plutarch *Eumenes* 8.4. Arrian *Events After Alexander* 1.40 for the clash at Sardis; Justin 14.1.7 and Plutarch *Eumenes* 8.6-7 for Eumenes' earlier visit to Sardis when brokering the marriage. More on Leonnatus' attempt at a union with Cleopatra in chapter titled *Lifting the Shroud of Parrhasius*.

56. Following the observation in Carney (1988) p 401 on Antipater's leniency; more on Cynnane's plight in chapters titled *The Silent Siegecraft of the Pamphleteers* and *Lifting the Shroud of Parrhasius*.

57. Curtius 3.1.11 for a vivid description of Celaenae and the surrounding countryside. Arrian 1.29 for the truce.

58. Arrian 1.29.3 for Antigonus 1,500 troops.

59. Cyrus had tasked his recruitment agents with finding Peloponnesians; Xenophon *Anabasis* 1.1.6 and 6.2.10. Parke (1933) p 29 for Isocrates' rendering of Xenophon's return.

60. Curtius 3.1.2-6 for a description of the River Marsyas and city walls.

61. Plutarch *Eumenes* 8.5-7 reported: 'Having promised to give his soldiers their pay within three days, he sold them the homesteads and castles about the country, which were full of slaves and flocks. Then every captain in the phalanx or commander of mercenaries who had bought a place was supplied by Eumenes with implements and engines of war and took it by siege; and thus every soldier received the pay that was due him.' From the Loeb Classical Library edition, 1919. Hatzopoulos (1996) p 332 for the status and garb of *philoi* and *hetairoi: purpurati* – 'clothed in purple'.

62. Plutarch *Eumenes* 8.6, translation from the Loeb Classical Library edition, 1919.

63. A translation of the recovered *Gothenburg Palimpsest* text can be found at http://www.attalus.org/translate/fgh.html.

64. Plutarch *Eumenes* 8.7-8, *Gothenburg Palimpsest* line 19 and Arrian *Events After Alexander* F1 41-42 associates Attalus and (the latter) Alcetas in negotiations with Eumenes; there is possibly a lacuna in Diodorus that lost additional detail; Wheatley (1995) p 435 and footnote 25. Diodorus 18.37.3-4, Arrian *Events After Alexander* 1.39 for Attalus' occupation of Tyre. Whether Ptolemy's annexation precipitated Attalus' departure or whether that came first is debatable.

65. Diodorus 18.39.7, Arrian *Events After Alexander* 1.43-44 and see discussion in Anson (2004) pp 125-127 for events at Celaenae, the failure of forces to combine and Eumenes' departure from Celaenae for Cappadocia. *Gothenburg Palimpsest* for Alcetas' enthusiasm; the incomplete text leaves leeway for seeing this as a cynical ruse by Alcetas.

66. Xenophon *On Horsemanship* 12.11 for the *machaera*. Xenophon's *Hipparchicus* advised the pointing forward of the lance between the horses' ears to make the approaching cavalry appear more fearsome; discussed in Hornblower (1981) p 198.

67. Thucydides 2.100.4-5 stated that in 429 BCE Macedonian cavalry wore corselets. The mosaic on the floor of the House of the Faun in Pompeii clearly shows Alexander in linothorax, but whether it was lined with metal is unknown. Curtius 4.13.25 for Alexander's reluctance to wear a cuirass.

68. Anderson (1961) p 143 for the cavalry mount armour and fuller discussion of Macedonian cavalry in Gaebel (2002) pp 161-196. Snodgrass (1967) p 90 for the construction of the linen corselet; Snodgrass (1967) p 115. Alexander wore an ornate linen corselet at Gaugamela captured from the Persians and in the Herculaneum mosaic depicting the battle at Issus he is shown in similar armour, though without a helmet. Curtius 9.3.22 suggested old armour was burned when new panoplies were issued in India, suggesting a combustible material was worn (linen or leather) and not simply metal; Curtius 8.5.4, Diodorus 17.95.4 for the new equipping before and in India, which rather suggests the burning mentioned by Curtius was as the army entered India, not well into the Indian campaign, unless these are two separate events.

69. Snodgrass (1967) p 104 for the use of the *petasos* as indicated by Xenophon.

70. Xenophon *Cyropaedia* 6.1.50, 7.1.2. Curtius 3.11.15 for the weighty protection of the Persian cavalry and 4.9.3 for description of the mailed cavalry. Cataphract, Roman *cataphracti*, stems from the Greek *kataphraktos* meaning 'fully enclosed'.

71. Sekunda (2012) p 10 for a prick-spur image.

72. Arrian 7.14.10. The hipparchy retained Hephaestion's name out of respect. Devine *Gabiene* (1985) p 93 for Eumenes' use of Alexander's cavalry techniques.

73. Plutarch *Eumenes* 9.1-2, translation from the Loeb Classical Library edition, 1919.

74. Justin 14.1.

75. Diodorus 18.40.1-6 for the two distinct defections and for Perdiccas' defection and subsequent capture by Phoenix of Tenedus; also Plutarch *Eumenes* 9.1-2.

76. Plutarch *Eumenes* 9.6, translation from the Loeb Classical Library edition, 1919; also Diodorus 18.40.8, Polyaenus 4.6.12.

77. Plutarch 57.1-3, Curtius 6.6.14-15, Polyaenus 4.30.10, Plutarch *Aemilius* 12.11 for Alexander's burning of the baggage. Diodorus 17.94.4 for the permission to plunder in India. Xenophon 4.1.12-13 burned his waggons before entering the mountains of Kurdistan in winter.

78. Diodorus 18.40.8 for Eumenes' losses. Anson (1977) p 251 footnote 1 for a discussion of the date of the battle at Orcynia.

79. *Anaklesis* is a flight from the battlefield. This episode is once more Plutarch-derived and Diodorus 18.41.1-4 made no such reference, though an earlier confrontation is possibly being described here; as it has been noted, Orcynia might have been a Cappadocian district and not a specific battleground. Only Diodorus 18.40-41 mentioned Eumenes' lost baggage train. It looks suspiciously as if Plutarch compressed the three battles into two and placed the doubling-back and funeral rites at Orcynia erroneously; see Diodorus 19.32.3.

80. Plutarch *Eumenes* 10.1 translation from the Loeb Classical Library edition, 1919. Also Justin 14.2, Diodorus 18.41.1-4, Nepos 5 for Eumenes' entry into Nora. Anson (2004) p 131 for the date the siege commenced. Diodorus 18.41.2 for 'lofty crag'.

81. Diodorus 18.41.4-6.

82. Diodorus 18.41.2-6 for the walls, ditch and pallisades; Plutarch *Eumenes* 11.1 simply mentioned 'a wall' was built around Nora.

83. Plutarch *Eumenes* 10.2-4.

84. See Heckel (2006) p 139 citing Hornblower (1981) p 6 and Diodorus 18.50.4.

85. Eumenes' 'demands' are consistently reported in both Plutarch's and Diodorus' accounts, so possibly Diodorus 18.41.7 compressed the moment for we would imagine the description of friendly relations and mutual respect was Hieronymus-derived.

86. Plutarch *Eumenes* 10.3-4, based on the translation in the Loeb Classical Library edition, 1919.

87. Plutarch *Eumenes* 10.2.

88. Diodorus 18.53.4-5 suggested the siege lasted a full year; Nepos 5.6-7 suggested six months. If both are approximations, the answer may lie in between; the dating of the battle at Orcynia is uncertain but if in spring of 319 BCE, after Eumenes had wintered in Celaenae, then Antipater's death came approximately six months later.

89. Plutarch *Eumenes* 12-13 for the oath; Nepos claimed Eumenes eluded Antigonus' officers but whether this means physically or psychologically with the oaths is uncertain.

90. Quoting Green (2007) p 36 referring to Euripides *Hippolytus* 6.12.

91. *Iliad* 9.312.

92. Plutarch *Eumenes* 12.1-2, Nepos 5.7.

93. Anson (1977) questioned the validity of the reporting of the changed oath. Anson (2004) p 136 considers it a fiction of Duris.

94. Plutarch *Eumenes* 12.3 for the return of hostages after Eumenes' release.

95. Eumenes' delay discussed in Anson (1977) p 253.

96. Plutarch *Eumenes* 12.3 and Diodorus 18.53.6-7 for Eumenes' re-gathering of forces.

97. The focus on the reporting of the battle was Eumenes' opportunity to seize Antigonus' baggage train, but in flight there is little chance Eumenes could have salvaged his own. Plutarch *Eumenes* 9.3 left it unclear whether Eumenes had the opportunity to take the enemy booty during battle or after he had doubled back from his flight to Armenia. The former is most logical when considering Menander's role.

98. Diodorus 18.59.1-2 for Menander's appointment to track down Eumenes. Strabo 14.5.10 described the location; for the Assyrian association see discussion in Bing (1973) pp 346-350. Modern excavations suggest a location on Mount Carasis high in the Taurus Mountains; discussed in Sayar (1995) pp 279–282. For the estimate of 20,000 talents see Roisman (2012) p 181. Quoting G Maspero's *History of Egypt, Chaldea, Syria, Babylonia, and Assyria,* The Grolier Society Publishers, Volume 8 part B, 1903, 'Some Assyriologists have proposed to locate these two towns in Cilicia; others place them in the Lebanon, Kundi being identified with the modern

village of Ain-Kundiya. The name of Kundu so nearly recalls that of Kuinda, the ancient fort mentioned by Strabo, to the north of Anchialê, between Tarsus and Anazarbus, that I do not hesitate to identify them, and to place Kundu in Cilicia.'

99. Diodorus 18.57.3-18.58.4, Plutarch *Eumenes* 13.1-3, Nepos 6.1-5, *Heidelberg Epitome* F 3.2 for the letters sent to Eumenes.

100. Diodorus 18.57.2-4 and 18.58.1-4. Arrian *Events after Alexander* 1.43-45 for the seventy elephants left with Antigonus and Antipater keeping the remainder; also Diodorus 19.23.2.

101. Diodorus 18.58.1-3 for the second letter offering funding and the Silver Shields. Also detailed in Plutarch *Eumenes* 13.1-2.

102. Diodorus 18.59.4-6 based on the translation from the Loeb Classical Library edition, 1947.

103. Diodorus 18.59.3 and Plutarch *Eumenes* 13.3-4. Roisman (2012) pp 177-236 for a useful study of the Silver Shields under Eumenes. Arrian *Events After Alexander* 1.38 for reference to Antipater giving Antigenes 3,000 of the most rebellious Macedonians to collect the treasure, or revenues, from Susa after Triparadeisus. For the origins of the Silver Shields see chapter titled *Sarissa Diplomacy: Macedonian Statecraft*. Heckel (1988) p 49 assumed the Silver Shields were already at Cyinda and Bosworth (2002) p 100 footnote 9 disputes this, suggesting Diodorus' reference to 'distance' placed them in Susa. Diodorus 18.58.1 however stated orders were issued to 'the generals and treasurers in Cilicia', which might suggest the Silver Shields were already billeted there. If so, the residue guard apparently feared for their safety after Eumenes departed; Diodorus 19.62.1-2. They were labelled 'troublemakers' here and it could be that the *ataktoi* and Silver Shields (both 3,000) were mistaken for one another though '3,000' appears a utility number used for a medium-sized body of men. For the formation of the *ataktoi* see chapter titled *The Reborn Wrath of Peleus' Son*. It is likely the Silver Shields were stationed in Cilicia when Perdiccas invaded Egypt in 320 BCE and enrolled them there; see Heckel (2006) p 30 (Antigenes) for discussion.

104. Billows (1990) p 277 for discussion of the *gazophylax* role and p 281 for the *phrouria* and *phrourarchoi*. Strabo 12.2.6 for his reference to the treasury of Sisines.

105. The legendary age of this veteran regiment stemmed from Diodorus 19.41.2 and was reinforced by Plutarch *Eumenes* 16.4, Justin 12.7.5 and the *Romance* 1.25.3-5 in which it was claimed the youngest of them was sixty and the oldest over seventy. The claims were repeated in other works, possibly in the belief this stemmed from an impeccable source: Hieronymus. The source was more likely Cleitarchus and as it has been pointed out, this is likely Hellenistic misinterpretation, or simple exaggeration. The *Romance* does suggest Alexander wanted to keep the elderly *hypaspistes* as instructors, which makes more sense and there is no reason to believe such elderly men still formed the active fighting ranks. Following the discussion by MCJ Miller in Watson-Miller (1992) pp 107-108.

106. Diodorus 18.60.3, translation from the Loeb Classical Library edition, 1947. Further discussion of the origins of the missives in the chapter titled *The Silent Siegecraft of the Pamphleteers*.

107. For the gift and refusal, see Diodorus 18.60.1-4.

108. Cicero *Laelius De Amicitia* 17 quoting Ennius on the fickleness of fortune. Diodorus 18.60.1.

109. Plutarch *Eumenes* 13.2, translation from the Loeb Classical Library edition, 1919.

110. Diodorus 18.60.6 for the show of insignia. Curtius 10.6.15 for Ptolemy's suggestion at Babylon. A *hieromnemon* was a religious official. It is unlikely Eumenes appealed to the soldiers themselves but the hierarchy above them; see discussion in Hornblower (1981) p 205. Diodorus 18.26.4 claimed the king's armour at least left Babylon with the funeral bier. Plutarch *Eumenes* 13.4-8, Polyaenus 4.8.2, Nepos 7.2-3, Diodorus 18.60.4-18.61.3, 19.15.3-4 for the dream vision and its employment.

111. See epilogue titled *The Return to Aegae* for more on the regalia found at Vergina and similarities (and differences) to those in extant texts.

112. Diodorus 17.16.4 for a description, for example, of the Tent of a Hundred Couches which was again more a pavilion enclosure. It was used to celebrate the departure from Macedonia in 335 BCE and taken on campaign; see Athenaeus 12.538c and 12.539d.; Aelian 9.3 described it as being held up by fifty gold pillars; the golden chair might have meant a 'throne' or represented one. Curtius 6.8.23 for the tent that housed over 6,000 men at the trial of Philotas.

113. Diodorus 18.60.4-18; Plutarch *Eumenes* 13.3-4.

114. Diodorus 18.60.6 for the insignia and throne; Arrian *Times After Alexander* 1.25 and 24.1 for the unsuccessful roles of Polemon and Attalus with the funeral bier. Diodorus 18.28.4, for example, did not refer to the insignia when describing the burial in Egypt, though we must recall Caligula allegedly took his breastplate and Caracalla seems to have taken some weapons; Suetonius *Caligula* 52, Cassius Dio 59.17.3 for Caligula taking the breastplate and *Epitome de Caesaribus Sexti Aurelia Victoris* 21.4. Herodian 4.8.9 for Caracalla's deposits and Cassius Dio 78.7.1 for his withdrawals. These (bogus) items could however have been deposited later by Ptolemy for propaganda purposes.

115. The Alexander cult on Rhodes discussed in the chapter titled *The Silent Siegecraft of the Pamphleteers.*
116. Diodorus 18.61.4.
117. Diodorus 18.61.4-5 for the recruitment drive and numbers. Xenophon *Anabasis* 1.1.8-11 for Cyrus' deception. Parke (1933) pp 231-232 for discussion of the pay to Cyrus' mercenaries. The gold daric was over ninety-five per cent pure.
118. Aristophanes *Peace* 1210 ff, written in 421 BCE. These numbers might have been comic exaggeration as an Athenian inscription of 415 BCE, just a few years later, gave prices of 2 drachmas for a secondhand javelin and 1.66 for a buttless spear. Snodgrass (1967) p 107 for detail. Anderson (1970) p 114 ff for the increasing appearance of peltasts.
119. Parke (1933) p 235 for the mercenary possessions popularised by the Greek poets. The Corinthian helmet was close-fitting and tailormade and thus might not fit a son of its original wearer. Aristophanes *Peace* 527, 1129 and *Acharnians* 1099-1101 for cheese and onions; see Anderson (1970) p 46.
120. Heckel-Jones (2006) pp 21-22 for discussion of Macedonian soldier pay rates. Curtius 5.1.45, Diodorus 17.64.6 being quoted.
121. See Billows (1990) p 262 for discussion of military costs; *misthos* for 40,000 infantry would have amounted to 2,435 talents per year but this excluded cavalry on higher pay. Parke (1933) p 233 for standard mercenary rates. Arrian for example mentioned 10-stater men at 7.23.3-5 and Sekunda (1984) pp 24-25 for discussion of double-pay men.
122. For Ptolemy's attempts to subvert the Silver Shields see Diodorus 18.62.5. Diodorus 18.62.4 for Antigonus' attempt to turn the Silver Shields; he almost succeeded as Teutamus had to be convinced by Antigenes to remain loyal to Eumenes. Diodorus 18.73.1 for Antigonus' departure for Cilicia.
123. Diodorus 18.63.6 suggested Eumenes was hoping to gather a fleet to send to Polyperchon; Polyaenus 4.6.9 reported that Phoenician crews were heading for a Cilician port laden with Eumenes' funds, presumably from Cyinda and perhaps to collect more, though we must question whether the ships were coming *from* Cilicia rather than heading to it. There is, in fact, a similarity here with Diodorus 18.52.7 describing Antigonus' assault of Ephesus where Antigonus again intercepted ships from Cilicia; we might wonder if Eumenes had sent the funds to Cleitus and was attempting to send more to him or to Olympias, perhaps via Polyperchon. Further detail of the victory over Cleitus at Polyaenus 4.6.8-9; more of Cleitus' and Arrhidaeus' defections and Olympias' pleas in chapter titled *The Silent Siegecraft of the Pamphleteers.*
124. Griffiths (1935) pp 297-316 for general discussion of mercenary pay rates. The numbers are taken from Griffiths (1935) pp 264-301 and rounded-up to account for provisions to feed the army. Discussion in Campion (2014) pp 183-184. Griffiths (1935) p 265 and p 283 for the ration allowance payments.
125. Diodorus 18.73.1 for the size of Antigonus' force. At that stage word of Peithon's aggression in the eastern provinces and the planned repercussions may well have reached Eumenes.
126. Diodorus 19.12.1-2 for Eumenes wintering in the villages of the Carians and sending out envoys to Seleucus. This could be a reference to Carrhae mentioned again at 19.91.1 where Seleucus later raised veteran troops and where Alexander had marched through on campaign; Diodorus 17.110.3.
127. Diodorus 19.13.7 and 19.15.5, translation from the Loeb Classical Library edition, 1947. Roisman (2012) p 193 footnote 40 for a discussion on the dating of this new letter; dispatch from Phoenicia seems a sound conclusion, before Eumenes headed east.
128. Heckel (2006) p 22 for discussion on Amphimachus' identity; probably 'brother of Arrhidaeus' in original manuscripts though later confused with King Philip III (Arrhidaeus). He was awarded with the governorship of Mesopotamia at Triparadeisus; Diodorus 18.39.6, Arrian *Events After Alexander* 1.35. We argue he came under the authority of Seleucus (or Perdiccas at Syria, see chapter titled *Lifting the Shroud of Parrhasius*), and yet was found operating under Eumenes at Paraetacene, Diodorus 19.27.4, so logically he defected at this point. Diodorus 18.51.1-2 and 18.72.2-3 for Arrhidaeus' activity in defiance of Antigonus.
129. Diodorus 19.12.1-3 for the failed overtures to Seleucus and Peithon and 19.12.4-19.13 for the confrontation that followed.
130. Diodorus 18.73.4 for Eumenes' numbers soon after. A useful discussion of the campaigns in Cilicia, Mesopotamia and Iran, and events surrounding its build up and aftermath, can be found in Bosworth (2002) pp 98-167. Tarn proposed Eumenes held the Babylonian citadel in October 318 BCE, see the Loeb Classical Library edition, 1919 (1968 reprint) of Diodorus 19.13.5 footnote 1 for detail.
131. Diodorus 19.15.4-6 for the continued invoking of Alexander's presence and the arrival of Eudamus with elephants.
132. For Peithon's installation of his brother see Diodorus 19.14.1-2. Diodorus used the general term 'upper satrapies' for the Eastern Empire. No satraps from the upper provinces were aligned

with Peucestas, though it was they who drove out Peithon. See chapter titled *Lifting the Shroud of Parrhasius* for further discussion.

133. Diodorus 19.13.7 explained that the forces from the regions under Peucestas' sway had already gathered to counter the threat of Peithon. We must assume Eumenes had heard of the gathering, for had he arrived in different circumstances, he might have received a rather colder reception. For the Persian lookout-post system see Diodorus 19.17.6-7 footnote 1 of the Loeb Classical Library edition, 1919 (1968 edition). Herodotus 5.52-53 for the Royal Road and courier messenger times. Also for variants on the system, Diodorus 19.57.5 and Aristotle *De Mundo* 398b 30-35 for the one-day delivery of messages to Susa and Ecbatana. Homing pigeons were in use in Greece from 776 BCE onwards when news of the Olympic Games was sent to villages this way; it is thought this was learned from Persia where Sargon employed them ca. 2,350 BCE. In Egypt their recorded use goes back to 2,900 BCE and Caesar later used them when campaigning in Gaul.

134. Herodotus 8.98, Xenophon *Cyropaedia* 8.6.17-18 and Diodorus 19.17.4-7 (amongst many others) for the Persian message system and Peucestas' summons.

135. Plutarch *Lysander* 19.5-7. A *skytale* is a tool used to perform a transposition cipher, consisting of a cylinder with a strip of leather wound around it on which is written a message. The Spartans in particular are said to have used this cipher to communicate during military campaigns. For the use of seals see Curtius 3.7.14.

136. Athenaeus 10.451d cited Apollonius as the original source. For Archilochus see FGrH 188 1-2.

137. See discussion in Collard (2004). Later references to the use of the *skytale* also appear in Plutarch, Aulus Gellius and Diodorus.

138. *Metz Epitome* 100, *Romance* 3.32.3 for Cassander contacting Antipater via a coded message from Cilicia. Whilst attached to the *Pamphlet* detail, it does suggest codes were used in such situations.

139. For the departure of Antigonus' forces from Media see Diodorus 19.24.4 and for his alliance with Peithon and Seleucus see Diodorus 19.17.2.

140. Plutarch *Eumenes* 14.2 (Pasitigris); Diodorus 19.18.3-8 (Coprates). The total number routed is closer to 10,000 but presumably many drowned in upturned boats and others escaped. Diodorus 19.18.3 for 4 *plethra* and 19.17.3 for 3-4 stades.

141. See chapter titled *The Reborn Wrath of Peleus' Son* and Plutarch 72 for the butchery of Cossaeans; Diodorus 19.19-20 for Antigonus' clash with the tribe.

142. Diodorus 19.21-22 for the geography of the journey to Persepolis and the festivities upon arrival.

143. Plutarch *Eumenes* 13.5, translation from the Loeb Classical Library edition, 1919.

144. Arrian 6.30.3 and 7.6.3 for Peucestas' adoption of the Persian language and Diodorus 19.48.5 for his popularity amongst the Persians. Strabo 15.3.9-10 confirmed Alexander ferried the wealth of Persis to Susa. Plutarch *Eumenes* 13.4 for the reference to the former friendship between Eumenes and Peucestas; Nepos 7.1 for their intense rivalry. This may be a device of Duris however to emphasise his later betrayal of Eumenes, for the reference is immediately followed by a damning description of Peucestas behaviour at 13.5-6. Heckel (1988) p 75 for 'high handed' and who agrees at the time we propose the *Pamphlet* was drafted, Peucestas showed little or no support for Eumenes; for his performance at Gabiene, Diodorus 19.42.4, Plutarch *Eumenes* 16.

145. Diodorus 19.23.2, Polyaenus 4.8.3. For Polyperchon's earlier offer to bring the army from Macedonia to support Eumenes should he need it, Diodorus 18.57.4. Diodorus stated the letter was in 'Syrian' but this presumably means 'Assyrian'. Diodorus often interchanged the terms geographically too. Arrian 3.8.5, Curtius 4.12.12 for Orontes at Gaugamela.

146. Diodorus 19.23.1-4, translation from the Loeb Classical Library edition, 1947. Diodorus 19.23.1-2 for the undermining of Sibyrtius. We might assume he fled to the enemy as Antigonus gave Sibyrtius the remnants of the Silver Shields after their capture at Gabiene; see below.

147. Diodorus 19.24.1-5.

148. Plutarch *Eumenes* 13.6.

149. Diodorus 19.24.5-5 for Eumenes' illness. Plutarch *Eumenes* 14.5-6 stated 'a few days' after the banquet, but Diodorus' account at 19.24.4-5 portrays the illness commencing once Eumenes heard of Antigonus breaking camp, so the actual timing is uncertain. Plutarch's coverage of the events that followed is far more detailed and colourful than Diodorus'.

150. Anson (2014) p 67 for discussion of the personal guard units of Eumenes, Peucestas, Leonnatus and Alcetas. Diodorus 19.29.5 and 19.28.3-4 for the guards of Eumenes and Antigonus at Paraetacene.

151. As noted and discussed by Bosworth (2002) pp 12-127 and J Roisman in Carney-Ogden (2010) pp 142-143. Arrian 6.12.1-6.13.3 for Alexander's behaviour after the Mallian battle.

152. Plutarch *Eumenes* 14.4-15.3, Diodorus 19.24.5-6.

153. Diodorus 19.25.1-3 for the relative encampments. Full battle tactics discussion in Devine *Paraetacene* (1985).

154. Diodorus 19.25.2-19.

155. Diodorus 19.26-27.
156. Diodorus 19.26.1-7.
157. *Aposkeue*, Greek for the baggage train; see discussion of its importance in Hornblower (1981) pp 188-189. It was variously referred to as *skeue, aposkeue* or *paraskeue* by Polybius, Cassius Dio and Appian, for example. Polyaenus 4.6.13 for the run-down of the baggage.
158. Diodorus 18.40.8.
159. Sekunda (1984) p 25 for supernumeraries and infantry baggage.
160. Engels (1978) p 12 for the absence of waggons, and Frontinus *Strategemata* 4.1.6. Engels (1978) p 21 for pack weights. Curtius 4.9.19-21 for a description of the pack contents for each soldier. Hanson (1991) p 39 for 70 lbs/31 kg weight of panoply alone.
161. Plutarch *Eumenes* 9.3 for the description of Antigonus' baggage train. Polyaenus 4.2 for a description of the Macedonian soldier's individual load.
162. Diodorus 18.30.2 for Craterus' promise to distribute Eumenes' baggage train. Eumenes' threat to harry the troops came after the battle with Craterus, and is recorded in papyrus PSI 12: 1284; see Goralski (1989) pp 95-96 for full transcription of the fragment and Bosworth (1978) for full discussion.
163. For discussion of possible malaria in Alexander's army and those of the *Diadokhoi*, see Borza (1987).
164. Finlay (1973) p 38 for the *philanthropon*.
165. Billows (1990) pp 286-290 for discussion on the tax system Antigonus maintained in Asia. Pseudo-Aristotle *Oikonomika* 2.1345. Arrian 1.16.7 for the tax remission for the fallen at the Granicus River.
166. Diodorus 19.27-32.
167. Diodorus 19.14.8-15.5 for Eudamus' reinforcements in which the total elephant number was 120, presumably some had perished since their arrival, and his payment of 200 talents. Diodorus 19.27-29 for the total troop numbers and formations. Bosworth (2002) p 114 views the 200 talents as a credible necessity for provisioning the elephants requiring a huge amount of food.
168. Diodorus 19.14.8. Compare this to Diodorus' description of Triparadeisus at 18.39.6 where Porus and Taxiles are left unmoved solely because it would have required a royal army to do so. This suggests Eudamus might have been encouraged to kill Porus. Arrian 6.2 1 for Porus' extended territory.
169. Diodorus 19.29.3 for Antigonus' Macedonian numbers and 27-28 for Eumenes' numbers. Diodorus simply stated Antipater had given the 8,000 Macedonians to Antigonus 'when he made him regent of the kingdom', which translates as commander-in-chief in Asia, at Triparadeisus. Additional Macedonians would have been present in the Companion Cavalry but numbers were not specified.
170. Double mounts were presumably horses carrying a spare or extra cavalryman, or, according to Livy 35.28.8, two horses per mount, and a title applied to the Tarentine cavalry who were described as skilled ambushers. Diodorus 19.29.5-6 reported that Antigonus used his own slaves as an advanced guard for his cavalry unit. Xenophon *Anabasis* 3.3.16 suggested the elliptical lead bullet flew twice as far as stones; Snodgrass (1967) p 84 for detail. Eumenes had two 50 cavalry-strong *ilai* of slaves accompanying him; see Diodorus 19.28.3. *Amphippoi* might be corrupted and even asthippoi or asphippoi; see chapter titled *Sarissa Diplomacy: Macedonian Statecraft* for discussion.
171. Billows (1991) p 310 for discussion of the *pantodapoi*, the unit mentioned at Diodorus 19.29.3. At Paraetacenae both Antigenes and Peucestas had their own cavalry *agema* as did Eumenes, and at Cretopolis Alcetas had his own pages and hypaspists, Diodorus 18.45.3. Plutarch *Eumenes* mentioned Eumenes' own bodyguard of 1,000 soldiers and Polyaenus 4.6.8 mentioned Antigonus boarding his best hypaspists on ships; following discussion in Anson (1988).
172. Following Heckel-Jones (2006) p 43 for the *syntagma* additions.
173. Hanson (1991) p110 ff for the construction of the *salpinx*.
174. Following Heckel-Jones (2006) p 43 for the *syntagma* additions.
175. An alternative view sees the *skytalis* attached to each fighter's wrist so the dead could be identified but the risk of losing the stick in battle would have been high; this and the muster roll discussed in Hanson (1991) pp 56-57.
176. Diodorus 19.31.5 for the death toll and wounded.
177. Diodorus 19.31.3-5. Eumenes' men would not occupy the battlefield to recover the dead due to their concern with the unguarded baggage train, leaving Antigonus able to do so and claim victory. But he himself was forced to send his baggage train on ahead to a neighbouring city for security; Diodorus 19.32.1-2.
178. Xenophon *Anabasis* 4.7.25 ff and Plutarch *Agesilaus* 19.2 and *Timoleon* 29.4 for examples of the *tropaion* being erected.
179. Polyaenus 4.6.10; the location of the battle is not specified but the circumstances sound like

Paraetacene.

180. Diodorus 19.34.1-6 for Ceteus' funeral and the cremation of his wife. Diodorus 18.32.2 for mention of a 'trophy' being set up after battle with Craterus.

181. Polyaenus 4.6.11 for the description of the land separating the armies. Diodorus 19.37-38 for the full account of their wintering and the relative distances between them at 19.34.8. The Gadamala mentioned at Diodorus 19.37.1 may well be the same Gamarga mentioned at 19.32.2.

182. Plutarch *Eumenes* 15.4-7 and Diodorus 18.38.1-4 for the ruses involving fire.

183. Diodorus 19.38-39 and Nepos 8-9 for the manoeuvring in the region of Gabiene and Plutarch *Eumenes* 15.6-15.7. Xenophon's *Hipparchikos* (*On Horsemanship*) provided lessons on how to make a small force appear large and surely both Eumenes and Antigonus were familiar with the text.

184. Plutarch *Eumenes* 15.3-4, Nepos 8.1-4 for the separation of Eumenes' troops. Eumenes' claim that he could gather his commanders in three to four days, suggesting as Roisman (2012) p 27 noted that the bulk of the army was close to Gabiene.

185. Diodorus 19.39-40.

186. Diodorus 19.82.3 for the ranks at Gaza. In musth, a sexually heightened state, males can become highly and uncharacteristically aggressive.

187. Samansiri-Weerakoon (2007) for elephant consumption. Diodorus 18.68.3 for Polyperchon's lack of supplies to see through the siege of Athens and Diodorus 19.49.2-3 for the death of the starved elephants at Pydna.

188. Roisman (2012) pp 98-99 for discussion of elephant logistics and Engels (1978) p 155. Engels (1978) p 16 for the average daily march of the army.

189. Herodotus 7.187, Diogenes Laertius 8.18 for the daily ration of 1 *cheonix* of grain in the Persian army.

190. Engels (1978) p 14 for mule and camels porterage figures and p 19 for pack animal estimates. Whilst Engels proposed one pack animal per fifty men, this is still significant and discounts baggage, any machinery and the tools of camp followers. Engels (1978) p 124 for the calorie and protein requirements of each soldier. The Persians had a history of eating camels and horses; Herodotus 1.133 and 4.143 ff.

191. Polyaenus 4.6.11 for the desert description and water cask numbers; also Diodorus 19.37.1-6, Nepos 18.8.4-9, Plutarch *Eumenes* 15.8-13.

192. Engels (1978) p 38 for crop consumption of the army on the march and pp 56, 38 and 27 for the foraging area; also discussed in Engels (1980) p 330; pp 145-149 for charts showing total weights of provisions required and army personnel sizes.

193. For Alexander's repayment of debt see Curtius 10.2.8, Diodorus 17.109.2 and quoting Justin 12.11.2-4. For the talent per man see Arrian 7.12.2. Whilst not necessarily restricted to infantry, it seems likely that they, and not the better-paid cavalry, accumulated the majority of the debt.

194. The roles of Nearchus and Menander discussed further in later chapters. Menander had been governor of Lydia since early in the campaign; see Arrian 3.6.7. He was reconfirmed at Babylon: Diodorus 18.3.1, Justin 13.4.15, Curtius 10.10.2, Dexippus FGrH 100 F8.2, Arrian *Events After Alexander* 1.6. Nearchus had likewise governed Lycia and Pamphylia early in the campaign, Arrian 3.6.6, Justin 13.4.15, whilst Nearchus' activity post-Babylon is unattested until he reappeared in the region of Telmessus in Lycia in 320/319 BCE; Polyaenus 5.35. Justin 13.4.15 alone granted Nearchus Lycia and Pamphylia at Babylon, which might once again be compression with earlier detail.

195. Discussed in Anson (1988) p 475; Diodorus 19.29-2-3 gave a description of the make up of Antigonus' mixed army. As pointed out by Roisman (2012) p 25, fresh recruits did not have baggage waggons to lose.

196. Plutarch *Eumenes* 16.1-3 for the planned and reported treachery at Gabiene; Antigenes was mentioned but his subsequent fate suggests Teutamus led the intrigue, see Heckel (2006) p 262 for discussion of *ignaris ducibus* suggested Antigenes' ignorance. For the possible *strategos* role see Heckel (1992) p 333.

197. Plutarch *Eumenes* 16.4-5; Diodorus 19.41.1-2, translation from the Loeb Classical Library edition, 1947. Eumenes is not directly credited with the plan, however it seems highly likely he was its architect when considering his other psychological ruses. Xennias' role is captured in papyrus PSI 12: 1284 See Goralski (1989) pp 95-96 for full transcription of the fragment and Bosworth (1978) for full discussion. Homer refers to Ares as 'Enyalius' in the *Iliad*. Sekunda (1984) for the origins of *Alalalai*.

198. Diodorus 19.40-43 for the battle and 19.43.5 for the Silver Shields blaming Peucestas' performance for the defeat. Plutarch *Eumenes* 16.5.5 for Peucestas' performance at Gabiene: 'lax and ignoble' translated from the Loeb Classical Library edition, 1919.

199. For explanation of *purgoi* in Homer see Van Wees (1994) p 4. Xenophon 3.1.36, 4.19-20, 4.19.28, 4.19.43; Anson (2013) p 50 for detail.

200. Polyaenus 4.6.13 suggested 300 losses compared with 5,000 for Antigonus; in fact Polyaenus reported Eumenes' soldiers were in high spirits at the end of the first day of battle until they learned of the loss of their baggage.
201. Justin 14.3 for the '2,000 women and a few children'; Plutarch *Eumenes* 18.1 for the Silver Shields' responses.
202. Kebric (1977) p 22, in contrast, sees Duris as generally laudatory to Eumenes, regarding his claim that he was a poor waggoner's son as a means to emphasise his achievement. The use of Duris is somewhat backed up by Plutarch's *Comparison of Eumenes with Sertorius* 2.3-4 in which he alleged the same.
203. Nepos 11.1, Plutarch *Eumenes* 18.2 for the instructions to guard Eumenes. Diodorus 19.42-44 and Plutarch *Eumenes* 16-18 for the outcome of battle at Gabiene; the pleas to spare him at Plutarch *Eumenes* 18.6, Nepos 10.3, Diodorus 19.44.2. Plutarch *Eumenes* 18.3 and 18.2 for the Silver Shields' claims to their baggage. Justin 14.3, possibly drawing from Duris, claimed Eumenes attempted to flee and only when captured again did he demand the right to deliver his final scathing speech. There is some confusion again between the accounts of Diodorus and Plutarch. The 'surrounded Silver Shields' in Plutarch's account are in the camp of Eumenes arguing the merits of fighting on. Additionally, the speech provided to them by Plutarch refers to the 'three nights' the captive wives with the baggage train had been 'sleeping with the enemy' which suggests a protracted period before Eumenes was finally given up to Antigonus.
204. Nepos 13 for Eumenes' age. Anson (2004) p 35 footnote 1 for age discussion.
205. Anson (2014) p 125 for discussion on the fate of Amphimachus and Stasander. See discussion of Stasander's role and identity in chapter titled *The Silent Siegecraft of the Pamphleteers*. Quoting Plutarch *Eumenes* 19.2, also Polyaenus 4.6.15, Diodorus 19.48.3-4; the remaining Silver Shields included those who betrayed Eumenes, so Teutamus might have been with them; Heckel (2006) p 262. Arrian related that Megasthenes spent time with Sibyrtius in Arachosia when visiting the court of Chandragupta.
206. Polyaenus 4.6.15, Diodorus 19.48.3, Plutarch *Eumenes* 19.3 and Justin 14.3.3-4 and 18 for the various fates of the disbanded Silver Shields. Bosworth (2002) p 235 theorised that the troops recruited from Carrhae, and with which Antigonus successfully stormed the citadel of Babylon in 311 BCE comprised brigade veterans. Roisman (2012) p 16 believes that Antigonus sent the Silver Shields to aid Sibyrtius and counter the rising power of Chandragupta, the Indian ruler. Disputed by Roisman (2012) p 237. But if they were that effective, why send them away?
207. Diodorus 19.35.5 for those under siege at Pydna.
208. Diodorus 19.49-52 for Olympias' end and quoting from the Loeb Classical Library edition, 1947 and from Justin 14.6, translation by Rev. JS Watson, 1853. Justin 14.6.1-13, Polyaenus 4.11.3 for further detail. Carney (2006) pp 104-105 for Olympias' burial and Aeacid reverence and Diodorus 17.118.2 for her corpse remaining unburied; Olympias' possible tomb discussed further in chapter titled *Lifting the Shroud of Parrhasius*.
209. Plutarch *Eumenes* 18.1 for the title given Eumenes: 'pest from the Chersonese'.
210. Following Anson (1980) for Alexander and Perdiccas shielding Eumenes from the full Macedonian prejudice. See Anson (2004) p 233 for Eumenes' open admittance of his 'handicap' referencing Plutarch *Eumenes* 1.3, Diodorus 18.60.3-4, Nepos 7.1-2.
211. Plutarch *Demetrius* 31; we know that Craterus amicably passed on his Persian wife Amastris to Dionysius of Heraclea.
212. Nepos 13, Plutarch *Eumenes* 19.1-2.
213. Plutarch *Eumenes* 1.3 and Arrian 7.4.6 for references to Eumenes' marriage to a daughter of Artabazus. The sources conflict on her name. Plutarch Eumenes 7.1 for Pharnabazus' support for Eumenes; he was the son of Artabazus. The identity of Eumenes' wife discussed in chapter titled *Lifting the Shroud of Parrhasius*.
214. For Philip II see Aelian 7.12; for Lysander see Diodorus 10.9.1 and Plutarch *Lysander* 8.4.
215. Plutarch *Moralia* 182a or *Remarkable Sayings of Kings and Commanders*, *Antigonus*, translated by W Hinton, Little Brown and Co., Boston, 1878.
216. Plutarch *Eumenes* 10.3, translation from the Loeb Classical Library edition, 1919.
217. According to Nepos 1, Eumenes was secretary to Philip for seven years before the king's death. Alexander's campaign headed south after the battle at Issus in 333 BCE leaving Antigonus to suppress remnants of Persian resistance. Nearchus headed to join Alexander in 331 BCE and Antigonus assumed control of a larger region including Phrygia, Lycia and Pamphylia in-between. Thus Eumenes could have only had perhaps two years of contact with Antigonus in the early campaign. See Diodorus 18.3.1 for detail.
218. 'Offstage' was a term used by Errington (1969) p 234. Bagnall-Derow (2004) p 1 for the decree of Priene. Arrian 2.1.3-3.2.7 for Pharnabazus' activities in Asia Minor. Curtius 4.1.34-35 and 4.15.13 recorded his campaign to mop-up remnants after the battle at Issus and his subsequent role in supporting battles in Cappadocia, Lycaonia and Paphlagonia. This included three battles

as well as skirmishes. Arrian 2.13.2-4 for the 8,000 escapees after Issus fleeing to Tripolis.

219. Tarn (1948) p 110 made the point that there was a bottleneck in the Royal Road where Cappadocia pressed upon it from the north. Engels (1980) p 331 for the description of the Royal Roads. Herodotus 5.52-53 for the number of relay stations and related distances.

220. Hornblower (1981) p 75 for Polyaenus' Macedonian descent. Polyaenus' book 4 focused on Antigonus' deeds. Polyaenus 4.6.1-20 for the list of Antigonus' stratagems.

221. Quoting Plutarch *Moralia* (*Sayings of Kings and Commanders*) 182a. See Anson (2004) p 189 for the timing of Eumenes' death. Anson concludes it was January 315 BCE. Diodorus' 19.44.2-4 accounts suggested very late 316 BCE though the delay between his capture and execution is not stated.

222. Heckel (2006) p 32 and p 234 (Ptolemy 2), p 224 (Antigonus' nephew, Polemaeus), p 156 (Marsyas) for the possible identity of Antigonus' siblings. Diodorus 19.62.7-9 for the actions of Antigonus' nephew Dioscorides and 19.74.1-2 and 19.87.1-3 for Telesphorus, possibly a third nephew; see Diogenes Laertius 5.79.

223. A full discussion of Antigonus' personality and physique in Hornblower (1981) pp 211-226. Plutarch *Demetrius* 28.3 for an example of Antigonus' voice and character.

224. For Antigonus' use of Asiatic cavalry see discussion in Anson (1988) p 475.

225. See discussion in Billows (1990) p 317. For Antigonus' stubborn streak see discussion in Hornblower (1981) pp 216-222. It was Plutarch who claimed that Antigonus would not let anyone in on his plans. The origins of castrametation discussed in Anderson (1970) p 59 ff.

226. Diodorus 18.62.4-6 and Diodorus 18.63-64.

227. Diodorus 18 73.1.

228. See discussion in Billows (1990) p 318; as an example Polyaenus 4.6.12, Diodorus 19.29.1, 19.26.7.

229. As examples, Polyaenus 4.6.19 in which Antigonus had a soldier announce the (false) arrival of allies before Eumenes' ambassadors; Eumenes in turn lit fires outside Gabiene to suggest he had a defensive battle order; Plutarch *Eumenes* 15.4-7 and Diodorus 18.38.1-4 .

230. Diodorus 19.29.1, translation from the Loeb Classical Library edition, 1947.

231. Devine *Gabiene* (1985) for full discussion of the battle and tactics.

232. Diodorus 18.50.1-3. Diodorus 19.56.5 for the income statement and 19.22.1 for his status.

233. Diodorus 19.7.3 and 19.18.1 made it clear that Eumenes, empowered by the 'kings', had previously ordered Xenophilus not to provide Antigonus with funds from the Susa treasury. Diodorus 19.48.5-8 for the removal of Xenophilus.

234. Diodorus 19.18.1 for Antigonus extending Seleucus' satrapal control to include Susiane, and Diodorus 19.48.6-8 for his stripping of the Susa treasure.

235. Herodotus 7.27; also Athenaeus 12.514f. The vine stood with a golden plane tree in the chamber of the Persian King.

236. Diodorus 19.46.6 for the 5,000 talents from Ecbatana and entering into Persia; 19.48.6 for the total of 25,000 talents.

237. Diodorus 19.46.1-4, Polyaenus 4.6.14 for Peithon's execution. Diodorus 19.55.2 for Antigonus' journey with the treasure to Babylon. Diodorus 19.48.8 for the sum of 25,000 talents in total removed by Antigonus from various treasuries. Following Billows (1990) pp 240-241 for discussion of Antigonus' empire strategy and p 257 for the use of Sardis (Polyaenus 4.9.4) and Pergamum (Strabo 13.623 and Pausanias 1.8.1) as treasuries.

238. Diodorus 19.55.2-3 for Antigonus' arrival in Babylon and treatment of Seleucus; Diodorus 19.55.4-6 and 19.56.1 for his flight to Egypt and confirmation of Seleucus' knowledge of the removal of Peithon and Peucestas. Diodorus referred to Babylon but nevertheless termed it the 'country' (19.55.3) suggesting Seleucus governed the whole province not the city. Appian *Syrian Wars* 53 claimed Seleucus punished a *hegemon* without Antigonus' permission, leading to the rift.

239. Diodorus 19.61.5 for the commencement and length of the siege of Tyre.

240. Diodorus 19.62.8-9 for the complement of Antigonus' navy and 58.2 for its construction.

241. Quoting Diodorus 21.1.2 and Diodorus 20.113 for Ptolemy's retreat back to Egypt from Sidon upon hearing false reports that Antigonus was advancing south.

242. Diodorus 20.112 for Cassander's troop losses; he had sent a previous contingent under Prepelaus. Diodorus 20.113.1 for the false letter proclaiming Antigonus' victory over Seleucus and Lysimachus, on which basis Ptolemy stopped his advance at Sidon.

243. Plutarch *Demetrius* 29.1-2 for Antigonus' fall. For his mood and usual countenance see Plutarch *Demetrius* 28-29. For the Chaldean prophesies see Diodorus 19.55.6-9. For Antigonus' state of mind before Ipsus see discussion in Hadley (1969) pp 142-152. For Hieronymus' use of *logoi* see Hadley (1974) p 56.

244. Diodorus 19.55.7.

245. The saying was attributed to Plato by General Douglas MacArthur's farewell address to the cadets at West Point in May 1962, yet the quote cannot actually be traced to any of the writings

of Plato. It could be read in G Santayana, *Soliloquies in England*, Scribners, 1924 p 102, Soliloquy 25, *Tipperary*, in a section which reads: 'Yet the poor fellows think they are safe! They think that the war is over! Only the dead have seen the end of war.' Santayana does not attribute the saying to Plato or anybody else for that matter. Yet the attribution again appeared on the wall of the Imperial War Museum in London.

246. Plutarch *Demetrius* 28.2. Heckel-Jones pp 14-15 for *sarissai* lengths; Polyaenus 2.29.2 suggested they had lengthened to 16 cubits or 24 feet by 300 BCE before being reduced in length gain after.

247. Plutarch *Demetrius* 28.3, Diodorus 20.110-113 for a description of the army and numbers, which vary somewhat.

248. See discussion in Billows (1990) p 181 and Diodorus 21.1.1-4 for remnants of the account of the battle.

249. Plutarch *Demetrius* 28.2, translation from the Loeb Classical Library edition, 1920.

250. Plutarch *Demetrius* 29.1-2, translation from the Loeb Classical Library edition, 1920.

251. Sources frequently mentioned that horses loathed the smell of elephants and would not readily approach them. See Plutarch *Demetrius* 29.3 for the line of elephants thrown in Demetrius' way.

252. Plutarch *Demetrius* has Antigonus aged 'little short' of eighty in 306 BCE. Porphyry of Tyre in FGrH 260 F32 claimed he was eighty-six when he died. Also Pseudo-Lucian *Makrobioi* 11. Diodorus 20.113.5 for his reference to the 'kings'. For the lifespan of the time see RA Gabriel and KS Metz, *The History of Military Medicine, Volume 1, From Ancient Times to the Middle Ages*, Greenwood Press, 1992, p 28.

253. Plutarch *Demetrius* 29.4-5; Diodorus 21.1.4b for the royal honours paid.

254. Following Billows (1990) p 315 for the propaganda failure of Ipsus.

255. Reiterating the observation made in Billows (1990) p 319 and quoting Plutarch *Demetrius* 30.1 for the carving up of the empire after Ipsus as if it were a 'great carcass'.

256. Pliny 35.90 and 96 recorded the paintings; discussion in Billows (1990) p 312. See discussion in Billows (1990) p 10; Antigonus was sensitive about his single eye though he joked about it. Plutarch *Moralia* 11b or *On the Education of Children* 14; Pliny 35.90 cited by Hornblower (1981) p 223.

257. Cicero *De Natura Deorum* 2.87.

258. Plutarch *Phocion* 29.1-2.

259. Polybius 31.2.11.

260. 'To live well is to live concealed', Ovid *Tristia* 3.4.25.

261. See Hornblower (1981) p 234 for details of Hieronymus' exile from his homeland. Also Diodorus 19.44.3-4 for his wounds.

262. Hornblower (1981) p 10 for discussion. Diodorus cited Hieronymus in action at 18.42.1,18.50.5, 19.44.3, and 19.100.2, in each case confirming him as historian of the wars.

263. Diodorus 19.96.4 ff and Plutarch *Demetrius* 7.1 for the Nabatean campaign and 19.100.1-4. *Mumiya* is Persian for asphalt. Billows (1990) p 288 for the harvesting of papyrus for ship cables (Pliny 13.73) and the frankincense trade, as described in Theophrastus *On Plants* 9.4.8.

264. Plutarch *Demetrius* 39.3-7 for Hieronymus' role at Thebes.

265. See chapter titled *The Silent Siegecraft of the Pamphleteers* for fuller discussion of Hieronymus' role at Nora. Diodorus 19.94-100 for the Syrian expeditions and 19.98-99 for Hieronymus' description of the asphalt extraction from the Dead Sea and 19.100.1-2 for Hieronymus' role in its collection. For his position as *Harmostes* at Thebes see discussion in Hornblower (1981) p 10 and p 12, Plutarch *Demetrius* 39.3-7 for that role in the interests of Demetrius and for detail of the Boeotian rebellion.

266. Diogenes Laertius *Zeno of Citium*. Polybius 5.10.10 for Antigonid claims to Argead descent and 8.36 for Persaeus' role at Corinth. Statues in the portico of Antigonus *Gonatas* (or *Doson*) on Delos began with Heracles. The name of Antigonus *Monophthalmos'* wife, Stratonice, was uniquely attested within the royal family.

267. Following the logic presented by Brown (1947) pp 694-695 for Hieronymus' treatment of *Gonatas*. Following Carney (2002) p 108 for the association of *Gonatas* with the Great Tumulus at Vergina; discussed in chapter epilogue titled *The Return to Aegae*. This covered five smaller earlier tumuli housing the tombs of the kings. Carney-Ogden (2010) pp 119-121 for Tomb III discussions. Adams (1991) p 28 for the format of the Great Tumulus. Plutarch *Pyrrhus* 26.6 and Diodorus 22.12 for the earlier looting by Gallic mercenaries.

268. Nearchus and Medius served with Hieronymus under Antipater after the battle at Gabiene. Hornblower (1981) suggested they might have been information sources for Hieronymus for events he was not himself an eyewitness to.

269. Diodorus 19.69.1 and 19.81.1 for his 'friend's advice' to avoid battle, thus confirming a relationship.

270. For the aftermath of Gaza and Ptolemy's chivalry and return of Demetrius' personal effects, Justin 15.1 and Diodorus 19.85.3. See Anson (2004) pp 23-25 for discussion. Anson does

however suggest Diodorus used his own vocabulary. Examples of the reciprocated chivalry can be found in Plutarch *Demetrius* 6.3 describing Demetrius' lenient treatment of the captured Cilles, a seeming repayment for the kindness of Ptolemy after Demetrius' defeat at Gaza. Diodorus 19.86.1-4 for the aftermath of Tyre.

271. Diodorus 20.73.1 for the death of Philip, Antigonus' son, and Diodorus 20.73.1-2 for Antigonus' invasion of Egypt.

272. Diodorus 20.75.1 ff for the bribes and desertions. Griffiths (1935) p 114 for the calculation of 5,000 Macedones at the core of Ptolemy's army. Ptolemy fought at Gaza with 18,000 infantry and 4,000 cavalry but captured 8,000 of Demetrius' men and had them sent to Egypt; Diodorus 19.85.5.

273. Diodorus 20.83.1-20.85.5 for the siege of Rhodes. See discussion of Hieronymus' eyewitness role in Brown (1947) p 685; the wounds and his participation in battles detailed at Pseudo-Lucian *Makrobioi* 22 suggest that Hieronymus could have given an eyewitness account of the battle and Antigonus' death.

274. Hieronymus' whereabouts at the time of Demetrius' death are unknown but if already serving Antigonus *Gonatas* he would certainly have known of the captivity of Demetrius, under Seleucus' guard, and would have received regular reports on his hopeless fate. Plutarch *Demetrius* 1.7: a description given when comparing Demetrius to Mark Antony. Plutarch *Demetrius* 19.6 reported that the Scythians would twang their bowstrings to 'summon back their courage when it is dissolved in pleasure'. He was in fact referring to Demetrius' earlier ability to immerse himself in both pleasure and preparations for war with equal effect and without compromising either. Phila had married Balacrus in the mid-330s BCE, Craterus in 322/321 BCE and finally Demetrius in 320 BCE. She bore three sons and a daughter.

275. Pausanias 1.9.7-8 cited Hieronymus as a source for the accusation that Lysimachus desecrated the graves of the Aeacids during the war with Pyrrhus. Pausanias (cf Carney (2006) p 77) did however voice his doubt and reported that Hieronymus was angered by the destruction of Cardia. Pausanias 1.9.8, Diodorus 22.12 and Plutarch *Pyrrhus* 16.6-7 blamed Pyrrhus' own Gallic troops. Pyrrhus was thrown out of Macedonia by Lysimachus two years later; discussion in Stewart (1993) pp 285-286.

276. Quoting WS Ferguson in his review of Tarn's *Antigonus Gonatas*, Classical Philology, Volume 9 No.3, July 1913, p 323. *Gonatas* had Philochorus the Attidographer executed for his anti-Macedonian stance; see discussion in Hornblower (1981) p 185. He also executed Oxythemis, probably the brother or nephew of Medius of Larissa; Billows (1990) p 414 for discussion. Stewart (1993) p 287 for *Gonatas*' association with Pan. Diogenes Laertius 2.127, 5.58, 5.67, 4.41 for *Gonatas*' association with philosophers. Athenaeus 13.578a-b for Medius' execution.

277. A citation in Strabo 11.530 suggested Medius wrote to some extent on the nature of the lands he campaigned in. See Billows (1990) p 401 for discussion.

278. Quoting Green (1990) p 143 for the 'first Stoic king'.

279. Quoting Rostovtzeff *Social and Economic History of the Hellenistic World, 1*, Oxford, 1941, p 2 and Brown (1947) pp 691-3 and p 688. Plutarch *Pyrrhus* 21.12 for proof that Hieronymus used Pyrrhus' memoirs when constructing his own history and Plutarch *Moralia* 119c-d (*Consolation to Apollonius*) and Aelian 3.5 for the death of *Gonatas*' son and his stoic acceptance.

280. Diodorus 19.44.1-4 and Plutarch *Eumenes* 18-19 for the expanded account.

281. Plutarch *Eumenes* 18.2 and 19.1.

282. Diodorus 19.48.5 for Peucestas' fate. Diodorus 19.22.2 stated Peucestas had chosen many Asiatic advisers.

283. Quoting Hornblower (1981) p 104; Antigonus *Gonatas* weeping for the death of Pyrrhus for example at Plutarch *Pyrrhus* 34.4. Plutarch *Eumenes* 7.8 for Eumenes weeping over Craterus.

284. See Billows (1990) p 28 on Duris' anti-Antigonid stance. Nepos 12 claimed a mutiny was brewing because Antigonus had kept Eumenes alive after the council that demanded his death; he was allegedly dispatched by his guards on the third day without food (Antigonus had already delayed seven days) and the guards had his body removed from camp without Antigonus' knowledge. Plutarch *Eumenes* 18-19 follows closely though Antigonus did order his execution on the third day.

285. Hornblower (1981) p 211.

286. Following Hornblower (1980) p 197 for comparisons to Odysseus and Spartan resourcefulness in which theft was encouraged, for example in Xenophon's *Hipparchikos* 5.11. Xenophon *Cyropaedia* 1.6.27 for the advice from Cyrus' father on generalship that promoted cunning. Also Polybius 12.27.10-11 and 12.28.1 for apparently well-known admiration of Odysseus and Pausanias 8.30.8; full discussion in McGing (2010) pp 129-130.

287. Diodorus 18.23.4 for Perdiccas' charges against Antigonus.

288. Diodorus 18.40.5-8, Plutarch *Eumenes* 9.2-3 for Apollonides' treachery and death. Also see Anson (2004) pp 128-130 for discussion of the events at Orcynia.

289. Discussed in *Bryn Mawr Classical Review* 30th June 2003 of the work by C Schäfer *Eumenes von Cardia und der Kampf um die Macht im Alexanderreich*, Buchverlag Marthe Clauss, Frankfurt, 2002, p 194.

290. Justin 14.1, Plutarch *Eumenes* 8.11. Discussed further in chapter titled *The Silent Siegecraft of the Pamphleteers*. The Samian appealed to Antigonus *Monophthalmos* for protection after the Polyperchon regime supported Athens' claim to the island in 319 BCE.

291. Diodorus 18.71.2 for Damis' experience and 18.71.6 for the siege at Megalopolis and Damis' defence; 19.83.2 and 19.84.1-3 for Ptolemy's use of caltrops at Gaza. Remains of a Lower Paleolithic elephant butchering site have been found near modern Megalopolis dating back to 300,000 to 600,000 years (Middle Pleistocene age); Science Daily, November 25th 2015.

292. Diodorus 18.74.1 for the contempt in which Polyperchon was held.

293. Diodorus 19.68.2 implied that Cassander expected Antigonus to cross to Europe and so he sent his own forces into Caria to distract him; Diodorus 19.66.1 pinned this action after a reference to the years 314/313 BCE based upon his Archon references.

294. See chronology arguments in Geller (1990) pp 1-7 and Wheatley (2002). Diodorus does mention an attack on Babylon by Demetrius that echoed that war. Diodorus 19.100.3-7 for details of Demetrius' entry into 'abandoned' Babylon. Also Bosworth (2002) pp 222-225.

295. Plutarch *Demetrius* 7.2-5.

296. The *Babylonian Chronicle* was first published with translation and commentary in 1924; see discussion in Hornblower (1981) pp 111-112. See Hornblower (1981) pp 111-114 citing Smith (1924) who proposed Berossus as author. The *Chronicle* covered the period from 320/19 to late 309 BCE. Further details in Bosworth (2002) p 21 and p 210.

297. Bosworth (2002) pp 227-226 for the dating of the battle at Gaza and Seleucus' return to Babylon. Diodorus 19.90-93 for the period under scrutiny. Diodorus 19.93.7 for Ptolemy's rape and destruction of the coastal cities of Phoenician Syria and Palestine.

298. This follows the reconstruction of Bosworth (2002) pp 216-230.

299. Quoting Wheatley (2002) p 46 for 'lightning raid'. Plutarch *Demetrius* 7.3 for the observation on his father's loss.

300. See chapter titled *Lifting the Shroud of Parrhasius* for discussion of Seleucus inheritance of Babylon.

301. Translation of both the astronomical diaries and *Babylonian Chronicle* in Geller (1990) pp 1-7. Geller argues the chronology slippage caused by Diodorus' method has confused historians and he placed the 'lost' campaign in 312/311. Discussed in detail in Hornblower (1981) pp 114-115 and in Bosworth (2002) pp 211-245. The exact date of the founding of Seleucia is uncertain and dates between 312 BCE and 305 BCE have been offered; if the destruction of the campaign of 310-308 BCE made Babylon irretrievable as a capital, then the date must have been post-308 BCE. Seleucia was sited on the confluence of the Tigris and a canal that flowed to the Euphrates, at the site of an old Babylonian settlement of Akshak. Wheatley (2002) p 41 outlines the conflicting dates of August-September 310 to January-February 309 BCE; Wheatley (2002) p 43 for the 'weeping and mourning' and p 44 for the final battle following Polyaenus 4.9.1 if attributable (not stated) to this date. Archibald-Davies-Gabrielson (2005) p 32 for the estimated size of Seleucia-on-Tigris.

302. Following the observation of Wheatley (2002) p 46.

303. Diodorus 19.100.3 for Antigonus giving up hope of gaining income from the lands east of Babylon.

304. Diodorus 19.105.1. His assistance to Seleucus was no doubt to produce a combined front that could contain Antigonus. In return Seleucus would have been asked for pledges of support if Egypt was invaded. Whilst Billows (2002) pp 242-243, for example, sees Lysimachus and Cassander abandoning Seleucus, whose recent revival was threatening, it is more likely Ptolemy still considered the principal threat came from Antigonus. Anson (2014) p 149 for Ptolemy being added to the 'peace' after the European-based satraps. For Ptolemy's late entry into the peace accord, see the letter from Antigonus to Scepsis; full discussion in Munro (1899).

305. Demetrius' murder of Dionysius did not feature in Diodorus but appeared in the *Suda*; see Simpson (1959) p 374.

306. Diodorus 18.73.3-5 for Seleucus' attack on Eumenes, and Diodorus 18.39.5-6 for Seleucus' confirmation as satrap of Babylonia and Arrian *Events After Alexander* 1.35. For the unreported campaign in Phoenicia, Polyaenus 4.6.8 and see discussion in Hornblower (1981) p 75. For the episode at Triparadeisus involving Seleucus, Arrian *Events After Alexander* 1.32-33, Diodorus 18.39.4 Polyaenus 4.6.4.

307. Diodorus 19.91.2-92.5 used these terms when describing the loyalty of the inhabitants of Babylonia, Susiane and Media.

308. Plutarch *Demetrius* 32.4-5.

309. Diodorus 19.90.4; Pyrrhus used a similar tactic in 288 BCE when invading Macedonia; Plutarch *Pyrrhus* 11.2.

310. Quoting Hornblower (1981) p 180 for the secular reference. Appian *Syrian Wars* 56 for the Didyma oracle.
311. Plutarch *Demetrius* 19.1-2 for Medius' dream vision concerning Antigonus' forthcoming campaign. Hadley (1969) for the detail of Hieronymus' use of portents and predictions. Examples at Diodorus 19.90, Appian *Syrian Wars* 56, Plutarch *Demetrius* 29.1-2, Justin 15.4.
312. See Hornblower (1981) p 107. It seems Hieronymus attributed much to *tyche* but avoided other divine digressions. The strategic use of superstition in a military capacity was however more interesting to him. Chapter titled *Sarissa Diplomacy: Macedonian Statecraft* for more on Polybius' quoting Demetrius of Phalerum.
313. Roisman (2012) p 18 and pp 9-30 for a discussion of the bias in Hieronymus.
314. Discussed in Brown (1947) p 685 citing Pseudo-Lucian *Makrobioi* 22; age 104 drawing from Agatharchides.
315. Macaulay (1828).
316. Diodorus 18.3.1. Arrian *Events After Alexander* 1.34-38, Justin 13.4.15, Curtius 10.10.2 As an example, the prosopography of Heckel (1988) attempts to triangulate the political leaning of the *Pamphlet's* author by comparing the satrapal allocations made in the *Pamphlet* Will with 'the historical situation' in 323 BCE. However that so-called historical situation is Hieronymus-derived.
317. Pausanias 1.13.8.
318. Marsyas of Pella was likely Antigonus' half-brother. A citation in Strabo 11.530 suggested Medius wrote to some degree on the lands he campaigned in. See Billows (1990) p 401 for discussion.
319. For Marsyas' career see Billows (1990) pp 399-400.
320. Lucian *How to Write History* 7 for the analogy to an isthmus. Billows (1990) pp 319-320 on Hieronymus' bias, which highlighted Antigonus' ambition. Also see discussion in Hadley (1969) p 149.
321. Antigonus II *Gonatas* was born to Demetrius *Poliorketes* by Phila, daughter of Antipater and sister of Cassander.
322. Roisman (2012) pp 9-30 for a discussion of Hieronymus' anti-Macedonian stance.
323. Examples of Hieronymus' hostile treatment of Peucestas at Diodorus 19.38.1, 42.2, 43.5; discussed in Hornblower (1981) p 155. Hornblower (1981) p 17 citing Pausanias for Hieronymus slandering Lysimachus and Pyrrhus. For Hieronymus' treatment of Peucestas see discussion in Roisman (2012) pp 13-14. See Justin 13.6.9 and Plutarch *Phocion* 23-25 for Polyperchon's behaviour after Antipater's death. Diodorus' portrait is one of a man who was manipulated by Cassander; see discussion in Wheatley (1998) p 12.
324. As proposed by Wheatley (1998) pp 13-14. For the death of Heracles, Diodorus 20.28, Justin 15.2.3, Pausanias 9.7.2 and for discussion of his identity see chapter titled *Lifting the Shroud of Parrhasius*. See Diodorus 18.74.1 for Polyperchon's failure at Megalopolis and 18.75.1-3 for his 'lack of energy and wisdom'; 20.20.1-3 for his ambition; 20.28.2 for his fickle character; 20.100.6 for his 'plundering' of Greece; 20.103.7 for his 'failure to come to aid'.
325. Herodotus noticed the symbiotic relationship of the crocodile and birds who picked leeches from its mouth to clean it, and then flew out unharmed; mentioned by Pliny 6.2.25.
326. Attributed to Charles Darwin, the quote cannot be found in his works in this form, and seems to be a summary of many conclusions found in his *On the Origin of Species*.
327. Following the argument of Shipley (2000) p 13.
328. It has been alternatively argued that the encomiastic treatment of Eumenes against a more neutral background in Diodorus' texts comes from Duris; namely Diodorus 18.57.3-4; 58.2-4; 59.3; 60.4-63.6; 58.1; Plutarch *Eumenes,* 1.4-5; 12.2-4; 12.6-7. As identified in Hadley (2001) p 32.
329. Aelian 3.23.
330. For Hecataeus' early career and use by Alexander see Diodorus 17.2.5 (and implied by Curtius 7.1.38) for his role in the crossing to Asia and assassination of Attalus. Nepos gave an explanation that in Greece, royal secretaries only came from a good family, which also argues against allegations of low birth, as does Plutarch *Eumenes* 1.2 that has Eumenes' father in a guest-friend relationship with Philip.
331. Aelian 12.43.
332. Athenaeus 1.17e-18a for reference to Cassander. The slander could have been linked to Antipater soon before his death and thus emerged as late as 319 BCE; it came from Hegesander and survives in Athenaeus 1.18a. The allegation applied to 319 BCE at the latest when his father died.
333. Athenaeus book 4.128a for reference to Duris studying under Theophrastus though this is a 19th century emendation and may not be accurate. This is not universally accepted: see Dalby (1991) for summary of the debate.

334. Proposed light-heartedly, though Kebric (1997) assumes Duris may have drawn detail from Lynceus for his own history. Duris' influence discussed in Hadley (2001). See Hornblower (1981) p 235 on their different perspective and Antigonid affiliations. Also Kebric (1977) p 5 for Duris' contact with Antigonus. Billows (1990) pp 333-336 for a summary of Duris' career; he might have only been a child when Antigonus came to power.

335. Plutarch *Eumenes* 1.1-2. Philip II first noted Eumenes' wrestling ability. See also Kebric (1977) p 2 for Duris' career and p 2 for his father's Olympic victory. Pausanias 6.13.5 believed a commemorative was to Duris' son who won the boy's boxing title; some scholars refute this and believe Duris was too young to have a son 'when the Samians were in exile' and so credit the boxing victory to his father.

336. Quoting Carney (2006) p 110 for 'scrap of partisan literature'.

11

THE SILENT SIEGECRAFT OF
THE PAMPHLETEERS

**Under what circumstances might the detail of
Alexander's testament and the conspiracy to kill
him have first been circulated, and for what specific
purpose?**

The tumultuous years between 320 and 315 BCE revealed the true nature
and subterfuges of the alliance between Eumenes, Polyperchon, Olympias
and Cleopatra, and also the extent of the opposition arrayed against it.

We analyse the specific detail within the *Pamphlet* and argue why the
Will and the conspiracy were constructed as we read them. Finally, we try
and pinpoint the timing of its release and why its incendiary claims never
achieved their intended outcome.

'Shut up there and surrounded by the enemy with a double wall, he [Eumenes] had no one to give him aid in his own misfortune. When the siege had lasted a year and hope of safety had been abandoned, there suddenly appeared an unexpected deliverance from his plight; for Antigonus who was besieging him and bent on destroying him, changed his plan, invited him to share in his own undertakings.'[1]

Diodorus *Bibliotheke*

'Where the skin of the lion does not reach, it must be patched with the skin of a fox.'[2]

Plutarch *Apophthegms* or *Sayings of Kings and Commanders*

In 1813 John Macdonald Kinneir, a captain in the service of the East India Company, explored an ancient stone fortress above a deep gorge known as both 'Yengi Bar' and 'Nour', and he was convinced it was Nora, a site referred to as 'Neroassus' in Strabo's day. In 1923 William Mitchell Ramsay published his *Military Operations on the North Front of Mount Taurus IV: The Campaigns of 319 and 320 B.C.* in which he recounted his own 1891 journey to discover the site at which Antigonus had fought Perdiccas' brother, Alcetas, in the 'funnel' of the Pisidic Aulon.[3] He noted the abundance of castle ruins close to the Taurus Mountains, even if, as he pointed out: 'Taurus was a general term given by the ancients to anything of a gigantic nature.'[4] Only one site exhibited natural springs, a necessary feature to align it with Plutarch's description of 'water in abundance' flowing down from a natural source. 'Neroassus' most likely translated as 'the castle of Nerreus' and the site did sit broadly where Plutarch related: a 'small… but wonderfully strong' grain-stocked stronghold for Eumenes to flee to following battle with Antigonus at Orcynia, another debated location and a name otherwise unknown.[5]

The exact location of Nora *remains* unidentified. Yet within that impregnable stone fortress in the Phrygian highlands, or on the confines of Lycaonia and the Cappadocian Plateau, contemplating his fate and the permutations of the outcomes with the odds stacked against him, Eumenes may well have conceived of the content of the *Pamphlet*.[6] The shockwaves from this precision-guided weapon targeted everyone then in power, with a range that reached from India to Epirus. Although its blast was short-lived, the fallout lingered on until it had been safely contained by Ptolemy's *Journal*. But its heat signature remained in what we have come to name *The Book of the Death and Testament of Alexander the Great*.

If the months of siege at Nora did inspire Eumenes to craft his path of retribution, when amongst his later invocations of the ghost of Alexander, the epistolary subterfuges, the forced campaign marches and the full-scale battles, did his unique *kykeon*, his propaganda cup, finally appear? Two significant factors hamper attempts at an exact dating: our sources' methodologies and the corruption of the texts which house the *Pamphlet* remnants today.

THEROS, TRYGOS, POLEMOS: SUMMER, HARVEST, WAR

Diodorus' *Biblotheka* remains the fullest coverage of events of the years 319-315 BCE in which the siege and its aftermath fell. What becomes clear from a comparison with the calculated length of Arrian's *Events After Alexander,* itself a précis of Hieronymus, is that Diodorus' compression was at times drastic.[7] Arrian needed ten books to cover the years 323 to 318 BCE whereas the same period occupies only Diodorus' eighteenth book.[8] Fragments of Duris suggest the Samian historian covered the same period at the pace of one and a half to two years per book, though he appears to have sped ahead with his narrative after Eumenes' death.[9]

Alongside the severe culling of detail we have the challenge of unravelling the order of events: Diodorus divided his chapters into synthetic campaign years in which little monthly or seasonal direction was provided, save his references to the hardships winter placed on operating; this was a method likely employed by Hieronymus himself, most likely following Thucydides and Xenophon before him.[10] And so *theros, trygos, polemos*, summer, harvest and war, all merged together in a less than coherent sequence. Diodorus additionally tried to synchronise the Roman consular year (January-January by his day) with the Athenian archon year (summer to summer) whilst attempting to adhere to Hieronymus' overall progression, but he filled gaps he found in his narrative – detail of affairs in Greece, for example, which Hieronymus did not personally witness – by drawing from other historians such as Diyllus.[11] In the process, Diodorus occasionally predated his entries against the eponymous archon change to more effectively introduce new subject matter, and as a result he was often six months or more off the pace. But only three of the five archon changes in the years 323-319 BCE were recorded, with no reference provided at all for the years 321/320 BCE and 320/319 BCE.[12]

Plutarch was even less concerned about being clinical on the sequence of events, as long as the resulting narrative satisfied his character development and the thematic shape he sought. So we have a conspicuous lack of syncronicity between his and Diodorus' account in which a lamentable lacuna sits between the *synedrion* at Triparadeisus, and the battle at Orcynia,[13] whilst almost all of the latter half of 320 BCE is 'passed over in silence'.[14]

Many scholars have dedicated lengthy studies to elucidating and solving the problem, noting that even the Triparadeisus settlement may have been wrongly dated; modern interpretations place the gathering of generals anywhere from summer 321 (the 'high' chronology, as suggested, imperfectly, by Diodorus' text) to mid-320 BCE (the 'low' chronology, suggested by the *Parian Chronicle* and *Babylonian Chronicle*, and which we follow), though hybrid theories place events somewhere in between. If the date of Perdiccas' death *can* be anchored down by the latter to May/June 320 BCE, the meeting of generals at Triparadeisus should have logically followed soon after.[15] But the *Babylonian Chronicle* and the *Parian Chronicle* only provide chronological safe anchorages here and there, and the latter is far from reliable.[16] As it has been pointed out, everything can be reinterpreted by the subtle shunting back and forward of a war council, a flotilla launch, or an envoy's arrival in between.

Nevertheless, studies of the *Liber de Morte Testamentumque Alexandri Magni*, which represents the *Pamphlet* in its modified form, have pinpointed two broad periods that best suit its original publication: 322-321 BCE, or better still, 319-316 BCE.[17] The latter period significantly commenced with the siege of Nora, and ended with Eumenes' death after battle at Gabiene (so the close of 316 BCE or beggining if 315 BCE). Within these dates, broadly occupied by the Second *Diadokhoi* War, several windows of opportunity, or moments of desperation, manifested themselves, and each could have precipitated the *Pamphlet*'s release. If we systematically break down its content, we can narrow down the moment at which the strategic rehash of Alexander's Will was broadcast to the fragmenting Macedonian-governed world.

'THE ARROGANCE OF THE FORTUNATE AND THE DESPAIR OF THE DESTITUTE'[18]

Eumenes' early attempts at a negotiated settlement at Nora failed; it seems he had been asking for more than his hopeless position deserved. Diodorus' text appears unequivocal on what happened next: Antigonus referred the matter back to Antipater, the royal regent in Pella. Eumenes also '... later sent envoys to Antipater to discuss the terms of surrender. Their leader was Hieronymus, who has written the history of the Successors.'[19] The reference to 'later' is vexing, but whenever Hieronymus undertook the journey as Eumenes' *presbeis*, he would have needed his besieger's blessing and potentially his protection, for Hieronymus may have been on the proscription list of Perdiccans drawn up at Triparadeisus if he was operating with Eumenes when Craterus was killed;[20] it is possible that Hieronymus departed Nora for Pella with Antigonus' own envoy, Aristodemus of Miletus.[21]

More confusing still is the implication that Antigonus, in his position as the Macedonian regent's *strategos* of Asia, was obliged to seek the regent's advice on Eumenes' fate; his mandate had given him plenipotentiary powers to hunt the Perdiccans down and put them to the sword, as the fate of others made quite clear. One possible explanation would be the fame of the siege, perhaps as notorious as Eumenes himself, for: 'No one else had been so much talked about in the army since the death of Craterus.'[22] If discussed from Pella to Persis and with a situation so unique, starving the occupants of Nora to submission, and executing the now powerless Eumenes without at least soliciting Antipater's blessing, might have broadcast ambition Antigonus was not quite ready to unveil: the *philotimia* and *philarchia* that Antipater already suspected.[23]

If Eumenes *was* pressing for his claims to be heard in Pella, he was simply buying time. No doubt he planned to ask Antipater, perhaps already known to be ill, to extend a similar offer of reconciliation to that he proferred to Eumenes before his confrontation with Craterus, terms Eumenes then rejected due to old enmities.[24] Although he had nothing to lose from diplomacy, Eumenes cannot have hoped for much: he had urged Perdiccas to repudiate Antipater's daughter, Nicaea, as a prelude to his invasion of Macedonia, he had widowed another of the regent's daughters (married to Craterus) and come close to a clash with Antipater himself at Sardis, a conflict saved only by a warning from Cleopatra's intelligence system. Moreover, he had bettered Antipater to an embarrassing extent in Lydia or Phrygia before taking Celaenae, if the content of the *Gothenburg Palimpsest* is reliable.[25] Any reply from Pella would likely be a death sentence and perhaps Antigonus knew it, explaining why he acquiesced to the embassy – as useful for Eumenes as bringing owls to Athens.[26] When considering that Eumenes remained incarcerated at Nora until *after* Antipater's death, we may conclude the answer from Pella was to continue the siege, assuming the embassy arrived before the regent expired.

When briefing Hieronymus for the journey, Eumenes would have tasked him with contacting Olympias who was still based in the Molossian region of Epirus, and possibly with getting word to Cleopatra who was now alone as an 'unofficial' hostage of Antigonus in Sardis.[27] If Eumenes expected a death sentence from the regent, he also knew he had an ally in Alexander's mother; Diodorus did report that some Molossians joined the Greek alliance against Antipater in the Lamian War, though their initial support ended in treachery soon after.[28] But there does exist a clear epistolary tradition that details Olympias' denigration of Antipater, and, in turn, it captures his complaints about her obduracy which had already prompted Alexander's famous quip: 'She was charging him a high rent for ten months' accommodation inside her womb.'[29]

Plutarch believed Alexander had even warned Antipater about a plot being laid against him, and if not specifically named, Olympias is a strong candidate as its architect, though this appears later embellishment to the tale that was possibly motivated (or supported) by the conspiracy detailed in the *Pamphlet*. Plutarch went as far as stating: 'Olympias and Cleopatra had raised a faction, Olympias taking Epirus, and Cleopatra Macedonia.' When he heard of it, Alexander allegedly commented that his mother had made the better choice, for '... the Macedonians would not submit to be reigned over by a woman'. More plausible is Antipater's deathbed caution: 'Never permit a woman to be *prostates* of a kingdom.'[30]

Antigonus notionally controlled the flow of information into Nora but it would have benefited him to reveal to Eumenes the gravity of his position. The proscribed Perdiccan confederates under Docimus, Attalus and Polemon were in a siege that was to last sixteen months in Phrygia and which would end with their deaths or defections.[31] The necrology may have included Laomedon, the displaced satrap of Coele-Syria, care of Ptolemy's annexation. Alcetas, faced with an impossible situation, finally committed suicide at Termussus in Pisidia and his body was posthumously mutilated, whilst Holcias and his 3,000 renegades had been rounded up more locally and their fate was in the balance.[32] Moreover, Eumenes had himself been served a painful reminder of his non-Macedonian origins at Orcynia, with significant defections from his ranks before, during, and after the battle; enlisting and retaining Macedonians was becoming the labour of Sysiphus for the Cardian Greek.

Antipater still dominated Pella and the dynastic stakes through a clutch of eligible daughters: the second-time widowed Phila, with an infant son by Craterus who had amicably passed on his Persian wife Amastris to Dionysius of Heraclea, remarried Antigonus' son, Demetrius, and Nicaea, following the rejection by Perdiccas, was sought by Lysimachus (probably before Antipater died).[33] Ptolemy had married a third wife, Eurydice, sometime in 321/320 BCE. The defeated pro-Perdiccan *Somatophylax*, Aristonus, had agreed to retire to Macedonia under Antipater's watchful eye, and Polyperchon had crossed to Europe with Craterus and supported Antipater in the Lamian War. Its successful conclusion saw the regent maintaining his stranglehold over Greece through the oligarchies he had installed over the previous fifteen years.[34] Additionally, White Cleitus, the former Perdiccan fleet commander, had been confirmed as satrap of Lydia at Triparadeisus in return for naval assistance given to the regent.[35]

Now, months into the siege, Eumenes cannot have truly fancied his chances of survival any more than a *thalamios* on a sinking trireme.[36] Supplies were dwindling and despite his ingenious mechanical device for exercising his horses, the military mounts must have looked more like meals even though Eumenes 'seasoned' what remained with 'charm and friendliness'.[37] 'Whatsoever friends asked to be dismissed because they could not endure the asperities of the place and the constraint in diet, all these he sent away, after bestowing upon them tokens of affection and kindness.' And underlining the plight of those who remained was the knowledge that Antigonus now commanded the most powerful force in Asia under a single Macedonian general: 60,000 infantry, 10,000 cavalry and thirty war elephants, with 'pay without end' if more were required.[38]

Cornelius Nepos, however, provided unique additional detail that might allow us to reconsider the true nature of Eumenes' plight: he claimed that: 'During that siege, as often as he desired, he either set on fire or demolished the works and defences of Antigonus.' Nepos further implied that Eumenes could have broken out, but he was awaiting spring and meanwhile 'pretended to be desirous of surrendering', and treating for terms.[39] If Eumenes was indeed playing a delaying tactic, it was to exploit any one of several outcomes: a new offer from Antigonus, the appearance of Perdiccan renegades still operating in the region, the death of Antipater, or as Nepos suggested, better breakout weather, for the mountain passes may well have been snowbound. The friends Eumenes dismissed may have been able to slip away individually and get word to supporters, and an escape in the planning explains the need to keep horses in shape. Antipater died first, and with him any death sentence appears to have expired, as Antigonus' next move suggests.

Having dealt with Alcetas, who had been attempting to install himself in Pisidia – perhaps more legitimately than historians have assumed – Antigonus was now on his way to his customary winter quartering at Celaenae when Aristodemus arrived with news of the regent's death; this points to late 319 BCE. Antigonus had reached Cretopolis ('city of the Cretans', most likely strategically located in Pisidia) and was reportedly 'delighted' at the turn of events, whereupon he prepared to make an offer to Eumenes, apparently prompted by the knowledge that Polyperchon had been appointed in Antipater's place.[40]

Hieronymus had either recently returned from Macedonia, perhaps in the company of Aristodemus once more, or he had already returned to Nora when he was summoned to hear Antigonus' terms.[41] Before agreeing to Eumenes' freedom, Antigonus unsuccessfully invited Hieronymus to join him with the promise of 'great gifts'. This raises several questions: was this offer independent of Eumenes' fate, or was Hieronymus being enrolled in order to turn his patron to Antigonus' cause? And had Hieronymus operated under the one-eyed general before in an otherwise undocumented career? We may never know, but Diodorus provided a typically stoic philosophical summation that was unlikely to have been wholly of his own design: 'For in the inconstancy and irregularity of events history furnishes a corrective for both the arrogance of the fortunate and the despair of the destitute.'[42]

With Antipater dead, Antigonus must have considered himself the foremost of *all* the surviving Macedonian generals, both in Europe and in Asia; and Polyperchon, as events were to prove, was maleable, and Antigonus must have known it. Furthermore, Cassander, always suspicious of Antigonus' plans, had been subordinated in the process to a role he would not accept: Polyperchon's second-in-command, one last evocation of the 'chiliarch' role.[43]

At the conclusion of negotiations, Antigonus invited Eumenes to 'share in his own undertakings', offering him a pardon, 'a greater satrapy besides' and 'gifts many times the value of what he had' before;[44] these are somewhat reminiscent of the terms Antipater had offered earlier.[45] Nepos claimed Eumenes only signed the (purportedly amended) oath of release at the approach of spring, thus early 318 BCE. The release date is sound as the likely distance from Nora to Celaenae (from summons to final agreement, a journey possibly twice made by Hieronymus) and the demands of winter travelling in the mountainous region, speak of a deal being brokered many weeks before.

Antigonus was now in his early sixties. The assimilation of an extended Asia Minor, and even the whole Asian empire, must have seemed possible to him. As Diodorus put it:

> Antigonus made up his mind to maintain a firm grip upon the government of Asia and to yield the rule of that continent to no one... Indeed he had in mind to go through Asia, remove the existing satraps, and reorganise the positions of command in favour of his friends.[46]

There was, however, much to marshal in Asia Minor in the first step of assimilation, and in-between Antigonus and Macedonia already stood an apparently accommodating Lysimachus in Thrace.[47] But there was one missing ingredient that would provide the approbation his muscle-flexing needed: official support of the Argead house. The royal line now potentially had Olympias as its figurehead, and Antigonus knew full well that she would return to the centre of Pellan policy with Polyperchon holding the regency for two incapable kings. Antigonus also knew that without approval of the 'kings' his men-at-arms did not constitute a royal army at all, for with the death of Antipater his own state mandate had lapsed. That meant royal treasuries were closed to him too, unless he went renegade. Eumenes must have positioned himself as the missing regal link in either scenario; had he maintained his support for Antigonus and not (allegedly) doctored the oath, the face of the Asian empire would have assumed a totally different complexion, as Plutarch pondered when comparing the fate of Eumenes with Quintus Sertorius.[48]

A 19th century view of Castle Lampron by Victor Langlois which appeared in *Voyage dans la Cilicie. La route de Tarse en Cappadoce*, Revue archéologique XXVI, 1856/7. Locally known as Namrun (earlier Nemrod), it sits amid the valleys that run from the Taurus Mountains' watershed to the sea and must be a contender for the unknown location of Nora, though other suitable and more remote peaks do exist. Sitting broadly where Plutarch described, Namrun guarded the pass leading to Cilicia, which may explain why it was already grain-stocked when Eumenes arrived. The ruins visible are of a Byzantine-period spur castle though signs of far earlier occupation exist, including a rock-hewn dry 'moat'. Its circumference broadly matches descriptions, as do water features and its impregnability.[49] Sheer cliffs leave one approachable path where Antigonus could have arranged his ditch and palisade. Greek inscriptions have been found carved into the rock.

APO MECHANES THEOS: LIKE GOD FROM THE MACHINE

Polyperchon the son of Simmias of the Macedonian Tymphaean aristocracy was a notable and high profile campaign veteran, yet he has been labelled 'a jackal among lions' for his performance and manoeuvrings in the Successor Wars.[50] And he does fit somewhat uneasily into the general scheme of things, if the portrait we see in Diodorus is anywhere near accurate.

Curtius claimed Alexander had once vocally rejected Polyperchon's advice (termed a subterfuge), likening it to the council provided by 'brigands and thieves'. This hostile treatment extended into the texts of Aelian who, indeed, termed him a brigand, and Athenaeus, who (drawing from Duris) described him as a 'dancer when drunk'. Curtius went as far as claiming Alexander once threw him in prison after he mocked a Persian performing *proskynesis*.[51] This sounds like propaganda, for Alexander entrusted Polyperchon with significant responsibilities; he became a *taxiarches* commanding a *taxeis* of some 1,500 *pezhetairoi* (plus thirty or so supernumeraries) from 330-325 BCE, operating alongside the likes of the prominent infantry commanders Coenus and Meleager. He was later designated second-in-command to Craterus when escorting some 10,000 veterans back to Macedonia from Opis.[52] Polyperchon's own son, Alexander, had been appointed a personal bodyguard to the new kings at Triparadeisus, and a year or two on in late 319 BCE, now likely well into his sixties, he was at Antipater's bedside when the failing regent passed away.[53]

Antipater had retained his position in Macedonia from an unexpected combination of events: the clamour for his continued regency by the infantry at Babylon, his eventual (though much assisted) victory in the Lamian War, and the early deaths of Leonnatus, Perdiccas, and then Craterus, any of whom could have challenged for the regency or even the throne. His alleged Aetolian secrets and his abrasive relations with Olympias aside, Antipater appears to have displayed nothing but loyalty to the Argead house until the end, despite the execution of his son-in-law, Alexander Lyncestis. The *Pamphlet* allegations, along with the regent's reported fear of being summoned to execution in Babylon, have led some scholars to conclude he had actually rebelled against Alexander in 323 BCE, but the evidence is scant and circumstantial.

Antipater had been among the first of Philip's generals to acknowledge Alexander as king upon his father's death, though as it has been aptly put, there is a difference between loyal service and devotion to an individual.[54] It was also claimed that Alexander maintained the affectionate salutation, *chairein* (formally 'greetings', less formally 'joy to you'), exclusively with Phocion in Athens with Antipater too, who presided over the Pythian Games in place of his king.[55] His presence had certainly helped Philip II rest more easily, if Plutarch's *Sayings of Kings and Commanders* are accurate (and by him): after oversleeping on campaign, Philip explained, 'I slept soundly because Antipater watched.'[56]

Antipater, in turn, had confidence in Polyperchon, entrusting him with the defence of the kingdom when campaigning in Greece in the Lamian War.[57] On his deathbed, and to the disgust of his son, Cassander, Antipater passed the regency to Polyperchon; he was now *epimeletes kai strategos autokrator*: the principal guardian of the kings *and* caretaker of the kingdom.[58] The choice was, in fact, unsurprising when reviewing his career, for 'Polyperchon, who was almost the oldest of those who had campaigned with Alexander, was held in honour by the Macedonians.'[59]

Unfortunately, this new arrangement in Pella both overestimated Polyperchon's ability and underestimated Cassander's ambition, which would feed off his father's well-established network of agents. Moreover, Cassander was to prove remarkably good at operating on limited resources, a skill he must have learned from his father.[60] This potentially fractious state of affairs doubtless added to Antigonus' delight, plotting as he was his own independence across the Hellespont. But understanding what took place next requires the unravelling of a severely knotted and tight-packed string of events that were formative to the shape, and the issue date, of the *Pamphlet*.

A disgruntled Cassander immediately aligned himself in Pella with Adea, now Queen Eurydice by virtue of her marriage to the mentally deficient Arrhidaeus, crowned King Philip III by the recalcitrant infantry at Babylon, though we argue that the crowning was in line with Alexander's wishes. It seems Eurydice exerted control over her husband despite Polyperchon's attempt to exploit the halfwit himself.[61] She was the daughter of Cynnane, Alexander's widowed warlike half-sister who reportedly slew the Illyrian queen, Caeria, with her own hands when in her mid-teens; it was perhaps a clan revenge killing on behalf of her Illyrian grandmother Audata, Philip's first or second wife who had also taken the regal title 'Eurydice'. Cynnane had never been afforded (as far as we know) a state-celebrated marriage by Philip like that given to Cleopatra and Alexander Molossus.[62] Her husband Amyntas, the son of former King Perdiccas III (thus Philip's nephew), was executed by Alexander on accusations of treason at Philip's death, but Amyntas had left Cynnane with child: Adea.[63] Alexander had attempted a useful new political match for Cynnane with Langarus, king of the Agrianians, before departing on campaign, but Langarus died before the marriage ceremony took place.[64] The Agrianians, a Paeonian tribe, nevertheless became an indispensable part of Alexander's campaigning army.

Sometime before Perdiccas' failed invasion of Egypt in 320 BCE, Cynnane raised her own corps of Macedonian soldiers (probably a modest bodyguard contingent despite Polyaenus' inference otherwise) and crossed the River Strymon into Thrace and onto Asia with Adea (who was not older than fifteen) against Antipater's wishes.[65] Previously living in obscurity in Macedonia under Antipater's watchful eye, Cynnane clearly saw their chance to re-enter the dynastic game; as Polyaenus put it, 'upon Alexander's death, his generals parcelled out his dominions among themselves, in exclusion of the royal family', or so it must have appeared to the Roman historians who never contemplated the historicity of the Will. Cynnane next demanded that Adea be presented as a bride to the newly elevated Arrhidaeus, and it was not the first time the hapless halfwit had been strategically targeted for marriage.[66]

Perdiccas, whose own position would be also undermined by Cynnane's move, had equal reason to block the passage of the Argead women, and so he sent his brother, Alcetas, to intercept them. The defiant Cynnane was killed and yet curiously Alcetas' men mutinied at this outcome and demanded that Adea be duly presented to King Philip III; some of them who '... at first paused at the sight of Philip's daughter', according to Polyaenus, could conceivably have seen Cynnane in action with her father in the Illyrian campaigns (mid-340s BCE).[67] Perdiccas was forced to agree to the match, and Adea boldly assumed the regal title 'Queen Eurydice'.[68] Unfortunately for the 'royalists' and the dynastically minded *Somatophylakes*, the daughter of Alexander's half-sister was now married to Alexander's half-brother (an 'Amazon and an idiot') and Eurydice became, as Heckel notes, the 'first true Macedonian queen in almost a generation'.[69]

With the new turn of events in Pella after Polyperchon assumed the regency, Eurydice, who seemingly harboured a hatred of Alexander's side of the Argead line (surely for the murder of her father; moreover, Alexander's former chiliarch was responsible for the death of her mother), had her new husband issue letters demanding Polyperchon deliver up his army to Cassander who was obviously promoting himself in the parallel role of regent to the kings.[70] Justin recorded that a similar demand for submission was sent to Antigonus in Asia, which presumably meant she and Cassander required his military support.[71] 'When everything necessary for his departure was ready', Cassander journeyed to Celaenae with the kings' edict, whereupon he secured for himself 4,000 infantry (probably Greek mercenaries) and a useful fleet of thirty-five of Antigonus' ships with which to return to Greece and build an opposition bridgehead.[72]

The assumption that Antigonus declared war on Polyperchon by agreeing to this requisition does not need to be made; he simply, though rather conveniently, complied with a directive from Pella. Cassander simultaneously reached out to Ptolemy (now his brother-in-law) in Egypt, and probably to Lysimachus as well (married to, or soon to wed, Nicaea).[73] With an oathless Eumenes now on the loose, and with the Cardian general and Polyperchon apparently corresponding with Olympias, Antigonus was only too happy to assist the old regent's son to embroil himself in a war with the new regent across the Aegean.[74] Antigonus' true intent was nevertheless clear:

> ... he pretended to be aiding him [Cassander] because of his own friendship for Antipater, but in truth it was because he wished Polyperchon to be surrounded by many great distractions, so that he himself might proceed against Asia without danger and secure the supreme power for himself.[75]

Polyperchon finally '... foresaw the serious character of the war that was to be fought with him.' According to Diodorus, he sought council approval before taking any actions and that 'many shrewd suggestions' were made about the war; the council was presumably the veneer of an Assembly, but here, with the Pellan royalty being tugged at from both sides, it was more likely a *synedrion* convened with *philoi*, court friends.[76] 'But it was clear that

Cassander, reinforced by Antigonus, would hold the Greek cities against them... since some of the cities were guarded by his father's garrisons and others dominated by Antipater's friends and mercenaries.'

Cassander must have promised his dying father he would serve Polyperchon well. He lied; as a direct result of his hostility, Polyperchon and his advisers '... decided to free the cities throughout Greece and to overthrow the oligarchies established in them by Antipater... for in this way they would best decrease the influence of Cassander and also win for themselves great glory and many considerable allies.'[77] Demades had pleaded with Antipater to take these steps himself, but his words had fallen on deaf ears; Cassander executed him in Pella after killing the orator's son standing at his father's side.[78]

Polyperchon's move in Greece appeared legitimate, perhaps even to some Macedonians; it was ostensibly a continuation of Alexander's earlier instructions to Craterus to 'guard the freedom of the Greeks', an edict closely linked to the Exiles Decree. Its central promise harked back even further to the battle at Gaugamela when Alexander had allegedly inferred that 'tyrannies were abolished and they might live under their own laws.'[79] In reality the slogan promised little; new oligarchs would replace the old under a 'Macedonian Peace' that offered no more a prospect of true independence than did the later *Pax Romana*. Certainly, after the battle of Megalopolis some thirteen years earlier, when the Spartan king, Agis, was aided by Peloponnesians, Antipater would have tightened his grip on the Greek city-states.

Future calls for 'freedom' would be repeated in the years to come for various political ends. We have Antigonus' 'Proclamation of Tyre' (315 BCE, he was by then in league *with* Polyperchon) which was similarly designed to challenge Cassander's oligarchs, and a proclamation by Ptolemy in response, though he too reinforced 'freedom' with garrisons, this time at Sicyon and Corinth. Antigonus' son, Demetrius *Poliorketes*, followed; he even revived Philip's League of Corinth in 302 BCE, but had garrisoned Athens by 295 BCE. These pledges of 'freedom' were by definition 'a declaration of power over their fate', or as Anson put it, the promise of freedom was a 'sound bite' to 'excuse war and revolution in the name of a broad philosophical ideal'.[80]

Here, in 318 BCE, 'many in fact obeyed' Polyperchon and 'there were massacres throughout the cities' whilst others 'were driven into exile; the friends of Antipater were destroyed, and the governments... began to form alliances with him.' Although Polyperchon had clearly been 'forced into a political stance that was diametrically opposite' to the Antipatrid regime in Greece, at no time was a declaration of war against Antigonus mentioned, a contention backed up by the fact that they would join forces three years later.[81] Polyperchon had, nevertheless, been manoeuvred into a position not of his own choosing, and he would have surely avoided a confrontation in Asia when Greece itself was now in turmoil. In this light the 'remarkable' missives he allegedly sent to Eumenes empowering him to wage war in the name of the kings look rather suspicious, especially so when recalling Eumenes' local deceits. Diodorus recorded the content of the avowed Pellan correspondence in the greater detail:

> He [Polyperchon] also sent to Eumenes, writing a letter in the name of the kings, urging him not to put an end to his enmity toward Antigonus, but turning from him to the kings, either to cross over to Macedonia, if he wished, and become a guardian of the kings in co-operation with himself, or if he preferred, to remain in Asia and after receiving an army and money fight it out with Antigonus who had already clearly shown that he was a rebel against the kings. He said that the kings were restoring to him the satrapy that Antigonus had taken away and all the prerogatives that he had ever possessed in Asia. Finally he set forth that it was especially fitting for Eumenes to be careful and solicitous for the royal house in conformity with his former public services in its interest. If he needed greater military power, Polyperchon promised that he himself and the kings would come from Macedonia with the entire royal army.'[82]

Polyperchon additionally compensated Eumenes for his losses providing him with a useful war chest and the crack infantry brigade:

> Eumenes, just after he had made good his retreat from the fortress [Nora], received the letters that had been dispatched by Polyperchon. They contained... the statement that the kings were giving him a gift of five hundred talents as recompense for the losses that he had experienced, and that to effect this they had written to the generals and treasurers in Cilicia directing them to give him... whatever additional money he requested for raising mercenaries and for other pressing needs. The letter also added that they were writing to the commanders of the three thousand Macedonian Silver Shields ordering them to place themselves at the disposal of Eumenes and in general to co-operate wholeheartedly with him, since he had been appointed supreme commander of all Asia.[83]

Polyperchon, under whose higher command the Silver Shields had once operated, must have appeared *apo mechanes Theos*, 'God from the machine', to everyone but Eumenes, for we suggest the true intervention was something less divine.[84] Diodorus obviously believed the correspondence to be genuine, but Hieronymus' pro-Eumenes hand was at work, we suggest.

Polyperchon could not have dispatched the letters in the format we read them; he would not have crossed to Asia from Macedonia when Cassander was recruiting an army in Greece and with Adea on the loose in Pella beckoning Cassander north and issuing her own 'king's' edicts. If Eumenes *had* elected to return to Macedonia, Polyperchon would have at once declared war on Antigonus through the missives and yet invited the only man capable of executing it away from the theatre of operations; it is a prospect rendered even more unlikely when considering the size of *Monophthalmos'* conglomerated army, and when factoring in the support the one-eyed veteran might receive from Ptolemy and Lysimachus, related as they now were.[85] And at none of the *synedria* Polyperchon held was there mention of open hostilities in Asia, or the inciting of other Asian satraps to rise against him, a wholly necessary step if he was to head an Asian counterchallenge. Polyperchon, the Tymphaean jackal, would have indeed then become a lion among the predatory *Diadokhoi*. So what was really couriered east from the beleaguered regent's desk?

First of all, the two missives were potentially one: a king's edict and a regent's covering letter, that is if Polyperchon sent anything at all, for at this point in his narrative, Nepos only mentioned correspondence and messengers from Olympias to Eumenes which outlined a dialogue both ways. In the accounts of Diodorus and Plutarch these dispatches appeared to have arrived together, so we might credit Olympias with covertly 'assisting' Polyperchon with his 'royal' directives on behalf of Eumenes' cause.[86] Additionally, Polyperchon's communications and pledges need to be considered in light of what was clearly reported to be faked correspondence drafted by Eumenes in the camp of Peucestas at Persepolis some two years on:

> Eumenes had fabricated a false letter… the purport of which was that… Olympias, associating Alexander's son with herself, had recovered firm control of the kingdom of Macedonia after slaying Cassander, and that Polyperchon had crossed into Asia against Antigonus with the strongest part of the royal army and the elephants and was already advancing in the neighbourhood of Cappadocia.[87]

As Roisman elegantly put it: 'In the murky world of Macedonian "constitutionalism" and legitimacy, a recent edict issued by the kings and their regent, and endorsed by Alexander's mother, carried more weight than a disinterred resolution of the Macedonian assembly sanctioned by the same kings.'[88] Realising just that, it seems more likely that Eumenes and Olympias between them had fully concocted, or partly exploited, an original letter from the regent in Pella and turned it into a mandate for war in Asia. As Eumenes also knew, this was not an age of high literacy or readily available writing materials, and so there was no widespread counterfeiting. The arrival of a state missive, penned in court officialese on fine parchment with an ornate Argead seal, and delivered by a suitably primed courier, would have carried the weight of unquestionable authenticity and an aura of royal gravitas for all but a privileged *syntrophos* more familiar with the royal secretariat.

Other deceits aside, fabricating *court* correspondence would have been too preposterously bold to contemplate, as would its repercussions, and those that knew how to carry it off were even rarer still. Anyone who might dare to challenge the veracity of a king's edict would be a brave man indeed, as the former king's secretary knew, and it was a state of affairs Eumenes now exploited. After all, he may well have crafted the bogus letters Philip II send out for Athenian 'interception' in 340 BCE during the siege of Byzantium; one falsely claimed Philip was abandoning the siege and it resulted in a Greek sea blockade being lifted, and a further letter to Antipater, again designed for capture, betrayed his army's (imaginary) position, duping the allied command guarding a strategic pass.[89]

THE DAGGER, THE ROPE AND THE HEMLOCK: OLYMPIAS' RETURN

There can be no doubt that Olympias would have wanted Eumenes back in Pella to help face the threat from Cassander once Asia Minor was secured, so *her* cry for help appears genuine at least. According to Nepos:

> Olympias… sent letters and messengers into Asia to Eumenes, to consult him whether she should proceed to re-possess herself of Macedonia… She then entreated Eumenes… not to allow the bitterest enemies of Philip's house and family to extirpate his very race, but to give his support to the children of Alexander; adding that, if he would do her such a favour, he might raise troops as soon as possible, and bring them to her aid; and, in order that he might do so more easily, she had written to all the governors of the provinces that preserved their allegiance, to obey him, and follow his counsels.[90]

By now Olympias had already reached out to Polyperchon, or possibly he to her, beset as they were by a mutual enemy. Alexander's son by Roxane was by now four years old and being referred to as one of the 'kings' (*symbasileos*, co-king) under the title of Alexander IV. Olympias, with Eumenes' support, was clearly planning to back her grandson over her despised dead husband's idiot offspring, Arrhidaeus, by Philinna of Larissa. We may question whether Olympias truly harboured grandmaternal feelings for Roxane's boy, but promoting him was her best route to survival. Strategically, that support made sense for Eumenes too: troops sent by Roxane's father, Oxyartes (now satrap of Bactria and, or,

Paropanisadae), *were* in the ranks of those assembled at Persepolis and they remained with Eumenes through the battles at Paraetacene and (we may assume) Gabiene.[91] So it is unsurprising that Roxane featured prominently in the *Pamphlet* in a 'tender' death scene in which it was made clear that she was the *foremost* wife at the king's court; her restraining Alexander from disappearing into the Euphrates may have been crafted to showcase her loyalty to her husband *and* his men.[92]

A blood feud was inevitable with Alexander's mother planning to return to Pella; it would have already taken place if Polyperchon's administration had any teeth. Nevertheless, after he once again 'had consulted with his friends', Polyperchon 'summoned Olympias, asking her to assume the care of Alexander's son'; she must have promised the desperate regent she would bring an Epirote army with her; and that is exactly what she did.

Nepos confirmed: 'Eumenes was moved with this communication', but not in the immediate direction Olympias might have wanted. Diodorus added that he '… at once replied to her advising her to remain in Epirus for the present until the war should come to some decision'; '… he therefore assembled troops, and prepared for war against Antigonus' in Asia.[93] Olympias was, however, active in rallying assistance: Diodorus was clear that the support of the Silver Shields held firm in the face of Antigonus' subversion because: 'Olympias, the mother of Alexander, had written to them that they should serve Eumenes in every way.'[94] She was also active in Greece; she sent instructions to Nicanor, Cassander's Macedonian *phrourarchos* of Munychia, demanding he return the strategic district and adjacent harbour at Piraeus to the Athenians.[95] On good terms with Phocion, Nicanor (possibly Aristotle's nephew) had strengthened his numbers and soon controlled the Great Harbour and the adjacent Bay of Phalerum along with the harbour booms; Athens was now landlocked.

Control of the harbours had been an essential part of Cassander's return with his new ships from his recruiting mission in Asia. But the Athenian Assembly, backed by an army under Polyperchon's son, Alexander, and Hagnonides who was once exiled by Antipater, now banished Phocion and prepared to oust the Macedonian garrison from Piraeus. This precipitated a chain of events that would result in the executions of *both* Phocion and Hagnonides, as well as the pro-Cassander Corinthian, Deinarchus, as the hopes of the city ascended to, and descended from, the high point of Polyperchon's promise of 'freedom', and then fell to a decade of 'tyranny' under the Cassander-installed Demetrius of Phalerum.[96] Cassander, in the style of Eumenes' counterfeiting in Asia, used forged letters to rid himself of the by now overly successful Nicanor who, it must have appeared to him (possibly with good cause), had been intriguing with Antigonus.[97]

Although Eumenes had cautioned Olympias to delay her return to

Macedonia and warned her against exacting revenge too soon, plans *were* clearly in place for just that: retribution.[98] His advice, 'not to stir until Alexander's son should get the throne', anticipated the execution of Eurydice and King Philip III in the coming months, perhaps to be carried out by the agency of the newly repatriated Holcias and his men.[99] But it seems that Olympias did return against Eumenes' advice, and thus potentially earlier than he had expected.[100] She journeyed towards Pella – possibly with Polyperchon already at her side – with the help of her nephew, Aeacides of the Molossian house (Pyrrhus' father), and in autumn 317 BCE she defeated the army of Queen Eurydice which was attempting to block the path out of the Pindus Mountains that separated Macedonia from the Molossian kingdom to the southwest.[101]

In the confrontation referred to by Duris as the 'first war between women', Eurydice the warrior (in the style of her mother) emblematically paraded herself in full battle armour, uniquely arranged according to Duris, while Olympias marched out as a worshipper of Dionysus to the sound of a tympanum. Eurydice's men, 'remembering the benefits that they had received from Alexander, changed their allegiance'.[102] The veterans were simply not ready to slay the mother of Alexander, who then rode into Pella and assumed her rightful place. Cassander was absent at the time in southern Greece. Olympias must have thought that her 'haste and timing' was justifiable after all; she may well have orchestrated trouble in the south to enable herself to strike.

Olympias immediately set about issuing orders to garrison commanders, directing generals and conducting personal vendettas.[103] Eurydice's fate was forced suicide; Olympias provided her a sword, a noosed-rope and hemlock: three deaths to choose from. Shunning these tools she is said to have hung herself with her own girdle, though she took the rope in another account. The half-witted King Philip III, presumably unable to decide on his fate, was put to the Thracian dagger after wearing the crown for six years and four months; that statement by Diodorus places his death in October 317 BCE, or possibly later according to the *Babylonian Chronicle*.

Alexander's mother and her former Cardian secretary were clearly working together on a bigger emerging picture, even if they did not concur on its timing; his experience at court and on campaign, and her role as head of the Argead house, formed a team with unique abilities, perhaps with Cleopatra facilitating their communication from Sardis; the new lower city lay astride the coast road (though not the Royal Road) to Ephesus some three days' travel away.[104] Thanks to the royal missives supposedly sent by Polyperchon, Eumenes had become the kings' commander-in-chief in Asia Minor, a role Nepos suggested Perdiccas had granted him before, though this time it was either *self-appointed*, or manipulated with the help of Olympias' hand. At this point, again thanks to Olympias' groundwork, the prospect of other satraps joining him was real. It was Antigonus who now appeared the 'rebel of the monarchy'.[105]

The unwitting Polyperchon was embroiled in the intrigues and cunning of all those vying for control of the kings, the throne and Asian empire: Cassander, Antigonus *and* Olympias with Eumenes. His chess was simply one-dimensional in the face of more complex gambits, but with an Antigonus-backed Cassander making headway in Greece, and a Eumenes-supporting Olympias now resident in Pella, what could Polyperchon possibly reverse?[106] Eumenes must have anticipated just that.

WORKING THE RESOURCES: CLEITUS' SILVER AND ARRHIDAEUS' RESCUE MISSION

It appears that two satraps in Asia Minor *were* activated by Olympias' call to arms, and their activity appears coordinated with a likely *initial* goal of facilitating Eumenes' eventual return to Macedonia. Had he not been hounded east out of Phoenicia after wintering in Cilicia, Eumenes may have headed north through Asia Minor and linked up with these newly defiant allies. The first was Arrhidaeus in Hellespontine Phrygia, probably the brother of Amphimachus who now governed Mesopotamia and who soon would link up with Eumenes when he made his way east. Arrhidaeus moved to garrison strategic cities of Cyzicus as a 'defensive measure'; he further dispatched a rescue force to free Eumenes from Nora.[107] These actions are more consistent with the trust Perdiccas placed in him when instructing him to oversee construction, and delivery, of Alexander's funeral bier at Babylon.

Basing their conclusions on Photius' severe compression of Arrian *Events After Alexander*, commentators generally accept that the bier's Syrian destination was a 'redirection' of its intended course, and so Arrhidaeus defied Perdiccas from the outset, as 'desertion' is mentioned. But this need not be so, and Hieronymus' rendering of the episode may well have made Arrhidaeus pay handsomely for his failure to assist Eumenes earlier, or to justify the Perdiccan loss of the corpse, or Arrhidaeus' help in its handing over to Ptolemy under a higher loyalty (Alexander's last wishes). For we have grounds to believe Perdiccas was himself based in Syria, so the cortege was being delivered to him as instructed, though no doubt Ptolemy's spies had advance knowledge of its route.[108]

Besides, if Alexander *had* requested burial in Egypt in his Will, its final destination was legitimate, the redirection aside; significantly no demands for the return of the body emerged. Arrhidaeus' elevation (alongside Peithon) to *epimeletes* at Triparadeisus suggests he was both held in high esteem and he had not alienated either side of the previously feuding armies.[109] He was demonstrably no lover of Antigonus, which is perhaps why Antipater confirmed him in Hellespontine Phrygia, so that any 'rogue' crossing of the Hellespont could be monitored by him.

Presumably, with his territory bordering the narrow seaway that separated the former Persian Empire from Europe, Arrhidaeus was the first governor in Asia to receive messages and instructions from Pella or Epirus. An attempt to break Eumenes out of Nora would have been a hugely ambitious undertaking as a sole initiative, but it is conceivable as part of a bigger emerging plan. It was too late, that is if the relief force ever reached the fortress, for its fate is unattested. But its timing confirms that Olympias was corresponding with satraps to solicit support when Eumenes was still incarcerated; Hieronymus' mission to Pella may well have been part of that. Intimate with the defences, the siege guard strength and the locations of Antigonus' army billeting, Hieronymus could have provided the detail that would have made a breakout possible; Nepos made it clear the perimeter was far from watertight.

If Antigonus harboured the belief that he alone was the architect of events unfolding in Asia, and potentially now those evolving in Greece, he would have been completely wrong on both campaign fronts. When Arrhidaeus moved against him, the second satrap to declare for the pro-Eumenes alliance, White Cleitus sailed to Macedonia after garrisoning *his* principal cities to inform Polyperchon of Antigonus' latest plans. Before returning to the Asian theatre of war he briefly generalled for the new regent and journeyed to Athens to oversee the execution of Phocion who had submitted himself to Polyperchon when Hagnonides, his arch-enemy, was reinstalled.[110]

In reply to these new threats, Antigonus dispatched 20,000 infantry and 3,000 cavalry to relieve Arrhidaeus' 'siege' of Cyzicus, and he journeyed himself with his remaining forces to take Ephesus in response to Cleitus' naval actions. Antigonus had opportunistically intercepted four ships under Rhodian captaincy carrying 600 talents of silver ostensibly destined for Polyperchon in Macedonia; this sounds like a shipment Eumenes might have dispatched from Cyinda. Was it in fact bound for the combined front of Cleitus and Arrhidaeus, rather than Macedonia?[111] Antigonus refused to give up the captured funds, claiming they were needed for the payment of mercenaries (perhaps the 4,000 he 'officially' furnished Cassander with); that he provided an explanation *at all* reinforces our contention that no *formal* war had been declared between himself and the Pellan regime under Polyperchon. Cassander's execution of Nicanor, who *had* returned from a coordinated action *with* Antigonus at the Hellespont, suggests there was little trust between the 'allies'; Antigonus was simply playing both sides of the discord.

Yet the reprimand Antigonus levied on the soon-defeated satrap of Hellespontine-Phrygia evidenced the weight he still placed on his

Triparadeisus-granted authority, despite Antipater's death: 'He sent envoys to Arrhidaeus, bringing against him these charges… he ordered him to retire from his satrapy and, retaining a single city as a residence, to remain quiet.'[112] Arrhidaeus took refuge in adjacent Bithynia and joined up with Cleitus' fleet upon its return from Macedonia; their new instructions were to block the crossing of enemy troops expected *from* Europe.

This statement is curious, for Cassander needed all the men he could muster in Greece, and Antigonus was already funding an army of immense size in Asia Minor. Was there the prospect of Lysimachus entering the frame?[113] After an early success, Cleitus' fleet was captured by Antigonus who employed typical cunning in the face of initial defeat; Cleitus was on the run though he was soon captured near the Bosphorus and he *was*, revealingly, executed by men operating under Lysimachus.[114] Nothing more was heard of Arrhidaeus, who either heeded Antigonus' demands, or was quietly dispatched. The Asia Minor initiative had collapsed; Eumenes and Olympias were left to face Antigonus and Cassander without the support they had hoped to muster.

It was worse in Macedonia. We are told that Olympias' immediate actions, the violent murder of Philip III and Eurydice alongside the pogrom she launched against Cassander's family and supporters, caused a popular revulsion against her, something Eumenes may well have feared. Olympias would have justified her actions under a Macedonian law that demanded the death of all those related by blood to those deemed guilty of a crime against the crown.[115] But more than one hundred of Cassander's supporters are said to have been hunted down, including his brother, Nicanor; Iolaos' grave was desecrated and his body mistreated in true Homeric style.[116] As a consequence, King Aeacides lost his support in Epirus and was soon expelled; his daughter, Deidameia, once pledged in marriage to Alexander's son by Roxane, would be destined for Demetrius *Poliorketes* instead.[117] The murdered Argead king and queen – the son and granddaughter of the still revered Philip II – along with her previously murdered mother, Cynnane, were later honoured by Cassander who held funeral games once he had disposed of Olympias and gained control of Macedonia a year or so on.[118]

'THE ENEMY OF MY ENEMY IS MY FRIEND' – THE FORTUNATE, INNOCENT FEW

In securing himself a release from Nora, Eumenes had given a masterclass in diplomatic chicanery, and it led to one of history's 'great reversals of fortune'. But now that the prospect of assistance from Cleitus and Arrhidaeus had evaporated, Eumenes and Olympias needed a more significant weapon that would galvanise other satraps into a coalition

– a mechanism that would advance the status of supporters, while undermining satraps and generals in the service of the enemy. The two-part *Pamphlet*, with its conspiracy allegations and the re-issued Will, was designed to achieve just that. Along with what were arguably Eumenes' 'self-issued' 'letters of marque and reprisal' that manoeuvred Polyperchon into the frame of war in Asia, it was a production only Eumenes and Olympias between them could pull off; if there was anyone in the empire who would have known the original uncorrupted content of Alexander's Will, and, moreover, who additionally bore long-term grudges against the family of Antipater, it was the former king's secretary and the dead king's mother.

When developing the shape of the *Pamphlet* and its regicidal finger-pointing, Eumenes and Olympias simply played on several well-known facts: Alexander's planned retirement of Antipater in favour of Craterus, the regent's subsequent (alleged) summoning to Babylon (both moves could be interpreted as a suspicion of treason), the subsequent arrival of Cassander in his place, the previous execution of Alexander Lyncestis (Antipater's son-in-law) and that well-documented bitterness between the regent and the queen mother. All this was neatly enveloped in the rising tensions at the court in Babylon; one of Plutarch's sources claimed Alexander physically and verbally assaulted the newly arrived Cassander, contemptuous of his behaviour and his double-sided arguments. Plutarch additionally stated that the king was now fearful of the threat posed by the presence of the regent's sons.[119]

Preceding the Will in the *Pamphlet* was a list of those at Medius' banquet at which Alexander was professedly poisoned; the enemies were being sighted in the coalition crosshairs by implication in the crime.[120] The *Pamphlet* also claimed: 'No one was unaware of what was afoot, with the exception of Eumenes, Perdiccas, Ptolemy, Lysimachus, Asander and Holcias.' The coalition of 'friends' being solicited by Eumenes and Olympias was clear.

The names of this select few, *hoi enkrithentes,* are more valuable to us than the identities of the guilty, for they represent a narrower focus of intent that might point to the *Pamphlet*'s dating. Moreover, these names are less corrupted. The first two, Eumenes and Perdiccas, need no explanation as a product of the authors' hands. Rather overtly, the *Pamphlet* beckoned Ptolemy and Lysimachus into the new order by stating they both were present at the drafting and the first private reading of the Will. Ptolemy had the vast resources of a veteran-strewn Egypt and Lysimachus could control the Hellespont and the route through Thrace to Macedonia.

The *Pamphlet* Will went on to grant them Argead wives: for Ptolemy it was Alexander's full-sister Cleopatra; his half-sister, Thessalonice, went to Lysimachus.[121] Most likely in her mid-twenties when Alexander died, she was the daughter of the Thessalian Nicesipolis of Pherae, one of Philip II's early brides who died soon after giving birth; remarkably Nicesipolis and Olympias seem to have struck up a lasting friendship.[122] Now a ward of Olympias, Thessalonice's Argead blood (and the Thessalian noble line) explains her continued spinsterhood in the campaign years, for she would have been a threat if powerfully wedded. But in these dangerous times, Olympias and Eumenes had had reason to use her to galvanise support. Furthermore, these Will pairings were clearly designed to undermine the marriages that Antipater had contrived when proffering his daughters.

By implication, the current plight of Cleopatra was being highlighted if she was now under 'house arrest' in an Antigonus-controlled Sardis. Carney might be correct in surmising that Cleopatra had come to an understanding with Antigonus: she would enter no foreign marriage negotiations if he and his son Demetrius did not themselves forcefully wed her.[123] Her attempt to unite with Perdiccas suggests that it was certainly within Eumenes' power to broker a new marriage between her and Ptolemy using his influence with Olympias, and it might have been a Ptolemaic-Argead-Aeacid line that Augustus saw terminated in Alexandria some three centuries later.[124]

If Olympias' vested interest in the *Pamphlet* is evident through its hostility to Antipater – though clearly both she and Eumenes shared that – the *hieros gamos*, the holy union suggested by the Will's opening claim that she sired Alexander with the god, if this is not later embellishment, points more firmly to her involvement. That in turn posed Alexander as a true reincarnation of Heracles, Theseus and Dionysus, each born of gods through mortal mothers; Alexander appears to have returned the favour in the hope for a 'consecration to immortality' for his mother.[125] Callisthenes had apparently claimed Olympias was *already* spreading 'lies' about Alexander's semi-divine status when he was compiling his book on campaign.[126] Her rejection of Philip was no doubt energised by her son's visit to the oracle of Ammon at Siwa (if not vice versa), where the propaganda for his own divinity was born. The search for that status was, in fact, inevitable and overdue: Lesbos had erected altars to his father, now Philippic Zeus, some years before.[127]

Furthermore, Plutarch recorded the tradition that Philip had been warned by the Delphic oracle to hold Zeus-Ammon (the god's Hellenised form) in special reverence, and he claimed that Philip had lost his eye as punishment for spying upon Olympias' Orphic rituals. This story was bound up with Philip's dream in which he put a seal upon Olympias' womb with a lion device, where she herself dreamed a thunderbolt fell upon her as Alexander was conceived. That was no doubt inspired by Euripides' *Bacchae* written at the Pellan court some eighty years before, which claimed the same occurred at the birth of Dionysus; Philip's fate further recalls the punishment of the maenads on Pentheus for banning the worship of Dionysus.[128] But Ammon's attachment to the *Pamphlet* Will was really something of a *fait accompli*. Of course, the well-documented commemoratives to Alexander's *mortal* father, rejected as part of the 'last plans' at Babylon, could not be fully dispensed with if a reissued Will was to appear genuine.

Could Olympias have authored the *Pamphlet* independently? Its structure certainly did require her support to fully realise the plans it was ushering in, and she would have added her designs to its more malevolent intent; she surely became an aggressive distributor of copies. In fact, the proposal that it was a Pella-sanctioned document was part of its expected efficacy, and because of that its origins would have been fairly obvious at the time. But the *Pamphlet* needed a military focus and an execution of martial policy that only Eumenes could provide. In that respect, some calls for help were obvious steps to take, but the complex web of military intrigues needed the experience only the campaigning Cardian and his satrapal intimacy could provide. The *Pamphlet*'s failure to feature the once 'Antipater-sponsored' Polyperchon, already bettered in Pella by Eurydice, reminds us that the new regent was neither the architect nor party to its design.[129]

Also on the 'innocent's' list is Asander, and the Will confirmed his inheritance of Caria. Named satrap of the region at Babylon, he received the Antipater-Craterus-Antigonus alliance that returned to Asia in 321/320 BCE 'as a friend', though resistance was probably futile in the face of such a dominant force.[130] Asander's confrontation with Alcetas and Attalus, in which he came off worse, suggests he might have been a reluctant Antigonid ally from the outset; this is supported by his defection to Ptolemy in 315 BCE.[131] Eumenes sensed Asander could be turned, and he was right, though his defection came too late. But we know little about his activity in the five or six years after Triparadeisus; he may well have withdrawn active support for Antigonus long before the final battle at Gabiene, as the war with Eumenes in the final two years was conducted far to the east of his own satrapy. The testament-provided gifts of 150 talents of silver to Cnidus and Miletus ought to be mentioned, as both cities resided in Caria; this looks like a promissory war chest with which Asander would conduct naval operations and incursions into Phrygia, or a bribe for neutrality, at least.[132]

The final guest salvaged from guilt alongside Perdiccas, Asander, Ptolemy and Lysimachus, was Holcias, whose fate must have been linked in some strategic way to the author's. His prominence in the Pamphlet reads:

> Over all the Illyrians, I appoint Holcias as governor and I award him a detachment of 500 requisitioned horses and 3,000 talents of silver coin, which he is to use for the making of statues of Alexander, Ammon, Athena, Heracles, Olympias and my father Philip. These he is to set up in the shrine of Olympia.[133]

Holcias commanded 3,000 'heavy' Macedonian infantry (Polyaenus termed them 'hoplites', so possibly hypaspists), and having defected from the ranks of Antigonus, he set about ravaging the Taurus Mountains bordering Lycaonia and Phrygia. That action in autumn 319 BCE coincided with Eumenes' incarceration at Nora, which, recalling Plutarch's geographical description, must once again have been located nearby.[134]

Holcias' brigade of renegades was potentially among the captives rounded up by Antigonus after battle at Orcynia, and who pledged their loyalty to their captor in the absence of immediate options. In which case their 'opportunistic defection' becomes more readily explainable. Alternatively, they may have been with the Macedonian 'friends' and soldiers Eumenes disbanded before entering the fortress, which does not discount their capture immediately after; as Plutarch described the start of the siege: 'As he wandered about and sought to elude his enemies, Eumenes persuaded most of his soldiers to leave him.'[135]

Now at large, and defying Antigonus' calls for their surrender, Holcias and his men may have been lingering in the vicinity waiting for either an opportune moment to storm the Nora palisade (in spring), or for Eumenes to negotiate his own freedom meantime. Other allies had remained in the region, as Diodorus' coverage of Eumenes' release some months on confirmed: 'Thus unexpectedly saved after a considerable time, he stayed for the present in Cappadocia, where he gathered together his former friends and those who had once served under him and were now wandering about the country.'[136] Holcias may even have attempted to get word to the Perdiccan faction under Alcetas, who was himself under siege at Cretopolis, or meeting a bloody end at Termessus where his tomb has now been identified.[137]

Antigonus hesitated to kill Holcias and his brigade when they were eventually lured out of the mountains and captured through a deception. He, along with two other 'leaders of the revolt', agreed to forced repatriation to Macedonia and to being chaperoned home by Leonidas who, curiously, had been the commander of the 3,000 *ataktoi*, the 'disciplinary unit' Alexander had formed after Parmenio's death. Yet this seems a rather quixotic amnesty from Antigonus and more so when we consider the eventual fate of the Silver Shields and their commanders who were executed at Gabiene.[138] Either Antigonus had his own plans for the brigade back in Macedonia, or they were freed as part of the bargaining between Eumenes and him at Nora, suggesting machinations yet to unfold.[139] It is not inconceivable that Antigonus envisaged Holcias and his men operating under Eumenes, who would then become his advocate with the royals at Pella.

From the perspective of the pamphleteers, however, once Holcias was back in Macedonia, he could give Olympias the personal army she had begged Eumenes to provide. The actual fate of he and his men is unknown; she may even have employed them well against the family of Cassander in her well-attested pogrom. The Will grant to Holcias included control of Illyria, and an additional 500 horses and 3,000 talents of silver, which was ostensibly a donation for the construction of statues, but presumably a campaign fund for waging war.

But why place him in Illyria? Well, the location was strategically opportune; the region did not encroach upon Lysimachus' satrapal grant or upon Macedonia itself, and yet it provided a 'local' staging point for operations against Pella. Holcias' authority may have been specifically aimed at suppressing any trouble in the region that could be stirred up by Eurydice with her Illyrian roots and claims that stretched back to King Bardylis.[140] If Eumenes and Olympias planned to remove Philip III and his queen in favour of Alexander IV, they might have expected the Illyrian regime to mount a new challenge to the throne, as they had done for generations when Macedonia was divided. This could now be mitigated and Illyrian support even harnessed; Holcias' own standing and legitimacy was being boosted by the Will's pairing of his sister, Cleodice, to the now-dead but useful Leonnatus, the prominent *Somatophylax* linked to the Lycestian royal house.[141]

Completing the rundown of those favourably dealt with by the *Pamphlet*, we have Craterus, the 'overseer of the whole Kingdom of Macedonia', for the Will granted him a wife of royal blood, suggesting posthumous respect. Eumenes may have genuinely offered to reconcile Perdiccas and Craterus before settling affairs in battle, and he certainly knew how important Craterus was to the veterans; as Plutarch put it, the death of '… Craterus… of all the successors of Alexander, was most regretted by the Macedonians.'[142] He had after all rivalled the first chiliarch in importance to Alexander: 'most affection for Hephaestion, most respect for Craterus.' His son of the same name went on to support his half-brother, Antigonus II *Gonatas*, and somewhat ironically he may have later befriended Hieronymus at *Gonatas'* court.[143] But it was *not* posthumous respect that was being displayed in the *Pamphlet*, and neither was Eumenes' post-battle contrition at Craterus' death anything more than contrived *sumpentheo*, a 'suffering togetherness', to defray immediate Macedonian anger. Eumenes cast the blame on Neoptolemus, who precipitated the clash, and he ensured Craterus' body was cremated and his bones returned to his widow, Phila, Antipater's influential daughter.[144]

Alexander's original Will most likely *would have* paired Craterus, the new regent-to-be, with an Argead woman, though it's questionable whether it was the choice proposed in the *Pamphlet*: Cynnane. But this was now a safe pairing to broadcast without repercussions since both of them were dead.[145] The match cast a shadow on both Antipater's extended regency and his offering Phila to Craterus, as it implied Cynnane had been displaced by the regent and rejected by Craterus too. The match would, nevertheless, provide an explanation for Cynnane's crossing to Asia with her daughter, for Craterus was then still based in Cilicia; if she *had* already been rejected, better prospects for their survival lay in Asia too in the form of the newly crowned King Philip III.[146] The *Pamphlet's* promotion of Cynnane additionally damned her killer, Alcetas, for he had all but abandoned Eumenes when refusing to work under him at Celaenae.[147]

Craterus' own inheritance of the regency was clearly too well attested to doctor in the new Will, but Eumenes may have found a subtler way to cast suspicion on the popular general. For the *Pamphlet* claimed that the central plotters against Alexander's life, Cassander and his brother Iolaos, had planned to meet up in Cilicia once the king was dead, and this was exactly where Craterus was still encamped with his 10,000 veterans. That smacked of complicity and it even called into question support Antipater had enjoyed from Polyperchon, for he too was in Cilicia with Craterus, as were the prominent commanders Polydamas (possibly a Thessalian noble and hence a close acquaintance of the 'guilty' Medius of Larissa), Gorgias and Antigenes who might be openly accused if they failed to unite with Eumenes.[148]

The *Pamphlet* testament allocated Cilicia to a Nicanor whom Eumenes must have been attempting to seduce into the coalition; he was plausibly the officer who was allocated Cappadocia at Triparadeisus. Sensing he too could be turned (he was obviously not at Medius' banquet or he would have named 'innocent'), Eumenes respectfully shunted him sideways to make way for his own reinstatement in the previously unconquered satrapy. The flattery didn't work; Nicanor appears to have served Antigonus well, possibly receiving Eumenes' final surrender at Gabiene, though a mutual respect *does* seem to have been in place: he is said to have allowed Eumenes his request to speak to his men before incarceration.[149] Nicanor *may* even have been subsequently elevated to *strategos* of Media and the upper satrapies after Peithon's execution in 315 BCE, though a dozen Nicanors are identified with Alexander's campaign.[150] Another credible alternative, in the context of the *Pamphlet's* courting of useful allies, is Nicanor the *philos* of Ptolemy who captured Coele-Syria from Laomedon and then garrisoned Phoenicia; an allied presence in Cilicia would give the coalition powerful naval bases and wider shipbuilding capability.[151]

Before we dissect the guilty list, Eumenes' release from Nora raises another fundamental question: could Antigonus *Monophthalmos*, who 'had in mind to go through Asia, remove the existing satraps, and reorganise the positions of command in favour of his friends', have been involved in the *Pamphlet's* birth, for much of its directed malice matched his aims?[152] Antigonus *did* go on to remove Peithon and Peucestas before targeting

Seleucus, and he may well have agreed to wipe out the house of Antipater had events taken a different path; in fact he did try, through Polyperchon, in a post-315 BCE realignment. Ptolemy and Lysimachus *were* initially in league with Antigonus. So the answer to *involvement* is 'yes', but not to the *Pamphlet* in the final format we see it, for too many of his friends (Nearchus, Medius and Menander, for example) were implicated in the treason. If it had been drafted *independently*, then Eumenes and Perdiccas would have fallen on the wrong side of conspiracy. But an 'early model' of the *Pamphlet* (like an early model of the oath) may well have been discussed as part of Eumenes' release mechanism at Nora, and had he chosen to join Antigonus then, the *Pamphlet*'s overall aims may well have become more fully realised.

If one of the central aims of the *Pamphlet was* to bring down Antigonus, why didn't the author(s) implicate him in conspiratorial guilt? Simply put, it would not have been credible; Antigonus had not been at Babylon and neither had he been associated with the other accused *hetairoi* in many years. Moreover, Antipater and Cassander maintained what appears to be a well-documented distrust towards Antigonus who was a hardly viable partner in their plot to murder the king.[153] Perhaps Eumenes was using the *Pamphlet* – potentially threatening to Antigonus through his associations but with no outright accusations yet made – to bring him to the bargaining table, and this time not as his 'better', but as an 'equal'.

THE FRIENDS OF THE ENEMIES OF THE PAMPHLETEERS

> Now, so not to appear evasive, I shall name those who were there, unlike Onesicritus who, in his desire to avoid controversy, refrained from telling. There was Perdiccas, Medius, Leonnatus, erat teon (sic), Meleager, theoclus (sic), Asander, Philip, Nearchus, Stasanor, Heracleides the Thracian, polydorus (sic), Holcias, Menander… (Peithon, Peucestas, Ptolemy, Lysimachus… Europius, Ariston of Pharsalus, Philip the engineer, Philotas).[154]

We should first address the oft-cited reference to Onesicritus and his reported fear of retribution in the *Metz Epitome* version of the *Liber de Morte* (T1), which has obviously suffered through time. Once again, we cannot be sure that the reference to Onesicritus is original content, though the same sentiment can be found in the Vulgate texts and so is potentially traceable back to Cleitarchus; that *does* suggest it could be *Pamphlet*-originating for the Vulgate absorbed its conspiracy detail.[155] It is widely held that Onesicritus published a book covering major aspects of the campaign before the other eyewitness sources, and earlier than Nearchus, who, it seems, found fault with Onesicritus' claims. Not associated with the military strife of the early Successor Wars, Onesicritus could have published an account – which touched upon Alexander's death (he may, or may not, have mentioned nameless rumours of foul play) – before the *Pamphlet* was released, a necessary conclusion if this extract is to be taken at face value.

The opening lines of this *Metz Epitome* allegation were written by someone who could only have been renowned as an eyewitness to events at Babylon. Here Eumenes may well have usefully contrived, and then attached, a fearful silence to the already famous court philosopher, in order to authenticate the *Pamphlet* allegations with a truly cynical and brilliant twist. This brings us to the men Onesicritus supposedly declined to name, and who were rather creatively represented (in what *was* most likely later embellishment) as the living parts of the gruesome creature brought to Alexander.[156]

The first of those named as guilty was Medius who became a central cog in the *Pamphlet*'s wheel of misfortune when he was cited as the complicit organiser of Alexander's final banquet. He and Aristonus had initially operated under Perdiccas when tasked with the invasion of Cyprus.[157] Their quick defeat by Antigonus may perhaps have been 'easy capitulation' for they came to immediate terms; Aristonus retired to Macedonia (though his allegiance remained intact) and Medius joined Antigonus, on the spot or sometime soon after.[158] Arrian believed that Iolaos, the bearer of the poisoned cup, was Medius' *eromenos*, his younger lover; if there was any truth in the claim, then Medius' role in the treason was easily fabricated and probably an inevitable association for the pamphleteers to make.[159]

The prominent Leonnatus was next heaped on the guilty pyre and it is not difficult to imagine why. Something resolved him to a course of action that was painted by Plutarch as underhanded: the abandoning of Eumenes in Asia Minor in a covert bid to claim Cleopatra's hand in an attempt to take the throne of Macedonia. Olympias *was* no doubt proffering her daughter to powerful men to 'spike Antipater's dynastic guns', and in Plutarch's version the offer *did* originate with Cleopatra who may then have enrolled Eumenes in the cause.[160]

Leonnatus did attempt to lure Eumenes into the scheme and promised to reconcile him with Hecataeus, the Cardian tyrant. Cardia had been founded on the Thracian Chersonese (today's Gallipoli peninsula) by settlers from the Greek city of Miletus (the founder of some ninety other settlements) and Clazomenae in the 7th century BCE. Philip II, who had already concluded a treaty of friendship with Cardia in 352 BCE, entered the picture more meaningfully in 343 BCE when Attic settlers arrived; unable to settle a boundary dispute by arbitration, he sent in troops to face Diopeithes' Attic mercenaries. References in Demosthenes' speeches confirm its subsequent independence from Athens, and Hecataeus,

Philip's agent, might have been installed then.[161] The likelihood of Eumenes accepting the offer of reconciliation was slim as 'hereditary distrust and political differences' existed, and Eumenes had repeatedly asked Alexander to remove Hecataeus.[162]

Although Leonnatus had travelled to Phrygia to meet Eumenes, Nepos claimed he attempted to kill the uncooperative Cardian who immediately decamped in the night with 300 cavalry, 200 armed camp followers and with the enormous sum of 5,000 talents, which, we assume, had been provided to Eumenes (from Cyinda?) by Perdiccas for the planned conquest of Cappadocia; that sum alone must have been a tempting target.[163] Withdrawing from the 'capricious man' of 'rash impulses', Eumenes reported Leonnatus' intentions to the chiliarch, gaining great influence with Perdiccas in the process. Diodorus' account was more compressed: Leonnatus' departure was in response to Antipater's request for assistance in the Lamian War, but this nevertheless defied Perdiccas' orders – that he assist Eumenes.

Moreover, Leonnatus had been promised another of the old regent's daughters no doubt in return for that help. His early death in the marshes of Thessaly was an outcome that apparently made Antipater 'rejoice'; it not only disabled Leonnatus' possible union with Cleopatra, but also saved the regent a useful daughter. All this made the deceased Leonnatus an easy target for Eumenes, and it opened up his satrapies (we propose he inherited a region far greater than Hellespontine Phrygia) for coalition assimilation.[164]

Next on the guilty list is the vocal Meleager, the most important infantry officer at Babylon (and, briefly, Perdiccas' *hyparchos*) and who had been executed for insurrection. He could be safely incriminated by the *Pamphlet* to good effect. The Will proposed he was the inheritor of Coele-Syria rather than Laomedon of Mytilene, though this was not philanthropy at work. Soon after Laomedon's *reconfirmation* to the region at Triparadeisus (as extant texts have Laomedan originally appointed at Babylon), Ptolemy had tried to buy him out of the province;[165] Ptolemy knew the strategic value of fortifying the route to Egypt whose borders had been recently tested by Perdiccas' invasion. Laomedon, a *hetairos* at the Pellan court and by now fluent in Persian, declined, and Ptolemy sent his general, Nicanor, to commence military operations which resulted in his capture. Laomedon managed to bribe his guards and escape to join Alcetas and the Perdiccan remnants in Caria.[166] They were finally cornered at Cretopolis and captured after fierce resistance. Laomedon may well have perished there for he was never mentioned again.

Branding the rebellious Meleager guilty, and yet posing him as the original satrap of Coele-Syria, justified both his execution by Perdiccas, and Ptolemy's annexation of the region, for it emphasised that Laomedon had not been the king's choice. The olive branch being proffered to Ptolemy was more of an olive bough, for it is difficult to imagine that Meleager would have challenged Perdiccas at Babylon 'on behalf of the passed-over infantryman' had he genuinely inherited the governorship of the influential region.

The prominent Menander based in Lydia was named with the guilty. Menander's long and well-attested tenure of the province (since 331 BCE) was dismantled when Perdiccas provided Cleopatra with a role in its governance at Sardis. He was sidelined again by Antipater at Triparadeisus and replaced by White Cleitus. As a result, the orphaned Menander became a useful Antigonid tool and we might imagine with the promise of reinstatement.[167] He had been hot on Eumenes' heels in his flight from Nora to Cilicia, and the Orcynian baggage-train charade at Menander's expense had no doubt added impetus to the chase. Though referred to as an 'old friend' of Eumenes by Plutarch (which may again simply mean 'former colleague'), Menander's early support for Antigonus and his reporting of the plan to see Perdiccas wed to Cleopatra, suggested the greater friendships resided on the other side of the Macedonian divide.[168] With no prospect of turning him, Eumenes branded Menander a traitor and may have scratched any reference to Lydia from the Will, as the region does not appear in the extant Will texts. He was never mentioned in action again, though Lydian troops did feature in later battles; his more enduring legacy was a painting by Apelles.[169]

Nearchus also suffered at the hands of the *Pamphleteers*. He was sufficiently distinguished by his naval voyage and his latter-day friendship with Alexander to have featured prominently in empire governance, so it is unlikely he would have been bypassed in the king's original Will.[170] Although the campaign governors were predominantly Macedonian, a few select Greeks *had* been chosen as satraps, though, notably, none of them originated from the mainland: Laomedon came from Mytilene and Stasander along with Stasanor were both Cypriots by birth. Nearchus, born on Crete – though his former residence of Amphipolis was now situated in an expanded Macedonia – had been appointed to Lycia and Pamphylia in the early campaign. Lycia would have been his most obvious satrapal inheritance for it would explain his mission there in 319/318 BCE to recover Telmessus, its largest city (modern Fethiye), though Polyaenus provided no date to this particular action.[171] Nearchus may additionally have been instrumental in establishing Cretopolis, the Cretan city in the strategic Telmessus passes linking Phrygia, Lycaonia and Cappadocia.[172]

What *is* beyond conjecture is his loyalty to Antigonus and Demetrius in campaigns that suggest he was steadfastly hostile to Ptolemy; perhaps this stemmed from their alleged conflicting interests in the Assembly at Babylon.[173] Nearchus fell on the *Pamphlet's* guilty list and he was targeted for removal, and any satrapal inheritance was scrubbed from history too. What became of him later in life is unknown; archaeologists scramble to reveal whether he and other prominent campaign figures were amongst the skeletons recently exhumed from the once magnificent Kasta Hill tomb at Amphipolis.[174]

Stasanor of Soli was implicated in the conspiracy as part of Eumenes' attack on Peithon, under whose mandate we propose the upper satrapies fell, thus his under-satraps were fair game too. There does seem to have been some confusion, however, between him and his neighbour, Stasander. Both were Greek Cypriots who (confusingly or mistakenly) exchanged the satrapies granted them at Babylon and Triparadeisus. Though Stasander sent troops and supported Eumenes in person at Paraetacene, Stasanor's presence was not mentioned at all.[175] Antigonus allowed Stasanor to retain Bactria-Sogdia after Eumenes' death, though Diodorus suggested that was simply due to the region's remoteness.

That acquiescence by Antigonus seems unlikely if the satrap had openly opposed him from what was a region renowned for effective fighters; from there Spitamenes had, for example, been bitterly opposed to Alexander to the end, rejecting honourable defeat and causing significant trouble for the Macedonian forces. Diodorus reported that over 120,000 Sogdians were killed in three successive revolts; this was a dangerous part of the empire unless its satrap was benign, and Antigonus certainly had generals capable of removing Stasanor if a threat, once Eumenes' forces had been assimilated.[176] Stasanor's good conduct towards the inhabitants of his region *was* clearly stated, tying in with what we read of his successful governance under Alexander; his distant neutrality seems to have allayed any fears Antigonus might have harboured.[177]

The most likely identification for the next plotter, Philotas (of the many so-named men associated with the campaign), is the Babylon-nominated satrap of Cilicia. Perdiccas had removed him in 320/321 BCE due to his well-attested friendship with Craterus, and he installed Philoxenus, his own man. That eviction would have sat uncomfortably with Antigenes, commander of the Silver Shields, and with the other remaining veterans Perdiccas had enrolled into the royal army on the way to attacking Egypt. Philotas was not reinstated at Triparadeisus (possibly due to his staunch support for the 'expansionist' Antigonus) where the apparently 'undistinguished' (and no doubt compliant) Philoxenus was reconfirmed to the province. Philotas was enrolled into Antigonus' ranks by 318 BCE, perhaps due to his experience in the region, and once again with the likely prospect of reinstatement. Philotas attempted to lure the *Argyraspides* from Eumenes in Cilicia and that may well have sealed his fate in the *Pamphlet*.[178]

We are on softer ground with the identifications of the less prominent banqueters because we are dealing with textual corruptions alongside a dearth of career information, and so focusing on them too sharply would to blur our perspective. Some names appear historical and broad deductions may be made.

If Polydorus can be identified as the physician from Teos, then it appears he was at some point a court guest of Antipater and thus was likely sympathetic (at that stage) to the Cassander-backing Antigonus. If this is a corruption of 'Polydamas' then he *was* possibly the prominent Thessalian *hetairos* with Craterus in Cilicia.[179] As far as Ariston, his Pharsalian origins were stated, and that makes him Thessalian with roots that might link him to Medius of Larissa as well. If it was the same Ariston who eventually delivered Craterus' remains to Antipater's daughter Phila, then his allegiance may well have resided with the opposing faction.[180]

Two Philips (possibly an engineer and a physician) are referred to in corrupted texts; one obvious identification is the brother of Cassander and Iolaos, thus he was another of the *paides basilikoi*, the royal pages and central to the plot, a role that was supported by his mention in Justin's account.[181] The other Philip is potentially the satrap of Parthia who was later killed by Peithon, but then assumed by the pamphleteers to be under his sway as part of his upper satrapy governance. The origins of a 'Philip the physician' might have come about on the back of earlier allegations of poisoning linked to Alexander's trusted doctor. But little save conjecture is known of Heracleides the Thracian; he may even have operated in Greece under the command of Cassander, and that could point to his being added to the list by Olympias.[182]

PEUCESTAS, PERSEPOLIS AND *PAMPHLET* PUBLICATION DATES

A key reference in dating the *Pamphlet*'s emergence is Plutarch's claim that it was some five years after Alexander's death that the conspiracy allegations first hit Greece (T10).[183] Although this is a less than clinical chronological guide, Eumenes' presence in Cilicia through the winter of 318 BCE becomes an attractive publication period when correspondence with Olympias was evidently taking place.

At this point, Seleucus' potential role in the emerging coalition needs explanation, because at first glance he does not appear in the list of Babylon banqueters. Diodorus never named him as one of Perdiccas' assassins in Egypt, nor is he amongst those Ptolemy felt indebted to after the event – the men then elevated to guardians of the kings.[184] In which case, we might suppose Eumenes had no cause to incriminate him; this would explain why he could have credibly solicited Seleucus' support when wintering in Babylonia in 317 BCE, although Peithon's presence would have undermined the negotiations.[185]

Nepos, on the other hand, *did* cite Seleucus as present in Egypt, and in the Υ recension of the *Romance* Seleucus *does* appear at Medius' party, though this text is derived from a far later (post-7th century) embellished manuscript. His attendance may also be supported by an otherwise unattested 'Europius' in the Armenian version of the *Romance* as this could be a reference to Seleucus' ethnic, for he was most likely born in Europus near the Axius River in Macedonia.[186] If Eumenes *was* implicating Seleucus in Alexander's death, a Cilicia-based early *Pamphlet* release date is unsupportable, because we cannot imagine Eumenes making overtures in 317 BCE if the accusations were already out.

What confounds historians is the observation that the *Pamphlet* Will bestowed Babylonia on Seleucus, as this appears to be another olive branch, because the mainstream texts (we propose Hieronymus-derived) claim Seleucus was only granted the province at Triparadeisus some three years on, either for his part in Perdiccas' execution, or for his defending Antipater against the angry mob being whipped up by Eurydice; that was the first of two 'mutinies' over back-pay Antipater would see before re-crossing the Hellespont.[187] Heckel has logically argued that the *Pamphlet* must therefore have a *terminus post quem* of May 320 BCE (thus Triparadeisus) for its author to have witnessed Seleucus' appointment. To the contrary, we argue that Babylonia was part of Seleucus' *original* and genuine Will-sanctioned *strategia*, and not a coalition 'gift', in which case such a prominent post could hardly be hidden by the architects of the *Pamphlet* now that Seleucus was back there governing.[188]

But recalling Plutarch's chronology, and following what Carney has termed a great public 'lamentation' in Macedonia which would have heralded in the *Pamphlet*'s release, we must consider how early Olympias could have 'glutted her rage with atrocities' from years of pent-up Antipatrid hatred,[189] because that was *supposed* to coincide: the *Pamphlet*'s accusation would vindicate Olympias' revenge killings, and no doubt the murders were supposed to imply that the *Pamphlet* content was genuine.[190]

This could have only taken place once Olympias had re-established herself in Pella after defeating and executing Eurydice and Philip III; so October 317 BCE or later if we adhere to Diodorus' statement on the length of the king's reign.[191] Release of the *Pamphlet* from Cilicia in late 318 BCE is perhaps still supportable, as news took time to travel, but it appears to be dangerously early, that is unless Olympias *did* imprudently (and so against Eumenes' advice) spread allegations of regicide when she was still in Epirus.[192] It would have been an unwise move that broadcast her intent, though we should ponder whether it was exactly these allegations that swayed the Cassander-backed army of Eurydice to Olympias' cause when she finally marched on Pella.

A more viable date for the *Pamphlet's* release would be when, or shortly before, Eumenes arrived in Persepolis and attempted to wrest command of the eastern coalition from Peucestas in the winter of 317 BCE, as by then Seleucus and Peithon had already united against him, and their *Pamphlet* incrimination (assuming Seleucus' name *was* present on the guilty list) would have logically followed.[193] Moreover, it was here that Eumenes' faked letter from Orontes 'arrived', and here that Eumenes brought false charges against Sibyrtius. Had the Persian satraps not already combined under Peucestas and had they not outnumbered Eumenes' own men, Eumenes may well have terminated the prominent Persian-speaking former Bodyguard right there.

This later release date requires that Eumenes was still hoping that Ptolemy and Lysimachus might join his cause; they had been meddlesome to his plans but no open hostilities had taken place. Eumenes' attempt to include them in an anti-Antigonus coalition was not altogether unrealistic considering Antigonus' rising power, for he was by then a formidable threat to *any* Asian satrap. Some two years on, Ptolemy was indeed assisting Seleucus in his bid to oust Antigonus from Babylonia, for with Eumenes' death came the unsuccessful demands from Ptolemy, Lysimachus and Cassander for a share of Asia Minor (the return of Babylon was required for Seleucus) and, curiously, Syria, along with the accumulated treasure seized in the war.[194]

If there still exist various other scenarios that could suit the *Pamphlet's* release, we do now have a broad *terminus post quem*: Eumenes' departure from Nora in spring 318 BCE, with a more obvious *terminus ante quem* established by his death in early 315 BCE or at Olympias' execution later the same year.

A depiction of Olympias on a large gold medallion commissioned to honour the Roman emperor Caracalla and representing him as a descendant of Alexander. The back (not shown) features a nereid (sea nymph), perhaps Thetis, the mother of Achilles, riding on a *hippocamp*, a mythical sea creature. Thus the medallion forms part of a double comparison: Caracalla is connected to Alexander, whilst Alexander is linked to Achilles. Found at Aboukir in Upper Egypt as part of a hoard of twenty similar medallions, they may originate from the mints at Ephesus or Perinthus. Walters Art Museum, Baltimore.

THE COMPLEX HYPOKEIMENA

The *Pamphlet* fired warning shots across the bows of the remaining satraps and their prominent supporting officers, whose guilt in Alexander's death, if not specifically mentioned, could be brought into question by association: those in Cilicia with Craterus, for example. That was Eumenes' own silent siegecraft, a clever intrigue that left doors open for future alliances, but with safety catches on.

If Olympias' hatred for her opponents is palpable, we should not underestimate Eumenes' own hunger for revenge, having been placed on a proscription list with fifty Perdiccan supporters. Reading the later Roman proscriptions demanded by Sulla in 82 BCE once he was appointed *dictator legibus faciendis et rei publicae constituendae causa* (dictator for writing the laws and restoring the state) makes for disturbing reading, as do the death lists of Antony and Octavian that heralded in the Second Triumvirate. That had been a period punctuated by *avaritas, crudelitas* and *per vim* ('by violence') if the *Periochae* preserving Livy's account can be relied on. The unbridled menace of a death list is shocking in an environment where political balances and voices of reason from such as Cicero (who was invited by Caesar to join the first coalition) were supposed to prevent tyranny, but they had this early Hellenistic example to draw from. Now, through the shockwave of the *Pamphlet*, Eumenes and Olympias were effectively returning the compliment with its widespread accusations of treason.

The *Pamphlet* was clearly a one-time bid for a huge prize: the lion's share of Asia should Antigonus fall, and complete control of Pella if Cassander could be silenced. But its virulence would mean a death sentence for both of its architects should the gambit fail, and so Eumenes and Olympias packed it with layers of purpose. The guilty and the innocent, and those wedded to Argead royalty were just the more prominent front lines of deeper, subtler ranks. The *Pamphlet* was built on complex *hypokeimena*, the political substrates lying beneath, some probably still eluding us today. Others are more obvious and they fit their joint predicament. The first was Perdiccas' position of authority in the Will:

> As for the areas lying between the boundaries of Babylonia and Bactria, the satraps should retain what they variously govern, and as commander-in-chief over them, I appoint Perdiccas, on whom I also bestow as a wife Roxane...[195]

From his reading of Hieronymus, Arrian interpreted that the outcome at Babylon entrusted Perdiccas with the 'care of the whole empire' in his capacity as the foremost of Alexander's *Somatophylakes*, acting chiliarch, and as the recipient of his ring.[196] But the compression of power suggested above sees him overseeing *only* what we propose were the regions inherited by Seleucus and Peithon, the most prominent of his murderers, *if* Nepos was correct.[197] And this suggested a clear motive for his assassination in Egypt: they wished to rid themselves of his overarching authority.

From the perspective of the pamphleteer, Perdiccas' marriage to Roxane legitimised the former chiliarch's authority over Bactria, whilst his earlier Susa marriage to the daughter of the Median satrap, Atropates (reinstalled by Alexander on campaign and reconfirmed after his death at Babylon, though now to Lesser Media), likewise justified an authority over Median regions as well.[198] A broader interpretation of the Babylon-Bactria mandate *could* include the Persian heartlands to the south, so Peucestas' domain. Either way, fencing in Perdiccas' authority to Babylon and eastwards released Ptolemy and Lysimachus (and Eumenes) from any overlord except the kings, whilst it legitimised Ptolemy's defence of Egypt by the suggestion that Perdiccas, who clearly had alternative plans for Alexander's corpse, was overstepping his mandate.[199]

According to the *Pamphlet* Will, before Alexander died he bade Perdiccas promise that he *and* Antipater would manage the affairs of the kingdom and empire and ensure the terms of his Will were properly concluded; this could have been a neat device that positioned it as a balanced testament and not one hell-bent on the destruction of the Antipatrids; Alexander was, after all, supposedly unaware of the plot against him when the Will was written (or amended) just before he died.

The section of the *Pamphlet* testament dealing with Asia Minor is the most corrupted in both the *Metz Epitome* and *Romance* texts (T1, T2), with the former involving Antipater in future government there.[200] The Halys is the proposed dividing line of administration, yet the river runs in a southwest-northeast arc on its way to the Black Sea, providing no clinical geographical division. The most obvious explanation, however, is that 'Antipater' should simply read 'Antigonus', in which case the Halys referred to the north and east borders of his Greater Phrygian authority. Whatever the intended name, governance east (or southeast) of the Halys remained free from any overlord, providing Eumenes in Cappadocia independence from their higher authority.

A curious gift in the testament is 'Syria as far as the so-called Mesopotamian Line', for this went to a Peithon, clearly not the hostile son of Crateuas who held the upper satrapies. If this referred to the prominent Peithon son of Agenor, who governed regions bordering on (and in) India on campaign and certainly until 320 BCE, then the pamphleteer had anticipated his return to Syria, which did take place in 314/313 BCE.[201] Peithon's whereabouts from Triparadeisus in 320 BCE to 315 BCE, when he was installed by Antigonus in Babylonia once Seleucus fled to Ptolemy in Egypt, remain unknown. If this is indeed our man, he too was being courted away from *Monophthalmos*.

The only other so-named candidate would be Peithon son of Antigenes whose importance is attested by the reference to the patronymic.[202] If the Antigenes referred to was the commander of the Silver Shields, Eumenes was granting his most important soldier honours and estates through his son; Antigenes himself now governed Susiane (though his service under Eumenes took him away from the province).[203] Events made it clear that Eumenes needed every coercive tool to keep the unruly Silver Shields brigade marching. Yet none of these identifications present ideal candidates.

A further possible identity – for what could have become corrupted to 'Peithon' – is Aristonus son of 'Peisaeus', though this would involve a lacuna that lost the *onoma* and saved the *patronymikon*, with a scribe reverting the name to more familiar *Somatophylax*. The loss of this type of detail must have occurred as patronyms would have been more widely employed, and they were certainly needed where the first name (*onoma*) was identical. Mistakes *were* often made: Arrian, for example, used varying *patronymika* for Leonnatus in four different passages.[204] Little is known of the campaign career of Aristonus, the seventh attested Bodyguard, apart from a reference to his *trierarchos* role with the Hydaspes-Indus fleet, and a wound in the Mallian city. Curtius proposed he had spoken out for Perdiccas at Babylon (T11) and we know he commanded his Cypriot invasion (the identity of the existing pro-Perdiccas governor remains unanswered), and so he ought to have featured in governance in a meaningful way, either in Alexander's Will, or (for the adherents to the intestacy) by virtue of Perdiccas' self-interested division of empire.[205]

The relative obscurity of Aristonus in the Alexander biographies suggests his contribution to the campaign was deliberately sidelined; in Ptolemy's account that may have been due to these 'royalist' sympathies and this may have influenced Cleitarchus. The unique references to him in Arrian's texts appear to come from Nearchus' *Indike,* and he is not mentioned by name (only inference) in the Susa honours list.[206] Aristonus was eventually murdered on Cassander's orders in 315 BCE after a brief resurgence the previous year when Olympias was confined to Pydna and he controlled Amphipolis.[207] References to him by Diodorus suggested he was popular and respected, in post-Alexander Macedonia at least.[208] If 'Aristonus son of Peisaeus' was truly being referred to as the inheritor of a part of Syria in the *Pamphlet* Will, it is not difficult to rationalise why. Either the pamphleteers were beckoning him out of forced retirement to operate in Macedonia or Asia once more (in which case he cannot have been present at Medius' banquet in Babylon or he would have been cited as an 'innocent'), or Alexander's *Somatophylax* did genuinely inherit a part of Syria (excluding the Coele-Syrian region) and the pamphleteers were conveniently returning it to him.[209]

RHODIAN SEDUCTION: A DIPLOMATIC *DIEKPLOUS*

Strikingly prominent in the *Pamphlet* is the favourable treatment of Rhodes, both within the main Will narrative and in Alexander's so-called 'Letter to the Rhodians' which preceded its bequests.[210]

This letter, as we read it today in the extant Will texts (T1, T2), could be the product of gradual embellishment. But to quote Bosworth on the issue: 'A single coherent document composed at a particular moment for a particular purpose is preferable to a composite production, growing layer by layer according to the interests of different groups at different times.'[211]

It would have benefitted Eumenes and Olympias to reach out to Rhodes, 'an aristocracy disguised as a democracy', to galvanise her naval resources to the planned alliance.[212] Rhodes was described by Diodorus as the 'best-governed city of the Greeks' and the island was strategically important: a seafaring power with a reputation for remaining politically neutral, with much of her wealth derived from tributes paid by those inclined for her to remain so. Additional income was earned from the renting out of Rhodian galleys (principally triremes) to clients lacking a fleet.[213] By now the smaller nearby islands and strategic mainland land tracts had become part of the Rhodian state. The Rhodian currency standard had eclipsed its Chian forerunner and it was uniquely maintained in the face of Alexander's adoption of the Attic standard, probably due to long-standing trade and shipping contracts.[214]

It is unlikely that the dying Alexander gave complete autonomy to the major Greek islands, despite the earlier rhetoric surrounding the 'freedom of the Greeks'; and if any of them in the eastern Aegean *did* consider themselves nominally independent, they were to soon lose their impartiality in the Successor Wars. Many examples survive of new law codes imposed by Antigonus, in particular on Kos, Chios and Lebedos, despite independent federations such as the Cycladic League of the Islanders which 'liberated' them in 313 BCE.[215] Any reference to their future at Babylon appears absent from Hieronymus' satrapal rundown, and the fate of strategically important Cyprus remains vexing; the island saw little activity during Alexander's campaign and it was never formalised into the empire, though its fleet assisted with the siege of Tyre. When Ptolemy later gained possession of the island in 315 BCE, he installed his brother, Menelaus, which perhaps suggests a gap in its governance still existed following the Perdiccan defeat.[216]

In contrast, the *Romance* bestowed Rhodes with authority over *all* other Greek islands (T2). If a relic of Alexander's original Will, it was a sound step, for a carefully chosen Macedonian *strategos* would have directed that Rhodian authority through the Aegean. Rhodes had already become directly answerable to Alexander and not to its ten former *strategoi*, and it had not been immune to Macedonian law, resulting in arrests in the campaign years.[217] If this is a design of the *Pamphlet*, then clearly a governor of some repute had held the island in Perdiccas' interest. Either way, Alexander's past attachment to Rhodes was being exploited by the pamphleteers.

Alexander had sported a belt of significance into battle taken from the Rhodian temple of Lindian Athena; it was a relic no doubt ascribed to a suitable hero or king, for thanks to the *Lindian Chronicle* we know the temple was a depository of heroic significance. Heracles, Persian kings (through their generals and satraps) and the kings of Egypt had made votive offerings of weapons and armour at Rhodian shrines, and after the battle at Gaugamela Alexander is said to have made a gift of caltrops and armour to the temple, just as he had at Troy. After all, Lindos, the daughter of Danaus (Alexander's ancestor) was worshipped on the island that named its templed city after her.[218] The island had always been closely associated with Heracles who visited it on his way from Egypt; Heracles' son, Tlepolemus, was the founding king of Rhodes. We also have evidence of a cult to Alexander, Heracles' alleged descendent, appearing on the island after his death; an inscription titling him 'Lord of Asia' was found in a Lindian temple,[219] so the Athena Poliouchus cult (to Athena 'Guardian of the city') might have resounded with a special significance.

The *Pamphlet* overtures to the powerful Rhodian confederation, made through the reworked Will, included 300 talents of gold, forty triremes, annual grain and wheat subsidies from Egypt and from the regions of Asia adjacent to Rhodes.[220] The island was promised its own 'freedom' with a pledge to have the garrison removed, a meaningless (yet symbolic) concession as it had already been expelled after Alexander's death, and it had more recently resisted Attalus' attempts to form a Perdiccan bridgehead there after Triparadeisus.[221]

Egypt's role in Rhodes' wellbeing was also being emphasised; Eumenes was bestowing Ptolemy with the 'honour' of providing the island with grain, the most influential currency in the empire.[222] Rhodes *did* become Ptolemy's most faithful ally in the Aegean with a relationship further strengthened by the enormous export, and to fund the grain subsidy the Will granted Egyptian priests 2,000 talents from the public purse.[223]

As conspicuous in the testament is Ptolemy's task of transporting Alexander's body to Egypt, for this justified his attack on the Perdiccan escort that was leading the bier elsewhere; a further 200 talents were to be used for the construction of the sarcophagus. The courting of Ptolemy continued; in the *Romance* text the Rhodian letter closed with an emphasis on his role as the executor of the Will:[224]

> I am quite sure you will obey my instructions. Ptolemy my bodyguard
> will take care of you: we have indicated to him what he must do for

you. Do not think this legacy was made lightly. The administrator of the kingdom will ensure there is no deviation from the instructions.

It was a golden handcuff: now Ptolemy was not only present at the Will's drafting, as were Holcias and Lysimachus, but he was also responsible for its enactment.

Olympias was granted the right to live on Rhodes.[225] Linking Alexander's mother to residency implied a 'guardianship' of the island, and any hostile move against it could result in a legitimate military response; this rather underpins the story of the doctored oath Eumenes allegedly signed when exiting Nora, as Eumenes would have known Antigonus would court Rhodes for the same reason he and Olympias planned to: the lack of a significant navy. It was a diplomatic *diekplous* that kept the islanders from a flanking action.[226] With Rhodes on board, and with Ptolemy annexing Coele-Syria and the Phoenician ports, the Eastern Mediterranean seaboard would be theirs to control.[227]

THEBES: THE WOVEN WEB, BANE OR BOON

Another visitor to the pages of the testament is Ismenias, apparently a Theban to whom the Will was entrusted for delivery to the city still in ruins.[228] An 'Ismenias' is mentioned earlier in verse in the *Romance* as the best of the Theban pipers ordered to play his shrill instrument while the city burned.[229] The name is firmly Theban in origin; the so-named god mentioned by Pausanias, Diodorus and Ovid, are all associated with the River Ismenas that washed the walls of Thebes, where a fountain allegedly ran with blood before Alexander destroyed the city.[230] In a surviving fragment of the third book of Callisthenes' *Hellenika* we have the reference '… that of Ismenas at Thebes: the trophonian oracle at Levadia.' Its existence is confirmed by Herodotus who claimed to have visited the sanctuary of Ismenias, or better, the Temple to 'Apollo Ismenias', and it is additionally referenced in a passage in the penultimate chapter of Plutarch's *Life of Lysander*.[231]

As far as a possible historic identification, Alexander did free Thessalicus, a son of Ismenias, after capturing the Theban and Greek envoys to Darius following the battle at Issus; Alexander's respect for Thessalicus' illustrious lineage was reportedly the reason for his release. Moreover, Pelopidas, the renowned general Philip II would have come to know well at Thebes, had been a member of the political party of Ismenias who was himself 'admired for valour' and for his ingenuity too, according to Aelian: he found a way to avoid *proskynesis* when visiting the Persian Great King.[232] Could a grateful *son* of Ismenias have joined Alexander's entourage, or have become a well-known agent in the Boeotian city with whom a copy of the Will was being entrusted?

Alexander is said to have regretted his destruction of Thebes, when children 'wailed piteously the names of their mothers', though Arrian gave his best shot at damning its past in the king's defence: he claimed its Greek enemies inflicted more damage than the Macedonians in the attack.[233] Alexander apparently feared the wrath of Dionysus (whose favourite city was Thebes – despite Euripides' portrayal of his hostility towards it), though this story might have emanated from Ephippus who claimed the god's anger was behind Alexander's death. The Theban ancestral oracle had nevertheless cryptically declared 'the woven web is bane to one, to one a boon' before he took the city.[234] Heracles himself was born there in legend, and so to hedge his bets on oracular fate, a donation of funds for the reconstruction of the ancient city (including the aforementioned temple) is not insupportable as one of Alexander's testament 'last wishes'.[235] The demand would have doubtless been cancelled by Perdiccas at Babylon and surely with little objection.

But restoration of the city by the *Pamphlet* architects is also credible; securing support of a renewed Boeotian confederacy headed by Thebes would turn central Greece against Cassander. Cassander knew it himself, and he embarked upon his own rebuilding programme after the death of Eumenes; many cities in Greece, Sicily and Italy pledged their support and 'played a part' in the city's rebuilding despite Antigonus' objection, for he demanded it be reversed in his proclamation from Tyre. As Crates had forewarned, a 'second Alexander' would surely seek to raze it to the ground.[236]

A NEW ARGIVE ODYSSEY

The *Pamphlet* Will requested a significant votive to Argos: Alexander's arms, insignia plus 1,000 talents of silver.[237] Divided texts direct the donation either to the Temple of Hera, or as 'first fruits of war for Heracles'.[238] The Argive Heraion was destroyed in 423 BC but had featured in the *Iliad*.[239] Heinrich Schliemann excavated the site in 1874 and the spurious Dictys of Crete claimed it was the site at which Agamemnon was chosen to lead the Argives against Troy. Alexander's lineage was traceable back to Argos and the returning Heracleidae, and so a bequest of this nature may be original.[240] But, once again, there was more reason for the Eumenes-Olympias-led coalition to exploit Polyperchon's position in Greece. Cassander had garrisoned Argos and yet the inhabitants offered to hand the city over to Polyperchon's son, Alexander, when its occupying general was absent campaigning elsewhere.[241] Although this was soon after Eumenes' death in Asia, it may have been the first opportunity the city had to show the support solicited by the promise of a significant financial gift.

The *Romance* text (T2) contains additional endowments not appearing in the *Metz Epitome* Will (T1): 3 talents apiece for 'feeble' Macedonian and Thessalian veterans due for repatriation.[242] Again, if based upon an original *Pamphlet* clause, Eumenes and Olympias were simply seeking to enrol the celebrated cavalry (whether in Thessaly or still in Asia) and other experienced Macedonian infantry into their ranks to help install Olympias in Pella, and potentially those resettled in Asia for Eumenes to muster. Antipater and Craterus must have destroyed much of Thessaly after the Battle of Crannon. This, along with much else in the document, only makes sense if Olympias and Eumenes were broadcasting their identity as the capable upholders of these *Pamphlet* pledges through their unique positions and mandates. Although 3 talents, equivalent to a total of almost fifty years' infantryman's pay, is clearly excessive, the *concept* was nevertheless sound once Eumenes gained control of a major Asian treasury.[243]

Overall verisimilitude would have demanded a testament that appeared complete. For that reason the collaborating pamphleteers left untouched what they could and what had no value in changing. Eumenes also knew he could not alchemise what was too widely known, indiscriminately elevating those who turned 'ally', for example, or downgrading those who opposed him, beyond a believable level. This is probably why the *Pamphlet* narrative appears to have referred to the suspicion that Alexander's death was being kept from the infantry which attempted to storm his bed chamber, for this likely correlated with what *did* take place at Babylon, though we must accept the possibility of its reverse origination: Cleitarchus incorporated this detail from the by then famous partisan publication.[244]

The passing of the ring to Perdiccas was clearly broadcast too, for this justified Eumenes placing initial support in him, and it reinforced the heinous nature of Perdiccas' murder in Egypt (in which Ptolemy was not implicated).[245] Eumenes would not, however, have been motivated to restate the grander untenable last wishes that were absorbed into Diodorus' 'last plans', for they were irreverently cancelled by Perdiccas at Babylon. The reasonable scale of Alexander's commemoratives is the carefully edited result, though they have since been contaminated in the surviving texts.[246]

Alexander's secretary, in collusion with Alexander's mother, was reissuing the Will as a genuine *Ephemerides*-recorded testament into a world in which knowledge of the original still carried dangerous connotations. Beside it they poured a toxic concoction of threat, bribery, exoneration and falsification into a deep propaganda cup, whose content was washed down with the fluid authenticity its complicitors could uniquely provide.

Ironically, Aristotle was at some later point dragged into the frame and not in a minor role; a Vulgate tradition embellishing the original conspiracy claims cited the great Peripatetic scholar in the role of providing the poison, and encouragement, to Antipater. By appointing the Macedonian regent as executor of his own Will, Aristotle might have unwittingly laid himself open for posthumous implication; it lent the plot a weighty audacity and something of a philosophical gravitas (T9, T10).[247] Before the *Pamphlet* was published, Aristotle's student and successor, Theophrastus, may have already published his *Enquiry Into Plants* in which he recommended disguising the bitter taste of the poison strychnine by serving it in undiluted wine, inspiring the *Pamphlet* authors' conspiratorial imaginations in the process.[248] After all, everyone knew that 'regicide was something of a Macedonian tradition'.[249]

THE LEGACY OF THE *PAMPHLET*

The immediate effect of the publication was short-lived, despite its contents reaching Greece. Cornered on a Macedonian chessboard himself, Eumenes had castled out of trouble with a folio of fakes, but he sacrificed too many pieces in the process. Once Cassander had engineered a guilty verdict at a sham trial of Olympias and overseen her execution near the fortified town of Pydna, the *Pamphlet* became as dangerous to quote as one of Callisthenes' sophisms.[250] Here Curtius' contention – echoed in other Vulgate texts – that 'whatever credence such stories gained, they were soon suppressed by the power of the people implicated by the rumour', finally comes to life.[251] In the vacuum that was left behind, Antigonus expediently broadcast his new 'royalist' side by demanding Cassander restore the imprisoned Roxane and Alexander IV 'to the Macedones'.[252] This was the veneer of loyalty and court-sanctioned legitimacy he had once hoped to obtain from an alliance with Eumenes, and Alexander's sons now started to glow with a lustre that failed to shine at Babylon.

In response, Cassander had his henchman, Glaucias, murder mother and son, possibly recalling the verse 'a fool is he who slays the sire and leaves the sons alive'.[253] Soon after, the polemical noises from Greece started haranguing the behaviour of the conquering Alexander, and that, suggested Tarn, was broadcast by the Peripatetics under Cassander's shield.[254] It was now 310 BCE, the 'seventh year of Alexander IV' according to the *Babylonian Chronicle* (here calculated from the death of Philip III, suggesting that had indeed been in 317 BCE), the same year that Antigonus commenced a concerted campaign to remove Seleucus from Babylon.[255] Diodorus described the mood:

> When Glaucias had carried out the instructions, Cassander, Lysimachus and Ptolemy, and Antigonus as well, were relieved of their anticipated

danger from the king, for henceforth, there being no longer anyone to inherit the realm, and each of those who had ruled over nations and cities entertained hopes of royal power…[256]

The short-lived 'Peace of the Dynasts' of 311 BCE had in fact been 'a disguised invitation to the jailers to eliminate any members of the family they held', and by 309/308 BCE, with the murder of Alexander's older son, Heracles, who was then approaching adulthood, and with Antigonus' execution of Cleopatra when she attempted to depart Sardis in 308 BCE to marry Ptolemy, the *Pamphlet* faded into romantic obscurity.[257] The original Will had now outlived its useful sell-by date and the royal charade was gone, almost, for Cassander had extracted the Argead Thessalonice at the conclusion of the siege at Pydna and took her as his bride, forcefully according to Antigonus, a potentially valid accusation when recalling she was Olympias' ward.[258]

Cassander's treatment of Olympias (he refused her a proper state burial), Roxane and Alexander IV (imprisoned and then executed) suggests, as one scholar put it, that he tried to categorise Alexander's 'branch of the Argeads as illegitimate' while seeding his own.[259] Cassander did, in fact, clear the way for the rise of the Ptolemaic, Seleucid and Antigonid dynasties when weeding the path for his own. Soon, once Pyrrhus had killed Cleopatra's son who reigned as Neoptolemus II in Epirus for five years (to 297 BCE, if that identification is correct), the only surviving males of any Argead blood were, ironically, the next generation Philip, Antipater and Alexander, Cassander's sons by Thessalonice.[260]

In his *Parallel Lives* we recall that Plutarch rather fittingly paired Eumenes with the brilliant Roman outcast, Quintus Sertorius, whose craft and ability was additionally compared to the achievements of Philip II, Antigonus *Monophthalmos* and Hannibal. Plutarch's obituary to both men is a fitting way to close the chapter:

> With him [Sertorius] we may best compare, among the Greeks, Eumenes of Cardia. Both were born to command and given to wars of stratagem; both were exiled from their own countries, commanded foreign soldiers, and in their deaths experienced a fortune that was harsh and unjust; for both were the victims of plots, and were slain by the very men with whom they were conquering their foes.[261]

The final lines were of course referring to the Silver Shields' treachery at Gabiene, when Eumenes had been 'unable to fly before being taken prisoner'.[262] The influential biographing historian from Chaeronea gave us a vivid picture of a man contemplating his fate upon hearing of the fermenting treachery:[263]

> … Eumenes… went off to his tent, where he said to his friends that he
> was living in a great herd of wild beasts. Then made his Will, and tore
> up and destroyed his papers; he did not wish that after his death, in
> consequence of the secrets contained in these documents, accusations
> and calumnies should be brought against his correspondents.[264]

This rather contradicts the allegation that followed from Plutarch:
Eumenes 'neither took good precautions against death, nor faced it well',
possibly echoing the continued hostility of Duris of Samos.[265]

What else did Eumenes have in the box of secret correspondence?
The blueprint of the grand plan he was hatching with Olympias? Perhaps
a copy of Alexander's *original* Will as a template to draw from? Or, possibly,
the first written copies of the *Pamphlet* and other homespun Pellan letters
of empowerment that were supposedly signed by Polyperchon and the
kings? We might guess who the counter-correspondents were apart from
Cleopatra in Sardis, Olympias in Epirus and then Pella: other promising,
but vacillating, satraps waiting to see which way to jump. And whom
would Eumenes have chosen to pass the incendiary folio to and then
appoint executor to his own Will? Hieronymus must be the obvious
choice on both accounts, in which case the Cardian historian became the
guardian of the knowledge of *two* vanished Wills.

Here it is tempting to pinpoint the third, and possibly the most
poignant, date for the release of the *Pamphlet*: before, or immediately
after, the final battle at Gabiene on the Iranian Plateau. Eumenes was not
immediately seized and handed over to Antigonus, for when negotiating the
return of their baggage the Silver Shields complained '… that their wives
should be spending the *third* night in a row in the arms of the enemy.'[266]
During this time and withdrawn in his tent, Eumenes had nothing to lose
by drafting the toxic document while destroying the evidence behind it.

'Among the wounded there was also brought in as a captive the
historian Hieronymus, who hitherto always had been held in honour by
Eumenes, but after Eumenes' death enjoyed the favour and confidence
of Antigonus.'[267] Did Hieronymus reveal the folio to his captor? Not
burdened himself with guilt in the *Pamphlet* and with his satrapies still
intact, and, moreover, intent on subduing those who *were* dammed by the
publication and yet still in league with those who were not, how much
would Antigonus have had to lose from letting the incendiary scrolls
past his sentries, or in passing the garnishing detail to Hagnon of Teos
(Hagnothemis) who is said to have first broadcasted it aloud, obviously
before his squadron was captured in a naval battle off of Cyprus?[268]

Following his victory at Gabiene, Antigonus must have heeded
Lysander's Spartan advice: 'Where the skin of the lion does not reach, it
must be patched with the skin of a fox', or perhaps in this case a jackal.[269]
For upon Eumenes' death, he certainly patched up his differences with

the now-bested Polyperchon and had him battling in his own interests *against* Cassander in Greece. This raises the question whether Antigonus himself was the source of the added slander against Aristotle, for he and Cassander's father had clearly been confidants.

Just a few years earlier, Antigonus' son, Demetrius *Poliorketes,* is said to have defied his father by saving Mithridates, a friend then under suspicion. Demetrius wrote in the sand with his spear without Antigonus noticing: 'Fly, Mithridates!' And he did, curiously to an unnamed stone fortress somewhere in Cappadocia.[270] 'Politics *is* history on the wing', Cicero is portrayed as declaring, and although 'unable to fly' at Gabiene, even though it was alleged he tried, what Eumenes may have initially conceived at Nora, and then sculpted into its final form sometime in the three following years, was indeed a masterstroke of mental warfare that rivalled the best Macedonian *machtpolitik.*[271]

NOTES

1. Diodorus 18.53.4-6, translation from the Loeb Classical Library edition, 1947.
2. Plutarch *Apophthegms* or *Sayings of Kings and Commanders* 8860 (5), *Lysander*.
3. The terrain is described by Polyaenus 4.6.7 and Diodorus 18.44.2-4.
4. Full title: JM Kinneir, *Journey Through Asia Minor, Armenia and Koordistan, In the Years 1813 and 1814, with Remarks on the Marches of Alexander and Retreat of The Ten Thousand*, John Murray, London 1818, pp 111-112, in which he stated he had interviewed locals of the region who identified an ancient stone fortress above a deep gorge as 'Nour'. Also quoted in Thirlwall (1845) p 305. It was also known as 'Yengi Bar'. For Neroasus see Strabo 12.2.17. For the reference to Taurus, Kinneir (1813) p 4.
5. Ramsay (1923) pp 1-10. For the battle at Orcynia see Plutarch *Eumenes* 18.9-10, Nepos 5 (battle name not mentioned) and Diodorus 18.39.7-18.40.4. As it has been noted, Orcynia might have been a Cappadocian district and not a specific battleground. Who stocked Nora, and why, has never been questioned but if it guarded the pass leading to the Cilician Gates, then it is more explainable as a permanently stocked fortress. Antigonus could have maintained its strategic value by keeping it provioned for just such a battle outcome; Eumenes could have likewise provisioned the fortress as a fallback option. Plutarch *Eumenes* 11.1 and Diodorus 18.41.3 for the water, firewood, grain and salt in abundance but, according to Plutarch, no other edibles. The *Journal of the Royal Geographic Society* of 1841 p 303 cited claims by Colonel Leake that Cybistra was Nora, though Cybistra is linked to Karahisar which appears too far west to be the location.
6. For the location see Plutarch *Eumenes* 10.1; Nepos 5 simply stated 'Phrygia'. Diodorus 18.41.1-3 did not state a specific location.
7. This was first made possible by Reitzenstein's 1888 translation of the two single leaves (a bifolium) of the Vatican palimpsest (ms. Vaticanus 495) and more recently Oxyrhynchus fragment *PSI 11* 1284; see Simpson (1959) p 377. This was published as *Arriani τῶν μετὰ Αλέξανδρον libri septimi fragmenta e codice Vaticano rescripto nuper iteratis curis lecto*, Breslauer philologische Abhandlungen Bd. 3, H. 3, Breslau 1888, S. 1-36. See Bosworth (1978) for full discussion. The fragment found at Oxyrhynchus in 1932 gave a detailed description of Eumenes in battle against either Craterus or, in Bosworth's opinion, Neoptolemus, which appeared to come from Arrian *Events After Alexander*. For details of the extract from the Vatican palimpsest see discussion in Goralski (1989) p 81 and for additional detail on surviving fragments of Arrian *Events After Alexander* see Goralski (1989) pp 81-83.
8. Errington (1970) p 73 and Bosworth (2002) p 22 for discussion on Arrian *Events After Alexander* filling ten books covering three years to Antipater's return to Macedonia sometime after Triparadeisus.
9. Goralski (1989) p 82 and Kebric (1977) p 52.
10. See discussion in Hornblower (1981) p 101 and Warner (1966) p 30 for dividing up the campaign year.
11. The Roman Consular Year was set at January 1st to December 29th from 153 BCE onwards. It had previously commenced in March and before that May. See explanation in Polo (2011) p 15. We have no idea how extensively Hieronymus covered events in Greece for example when based in Asia; the coverage of the double-burial of Philip III and Eurydice at Diodorus 19.52.5, as an example, seems Diyllus-sourced as it closely matches Athenaeus 4.155 citing Diyllus.
12. See Anson (2004) p 18 for discussion of Diodorus' chronology. For the archon dating see Hornblower (1981) pp 108-109. Also expanded in Anson (1986) pp 208-217. Full discussion of the chronological problems and the omission of archon years in Anson (2004) p 77 footnote 2 and Smith (1961) p 283 ff; also Goralski (1989) p 102.
13. See discussion in Anson (1977) p 251 for the dating of the battle at Orcynia.
14. 'Passed over in silence' quoting Billows (1990) p 347. Diodorus occasionally confused himself with his method. One result is the conflicting claim that Eumenes' victory over Craterus in 321 BCE provided Perdiccas with the confidence for his invasion of Egypt (18.33.1) whereas just several pages later he stated news of that battle arrived only *after* Perdiccas' death in May/June 320 BCE (18.37.1), although Eumenes' victory could refer to that over Neoptolemus some ten days before. Plutarch *Eumenes* 8.2 supported Diodorus' latter claim. Earlier, a more generalised approach to time-framing by Diodorus placed Alexander's Exiles Decree 'a short time before his death' (18.8.2) and yet he went on to state it was proclaimed at the Olympic Games of 324 BCE (17.109.1) thus almost a full year earlier.
15. Anson (2014) pp 58-59 and pp 116-121 for the relative chronologies. Also Hauben (1977) pp 85-120. He cites Manni and others who date Triparadeisus to 321 BCE (the 'high' chronology, supported by Diodorus' event order). The date of Perdiccas' death, May/June 320 BCE, is backed up by the *Babylonian Chronicle* extract BM 34, 660 Vs 4 which suggests 320 BCE for

the conference (the 'low' chronology, also backed by the *Parian Chronicle*). Also discussed in Errington (1970) pp 75-80. Anson (1986) pp 208-217 made a convincing case that Triparadeisus took place in 320 BCE. For references to the astronomical records of Babylon see Geller (1990) pp 1-7.

16. See Bosworth (2002) pp 20-21 for discussion and in particular Bosworth (2002) pp 55-81 and p 74 for the inaccuracy of the *Parian Chronicle*; also Wheatley (1995) p 434. Goralski (1989) p 103 for a full translation of the *Parian Chronicle*.

17. The dates and authorship discussed in detail in chapter titled *Guardians and Ghosts of the Ephemerides*.

18. Diodorus 18.59.6 describing Eumenes' change of fortune.

19. Diodorus 18.41.7-18.42.1.

20. Arrian *Events After Alexander* 1.39, Diodorus 18.37.1-3, Justin 13.8.10-14.1.1, Appian *Syrian Wars* 53 for the proscription of the Perdiccans. Hornblower (1981) p 11 agreed that Hieronymus would have needed Antigonus' permission to leave the fortress.

21. Diodorus 18.47.4-5. It was Aristodemus who later brought news to Antigonus of Antipater's death. One modern interpretation assumed the journey to Macedonia was in response to Eumenes' immediate demands, whilst another considers it took place late in the siege when Eumenes saw little hope with local negotiations. See Anson (2004) p 137 and compare to Billows (1990) p 77, accepting Diodorus' version at 18.41.7. Considering the distance to be covered, and the timing of Antipater's death; it seems the journey was more likely linked to the early demands. For the first offer see Diodorus 18.41.5-7. Also Diodorus 18.53.2-7 for the bargaining and release. For the full year of the siege, Diodorus 18.53.4-5. For six months, Nepos 5.6-7; either scenario is possible, that is until news of Antipater's death in late 319 BCE arrived in Phrygia.

22. Plutarch *Eumenes* 10.4 for Eumenes' fame.

23. Literally translated as either 'the love of honour' or the 'urge to be thought superior' and 'love of power'. Aelian 12.16 and 14.47a suggested Alexander had also been alarmed at the extent of his *philotimia* and *philarchia* before Antipater was.

24. Plutarch *Eumenes* 5.4-7 for Antipater's offer of an alliance with Eumenes in defeating Perdiccas. Eumenes rejected the offer stating they were old enemies.

25. For Sardis see Arrian *Events After Alexander* 1.40 and 24.8, Plutarch *Eumenes* 8.6-7. Justin 14.1.7-8 for the prestige hoped for. *Gothenburg Palimpsest* for detail of Eumenes bettering Antipater in Lydia or Phrygia; discussed in chapter titled *The Tragic Triumvirate of Treachery and Oaths*.

26. 'Owls to Athens' taken from the Greek proverb describing a pointless action or journey; owls roosted in the 'old' Xerxes-burned Parthenon. As a symbol of Athens, owls appeared on coins it minted. Thus to bring an owl to a city full of them was idiomatically 'a pointless journey'.

27. Diodorus 20.37.5 confirmed Antigonus' governor of Sardis had been instructed not to let Cleopatra leave. Diodorus 18.49.4 for Olympias' fleeing Pella and Blackwell (1999) p 94 for its dating.

28. Diodorus 18.11.1 for Molossian support of Greeks in the Lamian War.

29. Arrian 7.12.5-6 and Curtius 10.4.3 for the correspondence from Olympias and Antipater and Alexander's quip about his mother. Other examples at Justin 12.14.3, Plutarch 39.7-14. Slanders from Olympias against Antipater were cited at Arrian 7.12.5, Justin 12.14.3, Plutarch 39.7-14. Diodorus 17.118.1. Diodorus 18.49.4 claimed she fled Pella because of her quarrel with Antipater.

30. Plutarch 39.11-13 for Alexander's warning to Antipater and quoting Plutarch 68.4-5. Diodorus 19.11.9 for Antipater's deathbed warning.

31. For the capture of Attalus, Polemon and Docimus, see Diodorus 18.44.1-1845.3, Polyaenus 4.6.7 and 19.16-17 for Alcetas' siege. Its final location in Phrygia is likely as Antigonus' wife was in the vicinity, possibly at Celaenae. An escape was attempted 'when Antigonus was heading to the East' (Diodorus 19.16.1-5) which suggests Eumenes had already headed into the upper satrapies in 317 BCE when it finished; this vouches for the year-plus siege of the Perdiccans and for a far shorter siege at Nora. Diodorus 19.16 for Docimus betraying his comrades.

32. For the mutilation of Alcetas' body, Diodorus 18.47.3. Antigonus did pardon Docimus, who had betrayed Alcetas and Polemon to him. Moreover, Docimus had also refused to serve under Eumenes. Plutarch *Eumenes* 8.4. Also Heckel (2006) p 115. Nothing more is heard of Polemon or Attalus who were likely executed.

33. Diodorus 18.25.3 stated Antigonus reported Perdiccas' designs on the Macedonian throne. Phila had been married to Balacrus who died in Pisidia; Photius 166. Diodorus 18.22.1 for his death; discussion in Heckel (2006) pp 68-69.

34. Arrian *Events After Alexander* 1.42; Anson (2004) p 138 for discussion. Alexander crossed the Hellespont in 334 BCE and Antipater had controlled Greece since then, thus fifteen years.

35. Justin 13.6.16 suggested Cleitus was cooperating with Alcetas, Perdiccas' brother, in 322/1 BCE; see Heckel (1992) p 186 for detail. Arrian *Events After Alexander* 1.26 (implied) Cleitus' alignment with Craterus and Antipater and 1.37 for his satrapy at Triparadeisus. For Aristonus' capitulation see Arrian *Events After Alexander* 24.6.

36. A *thalamios* was a rower on the bottom deck of the three-decked trireme, thus with the least chance of survival in the event of its sinking.

37. Diodorus 18.41.4-5 for confirmation of Antigonus' military strength. Plutarch *Eumenes* 11.7-9 and Nepos 5.4-6 for the exercising contraption. For Eumenes' charm and friendliness that 'seasoned' the meals they had, Plutarch *Eumenes* 11.1.

38. Plutarch *Eumenes* 10.1-3 for the suffering of the men, translation from Loeb Classical Library edition, 1919. Diodorus 18.50.1-3 for Antigonus' strength.

39. Nepos 5 for Eumenes' delaying and his sorties on the palisade.

40. Diodorus 18.47.4-5, 18.50.1 and Plutarch *Eumenes* 12.1-2 for news of Antipater's death arriving. Cretopolis has never been formally identified. See discussion of its location in Sekunda (1997). For Alcetas' legitimacy in Pisidia see chapter titled *Lifting the Shroud of Parrhasius.* Diodorus 18.44-5-18.45.3 for Alcetas' activity in Pisidia.

41. Billows (1990) p 80; Anson (2004) p 135. Billows and Anson have differing views on Hieronymus' whereabouts.

42. Diodorus 18.59.4-6, translation from the Loeb Classical Library edition, 1947.

43. Antipater had appointed Cassander second-in-command or chiliarch to Antigonus 'so that the latter might not be able to pursue his own ambitions undetected'; Diodorus 18.39.7 and also Arrian *Events After Alexander* 1.38. The *Heidelberg Epitome* 1.4 reported Cassander urged his father to remove the kings from Antigonus' custody, though this makes little sense when Antipater took the kings back to Pella and did not leave them in Asia. This might however be a reference to Heracles based in Pergamum.

44. Diodorus 18.53.5, Plutarch *Eumenes* 12.2-3, Nepos 5.7 and Diodorus 18.50.4-5, translation from the Loeb Classical Library edition, 1947 for the terms of Eumenes' release.

45. Plutarch *Eumenes* 5.4-6 for Antipater's offer of an alliance with Eumenes in defeating Perdiccas.

46. Diodorus 18.47.5 and 18.50.5, based on the translation from the Loeb Classical Library edition, 1947.

47. Lysimachus was to assist the Antigonid cause in 318 BCE when capturing and killing White Cleitus who had aligned with Arrhidaeus, satrap of Hellespontine Phrygia; Diodorus 18.72.5-9 for events leading up to Cleitus' capture. Lysimachus was satrap of Thrace, although Heckel suggested he had a wider *strategos* role. See Heckel (2006) p 155 and Curtius 10.10.4, Diodorus 18.3.2, Arrian *Events After Alexander,* 1.7, Justin 13 4.16, and Dexippus F8.3. Lysimachus must have initially relied upon the network of 'agents' and tyrants Antipater had installed over the previous decade and he had his hands full with the rebellious Thracian king, Seuthes. For the first clash with Seuthes see Diodorus 18.14.2-15 and for the second referenced battle 19.73.8. Also Arrian *Events After Alexander* 1.10, yet here Lysimachus is incorrectly reported as slain in the battle.

48. Plutarch *Eumenes, The Comparison of Sertorius with Eumenes* 2; the text heads the chapter titled *The Tragic Triumvirate of Treachery and Oaths:* 'If Eumenes could have contented himself with the second place, Antigonus, freed from his competition for the first, would have used him well, and shown him favour.'

49. Full discussion of excavations at Lampron Castle in Robinson-Hughes (1969).

50. Heckel (1988) p 48 and Heckel (2006) p 226 for a summary of Polyperchon's lineage. Heckel (1992) p 188 for the label 'jackal among lions'.

51. Curtius 4.13.7-10 for Alexander's vocal rejection of Polyperchon's advice. This appears a Cleitarchean device to denigrate an opponent of Ptolemy. Aelian 12.43 for his living as a brigand, Athenaeus 4.155c for Duris' claim that he danced when drunk; see Heckel (1992) p 188 for citations. Curtius 8.5.22 for the *proskynesis* incident.

52. Polyperchon operated at Gaugamela as taxiarch of the Tymphaean battalion; Diodorus 17.57.2 and Arrian 3.11.9, Curtius 4.13.28. He was involved in various other missions with Meleager, Amyntas and Coenus and later under Craterus in India; Heckel (2006) pp 226-227 for a career summary. He was appointed second-in-command to Craterus at Opis, Diodorus 18.48.4, 47.4, Plutarch *Phocion* 31.1, Plutarch *Eumenes* 12.1. Arrian 7.12.1 stated there were about 10,000 veterans to return under Craterus, Diodorus 17.109.1, 18.4.1 and Diodorus 18.16.4 suggested the make-up of the 10,000 was 6,000 who originally crossed to Asia with Alexander and 4,000 enlisted on the march. Further, '1,000 Persian bowmen and slingers and 1,500 horsemen' are also mentioned although their role and destination is unclear.

53. Arrian *Events After Alexander* 1.38 for the appointment of Polyperchon's son as a bodyguard to the new kings.

54. Plutarch 49.14-15 reported that Antipater had entered into secret negotiations with the Aetolians after Alexander's execution of Parmenio, fearing for his own life. Yet an alliance with Aetolians was unlikely to have offered much protection against the agents of Alexander. For Antipater's acknowledging Alexander see Arrian *Events After Alexander* 25.1, Curtius 3.1.6-7, Justin 11.1.8, 11.2.2, Diodorus 17.2.2. Quoting Blackwell (1999) p 35 on devotion. Alexander Lyncestis was held in captivity for three years and executed; he was Antipater's son-in-law; Justin 11.2.1-2 and Curtius 7.1.6-7; Curtius 7.1.5-9, Diodorus 17.80.2, Justin 12.14.1 for his execution. Blackwell (1999) p 156 for discussion of Antipater's fear of Alexander; Bevan and Berve believe he rebelled in 323 BCE.

55. Plutarch *Phocion* 17.10.

56. Plutarch *Apophthegm* or *Sayings of Kings and Commanders* 179b. Antipater presided over the Pythian Games on behalf of Philip in the 430s BCE; dicussion in Blackwell (1999) p 34.

57. For Polyperchon being entrusted with the defense of Macedonia in the absence of Craterus and Antipater see Justin 13.6.9 and Diodorus 18.25.4-5

58. Anson (1992) p 41 for detailed discussion of the title and its relative authority.

59. Arrian 7.12.4, Justin 12.12.8 for Polyperchon's role under Craterus' returning veterans. Diodorus 18.48.4 for his reputation and standing in Macedonia.

60. Following the observation on their respective abilities in Roisman-Worthington (2010) p 212. For Antipater's skill at operating on limited resources, and Cassander's after him, see Adams (1985).

61. Justin 14.5.2-4 for the alliance between Eurydice and Cassander.

62. Arrian *Events After Alexander* 1.22. Also discussed in Carney (1987) pp 497-498 referencing Adea's warlike upbringing; and Carney (1988) pp 392-393 following Polyaenus 8.60. Musgrave-Prag-Neave-Lane Fox (2010) section 9.1.3 argues an undocumented wedding would have taken place in 337/6 BCE. Further discussion of Cynnane's age in chapter titled *The Return to Aegae.*

63. Polyaenus 8.60 suggested the marriage ended 'swiftly' to illustrate her independent spirit.

64. Arrian 1.5.2-3. The Agrianians were from the Paeonian region of Thrace bordering the Macedonian northern frontier.

65. Polyaenus 8.60 for the crossing of the Strymon in the face of Antipater's wishes. Musgrave-Prag-Neave-Lane Fox (2010) section 9.1.3 for arguments for Adea's age.

66. Philip had supposedly pledged him to the daughter of Pixodarus, the Carian dynast, some years before; see Plutarch 10.5.1; Alexander's intervention led to his exile.

67. Arrian *Events After Alexander* 1.22, Polyaenus 8.60.

68. Arrian *Events After Alexander* 1.23 suggested Perdiccas brought about the marriage but surely under duress; it was not by his design. See discussion in Anson (2004) p 111. Adea's father was the son of King Perdiccas III (Philip II's older brother) of the Argead line, and her mother was the daughter of Philip II by Audata-Eurydice, thus she was three-quarters Argead. Arrian *Events after Alexander* 1.22 for confirmation that Audata, Philip's Illyrian wife, was renamed Eurydice. Philip's mother had been named Eurydice too.

69. Quoting Bosworth (1993) p 425 for 'Amazon and an idiot' and Heckel (1978) p 157.

70. Arrian *Events after Alexander* 1.43-45 for the seventy elephants left with Antigonus and Antipater keeping the remainder; also Diodorus 19.23.2.

71. Justin 14.5 for Eurydice's demands to Polyperchon and Antigonus though in Justin's narrative this move appears to take place later; it makes more sense that Cassander had her draft the royal demands before he departed for Asia. Some commentary such as Heckel-Yardley-Wheatley (2011) footnotes to Justin 14.5 see this as being directed at Eumenes, providing Antigonus with authority to take over his royal army. But he had already achieved that before the siege at Nora. Rather than 'deliver up the army' the letter might have simply demanded Antigonus' military backing for their regime. Justin appears to place Cassander's alliance with Eurydice far later in events but it makes more sense that Cassander made the alliance *before* journeying to Antigonus at Celaenae. Diodorus made it clear that he was *looking back* to events in Europe having progressed them to a far more advanced stage in Asia in his text. So the timing is typically out of sync.

72. Diodorus 18.54.3-4 for Antigonus provisioning Cassander and Diodorus 18.54.3 for the pre-departure planning. Diodorus 18.68.1 for the size of Cassander's new force.

73. For Cassander's activity after the death of Antipater, Diodorus 18.49.1-2, Plutarch *Eumenes* 12.1, Plutarch *Phocion* 31.1 and 32.2. For the hostility between Cassander and Polyperchon, Plutarch *Phocion* 31.1. Diodorus 18.49.3 for the attempts to renew an alliance with Ptolemy. Diodorus 18.58.1-2 for Cassander's expectations and the strength of his father's oligarchs in Greece.

74. Diodorus 18.57.2 and 18.49.4 appear to suggest Polyperchon invited Olympias twice to Macedonia.

75. Diodorus 18.54.4 for Antigonus' covert intentions, translation from the Loeb Classical Library edition, 1947.

76. Diodorus 18.49.4 and 18.55.1-2 for Polyperchon taking council before making policy decisions, and his appreciation of the gravity of what he had done.

77. Diodorus 18.55.2-4 and repeated at 18.57.1-2 and 18.64.3. Diodorus 18.69.4 for the consequences. Translations from the Loeb Classical Library edition, 1947.

78. For Demades' execution see Diodorus 18.48.1-4 (no mention of Cassander here, just 'men in charge of punishments' and a 'common prison'), Arrian *Events After Alexander* 1.14 , Plutarch *Phocion* 30.8-9, Plutarch *Demosthenes* 31.4-6; Antipater was already ill and Cassander was, it appears, giving the orders.

79. Plutarch 34.2 for the declaration of Greek freedoms.

80. Anson (2014) p 134; Diodorus 19.61.1-3 for the contents of Antigonus' proclamation.

81. For Polyperchon's later hostility to, and warring with, Cassander, see Diodorus 19.11-36, 19.49-75, 19.50-19.64. Following the discussion and observations in Heckel (1992) p 194. The two war councils mentioned at Diodorus 18.49.4 and 18.55.1 focused on dealing with Cassander. Hostilities against Antigonus are not mentioned at either.

82. Diodorus 18.57.3-4, translation from the Loeb Classical Library edition, 1947; also see Plutarch *Eumenes* 13.1-3.

83. Diodorus 18.58.1-3, translation from the Loeb Classical Library edition, 1947. Reiretated in Plutarch *Eumenes* 12.1-3.

84. Diodorus 18.58.1 and Plutarch Eumenes 13.1 suggest Eumenes only received news of Polyperchon's new mandate for him *after* his release from Nora; see full discussion in Anson (1977) p 253. Polyperchon had been second-in-command to Craterus from Opis to Cilicia.

85. Ptolemy had married Antipater's daughter, Eurydice, and Lysimachus may have already concluded his marriage to Nicaea, Perdiccas' widow (if they ever married) and another of the regent's offspring. Antigonus' son Demetrius had recently married Phila, Craterus' widow and a further daughter of Antipater; Diodorus 19.59.3-6. Antipater's daughters were of course Cassander's sisters.

86. See Rozen (1967) pp 29-32 for the order of the letters and the possibility of a single edict and a regent's covering letter. Nepos 6 for messengers and correspondence; also Diodorus 18.58.2-4, Plutarch *Eumenes* 13.1-2.

87. Diodorus 19.23.2, translation from the Loeb Classical Library edition, 1947. Also Polyaenus 4.8.3 for the later episode involving a faked letter from Pella. Discussion of the possibility that these were false letters in Roisman (2012) pp 179-180.

88. Quoting Roisman (2012) p 186.

89. Theopompus fragment 217 and Polyaenus 4.2.8: discussion in Gabriel (2010) p 198 and p 211. If Eumenes served Philip for seven years before his king's assasination, he was potentially acting as secretary on campaign.

90. Nepos 6-7, translation by Rev. JS Watson, George Bell and Sons, London, 1886. This parallels the letter at Diodorus 18.58.2-4.

91. Diodorus 19.14.6 and 19.27.5 for the troops sent from Parapamisadae by Oxyartes. Curtius 9.8.9-10 referred to Oxyartes as *praetor Bactrianorum*. This in fact makes more sense than appointing him to a foreign province: Paropanisadae according to Arrian 6.15.3.

92. 'Tender' quoting Heckel (2006) p 242. *Metz Epitome* 101-102, 100, 112, *Romance* 3.32.4-7, Arrian 7.27.3 for Roxane's role at Alexander's death. *Metz Epitome* 115 was clear that the son of Roxane 'before all others' was to be the king of Macedonia; restated in the *Romance* 3.32. Her stopping Alexander throwing himself in the Euphrates reinforced that notion.

93. Nepos 7.1, translation by Rev. JS Watson, George Bell and Sons, London, 1886; Diodorus 18.58.3-4.

94. Diodorus 18.62.2 for Olympias writing to the Silver Shields.

95. Diodorus 18.64-65 for Nicanor's receipt of Olympias' instructions and his response. Heckel (2007) for discussion of Nicanor's identity. See chapter titled *Sarissa Diplomacy: Macedonian Statecraft* for more on Nicanor and *Aristotle* by G Grote, John Murray, 1880, footnotes 23-24 with Heckel (2007) for further arguments on his identity.

96. Plutarch *Phocion* 29-38 for the chain of events; also Diodorus 18.65.6, Nepos *Phocion* 3 ff. For Nicanor's execution by Cassander see Diodorus 18.75.1-1, Polyaenus 4.11.2.

97. Polyaenus 4.11.2 for the forged letter. Nicanor had been involved in coordinated action with Antigonus at the Hellespont, see below.

98. Nepos 6, Diodorus 18.58.2-4 for Eumenes' advice to Olympias on her return to Macedonia.

99. Diodorus 19.11.6-7, Aelian 13.36 for the capture and execution (forced sucide) of Eurydice and King Philip III (Arrhidaeus). More on Holcias' role below.

100. Nepos 6 for Olympias' failure to heed Eumenes' advice to wait until the situation was safer. Anson (2014) p 129 for the treasury sum. As Olympias and Polyperchon combined forces at the battle, he may have journeyed to Epirus after failures in the Peloponnese.

101. Aeacides supported Olympias' return to Macedonia, Diodorus 19.11.2, Justin 14.5.9.

102. Diodorus 19.11.2 for the victory of Olympia and Polyperchon over Eurydice. Carney (2006) pp 79-80 for the chronology. A tympanum is a drum used in Dionysiac rites; Carney (2006) p 97.

103. Athenaeus 13.560f for Adea's battle dress; Kechel (2006) p 229 sees this as a fabrication of Duris. Following the observation about Olympias' activity in Anson (1992) p 40; examples of Olympias' political activity are found in Diodorus 18.49.4, 18.57.2, 18.65.1, 19.11.8-9, 19.35.3-5, 19.50.1, 19.50.8. Athenaeus 13.560f following the observation in Carney (2006) p 74 for the 'first war between women'.

104. Herodotus 5.53 for the three days from Ephesus to Sardis on the Royal Road.

105. Diodorus 18.62.3-4 for 'rebel of the monarchy' and Nepos 3.1-2 for the suggestion that Perdiccas granted him authority from Mount Taurus to the Hellespont.

106. See Roisman (2012) p 180 footnote 8 for discussion. Briant also believed the letters from Polyperchon were partially forged.

107. Diodorus 18.51.3 for the siege of Cyzicus and 18.52.4 for Arrhidaeus' rescue mission. Justin 14.2.4 reported an unlikely story that Antipater sent aid to Eumenes at Nora; it is more likely Justin confused 'Arrhidaeus' for 'Antipater', or confused references to the old and new 'regents', believing Polyperchon (probably under instruction from Olympias) sent the aid.

108. For Arrhidaeus' instructions at Babylon, Diodorus 18.3.5, Justin 13.4.6; for his collusion with Ptolemy, Arrian *Events After Alexander* 1.25. See chapter titled *Lifting the Shroud of Parrhasius* for Perdiccas locating himself in Syria.

109. Diodorus 18.36.6-7 for Arrhidaeus' elevation to *epimeletes* following Perdiccas' death.

110. Diodorus 18.52.6-7 for Cleitus' preparations for an attack and his departure for Macedonia and Antigonus' seizure of 600 talents. Plutarch *Phocion* 34-37 for Phocion's execution; Diodorus 18.72.2-4 for Cleitus' naval action against Nicanor and 18.52.5-8 for his role in Greece.

111. Diodorus 18.63.6, Polyaenus 4.6.9 for Eumenes shipping funds from Cilicia. There is in fact a similarity here with Diodorus 18.52.7 describing Antigonus' assault of Ephesus where Antigonus again intercepted ships from Cilicia; we might wonder if Eumenes had sent the funds to Cleitus and was attempting to send more to him or to Olympias, perhaps via Polyperchon.

112. Diodorus 18.52.2-4 for Antigonus reprimanding Arrhidaeus, translation from the Loeb Classical Library edition, 1947.

113. Diodorus 18.51-52 for Arrhidaeus' failure in Hellespontine Phrygia and 18.72.2-3 for his linking up with Cleitus. The origin of the troops they were instructed to block is not specified. Either Cassander was already pouring troops into Asia in support of Antigonus, or Antigonus had hired mercenaries, or this referred to Nicanor's fleet from Piraeus. Some three years on an army of Cassander's was however besieging Amisus in Cappadocia against the forces of Antigonus; Diodorus 19.57.4. Antigonus had all the men he needed in Asia and was soon having to raid treasuries to pay them. It is unlikely he was recruiting in Europe when we consider that he had sent Cassander aid in Greece.

114. Diodorus 18.72.5-9 for Cleitus' defeat and execution.

115. Following Carney (2006) p 63 and p 77 for the Macedonian law recorded by Curtius 6.11.20 and 8.6.28 and the great 'lamentation' from the *Romance* 3.33.

116. Plutarch *Alexander* 77.1-2 linking Olympias' pogrom to the conspiracy rumours; also Diodorus 19.11.8-9. As Carney (2006) pp 85-96 points out, the mistreatment of the bodies of the dead featured prominently in the *Iliad*; 22.395-404 for Achilles' maltreatment of Hector, 23.20-3 and 24.14.21 as the most notable examples.

117. Diodorus 19.11.9, Justin 14.6.1 for the hostility caused by Olympias' actions. Plutarch *Pyrrhus* 2.1 for Aeacides' expulsion. Plutarch *Demetrius* 25.2 for Demetrius' marriage to Deidameia.

118. Diodorus 19.49-52 for the fate of Olympias and Diodorus 19.11.1-9, Justin 14.5.8-10, Aelian 13.36 for the deaths of King Philip III and Eurydice. Diodorus 19.11.5 for the length of his reign; Justin 14.5.10 stated 'six years'. Aelian claimed Eurydice chose the rope. Diodorus 19.52.5, Athenaeus 4.155a (using Dyllus) for Cassander's burial honours. Alexander died 10/11 June 323 BCE and Arrhidaeus was proclaimed king a week or so after; six years and four months later in mid-October 317 BCE. See chapter titled *Babylon: the Cipher and Rosetta Stone* for discussion of a possible reconciliation of the term of Philip III's reign.

119. Plutarch 74.2-6 and *Moralia* 180f for the hostility between Cassander and Alexander.

120. See Heckel (1988) p 10 for a discussion of those at the banquet and *Metz Epitome* 97-98 for the full list given in Heckel-Yardley (2004) p 283.

121. *Romance* 3.32 and *Metz Epitome* 116-117 for the marriage pairings. *Romance* 3.32, *Metz Epitome* 111 and 103 for Alexander's instructions to Ptolemy and Lysimachus and their presence at the drafting and first reading of the Will.

122. Athenaeus 11.784c, 13.557c for Thessalonice's maternal side. Plutarch *Moralia* 141b-c for Olympias' admiration of Nicesipolis.

123. Diodorus 20.37.5 confirmed Antigonus' governor of Sardis had been instructed not to let Cleopatra leave; a state of affairs which most likely went back to Triparadeisus. This does suggest she was an unofficial hostage. Following Carney (1988) p 402.

124. Diodorus 18.23.1, Arrian *Events After Alexander* 1.21, Justin 13.6.4 for Perdiccas' courting of Cleopatra. Eumenes had journeyed to visit Cleopatra at Sardis with gifts from Perdiccas. Moreover his close relationship to Olympias suggests Cleopatra had complete trust in him.

125. *Romance* 3.31.1, *Metz Epitome* 87 for Olympias' pleas. The Will opens by confirming Alexander's parentage; *Metz Epitome* 113, *Romance* 3.32; reiterated at *Metz Epitome* 116 and in the *Romance*. Curtius 9.6.26 for Alexander requesting Olympias' consecration to immortality.

126. Arrian 4.10.2 and Plutarch 3.2-3, Justin 11.11.3-4 for Callisthenes' claim that Olympia was spreading 'lies' about Alexander's alleged immortal father.

127. Discussion of the cults to Philip and Alexander in Briant (1974) pp 135-137.

128. Plutarch 2-3 for the dreams and oracles of Philip and Olympias. Euripides *Bacchae* 1. In the play Dionysus lured Pentheus to the forest where the maenads tore Pentheus apart limb from limb.

129. Diodorus 19.11.1 stated that Eurydice 'assumed the administration of the regency' from Polyperchon.

130. Diodorus 18.3.1, Curtius 10.10.2, Arrian *Events After Alexander* 1.6, Dexippus FGrH 100 F8 §2, *Metz Epitome* 117 for Asander's satrapal grant. Arrian *Events After Alexander* 25.1 for his possible family relations to Antigonus. For his defection to Perdiccas see Arrian *Events After Alexander* 25.1, where Photius' epitome stated 'Asander the satrap of Caria welcomed him as a friend.' Diodorus 19.62.2 for his subsequent defection to Ptolemy.

131. Arrian *Events After Alexander* 1.41 for Asander's poor performance against the Perdiccans.

132. See Heckel (1988) p 17 and Heckel-Yardley (2004) p 288 for the *Metz Epitome* 120 Will translation, and Stoneman (1991) p 155 for the *Romance* translation.

133. *Metz Epitome* 122.

134. Polyaenus 4.6.6 confirmed this took place when Antigonus was wintering in Cappadocia but suggested there was campaigning earlier, before Holcias' capture. The same entry mentioned Holcias' subsequent repatriation to Macedonia.

135. Plutarch *Eumenes* 10.1. This detail is paralleled in Justin 14.2.1-3; also Diodorus 18.41.1-4 and Nepos 5 for Eumenes' entry into Nora.

136. Diodorus 18.53.6. The numbers do look suspiciously like the defectors (under a general named Perdiccas) before the battle at Orcynia that were rounded-up by Eumenes' general, Phoenix of Tenedos.

137. Diodorus 18.45-46 for the fullest account of the fate of Alcetas and the Perdiccan remnants. Roisman (2012) p 29 footnote 48 for identification of Alcetas' tomb. Polyaenus 4.6.6 did suggest Antigonus was worried they would link up with Alcetas. Diodorus 19.16.2 for Attalus, Polemon and Docimus hoping for Eumenes' support. Stewart (1993) p 312 for Alcetas' tomb.

138. Polyaenus 4.6.6 for the capture of Holcias and his being escorted to Macedonia by Leonidas. The fate of the Silver Shields discussed in chapter titled *The Tragic Triumvirate of Treachery and Oaths*.

139. The timing of Holcias' release and Eumenes' release bargaining is supported by reports that their winter campaigning was followed by a ruse to lure them from their stronghold, their subsequent capture and parole. Anson (2004) p 121, footnote 21 and p 124 for a discussion of the timing of Holcias' campaign and capture. If Leonidas can be identified as the commander of the *ataktoi,* the 'disciplinary unit' Alexander formed after Philotas' trial and execution, then his value with 'renegades' had again been appreciated. See Heckel (2006) p 147 for discussion on Leonidas' identity.

140. Cynnane was the granddaughter of King Bardylis of Illyria (through her mother Audata-Eurydice), Athenaeus 13.557b-c, Arrian *Events After Alexander* 1.22.

141. For Cleodice's marriage to Leonnatus in the Will see *Metz Epitome* 119, *Romance* 3.34.14, Julius Valerius 3.58, a Latin translation of the *Romance*. Heckel (2006) p 146 for Leonnatus' royal links.

142. Plutarch *Eumenes* 5.4-6 for Eumenes' offer to reconcile Perdiccas and Craterus. Plutarch *Demetrius* 14.2, Plutarch *Eumenes* 6.2,6.7,7.1 for Craterus' popularity.

143. Plutarch *Moralia* 250f-253q, 486a, Polyaenus 2.29.1, Frontinus *Stategemata* 3.6.7 for Craterus' son supporting *Gonatas*. Plutarch 47.10 for the quote on comparative affection and respect and for Alexander's statement that they were the two men most loved by Alexander. Diodorus 17.114.1-2 for Craterus rivalling Hephaestion for Alexander's affections.

144. For Eumenes' treatment of Craterus see Plutarch *Eumenes* 7.6-13, Nepos 4.4, Diodorus 19.59.3.

145. Discussion of the royal pairing in the original Will in chapter titled *Lifting the Shroud of Parrhasius*.

146. *Metz Epitome* 116, *Romance* 3.32 for Craterus' appointment in Macedonia and his marriage pairing. Phila's husband Balacrus was killed in Pisidia; Diodorus 18.22.1. More detail on the fate of Cynnane at Arrian *Events After Alexander* 1.22-23, Polyaenus 8.60.

147. Alcetas disregarded orders to serve under Eumenes: Diodorus 18.29.2, Justin 13.6.15; Plutarch *Eumenes* 5.3.

148. *Metz Epitome* 100, *Romance* 2.32.3 for Cassander's plan to wait for Iolaos in Cilicia. Heckel (1988) p 10 discusses the later embellishments of Cassander's and Iolaos' roles. Justin 12.12.8 for Polyperchon, Polydamas, Gorgias departing Opis with Craterus. See discussion of Craterus' activity in Cilicia as linked to the so-called 'last plans' in chapter titled *Babylon: the Cipher and Rosetta Stone.*

149. Plutarch *Eumenes* 17.2 for Eumenes' speech when he was under the escort of Nicanor. He was unlikely to be the son of Balacrus who had family ties with Antipater; Heckel (2006) pp 68-69 for background.

150. Diodorus 18.39.6, Arrian *Events After Alexander* 1.37, Appian *Mithridatic Wars* 8, for Nicanor's grant of Cappadocia at Triparadeisus. Heckel (2006) p 178 Nicanor (10) and (12) for possible identification. Plutarch *Eumenes* 17.2 for Eumenes' surrender to Nicanor at Gabiene. For his possible role in the upper satrapies see Diodorus 19.92.1-5, 100.3, Appian *Syrian Wars* 55, 57. Heckel (2006) pp 176-178 for the identifications of various Nicanors.

151. Diodorus 18.43.2 for Nicanor's operations in Coele-Syria and Phoenicia; see Heckel (2006) p 178, Nicanor (11) for his career.

152. Diodorus 18.47.5 and 18.50.5 for the statements of Antigonus' intent.

153. Antipater had assigned Cassander to watch over Antigonus after Triparadeissus; Diodorus 18.39.7, Arrian *Events after Alexander* 1.38. The *Heidelberg Epitome* 1.4 went further stating Cassander urged his father to remove the kings from Antigonus' control.

154. *Metz Epitome* 97 provided eleven identifications as well as corrupted names; see Heckel (1988) pp 34-35. The Armenian *Romance* version backs up the Greek *Romance* 3.31.8 though peripheral names vary in different recensions.

155. 'Fearful' historians are suggested at Curtius 10.10.18-19, Diodorus 17.118, Justin 12.13.

156. The Scylla discussed in chapter titled *Guardians and Ghosts of the Ephemerides.* It appears at *Romance 3.30* and *Metz Epitome* 90-94: Scylla was a part-human part-beast monster from Greek mythology; here was a baby born as a human boy from the belly up, below which it was part-lion, panther, dog and boar. As Merkelbach and Heckel (1988) p 9 agree, the beast represented Alexander's own men and their betrayal and not his subject nations as translations suggest.

157. Arrian *Events After Alexander* 24.6.

158. Aristonus supported Polyperchon and the Olympias faction after Antipater's death; see Diodorus 19.35.4, 19.50.3-8, 19.51.1. Medius took part in Antigonid actions against Ptolemy both for Perdiccas and Antigonus.

159. Arrian 7.27.2 for Medius' relations with Iolaos. For Medius' career under Antigonus see Arrian *Events After Alexander* 24.6, Diodorus 19.69.3, 19.75-3-4, 19.97.7-8, 19.77.2-5, 20.50.3, Plutarch *Demetrius* 19.1-2.

160. Quoting Errington (1970) p 60 and Plutarch *Eumenes* 3.3-7 for Leonnatus' bid to unite with Cleopatra.

161. For Miletus' settlement activity, Hammond (1994) p 64; Brown (1947) p 690 for Demosthenes' references to Cardia.

162. Diodorus 18.14.4-5 for Hecataeus' envoy role to Leonnatus and Plutarch *Eumenes* 3.3-7 for the whole episode including Eumenes' flight. Also see discussion in Anson (2004) p 45. How long Hecataeus had governed Cardia is uncertain. Alexander sent a Hecataeus to Asia to murder Attalus soon after gaining the throne, see Diodorus 17.2.5-6 and implied by Curtius 7.1.38. They are likely one and the same man, and thus Hecataeus had been an agent of Alexander, and was likely a client of Philip II before. See discussion in Heckel (2006) p 131. For Hecataeus' earlier attempt to reconcile Eumenes with Antipater see Plutarch *Eumenes* 5.4-5.

163. Nepos 2.4-5 and Plutarch *Eumenes* 3.11 for Eumenes' troop numbers. Plutarch suggested Eumenes was either afraid of Antipater or 'despaired of Leonnatus as a capricious man' (translation from the Loeb Classical Library edition, 1919) when explaining his decampment and his rejection of Leonnatus' offer to join his cause. Leonnatus must have coveted Eumenes' campaign funds too.

164. Justin 13.6 for Antipater rejoicing. For Leonnatus' multi-satrapal inheritance in the Will see chapter titled *Lifting the Shroud of Parrhasius.*

165. For Laomedon's grant of Coele-Syria see Arrian *Events After Alexander* 1.5, Diodorus 18.3.1, Curtius 10.10.2, Justin 13.4.12, Appian *Syrian Wars* 52, Dexippus FGrH 100 F8 2. 'Coele' literally translated as 'Hollow', an association first made by Arrian 2.13.7, the region later disputed by the Ptolemaic and Seleucid dynasties. Appian *Syrian Wars* 52 for reference to the 'buying' of the satrapy. Diodorus 18.43.1-2 and Pausanias 1.6.4 for Ptolemy's hostility.

166. Arrian 3.6.6 for Laomedon's language ability. Laomedon was banned by Philip from Macedonia in spring 336 BCE along with his brother Erygius, Ptolemy and Nearchus; see Arrian 3.6.5 and Plutarch 10.4. He was also appointed a *trierarchos* on the Hydaspes; Arrian *Indike* 18.4. For his

flight to Alcetas see Appian *Syrian Wars* 52. Alcetas opposed Eumenes' suggestion of a marriage to Cleopatra, favouring Nicaea, Antipater's daughter. Arrian *Events After Alexander* 1.21. He also killed Cynnane; Diodorus 19.52.5, Arrian *Events After Alexander* 1.22-23; and disregarded orders to serve under Eumenes: Diodorus 18.29.2, Justin 13.6.15; Plutarch *Eumenes* 5.3.

167. Arrian 3.6.7 and 7.23.1 for Menander's appointment to Lydia. Diodorus 18.59.1-2 for Menander's attempts to capture Eumenes. Arrian *Events After Alexander* 25.2 suggested, but did not specifically state, that Perdiccas subordinated Menander to Cleopatra. For events at Sardis see Arrian *Events After Alexander* 1.26. A separate fragment of Arrian *Events After Alexander* preserved in the *Vatican Codex* suggested a conflict between Menander, Cleopatra and Perdiccas resulting in Eumenes' flight.

168. Diodorus 18.23.1, Arrian *Events After Alexander* 1.21, Justin 13.6.4 for Perdiccas' seeking the hand of Cleopatra. Only the *Heidelberg Epitome* FGrH 155F-4 suggested the marriage took place. Plutarch *Eumenes* 9.4 for the alleged former friendship with Menander. See discussion in Billows (1990) p 59 and p 63 for Menander's possible early collusion with Antigonus and 401-402 for his career; also Anson (2004) pp 91-91. Billows (1990) p 77 for discussion of his role at the Battle of Orcynia as per Diodorus 18.59.1-2 and Plutarch *Eumenes* 9.2-6. Menander had control of Antigonus' baggage train that Eumenes almost captured. Plutarch *Eumenes* 9.2-6 gave a very different account. Diodorus did not mention Menander at the battle.

169. See Heckel (2006) p 163 for references citing Pliny 35.93; the identification may be incorrect. Lydia is not referenced in either the surviving *Metz Epitome* or *Romance* texts, though it is possible an early textual lacuna is responsible. Diodorus 19.29.2 for Lydian troops present at Paraetacene. Diodorus 19.60.3 brings Lydian operations into the narrative but again Menander was not mentioned.

170. Nearchus' naval voyage and his reuniting with Alexander made him a prominent and celebrated commander during Alexander's lifetime. He was crowned for his services at Susa and was also illustriously paired in marriage to 'a daughter of Barsine'; Arrian 7.4.6 and also suggested by Arrian *Indike* 42.9.

171. Arrian *Indike* 18.4 cited Nearchus as coming from Amphipolis. Nearchus' whereabouts and affiliations from Babylon, to his reappearance operating under Antigonus, are unknown. He seems to have avoided the early conflict, perhaps as governor of Lydia or Pamphylia, or he was deliberately bypassed by Hieronymus' texts. For his undated mission to recover Telmessus see Polyaenus 5.35. See Heckel (2006) p 173 and Heckel (1988) p 36 for discussion. Although supposedly an action carried out on Antigonus' orders, he may have been, with consent, reacquiring his nominated satrapy after activity elsewhere. Nearchus had governed satrapies bordering Antigonus' sphere of activity in 334 BCE. Justin 13.4.15 did position Nearchus in both Lycia and Pamphylia after Babylon.

172. The founding of Cretopolis discussed in Sekunda (1997) though the suggestion is that this took place before Nearchus was recalled east by Alexander in 329/328 BCE.

173. Diodorus 19.69.1 for Nearchus' later service under Demetrius. See chapter titled *Babylon: the Cipher and Rosetta Stone* for detail of Nearchus' speech at Babylon. Nearchus fought against Ptolemy after his reappearance in 317/316 BCE and is unlikely to have been pro-Ptolemy before.

174. The lion monument at Amphipolis was originally thought to sit above the tomb which held the remains of Nearchus, Laomedon or Androsthenes, each born or resident at some point; see chapter titled *Lifting the Shroud of Parrhasius* for detail. Recent excavations suggest a grander tomb than first thought leading some historians to ponder whether Roxane and Alexander IV were entombed in Amphipolis after their murder by Cassander. Archaeologists now conclude the lion was too heavy and adorned another nearby tomb. It has long been thought that Tomb III at Vergina, possibly constructed by Cassander, held the remains of Alexander IV; Carney-Ogden (2010) pp 118-119.

175. Heckel (2006) p 235 sees Stasanor as a supporter of Eumenes and supplying troops. However there is considerable confusion between the switched roles and relationships of Stasander and Stasanor, both Greek Cypriots who alternatively governed Areia-Drangiana and Bactria-Sogdia between Babylon and Triparadeisus (Diodorus 18.39.6). We propose the troops came from Stasander who either levied Bactria himself or Diodorus was again confused. If Stasanor was vilified in the *Pamphlet*, it would be surprising to see him and Eumenes join forces; though here that alliance was initially forged in the name of Peucestas. Diodorus 19.14.7 for Stasander's support for Peucestas' original alliance and 19.27.3 for his support for Eumenes. For Peithon's arena of authority discussed in the chapter titled *Lifting the Shroud of Parrhasius*.

176. Arrian 4.1.5. Spitamenes refused to attend a conference in Bactria. See Heckel (2006) p 254 for discussion. Curtius, 7.6.14-15 for his continued resistance and for his siege of the Macedonian garrison, Arrian 4.3.6, 5.2.3. For his ambush of the Macedonian forces see Arrian 4.5.4-9. Then he fled to Bactria; see Curtius 7.9.20. He attacked a Macedonian fort; see Curtius 8.1.3-5, Arrian

4.16.5. For his betrayal by the Massagetae see Arrian 4.17.7, Curtius 8.3.1-16, Strabo 11.11.6. Diodorus Introduction to book 17, contents part 2, for the 120,000 Sogdian casualties.

177. Diodorus 19.48.1-2 for Antigonus' decision not to remove Stasanor. For his career in the East under Alexander, Arrian 3.29.5, 4.18.1, 4.18.3, 6.27.3, 6.27.6, 7.6.1-3, Diodorus 18.3.3, 18.39.6, Justin 13.4.22-23. The career of Spitamenes and Alexander's (and Persian) actions against the nomadic Massagetae suggested the region's (and bordering provinces') abilty to provide effective fighters.

178. For Philotas' appointment to Cilicia at Babylon, Diodorus 18.3.1, Justin 14.4.12, Arrian *Events After Alexander* 1.5, Dexippus FGrH 100 F8 2. Photius' text uniquely placed Philoxenus in Cilicia but this appears a corruption. See Heckel (1988) pp 71-75 for discussion and suggestion that his Antigonid support might explain his being passed over at Triparadeisus. Also see Arrian *Events After Alexander* 24.2; Justin 13.6.16 for references to Philotas' loyalty to Craterus. Cilicia went to Philoxenus: Arrian *Events After Alexander* 1.34, Diodorus 18.39.6. For Philotas' attempt to lure the Silver Shields away from Eumenes, Diodorus 18.62.4, and for the outcome 18.62.5-18.63.5. Arrian *Events After Alexander* 24.2 termed Philoxenus 'undistinguished'.

179. Heckel (2006) pp 225-226 for the carers of Polydorus and Polydamas; the latter had carried the orders for Parmenio's execution.

180. Athenaeus12.548e for Polydorus' association with Antipater. Diodorus 19.59.3 for Ariston's actions after the death of Craterus (or even after the death of Eumenes). Heckel (2006) p 213 for discussion of Philip (8).

181. Justin 12.14.1-3 for Philip's collusion with Iolaos.

182. Philip (though Philotas in Diodorus 19.14.1, probably a corruption, see Heckel (2006) p 214) had been satrap of Bactria and Sogdia and was moved to Parthia at Triparadeisus; Diodorus 18.3.3, Dexippus FGrH F8 6, Diodorus 17.31.5-6. For Philip the physician and the earlier accusations of poisoning see Arrian 2.4.9-10, Plutarch 19.5-10, Curtius 3.6.4-17, Justin 11.8.5-8, Valerius Maximus 3.8 extract 6, Seneca *de Ira* 2.23.2. Following Heckel (2006) pp 214-215 for the rationale for implicating Philip the physician. For Philip who became satrap of Parthia at Triparadeisus, see Heckel (2006) p 214, and p 215 for Philip the engineer. Heckel (1988) p 44 and (2006) p 137 and for a possible identification of Heracleides.

183. Plutarch *Alexander* 77.1-2. Plutarch 77.3-4. By then Antigonus was referred to as 'king' but this does not necessarily mean the rumours circulated after 306 BCE when he was formally crowned. By Plutarch's day the differentiation between when Antigonus was considered a dynast and king was probably blurred.

184. Only Nepos 5.1 cited Seleucus amongst Perdiccas' murderers, but Antigonus, clearly not present, was mentioned too. This could be a corruption of Antigenes, commander of the Silver Shields, or alternatively Nepos was summarising events at Egypt with Triparadeisus where Seleucus did appear alongside Antigonus. Moreover this was some weeks later and he could have journeyed west from Babylon upon hearing of the failed attack on Egypt (chapter titled *Lifting the Shroud of Parrhasius* for explanation of Seleucus in Babylon). Arrian *Events After Alexander* 1.33 for Seleucus' role in saving Antipater from the crowd at Triparadeisus. He is not mentioned alongside either Peithon or Arrhidaeus. In fact Seleucus is not associated with Perdiccas' campaigning from Babylon to his death in 320 BCE in any of the sources. Diodorus 18.36.6-7 for the aftermath of the battle with Perdiccas and the nomination of Peithon and Arrhidaeus as supreme commanders and guardians of the kings.

185. Diodorus 19.12.1 for Eumenes' overture to Seleucus in Babylonia.

186. Heckel (1988) Introduction p1 footnote 1 for a list of extant texts housing the *Liber de Morte* including the Armenian *Romance* text, and pp 34-35 for a comparison list of conspirators. The possible attachment of Europius and Seleucus' ethnic discussed in Heckel (2006) p 246 and Heckel (1988) pp 40-41. Moreover this reference sits amongst the named *Somatophylakes* in the list of attendees given in by the *Metz Epitome*. In another recension of the *Romance*, Seleucus is indeed placed on the guilty roster; Stoneman (1991) p 29 and p 150 footnote 120, for explanation of the 'Y' recension. Other examples of manuscript corruption would certainly accommodate the deterioration and loss of the *onoma*, the personal name, and *patronymikon* of the father. As an example, Arrian gave Leonnatus four different patronyms through his account; discussed in Heckel (1978) pp 155-158.

187. Diodorus 18.39.3-4, Arrian *Events after Alexander* 1.33, Polyaenus 4.6.4 for Seleucus' defence of Antipater at Triparadeisus. Heckel (1988) p 41 for the 320 BCE *terminus post quem*; a proposed date for Triparadeisus at which Seleucus was 'first' confirmed in Babylon, as the pamphleteer could not have anticipated the appointment before.

188. Full discussion on Seleucus' original Will grant in the chapter titled *Lifting the Shroud of Parrhasius*.

189. Diodorus 19.11.8-9 for Olympias' pogrom and Diodorus 19.51.5 where the pogrom is again

referred to and it is implied that Olympias was 'revenging Alexander's death thus suggesting the *Pamphlet* was by then *possibly* first circulating.

190. Plutarch *Alexander* 77.1-2 linking Olympias' pogrom to the conspiracy rumours; also Diodorus 19.11.8-9. As Carney (2006) pp 85-96 points out, the mistreatment of the bodies of the dead featured prominently in the *Iliad*; 22.395-404 for Achilles' maltreatment of Hector, 23.20-3 and 24.14.21 as the most notable examples.

191. Diodorus 19.11.5 for the length of his reign; Justin 14.5.10 stated 'six years'. Aelian claimed Eurydice chose the rope. Diodorus 19.52.5, Athenaeus 4.155a (using Dyllus) for Cassander's burial honours. Alexander died 10/11 June 323 BCE and Arrhidaeus was proclaimed king a week or so after; six years and four months later in mid-October 317 BCE.

192. Diodorus 18.58.3-4 for Eumenes' advice to Olympias not to make a move until the war in Asia had been decided.

193. Diodorus 19.12.1 for the envoys to Seleucus and Peithon and Seleucus' response.

194. Diodorus 19.57.1-3 for the envoys to Antigonus from Ptolemy and Lysimachus demanding their share of Asia Minor and Syria. Also detailed at Justin 15.1.

195. *Metz Epitome* 118.

196. Arrian *Events After Alexander* 1.3-4 for Arrian's interpretation of Perdiccas' role.

197. Nepos 5.1 alone included Seleucus in the list of Perdiccas' murderers. This section of the *Romance* Will is corrupted, placing Perdiccas in Egypt and a Phanocrates as governor from Babylon to Bactria. We would imagine Phanocrates ought to be Perdiccas; a Persian would not have been granted such a pivotal role.

198. Arrian 4.18.3 for Atropates' reinstallment in Media and again at 7.4.1. Arrian 7.4.5 for Perdiccas' marriage to his daughter. Diodorus 18.3.3, Justin 13.4.13 for his reconfirmation in Lesser Media at Babylon.

199. See chapter titled *Lifting the Shroud of Parrhasius* for Perdiccas' plans for Alexander's body.

200. *Metz Epitome* 110 for the instructions to Perdiccas and Antigonus and 117 and *Romance* 3.33.15 for Antipater's governorship west of the Halys.

201. Peithon son of Agenor was appointed satrap of 'lower' India bordering the Indus; Arrian 6.15.4; reconfirmed by Justin 13.4.21 in his account of Babylon. Heckel (2006) p 196 sees a move to the Cophen satrapy as per Diodorus 18.3.3, Dexippus FGrH 100 F8, a region reconfirmed as Triparadeisus in Diodorus 18.39.6, Arrian *Events After Alexander* 1.36, Justin. Diodorus 18.3.3 for his installation in the region between Parapamisus and the Indus. Peithon appeared in Syria in 314/313 BCE advising Demetrius; Diodorus 19.69.1, 19.82.1.

202. *Metz Epitome* 117 for the grant of Syria to Peithon. The son of Antigenes was mentioned in Arrian's *Indike* 15.10; Heckel (2006) p 194 for the possible identification (Peithon 1). Diodorus 19.56.4 for Antigonus installing Peithon son of Agenor in Babylonia.

203. Antigenes was granted Susiane at Triparadeisus (Diodorus 18.39.6, Arrian *Events After Alexander* 1.34) and the Will suggested all lands between Babylon and Bactria should retain the same governors.

204. Heckel (1978) p 155 for Leonnatus' various patronyms at Arrian 3.5.5, 6.28.4, *Events After Alexander* 1a.2, *Indike* 18.3.

205. For Aristonus' identity and roles on campaign Arrian 6.28.4; this may have come from Nearchus' list of trierarchs of the Hydaspes-Indus fleet; see the *Indike* 18.4 and Arrian *Events After Alexander* 1.2-3. Curtius alone cited him protecting Alexander in the Mallian campaign 9.5.15-18 and again at the assembly in Babylon at 10.6.16 ff. Heckel (2006) p 50 for explanation of Ptolemy's omission and Errington (1969) pp 233 and 242 for a similar argument. For his Successor War roles, Arrian *Events After Alexander* 24.6 (*Vatican Palimpsest/Codex* 6) for his leading the Perdiccan invasion force to Cyprus and for activity and support of Olympias see Diodorus 19.35.4 and 19.50.3-19.51.1.

206. Arrian *Anabasis* 7.5.6 suggested the Bodyguards each received a gold crown, yet only the *Somatophylakes* Leonnatus, Peucestas and Hephaestion were named. Nearchus and Onesicritus were also named in the honours list. See Heckel (1988) p 50 for discussion of other possible corrupted references to Aristonus.

207. Aristonus supported Polyperchon and the Olympias faction after Antipater's death, see Diodorus 19.35.4, 19.50.3-8, 19.51.1, Diodorus 19.49-51.1 for Aristonus' murder and his control of Amphipolis.

208. Diodorus 19.51.1 for Aristonus' high standing amongst the Macedonians.

209. A wider discussion of the Syrian satrapal grant in chapter titled *Lifting the Shroud of Parrhasius*.

210. Quoting Stoneman (1991) Introduction p 12 for 'clotted officialese'. *Metz Epitome* 110 for the roles of Perdiccas and Antipater. Heckel (1988) pp 12-14 for full discussion referring to Recension A of Pseudo-Callisthenes and Heckel-Yardley (2004) p 285 for a full translation of

the *Metz Epitome* version of the Rhodian 'interpolation'. Bosworth-Baynham (2000) p 213 agrees the Rhodian issue could have formed part of the original *Pamphlet* Will. See Stoneman (1991) pp 152-153 for a translation of the *Romance* version of the Letter to the Rhodians. The Letter to the Rhodians is concurrent in Pseudo-Callisthenes A. Fraser (1996) p 212 for the boule and demos and discussion on the Latin manuscript in which the letter appeared separately. Discussed in further detail in chapter titled *The Silent Siegecraft of the Pamphleteers*.

211. Bosworth-Baynham (2000) p 213.
212. Berthold (1984) p 39 on Rhodian government.
213. Diodorus 20.81.2 and discussed in Berthold (1984) p 38. Polybius 33.16.3 and Strabo 14.2.5 amongst others reiterated the same sentiment though without stating the date or Hellenistic period they were referring to. Rodgers (1937) p 262 for the renting out of Rhodian *trieres*.
214. Berthold (1984) pp 42-43 on Rhodes' expansion and state governance and pp 48-49 for the continuation of the Rhodian coinage weight after Alexander adopted the Attic standard. Rhodes had seceded early from the Delian League controlled by Athens, remaining neutral for example in the Peloponnesian War.
215. O'Neil (2000) p 425 for discussion of the law codes imposed and Billows (1990) p 220 for the League of the Islanders.
216. Arrian 2.20.2 for Cypriot assistance at Tyre. Diodorus 19.62.4, 20.47.3, Pausanias 1.6.6 for Menelaus' early role in Cyprus before his removal after the battle at Salamis in 306 BCE.
217. Berthold (1984) p 34 for discussion of Rhodian independence from Caria. The arrests of the Rhodian brothers Demaratus, Sparton and Harpalus' treasurer, probably by Philoxenus, demonstrated the reach of Alexander's authority over Rhodes.
218. For a description of caltrops at the battle of Gaugamela see Curtius 4.13.36. Also see *Lindian Stele Votive* 38 and discussion in Higbie (2003) pp 134-5; 234-235 for Persian votives. Spiked iron caltrops were used to maim horses and protect ground littered with them against cavalry charges. In legend, Danaus had fifty daughters, one of whom was Lindos and worshipped on Rhodes taking her name for its city; Diodorus 5.38 and Strabo 14.2.6 for the legend that Danaus had founded the sanctuary of Athena Lindia on his way to Egypt.
219. Discussed in Stewart (1993) p 220, and Lindian subtext at p 237. More detail about the cult on Rhodes in Brandt-Iddeng (2012) p 255. Lock (1977) p 100 and Tarn 1 (1948) p 59 for the Lindian inscription. Also Shipley (2000) p 37 and Tarn 1 (1948) p 59 for inscriptions on Rhodes.
220. *Metz Epitome* 118-119.
221. Arrian *Events after Alexander* 1.39 for Attalus' attack on Cnidus, Caunus and Rhodes where he was repulsed; Diodorus 18. 37.3-4 for his rounding up orphaned Perdiccans.
222. See Casson (2001) p 32 for grain discussion and Egyptian supply.
223. Quoting Brandt-Iddeng (2012) p 255 for Rhodes' long-standing alliance with Ptolemy.
224. *Romance* 3.33.9; see Stoneman (1991) p 154 for translation and Heckel (1988) pp 12-13 for discussion. Ptolemy's executor role reiterated in Lucian's *Dialogues of the Dead* 13.
225. *Metz Epitome* 116, *Romance* 3.23.
226. Diodorus 19.58.1-6 for the state of Antigonus' naval power.
227. Diodorus 18.43.1-2 for Ptolemy's annexation of Coele-Syria.
228. *Metz Epitome* 109.
229. *Romance* 1.46.
230. Ismenas the son of either Oceanus and Tethys or Asopus and Metope and who settled on the banks of the Rriver Ismenus in Boeotia. For examples see Plutarch *Demetrius* 1.6 for the musician of Thebes and for the 4th century BCE statesman by the same name, and Xenophon *Hellenika* 2.31 for another Ismenias; the name also appears in Plato *Meno* 90a as well as Plato *Republic* 336a. *Romance* 1.46, Pausanias 9.10.6, Ovid *Metamorphoses* 3.169, Callimachus *Hymn 4 to Delos* 77, Diodorus 4.72.1, 31.12.6. Aelian 12.57 for the portents at Thebes.
231. Herodotus 5.58-61. Plutarch *Lysander* 29.
232. Arrian 2.15.2-5 for the reference to the son of Ismenias, an envoy from Thebes and his lineage. Plutarch *Pelopidas* 5.1 for Pelopidas' membership of Ismenias' party. Ismenias was put to death at Sparta (*Pelopidas* 5.4), an outcome that possibly endeared him to Philip, if the same man. Also Diodorus 15.71.2-3 and Plutarch *Pelopidas* 27.1, 27.5 for Ismenias' repuation and relations with Pelopidas. Aelian 1.21; Ismenias dropped a ring as his excuse for kneeling to the Persian king.
233. Plutarch 13.5, *Moralia* 181b, Justin 11.4.9 and Arrian 2.15.3-4 for Alexander's later regret for such harsh treatment of Thebes. Diodorus 17.13.3. Arrian 1.8.8 for his defence of Alexander's actions by outlining the list of Theban treachery when aligning with Persia.
234. Athenaeus 434 a-b for Ephippus' remark. Diodorus 17.10.3, translation from the Loeb Classical Library edition, 1963.

235. Justin 10.4.5-6 for Heracles' birth in Thebes.
236. Diodorus 19.54.1 for the list of cities that pledged support for the rebuild. Diodorus 19.61.3 for Antigonus' demand that the reconstruction of Thebes be reversed. Diodorus 19.61.1-3 for Antigonus' proclamation. Aelian 3.6 for Crates' prediction.
237. *Metz Epitome* 120; the *Romance* 3.32 stated 50 talents of coined gold; that suggests a gold to silver ratio of 1:20 when the actual ratio was between 1:10 and 1:12 in the early Hellenistic period.
238. The *Metz Epitome* translation in Heckel (1988) p 17 claimed 1,000 talents for the temple of Hera at Argos. The *Romance* has Alexander's armour plus 50 talents, see Stoneman (1991) p 155 for translation. Bosworth-Baynham (2000) p 221 cites 150 talents. Variations in the texts range from the 'Temple of Hera' to 'the first fruits of war for Heracles'.
239. Homer *Iliad* 4.50-52
240. Pausanias 10.10.5 for the proposed lineage of the Argives and see discussion in chapter titled *The Rebirth of the Wrath of Peleus' Son*. The essence of the story was captured by Euripides in his *Heracleidae*. See Diodorus 12.75.5-6 for the significance of the legend to Argos. The Return of the Heracleidae is also known as the Dorian invasion when the scattered sons of Heracles come home to claim their rightful ancestral lands, including Sparta; see Pausanias 4.30.1 and Herodotus 8.73
241. Diodorus 19.63.1-5 for the confrontation at Argos.
242. *Romance* 3.32
243. See chapter titled *The Tragic Triumvirate of Treachery and Oaths* for the value of 1 talent vs infantry remuneration.
244. *Metz Epitome* 104-105, *Romance* 3.32.12-13 for the rumour of Alexander's death causing a troop uproar.
245. The discord at Babylon was captured; *Metz Epitome* 104-106 and 113, *Romance* 3.32. Cleitarchus could have of course embellished what they read in the *Pamphlet* when developing his book conclusion.
246. Roman contamination discussion in Tarn (1948) pp 378-398.
247. Arrian 7.27, Plutarch 7.27 for Aristotle's involvement.
248. Theophrastus *Enquiry into Plants* 9.16.2 and for hemlock 9.16.8.
249. Quoting Green (2007) p 2. As Champion (2014) p 4 noted of the last eleven Argeads, they were either assassinated or executed.
250. For Olympias' death on Cassander's orders, Diodorus 19.51.5, Justin 14.6.6-12, Pausanias 1.11.4, 25.6, 9.7.2 (for stoning to death); Carney (2006) pp 81-85 for discussion of the various accounts of her death.
251. Quoting Curtius 10.10.18-19. The theme of 'fearful historians' is reiterated in the Vulgate texts by Diodorus 17.118.2, Justin 12.13.10.
252. Diodorus 19.61.1-4, Justin 15.1.
253. The anonymous verse was quoted at Polybius 23.10.10 and 15 and allegedly repeated by the later King Philip V of Macedonia preparing to face Rome in the 149th Olympiad, so 183/182 BCE.
254. Tarn (1949) p 297.
255. Bosworth (2002) p 217 for the dating discussion according to the *Babylonian Chronicle*.
256. Diodorus 19.105.3-5 for the extracting of Thesalonice and Justin 15.2.2-5. Pausanias 9.7.2 for the murder of Roxane and Alexander IV.
257. Quoting Grainger (2007) p 116. For the death of Heracles, Diodorus 20.28, Justin 15.2.3, Pausanias 9.7.2 and for its dating Carney-Ogden (2010) p 118 and Wheatley (1998) p 13 and footnotes; it may have been 308 BCE. Diodorus 20.37.3 for Cleopatra's leaving Sardis to join Ptolemy and her execution.
258. For Heracles' death Diodorus 20.28, Pausanias 9.7.2-3, Justin 15.2.3. Antigonus claimed Cassander forced Thessalonice into marriage, Diodorus 19.52.1. and 61.2, Pausanias 8.7.7, Justin 14.6.13. For the death of Cleopatra on Antigonus' orders, Diodorus 20.37.5-6.
259. Quoting Carney (2006) p 84 on Cassander's attempt to de-legitimise Alexander's Argead branch.
260. Plutarch *Pyrrhus* for Neoptolemus' death, though his identity is challenged; see Heckel (2006) p 175. Also see Carney (2006) p 67 and footnote 25 (p 169); whilst not specifically attested as her children, Neoptolemus is mentioned as their father, though as Carney argues, this could mean 'descendants' and thus grandchildren, for Neoptolemus was the father to Alexander of Epirus, Cleopatra's husband.
261. Plutarch *Sertorius* 1.4, translation from the Loeb Classical Library edition, 1919, for comparisons with Philip, Antigonus and Hannibal and quoting 1.6
262. Plutarch *The Comparison of Sertorius with Eumenes* 2.3-4.
263. Whilst Plutarch painted a picture of Eumenes' pre-battle contemplations, this episode may well have taken place once he took council and the outcome of the battle looked doubtful once the Silver Shields had been surrounded, as Diodorus clarified that a council took place immediately before his arrest.

264. Plutarch *Eumenes* 16.2.

265. Plutarch *Comparison of Eumenes with Sertorius* 2.4.

266. Plutarch *Eumenes* 18.2 for the Silver Shields' complaint and 16-18 for the outcome at Gabiene.

267. Diodorus 19.44.3 for Hieronymus' capture and new employment.

268. See chapter titled *Guardians and Ghosts of the Ephemerides* for discussion of Hagnothemis' role. See Billows (1990) pp 387-388 for Hagnon's final activity; the date of the battle off of Cyprus is disputed, 315/314 BCE is proposed, though this conflicts with Diodorus 19.58.1 which claimed Antigonus had no naval force then (also see 19.59.1 and 19.62.3-4 for the possible engagement). Hagnon had been granted citizenship of Ephesus in 321/320 BCE.

269. Plutarch *Apophthegms* or *Sayings of Kings and Commanders* 8860 (5), *Lysander*.

270. Plutarch *Life of Demetrius* 4. Demetrius was described as a young man, so dating is not exact. But if born in ca. 336 BCE he would have been seventeen when Eumenes was at Nora, thus it is likely the episode took place before Eumenes' death at which point Demetrius would have been close to twenty. Heckel (2006) p 109 for discussion of Demetrius' age. Cicero's supposed line taken from R Harris *Imperium*, Pocket Books, 2006 p 262.

271. 'Unable to fly' quoting Plutarch *Comparison of Eumenes and Sertorius* 2.4. Justin 14.3, possibly drawing from Duris, claimed Eumenes attempted to flee and only when captured again did he demand the right to deliver his final scathing speech. The use of Duris is somewhat backed up by Plutarch's *Comparison of Eumenes with Sertorius* 2.3-4 in which he alleged the same.

12

THE PRECARIOUS PATH OF
PERGAMENA AND PAPYRUS

**What did it take for ancient manuscripts to survive,
how were they manipulated in the process, and how
closely does today's library represent the original texts?**

The 2,340 years since Alexander died have seen the loss of classical libraries, books change in materials and format, and witnessed the emergence of religions and philosophies that tugged at the consciences of those who decided which of them would survive.

The evolving classical library also gave rise to an industry of damaging imitations and outright fakes; the authenticity of some of the books we read today is still open to question.

Adding to these challenges was the gradual metamorphosis of the classical and vernacular languages into which texts had to be translated, and this provided further latitude for interpolation, well-meaning or otherwise.

So how closely does our extant library approximate the original authors' intent, and how relevant is this to any study of Alexander and his times? We review the precarious path of the book, from its origins in Egyptian papyrus to the age of the printing press.

'I have turned my attention to Greek. The first thing I shall do, as soon as the money arrives, is to buy some Greek authors; after that, I shall buy some clothes.'[1]

Erasmus *Letter to Jacob Batt*, 12th April 1500

'But one thing the facts cry out, and it can be clear, as they say, even to a blind man, that often through the translator's clumsiness or inattention the Greek has been wrongly rendered; often the true and genuine reading has been corrupted by ignorant scribes, which we see happen every day, or altered by scribes who are half-asleep.'[2]

Erasmus *Epistle* 337

'We can claim to have learnt reasonably well how to detect forgeries of ancient texts made either in the Middle Ages or in the Renaissance or later… On the other hand, it would be fatuous to maintain that we can readily expose a forgery when the forgery was made in Antiquity. Indeed in this case the name of forgery becomes a problem. What we are tempted to label as a forgery, may, on closer examination, be a perfectly honest work attributed to the wrong author.'[3]

Arnaldo Momigliano *Studies in Historiography*

Erasmus, the Dutch theologian, manuscript collector and so-called prince of the humanists, was so irked by 'clumsy translators' that he mastered 'pure' Latin, a skill he employed to unify the parallel Greek and Latin traditions of the *New Testament*. His new publication, followed by Martin Luther's (reputedly) nailing his *Ninety-Five Theses on the Power and Efficacy of Indulgences* on the door of the Church of All Saints on 31st October 1517, became a landmark that heralded in the Reformation which posed a challenge to the doctrine of the Catholic Church.[4]

A year earlier, Thomas More, a friend to Erasmus, published his Latin *Utopia*, which, as well as satirising the society of the day, had espoused religious tolerances through descriptions of an Arcadian isle; it embodied something of Lucian's wry sense of humour beside elements of Plato's *Republic*.[5] In one of the many ironies, tragedies, twists and turns of this troubled 'humanist' era, More became vigorously opposed to Protestantism, claiming Catholicism was the one true faith in his *Dialogue Concerning Heresies*. He perhaps failed to appreciate that its 'sacred history was Jewish, its theology was Greek', and 'its government and canon laws were, at least indirectly, Roman'.[6]

Erasmus' *Novum Instrumentum Omne,* dedicated to Pope Leo X, was 'rushed' into print in 1516; it was a task spurred on by the discovery in 1504 of Laurentius Valla's *New Testament Notes*.[7] The new edition stabilised

(Erasmus said 'purified') the Greek, Byzantine and Vulgate biblical texts in the same way the Alexandrian librarians had anchored down the fluid Homeric epics from their 'limpid formulaic style'.[8] For through his correspondence with numerous influential scholars of his day, many of whose methods he openly criticised (the Lutherans especially), Erasmus had seen first-hand the damage being done to ancient manuscripts at the scriptoriums across Europe. But despite his pedantic spirit, Erasmus' new influential and polished Latin translations ignored the older and better manuscripts to avoid what he termed the 'erratic' texts that conflicted with his direction. As a result, his Greek *New Testament* was demonstrably inferior, for example, to the *Complutensian Polyglot Bible,* a translation from 1514 originating in Alcala in Spain.[9]

Manuscript corruptions were occasionally deliberate when religiously or politically contrived, but more often than not they were due to the simple blind incompetency and lawlessness of ill-trained scribes. Erasmus' linguistic skills highlighted many, and he pertinently coined the adage 'in the land of the blind, the one-eyed man is king'.[10] But it was Petrarch (1304-1374), born in exile at the close of the High Middle Ages (or High Medieval Period, ca. 1000-1300) who was 'the first man since antiquity to make a systematic collection of Latin classical manuscripts'. In his attempt 'not to fashion fables but to retell history', he opened the pages of old once more as a fascination took hold with all things *alle romana et alla antica*, though in the case of Alexander, Petrarch thought he died in Babylon 'effeminate' and 'transformed into some kind of monster'.[11] Although the knowledge of Latin had improved, with much of its purity preserved by the Church, scholars' dexterity with classical Greek lagged far behind; as Momigliano reminds us, there was once a time when the *Bible* was *only* available in Greek but at the beginning of the Renaissance almost *none* existed.[12]

Edward Gibbon, whose own later English prose was still 'steeped in the cadences of Ciceronian Latin', recorded that Petrarch admitted similar linguistic shortcomings with Greek had hampered his own translation efforts, lamenting of a rare Homer manuscript that had been presented to him: 'Alas! Either Homer is dumb or I am deaf, nor is it within my power to enjoy the beauty I possess.'[13] Gibbon himself complained of the Byzantine-influenced Greek being spoken in his day: 'The modern Greeks pronounce the β as a V consonant, and confound three vowels and several diphthongs.'[14] Although Petrarch's earlier attempt to learn more than the rudiments of Greek from the Calabrian monk Barlaam came too late in his own life to be completely successful, his younger friend, Giovanni Boccaccio (1313-1375), *did* master the classical language before his reconversion to Church doctrine, and he saw to it that the Leontios Pilatos (locally Leonzio Pilato, died 1366) became the first professor of the neglected tongue in Western Europe by 1360 (though this was, in fact, Byzantine Greek too).[15]

A new generation of Graeco-Romans was being born, despite the diversion of wars, Crusades and the Black Death of 1348 which indiscriminately took scholar and pauper with it. In the re-educational process, the European languages were enriched with Greek and Latin loan words and attached phraseology, because the 'poorer' vernacular languages had previously evolved around purely practical, though rarely intellectual, vocabulary. This, in turn, broadened the translator's style as the new literary devices and linguistic structures entered the target language through 'positive paganism' at last.[16] Arguably, Dante's *Divine Comedy,* written in exile between ca. 1308-1320, had already helped to bridge a gap between the Christian doctrine and the values of the pagan Graeco-Roman tradition, in this case with the guidance of a reincarnated Virgil.[17] English was to benefit through the well-travelled Chaucer (ca. 1343-1400) and his translation of Boethius' *The Consolation of Philosophy* (the original written ca. 523 CE).

The *Bible* went through similar transmutations into English once the outcome of the Reformation finally permitted publication of Greek gospels and Latin sermons into the modern languages. Inspired by Luther's German translation, Tyndale principally used Erasmus' 1522 edition (along with the Latin Vulgate and Hebrew texts) for his 1526 *English New Testament*. It inclined to a very personal translation to ensure he would: '… cause the boy that drives the plow to know more of the Scriptures than the Pope himself!'[18] Published in secret in Germany (where Tyndale had been given safe haven by Luther), it came replete with idioms stemming from his native Gloucestershire patois, framing Latinate words in Anglo-Saxon and creating a rhythm that appealed to the humble masses, though it would cost Tyndale his life. The result was a new 'Vulgate' edition that remained largely intact in the King James Bible of 1611, giving us many of the influential words we use today.[19]

The Renaissance additionally saw a 'humanist' enlightenment that returned the individual to the centre stage as Hellenistic philosophies came under scrutiny with their templates of personal virtue and vice. Erasmus inspired fellow Dutchman, Jeroen de Busleyden, to found the Collegium Trilingue to promote the teaching of Greek, Latin, and Hebrew to better arm scholars resuscitating ancient texts. This was not for purely esoteric purposes; as Momigliano put it, men emerging from the 'ruins of a feudal system' were anxious to get 'all the advice they could' when searching for new 'political and military machinery' from the classical thinkers.[20] Enlightened Europeans knew they needed the lessons from the past to plot the path of a learned future.

But scholarship *was* still weighted down by the religious intolerances of the Holy Roman Empire and the threat of Ottoman invasion, so religious works dominated the scriptoriums located at abbeys and monasteries at the expense of the 'heathen' classics that preceded Christianity. Original Greek and Christian texts were ferried westwards as Byzantium (Constantinople) threatened to fall, and then they were chaperoned to safety by private collectors such as Cosimo de' Medici (1389-1464), Erasmus, and Poggio Bracciolini, who described how he found manuscripts in 'leaky rat-ridden monastery attics'... 'looking up at him for help' like 'friends in a hospital or a prison'; Boccaccio had similarly burst into tears at seeing the state of the library at Monte Cassino.[21]

The likes of Valla (1406-1457) and Machiavelli (Niccolò di Bernardo dei Machiavelli, 1469-1527) nevertheless, revived a wider philosophical curiosity that was inspired by these classical manuscripts, and finally universities and new libraries emerged, including the Vatican Library founded by Pope Nicholas V (reigned 1447-1455) whose eight years in office saw 5,000 volumes emerge from the hands of copyists and scholars.[22]

The momentum behind Renaissance 'enlightenment' led to a rising demand for previously neglected manuscripts from the classical past, and, ironically, this led to the start of a new industry in politically opportune and profitable forgeries. Pope Leo X was paying handsomely for new Greek and Latin texts, and Maffeo Vegio (1407-1458) wrote a thirteenth book to the *Aeneid* at the tender age of twenty-one, unsatisfied as he was with the original conclusion of Virgil. Bishop Gavin Douglas used Vegio's homespun edition when first translating the *Aeneid* to Scots in 1553, and he was followed by Thomas Twyne and his English edition published in 1584. In 1583 another unsatisfied scholar, Carlo Sigonio, declared he had discovered a complete copy of *De Consolatione* by Cicero; when challenged on its authenticity, he indignantly replied that if not genuine, it was at least *worthy* of Cicero.

The authenticity of Tacitus' *Annals* was soon called into question and Poggio Bracciolini, possibly because of their loud 'calls for help', was accused of being their fabricator. Bracciolini 'who rose to high posts in public affairs and won imperishable fame in letters' after he had fortuitously stumbled upon a genuine hoard of lost Latin texts some fifty years before, including (amongst others) the masterpieces of Cicero, Quintilian and Vitruvius the Roman civil engineer.[23] Debate on whether we have the fully genuine article for Tacitus' books 1-6 and 11-16 still has an audience, though JW Ross in his 1878 treatise on the matter was in no doubt:

> I give a detailed history of the forgery, from its conception to its completion, the sum that was paid for it, the abbey where it was transcribed, and other such convincing minutiae taken from a correspondence that Poggio carried on with a familiar friend who resided in Florence.

Ross went on to explain why not all agreed with the conclusion: 'The cause is obvious: the forger fabricated with the decided determination of defying detection.'[24] Bracciolini was not against using bribery to obtain the manuscripts he wanted, or attacking his contemporaries with compositions that led to a decade of invectives between him and Laurentius Valla. He superficially remained an austere scholar who dedicated his life to the papal *curia*. Whether the accusations are founded or not we may never know, but his sale of a Livy manuscript in 1434 enabled him to build a villa and adorn it with fine antiques.

THE LEAD BLADE FROM THE IVORY SCABBARD[25]

This brings us to the career of Johannes Annius of Viterbo (ca. 1432-1502), one of the 'great crop of forgers bred of the dark earth'. Although Annius' story is far removed from the death of Alexander, it remains potently pertinent too,[26] for his is a tale of contemporaneous historical forgery and creative historiographical method rolled into one. It raises the obvious question: has the history of Alexander survived with any more, or less, integrity? Documentary fakes and political frauds have changed the course of history, and many, we must speculate, remain undetected. Furthermore, by now, these historical traditions have inertias that make them difficult to reconsider any other way, and so they *remain* unchallenged. Given a following wind and with less talented philologists in circulation, Annius may have well become a hero of Italian Renaissance historiography, and for a while he was. Instead the man who claimed to read Etruscan is remembered today as a fraud.[27]

Annius was a Dominican preaching monk as well as an archaeologist and meddler in antiquity who held an apocalyptic view of the struggle between Christianity, Islam and Judaism. He perceived the worlds of Europe and Asia as historically irreconcilable and as culturally opposed as Alexander had once found them some 2,000 years before him, though some scholars romantically maintain that Alexander was attempting to change just that.[28] In the late 1490s Annius faked a number of Etruscan inscriptions giving pseudoarchaeology a new birth, and his *magnum opus* was an anthology of seventeen classical manuscripts he claimed to have 'unearthed' at Mantua.

Annius was probably inspired by Poggio Bracciolini and a hoard of new 'finds', all written by Annius himself, were published as *Antiquitatum Variarum*. His attendant commentaries, which first saw light in Rome in 1498, lent a fine verisimilitude to the whole affair, and the collection soon became famous as *The Antiquities of Annius* and it had Europe talking for a century or more.[29]

Annius' elaborate fabrications, which supposedly stemmed from ancient narratives leading back to the biblical Creation, were falsely attributed to Berossus the Chaldean priest of Babylonian Bel-Marduk, to a Persian, Metasthenes, and the Egyptian priest Manetho (3rd century BCE), alongside fragments from Xenophon and Cato the Elder; in other words, writers whose influential accounts shaped our knowledge of the classical world. Along the way, Annius placed his hometown of Viterbo on the site of Fanum Vultumnae and thus as the capital of the Etruscan Golden Age.

For good measure, Annius proposed that the Roman emperor Augustus had founded Florence, so enhancing the state ideology of the Medici.[30] This was a civic elevation synonymous with earlier classical claims by the Greek historian Ephorus, who proposed that Cyme, *his* home city in Aeolis (modern Nemrut in Turkey), was the birthplace of Homer and Hesiod.[31] Although he was eventually exposed, Annius' deceits were initially influential and he dedicated them to Ferdinand V and Isabella of Spain with a bold preface assuring the reader that as a theologian he had a particular duty to respect the truth; it was a 'denunciation of mendacity' that gave his 'discoveries' an 'air of moral as well as factual superiority'.[32]

In the fraudulent process, Annius' work paradoxically gave us the valuable concept of primary, secondary, and tertiary sources, the foundation of the methodology that distinguishes 'eyewitnesses' from those who drew from their *testimonia,* while relegating to 'tertiary' the writers even further removed from events. As it has been pointed out, though devoted entirely to fakes, his categorisation is the earliest extant Renaissance epigraphic treatise.[33] Annius' emphasis on chronology and inscriptions, and his rules of historical evidence alongside his linguistic theories, were all adopted in some form in later historiographical methods, the disciplines that ironically sealed his own fate. He was indeed a lead blade that slipped out of the ivory scabbard housing classical literature.

Contemporary with Annius was Abbot Johannes Trithemius, a theologian, moralist and antiquarian born in 1462. Trithemius concocted a history of the Franks from the fall of Troy up to King Clovis (ca. 466-511 CE) who first united them, claiming ancient Frankish manuscripts as his unimpeachable source. He managed to 'trace' the Habsburg House back to Noah, enabling the Emperor Maximilian I, with whom he was on good terms, to follow his illustrious line back to Theodoric and King Arthur.[34] As Trithemius noted: 'everyone was trying to find himself a Trojan ancestor', as Alexander had himself.[35]

But the likes of Erasmus were hot on the heels of duplicity. He set a tone of enlightenment when exposing the apocryphal correspondence known as the *Epistles of St Paul;*[36] it was long overdue according to Arnaldo Momigliano who noted that the letters between the apostle and Seneca were written in atrocious Latin when perhaps more convincingly Greek would have been used.[37] But there is an irony in implicating Seneca in the correspondence, for the stoic philosopher had stated of historians in general: 'Some are deluded, some delighted, by falsehood... the whole clan of them have this in common; they fancy their work cannot merit approval, and become popular unless they freely interlard it with lies.'[38]

Annius' fall from grace came in the form of Johannes Goropius Becanus (1519-1572) and Joseph Scaliger who brought their deep knowledge of classical Greek and Latin to bear on his *Antiquities*; their philological autopsies were capitalising on developments in Renaissance historiography and laying the foundations of *Quellenforschung*.[39] But these developing historiographical processes did not kill the industry of falsification; they simply sharpened the wits of future pretenders peddling their wares; as more deceptions and fakes fell out of the closet, some occasionally fell in. Laurentius Valla had already exposed the *Donation of Constantine*, a forged decree that placed a good deal of the Western Roman Empire under the authority of the Pope.[40] The 'donation' enjoyed a long legacy; it helped legitimise the 'returning' of lands by the Frankish king, Pepin the Short, to papal control in 756 CE and it was not acknowledged by the church as spurious until 1440. It nevertheless took the Catholic fathers 500 years to 're-donate' the Papal States back to Italy in 1929, the year the Lateran Accords recognised the Vatican as an independent state.

BARTHOLOMEI PICERNI DE
*monte Arduo, ad Iulium. II. Pontificè maxi
mum præfatio edicti siue donationis diui
Constantini,quam è græco in latinã
se asseuerat conuertisse.*

CVm inter legendum in hac tua celeberrima
bibliotheca,beatissime pater, occurrisset mi
hi libellus quidam græcus,qui donationem Costanti
ni continebat:æquum mihi uisum est, illü è græco in
latinum conuertere, & cum tibi sanctissime pater
inscribere debere,qui uicarius Christi,& Petri, ac
Siluestri successor existis.Quippe cü multi sint, qui
falsam Constantini donationé esse asseruerint:inter
quos est Laurëtius Vallensis,uir haud sanè inerudi-
tus, qui librü de falsa donatione Costätini scribere
ausus sit.Cuius opinionibus optime refragatur reue
ren.Cardinalis Alexãdrinus Iuris utriusq; cösultissi
mus,& illius obiecta diligëtissime cösutat. Existi-
mabat uir ille fortasse,ut quod ipse non legerat,nõ
posset apud alios reperiri. Nec mirum, cum tantæ
mordacitatis extiterit, ut Aristotelë philosophorü
principé carpere nõ dubitarit:& oës linguæ latinæ
autores ita taxare,ut nemini pepercerit. Sed ne lõ-
gior sim, Constätinü um ipsum audiamus.

Valla

A page from Laurentius Valla's *De falso credita et ementita Constantini Donatione declamatio*. Described as one of the 'monuments of historical criticism', Valla attacks the *Donation of Constantine*, an 8th century forgery which supported the papacy's claim to supreme political authority in Europe. Valla's work made it clear that the text could not have been written in the fourth century, the age of Constantine the Great, by revealing many anachronisms in form and content. This annotated edition was printed in Basel in 1520. Digitised by the CAMENA Project, Heidelberg-Mannheim.

The son of an Italian scholar portentously christened Julius Caesar, Scaliger, who was the first person to identify Indo-European linguistic groupings, is remembered for his appreciation that classical historiography should include the Persian, Babylonian, Jewish and Ancient Egyptian records, beside the Greek and Roman accounts that dominated Western interpretations of the classical age.[41]

Somewhat inevitably, the 'barbarian' finds of Annius, those credited to Berossus, Metasthenes and Manetho, for example, eventually came under scrutiny. In fact these 'rediscovered' historians were broadly contemporary with Alexander, if we accept that Megasthenes the Greek travelographer, rather than the otherwise unattested 'Metasthenes', was Annius' intended reincarnation. Perhaps this was a correction supposed to reinforce his pedantic philological zeal, for 'to throw together the real and the fictitious is an old device of verisimilitude and deceit', and it may explain Annius' own contention: 'Authors can both deceive and be deceived but an imposed name cannot.'[42]

As for the fate of Annius, he was (it is claimed) finally – and philologists might deem fittingly – poisoned by Cesare Borgia. Cesare's *alleged* father, Rodrigo Borgia, had already furnished the living quarters in the Vatican with images of the great Macedonian conqueror; indeed when elected Pope in August 1492 he assumed the name 'Alexander VI'.[43] Annius had placed an importance on onomastics, the derivation of proper names in the historical framework that provided him with his 'irrefutable arguments'.[44] He had etched-on with his own hand many of the Etruscan inscriptions he claimed to have found, and so we may reflectively deem them 'primary fabrications' of pseudoarchaeology. His real name was Giovanni Nanni though he had adopted a title more reminiscent of the Roman golden age; like Alexander, he was attempting to fuse his own imagery with another heroic past.

IN NOMINE PATRIS, DIAIREI KAI BASILEUE[45]

Annius' own deceits unwittingly motioned the wheels of historiographical method and provide us with 'an organon for arriving at historical truth'. Although the later proponents of *Quellenforschung* have done much for historiographic methodology, even if they exhibited bias when doing so,[46] its operators have not, and it *was* the heavy hand of religious doctrine that played the weightiest role in the loss of what once graced the library shelves. The sobering truth behind our library of classics is a stark one: we have nothing more than a very narrow cross-section of the literary output of the creative minds of antiquity. We might ponder what remained after Caliph Omar (579-644 CE) burned the 'infidel' Library at Alexandria (ca. 641 CE) and fuelled the 4,000 furnaces heating the city's bathhouses for over six months from the contents, though the historicity of the infamous destruction cannot be confirmed.[47]

Much of the polemical noise emerging in the Renaissance was piously motivated, for the new age of rational analysis still fought a stubborn tradition of faith, so the 'enlightenment' was not seen as a universally popular movement.[48] Goropius was ridiculed by Scaliger for his attempt at palaeolinguistics in which he claimed that Antwerpian Brabantic (a Dutch dialect) was the oldest (and so the 'father') of all languages (anticipating Indo-European linguistic theory) and so spoken in Paradise by Adam. Even Scaliger felt the backlash of his own autopsies; the Jesuits attacked him for exposing the authenticity of their *New Testament* compilations and their associated chronologies in his *De emendatione temporum* (1583) and *Thesaurus temporum* (1606). There commenced a literary battle with his former friend and church defender, Gasparus Scioppius, who published his retort, the *Scaliger Hypobolimaeus*, in which polemics and refutations were hurled back and forth.[49]

In October 1623 Digory Whear dedicated a treatise titled *De Ratione et Methodo Legendi Historias dissertatio* to fellow historian William Camden.[50] Summing up the extant accounts, and mentioning Annius' deceipts, Whear's 'plan and method' for reading history cited the Roman antiquarians Varro and Censorinus (3rd century CE) who proposed three distinct epochs had existed: the Creation to the flood, which they named 'the unclear'; the flood to the first Greek Olympiad, termed 'the mythical'; and the first Olympiad down to the Roman Caesars, which they sensibly proposed was 'the historical'.

In contrast to the *Varronian Chronology*, which had creatively anchored down Rome's own founding (April 21st 753 BCE) and the city's past by inserting 'anarchic' and 'dictatorial' years to fill chronological gaps,[51] Whear saw the first epoch as 'clearer than the noonday sun', citing the first six chapters of *Genesis* as an impeccable source of these 1,656 years. He next argued away the mythical, suggesting the holy secretaries, Moses and the prophets, had provided a 'sufficiently ample history' of that period. Ironically, Whear then challenged the integrity of the final 'historical' epoch, admitting, however, that it was 'distinguished by exact dates'. He rounded off with: 'All of these are to be read after biblical history, which is the oldest of all, and the truest.'[52]

Whear would have been mortified to hear that, 'arguably the most distinctive feature of early Christian literature is the degree to which it was forged', for 'orthodoxy and its faithful follower, persecution, encouraged literary dishonesty'.[53] This is a contention that explains why publications like Speyer's 300-page *Die Literarische Fälschung im heidnischen und christlichen Altertum* were needed to keep track of them.[54] Speyer was able to identify twenty-six Greek linguistic terms, with Latin parallels such as *adultere, configure, falsare* and *supponere*, associated with the act of forgery, suggesting a fraudulent tradition had already proliferated the classical world.[55]

The Christian Church, or rather religion *per se*, had a legacy of 'pious fraud' (a term first used by Gibbon) to protect the potency of its proprietary texts and so the continued loyalty (and donations) of its congregation. It explains the fervour with which Scioppius defended Catholicism and the zeal with which the Church issued the *Index Librorum Prohibitorum*. From spurious reincarnations of biblical scrolls, the *Sibylline Oracles* and *Gnostic Gospels*, elements of *The Apostolic Constitutions*, the aforementioned epistolary corpus between St Paul and Seneca and the *Decretals of Pseudo-Isidore*, religious falsification spurred a literary genre of erudite pious defence and attack. Much of *that* corpus took the form of forgery and counter forgery too.[56]

Eusebius, whose lost *Kronographia* was diligently reconstructed by Scaliger, had added to the problem long before. In his *Ecclesiastical History* (ca. 312 CE) he declared: 'We shall introduce to this history, in general, only those events, which may be useful first to ourselves and after to prosperity.'[57] Gibbon attacked Eusebius for proposing that falsifications were a lawful and necessary 'medicine' for historians.[58] It did Gibbon little good; although the first volume of his own book (published 1776) was so well received that it was 'on every table and on almost every toilet', he credited Christianity with a big part in the fall of Rome, an event which 'annihilated the noisesome recesses in which lurked the seeds of great moral maladies', leaving the Church fathers no option but to add his epic to the *Index Librorum Prohibitorum*.[59]

A copy of the *Index Librorum Prohibitorum* containing a list of publications banned by the Catholic Church and first enforced by Pope Paul IV in 1559. This edition was produced in the reign of Philip II of Spain and dated 1570. The Index was not formally abolished until 1966 in the papacy of Pope Paul VI.

Eusebius claimed that a document had appeared early in the 4th century purporting to be the *Pagan Acts of Pilate* filled with slanders against the character of Jesus. The author, possibly Theotecnus, a violent persecutor of the Church at Antioch, issued an edict that schoolmasters should have their pupils study and memorise the contents.[60] There were however many *Acta Pilati* entering circulation including those which came to be known as the *Gospel of Nicodemus,* and they were collected by the scholar Constantin von Tischendorf in his 1853 *Evangelica Apocrypha.* Pontius Pilate, the prefect or procurator of Judea from 26-36 CE and the infamous judge of Jesus, is, however, a vexatious character himself. Conflicting texts pose him as Dacian, Sarmatian, Samnite, and even of Scottish descent. The 'Roman' Tacitus, who possibly hailed from Gaul, linked Pilate to misfortune at the hands of the Emperor Caligula with a tragic death in Vienne (Vienna). In fact, solid proof of Pilate's historicity outside of (principally) biblical texts evaded us until the so-called Stone of Pilate was unearthed near Caesarea in 1961.[61]

Eusebius, once again setting out to undermine paganism, found use for a regurgitation of the already semi-fictional work named *Phoenician History* by Philo of Byblos (ca. 64-141 CE); he slanted it with his own evangelical agenda leaving us wondering whether Philo's source, a certain Sanchuniathon, really existed or not.[62]

In the Hellenistic era, and then later in the twilight years of the Roman Empire, new philosophies were fighting for recognition, and old ones for survival; religions too ('fossilised philosophies' in which the 'questioning spirit has been supressed') were fighting for the souls of kings, tyrants and emperors.[63] One of the bolder attempts at self-promotion came in the form of the so-called *Letter of Aristeas,* a sophisticated subterfuge explaining the origins behind the translation of the *Pentateuch,* the first five books of the *Septuagint,* the Hebrew *Bible.* It was written in the *koine* Greek, now the *lingua franca* of the Eastern Mediterranean. Seeking to promote Jewish interests in Alexandria, the letter, supposedly written by a gentile, Aristeas, to his brother, Philocrates, detailed the role of its seventy-two translators (six from each of the twelve tribes of Israel) with their deep philosophical knowledge.

Central to the letter is an ingenious documentary dialogue between Demetrius of Phalerum and Ptolemy II *Philadelphos,* in which the former sought to acquire Jewish texts for the Alexandrian Library in an attempt to elevate their significance.[64] Demetrius, who compiled the *Lopson Aisopeion sunagoga,* a collection of the fables of Aesop for use by orators, had allegedly advised his king: 'It is important that these books, duly corrected, should find a place in your library, because this legislation, in as much as it is divine, is of philosophical importance and of innate integrity.'[65] Over twenty manuscripts of the letters survived, the first mentioned in Josephus' *Jewish Antiquities,* and though it has now been convincingly exposed (after 1522), the *Letter of Aristeas* remains the oldest surviving document attesting to the existence of the great Alexandrian Library within the Museion founded by the Ptolemies.[66] *Tantum religio potuit suadere malorum* – 'such are the crimes to which religion leads', the Epicurean poet Lucretius reflected in his *On the Nature of Things*.[67]

'SPIN ME A THREAD FROM THE WORLD'S BEGINNING'.[68]

Aware as we are that that no primary source material survived for the period under our particular scrutiny – the 'books' written by the eyewitnesses to Alexander's campaigns and the era of the *Diadokhoi* – we need to further appreciate that neither did the *original* scrolls and codices of the secondary and tertiary historians who preserved them. Although manuscripts credited to these Hellenistic and Roman-era historians sat in medieval libraries across Europe, they were more often than not poor translations of much earlier vellums and papyri that had themselves been survivors of an earlier discriminatory process.

At the Library in Alexandria *kritikoi* had been employed to oversee the process of separation and judgment (the *krisis*) which decided what scrolls were to be copied and have a chance of survival as a result. So the antiquated books we enjoy today are the survivors of a selection process that commenced far earlier in our story, one that was itself at times judicious, occasionally malicious, and more often, grossly negligent too. The lucky manuscripts became *hoi enkrithentes*, the 'admitted few', which, if they were fortunate enough, were copied from papyrus to parchment and eventually into industrial print. This was a perilous journey that shaped the canon of what we read today.

The establishment of the two great public libraries at Alexandria and Pergamum (modern Bergama in Western Turkey) in the Hellenistic era created a massive demand for the works of famous authors, predating the Renaissance industry in fakes by some 1,500 years. Galen, the Greek self-titled 'doctor-philosopher' who cut his teeth patching up gladiators in Pergamum, reported that 'the recklessness of forging books and titles began' when the kings of Egypt and the Attalids sought to outdo one another in the number of scrolls on their competing library shelves, '… for there were those who, to increase the price of their books, attached the names of great authors to them and then sold them to nobility.'[69]

It was Callimachus and his *Pinakes* (literally, 'tables'), the 120-volume list of the genuine against the 'pseudos', which brought some kind of order to the growing corpus of works being catalogued and copied in Alexandria.[70] The Ptolemies, voracious collectors, confiscated original books from the incoming vessels and marked them *ex ploion*, 'from the ships', compensating the owners with a new *ex scriptorium* copy.[71] Ptolemy III *Euergetes* later swindled the Athenians out of many of their originals, forfeiting a fifteen-talent bond.[72] Financial rewards were offered for the more valuable texts and in consequence many imitations of ancient works were passed off as genuine, especially those of Alexander's teacher, Aristotle, a prized catch according to Ammonius Saccas, the 3rd century Alexandrian philosopher.[73] Certainly Aristotle's *De Mundo,* once thought to be a dedication to Alexander, fell apart under the Renaissance scrutiny of Daniel Heinsius (1580-1655), Scaliger's gifted pupil, and Isaac Casaubon, a regular correspondent with the by-now-famous philologist who provided the attendant commentaries. Casaubon went on to edit a number of classical works that feature in our study and his *magnum opus* was a commentary of Athenaeus' *Deipnosophistae, The Dinner Philosophers,* a rich source of historical detail found nowhere else.

Galen, prodigious in his writing, indignantly described how both his own medical works and the writings of Hippocrates had been corrupted by the interpolations of unscrupulous and careless editors; it prompted him to publish *On His Own Books* to help identify the works truly his. This may have assisted Diogenes Laertius when gathering the doxographies for his *Lives and Opinions of Eminent Philosophers,* that is if he did not simply plagiarise Diocles of Magnesia (2nd or 1st century BCE), as Friedrich Nietzsche supposed. Though the collection remains a rich biographical potpourri, we must assume much misattribution occurred, a suspicion reinforced by Diogenes himself who pointed to the frequent contradictions in his sources.[74] Winding up his *Life of Aristotle,* Diogenes commented: 'There are, also, a great many other works attributed to him, and a number of apophthegms which he never committed to paper.'[75]

Eusebius' *Praeparatio Evangelica* later recalled the objections of Apollonius 'The Grammarian' (amongst others) to the plagiarism of Theopompus and Ephorus, and he also brought to our attention the books with telling titles: Latinus' six books *On the Books of Menander that were Not by Him* and Philostratus' treatise *On the Plagiarisms (or Thefts) of Sophocles.*[76] Some misattribution was of course innocent and later writers repeatedly misidentified authors of the same name; as many as twenty writers named Dionysius or Ptolemy are known to us, a situation which prompted Demetrius of Magnesia, a tutor to Cicero, to publish *Of Poets and Writers of the Same Names,* which sought to differentiate them.

The real identities of the Pseudo-Callisthenes attached to the *Romance* and of the Curtius Rufus who biographed Alexander, remain just as obscure; *both* may prove to be classic cases of mistaken identity. But these are not unique; the Byzantine encyclopaedia we know today as the *Suda,* possibly deriving from the Greek *souda* meaning 'fortress' or 'stronghold', was thought by Eustathius (ca. 1110-1198) the Archbishop of Thessalonica, to be named after its compiler, Suidas. This is a worrying state of affairs as Eustathius presented himself as a scholar on things Homeric.[77] In truth, we don't know its etymology; although Strabo mentioned a Suidas as author of a separate work on Thessaly, the 10th century lexicon, with its 30,000 entries, remains essentially orphaned.

Even the venerable tales of Homer and the Epic Cyle were surrounded by confusion and they were not beyond early exploitation. From the fall of Troy to the Persian Wars, Greek history was 'covered with an obscurity broken only by dim and scattered gleams of truth'.[78] It was an environment bound to give birth to legends, lies and folklore; after all, 'the truest poetry is the most feigning'. As for the view of Plato on the matter: 'Hesiod and Homer and the other poets… composed false stories which they told people and are still telling them.'[79] Although his pupil, Aristotle, concluded: 'It is not the poet's function to describe what has actually happened, but the kinds of thing that *might* happen',[80] the pre-Socratic philosopher, Heracleitus of Ephesus (ca. 535-475 BCE), declared: 'Homer deserved to be expelled from the contests and flogged.' Herodotus argued that Homer exaggerated because he was a 'poet' when his *own* father had been an epic poet too; even Thucydides couldn't resist taking a stab at the author from pre-history.[81]

Despite these criticisms, or perhaps *because* of their underlying allegations, newly manipulated accounts of the war for Troy had surfaced by two supposed participants. The anonymous composers, the 'charlatans [who] cloak their non-existence with names well-tailored to their roles in the accounts of dramatic historians', were apparently exercising their rhetorical skills through the eyewitness accounts of Dares of Phrygia, a Trojan ally, and Dictys of Knossos on Crete who arrived with the invading Greeks.[82] The diary of Dictys, written in Punic, was ferried from Crete back to the philhellene emperor Nero who enthusiastically commissioned a translation into Greek.[83]

Paralleling Dictys' tale, and supposedly unearthed when an earthquake revealed his tomb, was the *De excidio Troiae historia* (*The History of the Destruction of Troy*) of Dares which contained an absurd precision of detail: the war for Troy lasted ten years, six months and twelve days, with 676,000 defenders and 886,000 Hellenic invaders taking part. Yet it fooled the influential Augustan-era historian Cornelius Nepos, an influential friend of the 'new poet' Catullus (ca. 84-54 BCE), and it even duped the sapient Cicero. Nepos wrote to his lettered friend Sallust explaining that he 'delighted' at finding a 'history written in Dares' own hand'; 'Thus my readers… can judge for themselves whether Dares the Phrygian or Homer wrote the more truthfully; Dares, who lived and fought at the time the Greeks stormed Troy, or Homer, who was born long after the War was over.'[84]

These newly appeared accounts were, however, more accessible than the originals of Homer, whose *Odyssey* had been translated into Latin as early as ca. 250 BCE by Livius Andronicus. Once translated into Latin by Nepos, these easy-to-read diaries with elaborate prefatory letters giving the precise circumstances of their discovery, were immortalised into the romances of the Middle Ages, for example in the form of Benoit de Sainte-Maure's *Le Roman de Troie*, inspiring Giovanni Boccaccio to his *Filostrato*, which was, in turn, adapted by Geoffrey Chaucer to his *Troilus and Criseyde*.[85] Elements of Dares and Dictys even entered a French edition of the *Iliad* by Jean Samxon in 1530.[86] Their continued popularity reflected their monopoly on information concerning the Trojan War, that is until Petrarch was able to acquire a 'very wooden' Latin translation of a genuine Homer manuscript from Constantinople in the 1360s. Remarkably the West had been blind to *original* Homer for almost 1,000 years. Luckily, as Polybius knew, 'justice has an eye'.[87]

Rome also fell for the *Batrachomyomachia, The Battle of Frogs and Mice*, a parody of the *Iliad* with probable Hellenistic origins but regarded as a genuine Homer work. Plutarch was less convinced and pinned the epic poem on Pigres of Halicarnassus who was of Carian royalty and thus an ally of the Great King Xerxes, and surely this better explained its blatant Trojan irreverence.[88] Recalling that Alexander once described a clash fought at Megalopolis between Antipater and a Sparta-led Greek coalition as a 'battle of mice', we may ponder whether the origins of the *Batrachomyomachia* were earlier still.[89]

Further evidence of manipulation of the Homeric epics comes from Strabo in his *Geography*. He proposed that a verse supporting Athens' claim to the island of Salamis had been inserted into the *Iliad* by Solon or by the tyrant, Peisistratus.[90] According to Herodotus, and somewhat suspiciously, Onomacritus, the friend and counsellor of Peisistratus, had been banished from Athens after it had been proven that he added his own material when editing the *Oracles of Musaeus*, the 6th century mystic seer, predicting the islands off Lemnos would disappear into the sea.[91]

Tampering with text was not the exclusive territory of historians and antiquarians. Legislation passed by Lycurgus the Athenian logographer and one of the so-named Ten Attic Orators, suggests creative interpolation had been damagingly interwoven into Greek drama. The new law demanded that actors should not deviate from the 'official' scripts as part of a move to preserve the integrity of the original plays of Aeschylus, Sophocles and Euripides. So liberated from the originals had the thespians' lines become that actors were threatened with losing their performing licenses if embellishment was detected.

But a precedent had already been set; some two centuries earlier Solon had berated Thespis (6th century), the first actor to perform on stage as a character from a tragedy, for telling blatant lies; Thespis predictably replied that there was nothing wrong with lying in a play.[92] Many of the new deviations were no doubt justified under the banner of *parrhesia*, freedom of speech, and they were later picked up by scholiasts in the Library at Alexandria proving Lycurgus' attempts were not altogether successful. But theatre was particularly susceptible to manipulation and misattribution; in Rome the prolific Varro judged 109 of 130 plays credited to Plautus to be falsely assigned, whilst the remaining twenty-one were termed 'Varronian' or 'Plautines' in recognition of the forensic success.[93]

Other early and more basic investigative models *had* existed to challenge the veracity of texts; Porphyry (literally 'the Purple'), for example, the Neo-Platonist philosopher of Tyre who, in the 3rd century CE, questioned a wide swath of literary and religious validity: from Homer's blindness in his *Homeric Questions*, to Christian texts and other pseudepigrapha. But to attribute deeper schematic thoughts on methodology to the ancient compilers of books would be to commit a 'hagiographical anachronism', to use Grafton's term.[94]

'HABENT SUA FATA LIBELLI' – FROM PAPYRUS TO THE MODERN CODEX[95]

We use the term 'book' liberally and certainly it is true that *habent sua fata libelli* – 'books have their own destiny'. Firstly, we should differentiate the handwritten *codices manu scripti*, which gave us our term 'manuscript', from *codices impressi*, the printed books that arrived in 1439 with Gutenberg's mechanical press and which immediately reduced the room for future transmission errors. Paper was first imported into Europe around the 10th century and was manufactured in the West from the 12th century onwards, with watermarks soon following. Until the development of the printing press and oil-based inks which led to the production of *editiones principes* – the first editions to exist outside of manuscripts – all written pieces of historical evidence, whether a mighty *Bibliotheke*, or a pamphlet of anecdotes, 'were exposed to all the chances and imperfections which attend the scribe and pen', so commented Falconer Madan in his 1893 treatise on the subject written at the Bodleian Library at Oxford University.[96]

Until 1500 (so convention has it) the *incunabula*, the books printed using wood blocks or moveable metal typographic sets, were laid out to replicate the manuscript format, complete with the diverse typefaces, abbreviated sentences, columns, margin notes and rubrications; with them were reproduced the decorative and much enlarged chapter-opening letters.[97] Although a print-press defect was an error immortalised in every future run, manuscripts were at least now 'crystallised' and could not decrepitate further. Mark Twain weighed up the merits of the device that lay behind the literary reinvigoration of the Renaissance:

> What the world is today, good and bad, it owes to Gutenberg. Everything can be traced to this source, but we are bound to bring him homage… for the bad that his colossal invention has brought about is overshadowed a thousand times by the good with which mankind has been favoured.[98]

But the story of the book, like the tale of Alexander, truly commenced in Egypt, the home of papyrus scrolls, with the earliest extant specimens dating to ca. 3,500 BCE.[99] Their preparation was lucidly described by the inquisitive Pliny in his *Natural History* (drawing from Theophrastus' earlier *Enquiry into Plants*), the compiling of which he viewed with a weighty gravitas: *'thesaurus oportet esse, non libros'*, 'there must be treasure houses, not books'.[100]

The inner rind, *biblos*, which gave us the word 'bible', was cross-braided and bound with glue and then pressed and dried and made ready for ink. Like modern textured paper, papyrus had a front and reverse, with one receptive to ink and the other coarser and less readily written on. This observation is helping modern researchers unravel the life cycles of newly found palimpsests; in one case, what was once considered the 'original text' recording a funeral oration we now frequently refer to as (the remarkably eloquent) *Hyperides over Leosthenes and his Comrades in the Lamian War*, written 322 BCE, the year following Alexander's death, has now been subordinated to a horoscope from 95 CE, for this occupied the 'right side' of the scroll.[101] The original would have benefited from having a *sillabos*, a reference tag explaining the content that Polybius termed a *prographe*.[102]

Papyri were best preserved rolled up and housed in jars, a state described by the Latin *volumen* which gives us our 'volumes'. In Rome, first-quality papyrus was once termed 'Augustan', second quality 'Livian' after the Emperor's wife, and the 'hieratic' grade used for administrative records came in third.[103] Formats continued to evolve as texts were copied to parchments, finely pressed animal skins, which included vellum from the Latin *vitulinum*, skin 'from the calf'. These were more hardwearing and had the added advantage of being scratchable for erasing mistakes. They were more expensive too but their emergence had been necessitated by the restrictions the Ptolemies placed on papyrus exports. In response to the squeeze, Eumenes II, the king of Pergamum where a competing library emerged, had the old art of parchment preparation perfected; they became known as *membrana* (or *charta*) *pergamena* in Latin.[104] Parchment *was* expensive and therefore copyists were fewer and more carefully chosen.

By Arrian's day the codex had arrived, the new book format that had developed from the old practice of stringing wooden writing tablets together. The codex was first described by the poet Martial in ca. 85/86 CE, when it began the gradual process of replacing the scroll.[105] A standard papyrus roll was made from twenty sheets glued together and was some 15 to 20 feet long when fully unravelled. Papyri of major works often ran to unwieldy lengths – 30 feet or more; the last two books of the *Iliad* alone ran to 25 feet.[106] The codices, representing the modern book format, were much more compact, as both sides of each leaf could be read in succession giving us *recto* and *verso* pages. The works of Homer, previously housed in fifteen thick scrolls, could be compressed to a practical size, and additionally, specific lines and middle chapters could be more easily accessed. Martial's amazement at the result is recorded: 'How small a tablet contains immense Virgil!'

But even the compact codices produced before the turbulence that followed the last of the Severan emperors (Alexander Severus, ruled 222-235 CE) which resulted in a division that produced the Eastern and Western Roman Empires, as well as the rise of the Sassanids, were not guaranteed to survive into the Byzantine era. Today only several of the oldest codices of Virgil survive, and just one copy of Homer. Primary materials that did survive through the 4th and 5th centuries had a better chance for further longevity if they were already 'codexed', as these books had the protection of leather covers where scrolled papyri did not. Works that had been hidden, or particularly well prepared, fared better.

The parchment skins of many of the Dead Sea Scrolls, for example, are still almost white rather than a faded yellow; it is thought they were treated with salt and flour to remove the hair, and then tanned with a gallnut liquid brushed on both surfaces. But the inks of this period were generally still charcoal-based and so were too easily erased by accident or were mendaciously amended. Reed pens gave way to quills in the 6th century, by which time the previously vulnerable ink of soot, gum and water, had evolved into a more permanent mix of gum, gallic acid and iron sulphate, a formula that was in fact used as early as the Herculaneum Scrolls, a collection of carbonised papyri unearthed in 1752 under the volcanic mud of Vesuvius and a find that has been described as the 'only intact library from antiquity'.

THE FATE AND FALL OF THE CLASSICAL LIBRARY

If political turmoil was often the catalyst behind a historian picking up a pen, sadly it was often the reason for the irrevocable loss of his output. In a sense, libraries were both the saviour and the nemesis of literature, for though their collecting and copying provided some order and safety to the few ancient texts in circulation, the delicate literary eggs were then all in one easily targeted basket. Libraries *were* prizes of war: Xerxes ferried Peisistratus' public library (the first in Athens) back to Persia before putting Athens to the torch in 480 BCE; King Perseus' Macedonian library at Pella went back to Rome with Aemilius Paullus; and Mark Antony gifted the entire contents of the Pergamum library (some 200,000 scrolls) to Cleopatra, in the process ending the literary legacy of the Attalids.[107] What was most likely a more modest library at Antioch found by the Seleucids (certainly by the reign of Antiochus III, 222-187 BCE) probably disappeared when Pompey annexed Syria in 64 BCE.

Although more robust parchments were creeping into the scriptoriums, a voluminous world history would have been prohibitively costly for a provincial library to procure on vellum despite the advent of awkward opisthographs, scrolls written on both sides to save space and materials before the codex arrived.[108] So cheaper but frailer papyrus remained the copyists' principal medium well past the arrival of skins, especially in Egypt.[109] This meant that the condition of the major Greek works demanded by the Roman literati was already poor. Neleus of Scepsis, to whom Theophrastus bequeathed his own library in his Will – some 232,808 lines of text and which include Aristotle's collection gifted with the school – absconded sometime around 287 BCE with the scrolls, though as a *metoikos* (foreign resident) in Athens, Aristotle was not technically able to 'own' the Peripatus and neither bequeath its contents in his Will.

The fate of the collection thereafter is uncertain: Neleus' heirs either had the scrolls hidden in a basement to prevent the princes of Pergamum from appropriating the collection, or as Athenaeus claimed, he sold them to Ptolemy II *Philadelphos* who imported the collection to the Alexandrian Library.[110] According to Strabo, however, around 100 BCE the mildewed and worm-eaten remnants of Neleus' library were sold to Apellicon of Teos, a minor Athenian military leader and a *philobiblos*, a lover of books. Apellicon, who had fled Athens after stealing a number of rare works to enrich his own shelves, tried to restore the volumes himself.[111] He only succeeded in damaging them further when inserting 'incorrect corrections' for missing fragments of pages, and otherwise poorly editing the works.'[112]

A 19th century engraving of the cataloguing of scrolls at the Library in Alexandria.

When the Roman consul and dictator Sulla 'liberated' the library to Rome, it needed much salvaging by Tyrannio whom Cicero later employed alongside a full staff to renovate his own private collection.[113] These works had already been subjected to editing by Andronicus of Rhodes (*floruit* ca. 60 BCE), the *scholarchos* and head of the Peripatetic school who organised Aristotle's work into the chapter and book divisions that survive today.[114] Although Diodorus confirmed the goldmine of resurrected sources when he arrived in Rome from Sicily, the damaging patching-up had already been done.[115]

Like so much associated with Rome, the admirable resided beside the lamentable. When Sulla died he dedicated his own memoirs to the 'just' Lucius Licinius Lucullus, the book collector and patron of the arts as well as praetor and great general of the East, along with the guardianship of Faustus, Sulla's wayward son.[116] Despite that, Faustus sold his father's collection, including the library of Apellicon, to pay off his gambling debts, which is an irony since the statutes of the *leges* (laws) *Cornelia*, *Titia* and *Publicia,* designed to curb gambling on sports, had been sponsored or supported by Sulla. Caesar's fire at Alexandria probably sealed the fate of many of the remaining manuscripts.[117] If they survived that, then Aurelian's fire in the 270s CE, the revolts that Diocletian suppressed in 272 and 295 CE, the earthquake beneath Crete that caused a tsunami to strike Alexandria in 365 CE, Bishop Theophilus' conflagration of the Serapeum in 390/391 CE, and the Muslim conquest in 642 CE onwards, surely finished them off.[118]

Julius Caesar never mentioned the burning of the famous Alexandrian Library in his memoirs. He *did* admit to setting the fleet alight in the harbour for his own safety, and stated that some arsenals were also burnt down, a claim that appears to be backed up by Cassius Dio, but many books were stored in harbour warehouses.[119] Caesar's additional comment, 'for Alexandria is in a manner secure from fire, because the houses are all built without joists or wood, and are all vaulted, and roofed with tile or pavement', has the hallmark of a guilt-ridden defence when considering that Lucan's *De bello civili* claimed that fire 'ran over the roofs like meteors through the sky'.[120] And that lingering sense of culpability might be why Caesar entrusted Varro with the establishment of a new library in Rome in 47 BCE,[121] though the proscriptions of Mark Antony were to soon deprive Varro of his books.[122]

But was the Alexandrian commentary truly Caesar's own? For the authorship of *The Alexandrine War* is heavily disputed; Suetonius, writing less than two centuries after the dictator's death, told us no one knew who wrote up Caesar's memoirs of the Spanish, African or Egyptian campaigns. Contenders are his legate, Aulus Hirtius (ca. 90-43 BCE), or perhaps his friend, Gaius Oppius, and no doubt both would have written

A 19ᵗʰ century drawing reconstructing ancient Pergamum.

under Caesar's direction. The quality of its construction was praised, especially by Hirtius, but that might have been a discreet vote of self-confidence.[123]

But time has taken its toll on the great dictator's legacy: in all copies of Suetonius' *Lives of the Twelve Caesars* the beginning of the *Life of Julius* is lost. This along with colophons, excerpts and cataloguing data, enables us to assume that all these copies go back to a lost *Codex Fuldensis* (which formed part of a library at Fulda in ca. 844 CE), a singular draft stemming from an earlier lost archetype.[124] Suetonius had himself questioned the authenticity of speeches later attributed to Julius Caesar, the *pro Metello,* for example.[125]

Historians are at odds over the scale of the Library at Alexandria and they even argue its origins, for there is no actual report of its founding. Aulus Gellius and Ammianus Marcellinus reported that at its height it contained 700,000 'books', whereas Seneca the Younger claimed 400,000 perished in the fire Caesar started, with other sources divided on the total number housed.[126] The Seneca manuscript from Monte Cassino actually reads 40,000, though this is an example of a 'composite scroll' that contained multiple works and so the numbers *may* be corrupted. A further 42,800 books are said to have been stored in a separate library (the Serapeiana) in the Temple of Serapis. What is clear is that Callimachus' *Pinakes*, in 120 volumes, could not have credibly systematically listed the larger numbers of works cited, and many papyri must have been so-called 'mixed rolls' that contained several works.[127] As a postscript to the library's fate Athenaeus mourned: '… and concerning the number of books and the establishment of libraries and the collection in the Hall of the Muses, why need I even speak when they are all in men's memory?'[128]

We cannot forget that Rome burned the library at Carthage which had housed a reported 500,000 volumes. It would have been a fascinating collection of Punic and barbarian works and their opposing views. Scipio Aemilianus, who later earned the agnomen 'Africanus the Younger', was there to oversee its final destruction in 146 BCE. He is said to have shed a tear for the fate decreed by the Roman Senate while quoting Homer's *Iliad* to Polybius, the historian standing beside him: 'A day shall come when sacred Troy shall perish and King Priam and his warriors with him.'[129] Polybius, possibly present in a technical capacity, is said to have accompanied the consul-general in a *testudo* formation attack on one of the city gates.[130] A notable philhellene and an avid reader of Xenophon's *Cyropaedia*, Scipio apparently foresaw the collapse of Rome itself.[131]

But careful as we are with the stuff of romance, we should see more of Polybius than Scipio in the general's recorded lament – which comes from Appian's later history – for it is distinctly anacyclotic, while '... to ponder, at such a moment, on the mutability of Fortune, showed a proper Hellenistic sensibility.'[132] And true to that destiny, by the time Leonardo Bruni Aretino reintroduced Polybius into Western Europe in ca. 1419 (Polybius had first entered Italy as a Roman captive in 167 BCE), only the first five of what we believe were forty books of *The Histories* remained entirely intact, so that we have to rely on the *Excerpta Antigua*, an abridgement compiled in the 10th century CE for the Byzantine emperor, Constantine VII *Porphyrogenitos*, for glimpses of their detail; in total we probably have about one-third of Polybius' original text.[133] His biography of the contemporary Greek statesman, Philopoemen (ca. 253-183 BCE), whose funeral urn he carried, and his military *Tactics* that must have impressed (or been inspired by) Scipio, have disappeared completely.[134]

The wealthy Greek port of Corinth was overthrown in the same year as Carthage; 'The two eyes of the seashore were blinded', lamented Cicero referring to the two maritime cities, and with the loss of the Punic library, history's vision never fully recovered; this was, rather aptly, the point at which Polybius terminated his history.[135] But perhaps Carthage had the last laugh, for she later gave Rome a Punic son, Septimus Severus, who espoused: 'Be harmonious, enrich the soldiers, and scorn all other men.' A product of the 'year of the five emperors' (193 CE), he ensured the Senate *was* scorned, and predictably it suffered.[136] Perhaps Septimus had taken Virgil's *Aeneid* at face value, punishing Aeneas and his Dardani Trojan descendants for abandoning Dido, the Queen of Carthage, generations before, even if the gods had commanded it.[137]

Modern wars have, of course, added to the loss of books. The parental 10th century *Metz Epitome* manuscript (*Codex Mettensis* 500 D) was destroyed in an allied bombing raid in 1944, so we now rely on two editions from 1886 and 1900.[138] But we might speculate that these *breviaria* themselves were largely responsible for the extinction of the original and far longer works they précised. The atthidographer Philochorus even précised his *own* work, the seventeen-book *Atthis*. The first known epitome of another's books was Theopompus' compression of Herodotus' *Histories*, a unique production for its time.[139] Thankfully the original survived the summary, but in Rome the opposite was more often the case; once Justin had boiled down Trogus to a fraction of its original size, the writing was, so to speak, on the wall for the forty-four volumes painstakingly compiled by the learned Romanised Gaul, while over 200 of Justin's manuscripts survive today.[140]

Perhaps the Romans had simply had enough of the extended epideictic texts. Lucius Anneaus Florus' *Abridgement of All the Wars for 700 Years* (*possibly* written 2nd century CE), otherwise known as the *Epitome of the Histories of Titus Livy* (in two books), is a work since termed 'a ferociously condensed Roman history', and the 4th century *Periochae*, itself probably based on an abridged edition of Livy's books, suggests the understandable desire to make the reading of history more succinct.[141]

But it was probably economic pressure and production practicality in the pre-print-press age that determined the need for the epitome. Diodorus' *Bibliotheke*, some forty books in length, and without which we would know far less of the Successor Wars, was itself a huge compression of its sources and it, too, may have helped to push the originals out of circulation. Yet Diodorus remains our central link to our knowledge of the lost histories of Hecataeus, Ctesias, Poseidonius, Agatharchides, Megasthenes, Ephorus and Hieronymus, amongst others. Hornblower proposed an epitaph: 'They faced the sentence of oblivion or the fate of being pickled...' in Diodorus' volumes.[142]

Diodorus' *Library of World History* did in fact survive intact in the imperial palace in Constantinople until the early Renaissance. The 1453 sack of the city has left us with just fifteen relatively intact books. Fifty-nine medieval manuscripts remain and they variously contain books one through five, and books eleven through twenty. Of the former, four 'prototypes' can be identified of the twenty-eight remaining manuscripts (containing books one through five) but they are all corrupted to some degree, although passages from the lost volumes are preserved in Photius' *Myriobiblion* and in Byzantine texts – George Syncellus' *Ekloge Chronographias*, for example.

The trend of précising reared its head again once the Renaissance had resurrected the ancient corpus; Jean Bodin's 1566 *Methodus ad facilem historiarum cognitionem* attempted to provide a method of easy absorption and comprehension in which the epitome was often recommended above the parental work itself. Digory Whear subsequently advised: 'If our reader wishes to remain engaged longer and more capaciously in universal history, [the epitome of] Justin can be read.' The dedication in Bodin's book (surely taken from Justin too) stated 'one should cull flowers from History to gather there of the sweetest fruits', and so history *was* indeed culled.[143]

FRICATIVES AND PALATISATION, *KOINE* AND VULGAR:
LINGUISTIC ALCHEMY AND NUMERICAL OBSTINACY

While the written book format was changing in response to supply and demand and to the price of raw materials, language was also evolving, and this played its part in the destiny of the book. In the late Roman Republic the literati were conscious of the progression in Greek and Latin prose style and aware of the resulting translation challenges. The first translation we know of from Greek to Latin was of the *Odyssey* by the Graeco-Roman poet Livius Andronicus ca. 250 BCE, and it was only a 'partly successful' attempt.[144] Cicero, who had already created something of a philosophical vocabulary when coining the terms *humanitas, qualitas* and *essentia* as he introduced Rome to concepts he had learned in Greece under Philo of Larissa and Poseidonius the prominent Stoic, took a practical line on textual transmission. He advocated a 'sense for sense' approach over a 'word for word' translation of Greek into Latin, considering that this better preserved the intent of the original author; his methodology placed an emphasis on what we would term today 'communication equivalence'.

The poet Horace, on the other hand, gave priority to methods that created 'impact' on the target language, thus a dynamic re-rendering of a text became the norm and literal fidelity suffered as a result, that is, if what we read is genuine.[145] Suetonius was dubious; in his *Life of Horace*: he explained: 'There have come into my possession some elegies attributed to his pen and a letter in prose, supposed to be a recommendation of himself to Maecenas, but I think that both are spurious.'[146] The fine line between tight transmission and a total rewrite was often tested when translators wished their labour to acquire a literary status of its own. This explains the widening gap between the grammatical structure of the 'linguistic arts' – poetry, history, oratory and rhetorical pursuits – and the language of the business, diplomatic and legal worlds where there was no latitude for literary license. That gap remains markedly visible today.

Alexander's eyewitness historians had a further translation challenge. Much of what they heard or extracted *en route* in Asia came from the myriad of races absorbed by the Persian Empire; it was a linguistic rainbow even though the administration of the Great Kings was probably conducted most widely in Aramaic and Parsi (and formerly in Old Persian).[147] Strabo preserved Onesicritus' meetings with the Indian gymnosophists, commenting that they translated their respective philosophical ideas through interpreters who 'knew no more than the rabble'. So expecting clarity on doctrines was 'like expecting clean water to flow through mud'. As one scholar pointed out, the Macedonians most likely arrived at their Indian translations through Bactrian or Sogdian interpreters, from which point a second polyglot would have turned this into Persian, with a third then rendering it into Greek.[148] So the opportunity for misunderstanding and oversimplifying, or perhaps 'Hellenising' an alien concept, precept or word, was ever present.

The Hellenic root languages were under scrutiny in the earliest scriptoriums as they were themselves shifting and occasionally clashing head-on. Zenodotus, the first head of the Alexandrian Library (ca. 280s), inherited materials in archaic Attic script and he had to transliterate them into the new Ionian alphabet adopted by Athens in 403 BCE. Archaic Greek texts were often written boustrophedonically (the direction and orientation of letters was reversed on alternate lines) which inevitably slowed the process, as presumably would have acrostics, which would be senseless after translation.[149] Orthographic decisions were complicated by three 'E' and three 'O' sounds that were not distinguished in the original alphabet.

The victory songs of Pindar, written between 498 and 446 BCE, suffered from this dilemma, and Zenodotus' imperfect understanding of the poet's rhythms ('a torrent rushing down rain-swollen from the mountains', thought Horace) violated the metrical scheme and chopped up his stanzas into irregular lines. Callimachus was confronted with the violations when he was later arranging the poems and the results were further 'disorganised' by Aristophanes of Byzantium (ca. 257-180 BCE), the head librarian from ca. 194 BCE.[150]

Zenodotus did, however, provide some standardisation to the Homeric epics in the reign of Ptolemy II *Philadelphos*, and Apollonius of Rhodes, the librarian's successor, provided further organisational commentaries so that some order finally fell upon the heroes of Troy.[151] He restricted Homer to the *Iliad* and *Odyssey* alone, though some 'Homerists' still believe the *Odyssey* is a product of a number of authors who gave it its final shape.[152]

Homer's *Iliad* contained Bronze Age words in Mycenaen dialect that had been preserved from the earliest oral tradition against a later Ionic linguistic background;[153] the antiquity of the battles being fought is apparent in that spears and arrowheads are being spoken of in bronze rather than iron.[154] Moreover, in Homer's day the Phoenician alphabet, initially termed *phoinikia grammata* by the Greeks, was starting to fill the void left when Mycenaean Linear B ended centuries before. How, then, were the epic Homeric tales to bridge the Greek Dark Age (broadly 1200-750 BCE) if not through oral recitation?[155]

The Hellenistic grammarian, Dionysius Thrax ('Thrax' – of Thracian descent, ca. 170-90 BCE), produced a *Tekhne grammatike* in a further attempt at rationalisation. He was a pupil of Aristarchus of Samothrace, another librarian working under the Ptolemies, whose harsh literary criticism gave rise to the term 'aristarch' to describe a severely judgmental commentator. True to Alexandrian tradition, his grammatical work appears syncretic and it's doubtful that the technical content we have represents Thrax's original.[156] The focus of his treatise was to finally facilitate the translation, with some systematic order, of Attic Greek (which became known as 'Alexandrian Greek') into Hellenistic *koine* which was still a *spoken* dialect only; yet it was too late to salvage the earlier works that had undergone operations at the hands of lesser surgeons. Soon, from the 1st century CE, Egyptian itself (hieroglyphic before) was being written in Coptic script, an adaption of the Greek alphabet that included signs from the demotic script to accommodate Egyptian sounds not represented in Greek, though its use in literature was principally confined to the output of priests.

Thrax, who, in turn, encouraged the learning of classical Greek, went on to teach rhetoric in Rhodes and Rome, perhaps even inspiring a young Apollonius Molon in the process, the orator employed by Caesar and Cicero to improve their method. The adoption of *koine* into literature would later prompt Phyrnichus Arabius (2nd century CE), a Bithynian rhetorician, to compile a Greek lexicon of *soloikismoi,* solecisms or grammatical deviations from the Old Attic standard that had taken place over the previous 600 years.[157]

In Rome Latin was evolving too; Polybius remarked that he had difficulty in translating an account of the first official treaty between Rome and Carthage which dated back to some twenty-eight years before Xerxes invaded Greece (thus ca. 508 BCE):

> I give below as accurate a translation as I can of this treaty, but the modern language has developed so many differences from the ancient Roman tongue that the best scholars among the Romans themselves have great difficulty in interpreting certain points, even after much study.[158]

Claudius later added three letters to the Latin alphabet to contribute to the linguistic shift. Although Robert Graves confidently gave us their names, this appears to be another modern interpolation as the identity of the letters was never revealed by Suetonius or Tacitus.[159] The diaskeuastic tendency to 'modernise' or 'clarify', 'abbreviate' and 'embellish', or as Dryden put it, 'lop off the superfluous branches', has never departed the hand of the historian, antiquarian or copyist.[160] Compare the 'innocent' admission by Robert Graves in his 1957 translation of Suetonius' *The Twelve Caesars*, which remains the popular Penguin Classics text; Graves stated he had cut out passages that seemed superfluous to the episode 'turning sentences and sometimes even groups of sentences inside out'.[161] Nietzsche admired what he termed the 'enviable abandon of the freedom enjoyed by Roman poets making new the works of the Greeks', and Graves was doing no less.[162]

Claudius was no doubt envious of Caesar and Augustus who rearranged the calendar year and inserted the eponymous months of Iulius (July, formerly Quintilis) and Augustus (August, earlier Sextilis). Faced with a replete calendar, Claudius the 'clod' settled for changing pronunciations instead, arguing that even the Greek alphabet did not evolve all at once.[163] In hindsight, he appears very un-clod-like, for he was the inspiration behind the revolutionary new harbour and canal system at the mouth of the Tiber (Portus, as Ostia could no longer handle the scale of shipping traffic). He next relegated 'Augustan' papyrus behind a 'Claudian' grade, and compensated by having Alexander's face replaced with Augustus' image on the paintings by Apelles that hung in the imperial forum.[164] Claudius decreed that his own literary works be read aloud every year in Alexandria from the beginning to the end; it was all in vain, for neither his Etruscan history, the *Tyrrenika,* nor his annals of Carthage, managed to survive.[165]

Robert Graves' richly embellished dramas of the first Roman emperor to be born outside of Italy, *I Claudius* and *Claudius the God,* penned through 1934-35, may in recent times have become more influential than Suetonius 'dryly indiscriminate' biography in filling the gap left by Tacitus' lost account.[166] This is another irony, for the full name of the English poet and novelist was Robert Von Ranke Graves; his mother was the great niece of Leopold von Ranke (1795-1886), the German historian who gathered up a wide swathe of source material and documentary facts in his attempt to show *wie es eigentlich gewesen,* 'how things actually were'. Von Ranke, who was responsible for the progression of *Quellenkritik,* source criticism, produced the first ever historical journal in the process, *Historisch-Politische Zeitschrift*, and he reinforced the value of working with original documentary evidence.[167] And if history is full of ironies, then the Muse Clio had a developed sense of the tragic too, for Suetonius, like many of those who preserved Alexander's tale, failed to mention who *his* sources were, the primary material *he* himself may have creatively 'upturned' in Rome between his alleged intimacies with Vibia Sabina, wife of the Emperor Hadrian.[168]

As the Alexandrian scholars had noted, the expansion of the Graeco-Macedonian and Roman Empires homogenised linguistic identity, though at the expense of classical linguistic purity. The term 'classical' entered modern English in the 16th century and by 1870 Wilhelm Siegmund Teuffel (1820-1878) had developed his philological classifications, which included the so-called Golden and Silver Ages of Latin: 83 BCE-14 CE and the years 14-117 CE respectively. Like all 'new' linguistic ideas, these built upon earlier less systematic models incorporating faulty systems of categorisation based upon political events rather than pure prose style.[169] In 1877 Charles Cruttwell refined the groupings by focusing on the progression of Roman literature through the republican and imperial periods in which it evolved from an 'immaturity of art and language', to 'ill-disciplined imitation of Greek poetic models', and finally to 'clear and fluent strength'.[170]

The Silver Age (broadly) witnessed the end of the true Roman Republic so that Diodorus, Trogus, Curtius, Plutarch and Arrian were publishing under successive Roman dictators and emperors. Despite that 'clear and fluent strength', Teuffel gave a scathing opinion on the loss of free speech through much of this period, particularly in the Julio-Claudian era (Augustus to Nero, 27 BCE-68 CE); it was a period of 'continued apprehension' when natural composition was subordinated to the desire to appear 'brilliant', 'hence it was dressed up with abundant tinsel of epigrams, rhetorical figures and poetical terms'. 'Mannerisms supplanted style, and bombastic pathos took the place of quiet power.'[171] Freedom of expression was apparently not the cure, for Teuffel credited the literature of the 'happier' 2nd century that followed as nothing less than a scandalous 'imitation'.

Able to appreciate the textual markers defined by these eras, modern scholars developed the tools of linguistic 'archaeology' to help decode the past and even gene-tag individual historians. Narratologists note that the classical writer had a literary pace, gait, or shuffle. In 1889 Dessau concluded the *Scriptores Historiae Augustae* were written in the time of Theodosius rather than Diocletian or Constantine (as the manuscripts claimed), noting 'the uniformity in phraseology and stylistic devices' which pointed to a single author, not six.[172] We can similarly identify where texts noticeably stride ahead or stumble from that uniformity, revealing what may be a historian's non-seamless switches between sources. When analysing texts dealing with Alexander, for example, Hammond pointed to Plutarch's change from 'florid' structures to 'restrained and artistic' prose and especially to clues in his rhythm, identifying 'iambic and spondaic runs and occasional tribrachs'.[173] He also observed Arrian's switches from narrative tenses when a new source was introduced, whereas Pearson saw 'Asianic rhythms' that betrayed the presence of genuine fragments of Cleitarchus.[174]

Sir Ronald Syme's linguistic studies concluded Curtius' style was 'sub-Livian and pre-Tacitan', whilst elements within the *Metz Epitome* place its authorship in the 4th or 5th century CE.[175] Only Curtius and the *Metz Epitome* employed the word *testudo* (tortoise) to describe the Greek shield formation.[176] The term didn't exist in Alexander's day or in Greek military history (aside from a mention of something similar in Xenophon's *Hellenika*), and so Curtius was delving into his own Latin vocabulary to describe an earlier, but now familiar, shield-locking tactic.[177] Using similar observations, linguists determined Carlo Sigonio's fragment of Cicero's

De Consolatione was a fake, as it employed terminology Cicero could not yet have himself been familiar with. Linguistic progression remains just as visible today; anyone reading the biographies of Alexander by Wheeler or Mahaffy cannot help chewing with difficulty on the prose laid down just a century ago, and Rooke's 1814 second volume of Arrian's *Anabasis* has already been described as 'archaic'.[178]

The classical Latin once spoken by the 'good' and noble families, the *sermo familiaris* and *sermo nobilis,* disintegrated to Vulgar Latin and then into the early Romance languages as the Roman Empire expanded and fragmented. As with Hellenistic Greek *koine*, *sermo vulgaris* was first spoken by soldiers, dispossessed townsfolk and slaves across the empire, resulting in marked differences between the spoken and written forms. Letters took on new sounds through palatisation, a process that produced the phonetic splits we read and hear in the romance languages of today. The loss of nasal inflection resulted in the dissimilation of voiceless consonants, and thus Platon became Plato.

The Greek 'K', which had become a 'C' in Latin though still pronounced as kappa, graduated to a soft 'S' before the vowels 'I' and 'E'. Cicero, originally pronounced 'Kikero' (we believe), and Caesar, pronounced 'Kaisar', took on the pronunciations we are more familiar with in English. In Hellenistic Greece, 'Y' and 'OI' were often written as a 'U', and later the distinction in vowel length was lost as part of a wider monopthongisation. Double consonants were reduced to single and aspirated voiceless stops were changed to fricatives by the 4th century. By the Byzantine period, sounds and their corresponding letters were further simplified when, for example, 'H' and 'EI' became 'I'. These processes played their part in textual infidelity as new translations were made.

The early Latin-from-Greek manuscripts, perhaps already incorporating corruptions from these linguistic challenges, went through further transmission processes as Western scripts developed; the latitude for confusion widened still further when Latin texts were translated into the 'modern' languages that were not rooted in Latin. When use of the capital and uncial scripts of the 4th and 5th centuries came to an end with what Petrarch termed another 'Dark Age', Christian copying of pagan literature halted for almost three centuries, so few manuscripts of this period survived. The so-called Carolingian Renaissance (late 8th to 9th century) saw a resurgence when monks once more started copying the oldest texts available to them into Carolingian miniscule. This lower case script, developed under the patronage of Charlemagne (never fully literate himself), had the advantage of spaces and punctuation, so liberating Latin from the confusing continuous flow of capitals in uncial texts.

New Latin transcriptions made during the 11th, 12th and 13th centuries attempted to restore some sense and order to already corrupted passages, but this, more often than not, further damaged the original prose. The aforementioned defective knowledge of classical Latin and Greek especially, and hence an ignorance of how to separate continuous script, led to nominative cases being confused with genitive and dative cases, and singulars with plurals, especially where the letters a, e, and diphthongs were concerned.[179] Add to this the mistaking of proper names with verbs, and the faulty extraction of numbers from uncial text, and we have some idea of the task facing scribes. Mistakes may have been innocent and well-intended but 'they were rich in the germs of future corruptions',[180] unlike the deliberate tampering of the later 14th and 15th centuries when religion held a heavy hammer over what survived and in what form.

A fragment of the *Codex Sinaiticus* (John chapter 21, verses 1-25) written in continuous Greek uncial script and dating to the 4th century CE.

As the works that had not been translated into Latin were in less demand in the Middle Ages, the Greek texts of Herodotus and Thucydides were largely bypassed. The case for the resuscitation of Herodotus was further challenged by the criticism heaped upon him in the texts that *had been* translated. As a result, it is estimated that there are just eight surviving manuscripts of Herodotus' *Histories*, whilst the extant manuscripts of Thucydides only date to some 1,300 years post his original. It was not until 1448-1452 that Valla produced a Latin edition of both the 'awe-inspiring' Thucydides, and the 'radiant' Herodotus (1452 through 1457) who was finally exhumed from his classical slashing with Stephanus' *Apologia pro Herodotus* published in 1566.[181] It was not an easy task, as Valla explained in his preface dedicated to Pope Nicholas V:

> … as everybody admits, Thucydides is steep and rocky, especially in the speeches, in which his books abound. This is clear from what Cicero, whom men of his time called 'the Greek', says in his *de Oratore*: Those speeches have many over-subtle thoughts that can scarcely be understood.[182]

Valla added: 'There you see, highest Pope, what Thucydides is like in Greek, and if you decide that in my translation he keeps this same dignity, I shall be oblivious of my labour.'[183]

But the labours were often divisive. A comparison of two manuscripts containing Livy's *Ad urbe condita libre* – the 5th century *Codex Puteanus* and the 9th century copy known as the *Codex Reginensis 762* – further illustrates scriptorium problems.[184] The *Reginensis* transcription was undertaken by eight separate scribes, each given a different section to work on. We even know the copyists' names as their signatures appear at the end of each quaternion, the manuscript unit of four double leaves. They were also of more than one nationality as evidenced by the repeated nature of the blunders they make and their non-identical ink types. Earlier divergent processes had already been at work on Livy; all manuscripts of the first ten books stem from the single recension commissioned by Quintus Aurelius Symmachus, a Roman consul, in 391 CE. Moreover, the emendation of the editor would have produced this version by selecting what was considered the best of the then extant earlier editions. Epigraphists have detected the hands, once again, of a number of scribes in the recensions that followed, one branch of which is known as the *Nichomachean* after the named subscribers.[185]

Fortunately, it is possible to determine if early book sections have been pieced together by different copyists, and whether pages have been lost, by studying the parchment on consecutive sheets, as the hair side of the skin is distinct from the flesh side and the double folding of the quaternion ought to produce matching textures. Von Tischendorf employed the techniques of codicology to highlight such discrepancies when describing the *Codex Sinaiticus*, believing that four separate scribes worked on the *manuscript*, with five 'correctors' amending the text at different times.[186] Recent paleographical studies of the codex do indeed confirm numerous scribes were employed.

The multiple-copyist methodology was, nevertheless, typical when a work encapsulating centuries of history had been either originally released by the author in 'packets' (as in the case of Livy's chapters) or had been packeted in later editions, when they were often separated into decade or pentad divisions that might be a wholly contrived new arrangement. But, understandably, Livy's 142 books were a challenge to read through without some kind of break; moreover, he had drifted into loquaciousness and repetitions, which, as Horace reminded us, 'are not well received'.[187] Barthold Georg Niebuhr (1776-1831), who finally gave us the *Römische Geschichte*, an ancient Rome that linked the fate of patricians and plebeians together,[188] supposed 'the declining quality of Livy's later books was the cause of their loss; they were considered less worthy of copying'.[189] In Livy's defence, the 'fountain that never trickles' had himself described the 'deep water' and 'vast depths' he was wading into from an inundation of recent detail, versus the 'shallow waters' of the earlier history of the city.[190] The result: only thirty-five books remain in reasonably complete form.

Supervisors or 'correctors' were on hand in the scriptorium to immediately edit the quaternions as they were completed, but this was an ink-upon-ink process and the inevitable dittographies, haplographies and parablepses, the scribal errors of repetition and omission, crept in.[191] If the corruptions manifested themselves in clear conflicts between what should have been identical manuscripts, we are least alerted, but when multiple texts are divided, we are on softer ground. For example, in Plutarch's *Life of Demosthenes* we cannot be sure if it is Theopompus, or Theophrastus, who refused to incriminate the orator, as various manuscripts cite both.[192] One scholar tackling the dilemma suggested a 'meddlesome' scribe made the error; he is no doubt correct, but which name should we amend?[193] Oratorical imitation was part of the classical education syllabus, and so the orators were vulnerable to having the speeches debased. We have six surviving letters supposedly written by Demosthenes; new analyses of an old debate suggest four are genuine and two are fakes, whilst roughly one-third of his extant speeches appear to be less than genuine too.[194]

Another ongoing debate is the relationship between Photius' references to the Ten Attic Orators in his *Myriobiblon*, and the ten *Lives* preserved in Pseudo-Plutarch. It has become unclear whether Photius used Pseudo-Plutarch directly, or an underlying source used *by* Pseudo-Plutarch, or whether Photius added material of his own or detail from a compilation that might have included *either* of the above. Although a study by Schamp targets an early 4th century common source, we don't know if the two sets of *Lives* developed from second or even third-generation transcripts.[195] But if we pay similar attention to Photius' own introduction to his collection of epitomes in the form of a letter to his brother, we note the admission: 'we engaged a secretary and set down all the summaries we could.'[196] The term 'we' recurs throughout, not 'I', leaving us to wonder how much of the epitomised work was Photius' own, and how much was compressed by the anonymous secretarial hand, or in fact summarised by members of the reading circle he ran.[197]

Besides scriptorium transmission errors, further loss of chronological precision resulted from the fluidity of the calendar year (in Greece especially), the loss of intercalary months (inserted to realign calendars with moon phases), along with the awkward synchronisation of archon years with consul elections; all troublesome detail for copyists trying to make sense of the order of events.[198] Additional slippage arose from the word-denoted and numeral-based counting systems of Greece and Rome, which lacked the numeric dexterity to efficiently deal with large numbers, fractions and percentages. As a result these were awkwardly presented as long sequences of letters and acrophonies, and this must partly explain the disparity in the treasury figures, and troop and casualty numbers we encounter in the battles of Alexander and his successors.

The 'plus', 'minus' and 'equals' symbols were still a millennium-and-a-half away, and the concept of 'zero' as a placeholder still eluded mathematicians. It was not until ca. 250 CE (an uncertain and debated date) in Alexandria that Diophantus, 'the father of algebra', and his *Arithmetica*, gave us an abbreviation for (and for powers of) the unknowns and a shorter means of expressing equations. But the use of true numbers in maths with succinct algebraic notation and symbolism – instead of long sentences of letters and words that Diophantus did still employ – made its way west later (in the 8th and 9th centuries CE as a refinement of the Hindu-Arabic system), and only then did it establish a useful and easily transmitted system to deal with and reproduce complex numbers

So, for a host of reasons, manuscripts were, as Digory Whear observed in 1623, 'interpolated by the hands of smatterers, and most basely handled'.[199] Petrarch bemoaned: 'What would Cicero, or Livy, or the other great men of the past, Pliny above all, think if they could return to life and read their own works?'[200] Here Petrarch was referring to the sad condition of the 'treasure house' of Pliny's *Natural History* that he had purchased in Mantua in 1350; some seven intact manuscripts survived, though none of them are earlier than 850 CE (older examples were either incomplete or survived as palimpsests).

But not everyone has shared his enthusiasm for poring over the past. In a posthumously written historical review of 1847, the English archaeologist, Sir William Gell, commented on the tedious job of copying newly found manuscripts and the Herculaneum Scrolls: 'If Omar, according to the tale, burned the library of Alexandria, we have doubts whether he ought not to be honoured as a benefactor of our race.' Gell followed with: 'The palimpsests so laboriously deciphered, have given us scarcely anything that is either of interest or value.'[201] And for all his efforts in educating scholars to adopt the opposite view, when Petrarch died, as his Will made no reference to his library of manuscripts, the collection was subsequently seized by the Lords of Padua and scattered across Europe.[202]

THE MASS GRAVES OF MICRO PRODUCTION

Time has lost more of Alexander and *his* literary heroes than it has preserved. Considering that it required thousands of hours for a skilled scribe to make a single copy of a set of papyri scrolls that constituted a modern book, the number of editions of the scrolls of Callisthenes, Onesicritus, Nearchus, Aristobulus and Ptolemy would have been initially limited to library commissions, state archives and wealthy private collectors, and from there into the damp basement of a wealthy senator to suffer the degenerative fate of Apellicon's worm-eaten collection. Duplicates were usually only made on demand and not as part of a production line. So we might question how many copies of the *Ephemerides*, that enigmatic and hotly-debated collection of *bematistes*' charts and measurements (via the *stathmoi*, 'stages'), ordnance accounts, troop movements, requisitions, and satrapal appointments which must have originally existed in some organised form, would have been made? In the case of the genuine campaign diaries the answer is probably none; it would have been a hugely laborious task with no commercial or didactic result.

Arrian's *Anabasis* has become almost the sole guardian of the very existence of the primary histories of Ptolemy and Aristobulus; some forty manuscript copies seem to have made it through, though none dating to earlier than ca. 1200. All of them stemmed from the *Codex Vindobonensis* (Vienna, Nationalbibliotek hist. gr. 4) so that each has a lacuna in chapter eight, the *Indike*, the account of Nearchus' voyage from the Indus delta to the Persian Gulf. What we consider to be Arrian's original wording therefore emanates from the hands of the copyist(s) behind that single manuscript. It is a wonder that we still have a corpus of Aristotle's 'student notes' via the five ancient manuscripts that were copied some 1,400 years after the polymath had died, and which preserve thirty-one of the 200 treatises he wrote; Diogenes Laertius calculated they once amounted to 445,270 lines.

In comparison, we are left with nothing but rare fragments of the writing of Demetrius of Phalerum, his prolific student.[203] Plato was unique; for a time it seemed that Thrasyllus, a friend of the emperor Tiberius and collector of the Platonist canon, had overdone it and assigned spurious works to the authentic, so providing Plato with a one hundred per cent plus survival rate.[204] The apocryphal were later thrown out and yet the tide is once again turning to reinstatement, reminding us that truth is anacyclotic too; even when analysing fragments, the pendulum of *communis opinio* is never still.

The weighty volumes titled *Philippika, Hellenika*, and *Makedonika* are lost to us.[205] The Sicilian historian Philistus, termed by Cicero 'the miniature Thucydides', has vanished without a trace even though admired by Alexander himself and possibly because Philistus had died in an epic sea battle; for all we know the Pellan court had procured the very last copy.[206] Of Theopompus' seventy books comprising his Greek and

Macedonian epics, Jacoby managed to collect 115 threadbare fragments, many from Athenaeus; Diodorus was clear that five of the fifty-eight books comprising the *Philippika* had already been lost by his day.[207]

Euripides was estimated to have written ninety-plus works yet only eighteen authenticated plays survive, an eighty per cent loss despite Lycurgus' advice to have them copied. Some won awards at the festivals of the Dionysia ('peep-shows for fools' according to the cynical Diogenes) and at the Panathenaia held at the Odeon situated dramatically at the foot of the Athenian Acropolis.[208] A more impressive credential is Plutarch's claim that after the military disaster at Syracuse, any Athenian captives able to quote Euripides had their liberty restored.[209]

Menander, whose comic drama and character portrayals Rome so loved and who counted Theophrastus, Demetrius of Phalerum and Ptolemy I *Soter* amongst his acquaintances, has a legacy of one play surviving (discovered in Egypt in 1957) against one hundred or more lost.[210] We are left with just three tragedians (four if *Prometheus Bound* can be pinned on Euphorion, Aeschylus' son), one comedian in Aristophanes (in eleven plays) and one lyric poet, Pindar (along with Sappho's complete *Hymn to Aphrodite*), and only seven of Aeschylus' ninety plays survive in complete form. The fickleness of micro production is clear for even the ivy-wreathed playwright. In the case of Aristophanes he might have sealed his own obscurity, for he was liberal in the accreditation of his works; his first three plays were staged in the names of Philonides and Callistratus, and two of his last were credited to his son, Ararus, to ensure his favourable public reception.[211]

Here the generosities appear to have been an open secret, yet in Rome a poet or playwright would lose all rights to his work once they had been accepted and paid for by the commissioner, and this often resulted in the complete loss of the author's name. So an inordinate number of anonymous works were floating around, possibly explaining why Varro doubted that 109 of the 130 comedies attributed to Plautus were genuinely his.[212] Varro's own work suffered; his *Imagines* is said to have contained 700 illustrations of the famous men he biographed, each provided with 'suitable epigrams'. The work was later epitomised but without the sketches, no doubt due to the labour required in their reproduction.[213]

What the copyists in churches and monasteries of Late Antiquity and the Middle Ages did give us in return were the bold and striking illuminations, the manuscript decorations in gold (gilding), silver and vibrant inks. These were ubiquitous in the Gothic period (principally the 13th and 14th centuries) but they had been produced from the fall of the Roman Empire through to the Renaissance. The border artistry often cramped texts, the two battling for territory on the pages, until a more disciplined approach placed the texts first and adornment only where gaps permitted. Rubricators who fashioned chapter headings and paragraph openings, usually in red ink, added further textual impact, and so an ornate and expensively illuminated book was inevitably treated with more reverence than a plainly bound sibling. As demand increased in the Renaissance, professional illuminators and freelance painters finally created the first early Italian 'mass' production lines.

Maps were the most challenging illustrations to reproduce. Claudius Ptolemy (ca. 90-168 CE), a Romanised Greek based in Alexandria who became known as the 'great geographer', produced a cartographic view of the known world (*Oikoumene*) in his *Geographia*. It has survived but in a textual form only, being rediscovered in time for the compilers behind the Waldseemüller map, the *Universalis Cosmographia,* to shock 16th century Europe. All cartographic diagrams from Ptolemy's work have departed from the surviving manuscripts; the last were seen sometime around 956 CE purportedly annotated with 4,530 cities and with over 200 mountains shown.

Future Ptolemaic maps were produced using the coordinates and instructions provided within his text, the first in 1295, some 300 years after the loss of the complete work. These, like the oriental names and descriptions provided in Marco Polo's travelogue, became hugely influential in the Renaissance despite the fact that Ptolemy had erred in using 500 *stadia* per degree (Eratosthenes calculated 700) with a grid

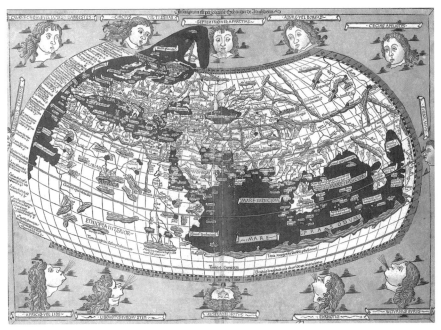

A 1482 engraving by Johannes Schnitzer depicting Ptolemy's known world or *Oikoumene* using detail and coordinated from Ptolemy's *Geographia*, though the original diagrams had by then been lost. This view of the continents completely ignored Herodotus' report of a Carthaginian circumnavigation of Africa.[214]

scheme that distorted both latitude and longitude. The misconceptions led Columbus (inspired to travel 'east' by Polo's book) to assume the lands of East Asia lay where he eventually found Cuba. Over the centuries the scribal errors made when transmitting the long tables of Ptolemy's numbers had in any case rendered the original topography unintelligible.

Ptolemy, also known as *ho megas astronomos*, the 'great astronomer', had proposed that simultaneous sightings of lunar eclipses was the best method of calculating longitude, whilst his astrological treatise, *Tetrabiblios* ('four books', known as the *Apotelesmatika* in Greek and *Quadripartitum* in Latin), explained how these celestial movements affected earthly matters. But Alexander's campaign had marked the end of the disciplined Babylonian astronomical diaries that Ptolemy might have called upon to verify his theories, when Babylon was ravaged in the Successor Wars. The technique would not have proved accurate anyway, for Ptolemy's *kosmos* was geocentric, but his astronomical treatise, the *Mathematike Syntaxis*, better known today as the *Almagest*, gave us the Ptolemaic System which was not replaced until Copernicus (Mikolaj Kopernik) published his heliocentric *De revolutionibus orbium coelestium* in 1543.[215]

Copernicus didn't live to see it banned by the Church and placed on the *Index Librorum Prohibitorum* for celestial heresy. He was simply reinstating the model of Aristarchus, the Greek father of 'western heliocentric' theory (whom he conspicuously failed to mention in his research), whose *On the Sizes and Distances of the Sun and the Moon* was likewise not thanked for its sun-centred observations, with their attendant theory that the Earth spun on its axis along the ecliptic; Cleanthes, the Stoic philosopher who studied paradoxes and pantheism, allegedly condemned him for impiety too.[216] The heavens were not to be challenged: Socrates had once been harangued for likening the sun to a stone, and Ephorus for claiming a comet had split in two.[217] It is altogether not surprising, in the light of our appreciation of history's infidelities, that Vedic Sanskrit texts had proposed the heliocentric idea half a millennium earlier.[218]

Despite a book's immediate impact, or the quality of the illuminations and the contemporary influence of their author, it still needed a well-connected admirer to be preserved, copied and ultimately printed. Plato had Augustine of Hippo but others were not so fortunate. Aurelius Augustinus Hipponensis, to quote his full title, is an example of how radically ideas might change in a single lifetime, and with them the direction of literary patrimony. Along his path from pagan hedonism to an austere Catholic faith (spurred on by his reading of Cicero's philosophical *Hortensius*), and with a period teaching rhetoric at Carthage and Rome in between, St Augustine famously uttered: 'Grant me chastity and continence, but not yet.'[219]

His admiration of Platonism, with its concept of eternity and the transmigration of souls, did not fully integrate into his new Christian doctrine (though he remained an admirer and adapted Neo-Platonist ideas to Christianity where he could), and in a tone that recalls Newton and Whear, he later exclaimed of non-pious men: 'They are deceived, too, by those highly mendacious documents that profess to give the history of many thousand years, though, reckoning by the sacred writings, we find that not six thousand years have passed.'[220] Augustine's library in the cathedral at Hippo Regius in modern Algeria narrowly missed destruction by the Vandals in 430 CE. But by then he may have dispensed with his early collection of pagan literature in favour of biblical texts, a reminder that a work stylistically out of synchronicity with the time would see neither parchment nor posterity, a social reality that has never truly ceased.

Another example of the waxing and waning of literary favour is Pliny's massive *Naturalis Historia*, one of the very first printed works. It was published fifteen times between the initial 'distinctly imperfect' translation of 1469 and 1500 when it was clearly in vogue in the inquiring spirit of the Renaissance.[221] In contrast, the 20th century saw less than half that number of new editions.[222] As for Pausanias' *Hellados Periegesis*, his *Guide to Greece*, there is no evidence it was read widely in classical times at all, possibly because its 'antiquarian sentiment' highlighted how far Greece had fallen from her glory.[223] A single reference to the work comes from the 6th century CE and several others from the Middle Ages; one single manuscript seems to have survived in the hands of Niccolo Niccoli (1364-1437) in 1418, and it was lost again by 1500. Three further copies survived but they are full of lacunae and errors, each loosely dated to the 15th century. It was not until Heinrich Schliemann was guided to the royal tombs at Mycenae by Pausanias' descriptions that classicists began to consider the work reliable; finally, after some 1,600 years and with his credibility reinstated (and Polybius' on his coat-tails), its publication widened.[224]

A century ago (found in 1879 and published in 1880) the sands of Egypt delivered to us what appeared to be Aristotle's lost *Constitution of the Athenians*, a copy evidently prepared by four different scribes and now in the British Library. It revealed a less than objective and rather prejudiced Peripatetic polymath.[225] And despite being referred to as 'the Attic bee because of the sweetness of diction', the reputation of Xenophon has declined since some 900 lines of the superior *Hellenika* of a 4th century historian known today as 'p' (for 'papyrus') were discovered at Oxyrhynchus in 1906, with further fragments published in 1946.[226] Similarly, Claudius' lucid *Letters to the Alexandrians* has reappeared, further regenerating his intellectual reputation. New finds are still possible; more recently an unearthed Archimedes palimpsest revealed a further ten pages of Hyperides' speeches under the new multi-spectral imaging techniques which are being brought to bear on previously illegible Herculaneum

Scrolls.[227] An exhumed Egyptian mummy was even found wrapped in the entire collected works of the Macedonian poet, Poseidippus, a fortuitous embalming in original Pellan prose.

But these are rare catches, like fisherman netting coelacanths, and unless a new hoard turns up we have to assume the process of source erosion is irreversible. For rarely in history do we meet individuals like Hagesitimus who recovered the history of the Lindian shrine of Athena and uniquely had the sources cast on a stele,[228] or orators like Lycurgus, whose superintendence of all things valuable bade the Athenians copy and preserve the works of Aeschylus, Euripides and Sophocles (seven of his plays remain) in a public place for posterity.[229]

THE ARTFUL ACCESSORISING OF THE *AUCTOR SUPPLEMENTORUM*

It is Curtius who provides us with the most comprehensive detail of events at Babylon immediately following Alexander's death, though his final chapter is lacunose. We have 123 codices of his work, all deriving from a single incomplete archetype dating back to the 9th century.[230] Notes from the colophons, literally the 'finishing strokes' at the end of a manuscript in which the copyist detailed his work, inform us that the earliest of them, referred to as the *Codex Parisinus 5716*, was written in the Carolingian period by a scribe named Haimo. This dates to the second-half of the 9th century in the vicinity of the Loire in France.[231] Unfortunately, Curtius' florid style had gained him early Middle Age meddling, whereas the drier pedantic Arrian was virtually forgotten until the more disciplined Renaissance had provided a better methodology for textual recovery and transmission. The 'base handling' of the diaskeuasts of this earlier period was less easily deciphered, when artful rather than informed filler damaged already wounded manuscripts.

Five of the Curtian manuscripts provided the basis of all modern translations, like Hedicke's influential 1867 edition, one of a number of informed copies to emerge.[232] All of the manuscripts were corrupted and most of poor quality, and as a result the *Codex Parisinus* is in places significantly different from the other four (*Bernensis, Florentinus, Leidensis, Vossianus*), giving us two textual traditions. Large lacunae existed in the books five, six and ten, and the first two chapters are missing completely, so the single and now lost archetype must have been similarly mutilated. We are still not sure how Curtius divided his work, and editions have been variously split into anything from eight to twelve chapters.[233] Whereas conscientious scribes were vigilant to the missing texts – *Codex 'P'* (Paris B N Lat. 14629) was, for example, translated by a scribe aware of the major lacuna between books five and six – others misleadingly ran the books together, often with a margin comment on 'some missing words', in this case creating a new edition with only nine books.[234]

No library in the Renaissance was considered well equipped unless a copy of Curtius sat on its shelves. The first translation from Latin to a modern language took place in 1483 by Pier Candido Decembrio in Milan and it existed in manuscript form until 1470/71 when the first *editio princeps* of Vindelinus Spirensis appeared in Florence (or Venice), often with spurious resurrections of the first two lost chapters.[235] Unfortunately, this became a trend; Decembrio called upon his knowledge of Arrian, Justin and Plutarch to propose a reconstruction of the missing text. One scholar recently warned on what we might consider akin to the 'holes in Homer' syndrome: 'Poets, antiquarians and historians drew on heroic narrative patterns to plug these gaps, places in the tale where objects or figures disappear from events.'[236]

Other scholars did adopt a more disciplined approach when supplementing lost texts, and they informed us when they did so. The first recorded *auctor supplementorum* was Christopher Bruno, whose edition was printed at Basel in 1545; certainly the *scholia* – the explanatory margin notes – were informative to the followers of a growing 'Curtiana'.[237] Analysis of a Curtius manuscript at Corpus Christi College, Oxford (*O 82*), revealed textual supplements that appear to have originated in France along with the redactions that preserved them. Here we find a patchwork of clear emulations of Seneca, Cicero, Josephus, Horace and Virgil, alongside elements of Julius Valerius' *Romance* translation, to name but a few. In this particular case margin notes *were* included, identifying the inspirational inserts; this was a 'transparent' attempt at *compilatio*. But the Curtius manuscripts, more often than not, became partnered by a process of 'anonymous fluidity', which, for example, absorbed elements of the *Roman d'Alexandre* by the 12th century poet Alberic de Pisancon.[238] Where margin notes are absent, we are left with an ever-present danger of assuming the style was Curtius' own, or an example of *his* emulation of the great literary stylists of the age.

Middle Age romance transmission was an even more difficult client itself, for its artistry was by definition anything but literal. Curtius *was* influential to both the romance genre and to the speculum literature of the Middle Ages, when alchemy rather than erudition walked the centre stage. The *Speculum Historiale* (*Mirror of History*) of Vincent de Beauvais was a monumental encyclopaedia that attempted to embrace the sum of all knowledge. It had relied on the similarly ambitious *Chronicon* of Helinand of Froidmont written sometime in the early 13th century for its references to Alexander, replicating all the mistakes therein, including extracts from the supplements of the Corpus Christi manuscript.[239] The popular edition of Johannes Freinsheim (1608-1660), which came with textual supplements and voluminous explanatory notes, was in fact reprinted up until the 20th century; his infills 'were so successful that we almost cease to lament the loss of the original'.[240] Efforts were finally made to standardise Curtius' text and highlight these interpolations: Zacher (1867), Thomas (1880) and Dosson (1887) published commentaries on these earlier manuscripts as the disciplines of *Quellenforschung* began to establish themselves.

THE SACRIFICE OF LINGUISTIC COMPROMISE

Commercial publication pressures eventually demanded that translations from Greek and Latin into vernacular languages were more readily available. If Aristotle had captured something of the essence of modern grammatical theory in his *Peri Hermeneias, On Interpretation*, neither he, nor Cicero and Horace who had been conscious of their methodology when undertaking translations, could have anticipated the shifting linguistic sands that would give rise to an industry of hermeneutical controversy. As John Dryden, Poet Laureate and celebrated translator, eloquently explained:

> '… the Words; when they appear (which is but seldom) literally graceful, it were an injury to the Author that they should be chang'd: But since every Language is so full of its own properties, that what is Beautiful in one, is often Barbarous, nay sometimes Nonsense, in another, it would be unreasonable to limit a Translator to the narrow compass of his Author's Words: 'tis enough if he chuse out some Expression which does not vitiate the Sense.'[241]

Dryden penned an illuminating preface to Ovid's *Episteles* in 1680. In it he 'reduced all translation to three heads': metaphrasing (word by word), paraphrasing (translation with 'latitude') and imitation ('the liberty to forsake' both 'words and sense'), a necessary means with which Dryden planned to tackle Latin texts: 'Tis almost impossible to Translate verbally, and well, at the same time; for the Latin (a most Severe and Compendious Language) often expresses that in one word, which either the Barbarity, or the narrowness of modern Tongues cannot supply in more.' Ovid wound up his *Metamorphoses* with a bold claim about the immortal nature of the work '… that nothing can destroy… not Jupiter's wrath, nor fire nor sword, nor devouring time.'[242] But Ovid had not factored in the challenges of translation.

Dryden's edition of Virgil (published 1697) and Alexander Pope's Homer (the *Iliad* was published between 1715 and 1720 and 'its wife', the *Odyssey* in 1726) became the authoritative and representative English classical texts of their era.[243] The latter followed Chapman's first English translation from Greek of 1611, which superseded an earlier attempt by

Hall (who spoke no Greek) from Spanish in 1581.[244] Yet the classical scholar, Richard Bentley, scoffed at Pope's efforts: 'It is a pretty poem Mr Pope, but you must not call it Homer.'[245]

Bentley had already gained notoriety when William Wotton (1666-1727), an accomplished linguist and classical scholar, requested that he expose the *Epistles of Phalaris,* whose authenticity had been long debated, once and for all. The *Epistles,* most likely an Alexandrian production of the 3rd century BCE, is purportedly a corpus of 148 Greek missives written by the ruthless tyrant of Agrigento in Sicily, who, according to the lyric poet Pindar, had a bronze bull made in which he roasted criminals alive.[246] Lucian suggested the bull's creator, Perilaus, designed it so the cries of agony could be heard like 'melodious bellowings' through pipes placed in the nostrils.[247] And though the *Epistles* painted Phalaris as a gentle ruler and patron of arts, he suffered a gruesome death when his subjects, seeing none of those worthwhile traits, finally revolted.[248]

Bentley's haughty scientific paper on the subject published in 1697 (which 'violently' exposed the corpora of the *Letters of Themistocles, Letters of Socrates* and *Letters of Euripides* at the same time) saw the eruption of a literary dispute with Charles Boyle and Francis Atterbury in the style of Scaliger and Scioppius; it was satirised by Jonathan Swift in *The Battle of the Books.*[249] Some years later, in 1742, Pope caricatured Bentley in *The Duncaid*, referring to the lack of humanity in his scholarship that led to his being satirised earlier.[250]

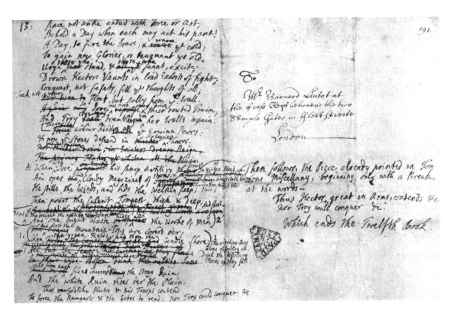

Alexander Pope's original handwritten draft of his *Iliad* translation published between 1715 and 1720, written on the back of a letter.

Dryden's translation of Virgil too was termed nothing less than 'alchemy'; in the words of Sir Walter Scott, Dryden managed to explain the '… sense … with the eloquence in his own tongue, though he understands not the nice turns of the original.' In Scott's view, Dryden '… cared not if minute elegancies were lost, or the beauties of accurate proportion destroyed, or a dubious interpretation hastily adopted on the credit of a *scholium*.'[251] He nevertheless concluded generously:

> … many passages that are faulty, many indifferently understood, many imperfectly translated, some in which dignity is lost, others in which bombast is substituted in its stead. But the unabated vigour and spirit of the version more than overbalances these and all its other deficiencies.

In the age of Dryden and Pope, the rhyming couplet was the standard choice for reconstruction of Homeric hexameter, whereas in more modern translations a six-beat line or iambic decasyllabic structure is employed, though any rigid adherence to method requires necessary liberties with structure to avoid what the Greeks termed *logoi pezoi*, 'pedestrian wording', where the spirit of the original gets lost.[252] Archaic poetry remains a conundrum because its metre may simply not exist in the target language, and perhaps this is why almost all Greek and Roman lyric poetry disappeared in the Dark Ages. A recent translator of the *Homeric Hymns* commented on early hexameter verse: 'As the Greek language operates very differently from English using a system in which the function of a word is generally signalled by its ending, rather than by its position in the sentence, a strict literal translation is often impossible or unsatisfactory.'[253] The result, as with the case of the Alexandrian attempts to modernise Pindar, is that the lilt, flow and formula, and ultimately the very essence and mood of the hymn in the mind's ear, is interrupted by the need to reposition the words.

Dryden had himself compared the translation of a classical work to a 'drawing after life', and yet one that should nevertheless retain recognisable facial features. He further proposed a middle methodological ground in translation, shunning both *verbum pro verbo* and imitation. John Denham had already proposed a similar approach in his 1656 preface to the *Destruction of Troy* though neither scholar's method was well defined. Dryden went on to admit: 'I am ready to acknowledge that I have transgress'd the Rules which I have given; and taken more liberty than a just Translation will allow.'[254] In contrast, Bardon's approach to reproducing Curtius has been described as 'misguided conservatism' in that it maintained corrupted Latin even when it made little sense.[255]

Any scholar who has read parallel translations of the classics can understand the challenge, and especially so in the case of Tacitus. Michael Grant remarked of the *Annals* when introducing his 1956 edition: 'The more prudent translators preface their efforts by apologetic reminders that Tacitus has never been translated and probably never will be.'[256] The translators were, and always are, faced with what has been termed 'the art of the correct sacrifice'.[257]

The above retrospections highlight the challenges posed to literature through the 'ages' that revolve around cosmetic chronological classifications with which we attempt to tidy up the past. Yet the terms 'modern', 'classic' and 'antiquated', are, of course, temporally relative.[258] Along with Teuffel's Silver and Golden Ages of Latin we bundle history into the 'Classical Period' and 'Late Antiquity', Droysen's 'Hellenistic Era' and the Roman 'Second Sophistic', a period first labelled by Philostratus (ca. 172-250) in his *Lives of the Sophists*. We have also established the label of a so-called Third Sophistic in the 4th century when Christian rhetoric found a string of brilliant rhetors and philosophers inspiring Augustine to his *De doctrina christiana*.

We gather up later events through Petrarch's 'Dark Ages', the 'Middle Ages', the 'High Medieval Period' and the enlightened 'Renaissance', the epithet coined by Jules Michelet in his 1855 *Histoire de France* which rather unsurprisingly claimed it was a French-inspired movement. We even have a 'Macedonian Rennaisance' for the dynasty based at Constantinople (broadly spanning 867-1056 CE) which ruled the Byzantine Empire. Commonly attributed to Basil I 'the Macedonian', but born in fact to a Thracian peasant family of alleged Armenian origin, the period saw a reinvigoration of arts when the iconoclasms of the Amorian dynasty were reversed for a while.[259] Yet these periodisations are too broad in breadth and too shallow in depth for such tentacular processes, which neither commenced, nor ended, with the succinctness we like to attribute to them. We have simply observed a cluster of cultural vintages originating from a common *terroir* and then deemed them an appellation.

It is said that every language and every era *does* have a different view of the world, synthesising its cultural background into idioms with unique connotations that may not necessarily be compatible with the originating archaic, or the modern target, language. 'The vocabulary of ancient languages reflects a cultural context that modern Europe left behind a long time ago.'[260] Take, for example, the Hippocratic Oath assigned to the famous doctor from Kos. Though Hippocrates would recognise the relics of an original in its modern form, the wording has evolved to cope with new ethical and technological practices. Gone are the pledges to share medical knowledge free of fees and the oath of non-violation of 'free' women 'or slaves'; the vow not to provide lethal drugs is today caveated with – most pertinently in countries permitting euthanasia – 'I tread with care in matters of life and death.'

Taking all this into account, what chance is there that Arrian, Diodorus and Plutarch accurately captured the intent of their earlier sources, no matter how well (or ill) meaning their attempts? How faithfully did Cleitarchus transmit the essence of his eyewitness sources, and how successfully did Curtius convert

Cleitarchus' Greek construction and the underlying thought processes into Latin? We may equally ponder how accurately their interpretations have been preserved in the centuries since with the attenuation of time. For a subtlety unappreciated, an inflection misused, sarcasms and witticisms taken too literally (any translator of Lucian's works, or Ovid's *Metamorphoses* would appreciate the dilemma), each diffuse the focus and nuances of the original.[261] Moreover, 'fiction, true, false or free-falling, is intimately bound up with figures of discourse such as metaphor and irony, and with speculation and hypothesis', all the elements vulnerable in translation.[262] Alongside them we find deep-lurking lacunae, scribal cut-and-pastes, scriptorium pastiches and the text-amending prejudices of pious distaste; and each, or any, one of them may have changed our very interpretation of history.

What of the limitations and even the errors of the ancient authors themselves that stemmed from their rudimentary working materials? For where a modern writer might ponder his prose and commit to words knowing he can instantly correct and erase, the classical writer could not readily do so. Where we have limitless scope to improve paragraphs, reintegrate chapters and replay syntax until the publication button is pressed, the ancient author committing to papyrus or vellum had almost no latitude for amendment. It is perhaps why the Homeric epics, optimised with each oral recounting, attained such poetical heights, whereas written texts, handcuffed to ink, essentially remained a 'first attempt'.

Cato, via Cicero, unwittingly articulated the overall challenge while commending the order stoicism brought: 'What is there, which is not so linked to something else, that all would collapse if you moved a single letter?'[263] This sounds like a premonition of the uncial script that caused so much confusion in scriptoriums, and the early Semitic languages that had no vowels at all.[264] The analogy helps explain the mistransmission of book titles, names, numbers and dates, and how, for example, Alexander's Will bequests could have become a part of the so-called last plans that were so curiously revealed in Babylon (T25), and why the lacunae that permeated Curtius' last chapter were sewn up with such poor stitching.[265]

But perhaps the better answer is Alexander's 'last words', which were his supposed response to questions on kingship. For the Vulgate-genre reply – *toi kratistoi*, 'to the strongest' – is suspiciously akin to *toi Krateroi*, 'to Craterus' (Greek, Krateros), Alexander's senior general who was entrusted to oversee the entire kingdom of Macedonia in the Will along with the dowry of an Argead wife, an observation not lost on historians (T6, T7, T8, T9).[266] If not exactly the point Cicero was making, when this is juxtaposed beside the stoic argument of Chrysippus, which proposed that 'every word is naturally ambiguous', we appreciate just how far removed we may be from the original testimony of the eyewitness historians who followed Alexander at the dawn of the Hellenistic Age.[267]

NOTES

1. *Collected Works of Erasmus, Letters 1-141* (1484-1500) Vol. 1, p 252, translation by RAB Mynors and DFS Thompson, University of Toronto Press, Toronto-Buffalo, 1974.
2. *Collected Works of Erasmus, Letters 1-141* (1484-1500) Vol. 1, p 134, translation by RAB Mynors and DFS Thompson, University of Toronto Press, Toronto-Buffalo, 1974.
3. Momigliano (1954) p 22.
4. Whether it was actually nailed to the door, rather than being distributed by hand, is disputed and may be myth; the Latin title of Luther's work is *Disputatio pro Declaration Virtutis Indulgentarium*.
5. The original full title of *Utopia* was *Libellus vere aureus, nec minus salutaris quam festivus, de optimo rei publicae statu deque nova insula Utopia*. Blackburn (2006) p 22 for the dating of Plato's *Republic*.
6. Quoting Russell (1946) p 7.
7. First published as *Collatio Novi Testamenti* in 1453. By his death in 1457 Valla had revised and improved the work now titled *In Latinum Novi Testamenti Interpretationem Annotationes*; it was first printed in 1505. Erasmus found a copy in the abbey of Parc outside Leuven in summer 1504; discussion in Rummel (2008) pp 18-22.
8. Quoting West (2008) Introduction viii. The 'erratic' nature of the early manuscripts Erasmus had to work with is discussed by Metzger (1992) p 102. *Instrumentum* was changed to *Testamentum* from Erasmus' second edition onwards.
9. Erasmus later drew from the *Complutensian Polyglot Bible* to improve his 4th edition text.
10. Erasmus *Adagia* (III, IV, 96) 'collection of proverbs' published first in Paris in 1500.
11. Quoting PG Naiditch and R Resinski *Philodemus and Greek Papyri: an exhibition 1 April – 31 August 1994*, UCLA, University Research Library, Dept. of Special Collections, April 1994. Following Grafton-Most-Settis (2010) p 30 for Petrarch's treatment of Alexander.
12. Momigliano (1977) p 109.
13. Quoting Highet (1949) p 113 for Gibbon's prose. Gibbon (1776) *The History of the Decline and Fall of the Roman Empire* chapter 8, quoting Petrarch *Epistlolae Familiares* 9.2.
14. Gibbon (1776) *The History of the Decline and Fall of the Roman Empire* cited in Highet (1949) Introduction p 17.
15. Highet (1949) Introduction p 16 for the first professor of Greek.
16. Highet (1949) pp 106-111 for the impact of purer Greek and Latin on the vernacular languages and following his observation on the reasons for the 'poorer' vocabulary and p 85 for 'positive paganism'.
17. Discussion of the significance of the *Divine Comedy* in Highet (1949) pp 70-80.
18. Quoting Tyndale's alleged defiant words when confronted by an ordained clergyman.
19. It is estimated that some eighty-four per cent of the *New Testament* and seventy-five per cent (of the first five chapters) of the *Old Testament* of the King James Bible stemmed directly from Tyndale's translation, as had Miles Coverdale's English bible edition for Henry VIII before it.
20. Quoting Momigliano (1977) p 76.
21. Quoting Highet (1949) Introduction p 15, following Bracciolini. Highet (1949) pp 91-92 for Boccaccio's visit to Monte Cassino.
22. Highet (1949) pp 17-18 for the Vatican Library.
23. Quoting from the Preface (line 1) to *Tacitus and Bracciolini, The Annal Forged in the XVth Century* by JW Ross, originally published anonymously in 1878.
24. Quoting *Tacitus and Bracciolini, The Annal Forged in the XVth Century* chapter 2.3 by JW Ross. Also Hochart (1889). The popular title *Annals* is in fact 16th century. Tacitus published his works as *Historiae* in fourteen books, and then wrote sixteen books titled *Ab excessu Divi Augusti*.
25. Following Diogenes of Sinope in Diogenes Laertius *Diogenes* 65-66. The riposte was in response to Diogenes hearing a handsome youth talking in an unseemly fashion; in other words the words or claims do not do justice to the source from which they emanate; thus the 'lead blade from the ivory scabbard'.
26. Quoting Homer *Odyssey* 11.362-6.
27. Annius was made Master of the Palace by Alexander VI. Ligota (1987) p 50 for discussion of Annius' claim to read Etruscan. Etruscan is not an Indo-European language and has not been fully deciphered. The *Pyrgi Tablets*, written in both Etruscan and Phoenician (Punic), have helped translate some rudimentary phrases and vocabulary. According to Suetonius *Claudius* 42.2. Claudius wrote a history of the Etruscans in twenty books; this has led some people to assume he spoke Etruscan but there is no corroborating text.
28. Chapter titled *The Reborn Wrath of Peleus' Son* for more on Alexander's alleged cosmopolitan views.
29. Full discussion of Annius' methods is given by Ligota (1987) chapter 3 footnote 11 – for reference to Cyme. Annius' *Antiquitatum Variarum* was first published under the title *Commentaria super*

opera diversorum auctorum de antiquitatibus loquentium, Eucharius Silber, Rome, 1498; discussed in Temple (2002). Also a series of essays on various aspects of Annius' career and his influence on Renaissance myth and the first interest in the Etruscans was collected in *Annio da Viterbo, Documenti e ricerche,* Multigrafica Editrice, Rome, 1981.

30. Discussed in Ligota (1987) p 44.
31. Herodotus 2.53 claimed Homer lived some 400 years before his own time, thus ca. 850 BCE. Estimates of the dating of Homer vary across sources with some preceding this by 250 years.
32. Discussion in Borchardt (1986) pp 27-35. Quoting Grafton (1990) p 61.
33. Quoting Weiss (1962) pp 101-20.
34. For full discussion see Borchardt (1986) pp 27-35.
35. Grafton (1990) p 23.
36. Discussed in detail in Grafton (1990) pp 78-81.
37. Momigliano (1966) p 145. Most educated Romans were expected to have mastered Greek.
38. Seneca *Quaestiones Naturales* 7.16, translation by J Clarke, 1910.
39. Scaliger's work was published as *De emendatione temporum,* discussed in Grafton (1975) pp 164-166.
40. Grafton (1990) p 116 for the legacy of Goropius. Valla exposed the fraud in 1440 in his *De falso credita et ementita Constantini Donatione.* For discussion of the *Donation of Constantine* see R Fubini (1996) p 80.
41. Discussion in Mallory (1989) pp 9-10.
42. Quoting Syme (1971) p 265 and taking Annius' contention from Ligota (1987) p 46.
43. Excerpt from the Catalogue of the Exhibition *Alexander the Great in European Art,* edited by Nicos Hadjinicolaou, Thessalonica, 22 September 1997 to 11 January 1998.
44. Ligota (1987) pp 52-53.
45. *Diairei kai basileue* (Greek Διαίρει καὶ βασίλευε), translated *divide and rule,* comes to replace, in this case, the Latin *divide et impera.*
46. Ligota (1987) for 'organon of the truth'. See discussion in Grafton (1990) pp 95-97. Casaubon, Porphyry and Reitzenstein each exhibited bias in their critiques.
47. Discussed in detail in Casson (2001) p 138; it was Edward Gibbon who proposed the material fueled the 4,000 baths for six months.
48. 'Rational analysis fought stubborn faith', quoting Glenn W Most, speech at the Israel Society for the Promotion of Classical Studies 42nd Annual Conference. Following Russell (1946) p 462 for the unpopularity of the Renaissance.
49. Scaliger (1583) *De emendatione temporum,* with a second edition in 1598. Between them Scaliger had published his *Epistola de vetustate et splendore gentis Scaligerae et JC Scaligeri vita* (1594). The *New Testament* preacher called into question was Dionysius the Areopagite. The Jesuit reply came in the form of Gasparus Scioppius' *Scaliger Hypobolimaeus* or *The Supposititious Scaliger,* a polemic against his character. A complete list of his works appeared in a biography by Jakob Bernays, Berlin, 1855. Discussed at length in Grafton (1983). Scaliger's response included the *Confutatio fabulae Burdonum.*
50. Digory Whear *De Ratione et Methoda Legendi Historias (On the Plan and Method of Reading Histories),* October 1623. Further discussion in Levine (1991) p 279.
51. Varro attempted to 'correct' the calendar inefficiencies by inserting both dictatorial years and anarchic years in Rome's past. Augustus canonised the system and had it inscribed in his Arch. Fragments of the inscription survive as the so-called *Fasti Capitolini.*
52. Digory Whear *De Ratione et Methoda Legendi Historias.*
53. Quoting Ehrman (2014) Introduction and Momigliano (1954) p 23.
54. This appears in the bibliography as Speyer (1971).
55. Following the observation made by Ehrman (2014) p 31 and Metzger (1972) p 13.
56. Full discussion at *The Freethought Exchange,* no. 37-38, 1998, article titled *Thirty Centuries of Forgeries* pp 1735-1837 now available online at christianism.com. The so-called *Angel Scroll* is an example of newly emerging deceptions. Summarising NC Gross *The Mystery of the Angel Scroll: Find of the Century or Elaborate Hoax?* Jerusalem Report, 11 October 1999. For a full discussion of their authenticity see Berry (1999) and Pagels (1979). The definitive study of the *Decretals of Pseudo-Isidore* is H Fuhrmann, *Einfluß und Verbreitung der pseudoisidorischen Fälschungen,* 3 vols. Schriften der Monumenta Germaniae Historica 24, i-iii, 1972-3.
57. Eusebius *Ecclesiastical History* 8.2.
58. E Gibbon *Vindication.* It was an attack on Eusebius' treatise on pseudos in his *Praeparatio Evangelica* 12.31.
59. Gibbon's own words about the popularity of his book cited in Highet (1949) p 344 and pp 352-354 for Gibbon's bias against Christianity. Quoting Macaulay's *History* from *Miscellaneous Essays and Lays of Ancient Rome,* first published in the Edinburgh Review January-May 1828, Longman, Rees, Orme, Brown and Green, London, 1828, p 358.

60. Eusebius *Praeparatio Evangelica* 9.5.1. For Theotecnus see Metzger (1972) pp 3-24.
61. Pilate discussed in Wroe (1999). Tacitus' origins discussed in Alonso-Núñez (1987) p 70.
62. Discussed in Attridge Oden (1981). References to Sanchuniathon are found in Eusebius' *Praeparatio evangelica* 1. 9-10.
63. Quoting Blackburn (2006) p 1.
64. Discussed in Grafton (1990) pp 14-16.
65. The *Letter of Aristeas* 10-11, translation from Bartlett (1985) pp 20-21.
66. Full discussion in Heller-Roazen (2002) p 141.
67. Lucretius *De Rerum Natura* 1.101.
68. Heading taken from Ovid *Metamorphoses,* Prologue.
69. Galen *Corpus Mediocorum Graecum* 9.1; full text in Heller-Roazen (2002) p 146; 'self-proclaimed' as Galen wrote a work titled *The Best Physician is also a Philosopher.*
70. Discussed in Grafton (1990) p 12 and pp 73-77; Callimachus' catalogue's full title was *The Tables of Persons Conspicuous in every Branch of Learning and a List of Their Compositions.*
71. Casson (1971) p 45. *Ex ploion* meant literally 'from the ships'.
72. 1 talent = 6,000 drachmas = 36,000 obols, equivalent to 6 obols per day for sixteen years; most infantrymen received 4 per day. Top pay would equate to 1/10 of a talent per man per year. In terms of 1 talent of silver, that was approximately 57 lb (26 kg) of silver, the equivalent of 6,000 drachmas which would have amounted to something like sixteen years of an infantryman's generous pay.
73. Galen reported competition between Pergamum and Alexandria. For references to Ammonius Saccas see Gudeman *Greeks* (1894) p 61. Full discussion in Metzger (1972).
74. Galen *On His Own Books* 2.91-92. Galen is said to have written over 600 treatises; see Kotrc-Walters (1979). A reading of the *Life of Diogenes* by Diogenes Laetius will, for example, illustrate the number of times a story was additionally credited to other individuals.
75. Diogenes Laertius *Aristotle* 13.
76. Eusebius *Praeparatio Evangelica* 10. As further examples, Eusebius accused Theopompus of stealing entire passages from Xenophon; Apollonius suggested he plagiarised Isocrates word for word. Lucian *How to Write History* 59, Eusebius *Praeparatio Evangelica* 10.3.1, Porphyry *The Study of Philology* Book 1: *On the Greeks as Plagiarists*, cited in Shrimpton (1991) p 5. Grafton (1990) p 78 for Apollonius' criticism of Theopompus and for Ephorus stealing 3,000 of Duris' lines.
77. Eustathius published extant commentaries of the Homeric works, the *Eustathii archiepiscopi Thessalonicensis commentarii ad Homeri Iliadem* 1194, published by Hildesheim G Olms, 1960.
78. Quoting Macaulay (1828).
79. Quoting Shakespeare *As You Like It*, scene III and Plato *Republic* 377d 4-6.
80. Aristotle *Poetics* 1451a36-8; translation from Gill-Wiseman (1993) p 182.
81. Diogenes Laertius *Heraclitus*. Herodotus 2.2.23; Herodotus' father discussed in Pitcher (2009) p 156. Thucydides' criticism of Homer discussed by JL Moles in Gill-Wiseman (1993) pp 100-101, citing Thucydides 1.9.3,10.1,10.3-5,11.1-2.
82. In the 4th century Q Septimius published *Dictys Cretensis Ephemeridos belli Troiani*, in six books, a work that professed to be a Latin translation of the Greek version. Dares' work was published as *Daretis Phrygii De excidio Troiae historia* and is dated to the 5th century. Aelian 11.2 reports that Dares' original *Iliad* predated Homer. Quoting Heckel (1987) p 114 on 'charlatans' referring to deceptive anonymae in general.
83. Discussion of Nero's part on the translation of Dictys' diary in Gudeman (1894) p 152.
84. Translation of Nepos' letter by RM Fraser from Martinez (2011) 2011 p 17. There is however a warrior named Dares in Homer *Iliad* 5.9; discussed in Highet (1949) pp 52-53.
85. Benoit de Sainte-Maure's *Le Roman de Troie* was one of the inspirations for Chaucer's *Troilus and Criseyde*. For full discussion see Nolan (1992). Highet (1949) p 55 for discussion of the later adaptations and p 104 for the Latin *Odyssey*.
86. Highet (1949) p 114 for Samxon's edition of the *Iliad*.
87. Polybius 23.10 for the proverb 'justice has an eye'. The Latin translation was by Boccaccio, a friend of Petrarch, aided by Leontius Pilatos, the first professor of Greek in Western Europe; quoting Highet (1949) Introduction p 15 for 'wooden'.
88. Plutarch *On the Malice of Herodotus* 43, or *Moralia* 873f.
89. Plutarch *Agesilaus* 15.4 for a 'battle of mice'; chapter titled *Sarissa Diplomacy: Macedonian Statecraft* for more on the battle at Megalopolis.
90. Strabo 9.1.10 and also implied at Plutarch *Solon* 10.1. The inserted verse referred to the *Iliad* 2.557-558.
91. Herodotus 7.6.
92. Casson (2001) pp 29-30 for discussion. The reference to Lycurgus comes from Pseudo-Plutarch *Lives of the Ten Orators* 841f. Metzger (1972) p 9 for *dramatis personae*. Also discussed in more detail in Gudeman *Greeks* (1894) p 55. Plutarch *Solon* 29.4-5 for Thespis' lies.

93. Aulus Gellius 3.3 quoted in Grafton (1990) p 13; termed Varronian as Varro used a sound method to detect the genuine plays.
94. Quoting Grafton (1990) p 118.
95. This partially quoted text fragment belongs to Terentianus Maurus (3rd century) and constitutes verse 1286 of his work *De litteris, De Syllabes, De Metris*. Full quotation text is *Pro captu lectoris habent sua fata libelli*, translated as 'According to the reader's capabilities, books have their destiny'.
96. Madan (1893) p 2.
97. Many books printed after 1500 followed this format but Bernhard von Mallinckrodt in his *prima typographicae incunabula* chose an arbitrary date of 1500 as the end of the 'infancy of printing', thus incunabula, Latin for 'cradles'.
98. From the German publication titled *Gutenberg-fest zu Mainz imjahre* 1900, quoting a letter Mark Twain had sent them to celebrate the opening of the Gutenberg Museum.
99. Kenyon (1899) p 14 for the dating of the oldest extant papyri.
100. Pliny 13.74-82; as an example see Theophrastus *Enquiry into Plants* for the many uses of papyrus.
101. First argued by Theodor Birt in his *Das Antike Buchwesen* (1882) and discussed in Madan (1893).
102. Pitcher (2009) p 2 for *Sillabos* detail. Polybius 11.1a.1-5. This was the contents list on the outside of a scroll and distinct from the *proekthesis*, an introductory narrative inside.
103. Pliny 13.74-82.
104. Discussed in Madan (1893) pp 8-12. Pliny 13.17 claimed parchment was invented at Pergamum but the differentiation to vellum is unclear. Pliny 13.21 for *charta Pergamena*. Herodotus 5.58 for its earlier development by the Ionians.
105. Martial first described the codex format and its handy compactness for travel in a series of poems written between 84-86 CE. Full discussion in Needham (1979) p 4 and following Casson (2001) p 126.
106. Kenyon (1899) pp 17-18 for the lengths of unrolled papyri.
107. Aulus Gellius 7.17 for the fate of the Pergamum library. Chapter titled *Sarissa Diplomacy: Macedonian Statecraft* for further discussion of the battle between King Perseus and the Roman general, Aemilius Paullus. Mark Antony gifted Cleopatra much of the Pergamum library; Plutarch *Antony* 58. Archaeological excavation suggests the library at Pergamum may have been large enough to hold 160,000 scrolls.
108. Discussed in Momigliano (1966) p 124.
109. Casson (2001) pp 125-127. Over seventy per cent of Oxyrhynchus finds have been on papyrus and less than 1.5 per cent in total were in the codex format.
110. Neleus' activity detailed in Athenaeus 1.4.3a-b, Strabo 13.1.54, Plutarch *Sulla* 26.1-2, Diogenes Laertius 5.52-56. Discussed in Fortenbaugh-Schütrumpf (2000) p 344 and Casson (2001) p 35.
111. Athenaeus 5.53.214d-e.
112. Quoting Harris (1999) pp 40-41.
113. Strabo 13, Plutarch *Sulla* 26. Also discussed in Casson (2001) pp 70-71.
114. Porphyry *Vita Plotini* 24 mentioned the classifications and arrangement that Aristotle's and Theophrastus' works were subjected to by Andronicus.
115. Diodorus 1.4.2.
116. Plutarch *Lucullus* 74.3 described his rule of Africa as carried out with 'the highest degree of justice'.
117. Plutarch *Caesar* 49.8. Aulus Gellius 7.17. Ammianus Marcellinus and Orosius concur that Caesar started the fire, though the burning of the Library was accidental.
118. Also Shipley (2000) p 235 for discussion and Casson (2001) p 138. The earthquake and subsequent tsunami were recorded by Ammianus Marcellinus 26.10.15-19.
119. Caesar *Civil Wars* Book 3.111. For Cassius Dio's claim see discussion in Casson (2001) p 46.
120. Caesar *The Alexandrian War* 1 and Lucan *De bello civili* 10.440 ff; 486-505. Full discussion in Heller-Roazen (2002) p 148.
121. Discussed in Casson (2001) p 79. Detailed discussion of the damage caused by Caesar and the final destruction of the Library at Alexandria in Heller-Roazen (2002) pp 147-149. There is some doubt as to whether the fire actually affected the Library at all; see Heller-Roazen (2002) pp 150-151.
122. Augustus later favoured Varro and his writing was again encouraged.
123. Suetonius *Julius Caesar* 56.1 and 56.3 for confirmation of Hurtius' praise.
124. The lost *Codex Fuldensis* discussed in Rolfe (1913) p 207.
125. Suetonius *Caesar* 55.
126. Other sources for the fire and book numbers destroyed are Orosius, 6.15.31-2, Aulus Gellius 7.17 and Seneca *On the Tranquillity of the Mind* 9.5, Ammianus Marcellinus *Roman History* 22.16.13-15; other citations: Pseudo-Aristeas (200,000 increasing to 500,000 echoing Demetrius of Phalerum's promise to Ptolemy), Orosius 6 (400,000), Epiphanius *Weights and Measures* 9 (54,800), Isidore of Seville *Etymologies* 6.3.3 (80,000), John Tzetezes *Prolegomena to Aristophanes*

(490,000). Full discussion of the size of the library and its traditions in Bagnall (2002).

127. Discussion of the composite scrolls in Heller-Roazen (2002) p 140. Following Bagnall (2002) p 356 for the doubt that Callimachus could have listed all the works. Boardman-Griffin-Murray (1986) p 392 for the Serapis library. Vrettos (2001) p 34 for the Serapeiana. Vrettos (2001) p 40 for the mixed rolls.

128. Athenaeus 5.203e.

129. Polybius 38.5.21. Also recorded in Appian *Hannibalic Wars* 132. Scipio's quote is from Homer *Odyssey* 6.448.

130. Polybius 38.19 made it clear he had advised Scipio on technical details. Ammianus Marcellinus 24.2.14-17 for the storming of the gate; see citation in McGing (2010) p 142; p 141 for the technical capacity and Polybius 38.19 for his presence at Carthage.

131. Cicero claimed Scipio Aemilianus was an avid reader of the *Cyropaedia*. See discussion in Pitcher (2009) p 152.

132. Quoting Hornblower (1981) p 104 and also the discussion on the 'weeping' of great generals in McGing (2010) p 27. Appian chapter 19 (or section 132, Punic Wars) for Polybius' tears.

133. The loss of Polybius' books discussed in McGing (2010) p 13.

134. Discussed in Green (2007) pp XXVII-XXIX and Momigliano (1977) pp 72 and 76. Plutarch *Philopoemen* 21.5 for Polybius' funeral role.

135. Quoting Digory Whear on Cicero in *On the Plan and Method of Reading Histories* 1623. Cicero expressed his regret for the destruction of Corinth in his *De Officiis* 1.11. He possibly took the analogy from Hegesias, who compared Thebes and Corinth to the 'two eyes of Greece'. Discussed in Pearson (1960) p 246. The 'two eyes of Greece' was a common analogy apparently; Anaximenes had used it for Athens and Thebes after Thebes' destruction by Alexander; see Pearson (1960) p 246 for discussion.

136. Septimus Severus was born in Leptis Magna south of Carthage and his father was of Punic or Berber origin; see the *Historia Augusta, Life of Septimus Severus* 1-3. Cassius Dio 77.15 for Severus' quote.

137. Virgil *Aeneid* 4.645. Dido, queen of Carthage, fell in love with Aeneas, who, in his quest to found a new dynasty in Italy, left her in Carthage, after which she committed suicide, pledging revenge and predicting eternal strife between the two races. Also Ovid *Metamorphoses* 14.75 ff for the story of Aeneas' arrival in Africa.

138. The fate of the *Metz Epitome* discussed in Baynham (1995) p 62. Texts now rely upon the editions of D Volkmann (Nuremberg, 1886) and O Wagner (Strasburg, 1900); more on the surviving editions in Thomas Review (1963).

139. Theopompus' epitome detailed in Flower (1994) p 35.

140. Discussed in Heckel-Yardley (1997) Introduction p 1.

141. Some manuscripts describe the work as an epitome of Livy but this is obviously inaccurate for its text provides post-Livy commentary.

142. Quoting Hornblower (1981) pp 19-20 and 28-29.

143. In the preface to his epitome of Trogus' forty-four books Justin followed his explanation of methodology with, 'I made a short work, comprised of the choicest flowers as it were…', translation by TJ Ryan from Baynham (1998) p 31.

144. Livius Andronicus' translation discussed in Highet.

145. Discussed in Baker-Saldanha (2009) p 35.

146. Quoting Grant (1995) p 97 and Suetonius *Life of Horace*.

147. Strabo 15.2.8 suggested the people of Ariana (Iran and Central Asia) including Persians, Bactrians, Medes and Sogdians as '… speaking approximately the same language. With slight variations.' Discussed on Olbrycht (2008) p 243.

148. Onesicritus' conversations with the Indian sages are preserved at Strabo 15.1.63-65; full discussion in Brown (1949) pp 38-39 and p 44 for the translation discussion.

149. An acrostic is a writing format in which the first letter, syllable, or word of each line, spells out a word or message.

150. Following and quoting from Nisetich (1980) pp 15-16. Highet (1949) pp 222-224 for Pindar's stanzas.

151. Discussed in detail in Casson (2001) p 43.

152. Discussed in Gudeman *Greeks* (1894) p 69. Fitzgerald (1998) p xii for the multiple-author theory behind the *Odyssey*.

153. Following Robbins (2001) p 79.

154. Discussion of the Bronze Age references in West (2008) p 76.

155. Robbins (2001) p 66. Herm (1975) p 180 for *phoinikia grammata* and its early Greek usage.

156. Discussed in Robins (1987).

157. The *Suda* identified a work titled *Selection of Attic Words and Phrases* that likely belongs to the grammatician.

158. Polybius 3.22, translation by Ian Scott-Kilvert, Penguin Classics edition, 1979.
159. Discussed in Revilo (1949) pp 249-257; cited in Tacitus 11.14 and Suetonius *Claudius* 41.
160. J Dryden *Preface concerning Ovid's Epistles* 16.
161. Grant (1979 p XI.
162. Nietzsche (1974) pp 137-8 and citing Nisetich (1980) p 73.
163. Tacitus 11.13 for Claudius' comment on the alphabet. He is often referred to as the 'Clod' thanks to Seneca's work best known today (thanks to Cassius Dio) as the *Apocolocyntosis*, a satire of Claudius' last days and his death attributed to Seneca; full discussion in chapter titled *Comets, Colophons and Curtius Rufus*.
164. See discussion on the Apelles portraits in Stewart (1993) p 27. Pliny preserved much of what we know about Apelles and his paintings, for example at 35.86-92 for his payment by Alexander; also Plutarch 4.3-4. For the claim that Alexander allowed none other to paint him Cicero *Ad Familiares* 15.12.7, Horace *Epistles* 2.1.239, Pliny 7.125, Valerius Maximus 8.11 ext. 2.
165. Pliny 13.74-82 and Casson (2001) p 111 for Claudius' works and recitals. According to Suetonius *Claudius* 42.2, Claudius wrote a history of the Etruscans in twenty books.
166. Discussed in Grant (1979) p IX.
167. Quoting from the Preface to Ranke's *Geschichte der romanischen und germanischen Völker von 1494 bis 1514*, 1824.
168. Suetonius is rumoured to have had an affair with Vibia Sabina, then married to Hadrian, according to the *Historia Augusta* 11.3. Suetonius was dismissed from office for it. This may be rumour and he may have simply been disrespectful, for we would have expected harsher treatment if true.
169. The earlier model being in the form of JF Bielfeld *The elements of Universal erudition, Containing an Analytical Abridgement of the Science, Polite Arts and Belles Lettres*, Vol. III, Published by J Robson, London, 1770.
170. Quoting Cruttwell (1877) p 7.
171. Quoting Teuffel-Schwabe (1892) pp 4-5.
172. Discussed by Momigliano (1954) p 27.
173. Hammond (1993) p 154.
174. Hammond (1993) p 190 and Pearson (1960) p 213.
175. Syme (1987) pp 111-114 and discussed by Baynham (1999) p 201. The *Metz Epitome* dating discussed in Bosworth-Baynham (2000) p 65; Baynham (1995) pp 63-65. *Testudo* also appeared in the *Metz Epitome* although the text is corrupt. However Wagner suggested the reference to the king's tunic employs a phrase rarely used in Latin and argues for a Hellenic original; for discussion see p 65. For the unique citations of the *Metz Epitome* see Heckel-Yardley (2004).
176. Curtius used *testudo* at 5.3.9 and implied its formation again at 5.3.21 and 7.9.3.
177. Xenophon *Hellenika* 3.1.7.
178. Wheeler (1902); Mahaffy (1888) and quoting Goralski (1989) p 83 on Rooke.
179. Discussed in Shipley (1903) pp 1-25.
180. Following Shipley (1903) pp 7-8.
181. Following the observation by Momigliano (1966) p 139 and quoting Momigliano (1966) p 134; and for Stephanus pp 139-140.
182. Valla's translation of Thucydides Preface 4. Valla was quoting Cicero *De Oratore* 9.30.
183. Valla's translation of Thucydides Preface 9.
184. Discussed in Shipley (1903) pp 1-25.
185. Full detail of Symmachus in Hedrick (2000) pp 181-182; for detail of the later recensions see Foster (1874) p 32. For details of the *Nichamachean* recensions see Hall (1913) pp 246-247 and Kraus (1994). The new copy bore the subscription *Victorianus emendabam dominis Symmachis* ('I Victorianus emended (this) by the authority of Symmachus'), thus anticipating the useful colophons, the publication and production notes, of the Middle Ages.
186. Discussed in Gregory (1886) pp 27-32.
187. Horace *Ars Poetica*.
188. Niebuhr seems to have appreciated the role of the common people after his term of residence in England. The *Römische Geschichte* was first published between 1827 and 1828. Also Grafton (1990) p 69 for comment on Niebuhr and Livy.
189. Quoting Niebuhr (1844) p 38 who proposed scribes refused to copy the later books of a by then 'old and loquacious' Livy.
190. For the description of Livy see Macaulay (1828). Livy 31 for the scale of the task before him.
191. A dittography is a scribal error in which a letter, syllable or word is accidentally repeated in the text; a haplography is an error where a word, syllable or letter is written just once instead of twice, a parablepsy is an error resulting from a distraction to the eye which causes an omission in the text.
192. Plutarch *Demosthenes* 14.4.

193. Discussion in Cook (2000) pp 537-547.
194. Discussion of Demosthenes' spuriously assigned speeches in Worthington (2000) p 1.
195. The debate is discussed in Schamp (2000) p 232.
196. Photius *Myriobiblion* Introduction.
197. Photius ran a reading circle at which summaries of histories were read; discussed by JR Morgan in Gill-Wiseman (1993) p 194.
198. Many of the Greek city-states used different names for the calendar months. Caesar abolished the lunar year and intercalary month, reverting to a solar year. Diodorus tried to synchronise the archon changes in Athens with the campaign years during the Successor Wars, causing as much as six months' slippage along the way. Discussion and citations for Caesar in Hannah (2005) p 98. Also discussed in more detail in chapter titled *The Silent Siegecraft of the Pamphleteers.*
199. Digory Whear *On the Plan and Method of Reading Histories* 1623.
200. Translation from JF Healy, *Pliny the Elder on Science and Technology*, Oxford University Press, 1999, Preface p VIII.
201. Taken from PG Naiditch and R Resinski *Philodemus and Greek Papyri: an exhibition 1 April-31 August 1994*, UCLA, University Research Library, Dept. of Special Collections, April 1994. This was read in a review of 1847, some eleven years after Gell had died. The Caliph Omar of Damascus is one of the suspects for the burning of the Library at Alexandria. Its actual fate is unconfirmed.
202. Following Bishop (1983) p 360 and p 366.
203. Aristotle's work is thought to be preserved through his lecture notes. The current organisation into treatises and sequences was certainly not his. Diogenes Laertius *Aristotle* 12 for the calculation of lines. For Demetrius of Phalerum see Reeve (2001) Introduction p 15; Diogenes Laertius *Demetrius* for detail of his output.
204. Diogenes Laertius *Plato* 55-61 mentioned Thrasyllus' collection and identifications. Well discussed in Gibson (1998).
205. Pliny preface 24.
206. Cicero *Ad Quintum,* fr 2.11.4 The full citation is *'paene pusillus Thucydides'* or 'almost a miniature Thucydides'.
207. Flower (1994) Introduction p 1. Diodorus 16.3.8 for the loss of five of Theopompus' books.
208. Diogenes Laertius *Diogenes* 24.
209. Plutarch *Nicias* 29.
210. Full discussion in Balme (2001).
211. Discussed in Gudeman *Greeks* (1894) p 72.
212. Discussed in Gudeman *Romans* (1894) p 161. Aulus Gellius on the other hand suggested there had been another comedian named Plautios and hence the confusion.
213. Details in Gudeman *Romans* (1894) p 159.
214. Herodotus 4.42 reads: 'For Libya shows clearly that it is bounded by the sea, except where it borders on Asia. Necho king of Egypt first discovered this and made it known. When he had finished digging the canal which leads from the Nile to the Arabian Gulf, he sent Phoenicians in ships, instructing them to sail on their return voyage past the Pillars of Heracles until they came into the northern sea and so to Egypt. So the Phoenicians set out from the Red Sea and sailed the southern sea; whenever autumn came they would put in and plant the land in whatever part of Libya they had reached, and there await the harvest; then, having gathered the crop, they sailed on, so that after two years had passed, it was in the third that they rounded the Pillars of Heracles and came to Egypt. There they said (what some may believe, though I do not) that in sailing around Libya they had the sun on their right hand.'
215. *Almagest* derived from the Arab superlative *megiste* preceded by 'al'.
216. Cleanthes' denunciation of Aristarchus was recorded in Plutarch's *Concerning the Face that Appears in the Orb of the Moon* 922F while Aristarchus' proposal of an axial spinning earth about the ecliptic was provided in the same text at 922F-923A. Diogenes Laertius *Cleanthes* additionally recorded that Cleanthes wrote a treatise named *Against Aristarchus*, a work in which presumably the denunciation sat.
217. See discussion in Pownall (2004).
218. Greek heliocentric theory discussed in Teresi (2002) p 130 and Heath (1913) pp 301-311. The view that ancient Greek astronomers and philosophers were ignorant of heliocentrism and adhered to a geocentric view is challenged in I Liritzis (2008) *Ancient Greek Heliocentric Views Hidden from Prevailing Beliefs?, Journal of Astronomical History and Heritage* 11 (1), pp 39-49.
219. St. Augustine *Confessions* book 8.7.17.
220. St Augustine *Of the Falseness of the History Which Allots Many Thousand Years to the World's Past,* from *The City of God* Book 12.10.
221. Discussed in JF Healy *Pliny the Elder on Science and Technology*, Oxford University Press, 1999.
222. PG Naiditch and R Resinski *Philodemus and Greek Papyri,* UCLA University Research Department, Exhibition Catalogue, 1994, quoting Sir William Gell.

223. Quoting Deane (1918) p 41 for 'antiquarian sentiment'.

224. Momigliano (1977) p 79 ff for discussion of Pausanias' reintroduction into Europe.

225. Casson (2001) p 57. For Aristotle's prejudice evidenced in the *Constitution of the Athenians* see Grant (1995) p 125.

226. A point made by Flower (1994) p 42. The 'Attic Bee' quote is from Digory Whear's historical treatise in 1623, a term previously used for Sophocles: see Athenaeus 13.598c. Barnes (2000) p 12; see discussion of the Oxyrhynchus historian in Warner (1966) pp 16-17 and Shrimpton (1991), Introduction, p XVIII. Warner (1966) p 30 for the suggestion that Cratippus may be the author. The historians appear to criticise Thucydides' use of speeches as part of the narrative; Sacks (1990) p 94 for Cratippus' opinion, from Dionysius of Halicarnassus *On Thucydides* 16.349. As the work appears to be a continuation of Thucydides' account (410 BCE onwards) a link is further established.

227. See further discussion of the finds at Oxyrhynchus in Green (2007) pp xxxiv-xxxv.

228. Discussed in Higbie (2003).

229. Pseudo-Plutarch *Lycurgus* 841f. Highet (1949) for the surviving plays.

230. They are listed by Dosson in his *Etude sur Quinte Curce*, 1887, pp 315-356.

231. McKitrerick (2004) p 28. Also a comprehensive summary of the Curtian manuscripts given in Curtius' *History of Alexander*, Loeb Classical Library edition, 1971 reprint, Introduction pp IX-XIV, translation by JC Rolfe.

232. J Mutzell had already published an influential well-informed edition in 1842 in Berlin in two volumes; discussed in Timpanaro-Most (2005) p 53. The two traditions was a distinction first made by Nikolaas Heinsius, the Dutch philologist and son of Daniel Heinsius, Joseph Scaliger's pupil.

233. Following Baynham (1998) p 37.

234. Discussed in Atkinson (1997) pp 3448-3449; also Curtius' *History of Alexander*, Loeb Classical Library edition, 1971 reprint, Introduction pp IX-XIV, translation by JC Rolfe.

235. Following discussions in Baynham (1998) pp 4-5, Berzunza (1941) p 133 and Curtius' *History of Alexander*, Loeb Classical Library edition, 1971, Introduction pp XXXII-XXXIII.

236. Quoting Higbie (2003) p 222.

237. Following Berzunza (1941) p 133.

238. 'Anonymous fluidity' taken from Townsend (1996) introduction p 23.

239. Full discussion of the supplements in Curtius and the associated MSS can be found in Smits (1987) pp 89-124.

240. Details in Smits (1987) p 90. The 1946 Loeb Classical Library edition of Curtius still houses Freinsheim's added text. The comment on Freinsheim's efforts preserved in the preface by WH Crosby in the 1854 Cellarius edition.

241. John Dryden *Preface Concerning Ovid's Epistles* 16

242. Ovid *Metamorphoses*, Epilogue, lines 871-874.

243. 'The *Iliad*'s wife' as proposed by Samuel Butler, see Fitzgerald (1998) p ix for discussion.

244. Highet (1949) pp 114-115 for the various *Iliad* translations.

245. Bentley's comment appeared in Samuel Johnson's *The works of the poets of Great Britain and Ireland* (1804) p 568.

246. This tradition was discounted by Timaeus (but upheld by Diodorus; see Diodorus 13.90.4-7 in which he attacked Timaeus' account).

247. Lucian *Phalaris*.

248. For Phalaris' cruelty see Pindar *Pythian* 1.96-98.

249. The definitive work on the *Epistles* was R Bentley's *Dissertation upon the epistles of Phalaris*, 1697, collected in *Works of Richard Bentley*, Dyce (1836) v.1-2. It included dissertations upon the epistles of Themistocles, Socrates and Euripides. Full discussion of the 'battle of the books' in Lynch (1998). Highet (1949) p 285 for Bentley's parallel exposures.

250. Discussed in Highet (1949) pp 285-286; see chapter titled *Spear-Won History: the Fable Agreed On* for the *Battle of the Books*.

251. *The Miscellaneous Prose Works of Sir Walter Scott*, 1848 Volume 1, *Life of John Dryden* p 318.

252. Following the observation of DS Carne-Ross in Fitzgerald (1998) pp lxi-lxiii on poetic structure.

253. Quoting Shelmerdine (1995) Preface iii. Highet (1949) p 200 for the loss of lyric poetry.

254. J Dryden *Preface Concerning Ovid's Epistles*, 1683 text, sections 12 and 19.

255. The comment on Bardon's edition came from WS Watt and is discussed in JE Atkinson's commentary p 23 on Curtius in *A Commentary on Q. Curtius Rufus' Historiae Alexandri Magni, Books 5 to 7, 2*, Acta Classica, Supplementum 1.

256. Grant (1956) p 25.

257. Quoting Wolfgang Schwadewaldt in the *Bryn Mawr Classical Review*, June 2010, review of Mindt N (2008) *Manfred Fuhrmann als Vermittler der Antike: ein Beitrag zu Theorie und Praxis des Ubersetzens*, Transformationen der Antike, Bd5, Berlin, New York.

258. Discussed in detail by Pitcher (2009) chapters 1 and 2.
259. Modern opinion credits Mikhaēl III (842-867) and the family councilor Theoctistus with the reforms that heralded in the 'Macedonian Renaissance', a name coined in the title of a book by K Weitzmann in 1948. For the various traditions relating to Basils I's roots see discussion in Tobias (2007). For the 'Third Sophistic' see Pernot (2000) p 206.
260. Quoting from the *Bryn Mawr Classical Review* June 2010 and its review of Mindt N (2008) *Manfred Fuhrmann als Vermittler der Antike: ein Beitrag zu Theorie und Praxis des Übersetzens.* Transformationen der Antike, Bd5, Berlin, New York.
261. Ovid alluded to many humorous comparisons that would be immediately identifiable to his audience in Rome, but which require additional explanation today to avoid them being taken literally and the wit overlooked. Discussion in Raeburn-Feeney (2004) translator's note xli. Lucian engaged in satiric dialogue, often turning facts on their head for humour. None of his works dated back earlier than the 9th century manuscripts. For a full list of the manuscripts see the commentary by AM Harmon to the 1913 Loeb Classical Library edition of *The Works of Lucian.*
262. Quoting M Wood from Gill-Wiseman (1993) Prologue xiii.
263. Cicero *De finibus honorum et malorum* 3.74; discussed in Long (1986) p 107.
264. Weill (1980) pp 158-159. The lack of vowels was particular to early Semitic languages.
265. More on the so-called last plans in chapter titled *Babylon: the Cipher and Rosetta Stone.*
266. See discussion in Shipley (2000) p 40. Quoting Atkinson (2009) p 146 for an alternative transmission into *Kalistei*, a pun on the message on the Apple of Discord from Homer, for Justin 12.15.11 suggested Alexander was tossing his men the Apple of Discord. Diodorus 17.117.4 and Arrian 7.26.3 for *kratistos*: 'the strongest or noblest'. Latin interpretation of that from Curtius 10.4.5 *qui esset optimus* (the 'best') and *dignissimus* (broadly the 'most worthy') from Justin 12.15.
267. Detail from Atherton (1993) p 298.

13

COMETS, COLOPHONS AND CURTIUS RUFUS

Who was the Roman historian, Curtius, and could his conspicuous dismissal of Alexander's Will have been self-interested and politically motivated?

Although we are heavily reliant upon Curtius' texts for our knowledge of the events at Babylon in the days following Alexander's death, his identity remains a mystery. Whilst both he and Diodorus knew of a tradition that linked the distribution of the empire to Alexander's Will, it was Curtius who uniquely went to the trouble of denying it was so.

Why? And what would he have gained from stating that, writing as he was some centuries later? Who *was* the Roman author, Curtius, when did he write, and what political and imperial pressures were influencing the direction of his account?

'Nothing is known about Quintus Curtius Rufus. To us he is only a name at the head of the book *De gestis Alexandri Magni*: he is never mentioned anywhere, and no other writing of his is known or even referred to: possibly the name was not even the author's real name. He presents a mass of problems, and the first is, why his book was ever written.'[1]

WW Tarn *Alexander The Great, Volume II, Sources and Studies*

'There is an unwritten law that the volume of scholarship on a subject is in inverse proportion to the evidence available', so wrote Brian Bosworth in his opening of a review of the elusive '*Quellenforscher*'s phantom', Cleitarchus.[2] The observation holds true for the *identity* of Curtius Rufus, for Tarn's chapter-heading remark – 'we know nothing for sure about Curtius' – is accurate and remarkable when considering the extent of his influence to the history of Alexander. Curtius' book is an extremely detailed monograph and it remains the richest account of events at Babylon surrounding Alexander's death. So it is equally vexing that '… no ancient reference is known to the *Historiae Alexandri Magni Macedonis,* or to a Q Curtius Rufus as the author of such a work.'[3] If he is not quite as obscure as the 'Pseudo-Callisthenes' of the *Greek Alexander Romance*, or even 'Suda' (or Suidas) as an individual compiler of the otherwise anonymous Byzantine lexicon, we may nevertheless have been sidetracked once more on identity.

'Lost historians' from the Hellenistic Age and the Silver Age of Roman literature are, paradoxically, not difficult to find, and they left legacies. Although little or nothing remains of their own works, fragments often proliferated later accounts, usually with a commentary on their style, whether laudatory, or more commonly, derogatory. The most relevant example is of course Cleitarchus, Curtius' principal (so convention has it), but not exclusive, source and about whom little is known.[4] Nevertheless, he was sufficiently influential in Rome for Strabo, Quintilian, Cicero, Athenaeus and Aelian to reference him directly. Curtius, on the other hand, represents a 'found historian' as far as his text (but not identity) with a lost literary past. The intrigue has inspired forensic attempts to salvage him from that anonymity, analyse his style and method, contemplate his other sources, and assess how influential he might have been to other writers of the day; and finally to ponder what day that might have been.

The identification of his full name as 'Quintus Curtius Rufus' appears one of a later age (in Hedicke's 1867 edition, for example), for the *praenomen* 'Quintus' did not appear against the title of the earliest extant manuscripts, but in the colophons, the copyist's endnotes. These were generally written in the first person and usually included the copyist's name, the title of the work, the date and place of the transcription and the patron ordering the edition. Amongst the five most intact texts, manuscript 'V' *also* omitted

'Quintus', leaving us with simply 'Curtius Rufus'. Alongside this dubiety, we cannot say the name of his book with any certainty.

The 123 surviving manuscripts are variously titled, including *Historiae, Historiae Magni Macedonis Alexandri* or *Historiae Alexandri Magni Macedonis*, with older scripts including *De rebus gestis Alexandri Magni libri* and *Cvrti Rvfi de rebvs ab Alexandro magno gestis*.[5] If this suggests a lack of clarity on the name from an early date, we should recall that Arrian's *Anabasis* and Livy's *Ab urbe condita libri* are as fluidly rendered in translations today.[6]

Titular uncertainty is not unique; somewhat relevant to arguments on Curtius' identity is an attribution made by Cassius Dio to what *he* termed the *Apocolocyntosis,* a play on the word 'apotheosis' in a 'pungent satire' at Claudius' expense, and it is attributed to Seneca who had been banished by Claudius to Corsica between 41 CE and 49 CE. The title suggests the deification of a 'pumpkin-head', though extant texts don't support that,[7] and surviving anonymous manuscripts are variously titled *Ludus de morte Divi Claudii,* the *Play on the death of Divine Claudius*, and *Divi Claudii Apotheosis per saturum* or *Satira de Claudio Caesare,* though nothing in the text alluded to the better-known title we use today. In fact, its connection to Seneca is even questioned: 'It is impossible to prove that it is his, and impossible to prove that it is not.'[8] His nephew, Lucan, wrote an account of civil war between Julius Caesar and Pompey, *De Bello civili,* and that is now better known as *Pharsalia.* But vexing as titles are, the greatest challenge with the Alexander monograph is to identify Curtius himself, for this might impact our debate on the Will that he so vocally assaulted (T11).

A 1695 second printed edition of Curtius' book by Christopher Cellarius titled *De rebus Alexandri Magni Rebus Historia Superstes.* The edition was subtitled with *Recensuit, etiam Supplemetis, Commentariis, Indicibus & Tabulis Geographicisbisque omnibus novis illustravit Christopher Cellarius.* Printed in 609 pages by Friederick Gleditsch, Leipzig. Author's collection.

THE POSSIBLE ROMAN *IGNOTUS*

The vigorous century-and-a-half-old debate on the dating and identification of the Roman *ignotus* remains vigorously inconclusive.[9] Although the subject matter has become 'a fine field for critical and uncritical revelry', it is generally agreed that the language and style of Curtius' prose places him in the first three centuries of the Roman Empire.[10] Studies have variously promoted publication dates as early as Augustus (ruled 27 BCE-14 CE) and as late as Constantine (emperor 306-337 CE) whilst more recent opinions incline to Claudius (emperor 41-54 CE) and Vespasian (emperor 69-79 CE).[11]

A superficially attractive identification is the senator named Curtius Rufus referred to by Pliny in his *Epistles* and by Tacitus in his *Annals*, in which case the biography of Alexander must have been published sometime between 31 CE and 53 CE, potentially in Claudius' term.[12] This Curtius had been a suffect consul under Claudius, holding a quaestorship (supervising public affairs, finances, army and officers), and then a senator and attaining a praetorship (magistracy, or in times of war, a military command) under Tiberius who appears to have described him as a 'self-made' man, well-meaning or otherwise.[13]

After administrating Germania Superior, the aforementioned Curtius Rufus made it to the prestigious governorship of Africa around year 53 CE when apparently in old age. He died shortly after, possibly early in the emperorship of Nero. Could this be our man? He *might* have been the rhetorician Q Curtius Rufus referred to by Suetonius in the index to his *De Grammaticis et Rhetoribus,* and if so, it reconciles that career path with a later senatorial post.[14] If the list of rhetors is arranged in chronological order, a Claudian dating does work. Rhetoric was a necessary device on the Roman *cursus honorum* on the road from tribune to consul, as Suetonius himself made imminently clear, and as Cicero had so eloquently proven. Yet, like the various individuals proposed as authors of the anonymous *Pamphlet*, neither identification fits the Alexander historian sufficiently well.[15]

By Augustus' day a senatorial career demanded upwards of one million *sestertii*, and despite the fact that the currency had been demoted from silver to a large brass coin, this was still a fortune, and it restricted who could aspire to the path.[16] Augustus had fixed the sestertius value at 1/100th of an aureus, which, at (broadly) current gold prices (the aureus was almost pure twenty-four carat gold) values a million *sestertii* at over 3,500,000 US dollars.[17] Later emperors melted down the 'old' sestertius to reissue the coins by then debased with bronze and lead, inevitably with an inflationary impact. The true magnitude of the financial requirement for such a political career becomes apparent when compared to the salary of a

1st century Roman legionary: around 900 *sestertii* per annum, half of which would have been deducted at source for maintenance and equipment. The low interest and interest-free loans we see provided by Brutus, Crassus and Caesar (800,000 *sestertii* to Cicero, for example) illustrate the requisite political alliances behind such funding, though other loans could be procured more expensively (and potentially without political strings) from *faeneratores*, professional moneylenders.[18]

The rubric for establishing *termini post quem* and *anti quem* for Curtius' publication has been to analyse references within his *basilikos logos*, the imperial encomium, that sits conspicuously in his final chapter in the midst of his narrative of infighting and settlement at Babylon; within it he referred to an unnamed *princeps* who may well have been identified at the beginning of Curtius' first book (books one and two have been lost) along with a preface and potentially a self-identification, all of which would have dovetailed neatly with the panegyric to the emperor. Tacitus, for example, identified himself in the opening of his book with a clear date reference (by naming the current consuls), and Pliny identified his *princeps*, Titus the son of Vespasian, with: 'This treatise, *Natural History*, a novel work in Roman literature, which I have just completed, I have taken the liberty to dedicate to you, most gracious Emperor…'[19] Pliny went on to further praise Titus (he termed him 'friend') and Vespasian as well as their respective patronage of the arts. His entry ended with a rundown of his methodology containing a list of his sources, the latter a unique acknowledgement, as he himself observed.[20]

Curtius did, however, make contemporary references to the powerful Parthian Empire. But this, along with the encomium, only acknowledges that his work was written between 27 BCE – when a *princeps* first appeared (when Octavian became 'Augustus') – and 224 CE – when the latter ended (with the fall of the Arsacid Parthian Empire, after which the Sassanids ascended) – though if Bruère's theory is correct and Silius Italicus (died ca. 101) knew of Curtius' work and drew inspiration from it for his *Punica*, then that corridor is narrowed significantly.[21]

Additional dating clues come from Curtius' references to the Phoenician city of Tyre, described as enjoying 'tranquillity under the merciful protection of Rome', and from the terminology he used to describe military units.[22] But these and the references to archers and archery, and to the *cataphracti* (heavy-mailed cavalry) all remain inconclusively dissected, as does the allusion to a 'civil war' that appears to have been averted by the emperor being eulogised.[23] But deeper textual themes of the Roman political arena permeated Curtius' work too, as does a linguistic style that displays notable similarities to the historians of the Gold and Silver Latin ages, as scholars have noted. This in itself isn't helpful, as establishing who emulated who, and whether they were influenced through an intermediary, remains problematic.

The Julio-Claudian age – the strongest contender for the publication date – arrived with additional historiographical challenges: 'The gradual concentration of political power within a smaller and smaller group, together with the secrecy and mystery which resulted, could not but affect the task of recording Roman history.'[24] If those holding the stylus were from privileged backgrounds, then the opening of Tacitus' *Annals* captured a dilemma that began with Augustus:

> Many historians… dealing with the Republic they have written with equal eloquence and freedom. But after the battle of Actium, when the interests of peace required that all power should be concentrated in the hands of one man, writers of like ability disappeared; and at the same time historical truth was impaired in many ways: first, because men were ignorant of politics as being not any concern of theirs; later, because of their passionate desire to flatter; or again, because of their hatred of their masters. So between the hostility of the one class and the servility of the other, posterity was disregarded.[25]

Tacitus added: 'Opposition there was none: the boldest spirits had succumbed on stricken fields or by proscription-lists while the rest of the nobility found a cheerful acceptance of slavery the smoothest road to wealth and office…'[26] This looks like a template for Plutarch's later polemic and for Cassius Dio's after him.[27] But setting out one's virtuous stall, as Tacitus did, and sitting on it, as Tacitus did not always, are different matters.[28]

An independent literary spirit was not impossible under the Julio-Claudians, as evidenced by the accounts of Aulus Cremutius Cordus under Tiberius, and Aufidius Bassus under Claudius, but imperial criticism was dangerous and more often than not it was fatal.[29] Lucan, once a favourite of Nero, published the benign first three books of his *De Bello civili* without initial repercussions, though his (now lost) *laudes Neronis*, read out at the first Greek-styled celebration of the quinquennial Neronia of 60 CE (with contests of music, gymnastics and riding), had clearly helped, for Lucan was crowned and appointed to the city augurate soon after.

As his *De Bello civili* advanced, however, the poem, influenced by Livy's republican nostalgia, increasingly appeared to attack the tyrannical excesses of his emperor, and this, alongside Lucan's brazenly vocalised critiques, saw the young prodigy dead at twenty-five in the wake of the Pisonian plot that was exposed in April 65 CE. Another example of the imperial danger was Claudius' early literary career, which had been cut short for being too critical of *his* emperor, Augustus; when he resumed his writing, now himself holding an imperial pen, he avoided the Triumvirate Wars altogether in which Octavian had risen to power.[30]

If Curtius was, indeed, aboard the *cursus honorum* then the expediency of his imperial sycophancy, a typical and frequent Roman *laudatio*, becomes clear: it was a simple necessity for survival, if not the genuine admiration of an emperor. Curtius' encomium has been dissected in the same way as the autopsies of Calpurnius Siculus' first *Eclogue*, and similar conclusions which link it to Nero's emperorship can possibly be drawn.[31] Positioned within the chaos of Macedonian 'civil war' that was manifesting itself at Babylon following Alexander's death, and set against a background of Curtius' 'contemplation of the public happiness' of his *own* day, his panegyric to an unnamed 'saviour' took the following form:

> But already by the Fates civil wars were being forced upon the Macedonian nation; for royal power desires no associate and was being sought by many. First therefore they brought their forces into collision, then separated them; and when they had weighted the body with more than it could carry, the limbs also began to give out, and an empire that might have endured under one man fell in ruins while it was being upheld by many. Therefore the Roman people rightly and deservedly, asserts that it owes its safety to its prince, who in the night which was almost our last shone forth like a new star. The rising of this star, by Heaven! rather than that of the sun, restored light to the world in darkness, since lacking their head the limbs were thrown into disorder. How many firebrands did it extinguish! How many swords did it sheath! How great a tempest did it dispel with sudden prosperity! Therefore our empire not only lives afresh but even flourishes. Provided that only the divine jealousy be absent, the posterity of that same house will continue the good times of this our age, it is to be hoped forever, at any rate for very many years.[32]

'OF COMETS OR BLAZING STARS, AND CELESTIAL PRODIGIES, THEIR NATURE, SITUATION, AND DIVERSE SORTS.'[33]

Curtius' laudation of his emperor, though it was typically thematic of the day and well exampled by Ovid's *Apotheosis of Julius Caesar*, which framed Augustus as a demi-god, contains some noteworthy pointers.[34] He compared his Emperor's arrival to a *novum sidus*, a 'new star', and one that shone in the night.[35] The 'star' seems to have become a frequent *topos* in panegyrics of the Julio-Claudian dynasty and one possibly continued through to Vespasian; in his *Satires*, Horace suggested its continued use was even being mocked.[36] It was a term of endearment apparently used at Caligula's accession, again by Seneca to describe Claudius in 43 CE, and Pliny the Younger used the symbolism for the dynasty of Trajan.[37] Lucan's *De Bello civili* described Alexander as an 'evil star of humanity' that brought disaster to mankind, where Curtius himself referred to Alexander as 'a star of Macedonia', with similar phraseology appearing in Livy and

Virgil.[38] More strikingly, Tacitus attached the motif (here 'ill-starred') to the final consulate of Galba (3 BCE-69 CE).[39]

If references to a *sidus* were a rhetorical commonplace, we might wish to take the stellar observation more literally and less metaphorically in the case of Curtius' encomium, for its luminous attachment to 'shining in a darkened world' suggests a further specificity. The same could be said of the reference to the 'putting-out of torches'. What could they be?

The classical world maintained a fascination with the night sky; it was viewed with an awe evoked by the scientifically unexplained and by prevailing superstitions, moreover, the celestial clarity from a lack of light pollution and emissions only enhanced the spectacle. The wonder and dread of moving stars (Greek, *planetai*, 'wanderers'), the Milky Way (from the Greek *galaxias kyklos*, milky circle) and a comet in particular (*kometes* in Greek, *crinitas* in Latin, a 'hairy' star) is well recorded; the astronomical theories of Pythagoras, Anaxagoras and Democritus had been well summarised in Aristotle's *Meteorologika*. Rome was equally curious about the phenomena as evidenced by Seneca's *De Cometis* in his *Quaestiones Naturales*, and by Pliny's frequent references in book two of his *Naturalis Historia*.[40] The most portentous celestial episode of all took place in Constantine's rule in the twilight of the Roman Empire, when, according to Eusebius, in the year 312 CE 'a most marvellous sign appeared to him from heaven'; it was a sighting by the emperor and his army that might have redirected the religious doctrine of the empire.[41]

Here, in Curtius' eulogy, *novum sidus* and dark nights could be references to comets and eclipses, for they satisfy both. Linking the 'new star' to a comet has already been pondered and such arguments pointed to, as one example, the *birth* of Alexander Severus.[42] However, it seems the attachment has not been fully exploited. If a clearly developed encomiastic device, *novum sidus* is conspicuous in its attachment to emperors whose imperial *tenancy* was linked to stars rising and to comets as well as eclipses; the appearance of the latter was considered biographically portentous, usually as a harbinger of death and to the end of an administration,[43] so they were often exploited by the successor.

Pertinent to the era under scrutiny, a comet appeared shortly after Julius Caesar's death in 44 BCE, and Virgil claimed in the first book of his *Georgica* when referring to Caesar's assassination and civil war: 'Never fell more lightening from a cloudless sky; never was comet's alarming glare so often seen.'[44] That cataclysmic scene begged a salvation by Augustus, to whom he dedicated a prayer early in the chapter and possibly more relevant still, both Suetonius and Cassius Dio reported a comet sighting four months prior to Claudius' death in 54 CE, thus heralding in Nero's imperium; as Suetonius described it, 'the principal omens of his death were the following: the rise of a longhaired star, commonly called a comet...'[45]

Seneca, Calpurnius Siculus and Tacitus mentioned a further comet which 'blazed into view' in 60 CE and it was visible for a full six months, with the latter historian commenting on its portent: 'The general belief is that a comet means a change of emperor. So people speculated on Nero's successor as though Nero were already dethroned', though in this case they were to be some eight years out (Nero died in 68 CE).[46] Another was seen in late 64 CE, the year of the great fire in Rome, and it was visible from July to September, with Tacitus commenting that it was 'a phenomenon to which Nero always made atonement in noble blood', for the emperor massacred selected nobility to appease the obviously angry gods.[47]

Suetonius recorded the presence of a comet, possibly Halley's in 66 CE (visible in January), and another graced the Jerusalem night and might have preceding the capture of the historian Josephus following the battle and siege at Jotapata.[48] A brilliant comet was visible for forty days in 72 CE, the year that followed Vespasian's accession, and a further sighting occurred in 73 CE, the year he expelled philosophers from Rome. One followed in 75 CE when Vespasian made a dedication to peace at the temple in which he housed the works of art he had dubiously amassed during his term.[49] And in 79 CE Vespasian is recorded as having declared, 'the "hairy star" is an omen not for me, but for the Parthian king, for he had long hair where I am bald'; portents are littered across Suetonius' biography of Vespasian.[50]

Solar eclipses carried similar predictive gloom, and with them came a verifiably 'darkened world'; it could cause panic in the ranks as it did with Darius III's troops at Gaugamela, when it provoked Sulpicius Galus to explain the phenomenon to the shaken Roman army amassed against the Macedonians at Pydna in 168 BCE.[51] So an eclipse potentially brought Curtius' 'last night' with it. According to Pliny, himself an ambitious politician who became a procurator,[52] a protracted eclipse also occurred shortly after Julius Caesar's death in 44 BCE, though modern calculations suggest none was visible from Europe until 49 CE; this has led some scholars to question the whole chronology of the Julio-Claudian era. A further solar eclipse was described by Cassius Dio as one of the portents of Augustus' death, though this cannot be substantiated by modern calculations either.

Cassius Dio further recorded a partial eclipse of the sun in 26 CE and a further event in Claudius' rule prompting the emperor to enquire of his astronomers the date of the next occurrence. It actually coincided with his birthday on August 1st (45 CE), and to forestall panic, Claudius issued a proclamation detailing the time and duration of the darkness, with a full scientific, though non-heliocentric, explanation.[53] Dio detailed a lunar eclipse that accompanied a comet before Vitellius' short emperorship in 69 CE.

Although two lunar eclipses would have been visible from Rome on April 25th and October 18th, modern reckoning dates the unusual *double-event* (eclipse and comet) to the summer of 54 CE, and once again this broadly coincided with the death of Claudius and the beginning of Nero's term. It has been further speculated, in the case of Curtius' encomium, that the use of *caliganti*, 'darkened', was a deliberate pun on 'Caligula' (alternatively Gaius) whose rule had ended in 41 CE, still recent enough to have the desired literary effect by a writer who might have published in the colourful imperium of Nero.[54]

So does Curtius' dual reference to 'new star' and 'darkened world' give us a more specific date? We should appreciate that encomia of this nature were two-dimensional at best, here relating to the breadth of an emperor's achievement and the 'height' of their exulted standing. We can hardly expect the author to embody any literal 'length' – the more useful chronological dimension – within a few lines. Thus, civil war, dark nights, peace and prosperity were rolled into a single paragraph in which a decade of colour might be compressed to a sycophancy as brief as a Spartan witticism. So where does this leave us?

EXITUS ILLUSTRIUM VIRORUM: ARGUMENTS FOR PUBLICATION UNDER NERO

> And in our own age, about the time when Claudius Caesar was poisoned and left the Empire to Domitius Nero, and afterwards, while the latter was Emperor, there was one [comet] which was almost constantly seen and was very frightful…[55]

Modern calculations confirm a comet would, indeed, have been visible at the accession of Nero in autumn 54 CE (Nero succeeded Claudius on October 13th); both Suetonius and Cassius Dio recorded the noteworthy sighting that 'lasted for a long time' and Pliny termed it 'frightful'.[56] Tacitus mentioned two further comets ('omens of impending misfortune') and a lacuna in the *Annals* would surely have included the Halley's Comet sighting in January 66 CE.[57] No one became more firmly associated with the night sky, stars, the sun god Apollo, and Helios the Charioteer streaking across the firmament, than Nero, in what has been termed his 'solar monarchy'.[58] And nowhere is this more evident than in the aforementioned *Apocolocyntosis* that eulogised him. One extract reads:

> He brings glad days, to muted law a tongue,
> As the Morning Star, setting the stars to flight,
> As the shining sun, when his chariot moves first from the line,
> So Caesar comes, so Nero appears to Rome,
> His bright face glowing with gentle radiance,
> His neck all beauty under his flowing hair.[59]

Comparisons with elements of Curtius' laudation are unavoidable despite varied liberal translations. The dawn of Nero heralded in an imperium that required new obeisance, for the dangerous *scaenici imperatoris*, the 'actor-emperor', managed thirteen years and eight months in the purple *trabea* despite his bankrupting the empire.[60] As Erasmus later noted, Dawn is a friend of Muses, who, Nero believed, could not rival his own sweet voice, and it is difficult to avoid the conclusion that one encomium drew inspiration (if not parallel wording) from the other.[61] But which came first?

The issue is complicated by the suggestion that this extract from the *Apolococyntosis* was a later addition to an original draft that had been published soon after Nero's succession in 54 CE, perhaps by Seneca himself, or by an anonymous compiler writing with the hindsight of events, possibly as late as 59 CE (or 60 CE) when laudation would still have been relevant. Because in that year Nero's true colours began to emerge following the death of his mother, the universally hated Agrippina (15/16-59 CE), the great-granddaughter of Augustus who had previously manipulated her way to becoming Claudius' fourth wife.[62] It was Agrippina who had Seneca recalled from exile, for she saw the value of his educating and counselling her impressionable son.

Agrippina crowning Nero with a laurel wreath. Agrippina carries a cornucopia, the symbol of plenty, whilst Nero is outfitted as a Roman commander. The scene suggests Nero's accession of 54 CE and certainly the imagery would be invalid after he murdered Agrippina in 59 CE. Aphrodisias Museum, Turkey. Image by Carlos Delgado; CC-BY-SA.

Nero *had* distinguished himself in the first five years of his rule (thus 54-59 CE), taking an interest in civic affairs: taxes were reduced, legal fees capped, he empowered freedmen and had corrupt officials arrested. Seneca's own reference to the comet of 60 CE (six years into Nero's emperorship) was *still* accompanied by 'in the happy principate of Nero'.[63] Striking likenesses were captured on coinage by the emperor's *caelatores* (engravers) and struck at the new mint at Lugdunum (Lyons), and though much of the 'happy' spin stemmed from his obsession with popularity, Trajan appears to have later commended Nero's early years too, whilst Otho used 'Nero' as a surname to boost his appeal.[64] Dio

Chrysostom recalled the nostalgia with which the populace, especially that in the East, mourned his eventual death in 68 CE.

Seneca's poem (if it *was* Seneca's), possibly written with genuine optimism, appears elegant with a completeness that suggests a smooth original composition and not one awkwardly absorbing a forerunner's prose.[65] If that is the case, Curtius' encomium (assuming one of the texts was inspired by the other) was published after. It is notable that Curtius' description of a state with limbs lacking a head contains striking similarities to Seneca's *Of Clemency* published in 56 CE.[66] Further, as Bosworth notes, Seneca and Curtius employed identical phraseology to describe Alexander's devastation 'of peoples so remote as to be unfamiliar with even their neighbours'; this is wording that does not appear anywhere else in literature.[67]

But what of the 'extinguishing of torches'? If we are associating Curtius' encomium with the term of Nero, we arrive inevitably at 'fire'. Yet fires were common; noteworthy conflagrations destroyed parts of the city under both Titus and Trajan. Yet the Great Fire of Rome of July 64 CE was exceptional, and so was Nero's part. On the night of July 19th, while the city burned, we have the popular image of Nero playing the fiddle, an instrument that was, in fact, developed some 1,500 years later; Nero was in fact a *citharoedo principe*, a player of the cithara (lyre), and a bad one according to Vindex, his rebellious governor in Gaul.[68] And though Suetonius and Cassius Dio claimed Nero was the arsonist who sang *The Sack of Ilium* while the fire spread (thus paving the way for his new-planned city, Neropolis), Tacitus claimed Nero organised a relief effort and paid for it himself.[69] He even opened his palace grounds to shelter the homeless and followed up with stringent fire codes governing new construction.

Conflicting reports have the conflagration raging anywhere from five to nine days, despite the 7,000 city *vigiles* of the fire brigade who were armed with two-handled water pumps, a fire-suppressing vinegar mix and fire-smothering patchwork quilts. The destruction recognised no class; starting close to the Circus Maximus, the blaze spread down the Triumphal Way to the Forum, decimating the finest villas and temples as well as the vulnerable crowded slum, the Suburra.[70]

Augustus had earlier divided Rome into fourteen administrative *regiones* and after the fire of 64 CE only four remained standing.[71] If blazes were common, so were scapegoats. Members of a mysterious sect called the *Chrestiani* were burned, crucified and thrown to the dogs.[72] The religious order was not popular; some years later under Trajan, Pliny the Younger, a 'moderate man' who befriended Tacitus and employed Suetonius, conducted show trials as a public prosecutor (Tacitus held the same post) and hunted down Christians, detailing the recommended methods of torture he used to exact the 'truth'.[73] Tacitus described the contemporary view of the religious sect: Christianity was a 'most mischievous superstition' … 'coming from Judaea, the first source of the evil' and 'a class hated for its abominations'.[74]

The great fire heralded in the most ambitious civil construction project ever undertaken in the city, and one that included a financially ruinous colossus of Nero in the new Domus Aurea. Nero's immediate financial fix was to rob the temples of their votive offerings. After his death, the statue's face was modified to represent Sol Invictus, the unconquered god, and moved by the Emperor Hadrian with the help of twenty-four elephants to a new home beside the Flavian Amphitheatre which became known as the Colosseum.[75]

Curtius' encomium additionally called for the 'long life' for the 'same house', a clear reference to the emperor's line. Pertinent to his final chapter on the Macedonian king, Curtius knew from his sources how short-lived the reign of Alexander's half-brother, King Philip III (formerly Arrhidaeus), had proved to be after the settlement at Babylon in 323 BCE, and recalling the fate of Olympias and Alexander's sons soon after, he was therefore obliquely beseeching the gods for a better destiny for *his* Roman emperor.

Like Caligula and Claudius before him, Nero was of the line of the much-loved Germanicus, whose suspicious death was still greatly lamented in Rome, despite the damage Caligula had done to the reputation of the so-called Julio-Claudians.[76] Whilst Curtius' phraseology suggested a *new* line of imperial hope, it was again a general motif that heralded in each new *princeps*. Nevertheless, he would have been unlikely to pin such hopes on emperors who were disinclined, or obviously unable, to produce heirs. Excluding female issue and adopted sons, that would rule out Galba (who was in his early seventies at the close of Nero's rule) and possibly Otho too, for both were rumoured to prefer males as partners. In Otho's case that meant Nero, perhaps with a similar affiliation to Caligula before him, though we must recall that Otho had two (now dead) sons, so whilst procreation was not impossible, his short tenure as emperor makes him a rather unlikely candidate for Curtius' wording. Notably, each of the 'five good emperors', comprising the Nervan-Antonian dynasty from Trajan to Marcus Aurelius, *were* no more than adopted sons.[77]

Interestingly, this state of affairs, partly stemming from infertility, has been recently blamed on poisoning from the lead-lined aqueducts and water pipes in Rome (*plumbum*, lead, is the root of 'plumbing'), as well as from lead-II acetate that was used to sweeten wine, and from *defrutum,* a food preserving must-reduction often boiled in lead pots. Despite a warning from the Roman architect Vitruvius and from Pliny who knew the risks of *morbi metallici,* recent tests of lead isotopes from the Tiber

River confirmed huge concentrations when compared to the spring water of the region.[78]

More relevant to Curtius' dynastic hope, Nero's second wife, the 'proud whore' Poppea Sabina, was pregnant in 65 CE with their second child, that is until Nero is recorded to have kicked her to death.[79] Poppea had been previously married to Otho who subsequently became emperor himself in 69 CE for three months until he killed himself after the battle of Bedriacum at which the historian Suetonius earned his equestrian spurs. Obsessed with Poppea Sabina, Nero had taken her first as mistress and then when he became emperor, he removed Otho from Rome by appointing him governor of Lusitania, a region more or less equivalent to modern Portugal.

Tacitus suggested Poppea deserved her fate for the intrigues that led to the death of Agrippina and Nero's first wife, the childless Claudia Octavia.[80] Although Tacitus, Cassius Dio and Suetonius each recorded versions of Poppea's violent death, their accounts might be nothing more than a polemical tradition, for fatal miscarriages were not uncommon. Nero mourned her lavishly; he embalmed her body in the fashion of the royalty of Egypt and had it incarcerated in the mausoleum of Augustus. Their first child, Claudia Augusta, had lived just four months; Nero was again childless and hopes for the continuation of his line now had particular relevance.

But what of the encomium's reference to the sheathing of swords? If truly a reference to civil war it would narrow the contending emperors down further to Augustus, Claudius, Galba, Vespasian, Nerva and Septimus Severus. But as it has been noted, the use of the verb *trepidare*, 'to tremble in anticipation', suggests a world on the brink and one waiting for something calamitous to happen, not a world that had *already* been torn apart; here the parallel 'brink' is the civil war averted by the eventual settlement at Babylon.[81] So the sheathing of swords could simply be a celebration of Nero's bloodless accession in contrast to the Praetorian bloodletting accompanying the accession of the unwitting Claudius. Perhaps more relevant was Nero's unravelling of the Pisonian Plot in April 65 CE.

Gaius Calpernius Piso, literary benefactor and statesman, had rounded up support for Nero's assassination amongst prominent senators and the joint-prefect of the Praetorian Guard. Yet support for Nero was far from extinct, especially amongst the equestrians who enjoyed his favour; if Piso had been successful there would have been collateral damage and recriminatory bloodletting.[82] Swords were certainly sheathed, most notably the emperor's which struck down the captured conspirators; the aftermath saw Lucan, Seneca, and the satirist, Petronius, summarily forced to commit suicide. After being denied tablets on which to write a Will, Seneca's last alleged words to his friends were: 'Who knew not

Nero's cruelty? After a mother's and a brother's murder, nothing remains but to add the destruction of a guardian and a tutor.'[83]

A 19ᵗʰ century illustration of the death of Seneca, following Nero's demand for his suicide. According to Tacitus, after severing his veins he resorted to taking hemlock.

Nero's behaviour is something of an irony against the cultural background, because the Second Sophistic, with its love of Greek culture and expressive freedom, is reckoned to have commenced with his emperorship. Josephus saw the retrospective problem when 'aiming for the truth':

> Many historians have written the story of Nero, of whom some, because they were well treated by him, have out of gratitude been careless with the truth, while others from hatred and enmity towards him have so shamelessly and recklessly revelled in falsehoods as to merit censure.[84]

What we now refer to as the *Exitus Illustrium Virorum,* a compendium written by Titinius Capito containing the names of those banished or killed by Nero, and the *Exitus Occisorum aut Relegatorum*, a parallel work by Gaius Fannius, were read by Pliny the Younger who coined the former name.[85] If published sufficiently early (its dating is uncertain), Tacitus might have used this material for his depiction of Seneca's death.

The 'sheathing of swords' was phraseology also used by Seneca in his *De Clementia*, once again suggesting Curtius could have drawn from his template; in fact Seneca 'communed' with Nero to restrain himself in his use of swords throughout book one in favour of the clemency he was advocating, and it rather suggests that Seneca had seen the writing on the wall, even though *De Clementia* was composed just two years into Nero's emperorship.[86]

The above extract from Seneca's *Apocolocyntosis* alluded to his emperor as a 'charioteer' who was moving 'first from the line'; if a literal link, it could refer to Nero's attested participation in the sport. He appeared in 65 CE at the Circus Maximus, an event that heralded in the *peregrinatio Achaica,* his tour of Hellas, and so it is likely that he was seen practising or participating in games and festivals in Rome before Seneca died (in 65 CE). Nero repeated his chariot performances at the Olympic Games of 67 CE, advancing them a full year to fit in with his travel plans. Inevitably, he was awarded a crown, despite falling from his ten-horsed carriage; we should note that Alexander was himself portrayed as a charioteer in the *Romance*.[87] Nero went on to become a *periodonikes pantonikes*, an 'all conquering champion' on the circuit of eiselastic games, and a guaranteed 'victor' who paid judges to adjudicate 'wisely'.[88] He returned to a triumph through a breach in Rome's wall, reportedly on the chariot Octavian had used a century before; the crowd now hailed their emperor as 'Nero Apollo'.[89]

As far as Curtius' references to Parthia, Nero responded vigorously to Parthian incursions into Armenia in the wars of 58-63 CE, and so a fascination with the East and the former Macedonian empire was inevitable at the time. Curtius' reference to the widespread skill of archery fits here too, for Nero's general, Gnaeus Domitius Corbulo, faced formidable Parthian mounted bowmen and he had to enlist auxiliary archers himself; no doubt when preparing for the campaign, the city was keenly aware of this requirement and we imagine training was being given to the Roman counterparts.[90] Nero was possibly encouraged to campaign in Asia by the *early* books of Lucan's *Pharsalia* published through 61-64 CE, and which recalled Alexander's legacy in the East with a nostalgia that embodied something of a challenge:

> ... Yet he fell in Babylon and Parthia feared him.
> Shame on us! That they dreaded more the *sarissa*
> Of Macedon than they do now the Roman javelin.[91]

As Bosworth points out, the *Pharsalia* also mentioned the frequent shipwrecking activities of the Nasamonians, detail Curtius also included in his geographical digression of Africa, and which may further point to a relevant *terminus post quem*.[92]

Nero's Parthian campaign was eventually successful, but it is possible that at the time Curtius was writing, the 'fates' still waited for Nero to subjugate the East, and Curtius' repeated references to Parthian power were magnifying the task facing his young emperor; he was potentially comparing his *novum sidus* to a young Alexander as a result. To cement Roman influence in the East, Tiridates was invited to Rome and crowned (client) king of Armenia by Nero in 66 CE. A Zoroastrian priest and founder of the Arsacid dynasty, Tiridates arrived with a grand entourage and much fanfare; it was a huge propaganda success and he too *publicly* worshiped Nero as the Sun – thus as Apollo or Helius.[93]

But despite the public obeisance, Tiridates was reportedly disgusted at seeing Nero playing the lyre when entering the city; Nero was, as Cassius Dio stated, 'ushering in his own career of disgrace'.[94] There are again clear overtones of Alexander's Eastern victories here, and Nero was just as attached to the heroic imagery of the past as Alexander had been: his thespian activities reinforced Homeric themes, and his paean to Troy as Rome burned, whether true or invented, was equally emblematic of that. Indeed, Virgil's *Aeneid* had vividly set the scene with his references to the 'last night' of Troy that saw Priam's city burned.[95]

The comparison with the Macedonian did not end there. The *Epistles* and *Suasoria* of Seneca and Lucan that followed the happier years of Nero's rule, as well as being badly veiled assaults on their present emperor, were also hostile to Alexander. Curtius' explicit correction of allegations that Alexander had caged Lysimachus with a lion, appears a further link to Seneca, for the allegation appeared most vividly in his *de Ira* and, once again, his *de Clementia*.[96] Many of Curtius' moral reflections, which permeated his book, also have parallels in Cicero's *epistulae* as well as Seneca's *declamations*, for these were *topoi* almost impossible to avoid when Alexander's imperial excesses begged all the rhetorical devices of the day. Motifs were recycled and declamatory exercises rolled out, re-treading the familiar literary Via Appia with a vocabulary that standardised biographical themes in Roman monographs. This is presumably why few scholars have associated Nero with the subject of Curtius' *basilikos logos*.

But if we are correct in the imperial association, and contemplating how precarious was his own fate in the wake of Nero's court-demanded suicides, Curtius' encomium was conspicuously reconstructed with due imperial care. He knew any implied comparison with Macedonian 'great' had to be conspicuously Nero-friendly, with any criticism directed at behaviour Nero did *not* adopt: Alexander's orientalisation, for example, and his massacres in the upper satrapy and in India, when, in contrast, Nero was developing friendly client-king relations in the East. So where Seneca and Lucan saw the Macedonian taking 'weapons all over the world' and 'plunging his sword through all peoples', in Curtius' account it was the 'best of Alexander' that Nero was supposed to see in himself. It was an exercise that anticipated Dio Chrysostom's dissections of Philip and Alexander in his *Kingship Orations* for *his* emperor, Trajan.[97]

Any unavoidable behavioural overlaps were defended in the character post-mortem Curtius provided Alexander a few pages before the imperial encomium, for much of its content and direction would have been equally valid for the young Nero whose mental energy could not be denied. Curtius philosophically wrote of the Macedonian conqueror, 'And, by Heaven! To those who judge the king fairly it is clear that his good qualities were natural, his faults due to his fortune or to his youth.'[98]

Curtius followed with a further *apologia* that pardoned Alexander for his lust for glory by taking into account his 'youth and achievements'. As virtues: his devotion to his parents, his mental energy, ingenuity and magnanimity 'barely possible at his age'. Notably, he also praised Alexander's sexual restraint. Fortuna is blamed for his assumption of divine honours and for Alexander giving credence to oracles. He interlaced Alexander's *irascundia* and *cupido vini* – irascibility and a love of wine – with his *clementia*, *benevolentia* and *consilium par magnitudini*,[99] where the faults were again credited to youth alone. The obituary ended with: '... the fates waited for him to complete the subjugation of the East and reach the Ocean, achieving everything of which a mortal was capable.'[100]

Nero had become emperor when he was just seventeen, and he was only twenty-two when he murdered Agrippina. Everyone, including Curtius, would have known of Nero's attachment to, and emulation of, Alexander, who also played the cithara, and though Trajan's admiration of the conqueror is often cited as the turning point in the reception Alexander's memory received in Rome, it appears it was earlier, at the imperial level at least.[101] For Nero formed a bodyguard he named The Phalanx of Alexander (which became the 1st Italica legion) and so the obituary in Curtius' final chapter could have fed that nostalgia. We should further recall that an Alexander of Aegae was allegedly employed as one of Nero's tutors.[102] Curtius may even have written his *Historiae* specifically as a gift to an emperor so enamoured.

On his Greek tour in 67 CE, Nero visited the Pythia at Delphi to request information on his fate, just as Alexander once had, and Suetonius claimed he was warned to 'beware the seventy-third year'; Nero, then aged thirty, rejoiced at forty-three more years of imperium and rewarded her with 400,000 *sestertii*. Less benign though unverifiable traditions exist, the darkest of which claimed he 'abolished the oracle, after slaying some people and throwing them into the fissure from which the sacred vapour arose', either because the god made 'unpleasant predictions', or because the Pythia had reproached him for his matricide. Pausanias more credibly reported that Nero couldn't resist ferrying 500 bronze statues from the sacred precinct back to Rome to grace his Golden House.[103] Prophetically, two years later, Galba, then in his seventy-third year, attained the emperorship.

The Torches of Nero by Henryk Siemiradzki, 1876. To the right of the painting the guilty culprits, the Christians, are depicted being torched as their punishment for starting the great fire that commenced on 18th or 19th of July 64 CE, based on the claims in Tacitus' *Annals* 15.42-45. Gallery of Polish Art at Sukiennice.

'FAST GRIPPED BY PURPLE DEATH AND FORCEFUL FATE'[104]

Curtius made a vexatious fourth-chapter reference to the city of Tyre and its tranquillity under Roman rule in his day. The city was definitely on Nero's list of banks to loot, as its lucrative murex industry provided the purple dye associated with Roman imperial dress. Nero took to wearing exclusively purple robes to reinforce his status, decreeing that any other doing so would be executed. If the comparison of Tyrian resurgence after its destruction by Alexander in 332 BCE was the underlying political message, the sentiment might even be traced back to Cleitarchus, as the city's trade *was* rekindled by the new harbour and naval requirements of the *Diadokhoi* in the decades following Alexander's siege; by 315 BCE Tyre was even able to sustain the fifteen-month siege of Antigonus *Monophthalmos*.

But the allusion to its more recent regained prosperity on the back of that, as well as its 'protection' by Rome, could have applied to any time period after Pompey's conquest of Judaea and its occupation in 63 BCE, and certainly the Syrian-born Ammianus Marcellinus referred to a flourishing Tyre when Pompey annexed the Levant.[105] Nero minted a new portrait coin, the Neronian Sela, at Antioch and possibly at Tyre as well.

The currency was most likely forced upon the population, which, until that time, had used the Tyrian shekel. If the move proved unpopular, then Curtius' intimation that the city enjoyed new prosperity was indeed more antique spin to smother a financial controversy. Inland from Tyre, the lush settlement of Caesarea Philippi was certainly named 'Neronia' in honour of the emperor by Agrippa II, the Rome-supported king of the region who commenced new palace construction, so the allusion to prosperity is explicable.[106] Judaea did, nevertheless, rebel in 66 CE expelling the Roman legions, whereafter the Jewish population minted their own silver currency until Vespasian and his son, Titus, quelled the uprising. Following that the Roman emperors adorned the obverse of the new coins, though familiar Tyrian motifs of Melquart and the Eagle of Egypt were still stamped on the reverse to partially appease the Phoenician population.

Finally, we have possible dating evidence in the undercurrent of Roman affairs that were expressed more generally through Curtius' narrative.[107] We have the aforementioned profiling of the halfwit king, Philip III, for example, a possible comparison with Claudius, and we have Perdiccas' Assembly behaviour which amounted to a 'Tiberian farce'.[108] Tiberius' laggard behaviour apparently justified the deathbed quip from Augustus: 'Alas for the Roman people, to be ground by jaws that crunch so slowly!'[109] And no doubt Tiberius' behaviour was recounted in Nero's day. In Curtius' portrayal of the Philotas affair of 330 BCE, Craterus' incrimination of the arraigned son of Parmenio displayed visible Roman themes, for the sham trial was depicted as a *fait accompli*, and this recalls the infamous trial of Asiaticus in 47 CE by Claudius and his ruthless wife, Messalina: clapped in chains without a Senate hearing, Asiaticus was essentially denied a defence.[110]

All this may provide a chronological triangulation of some relevance and with a *terminus post quem* positioned at the end of Claudius' rule when the almost simultaneous comet and eclipse provided a uniquely exploitable portent. The Great Fire of 64 CE, a foiled plot in 65 CE, Halley's Comet in 66 CE and perhaps allusions to the successful Parthian War (the 'safety of Rome' and a 'tempest dispelled') might all be found in Curtius' encomium. Moreover, we have the manifest emulation of Alexander that cannot have gone unnoticed by historians attempting to please Nero.

If we *were* to attach Curtius' encomium to Nero – and if the 'sheathing of swords' did not, in fact, allude to the new peace in the East – the book's publishing would fall somewhere between the Pisonian plot of spring 65 CE and the brewing of the Vindex rebellion in late 67 or early 68 CE, which finished Nero off. The statement from Curtius that preceded his eulogy – 'a throne is not be shared and several men were aspiring to it' – would have captured Nero's early suspicions of M Junius Silanus, Rubellius Plautus and Faustus Sulla, all of whom he was to eventually 'remove'. The expression would have been equally relevant to Nero's fear of those already supporting the causes of the four emperors that came to power in the year that followed his death.[111] If this timing is correct, then Curtius clearly knew the intimacies of political affairs in Rome.

Of course, much of the chronology debate can be explained away as simple encomiastic plagiarism; the textual similarities between Seneca, Lucan and Curtius' history of Alexander have been well explored.[112] The histories of Tacitus and Pliny can be similarly connected as imperial ideograms were rehashed. Their careers, and those of Josephus, Pliny the Younger and Suetonius, followed on from one another in close succession and with significant thematic overlaps. Each was an accomplished rhetorician and each lived in, or immediately after, Nero's emperorship.[113]

Here the allegation that a gradual concentration of political power (and we might add 'politically backed' *literary* power) resided within an ever-smaller group, appears justified.[114] And somewhere in the middle most likely lay our Curtius Rufus; we recall Sir Ronald Syme concluded his style was sub-Livian and pre-Tacitan. Livy published in Augustus' administration (27 BCE-14 CE) and Tacitus' works appeared towards the end of the 1st century.[115] It appears that much of Curtius' style and imagery was adopted from Livy's much admired *Ab Urbe Condita Libri*, with frequent use of the same modes of expression, with some reused almost verbatim, so that today 'nobody doubts Curtius studied Livy'.[116]

An exemplum appears to be a direct Curtian extraction from a Livian text that pondered Rome's ability to deal with the Macedonian *sarissa*. We recall that Livy mused that if Alexander had faced Rome 'he would often have been tempted to wish that Persians and Indians and effeminate Asiatics were his foes' instead. Curtius similarly described how, at his death, Alexander of Epirus (Alexander's uncle and brother-in-law) reflected that where he had faced real soldiers in Italy, Alexander had fought women in Asia; this was a theme curiously reiterated by Arrian.[117] Curtius' *contio* was attached to the accusations emanating from Cleitus' fatal speech, though this is hardly credible as an original utterance for such an occasion for it would have undermined Cleitus' own argument that Alexander's men (and father) were responsible for a great deal of his hard-fought success.[118] The reading of Livy's epic (and Virgil's) was nevertheless *sine qua non* for anyone on the *cursus honorum* and so Curtius, showing due respect, followed their lead.[119]

But there may well be one final – and perhaps the most relevant – clue to a publication under Nero: Curtius' noteworthy denial of Alexander's Will: '… some have believed that the provinces were distributed by Alexander in his Will, but I (or 'we') have ascertained that this report, though handed down by some authorities, was false.'[120] Curtius was attempting to suppress any further debate on the matter with his emphatic wording, and the relevance of this stems from the lingering rumour that

Nero had poisoned Claudius, with Agrippina dispensing with the Will that would have publicly reconfirmed as his successor the fourteen-year-old Britannicus, Claudius' son by his former wife, Messalina.[121] Moreover, as Milns points out: 'Both Alexander and Nero had domineering mothers, both of whom were suspected of complicity in the deaths of the two fathers and accessions of the sons.'[122] Curtius' idiomatic Will denial seems aggressively penned in the context of distant Alexander, when he could have simply stated he knew of the tradition, just as Arrian had dismissively referenced the *Pamphlet* conspiracy. But Curtius' emphatic and clearly targeted forensic denial would have resonated loudly as a rumour-buster, or a suppressant at least, for allegations still pointing at Nero. And if it did not, it would still have earned Curtius imperial points.

PROBLEMS WITH TACITUS' CURTIUS RUFUS

If these parallels assist a dating, they also argue for a familiarity between the historian and his emperor; Curtius' description of 'the night that was almost our last' could suggest more than observer status, and, potentially, to personal political involvement. To suppose that the senatorial Curtius Rufus identified by Tacitus might find himself in imperial company, is reasonable, but he appears to have died of old age in Africa late in Claudius' rule, or very early in Nero's. He becomes an even less adequate candidate when we consider that: 'It has long been recognised that there are many verbal similarities between Tacitus and Quintus Curtius Rufus';[123] in 1887 Friedrich Walter identified some 600 examples that suggest one repeatedly borrowed from the other, and if widely held dating contentions are correct, Tacitus was obviously plagiarising Curtius.[124] Walter saw further textual parallels between Curtius' obituary to Alexander and Tacitus' summation of Germanicus' qualities, as well as similarities detailing the mourning following their respective deaths.[125] This emulation of Curtius perhaps justifies Macaulay's summary of Tacitus' style: 'He tells a fine story finely, but he cannot tell a plain story plainly.'[126]

As a recent study concluded, this provides no more than a *terminus ante quem* for Curtius' publication, for Tacitus commenced his own literary career with the *Life of Agricola* and *De origine et situ Germanorum* in 98 CE, with the *Histories* and *Annals* following in 105 CE and 117 CE. But, at the same time, this would indicate that Tacitus held Curtius in high esteem, or at least worthy of emulation. If we can agree with Tarn's opinion of Curtius – 'he can make epigrams which might pass for Tacitus on a day when Tacitus was feeling not quite at his best' – then Tacitus not only borrowed from Curtius, but, on the whole, he bettered him by far.[127]

Here we encounter the major problem with the aforementioned Curtius Rufus, for the senator who died in Africa around 55 CE was rather vilified by Tacitus who afforded him the following: 'As to the origin of Curtius Rufus, whom some have described as the son of a gladiator, I would not promulgate a falsehood and I am ashamed to investigate the truth.'[128] In the previous paragraph Tacitus recounted the omen that foretold Curtius' praetorship in Africa, his career under Tiberius, and his unsuccessful mining activities that led his men to secretly petition the emperor to grant *advance* triumphal distinctions *ahead* of their toil; this cast a shadow on Curtius' overzealous activity in dangerous subterranean conditions. Tacitus summed up his career with:

> Afterwards, long of life and sullenly cringing to his betters, arrogant to his inferiors, unaccommodating among his equals, he held consular office, the insignia of triumph, and finally Africa; and by dying there fulfilled the destiny foreshadowed.[129]

Reiterating the poignant observation in a parallel source autopsy, would a literary 'mountain' like Tacitus have been moved by a relative 'molehill', and one he seems to have afforded such little respect?[130] Moreover, Tacitus' narrative gave no hint of *this* Curtius Rufus having a literary career, and neither did the index to Suetonius' *De Grammaticis et Rhetoribus* link the similarly named rhetorician to any historical monograph; he was listed as a '*rhetores*' but not as a '*grammatici*'.

If these individuals are to be discounted, do we have alternative historians who might fit the bill and who *were* respected by Tacitus, recalling that the *praenomen*, Quintus, is absent from early manuscript headings? Tacitus cited two historians who provided detail for his *Annals*, the work that covered the Julio-Claudian emperors: Fabius Rusticus, 'an angry outsider', and more interestingly, a Cluvius Rufus, a 'dispassionate insider'.[131] Both were of equestrian rank and both were intimately involved in the politics of the day.

'*VÆ, PUTO DEUS FIO!*' – ARGUMENTS FOR A FLAVIAN PUBLICATION DATE[132]

Before we argue for an alternative identity we should take a look at the Flavian dynasty, for Vespasian's rule included many of the ingredients to challenge Nero's as a Curtian publication period, though it conspicuously lacked some too. But we should also consider the probability that the *Historiae Alexandri Magni Macedonis* was the product of many years' work, potentially spanning the terms of more than one emperor, and for all we know, the final chapter might have been redrafted numerous times to fit the occasion before finally being published.

After Nero and the 'year of the four emperors' (69 CE), Vespasian came to power for ten years and he brought the first true political calm since Tiberius' death over thirty years before. The intervening years had witnessed the intrigues associated with Caligula, Claudius, Nero, Galba, Otho and Vitellius. On December 20th 69 CE, Vitellius was defeated, and Vespasian, already proclaimed emperor by his troops in Egypt and Judaea that July, could now enter Rome and end civil war. So here we find a good home for Curtius' 'sheathing of swords'.[133] The chaotic advance of Vespasian's troops under the command of Antonius Primus did result in a fire that again destroyed much of Rome, though no doubt the conflagration was easily attributed to retreating forces. Calm was restored and so 'torches' were metaphorically doused. And to quote Suetonius, Rome *was* 'given stability by the Flavian family'.[134] But as Milns and Bosworth remind us, the use of *trepidare*, along with 'rhetoric' 'too tame' for the structure, suggest an event *yet to happen*, and that seems to rule Vespasian out.[135]

However, a 'flourishing empire' did follow in which much of the capital was rebuilt without the Neronian excesses, including a Temple of Peace.[136] Coinage was minted with the slogan *Roma resurgens* and Vespasian was remarkably 'down to earth' compared to the imperium of the previous decades. Much of the rustic virtue of Cato resurfaced in him, minus the republican zeal. Vespasian had suffered his own humiliations: Caligula had once filled his aedile toga with mud.[137] Furthermore, he is recorded as being tolerant of criticism and supportive of the literati and the arts, providing salaries from the Privy Purse to poets and teachers of rhetoric including Quintilian who was soon elevated to consul.[138] Vespasian even had a sense of humour; his alleged last words 'Væ, puto deus fio! – 'Oh dear, I think I am turning into a god!'– epitomised what was purportedly an extremely dry wit.[139]

Benign historians such as Josephus flourished; he was the remarkable sole survivor of forty fighters besieged at the hillside town of Jotapata (Yodfat) in Judaea in 67 CE, a siege in which Vespasian himself almost lost his life.[140] As the walls fell to the Roman *ballistae* and battering rams on the forty-seventh day, the last survivors drew lots as part of a collective suicide pact. The last lot fell to Josephus, who, after talking the second-to-last man out of death, was presented to Vespasian and then offered his services, predicting his captor would some day become emperor at Rome. It was prophetic, and Josephus, a renowned academic and prodigy from an early age, began his new career under the Flavians with free imperial lodging with an income as a Roman citizen.[141]

Vespasian is likely to have fostered an environment in which an imperial history might be published, if it sidestepped the complex web of intrigues of the recent civil wars.[142] Thus an account of Alexander could have been circulated then. Philosophers were not so fortunate, and Helvidius Priscus, outspokenly pro-republic, *was* put to death, though according to Suetonius, it was reluctantly called for by the emperor.[143] Curtius' hopes for the longevity of 'the line of this house' would equally relate to the Flavians. Moreover, Curtius' prayer for a 'long duration' hinted at an exacerbation born of recent turbulence that immediately preceded Vespasian's term. Tacitus' own introduction to the year 69 CE suggested it was almost the last for Rome, thus the 'last night' finds its place comfortably.

Taken at face value, the prosperity of Tyre remains a problem, for the Jewish Wars brought upheaval to the region even if the thirteen references to the city in Josephus' *Jewish Wars* never mention Tyre's part; the Phoenician city remained neutral, or arguably loyal to Rome, perhaps for the commercial benefit that came from supplying the legions.[144] But, as we noted, Curtius' was an encomium constructed when the need to mollify outweighed the literal truths, and when a *Pax Romana* could be invoked in a largely rhetorical sense.[145] Josephus confirmed that Vespasian had visited the region in 67 CE in the company of Agrippa II, king of the adjacent provinces.[146] If this later Flavian publication date can be successfully argued for, then the Curtius Rufus who died in Africa around 55 CE can once again be discounted as our historian.[147]

Marble bust of Vespasian. The most enduring epitaph of his emperorship was the Flavian Amphitheatre, otherwise known as the Colosseum, started by him and finished by his son, Titus.

ALIQUID STAT PRO ALIQUOT: A POSSIBLE NEW IDENTITY

Numerous scholars credit much of the material Tacitus used for his biographical detail of Caligula, Claudius, Nero, and the 'year of the four emperors', to the much admired Cluvius Rufus, a historian whose name appeared again in the accounts of Plutarch, Pliny, Suetonius, Cassius Dio and most likely Josephus; the citations made it clear that he was their source as well as, significantly, their subject matter.[148]

Josephus' coverage of the deaths of Caligula (which occupied three-quarters of his nineteenth book) and the Claudian coup is certainly the most detailed surviving account in the absence of Tacitus' books seven to ten; it was penned with the confidence of a historian drawing on at least one impeccable 'inside source', and it is replete with the dialogue of conspirators reproduced in a verbatim and non-rhetorical style. As early as 1870 Mommsen proposed Cluvius Rufus *was* the 'inside source' who provided this detail. Josephus, whose *praenomen*, incidentally, also remains unknown, professed the importance of *akribeia*, 'exactness', in Thucydidean style, in his preface.[149] Assuming he adhered to his own methodology (never a safe assumption), then his choice of source would have mirrored that requirement; if Mommsen was correct, then Josephus also held Cluvius Rufus in high esteem.

Cluvius Rufus was also most likely the archetype for Suetonius' detail for the assassinations of Caligula, Claudius, and Nero, and he provided detail for Plutarch's biographies of Galba and Otho, that is assuming Plutarch did not simply extract from Tacitus.[150] Suetonius had initially been well placed to access the court archives when he was given the freedom of the imperial library under Trajan, then holding the office of *ab epistulis*, secretary, under Hadrian. However, his verbal indiscretion, or physical affair, with the empress Vibia Sabina, lost him imperial favour (and most likely his *jus trium liberorum* too), so Suetonius must have resorted to using *testimonia* from earlier historians such as Cluvius Rufus thereafter.[151]

The unnamed common source was clearly an *eyewitness* to events and we know that Cluvius Rufus *had been* an intimate of Nero and at the centre of the post-Nero intrigues of Galba, swiftly moving his allegiances to Otho and Vitellius after him; he needed to reassure the latter of his innocence in the charges brought against him, and what was obviously an eloquent defence resulted in a new imperial post. Cluvius was once again in imperial favour: he was one of two witnesses (with Silius Italicus) party to the surrender pact being discussed by Vitellius and Flavius Sabinus, the prefect of Rome and the city's cohorts (he was actually the brother of Vespasian), when surrounded by Vespasian's forces in late 69 CE.[152]

It would be specious to create a link to the author of Alexander's history through the similarity in name alone, but other parallels do exist. Cluvius is a 'lost historian' in that none of his works survive and his *praenomen* is also uncertain.[153] His identification with the senators referred to by Suetonius and Tacitus confirmed he too followed the *cursus honorum* in the Julio-Claudian era as a political *nobilis*.[154] He was born as late as 8 CE and was an ex-consul by year 65 CE (and as early as 41 CE if a 'Cluitus' mentioned by Josephus actually refers to Cluvius), possibly acting variously as a suffect consul under Caligula, then as a senator, and later as a governor appointed by Galba (if not Nero himself before his death) to Hispania Tarraconensis in 68 CE, the province Galba had previously governed under Nero.[155]

This lucrative region of northern Spain was an expansion of the former province of Hispania Citerior, the mines of which were so lucidly described by Pliny who became Procurator of the region during the 'gold rush' of 73 CE.[156] And it seems that Cluvius *did* take some part in Caligula's assassination, if an episode recorded by Josephus is accurate and if the same Rufus *is* being referred to. If so, he was a careful operator; when questioned on rumours of political change by a senator sitting beside him – who then confided in him that 'the programme for today will include the assassination of a tyrant' – Cluvius denied any knowledge of it and quoted a line from Homer: 'Quiet, lest one of the Achaeans should hear your word.'[157]

Although his work is lost, we *do* know that Cluvius Rufus published historical accounts; Plutarch's *Roman Questions* cited him as the source for an answer on Dionysiac origins, so he appears something of an antiquarian; in this case his knowledge stretched back to a plague of 361 BCE, the time of Alexander's father's reign.[158] Pliny preserved a dialogue between Cluvius and the veteran governor of Germania Superior, curiously named Lucius Verginius Rufus, who had quelled the Vindex rebellion of 68 CE for Nero; Cluvius made an insincere-looking *apologia* pertaining to elements of his book that the governor might disapprove of:[159]

> You know, Verginius, how binding is objectivity in writing; thus, if in my *Histories* you happen to read anything not to your liking, I ask that you forgive me. And he to him, 'Why don't you know Cluvius, that what I did I did only that you may be free to write what you deem right?'[160]

The dialogue has spawned many different interpretations, each involving the intrigues behind Nero's fall and the calamitous year that followed.[161] Late in Nero's term, Verginius' legions had twice attempted to elevate him to the emperorship, and he had twice declined the role, so his riposte underpins his philosophical position on the usurpation of power. It seems the two men in the dialogue were central to those intrigues.

Pliny later described Verginius' 'double-vocation of history' with he was '… one who outlived his moment of glory by thirty good years: he read poems and histories about himself and became a member of his own posterity.'[162] Cluvius' reference to his own *Histories* suggested he published more than one account, or at least biographed more than a single emperor or period. His care with imperial issues suggests these were unlikely to have been accounts of those *then* in power.[163] It also raises a further question: were Lucius Verginius Rufus and Cluvius Rufus related?

The Cluvii were situated in Capua in the 3rd century BCE and moved to Puteoli in Campania (a region now centred on Naples) a century later, enjoying a long history of commerce with Greeks and political success as praetors, senators, consuls and governors.[164] Virginius Rufus is attested as hailing from Mediolanum, modern Milan in Northern Italy, so if they were related, it would have been a 'new' family attachment. But name alone is an uncertain prosopographic method of establishing blood ties. The traditional *tria nomina* (*praenomen, nomen, cognomen*) evolved as ambitions widened, and when, to reinforce status or ancestry, new naming conventions were used. Genealogies were further clouded by adoption within the aristocratic classes and by the confusion between *nomon gentile* (clan name) and *cognomen* (the line within the gens) in later manuscripts.

Uncertainty aside, the careers of Verginius Rufus and Cluvius Rufus bear remarkable resemblances to one another through this period. Both were political survivors *par excellence*; Verginius Rufus, regarded as a *novus homo,* a 'new man' in Rome, came from humble origins: *equestri familia, ignoto patre* – a 'mere equestrian family, and a father unknown to fame' – according to Tacitus.[165] He was honoured with a consulship by Otho and elevated again thirty years later by Nerva (30-98 CE), the consul then beside him. Verginius penned poetry from the literary salon of his villa at Alsium in between, and he enjoyed intimate friendship with (and guardianship of) Pliny the Younger, whose letter, *To Voconius Romanus,* eulogised him; an admiring Tacitus eventually delivered his funeral oration.

As far as Cluvius Rufus' career, Tacitus stated he received the following treatment from the Stoic philosopher Heldivius Priscus: 'So he began his speech by praising Cluvius Rufus, who, he said, though just as rich and just as fine an orator as Marcellus, had never impeached a single individual in Nero's time.'[166] If Cluvius evidently blew with the political wind, or rather set his sails to gybe past the squalls that whipped through those years, his oratory must have been politically neutral too, perhaps in the style of Quintilian's *Institutio Oratoria,* which also sidestepped the traditional polemics on tyrants, dictators, and trappings of absolute power. But that would not have prevented Cluvius profiling Alexander, with the aforementioned discretion and care attached to any imperial comparisons.

Priscus' praise, if it *was* praise and not a slight, suggests that although Cluvius' tact prevailed through Nero's emperorship, it did not exclude him the odd *declamatio* thereafter. The delayed polemic could be backed up by a further explanation from Tacitus on the source challenge behind his *Annals*:

> But, while the glories and disasters of the old Roman commonwealth have been chronicled by famous pens, and intellects of distinction were not lacking to tell the tale of the Augustan age, until the rising tide of sycophancy deterred them, the histories of Tiberius and Caligula, of Claudius and Nero, were falsified through cowardice while they flourished, and composed, when they fell, under the influence of still rankling hatreds.[167]

Though by now these are quite familiar themes, they were acutely relevant here.

A 1960 study by Townend proposes the frequent use of Greek in Suetonius' biographies of the Caesars could be traced to Cluvius Rufus, passages conspicuous in that they 'attribute the worst excesses to the main characters'.[168] Campania was the most Hellenised part of Italy and it is possible that Cluvius was a philhellene himself with his attested Greek ties. If correct, this suggests he *was* prepared to become a 'sensational and polemical writer' when the political climate permitted.[169] This *chronique scandaleuse*, based around the court secrets he was privileged to, does not, as Wiseman has pointed out, preclude the lurid and scandalous being true.[170]

However, it is just as likely, or perhaps more probable, that Cluvius was the source of Tacitus' more lenient treatment of Nero, displaying the tact, not sensationalism, which Priscus attached to him; Cluvius was, indeed, maintaining the 'golden mean.'[171] In which case the source of Suetonius' Greek is more likely Pliny (also from the Como-Milan region) who tagged Nero an 'enemy of mankind'.[172] Pliny used Greek extensively, both isolated words and longer phraseology, because there were often no direct Latin equivalents for the subtle undertones of many Greek words and terms he found in his sources.[173] But sprinkling *Graeci* onto Latin prose was a running theme through the Silver Age, providing texts with an archaic charm, especially using extracts from poetry, to impress an educated audience. It may also have been a necessary means of implication and innuendo when simple straight-talk was not always possible.[174]

Moreover, Cluvius Rufus had been part of Nero's inner circle, acting as the emperor's herald or master of ceremonies at the new Greek-style artistic contests, the Neronia, where he announced the emperor would be singing the story of *Niobe*.[175] And he accompanied Nero on his artistic tour of Greece in 66-67 CE, probably when Cluvius was in his fifties.[176] Notably, the future emperor, Vespasian, accompanied them too, falling out of favour with Nero for the apathy he showed towards his performances.[177] So Cluvius was unlikely to have later published a biography that painted Nero as the monster Suetonius portrayed, for this would have called into question his own close association. His account was indeed most likely another quarantine affair. Tacitus was clear that Cluvius, possibly as an eyewitness, credited Agrippina with incestuous behaviour towards her son (possibly when she sensed she was losing authority over him), when others claimed the roles had been the reverse.[178] And though Claudius' suspicious death from the 'food of the gods' became a popular comical theme in Rome, it remains an allegorical episode and one Tacitus (possibly influenced by Cluvius' account) curiously refused to endorse.[179]

In complete contrast to his treatment of the governor of Africa, Tacitus, whose style was also visibly influenced by Sallust and Virgil, referred to

Cluvius Rufus as 'an eloquent man'. Cluvius appears to have capably bottled essences from the Golden Age of Latin in his *Histories*; 'eloquent' was a term afforded to Tacitus himself by Pliny the Younger.[180] We don't know when Cluvius Rufus died; 70 CE has been suggested because Tacitus stated Spain was left vacant by his absence, but this does not require his death, only his retirement from the region.[181] We have four fragments and one anecdote of Cluvius' work.[182] Nonetheless, 'Cluvius has been recognised more and more as a literary artist' and that is consistent with the style, or the attempted *eloquentia*, we read in Curtius Rufus' *Historiae Magni Macedonis Alexandri*.[183]

Oratory was, as we know from Cicero, a close cousin of history, and so Cluvius was well placed to litter a non-contemporary account with epideictic speeches. The 'striving for rhetorical *tour de force*' is evident in a number of speeches found in Josephus' coverage of the downfall of Caligula and the accession of Claudius.[184] If Josephus' vivid recounting of the aftermath and the plight of the people is truly based on Cluvius' style and vocabulary, and if Suetonius' description of Nero's last hours was likewise sourced, then we have further evidence of a technique reminiscent of that narrating the chaos at Babylon in the wake of Alexander's death.[185]

AUDIATUR ET ALTERA PARS: CVRTI OR CLVVI? – A CASE FOR CONFUSION

If Cluvius Rufus *is* a candidate for the authorship of the Alexander monograph, how could the confusion with a 'Curtius Rufus' have originally arisen? Well, firstly, the career similarity with the widely favoured candidate is striking. The Q Curtius Rufus referred to in the index to Suetonius' *De Rhetoribus* was an eloquent rhetor, and Tacitus' African governor was a well-connected politician. Cluvius Rufus was both it seems, and he was without doubt a historian.[186]

The Latin alphabet then had twenty-three capital characters. The letters J, U and W were added in the Middle Ages (or later) to facilitate use of the Roman alphabet in languages other than Latin, and 'U' sounds would have previously been written as V. Hence Curtius Rufus would have appeared as CVRTII RVFI when pertaining to ownership of the manuscript title; we still see this in the 1623 *Cvrtii Rvfi de rebvs ab Alexandro magno gestis* manuscript from Mattaus Rader in Germany, for example. 'Cluvius' Rufus, appearing as CLVVII RVFI in similar circumstances, resided as close then to 'Curtius' as it does today, and possibly with more scope for confusion, as would CVRTIVS and CLVVIVS written as standalone names.

We still don't know when an uncorrupted Curtius manuscript was last available for reference, but certainly it was some time before the 9th century *Codex Parisinus 5716* was produced. Neither do we know when

'Quintus' first appeared in the colophons. However, if a medieval scribe or his overseer was attempting to link the author to a historical figure, and one known to be a high ranking equestrian from the Claudian age with a rhetor's eloquence, then the Curtius Rufus so conspicuously investigated by Tacitus and appearing in Suetonius' *De Rhetoribus*, was an obvious choice, with the 'Q' (most obviously 'Quintus') for his *praenomen* being erroneously attached following the latter.

Other misidentifications in the biographing of Alexander are not difficult to pinpoint and we might even have another example of the corruption of Cluvius. The aforementioned and otherwise unattested 'Cluitus' was cited in Josephus' *Jewish Antiquities* in a text concerning the murder of Gaius, the emperor better known by his *agnomen*, Caligula. Mommsen argued that the identity in Josephus' original Greek manuscripts should be corrected to 'Cluvius', recalling the historian's own advice to a praetor that he keep quiet on the planned treason.[187] Again the arguments are not conclusive and were rejected by some later scholars, but the parallels are striking.[188]

The poet Martial curiously suggested that a colourful writer named Canius Rufus had covered the lives of Claudius and Nero:[189]

> Tell me, Muse, what my Canius Rufus is doing: is he putting on paper the acts of Claudian times for posterity to read, or the deeds which a mendacious writer ascribed to Nero? Or does he emulate the fables of rascal Phaedrus?[190]

Canius Rufus was cited as a 'poet and historian from Gades', modern Cadiz. Martial himself came from Hispania Tarraconensis, northeast Spain, and it is tempting to link Canius Rufus to Cluvius once more due to his Spanish presence, though in the northern region and not Gades. Yet the cognomen was common; Martial mentioned the name 'Rufus' thirty-three times in his *Epigrams*; a century earlier Cicero wrote to his young protégé, Marcus Caelius Rufus, who appears to have even been an avid reader of Cleitarchus, Curtius' principal source. Caelius was the talented author of some of the more prominent letters in Cicero's epistolary *ad Familiares*.[191] Catullus may have been referring to him in his *Rufus*, and if so, the references support a controversial figure that needed Cicero's defence: the *pro Caelio*.[192]

Yet the addition of the poet from Gades places us in a position in which we must accept, if names have indeed been transmitted intact (and Josephus' 'Cluitus' aside), that both a Cluvius Rufus and a Canius Rufus, each well connected and linked to regions of Spain, penned accounts of Claudius and Nero, whilst the clues in Curtius Rufus' imperial encomium arguably fit Nero's emperorship. Additionally, the works of all three have either disappeared or exist without any background to the historian.

Interestingly, the 'Phaedrus' referred to in Martial's *Epigram* is likely Gaius Julius Phaedrus, a Romanised Macedonian contemporary who wrote between 43 CE and 70 CE, and who Latinised the books of Aesop's fables. His largest collection bears the name *Romulus* and a prose manuscript dating to the 10th century is addressed *Aesopos ad Rufum*, suggesting a dedication by the compiler to a 'Rufus'.[193] Was that to Canius Rufus with whom Phaedrus might have been acquainted?

The fact remains that there is no evidence that Cluvius Rufus published a book on Alexander. This would be troublesome if much else was known about his work, but save his own reference to the *Histories*, nothing is. His subject matter is not described, only implied by the citations in the sources, and neither was he mentioned in Quintilian's list of the literati that appeared in his *Institutio Oratoria*, yet this remained incomplete as Quintilian himself admitted; neither Pliny the Younger nor other writers mentioned by Tacitus featured in his famous line-up.[194] As Syme has remarked, surviving detail on historians publishing in the long interval between Livy and Tacitus is sparse.[195]

We do not even know where, or when, Tacitus, the mighty Roman annalist, was born, or in fact, *his praenomen*: only books one to four of Tacitus' fourteen-book *Histories* are preserved complete. The first half of his *Annals* survived in a single copy of a manuscript from Corvey Abbey, and books eleven to sixteen (and what remained of his *Histories*) are reproduced from a single manuscript found in the Benedictine Abbey at Monte Cassino – a 'barbarous script' commented Poggio Bracciolini. The latter, the *Codex Mediceus II*, written in the Langobard script of the mid-11th century (though evidence suggests it derives from a 5th-century Rustic Capitals manuscript, possibly through an intermediary),[196] gave Tacitus' *praenomen* as 'Publius', whereas Apollinaris Sidonius (ca. 430-489 CE), a learned Gallo-Roman aristocrat, named him 'Gaius.'[197]

The paucity of Tacitus' material likely reflects the disfavour of both the late Caesars and the Church fathers, for he was openly contemptuous of the 'new' religion, as well as the tyranny of the early emperors. We may also question whether his last annalistic work was to be titled *Annals* for he actually named the former *Ab excessu divi Augusti*. We do not even know if it was, in fact, designed to be distinct from what we call his *Histories,* though the temporal divide between past and contemporary history did likely separate them.

In Momigliano's view, Cluvius Rufus was not just *a* source; he was the *principal* source for Tacitus' own *Historiae* and for much of his *Annals*, hence Momigliano concluded: 'The surviving books of Tacitus' *Annals* are the most conspicuous example of a great work of history written with the minimum amount of independent research.'[198] If, as it has recently been argued, the textual similarities suggest that Tacitus drew from Curtius' *Historiae* of Alexander, we should give credence to the fact that Curtius and

Cluvius are one and the same author. If not, then the evidence requires we accept that Tacitus, the 'Roman Thucydides', took detail and style from both a Cluvius Rufus and a Curtius Rufus. Has Nineveh become Babylon once again?

COLOPHONEM ADDERE – THE FINISHING TOUCH[199]

Although we could ourselves be accused of attempting to 'tidy up' history too neatly here, a few loose ends do need comment before we close the chapter. Much of this debate has focused on the so-called Julio-Claudians. This, it could be argued, is a modern anachronism, and to quote one scholar's view of the issue: 'There never was such a thing as the Julio-Claudian dynasty.' Claudius was an imposter to the Julian line (he 'was not a Caesar either by blood or by adoption') and the label heralds back to a reference in a speech given by Galba as another rhetorical device.[200]

As for common interpretations of Josephus' fortuitous outcome at Jotapata, it has been argued that rather than a lucky survivor of a 'Roman roulette', the mathematical outcome of which is still known today as the 'Josephus Permutation', he simply sold out his comrades to buy his own survival, an action that has been termed 'a shocking duplicity'. Perhaps the conclusion to the siege was aided by his Pharisee training for it resembled the Greek Stoic doctrine on the path to death.[201] The detail behind the outcome, which recorded 40,000 deaths (archaeologists suggest more likely 7,000), will never be unravelled, for it, along with the portrayal of Titus' and Vespasian's subjugation of the Jews, was recorded by Josephus himself; his remains the sole account of the unique detail concerning the wars in Judaea.[202]

The word 'colophon' ('summit') which denoted a copyist's final note and which preserved Curtius' *praenomen*, might have derived from the so-named city in Lydia, birthplace of Deinon, Cleitarchus' father. For Strabo mentioned that the roots of the proverb *colophonem addere*, 'to put a finish to anything', stemmed from the superlatives afforded to the Lydian cavalry that usually brought victory to its allies. And to sum up the fate of Curtius' identity, a colophoned 'Quintus', and a career that paralleled a disrespected senator who died governing Africa, might have led to the misattribution of one of the most important books ever written about Alexander and to the historicity of his Will called into question within it.

NOTES

1. Tarn (1948) p 91.
2. Quoting Bosworth (1996).
3. Quoting Fears (1976) p 214.
4. Curtius referenced Cleitarchus as a source at 9.5.21 and 9.8.15. The stylistic accord of Diodorus, Curtius and Justin's epitome of Trogus suggested a common source for much of their works. See chapter titled *Hierarchic Historians and Alexandrian Alchemy* and *Classicus Scriptor, Rhetoric and Rome* for further detail on their relationship.
5. The 123 manuscripts are listed by Dosson in his *Etude sur Quinte Curce*, 1887, pp 315-356. The titles are discussed in *Quintus Curtius Rufus, The History of Alexander*, Penguin, London 1984, Introduction by W Heckel p 1. An author-owned 1623 edition from Mattaus Rader in Germany carries this final title.
6. Printed English editions of the *Ab urbe condita* range from *The Early History of Rome* to the *Dawn of the Roman Empire*. Arrian's *Anabasis* is most commonly named *The Campaigns of Alexander* though 'campaigns' is far from a literal translation.
7. Cassius Dio 60.35; thus the title suggested Claudius had an apotheosis into a pumpkin, though modern interpretation suggests it implied 'pumpkin head'. Full discussion in Sullivan (1966).
8. Quoting WHD Rouse's 1920 translation of Seneca's *Apocolocyntosis.*
9. A comprehensive list of studies dedicated to the theme can be found in Atkinson (2009) introduction pp 3-19, Baynham (1998) pp 200-219 and *Quintus Curtius Rufus, The History of Alexander*, Penguin Classics edition, 1984, Introduction pp 1-4.
10. Quoting Steel (1905) pp 402-423 and following Hamilton (1988) p 445 for the dating.
11. Dating arguments well summed up by Atkinson (2009) pp 3-9 and Baynham (1998) p 206, especially for Claudian supporters. Also see Tarn (1948) pp 111-116 for late dating arguments.
12. Pliny *Epistles* 7.27.2-3, Tacitus 11.20.4-11.21.4. See full discussion in the introduction of Heckel (1984). For similar arguments see Fears (1976) p 447.
13. Tacitus 11.21.2.
14. Suetonius *De Grammaticis et Rhetoribus*, Index 1.28. Q Curtius Rufus appeared between M Porcius Latro and L Valerius Primanus in Suetonius' *De Rhetoribus.*
15. Milns (1966) p 504 for the dating based on the list of rhetors. Suetonius' father was a tribune of equestrian rank and he himself became an intimate of Trajan and Hadrian. A further Q Curtius (not Rufus) is thought to have been mentioned by Cicero who complimented his prosecution skills, though his letter dates to ca. 55 BCE. But as Milns points out, this on 'stylistic grounds, though inconclusive in many ways, must also exclude him, since it is obviously post-Ciceronian and has strong affinities with the Latin of the rhetorical schools of the first century AD'. Moreover, as another scholar comments, the name was actually penned as Q Acutius, not Curtius! Nevertheless in Milns' view, due to 'the comparative rarity of the name in Imperial times there is a strong possibility' that the historian is one of these three. Milns (1966) pp 504-5. The rejection of the name comes from JW Bussman, Quintus Curtius Rufus' *Historiae Alexandri: The Question of Authorial Identity and Intent.*
16. Summarised in Wells (1984) p 8.
17. Augustus fixed the sestertius at 1/100th of an aureus, thus 1 million *sestertii* equated to 10,000 aureii, each of which was approximately 8 grams in weight of gold. At a gold price of US $40 per gram, that gives a present-day gold standard value of approximately $3,600,000.
18. The loans of the Roman nobility discussed in Finlay (1973) pp 53-57.
19. Tacitus *Histories* 1.1.
20. Pliny Preface.
21. Parthian references can be found at Curtius 5.7.9, 5.8.1, 6.2.12, 7.12.11 describing their dominance over former Macedonian territory and 'everything beyond the Euphrates'. Following Milns (1966) for the broad dating argument though he mentioned 227 CE as the fall of Arsacid Parthia. RT Bruère, *C.Ph.* 47 (1952) cited in JW Bussman, Quintus Curtius Rufus' *Historiae Alexandri: The Question of Authorial Identity and Intent.* Silius' Italicus' knowledge of Curtius also discussed in Fears (1976) p 215 ff.
22. Curtius 4.4.21.
23. The statement that archery was still a widely practised skill at Curtius 7.5.42. Curtius 3.11.15, 4.9.3 for *cataphracti*; impact on dating arguments discussed in Fears (1976) pp 222-223.
24. Quoting Wilkes (1972) p 178.
25. Tacitus *Histories* 1.1, translation from the Loeb Classical Library edition, 1925.
26. Tacitus 2.1.
27. Cassius Dio 53.19.2 ff; cited in full in Wilkes (1972) p 186.

28. Discussion of the less than frank rendition of speeches by Tacitus and Livy, for example, in Gudeman *Romans* (1894) p 145.
29. See discussion in Morford (1973) p 210. Tacitus 4.43.1 for the comparison to Cordus.
30. Discussed in Scramuzza (1940) p 39.
31. In particular the study of Wiseman (1982) linked both the first *Eclogue* and Curtius to Nero's emperorship.
32. Curtius 10.9.1-6, translation from the Loeb Classical Library edition, 1946.
33. Pliny 2.25.
34. Ovid *Metamorphoses* book 15 lines 745-870.
35. Curtius 10.9.1-6. For a full discussion on the chronology issues see Baynham (1998) Appendix pp 201-220, Heckel (1984) Introduction pp 1-4 and Atkinson (2009) pp 203-214.
36. For a useful summary of historical references to 'star' and 'last night' see Atkinson (2009) Introduction pp 207-208. Horace *Satires* 1.7.23-36; following Fears *Solar* (1976) p 495.
37. Hamilton (1988) pp 459-451 for the use of *sidus* and citing Pliny *Panegyricus* 19.1 for its attachment to Trajan.
38. Lucan *Pharsalia* 10.35-36. Curtius 9.6.8; for similarities to Virgil see Steele (1915) pp 409-410.
39. Tacitus *Histories* 1.38.
40. The theories and sighting are summarised in Barrett (1978). See Atkinson (2009) p 7; Pliny made 75 references to comets in his second book and mentioned the allusion to a hairy star frequently; at 2.25 for example.
41. Eusebius *The Life of Constantine* 28. Recent geological surveys might have pinpointed the crater of a meteorite that could be related to the sighting. Theories suggest a mushroom cloud could have constituted the 'cross' in the sky. See Dr David Whitehouse *Space impact saved Christianity*, BBC NEWS, 23rd June 2003.
42. This was first proposed in Steel (1915).
43. As an example of the significance attached to comets see Suetonius *Nero* 35.
44. Virgil *Georgics* book 1 lines 487-488.
45. Suetonius *Claudius* 46. The comet following Caesar's death also alluded to in Ovid's *Metamorphoses*, chapter 15, *The Apotheosis of Caesar* line 786. Suetonius *Claudius* 46, Cassius Dio 61.35 for the comet heralding in Nero.
46. Seneca *Quaestiones Naturales, De Cometis* 7.21.3. Quoting Tacitus 14.22. Calpurnius Siculus *Eclogues* 1.77.79 if they can be dated to 60 CE and not 54 CE; discussion in Barrett (1978) pp 99-100. The *Octavia* 231-232, wrongly ascribed to Seneca, also recorded the sighting; discussion in Barrett (1978) p 99.
47. Tacitus 15.47 translated by AJ Church and WJ Brodribb (1864) Macmillan and Co. Seneca also confirmed the sighting 'when Paterculus and Vopiscus were consuls…' in his *Quaestiones Naturales, De Cometis* 7.28.3; see Barrett (1978) p 99 for the full entry.
48. Suetonius *Nero* 36 for the 66 CE sighting. Josephus *Jewish War* 6.289 for the Jerusalem sighting; the comet appeared 'like a sword' hanging over Jerusalem. The fact that it was allegedly visible for a whole year has made scholars question whether it was in fact Halley's Comet of three years earlier used for rhetorical effect. Pliny 2.89 also recorded a comet in 76 CE in Titus' fifth consulship.
49. Sir David Brewster *The Edinburgh Encyclopaedia*, 1832, Volume 9 p 427. For the works of art see Pliny 34.84. Suetonius *Vespasian* described Vespasian's dubious financial dealings.
50. Suetonius *Vespasian* 5-6 for a list of portents and 7.2 for prediction of his alleged healing powers. Sextus Aurelius Victor *De Caesaribus* 9 recorded it but appears to be following Suetonius as well as Cassius Dio 66.17.2.
51. More on the eclipse at Gaugamela in chapter titled *The Reborn Wrath of Peleus' Son* and Salpicius Galus and the sighting in chapter titled *Sarissa Diplomacy: Macedonian Statecraft*.
52. For a summary of Pliny's career see Champlin (2003) p 41.
53. Cassius Dio 60.26.
54. Following the proposal of Atkinson (2009) p 209; rejected by Milns (1966) p 502, though neither linked this to Nero's term.
55. Pliny 2.92-93, translation from J Bostok and HT Riley, Taylor and Francis, 1855. This may not relate the comet seen at Nero's accession but to a later sighting.
56. Suetonius *Claudius* 46; quoting Cassius Dio 61.35.
57. Tacitus 14.22 and 15.47. The sighting of 66 CE might have been a super nova as it had no tail according to Chinese astronomers.
58. See Atkinson (2009) pp 207-208 for a summary of Nero's relationship to Roman Apollo; discussion in Champlin (2003) pp 112-113 for Nero's associations with the heavens. The view and 'solar monarchy' is challenged by Fears *Solar* (1976).
59. Seneca *Apolocyntosis* 4, translation from Sullivan (1966) pp 383-384.
60. 'Actor-emperor' was a term used by Pliny the Younger in his so-called *Panegyricus Trajaini* 46.4.

61. Quoting Desiderius Erasmus *De Ratione Studii*.
62. For the reporting of the death of Agrippina see Tacitus 14.1-8, Suetonius *Nero* 34, Cassius Dio 63.11-14.
63. Seneca *Quaestiones Naturales, De Cometis* 7.28.3.
64. Trajan's praise of Nero's first five years is mentioned in Aurelius Victor *The Style of Life and the Manners of the Emperors*, and in the anonymous epitome *de Caesarbus* 5. For his civic activity see Suetonius *Nero* 17 for the limit on legal fees; Tacitus 13.26 for his support for freedmen; and for the impeachment of government officials, Tacitus 13.30,14.18, 14.40,14.46. For Otho's emulation of Nero see Plutarch *Otho* 3.2.
65. Following the observation of Champlin (2003) pp 116-117.
66. See Atkinson (2009) pp 209-210 for discussion of the similarity of Seneca *Of Clemency*.
67. Bosworth (2004) p 553.
68. *Citharoedo principe* was a term used by Juvenal in the *Satires* 8.198.
69. Suetonius *Nero* 38; Cassius Dio 62.16. Tacitus 15.39. He nevertheless reported there were rumours of Nero playing his lyre.
70. Tacitus 15.40 claimed five days; Suetonius *Nero* 38 claimed six days and seven nights and a pillar erected by Domitius claimed nine days.
71. Tacitus 15.40.
72. Tacitus 15.42-45.
73. For Pliny's treatment of the Christians see Pliny *Epistulae* (to Trajan) 10.96. Tacitus 15.42-45 for the guilt heaped upon the Christians.
74. Tacitus 15.44.
75. For the use of elephants see Spartianus *Life of Hadrian* 19.
76. For Germanicus' attributes and his suspicious death see Suetonius *Caligula* 1-5.
77. For Otho's homosexual relations with Nero see Suetonius *Galba* 22.
78. Vitruvius *De Architectura* 8.6.10-11, Pliny 34, 54.175-178. The principal claim that lead contributed to the fall of Rome was published by JO Nriagu in March 1983 titled *Saturnine gout among Roman aristocrats. Did lead poisoning contribute to the fall of the Empire?* A more recent paper by H Delile titled *Lead in ancient Rome's city water* confirmed the high levels, published by the University of Utah, Salt Lake City March 2014. The claim that lead contributed to the fall of the Roman Empire is generally considered extravagant, though the effects of lead poisoning on long-term users of lead cookware in Rome is not denied; this can result in insanity as well as infertility.
79. Suetonius *Nero* 35.3. Tacitus 16.6 recorded the same but attributed it to a casual outburst. Cassius Dio 63.27 suggested it could have been an accident.
80. For the various versions of Poppea's death see Tacitus 16.6, Cassius Dio 63.27, Suetonius *Nero* 35.3.
81. Following Milns (1966) p 491 for arguments on the use of *trepidare* and an event yet to happen.
82. The main source for the Pisonian plot is Tacitus 15.47-65.
83. Quoting Tacitus 15.62; the 'brother' was a reference to Nero's step-brother (and former brother-in-law), Britannicus, the heir designate who died mysteriously just a month before he would assume manhood and thus the emperorship and one day before his fourteenth birthday. Tacitus 13.14-16 and Suetonius *Nero* 33-34 claimed it was the work of Nero's poisoner, Locusta.
84. Josephus 20.154-156. Compare with Tacitus 2.1.
85. Ker (2009) p 53. Pliny the Younger's citation is from *Epistulae* 8.12.4-5 and references to Fannius at 5.5.3.
86. Seneca *De Clementia* 1.1; there are ten sentences connected to 'swords' (sheathing or drawing) in book 1.
87. Suetonius *Nero* 24.2. *Romance* 1.18-19 as an example of Alexander's charioteering.
88. Champlin (2003) p 55 for fuller discussion on Nero's entries into the games of Greece.
89. Suetonius *Nero* 25, Cassius Dio 63.20-21.
90. Tacitus 13.40 for the role of the archers against Tiridates in the campaign.
91. Lucan *Pharsalia* 10.2.
92. Bosworth (1983) p 152 citing Lucan *Pharsalia* 9.439-444 and Curtius 4.7.19.
93. See full accounts of Tiridates' entry into Rome in Champlin (2003) pp 228-234 and also Cassius Dio 62, Tacitus 15, Pliny 30.6.16 all recorded elements of the events. For Nero's attachment to Apollo see discussion in Champlin (2003) pp 276-286. Greek Helios was Latinised to Helius and Apollo to Apollo; both were associated with the Sun.
94. Cassius Dio 63.1-6.
95. Virgil *Aeneid* 5.190, 6.502,6.513; Bosworth (2004) p 553 for discussion.
96. The episode of Lysimachus' caging with a lion appeared in Justin 15.3, Seneca *de Ira* 3.17.2, *de Clementia* 1.25, Pliny 8.16.21; he was most likely Alexander's school teacher, not the *Somatophylake*. Heckel (2006) p 154 for the alternative identification of Lysimachus, discussed

in chapter titled *Classicus Scriptor, Rhetoric and Rome*. For other similarities between Seneca and Curtius see Hamilton (1988) though Hamilton proposes Seneca followed Curtius.

97. If Seneca was following Curtius (as Wiedemann argued a century and a half ago) then it was Curtius who wrote in the untroubled days of Nero's early term, though this argues against much we find in his encomium. What seems clear from other similarities is that one of them borrowed phraseology from the other. Hamilton (1988) p 447 for discussion of Wiedemann's views. Seneca *Epistle* 94.62 '*Toto orbe arma circumfert*' and Lucan *Pharsalia* 10.31 ff, '*gladiumque per omnes Exegit gentes*'. Hamilton (1988) pp 447-456 for the similarities, especially Seneca's Epistles 56 and 59. For Chrystrom's orations see SR Asirvatham in Carney-Ogden (2010) pp 196-200.

98. Curtius 10.5.26, translation from the Loeb Classical Library edition, 1946.

99. For discussion on the use of these terms see Balot (2001) p XI, and p 291. Also see McKechnie (1999) p 103 for Curtius' necrology and its vocabulary at 10.5.26-34.

100. Curtius 10.5.37.

101. Nero's associating himself with Alexander discussed in chapter titled *Classicus Scriptor, Rhetoric and Rome* and *Mythoi, Muthodes and the Birth of Romance*. See Whitmarsh (2002) p 175 for the comment on Trajan and the transition in Roman opinion. Aelian 3.32 for Alexander playing the cithara.

102. Suetonius *Nero* 19 for the phalanx. Suda α 1128= FGrH 618 T2 for Alexander of Aegae.

103. Pausanias 10.7.1 and 10.19.2 for the looting of statues and Cassius Dio 63.14 for the blocking up of the fissure. Full discussion of other sources in Champlin (2003) pp 133-134.

104. Homer *Iliad* 5.83, the original lines referring to the death of minor status Trojan soldiers.

105. Ammianus Marcellinus 4.8.10; discussed in Fears (1976) p 221.

106. Josephus *Jewish Wars* 2.95, and Josephus 17.319, 18.28 for the renaming to Neronia.

107. See discussion in McKechnie (999) p 49.

108. Discussed in more detail in chapter titled *Babylon: the Cipher and Rosetta Stone*.

109. See Errington (1970) pp 50-51 for comparisons between Arrhidaeus and Claudius. For Tiberius' reticence to assume power see Suetonius *Tiberius* 24 and for the quip *Tiberius* 21.2.

110. Tacitus 11.2.1-11.5 for the trial of Asiaticus and the indictments that followed, and following the discussion in Baynham (1998) p 174.

111. Curtius 10.9.1 and quoting Atkinson (2009) p 205 on its relevance to Nero's suspicions of conspirators if indeed Curtius' words were related to the encomium.

112. For arguments against Seneca and Lucan drawing from Curtius see Fears (1976) pp 216-217. In contrast, their use of Curtius has been recently upheld by Hamilton (1988) p 445. Also see Bosworth (2004) p 553 citing Seneca's *Epistle Morales ad Lucillium* 59.12 for more arguments.

113. See discussion of the sources and dates in Champlin (2003) pp 38-44.

114. Revisiting the comment by Wilkes (1972) p 178.

115. Syme (1987) pp 111-114 and discussed by Baynham (1998) p 201.

116. Quoting Baynham (1998) p 20 on 'no one doubting' Curtius used Livy. A full discussion of Livian influence can be found at pp 20-25, 35 and 75-76. Also see Oakley (2005) pp 661-662; and especially the introduction to Atkinson-Yardley (2009) and also well summarised by W Heckel in the introduction to the 2004 Penguin Books edition of Curtius and quoting Heckel on 'modes of expression'. Fuller discussion of the similarities to Livy in Steele (1915) pp 402-409.

117. Arrian 2.7.5 for the effeminacy of the Asian troops the 'most warlike' of Europeans would face.

118. Livy 9.19.10 for the comparisons of the foes of each Alexander and Curtius 8.1.37 for its reiteration at Cleitus' death.

119. As an example of Curtius taking phrases from Virgil see Curtius 4.6.25-29 and Alexander's treatment of Baetis following the siege of Gaza which emulated Virgil's treatment of Hector's mutilated body.

120. Curtius 10.10.5-6. As far as Curtius' own dismissal, and reiterating Chugg (2009) p 5 who refuted the use of the first personal singular in favour of the first person plural, in other translations 'we' is used; as an example the translation by JC Rolfe in 1946 published by the University of Michigan. Nevertheless it was not unusual for an author to use the plural 'we' when referring to his own efforts and this does not convincingly argue that Curtius paraphrased Cleitarchus, for example. Diodorus (for example 1.83.9) and Polybius, in particular, switched between singular and plural where emphasis demanded it and in particular to stress the veracity of either eyewitness reporting or personal vouching for facts; discussion in Marmodoro-Hill (2013) pp 199-204. Of course 'we' is still commonly used today, and by the author in this book.

121. See Suetonius *Claudius* 43-46, translation from the Loeb Classical Library edition, 1914, and extract discussed in chapter titled *Wills and Covenants in the Classical Mind*. Britannicus had become the heir designate of Claudius under the name Tiberius Claudius Germanicus.

122. Milns (1966) p 502.

123. Following the observation in Bosworth (2004) p 551.

124. F Walter *Studien zu Tacitus Und Curtius*, H Kutzner, Munich 1887. For discussion of the similarities see Bosworth (2004).

125. Bosworth (1994) p 559 and for the mourning p 562.
126. Macaulay (1828).
127. Tarn (1948) pp 91-92, see McKechnie (1999) pp 44-46 on Tarn's treatment of Curtius.
128. Tacitus 11.21, translation from the Loeb Classical Library edition, 1937.
129. Tacitus 11.20 for Curtius' mining activities and 11.21 for the summation; translation from the Loeb Classical Library edition, 1937.
130. Following the title and theme of Bosworth (2004).
131. 'Insider and outsider' quoting Champlin (2003) p 44.
132. Cassius Dio 66.1 for Vespasian's alleged last words.
133. Suetonius *Vespasian* 6.3 for the July accession.
134. Suetonius *Vespasian* 1.
135. Milns (1966) p 491 for *trepidare* and quoting Bosworth (1983) p 151.
136. Suetonius *Vespasian* 8-9.
137. Cassius Dio *Vespasian* 59.12.3.
138. Suetonius *Vespasian* 18.
139. 'Oh dear' is a Robert Graves translation from the Penguin edition of the *Life of the Twelve Caesars-Vespasian* 1957, of what is more traditionally worded 'woe is me'.
140. Josephus' comments in *Against Apion* 9 are a good example of Vespasian's tolerance to historical works that painted him in a favourable light. For the siege at Jotapata see Josephus *Jewish Wars* 3.6 ff.
141. Josephus' treatment in Rome discussed in Wiseman (1991) Introduction p ix.
142. See discussion on Vespasian's censorship in Townend (1964) pp 340-341.
143. Suetonius *Vespasian* 15.
144. Milns (1966) p 493 for Tyre's stance in the war.
145. Fears (1976) p 220.
146. Josephus *Jewish War* 3.3 ff.
147. See discussion in Heckel's introduction to the Penguin edition of *Quintus Curtius Rufus, The History of Alexander the Great,* Penguin, London, 1984, pp 1-4.
148. References to Cluvius Rufus are found at Josephus 19.1.13, Suetonius *Nero* 21, Pliny the Younger *Epistulae* 9.19, Plutarch *Otho* 3, Tacitus 12.20 and 14.2, Tacitus *Histories* 1.8, 2.58, 2.65, 3.65, 4.39 and 4.43, Cassius Dio 68.14.
149. Josephus' account and his sources are discussed in detail in Wiseman (1991) Introduction p XIV.
150. Proposed by Syme and discussed in Townend (1964) pp 337-377. Rejected by LH Feldman (editor) *Josephus the Bible and History,* EJ Brill, Leiden, 1988, p 404.
151. Suetonius is rumoured to have had an affair with Vibia Sabina who was married to Hadrian, according to the *Historia Augusta* 11.3. Suetonius was dismissed from office for it. This may be rumour and he may have simply been disrespectful, for we would have expected harsher treatment if true. The *jus trium liberorum,* literally 'the right of three children', were exemptions and privileges awarded to citizens who bore three children, ostensibly to repopulate the dwindling upper classes, but more invidiously to encourage procreation of a favourable gene pool. It later became a privilege of those considered meritous for good military of political deeds, regardless of offspring.
152. Tacitus *Histories* 1.76.1 for his support of Vitellius and 2.65.1 for the charges brought against him, 3.65 for Cluvius' presence with Vitellius.
153. References to a 'Marcus' Cluvius Rufus appear unfounded and the sources mentioned a 'Cluvius Rufus' only. See Cornell (2013) p 550 footnote 3 citing a mistranslation of Tacitus *Histories* 2.65.1 from which the 'Marcus' stemmed. It is possibly because the translator had Marcus Caelius Rufus, protégé of Cicero, on his mind. His identity is discussed later in the chapter.
154. Suetonius *Nero* 21.1 and Tacitus *Histories* 1.8.1. See Wiseman (1991) p 111 for the *nobilis* discussion.
155. Suetonius Nero 21.1, Cassius Dio 62.14.3 for Cluvius' ex-consulship. See below for 'Cluitus'; Tacitus *Histories* 1.8 for his role in Hispania.
156. Full chronology discussion for dating Cluvius in Wiseman (1991) p 111. Pliny 33.
157. Josephus 19.1.13. Taken from *Iliad* 14.90-91.
158. Plutarch *Roman Questions* 107; Livy 7.2 recorded the same incident.
159. The disapproval – and its origins – is the opinion of Shorter (1967) pp 370-381.
160. Pliny the Younger *Epistles* 9.19.5, translation from Marchesi (2008) p 146.
161. As an example of the interpretations see the opinions of Levick (1985) pp 318-346.
162. Pliny *Epistles* 2.1.2, translation from Marchesi (2008) p 146 and quoting Marchesi on 'double vocation of history'.
163. Discussed in Marchesi (2008) pp 145-146.
164. The origins of the Cluvii discussed in Wiseman (1991) p 111 and Cornell (2013) p 550 for the early Capua origins.

165. Tacitus *Histories* 1.52-54.
166. Tacitus *Histories* 2.65.1 for Cluvius' oratorical skills.
167. Tacitus 1.1.
168. See Townend (1960) pp 98-100; the theme was picked up again in Townend (1964) p 342 for discussion on sources on the year 69 CE.
169. Townend (1964) p 346.
170. See Wiseman (1991) p 115 for discussion of Townend's conclusions.
171. For Cluvius' lenient treatment of Nero see Wilkes (1972) p 202. Cornell (2013) p 558 for 'golden mean'.
172. Pliny 7.45 ff.
173. For a full discussion of Pliny's use of Greek see Deane (1918) pp 41-44.
174. Discussed extensively in Teuffel-Schwabe (1892) and Sandy (1921) pp 824-826.
175. Suetonius *Nero* 21.
176. For Cluvius' age see discussion in Wiseman (1991) p 111.
177. Suetonius *Vespasian* 4.4.
178. Tacitus 14.2; also discussed in Wiseman p 112.
179. For 'food of the gods' see Suetonius *Nero* 33. Pliny 7 reported that Agrippina used poisoned mushrooms on Claudius; also Tacitus 12.66; Suetonius *Claudius* 44, Cassius Dio 61.34 for the account of his death. Josephus 20.8.1 was more ambivalent. Additionally Cassius Dio 61.35 and Suetonius *Nero* 33 claimed Nero knew of the murder, whilst Tacitus 12.65 and Josephus 20.8.1 mentioned Agrippina only and not Nero's involvement.
180. Tacitus *Histories* 4.43.1, Pliny *Epistles* 2.11.17.
181. Tacitus *Histories* 4.39.4, following Cornell (2013) p 552.
182. Townend (1964) pp 111-113 and Wiseman (1991) p 111 for a list of fragments and anecdotes. The four fragments appear in Tacitus 13.20, 14.2, Plutarch *Otho* 3, Plutarch *Roman Questions* 107 and the anecdote in Pliny the Younger *Letters* 9, 19.5.
183. Quoting Champlin (2003) p 50.
184. Discussed and developed through Townend (1964) and Wiseman (1991) pp 114-115.
185. Compare Josephus 19.127-157 to Curtius' coverage of Babylon at 10.5.7-15.
186. Confirmation that he wrote a history comes from Pliny *Epistle* 9.19.5.
187. Mommsen (1870) pp 320-322 republished in *Gesammelte Schriften* 7, Berlin, 1909, p 248. The extract is from Josephus 19.91-92.
188. Complete discussion of the arguments in Feldman (1996) pp 165-168. Feldman refutes the claim. Also disputed by Wardle (1992) pp 466-482.
189. The identity of a Canius Rufus is also discussed in Nauta-van Dam-Smolenars (2006) pp 315-328.
190. Excerpt from Martial *Epigrams* Book 3.20 *On Canius*, sections 1-4, Bohn's Classical Library, 1897. The translation, modified by the author, comes from Champlin (2003) p 36.
191. See discussion in Williams (2004) p 60. For Caelius Rufus see Cicero *De legibus* 1.7. Cicero also mentioned a Q Curtius (though not Rufus) in his *Epistulae ad Quintum fratrem*, confirming his, and his brothers' like of the man they were attempting to advance with a military tribuneship from Julius Caesar.
192. Sentiment captured in Cicero *Epistulae ad Familiares* 5.12.4-6; discussed in Dominik (1997) p 218.
193. See discussion in Adrados (2000) p 540.
194. Quintilian 10.1.102-105.
195. Syme (1964) pp 408-424.
196. The codex is also referred to as Laurentianus 68,II. Langobard, thus from the Lombards, is also known as Beneventan Script used from around the mid-8th century until the 13th century, although there are later examples. There were two major centres of Beneventan usage: the monastery on Monte Cassino and Bari.
197. Apollinaris Sidonius *Epistle* 4.14.1 and 22.2 .
198. Discussed in detail in Wilkes (1972) pp 179-180 and quoting Momigliano (1966) p 131.
199. In translation 'to put a finish to anything'.
200. Quoting Wiseman (1982) p 67 and p 58. As has been pointed out, the issue is perhaps not as clear-cut as the conclusion of Wiseman. Tiberius, a Claudian, was adopted by Augustus, a Julian (by adoption), hence 'Julio-Claudian'. Claudius was not related to Julius Caesar, but he was an integral part of the extended family that included (adopted) Julians and Claudians. So 'Julio-Claudian' is a valid term.
201. See discussion of Josephus' training and Pharisee teaching in Wiseman (1991) Introduction p ix.
202. Quoting Mordechai (2007) with full discussion of events at pp 372–384.

14

LIFTING THE SHROUD
OF PARRHASIUS

**What might Alexander's *original* Will have contained,
how would it have distributed the empire, and how
much of its content might be retained in the testament
read today?**

Guided by the settlements at Babylon and Triparadeisus and by the behaviour of the *Diadokhoi* in the wars that followed, we attempt to rebuild the content of Alexander's original Will.

We question whether the testament that appeared in the *Pamphlet* mirrored the true division of the empire and the intended position of the royal women and Alexander's sons. Finally, we contemplate how the so-called 'last plans' might be reconciled with extant Will texts and with an original.

'For illustrious men have the whole of the earth for their tomb.'[1]

Thucydides *The History of the Peloponnesian War*

'Let no one without knowledge of geometry enter.'[2]

Written above the entrance to Plato's Academy

Philosophy and geometry were close relatives in the ancient Greek world, though they were not always happy partners: Diogenes the Cynic had no time for mathematicians '… who fixed their eyes on the sun and moon yet overlooked what was under their feet.'[3] Nevertheless, squaring the circle, doubling the cube, and trisecting the angle, remained the three great geometrical mysteries, despite the theories and arguments that had been advanced by Pythagoras, Thales of Miletus, Hippocrates of Chios and the polymaths who followed them.

Triangulating the content of Alexander's original testament is no less of a task; we have what Euclid (*floruit* ca. 300 BCE) might have termed a *porisma*.[4] For Alexander was an elusive equation: a calculable axiom of Aristotle's empirical and categorising present, and an indefinable irrational number from the Homeric past. He was a mythopoeic conqueror who at once lived by the tenets of the strategically sound and the proportionally outrageous; a tribal leader recalling heroic deeds, and a mortal seeking apotheosis through his progression from Macedonian king, to Greek *hegemon*, pharaoh of Egypt and *basileus basileon*, a Persian king of kings. Indeed his was blood and *ichor* mixed in one and we suggest the content of his testament would have been no less.

Euclid worked in Alexandria during the kingship of Alexander's general, Ptolemy I *Soter*, where he published his geometry as *Stoicheia*, *Elements*, which systemised and tightened up the earlier propositions of Eudoxus of Cnidus, Theaetetus of Athens, and other mathematical works that may have carried similar titles.[5] Euclid and Ptolemy undoubtedly knew one another; the neoplatonist philosopher Proclus the Successor (412-485 CE), who wrote a commentary on the treatise, claimed Ptolemy asked Euclid if there were quicker mathematical solutions than those he illustrated, to which the mathematician allegedly replied, 'there is no royal road to geometry'.[6] One had Pi to vex him and the other had an equally distracting geometrical dilemma: how to reshape a page of history in order to hide the outline of a royal Will. Eumenes and Olympias had already pointed the way with its tactical folding in the *Pamphlet*. So, recalling Alexander's solution to the Gordian Knot, and defying Euclid's prolix equations, Ptolemy found the quick route: he unyoked the Will altogether from Alexander's death.

Euclid's original treatise is lost to us in its complete form, and he himself suffered a similar fate when Arab scholars alchemised his name to 'Uclides' claiming its roots in *ucli* and *dis*, the Arabic words that combine to suggest the 'key of geometry'. It was a more creative identity theft than afforded him by the Middle Ages translators: they simply confused Euclid with the same-named philosopher from Megara.[7] Name exploitation was common, however; Aristippus explained Pythagoras' name derived from his celebrated wisdom – 'he spoke the truth, *agor*, no less than did the Pythian, *pyth*'.[8] If each could have anticipated Galen and Demetrius of Magnesia they might have wound up their careers with treatises titled *On My Own Name.*[9]

The geometric tales from Alexandria, however, like so many stories attached to Alexander and his *Diadokhoi,* have similarly doubtful origins, and whether Ptolemy actually benefited from Euclid's advice on the 'royal road' is unlikely. An earlier mathematician, Menaechmus, reportedly provided an identical retort when tutoring the young and impatient Alexander.[10]

Found by Grenfell and Hunt at Oxyrhynchus in 1896/7, this is one of the oldest complete diagrams from Euclid's *Elements* explaining Proposition 5 from book 2, this fragment possibly dating to 75-125 CE. The geometric formulation would be rendered in algebra as $ab + (a-b)^2/_4 = (a+b)^2/_4$ though Euclid did not yet possess algebraic method. The papyrus now residing in the University of Pennsylvania reads: 'If a straight line be cut into equal and unequal segments, the rectangle contained by the unequal segments of the whole together with the square on the straight line between the points of section is equal to the square on the half.' Like many finds from the period, the continuous capital letters hampered translations and gave rise to numerous scribal mistakes. Information source www.math.ubc.ca.

We have sought to explain the man, the motive and mechanisms behind the origination of the *Pamphlet*. In doing so we have argued why the re-emergence of a Will could have been so potent. But with no sacred geometry at hand, any attempt to trace the outline of Alexander's *original* testament remains as precarious as charting the coastline of Britain from the gnomon readings in Pytheas' *On the Ocean*, or navigating the coast of West Africa from Hanno's *Periplous*, both historically challenged sources with attachments to Alexander's day.[11] Corruptions and later embellishment of the *Romance* and *Metz Epitome* Wills leave them laden with diversional traps, like ship-wreckers' lanterns beckoning historians to perilous harbours of deduction. We know the problems and we have our theories, yet many can be argued in various directions so that we are often ourselves immersed in *dissoi logoi,* double arguments; moreover, facts, even when stated plainly, are sometimes bilingual.[12]

It was Zeno of Elea who 'invented' (better, 'developed') dialectics, the art of arguing on both sides of an issue, and its spirals of debate have led us here.[13] The *Skeptikoi*, who proposed human knowledge never amounts to certainty but only probability, would have termed it something of an acataleptic exercise.[14] Yet Euclid also coined the axiom that all non-parallel lines will eventually meet, and here it seems they do, and it completes an investigative *trivium* in which we attempt to give some form to the lost *first* testament of *Megas* Alexander.[15]

A STRATEGY FOR *STRATEGOI*: THE EMPIRE'S CENTRIPETAL STRINGS

When considering the distribution of Alexander's empire at his death, an impartial read of the list of appointed satraps, with its twenty-four-plus governors answering to no clear *local* hierarchy structure, transmits the inevitability of fragmentation; it was a fate underlined by Alexander's alleged prediction of posthumous *epitaphios agon,* the immortal 'funeral games'.[16] Despite the superficial simplicity of such an arrangement, regional administration would have been further complicated by the divided responsibilities of satraps, garrison commanders and citadel officers-cum-treasurers, with their reporting lines to absent kings, a roving *chiliarchos*, and no doubt, local bureaucrats. Thus we read of the *gazophylakes, phrourarchoi, hyparchoi, diskastai* and *dioiketai*, the titles frequently attached to these posts under the overarching authority of an *epistates, epitropos* or *epimeletes, hyparchos, hegemon* or *strategos autokrator*.[17]

We have further epigraphic evidence of the titles and roles of Macedonian-governed city magistrates that we assume operated under them: the *gymnasiarchoi, politarches* and *exetastai,* for example.[18] But if this represented the true state of the administrations of the empire in Asia, loyalties would have crossed borders with bureaucratic bottlenecks, factions would have aggregated, garrisons would have walked out and locally recruited mercenaries could have poured in; each satrap's own designs would have paid scant heed to the bigger picture.

Some further regional cohesion was required, the centripetal strings that would hold those 'centrifugal forces' at bay.[19] And when considering the locations of royal treasuries and mints scattered unevenly across the empire, counter balances must have been in place to ensure the accumulated wealth and incoming tribute, now nominally belonging to the kings in Pella, was not squandered by the local administration, or appropriated by a local warlord. This required pan-provincial governance that prevented accounting anarchy, and which, for example, *did* keep the treasuries broadly intact until 316/5 BCE; any financial extraction before that was mandated (genuinely or contrived) by the *chiliarchos* or the acting Macedonian regent on behalf of the kings.[20]

Our explanation of the missing cohesive glue is relatively simple: Alexander appointed the *Somatophylakes* along with the most prominent of generals as regional *strategoi autokratores* in his Will; Ptolemy's proposal that a select few Bodyguards – those Alexander customarily relied on for advice – should make crucial decisions on governance in his 'group rule' speech at Babylon, is a relic of just that.[21] These super-governors oversaw their surrounding satraps, so binding the empire together in perhaps nine, or ten, pan-provincial jurisdictions (if we include a 'greater' Macedonia itself), in roles in which, according to Justin, they 'became princes instead of prefects'.[22] And to head up this arrangement Alexander nominated Perdiccas as the overseer of the new Asian empire, with Craterus in a similar position in Europe, with their responsibilities overlapping in their guardianships of Alexander's sons.

The greater cohesion this implies would have ensured the borders of the Macedonian-governed empire, stretching from Scythia in the north to the Indus in the east, from Arabia and Ethiopia in the south to the Adriatic in the west, did not soften under incompetent or secession-inclined satraps, to use the Persian term. It is highly probable that the men selected had already been groomed for the roles, so that Alexander could venture westward from Babylon leaving Asia distributed securely behind him. Perhaps the crowning of the unified body of *Somatophylakes* at Susa was a step towards this public declaration of intent.[23]

Pan-provincial administrators *had* necessarily been installed throughout the Asian campaign. Philoxenus, who replaced the treasurer, Harpalus, after his first flight with funds, had an overarching authority west of the Taurus range as *strategos* of coastal forces and as *hyparchos* of the region; he potentially operated as *dioiketes* directing financial affairs in addition.[24] Balacrus, a former *Somatophylax*, had enjoyed similar responsibilities stemming from his long tenure of Cilicia and certainly Antigonus enjoyed a regional mandate in the hinterland of Asia Minor from the Battle of Issus onwards (Curtius termed him *praetor praerat* – broadly 'supreme commander').[25] Parmenio exercised similar power in all directions from Ecbatana with Alexander in the East, and Black Cleitus looks to have been appointed in a similar role in the upper satrapies shortly before his death at Alexander's hand. Craterus had operated in a regional capacity from Bactria-Sogdia when Alexander was absent on expeditions.[26] Moreover, we imagine that the Persian satraps, Mazaeus for example at Babylon, Abulites in Susiane, Phrasaortes in Persis and Phrataphernes in Parthia, as well as Artabazus and then Oxyartes (father of Roxane) in Bactria (later Parapamisadae), *must* have always answered to the Macedonian regime through these regional overseers.[27]

Could such a fundamental command structure remain buried beneath the literary topsoil for so long? Well, to consider matters in archaeological parallels with an epigraphical and papyrological perspective, knowledge of the forgotten Hittite Empire remained underground (literally) for over 3,000 years, despite its profusion of cuneiform tablets and its contact with the three great kingdoms of antiquity; we only discovered the great Indus valley civilisation, larger than that of Mesopotamia, in the 1920s. Egyptian hieroglyphs remained substantially undeciphered until Champollion published his *Précis du système hiéroglyphique* in 1824, and the identity of the 'sea people', who caused such destruction at the end of the Bronze Age, still eludes us today.

The name 'Aegae' was only uttered with any confidence again after excavations in 1977, the locations of Nora, Orcynia, and Alexander's tomb remain unknown, as does the identity of the original occupant of the Alexander Sarcophagus; there remains no proof of gardens 'hanging' at Babylon to this day. Papyri fragments from excavations in Egypt over the past century have reminded us of the literature lost, and only now are the new tomb finds at Amphipolis, Katerini and Pella revealing more of Macedonia's own past.

How, and why, these regional over-arching roles were condensed to plainer governorships and core satrapies in texts is not difficult to explain. Hieronymus' original extended detail may have simply been compressed by Diodorus and epitomisers into what we have today, just as the patronyms attached to important individuals were lost along the way. But we must also factor in the possibility, or even the probability, that Hieronymus' Antigonid-sponsored book had no interest in reinforcing knowledge of the huge Will-mandated remits of the territorial stakeholders who remained steadfastly opposed to his patrons. But, as today's 'standard model' of Alexander and his administration stands intimidating as ever, proposing a radical overhaul is inevitably controversial.

If we take a closer look at the satrapal boundaries broadcast at Babylon, however, Ptolemy's grant *does* appear extended. It included 'all the Libyan peoples subject to Macedonia' *and* 'part of Arabia bordering Egypt', presumably the Sinai. Similarly, Lysimachus received 'Thrace, the Chersonese and the peoples bordering Thrace as far as the sea at Salmydessus on the Euxine' as well as 'the neighbouring tribes of the Pontic Sea'. The *only* other mandate that looks pan-provincial, or at least as expansively well-defined, is Eumenes' Cappadocia, Paphlagonia, and 'the country on the shore of the Euxine as far as Trapezus', alternatively transmitted as 'all the lands bordering these that Alexander did not invade'.[28]

The original *Pamphlet* in its less abbreviated form (and recalling that names *were* corrupted) may have likewise expanded on these regions, for the correlation between these governors, and the *Pamphlet*'s 'coalition team', should not be ignored. Antigonus' control of Lycia, Pamphylia and Greater Phrygia is significant too, but Hieronymus had every reason to broadcast it once in Antigonid employ. So we may see in the Hieronymus-originating satrapal rundown given at the Babylonian settlement (T16, T17, T18, T19, T20) something of the *original* Will, something of the *Pamphlet*, and something of Hieronymus' duty to his two early patrons as well.

Ptolemy's authority in 'Libya' suggests his continued 'annexation' of Cyrene was possibly more legitimate (in the eyes of the *Diadokhoi*) than historians have assumed.[29] At Triparadeisus, Antipater did not demand Ptolemy's withdrawal from the region, rather: 'Egypt and Libya and all the territory that had been conquered to the West went to Ptolemy...'[30] Cyrene had offered its supplication to Alexander on his way to the Siwa Oasis in 331 BCE and thereafter Cyrenaica enjoyed (almost) uninterrupted Ptolemaic rule for over two centuries until it passed to Rome.[31]

Under the terms of Alexander's original Will, Craterus would have enjoyed authority over a Macedonia that controlled its immediate Balkan neighbours (including Illyria, the Triballians, Paeonians and Agrianians), a domain that was referred to as 'the Kingdom of Arrhidaeus' (Philip III). The Epirus of Olympias and Cleopatra would have been dealt with respectfully but was for all intents and purposes now a vassal state, while oligarchs and garrisons in Greece further extended Macedonia's political arm, though regime change (away from the Antipater-installed oligarchs) was clearly afoot with Craterus' planned return.[32] His reported emulation of Alexander certainly suggests he felt endowed with an authority beyond a blunt *prostasia*, which, due to unforeseen demands at Babylon, manifested itself as Antipater's second-in-command, a regent-in-waiting and joint *epimeletes* to the kings.[33]

Perhaps more appropriately, Photius' epitomes described Craterus' intended office as *protiston times telos,* 'the highest honour'.[34] The new guardian of the kingdom even invited Diogenes the Cynic to dine with him: 'I would rather lick salt in Athens', came the reply.[35] Craterus' monument by Lysippus and Leochares overlooking the terrace of the Temple of Apollo at Delphi, replete with a hunting scene bronze from Asia depicting him coming to the aid of Alexander who was attempting to down a lion (lion hunts had taken place in Syria and Sogdia) – the earliest and possibly the most significant of all the successor monuments (though likely completed by his son) – suggested the same; its surviving stone niche is over 50-feet long and 20-feet wide.[36]

Peucestas was already administering what we argue was a pan-provincial Persia centred on the Achaemenid capitals of the now partly charred Persepolis (the palace complex at least) and Pasargadae before Alexander died.[37] We propose his regional authority extended over the bordering lands that stretched eastwards to the Indus; the universal sentiment that in the East the governors were to remain unchanged is no doubt accurate, for Peucestas was popular and he commanded widespread loyalty. His new role may have cost him dearly if adhering to the old rites: Persian tradition obliged the ruler of ancient Parsa (the Persepolis region) to pay each matron a gold coin when they entered the province; this resulted in infrequent visits and Artaxerxes III Ochus, it is said, never set foot in his own homeland once he had been crowned.[38]

In the case of Peithon and Seleucus, the clues to their original expansive and pan-provincial grants lie in the Successor Wars.

PEITHON THE REVOLUTIONARY AND *HIS* MERCENARY REVOLT

> The Greeks who had been settled by Alexander in the upper satrapies, as they were called, although they longed for Greek customs and manner of life and were cast away in the most distant part of the kingdom, yet submitted while the king was alive through fear, but when he was dead they rose in revolt.[39]

Soon after news of Alexander's death reached the upper satrapies, 20,000 discontented Greek mercenary infantrymen and 3,000 allied cavalry, 'all of whom had many times been tried in the contests of war and were distinguished for their courage', were making their way through the 'upper satrapies' (not Media) in a state of revolt under an Athenian general, Philon. This was the second mass defection of mercenary garrisoneers; the first wave had successfully returned to Greece from Bactria.[40] Peithon son of Crateuas, the prominent *Somatophylax* who, we are told, was given Media to govern (T16, T17, T18, T19, T20) at Babylon, was charged with quelling the uprising.[41] He 'was a man of great ambition, [who] gladly accepted the expedition, intending to win the Greeks over through kindness, and, after making his army great through an alliance with them, to work in his own interests and become the ruler of the upper satrapies', so Diodorus concluded from his reading of Hieronymus.[42]

Upon departing Babylon, Peithon's troop numbers were insignificant; from the royal army he had been supplied with just 3,000 Macedonian infantry (of perhaps 13,000 then in Babylon) and 800 Macedonian cavalry (of possibly some 2,000 remaining), all chosen by lot and many surely unwilling to head back to the East. Perdiccas provided Peithon with letters to the satrapal governors ordering them to furnish him with a further 10,000 Asiatic foot soldiers and 8,000 cavalry.[43]

Firstly, the numbers look suspicious. Alexander and his generals knew full well no Asiatic force, even with 3,000 Macedonian infantry at its heart, could take on 20,000 Greek mercenary hoplites. In disciplined phalanx formation they would have pierced the more lightly armed Asiatic ranks and outflanked the opposing phalangites, assuming the Macedonian contingent were *pezhetairoi* unsupported by *hypaspistai*. If the 3,000 Macedonians *were* in hoplite panoply, and not pike-bearers, then no 'first-strike' weapon had been provided to Peithon; there is no mention of a further 10,000 *sarissai* being collected along the way with which to equip those local recruits, that is if they had even been *trained* in the use of the pike as the Susa *epigonoi* had presumably been.[44] Mounted troops would not have been able to charge a tight infantry formation with spears arrayed forward unless they were equipped as *sarissophoroi* and accomplished in the flying wedge (and perhaps not even then), and if Peithon's mounted ranks simply acted as static cavalry guarding the infantry flanks, they would have been vulnerable themselves.[45]

Perdiccas' distrust of Peithon had led him to issue orders to the effect that all the renegades were to be slaughtered, suspecting he might indeed raise a private army from their ranks.[46] This raises the question: why task Peithon with the mission in the first place? Diodorus believed his personal ambition and intriguing was real, the 'revolutionary behaviour' Aelian picked up on.[47] But Hieronymus may have swung the episode around a little unconvincingly, for Peithon quelled the uprising and managed to rejoin Perdiccas, either in time for the conquest of Cappadocia and Pisidia (if so, he was never mentioned), or before the ill-fated invasion of Egypt where he murdered the chiliarch.[48]

Although 3,000 Greek infantry were reportedly persuaded by Peithon to betray their comrades, the mercenary numbers look grossly inflated, for it is difficult to imagine that the remaining 17,000 who were 'distinguished for their courage' – a formidable army in any circumstances – took flight in confusion, as the text claims. Peithon supposedly gained a victory over them (no detail of how he accomplished this is given) and sent a herald to the 'conquered' mass offering false terms of satrapal repatriation if they laid down their arms. Diodorus claimed the Macedonians, remembering Perdiccas' instructions, were able to 'shoot them all with javelins' after betraying the trust of the Greeks. This sounds dubious despite Diodorus' claim that the Macedonians 'set upon them unexpectedly' (which would have been difficult to pull-off as it was against Peithon's alleged objective) and caught 'them off their guard', because the text additionally stated that the unwitting Greeks '... were interspersed among the Macedonians', hardly a situation in which javelins could be hurled.[49]

We recall how reluctantly hoplites ever gave up their shields, especially to what must here have been a largely Asiatic force half the size of their own. If the Greeks *were* still equipped with their *hopla* and grouped together, to quote one scholar on the issue: 'Missile weapons seem, in fact, to have been comparatively ineffective against the hoplite phalanx', and as Tarn pointed out, the day of the Persian archer had ended at Plataea.

We may imagine what was deemed a hostile mass of '20,000' was, in fact, made up from predominantly non-combatants – the families of the forced settlers, and their baggage train – and they were the vulnerable target being threatened in the negotiations.[50] Their possessions *were* plundered; we imagine what amounted to just few thousand remaining infantry *were* set upon at Peithon's orders once they were isolated, and the 3,000 complicit hoplites were probably sent back to their satrapies (Peithon did not entirely lose the potential future army) and the surviving women and children were left to march with them.

Peithon's mission becomes more credible, and explainable, if we accept that he had already become *strategos* of the upper satrapies, with his authority *centred* on a Media Major and extending to the Caspian Gates to the west, and to India to the east (authority *in* India is less clear, Peithon son of Agenor, or Philip son of Machatas – thus Harpalus' brother – *may* have governed a region in a similar role).[51] So it was *his* 'upper satrapy' regional revolt to deal with, whether Perdiccas liked it or not.[52] The contention that this authority was a genuine Will inheritance, and not one of Perdiccas' designs, is strengthened when we recall that Atropates, Perdiccas' father-in-law since the Susa weddings, was only granted Lesser Media at Babylon when he appears to have previously governed Media complete, a more powerful mandate his son-in-law could have readily reconfirmed (T16, T20).[53] A later statement by Diodorus seems to further support the expanded role: 'Peithon had been appointed satrap of Media, but when he became general of all upper satrapies, he put to death Philotas, the former general of Parthia, and set up his own brother Eudamus in his place.'[54] What is seen as unbridled ambition by Diodorus may have had more legitimate foundations.

It appears that Peithon was nevertheless testing the patience of his subordinate governors and his arrogance soon backfired. But as Anson points out, that Seleucus provided him sanctuary in Babylonia indicates *he* was not troubled by his colleague's cross-provincial meddling.[55] Although Diodorus explained the 'upper satraps had concentrated their armies in a single place' (in response to the threat from Peithon), the coalition that Eumenes met was principally conglomerated from the forces from what we argue was Peucestas' domain: in other words those 'lower' eastern satrapies comprising Peucestas' own Persian archers and slingers alongside troops from Susiane, Carmania, Arachosia, Areia, Drangiana and Paropanisadae.[56] An addition to their ranks was Eudamus who had taken control of the Paurava region in India.[57]

Diodorus employed the term 'upper' loosely when referring to the eastern provinces. But what does remain clear is a clinical regional divide: Peucestas' coalition did not, for example, feature Peithon son of Agenor, the satrap of the northern Indus region bordering Paropanisadae, who later joined Antigonus. Neither were troop contingents mentioned from Hyrcania or regions north of Bactria and Sogdia, under Stasanor, for example, who was vilified by the *Pamphlet*, for these were the regions that fell under Peithon's pan-provincial mandate.[58] Though some troops do appear to have originated from Bactria itself, these were raised by Stasander, the satrap of Areia-Drangiana, and he was probably able to achieve this because he had (curiously) *previously* governed Bactria and still had loyal contingents.

This geographical division of allies appears less than coincidental and falls neatly in line with the regional *strategia* we propose. In which case the two gold-crowned *Somatophylakes*, Peucestas and Peithon son of Crateuas, were the overseers of the further-eastern empire to India with its named satrapal governors under them, and there is much evidence that neither had plans of abandoning their considerable inheritances.[59] Any confusion within these eastern subdivisions are understandable: Bactria and Media 'embraced many regions with distinctive names' and, moreover, they 'afforded an ejected commander many refuges and retreats'.[60] Atropates himself is one example in northwest or 'lesser' Media. He eventually declared himself king and his territory was thereafter referred to as Media Atropatene, and that came, significantly, after Peithon's execution by Antigonus in 315 BCE, though Polybius believed this region had never been previously conquered.[61]

Following Peithon's removal, Antigonus granted Nicanor (and possibly Hippostratus before him), potentially the general who received Eumenes' surrender at Gabiene, *strategia* over what Diodorus clearly stated as all the 'upper satrapies'.[62] More telling still was his *failure* to unite the remaining governors to the south, for Peucestas had by then also been removed. It appears the southern and central satraps of the East were reluctant to unite under a non-legitimate *strategos*, or one who had not adopted their customs. In this newly fragmenting environment it was no surprise that Seleucus was able to inflict a crushing defeat on Antigonus' divided forces when they put up a 'perfunctory and negligent guard'.[63]

BABYLONIA AND BEYOND: SELEUCUS' HIDDEN INHERITANCE

There is scarcely a mention of Seleucus in the extant texts between Alexander's death and his re-emergence at Triparadeisus some three years later when a 'new' satrapal role was supposedly confirmed on him: the governorship of Babylon. We have already argued why Hieronymus had little interest in featuring his patrons' opponent and his regional inheritance more prominently. But when Antigonus threatened Seleucus' tenure of the region after Eumenes' death in 315 BCE, Diodorus stated that Seleucus claimed he had been given 'the country' (not just city) in 'recognition of his services rendered while Alexander was alive.'[64]

The reference to 'Macedonians' bestowing the role on him discounts it being the manipulative hand of Perdiccas alone. Superficially, at least, it is more representative of either the endorsement of Seleucus' inheritance at the original Assembly at Babylon, or his reconfirmation at Triparadeisus in 320 BCE; in fact, reminding Antigonus of either of these events would have been a better repost than 'as per the testament of Alexander', for Antigonus had already demonstrated by then that he completely ignored satrapal boundaries established by *any* regal authority.

Diodorus was under the impression that Seleucus had been granted the hipparchy of the Companion Cavalry by Perdiccas at Babylon in 323 BCE, the command Perdiccas had himself inherited at Hephaestion's death (T16). This is supported by Justin who more generally stated Seleucus received 'chief command of the camp' (T20), and it is perhaps strengthened by the fact that Seleucus had already commanded the Royal Hypaspists after Hephaestion was promoted to hipparch, probably in 330 BCE (when Philotas was executed).[65] That this post, previously held by the king's chiliarch, was separated out, clearly indicates that Perdiccas' own continued 'chiliarchy' is to be interpreted as the higher-functioning quasi-regent post, and not the cavalry command. Like the authority it had vested in Hephaestion before him, the title equated to administrator of the kings and their realms and with no power above, save *basileia*.[66]

Diodorus further accepted that a more obscure Archon was appointed as the principal Babylonian governor.[67] But Seleucus' hipparchy command cannot be compared to Ptolemy's inheritance of the ancient land of Egypt, deemed 'the best' due to its revenues, a sentiment no doubt originating with the Alexandrian Cleitarchus; and neither was it equal to Peithon's governance of Media, also referred to as 'the greatest of all' due to its regional diversity.[68] It did not match Peucestas' control of the ancient

Persian heartlands, or even, for that matter, Eumenes' grant centred on Cappadocia, which hosted the Royal Road on its northern route from Susa to Sardis.[69] Although Justin interpreted Seleucus' new post as 'second-in-command' (in Perdiccas' immediate camp), he would have been witnessing his colleagues exploit their new chunks of the empire when he had nothing but the prestige of serving Perdiccas on horseback. Named amongst the most eminent of cavalry leaders at Babylon, would Seleucus, the future builder of the most expansive of all the successor empires, have truly been excluded from the territorial honours list in Alexander's Will?[70] Or could Perdiccas himself, in the accepted intestate scenario, have really orchestrated this estateless role?

In contrast, we know the *Pamphlet*-based Will, which had every reason to pass Seleucus over (he was clearly not named 'innocent' of regicide, thus not on the coalition team), appears to have unambiguously allocated him Babylonia – city, province and 'territory adjoining it'; and here the *Romance* and *Metz Epitome* texts are in clear accord (T1, T2).[71] In which case Archon, and potentially Arcesilaus too, if Mesopotamia came under a Babylonia-centred expansive remit, were operating *under* Seleucus as subordinate governors.[72] Under-governors usually appeared in Diodorus' narrative when their overlords were on campaign; Seleucus appointed Patrocles to Babylon, for example, when campaigning in Media against Nicanor in 312 BCE.[73] If Mesopotamia was a part of that territorial grant, then Amphimachus (appointed at Triparadeisus and also over the Arbelitis region) and Blitor who assumed a similar post after him, operated in similar subordinate roles later. Amphimachus appears to have joined Eumenes when he passed through the region in winter 317 BCE, following which Seleucus replaced him with Blitor who facilitated Seleucus' escape from Antigonus in 315 BCE.[74]

Mesopotamia was never mentioned as a distinct satrapy until the dispensation of governorships at Babylon; the name was after all a Greek construction: broadly 'land between rivers', the Tigris and Euphrates.[75] Sumer, Akkad and Babylonia had once comprised 'Assyria' which later denoted the northern part of Mesopotamia, and it was the name the Achaemenid kings would have still used for the region. If our deduction about Seleucus is correct, he was to govern what is broadly Iraq today, and there is evidence that Antigonus did, in fact, combine these satrapies into a single regional mandate once Seleucus fled the territory in 315 BCE.[76]

So who was Archon? He had been named as a *trierarchos* of the Hydaspes-Indus fleet but he is otherwise unattested on campaign.[77] Perdiccas replaced him with Docimus, and Archon was supposed to retain the role as collector of revenues in the province, a demotion Perdiccas may have assumed (and wished) he would never accept. Archon may have colluded in the interception of Alexander's funeral hearse by Ptolemy, presumably with the blessing of Seleucus, thus prompting his removal. Enmity was clear; he and Docimus ended up fighting it out for control and Archon lost his life.[78] *Reconfirmed* at Triparadeisus, Seleucus entered the city unopposed when Docimus, now a proscribed Perdiccan, fled to join the 'royal rebel' cause.[79] None of this excludes Seleucus inheriting the honorific *hipparchos* of the First (Hephaestion's) *chiliarchia* of the Companion Cavalry in Perdiccas' royal army, or attending to the administration of his wider region. This would explain why he was absent from Babylon when Docimus was installed, and, moreover, why he claimed the region was his 'by right' when confronting Antigonid expansion in 315 BCE.

How could Diodorus have arrived at his conclusions about Seleucus' hipparchy post? The first explanation would once again be to assume Hieronymus omitted his regional mandate as payback for his long history of hostility; publishing his account some fifty years after events, this demotion was easily made, though carefully reconstructed to rebroadcast that he had become Perdiccas' 'number two'. Yet we do have a contradiction, for in Photius' epitome (of Dexippus' summary) of Arrian's *Events After Alexander*, which is ultimately Hieronymus-sourced, we read that Seleucus *did* indeed receive control of Babylon from the outset (T18), though this may simply be an epitomised merging of the appointments at Babylon and Triparadeisus once more. Unfortunately, in Photius' own direct précis of Arrian a lacuna has swallowed this part of the satrapal list robbing us of a useful comparison, whilst a lacuna (we imagine) resulted in the total loss of references to Babylonia in Curtius' run down, which is otherwise inexplicable when considering the space he dedicated to the infighting at Babylon (T17).[80]

We cannot discount a further (and perhaps the most obvious) explanation: Diodorus simply misunderstood Hieronymus' original wording, and it is not difficult to imagine a sufficiently ambiguous statement:

> Seleucus campaigned with Perdiccas in the role of hipparch of the Companion Cavalry, a prestigious role amounting to a second in command and formerly held by Perdiccas and Hephaestion before him, and in his absence Archon was appointed governor of Babylon.[81]

Whatever the cause of the compression of Seleucus' role, Diodorus' explanation has been formative to interpretations ever since.

LANDS WEST OF THE HALYS: LEONNATUS' HIDDEN INHERITANCE

The extant sources unanimously stated that Leonnatus was allocated Hellespontine Phrygia at Babylon (T16, T17, T18, T19, T20).[82] Leonnatus was a *syntrophos* raised with Alexander at the Pellan court and a decorated

Bodyguard credited with saving the king's life.[83] His father, Anteas, was a relative of Eurydice, the mother of Philip II; Leonnatus was therefore a member of the Lyncestian royal house and his correspondence with Cleopatra hints that he felt every bit as regal as his heritage suggested.[84] Additionally, at Babylon, Leonnatus was clearly chosen beside Perdiccas to be a guardian of the unborn king, and Curtius positioned him as the second most important of the *hetairoi* then present.[85]

In traditional interpretations, Leonnatus and Antigonus were tasked by Perdiccas with assisting Eumenes in his pacification of the geographically vast and important unconquered Cappadocia, when Leonnatus' own authority was restricted to the relatively diminutive (in size) Hellespont-bordering province once governed by a 'son of Harpalus', possibly a relative of the controversial treasurer; the region's principal importance lay in its bordering the narrow sea-crossing to Europe, though its boundaries are less than clinically outlined by our sources.[86] Once again we need to question whether Alexander would have really carved up the empire so disproportionately when considering the *accepted* territorial grants of Ptolemy, Peithon, Peucestas, Lysimachus, Antigonus and Eumenes. Again we need to similarly challenge the notion that Perdiccas could have attempted the same, for he and Leonnatus were in action together as far back as Philip II's death in Aegae some thirteen years before.[87]

Alexander would surely have bestowed a grander role on Leonnatus that recognised his true importance: logically this was authority over northwest Asia Minor governed *from* Hellespontine Phrygia, just as Antigonus had initially operated in a wider role from his own early 'capital' at Celaenae in Phrygia. Asia Minor had never been governed under a single mandate; with Alexander campaigning east, Antigonus was supplemented by Balacrus in Cilicia, Nearchus south of the Taurus (to the west of Cilicia), with Calas and Asander in the Hellespontine region and Lydia.[88] If the bulk of Asia Minor was to be divided between them now, then Leonnatus' authority could have spanned the still nominally independent Bithynia (alongside Mysia and the Troad region), Lesser Phrygia, Lydia and Caria, with lesser governors under him.[89]

Antigonus would have then received the adjoining hinterland and much of the south: Greater Phrygia, Lycia, Pamphylia and Lycaonia.[90] Pisidia and Cilicia as far as the Cilician or Amanian Gate bordering Syria (so southeastern Asia Minor) appear to have fallen outside his mandate, as they had before. This division of power explains why *both* Leonnatus and Antigonus were charged with helping Eumenes pacify Cappadocia and presumably Paphlagonia (separated from Bithynia by the Parthenius, the modern Bartin River); quite credibly Eumenes was also a pan-satrapal *strategos* whose own region would have stretched eastwards through Armenia.[91]

Armenia may have been bestowed upon Neoptolemus on similar conditions to Eumenes' region: the territory first needed subduing, and a similar reciprocal arrangement for assistance might have been demanded. Perdiccas '... sent Eumenes back from Cilicia, ostensibly to his own satrapy [Cappadocia], but really to reduce to obedience the adjacent country of Armenia, which had been thrown into confusion by Neoptolemus.' And so it *is* tempting to join Armenia to Eumenes' wider mandate, as this would explain Neoptolemus' resentment of the 'man who followed Alexander with a pen'. Peucestas' friend, Orontes, had either claimed the region, or later been reinstated as satrap.[92] If Armenia *was* part of Eumenes' genuine inheritance, or even if it was a more-duplicitous *Pamphlet*-Will grant, it would better explain why Eumenes' ruse involving the unwitting Orontes worked so convincingly at Persepolis, helping him wrest regional control from the equally unwitting Peucestas.[93] Eumenes' governance of Armenia would have then logically extended his authority towards the Caspian whence Peithon's own governance commenced from Media and stretching eastward, and it would have been neatly bordered by Mesopotamia in the south.

In the aftermath of the Second *Diadokhoi* War ending 315 BCE, Lysimachus demanded Hellespontine Phrygia when he, Cassander and Ptolemy sent envoys to Antigonus. The satrapy was vacant following the defeat of Arrhidaeus, and the same delegation of envoys demanded Lycia for Cassander along with Eumenes' Cappadocia.[94] 'Lycia' should surely read 'Lydia', the satrapy left ungoverned since the death of White Cleitus, for with Leonnatus dead, the region had been become divisible at Triparadeisus.

At this point, 315 BCE, Cassander was the *de facto* ruler of Macedonia, for he had King Alexander IV and his mother under lock and key at Amphipolis. *His* role in the defeat of Eumenes had been restricted to distracting Polyperchon in Greece, and yet he seems to have already sent advanced forces into Cappadocia, besieging the city of Amisus (modern Samsun in northern Turkey), *possibly* to distract Antigonus from invading Macedonia.[95] But why here specifically? As Cassander had no experience in Asia and no previous Asian claims, we might conclude it was the publication of the *Pamphlet*, with its obvious authorship, that incited him to occupy Eumenes' inherited region. Whether this led to the rift between him and Antigonus, who realigned with Polyperchon, or whether it followed it, is unclear, but Antigonus had no intention of letting Cassander stay on Asian soil.

PERDICCAS: HOLLOW PROMISES FOR A GREATER SYRIA

With Craterus appointed to govern the Macedonian kingdom as the principle resident guardian of the kings, and with Alexander's

Somatophylakes spread through the vast provinces of the former Persian Empire they would now govern, tax and harvest, we should pose a huge but as yet unarticulated question: where Perdiccas, the supposedly itinerant overseer of the empire, was supposed to base himself? The one hugely important region, greater in significance than those assigned to govern it and less than satisfactorily accounted for in the divisions listed at Babylon, is a 'Greater Syria' that would link Egypt, Arabia, Mesopotamia-Babylonia and Asia Minor (through Cilicia and Pisidia) together. The only reference to Syria in the Babylonian settlement, or at Triparadeisus, was a governorship linked to Laomedon, and that was more convincingly Coele-Syria, as Diodorus and other satrapy-citing texts later clarified; Arrian was clear that his territory bordered Egypt and Justin additionally stated: 'Laomedon of Mytilene was allotted Syria, which bordered on Ptolemy's province' (T17, T20).[96]

Coele-Syria was itself ambiguously referenced throughout history though it was more specifically delineated in the *Pamphlet*-originating Wills. In *koine* Greek, *Coele* (*koile*) meant 'hollow', and this referred to the fertile Bequaa Valley in modern eastern Lebanon, or, as some scholars interpret it, broadly modern Israel.[97] Diodorus' Hieronymus-inspired digression on the geography of the empire was clearer on the constituent Syrian parts:

> Next to Mesopotamia are Upper Syria, as it is called, and the countries adjacent thereto along the sea: Cilicia, Pamphylia, and Coele Syria, which encloses Phoenicia. Along the frontiers of Coele Syria and along the desert that lies next to it, through which the Nile makes its way and divides Syria and Egypt...[98]

Diodorus often referred to the region bordering Egypt as 'lower' Syria. A 'Greater Syrian' governorship might then have encompassed lower Syria, Coele-Syria (encompassing Phoenicia) and Upper Syria (in total, broadly modern Israel, Lebanon, Jordan and Syria) to the Mesopotamian Line (thus including 'Mesopotamian Syria') which we assume was the River Euphrates, and it would have been a strategically sound base of operations, linking as it did the major Asian regions.[99] On this basis the division of what we might term the 'Levant' today is clear-cut. The extended domain, as far north as Cilicia and eastern Pisidia, operated as a buffer zone through which any army would need to pass if it were to invade another. Certainly Cilicia *was* carved out of Asia Minor in texts: following battle at Gaugamela, Alexander appointed Menes in a role that was to govern from Babylon (probably again though Syria and Phoenicia) to the Taurus.[100] So the Taurus Mountain range was the natural cut-off of a cohesive region that was still in existence when Mark Antony and Cleopatra allocated it to their son, Ptolemy II *Philadelphos* under the Donation of Alexandria in 34 BCE.[101]

It is generally supposed that Eumenes returned to Babylon to report to Perdiccas once Leonnatus and Antigonus refused to assist his pacification of Cappadocia.[102] Yet his and Perdiccas' whereabouts are not actually stated; the urgency of Antigonus' flight, and the speed with which a new campaign against Ariarathes was initiated – 'moreover, a little while after he [Eumenes] was conducted into Cappadocia with an army which Perdiccas commanded in person' – suggest the chiliarch might have been rather closer, and northern Syria is a strategically sound option. It does appear that Perdiccas was based just to the north of Syria, in Cilicia, when he ordered Eumenes to take control of Armenia with plenipotentiary powers, and this further explains Perdiccas' own hostile campaign in the region, and why his brother, Alcetas, was cited at Cretopolis and Termessus.[103]

Perdiccas' tasking Arrhidaeus with the construction of the dead king's funeral bier indicates that he was not based at Babylon, otherwise he could have overseen it himself, and Arrhidaeus had no technical or engineering background that we know of; if its destination was Syria (it was hijacked near Damascus) then, as we previously posed, Arrhidaeus did not 'redirect' its path at all. As Atkinson points out, the wording Diodorus used – 'return journey' and 'home' – clearly indicates that Perdiccas eventually planned to send the body to Aegae.[104]

Perdiccan-Syria, it appears, was to be the temporary home of Alexander while the dust from the recent tensions settled and until Perdiccas could launch his own 'invasion' of Pella. Routing the cortège though Damascus conforms to no practical route to Macedonia; the more direct journey to the Hellespont from Babylon, and the one best served by established roads, would have been to follow the Euphrates north, or better, the western bank of the Tigris, to connect with the Royal Road network in upper Mesopotamia and then northwest through Asia Minor. It is possible that Alexander's throne, weapons and panoply (a 'set' of which later resurfaced with Eumenes) had originally travelled with it.[105] But loading an enormously weighty sarcophagus – housed in an ornate 'ionic temple' – on a ship would have been a tricky business for even the best of engineers in the most peaceful of times, and this suggests the funeral hearse was never constructed with a maritime voyage in mind. Then again, the Macedonians had witnessed Alexander in action and they were now hardly deterred by such challenges: elephants were just as much of a transportation headache, and Antipater managed to take some seventy of them back with him across the Hellespont.[106]

Further clues to Perdiccas' extended presence in a Greater Syria exist. He is recorded as having founded (or refounded) the city of Samaria (now northern Israel), probably during this period, and he launched his campaign against Ptolemy from Damascus. It was here that the ancient network of roads converged: the *Old Testament* 'way of the Philistines' (or the 'way of the sea'), 'way of the kings' which had an offshoot – the 'way of the wilderness' from Babylonia to Egypt and across the Sinai and Negev.[107] Damascus, Alexandria ad Issus (Roman Alexandretta, modern Iskenderun) and Beroia (today's Aleppo) to the north were similarly connected and therefore strategically sound choices as bases for empire administration. Diodorus described the location as '... naturally well adapted for watching over Babylon and the upper satrapies, and again for keeping an eye upon lower Syria and the satrapies near Egypt.'[108] Antigonus would later learn the strategic value of Syria when founding Antigonea-on-the-Orontes near Antioch, his residence from 306-302 BCE.[109] Seleucus later positioned the city of Apamea in calculated fashion on the right bank of the Orontes as part of a Syrian tetrapolis.[110]

Following Perdiccas' death in Egypt, and as further evidence of his regional governance, Archelaus, the garrison captain at Tyre, handed over the 800 talents to Attalus that Perdiccas had there for safekeeping. As one scholar noted, this was a transaction that appeared to take place independently of the local authority of Laomedon, suggesting an overarching authority at work.[111] We know Ptolemy offered to buy Laomedon out of Coele-Syria (in previous times annexed, along with Phoenicia, by the Egyptian pharaohs) to better secure his border and gain the Phoenician ports.[112] Diodorus' account of the episode is brief; either a lacuna exists or Hieronymus' oversimplified the rationale behind Ptolemy's move.[113]

If we *are* correct in identifying these wider roles for the *Somatophylakes*, a financial offer would have only been acceptable to the remaining *Diadokhoi* if it did not infringe upon a living *strategos*. That implies a new absence of that overarching authority in the Syrian region following Perdiccas' death. For unless we introduce a missing mechanism, Ptolemy's annexation would have appeared controversial and indeed expansionist, and yet no challenge emerged. The region was not contested until Eumenes 'thought to recover for the kings Phoenicia' in early 317 BCE.[114] In 315 BCE, after war with Eumenes was concluded, Ptolemy's envoy to Antigonus demanded '*all* Syria' be granted for the part he played in the victory; once again this suggests there was no *de jure* governor of the Greater Syrian region.[115]

Perdiccas may well have initially succeeded in surrounding himself with trusted governors and potentially with Alexander's approval in the name of stability: Aristonus could have governed a northern part of Syria 'to the Mesopotamian Line' (therefore close to Cilicia from where he set off on the failed Cypriot invasion), Arcesilaus in Mesopotamia itself, Laomedon in Coele-Syria, Philoxenus in Cilicia, and his brother Alcetas in Pisidia; no doubt Docimus in Babylonia, Cleomenes in Egypt and

Eumenes in eastern Asia Minor were supposed to report on developments across the immediate borders.[116]

Why then was Hieronymus not more lucid on Perdiccas' Syrian mandate? Diodorus could have misunderstood the role of the roving chiliarch, as he did that of Seleucus, or, quite simply, it did not benefit Hieronymus to broadcast it, for once he had made it clear Perdiccas enjoyed foremost authority at Babylon he had achieved all he needed to legitimise Eumenes' early career. Syria was after all raped and torn apart by Hieronymus' own patrons in their bid to secure Phoenician ports and a path south to Egypt.

Could the other still-debated coffin, the so-called 'Alexander Sarcophagus' that was discovered in Sidon, and which is still widely linked to Abdalonymus (or as Heckel suggests, Mazaeus), have actually been crafted for Perdiccas, perhaps after the conference at Triparadeisus, itself in Upper Syria? His brother-in-law, Attalus, was close by gathering up any soldiers who made it out of Egypt, and Eumenes could have even commissioned the 'highly conflicted' coffin when he passed through the region in early 317 BCE with his pockets full from Cyinda. It is noteworthy that carved on one pediment (the top of short side 'A') is a relief reckoned by some scholars to depict Perdiccas' murder; an unarmed man is being attacked by what appear to be three armed Macedonians (Antigenes, Peithon, Seleucus, or even a bearded Philip III?). A second victim (perhaps his sister, Atalante) looks to be holding a shield for protection, and one attacker has fallen implying a spirited defence. If that theory is correct, this would hardly be a fitting commemorative for anyone else but Perdiccas.[117]

A scene from the so-called Alexander Sarcophagus (short side 'A') which may depict the murder of the unarmed Perdiccas. Istanbul Archaeology Museum.

A TESTAMENTAL MIRROR: THE IMPORTANCE OF TRIPARADEISUS

At the reconvening of generals at Triparadeisus in late summer of 320 BCE, the discord from Babylon re-emerged, incited by Eurydice and stirred by 'accusations' delivered in her speech, though the unexpected presence of Attalus and his fleet (perhaps moored nearby, but surely not *at* the convocation where he would have been seized and executed), may have added to the tension. Eurydice was fanning a fire lit by grievances related to pay and promised bonuses (and probably more besides), a crisis finally defrayed by Antigonus and Seleucus.[118] With Perdiccas, Craterus and Leonnatus now dead, and with Eumenes along with the remaining Perdiccans scattered under sentence of death, and with Peithon, Antigenes, and possibly Seleucus having recently shown their deadly dissatisfaction with the state of Perdiccan affairs, the empire could have been *completely* redistributed.[119]

This was also the perfect opportunity to take a second and perhaps more legitimate vote on the accession of the princes; Antipater, we should recall, arrived with a Macedonian army not tainted by Babylonian Assembly politics or by years of service under the *Somatophylakes*. Moreover, the principal backers of Arrhidaeus – Meleager and his supporters – were dead or firmly outnumbered.[120] A completely new order could have emerged, and yet it did not.

The most significant of the territorial grants made by Antipater at Triparadeisus matched the original satrapal appointments supposedly orchestrated by Perdiccas at Babylon. The few changes that were made simply plugged the gaps left by the dead or by the clearly untrustworthy. Ptolemy, Laomedon, Lysimachus, Antigonus (though now with wider powers), Asander, Peithon, Peucestas, and we propose Seleucus too, all retained control of their original regions, as did the majority of the eastern satraps.[121] If Alexander had made no effort to formalise the governance of the empire, this would be a vexing *status quo*, and it is far better explained as adherence to his Will that no one dared challenge at that stage. Besides, the *Somatophylakes* did not wish to challenge their inheritances, for they had surely been discussed, shaped, and agreed upon well before Alexander's death.

'WHERE THERE IS GAIN, 'GAINST NATURE'S DICTATES MUST ONE WED': MACEDONIAN WOMEN, ROYAL-BORN AND REGENT-BRED[122]

... once the father is dead, heirs are for practical purposes (assuming they are well below the age of maturity) no man's sons, and can do no would-be-dynast any more than short-term good, whereas the king's sisters can be married and thus, legitimise the seizure of royal or quasi-royal power. Better yet, a king's sister may produce children of the blood of the royal house, as well as the new.[123]

This extract from a study of Argead women by Elizabeth Carney has particular relevance to the situation Alexander was faced with on his deathbed in Babylon, and to the struggles of ascendancy his successors were faced with after. The contribution of women in Macedonian dynasties is well-documented, and the Hellenistic Age was 'strewn with' Stratonices, Berenices, Laodices, Arsinoes, and of course, Cleopatras, all of whom played significant political roles at the royal courts of their day.[124]

There is evidence that Olympias and Cleopatra were executing Alexander's policy in their role as *prostates* throughout his absence on campaign, an arrangement wholly abrasive to his embattled regent, Antipater. Alexander's mother and sister were listed as recipients on grain shipments from Cyrene (without patronymic, suggesting a head of state and probably in the famine years of 330-326 BCE) alongside other dignitaries.[125] After the death of her husband, Alexander Molossus, Cleopatra may have been acting *prostates* in Epirus where women appear to have enjoyed a higher social status (as they did in Etruria), and where roles akin to 'presidents' were attested in the absence of a king. Cleopatra may well have held the office of *thearodochos* (an official who received sacred envoys) for the Epirote League; it has been argued that the whole Argead clan possessed this sacral power, and Olympias had certainly taken over custody of the oracle of Dodona during her tenure of Epirus, warding off Greek interference in the process. She had also attempted to intervene in the Harpalus affair by demanding he be surrendered up when he fled to Athens in 324 BCE, for she would surely have preferred to take control of the Asian treasury funds he absconded with rather than letting them be scooped up by Antipater.[126]

In the post-Alexander world, Phila the sagacious daughter of Antipater, Cynnane the daughter of Philip II, her daughter Adea and Polyperchon's daughter-in-law Cratesipolis were all involved in military actions or state decision-making.[127] Stratonice the wife of Antigonus had a role in the conclusion of the siege of the Perdiccan rebels in Pisidia, and a generation on, the Successor Wars were permeated by intermarriages between more of these remarkable Macedonian women – the daughters of the *Diadokhoi* – as families sought dynastic advancement and protection from rivals. And none of them '… could be reproached either for cowardice or for scrupulousness.'[128]

The Will preserved in the *Romance* and *Metz Epitome* is Greek in style, an endogamous document that saw the pairing of the royal women and the king's leading men. But do any of these arrangements reflect Alexander's *original* wishes, or are they the political machinations of the pamphleteers? Alexander appears to have trusted two men above all: Craterus and Perdiccas, though they inconveniently mistrusted one another, and despite allegations to the opposite, Alexander relied upon two women to protect his interests: Olympias and Cleopatra.[129] Both men and women could presumably be counted as guardians of Alexander's sons. 'Macedonian kings arranged marriages for themselves *and* their offspring', and Alexander would have wanted to stage-manage exactly that through his Will.[130]

Although overwhelmingly influential, Olympias was past childbearing age and she could not in any case produce an Argead heir being Molossian in origin, now that there were no surviving or suitable Argead males. Cleopatra was in her early thirties when Alexander died and sources suggest was already the mother of two children; as the daughter of Philip II she *could* still provide a half-Argead heir.[131] Contemplating their respective positions, Olympias saw the two obvious means to surviving the turmoil: find Cleopatra a powerful husband 'complete with a Macedonian army', and establish herself as principal guardian of the young Alexander IV.[132] It appears she attempted both.

With the strongest contenders – Perdiccas, Leonnatus and Craterus – dead by 320 BCE, Cleopatra courted, or was variously courted by, Cassander, Ptolemy, Lysimachus, and possibly even by Antigonus, during her twelve years at Sardis.[133] If Perdiccas' approach to Cleopatra (brokered through Eumenes) had led to war with Antipater – suggesting *this* match was not endorsed or demanded by Alexander's Will – and when considering that no other suitor appeared immediately after to claim the 'right' to her hand, then it follows that she was most likely paired with either the already dead Leonnatus or Craterus; it would further explain why Antipater was relieved when Leonnatus fell at Lamia. If Cleopatra *had* been paired with the fallen *Somatophylax*, then her correspondence with Leonnatus carried a legitimacy that has been lost or deliberately camouflaged; her overtures to Perdiccas and her crossing to Asia did only take place once Leonnatus had fallen in Thessaly.

The pairing of Cleopatra with Craterus is more troublesome, for we would have to assume that he rejected Alexander's sister in favour of Phila after considering the permutations and after crossing to Greece to assist Antipater in the Lamian War. Although Craterus does seem to have initially delayed his departure and only journeyed upon realising Leonnatus had not turned the tide,[134] Arrian's *Events After Alexander* makes it clear that once Menander revealed Perdiccas' designs on Alexander's sister, Craterus (and Antipater) was 'more than ever determined to make war on Perdiccas', hardly a position Craterus could adopt if he had himself rebuffed her, that is assuming our understanding of the event order is accurate.

It seems even more unlikely that Cleopatra would have rejected Craterus, for his 'bride price' would have included his 10,000 veterans and an imminent Macedonian regency to underscore the guardianship of her and Alexander's children, though Perdiccas and his royal army was equally attractive; logic demands, therefore, that we accept the (unlikely) possibility that Craterus' increased determination to meet Perdiccas in battle was because of his undermining the union Craterus had yet to conclude.

What of Thessalonice, Alexander's half-sister who was paired with Lysimachus by the *Pamphlet* (T1, T2)? Cassander is said to have forced Thessalonice into marriage following her capture at Pydna; this clearly highlights Carney's contention and the danger posed by the continued availability of an unmarried daughter of an Argead king. For exactly this reason, Olympias, most likely with Alexander's approval (despite reports of the contrary), had murdered Europa, a daughter from Philip's seventh marriage, upon Alexander taking the throne.[135] Antipater had probably kept Thessalonice carefully quarantined at Pella (as he tried with Cynnane), just as Antigonus had attempted to keep Cleopatra 'safe' from marital intrigue at Sardis.[136] Alexander would have likewise been cautious and planned a 'safe' pairing for Thessalonice in his Will. Lysimachus *was* a credible option as were several prominent others. But there is no evidence he 'claimed' his inheritance either; he married another of Antipater's daughters becoming Cassander's brother-in-law, and so this pairing does appear to be a *Pamphlet* overture to the satrap of Thrace and its bordering regions.

What the early years of the Successor Wars made abundantly clear is that Antipater's long control of Macedonia and Greece made his daughters desirable currency, and especially so in the face of an Argead dynasty promising a half-Asiatic and only one-quarter Argead princes (Alexander was half-Epirote) or a halfwit married to a troublemaking queen with Illyrian roots. Antipater's daughters initially cemented a brief accord with Antigonus (via Demetrius), Craterus and Ptolemy, with Perdiccas and Leonnatus apparently being invited to join the fold to stave off immediate challenges; with the exception of Antigonus, these were effectively the surviving 'guardians' appointed at the Assembly at the Babylonian settlement, or, in Ptolemy's case, the guardianship offered following Perdiccas' death in Egypt (T11, T12).[137] Clearly, Alexander would not have orchestrated, or condoned, this Antipatrid family dominance.

In contrast to this early nuptial nepotism, none of the *Diadokhoi* or their offspring intermarried until after the battle at Ipsus in 301 BCE, when in quick succession Lysimachus took Arsinoe, a daughter of Ptolemy, and another, Lysandra, for his son Agathocles. Upon the death of his wife Deidameia (the sister of Pyrrhus) soon after, Demetrius was betrothed to a further daughter of the Egyptian dynast (though he married her twelve years later) and Seleucus asked for the hand of Stratonice, Demetrius' own daughter by Phila (thus Antigonus' granddaughter and Cassander's niece). Cassander, in turn, later arranged for his young sons to marry daughters of both Ptolemy and Lysimachus; even the Epirote royal line was to marry into the ranks of the Macedonian *Diadokhoi*.[138] The royal women, then, were indispensable to the survival of dynasties, and they would not have been bypassed in Alexander's Will.

THE HALFWIT KING AND THE HALF-ARGEAD PRINCESS

The testaments found in the *Romance* and *Metz Epitome* positioned the newly elevated King Philip III as a 'caretaker king' acting in the name of the juvenile Alexander IV: 'In the *interim* Arrhidaeus, son of Philip, should lead the Macedonians.'[139] Why would the pamphleteers have thrown what amounted to an idiotic spanner into their artful works?

Bearing in mind Olympias' hostility to Philip III and Queen Eurydice, this must have been an original Will edict that simply could not be hidden, a regal appointment already notorious for the conflict it caused in Babylon and further publicised by the antics of Eurydice at Triparadeisus. Alexander had presumably designed his half-brother's role exactly as outlined in the extant Wills: it was a temporary regnum to housesit for his sons under the benign and trusted *prostasia* of Craterus to thwart any rivals coveting an empty throne; the office of *prostates* appears to be an extraordinary role only ever linked to the Macedonian court when the monarch was deemed incapable of immediate rule.[140] Perdiccas' charge of Roxane, whether their marriage was truly demanded or not, represented a balance that provided Alexander's sons with a further guardian.

Philip III was presumably physically developed and able to procreate (a fear that never materialised, as far as we know), so the pairing would be precipitous if they produced a son, and not much less dangerous if a daughter was born to them. So it is unlikely that Alexander would have provided Arrhidaeus with a bride in his Will, and certainly not an ambitious one who was hostile to his name. Eurydice was 'no cipher to be manipulated at will'; her presence at Triparadeisus where her 'rabble-rousing' almost resulted in Antipater's death, to her final face-off against Olympias' army in 317 BCE, demonstrated how dangerous she was.[141] Too young to be a threat when Alexander departed for Asia, she may well have been targeted for 'removal' in his *private* 'last wishes'.

THE PERSECUTORS AND PROTECTORS OF ALEXANDER'S BARBARIAN FAMILY

Alexander would have additionally needed to provide for the welfare of his Asiatic wives and mistresses: Parysatis a daughter of Artaxerxes III

Ochus, Stateira a daughter of Darius III, the already accounted for Roxane the daughter of Oxyartes, and Barsine who we are told was a daughter of Artabazus. The last two required special attention, as they were mothers of Alexander's children. The noise from Babylon suggests Roxane was placed under Perdiccas' protection (a contention reinforced by Meleager's speech), and she could have credibly been pledged to him in marriage, as the extant Wills suggest. Macedonian tradition was indeed to appoint a *relative* of an immature king as guardian-cum-regent.[142] If Barsine and her son Heracles were to remain in the region of Artabazus' family estates in Hellespontine Phrygia, then Leonnatus would have been expected to assume the role of *prostates*; if he *was* paired with Cleopatra, then the 'relative' status held.

Assuming that a prominent former Bodyguard was to safeguard the welfare of the remaining childless Achaemenid wives, that role would have likely fallen to the Persian-speaking Peucestas, controlling as he did the Achaemenid homelands.[143] Stateira and her younger sister Drypetis (Hephaestion's widow) were reportedly murdered in Babylon by Roxane and Perdiccas, possibly for that reason; their unfortunate fates had been determined by their recognition – so legitimisation – in marriage at Susa. Parysatis may have been executed too for she was never mentioned after, for the daughters of the last two Great Kings could have been influential Persian rallying points in the forthcoming uncertainty.[144]

If so, it suggests an attack on Darius' branch of the Achaemenid line had already commenced. Sisygambis, Alexander 'second mother', passed away with grief-laden suicide, which raises the question: was it suicide at all?[145] Or did a quiet pogrom take place that has almost eluded history's pages? Did Sisygambis' dark reflections, fuelled by memories of Ochus' onslaught of her eighty brothers a generation before, now anticipate a re-run at Macedonian hands?[146] Ochus, Darius' own son, was never again mentioned,[147] and Darius' brother, Oxyathres, who had been one of Alexander's court *hetairoi*, disappeared from the texts; he was likely Sisygambis' only remaining child.[148] Although the prominent Asiatic wives of the *Diadokhoi did* feature in the new order – Oxyathres' daughter Amastris, for example (she was briefly the wife of Craterus and later Lysimachus) – the women who were widowed or rejected faced far bleaker prospects with Alexander dead.

In this period many attested children would have vanished with their parents: Eumenes' children were never referred to after his death, and the daughters of Attalus by Perdiccas' sister, Atalante, were captured with Thessalonice at Pydna and never reappeared.[149] We may wonder what became of the myriad half-Asiatic offspring sired by Alexander's soldiers and born in the wake of the decade long campaign. They must have had an estate claim or two in the name of their fathers, and surely this is one of the reasons why Alexander forbade their repatriation to Macedonia; the fear for their integration into families 'at home' was mentioned too. Although promises were provided by Alexander for their eventual return, it is difficult to imagine that such prejudice in Macedonia would change, and it sounds a rather hollow-sounding pledge bearing in mind these *epigonoi* were the most likely descendants to accept Alexander's own half-caste sons as overlords in Asia.[150]

When pondering the sons, now-stranded or forgotten at Alexander's death, we inevitably arrive back at the identity of Heracles, Alexander's eldest, and whose mother was, we are told, descended from a branch of the Achaemenid line, though sources suggest Alexander never legitimised Heracles as he could have, by marrying Barsine.[151]

THE FORGOTTEN SON AND HIS MISIDENTIFIED MOTHER

A read through the accounts of the Successor War years suggests it was Polyperchon alone who recalled the existence of Heracles, a figure so obscure that many historians have dubbed him a fraud.[152] The boy did not feature at all in the main biographical narratives of Alexander; Curtius, and thus we suppose Cleitarchus, first brought him into the debate during the Assembly at Babylon after the king's death. Yet Heracles and his mother featured briefly, though significantly, in Diodorus' later books when we may reasonably assume he was still following Hieronymus' narrative of events.

After Cassander executed Olympias sometime in 315 BCE, the barometer dropped on the Antipatrids and a new Polyperchon-Antigonus alliance was cobbled together against him in the Peloponnese. Duplicities followed which saw sons turned and then assassinated in the next five years in which Polyperchon's power and credibility was whittled away; he faded into a relative obscurity that bordered on 'retirement', and the peace treaty of 311 BCE in which he didn't feature essentially isolated Polyperchon from any wider role.[153] His last bid for power was to bring Heracles, and so himself, out of that obscurity in 310/309 BCE.

Polyperchon was now past seventy and without the support of his own son, Alexander, who had been murdered in 314 BCE, and he also lacked the support of Alexander's remarkable wife, Cratesipolis (literally 'conqueror of cities'), a renowned beauty who had held the leaderless army together.[154] Yet Polyperchon managed to extract Heracles from Pergamum and raise an army of 20,000 infantry (including Antigonus' allies, the Aetolians) with 1,000 cavalry, to launch an invasion of Pella from his native canton of Tymphaea in Upper Macedonia. None of this could have been possible, as Tarn and others have since concluded, without the support of Antigonus who was once again attempting to undermine

Cassander and his allies (Ptolemy, Lysimachus and Seleucus) in the wake of the failed peace.[155]

Heracles was most likely 'about' seventeen by 310/309 BCE, so he had been born ca. 327/326 BCE when Alexander had been campaigning in the upper satrapies or planning to enter India.[156] When Polyperchon tried to promote the youth, '… the Macedones regarded the restoration of the king without disfavour.'[157] The terms Diodorus associated with this episode – 'ancestral throne' and 'regal title' – suggest Hieronymus recognised the legitimacy of the boy, or the legitimacy others attached to him. Tarn argued that because Hieronymus published in the rule of Antigonus II *Gonatas* he never revealed the role of his king's grandfather (*Monophthalmos*) in the venture; moreover, this is why Hieronymus omitted to mention that Pergamum, where Heracles had been installed years before, was under Antigonus' control.[158]

We may speculate whether Cassander, who had implored his father 'not to get too far away from the kings' after the conference at Triparadeisus in 320 BCE, was also thinking of the danger that Heracles posed in hostile hands, otherwise the warning is vexing, for Diodorus made it clear that Antipater kept the infant Alexander IV and the half-witted Philip III with him on his way back to Pella. The one short time Antipater *might* have deposited these two in temporary custody with Antigonus was during what reads in the *Gothenburg Palimpsest* as a humiliating campaign against Eumenes.[159]

Tarn further suggested that Hieronymus knew full well Alexander had no second son, implying that any mention of Heracles at Babylon was part of a later fabrication.[160] Other scholars have effectively turned the 'intruder' arguments back on themselves, and surely it would have been foolhardy for someone of Polyperchon's standing (and that of Antigonus behind him) to try and dupe the remaining *Diadokhoi* with a late-entry pretender, for all would have been familiar with Alexander's past liaisons and presumably with their results.[161] Cassander was clearly unsettled by the move, and now that rumours (or open knowledge) of his recent execution of Alexander IV and Roxane were circulating, he could not trust Macedonian sentiment. With promises of reinstatement as his general in the Peloponnese with a share in power, Cassander convinced Polyperchon to murder the boy rather than grasping the opportunity to expose him as a fraud himself, which, as Errington has argued, is an argument *for* Heracles' legitimacy.[162] The conclusion to the sad affair, like all character-exposing outcomes, provided useful epideictic material for Plutarch's *On Compliancy* in his *Moralia*.[163]

But Heracles' story began some twenty-four years earlier and in far less tragic times for Macedonia. Following the Persian defeat at Issus in November 333 BCE, the royal family of Darius III was captured and it included his wife Stateira, his mother (Sisygambis), two *adultae virgines* (his daughters Stateira and Drypetis), and a 'not yet past his sixth year' son (Ochus).[164] Immediately after Issus, Parmenio captured other notable Persian women at Damascus, including the wife and the three 'maiden' daughters of the former Great King known as Artaxerxes III Ochus, whose son (Arses, Artaxerxes IV) Darius had deposed with the help of the eunuch Bagoas. We may assume one of these daughters was Parysatis, Alexander's later bride at Susa, though the other two remain anonymous. Also listed in this set of captives was the daughter (probably Amastris) of Oxyathres the brother of Darius III. To the tally of captured women we need to add the Great King's concubines, allegedly 329 in number.

Additionally apprehended were the wife and son of Pharnabazus (the son of Artabazus) who had been given supreme Persian command of the Aegean coast by Darius, along with the three unnamed daughters of Mentor, the some-years-dead Rhodian mercenary who had fought both against, and then for, Artaxerxes III. Next were listed the 'wife and son of the renowned general Memnon'; he was Mentor's brother and Alexander's most talented opponent in Asia Minor who had died of illness much more recently. We are led to believe that this captured wife, Barsine, became Alexander's mistress; we are told she was a daughter of Artabazus, the 'chief of courtiers' and the former Persian satrap of Hellespontine Phrygia (grandson of Artaxerxes II and nephew of Artaxerxes III). Artabazus' son (Ilioneus) and wife were also in the group; she was *possibly* the Rhodian sister of Mentor and Memnon who had borne to Artabazus eleven sons and ten daughters, that is if a later bride was not being referred to here as might be suggested by Ilioneus' immaturity. Alongside this royal haul at Damascus, hostile Spartans and Athenians had been rounded up along with a useful cache of 2,600 talents of coined money, 500 pounds of wrought silver and 7,000 loaded pack animals.[165]

Artabazus had initially refused to recognise his uncle, Artaxerxes III, whose pogrom wiped out his brothers' rival lines (when eighty of Sisygambis' brothers by various concubines were killed in a single day) as he ascended the throne in 358 BCE; the new Great King then issued a royal edict that the mercenary armies of the satraps were now to be disbanded. Although assisted by his Rhodian brothers-in-law in the so-called Great Revolt of the Satraps, Artabazus was finally defeated and took refuge with his family at the court of Philip II in Macedonia in 349/348 BCE, along with Memnon.[166] So he, along with his large clutch of offspring and his talented son-in-law were well known to (the then young) Alexander;[167] his 'honourable' surrender to the Macedonians in Hyrcania some three years after Issus, and the reported warmth between him and his captor, stemmed from this former 'guest exile', whereupon Alexander appointed Artabazus as his new satrap in Bactria. Memnon had fared worse; he had died when still in opposition to the Macedonian invasion of Asia.[168]

The dense and intertwined branches of the line of Artabazus with the Rhodian brothers and sister, the inter-related Achaemenids and the captive lists from Issus and Damascus with their female *anonymae*, were bound to provide latitude for confusion to historians.[169] For here we have three daughters of Artaxerxes III Ochus, three of Mentor, two of Darius, and ten of Artabazus; most were unnamed and all of them could be referred to as 'royal'.[170] To add further scope for misidentification, Justin described the allure of these regal women: 'He [Alexander] fell in love with his captive Barsine for her beauty, by whom he had afterwards a son that he called Heracles', though Justin later linked Heracles to Roxane in his careless epitomising form, whilst Porphyry erroneously stated Roxane was the daughter of Darius.[171] But it seems *all* prominent royal women were described as visually prepossessing: Darius III's two daughters were also complimented this way, whilst his wife was voted 'the most beautiful woman in all Asia', with Roxane a runner up; Plutarch additionally stated that Darius' daughters resembled their handsome parents.[172]

Plutarch's rundown of Barsine's qualities included her 'agreeable disposition', and thus 'Alexander determined (at Parmenio's instigation, claimed Aristobulus) to attach himself to a woman of such high birth and beauty.'[173] But, once again, this description could fit the daughters of both Great Kings, and, in particular, the daughter of Darius who *was* curiously named 'Barsine' by Arrian.[174] Tarn convincingly argued that the 'beautiful captive' Parmenio urged Alexander to marry *was* one of Darius' two daughters, for that would clearly provide the legitimacy the Macedonian king sought in Asia.[175] Darius *had* reportedly proffered his daughter to Alexander previously, along with a portion of his empire, and Parmenio urged him to accept the olive branch.[176]

The bold rejection we read of may not in truth have been so confidently drafted, as the marriage would have been attractive to a man who had now conquered the western satrapies of the Persian Empire and who now sought legitimacy in the East. Alexander allegedly replied with: 'That which was offered was already his.' The result was that he had Darius III's daughters with him for perhaps two years after Issus and may have come to know them well, despite Plutarch's claim that the women continued 'to live as though guarded in sacred and inviolable virgins' chambers instead of in an enemy's camp, apart from the speech and sight of men.'[177] Leaving them at Susa in 331 BCE, Alexander ordered that the princesses be given a Greek education, which in itself suggests he had unique future plans for the girls: he and Hephaestion married them when they returned to Susa some seven years on.[178]

It was Plutarch (uniquely it seems) who claimed Heracles' mother was one of the *daughters* of Artabazus, who was already in his late sixties when Barsine was captured post-Issus in 333 BCE (though Curtius implied he was around ninety).[179] To truly entangle matters, Plutarch stated Barsine had been the wife of Memnon (Tarn thought he had followed the inaccurate Duris in this; Curtius and Diodorus never named Memnon's widow), but Arrian stated that Barsine had a daughter by Mentor; this would suggest (Tarn called it 'a modern invention') that Barsine had married her dead husband's brother, unless he, or later scribes, were confused by their similar names (Strabo may have made the same mistake). Plutarch's statement reads:

> But Alexander, as it would seem, considering the mastery of himself a more kingly thing than the conquest of his enemies, neither laid hands upon these women, nor did he know any other before marriage, except Barsine. This woman, Memnon's widow, was taken prisoner at Damascus. And since she had received a Greek education, and was of an agreeable disposition, and since her father, Artabazus, was son of a king's daughter...[180]

Here the Greek education rears its head again. Plutarch believed Barsine was the *only* woman Alexander had consorted with before his marriage to Roxane in 327 BCE; this is a romantic, and yet highly unlikely, proposition, and more so if we give any credence to Diodorus' claim that Alexander consorted with concubines from Darius' harem; he also detailed his (less likely) thirteen-day tryst with the Amazon queen, Thalestris.[181] There is no further evidence that the widowed Barsine remarried Memnon; only a nameless 'widow' of that Rhodian commander was mentioned in the captive list by Curtius and Diodorus.[182] Perhaps because Mentor's wife was not listed, Plutarch (or his source) concluded Memnon was caring for his brother's three orphaned daughters and thus he had married Barsine for the practical application of that. This may have further led Plutarch to conclude Memnon's young son was born from the new union.[183]

Clearly, judging by these associations, Barsine already had a number of children by the time she was captured. Taking this into account, Tarn quite reasonably concluded she was a woman of a different (older) generation to Alexander who was aged twenty-three when he captured her. The reasoning is further supported by evidence that a son of Mentor (if Barsine was his mother too) may have been mature enough for battle in 327/6 BCE; Memnon also had sons fighting beside him at the Granicus River in 334 BCE, though Plutarch must have assumed these were from a previous marriage (if indeed his above text originally referred to 'Memnon' and not 'Mentor').[184] Moreover, there is no mention that *this* Barsine accompanied Alexander for the next six years, or longer, until 327-326 BCE, the time Heracles would have been born.[185] We also know from Arrian, who stated that he was taking some of his detail from Aristobulus at this point (and probably from Ptolemy too) that one of

Barsine's daughters had attained marriageable age by 325 BCE at the Susa weddings:[186]

> … to Ptolemy the Bodyguard and Eumenes the Royal Secretary he gave two daughters of Artabazus, Artacama to Ptolemy and Artonis to Eumenes; to Nearchus the daughter of Barsine and Mentor…[187]

The inference given by Plutarch when describing the same Susa weddings was that the Barsine who consorted with Alexander had *only* two sisters, and not two of ten, if this is not a misleading translation:

> For Barsine the daughter of Artabazus, the first woman whom Alexander knew in Asia, and by whom he had a son, Heracles, had two sisters; of these Alexander gave one, Apame, to Ptolemy, and the other, also called Barsine, to Eumenes.[188]

The names Plutarch provided for the brides of Ptolemy and Eumenes (Apame and Barsine) are different from those given by Arrian (Artacama and Artonis) and it is unlikely (though not impossible) that Artabazus named two daughters 'Barsine'. However, 'Apame' was a well-established Achaemenid name and one also attached to Seleucus' bride.[189] How could such confusion arise when eyewitness historians presumably passed down their identities? Ptolemy was a bridegroom at Susa and Aristobulus may well have been. Tarn, who paradoxically concluded Ptolemy's detail came from the Eumenes-compiled court *Journal*, simply quipped: 'One may suppose that they knew their wives' names.'[190]

Identifications within the interwoven royal lines of Persia *are* perilous; a read of Plutarch's *Artaxerxes* (III) reveals the recurring use, through the generations (though not for two coeval daughters), of these traditional Achaemenid names, including Oxyathres, Apame, Stateira and Parysatis. Darius III himself had married a 'Stateira', his second wife, who was in fact his sister (or half-sister).[191] He had been previously married to a sister of Pharnaces (*possibly* related to Artabazus), the Persian commander who died in battle at the Granicus River, and he probably had a daughter by her.[192] And as it has been pointed out, when considering wives beside concubines, Darius III could have had many more than the three children who were named, and his mother, Sisygambis, may have had as many as seven children herself.

A seemingly unexploited conclusion, surrounding the identity of Barsine, is that we are dealing with sisters from more than one generation of Artabazus' line, with the confusion surely arising from what were ambiguous original references to 'nieces', 'sisters-in-law', 'aunts' and 'uncles', and probably 'cousins' too. For if Mentor had married a daughter of Artabazus, and recalling that Artabazus had in turn married Mentor's

Rhodian sister, then Mentor married his niece. This exhibits a true strategic bonding of the two families, and judging by the attested children from both sides it had proved a highly successfully union.

This dynastic interweaving would make it quite probable that Memnon had also married another of Artabazus' ten daughters. Furthermore, Mentor's own three daughters by Barsine would have also been termed Memnon's 'nieces', and vice versa, as well as them being the nieces of Artabazus' wife (their sister). Barsine's three daughters (assuming Mentor's girls were by her) were additionally nieces to the remaining nine of Artabazus' girls, whose own daughters (not mentioned but surely existing) were in turn the nieces of Barsine. In fact, the two unnamed daughters of Artaxerxes III Ochus (Parysatis was the third) were cousins of Artabazus.

The potential age ranges of the captives, both the youngest daughters of Artabazus and the oldest of his granddaughters, could well have made them suitable for intimacy with their captors between Damascus in 333 BCE and Susa in 325 BCE, moreover, marriages between mature men and far younger women were commonplace then.[193] It seems doubtful in this environment that Alexander would have chosen an older woman who was already the mother of numerous children as his mistress when far younger, equally royal and illustrious *virgines filias* were available to him.[194]

It is quite possible that more of Artabazus' ten daughters, who now depended upon Alexander for their wellbeing in the new Macedonian-ruled empire, were present at the Susa weddings. If 'Barsine' was a traditional family name, or title, it could have proliferated through their offspring. So a creditable explanation for two same-named girls is to conclude one of the three daughters by Barsine and Mentor was named after her mother, in which case she is a more credible candidate as the mother of Heracles. Considering the many corruptions that crept into manuscript transmission over two millennia or more, could a single archetypal sentence, stripped of its precision, have led to the different names given by Arrian and Plutarch? Well, the wording below, unpunctuated to highlight its potential ambiguity, could (along with other permutations) achieve just that:

> ... to Ptolemy the Bodyguard and Eumenes the Royal Secretary he gave sisters of Barsine the daughter of Artabazus and to Nearchus Alexander gave a daughter of Mentor and Barsine who had two sisters including Alexander's mistress also named Barsine to Eumenes Artonis Artacama to Ptolemy Apame to Seleucus the daughter of Spitamenes...[195]

Without punctuation, the double references to Eumenes and Ptolemy look awkward, that until a break after the second mention of 'Barsine' would suggest the source was proceeding to name the aforementioned anonymous women. This wording would justify Plutarch's belief that Heracles' mother had *two* sisters (so accounting for the three daughters of Mentor, one named Barsine after her mother) and it overcomes Tarn's objection that '… these women all belonged to an older generation.' It would explain the presence of *two* Barsines, and the corruption (or loss) of punctuation would explain how both Nearchus and Eumenes were linked to a Barsine as well. Plutarch would then have believed the 'stranded' names of Artonis and Artacama were the remaining two (non-paired) sisters of Nearchus' wife.

The same ambiguity could additionally indicate how Ptolemy and Seleucus were linked in marriage to Apame, and explain why Strabo thought Apame was a daughter of Artabazus, where Arrian believed Seleucus' unnamed wife was the daughter of Spitamenes.[196] Strabo frequently used Aristobulus as a source and Aristobulus was the only source named by Arrian for detail of the Susa weddings, so perhaps it was he who provided the original unifying text.

In this nexus of Persians, progeny and 'beautiful' prisoners, it seems a spurious bridge or two was built, with the mother of Heracles sitting somewhere in its span. What *does* appear to have happened, either through marriages to the daughters or granddaughters of Artabazus, is that Ptolemy, Nearchus and Eumenes became related through Heracles. Unfortunately, as events made clear, they thought it of little significance. Nearchus' alleged speech at the Assembly in Babylon in which he made a case for the boy, certainly supports the connection, if it was not a back-construct of Cleitarchus. Eumenes also appears to have gained family loyalty, for Pharnabazus fought for him in 321/320 against Craterus.[197] But we must recall that Heracles himself never featured in the *Pamphlet* Will, and this would appear counterproductive to Eumenes in the circumstances, that is until we recall Antigonus was in control of the boy. In which case Heracles' absence from the testament was an attempt to neutralise exactly that, while it promoted the cause of Alexander IV who was in Olympias' custody in Pella.

The claim that Heracles was based at Pergamum in 323 BCE (T11), rather than Susa, for example, further supports his descent from Artabazus, for the family estates did reside in Hellespontine Phrygia with its southern border falling just to the north of the city.[198] The family condottieri, Mentor and Memnon, had also been granted substantial estates in the Troad, probably for helping Artabazus to reclaim his father's lands from Autophradates.[199] And we can assume that following Artabazus' voluntary retirement from service under Alexander, he and his family returned to their lands. It is tempting to credit his retirement and Barsine's departure from the court and the king's bed, to Alexander's marrying Roxane, for according to Curtius, Roxane's father, Oxyartes, was granted the governance of Bactria, the very satrapy Alexander had previously bestowed on Artabazus. But this appears to have taken place a little later, though much chronological confusion exists at this point in the extant texts.[200]

It is universally assumed that Alexander never married his mistress, Barsine, so Heracles remained an unrecognised bastard son; this would of course go some way to explaining his rejection at Babylon. But at Susa, Alexander was demonstrably 'marriage-minded' in the face of whatever objections Roxane may have thrown up or the fears she harboured, for there he took the hand of Stateira the daughter of Darius III, and Parysatis the daughter of Artaxerxes III Ochus.[201] If Heracles' mother was descended from an Achaemenid line, there remains the question of why he did not legitimise his (then) only son.[202] We cannot in fact be sure he did not, for a slight amendment to Arrian's statement (or Aristobulus' before him) changes the context of the marriages altogether, and explains why Arrian named Darius' daughter 'Barsine' when the Vulgate texts gave us the more convincing 'Stateira'. Consider the text as it stands relating to the weddings at Susa:

> He [Alexander] himself married Darius' eldest daughter Barsine, and according to Aristobulus, another wife as well, Parysatis, the youngest daughter of Ochus (he was already married to Roxane, the daughter of Oxyartes of Bactria).

Although this represents a modern translation descended from Arrian's Greek, it once again requires no more than a punctuation change, with a comma or break to be placed after 'Darius' eldest daughter' to suggest that *three* marriages took place including one to Barsine whose identity had already been established in texts above relating to the *hetairoi* marriages.[203] The loss of punctuation (or spacing) led to Arrian's confusion. When dealing with this grand event, whether Aristobulus was the *sole* source for Plutarch, Arrian, and Cleitarchus before them, or simply an *auxiliary* source for *extra* detail (as the above text could imply), we have shown that a single archetypal statement *could* in fact have provided the different conclusions we read.

It is possible that Ptolemy avoided commentary at this point, as he did not wish to boost either the profiles of his Successor War opponents or the status of Alexander's children and their politicking guardians. Ptolemy's alleged Babylon speeches and his rejection of Asiatic unions could support that conclusion; after Alexander died Ptolemy married solely Greek and Macedonian wives despite his attempts to integrate his kingship into the Egyptian dynastic mode.

Other solutions have been proffered to explain Arrian's 'slip'; one of them supposes that because his source, Aristobulus, wrote late in life he was by then confused on names.[204] But this seems extremely unlikely; if the Cassandreian engineer-cum-historian was lucid enough to pull together a history of the campaign, then the detail as momentous as the Macedonian king's brides would have surely remained unsullied in his mind. If he *was* that unreliable, Arrian would surely have highlighted many more obvious discrepancies and probably questioned his veracity in his opening rundown of his sources.

A second solution, backed by recent studies of Persian tradition, suggests Darius' daughters may have been referred to under different titles at different stages of their lives: formal court monikers and informal family names.[205] Thus a daughter of Darius, referred to as 'Barsine' in early life, could have assumed the royal title 'Stateira' (or vice versa) once proclaimed a queen, either of which could have more generally denoted 'royal daughter', or 'queen to be'.[206] We recall Adea became 'Eurydice', a name by then synonymous with Macedonian queens; Audata, Philip's first Illyrian wife, his mother, and possibly Cleopatra, his last wife, had assumed the title too.[207]

Another onomastic parallel might exist: the name of Candace (*Kandake*), the legendary Queen of Nubia (or Kush) with whom Alexander had a *Romance* affair, was, it seems, derived from the Meriotic *ktke,* or *kdke,* meaning 'queen mother', and it was used for *all* Ethiopian female sovereigns.[208] We know 'Semiramis' was attached to prominent Assyrian queens, and, according to Strabo, a host of monuments across the western Persian Empire.[209] Alexander's mother, Olympias, had at youth been called 'Polyxena' (named after a Trojan heroine), after marriage (or as a girl) 'Myrtale' (perhaps from Myrtle, *Myrtos*, the sacred plant of Aphrodite), and later in life she was known as both 'Olympias' (possibly after Philip's victory at the Olympic Games at the time Alexander was born) and as 'Stratonice'; presumably she was never given the title 'Eurydice' herself as Audata (now Eurydice) was still residing at the Pellan court when she married Philip.[210]

Heracles' maternal identity aside, could a true son of Alexander have really been ignored for so long? This was a bone of contention that persuaded Tarn to conclude the boy was a pretender. But Heracles may not have been 'forgotten' at all, neither at Babylon as evidenced by Nearchus' speech (and its rejection), and surely he was never forgotten by Perdiccas and Roxane either; no doubt Eumenes and Olympias pondered his part, or removal, in their developing plans. It was simply Hieronymus' later literary silence on Antigonus' tenure of the boy at Pergamum that made Heracles' re-emergence appear 'sudden'.

But what of Heracles' fate in Alexander's *original* Will? As the outcome of Roxane's pregnancy was unknown in summer 323 BCE, Alexander would have recognised his existing son. If he was to have two boys, the immortal

Vulgate lines, 'to the strongest', or 'to the most worthy' (T6, T7, T8, T9), if ever truly uttered, were perhaps an answer to the question posed to a dying king on which son he wished to eventually take the diadem when of throne age. Justin concluded his narrative of the Babylon settlement with: 'A portion of the empire was reserved for Alexander's son, if a son should be born' (T20). Though this clearly referred to Roxane's child, and supposedly to the compromise reached, such a concession for *two* princes would not have been without precedent. For in his testament Cyrus appointed one son, Cambyses, as king, and he granted the other a 'portion of the kingdom' to avoid an inevitable conflict. Insightfully, Xenophon's reinvented Cyrus predicted more happiness for the son without the crown – free from the 'plots and counter plots' that plagued Persian politics.[211]

Likewise, two sons raised at Pella would have been a recipe for court intrigue and yet more Macedonian fratricide that would pit one guardian against another. Moreover, the sons each had family claims in different regions, Alexander IV with hereditary residencies in Bactria (or Sogdia) and Heracles in Hellespontine Phrygia. But what testament strategy was not dangerous in Babylon, given one full-sister, two half-sisters, two sons, three or possibly four wives, and at least seven ruthlessly ambitious Bodyguards overseeing even more regional satraps with discontented garrisoned veterans and mercenaries accumulating under them? And what alternatives existed? In his heart Alexander himself may have doubted whether his half-barbarian sons would ever be named as kings of Macedonia. But if he *was* to truly defy Themistocles' words and so challenge the gods and heroes with an 'ungodly pride' by ruling Europe *and* Asia, it would now take sons of royal blood from both sides of the Aegean to carry the title 'King of Kings'.

DONATIVES, TEMPLES AND MAUSOLEUMS: SOUND PLANNING FROM AN UNSOUND MIND

Can the references to temples, statues and the tombs Alexander demanded in the 'last plans' 'discovered' at Babylon be reconciled with the surviving Will texts (T1, T2)? They can, but only if we accept corruption at the edges: *Romance* accretion and Roman-era contamination from one side, and deception in the *Pamphlet* on the other, for the pamphleteers had a clear agenda and it was not to bring attention to any Will-demanded monuments that Perdiccas had cancelled.[212]

In return for their hardly unexpected 'gifts from the fates', the extant Will texts demand that the most notable of the *hetairoi* erect statues of Alexander, Heracles, Olympias, Ammon, Athena and Philip II in their respective territories, whilst offerings were to be sent to other notable religious sites such as Delphi and Olympia. Ambitious, but not unreasonable, this is the content we would have expected the pamphleteer(s) to preserve in a testament focusing on satraps and satrapies and not diversionary costly commemoratives. So the temples we see in the 'last plans' to be built at Delos, Delphi, Dion (the most important centre of worship of Zeus at the foot of Mt Olympus), Dodona, Cyrnus (Thrace) and Amphipolis, with one to surpass them all at Troy, appear to have been expediently dumped, if they were indeed from Alexander's original Will (T25).[213]

The testament may well have attempted a sound strategy for what were nevertheless fundamentally unsound circumstances. If our conclusions are valid, it featured the sensible deployment of the *Somatophylakes* and the leading generals as empire pan-provincial governors with multiple satraps under them, power counterbalanced by strategic Argead marriages at the top of the chain of command. On the other hand, those grandiose last plans – that conglomerate of untenable Will demands and campaign projects – were the product of a deeply troubled man whose sense of scale had been corrupted by Tyche's unswerving companionship, the poetasters' fawning verses, and by the profound but not bottomless depths of the Great Kings' treasuries. 'For whilst Fortune blinds herself, as a rule she even blinds those whom she has embraced.'[214]

Whilst 'the mind boggles' at the arrangements Alexander 'might have made for his own obsequies', a laconic, humble and yet piercing inscription found on Cyrus' single-storey tomb was said to have deeply moved Alexander; he was 'reminded of the uncertainty and mutability of life.'[215] Aristobulus stated he was recalling the carved epitaph 'from memory' in his book:

> Passer-by! I am Cyrus son of Cambyses,
> who founded the Persian Empire,
> and was King of Asia.
> Grudge me therefore not my monument.[216]

Poignant as it reads, laconic philosophical epitaphs of this nature were not the norm on Achaemenid funerary architecture.

Other 'modest' inscriptions do exist elsewhere at Pasargadae and they possibly provided the model for Aristobulus' claim. Cyrus' unassuming monument with six steps, a stone-roofed chamber and an entrance door 'so small that even a short man would struggle to pass through it', was portrayed by Onesicritus as a 'tower with ten stories' with Cyrus occupying the top floor.[217] When Alexander wished to pay honours to the corpse within, rather than finding the golden couch and coffin, table, robes and gem-studded earrings they had once seen in the tomb guarded by the Magi, or the 3,000 talents of gold and silver allegedly buried with his insignia, he found 'Cyrus' decomposing shield, two Scythian bows and a scimitar.' It had been looted – by Polymachus of Pella said Plutarch, or by the satrap Orsines implied the scheming eunuch Bagoas, recently snubbed by him.[218] Ultimately, it was Alexander's upheaval that was to blame for the sepulchral chaos, but the Magi were summarily tortured and the entrance was resealed.

The small stone monument in what was once a royal park surrounded by a plantation of trees and irrigated lawns, sits in what is today the Murghab Plain, one kilometre southwest of Pasargadae. It is commonly known as the Ma`shad-e Madar-a Solayman, 'the Tomb of Solomon's Mother' and the only remaining inscription is a verse from the *Qur'an*.[219] A proposed dam that would flood the plain between Pasargadae and Persepolis has put the tomb's fate in peril, just as the Ataturk Dam inundated Lucian's birthplace in Samosata on the Upper Euphrates.[220] Engineers claimed Cyrus' monument would sit above the water line, archeologists claimed humidity would nonetheless destroy it. Construction of the dam finally commenced in April 2007.[221]

A 19th century photo of the tomb of Cyrus the Great on the Murghab Plain near Pasargadae.

A short distance down the Euphrates, the Birecik Dam dealt the same fate to the ancient river crossing at Thapsacus, possibly identifiable with Seleucia-on-the-Euphrates or with the later Roman Zeugma.[222] Gone is the site which witnessed Alexander's shipwrights reassembling two quinqueremes, three quadriremes, twelve triremes and some thirty light galleys (triaconters) they had portered in pieces overland from Phoenicia, a nautical feat recommissioned by the Duke of Wellington in 1835-37 to explore the ancient watercourses by steamship as a shortcut to India. Also gone are the bridge chains that Pliny thought were a relic of Alexander's river crossing after the battle at Issus in 333 BCE, the same chains Pausanias described as covered in ivy and vine and used by the god Dionysus himself on his way to India.[223]

The upturning of the past, whether deliberate plundering or well-intentioned excavation, has never truly ceased; the Tomb of Eurydice at Vergina was robbed of artefacts as recently as August-September 2001. Even the new excavations at Amphipolis risk causing imminent damage: it is feared that in the face of political turmoil the slowdown in the project leaves the exposed tomb vulnerable to landslides and poor drainage. These are rather symbolic examples of how our responsibilities as guardians of the past have always been subordinated to the needs of the present, a sobering reflection that explains much behind the disappearance of Alexander's testament, and no doubt *his* tomb as well. Rather fittingly, that places the Macedonian king alongside Xerxes, Darius III and Augustus as '... celebrated rulers whose last resting places were now unknown.'[224]

Naqsh-e Rustam in Shiraz, close to Persepolis. The site once contained the tombs of four Achaemenid kings, including Darius I and *possibly* Xerxes. Image by Amir Hussain Zolfaghary.

CLOSING THE SOCRATIC *ELENKHOS*

In an attempt to better understand the Macedonian-dominated world before, during, and after the death of Alexander, we have been stripping back layers of social, political, rhetorical and philosophical debris that cling to the extant accounts. Somewhere below that exoskeleton lies the bare-boned truth. As a riposte to the acataleptic dogma of the Sceptics that was taking hold of Athens, Aristotle once reasoned that the '... proper object of unqualified scientific knowledge is something which cannot be other than it is.'[225] Without being able to subpoena a primary witness and one who could prove his unswerving neutrality on the matter to avoid the *amphidoxon*, we must acknowledge that our conclusions fall short of Aristotle's stringent definition.[226] Like all studies of Alexander's life and the times of his successors, ours is a brief CAT scan of an infinitely complex body, that dimly lit candle flickering above that still damn dark abyss.[227]

Aristotle also warned that 'men are duped through certain likenesses between the genuine and the sham'; it was a proposition that may well have been known to Eumenes, written, as his *Sophistical Refutations* was, around 350 BCE.[228] Rome similarly had to tackle *verum* and *verisimile*, and today's investigative methodologies can still be thus fooled, for scholars have at times picked out brail-like contours in obscure sources and blindly joined the dots, bringing down the heavy hammer blows of *Quellenforschung* on the frailest of fragments in a hermeneutical *tour de force*. We forget the inaccuracies of the original texts themselves, and those of opinioned epitomisers, careless copyists and undisciplined diaskeuasts who render these forensic efforts comparable to an archaeologist reverently restoring words on a wall covered in nothing more than graffiti. As Friedrich Nietzsche wrote of 'we philologists', 'one imitates something that is purely chimerical' and one 'chases after a wonderland that never existed'.[229] And that somewhat epitomises the enduring 'standard model' of Alexander.

It was Aristotle who, in his two *Analytics*, introduced and developed letters as placeholders in chains of logic.[230] If he were here to conclude our investigation, he would encourage us to consider that if 'a' is opposed to 'b' and either is proved false, then the other may be true. But if both 'a' and 'b' appear to be fallacious, then 'c' must exist as an alternative to them both. Chrysippus, if he had survived a fourth dose of hellebore, would have used numbers in his argument-schemata to come to similar conclusions, and 'if the gods studied logic, it would be the logic of Chrysippus.'[231] But whether Peripatetic syllogisms, Stoic non-demonstrables or Epicurean canons are employed, logic *does* demand we ask a central question once again: if the *Journal* appears to be a fake and last words in the Vulgate genre read as pure theatre, why has history never reincarnated an alternative tradition?[232]

Are we justified in such extended controversy, or are we, like Diogenes, simply rolling our wine jar up and down the Craneion to appear to be doing something useful?[233] Well, scholars have demolished just about every other vivid episode linked to Alexander's life, but little to date has probed beneath the rubble of his intestate death. Until something momentous turns up, Cleitarchus will 'haunt the courts of history' and be its 'unhappy gibbering shade', and Curtius will remain 'decked in false tinsels' in the absence of an identity.[234] And though we are all frogs staring at the same historiographical pond, this ought not to preclude us searching for new streams of thought, even at the risk of appearing eristic, for still water inevitably stagnates.

In a study of the 'fact' and 'fiction' embedded within the conqueror's story, Brian Bosworth observed that: 'One is constantly looking back to Alexander's reign to explain what happened after his death and conversely interpreting his reign by references to later events.'[235] This is exactly the case, and, of course, a flaw in the former perpetuates a defect in the latter. The irrationalities of the Successor Wars are forever divisible recurring numbers when considered in the light of intestacy.

If events at Babylon remain cloaked by a literary 'shroud of Parrhasius' that *Quellenforschung* has not yet lifted,[236] and if the nets and tridents of rhetorical entrapment still loom large as ever, the great rubbish dump at Oxyrhynchus *is* giving up lost Sophocles, Euripides and Hesiod and the odd mummy embalmed in Pellan prose.[237] But we ask, as part of our *elenkhos* in Socratic debating style, if Hieronymus' opening pages were now unearthed listing satrapies linked to a Will, would today's scholars truly accept a new testate scenario?[238] If the sands of Egypt exhaled a new papyrus in which Seleucus inherited by testament the satrapy of Babylonia, would historians not dismiss it as a closing fragment of the *Romance*? And if Perdiccas' body were to be exhumed beside a similarly inscribed vellum, would they see a man facing off his assassins with the very mandate that empowered him, or simply an early *Pamphlet* draft?

To reiterate our central contention when autopsying the *Pamphlet*: rebroadcasting the existance of Alexander's testament in the early years of the Successor Wars and the deadly 'funeral games' would have only been a tenable strategy if knowledge of the original – or hearsay and rumour, to those not at Babylon – was circulating in the *Diadokhoi* armies and their courts. And Alexander *was* ever Alexander; facing death at Babylon, a Will by which his sons would rule under the protection of his few trusted men was the *only* route to immortality when requests for divinity and *isotheos* had been so hard to come by in his life.[239] So it is high time that the discredited document was de-accessorised of portents and accusations of conspiracy, and extracted from the clutches of 'romance'. It could bring coherency to Alexander's 'last words' and his 'last plans', and it would explain the mechanism behind the division of the empire, as well as the references to the Will made by Curtius and Diodorus.[240] Finally, it would demystify the intent of the *Pamphlet* itself.

We have already noted that 'the argument about the "truth" revolves around the degree of trust we place in the instincts of our secondary sources and *their* immunity to seduction.' An example of how problematic this is can be evidenced by the above reference we made to Pytheas who possibly made an epic voyage to Thule (perhaps Orkney or Shetland, Norway, or even Iceland) in years not far removed from Alexander's death, as his story is instructive. Polybius called the explorer from Massilia (modern Marseilles) a liar, preferring instead to believe the geography of Euhemerus, no doubt to preserve the reputation of Polybius' own extensive travels.[241] The fabled isles beyond Albion and Ierne – Britain and Ireland – existed, and yet they were branded a fanciful fiction, but Eratosthenes, who accurately calculated Earth's circumference, never had any doubts about Pytheas' log.[242]

Pliny offered little more credulity to Hanno of Carthage who penned a *paraplous* of the west coast of Africa, and this is paradoxical considering that Herodotus had long before recorded the Carthaginian trading customs with African tribes in some detail.[243] Whilst Pytheas' return is unattested, his log did survive through the classical era. Hanno's stele in the Temple of Baal in Carthage was destroyed when Rome rubbed salt in the city's wounds, and yet fragments of his journal also survived.[244] Pytheas and Hanno have been lucky, and modern confirmation of the accuracy of their observations has finally salvaged them and their voyages from earlier doubt.

The votive stele dedicated to Baal Hammon by Hanno the Carthaginian, son of Adonibal, 6th century BCE in Phoenician Punic, from Lilybaeum, and a fragment of Hanno's *Periplous* of Africa. Once written on a stele at the Temple of Baal at Carthage, it is now preserved in a single manuscript, *Codex Heidelbergensis 398*. The full title of the Greek translation of the Punic is *The Voyage of Hanno, commander of the Carthaginians, round the parts of Libya beyond the Pillars of Heracles, which he deposited in the Temple of Cronus*. The account was known to the Romans and Arrian ended his account of Nearchus' voyage, *Indike*, with a reference to Hanno's journey which took place ca. 500 BCE. Source: Heidelberg University Library.

In contrast, Alexander's testament has lacked a cartographer with the conviction to navigate by the waypoints scattered over the histories of the successors, and hopefully our conclusions provide a gnomon and lodestone for others to do just that.[245] Because the entertaining though implausible, corroborating though more often conflicted, the largely intact but irrevocably damaged and inspiring yet troubling portraits of Alexander we gaze upon today, were framed by those extracting something useful from his life, whether for political, territorial or philosophical gain. The guilty finger might also point at Olympias and Eumenes, whose attempt at reintroducing a Will linked to an indigestible court conspiracy killed any chance the original had of finding a serious literary home. So along with those agenda-laden primary historians and those who later came under their sway, and beside the philosophers and rhetoricians who wished to add their brushstrokes to the art, it is their iconograph, and not Alexander's, that has been hanging in history's gallery. *Ars longa, vita brevis*, as Hippocrates once proposed.[246]

NOTES

1. Thucydides 2.34-46, from Pericles' panegyric to the Athenian dead.
2. The inscription, according to legend, was engraved above the entrance to Plato's Academy. Quoted in Elias of Alexandria's commentary on Aristotle's *Categories*.
3. Diogenes Laertius *Diogenes* 6.4.
4. Pappus of Alexandria described Euclid's *porismata* as neither theorems nor problems but some kind of intermediate. See discussion in Pycior (1997) p 275.
5. See Proclus *Commentary on the First Book of Euclid's Elements* 66.7 ff for the titles of earlier works. Euclid's contribution and reliance on earlier works discussed in Shipley (2000) p 356.
6. Proclus on Euclid *Elements* 1 and 6-20, cited in Heath (1913) p 68 and p 354.
7. Heath (1913) p 355.
8. Riedweg (2002) pp 5-6, 59, 73.
9. Galen published *On His Own Books* to identify works truly his; Demetrius of Magnesia (1st century BCE) wrote the philological treatise *On Poets of the Same Name* which is much quoted in Diogenes Laertius' doxographies; both discussed in chapter titled *The Precarious Path of Pergamena and Papyrus*.
10. Discussed in Boyer (1991) pp 100-119; the variant originated with Stobaeus, a Macedonian compiler of the late fifth century.
11. Pytheas was reckoned to have journeyed to Thule sometime around 320 BCE; see Roseman (1994) p III and Cunliffe (2001) p VII. Details of Hanno's journey were mentioned at the end of Arrian's *Indike* 43.11-12. Antonius Diogenes wrote *The Wonder Beyond Thule* in the 2nd century as a book of *fabulae* and did link it to Alexander at Tyre which might reconfirm the broad timeframe in which it was known to have been published.
12. Following Worthington (2000) p 160 for facts being potentially 'bilingual'.
13. Diogenes Laertius *Zeno the Eleactic* 4; this was according to Aristotle *The Sophist*.
14. 'Acataleptic' is derived from the Greek word meaning 'incapable of being comprehended or ascertained' pertinent to the doctrine held by the Sceptic philosophers, which proposed human knowledge never amounts to certainty but only to probability.
15. The Trivium comprised the group of literary disciplines: rhetoric, grammar and dialectic or logic, all concerned with the art of discourse. It was distinct to the quadrivium, which comprised scientific disciplines.
16. *Heidelberg Epitome* 1.2 for twenty-four satrapies.
17. A good summary of the various satrapal lists can be found in Goralski (1989) pp 104-105. Anson (2014) p 49 and p 189 for discussion on the division of responsibilities. Billows (1990) p 276 and p 278 for the various satrapal posts. Anson (2013) p 65 for the *epistates* role and pp 141-146 for the layers of administration; full discussion of titles in Anson (1992).
18. Hatzopoulos (1996) p 156 for magistrate titles and roles.
19. Quoting Hornblower (1981) p 103 on 'centrifugal forces'.
20. Notably, some four or five years after Alexander's death, Eumenes was still able to access the treasury at Cyinda in western Cilicia. It remained intact, as did the treasury at Susa, which Eumenes planned to use to pay his troops when wintering in Babylonia in 317 BCE with his mandate from the 'kings'. Hieronymus pointed out that Antigonus benefited from an annual income of 11,000 talents after his defeat of Eumenes and assuming control of Cilicia in 315 BCE. Bellinger (1979) p 83 for a list of mints across Asia Minor.
21. Curtius 10.6.15 for Ptolemy's proposal of group rule. We propose Seleucus was included in this line-up. Whilst Arrian 6.28.4 did not list him amongst the Bodyguards, he was listed as amongst the most important of the generals in Arrian *Events After Alexander* 1.2; it is not impossible he replaced Hephaestion who died in 324 BCE, as a new 'eighth'.
22. Justin 13.4 for 'princes to prefects'.
23. Arrian 7.5.4-6 for the crowning of the Bodyguards.
24. Arrian 3.5.4, Plutarch 22.1, Polyaenus 6.49, Plutarch *Moralia* 333a for Philoxenus' role from 333 BCE.
25. Curtius 4.1.34-35 for a description of Antigonus' role and task in Lydia, here referring to the old Lydian kingdom of Asia Minor west of the Halys. Also Arrian 1.29.3, Justin 13.4.14 for Antigonus' previous regional command. For Balacrus' career see Heckel (2006) pp 68-69.
26. See Heckel (2006) pp 96-97 for Craterus' roles in Alexander's absence.
27. Diodorus 17.80.3 confirmed Parmenio's administrative role and guardianship of the 180,000 talents at Ecbatana. Black Cleitus was to govern the upper satrapies of Bactria and Sogdia, Curtius 8.1.19-21. Mazaeus had played a valuable role in Darius' battles, especially Gaugamela; he was made satrap of Babylon soon after Gaugamela until his death in 328 BCE; Arrian 3.16.4, Curtius 5.1.44, Diodorus 17.64.5-6; he surely reported to a Macedonian general: Parmenio once

installed. Phrataphernes was possibly reinstated in Parthia and possibly Hyrcania by Alexander after Darius' death; Arrian 3.23.4, 3.28.2. At Babylon he was reconfirmed; Diodorus 18.3.3, Justin 13.4.23, a position implied in the *Pamphlet* Will, *Metz Epitome* 121. Arrian 3.16.9 and 3.18.11 for Abulites and Phrasaortes; Anson (2013) pp 141-142 for discussion of the layers of satrapal government.

28. Curtius 10.10.1-5 and Dexippus FGrH 100 F8 for Ptolemy's regional grant. Curtius 10.10.1-5, Dexippus FGrH 100 F8, Justin 13.4-5 and Diodorus 18.3.1-3 for Lysimachus' territories.

29. The grain trade from Cyrene discussed in Carney (1995) p 386. Justin 13.7 for the history of Cyrene. Bagnall-Derow (2004) pp 3-4 for the list of grain shipments from Cyrene.

30. Arrian *Events After Alexander* 1.34.

31. Diodorus 17.49.2-4 for the embassies from Cyrene that met Alexander on his way to the oasis at Siwa. For detail of Ptolemy's annexation of Cyrene see Diodorus 18.21.7 and Arrian *Events After Alexander* 1.17. This is following Harpalus' unsuccessful flight to Athens as Alexander re-emerged from Gedrosia. Thibron, leader of his mercenary force, fled from Cyprus to Cyrene. After initial defeats, the population was divided on how to deal with him and Ptolemy sent his general Ophellas of Pella, a former *trierarchos* of Alexander's Hydaspes-Indus fleet, to restore order. Thibron was eventually captured and handed over to the populace for execution and Ophellas continued to govern the region until his misadventure with Agathocles, tyrant of Syracuse (361-289 BCE) in 309/308 BCE. Ophellas was fatally betrayed and his wife Eurydice returned to Athens, marrying Demetrius *Poliorketes*. For his death see Diodorus 20.42.3-5, Justin 22.7.5-6, *Suda* O994. Cyrene was for a time ruled by Demetrius the Fair, youngest son of Demetrius *Poliorketes*, yet he was related to the Ptolemaic regime through his maternal grandfather, Ptolemy *Soter*.

32. Arrian *Events After Alexander* 1.3-4 for the 'kingdom of Arrhidaeus' and reiterated in Dexippus FGrH 100 F8 4. For Craterus being charged with safeguarding the freedom of the Greeks and thus a regime change was suggested, cosmetic or otherwise, Arrian 7.12.4.

33. Bosworth (2002) pp 10-11 for discussion of Craterus' emulation of Alexander. Also see the full text of Demetrius of Phalerum *On Style* 289 in Fortenbaugh-Schütrumpf (2000) p 43. Craterus apparently received Greek emissaries on a raised golden couch dressed in purple robes.

34. Arrian *Events After Alexander* 1a.3, Dexippus FGrH 100 F 8.4 *for protiston times telos*; discussed in Anson (1992) p 39.

35. Diogenes Laertius *Diogenes* 6.57 for Diogenes' reply to Craterus. The episode is not dated but the only period Craterus was back in Greece or Macedonia was either side of the Lamian War.

36. Plutarch 40.5 reported that a hunting scene in which Alexander fought a lion was represented on Craterus' monument at Delphi. Also Pliny 34.64 for the monument; Borza-Palagia (2007) p 97 for its significance and pp 90-103 for lion hunts and their representation; pp 101-202 for Craterus' monument and dedication. Curtius 8.1.11-18, 8.1.14-18, 8.6.7, 8.8.3, Arrian 4.13-14, Plutarch 55 for additional hunting incidents involving Alexander. See discussion and measurements in Stewart (1993) p 270 and descriptions on p 390.

37. Diodorus 18.3.3, Justin 13.3.23, Dexippus FGrH 100 F8 6.

38. Plutarch 69.1 for the Persian payment tradition.

39. Diodorus 18.7.1-3, translation from the Loeb Classical Library edition, 1947.

40. Diodorus 18.4.8, 18.7.1-9 and the new revolt and Curtius 9.7.1-12 for the previous uprising.

41. For T20, so Justin 13.4, there appears a lacuna that swallowed Peithon's name, for Perdiccas' father-in-law, Atropates, is clearly given Lesser Media.

42. Diodorus 18.7.4, translation from the Loeb Classical Library edition, 1947 for the mercenary revolt.

43. Diodorus 18.7.3-18.8 for the troop numbers and outcome.

44. Numbers were often misrepresented. For example it remains just as unlikely to interpret from Arrian 1.16.2-3 and Plutarch 16.12-15 that 18,000 mercenaries were slaughtered at the Granicus River. Arrian 1.14.4 suggested a similar number ('little less') of mercenaries to the Persian cavalry stated at 20,000, and that all died bar 2,000 prisoners; 1.16.2. The Macedonians allegedly lost only eighty-five cavalry and thirty infantry (less according to Aristobulus, so claimed Plutarch). Modern interpretations suggest more like 5,000 mercenaries were present. Discussion in Parke (1933) p 180.

45. Discussed in Gabriel (2006) p 114.

46. Diodorus 18.7.4-9.

47. Aelian 14.47a.

48. Diodorus 18.4.8 and 18.7-8 for Peithon's actions quelling the revolt.

49. Diodorus 18.7.5-9 for the battle and its outcome.

50. Diodorus 18.7.8. Quoting JK Anderson in Hanson (1991) p 21 and Tarn 1 (1948) p 15 footnote 1.

51. Heckel (2006) p 196 (Peithon 4) for the governorship of the Indus region and to the sea and p 212 (Philip 5).

52. See discussion of Peithon's role in Heckel (1988) p 61 footnote 8 citing the *Metz Epitome* 118 and *Romance* 3.33.15. Heckel (2006) p 195 concedes that 'special powers' were provided to Peithon to carry out this task. Heckel (2006) p. 195. Arrian *Events After Alexander* 1.35 mentioned the Caspian Gates as the boundary of Media in the west.

53. Justin 13.4.13, for Atropates' grant of Lesser Media; implied at Diodorus 18.2.3 here Peithon is mentioned in Media first; see Strabo 11.13.1 for confirmation. Arrian 3.8.4, 4.18.3, 7.4.1 for his previous governance and Arrian 7.4.5, Justin 13.4.13 for Perdiccas' marriage to his unnamed daughter.

54. Diodorus 19.14.1, translation from the Loeb Classical Library edition, 1947. Diodorus 18.39.6 named the governor of Parthia 'Philip' yet he referred to him as 'Philotas' at 19.14.1; Heckel (2006) p 214 for the identity discussion.

55. Anson (2014) p 101 for the observation on Seleucus' acceptance of Peithon.

56. Quoting Diodorus 19.14.4. See Heckel (1988) pp 60-61 and Goralski (1989) pp 104-105 for a useful full list and comparison of satraps and *Pamphlet*-nominated names.

57. Diodorus 19.14.8. Compare this to Diodorus' description of Triparadeisus at 18.39.6 where Porus and Taxiles are left unmoved solely because it would have required a royal army to do so. This suggests Eudamus might have been encouraged to kill Porus. Arrian 6.2 1 for Porus' extended territory.

58. Diodorus 19.14.1-2. For Peithon son of Agenor's appointment to the northern Indus bordering region; see Diodorus 18.3.3, Dexippus FGrH 100 F8, and for reconfirmation at Triparadeisus, Diodorus 18.39.6, Arrian *Events After Alexander* 1.36, Justin 13.4.21. Forces from Bactria are also mentioned at Diodorus 19.14.7. See chapter entitled *The Silent Siegecraft of the Pamphleteers* for discussion of Stasanor and Stasander.

59. Arrian 7.5.6. Peucestas is mentioned by name but Arrian suggested *all* of the Bodyguards received gold crowns.

60. Quoting Diodorus 18.5.4 and Plutarch *Demetrius* 46.4.

61. For Atropates' appointment to Lesser Media see Justin 13.4.13, Diodorus 18.3.3. Arrian 7.13.2 and 6 for the 'Amazon' episode. Discussion in Heckel (2006) pp 61-62 and Bosworth-Baynham (2000) p 300. Diodorus 19.46.1-6 for events surrounding the removal of Peithon. Heckel (2006) p 62 for discussion and Strabo 11.13.1 for Atropates' kingship and new title. Polybius 5.55.9-10 for Media Atropatene.

62. Diodorus 19.92.1-5 and 100.3-4, Appian *Syrian Wars* 55 and 57 for Nicanor's installation as *strategos* of Media and the upper satrapies, Peithon's previous domain. See identification discussion in Heckel (2006) p 178 (Nicanor 12) and Billows (1990) pp 409-410. Anson (2014) p 125 following Billows (1990) p 393 suggested Hippostratus assumed this role first, though Diodorus 19.46.5 seems to have suggested that role (*strategos*) applied to Media only. Hippostratus may have replaced him due to his poor performance when attacked; Diodorus 19.47.1-3.

63. Diodorus 19.92.3 for the negligent guard and 19.100.3 for Antigonus giving up hope of gaining income from the lands east of Babylon.

64. Diodorus 19.55.3 for Seleucus rebutting Antigonus' demands. Diodorus referred to Babylon but nevertheless termed it the 'country' suggesting Seleucus governed the whole province not the city.

65. Following Heckel (2006) p 247.

66. Collins (2001) pp 270-273 for discussion of the chiliarch's peripheral roles

67. Diodorus 18.3-4, Justin 13.4.17 and 13.4.23 for Seleucus' appointment and Archon's role.

68. Diodorus 18.6.3 described Egypt as the 'best due to its revenues' and Diodorus 18.5.4 described Media as the 'greatest of all the satrapies'; the importance of the treasury at Susa and Persepolis, coming under Peucestas' authority, made them desirable.

69. Justin 13.4.17; Diodorus 18.3.4 terms Peucestas' appointment 'a most distinguished office'.

70. Arrian *Events After Alexander* 1.

71. The *Metz Epitome* and *Romance* are in accord on Seleucus' inheritance. Heckel (1988) p 16 for the *Metz Epitome* 118 and Stoneman (1991) p 154 for the *Romance* translation.

72. For Arcesilaus' role (a probable Perdiccan) see Diodorus 18.3.3, Justin 13.4.23; Dexippus FGrH 100 F8 6 called him Archelaus.

73. Diodorus 19.100.5 for Patrocles and 19.99.3-4 for Seleucus' campaign into Media.

74. Appian *Syrian Wars* 53.269 for Blitor and Seleucus' escape. Nothing else is known about him. For Amphimachus' appointment see Arrian *Events After Alexander* 1.35, Diodorus 18.39.6. Heckel (2006) p 22 and 53, and Bosworth (2002) p 113 for discussion on Amphimachus' identity; probably 'brother of Arrhidaeus' in original manuscripts though later confused with King Philip III (Arrhidaeus). He was awarded the governorship of Mesopotamia at Triparadeisus; Diodorus 18.39.6, Arrian *Events After Alexander* 1.35. He was unlikely to have been the brother to the new King Philip III and was more likely brother of Arrhidaeus who became satrap of Hellespontine Phrygia and sources (Justin in particular) confused the identity of 'Arrhidaeus'. Amphimachus' later support for Eumenes at Gabiene suggests the latter too. As a governor of Mesopotamia,

Amphimachus would have nevertheless been subordinate to Seleucus the regional *strategos* (or to Perdiccas in Syria), and yet was found operating under Eumenes at Paraetacene, Diodorus 19.27.4, so logically he defected at this point if not under Perdiccas' authority; discussion in chapter titled *The Tragic Triumvirate of Treachery and Oaths.*

75. Mesopotamia is derived from 'middle' (*mesos*) and 'river' (*potamos*). See Diodorus 18.6.3 for confirmation of the origins.
76. Billows (1990) p 272 for discussion on Antigonus' amalgamated governance of Mesopotamia and Babylonia under Peithon son of Agenor from 315 BCE onwards.
77. Arrian *Indike* 18.3.
78. The conflict between Docimus and Archon covered at Arrian *Events After Alexander* 24.3-5.
79. Diodorus 18.39.6 for Seleucus' 'reconfirmation' as satrap of Babylonia. Diodorus 18.37.1-3, Arrian *Events After Alexander* 1.39, Justin 13.8.10-14.1.1, Appian *Syrian Wars* 53 for the sentence on the Perdiccans.
80. The lacuna would follow Arrian *Events After Alexander* 1.8 and before the reference to Roxane. Goralski (1989) pp 10-5 and Heckel (1988) p 61 for the relative satrapal references to Babylon; Photius' epitomes of Arrian suggest these three sources clearly stated Seleucus inherited the governorship of Babylon at least. The confusion with detail from Triparadeisus is supported in Photius' positioning Arrhidaeus in Hellespontine Phrygia.
81. Compare this reconstruction with Diodorus 18.3.3-4 where Archon and Seleucus are mentioned in bordering sentences.
82. Diodorus 18.3.1 and 18.14.4. At 18.12.1 Diodorus mistakenly named 'Philotas' as satrap of the region, but this is usually corrected to 'Leonnatus.' Also Arrian *Events After Alexander* 1.6, Dexippus 82,62B, Curtius 10.10.2, Justin 13.4.16. Photius' epitome of Arrian *Events After Alexander* has Arrhidaeus in the region but presumably this is again mistaking or compressing the detail of his appointment at Triparadeisus.
83. For Leonnatus' decoration for saving Alexander's life see Arrian 7.5.4-5.
84. Leonnatus' heritage discussed in Heckel (2006) p 147. Plutarch *Eumenes* 3.5 for Leonnatus' bid to take the throne.
85. Curtius 10.7.8 for recognition of Leonnatus' royal stock and guardianship role, 10.7.20 for his cavalry command and 10.8.23 for a reiteration of the 'two' guardians of the king then in Babylon, the third being Meleager, by negotiation.
86. Heckel (2006) p 150 suggests Leonnatus would have been 'disappointed' but goes no further. Many modern historians believe it was a manipulation by Perdiccas. Arrian 1.17.1-2, 1.25.2 for its governance by a son of Harpalus, Calas; Heckel (2006) pp 74-75 and footnote 163 for identity discussion.
87. Leonnatus and Perdiccas are attested together in chasing Pausanias, Philip's assassin; Diodorus 16.94.
88. Arrian 2.12.2 for Balacrus, Arrian 1.17.1,2.4.1, Curtius 4.5.13 for Calas, Arrian 3.6.6 for Nearchus, Arrian 1.17.7 for Asander.
89. Bithynia was ruled by Zipoetes who formally became king in 297 BCE; no conflict between him and the Macedonians is recorded. The Hellespontine Phrygia region may have still encompassed Bithynia, the Troad and Mysia, as it did after the conquests of Cyrus the Great, when Hellespontine Phrygia controlled the Asian shores of the Propontis from its capital at Dascylium.
90. Bithynia is not mentioned as a separate territory at this point by the sources. Arrian *Events After Alexander* 1.37 for confirmation that Lycaonia fell within Antigonus' mandate from outset.
91. Plutarch *Eumenes* 3.3 for Antigonus' rejection of Perdiccas' orders. More below on how far east Eumenes governance might have reached.
92. For Neoptolemus' opposition see Plutarch *Eumenes* 5.4, Diodorus 18.29.4-5 and Arrian *Events After Alexander* 1.27. Quoting Plutarch *Eumenes* 4.1-2 for reference to Neoptolemus' presence in Armenia and for his career, see discussion in Heckel (2006) p 174, and for Orontes, Heckel (2006) p 185 citing Dexippus' corrupt epitome FGrH 100 F8 6 which stated Neoptolemus' inherited Armenia. Heckel (1988) pp 61-63 for corruptions in satrapal and governor names. It remains unclear whether Orontes, the Armenian satrap under Darius III, ever made terms with Alexander, or whether the province remained unconquered. Orontes fought for Darius III at Gaugamela, see Arrian *Anabasis* 3.8.5. He escaped and is heard of next in 317 BCE back in Armenia as a friend of Peucestas, whom he may have met in Macedonia originally. See Diodorus 19.23.3. Armenia had not been conquered despite Alexander attempting to install Mithrines after the battle at Gaugamela; Diodorus 17.64.6, Curtius 5.1.44, Arrian 3.16.5. Neoptolemus' appointment however in 323 BCE suggests plans were afoot for just that, as in Cappadocia. For later references to Orontes see Diodorus 19.23.3, Polyaenus 4.8.3. See Plutarch *Eumenes* 7.5-8, Diodorus 18.29.4 for the battle with Neoptolemus.
93. Diodorus 19.23.1-4 for details of the ruse and see chapter titled *The Tragic Triumvirate of Treachery and Oaths.*
94. Diodorus 19.57.1-3 for the envoys to Antigonus, also Justin 15.1.

95. Diodorus 19.57.4 for Cassander's incursion into Cappadocia. See chapter titled *The Tragic Triumvirate of Treachery and Oaths* for Antigonus' possible planned invasion.

96. Diodorus 18.43.1-2 clearly stated that Laomedon was removed from Coele-Syria, thus enabling Ptolemy to acquire Phoenicia too; reiterated at Justin 13.4. The Will references reinforce it. The *Metz Epitome* 117 and *Romance* 3.32 both have Meleager in Coele-Syria rather than all Syria.

97. McGing (2010) p 98 for an example of Israel being cited as Coele -yria.

98. Diodorus 18.6.3 for the geographical digression referring to Syria. That Coele-Syria included Phoenicia is reiterated by Diodorus at 18.43.2.

99. Arrian 3.8.6 and 5.25.5 as an example of 'Mesopotamian Syria' being referred to.

100. Diodorus 17.64.5 for Menes' appointment.

101. Chapter titled *Wills and Covenants in the Classical Mind* for the Donation of Alexandria by Antony and Cleopatra.

102. Plutarch *Eumenes* 3.6 stated Eumenes fled to Perdiccas but no location was given.

103. Diodorus 18.23.4 for Antigonus' flight; Plutarch *Eumenes* 4.1 for the suggestion that both he and Eumenes were together in Cilicia. Diodorus 18.44-45, 50.1 and 18.45.2-47.3 for Alcetas' actions at Cretopolis and Termessus.

104. Atkinson (2009) p 40 footnote 61 for Diodorus' wording concerning the fate of the funeral bier.

105. Diodorus 18.60.6 for Eumenes' possession of Alexander's throne, sceptre, weapons and insignia.

106. Arrian *Events after Alexander* 1.43-45 for the seventy elephants left with Antigonus and Antipater keeping the remainder.

107. Arrian *Events After Alexander* 1.28 for Perdiccas launching his campaign against Ptolemy from Damascus. Hill-Walton (1991) p 49 for description of the ancient network of roads converging on Damascus. Samaria was garrisoned or settled by Alexander after the siege of Gaza; Curtius 4.8.10. St Jerome *Kronographia* 1685 for its founding by Alexander and 1721 suggesting Perdiccas refounded it.

108. Diodorus 20.47.5 translation from the Loeb Classical Library edition, 1954.

109. Billows (1990) p 297 for Antigonus' tenure.

110. Strabo12.8.15 and Livy 38.13.5 for the founding of Apamea. Appian *Syrian Wars* 57 stated Seleucus *Nikator* named three cities after her; also Strabo 16.2.4. The Syrian tetrapolis consisted of Antioch, Apamea, Seleucia in Pieria and Laodicea.

111. Diodorus 18.37.3-4 for Alcetas' recovery of money from Tyre. Bellinger (1979) p 84 for the observation on Laomedon's non-involvement.

112. For Laomedon's grant of Coele Syria see Arrian *Events After Alexander* 1.5, Diodorus 18.3.1, Curtius 10.10.2, Justin 13.4.12, Appian *Syrian Wars* 52, Dexippus FGrH 100 F8 2. Appian *Syrian Wars* 52 for reference to the 'buying' of the satrapy. Diodorus 18.43.1-2 and Pausanias 1.6.4 for Ptolemy's hostility. See temporal discussion in Wheatley (1995) pp 433-440. The likely date of Ptolemy's annexation was 321 BCE and very shortly after the conference at Triparadeisus; Wheatley (1995) for dating discussion.

113. See Wheatley (1995) p 437 for discussion of the lacuna after Diodorus 18.39.

114. Diodorus 18.73-74 for Eumenes entering Phoenicia.

115. Diodorus 19.57.1-2 for Ptolemy's and Cassander's envoy and demands to Antigonus.

116. Arrian *Events After Alexander* 24.2, Justin 13.6.16 for Philoxenus' installation by Perdiccas. He was reconfirmed at Triparadeisus: Diodorus 18.39.6, Arrian *Events After Alexander* 1.34. The 'Mesopotamian Line' is referred to in the *Metz Epitome* 117; for Aristonus' possible role see chapter titled *The Silent Siegecraft of the Pamphleteers* and Arrian *Events After Alexander* 24.6 for the Cyprus affair.

117. Stewart (1993) pp 294-295, 297, 301 for analysis of the sarcophagus and description of the unarmed man being murdered, thought to be Perdiccas. For the panel on the Alexander Sarcophagus, and Arrhidaeus' possible portrayal, see discussion by VA Troncoso in Carney-Ogden (2010) p 21 and footnote 53 and doubted in Heckel Sarcophagus (2006) pp 386-388.

118. Arrian *Events After Alexander* 1.33 and Polyaenus 4.6.4 focused on money being the central grievance. Arrian *Events After Alexander* 1.33,1.39 for Attalus' presence at Triparadeisus. Many scholars accept Attalus, the Perdiccan general that commanded the fleet supporting the Egyptian invasion, was present; he later failed to unite with Eumenes. That seems unlikely. He may have managed to send communications to Eurydice but as Alcetas had killed her mother, any Perdiccan support seems unlikely, especially with Peithon and Antigenes present, the murderers of Perdiccas.

119. The dissatisfaction of Peithon, Seleucus and Antigenes refers to their murder of Perdiccas; discussed in chapter titled *The Silent Siegecraft of the Pamphleteers*.

120. Antipater would have benefited from the remnants of Leonnatus' troops and those of Craterus that had either crossed from Cilicia to Thessaly, or remained in Cilicia.

121. The similarity between Peithon and the 'son of Agenor' seems to have confused Diodorus, or a translator, when referencing Media. If Stasander and Stasanor were similarly confused, rather than strangely 'swapping' satrapies, they remained in place too. See further discussion in chapter titled *The Silent Siegecraft of the Pamphleteers*.

122. Euripides from Plutarch *Demetrius* 14.1-3; Antigonus apparently quoted the line to his young son, Demetrius, whom he was encouraging to marry to the older Eurydice, widow of Ophellas of Cyrene and a descendent of the Athenian general Miltiades, for political gain. Apparently Antigonus substituted 'wed' for 'serve' when whispering the lines to Demetrius.

123. Quoting Carney (1988) p 385.

124. Quoting Green (2007) p 11. Blackwell (1999) for further discussion of their roles.

125. The significance of the lack of patronymic observed and commented on in Carney-Ogden (2010) p 44; Finlay (1973) for the specific grain deliveries 76,000 Attic *medimni* to Olympias and 50,000 to Cleopatra. Hammond (1985) p 160 for Olympias' prostates role. Bagnall-Derow (2004) pp 3-4 for the translated list of the grain shipments.

126. Discussion on the roles of Olympias and Cleopatra in Epirus and Macedonia in Alexander's final years in Carney (1988) pp 396-397, Blackwell (1999) pp 81-105, Anson (2013) p 35. Plutarch 68.11 went as far as stating Olympias and Cleopatra planned to take over Epirus and Macedonia from Antipater's control. Diodorus 17.108.7 for Olympias' involvement in the Harpalus affair. Blackwell (1999) p 86 for Cleopatra's *prostasia* and pp 81-105 for full discussion on Olympias' role and p 88 for the status of women in Epirus. Blackwell (1999) pp 89-91 for the grain shipments. For the death of Alexander Molossus see Justin 12.2.4 and Blackwell (1999) p 90 for Cleopatra's office as thearodoch. Blackwell (1999) p 103 the possible greater autonomy of the Epirote League states. Anson (2013) p 21 for discussion on the sacral power vested in the Argead clan. Flower (1994) p 190 for evidence of the higher social status of Etruscan women. Carney (2006) pp 91-92 for Olympias' stance on Dodona. Hammond (1985) p 156 and Thucydides 2.80.5 and the presidential role in Epirus.

127. Diodorus 19.59.4 reported that Antipater valued Phila's wisdom and consulted her on policy; she was charged with the defence of Cyprus late in Demetrius' reign, Diodorus 19.67.1, and she acted as a diplomat for Demetrius to Cassander, Plutarch *Demetrius* 32.4. For Cratesipolis' actions at Sicyon, see Diodorus 19.67 and 20.37, Polyaenus 8, Plutarch *Demetrius* 9. The roles of Phila, Cratesipolis, Cynnane and Olympias are discussed in Carney (1995) p 389. Diodorus 19.16.4-5 for Stratonice's role in the sixteen-month siege that saw Docimus and Attalus finally captured, probably in Pisidia, though the location is not stated.

128. Quoting from Bury-Barber-Bevan-Tarn (1923) p 11.

129. Plutarch 39.11 implied Alexander warned Antipater that Olympias might be planning to kill him and that Alexander kept her away from state affairs.

130. Quoting S Ruzicka in Carney-Ogden (2005) p 9.

131. See Heckel (2006) p 90 for discussion of Cleopatra's age. See Carney (1988) p 398 for Olympias and Cleopatra's ability to provide offspring. She had two children by Alexander of Epirus according to Plutarch *Pyrrhus* 5.11: Cadmea and Neoptolemus.

132. Following the logic of, and quoting, Carney (1988) p 399.

133. Diodorus 20.37.3-4 for confirmation of her suitors. As Anson (2014) p 153 noted, any approach by Cassander must have been before he murdered Olympias in 315 BCE and thus before he married Thessalonice soon after.

134. For Craterus' delay in crossing to Greece see Heckel (2006) p 98 and footnote 258.

135. Europa (or Caranus) was born just days before Philip died according to Athenaeus 13.557e in mid-summer 336 BCE according to Diodorus 17.2.3. According to Justin 9.7.12 she (or he) was murdered in her mother's arms by Olympias who forced her mother to commit suicide by hanging, whilst Pausanias 8.7.5-7 claimed mother and daughter were burned in an oven or dragged over a brazier without Alexander's approval; Plutarch 10.8 confirmed Alexander's anger at treating her 'savagely'. The sex of the baby and whether there were more than one is debated: see Musgrave (1991) p 7 footnote 23 for details and Lane Fox (2011) p 385. A full discussion on the significance of Alexander's sisters is given in Heckel (1988) pp 55-59.

136. Diodorus 20.37.5 confirmed Antigonus governor of Sardis had been instructed not to let Cleopatra leave.

137. Diodorus 18.36.6 for Ptolemy being chosen as a guardian to the kings.

138. Plutarch *Demetrius* 31.3-32.3 for a concise picture of the various intermarriages post-Ipsus. Ptolemy married Ptolemais to Demetrius *Poliorketes* (Plutarch *Demetrius* 32), Lysandra to Alexander V of Macedonia (Cassander's youngest son by Thessalonice), Porphyry FGrH 695), Eirene to Eunostus king of Soli on Cyprus (Athenaeus 13.576e) and Arsinoe to Lysimachus (Pausanias 1.10.3); Carney-Ogden (2010) p 131 and footnote 63 for detail. Pyrrhus married Antigone, a daughter of Ptolemy, and Demetrius *Poliorketes* married Deidameia, a daughter of Aeacides, so Pyrrhus' sister.

139. Quoting *Metz Epitome* 115, also *Romance* 3.32.

140. Following the argument of Anson (1992) p 39; this is contra Hammond (1985) p 158 who believed Olympias carried the title in Alexander's absence.

141. Quoting Bosworth *A to A* (1988) p 12. Diodorus 18.39.2; Arrian *Events After Alexander* 1.30-31 for Eurydice's behaviour at Triparadeisus.
142. Full discussion of the role of *prostasia* in Anson (1992).
143. Arrian 6.30.3 for Peucestas' ability to speak Persian.
144. Plutarch 77.6-7 for the death of Stateira and Drypetis.
145. Sisygambis allegedly died from self-imposed starvation five days after hearing of Alexander's death, see Curtius 10.5.19-25, Diodorus 17.118.3, Justin 13.1.5; for the Vulgate depiction as Alexander's second mother, Curtius 3.12.17, 5.2.22, Justin 13.1.5.
146. Curtius 10.5.23 for Sisygambis' reflections on the previous pogrom. For Ochus' pogroms see Justin 10.1-10.3, Valerius Maximus 9.2.7.
147. See Heckel (2006) p 181 for discussion. Ochus was left at Susa with Sisygambis and his sisters were never heard of again; see Curtius 5.2.17, Diodorus 17.67.1.
148. Curtius 10.5.23 suggested Sisygambis lamented that she had only one remaining child alive.
149. Plutarch *Eumenes* 19.1-2 for Eumenes' children. Diodorus 19.35.5 for the daughters of Attalus; Heckel (2006) pp 276-277 for discussion (F38-39).
150. Arrian 7.12.2 for Alexander's refusal to let the Asiatic children be repatriated to Macedonia. This is reinforced by Diodorus 17.110.3 detailing the fund Alexander left for their upbringing and schooling.
151. For Heracles' link to Barsine see Diodorus 20.20.1, 20.28.1, Justin 11.10.3, Plutarch *Eumenes* 1.3, Curtius 10.6.11, 10.6.13, Justin 13.2.7, 15.2.3, Pausanias 9.7.2.
152. Heracles' authenticity discussed in Billows (1990) pp 140-141 citing the initial work by Tarn and Brunt. Also see Tarn (1948) p 330 relating to his earlier article: Tarn (1921). Whereas Errington (1970) p 74 and Brunt (1975) pp 22-34 accepts the child could have been legitimate, Pearson (1960) p 117, Jacoby, Berve, Beloch and Hamilton concluded he was an imposter. Tarn dismisses the boy on a number of principles: his age, and conversation between Polyperchon and Cassander that Tarn concluded alluded to the boy as a 'pretender', along with the boy's previous long-term obscurity. However these contentions are open to reinterpretation. As it has been pointed out, Tarn took a moralistic stance in his interpretations of Alexander's career, here defending him from accusations of a liaison (and its outcome) with an unofficial concubine, Barsine. Heracles' existence and/or his relationship to Alexander was recorded by Diodorus 20.20.1, 20.28, Justin 11.10.3, Dio Crysostom *Discourse* 64.23, Pausanias 9.7.2 and Appian *Syrian Wars* 52, Curtius 10.6.11, 10.6.13 and Plutarch *Eumenes* 1.3.
153. Diodorus 19.64.3-5 for Cassander's turning of Polyperchon's son and Diodorus 19.66.7 for his son's assassination. See Heckel (2006) p 230 for 'retirement'. Billows (1990) p 140 for his powerlessness. Following Tarn (1921) p 22 for Polyperchon's isolation.
154. Diodorus 19.67.1. For Cratesipolis' actions at Sicyon, see Diodorus 19.67 and 20.37, Polyaenus 8, Plutarch *Demetrius* 9.
155. Antigonus' likely role in the affair as stated in Tarn (1921) pp 18-21, Tarn (1948) pp 330-337 and re-stated in Billows (1990) p 141.
156. Diodorus 20.20.1 for Heracles' being aged seventeen and Justin 15.2.3 has Heracles in his fifteenth year. See discussion in Heckel (2006) p 138. Brunt (1975) p 28 suggests Heracles could have been born as early as 328 BCE. Considering Justin's poor track record with identities, aged seventeen is more convincing than fourteen; Justin's confusion (see 14.6.2 and 14.6.13), in which he claimed Heracles and his mother were murdered together, was actually a reference to Roxane and her son Alexander IV who, in 310 BCE, would have been close to his thirteenth year; see Wheatley (1998) p 19 for discussion.
157. Diodorus 20.20.1-2 for Polyperchon's reintroduction of the boy and Diodorus 20.28.1 for the reception in Macedonia. Justin 15.2 suggested both mother and son must have travelled to Macedonia as both were later secretly killed.
158. Tarn (1948) p 332.
159. Arrian *Events After Alexander* 1.43 for Cassander urging his father not to 'get too far from the kings'. Arrian *Times After Alexander* 1.38 suggested Antigonus took custody of the kings but this should more logically read Antipater as there is no evidence of this, he was after all heading for war with Eumenes, and it was Antipater who took the kings back to Macedonia; however, Antigonus' custody might be a reference to Heracles based in Pergamum. Cassander urged his father not to 'get too far from the kings.' The one time Antipater may have given them up, temporarily, is when confronting Eumenes in a short campaign uniquely mentioned in the *Gothenburg Palimpsest*; discussed in chapter titled *The Tragic Triumvirate of Treachery and Oaths*.
160. Tarn's theory proposes that Nearchus' own book promoted the boy as genuine, and so too his part in the boy's promotion at the Assembly, when he was writing at the Antigonid court some years later. It has been argued that Antigonus' influence over Nearchus, who operated under him from 317/6 BCE onwards, paved the way for a publication that perpetuated the claim of Heracles; inevitably it was for Antigonus' own dynastic ends, care of a compliant Polyperchon who was by then desperate for alliances in Greece.

161. Brunt (1975) pp 22-34 concurs.
162. For Cassander's actions see Diodorus 20.28.1-4. Curtius 10.6.10-13 preserved Nearchus' speech proposing Heracles be recognised as an heir. Errington (1970) p 74.
163. Plutarch *Moralia* 530b-d and Diodorus 20.28.2 for Polyperchon's murder of Heracles: Polyperchon handed him over to Cassander for 100 talents and a share of power, which amounted to little.
164. Curtius 3.11.24-25 for their respective ages, Diodorus 17.36.2, Justin 11.9.12, Plutarch, 21.1 and Arrian 2.11.9 for the confirmation that Darius' wife was his sister.
165. Curtius 3.13.12-17 for the captive list. Diodorus 17.23.5 for Mentor's sending his wife and children to Darius' care. Diodorus 16.52.3-5 and Arrian 2.1.3 mentioned Memnon appointed Pharnabazus, son of Artabazus, as his own replacement. See Heckel (2006) p 70. Mentor was last heard of in 342 BCE; for Memnon's death see Diodorus 17.29.3-4, Arrian, 2.1.3, Curtius 3.1.21 and 3.2.1. Diodorus 16.52.4 for the eleven sons and ten daughters; Curtius 6.5.4 mentioned nine sons (Arrian 3.23.7 named three of them) were with him when he surrendered to Alexander in Hyrcania at age ninety-five; perhaps two had died earlier or were operating elsewhere. Ilioneus is named 'Hystanes' by Hedicke in some Curtius editions; amended by Heckel (2006) p 143.
166. Curtius 5.9.1 and 6.5.2 for Artabazus taking refuge in Macedonia. The date of the arrival at Pella is uncertain; see Heckel (1987) p 116 footnote 4. Alexander would have still been young (perhaps eight) when Artabazus and family departed ca. 348 BCE as suggested at Diodorus 16.52.1-4 (16.5.2.3 for Memnon's presence in Macedonia); the archonship of Callimachus is referred to 349/348 BCE though communications, pleas and exonerations would have taken time, so we may add a year or so to the departure of Artabazus from Macedonia. Heckel (2006) p 275 (F12) for discussion of the wife captured at Damascus.
167. See Heckel (2006) pp 55 and 70 for discussion, as well as Diodorus 16.52.3-4.
168. For Barsine's intimacy with Alexander see Curtius 3.13.14, Plutarch 21.7-9, Justin 11.10.2-3, Plutarch *Eumenes* 1.3. For Artabazus' surrender see Curtius 6.5.2-6; Arrian 3.23.7, and for Bactria, see Curtius 8.1.10 and Arrian 3.29.1 Artabazus was the son of the daughter of the Great King Artaxerxes II; see Plutarch 21.9.
169. See Heckel (1987) for a list of these and other *anonymae* and their backgrounds and Heckel (2006) pp 274-275.
170. For the Rhodian connection for Artabazus' wife and family links see Demosthenes 23.154, 23.157 (these suggest an 'in-law' relationship). Diodorus 16.52.4 was more specific that Artabazus sired his children with their sister; Heckel (2006) p 275 for details. Heckel (1987) pp 114-116 provides a study of these interwoven lines. Also Mentor had married a daughter of Artabazus, who was himself the son of an Achaemenid princess.
171. Quoting Justin 11.10.2-4; for Roxane's misidentifications see Justin 14.6.2 and 14,6,13, Porphyry fr.3.1; see Tarn (1921) p 27 for discussion.
172. Curtius 3.12.21-23 for Barsine's descriptions and Arrian 4.19 for similar descriptions of both Roxane and Darius' wife. Discussed at Tarn (1948) p 333, Plutarch 21.6.
173. Plutarch 21.6-7.
174. Arrian 7.4.4 for naming Darius' daughter Barsine. Tarn (1948) p 334 disagrees with her having royal blood, and this is one of his principal arguments for Heracles being a 'pretender'. Brunt (1975) p 24 reversed the claim. She (a daughter of Darius) cannot have been the mother of Heracles for various reasons: Stateira was reportedly murdered by Roxane in Babylon, as Plutarch 77.6 claimed, and if Heracles' mother was murdered *with him* in Macedonia fourteen years on, as Justin 15.2.3 stated, then obviously Heracles cannot have been Darius' grandson. It would also fail to explain Nearchus' promotion of the boy at Babylon and fail to explain why Perdiccas did not have the boy killed when Antigonus vacated Asia Minor. We would further imagine that Heracles' descent from the Great King would have been a widely discussed *topos*. And it was not.
175. Tarn (1948) pp 335-336.
176. Brunt (1975) pp 28-29 refutes Parmenio's advice and sees it as fiction. Tarn (1948) p 335 sees it differently and argues Parmenio was referring to the Persian princess, citing a mistaken identification by Plutarch. The offer of marriage to Barsine and the division of empire is positioned in Curtius after the capture of Tyre. See Curtius 4.5.1-8 and Justin 11.12.3-3.
177. Plutarch 29.4, Curtius, 4.5.1, Justin 11.12 for Alexander's reply; quoting Plutarch 21.5.
178. Diodorus 17.67.1.
179. Curtius 6.5.4 stated Artabazus was ninety-five when he surrendered to Alexander ca. 330 BCE in Hyrcania; Heckel (2006) p 55 for age discussions. Curtius 8.1.19, Arrian 4.17.3 for his retirement due to old age.
180. Plutarch 21.8-9, translation from the Loeb Classical Library edition, 1919. Tarn (1948) p 333 for the Duris link and p 334 for a similar (possible) misidentification at Strabo 13.610. See below for Arrian 7.4.6 linking Barsine to Mentor.

181. Diodorus 17.77.7 and Justin 12.3.11-12 for Alexander's incorporation of concubines into his retinue and Justin 12.3.7-8 and Diodorus 17.77.3 for his thirteen-day tryst with Thalestris.

182. Curtius 3.13.14, Diodorus 17.23.5.

183. Tarn's statement in the *Journal of Historical Studies* xli 18 ff, quoted in Todd (1985) p 283 considered this 'a purely unfounded conjecture of modern writers'. Heckel supposes two separate Mentors are being referred to. Brosius (1996) p 95 has Barsine as the daughter of Arses.

184. Tarn (1948) p 333 for the generation statement. Arrian 1.15.2 for Memnon's sons at the Granicus. Tarn (1921) p 24 for discussion of Mentor's son; an Athenian inscription honouring a 'Memnon' may also suggest Mentor's son was old enough to have seen action though he could be from an earlier marriage. This fragmentary stele on pentelic marble dating to 327 BCE seems to support 'a family relationship', though not conclusively *this* one. Full details of the inscription in Todd (1985) pp 281-284; it honours a Mentor for saving Greek lives in Egypt during the Persian invasion in 343 BCE; see Heckel (2006) p 162 for discussion and p 318 footnote 42, and Brunt (1975) pp 26-27.

185. Diodorus 20.20.1 for Heracles being aged seventeen and Justin 15.2.3 has Heracles in his fifteenth year; Tarn (1948) pp 333-334 concurs, yet sees this as proof that the boy was an imposter, terming the links a wholesale 'tissue of absurdities'.

186. That Barsine had a daughter sufficiently old enough for marriage by 325 BCE only need, in extremis, put her in her mid-twenties in 333 at Issus, assuming, for example, she gave birth to that daughter when she was sixteen and that daughter in turn was sixteen when being married to Nearchus in 325 BCE. But the reference to several children and the ages of Mentor's children, if by her, would clearly make her far older, unless sources only *assumed* she birthed the other children with the brothers.

187. Arrian 7.4.6, translation from the Oxford World Classics edition, 2013.

188. Plutarch *Eumenes* 1.3, translation from the Loeb Classical Library edition, 1919.

189. The name 'Apame' was attested in Artabazus' family; his own mother had been so called: Plutarch *Artaxerxes* 27.4, Xenophon *Hellenika* 5.1.28, Plutarch *Agesilaus* 3.3. Plutarch, Arrian and Strabo were unclear over the identity of the bride of Seleucus. Arrian 7.4.6 stated he married the daughter of Spitamenes of Sogdia-Bactria, but he failed to mention her name. In his *Life of Demetrius* 31.5 Plutarch named Seleucus' wife 'Apame' 'the Persian', the correct name for a number of Seleucid cities that were later named after her, but Plutarch failed to say whose daughter she was. Strabo thought Apame was a daughter of Artabazus, and the above text explains why. The *Metz Epitome* termed her *quaedam Bacrtrina*; see Heckel (1987) p 117 for discussion. Whilst Alexander was able to forgive and elevate those who opposed him (Roxane's father for example) accounts of Spitamenes' death, and the unique detail of Spitamenes' flawed character at Curtius 8.3.1-12 (he took concubines and banished his own wife), make his daughter a strange choice of bride; unless this Apame was really Achaemenid and her true identity was hidden by Ptolemy?

190. Arrian 7.4.4-6 named Aristobulus as his source for the name matches at the Susa weddings. Sources of the Susa wedding lists discussed at Tarn (1948) p 333 footnote 1. Aristobulus is not mentioned by name as a groom in Arrian 7.4.6 but eight pairings are, as well as a reference to Companions. Chares' description of the wedding banquet suggested ninety-two marriages were to take place for ninety-two bedchambers were prepared, see Athenaeus 12.54P, 538B-539A, full text in Robinson (1953) p 79. Aelian 8.7 claimed ninety brides.

191. Justin 11.9.13.

192. Arrian 1.15.7 mentioned Mithridates was Darius' son-in-law. Thus we assume he had a daughter apart from the 'virgins' Stateira and Drypetis, both from his second wife Stateira. Heckel (2006) p 274 (F5) for Darius' previous wife and F8, F9, for other unnamed daughters. Heckel (2006) p 206 for Pharnaces' possible identification.

193. The contention at Curtius 6.5.3 that Artabazus was ninety-five by the time he surrendered to Alexander is termed 'absurd' by Tarn, see Brunt (1975) p 25. Tarn suggested he was 'well over sixty'. As he married before 362 BCE and had twenty-one children by 342/1 BCE, and as nine of his sons were old enough for military campaigning against Alexander, and as we have no gender order for their birth, it is quite possible Mentor's daughters by Barsine, who was possibly an earlier older child of Artabazus, could have been past puberty.

194. Curtius 4.11.5-6 stated Darius demanded the return of his two daughters, *duas virgines filias*.

195. Based upon Arrian 7.4.6 and incorporating the claims of Plutarch *Eumenes* 1.3.

196. Strabo 15.8.15 for Apame being a daughter of Artabazus.

197. Plutarch *Eumenes* 7.1 for Pharnabazus' support for Eumenes.

198. Also Heckel (2006) p 54. Artabazus' father, Pharnabazus, had been the satrap of Hellespontine Phrygia. Justin 13.2 for Heracles at Pergamum.

199. Demosthenes *Against Aristocrates* 23.154; Strabo 13.1.11.

200. Curtius 8.1.19, Arrian 4.17.3 for Artabazus' retirement. Heckel (2006) p 187 (Oxyartes) and pp 241-242 (Roxane) for a summary of the confusion with dates and sieges surrounding the capture of Roxane and her father. Curtius 9.8.9-10 referred to Oxyartes as *praetor Bactrianorum*. This in

fact makes more sense than appointing him to a foreign province: Paropanisadae according to Arrian 6.15.3; was Arrian's source, Ptolemy undermining Roxane's family power? See Heckel (2006) pp 187-188 for discussion of Oxyartes' appointment.

201. Arrian 7.4.4 and Curtius 10.3.11-13 for Alexander's additional marriages to Parysatis and the daughter of Darius III.

202. See Heckel (2006) p 379 for the stemma of Artabazus.

203. At Curtius 10.3.11-12 a highly rhetorical speech, in which Alexander is chastising his men at Opis and explaining his integration of Persian troops (and wives) into his ranks, only mentioned Roxane and 'a daughter of Darius', failing to mention Parysatis too; this could have come from his sources (or Cleitarchus alone) or from his own understanding of events.

204. Arrian 7.4.4. For the marriage of Stateira see Arrian 7.4.4. Justin 12.10.9, Diodorus 17.107.6, Plutarch *Moralia* 338d, Curtius 10.3.11-12. Heckel (2006) p 341 footnote 695 suggested Aristobulus was Arrian's source, and that when writing 'late in life' (well after Ipsus in 301 BCE we propose) he was no longer clear on detail; thus, he had confused the great king's daughter with Alexander's mistress.

205. Brosius (1996) p 185.

206. Brosius (1996) p 95.

207. Adea's own grandmother, Philip's Illyrian wife, had probably been renamed 'Eurydice' before her; Arrian *Events after Alexander* 1.22; discussed by O Palagia in Carney-Ogden (2010) p 35. Arrian 3.6.5 named Cleopatra, niece of Attalus, as 'Eurydice' where elsewhere she was named Cleopatra; discussed in Heckel (1978).

208. For Candace's meeting with Alexander, *Romance* 3.18-22, and for the origins of the name see full discussion in Arthur-Montagne (2014) p 9.

209. Strabo 16.1.2.

210. The change of name discussed in Heckel (2006) p 181 and Heckel (1978) pp 155-158; also Carney-Ogden (2010) p 35 for Olympias' changes of name as well as Tarn (1948) p 334 footnote 4; Plutarch *Moralia* 401a-b, Justin 9.7 and Carney (2006) pp 93-94 for the adoption of the name 'Myrtale' and p 95 for Olympias.

211. Xenophon *Cyropaedia* 8.7.9-12.

212. Tarn (1948) pp 378-399 clearly demonstrated later Roman corruptions of the so-called last plans.

213. For the importance of the lesser known Dion see Arrian 1.11.1-2 and Diodorus 17.16.3-4. For Heracles' former possession of Amphipolis and Olynthus see Carney-Ogden (2010) p 74.

214. Quoting Cicero *Laelius De Amicitia* 15.

215. Quoting Bosworth *A to A* (1988) p 203 and Plutarch 69.5 for the 'uncertainty and mutability of life'. Compare this to Onesicritus' version given at Strabo 15.3.7: 'Here I lie, Cyrus, king of kings'; translation from Pearson (1960) p 165.

216. The inscription was recorded by Arrian 6.29.5-8 and with minor variations by Plutarch 69.3 and Strabo 15.3.7.

217. Strabo 15.3.7 for Onesicritus' descriptions of the tomb.

218. Alexander, or Aristobulus at least, had visited the tomb earlier, before it had been robbed, and they found 'a golden couch, table with cups, a golden coffin, a large quantity of garments and dresses ornamented with precious stones'; a description corroborating Arrian's and Strabo's accounts. Plutarch 69.3 for the looting of the tomb. Polymachus was a prominent Macedonian from Pella. Curtius 10.1.31-32 for the tomb's content and 10.1.35 for Bagoas' references to Orsines; Curtius 10.1.26 for Orsines snubbing Bagoas.

219. Arrian 6.29.4 for the plantation description. D Stronach *Excavations at Pasargadae*, Second Preliminary Report in *Iran* 2, 1964, p 2139.

220. The ancient ruins at Samosata, Lucian's birthplace, were flooded in 1989 by the Ataturk Dam project. For inundation details see P MacQuarrie (Revised 2004-2-26) *Water Security in the Middle East Growing Conflict Over Development in the Euphrates – Tigris Basin, New York Times*.

221. The site is most likely Zeugma; see Gawlikowski (1996) pp 123-133. The flooding was discussed in *Sivand Dam Waits for Excavations to be finished*, Cultural Heritage News Agency, 26 February 2006, and *Ancient Pasargadae threatened by construction of dam*, Mehr News Agency, 28 August 2004.

222. Or Seleucia-at-the-Zeugma, its location is disputed.

223. Arrian 7.19-20, Strabo 16.1.11 for Alexander's shipbuilding. Full discussion of identifications in Gawlikowski (1996) pp 123-133 with references taken from Pliny 34.15 and Pausanias 10.29.4; Gawlikowski (1996) p 125 for the Duke of Wellington's commission.

224. Quoting from Erskine (2002) p 178 for the lost resting places of celebrated rulers. Arrian 3.22.1 reported that Alexander sent Darius to be buried 'amongst the royal tombs' at Persepolis but where is not clear and the tomb has been lost; it may be a fifth unfinished tomb at Naqsh-e-Rustam some 7.5 miles to the northwest. Although Augustus was buried in the Mausoleum of Augustus, barbarian invasions scattered his remains.

225. Aristotle *Posterior Analytics* book 1.2.

226. *Amphidoxon*, the ambiguous, or, that with doubt attached.

227. A statement possibly originating with WS Holt, professor of history at Washington University, or Charles Beard, cited in a communication by RF Smith, *American Historical Review* 94, October 1989, 1247.

228. Aristotle *Sophistical Refutations* 1, discussed in Reeve (2001) p 208.

229. F Nietzsche *Wir Philologen* 7.1; full text and citation in Heller-Roazen (2002) pp 151-153.

230. Referring to principles outlined in Aristotle *Prior* and *Posterior Analytics*.

231. Diogenes Laertius *Chrysippus* 2 for the divine reference: 'if the gods studied logic, it would be the logic of Chrysippus'. The reference to hellebore is not to suggest he died of poisoning – but he died either of laughter, or from undiluted wine – according to Diogenes Laertius. Chrysippus used hellebore as a purge three times, and although Lucian did say he was banned from reaching the Isle of the Blessed until he had taken a fourth dose, this is just a joke.

232. In his *True History* 2.18, and also *Sale of Lives* 23, Lucian suggested Chrysippus had been banned from reaching the Elysian Plain until he had taken a fourth dose of hellebore as a cure for insanity. For a summary of Hellenistic logical argument see *The Oxford History of Greece and The Hellenistic World*, Oxford University Press, Oxford, 1986, chapter 15 p 421 ff.

233. Lucian *How to Write History* 3-4 and 63. As Philip II approached Corinth and fear gripped the city, the citizens frenzied themselves with defence preparations. Diogenes had nothing to do and so repeatedly rolled his wine jar, in which he was living, through the Craneion, a wealthy district of the city, to look busy.

234. Quoting Tarn as cited in Bosworth (1996) though all Tarn's analogies applied to Cleitarchus.

235. Bosworth-Baynham (2000) p 14.

236. According to Pliny 36.9-10 in a competition (4th century BCE) between Parrhasius and Zeuxis, two of the foremost painters then living in Greece, Zeuxis removed the shroud draped over his canvas to reveal a bunch of grapes painted so realistically that birds pecked at them, but Parrhasius invited Zeuxis to remove the shroud covering his own work. When Zeuxis attempted to, he realised the shroud was itself the painting, so lifelike that it had fooled him. Parrhasius won the competition.

237. Posiedippus of Pella's work was discovered bound around an Egyptian mummy.

238. Scholars usually employ the Latin form, *elenchus*, when referring to Socratic debating or method of enquiry involving cross examination, disproof and refutation as part of the testing of an argument.

239. Requests for divinity aside, Arrian 7.29.4 confirmed Alexander saw himself as the son of Ammon and 7.20.1 with Strabo 16.1.11 stated he planned to attack the Arabs to be worshipped as a third god. For the Athenian Assembly's refusal to grant Alexander's deification see Polybius 12.12b.3, Deinarchus *Against Demosthenes* 1.94 and for the fine to Demades who proposed the bill, Athenaeus 6.251b, Aelian 5.12. Aelian 5.12 and Strabo 16.1.11 cited Aristobulus as confirming Alexander had laid claims to divinity. However Flower (1994) pp 259-260 points out that Theopompus seemed to have known of an Alexander cult in Asia Minor worshiping him as Alexander-Zeus in his lifetime.

240. Diodorus 20.81.3 for the Will reference.

241. See discussion in Walbank (1962) p 10. Polybius 3.281 claimed a reputation for 'opening up' the known Western world with his own travels. His attack on Pytheas is found at 34.5-7 and confirmed by Strabo 2.4.1-2; Scipio had likely given Polybius a ship to explore beyond the Pillars of Hercules (straits of Gibraltar) after the fall of Carthage; McGing (2010) p 144. Strabo 1.4, Pliny 2.75 claimed Pytheas reported Thule was six days north of Britain but this could refer to Orkney. Yet he described the phenomenon of the midnight sun.

242. See discussion in Green (2007) pp 19-21. Pytheas' references to Thule appeared in Vergil's *Georgics* 1.30 (*Ultima Thule*), Pliny 2.75, in a novel by Antinius Diogenes, *The Wonder Beyond Thule*, amongst others, which referenced the midnight sun.

243. See Oikonomides-Miller (1995) pp 1-5 Herodotus 4.196 for Carthaginian trading along the African coast.

244. Two copies of Hanno's log or *Periplous* survive dating back to the 9th and 14th centuries; one is the *Palatinus Graecus 398* at the University Library of Heidelberg. The other text is the so-called *Vatopedinus 655*; parts of it are in the British Museum and in the Bibliotheque Nationale in Paris. The fully translated title is *The Voyage of Hanno, commander of the Carthaginians, round the parts of Libya beyond the Pillars of Heracles, which he deposited in the Temple of Cronus*. This was known to Pliny and Arrian who mentioned it at the end of his *Indike* VIII.

245. A gnomon is an early form of upright sundial used by the Greeks for navigational purposes. Diogenes Laertius *Anaximander* 2.1 credited its introduction from Babylon to Anaximander of Miletus. A lodestone was a primitive magnetic compass formed from magnetite, naturally magnetic rock. Thales of Miletus first mentioned its properties.

246. Translates from Latin: 'art is long, life is short'. The saying is attributed to Hippocrates, as exampled in Lucian's *Hermotimus or on Philosophical Schools* 1.

POSTSCRIPT

OF BONES, INSIGNIA AND WARRIOR WOMEN: THE RETURN TO AEGAE

A continuation to the Press Release: The Bones of Philip II Found

Any dissection of Alexander's testament, and his own plans for commemoratives, brings us back to the royal burial grounds at Aegae, a necropolis he may himself have rejected once he deemed his own father too mortal, relegating him to 'co-father' with Zeus-Ammon.[1] Although there is strong circumstantial evidence that Tombs I, II and III *are* appropriately termed the 'royal burial cluster of Philip', there is as yet no *absolute* proof for the identities of their occupants. As it has been pointed out, the cluster need not be Argead at all: the Antipatrids and the Antigonids would not have denied themselves significant burials, and potentially with artefacts that predated their own regnum.[2]

The least controversial identification within the cluster surrounds the adolescent (estimated to be aged twelve to fifteen at death) male occupant of Tomb III, whose cremains were found in a silver hydria (a water jug, now used as a funerary urn), along with regalia suitable for that identification: a royal robe, a linen cuirass, gilded bronze greaves, a spear with gold casing (possibly a sceptre), a gold oak wreath and a marble throne.[3] For it has been 'universally' accepted that the inhabitant was Alexander IV, the teenage son of Alexander by Roxane, and who was killed on Cassander's orders ca. 310 BCE. But the double execution of Alexander IV and his mother was reportedly concealed on Cassander's orders. So this conclusion requires that their hidden remains were found and exhumed by someone seeking credibility as a legitimate Argead successor, and, moreover, someone prepared to highlight Cassander's termination of Alexander's branch of the Argead line by building an impressive resting place that closely resembled Tomb II.[4]

Although the conclusion of an early report by Xirotiris-Langenscheidt (1981) was that the bones are too fragmentary for any reasonable age range to be determined,[5] the presence of a male teenager *would* support the conclusion that we have the line of Philip II in the cluster, but we still need to explain the unique and remarkable double (or multiple) burials in Tombs I and II. They appear 'remarkable' because kings and their wives inevitably died at different times (natural disasters and epidemics aside), potentially decades apart and with separate burials, hence the necropolis of the kings is separate from the so-called 'cluster of the queens'. So it appears that the inhumations (Tomb I) and cremations (Tomb II) were the results of exceptional circumstances.[6]

TOMB II: PHILIP II OR PHILIP III?

As recent press releases illustrate, ever since Tomb II was first uncovered in 1977 scholars have been divided on the identity of the male occupant, with one camp arguing that the main chamber bones are those of Philip II, and another upholding the case for Philip III, his half-witted son.[7] The identification process has not been helped by the fact that both Philip II and his son (formerly named Arrhidaeus) were in their mid or early forties when they died. Moreover, their wives were both teenagers or in their early twenties when the kings were murdered.[8]

A most recent and controversial study led by Antonis Bartsiokas in 2015 proposed that the scattered bones in Tomb I, known as the 'Tomb of Persephone' after the remarkable fresco that occupies the whole of its northern wall, included Philip II's remains.[9] Though this is a smaller cist tomb (a cavity dug into the ground rather than a vaulted chamber) the remarkable decoration points to the importance of its inhabitant, previously thought to be King Amyntas III, Philip II's father, or Philip's older brother, King Alexander II.[10]

Recent studies therefore put great store in evidencing the wounds Philip II suffered in various battles. The injuries were clearly described by Demosthenes for the 'shattered remnant' (so he termed Philip) in his *On the Crown*, and included the loss of an eye, a broken clavicle (collarbone) and a mutilated arm (or hand) and leg. But even the veracity of these wounds has been called into question, for they either conflict with other texts, or they are barnacled with anecdote that accompanied rhetorical agenda. As Professor Theodore Antikas has, for example, pointed out, if the arrow had actually entered Philip's eye at Methone (as some examining the trauma seem to assume), he would have died instantly, where texts actually suggest that rather his vision was only impaired.[11] Unsurprisingly, the early forensic teams employed by Andronikos came to completely opposite conclusions on what they found; the part-healed eye-socket injury by an arrow or catapult-bolt (thus 'proof' it was Philip) was later attributed to taphonomy – in this case bone cracking during cremation.[12]

Supporting the case for the burial of Philip III, which took place in 316/315 BCE, some twenty years after his father's death, are well-constructed arguments from Eugene Borza and Olga Palagia, amongst others, which rest on a number of key premises. The first is the conclusion that the iconography of the multiple-quarry big-game hunt seen on the fresco above the entrance of Tomb II was inspired by the well-stocked Persian game parks witnessed on Alexander's campaigns.[13] This, they argue, is supported by its depiction of lions, for their presence in Macedonia is questioned.

Those upholding the case for Philip II, on the other hand, believe that within the hunting fresco is Philip's likeness (bearded and showing his left profile, thus avoiding his disfigured right eye) and also that of a young clean-shaven Alexander.[14] Additionally, as Hammond, Fox, and other scholars have demonstrated, there is clear evidence for the presence of lions in Macedonia in the (earlier) 5th century BCE, along with the danger they presented; Pausanias and Xenophon placed them in the region, and Herodotus recorded that lions preyed upon Xerxes' camels when his army was transiting Macedonia in 480 BCE. If Herodotus' entry was perhaps allegorical as a 'symbol of fierce resistance', lions are nevertheless attested to have roamed 'near' the country's borders (Mount Pangaeum, Mount Crittus and Thrace) and on Mount Olympus; a lion hunt also adorned the coins of King Amyntas III, Alexander's grandfather. Just as Homeric themes lived on, the Tomb II mural might have captured the essence of the once-iconic test of bravery, even if by the 4th century it was wild boar that were actually hunted to symbolise that rite of passage; the lion and boar *were* considered a pair in ferocity.[15]

The art-linked argument for the later dating of the tomb is also undermined if we recall that Macedonia had been annexed by Persia for much of the 6th and early 5th centuries BCE, when Eastern influences in art and architecture surely left their mark; the sister of Alexander I had married the Persian ambassador Bubares, and sanctuary had been given to Persian royalty – the family of Artabazus – by Philip II when Alexander was a child.[16]

Additional arguments for Philip III in a later-dated chamber speculate that the more elaborate barrel-vaulted 'Macedonian' tomb design (Tombs II and III) originated with the architects of Alexander's generation, possibly incorporating building techniques they had seen in Asia, so once again post-dating the reign of his father. But the discovery in 1987 of a similar structure believed to have housed Philip's mother, Eurydice (dubbed the 'Tomb of Eurydice'), with artefacts within it dating to ca. 344/3 BCE, as well as the description of the ideal mausoleum found in Plato's *Laws* (written ca. 360 BCE) appear to contest that; Plato's recommendations may in fact have been influenced by even earlier burial practices of Macedonia.[17]

We cannot be *sure* the aforementioned tomb housed Eurydice, as the pottery evidence recovered only provides a *terminus post quem*, and such prized items may have been handed down through the generations.[18] Besides, in light of allegations that Eurydice consorted with Ptolemy of Alorus who was clearly a threat to the line of Philip II, and, further, if there is any truth behind allegations that Eurydice killed his brother, Alexander II (her own son), such an ornate tomb seems a remarkable act of reverence in the face of major indiscretions and even complicit filicide. But typifying the uncertainty that surrounds the Argead line, we have evidence to the contrary which suggests Eurydice was a devoted mother who negotiated her sons' accessions in the face of major adversity; the likely inclusion by Philip II of her statue in the Philippeion at Olympia recognised her place in the royal family, as well suggesting the semi-divine status of Philip's line.[19]

The Tomb II debate further focuses on the king's regalia, for the diadem, armour, and an illusive sceptre Andronikos (initially) claimed to have found in Tomb II, do *resemble* descriptions of the regal items on display at Babylon, as well as the insignia later used for propaganda purposes in the Successor Wars.[20] Similar regalia were also listed amongst those destined for burial with Alexander's corpse within the lengthy description of his funeral bier, and this suggests an established Macedonian funerary custom.[21] Once again, this could point to a post-Philip II tomb. But the objects described are not *fully* reconcilable with Alexander's originals[22] and though the diadem, in particular, follows the Persian regal tradition adopted by Alexander after the defeat of Darius III, in Persia it likely took the form of a cloth ribbon and not a gilded silver band like that found in Tomb II.[23]

The presence of a (now illusive) sceptre in Tomb II, it is argued, would have had specific significance to the dating debate, for the sceptre would surely have been passed down through the line of kings, and thus Philip II would not have been buried with his, though a *last* king of his direct line may well have been (so Philip III). Certainly the sceptre tradition is archaic and was maintained through the Argead line. In the *Iliad* 'the son of Peleus dashed his gold-bestudded sceptre on the ground', and in what might have been yet another emulation of Achilles, the so-called Porus Medallion appears to show Alexander holding a sceptre.[24] If the Macedonian custom of burying *soldiers* with their *weapons* under a tumulus was well established, this practice needs to be distinguished from Livy's description of the annual spring festival of Xandika at which the army was preceded by the 'arms and insignia of *all* past kings from the founding of Macedonia'. So clearly a 'ceremonial' set (or sets) of regalia and weapons must have existed quite apart from any buried with the kings, like those on display in the Assembly in Babylon, and potentially those Eumenes later employed to beguile the Silver Shields.[25] This too renders late-dating arguments inconclusive. Moreover, the exquisite contents of Tomb II speak of a truly revered warrior king; the half-witted Philip III was anything but that.

At the core of the ongoing debate remain the various osteoarchaeological analyses from Tombs I and II which have seen, for example, scholarly opinion shift back and forth after the published and conflicting conclusions of teams led by Langenscheidt and Xirotiris and by Musgrave and Bartsiokas, in particular, over the past two decades. The most recent 2015 study of the Tomb I bones by the Bartsiokas team appears to have engendered more controversy than it set out to finish.[26] The 2014 report from the team led by Theodore Antikas had itself turned up unexpected finds and a new conundrum.

This comprehensive and disciplined 2014 analysis of the bones in Tomb II discovered, and reconfirmed, the existence of a number of compelling clues that point to Philip II. It revealed previously unseen trauma to the male body (chronic frontal and maxillary sinusitis, and soft-tissue eye trauma with chronic pathology on several ribs), which broadly match the wounds credited to Philip II.[27] Antikas' report additionally confirmed the corpse had undergone a flesh-boned cremation, and there is textual evidence that Philip was provided with just that, for Justin claimed that the friends of the assassinated king '… grieved that the same torch that had been kindled at the daughter's wedding should have started the funeral pyre of the father.' But, as scholars have pointed out, this was a well-used poetic simile and both Ovid and Propertius used similar lines, so it is not conclusive proof of cremation, and other sources simply referred to a 'burial.'[28] Justin's claim that: 'A few days after, she [Olympias] burnt the body of the assassin [Pausanias], when it had been taken down [from hanging on a cross], upon the remains of her husband, and made him a tomb in the same place', is likewise suggestive of Philip's cremation but could equally refer to the evidenced ceremonial fire on the roof of the tomb.[29]

There is additional new and compelling evidence that the cremation of the male in Tomb II was part of a highly ritualised ceremony, as melted gold has been identified (thought to be from a crown, though gold death masks have been discovered in graves at Mycenae, not burned, however) and the white mineral huntite, which, along with purple porphyry, suggests that a funerary mask covered the face before the pyre was set ablaze. We should also bear in mind that the throwing of armour into the fire, as well as gold and silver likenesses (*eidola*), seems to have been a tradition, as evidenced by Alexander's plans for Hephaestion's funeral.[30]

The so-called Mask of Agamemnon discovered at Mycenae in 1876 and so labelled by its discoverer, Heinrich Schliemann who thought he had found the body of Agamemnon who led the Greek coalition to Troy. Hammered out of a single gold sheet, it dates to 1550-1500 BCE, too early to belong to the traditional dating for Agamemnon, and was one of several funerary masks found in the shaft graves. Now in the National Archaeological Museum of Athens.

In contrast to the ritualised interment of the male in Tomb II, Pausanias reminds us that Philip III was never destined for honorary funeral rites, for Olympias, on whose orders he was brutally executed, did 'unholy' (*anosia*) things to his body, and no formal cremation was ever mentioned, or was ever likely to have been provided for his remains.[31] It is equally doubtful that any of the supporters of Philip III, or more likely the supporters of his simultaneously executed wife, Queen Eurydice, would have dared to cross Alexander's mother and exhume their still-fresh bodies for cremation. Doing so at a sufficiently later date would have resulted in a 'dry-boned' result (visibly distinct from flesh-boned remains). It is noteworthy, then, that the bones from Tomb I exhibit no signs of cremation and this suggests that Philip III is still a candidate for burial there, that is if we accept

Cassander's reburial was sufficiently delayed for Philip to have remained in the ground and become completely skeletal before exhumation.[32]

Antikas' study led to two further thought-provoking developments. The first is the revising of the age of the female occupant of the antechamber of Tomb II, for the bone analysis included, in particular, her pubic symphysis, which was not seen by earlier researchers; she is now believed to have been aged thirty to thirty-four when she died. Here we have the conundrum, as this rules out Philip II's last wife, Cleopatra, *and* the equally young Queen Eurydice the wife of Philip III, both believed to be in their late teens (or early twenties) when they died.[33]

The second development was the discovery of hundreds of new bone fragments that had been bagged, stored and never examined for over thirty-five years, and which were labelled as originating in Tomb I. Seventy of these bones were analysed and they suggest the tomb contained the remains of at *least* seven individuals: an adult male, a female, a child (mirroring the conclusions of the previous bone analyses), as well as four babies aged eight to ten lunar months and one foetus of six-and-a-half lunar months; there were additionally several species of sacrificial animal.[34] If they *did* originate in Tomb I, as indicated, then the earlier examinations, though on the whole meticulously carried out, were based on less than ten percent of the evidence.[35]

Assuming we *are* dealing with the cluster of Philip II, and if we *are* prepared to accept that the previously analysed Tomb I adult bones belong to the original occupants, even if irreverently scattered about the tomb (Plutarch described the despoliation at Aegae ca. 274 BCE with 'the treasure they plundered, the bones they insolently cast to the winds'),[36] and, additionally, noting their estimated ages at death – a male in his mid-thirties to early or mid-forties (analyses conflict), and a woman ca. twenty – what conclusions might we reach?

Firstly, we can probably rule out Philip II's elder brothers, King Alexander II (assassinated in his late teens) and King Perdiccas III too, if we conclude that his body was unlikely to have been retrieved from the bloody battle against the Illyrians where 4,000 Macedonians were reportedly slain. We can also rule out Philips II's father, King Amyntas III, who would *likely* have been approaching fifty when he died after a reign of twenty-four years. The inhumation rather than cremation of the bodies rules out Philip II too, if Justin's reference to cremation is accurate. With Alexander buried in Egypt (and as Roxane was far more mature than twenty when she was executed), the remaining candidates from that branch of the Argead line for the *adult* remains of Tomb I *are* Philip III and Queen Eurydice, though questions still hang over the infant and foetal remains.

But how can we explain the (original) *double* burials in Tombs I and II?[37]

THE CONUNDRUM OF THE TOMB II FEMALE

Scholars dissecting the latest reports from Vergina may not have been surprised when they learned that the revised age of the Tomb II female (thirty to thirty-four) rules out Philip's last wife, Cleopatra, the niece of Attalus, as sources tell us Olympias either forced her to hang herself, or she dragged Cleopatra across a brazier with her new-born baby in her arms. Attalus, her influential uncle, was soon executed on Alexander's orders, and Justin (quite credibly) claimed that his whole family was killed.[38] Murdered perhaps a year after Philip's death, Cleopatra's mistreated body was most likely 'insolently cast to the winds' too and her bones would never have seen a tomb.

Hammond first argued in detail that the remains of the Tomb II female may be those of a more obscure wife of Philip II: either Meda his Getic (Thracian) wife, or a daughter of King Ataias of the Thrace-bordering Scythians who once offered to appoint Philip as his successor through adoption. The obvious link to the latter is the Scythian gold *gorytos* (quiver) and the remains of seventy-four arrows (though no evidence of a bow) that were found in the antechamber. Moreover, an image of a Scythian *gorytos* did appear on King Ataias' coins.

Prof. Antikas upholds the latter identification and his report further revealed that the tailor-made greaves, one shorter than the other, belonged to the female, for she had experienced a major fracture to her left tibia.[39] This is suggestive that the other weapons belonged to the horse-riding 'warrior woman' as well. The relationship between Ataias and Philip broke down, but it is argued that his daughter, given freely or captured (some 20,000 prisoners were allegedly brought to Macedonia following Ataias' defeat), would have then become Philip's concubine (*pallakis*) or *possibly* his seventh wife of what would then be an eventual eight. In the tradition of the Scythian tribes (and some Thracians and Getae too), she could have taken her own life upon her husband's death.[40]

This is a viable explanation, and yet the Scythian identity still relies on a marriage, or liaison, never mentioned by our sources and in Satyrus' fulsome rundown of Philip's wives, in particular.[41] And though Ataias once planned to 'adopt' Philip to secure an alliance, we read that he later retracted the offer.[42] Moreover, proffering a daughter in marriage would have been the more obvious and the higher profile route. Apart from failing to mention a union with a Scythian, there is no mention of Philip being interred in his tomb with *anyone* at his death. As the care with which Alexander attended to his father's funeral *is* detailed, as well as the executions above the tomb (with the accused assassins even named, though Justin and Diodorus disagree on the events order), we would expect to see some reference to the woman being cremated beside the king.[43]

Justin claimed that no gold or silver was captured in Philip's victory over Ataias,[44] in which case the Scythian artefacts found in the antechamber of Tomb II could have been trophies of war or gifts of alliance from a number of campaigns; Cyrus the Great was entombed with two Scythian bows at Pasargadae and various Scythian envoys had met with Alexander as he campaigned in the depths of Asia when similar gifts were likely received.[45] But not all of the items from the antechamber *are* Scythian; apart from the ceremonial *gorytos* and presumably the arrows, we have greaves, a linothorax and pectoral, and these are more symbolic of a Hellenic-outfitted warrior.

Unless we are prepared to accept that a (never-mentioned) surviving wife of Philip II in her thirties was ceremonially killed or committed suicide at his death, the age of the Tomb II female (broadly) matches only one remaining relative who we know *was* buried at Aegae: Philip's daughter, Cynnane, given funeral rites by Cassander after he had dealt with Olympias.[46] Cynnane's attested warrior upbringing would explain the presence of iconic warrior weapons and panoply. Her exact birthdate is uncertain, but she was born of an Illyrian mother, Audata, sometime following Philip's victory over King Bardylis ca. 358 BCE, after which a 'noteworthy' truce had been concluded. So Cynnane was potentially born ca. 357/356 BCE.[47]

From Polyaenus we additionally know that by ca. 344/343 BCE she was old enough to accompany Philip on another Illyrian campaign in which she reportedly killed their queen, Caeria.[48] Remarkably, that dating indicates Cynnane was still in her early or mid-teens when she did that, though the 'slaying' referred to may well have been court propaganda, or a show execution as part of an Illyrian tribal vendetta, perhaps on behalf of her mother. But we should also bear in mind that her daughter, Adea, was able to cause ferment at Triparadeisus at the 'marriageable' age of just fifteen (or perhaps even fourteen, 'high' or 'low' chronologies depending).

Adhering to these dates, Cynnane would have been in her mid-thirties when she was killed by Perdiccas' brother, Alcetas, in the vicinity of Ephesus in 322/321 BCE.[49] And though we may assume she crossed to Asia with few of her possessions about her, as the daughter of Philip II she must have owned precious chattels that were retained in her royal quarters at Pella, and these would have surely been buried with her, some of which potentially came from her mother, Queen Audata, Philip's Illyrian wife.

To reason that Cynnane's remains could credibly be those of the female in Tomb II requires that her body was handled reverently by Alketas' men and immediately cremated, probably on the insistence of her headstrong daughter who would, as events showed, have been supported by Alcetas' indignant troops; Cynnane's bones were most likely returned to Macedonia with Adea (by now Queen Eurydice) and Philip III in the entourage of Antipater. Such posthumous respect certainly appears plausible when we consider that the corpses of Craterus and Eumenes were similarly dealt with and returned to their relatives.[50] Alcetas and his men were on the move (they 'intercepted' Cynnane on her way to meet the royal army), so an immediate flesh-boned cremation, rather than inhumation followed by the later retrieval of dry bones, is a sound conclusion. The 2014 report by Antikas' team did note that the female bones from Tomb II had been subjected to *different* funeral pyre conditions and with less care taken in their collection when compared to those of the male.[51]

As Cynnane and Adea had crossed to Asia against Antipater's wish, and as Adea had caused such trouble for him at Triparadeisus, almost resulting in his death, and, further, as the pro-Olympias Polyperchon had assumed the Macedonian regency in Pella following Antipater's death in autumn 319 BCE (which brought with it the prospect of Olympias returning to Pella at any time), Adea, now titled Queen Eurydice, may well have been unable to immediately entomb her mother's remains at Aegae in any meaningful way. So how could Cynnane's remains have ended up in the same tomb as her father?

Texts confirm that soon after Cassander gained control of Macedonia, either in late 317 or in 316 BCE, and as part of his highly choreographed show of posthumous reverence to the offspring of Philip II (excluding the immediate line of Alexander III), he exhumed and reburied the bodies of Philip III and Eurydice after funeral games had been held; commentators believe this was between six and seventeen months after Olympias ordered their deaths. Cassander also interred the remains of Cynnane, but nowhere is it specifically stated that mother and daughter were buried *together*, either physically or temporally, though some scholars have assumed just that.

Never the wife of an *enthroned* king herself (unlike her daughter), Cynnane would not have merited a tomb in the cluster of the queens.[52] But the gold diadem found in the antechamber of Tomb II suggests *basileia*. If not passed to Cynnane by Audata (or by Alexander when he pledged her in marriage to the Agrianian king, Langarus), then the finely crafted diadem would have subtly and usefully symbolised that Philip had, in fact, usurped the right to the throne from his nephew, Amytas Perdicca, Cynnane's first husband, to whom many were inclining (in place of Alexander) at Philip's death.[53]

If we accept (as texts imply) that Philip II was *not* buried with a wife, Cassander would have had good reason to seek approbation from the veteran supporters of the still-revered Argead king (Cassander's ultimate aim) by interring Cynnane with her father in the unoccupied large antechamber of Tomb II. Moreover, by doing so he had everything to gain from reminding Macedonia of the brutality of Olympias who murdered Philip II's son as well as his granddaughter, and his last wife with her child. That, in turn, would have underscored Olympias' recent wider pogrom against Cassander's own family, all of which was aimed at justifying *his* orchestrating her recent execution at Pydna (though ostensibly it was Assembly sanctioned).[54] And perhaps in retaliation to the regicidal allegations that we argue were lodged against him by Olympias and Eumenes through the *Pamphlet*, Cassander simultaneously resuscitated rumours that Olympias and Alexander were complicit in Philip's assassination.

The site of Philip II's tomb was most likely chosen well in advance of his death; his two full-brothers had untimely deaths and it may have become a normal practice to have at least a basic funerary structure in place, and significantly more constructed in the case of Philip's extensive twenty-three-year reign.[55] With this in mind, it is perhaps noteworthy that the main chamber of Tomb II was originally sealed unfinished with internal walls left un-plastered, and with the preparation of the antechamber appearing delayed; the external hunting scene appears partly painted *al fresco* (on wet plaster) and partly not. Additionally, the brick structure built above the vaulted roof of the main chamber (to house a pyre and stage executions) was similarly placed on wet plaster.

These clues suggest that whoever was overseeing the *original* funeral rites, the executions, and the sealing of the tomb, was more concerned with rapidly moving on than paying extended reverence to the occupant within.[56] That observation could certainly fit the behaviour of Olympias and Alexander at Philip's death in 336 BCE (whether they were complicit in Philip's murder, and/or, beset as they were by immediate threats) and the agenda of Cassander some twenty years on; the façade above the entrance and the remarkable frontage of 'illusionist' Doric columns, would have nevertheless fulfilled Cassander's aim of a very public spectacle, assuming it remained uncovered by a tumulus for a time.[57]

It would have taken no great effort by Cassander to unseal the marble door that formed the entrance to the antechamber which was three-quarters as large as the main chamber itself, if the tomb was still tumulus-free.[58] And though Justin stated Philip's assassins were killed on the orders of Alexander *ad tumulum patris*, what appear to be the remains of the Homeric-styled ceremonial execution of Philip's assassins were found directly on the roof of the vault, and not in the remains of the tumulus debris covering it.[59] Even if there existed an easily-penetrated small mound that ended abruptly to accommodate further tombs (as Plato's *Laws* recommended), the opening of the tomb as a public gesture is far from implausible. In fact, any scholar who initially concluded that the female in the antechamber was Philip's last wife, Cleopatra, must have accepted the same (a delayed tumulus), for she was not killed *immediately* upon his death, for Alexander was away campaigning when he heard she had been murdered by Olympias.

Cassander could have taken an equally (financially) pragmatic approach to the burial of Philip III and Queen Eurydice as he did for her mother, in this case their interment together in the one simpler cist tomb. Eurydice had sported ceremonial weaponry when she emblematically paraded herself in full battle armour when facing the army of Olympias in 317 BCE, and it is alluring to picture it stacked in Tomb I before it was plundered.[60] In this scenario it remains possible that any weapons buried there (and not impossibly those in the antechamber of Tomb II, if the female remains are those of Cynnane) *were* trophies of Alexander's campaigns: the weapons, armour and regalia could have made their way back to Macedonia with Antipater, with the kings in tow.[61] It is noteworthy that Nicomachus of Thebes, the artist who is suspected of painting the scene adorning the northern wall inside Tomb I, was known for his rapidity and economy with oil and colour which produced an '*al fresco*' technique and 'restrained palette'.[62] Could he have painted the Tomb II hunting scene as well?

In these interpretations, Tomb II (though perhaps not its painted façade) pre-dates the simpler structure of Tomb I, which was nevertheless exquisitely painted inside with the images of the Abduction of Persephone, a theme depicted so prominently in the Homeric *Hymn to Demeter* (with origins in the 7th century);[63] the simplicity of the later structure (though counterintuitive to a 'progression' of style and architectural sophistication) was, then, decided by Cassander's financial position and his immediate political needs. That is, if Tomb I had not been sitting empty for many years because its intended occupant died elsewhere. Close by Tomb I is the also looted *heroon* built from the same porous ashlar blocks (Plato recommended porous stone for tombs); with foundations measuring some 31.5 x 26.25 feet, the shrine *does* point to the established worship of the cluster.[64]

But for all we know, and if Justin is to be believed, this may have been Olympias' cynical offering to Philip's assassin, Pausanias: '… she burnt the body of the assassin, when it had been taken down, upon the remains of her husband, *and made him a tomb in the same place*; she also provided that yearly sacrifices should be performed to his manes…' (author's italics).[65]

Finally, after Cassander had achieved his publicity goals, and to mark the end of an era that would herald in his own dynasty through Philip's other daughter, Thessalonice (whose tomb may also reside in the cluster of the queens), Cassander could have symbolically raised the first 65.6-foot-in-diameter tumulus that we know originally covered Tombs I and II (and possibly the *heroon*), with Tomb II broadly at its centre.[66]

The line of Philip II and Alexander III was proverbially buried for good, so Cassander may have initially thought, until Polyperchon reintroduced Heracles, Alexander's son by Barsine.

The extraction of DNA from the bones could establish genetic links between the occupants of the tombs, and cremated bones do provide a sterile and favourable environment for DNA survival. Prof. Antikas' anthropological research team in collaboration with the National Centre for Scientific Research 'Demokritos' applied to the Greek Ministry of Culture for a permit to run DNA, C14 and standard isotope tests on bones from tombs I, II and III of the Great Tumulus and from the cremains in the Agora in 2014. The ministry has now issued a permit to run a pilot study on the bones from Tomb I and the Agora ahead of any similar analyses of the bones from tombs II and III.[67] But, in a wholly appropriate impasse for a decades-old debate, this would still not conclusively reveal who was who, as all those under scrutiny – Philip II, Philip III, Eurydice, Cynnane and Alexander IV – were genetically related. The results could, nonetheless, justify the site being referred to as the 'cluster of Philip II'.

THE GREAT GUARDIAN OF THE TOMBS

It is widely held that it was either Lysimachus, who briefly became king of Macedonia ca. 285 BCE (though he had influence there from 288 BCE when Pyrrhus was installed), or Antigonus II *Gonatas*, a decade or more later, who raised the Great Tumulus at Aegae. Either *Gonatas* or his father, Demetrius *Poliorketes*, could have built Tomb III for the teenage Alexander IV to highlight Cassander's collateral damage, and to stake a new claim to post-Argead legitimacy.[68] Moreover, Antigonus *Monophthalmos* had once (self-servingly) called for Cassander to release Alexander IV and his mother, Roxane, from captivity. *Poliorketes'* reign was beset by instability and his financial focus was firmly on a reinvasion of Asia, and it was *Gonatas* who was most concerned with appearing the legitimate Macedonian royal heir.[69] It has been proposed that a further tomb ('Tomb IV') discovered in 1980 may well house his remains.[70]

The case for the raising of the Great Tumulus over the tombs before any looting took place has advantages over claims that the lesser tumuli were covered by it *after* the Gallic looting ca. 274 BCE, for that raises the question of why were Tombs II and III, similarly rich in regalia, not opened and raped of possessions like other burial sites at Aegae. Individual tumuli do not hide a tomb's presence; in fact they broadcast it, even if hindering immediate access.

Knowing of the destruction the Gauls had already wrought in Greece through 279/278 BCE which may have included the pillaging of Delphi, *Gonatas* could more credibly have raised the Great Tumulus following his victory over the remnants of the once 85,000-strong invading Gallic army in 277 BCE.[71] Because the rich tomb cluster that the looters under Pyrrhus were targeting (clearly guided by 'insider knowledge') some three years later (274 BCE) lay at the outer rim of the recently thrown-up great mound, a horizontal shaft would have been sufficient to intercept the prize. The *heroon*, closest to its perimeter, was located and looted first, and then Tomb I, whose own riches may have convinced the Gauls that they had found the prize they sought. In which case the reddish-brown sediment covering the bones inside Tomb I was a result of the infill from that probing horizontal shaft.[72]

Tombs II and III lay on a different line and so were never intercepted. We may speculate that the scar this incision made into the Great Tumulus was finally smoothed over by *Gonatas* once the looters had departed; it was potentially then extended to cover his own burial site (potentially Tomb IV). The 9.8-foot-thick layer of rocks at its base emphasises the protective nature of the 360-foot-wide and 40-foot-tall mound.[73] Broken *stelae* below the surface (though above the original tumuli) bore the names of leading Macedonians, so facilitating their dating to ca. 330–275 BCE, and this broadly matches the *Gonatas* proposition. Another important structure appears to have been built at the centre of the mound, possibly a stoa or cenotaph tumulus, which Hammond postulated may have been dedicated to Alexander, before its contents were removed ahead of the Great Tumulus being raised over it.[74]

The depiction of the Abduction of Persephone by Hades (Pluto) on the north wall on the interior of Tomb I is imagery also found on the marble throne in the Tomb of Eurydice in the cluster of the queens, though here Persephone and Hades are painted together in a 'relationship equality'.[75] Very similar funerary theology can be found in the floor mosaic in the second chamber of the Kasta Hill tomb at Amphipolis, discovered in 2014 under the mound now considered a natural hill (nevertheless sculpted) rather than a man-made tumulus. Philip II was already being worshipped 'as a god' at Amphipolis as his father, Amyntas III, had been at Pydna.[76] It remains uncertain whether the depictions can in any way connect these burial sites more specifically. The common art – the Abduction of Persephone – does suggest a link to the Orphic faith; a Thesmophorion has been excavated at Pella (the female-dominated festival of Thesmophoria was traditionally held there) where the cult of Persephone is attested.[77]

The absence of any regalia and precious artefacts at Amphipolis, and the broken marble doors (which show signs of heavy use, thus possibly suggesting a crypt once on display), with the removal of entry stones, as well as the scattered and fragmented nature of the bones, suggest Pyrrhus' Celtic Gauls may have ransacked this site too, before it was resealed, that is if the Romans under Aemilius Paullus, who entered Amphipolis in 167 BCE, were not responsible.[78]

The tomb finds included the bones of a woman aged sixty or over and a little under 5 feet 2 inches tall, a newborn child, fragments of a cremated adult (sex as yet undefined) and the bones of two men aged thirty-five to forty-five and approximately 5 feet 4 inches to 5 feet 6 inches tall, the younger of them appearing to have suffered mortal wounds to the chest. Olympias, aged somewhere around sixty when she was executed, had been initiated into the Orphic mysteries that were linked to Demeter (who was also featured on the east wall of Tomb I) and her daughter Kore, otherwise known as Persephone of the underworld, the patroness of the Eleusinian Mysteries.

Philip's mother, Eurydice, was renowned as a politically active queen with links to Eucleia, the female spirit of good repute (the chaste bride) who had a shrine at Aegae that was possibly erected by Philip; inscribed dedications to Eurydice have been found in the temple remains.[79] Eucleia was frequently depicted amongst the handmaidens of Aphrodite (she, with Persephone, was the Maiden form of the Earth-goddess) and one of the *Kharites* (Graces) who were associated with the Greek underworld and Eleusinian Mysteries as well. As Carney has pointed out, after her scandal with Ptolemy of Alorus, Eurydice may have been attempting to salvage her reputation for the sake of her surviving sons.[80]

A tomb in the cluster of the queens linked to one of the wives of King Alexander I contained at least twenty-six figurines of Demeter and Kore. Discovered in 1938, another burial site close to the Tomb of Eurydice contained a marble throne adorned with the representations of sphinxes like those at Amphipolis. Never covered by a tumulus, this tomb may not have been occupied by its intended resident; could it have been originally built for Olympias?

Though a common motif on Greek pottery, the Abduction of Persephone and images of Demeter and Kore seem unique to these Macedonian burial sites, whilst sphinxes (and griffins) were clearly associated with late 4th century BCE Macedonian queens.[81] The aforementioned traces of huntite and porphyry suggest the male of Tomb II was cremated in an Orphic funeral mask that could suggest his role as chief priest of Orphic rites, or, if the remains *are* those of Philip II, then of Olympias' (perhaps less likely) influence in his funeral as a priestess of the mystery religion, for women had a prominent role in burial preparations.

Orphic symbolism in the form of the myth of Persephone confirmed the hope for a rebirth and thus an afterlife as both Demeter and Persephone were associated with immortality; the Macedonians may have accepted the afterlife in more literal terms than their Greek counterparts.[82] As far as the iconography of 'abduction', it was attached to wedding rituals in which the bride was symbolically carried off on a chariot denoting her new fettering to her husband; could the polygamy of the Argeads, and Philip in particular, have added to this emphasis?[83]

When Cassander contrived to have Olympias executed at the conclusion of the siege at Pydna, her body was left unburied by the relatives of her victims, but there is no mention that it was hidden (unlike the fate of the bodies of Alexander IV and Roxane); rather, the public humiliation of her corpse would have been a useful warning to any new challengers. Edson and Carney have suggested that Pyrrhus of the Aeacids, the royal clan of Epirus from which Olympias was descended, may have later provided her with grander burial honours close to Pydna when briefly in control of the region, if a now-lost grave inscription nearby was accurate. After all, Pyrrhus hardly seems to have respected the Argead necropolis at Aegae, if the allegations that he failed to stop his Gallic mercenaries from plundering the graves are true.[84]

If Olympias' complicity in Philip's murder *was* still suspected or had been broadcast (and bearing in mind she additionally executed his surviving family), then Aegae was an inappropriate resting place regardless of any posthumous self-serving reverence to be paid. Could her remains have finally been transferred to Amphipolis? Olympias could herself have expressed a desire to be interred in grander style than she now merited at Aegae, preferring an attachment to her son's 'divinity' rather than her late husband's mortal line; we recall that Alexander is said to have promised her 'a consecration to immortality'.[85]

New reports from Katerina Peristeri, the lead site archeologist, claim a further monogram of Hephaestion has been found inside the tomb, giving additional significance to similar inscriptions recovered from the close-by River Strymon in the early 20th century.[86] The king's closest companion and first chiliarch would have been in his early thirties when he died in 324 BCE, thus archaeologists are pondering whether the styling at Amphipolis is resonant of the Rhodian architect Deinocrates for it is said Alexander longed to employ him to build a monument for Hephaestion.[87] That connection is unsubstantiated, though Amphipolis certainly appears in the extant Will texts as one of the sites at which Alexander requested commemoratives; as Hammond points out, even the Great Tumulus at Aegae could broadly represent the 'memorial to match the greatest pyramid' found in Alexander's 'last plans'.[88]

So could the Lion of Amphipolis have once stood before (if not above) the subterranean Amphipolis tomb, matching the sepulchral and still-standing lion monument at Ecbatana (modern Hamadan) reputed by some to be a commemorative to Hephaestion?[89] Once again, it is an alluring idea, but the graffiti seen at Amphipolis is common at burial sites. Nor should we forget that a Companion Cavalry hipparchy was named after Hephaestion, so it is likely that any former-serving cavalry officers would have exploited their participation in the elite *agema* in their own commemoratives. Furthermore, as the Assembly vote at Babylon had clearly shown, no one save Alexander was interested in spending further treasury funds on the memory of Hephaestion.[90]

It remains possible that Amphipolis was, or became, a *polyandreion* for illustrious former Companions of Alexander; its construction may have commenced on his instruction, or after his death, when it may have been initially overseen by Antipater or by Olympias upon her return to Macedonia, possibly aided by Polyperchon and Aristonus, or by a later Antigonid king once more exploiting the suggestion of Argead ties.

Notable candidates for the male bones, and who were linked in some way to both Alexander *and* Amphipolis, include Alexander's *hetairos* Laomedon, the trierarch Androsthenes, Olympias' supporter and final defender of the city, Aristonus, and the celebrated Nearchus who would have been around the age of forty-five if he perished in battle at Gaza in 312 BCE.[91] Although the Amphipolis construction has been recently labelled 'cheap', the sphinxes, caryatids with traces of coloured paint with the accomplished mosaic floor, as well as the 1,630-foot marble circular perimeter wall (*peribolos*) around the 508-foot-in-diameter mound, point to a construction of considerable scale and detail.

When considering further candidates for the additional significant tombs at Aegae such as the Tomb of Palatitsia, and for the 'non-royal' graves under the Great Tumulus, we should not forget the other campaign notables whose burial places have never been identified, and whose remains *were* likely sent back to Macedonia: Leonnatus who fell at Lamia relieving Antipater, and Craterus whose cremated remains were returned to his former wife, Phila (his monument at Delphi was not a tomb).[92] As Hammond pointed out, some forty-seven funerary headstones (though without graves) found in the upper layers of the Great Tumulus 'emphasise the attachment of deceased warriors' to Alexander. The newest tomb finds being investigated by Prof. Antikas' team at Pella and Katerini may also reveal surprise occupants; one day we might even see the tragic lines of Euripides gracing a stone that marks his own resting place.

'Death is a debt we all must pay.'[93]

Euripides *Alcestis*

NOTES

1. Some scholars argue that Alexander truly believed he was the son of both Philip and Zeus; discussed in Carney (2006) p 103.
2. Following Bosworth's comment in Borza *Tombs* (1987) p 105 footnote 2 on possible Antipatrid self-recognition.
3. Adams (1991) p 27 for the 'universal' acceptance that Alexander IV occupied Tomb III. Hammond *Tombs* (1991) p 77 for the items found in Tomb III.
4. Diodorus 19.52.4, Justin 14.6.13, 15.1.3 for the incarceration of Roxane and Alexander IV at Amphipolis by Cassander. Diodorus 19.105.2, Justin 15.2.5 for the concealment of their murder (Justin confused Heracles for Alexander IV, as he did at 14.6); Pausanias 9.7.2 stated Alexander IV was poisoned.
5. Xirotiris-Langenscheidt (1981) pp 156-157.
6. Borza *Tombs* (1987) p 105-107 for the uniqueness of the double burial. Also Borza-Palagia (2007) p 84 for discussion of antechambers being used as a repository for grave goods, and not double burials.
7. A thorough summary of the ongoing controversy and attached opinions can be found in a thesis titled *Understanding the Bones: The Human Skeletal Remains from Tombs I, II and III at Vergina* by Jolene McLeod, University of Calgary and available online at http://theses.ucalgary.ca/bitstream/11023/1562/2/ucalgary_2014_mcleod_jolene.pdf.
8. Arrhidaeus was likely born in 358/357 BCE, thus late thirties or potentially early forties when executed in 317 BCE by Olympias; Heckel (2006) p 52 for detail. Plutarch 9.6 stated Cleopatra was a maiden when she married Philip.
9. The remains of three individuals studied earlier exclude the already bagged bones located elsewhere and found by Antikas' teams. The evidence and findings of the Bartsiokas-Arsuaga-Santos-Algaba-Gómez-Olivencia (2015) report have been called into question.
10. Tomb I measures 3.5 x 2.09 x 3 metres high: 11.55 x 6.9 x 9.9 feet. The wall painting depicts the Abduction of Persephone; it is the oldest cist tomb in Macedonia decorated with a mythological scene; following Borza-Palagia (2007) p 82. Plinius 35.108 credited Nicomachus with painting the Abduction of Persephone in a style that used only four colours. Hammond (1978) first argued that Tomb I held Amyntas; the additional remains must therefore be 'secondary burials' placed in a looted and exposed tomb. He also argued for Alexander II: Hammond *Tombs* (1991) pp 77-78.
11. Personal correspondence with Professor Theodore Antikas. For the wound at Methone, Justin 7.6.14 (and mentioned without place or date at Plutarch 3.2).
12. Demosthenes *De Corona* 18.66-67; the veracity of Philip's alleged wounds discussed in Riginos (1994); a full list of the sources citing the wounds is provided on p 106. Borza-Palagia (2007) p 107 for the conflicting opinions of the Langenscheidt-Xirotiris team and Prag-Neave-Musgrave team on the trauma to Philip's eye socket; Philip was blinded by a projectile during the siege of Methone in 354 BCE. For a thorough rundown and discussion of Philip's wounds see *Understanding the Bones: The Human Skeletal Remains from Tombs I, II and III at Vergina* by Jolene McLeod, University of Calgary and available online at http://theses.ucalgary.ca/bitstream/11023/1562/2/ucalgary_2014_mcleod_jolene.pdf p 70 ff.
13. Borza-Palagia (2007) pp 90-103. Cohen (2010) p 238 ff for its detail and additional arguments.
14. Hammond *Tombs* (1991) p 75 for discussions of the royal hunt fresco and suggested likenesses.
15. The presence of lions discussed at Herodotus 7.124-126, Xenophon *Kynegetikos* 11.1, Pausanias 6.5.5 ff; see discussion in Fox (2011) pp 10-11 and Hammond *Tombs* (1991) p 80. Pliny 8.17 and Aristotle *History of Animals* 579b5-8, 606b14-14 also mentioned lions in the region. The coins of Amyntas III are rejected as proof by Borza-Palagia (2007) p 93 ff and p 96. Athenaeus 1.18a, Pseudo-Aristotle *Physiognomics* 806b8-11, Herodotus 1.36-43 for the importance of the boar hunt; discussed in Cohen (2010) p 71 and p 240.
16. Herodotus 5.17-21 for Macedonia first accepting Persian dominance. Justin 7.4.1-3 for Xerxes placing Alexander I in command of an expanded Lower Macedonia, stemming from the marriage of Bubares, a Persian ambassador, to his sister. Demosthenes 4.48 reported Philip II sending envoys to Artaxerxes III in 351/350 BCE; this may have reconciled Artabazus, taking refuge in Macedonia, with the Great King. Artabazus and his family resided at Pella in, or from, 349/348 BCE; Hammond (1994) p 57 for discussion. Demosthenes 6.11 termed Alexander I 'a traitor'. Herodotus 7.173, 8.34, 8.136-144, 9.44-45 for Alexander I's participation in the Persian invasion. In the wake of the Persian Wars lower Paionia with Pella, Ichnai, Mygdonia beyond the Axius (Thracian) and territories to the Strymon River were added to the kingdom: Hatzopoulos (1996) p 106. Hammond (1991) pp 16-19 for the politics of the Persian occupation. See chapter titled *The Reborn Wrath of Peleus' Son* for more on Persian influences on the Macedonian court.

17. Plato *Laws* 947D, quoted in Hammond *Tombs* (1991) p 73; he suggests Euphraeus, Plato's pupil, reported on the burials. The late date for barrel-vaulted tombs is refuted by Fredericksmeyer (1981) p 333 and Hammond (1978) p 338 and Hammond *Tombs* (1991) pp 73 and 79-80; fuller discussion in Saatsoglou-Paliadeli (1999) p 357 ff. Also Borza *Tombs* (1987) pp 107-109 and Borza-Palagia (2007) p 83 and pp 86-89 for the relative dates of tomb design and the dating of the Tomb of Eurydice; pp 107-117 for the royal paraphernalia.

18. Pottery fragments dating to 344/3 BCE (the Athenian archonship of Lyciscus) provide a *terminus post quem* for Eurydice's death; see Borza-Palagia (2007) p 86 ff for discussion.

19. See chapter titled *Sarissa Diplomacy: Macedonian Statecraft* for more on Ptolemy of Alorus. Pausanias 5.17.4, 5.20.9-10 for the Philippeion. Carney (2006) p 101 for its suggestion of divinity. After the death of King Amyntas III in 370/369 BCE, Ptolemy of Alorus, a possible envoy to the king (an alliance with Athens in 375-373 BCE mentioned the name) and possibly the son of Amyntas II (Diodorus 15.71.1; thus descended from the line of Menelaus, son of Alexander I) started a liaison with Amyntas' widow, Eurydice, and he may in fact have married her and ascended to the throne. In 368/367 BCE Ptolemy allegedly assassinated Alexander II (Diodorus 16.2.4 and 15.71.1-2 but Demosthenes *On the False Embassy* 19.194-95 stated an Apollophanes was executed for the murder) after less than 2 years on the throne (Diodorus 15.60.3 stated 1 year), and became guardian (*epitropos*) for the immature Perdiccas III (Aeschines *On the Embassy* 2.29, Plutarch *Pelopidas* 27.3), a role that saw him become regent of the kingdom until Perdiccas killed him in 365 BCE and then reigned for 5 years (Diodorus 15.77.5). Diodorus 15.71.1, 15.77.5, Eusebius *Kronographia* 228, stated Ptolemy was in fact *basileus*, king, for 3 years, but the use of the demotic, Alorus, and the absence of coinage in his name, speak otherwise. Moreover his marriage to Eurydice (Justin 7.4.7, Aeschines 2.29) and previously to her daughter, Eurynoe, (Justin 7.4.7-7, 7.5.4-8 stated Ptolemy and Eurydice were lovers even then), suggest he needed legitimacy his heritage did not provide. According to Justin, the intrigue was revealed by Eurynoe. Why Eurydice intrigued with Ptolemy remains unclear (Justin 7.5 claimed she had previously plotted against Amyntas who spared her for the sake of their children); it may have been to undermine Alexander II, or the line of Amyntas on behalf of a foreign regime, or simply lovers intriguing to put Ptolemy in power, even above her sons. However, neither Diodorus nor Plutarch included her in any plotting with Ptolemy, so her involvement may be fiction; Carney (2006) p 90 argues that there is evidence she was a loyal and devoted mother. Pelopidas who had already driven the Macedonian garrisons installed by Alexander II from Thessaly, was called in to arbitrate (Plutarch *Pelopidas* 26.3, Diodorus 16.67.4). Pelopidas was offered, or took, hostages for good behaviour, including Philip II.

20. Curtius 10.6.4 for the regalia at Babylon. Diodorus 18.61.1 for Eumenes' use of Alexander's regalia and implied at 19.15.4.

21. Diodorus 18.26-27 for the full description of Alexander's funeral bier; discussed in Hammond (1989) p 219. A sceptre was apparently discovered by Andronikos in Tomb II in 1977 and featured in his first reports: 'It seems almost unavoidable to interpret it as a sceptre.' It appears to have been 6.56 feet tall with a bamboo core wrapped in alternate layers of cloth and gold. The sceptre itself and all mention of it disappeared from Andronikos' later reports; see Hammond (1978) p 225 and Borza-Palagia (2007) p 108 ff.

22. Hammond (1989) p 221 for the helmet differences, principally the plumes; cf. Borza-Palagia (2007) p 111 for the similarities to the iron helmet described by Plutarch. Hammond (1989) p 222 for the cuirass differences.

23. Lehmann (1980) pp 529-530 for discussion of the diadem. Arrhidaeus wore the diadem at Babylon in June 323 BCE; Curtius 10.8.20; more on the regalia in chapter titled *Babylon: the Cipher and Rosetta Stone*. Hammond (1989) pp 218-218 for discussion of the throne, diadem, signet ring, robe and arms. Fredericksmeyer (1981) p 332 and Hammond *Tombs* (1991) p 81 refutes the gilded diadem as stemming from Persian tradition.

24. Homer *Iliad* 1.245, translation by Samuel Butler; references to sceptres appear frequently in the *Iliad* and this is just one example. Borza *Tombs* (1987) p 116 for the Porus Medallion. One of the painted tablets within the golden colonnade of Alexander's funeral bier, itself resonant of a barrel-vaulted tomb, depicted Alexander holding a sceptre in his hands, as (likely) does the so-called Porus Medallion (a minted silver decadrachm) discovered in Afghanistan, potentially the sole surviving depiction of Alexander produced in his lifetime.

25. Arrian 1.16.5 and Curtius 7.9.21 confirmed Alexander had himself followed the 'custom' of burying the dead with their weapons; discussed in Hammond (1978) p 332, Hammond (1989) p 217. Livy 40.6.2 for the Xandika and Hammond (1989) p 218. Curtius 10.6.5, 10.7.13, 10.8.20, 10.10.13 for the insignia in Babylon; Diodorus 18.2-27 for them reappearing in the funeral bier. Diodorus 18.60.6 and 18.61.1 for Eumenes' exploitation of similar items on campaign ca. 318/317 BCE; see chapter titled *The Tragic Triumvirate of Treachery and Oaths* for more detail and several sets of regalia potentially being in circulation.

26. Nikolaos Xirotiris was the first physical anthropologist to examine the remains, along with Franziscka Langenscheidt and a team of specialists in *Cremations from the Royal Macedonian Tombs of Vergina*, Archaiologike Ephemeris 1981. A number of studies followed (see *Understanding the Bones: The Human Skeletal Remains from Tombs I, II and III at Vergina* by Jolene McLeod, University of Calgary and available online at http://theses.ucalgary.ca/bitstream/11023/1562/2/ucalgary_2014_mcleod_jolene.pdf for a rundown of the studies and conflicting conclusions). More recently, in 2000, emerged A Bartsiokas *The Eye Injury of King Philip II and the Skeletal Evidence from the Royal Tomb II at Vergina*, Science 288, pp 511-514, 2000 which was answered a decade later by JH Musgrave, AJNW Prag, RAH Neave, R Lane Fox, and H White. 2010, *The Occupants of Tomb II at Vergina. Why Arrhidaios and Eurydice must be excluded*, International Journal of Medical Science 7(6), pp 1-15. The most recent study – Bartsiokas-Arsuaga-Santos-Algaba-Olivencia (2015) *Results* – has been called into question as it introduced bones never seen before or described in the diaries or illustrations of the initial excavators including 'a remarkable flexional ankylosis of the left knee, which resulted in the fusion of the tibia with the femur.'

27. For a thorough rundown and discussion of Philip's wounds see *Understanding the Bones: The Human Skeletal Remains from Tombs I, II and III at Vergina* by Jolene McLeod, University of Calgary and available online at http://theses.ucalgary.ca/bitstream/11023/1562/2/ucalgary_2014_mcleod_jolene.pdf p 70 ff.

28. Quoting Justin 11.1.4, however, following the observation in Borza-Palagia (2007) p 84, this is far from proof of the ritual being performed at Aegae.

29. Justin 9.7.11

30. Director of Research and Head of the Laboratory of Archaeometry at the Democritus Institute, Giannis Maniatis, who conducted the analysis, believes that these residues are from a mask 'of complex design, using laminated fabric that is found for the first time in Macedonia, meticulously crafted from six or seven layers of huntite and porphyry, and which Philip wore during religious ceremonies, possibly as high priest of the Orphic mysteries': quoting Archaeology News Network. See opening text, *Press Release, the Bones of Philip II Found* for more detail on the funeral mask findings. Aelian 7.8 for the armour, gold and silver on Hephaestion's funeral pyre. Diodorus 17.115.1 for the gold and silver likenesses being prepared for the funeral of Hephaestion.

31. Pausanias 1.11.3-4, 8.7.7 for Olympias' treatment of Arrhidaeus' body, also Justin 14.5.10 and Diodorus 19.11.5; discussed in Carney (2006) p 76. Musgrave-Prag-Neave-Lane Fox (2010) section 9.1.2 for related pollution and contamination discussion issues.

32. Bartsiokas-Arsuaga-Santos-Algaba-Olivencia (2015), Abstract, also concludes the bones in Tomb I were inhumed, though this evidence may inevitably be called into question after the recent controversy. Cassander could in fact have exhumed Philip II's body before it became completely skeletal if that took place at the earlier end of estimates of reburial between six and seventeen months after Olympias ordered their deaths.

33. Earlier analyses suggested the bones were of a twenty-to-thirty-year-old female; see Musgrave-Prag-Neave-Lane Fox (2010) section 6 for summary of earlier conclusions. Antikas-Wynn Antikas (2014) *Results* for the new proposed age. Diodorus 17.2.3 confirmed Cleopatra was Philip's last wife.

34. A young archaeologist working on his thesis at Vergina found three wooden crates in a storage place filled with bone fragments and artefacts from Tomb I in three plastic bags containing well over one hundred bone fragments never-before studied; Dr Theodore Antikas, private communication.

35. Referring, for example, to the previous analyses of Musgrave (1990) and Xirotiris-Langensheidt (1981)

36. Plutarch *Pyrrhus* 26.6; evidence unearthed in 2013 suggests other tombs at Aegae were looted at the same time.

37. Borza *Tombs* (1987) pp 105-107 for the uniqueness of the double burial. Also Borza-Palagia (2007) p 84 for discussion of the antechamber as a repository for grave goods and not a second person.

38. Europa, according to Athenaeus 13.557e and Justin 9.7.12 was born just days before Philip died; Diodorus 17.2.3. According to Justin 9.7.12 she (or he, or even 'they') was murdered in her mother's arms by Olympias who forced her mother to commit suicide by hanging, whilst Pausanias 8.7.5-7 claimed mother and daughter were burned in an oven or dragged over a brazier without Alexander's approval; Plutarch 10.8 confirmed Alexander's anger at Olympias treating her 'savagely'. The sex of the baby, and whether there was more than one child, is debated as Justin 11.2.3 suggested Alexander killed the son (Caranus) of his mother-in-law, thus we may assume Cleopatra: see Musgrave (1991) p 7 footnote 23 for details and Lane Fox (2011) p 385; also Heckel (2006) p 78 (Caranus 1). Diodorus 17.5.2, Curtius 7.1.3 for Attalus' execution. Justin 11.5.1 for the murder of the whole of Attalus' family.

39. Antikas-Wynn Antikas (2014) *Introduction* and *Paleopathology* for the leg fracture and *Results* for the regular horse-riding.

40. Antikas-Wynn Antikas *Discussion* for arguments promoting the female identity as King Ataias' daughter; Justin 9.2.1-6 for Ataias' loss of 20,000 captives and for Ataias' adoption offer, and Diodorus 16.4-5 for Ataias' defeat. Hammond *Tombs* (1991) p 77 for Ataias' coins being adorned with quivers. Hammond *Tombs* (1991) p 76 for burial rituals of Scythians, Getae and some Thracian tribes. Other candidates for the female, besides Eurydice the wife of Philip III, are Philip's Illyrian warrior queen, Audata (renamed Eurydice, date of death unknown) or more likely Meda, the daughter of the Getic Thracian king, Cothelas. Early discussion of the contents of the tomb in detail in Hammond (1978) and pp 336-337 for discussion of the daughter of Ataias and the tribal tradition of being buried beside their men. Herodotus 4.71.2-4 for Scythian burial customs including strangulation of a concubine and servants, Herodotus 5.5 for a similar tradition in Crestonia, Thrace.

41. Athenaeus 13.557b-e for a rundown of Philip's wives, as provided by Satyrus, and the political motivation behind the marriages.

42. Justin 9.2.3.

43. Diodorus 17.2.1 confirmed Alexander 'dedicated himself' to his father's funeral. Diodorus 17.2.1 stated Alexander dealt with the assassins and their conspirators before overseeing the funeral where Justin 11.2.1 claimed they took place together; this is not necessarily a conflict if we consider there may have been many conspirators, real or accused for political convenience, who needed tracking down and killing.

44. Justin 9.2.6.

45. Plutarch 46.3, Arrian 7.13.1-4, 4.1-3, 4.15.1,7.15.4 for embassies from the Scythians; discussed in detail in chapter titled *Mythoi, Muthodes and the Birth of Romance*. Curtius 10.1.31-32 for the contents of Cyrus' tomb; other versions at Strabo 15.3.7 and Arrian 6.29.5.

46. Diodorus 19.52.2, Athenaeus 4.155a (from Diyllus) for Cynnane's remains being returned to Macedonia for later burial.

47. Polyaenus 8.60 for Cynnane's warrior past and Athenaeus 13.560f for her training her daughter in the arts of war. Diodorus 16.4.1 named Eucharistus as archon at Athens in the year of Philip's campaign against Bardylis; if as Heckel (2006) p 64 (Audata) concludes, Philip married Audata as part of the 'noteworthy peace' (Diodorus 16.8.1) with the Illyrians which followed, then it is unlikely that Cynnane was born before 357/356 BCE.

48. Polyaenus 8.60 stated she was a leader of armies and charged ahead of them into battle but these actions do not necessarily relate to the earlier Illyrian campaign. It may of course be court propaganda, or simple exaggeration.

49. Adea was likely born in 336 BCE as her father Amyntas was killed by Alexander, probably soon after Philip's death; according to Arrian 1.5.4 Amyntas was definitely dead by spring 335 BCE; Heckel (2006) p 4. See discussion on the 'high' and 'low' chronologies of events post-Babylon, which renders dating uncertain, in chapter titled *The Silent Siegecraft of the Pamphleteers*.

50. Nepos *Eumenes* 13, Plutarch *Eumenes* 19.1-2; upon Eumenes' death his ashes were returned to his wife, children and mother. For Craterus' death see Plutarch *Eumenes* 7.13, Arrian *Events After Alexander* 26, Nepos *Eumenes* 4.4, Diodorus 19.44.2, 19.59.3. Arrian *Events After Alexander* 1.23 confirmed Alketas' troops were indignant at Cynnane's death.

51. Antikas-Wynn Antikas (2014) *Results* for the different pyre conditions.

52. Cassander's double burial of Philip III (Arrhidaeus) and Eurydice in ca. 316 BCE is found in Athenaeus 4.155a (Diyllus 73 F 1), Diodorus 19.52.5; see discussion in Musgrave-Prag-Neave-Lane Fox (2010) section 7.1 and 9.1.2 for the delay between deaths and burial, though the same report concluded mother and daughter would have been buried together. Cynnane had been briefly married to Amyntas, son of King Perdiccas III, but he yielded the throne to Philip due to his youth; it is unlikely he was ever on the throne, see Heckel (2006) p 23 for discussion.

53. See chapter titled *The Reborn Wrath of Peleus' Son* for more on the collateral damage at Philip's death.

54. For Olympias' death after an Assembly, Diodorus 19.51.1-4 and Justin 14.6.6-13; both recorded a judicial proceeding in the form of an Assembly gathering. Discussed in detail in Hatzopoulos (1996) pp 274-275.

55. Hammond (1978) p 348 for the preconstruction of tombs. Diodorus 16.1.3 stated a twenty-four-year reign; the additional year depends upon whether he initially acted as regent for his nephew, Amyntas, or immediately proclaimed himself king.

56. Hammond *Tombs* (1991) p 76 and p 82 for the unfinished features of Tomb II and delayed preparation of the antechamber. Cohen (2010) p 237 for the preparation of the plaster.

57. Quoting Stella Miller-Collet for 'illusionist' columns from Borza-Palagia (2007) p 87.

58. Borza-Palagia (2007) pp 83-85 for discussion of the relative size of the antechamber and its significance.

59. Hammond *Tombs* (1991) p 79 for the ceremonial remains on the top of the vault, and Justin 11.2.1 for the executions at the burial place though in some translations this reads as 'tumulus'. The executions were 'Homeric' as in the *Iliad* 23.171-176; some twelve young Trojans were sacrificed at Patroclus' funeral, see Hammond (1978) p 350. Other examples, as Carney (2006) pp 85-96 points out, *Iliad*; 22.395-404 for Achilles' maltreatment of Hector, 23.20-3 and 24.14.21 as the most notable examples.

60. More on their confrontation in chapter titled *The Silent Siegecraft of the Pamphleteers*. Athenaeus 13.560f for Adea's battle dress; Kechel (2006) p 229 sees this as a fabrication of Duris.

61. Whilst the suggestion that the weapons and armour found in Tomb II once belonged to Alexander goes back to Eugene Borza (1987), other scholars such as Hammond (1989) refute the argument and propose such items were the standard insignia destined for burial with every Argead king.

62. Andronikos-Fotiadis (1978) p 35 for the suggestion of Nicomachus; Pliny 35.108 related that he used only four colours and painted rapidly. Quoting Borza-Palagia (2007) p 82 of the artist's technique.

63. Cohen (2010) p 190 for the origins of the *Hymn to Demeter* and its setting.

64. Adams (1991) p 28 for the *heroon* close to Tomb I; Hammond *Tombs* (1991) p 74 for its dimensions. Bartsiokas-Arsuaga-Santos-Algaba-Olivencia (2015) *Abstract* for the rock of the *heroon* and Tomb I. Plato *Laws* 947D for the porous recommendation; Hammond *Tombs* (1991) p 73 for discussion and p 75 for the dating of the secondary tumulus originally covering both tombs. Hammond *Tombs* (1991) p 74 for the secondary burials in Tomb I.

65. Justin 9.7; 'manes' is a Roman term for the chthonic deities associated with the soul of the deceased.

66. Hammond (1978) pp 332-333 for the original double-tumulus; Hammond *Tombs* (1991) p 75 believed that as Tomb II lay broadly at its centre, the double-tumulus was built after Tomb II; this does not *necessarily* follow, as it could have been extended geometrically with this intention. www.Aigai.gr (necropolis) for Thessalonice's possible tomb.

67. Dr Antikas, personal communication; this however does imply that Antikas agrees with the author that Cynnane is a candidate as the Tomb II female.

68. For Lysimachus see Hammond (1991) p 78 and following Carney (2002) p 108 for the association of *Gonatas* with the Great Tumulus; Adams (1991) p 28 for the format of the Great Tumulus. Plutarch *Pyrrhus* 26.6 for the earlier looting by Gallic mercenaries. Also see Andronikos-Fotiadis (1978) p 35 for *Gonatas'* own tomb and his rationale for building the Great Tumulus.

69. Diodorus 19.61.1-4, Justin 15.1 for Antigonus' call for the release of Roxane and Alexander IV; discussed in chapter titled *The Silent Siegecraft of the Pamphleteers*. See chapter titled *Sarissa Diplomacy: Macedonian Statecraft* and *The Tragic Triumvirate of Treachery and Oaths* for the Antigonid bid for legitimacy.

70. Borza-Palagia (2007) p 82 footnote 5 for detail of Tomb IV and its dating.

71. The accounts of the Gallic attack on Delphi conflict; Justin 24.7-8 and Pausanias 10.23.1-14 claimed the Gauls were defeated at Delphi, but Strabo 4.1 provided detail for Roman tradition of the fabled 15,000 talent *aurum Tolosanum*, the cursed gold of Tolosa looted from Delphi.

72. Bartsiokas-Arsuaga-Santos-Algaba-Olivencia (2015) *Methods* for the reddish-brown sediment and horizontal shaft. If there was no Great Tumulus covering both tombs, looters would not have needed to dig a subterranean shaft from the *heroon*. Hammond *Tombs* (1991) p 79 and Hammond (1978) p 334 more logically argues that it was constructed before the Gallic raids, possibly by Lysimachus.

73. Hammond *Tombs* (1991) p 79 for the layers of rock.

74. Hammond (1978) p 334 for the *stelae* and dating. Hammond *Tombs* (1991) p 78 for the possible stoa and cenotaph at its centre.

75. Quoting Cohen (2010) p 233 on a 'relationship of equality'.

76. Hammond (1978) p 333 for the worship of Philip at Amphipolis and Hammond *Tombs* (1991) p 74 points out that Amyntas, Philip's father, was also worshipped at Pydna at a *heroon* known as the Amyntaion. Excavations at Pella have turned up the so-called House of the Abduction of Helen, ca. 325-300 BCE, though this was not funerary.

77. Hammond (1978) p 338 for linking the mural of Persephone to the Orphic faith. Cohen (2010) p 188 ff for the myth behind the scene and p 213 for the Thesmophorion.

78. Livy 45.32.3-11, Polybius 26.4-9 for Aemilius Paullus' proclamation and victory games at Amphipolis.

79. A further inscription dated to 340 BCE and dedicated to Eurydice has been found at Vergina; Carney (2006) pp 90-91. Olympias probably married Philip in 357 BCE – Heckel (2006) p 181 – so she and Alexander would have known Philip's mother, Eurydice, for well over a decade before her death.

80. Carney (2006) p 91 for Eurydice's possible attempt to salvage her reputation.

81. In a tomb dating to one of the wives of Alexander I (498-454 BCE) were clay heads depicting Demeter and Kore; see the official outline at Aegae.gr/necropolis. Cohen (2010) p 94 ff for griffin iconography.

82. Carney (2006) p 88 for the role of women in burial rites and p 98 for Orphic symbolism and rebirth. Cohen (2010) p 198 for the themes of immortality.

83. Cohen (2101) pp 230-233 for the link of abduction to marriage rites.

84. Carney (2006) p 104 for the site and once fragmentary inscription marking Olympias' tomb near Pydna; further discussion in Edson (1949). Also see http://www.ascsa.edu.gr/pdf/uploads/hesperia/146994.pdf; and ALN Oikonomides *The epigram on the tomb of Olympias at Pydna,* Chicago. Diodorus 17.118.2 (and Porphyry FGrH 2.260 3.3) claimed Cassander 'threw her body out without burial'. Plutarch *Pyrrhus* 26.6-7 and Diodorus 22.12 for the tomb-raiding by Pyrrhus and, or, his men.

85. Curtius 9.6.26 for Alexander requesting Olympias' consecration to immortality; see chapter titled *The Silent Siegecraft of the Pamphleteers* for the circumstances.

86. What are believed to be Hephaestion monograms were dredged from the River Strymon in the early 20th century but thought to have originally formed part of the circular wall of the tomb; a further monogram was recently found above the Persephone mosaic.

87. Plutarch 72.5 for Deinocrates; chapter titled *Babylon: the Cipher and Rosetta Stone* for more on Deinocrates.

88. Hammond (1978) p 334 linking the Great Tumulus to Alexander's last wishes. Alexander had already constructed a large tumulus some 125 feet (38 metres) high and 'great in circumference' for Demaratus of Corinth, Plutarch 56.2; a tumulus for Hephaestion, Plutarch 72.5; and a first modest tumulus for Philip upon his death, Justin 11.2.1.

89. Archaeologists note its 'cheap' construction and believe the tumulus could have in no way supported the 25-foot-tall Lion of Amphipolis found nearby some decades ago in the Strymon River; but recently the mound has been judged natural and not manmade which may change opinion.

90. See chapter titled *Babylon: the Cipher and Rosetta Stone* for the cancellation of plans including Hephaestion's funeral pyre.

91. Arrian *Indike* 18.4 listed Nearchus as from Amphipolis; chapter titled *The Silent Siegecraft of the Pamphleteers* and *Hierarch Historians and Alexandrian Alchemy* for Nearchus' career under Antigonus and his possible death at Gaza and other generals linked to Amphipolis. Laomedon was also associated with the city; his brother, Erygius, died in Sogdia in 328/7 BCE.

92. For Eumenes' treatment of Craterus see Plutarch *Eumenes* 7.6-13, Nepos 4.4, and Diodorus 19.59.3 suggests that by the time Craterus' bones were finally returned to Phila by Ariston she was married to Demetrius *Poliorketes* but her whereabouts were not stated. Hammond *Tombs* (1991) p 70 for the Tomb of Palatitsia at Vergina.

93. Euripides *Alcestis* line 419.

BIBLIOGRAPHY

The English titles of ancient works are often the result of a very liberal translation process. I have used the most popular and accepted names.

ABBREVIATIONS – ANCIENT AUTHORS

Aelian : *Historical Miscellany* (*Varia Historia*).

Ammianus Marcellinus : *Historical Events* (*Res Gestae*).

Arrian : *The Campaign of Alexander* (*Anabasis Alexandrou*).

Athenaeus : *The Dinner Philosophers* (*Deipnosophistae*).

Aulus Gellius : Attic Nights (*Noctes Atticae*).

Cassius Dio : *Roman History* (*Historia Romana*).

Curtius : *History of Alexander the Great* (*Historiae Alexandri Magni*).

Dexippus : précis by Photius of Dexippus' epitome of Arrian *Events After Alexander*.

Diodorus : *Library of World History* (*Bibliotheke*).

Diogenes Laertius : *Lives and Opinions of Eminent Philosophers* (*Bioi kai Gnomai ton en Philosophia Eudokimesanton*).

Eusebius : *Ecclesiastical History* (*Historia Ecclesiastica*).

Herodian : *History of the Empire From the Death of Marcus Aurelius* (*Historia de Imperio post Marcum Aurelium*).

Herodotus : *The Histories* (*Historiai*).

Josephus : *Jewish Antiquities* (*Antiquitates Iudiacae*).

Justin : *Epitome of the Philippic History of Pompeius Trogus* (*Epitoma Historiarum Philippicarum*).

Juvenal : *Satires* (*Satirae*).

Livy : *The Early History of Rome* (*Ab Urbe Condita Libri*).

Metz Epitome : (*Epitoma Rerum Gestarum Alexandri Magni et Liber de Morte Eius*).

Nepos : *Eumenes*; *Lives of Eminent Commanders* (*Vitae Excellentium Imperatorum*).

Orosius : *Seven Books of History Against the Pagans* (*Historiarum Adversum Paganos*).

Ovid : *Transformations* (*Metamorphoses*).

Pausanias : *Guide to Ancient Greece* (*Hellados Periegesis*).

Pliny: *Natural History* (*Naturalis Historia*).

Plutarch : *The Life of Alexander* from his *Parallel Lives* (*Vitae Parallelae*).

Plutarch *Fortune* : *On the Fortune or the Virtue of Alexander The Great* (*De Alexandri Magni Fortuna aut Virtute*).

Polyaenus : *Stratagems of War* (*Stratagemata*).

Polybius : *Histories* (*Historiai*).

Quintilian : *Institutes of Oratory* (*Institutio Oratoria*).

Romance : The *Greek Alexander Romance* or Pseudo-Callisthenes (probably first circulated as *Istoria tou Megalou Alexandrou*, better known by its early Latin name *Historia Alexandri Magni*).

Strabo : *Geography* (*Geographika hypomnemata*).

Suetonius : *About the Life of the Caesars* (*De Vita Caesarum*).

Tacitus : *Annals* (*Annales* originally, *Ab excessu divi Augusti*).

Thucydides : *History of The Peloponnesian War* (*Historiai Peloponnesiakos Polemos*).

Valerius Maximus : *Nine Books of Memorable Deeds and Sayings* (*Factorum ac Dictorum Memorabilium*).

Xenophon : *The Education of Cyrus* (*Cyropaedia, Kyrou Paideía*).

MODERN ABBREVIATIONS

FGrH : *Fragmente der griechischen Historiker*, F Jacoby (1926-1958) Leiden.

BIBLIOGRAPHY

Where more recent editions of older works have been used, I have, nevertheless, cited the original publication date in the footnotes, and referenced the edition being used in this bibliography. This seems more respectful than referencing, for example, 'Gibbon (1996)' for the *History of the Decline and Fall of the Roman Empire* first published between 1776 and 1789. For clarity, only the publication being referred to in the book is italicised, though convention would also italicise the journal or publication in which the article appeared.

Adams (1980) : WL Adams, *The Royal Macedonian Tomb at Vergina: An Historical Interpretation*, The Ancient World 3, 1980, pp 67-72.

Adams (1985) : WL Adams, *Antipater and Cassander, Generalship on Restricted Resources in the Fourth Century*, The Ancient World 10, 1985, pp 79-88.

Adams (1991) : WL Adams, *Cassander, Alexander IV and the Tombs at Vergina*, The Ancient World 22, no. 2, 1991, pp 27-33.

Adams (1996) : WL Adams, *In the wake of Alexander the Great: the impact of conquest on the Aegean world,* The Ancient World 27, no, 1, 1996, pp 29-37.

Allen (1912) : TW Allen, *Lives of Homer*, The Journal of Hellenic Studies, 32, 1912, pp 250-260.

Alonso-Núñez (1987) : JM Alonso-Núñez, *An Augustan World History: The Historiae Philippicae of Pompeius Trogus,* Greece and Rome, Second Series, 34, 1987, pp 56-72.

Anderson (1961) : JK Anderson, *Ancient Greek Horsemanship*, University of California Press.

Anderson (1970) : JK Anderson, *Military Theory and Practice in the Age of Xenophon*, University of California Press.

Andronikos (1970) : M Andronikos, *Sarissa*, Bulletin de Correspondence Hellénique 94, no.1, 1970, pp 91-107.

Andronikos (1977) : M Andronikos, *Vergina: the Royal Graves in the Great Tumulus,* Athens Annals of Archaeology 10, 1977, pp 59-60.

Andronikos (1981) : M Andronikos, *The Finds from the Royal Tombs at Vergina*, Oxford University Press.

Andronikos (1987) : M Andronikos, *Vergina: The Royal Tombs and the Ancient City*, Ekdotike Athenon, 1987, pp 221-222.

Andronikos-Fotiadis (1978) : M Andronikos and M Fotiadis, *The Royal Tomb of Philip II: An unlooted Macedonian grave at Vergina*, Archaeology 31, no. 5, September/October 1978, pp 33-41.

Anson (1977) : EM Anson, *The Siege of Nora: A Source Conflict*, Greek, Roman and Byzantine Studies, 18, 1977, pp 251-256.

Anson (1980) : EM Anson, *Discrimination and Eumenes of Cardia*, The Ancient World 3, 1980, pp 55-59.

Anson (1984) : EM Anson, *The Meaning of the Term Makedones*, The Ancient World 10, 1984, pp 67-68.

Anson (1985) : EM Anson, *The Hypaspists: Macedonia's Professional Citizen-Soldiers*, Historia 34, 1985, pp 246-248.

Anson (1986) : EM Anson, *Diodorus and the Dating of Triparadeisus*, The American Journal of Philology 107, no. 2, 1986, pp 208-217.

Anson *Argyraspides* (1988) : EM Anson, *Hypaspists and Argyraspids after 323 BCE*, The Ancient History Bulletin 2, no.6, 1988, pp 131-133.

Anson (1988) : EM Anson, *Antigonus, the Satrap of Phrygia*, Historia: Zeitschrift für Alte Geschichte 37, no. 4, 1988, pp 471-477.

Anson (1991) : EM Anson, *The Evolution of the Macedonian Army Assembly (330-315 BC)*, Historia: Zeitschrift für Alte Geschichte 40, no. 2, 1991, pp 230-247.

Anson (1992) : EM Anson, *Craterus and the Prostasia*, Classical Philology 87, January 1992, pp 38-43.

Anson (1996) : EM Anson, *The 'Ephemerides' of Alexander the Great*, Historia: Zeitschrift für Alte Geschichte 45, no. 4, 1996, pp 501-504.

Anson (2003) : EM Anson, *The Dating of Perdiccas' Death and the Assembly at Triparadeisus*, Greek, Roman and Byzantine Studies 43, 2003, pp 373-390.

Anson (2004) : EM Anson, *Eumenes of Cardia: A Greek amongst Macedonians*, Brill.

Anson (2013) : EM Anson, *Alexander the Great, Themes and Issues*, Bloomsbury.

Anson (2014) : EM Anson, *Alexander's Heirs, the Age of the Successors*, Wiley Blackwell.

Antikas (2005) : TG Antikas, *Bucephalas, Common Burials of Horses and Heroes in Antiquity*, Ichor Journal 55, 2005, 55, pp 86-97.

Antikas-Wynn Antikas (2014) : TG Antikas and LK Wynn-Antikas, *New finds from the cremains in Tomb II at Aegae point to Philip II and a Scythian princess*, International Journal of Osteoarchaeology, 2014.

Arnaoutoglou (1998) : I Arnaoutoglou, *Ancient Greek Laws*, Routledge.

Archibald-Davies-Gabrielson (2005) : Z Archibald, J Davies and V Gabrielsen (editors), *Making, Moving and Managing, The New World of Ancient Economies 323-31 BC*, Oxbow.

Arthur-Montagne (2014) : J Arthur-Montagne, *Persuasion, Emotion, and the Letters of the Alexander Romance*, Ancient Narrative 11, 2014, pp 159-189.

Atherton (1993) : C Atherton, *The Stoics on Ambiguity*, Cambridge University Press.

Atkinson (1963) : JE Atkinson, *Primary Sources and the Alexanderreich*, Acta Classica 6, 1963, pp 125-137.

Atkinson (1994) : JE Atkinson, *A Commentary on Q. Curtius Rufus' Historiae Alexandri Magni, Books 5 to 7.2*, Acta Classica, Supplementum 1.

Atkinson (1996) : JE Atkinson, review of AB Bosworth, *Alexander and the East: the Tragedy of Triumph,* Clarendon Press.

Atkinson (1997) : JE Atkinson, *Q Curtius Rufus' Historiae Alexandri Magni,* Aufstieg und Niedergang der römischen Welt II, no. 34.4, 1997, pp 3447-3483.

Atkinson (2009) : JE Atkinson, *Alexander's Last Days: Malaria and Mind Games,* Acta Classica 52, 2009, pp 23-46.

Atkinson-Yardley (2009) : JE Atkinson and JC Yardley (translator), *Curtius Rufus, Histories of Alexander the Great, Book 10,* Oxford University Press.

Attridge-Oden (1981) : HW Attridge and RA Oden, *Philo of Byblos: Phoenician History, Introduction, Critical Text, Translation, Notes,* Catholic Biblical Quarterly Monograph Series 9.

Ausfeld (1895) A Ausfeld, *Das angebliche testament Alexanders des Grossen,* Rheinisches Museum Für Philologie 50, 1895, pp 357-366.

Avcioğlu (2011) : N Avcioğlu, *Turquerie and the Politics of Representation 1728-1876,* Ashgate Publishing Company.

Avramović (2006) : S Avramović, *The Rhetra of Epithadeus and Testament in Spartan Law,* University of Belgrade School of Law, Alan Watson Foundation.

Badian (1958) : E Badian, *Alexander the Great and the Unity of Mankind,* Historia: Zeitschrift für Alte Geschichte 7, no. 4, October 1958, pp 425-444.

Badian (1963) : E Badian, *The Death of Philip II,* Phoenix 17, 1963, pp 244-50.

Badian (1964) : E Badian, *Alexander the Great and the Loneliness of Power,* in Studies in Greek and Roman History, Blackwell pp 192-205.

Badian (1968) : E Badian, *A King's Notebooks,* Harvard Studies in Classical Philology 72, 1968, pp 183-204.

Badian (1975) : E Badian, *Nearchus the Cretan,* Yale Classical Studies 24, 1975, pp 147-1870.

Bagnall (1976) : RS Bagnall, *The Administration of the Ptolemaic Possessions outside Egypt,* Leiden.

Bagnall (2002) : RS Bagnall, *Alexandria: Library of Dreams,* American Philosophical Society 146, no. 4, December 2002, pp 348-362.

Bagnall-Derow (2004) : RS Bagnall and P Derow (editors), *The Hellenistic Period, Historical Sources in Translation,* Blackwell.

Bailey (1978) : S Bailey (editor), *Cicero: Selected Letters,* Penguin.

Baker-Saldanha (2009) : M Baker and G Saldanha (editors), *Routledge Encyclopedia of Translation Studies,* Routledge.

Balme (2001) : M Balme, *Menander, The Plays and Fragments,* Oxford University Press.

Balot (2001) : RK Balot, *Greed and Injustice in Classical Athens,* Princeton University Press.

Barber (1993) : GL Barber, *The Historian Ephorus,* Ares Publishers.

Barker (1990) : N Barker, *Fake? The Art of Deception,* University of California Press.

Barker-Rasmussen (2000) : G Barker and T Rasmussen, *The Etruscans,* Blackwell Publishing.

Barnes (1995) : J Barnes, *The Cambridge Companion to Aristotle,* Cambridge University Press.

Barnes (2000) : J Barnes, *Aristotle, A Very Short Introduction,* Oxford University Press.

Barrett (1978) : AA Barrett, *Observations of Comets in Greek and Roman Sources Before AD. 410,* Journal of the Royal Astronomical Society of Canada 72, 1978, pp 81-105.

Bar-Sharrar (1991) : B Bar-Sharrar, *Vergina Tomb II : Dating the Objects,* The Ancient World 22, no. 2, 1991, pp 11-15.

Bartlett (1985) : JR Bartlett, *Jews in the Hellenistic World, Josephus, Aristeas, The Sybilline Oracles, Eupolemus,* Cambridge University Press.

Bartsiokas-Arsuaga-Santos-Algaba-Gómez-Olivencia (2015) : A Bartsiokas, J-L Arsuaga, E Santos, M Algaba, A Gómez-Olivencia, *The Lameness of King Philip II and Royal Tomb I at Vergina, Macedonia,* first published in Proceedings of the National Academy of Sciences, June 2015.

Baynham (1995) : EJ Baynham, *An Introduction to the Metz Epitome: its Tradition and Value,* Antichthon 29, 1995, pp 60-77.

Baynham *Romance* (1995) : J Baynham, *Bucephalus, Various Versions of Alexander's Taming of his Horse,* Ancient History Bulletin 9, no.1, 1995, pp 1-13.

Baynham (1998) : EJ Baynham, *Alexander the Great, The Unique History of Quintus Curtius,* University of Michigan Press, 2004 edition.

Baynes (1926) : NH Baynes, *The Historia Augusta. Its Date and Purpose,* Oxford University Press.

Beaulieu (2006) : PA Beaulieu, *Berossus on Late Babylonian History,* Special Issue of Oriental Studies.

Bellinger (1979) : AR Bellinger, *Essays on the Coinage of Alexander the Great,* Sanford J Durst Numismatic Publications.

Bentley (1697) : R Bentley, *Dissertation upon the epistles of Phalaris, Volumes 1 and 2,* Dyce, 1836 edition.

Behrwald (1999) : R Behrwald : review of J Engels *Augusteische Oikumenegeographie und Universalhistorie im Werk Strabons von Amaseia,* Geographica Historica 12, 1999, p 464.

Berry (1999) : P Berry, *Correspondence between Paul and Seneca, A.D. 61-65,* Edwin Mellen Press.

Berthold (1984) : RM Berthold, *Rhodes in the Hellenistic Age,* Cornell University Press.

Berve (1926) : H Berve, *Das Alexanderreich auf prosopographischer Grundlage,* CH Beck.

Bevan (1902) : ER Bevan, *The House of Seleucus,* Ares Publishers, 1985 edition.

Bevan (1913) : ER Bevan, *Stoics and Sceptics,* Clarendon Press.

Bevan (1927) : ER Bevan, *The House of Ptolemy: A History of Egypt under the Ptolemaic Dynasty,* Ares Publishers, 1968 edition.

Berzunza (1941) : J Berzunza, *Preliminary Notes of the Three Italian Versions of Quintus Curtius Rufus' Historiae Alexandri Magni,* Italica 18, no. 3, 1941, pp 133-137.

Billows (1990) : RA Billows, *Antigonos the One-Eyed and the Creation of the Hellenistic State,* University of California Press, 1997 edition.

Bing (1973) : JD Bing, *A Further Note on Cyinda /"Kundi",* Historia: Zeitschrift für Alte Geschichte 22, no. 2, 2nd qtr., 1973, pp 346-350.

Bishop (1983) : M Bishop, *Petrarch and his World,* Indian University Press.

Blackburn (2006) : S Blackburn, *Plato's Republic, A Biography*, Atlantic Books.

Blackwell (1999) : CW Blackwell, *In the Absence of Alexander, Harpalus and the Failure of Macedonian Authority,* Peter Lang Publishing.

Blackwell (2005) : CW Blackwell, *Athens and Macedonia, in the Absence of Alexander*, in CW Blackwell (editor), *Dēmos: Classical Athenian Democracy*, July 1, 2005.

Blyth (1906) : AW Blyth, *Poisons: Their Effects and Detection,* Charles Griffin and Company.

Boardman (1964) : J Boardman, *The Greeks Overseas, Their Early Colonies and Trade*, Thames and Hudson, 1999 edition.

Boardman-Griffin-Murray (1986) : J Boardman, J Griffin , O Murray, *The Oxford History of Greece and The Hellenistic World*, Oxford University Press.

Boiy (2004) : T Boiy, *Late Achaemenid and Hellenistic Babylon,* Peeters Publishers and Department of Oriental Studies.

Borchardt (1986) : FL Borchardt, *Forgery, False Attribution, and Fiction: Early modern German History and Literature*, Studi Umanistici Piceni 6, 1986, pp 27-35.

Borza *Tombs* (1987) : EN Borza, *The Royal Macedonian Tombs and the Paraphernalia of Alexander the Great*, Phoenix 41, no. 2, summer 1987, pp 105-121.

Borza (1987) : EN Borza, *Malaria in Alexander's Army*, Ancient History Bulletin 1, 1987, pp 36-38.

Borza (1990) : EN Borza, *In the Shadow of Olympus, The Emergence of Macedon*, Princeton University Press.

Borza (1991) : EN Borza, *Commentary*, The Ancient World 22, no. 2, 1991, pp 35-40.

Borza (1995) : EN Borza, *Makedonika, Essays by Eugene N Borza*, Regina Books.

Borza (1999) : EN Borza, *Before Alexander: Constructing Early Macedonia*, Regina Books.

Borza-Palagia (2007) : EN Borza and O Palagia, *The Chronology of the Macedonian Royal Tombs at Vergina*, Jahrbuch des Deutschen Archäologisches Instituts 122, 2007, pp 81-125.

Bosworth-Baynham (2000) : AB Bosworth and EJ Baynham, *Alexander the Great in Fact and Fiction,* Oxford University Press.

Bosworth (1971) : AB Bosworth, *The Death of Alexander the Great: Rumour and Propaganda*, Classical Quarterly, New Series 21, no. 1, 1971, pp 111-136.

Bosworth (1976) : AB Bosworth, *Errors in Arrian*, Classical Quarterly, New Series 26, no. 1, 1976, pp 117-139.

Bosworth (1978) : AB Bosworth, *Eumenes, Neoptolemus and PSI XII 1284*, University of Western Australia, 1978.

Bosworth (1981) : AB Bosworth, *A Missing Year in the History of Alexander the Great*, The Journal of Hellenic Studies 101, pp 17-39.

Bosworth (1983) : AB Bosworth, *History and Rhetoric in Curtius Rufus, A Commentary on Q. Curtius Rufus' "Historiae Alexandri Magni", Books 3 and*

4 by JE Atkinson, review in Classical Philology 78, no. 2, April 1983, pp 150-161.

Bosworth *A to A* (1988) : AB Bosworth, *From Arrian to Alexander: Studies in Historical Interpretation*, Clarendon Press.

Bosworth (1988) : AB Bosworth, *Conquest and Empire, The Reign of Alexander The Great*, Cambridge University Press.

Bosworth (1992) : AB Bosworth, *Philip III Arrhidaeus and the Chronology of the Successors*, Chiron 22, 1992, pp 55-81.

Bosworth (1993) : AB Bosworth, *Perdiccas and the Kings,* Classical Quarterly 63, 1993, pp 420-427.

Bosworth (1996) : AB Bosworth, *In Search of Cleitarchus*: Review-discussion of Luisa Prandi: *Fortuna è Realtà dell' Opera di Clitarco,* Historia Einzelschriften 104, 1996, pp 203.

Bosworth *A in the East* (1996) : AB Bosworth, *Alexander in the East, The Tragedy of Triumph,* Oxford University Press.

Bosworth (2002) : AB Bosworth, *The Legacy of Alexander, Politics, Warfare and Propaganda under the Successors*, Oxford University Press.

Bosworth (2004) : AB Bosworth, *Mountain and Molehill? Cornelius Tacitus and Quintus Curtius,* Classical Quarterly, December 2004, pp 551-567.

Boyer (1991) : CB Boyer, *Euclid of Alexandria, a History of Mathematics,* J Wiley and Sons.

Brandt-Iddeng (2012) : JR Brandt and JW Iddeng, *Greek and Roman Festivals, Content, Meaning and Practice,* Oxford University Press.

Braudel (1969) : F Braudel, *On History,* University of Chicago, 1980 edition.

Braudel (1973) : F Braudel, *The Mediterranean in the Ancient World*, Allen Lane, Penguin, 2001 edition.

Briant (1973) : P Briant, *Antigone le Borgne,* Annales littéraires de l'Université de Besançon 152, 1973, pp 366-368.

Briant (1974) : *Alexander the Great and his Empire, A Short Introduction*, Princeton University Press, 2012 edition.

Brickhouse-Smith (2001) : TC Brickhouse and ND Smith, *The Trial and Execution of Socrates*, Oxford University Press.

Brosius (1996) : M Brosius, *Women in Ancient Persia (559-331 BC),* Oxford University Press.

Brouwer (2011) : R Brouwer, *Polybius and Stoic Tyche*, Greek, Roman and Byzantine Studies 51, 2011, pp 111-132.

Brown (1946) : TS Brown, *Euhemerus and the Historians,* The Harvard Theological Review 39, no. 4, October 1946, pp 259–274.

Brown (1947) : TS Brown, *Hieronymus of Cardia*, The American Historical Review 52, no. 4, pp 684-696.

Brown (1949) : TS Brown, *Onesicritus A Study in Hellenistic Historiography*, Ares Publishers, 1981 edition.

Brown (1950) : TS Brown, *Clitarchus,* The American Journal of Philology 71, no. 2, 1950, pp 134-155.

Brown (1959) : TS Brown, *Timaeus and the Aeneid*, The Vergilian Society 6, 1959-fall 1960, pp 4-12.

Brown (1962) : TS Brown, *The Greek Sense of Time in History as Suggested by Their Accounts of Egypt,* Historia: Zeitschrift für Alte Geschichte 11, no. 3,

July 1962, pp 257-270.

Brunt (1975) : PA Brunt, *Alexander, Barsine and Heracles,* Rivista di Filologia di Instruzione Classica 103, 1975, pp 22-34.

Brunt (1974) : PA Brunt, *Notes on Aristobulos of Cassandria,* Classical Quarterly 24, 1974, pp 65-69.

Brunt (1980) : PA Brunt, *On Historical Fragments and Epitomes,* Classical Quarterly, New Series 30, no.2, 1980, pp 477-494.

Bryce (1977) : TR Bryce, *Ahhiyawa and Troy: A Case of Mistaken Identity?* Historia: Zeitschrift für Alte Geschichte 26, no.1,1ˢᵗ quarter 1977, pp 24-32.

Burke (1991) : P Burke, *The French Historical Revolution: The Annales School, 1929-1989,* Stanford University Press.

Burstein (1976) : *Alexander, Callisthenes and the Source of the Nile,* Greek Roman and Byzantine Studies 17, 1976, pp 135-146.

Bury-Barber-Bevan-Tarn (1923) : JB Bury, EA Barber, E Bevan, and WW Tarn, *The Hellenistic Age: Aspects of Hellenistic Civilization,* Cambridge University Press.

Cahn (1990) : M Cahn, *Reading Rhetoric Rhetorically: Isocrates and the Marketing of Insight,* Rhetorica 8, 1990, pp 103-118.

Carney (1987) : ED Carney, *The Career of Adea-Eurydike,* Historia 36, 1987, pp 496-502.

Carney (1988) : ED Carney, *The Sisters of Alexander the Great: Royal Relicts,* Historia: Zeitschrift für Alte Geschichte 37, no. 4, 1988, pp 385-404.

Carney (1991) : ED Carney, *The Female Burial in the Antechamber of Tomb II at Vergina,* The Ancient World 22, no. 2, 1991, pp 17-26.

Carney (1995) : ED Carney, *Women and Basileia: Legitimacy and Female Political Action in Macedonia,* The Classical Journal 90, no. 4, 1995, pp 367-391.

Carney (1996) : ED Carney, *Macedonians and Mutiny,* Classical Philology 91, 1996, pp 19-44.

Carney (2000) : ED Carney, *Women and Monarchy in Macedonia,* University of Oklahoma Press.

Carney (2006) : ED Carney, *Olympias, Mother of Alexander the Great,* Routledge.

Carney-Ogden (2010) : ED Carney and D Ogden (editors), *Philip II and Alexander the Great, Father and Son, Lives and Afterlives,* Oxford University Press.

Carr (1961) : EH Carr, *What is History?,* Cambridge University Press.

Carr (1987) : EH Carr, *What is History?* incomplete 2ⁿᵈ edition, Penguin.

Cartledge (2003) : P Cartledge, *The Spartans: The World of the Warrior-Heroes of Ancient Greece,* The Overlook Press.

Cartledge (2005) : P Cartledge, *Alexander the Great: The Hunt for a New Past,* Pan Macmillan.

Caspar (1993) M Caspar, *Kepler,* Dover Publishing.

Casson (1971) : L Casson, *Ships and Seamanship in the Ancient World,* Princeton University Press, 1995 edition.

Casson (2001) *Egypt*: L Casson, *Everyday Life in Ancient Egypt,* The John Hopkins University Press, expanded edition from the original published in 1975 as *The Horizon Book of Daily Life in Egypt.*

Casson (2001) : L Casson, *Libraries in the Ancient World*, Yale University Press.

Cartledge (2004) : P Cartledge, *Alexander the Great*, The Overlook Press.

Cawkwell (1979) : G Cawkwell, Introduction to *Xenophon, A History of My Times,* Penguin.

Champion (2000) : C Champion, *Romans as BAPBAPOI: Three Polybian Speeches and the Politics of Cultural Indeterminacy*, Classical Philology 95, no. 4, October 2000, pp 425-444.

Champion (2014) : J Champion, *Antigonus the One-Eyed, Greatest of the Successors*, Pen and Sword Military.

Champlin (2003) : E Champlin, *Nero,* The Belknap Press of Harvard University Press.

Chroust (1964) : AH Chroust, *Aristotle and the Philosophies of the East,* The Review of Metaphysics 18, no. 3, March 1964, pp 572-580.

Chroust (1967) : AH Chroust, *Aristotle's Last will and Testament*, Wiener Studien 80, 1967, pp 90-114.

Chroust (1970) : AH Chroust, *Estate Planning in Hellenic Antiquity: Aristotle's Last Will and Testament*, Notre Dame Lawyer 45, pp 629-662.

Chroust (1973) : AH Chroust, *Aristotle: New Light on his Life and on Some of his Lost Works, Volume 1, some novel interpretations of the man and his life*, Routledge, 2016 edition.

Chugg (2002) *The Sarcophagus of Alexander the Great?* Greece and Rome 49. no.1, 2002, pp 8-26.

Chugg (2004) : AM Chugg, *The Lost Tomb Tomb of Alexander the Great,* Periplus Publishing.

Chugg (2006) : AM Chugg, *Alexander's Lovers,* Lulu.com.

Chugg (2007) : AM Chugg, *The Quest for the Tomb of Alexander the Great,* Lulu. com.

Chugg (2009) : AM Chugg, *The Death of Alexander the Great, a Reconstruction of Cleitarchus,* AMC Publications, 2010 edition.

Cilliers-Retief (2000) : L Cilliers and FP Retief, *Poisons, Poisoning and the Drug Trade in Ancient Rome*, Akroterion 45, 2000, pp 88-100.

Clayton-Price (1989) : PA Clayton and MJ Price, *The Seven Wonders of the Ancient World*, Routledge.

Cohen (1973) : GM Cohen, *The Marriage of Lysimachus and Nicea*, Historia 22, 1973, pp 354-356.

Cohen (2010) : A Cohen, *Art in the Era of Alexander the Great*, Cambridge University Press.

Collard-Cropp-Gilbert (2004) : C Collard, MJ Cropp, J Gilbert, *Euripides, Selected Fragmentary Plays II*, Oxbow.

Collard (2004) : B Collard, *La Cryptographie dans l'Antiquite greco-romaine,* Folia Electronica Classica, Louvain-la-Neuve, no. 7, January-June 2004.

Collins (2001) : AW Collins, *The office of Chiliarch under Alexander and the Successors*, Phoenix 22, 2001, pp 259-283.

Collins (2008) : D Collins, *Magic in the Ancient Greek World,* Blackwell Publishing.

Cook (1983) : JM Cook, *The Persian Empire*, Schochen Books.

Cook (2000) : BL Cook, *Theopompus not Theophrastus: correcting an Attribution in Plutarch Demosthenes 14.4,* The American Journal of Philology 121, no. 4, winter 2000, pp 537-547.

Copenhaver (1992) : BP Copenhaver (editor), *Hermetica: The Greek Corpus Hermeticum and the Latin Asclepius in a New English Translation,* Cambridge University Press.

Cornell (2013) : TJ Cornell, *The Fragments of the Roman Historians,* Oxford University Press.

Costa (1997) : CND Costa (translator), *Seneca On the Shortness of Life,* Penguin.

Costa (2005) : CND Costa, *Lucian Selected Dialogues,* Oxford University Press.

Crake (1940) : JEA Crake, *The Annales of the Pontifex Maximum,* Classical Philology 35, no. 4, October 1940, pp 375-386.

Cruttwell (1877): CT Cruttwell, *A History of Roman Literature from the Earliest Period to the Death of Marcus Aurelius,* C Griffin and Company, 1877, republished by Forgotten Books in 2008.

Cumont (1911) : F Cumont, *The Oriental Religions in Roman Paganism,* The Open Court Publishing Company.

Cunliffe (2001) : B Cunliffe, *The Extraordinary Voyage of Pytheas the Greek,* Walker and Company.

Cunningham (1884) : A Cunningham, *Coins of Alexander's Successors in the East,* Argonaut Inc. Publishers, 1884 and 1969 reprint.

Dalby (1991) : A Dalby, *The Curriculum Vitae of Duris of Samos,* Classical Quarterly 41 no.2, pp 539-541.

Dalley-Oleson (2003) : S Dalley and JP Oleson, *Sennacherib, Archimedes, and the Water Screw: The Context of Invention in the Ancient World,* Technology and Culture 44. no.1, January 2003, pp 1-26.

Dalley (1994) : S Dalley, *Nineveh, Babylon and the Hanging Gardens: Cuneiform and Classical Sources Reconciled,* Iraq 56, 1994, pp 45-58.

Dalley (2013) : S Dalley, *The Mystery of the Hanging Garden of Babylon: an Elusive World Wonder Traced,* Oxford University Press.

Davis (1914) : WS Davis, *A Day in Old Athens,* IndyPublish.com.

Deane (1918) : SN Deane, *Greek in Pliny's Letters,* The Classical Weekly 12, no. 6, 1918, pp 41-44.

De Mauriac (1949) : HM de Mauriac, *Alexander the Great and the politics of "Homonoia",* Journal of the History of Ideas 10, no. 1, January 1949, pp 104-114.

de Polignac (1999) : F de Polignac, *From the Mediterranean to Universality? The Myth of Alexander, Yesterday and Today,* Mediterranean Historical Review 14, no. 1, 1999, pp 1-17.

Delbrück (1920) : H Delbrück, *History of the Art of War* (originally published as *Geschichte der Kriegskunst im Rahmen der politischen Geschichte*), Bison Books, 1990 edition.

Depuydt (1997) : L Depuydt, *The Time of Death of Alexander the Great 11 June 323 B.C. (-322), ca. 4:00-5:00 PM,* Die Welt des Orients 28, 1997, pp 117-135.

Devine (1983) AM Devine : *EMBOΛON: A Study in Tactical Terminology,* Phoenix 37, no. 3, autumn 1983, pp. 201-217.

Devine *Paraitacene* (1985) : AM Devine, *Diodorus' Account of the Battle of*

Paraitacene (317 BCE), The Ancient World 12, nos. 3-4, 1985, pp 75-86.

Devine *Gabiene* (1985) : AM Devine, *Diodorus' Account of the Battle of Gabiene*, The Ancient World 12, nos. 3-4, 1985, pp 87-96.

Doherty (2004) : P Doherty, *Alexander the Great, Death of a God*, Constable.

Dominik (1997) : WJ Dominik, *Roman Eloquence, Rhetoric in Society and Literature,* Routledge.

Duggan (2001) : JJ Duggan *The Romances of Chrétien de Troyes*, Yale University Press.

Drews (1975) : R Drews, *The Babylonian Chronicles and Berossus*, Iraq 37, no. 1. spring 1975, pp 39-55.

Droysen (1877) : JG Droysen *Geschichte des Hellenismus* I, *Geschichte Alexanders des Grossen*, Gotha.

Eckstein (1992) : AM Eckstein, *Notes on the Birth and Death of Polybius*, The American Journal of Philology 113, no. 3, autumn 1992, pp 387-406.

Ehrman, (2014) : BD Ehrman, *Forgery and Counterforgery; The Use of Literary Deceit in Early Christian Polemics,* Oxford University Press.

Eidinow-Kindt (2015) : E Eidinow and J Kindt, *The Oxford Handbook of Ancient Greek Religion*, Oxford University Press

Ellis (1994) : WM Ellis, *Ptolemy of Egypt*, Routledge.

Edson (1949) : C Edson, *The Tomb of Olympias*, Hesperia, The Journal of the American School of Classical Studies at Athens 18 no. 1, The Thirty-Sixth Report of the American Excavations in the Athenian Agora, January-March, 1949, pp. 84-95.

Engels *Note* (1978) : DW Engels, *A Note on Alexander's Death*, Classical Philology 73, no. 3, 1978, pp 224-228.

Engels (1978) : DW Engels, *Alexander the Great and the Logistics of the Macedonian Army,* University of California Press.

Engels (1980) : DW Engels, *Alexander's Intelligence System*, Classical Quarterly 30, 1980, pp 327-340.

Errington (1969) : RM Errington, *Bias in Ptolemy's History of Alexander*, Classical Quarterly, New Series 19, 1969, pp 233-242.

Errington (1970) : RM Errington, *From Babylon to Triparadeisus: 323-320 BC*, Journal of Hellenic Studies 90, 1970, pp 49-77.

Errington (1990) : RM Errington, *A History of Macedonia*, University of California Press.

Erskine (2002) : A Erskine, *Life After Death: Alexandria and the Body of Alexander*, Greece and Rome 49, no. 2, October 2002, pp 163-179.

Fears (1976) : JR Fears, *Silius Italicus, Cataphracti, and the Date of Quintus Curtius Rufus*, Classical Philology 71, no. 3, 1976, pp 214-223.

Fears (1976) : JR Fears, *The Solar Monarchy of Nero and the Imperial Panegyric of Q. Curtius Rufus*, Historia: Zeitschrift für Alte Geschichte 25, no. 4, 4th quarter 1976, pp 494-496.

Feldman (1996) : LH Feldman, *Studies in Hellenistic Judaism,* Brill.

Finkel (1988) : IL Finkel, *The Hanging Gardens of Babylon*, in PA Clayon and M Price (editors), *The Seven Wonders of the Ancient World*, Routledge.

Finlay (1973) : MI Finlay, *The Ancient Economy*, University of California Press, second edition, 1985.

Fitzgerald (1998) : R Fitzgerald (translator) Homer, *The Odyssey*, Farrar, Straus and Giroux.

Flower (1994) : MA Flower, *Theopompus of Chios, History and Rhetoric in the Fourth Century BC*, Clarendon Press.

Flower (1998) : MA Flower, *Simonides, Ephorus and Herodotus on the Battle of Thermopylae*, Classical Quarterly, New Series 48, no. 2, 1998, pp 365-379.

Fortenbaugh-Schütrumpf (2000) : W Fortenbaugh and E Schütrumpf (editors), *Demetrius of Phalerum*, Transaction Publishers.

Foster (1874) : BO Foster, *Livy*, Trollope Press, 2008 edition.

Fredericksmeyer (1981) : EA Fredericksmeyer, *Again the So-Called Tomb of Philip II*, American Journal of Archaeology 85, no. 3, July 1981, pp 330-334.

Fredericksmeyer (1990) : EA Fredericksmeyer, *Alexander and Philip: Emulation and Resentment*, Classical Journal 85, no.4, April-May 1990, pp 300-315.

Fraser (1996) : PM Fraser, *Cities of Alexander the Great*, Clarendon Press.

Freese (1920) : JH Freese, *The Library of Photius*, Society for Promoting Christian Knowledge.

Frier (1979) : BW Frier, *Libri Annales Pontificum Maximorum : The Origins of the Annalistic Tradition*, University of Michigan, 1999 edition.

Frolov (2013) : RM Frolov, *Public Meetings in Ancient Rome: Definitions of the Contiones in the Sources*, Graeco-Latina Brunenesia 18, no.1, 2013, pp 75-84.

Frost (1979) : F Frost, *The Dubious Origins of the Marathon*, American Journal of Ancient History 4, 1979, pp 159-163.

Fubini (1996): R Fubini, *Humanism and Truth: Valla Writes Against the Donation of Constantine*, Journal of the History of Ideas 57. no.1, January 1996, pp 79-86.

Fuhrmann (1972-3) : H Fuhrmann, *Einfluß und Verbreitung der pseudoisidorischen Fälschungen*, 3 vols, Schriften der Monumenta Germaniae Historica 24, nos. 1-3.

Gabriel (2006) : RA Gabriel, *Soldiers' Lives through History* – The Ancient World, Greenwood.

Gabriel (2010) : RA Gabriel, *Philip II of Macedonia, Greater than Alexander*, Potomac Books Inc.

Gaebel (2002) : RE Gaebel, *Cavalry Operations in the Ancient Greek World*, University of Oklahoma Press.

Garraghan (1946) : GJ Garraghan, *A Guide to Historical Method*, Fordham University Press.

Gawlikowski (1996) : M Gawlikowski, *Thapsacus and Zeugma. The Crossing of the Euphrates in Antiquity*, Iraq 58, 1996, pp 123-133.

Geiger (1979) : J Geiger, *Cornelius Nepos, De Regibus Exterarum Gentium*, Latomus 38, July-September 1979, pp 662-669.

Gelb (1955) : IJ Gelb, *The Name of Babylon*, Journal of the Institute of Asian Studies 1, 1955, pp 1-4.

Geller (1990) : MJ Geller, *Astronomical Diaries and Corrections of Diodorus*, Bulletin of the School of Oriental and African Studies, University of London 53, no. 1, 1990, pp 1-7.

George (1992) : AR George, *Babylonian topographical texts,* Orientalia Lovaniensia Analecta 40, Department Orientalistiek and Peeters.

Gershevitch-Fisher-Boyle (1968) : I Gershevitch , WB Fisher, JA Boyle (editors), *The Cambridge history of Iran*, Cambridge University Press.

Gibbon (1776 to 1789) : E Gibbon, *History of the Decline and Fall of the Roman Empire,* Penguin, 1996 edition; originally published as vol. I, 1776; vols. II, III, 1781; vols. IV, V,VI, 1788–1789.

Gibson (1998) : T Gibson, *The Platonic Canon*, the APA Newsletter 98, no. 1, 1998.

Gill-Wiseman (1993) : C Gill and TP Wiseman (editors), *Lies and Fiction in the Ancient World*, University of Exeter Press.

Goralski (1989) : J Goralski, *Arrian's Events after Alexander, Summary of Photius and Selected Fragments*, The Ancient World 19, nos. 3-4, 1989, pp 81-108.

Gottschalk (1980) : HB Gottschalk, *Heraclitus of Pontus*, Oxford University Press.

Goukowski (1978) : P Goukowski, *Essai sur les origins du mythe d'Alexandre, vol 1*, Publications de l'Universite de Nancy.

Grafton (1975) : A Grafton, *Joseph Scaliger and Historical Chronology*, History and Theory 14, 1975, pp 156-185.

Grafton (1983) : A Grafton, *Joseph Scaliger: A Study in the History of Classical Scholarship*, 2 volumes, Oxford University Press.

Grafton (1990) : A Grafton, *Forgers and Critics: Creativity and Duplicity in Western Scholarship*, Princeton University Press.

Grafton-Blair (1998) : A Grafton and A Blair (editors), *The Transmission of Culture in Early Modern Europe*, Shelby Cullom Davis Center for Historical Studies series, University of Pennsylvania Press.

Grafton-Most-Settis (2010) : A Grafton, GW Most, S Settis, *The Classical Tradition*, Harvard University Press.

Grainger (2007) : JD Granger, *Alexander the Great Failure,* Continuum Books.

Granier (1931) : F Granier, *Die makedonische Heeresversammlung: Ein Beitrag zum antiken Staatsrecht,* (Munchener Beitrage zur Papyrusforchung), 13, Munich, CH Beck.

Grant (1956) : M Grant (translator), *The Annals of Cornelius Tacitus*, Penguin.

Grant (1979) : M Grant, *Introduction to Suetonius the Twelve Caesars*, Penguin.

Grant (1995) : M Grant, *Greek and Roman Historians, information and misinformation*, Routledge.

Graves (1955) : R Graves, *The Greek Myths*, Penguin, 1992 edition.

Gray (1987) : V Gray, *Mimesis in Greek Historical Theory*, The American Journal of Philology 108, no. 3, autumn, 1987, pp 467-486.

Green (1970) : PM Green, *Alexander the Great*, Book Club Associates, 1973 edition.

Green (1974) : PM Green, *Alexander of Macedon, 356-323 BC: A Historical Biography*, University of California Press, 1991 edition.

Green (1990) : PM Green, *Alexander to Actium: The Historical Evolution of the Hellenistic Age,* University of California Press.

Green (2007) : PM Green, *The Hellenistic Age: A Short History,* Random House, London.

Greenwalt (1985) : W Greenwalt, *The Introduction of Caranus into the Argead King List*, The University of Santa Clara, January 1985.

Greenwalt (1999) : W Greenwalt, *Why Pella?*, Historia: Zeitschrift für Alte Geschichte 48, 2nd quarter, 1999, pp 158-183.

Gregory (1886) : CG Gregory, *The Quires in Greek Manuscripts*, The American Journal of Philology 7, no. 1, 1886, John Hopkins University Press.

Griffith (1935) : GT Griffiths, *The Mercenaries of the Hellenistic World*, Ares Publishers, 1984 edition.

Griffin (1986) : M Griffin, *Philosophy, Cato and Roman Suicide*, Greece and Rome 33, no. 2, October 1986, pp 192-202.

Grimal (1965) : P Grimal, *Hellenism and the Rise of Rome*, Delacorte Press.

Grmek (1989) : MD Grmek, *Diseases in the Ancient Greek World*, The John Hopkins University Press, 1989.

Gudeman *Greeks* (1894) : A Gudeman, *Literary Fraud Amongst the Greeks*, in Classical Studies in Honour of Henry Drisler, Macmillan, pp 52-74.

Gudeman *Romans* (1894) : A Gudeman, *Literary Fraud Amongst the Romans,* Transactions of the American Philological Association 25, 1894, pp 140-164.

Guthrie (1971) : WKC Guthrie, *The Sophists*, Cambridge University Press.

Guthrie-Fideler (1987) : KS Guthrie (translator) and D Fideler (editor), *The Pythagorean Sourcebook and Library*, Phanes Press.

Gutierrez (2012) : A Gutierrez, *The Seasons of Alternative Dispute Resolution: A Study of Mediation Tactics in the context of Ancient Greek Mythology*, The American Journal of Mediation 6, 2012.

Habicht (1999) : C Habicht, *Athens from Alexander to Antony*, Harvard University Press.

Hadjinicolaou (1997) : N Hadjinicolaou, *The Disputes about Alexander and his Glorification in the Visual Arts*, in N Hadjinicolaou (editor) catalogue of the exhibition Alexander the Great in European Art, Thessaloniki, 22 September 1997 to 11 January 1998.

Hadley (1969) : RA Hadley, *Hieronymus of Cardia and Early Seleucid Mythology*, Historia 18, 1969, pp 142-152.

Hadley (1974) : RA Hadley, *Royal Propaganda of Seleucus I and Lysimachus*, The Journal of Hellenic Studies 94, 1974, pp 50-65.

Hadley (2001) : RA Hadley, *A Possible Lost Source for the Career of Eumenes of Kardia*, Historia: Zeitschrift für Alte Geschichte 50, no. 1,1st quarter 2001, pp 3-33.

Hale (1961) : JR Hale, translator, *The Literary Works of Machiavelli*, Oxford University Press.

Hall (1913) : FW Hall, *A Companion to Classical Texts*, Clarendon Press.

Hamilton (1961) : JR Hamilton, *Cleitarchus and Aristobulus*, Historia 10, 1961, pp 448-458.

Hamilton (1971) : JR Hamilton, introduction to *Arrian, The Campaigns of Alexander*, Penguin.

Hamilton (1988) : JR Hamilton, *The Date of Quintus Curtius Rufus*, Historia: Zeitschrift für Alte Geschichte 37, 1988.

Hammond (1978) : NGL Hammond, *Philip's Tomb in Historical Context*, Greek, Roman and Byzantine Studies 19, no.4, 1978, pp 331-350.

Hammond *Cavalry* (1978) : NGL Hammond, *A Cavalry Unit in the Army of Antigonus Monophthalmus: Asthippoi*, Classical Quarterly 29, no. 1, 1978, pp 128-135.

Hammond (1980) : NGL Hammond, *Training in Use of the Sarissa and its Effect in Battle*, Antichthon 14, 1980, pp 53-63.

Hammond (1985) : NGL Hammond, *Some Macedonian Offices: c. 336-309 BC*, Journal of Hellenic Studies 105, 1985, pp 156-160.

Hammond (1988) : NGL Hammond, *The Royal Journal of Alexander,* Historia 37, 1988, pp 129-150.

Hammond *Journal* (1989) : NGL Hammond, *Aspects of Alexander's Journal and Ring in His Last Days*, The American Journal of Philology 110, no. 1, spring 1989, pp 155-160.

Hammond (1989) : NGL Hammond, *Arms and the King: The Insignia of Alexander the Great*, Phoenix 43, no. 3, autumn 1989, pp 217-224.

Hammond (1991) : NGL Hammond, *The Miracle that was Macedonia,* Sidgwick and Jackson.

Hammond *Tombs* (1991) : NGL Hammond, *The Royal Tombs at Vergina, Evolution and Identities*, The Annual of the British School at Athens 86, 1991, pp 69-82.

Hammond (1993) : NGL Hammond, *Sources for Alexander the Great: An Analysis of Plutarch's Life and Arrian's Anabasis Alexandrou.* Cambridge University Press.

Hammond (1994) : NGL Hammond, *Collected Studies III, Alexander and his Successors in Macedonia*, Adolf M Hakkert.

Hammond *Philip* (1994) : NGL Hammond, *Philip of Macedon*, Duckworth, 2002 edition.

Hammond (1996) : NGL Hammond, *The Early History of Macedonia*, The Ancient World 27, no.1, 1996, pp 67-71.

Hammond (1998) : NGL Hammond, *Portents, Prophesies and Dreams in Diodorus books 14-17*, Roman and Byzantine Studies, 39, no. 4, 1998, pp 407-428.

Hammond (1999) : NGL Hammond, *What May Philip Have Learnt as a Hostage in Thebes?*, Greek Roman and Byzantine Studies 38, no. 4 1997, pp 355-372.

Hammond-Griffith (1979) : NGL Hammond and GT Griffith, *A History of Macedonia: Volume II : 550-336 B.C.*, Oxford University Press.

Hammond-Walbank (1988) : NGL Hammond and FW Walbank, *A History of Macedonia*, Oxford University Press.

Hammond-Atkinson (2013) : M Hammond (translator) and J Atkinson (introduction and notes), *Alexander the Great, The Anabasis and the Indica*, Oxford University Press.

Hannah (2005) : R Hannah, *Greek and Roman Calendars, Constructions of Time on the Classical World,* Gerald Duckworth and Company.

Hansen (1999) : MH Hansen, *The Athenian Democracy in the Age of Demosthenes, Structure, Principles and Ideology,* University of Oklahoma Press.

Hanson (1991) : VD Hanson (editor), *Hoplites, The Classical Greek Battle Experience*, Routledge.

Harris (1999) : MH Harris, *History of Libraries in the Western World*, 4th edition, Rowman and Littlefield Publishers Inc.

Harris (1986) : R Harris, *Selling Hitler*, Faber & Faber.

Harris (2009) : WV Harris, *Dreams and Experience in Classical Antiquity*, Harvard University Press.

Harris (1911) : VM Harris, *Ancient Curious and Famous Wills*, Little Brown and Company.

Hatzopoulos (1996) : MB Hatzopoulos, *Macedonian Institutions under the Kings 1, A Historical and Epigraphic Study*, Meletemata 22, 1996.

Hauben (1977) : H Hauben, *The First War of the Successors (321BC): Chronological and Historical Problems*, Ancient Society 8, 1977, pp 85-120.

Heath (1913) : Sir Thomas Heath, *Aristarchus of Samos, The Ancient Copernicus*, Clarendon Press.

Heckel (1978) : W Heckel, *Kleopatra or Eurydike? Phoenix* 32, no.2, 1978, pp 155-158.

Heckel *Somatophylakes* (1978) : W Heckel, *The "Somatophylakes" of Alexander the Great: Some Thoughts,* Historia: Zeitschrift für Alte Geschichte 28, no. 1,1ˢᵗ quarter 1978, pp 224-228.

Heckel *A and A* (1978) : W Heckel : *On Attalus and Atalante*, Classical Quarterly 28, no. 2, 1978, pp 377-382.

Heckel (1984) **:** W Heckel, Introduction to *Quintus Curtius Rufus, The History of Alexander*, Penguin.

Heckel (1987) : W Heckel, *Fifty-Two Anonymae in the History of Alexander*, Historia: Zeitschrift für Alte Geschichte 36, no.1, 1ˢᵗ quarter 1987, pp 114-119.

Heckel (1988) : W Heckel, *The Last Days and Testament of Alexander the Great*, Franz Steiner Verlag GMBH.

Heckel (1992) : W Heckel, *The Marshals of Alexander's Empire,* Routledge.

Heckel (1993) : W Heckel, review of NGL Hammond, *Sources for Alexander the Great: An Analysis of Plutarchs' Life and Arrian's Anabasis Alexandrou*, Cambridge University Press, in the Bryn Mawr Classical Review 97.4.8., 1993.

Heckel (2006) : W Heckel, *Who's Who in the Age of Alexander the Great,* Blackwell Publishing.

Heckel *Sarcophagus* (2006), W Heckel, *Mazaeus, Callisthenes and the Alexander Sarcophagus*, Historia: Zeitschrift für Alte Geschichte 55, no. 4, pp 385-396.

Heckel (2007) : W Heckel, *Nicanor son of Balacrus*, Greek, Roman and Byzantine Studies 47,2007, pp 401-412.

Heckel (2008) : W Heckel, *The Conquests of Alexander the Great,* Cambridge University Press.

Heckel-Yardley (1997) : W Heckel and JC Yardley, *Justin, Epitome of the Philippic History of Pompeius Trogus, Volume 1, Books 11-12*, Clarendon Press.

Heckel-Yardley (2004) : W Heckel and JC Yardley, *Alexander the Great: Historical Sources in Translation,* Blackwell Publishing.

Heckel-Yardley-Wheatley (2011) : *Justin: Epitome of the Philippic History of Pompeius Trogus, Volume II: Books 13-15: The Successors to Alexander the Great,* Clarendon Press.

Heckel-Jones (2006) : W Heckel and R Jones, *Macedonian Warrior, Alexander's elite infantryman*, Osprey Publishing.

Hedrick (2000) : CW Hedrick, *History and Silence; Purge and Rehabilitation of Memory in Late Antiquity*, University of Texas Press.

Hegel (1837) : GWF Hegel, *Lectures on The Philosophy of History,* originally delivered as lectures at the University of Berlin, 1821, 1824, 1827, 1831. First published by Eduard Gans in 1837 and by Karl Hegel in 1840 and first full English edition by HB Nisbet in 1974, Cambridge University Press.

Heisserer (1973) : AJ Heisserer, *Alexander's Letter to the Chians: A Redating of ?*, Historia: Zeitschrift für Alte Geschichte 22, no. 2, 2nd quarter 1973, pp 191-204.

Heller-Roazen (2002) : D Heller-Roazen, *Tradition's Destruction: On the Library of Alexandria,* October 100, Obsolescence, spring 2002, pp 133-153.

Herm (1975) : G Herm, *The Phoenicians, The Purple Empire of the Ancient World*, William Morrow and Company.

Hernandez (2009) : JPS Hernandez, *Procles the Carthaginian: A North African Sophist in Pausanias' Periegesis*, Institute for the History of Ancient Civilizations, Northeast Normal University.

Higbie (2003) : C Higbie, *The Lindian Chronicle and the Greek Creation of Their Past,* Oxford University Press.

Highet (1949) : G Highet, *The Classical Tradition, Greek and Roman Influences on Western Literature*, Oxford University Press.

Hill (2002) : J Hill, *The Ephemerides of Alexander the Great: Fact and Fiction*, Daedalus 3, no. 2, July 2002, pp 11-17.

Himmelfarb (1986) : G Himmelfarb, *Who Now Reads Macaulay?*, in his *Marriage and Morals Among The Victorians. And other Essays,* Faber and Faber, pp 163-177.

Hochart (1889) : P Hochart, *De l'Authenticite des Annales et des Histoires de Tacite*, G Gounouilhou.

Hojte (2009) : JM Hojte, *The Death and Burial of Mithridates,* in his *Mithridates VI and the Pontic Kingdom*, Aarhus University Press, pp 121-130.

Holt (1996) : FL Holt, *Euktratides of Baktria,* The Ancient World 27, no. 1, 1996, pp 72-76.

Holt (2005) : FL Holt, *Into the Land of Bones, Alexander the Great in Afghanistan,* University of California Press.

Hornblower (1981) : J Hornblower *Hieronymus of Cardia*, Oxford University Press.

Hornblower (2004) : S Hornblower, *Thucydides and Pindar. Historical Narrative and the World of Epinikian Poetry*, Oxford University Press.

Howell- Prevenier (2001) : M Howell and W Prevenier, *From Reliable Sources, An Introduction to Historical Method*, Cornell University Press.

Huffman (1993) : C Huffman, *Philolaus of Croton Pythagorean and Presocratic: A Commentary on the Fragments and Testimonia with Interpretive Essays*, Cambridge University Press.

Hutchinson (1997) : G. Hutchinson, *Poison Arrows*, British Medical Journal, 8th March 1997.

Ifrah (2000) : G Ifrah *The Universal History of Numbers, from Prehistory to the Invention of the Computer,* John Wiley and Sons.

Iglesias-Zoido (2010) : JC Iglesias-Zoido, *The Pre-Battle speeches of Alexander at Issus and Gaugamela,* Greek, Roman, and Byzantine Studies 50, 2010, pp 215-241.

Iossif-Chankowski-Lorber (2007) : PP Iossif, AS Chankowski, CC Lorber (editors), *More than Men, Less than Gods, Studies on Royal Cult And Imperial Worship,* Studia Hellenistica 51, Proceedings of the International Colloqium Organised by the Belgian School at Athens, November 1-2, 2007.

Jacoby (1923-1958) : F Jacoby, *Die Fragmente der griechischen Historiker I-II* (FGrHist), Berlin.

Jaeger (1939) : W Jaeger, *Paideia, The Ideals of Greek Culture,* Oxford University Press, 1965 edition.

Jarde (1997) : A Jarde, *The Formation of the Greek People,* Routledge, 1997 edition.

Jenkins (1991) : K Jenkins, *Rethinking History,* Routledge.

Jobes-Silva (2001) : K Jobes and M Silva, *Invitations to the Septuagint,* Paternoster Press.

Jones (1868) : WHS Jones, *Hippocrates Collected Works I,* Harvard University Press.

Jones (1783) : Sir William Jones, *On the Gods of Hellas, Italy and India,* extracted from *Asiatic Researches,* 1788, pp 221-75.

Kagan (1965) : D Kagan (editor), *The Great Dialogue: A History of Greek Political Thought from Homer to Polybius,* The Free Press.

Kamen (2013) : D Kamen, *Status in Classical Athens,* Princeton University Press.

Kaufman (1932) : DB Kaufman, *Poisons and Poisoning Among the Romans,* Classical Philology 27, no. 2, April 1932, pp 156-167.

Kebric (1977) : RB Kebric, *In the Shadow of Macedon: Duris of Samos,* Franz Steiner Verlag GMBH.

Kennedy (1989) : GA Kennedy, *The Cambridge history of literary criticism: Volume 1, Classical criticism,* Cambridge University Press.

Kenyon (1899) : G Kenyon, *The Paleography of Greek Papyri,* Ares Publishers, 1998 edition.

Ker (2009) : J Ker, *The Death of Seneca,* Oxford University Press.

Kern (1999) : PB Kern, *Ancient Siege Warfare,* Indiana University Press.

Keyser (1994) : PT Keyser, *The Use of Artillery by Philipp II and Alexander the Great,* The Ancient World 25, no.1, 1994, pp 27-59

Keyser (2011) : PT Keyser, *The Last Will and Testament of Ajax,* Illinois Classical Studies 33-34, 2011, pp 109-126.

Kimball (2000) : R Kimball, *Plutarch and the Issue of Character,* The New Criterion Online 19, no. 4, December 2000.

Koldeway (1913) : R Koldeway, *Das wieder erstehende Babylon,* JC Hinrichs.

Kotrc-Walters (1979) : RF Kotrc and KR Walters, *A bibliography of the Galenic Corpus. A newly researched list and arrangement of the titles of the treatises extant in Greek, Latin, and Arabic.* Transactions and Studies of the College of

Physicians of Philadelphia 1, no. 4, December 1979, pp 256-304.

Kraus (1994) : CS Kraus (editor), *Ab Urbe Condita Book VI*, Cambridge University Press.

Kuhrt (1983) : A Kuhrt, *The Cyrus Cylinder and Archaemenid Imperial Policy,* in Journal of Studies of the Old Testament 25, 1983, pp. 83-97.

Lane Fox (1973) : R Lane Fox, *Alexander the Great*, Penguin, 1986 edition.

Lane Fox (1980) : R Lane Fox, *The Search for Alexander*, Little Brown and Company.

Lane Fox (2011) : R Lane Fox (editor), *Brill's Companion to Ancient Macedon, Studies in the Archaeology and History of Macedon, 650 BC-300AD*, Brill.

Lattey (1917) : C Lattey, *The Diadochi and the Rise of King-Worship*, The English Historical Review 32, no. 127, 1917, pp 321-334.

Lattimore (1953) : R Lattimore, introduction to *Aeschylus Orestia,* The University of Chicago Press.

Lazenby (1987) : JF Lazenby, *The Diekplous*, Greece and Rome, Second Series 34, no. 2, October 1987, pp 169-177.

Leckie (1906) : EH Leckie in JB Bury (editor), *The History of the Decline and Fall of the Roman Empire*, Fred De Fau and Company.

Lehmann (1980) : PW Lehmann, *The So-Called Tomb of Philip II: A Different Interpretation*, American Journal of Archaeology 84, no.4, October 1980, pp 527-531.

Lenden (2005) : JE Lenden, *Soldiers and Ghosts, A History of Battle in Classical Antiquity*, Yale Press.

Levene (1993) : DS Levene, *Religion in Livy*, Brill.

Levick (1985) : B Levick (1985) *L Verginius Rufus and the Four Emperors,* Rheinisches Museum für Philologie 128, 1985, pp 318-346.

Levine (1991) : MJ Levine, *The Battle of the Books: History and Literature in the Augustan Age*, Cornell University Press, 1994 edition.

Ligota (1987) : CR Ligota, *Annius of Viterbo and Historical Method, Journal of the Warburg and Courtauld Institutes* 50, 1987, pp 44-56.

Lincoln (2002) : B Lincoln, *Isaac Newton and Oriental Jones on Myth, Ancient History and the Relative Prestige of Peoples*, History of Religions 42, no. 1, August 2002, pp 1-18.

Lock (1977) : R Lock, *The Macedonian Army Assembly in the Time of Alexander the Great*, Classical Philology 72, no. 2, 1977, pp 91-107.

Long (1986) : AA Long, *Hellenistic Philosophy, Stoics, Epicureans, Sceptics*, University of California Press.

Luch (2009) : A Luch (editor) *Molecular, Clinical and Environmental Toxicology, Volume 1: Molecular Toxicology*, Birkhäuser Verlag AG.

Lynch (1998) : J Lynch, *Preventing Play: Annotating the Battle of the Books*, Texas Studies in Literature and Language 40, no. 3, 1998, pp 370-388.

Macaulay (1828) : TB Macaulay, *History,* (a review of H Neele's *The Romance of History*) first published in the Edinburgh Review May 1828, p 361, reproduced by H Neele (1889) *The Miscellaneous Writings and Speeches of Lord Macaulay*, Longmans, Green and Company.

Madan (1893) F Madan, *Books in Manuscript*, Kegan Paul Trench, Trubner and Company.

Magee (1998) : B Magee, *The Story of Philosophy*, Dorling Kindersley Ltd.

Mahaffy (1888) : JP Mahaffy, *Alexander's Empire*, T Fisher Unwin.

Mallory (1989) : JP Mallory, *In Search of the Indo-Europeans, Language, Archeology and Myth*, Thames and Hudson.

Malkin (1998) : I Malkin, *The Returns of Odysseus, Colonization and Ethnicity*, University of California Press.

Malthus (1798) : T Malthus, *An Essay on the Principle of Population*, originally published anonymously and printed for J Johnson in St. Paul's Churchyard.

Manfreddi (2001) : M Manfreddi, *Alexander, Child of a Dream, Alexander The Sands of Ammon: Alexander, The Ends of the Earth*, McMillan.

Manning (2005) : JG Manning, *Land tenure, rural space, and the political economy of Ptolemaic Egypt (332 BC-30 BC)*, Princeton/Stanford Working Papers in Classics, May 2005.

Manti (1992) : PA Manti, *The Sarissa of the Macedonian Infantry*, The Ancient World 25, no. 1, 1992, pp 30-42.

Marasco (2011) : G Marasco (editor), *Autobiographies and Memoirs in Antiquity*, Brill.

Marchesi (2008) : I Marchesi, *The art of Pliny's letters: a poetics of allusion in the private correspondence*, Cambridge University Press.

Margotta (1968) : R Margotta, *The Story of Medicine*, Golden Press.

Markle (1977) : MM Markle, *The Macedonian Sarissa, Spear and Related Armour*, American Journal of Archaeology 81, 1977, pp 323-339.

Marmodoro-Hill (2013) : A Marmodoro and J Hill (editors), *The Author's Voice in Classical and Late Antiquity*, Oxford University Press.

Martí-Ibáñez (1961) : F Martí-Ibáñez, *A Prelude to Medical History*, MD Publications Inc.

Martinez (2011) : J Martinez, *Fakes and Forgers of Classical Literature*, Alfonso Martinez Diez.

Marsden (1971) : EW Marsden, *Greek and Roman Artillery, Technical Treatises*, Oxford University Press.

Mayor (2003) : A Mayor, *Greek Fire, Poison Arrows and Scorpion Bombs, Biological and Chemical Warfare in the Ancient World*, Overlook Duckworth.

Mayor (2010) : A Mayor, *The Deadly River Styx and the Death of Alexander*, Princeton/Stanford Working Papers in Classics, version 1.2, September 2010.

Mayor (2014) : A Mayor, *The Amazons, Lives and Legends of Warrior Women across the Ancient World*, Princeton University Press.

McCullagh (1984) : CB McCullagh, *Justifying Historical Descriptions*, Cambridge University Press.

McDowell (1972) : J McDowell, *Evidence that Demands a Verdict*, Nelson Publishers.

McGing (2010) : B McGing, *Polybius' Histories*, Oxford University Press.

McGroaty (2006) : K McGroaty, *Did Alexander the Great read Xenophon?*, Hemathena 181, winter 2006, pp 105-124.

McKechnie (1995) : P McKechnie, *Diodorus Siculus and Hephaestion's Pyre*, Classical Quarterly, New Series 45, no. 2, 1995, pp 418-432.

McKechnie (1999) : P McKechnie, *Manipulation of Themes in Quintus Curtius*

Rufus Book 10, Historia Zeitschrift für Alte Geschichte 48, no. 1, 1999, pp 44-60.

McKitrerick (2004) : R McKitrerick, *History and Memory in the Carolingian World*, Cambridge University Press.

McInerney (2007) : J McInerney, *Arrian and the Greek Alexander Romance*, The Classical World 100, no. 4, summer 2007, pp 424-430.

Meiggs (1982) : R Meiggs, *Trees and Timber in the Ancient Mediterranean World*, Clarendon Press.

Meijer-Nijf (1992) : F Meijer and O van Nijf, *Trade, Transport and Society in the Ancient World*, Routledge.

Merkelback (1954) : R Merkelback, *Die Quellen des griechischen Alexanderromans*, CH Beck, second edition 1977.

Merzbach-Boyer (1968) : CB Boyer and UC Merzback, *A History of Mathematics*, John Wiley and Sons, third edition 2011.

Metzger (1972) : BM Metzger, *Literary Forgeries and Canonical Pseudepigrapha*, Journal of Biblical Literature 91, no 1, 1972, pp 3-24.

Metzger (1992) : BM Metzger, *The Text of the New Testament. Its Transmission, Corruption and Restoration,* Oxford University Press.

Miller (1991) : MCJ Miller, *The Regal Coinage of Kassander*, The Ancient World 22, no. 2, 1991, pp 49-55.

Milns (1966) : RD Milns, *The Date of Curtius Rufus and the "Historiae Alexandri"*, Latomus 25, no. 3, July-Sept 1966, pp 490-507.

Milns (1968) : RD Milns, *Alexander the Great*, Robert Hale.

Milns (1971) : RD Milns, *The Hypaspists of Alexander III, Some Problems*, Historia 20, 1971, pp 186-195.

Milns (1981) : RD Milns, *'Asthippoi' Again*, Classical Quarterly, New Series 31, no. 2, December 1981, pp 347-354.

Mitchell (2007) : L Mitchell, *Born to rule? Succession in the Argead royal house*, in W Heckel, L Tritle, P Wheatley, *Alexander's Empire: Formulation to Decay*, Claremont, pp 61-74.

Mixter (1992) : JR Mixter, *The Length of the Macedonian sarissa during the reigns of Philip II and Alexander the Great,* The Ancient World 23, no.2, 1992, pp 21-29.

Momigliano (1954) : AD Momigliano, *An Unsolved problem of Historical Forgery: The Scriptores Historiae Augustae,* Journal of the Warburg and Courtauld Institutes 17, no 1-2, 1954, pp 22-46.

Momigliano (1966) : AD Momigliano, *Studies in Historiography*, Harper Torchbooks.

Momigliano (1977) : AD Momigliano, *Essays in Ancient and Modern Historiography*, Blackwell.

Mommsen (1870) : CMT Mommsen, *Cornelius Tacitus und Cluvius Rufus*, in Hermes 4, 1870, pp 320-322, republished in Gesammelte Schriften 7, 1909, pp 210-215.

Mordechai (2007) : A Mordechai, *The Archeological Illumination of Josephus' Narrative at the Battles of Yodefat and Gamla*, in Z Rodgers, *Making history: Josephus and historical method,* pp 372–384, Brill.

Morford (1973) : M Morford, *The Neronian Literary Revolution*, The Classical Journal 68, no. 3, 1973, pp 210-215.

Morrison-Coates-Rankov (2000) : JS Morrison, JE Coates, NB Rankov, *The Athenian Trireme, The History and Reconstruction of an Ancient Greek Warship*, Cambridge University Press.

Mossman (1988) : JM Mossman, *Tragedy and Epic in Plutarch's Alexander,* The Journal of.Hellenic Studies 108, 1988, pp 83-93.

Muller (1841) : CW Muller, *Fragmenta Historicorum Graecorum, vol. I*, Firmin-Didot.

Muller (1853-1870) : CW Muller, *Fragmenta Historicum Graecorum*, Firmin-Didot.

Munro (1899) : JAR Munro, *A Letter from Antigonus to Scepsis, 311 B.C.*, The Journal of Hellenic Studies 19, 1899, pp 330-340.

Murray (1915) : G Murray, *Stoic Philosophy*, Conway Memorial Lecture delivered March 16th 1915, GP Putnams and Sons.

Murray (2012) : WM Murray, *The Age of Titans, The Rise and Fall of the Hellenistic Navies*, Oxford University Press.

Musgrave (1991) : JH Musgrave, *The Human Remains from Vergina Tombs I, II and III: An Overview*, The Ancient World 22, no. 2, 1991, pp 3-9.

Musgrave-Prag-Neave-Lane Fox (2010) : JH Musgrave, AJNW Prag, R Neave, R Lane Fox, *The Occupants of Tomb II at Vergina. Why Arrhidaios and Eurydice must be excluded*, International Journal of Medical Science 7, no. 6, 2010, pp 1-15.

Mylonas (1964) : G Mylonas : *Priam's Troy and the Date of its Fall,* Hesperia 33, 1964, pp 52-380.

Nauta-van Dam-Smolenars (2006) : RR. Nauta, HJ van Dam, JJL Smolenars, *Flavian Poetry*, Mnemosyne Supplementum 270, 2006, pp 315-328. Brill.

Needham (1979) : P Needham, *Twelve Centuries of Bookbindings 400-1600*, The Pierpont Library, Oxford University Press.

Neugebauer (1957) : O Neugebauer, *The Exact Sciences in Antiquity*, Dover Publications, 1969 edition.

Nolan (1992) : B Nolan, *Chaucer and the Tradition of the Roman Antique*, Cambridge University Press.

Niebuhr (1844) : BG Niebuhr, *The History of Rome, Volume III*, Lea and Blanchard.

Nietzsche (1974) : F Nietzsche, *The Gay Science,* Vintage Books.

Nisetich (1980) : FJ Nisetich, *Pindar's Victory Songs*, John Hopkins University Press.

Nutton (1984) : V Nutton, *From Galen to Alexander, aspects of medicine and medical practice in late antiquity,* Dunbarton Oaks Papers.

Oakley (2005) : SP Oakley, *A Commentary on Livy VI-X: Volume 3, Book 9*, Clarendon Press.

Oates (1979) : J Oates, *Babylon*, Thames and Hudson.

Ober (1998) : J Ober, *Political Dissent in Democratic Athens, Intellectual Critics of Popular Rule*, Princeton University Press.

Ogden (2001) : D Ogden, *The Ancient Greek Oracles of the Dead*, Acta Classica 44, 2001, pp 167-195.

Oikonomides-Miller (1995) : AN Oikonomides and MCJ Miller, *Hanno the Carthaginian, Periplus or Circumnavigation (of Africa)*, Ares Publishers.

Olbrycht (2008) : MJ Olbrycht, *Curtius Rufus, The Macedonian Mutiny at Opis and Alexander's Iranian Policy in 324 BC,* in Jakub Pigón (editor) *The Children of Herodotus: Greek and Roman Historiography and Related Genres,* Cambridge Scholars Publishing, pp 231-252.

Ormerod (1997) : HA Ormerod, *Piracy in the Ancient World,* The John Hopkins University Press.

O'Neil (2000) : JL O'Neil, *Royal Authority and City Law Under Alexander and his Hellenistic Successors,* Classical Quarterly 50, no. 2, 2000, pp 424-431.

O'Sullivan (2009) : L O'Sullivan, *The Regime of Demetrius of Phalerum in Athens, 317-307 BCE,* Brill.

Pagels (1979) : E Pagels, *The Gnostic Gospels,* Random House.

Parke (1933) : HW Parke, *Greek Mercenary Soldiers,* Ares Publishers.

Parke (1985) : HW Parke, *The Massacre of the Branchidae,* The Journal of Hellenic Studies 105,1985, pp 59-68.

Pearson (1955) : L Pearson, *The Diary and Letters of Alexander the Great,* Historia: Zeitschrift für Alte Geschichte 3, no. 4, 1955, pp 429-455.

Pearson (1960) : L Pearson, *The Lost Histories of Alexander the Great,* The American Philological Association.

Pernot (2000) : L Pernot, *Rhetoric in Antiquity,* The Catholic University of America Press, 2005 edition.

Pitcher (2009) : L Pitcher, *Writing Ancient History,* IB Tauris.

Polcaro-Valsecchi-Verderame (2008) : VF Polcaro, GB Valsecchi, L Verderame *The Gaugamela Battle Eclipse, An Archeoastronomical Anaylsis,* Mediterranean Archeology and Archeometry 8, no. 2, 2008, pp 55-64.

Polo (2011) : FP Polo, *The Consul at Rome, The Civil Functions of the Consuls in the Roman Republic,* Cambridge University Press.

Pollitt (1972) : JJ Pollitt, *Art and Experience in Classical Greece,* Cambridge University Press.

J Porter (2006) : J Porter (editor), *Classical Pasts, The Classical Traditions of Greece and Rome,* Princeton University Press.

Potter (2006) : DSA Potter, *Companion to the Roman Empire,* Blackwell Publishing.

Powell (1939) : JE Powell, *The sources of Plutarch's Alexander,* Journal of Hellenic Studies 59, 1939, pp 229-240.

Pownall (2004) : F Pownall, *Lessons from the Past: The Moral Use of History in Fourth-Century Prose,* Ann Arbor, University of Michigan Press.

Pycior (1997) : HM Pycior, *Symbols, Impossible Numbers and Entanglements; British Algebra Through the Commentaries on Newton's Universal Arithmetick,* Cambridge University Press.

Raeburn-Feeney (2004): D Raeburn (translator) and D Feeney (introduction), *Ovid, Metamorphoses,* Penguin.

Rahe (1981) : P Rahe, *The Annihilation of the Sacred Band at Chaeronea,* American Journal of Archaeology 85, no.1, 1981, pp 84-87.

Ramsay (1923) : WM Ramsay, *Military Operations on the North Front of Mount Taurus (Continued),* The Journal of Hellenic Studies 43, no. 1, 1923, pp 1-10.

Reeve (2001) : CDC Reeve, *Introduction to The Basic Works of Aristotle,* The Modern Library.

Reade (2000) : J Reade, *Alexander the Great and the Hanging Gardens of Babylon*, Iraq 62, 2000, pp 195-217.

Renault (1969,1972, 1981) : M Renault, *Fire from Heaven; The Persian Boy; Funeral Games,* Penguin.

Renault (1975) : M Renault, *The Nature of Alexander*, Pantheon Books.

Revilo (1949) : OP Revilo, *The Claudian Letter I* , American Journal of Archaeology 53, no. 3, 1949, pp. 249-257.

Reynolds-Tracy (1990) : FE Reynolds and D Tracy (editors), *Myth and Philosophy*, University of New York Press.

Rhodes-Osborn (2003) : PJ Rhodes and R Osborn (editors), *Greek Historical Inscriptions, 404-323 BC.*, Oxford University Press.

Riginos (1994) : AS Riginos, *The Wounding of Philip II of Macedon: Fact and Fabrication*, The Journal of Hellenic Studies 114, 1994, pp 103-119.

Riedweg (2002) : C Riedweg, *Pythagoras, His Life, Teachings and Influence*, Cornell University Press.

Robins (1987) : RH Robins, *The Techne Grammatike of Dionysius Thrax in Historical Perspective*, in P Swiggers and W van Hoecke (editors) *Mots et Parties du Discours*, Leuven University Press, pp 9-37.

Roberts (1984) : RW Roberts, *City of Sokrates: an Introduction to Classical Athens*, Routledge, 1998 edition.

Robbins (2001) : M Robbins, *The Collapse of the Bronze Age, The Story of Greece, Troy, Israel, Egypt an the People of the Sea*, Authors Choice Press.

Robinson (1953) : CA Robinson, *The History of Alexander the Great: a Translation of the Extant Fragments and the Ephemerides of Alexander's Expedition*, Ares Publishers.

Robinson-Hughes (1969) : FCR Robinson and PC Hughes, *Lampron : Castle of Armenian Cilicia*, Anatolian Studies 19, 1969, pp 183-207.

Rodgers (1937) : WL Rodgers, *Greek and Roman Naval Warfare, A Study of Strategy and Ship Design from Salamis (480 B.C) to Actium (31 B.C)*, Naval Institute Press, 1977 edition.

Rodrigues Adrados (2000) : FR Adrados, *History of the Graeco-Latin Fable II, The Fable during the Roman Empire & in the Middle Ages,* Brill.

Roisman (1994) : J Roisman, *Ptolemy and his Rivals in the History of Alexander*, Classical Quarterly 34, 1994, pp 373-385.

Roisman (2012) : J Roisman, *Alexander's Veterans and the Early Wars of the Successors*, University of Texas Press.

Roisman-Worthington (2010) : J Roisman and I Worthington (editors), *A Companion to Ancient Macedonia*, Wiley-Blackwell.

Rolfe (1913) : JC Rolfe, *Suetonius and His Biographies*, Proceedings of the American Philosophical Society 52, no. 209, April 1913, pp 206-225.

Roller (1997) : MB Roller, *Color-Blindness: Cicero's Death, Declamation, and the Production of History*, Classical Philology 92, no. 2, April 1997, pp 109-130.

Roller (1981) : LE Roller, *Funeral Games in Greek Art*, American Journal of Archaeology 85, no. 2, 1981, pp. 107-119.

Romane (1987) : JP Romane, *Alexander's Siege of Tyre*, The Ancient World 16, nos. 3-4, 1987, pp 79-90.

Romm (1988) : JS Romm, *Herodotus*, Yale University Press.

Romm (2011) : JS Romm, *Ghost on the Throne, The Death of Alexander the Great and the War for Crown and Empire*, Alfred A Knopf.

Roseman (1994) : CH Roseman, *Pytheas of Massalia, On the Ocean*, Ares Publishers.

Rostovtzeff (1936) : MI Rostovtzeff, *The Hellenistic World and its Economic Development*, The American Historical Review 41, no. 2, January 1936, pp 231-252.

Ross (1878) : JW Ross, *Tacitus and Bracciolini, The Annals Forged in the XVth Century*, originally self-published in London in 1878 and now available from Project Gutenberg EBook at http://www.dominiopublico.gov.br/download/gu009098.pdf.

Rozen (1967) : K Rozen, *Political Documents on Hieronymus of Cardia (323-302 BC)*, Acta Classica 10, 1967, pp 41-94.

Roussineau (2001) : G Roussineau, *Le Roman de Perceforest*, published through 1987-2001, Droz.

Rummel (2008) : E Rummel, *A Companion to Biblical Humanism and Scholasticism in the Age of Erasmus*, Brill.

Russell (1946) : B Russell, *History of Western Philosophy*, Routledge, 2004 edition.

Ryder (1975) : TTB Ryder, *Demosthenes and Aeschines*, Penguin.

Sachs-Hunger (1988) : A Sachs and H Hunger, *Astronomical diaries and related texts from Babylon* 1, Verlag der Osterreichischen Akademie der Wissenschaften.

Sacks (1990) : K Sacks, *Diodorus Siculus and the First Century*, Princeton University Press.

Saggs (1962) : HWF Saggs, *The Greatness that was Babylon*, The New American Library.

Saggs (1984) : HWF Saggs, *The Might that was Assyria*, Sidgwick and Jackson.

Samansiri-Weerakoon (2007) : KAP Samansiri and DK Weerakoon, *Feeding Behaviour of Asian Elephants in the Northwastern Region of Sri Lanka*, Gajah: Journal of the International Union for Conservation of Nature/Special Survival Commission Asian Elephant Specialist Group 2, 2007, pp 27-34.

Samuel (1986) : AE Samuel, *The Earliest Elements in the Alexander Romance*, Historia: Zeitschrift für Alte Geschichte 35, no. 4, 4th quarter 1986, pp 427-437.

Sandy (1921) : JE Sandy, *A Companion to Latin Studies edited for the Syndics of the University Press (3rd edition)*, Cambridge University Press.

Saatsoglou-Paliadeli (1999) : C Saatsoglou-Paliadeli, *In the Shadow of History: The Emergence of Archaeology*, The Annual of the British School at Athens 94, 1999, pp 353-367.

Sayer (1995) : MH Sayar: *A recently discovered seleukidische mountain fortress in the ostkilikischen Taurus*, Antique World 26, 1995, pp 279-282.

Schachermeyr (1944) : F Schachermeyr, *Indogermanen und Orient, Ihre kulturelle und machpolitische Auseinandersetzung im Allertum*, W Kohlhammer.

Schachermeyr (1949) : F Schachermeyr, *Alexander der Grosse: Ingenium und Macht*, Pustet.

Schachermeyr (1970) : F Schachermeyr, *Alexander in Babylon und die reichsordnung nach seinem Tode*, Verlag der Osterreichischen Akademie der Wissenschaften.

Schäfer (2002) : C Schäfer, *Eumenes von Kardia und der Kampf um die Macht im Alexanderreich*, Buchverlag Marthe Clauss.

Schamp (2000) : J Schamp, *Les Vies des dix orateurs attiques*, Editions Universitaires, Fribourg.

Schoff (1915) : WH Schoff : *The Eastern Iron Trade of the Roman Empire*, Journal of the American Oriental Society 35, 1915, pp 224-239.

Schep-Slaughter-Vale-Wheatley (2013) : RL Schep, RJ Slaughter, AA Vale, P Wheatley, *Was the Death of Alexander the Great due to poisoning? Was it Veratrum album?*, Clinical Toxology 52, no.1, 2013, pp 72-77.

Schliemann (1881) : H Schliemann, *Ilios, the city and country of the Trojans*, Harper & Brothers.

Schmeling (1996) : GL Schmeling (editor), *The Novel in the Ancient World*, Brill.

Schwenk (1985) : Schwenk, *Athens in the Age of Alexander, The Dates, Laws and Decrees of the Lykourgan Era 338-322 B.C.*, Ares Publishers.

Scott (1928) : K Scott, *The Deification of Demetrius Poliorcetes,* Part 1, The American Journal of Philology 49, no. 2, 1928, pp 137-166.

Scramuzza (1940) : V Scramuzza, *The Emperor Claudius*, Harvard University Press.

Shafer (1974) : RJ Shafer, *A Guide to Historical Method*, The Dorsey Press.

Schamp (2000) : J Schamp, *Les Vies des dix orateurs attiques*, editions Fribourg Universitaires.

Seeley (1881) : JR Seeley, *Livy, Book 1, with introduction, Historical Examination and Notes*, 3rd edition, Clarendon Press.

Sekunda (1997) : NV Sekunda, *Nearchus the Cretan and the Foundation of Cretopolis*, Anatolian studies 47,1997, pp 217-222.

Sekunda (1984) : NV Sekunda, *The Army of Alexander the Great*, Osprey Publishing, 2008 edition.

Sekunda (2001) : NV Sekunda, *The Sarissa*, Acta Universitatis Lodziensis, Folia Archaeologica 23, 2001, pp 14-31.

Sekunda (2012) : NV Sekunda, *Macedonian Armies after Alexander 323-168 BC*, Osprey Publishing.

Seltman (1938) : CT Seltman, *Diogenes of Sinope, Son of the Banker Hikesias*, in Transactions of the International Numismatic. Congress 1936, London.

Shelmerdine (1995) : SC Shelmerdine, *The Homeric Hymns*, Focus Publishing, R Pullins and Company.

Shilleto (1874) : R Shilleto, *Demosthenis De Falsa Legatione*, Deighton, Bell and Company.

Shipley (1903) : FW Shipley, *Certain Sources of Corruption in Latin Manuscripts: A Study Based upon Two Manuscripts of Livy: Codes Puteanus (Fifth Century), and its Copy, Codex Reginensis 762 (Ninth Century)*, American Journal of Archeology 7, no.1, January-March 1903, pp 1-25.

Shipley (2000) : G Shipley, *The Greek World After Alexander 323-30BC*, Routledge.

Shipley (2011) : G Shipley, *Pseudo-Skylax's Periplous: the Circumnavigation of the Inhabited World*, Phoenix Press.

Shorter (1967) : DCA Shorter, *Tacitus and Verginius Rufus*, Classical Quarterly, New Series 17, no, 2, November 1967, pp 370-381.

Shrimpton (1991) : GS Shrimpton, *Theopompus the Historian*, McGill-Queen's University Press.

Siebert (1969) : J Siebert, *Untersuchungen zur Geschichte Ptolemaios' I*, Munchener Beitrage zur Papyrusforchung und antiken Rechtgeschichte 56, 1969.

Sihler (1995) : AL Sihler, *New Comparative Grammar of Greek and Latin*, Oxford University Press.

Simpson (1959) : RH Simpson, *Abbreviation of Hieronymus in Diodorus*, The American Journal of Philology 80, no. 4, 1959, pp 370-379.

Simpson (1957) : RH Simpson, *A Possible Case of Misrepresentation in Diodorus XIX*, Histroria: Zeitschrift für Alte geschichte 6 no. 4, 1957, pp 504-505.

Smith (1981) : LC Smith, *The Chronology of Books XVIII-XX of Diodorus Siculus*, American Journal of Philology 32, 1981, pp 283-290.

Smits (1987) : ER Smits, *A Medieval Supplement to the Beginning of Curtius Rufus's Historia Alexandri: An Edition with Introduction*, Viator 18, 1987, pp 89-124.

Snodgrass (1967) : AM Snodgrass, *Arms and Armour of the Greeks*, Thames and Hudson, 1982 edition.

Spencer (2002) : D Spencer, *The Roman Alexander*, University of Exeter Press.

Speyer (1971) : W Speyer, *Die literarische Fälschung im heidnischen und christlichen Altertum*, CH Beck.

Sprague de Camp (1972) : L Sprague de Camp, *Great Cities of the Ancient World*, Dorset Press.

Srinivasan-Sinopoli-Morrison-Gopal-Ranganathan (2009) : S Srinivasan, CM Sinopoli, KD Morrison, R Gopal, S Ranganathan, *South Indian Iron Age iron and high carbon steel: with reference to Kadebakele and comparative insights from Mel-siruvalar*, in *Metallurgy and Civilization: Eurasia and Beyond*, Archetype, 2009, pp 116-122.

Stadter (1967) : PA Stadter, *Flavius Arrianus: The New Xenophon*, Greek, Roman and Byzantine Studies 8, 1967, pp 155-161.

Steele (1915) : RB Steel, *Quintus Curtius Rufus*, The American Journal of Philology 36, no. 4, 1915, pp 402-423.

Stewart (1993) : A Stewart, *Faces of Power, Alexander's Image and Hellenistic Politics*, University of California Press.

Stoneman (1991) : R Stoneman, *The Greek Alexander Romance*, Penguin.

Stoneman (1994) : R Stoneman, *Legends of Alexander The Great*, Everyman-JM Dent.

Stoneman (1997) : R Stoneman, *Alexander the Great*, Routledge.

Stoneman (2012) : R Stoneman (translator), *The Book of Alexander the Great, Life of the Conqueror*, IB Tauris.

Strassler (1996) : RB Strassler (editor), *The Landmark Thucydides, a Comprehensive Guide to the Peloponnesian War*, Simon and Schuster

Striker (1996) : G Striker, *Essays on Hellenistic Epistemology and Ethics*, Cambridge University Press.

Sullivan (1966) : JP Sullivan, *Seneca: The Deification of Claudius the Clod*, Arion: A Journal of Humanities and the Classics 5, no. 3, autumn 1966, pp 376-399.

Sundberg (1958) : AC Sundberg, *The Old Testament of the Early Church (A Study in Canon)*, The Harvard Theological Review 51, no 4, 1958, pp 205-226.

Syme (1939) : R Syme, *The Roman Revolution,* Oxford University Press.

Syme (1964) : R Syme, *The Historian Servilius Nonianus*, Hermes 92, no. 4, 1964, pp 408-424.

Syme (1971) : R Syme, *Emperors and Biography: Studies in the Historia Augusta,* Oxford University Press.

Syme (1987) : R Syme, *The Word 'optimus': - not Tacitean*, Eranos 85, 1987, pp 111-114.

Tarbell (1920) : FB Tarbell, *Centauromachy and Amazonomachy in Greek Art: The Reasons for Their Popularity*, American Journal of Archeology 24, no. 3, July-September 1920, pp 226-231.

Tarn (1910) : WW Tarn, *The Dedicated Ship of Antigonus Gonatas*, The Journal of Hellenic Studies 30, 1910, pp 209-222.

Tarn (1921) : WW Tarn, *Heracles Son of Barsine*, Journal of Hellenic Studies 41, 1921, pp. 18-28.

Tarn (1923) : WW Tarn, *The Hellenistic Age. Aspects of Hellenistic Civilisation, The Social Questions in the 3rd Century*, Norton & Comp.

Tarn (1927) : WW Tarn, *Hellenistic Civilisation*, The New American Library, 1961 edition.

Tarn (1939) : WW Tarn, *Alexander's Plans*, Journal of Hellenic Studies 59, no. 1, 1939, pp 125-135.

Tarn 1 (1948) : WW Tarn : *Alexander the Great 1, Narrative*, Cambridge University Press, 1979 edition.

Tarn (1948) : WW Tarn, *Alexander The Great, Volume II, Sources and Studies*, Cambridge University Press, 1979 edition.

Tarn (1968) : WW Tarn, *A King's Notebooks*, Harvard Studies in Classical Philology 72, 1968, pp 183-204.

Tarn-Griffith (1952) : WW Tarn and GT Griffith, *Hellenistic Civilisation*, 3rd edition, Meridian Books.

Temple (2002) : N Temple, *Heritage and Forgery: Annio da Viterbo and the Quest for the Authentic*, Public Archaeology 2, no.3, 2002, pp 151-162.

Teresi (2002) : D Teresi, *Lost Discoveries, The Ancient Roots of Modern Science - from the Babylonians to the Maya*, Simon and Schuster.

Teuffel-Schwabe (1892) : WS Teuffel and L Schwabe, *Teuffel's History of Roman Literature Revised and Enlarged, Volume II, The Imperial Period*, Deighton, Bell & Company.

Thirlwall (1845) : C Thirlwall, *A History of Hellas, Volume 2*, Harper and Brothers.

Thomas *Review* (1963) : Review by CL Howard of PH Thomas, *Incerti auctoris epitoma rerum Gestarum Alexandri Magni cum libro de morte testamentoque Alexandri*, Classical Philology 58, no. 2, April 1963, pp 129-131.

Thomas (1968) : CG Thomas, *Alexander the Great and the Unity of Mankind*, The Classical Journal 63, no. 6, March 1968, pp 258-260.

Thomas (2007) : CG Thomas, *Alexander the Great in his World*, Blackwell Publishing.

Thorpe (1966) : L Thorpe, *Geoffrey of Monmouth, The History of the Kings of Britain*, Penguin.

Timpanaro-Most (2005) : S Timpanaro and GW Most, *The Genesis of Lachman's Method*, University of Chicago Press.

Tobias (2007) : N Tobias, *Basil I, Founder of the Macedonian Dynasty: A Study of the Political and Military History of the Byzantine Empire in the Ninth Century*, Mellen Press.

Tod (1985) : MN Tod (editor), *Greek Historical Inscriptions*, Ares Publishers.

Townend (1960) : GB Townend, *The Sources of the Greek in Suetonius*, Hermes 88, 1960, pp 98-100.

Townend (1964) : GB Townend, *Cluvius Rufus in the Histories of Tacitus*, The American Journal of Philology 85, 1964, pp 337-377.

Townsend (1996) : D Townsend (translator), *The Alexandreis of Walter of Chatillon, A Twelfth Century Epic*, University of Pennsylvania Press.

Van der Mieroop (2004) : M Van de Mieroop, *A Tale of Two Cities: Nineveh and Babylon, Iraq* 66, 2004, pp 1-5.

Van de Mieroop (2005) : M Van de Mieroop, *King Hammurabi*, Blackwell Publishing.

Van der Spek (2003) : RJ Van Der Spek, *Darius III, Alexander the Great and Babylonian Scholarship*, Achaemenid History 13, 2003, pp 289-346.

Von Ranke (1905) : Leopold Von Ranke, *History of the Reformation in Germany*, George Rutledge & Sons Ltd.

Van Wees (1994) : H Van Wees, *The Homeric Way of War: The 'Iliad' and the Hoplite Phalanx (1)*, Greece and Rome, Second Series 41, no 1, April 1994, pp 1-18.

Vezin (1907) : A Vezin, *Eumenes von Kardia*, Aschendorff.

Verbrugghe-Wickersham (2000) : GP Verbrugghe and GP & JM Wickersham, *Berossus and Manetho Introduced and Translated: Native Traditions in Ancient Mesopotamia and Egypt*, University of Michigan Press.

Vrettos (2001) : T Vrettos, *Alexandria, City of the Western Mind*, The Free Press.

Walbank (1962) : FW Walbank, *Polemic in Polybius*, The Journal of Roman Studies 52, nos.1 and 2, 1962, pp 1-12.

Walbank (1981) : FW Walbank, The *Hellenistic World*, Harvard University Press, 1993 edition.

Wallis Budge (1896) : EA Wallis Budge, *The Life and Exploits of Alexander the Great being a Series of Translations of the Ethiopic Histories of Alexander by the Pseudo Callisthenes and Other Writers*, J Clay and Sons.

Wardle (1992) : D Wardle, *Cluvius Rufus and Suetonius*, Hermes 12, no. 4, 1992, pp 466-482.

Wardle (2005) : D Wardle, *Valerius Maximus on Alexander the Great*, Acta Classica 48, pp 141-161.

Wardy (1996) : R Wardy, *The Birth of Rhetoric: Gorgias, Plato and Their Successors*, Routledge.

Warner (1949) : R Warner (translator), *Xenophon, The Persian Expedition*, Penguin.

Warner (1966) : R Warner (translator), *Xenophon, A History of My Times*, Penguin.

Watson-Miller (1992) : JS Watson and MCJ Miller (editors), *M. Junianus Justinus, Epitoma Historiarum Philippicarum, Books VII-XII Excerpta de Historia Macedonia*, Ares Publishers.

Weill (1980) : R Weill, *Phoenicia and Western Asia to the Macedonian Conquest*, Ares Publishers.

Weiss (1962) : R Weiss, *An Unknown Epigraphic Tract by Annius of Viterbo*, in CP Brand (editor) Italian Studies presented to ER Vincent, Heffer, 1992 edition, pp 101-20.

Wells (1984) : MC Wells, *The Roman Empire*, second edition, Harvard University Press.

West (2008) : ML West (translator), *Hesiod, Theogeny and Works and Days*, Oxford World's Classics.

Wheatley (1998) : PV Wheatley, *The Date of Polyperchon's Invasion of Macedonia and Murder of Heracles*, Antichthon 32, 1998, pp 12-23.

Wheatley (1995) : PV Wheatley, *Ptolemy Soter's Annexation of Syria 320 B.C.*, Classical Quarterly, New Series 45, no. 2, 1995, pp 433-440.

Wheatley (2002) : PV Wheatley, *Antigonus Monophthalmus in Babylonia, 310-208 BCE*, Journal of Near Eastern Studies 61, no. 1, January 2002, pp 39-47.

Wheeler (1902) : IH Wheeler, *Alexander The Great, The Merging of East and West in Universal History*, GP Putnam's Sons.

Whitehead (1987) : I Whitehead, *The Periplous*, Greece and Rome, Second Series 34, no. 2, October 1987, pp 178-85

Whitehead (1929) : AN Whitehead, *Process and Reality*, MacMillan.

Whitehead-Blyth (2004) : DP Whitehead and PH Blyth, *Athenaeus Mechanicus on Machines*, Historia Einzelschriften 182, Franz Verlag GMBH.

Whitmarsh (2002) : T Whitmarsh, *Alexander's Hellenism and Plutarch's Textualism*, Classical Quarterly 52, no. 1, 2002, pp 174-192.

Wilcken (1931) : U Wilcken, *Alexander the Great*, W W Norton and Company; first published as *Alexander Der Grosse* in 1931, 1967 edition.

Wilkes (1972) : J Wilkes, *The Julio-Claudian Historians*, The Classical World 65, no. 6, 1972, pp 177-192, 197-203.

Wilkins-Hill (2006) : JM Wilkins and S Hill, *Food in the Ancient World*, Blackwell Publishing.

Williams (2004) : CA Williams (translator, commentary), *Martial, Epigrams Book II*, Oxford University Press.

Winiarczyk (2013) : M Winiarczyk, *The Sacred History of Euhemerus of Messene*, Walter de Gruyter GmbH.

Winn Leith (1998) : MJ Winn Leith, *Israel among the Nations: The Persian Period*, in MD Coogan, *The Oxford History of the Biblical World*, Oxford University Press, pp 276-316.

Wiseman (1982) : TP Wiseman, *Calpurnius Siculus and the Claudian Civil War*, Society for the Promotion of Roman Studies 72, 1982, pp 57-67.

Wiseman (1991) : TP Wiseman, *Death of an Emperor, Flavius Josephus*, Exeter Studies of History no 30, University of Exeter Press.

Wood (1985) : M Wood, *In Search of the Trojan War*, BBC Books.

Wood (2005) : M Wood, *In Search of Myths and Heroes: Exploring Four Epic*

Legends of the World, University of California Press.

Womersely (1994) : D Womersley, *Edward Gibbon – The History of the Decline and Fall of the Roman Empire, volume 2*, Penguin.

Worthington (2000) : I Worthington I (editor), *Demosthenes Statesman and Orator*, Routledge.

Worthington (2007) : I Worthington (editor), *A Companion to Greek Rhetoric*, Blackwell Publishing.

Wright (1995) : A Wright, *The Death of Cicero: Rhetorical Invention in Ancient Historiography*, Humanities Research Centre, Australian National University, 12-14 July 1995.

Wroe (1999) : A Wroe, *Pilate: The Biography of an Invented Man*, Jonathan Cape Ltd.

Yardley (2003) : J Yardley, *Justin and Pompeius Trogus*, University of Toronto Press.

Xirotiris-Langenscheidt (1981) : NI Xirotiris and F Langenscheidt, *The cremations from the royal Macedonian tombs of Vergina*, Archaiologiki Ephemeris, 1981, pp 142-60.

Yonge-Seddon (2008) : CD Yonge and K Seddon : *An Outline of Cynic Philosophy: Antisthenes of Athens and Diogenes of Sinope*, based on the translation by CD Yonge in 1853, 2008 edition, Lulu.com.

INDEX

The Index relates to names appearing in the main chapter text only, not footnotes, except where they *only* feature in footnotes.